A NEW CORNISH-ENGLISH AND ENGLISH-CORNISH DICTIONARY

Dhe gof

CARADAR,

Ow hesoberor skentyl ha dywysyk dres
lyes bledhen ow-whylas dry golow
a-berth yn tylleryow tewl
an Yeth Kernow.

GERLYVER NOWETH KERNEWEK-SAWSNEK HA SAWSNEK-KERNEWEK

GANS

R. MORTON NANCE

Published by Agan Tavas
The Society for the Promotion of the Cornish Language
Gordon Villa, Sunnyvale Road, Portreath, Redruth,
Kernow/Cornwall TR16 4NE
1999

First published 1990
Second impression 1994
Third impression 1999
Memorial Edition Reprinted 2003

This edition published by Agan Tavas with the permission of
The Federation of Old Cornwall Societies
ISBN 1 901409 03 1

Printed and Bound by Short Run Press Ltd. Exeter

INTRODUCTION TO THE MEMORIAL EDITION

This second reprint of the combined 1938 Cornish-English and the 1952 English-Cornish Dictionary has been produced by Agan Tavas (The Society for the Promotion of the Cornish Language) with the permission of the Federation of Old Cornwall Societies, the first publishers.

The first and second impressions were printed due to the foresight of the late Len Truran of Dyllansow Truran. A true Cornishman, he had a proper respect for the work of the earlier language revivalists. This impression is printed as a memorial volume to mark the 40th anniversary of the death of Robert Morton-Nance 1873-1959. It also marks the 70th anniversary of the publication by Nance of **Cornish For All**, the text book which first introduced the **Unified** system of spelling which made revived Cornish accessible to many more people than before.

Other systems of Cornish orthography have been introduced during the last 15 years but Unified is still considered to be the preferred system of Cornish for anyone wishing to learn the language. This has been confirmed by the recent study undertaken by Dr Nicholas Williams of University-College Dublin, the first professional Celtic linguist to study revived Cornish in depth.

Those who have used both the 1938 and 1955 Cornish-English dictionaries will confirm that the 1938 version is superior in many ways. It provides the derivations of words as well as their meanings and examples of uses. The 1938 dictionary also included other useful material such as a number of uncommon words from texts, some words derived by analogy from Welsh and Breton and the numerous appendices which added so much value to the original dictionary.

Of course the 1955 version contained a number of extra words that had been discovered or had come into use since 1938. These have been listed in the enlarged addenda prepared by Richard Jenkin and printed in this volume so that readers can have all the material available in both versions.

Agan Tavas is honoured to be able to publish this *memorial edition* of the Robert Morton-Nance dictionary as a classic and irreplaceable publication and as the standard Cornish language reference work.

We express our thanks to all those, both individuals and societies, who have provided much of the funding which has enabled this edition to be printed. Their names are too numerous to be listed in this brief introduction.

INTRODUCTION

THIS NEW CORNISH-ENGLISH DICTIONARY aims at including every known word of the Cornish Language, but as chance must have prevented many of its words from coming down to us and as this dictionary is primarily intended for people of Cornish nationality who wish to make use of their own Celtic language or to interpret its surviving relics in place-names and dialect words, it also includes many words which can only be *presumed* to have formed part of the language. Such words are distinguished clearly from those of recorded Cornish.

An acceptable standard spelling has been aimed at. This is based on the Middle Cornish of the *Ordinalia* and *Passion Poem*, which is the most perfect form of the language as well as being the one best known, but apart from the re-spelling, to match Middle Cornish, of words known only as Old Cornish or Late Cornish, i.e., roughly either older than 1300 or later than 1600, some irregularities or ambiguities of Middle Cornish itself have been removed: thus *th* and *dh*, *g* and *j*, *u*, *v* and *w* are all here distinguished, and an attempt has been made at separating *e* and *y*, *f* and *v*, *ou* and *ow*, etc. Actual spellings and variants are added in brackets, but the phonetic symbols of Lhuyd are represented in ordinary type, and the words of illustrative quotations are given the unified spelling. Words from Old Cornish are distinguished by the dagger (†). A few variant or contracted Middle-Cornish spellings are recognised as optional, the form first given being usually preferable, even when it differs from that hitherto most usual. Hyphens are generally used to link words that are translated by one word in English, or to separate the parts of words that without them might be misread. They will be useful at least until the language becomes more familarly known than it now is.

Where this unified spelling differs from that of the older Cornish-English dictionary, the Rev. Robert Williams' *Lexicon Cornu-Brittanicum* of 1865, it does so chiefly in keeping the characteristic Middle-Cornish *k*, *p*, *th* where he preferred *g*, *b*, *dh*; keeping Middle-Cornish *k*, *gh*, *y* where he preferred Old-Cornish *c*, *ch*, *i*, and representing the unstressed final *e* of the older texts by the *a* of later ones. In the necessary replacement of so many missing genders, plurals, infinitive-endings and inflected parts of verbs, too, the suggestions of Breton have usually been taken as preferable to those of the more distant Welsh. Certain vowels are given diacritical signs in the dictionary, but like the accents and the diacritical numerals referring to mutation, these markings are not suggested for imitation in ordinary use.

Space would not allow of following Williams' unusual though helpful plan of giving separate insertion to each variant spelling of a word, or of following up its varying initial through all states of mutation; and to find every inflection of a verb, or every person of a pronominal preposition, the search must here be extended to the APPENDICES. Text-references are given chiefly for the less common words, and quotations either to illustrate idioms, or to amend the old. translations. Linguistic comparisons are made only when some such explanation seems called for, and not as a general rule.

Still there are some compensating advantages which any new dictionary, however concise, is bound to have over the old one. Not only has far greater accuracy of definition been made possible since 1865 by the critical studies of later Celtic philologists, especially those of Joseph Loth and Whitley Stokes; the texts of the *Passion Poem* and *The Creation of the World*, only then known as they were crudely put forth by Davies Gilbert, have since been more correctly printed and translated in the Stokes editions, and sources of words then all untapped have since been made available for study, including the very important *Life of Meriasek*, based on the Latin life of the Saint, with added legendary matter, the interesting little *Charter Endorsement Fragment*, the various Lhuyd, Borlase, Tonkin, and Gwavas manuscripts, and several odd fragments of Cornish of different periods, none of which had been seen by Williams. Besides drawing on so much fresh material, a comparison of the *Old Cornish Vocabulary* with Aelfric's practically word-for-word Old-English model for it has explained many difficult words from this source.[1] Lhuyd's manuscript vocabulary (Llanstephan MS. 84, Nat. Lib. Wales, Aberystwyth) has contributed many words otherwise unrecorded.[2] The writings of Leland, Carew, Symonds, Mundy and Ray have yielded others, and the many suggestions of Cornish place-names or living traditional fragments of spoken Cornish have been taken whenever it seemed reasonably safe to use them, as I ave also those of some hundreds of local dialect survivals of the language, of which most have been noted only since the *English Dialect Dictionary* was printed.[3]. No trouble has been spared in giving all these words the most accurate definition that seems as yet attainable.

It has also been recognized that hosts of words passed over by Williams as irrelevant, because of their non-Celtic origin, are nevertheless as much a part of Cornish as the non-Teutonic ' joy " or "beauty," "mustard" or "beef" are a part of English, so that a Cornish dictionary is only impoverished, and not purified, by their omission. Non-Celtic loan-words are by no means a symptom of decay in the language during its later stages of gradual desertion. Old Cornish had already taken over several Teutonic words from Old English (here marked O.E.), or even from Frankish, by way of Old French, and Middle Cornish not only borrowed occasionally from West-Country English, but took to itself the Anglo-French adornments of cultivated Middle English still more readily. Such words (marked M.E.) are rarely in such frequent use as Celtic ones, some may be preferred here and there for variety's sake, others seem dragged in only as rhymes, and in attempting to write "unified" Cornish we may shun those of them which most resemble current English ; yet it is true that a well-chosen Chaucerian word can look more at home in a Middle-Cornish sentence than a new-made compound built up of Cornish elements, or a re-spelt Old-Cornish word, or a pedigree Celtic one that is backed by Welsh and Breton together.

This is not of course to suggest that would-be users of Cornish should avoid new Celtic compounds or restorations. They could not indeed get very far without some of them, and a good many ready-made compounds based on those current in Welsh or Breton, marked (B.) or (W.), have been given, though the temptation to adapt them by the score has been resisted and some very obvious ones have been left to suggest themselves. When Welsh and Breton both keep some word that as Cornish is either lost or unrecorded, this is admitted in a deduced Cornish spelling, but starred (*) and followed by (W., B.). When such words seem to have been definitely replaced by others, this is stated. A few similarly starred words are likely borrowings from Middle English.

To add, only to explain them away, the masses of words that have mistakenly been accepted as Cornish by Hals, Gwavas, Tonkin, Borlase, Pryce and Polwhele would only have caused annoyance to most users of the dictionary ; these are simply omitted, but Appendix I. contains a short list of words, difficult or even dubious but not necessarily spurious, most of them Old Cornish.

---

1. O. Eng. words are quoted in the spelling of Vocabulary X. in Wright and Wülke's *Anglo-Saxon and Old English Vocabularies*, 1884. The word-order in this is very close to that of Cor. Voc., as it is also in their "Semi-Saxon" vocabulary XIII., and as it must have been in the *Dictionarium Latino-Saxonicum* seen at Glastonbury by Leland in 1542, as shown by his running extracts of its words in his *Collectanea*, 1774, Vol. IV., p. 134 (Glastonbury Catalogue, p. 155). The Old-Cornish version has 22 words that are not in Aelfric, but by missing out others that are there and by breaking off suddenly it has lost a far greater number. Recent scholarship has thrown suspicion on several of its words, e.g., *maur*, *euiter*, as having been re-spelt as Welsh by the Welsh copyist of a lost Cornish original. This original was evidently written in "Anglo-Saxon" script, which the transcriber sometimes puts incorrectly into his own Lombardic handwriting.
2. Many of Lhuyd's needless borrowings elsewhere from Welsh or Breton have been omitted.
3. Some of the richest sources of Celtic survivals were almost neglected by the earlier collectors of Cornish dialect words, particularly St. Just, St. Ives, Newlyn, Mousehole and the fishing-coves in general. Such words are often known only to a few persons in one particular place. Many have been omitted that may eventually prove to be Celtic, but are not yet satisfactorily identified as such. The same applies to many place-name vocables.

The remarks on pronunciation which follow add to what it was possible to say in the body of the dictionary. In the absence of any native-speakers of Middle Cornish to give us certainty, or of perfect agreement even among expert philologists as to its probable sounds, they have to be based largely on the traditional sounds as still heard in place-names and dialect survivals, and failing these, on hints taken from the allied tongues, or from rhymes and stresses in the texts themselves. Rhymes are there often forced or conventional, and natural stress is often violated, especially is order to get the desired beat on the end syllable of a line, which was required by the chosen verse-form, but left Cornish rather short of real rhymes. This makes it difficult at times to judge whether a long vowel which by analogy should be short was really made long in common speech, and even more difficult to say if an accent had really shifted off its normal stance on the penultimate syllable, or whether Cornish verse was not rather delivered without much regard for natural stresses or vowel-lengths, but in a chanting tone, and varied only by the cadences that added meaning to its sentences as they still do in the musical English-speaking of those extremities of Cornwall where the language was last popularly spoken. Just as English-speakers in Ireland, the Highlands of Scotland, the Isle of Man or Wales, and French-speakers in Brittany, whether they know the old Celtic language or not, still speak with the intonation that belongs to it, so those who keep this West-Cornwall intonation are obviously still using an important and distinguishing part of the Cornish language, perhaps the part about which we can feel more certain than about any other. As we thus hear it applied to English words, the general sound of Cornish is, to ourselves at least, a most pleasing one, but it is as unlike the sound of any other Celtic language as it is unlike that of any sort of English dialect, except for the fact of being half-chanted, though to a Celtic tune of its own. Its nearest resemblance seems curiously to be to the sound of southern Irish rather than to the sound either of Welsh or of Breton. Though Cornish changed much from the 12th to the 15th century, the suggestion made by contemporary spellings of place-names is that, apart from a few well-known substitutions to be mentioned in their place, the sounds of Cornish have not very materially altered from the 15th century onward, and that the singing tones which characterized the language in its latest phase were probably no new feature either, but had evolved gradually through the ages. Cornish borrowed non-Celtic words freely, but on the other hand it had vitality enough to preserve many Celtic words that have long been obsolete in Welsh or Breton, and even in its days of worst neglect, when scarcely any but a few miners and fishermen spoke it, it never became a hybrid Anglo-Celtic dialect, but remained a Celtic language.

PRONUNCIATION

Syllable stress and division tend to follow meaning, stressed stems and unstressed endings being clearly separated in sound; e.g., *cana*, *kerdhes*, *tenna* are pronounced ***can-a***, ***kerdh-es***, ***tenn-a***, not ***ca-na***, ***ker-dhes***, ***ten-na***.

Consonants. But for the absence of *x* and *z* (used only in borrowed words), the consonants are very much as in English, but with some distinctions.

b as final commonly hardens to *p*, as in *heb* to *hep*, *mab* to *map*, *ryb* to *ryp*, but may remain *b* before following initial vowels, though M. Cor. MSS. make no such discrimination. Final *b* is actually commoner in all but *Ordinalia* spelling.

c, k commonly represent one sound, hard as in "*cake*," **c** being used before *a*, *o*, *u* and consonants *l*, *r*, and *k* before *e*, *y*, consonants other than *l*, *r*, and as final; initial *k* is sounded separately before *n*, almost as *ken*; *qu* replaces *kw*; when *c* is used before *e* or *y*, as in a few non-Celtic words, it is sounded as *s*.

d as final in a non-Celtic word may become *t*, as in ***sat***, ***sadt***, ***sad***; ***spet***, ***spedt***, ***sped*** (3 s. pres.-fut. of ***spedya***); see also **j**.

f as final may be sounded as *v*, especially before a following initial vowel, or may even be silent, as *lavara'* for *lavaraf*; in positions where mutable consonants are softened, too, it is usually sounded as *v*, though except in place-names not so spelt; e.g. *an fenten*, but place-name Park an Venton. The distinction between *f* and *v* is less marked than in English and in MSS. *ff* is often used between vowels to express a decided *f*, while *f* is sometimes written for ***v***.

g is always hard as in "*gag*"; it is sounded before *n* in Celtic ***gnas***, ***gowegneth***, but only lengthens the vowel in non-Celtic ***regnya***; as final it commonly sharpens to *k* unless before initial vowels, final *g* being more characteristic of C. Voc. and Late Cornish.

h is usually sounded, but as initial may be mute in unstressed words, as ***ha***, ***hy***, and in verbs also, these taking the particles *owth-*, *yth-* used before vowels. In spelling, a silent *h* is occasionally inserted between vowels to ensure their separate pronunciation, as in ***rohow*** for *roow*, cf. C. Voc. *gouhoc* for *gowak*, etc. In words of Anglo-French origin silent *h* is often unspelt, as in ***ertach***, Fr. *heritage*, *omajer*, Fr. *hommager*, etc.

j represents the soft sound of *g* in "*g*inger," tending towards that of *z* in "azure." In M. Cor. MSS. it is usually spelt *i* or *g*, and as variant pronunciation occasionally *y*, as in ***venyons***, ***yunnya***. It is used (a) in non-Celtic words, as ***jujja***, and (b) in Celtic words as a softening of *s*, as in *nyja*, of *sw*, as in *ajy*, of *d* after *n* and before *y* or *e*, as in *y'n jeth*, *an jawl*, or of *ch* by mutation as in y^2 *jy*. In *densa* (*dēn*, *da*), *j* as result of *d* after *n* is spelt *s*. Dialect "jank," "jale" (see *dyank*, *dehelghya*) suggest that *dy* was sometimes sounded as *j* where it is never found so spelt. *Golowan* seems to show that the O. Cor. pronunciation of *Jowan*, John, was *Yowan*, as W. *Ioan*, B. *Ian*, though this had become obsolete in M. Cor.

k, see **c**.

m, **n**, following a stressed short vowel or *ü*, later developed *b*, *d*, respectively before them; e.g., *cam* became *cabm*, *pen* became *pedn*, while *mm* became *bm* and *nn* became *dn*; the latter was the first to be acknowledged in spelling and already in B.M. *bednath* for *bennath* occurs twice. Though no distinct *b* or *d* is elsewhere implied in M. Cor. MSS., sounds between *mm*, *nn* and *bm*, *dn* are probable. In latest Cor. we find *bb*, *dd* replacing *mm*, *nn*, as in *ubba* for *omma*, *hodda* for *honna*.

q is used before *u* in both Celtic and non-Celtic words. In the former *qu* replaces *kw* as a mutation of *gw*.

r is not trilled, but has a "reverted" sound approaching that of south-western English *r*, and heard most strongly before consonants. Before vowels it is a pronounced but less reverted *r*.

s as unaffected initial or before a consonant other than *v*, *w*, *y*, and in words from Middle English, e.g., *forsakya*, *hansel*, *person*, is like *s* in "*s*ister." Before a vowel in a Celtic word, or in a position which causes softening of mutual consonants, it is sounded as *z* in "lazy" or *s* in "rai*s*e," and may be sounded between vowels more softly still as *zh* (*s* in "lei*s*ure" or *z* in "azure") or as *j* in "ajar," or even latterly as *y*, as in *falya* (Lh. *fallia*) for *falsa*. The *j* sound is often spelt as *g* in MSS., *ss* being necessary between vowels to express a decided *s*, as especially in non-Celtic words like *grassyes*, *passya*. As final, *s* is sounded as Eng. *ss* or *ce* in non-Celtic words like *fas*, *gras*, *plas*, *rychys*, *servons*, *spas* (in all of which it alternates with *th*) and occasionally in Celtic words, especially when following a short vowel, as in *bys* (prep.), *plos*, *eglos*, or before the initial consonant *b*, *c*, *d*, *f*, *g*, *k*, *p*, *q*, *s*, *t*, *th*, *v* of a following word. In words from Middle English, e.g., *nasyon*, *temptasyon*, *s* before *y* consonant is sounded as *sh*. In Late Cornish, *s* between vowels is sometimes replaced by *r*; e.g., *era* for *esa*, *gara* for *gasa*, *gorowes* for *gos(l)owes*: doubled *ss* evidently tended to become *ch* (Lh. *tsh*), as in *pyskecha* (*pysgetsha*, Lh.) for *pyskessa*, or Letcha, place-name, older Lesshe. M. Cor. *s* often represents an O. Cor. *d* or *t*.

y is a consonant before vowels except in *yu* (*yw*, *ew*), or in words where an accented long *ȳ* is followed by an unaccented vowel; e.g., *skȳans*, *lȳes*, or in which *y* is a stem-vowel; e.g., *babÿow*, *dustunÿow*, *golÿa*, *gwarÿes*, *ylÿa*. After *w*, *l*, *r* it is sometimes practically silent; e.g., *sylwyans*, *dyskyblyon*, *lyfryow*, *gwyryoneth*, also spelt *sylwans*, *dyskyblon*, *lyfrow*, *gwyroneth*. In the verbs from English, *marya*, *tarya*, *varya*, it remains a consonant after *r* except when final, perhaps imitating *carya* with stem *car*, but cf. also "carr," to carry, in western English dialect, the reverted *r* there absorbing the *y*.

ch is as in "*ch*ur*ch*": it represents, (a) an altered sound of *t* before *y*, as in *chy*, older *ty* (which on losing stress in a compound name like Chyanhals, Chyandowr is sounded together with the following *an* as *shun*), (b) in loan-words a non-Celtic sound as in *chanjya*, *cachya*, and (c) the sharpening of a non-Celtic final *j* (*-ge*), as in *maryach*, *ymach*; as initial it may soften by mutation to *j*.

dh is like soft *th* in "*th*i*th*er": as final or before consonants other than *l*, *r*, *w* (doubtfully *v*), and in situations causing hardening, it becomes hard *th* as in "*th*ink*eth*"; e.g., *dewedha*, inf.; *dewedhes*, adj.; *deweth*, 2 s. imp. and 3 s. pres.-fut.; *dewetho*, 3 s. subj.; *dewethsa*, 3 s. plupf.; *deweth*, noun, and *dewetha*, comp. adj. Until Lhuyd introduced this spelling from contemporary Welsh, *dh* was not distinguished from *th*, though in the M.C. MS. the tailed *z* that in MSS. occasionally represents also *y*, *th*, *gh* and *z* was generally reserved for *dh*. In Late Cornish *dh* following *r* is occasionally silent; e.g., *gworria* for *gordhya*, *furu*, (*Tre*)*vorrow* for *fordhow*, *morraz* for *mordhos*. The M.C. spellings *yn mezy*, *yn meza*, *yn meze*, *laze*, beside *yn meth an*, *yn meth y wrek*, suggest that before the enclitic suffixed prons. *e* and *y*, final *dh* remains unchanged to *th*, the prons. being treated as part of the vb.

gh is often made *h* or omitted altogether in MSS.; when sounded it is hardly more guttural than *h*, and is practically as silent as in "throu*gh*out," "kni*gh*t," "Hu*gh*," except as final after *l*, *r* as in *golgh*, *margh*, or when it is followed by an initial vowel, as in *sagh a ȳs*, or internally when it separates a stressed long vowel from an unstressed short or obscure one, as in *flēghes*. What is historically the same sound (Welsh *ch*, Breton *c'h*) is spelt *wh* when combined with *w* (Welsh *chw*, Breton *c'ho(u)*), and *h* as a mutation of *c*, *k*; e.g., EWH*a*(*th*), WHEGH, *try*H*ans*, represent Welsh ECHW*ydd*, CHWECH, *tri*CH*ant*, Breton *ec'*H*oaz*, C'H*ouec*'H, *tric'*H*ant*. Final *gh* is occasionally represented in MSS. by *g* alone, and final *g* by *gh*, but these are mere mis-spellings: *ghwh* together are apt to be sounded as *w*; e.g., *ough-whȳ* as *owȳ·*.

gw usually has a just perceptible sound of *w* before *l*, *r*, and a distinct one before the vowels *a*, *e*, *y*. The *w* has disappeared before *o*, *u* even in spelling; e.g., *gōn*, *gūsen*: *gw* hardens to *qu* by mutation (*ow-queles*) or as the effect of a previous *s* or *th* (*pesquyth*, *bythqueth*).

sh occurs in some English loan-words; e.g. *myshyf*, *shara*: it often replaces *sch* of the texts, though this may also represent *sk*.

th is always hard, as in "*th*inke*th*": between vowels, after *r*, or as final it may become silent, as in *lon* for *lothen*, *banal* for *banathel*, *marejyon* for *marthejyon*, *vor*, *por* in place-names, for *forth*, *porth*; final *th*, especially as representing older *dh*, is sometimes ignored in spelling, as in *ewha*, *kerensa*, *notha*; occasionally a final *th* of Middle-English loan-words is a lisped variant of *s*, as in *fath* for *fas*, etc., see **s**; in *Ordinalia* MS. final *th* is sometimes contracted to *t* followed by an oblique stroke ignored in the printed copy. In late forms of place-names final *gh* is sometimes represented by *th*, as in Carn Yorth (*yorgh*): Croft an Verth (*mergh*), the reverse is found in the C.W. spelling *blygh* for *blyth*.

v has a tendency to become *f* before *l*, *r*, and after *s*, *th*, *gh*. In a very few words *v* or *f* has become *w*; e.g., *hewas*, *cawas* for *havos*, *cafos*, cf. *saun*, "zawn," W. *safn*, also in western English "hawn" for "haven."

wh, see **gh**.

MUTABLE CONSONANTS. In Cornish, as in all Celtic languages, certain consonants are subject to "Initial Mutation"; what in other languages are quite other consonants being accepted as their "soft," "breathed" or "hard" forms, which they assume according to rules defined by grammar, though not precisely the same even in Cornish, Breton and Welsh. To find the meaning of any Cornish word which at first glance seems missing from its expected place in the dictionary, those not already familiar with these rules are referred to the following table, and as a further help, words which cause such grammatical change of initial in the immediately following word are marked in the dictionary with a diacritical numeral showing the state of mutation caused by them, as *a*^{2}-, *hy*^{3}, *ow*^{4}-, *yn*^{5}-. To find the dictionary or radical initial (column 1) of a word in mutation, as *a*^{2}*-dhanvon*, *hy*^{3} *thas*, *ow*^{4}*-queles*, *yn*^{5}*-fras*, one must hark back from the **dh** of column 2, the **th** of column 3, the **qu** of column 4, or the **f** of column 5, to the corresponding **d**, **t**, **gw**, and **b** or **m** of column 1, when *danvon*, *tās*, *gweles*, *brās* will each be found defined in its alphabetical place. The second state or soft mutation is by far the commonest and results sometimes from a general cause rather than from any particular preceding word. Place-names give familiar examples of the way in which, for instance, the second word of a compound or an adjective or a personal name immediately following a feminine noun suffer this mutation, *tre* becoming *dra* in Hendra, *byghan* in Carn Bean becoming *vyghan* in Camborne Vean, *Myghal*, *Budhek* (Budoc), *Casek* (Cadoc) becoming *Vyghal*, *Vudhek*, *Gasek* in Lanvyghal, Plu Vudhek, Tregassick, etc.

TABLE OF INITIAL MUTATIONS

1	2	3	4	5
b	v	.	p	f, v
c, k	g	h	.	.
ch	j	.	.	.
d	dh	.	t	t
g	–, w	.	c, k	h
gw	w	.	qu	wh, w
m	v	.	.	f, v
p	b	f	.	.
qu	gw	wh	.	.
t	d	th	.	.
Radical	Soft	Breathed	Hard	Mixed

In the table a dot or period (.) signifies that the corresponding radical initial consonant (column 1) is unchanged.

A word with radical initial *g* normally loses this *g* altogether in soft state (column 2), this loss being expressed by the minus sign (–) there. When followed by *ew*, *o*, *u*, or *r*, however, *g* is affected as if it were *gw* and is replaced by *w*. In mixed mutation (column 5) *v* and *w* are less common softened variants, found especially after pron. *'th*.

In addition to the written mutations, *f* and *s* (unless *s* is followed by a consonant) have respectively the sounds of *v* and *z* as second or soft state, caused in exactly the same way but except in Late Cornish (and so in place-names, as Trevose, Penzance, etc.) not written ; e.g., *an*² *fenten*² *sans*, the holy well, is pronounced *an venten zans*.

Relics of a former nasal mutation of *d* to *n* are found in *nor*, *unnek*, but this is otherwise lost.

OBSTACLES TO MUTATION. The rules set out in the table are occasionally counteracted ; thus a final *s* or *th* will usually prevent mutation of a following c or *k*, *d*, *p*, *t*, while *l*, *n*, *r* after c or *k*, *g* usually prevent mutation of these to *h* ; *l*, *n* usually prevent mutation of a following *d* ; this especially, but not exclusively, after *del*, *fatel*, *kettel*, *pan*, *aban*, *yn-dan*.

Mutations may also be neutralized, or irregular ones may be caused, by a clash of consonants, as often illustrated by place-names. In such clashes either both of two soft sounds harden themselves, or the softer adapts itself to the harder ; e.g., *bd* changes to *pt*, *bp* to *pp*, *ghd* to *ght*, *kd* to *ct*, *kt*, *sb* to *sp*, *sd* to *st*, *sg* to *sc*, *sk*, *sgw* to *squ*, *thgw* to *thqu*, *thd* to *tht* and further to *tt*, *vd* to *ft*, *dhs* to *ths* and then *ss*, *dhv* to *thv*, *dhf* to *thf* and then *ff*, and (in *wheffes*) *ghv* to *ghf* and then *ff*. After *n*, *d* occasionally becomes *j* ; e.g., *nownjek*, *an jeth*, *an jawl*, *a-n-jeva*. In place-names we often find what seems to be an otherwise obsolete breathed mutation after the fem. nouns *tre*, *lan*, *car* (*kēr*) ; e.g., Tretheage (*tēk*), Lanhevern (Kevern), Carharrack (*carrek*), though nothing like it is found in the texts.

Mutations may further be ignored for practical reasons when writing or speaking the unfamiliar names of persons or places, or they may be prevented in adjectives by any construction that tends to separate them from their noun ; e.g., *un alter tek ha da*, a fair and good altar, without mutation, O.M. 1170, though *alter*² *dek da*, would be "a fair, good altar," as *alter* is fem.

In compound words mutation usually follows the gender of the element which is a general term, but there is a tendency for it to follow the distinguishing element instead. It seems likely that for mutation each element was taken separately ; e.g., *an*² *growspren bras* (*crows* f., but *pren* m.).

ELISION AND METATHESIS. Pronunciation is occasionally made easier by sacrificing or transposing consonants, thus *k* is elided between two *s*'s in *dyssys* for *dys*(*k*)*sys*, etc. ; an elided *r* may take an inorganic *e* with it, sharpening the previous consonant; e.g., ***deb(er)sa*** becomes *depsa*, ***lad(er)sa*** becomes *latsa*, *hag(er)der* becomes *hakter*, etc., and by metathesis we get *delyrf* for *delyv(e)r* and then *delyrsa* for *delyr(f)sa*; *drefa* for *drehef*; a variant *whelth* for *wheth(e)l*; *gawlsons* for *gal(o)wsons*.

Vowels. Cornish words are usually accented on one syllable only, the vowel of this syllable being stressed at the expense of the vowel or vowels of any other syllable, so that these tend to lose their clear sounds, becoming more or less obscure.

Stressed **a, e, y, o, u,** when unmarked in this dictionary with the long sign, have their short sounds as in English "h*a*t," "h*e*n," "h*y*mn," "h*o*t," "h*u*t" (*i* being *y* in Mid. Cor. spelling). Before *r* they may acquire much the same modifications as in English "f*a*r," "h*e*r," "m*y*rrh," "f*o*r," "c*u*r." There is always much less difference between short *e* and short *y* than in English, and in Middle-Cornish MSS. these are practically interchangeable, with in M.C. a preference for *e*. In the later spelling also, *y* is oftener replaced by *e* than by *i*, though *i* is used for the *y* consonant of *-yon*, *-yas*, *-ya*, etc.

When unstressed, short **a, e, o** usually take the obscure sound of short **u**; obscure **e** as final being here spelt **a** (exceptions *e*, him, *dhe*, to, *re-*, particle). Even when stressed, **o** is apt to take this obscure sound, as in English "L*o*nd*o*n," "*o*nion." Short **y** occasionally becomes obscure when unstressed, as in *yth-*, *yma·*, but is oftener unchanged.

An inorganic, obscure, unaccented vowel is inserted between two final consonants the latter of which is *l*, *n*, *r* or *w*: e.g., *whethel*, *gwethyn*, *tardar*, *galow*, *hanow*, *garow*, W. *chwedl*, *gwydn*, *taradr*, *galw*, *enw*, *garow*, B. *keal*, *gwevn*, *tarar*, *galv*, *hano*, *garo*. This vowel disappears on adding a syllable that begins with a vowel, as *whethlow*, *gwethna*, *tardra*, *galwans*, *hynwyn*, *garwa* (exception O.C. *ara·deror*), but remains if it begins with a consonant, as in *whe·rowder*, W. *chwerwder*, B. *c'houervder*, etc.

Short unstressed vowels may disappear completely, as in *tewl*, *tenwennow* for *tew·(a)l*, *ten(e)we·nnow*, and especially as second syllable of a trisyllable, usually non-Celtic, that is accented on the first syllable; e.g., *tardar*, *consler*, *marner*, *prysner*, *felshyp*, for *ta·r(a)dar*, *co·ns(e)ler*, *ma·r(y)ner*, *pry·s(o)ner*, *fe·l(ow)shyp*.

Stressed **a** before *ls*, and in some words before *r*, has the sound of long *ō*: e.g., *als*, *cals*, *fals*, *pals*, *gwartha*, *war*, *gwarnya*. In *gwalgh*, *gwaneth*, *gwandra* it has the sound of short *o*.

The sound of ü (often *ue*, *eu* in MSS., also *uy*, *ey*, *e*) is practically that of **ee** in "s*ee*n," or (before *r*) in "s*ee*r." In many words, however, *ü* is alternated with or permanently exchanged for *ē*. It most often represents an Old-Cornish *o* (W. *aw*, B. *eu*), as *lür*, *lüf*, *düf* *scüs* or *skēs*, O. Cor. *lor*, *lof*, *dof*, *scod*, but it may remain uuchanged from O. Cor. *u* (W. and B. *u*), as in *für*, *crük*, *cül*. When made obscure it may be spelt *o* or *e*; e.g., *porres*, *covva*, *marthejyon*. In unstressed final syllables it is usually pronounced, and often spelt, as short *y*; e.g., *gothys*, *marthys*, but in the verbs *bos* and *dos*, final *ü*, *ē*, on loss of stress after an added syllable becomes *a*; e.g., *dufa*, *a-n-jeva*, while stressed *bü*, *bē*, is itself conventionally rhymed with obscure *e*.

Long **ā** (often *ay* in MSS.) is the *aa*, approximating to *ēa*, *aya*, of West-Cornwall dialect "br*aa*ve." With loss of stress it becomes short *a*, as *brās*, comp. *brassa*. In this one word, *brās*, it became long *ō* in Late Cornish, spelt *brawze*, etc. A conventional rhyme of *ās* with *as*, etc., is often found in MSS.

Long **ē** (often *ey* in MSS.) is like *ay* in "d*ay*," unstressed becoming short *e*, or as final, obscure *e*, here spelt *a*; it often alternates, however, with *ȳ* or *ü*, and *ēr* especially, as shown by the later spellings *eer*, *eare*, *ere*, tended to the sound of *ür*, *ȳr*, still heard in "Gear" (*an gēr*), etc. In verse, *ē* often seems shortened to make a conventional rhyme; e.g., *trē* is rhymed with short *a* or obscure *e*.

Long **ȳ** (often *ey* in MSS.) is like *ee* in "s*ee*n," but is apt, in some words especially, to alternate with *ē* (cf. *ü*); with loss of stress it becomes short *y*, or even obscure. In Late Cornish *ȳ* is often found to have taken the sound of *ey*, especially in stressed monosyllables; e.g., *chei*, *nei* for *chȳ*, *nȳ*.

Long **ō** (often *oy* in MSS.) is like *aw* in "s*aw*," unstressed becoming short *o* and as final or before *gh* becoming the close long *o* of "so." As unstressed final, this *o* tends to become obscure, so that in MSS. it is sometimes spelt *a*. In Late Cornish *ō* sometimes becomes *ū*, especially in monosyllables ending in an *s* that represents an older *d* or *t*; e.g., *bōs* (food), *cōs*, *trōs*, *lōs* become *būz*, *cūz*, *trūz*, *lūz*.

Long **ū** is the *oo* of "root," unstressed becoming the *u* of "put," but as stressed final and before *gh*, and also in non-Celtic words having this sound, e.g., in *tū*, *dū*, *a-ūgh*, *ūsya*, it becomes the *ew* of "few."

au is like *aw* in "saw"; this sound is usually represented by *ō*, but *au* is used in a few words; e.g., *laun* (W. *llafn*, B. *laon*), *cauns*, etc.

aw is like *ow* in "now"; with stress it may take the sound of stressed *ow*.

ay (often *ey* in MSS.) is like *ay* in "day"; as a contraction of *a*, *y* in *a'y*, *ha'y*, *na'y*, *may* the sound is the same, but in *may* it inclines to obscure *a*, as shown by variant spellings *ma teth*, *math yllyf*, *ma fo*.

eu, ew, yu, yw are all like *ew* in "dew." In Late Cornish this vowel in a few words became *ow*; e.g., *bownas*, *clowas*, *rowl*, *towlal*, for *bewnans*, *clewes*, *rewl*, *tewlel*.

ey is like the *y* of "fly." In Middle-Cornish spelling *ey* in some words may stand for *ē* or *ay*, in others for *ȳ* or *ŭ*, and in over a score for a sound apparently hovering among these; e.g., *creys*, *cres*, *crys*, etc., are variant spellings used for the same word by the same writer. It is not certain that the sound here given to *ey* was current in identical words in Middle Cornish, for in Late Cornish it often replaced what had definitely been *ȳ*. The benefit of the doubt has occasionally been given, however, to the sound most familiar in place-names; e.g., *meyn*, *dreyn* (C. Voc. *drein*), etc.

ou is like *oo* in "root," and most used in non-Celtic words, the chief Celtic exceptions being *gour*, *mousak*. In Middle Cornish spelling *ou* so often represents the sound of *ow* that it has been accepted as an alternative for this in several words; e.g., *dour*, *dout* for *dowr*, *dowt*.

oy is like *oy* in "boy," but as final the *y* seems to predominate: late spellings of *moy* are *muy*, *mouy* (cf. W. Cor. dialect "booy," "booay" for "boy") and *oy*, *joy*, *moy* are invariably rhymed with *ȳ*, though this is perhaps a forced rhyme (cf. those of *dry*, *fey*; *joy*, *pray*; *bay*, *vy*, P.C. 1993, M.C. 21, B.M. 508) in which the *y* is separated from the diphthong.

ow when stressed is commonly the diphthong *ēū* (ayoo) of dialect "daown"; unstressed, or as pl. in place-names it is like *ow* in "barrow," somewhat approaching *ou*, *ū*; but with artificial end-of-line stress in verse, pl. *-ow*, *-yow* is allowed, by splitting the diphthong, to rhyme with *pow*, *gow*. Stressed *öw* in *golowan*, *lowarth*, *lowen*, *jowal*, *Jowan*, *bowyn*, *towargh*, *voward* is the *ow* of "lower" with a tendency in Late Cornish to *ū*, as shown by the spellings *looar*, *looan*, *Jooan*, Lh. *lūar*, etc., and a further tendency of *owa*, *owe* to contract before *r*, *s*, *th* into *ō* or *ū*, as in *loare* (*lowarth*), *lorn* (*lowarn*), *pour* (*power*), *toor* (*towargh*), *mōs* (*mowes*), etc.

In unified spelling, the device of marking the lengthening of vowels by adding *y* which adds confusion to Middle-Cornish spelling is quite abandoned, neither is any sound represented by doubling vowels; e.g., the *o*'s of *roow* are pronounced as separately as in the variant *rohow* with silent *h* inserted, and the *e*'s of *eef* are equally distinct.

Stem-vowels, if long, will commonly shorten on adding a plural or other ending; e.g., *gēr*, pl. *geryow*, *drōk*, comp. *drocca*, and whether short or long they may change in plural; e.g., *sans*, pl. *syns*, *flōgh*, pl. *flēghes*. Vowels are apt to shorten in both elements of compounds; e.g., *hēn*, *trē* together make *he·ndra*; *mēn*, *hȳr* with pl. ending *-yon* make *menhy·ryon*. In verbs, the long stem-vowel of 2 s. imp. or 3 s. pres.-fut. is similarly shortened elsewhere, and whether long or short, a stem-vowel may alter in sympathy with an added ending of tense and person; e.g., *gās* has infinitive *gasa*, but elsewhere *geseugh*, *gyssys*, etc. Specimen altered forms are usually given in the dictionary with a reference to the heading under which they are explained.

STRESS. The principal stress or tonic accent normally falls on the syllable before the last, but also follows to some extent the meaning; e.g., in compound place-names the accent, here marked by a turned period (·) after its vowel, falls on the descriptive adjective or noun rather than on the general term, as Gunwy·n, Tregea·r (When taken as surnames these were often deliberately Anglicized by shifting the accent, as Keigwin, pr. *ke·gwin*, though as place-name Kegwy·n, Kegwy·dn, La·nyon, as place-name Lani ne, etc.); in compound prepositiosn, adverbs, conjunctions and pronouns the accent similarly falls on the more important element, as *dera·k*, ***bytege·ns***, *warle·rgh*, *aba·n*, *pyna·k*. In loan-words from Middle English the accent remains as in the lending language, ***dyske·vera***, *tre·tury* (the penultimate vowel often fading out in consequence, as *e·mprour* for *e·mperour*, *ra·fsys* for ***ra·vys(h)ȳes***, etc.). Whether the presence in the language of many such loan-words modified the penultimate rule for some Cornish words also is not certain; neither do we know how far misplaced accents were admissable in Cornish verse. If, as usually accepted, the common seven-syllable line of the ***Passion Poem*** and most of the *Ordinalia* regularly matched Milton's line, "These delights if thou canst give," but with a strong beat on "give," then either natural accents were discarded in favour of a level chanting pronunciation, which is very possible, or else by preponderating evidence we must assume that the penultimate accent regularly shifted back from the first syllable of a two-syllabled suffix. It did so naturally in the borrowed *-ury* of *tre·tury*, ***fa·lsury***, etc., and may have done so regularly in ***-adow***, ***-ethes***, ***-ȳeth***, ***-yjy***, *-ynsy*. In words with compound suffixes a verse-scansion majority would support the unorthodox ***cow·sesow***, *ske·ntoleth*, ***gene·sygeth***, *pe·ghosow*, *mow·ysy*, *gla·nythter*, *u·thekter*, ***me·ppygow***, *dyalwhe·dhygow*, also, and ***cara·dewder***, *cara·dowyon*, *tymmy·nygow*, ***fleghe·sygow***, together with *a·rlydhy*, *a·nkensy*, *ca·rrygy*, *mou·segy* and other such words ending in ***y***, and usually *a·lwhedhow*, *da·rrajow*, *dew·olow*, *go·lewder*, *my·gylder*, ***yow·ynkneth***, ***yow·ynksys***, with sometimes even ***otho·mogyon***, *bogho·sogyon*, *ty·oryon*, ***pegha·dores***. *O·nester*, *go·kyneth* may be explained by their Middle-English origin, and others perhaps by the needs of verse, but some of these unexpected accents are represented even in spelling by an obscuration of an unstressed vowel and must at least have been recognized variants; e.g., we find both *maro·gyon* and *ma·rregyon*; ***skye·ntoleth*** and *ske·nteleth*, ***ske·ntuleth***; ***ponvo·tter*** and *po·nveter*; *darra·jow* and ***de·rggawe***; *dewo·low* and *jaw·low*; ***tewo·lgow*** and ***tew·lgow***.

Nothing, however, is known with certainty on this point, and though one finds in verse, e.g., forty times ***-adow*** to four times *-a·dow*, this is less than definite proof of the normal prose accent. Unfortunately this was not realized in time to prevent several such apparently unorthodox accents from being printed in the earlier pages of the dictionary as if established (see **corrigenda**). Verified exceptional stresses are of course found in all verbs with infinitive-ending *-hē*, and in some with prefix *om-*, as well as in the compounds noted above. Whether a common prefix, as ***an-***, *dy-*, *ke-*, *kes-*, ***go-***, ***gorth-***, etc.., ever lost the accent in words of two syllables is uncertain. Dialect survivals and place-names give *gorgē* as "gu·rgy" and *gobans* as "Go·bbens," but ***kedryn*** as "cudri·dn" and *godram* as "godra·bm." Verse-scansion is here impartial and it may be that the accent in some words was variable; e.g., that one said *dyne·rth* as well as *dy·nerth* (either pronunciation is at some times or places favoured in W. *dinerth*, B. *dinerz*, the latter seeming more ancient), apart from proved exceptions, however, the safer and simpler plan for those who use unified Cornish will be to assume a general penultimate accent.

Abbreviations and Signs

abst. abstract noun
abst. pl. plural used as abstract singular
adj. adjective
adv. adverb
art. article
aux. auxiliary
B. Breton
B.M. *Bewnans Meryasek*
card. num. cardinal numeral
cf. compare
col. collective (sing. used of many together)
colloq. colloquial
comp. comparative
conj. conjunction
C. Voc. (Voc. Cor.) *Old-Cornish Vocabulary*
C.W. (Cr. or G.B.) *Creation of the World*
D. Dialect Survival
d. dual (used of two alike)
D.E. Dialect English
def. defective
dem. demonstrative
dim. diminutive
E. English
E. Cor. East Cornwall

E.D.Dic. *English Dialect Dictionary*
e.g. for example
equat. equative
exclam. exclamative
f. feminine
Fr. French
fut. future tense
Gw. Gwavas MSS. (Brit. Mus. and others)
Gael. Scottish Gaelic
imp. imperative
impf. imperfect tense
inf. infinitive or verbal noun
intens. intensive
interj. interjection
interr. interrogative
Ir. Irish
irreg. irregular
Late Late or "Modern" Cornish
Lh. Lhuyd, *Archaeologia Britannica* and MSS.
lit. literally
m. masculine noun
M.B. Middle Breton
M.C.(P.) *Passion Poem* ("*Mount Calvary*")
M. Cor. Middle Cornish
M.E. Middle English
Med. Lat. Mediaeval Latin
neg. negative
O.B. Old Breton
O. Cor. Old Cornish
O.E. Old English (Anglo-Saxon)
O. Fr. Old French
O.M.(O.) *Origo Mundi*
Ord. (A.C.D.) *Ordinalia* in *Ancient Cornish Drama*
ord. num. ordinal numeral
P. Pryce, *Archaeologia Cornu-Britannica*
P.C.(D.) *Passio Christi*
perf. perfect tense
pl. plural
plupf. pluperfect tense
poss. possessive
p. pt. past participle
pr. pronunciation
pres. present tense
pret. preterite tense
priv. privative
pron. pronoun
q.v. which see
rel. relative
R.D. (R.) *Resurrectio Domini*
s. singular
subj. subjunctive (when alone pres.-fut.)
superl. superlative
s.v. under the word
V. Vannes Breton
var. variant
vb. verb
W. Welsh
W. Cor. West Cornwall
* word adapted
† word (usually respelt) from Old Cornish
2, 3, 4, 5 after words indicate mutations they cause
· turned period after vowel to indicate stress other than on penultimate syllable
·· dots over vowel other than ü to indicate its separate pronunciation

N.B. For convenience the double reference-letters used by Williams for Cornish texts have been kept, though M.C. and C.W. refer here to the Stokes editions, and not to those of Davies Gilbert. The single reference-letters also in use are added in brackets. The references Lh., Gw. and P. cover the collected writings of many others whose names are not usually added. The reference D. covers MS. collections as well as printed glossaries of Cornish Dialect.

A NEW CORNISH-ENGLISH DICTIONARY

Gerlyver Noweth Kernewek Ha Sawsnek

A NEW CORNISH-ENGLISH DICTIONARY

-a, *suffixed pron.*, I, me; also used for **-e.**

a^{2}, *prep.*, of, by, from, on, concerning: with *clewes, scryfa*, etc., about; with *prena, gwertha*, for; with *ry cumyas, grath, danvon, sconya, erghy, bos prys, cusulya* before inf., to; of parts of body, in; combines with preps, see APPENDIX V., and causes contraction in following *an, un* and possessive prons., as *a'n, a'm, a'gas*, etc.

A, a^{2} *interj.*, O, oh, ah: mutation affects common nouns and their prefixed adjs. or nums., *A vester*, (O)master (vocative), *A bur-debel-venen*, O most wicked woman, *A dheu-atla*, O two rascals. Proper names are not usually affected in spelling, though they may always be so in pronunciation.

a-^{2} *rel. and interr. verbal particle*: for uses see APPENDIX VII.

a^{4}, *conj.*, if: used directly before subjunctive and of what is unlikely or impossible; prons. are infixed, as *a's-dysken*, if I were to take it off, R.D. 1941; see **mar(s).**

ā, see **mōs**, APPENDIX VIII.

a', see **an.**

abajes, *f.*, *pl.* **-ow**, abbess (W., B.).

aba'n^{2}, *conj.*, *adv.*, since: for uses see **pan.**

a-barth, aba'rth, aba'r' (*aberth*), *prep.*, beside, in the name of, for the sake of, on the part, side, or behalf of: *a. a-woles*, down below, *a. a-wartha*, up above; *a. an Tas*, in the name of the Father; *kerens a. tas, mam*, paternal, maternal, relatives; *a. -dhon* (*barthone*, Paul Register), bastard; see **parth.**

†abas (C. Voc. *abat*), m., pls. **-ow, ebes,** abbot, *abbod, faeder* Aelfric.

a'batty, *m.*, *pl.* **-ow**, abbey (W., B.).

a'battȳr, *m.*, *pl.* **-ryow**, abbey-land (W.).

abel, *adj.*, able, B.M. 2495 (E.).

a-bell, *adv.*, afar, far off: see **pell.**

†aber, *m.*, *pl.* **-ow**, confluence, meeting of waters, mouth of river, C. Voc., *wael* Aelfric.

***aberth,** *m*,. *pl.* **-ow**, sacrifice (W., B.): replaced by *sacryfys.*

a-berth-yn, abe'rth-yn, a b e'r' - y n, 'berth-yn (Late *abera, bera*), *prep.*, in, within: combines with prons. as **yn,** APPENDIX V.

a-berveth (*a*^{2}, *perfeth*), *adv.*, in, inside; **a.-yn,** *prep.*, within, inside: see **perveth.**

a-blē, a-bȳla, 'bȳla (*a*^{2}, *py, le*), *adv.*, whence, from what place: unlike **plē(th),** which always takes the *th* of the indefinite particle *y(th)-* before vowels in *bos* and *mos*, this is followed by the implied relative particle *a-* before vowels in *bos* (and presumably *mos*), e.g., *a-ble ota-jy*, M.C. 44, *a-byla osa*, P.C. 2179, *'byla es*, C.W. 552; *a by le yu*, from what place is it, is likely to be the origin of this, thus accounting for the following implied *a-*, that, before the vb.; see **plē(th), pȳla.**

abostol (C. Voc., Aelfric *apostol*), *m.*, *pl.* **abe'stely,** *col.* **abe'steleth,** apostle: col. is used chiefly in addressing assemblies.

abostolek, adj., apostolic.

†abrans, *m.*, *pl.* **-ow, -njow,** *d.* **deuabrans,** eyebrow, C. Voc., *ofer bruwa* Aelfric.

a-brȳs, *adv.*, in (good)time, early, timely: *a vrys*, O.M. 1229 must be intended for this, "I had as lief die betimes, before an ill death comes," see **prȳs.**

a-bȳla, see **a-blē.**

achēson, chēson, *m.*, *pl.* **-ys,** occasion, cause, reason, motive for action, charge against person (M.E. *achesoun, chesoun*): *hep guthyl namoy c.*, without showing any further reason, R.D. 460.

aco'nt, *m.*, *pl.* **-ys,** account (M.E.).

acontya, *vb.*, to count, reckon, esteeem (M.E.).

acō'rd, *m.*, agreement, harmony, accord (M.E.).

acōrdya, *vb.*, to agree, accord (M.E.): *bos acordys orth*, to be in agreement with, approved by, B.M. 494.

acūsya, *vb.*, to accuse (M.E.).

a-dal (*dalh*, Gw.), *prep.*, opposite, facing, fronting: see **tāl.**

***a'damant,** *m.*, *pl.* **-ans, -tys,** diamond (M.E.).

adar, ader, ater, *prep.*, *conj.*, *adv.*, without, away from, out of, outside, except: *a.medhelhés bras ough*, except for your being greatly weakened, B.M. 4311; *ater*, B.M., 3631, seems only a variant spelling; "atter," outside, is traditional Cor.; Galladder, *gwel ader*, field-name.

†aden, *f.*, *pl.* **edyn**, leaf of a book, *leaf* Aelfric: lit. "wing," W. *adain*.

a-denewan, *adv.*, aside, sideways, O.M. 2063.

a-dermyn, *adv.*, in time, punctually: see **termyn**.

a-dhan², *prep.*, from under, from beneath: combines with prons. as **yn**, APPENDIX V.; see **dan**.

a-dhe-drō·, *adv.*, about: see **trō**.

a-dhelergh, **adhelergh**, *adv.*, behind, aft, behindhand, in arrear, B.M. 3333: see **delergh**.

a-dhera·k(g), **adhera·k(g)**, *prep.* before, in the presence of, in front of: combines with prons. as **rak(g)**, APPENDIX V.; see **derak(g)**.

a-dhesempys, *adv.*, suddenly, immediately: see **desempys**.

a-dhevȳ·s, *adj.*, exact, just, right, elegant, complete: see **devȳs** (M.E.).

a-dhewha·ns (*a thyhons* O.M. 2810), *adv.*, immediately: see **dewhans**.

***adhüly**, *vb.*, to adore (W., B.): replaced by **gordhya**.

adhves, see **athves**.

a-dhyfüna, *adv.*, awake, when not sleeping, B.M. 1785 (*a thyuvne*): see **dyfüna**.

a-dhy(gh)ow, **a-dhy(gh)owbarth**, *adv.*, on the right hand: see **dy(gh)ow, parth**.

a-dhystough, *adv.*, immediately: see **dystough**.

a-dhywa·r², *prep.*, from on, from over: combined with prons. as **war²**, APPENDIX V.; see **dywar²**.

a-dhywo·rth, (Late *dhort*, *dhurt*, *adhor*), *prep.*, from, away from, (after *bos rewardyes*) by: combines with prons. as **(w)orth**, APPENDIX V.; see **dyworth**.

adla, see **atla**.

†adlen, see **ēthlen**.

a-drē (also, by rhymes, *a-dra·*), *adv.*, from home, away: see **tre**.

a-dre-drō·, **a-der-drō·**, *adv.*, all around, round about: see **trō**.

a-drēs, *adv.*, from beyond, from over, R.D 1477: see **drēs**.

a-drō, **adrō·**, (Late corruption *ter*, Lh.), *adv.*, around, concerning, on, about, upon a part of the body (Lh. of clothing); *adj.*, in *gwyns a.*, whirlwind: *a -dhe²*, about, around, *dhe wonys a.-dhodho*, to work about it, O.M. 1000; *evyn pup-oll a.*, let's all drink round, O.M. 2627; see **tro**.

a-drōs, *adv.*, afoot, Lh.: see **trōs**.

a-drüs, **adrüs**, *adv.*, across, athwart, contrarily: *cows a.*, talk beside the point; *a. hag a-hes*, far and wide, to the greatest extent; *a.-dhe²*, across, athwart; *a.-kēn*, thwartwise; see **trüs**.

a-dryf, **adryf.**, **adref.**, *adv.*, *prep.*, behind: *a. tus*, clandestinely; *a. ow chy*, behind my house, but takes *dhe* before prons. other than possessive, *a. dhodho*, behind him, etc.

af-, see **an-**, APPENDIX II.

afla·n, **aflaneth**, **avla·n -eth**, *adj.*, unclean (W.).

†aflavar, **avlavar** (C. Voc. and *omlanar*, M.C. 25, miswritten for this), *adj.*, speechless, dumb, mute; *m.*, *pl.*, **-yon**, dumb person.

aflythys (*avlethis*, C.W. 1152), *adj.*, hardened, not of tender age, obdurate (P.C. 451); *m.*, *pl.* **-yjyon** (O.M. 2745), ruffian, callous person: see ***lȳth**.

afȳa, *vb.*, to affirm: *del afyas*, as he affirmed (M.S. *dalafias*), P.C. 1845 (M.E. *affy*).

afydhya, *vb.*, to assure, confirm, vouch for: *my a-n-afyth dhyso-jy*, I affirm it to thee, O.M. 1788.

afȳna, *vb.* to adorn, make fine (M.E. *affine*).

afȳna (*avyna*), *adv.*, completely, entirely, from end to end, O.M. 1758, M.C. 135 (M.E. *afyne*).

aga, *poss. pron.*, their; contracts to **'ga** after *a*, *na*, *ha*, *y'*.: a noun that names a relative, a part of the body, or a thing possessed, of which no-one can have more than one, is usually made sing. after *aga*, *agan*, *agas*, a following pron. agreeing, e.g., *a'gan enef pys ma n-jeffo salvasyon* pray for our *souls* that *they* may have salvation, B.M. 1248; *aga*, etc., can however be followed by dual, and sometimes by pl., even in nouns of the sort usually made sing., e.g., *agan corfow*, (both of) our bodies; *a. naw*, the nine of them, etc.

agan, *poss. pron.*, our; contracts rarely to **'an**, commonly to **'gan** after *a*, *na*, *ha*, *y'*, and (late) to **'n** after all vowels: see **aga**.

-agan-, **-'gan-**, *infixed pron.*, us.

agas, *poss. pron.*, your; contracts to **'gas** after *a na*, *ha*, *y'* and (late) to **'s** after all vowels: *a. try*, the three of you; see **aga**.

-agas-, **-'gas-**, *infixed pron.*, you.

agen, *f.*, the stomach of an animal, especially of a pig (Borlase, cf. D. "meagan," "mea," pig's stomach).

agensow, *adv.*, lately, just now, recently, a short time ago: see **degensewa, degensow, kensow.**

age·s, es, *conj.*, than: combines with prons. as **yn**, Appendix V., *s* being doubled in 3rd person.

†**agh** (C. Voc. *ach*), *f.*, *pl.* **-ow**, progeny, race, offspring, *bearn* Aelfric; pl. genealogy, pedigree (Lh., W.).

agh, *interj.*, fie! ah! (W., B., D.).

agha, *m.*, dread, awe (M.E. *aghe*): see **dyagha** and cf. **lagha.**

a-glēth, *adv.*, on the left hand, M.C. 236: *a. dhe*², on the left of; see **clēth.**

agolen, *f.*, *pl.* **-now**, whetstone, hone (Lh.).

ago·r, *m.*, opening; *adj.*, open (W., B.).

ago·r, see **egery**.

ago-mar(gh)ogyon, *f.*, knight-service, feudal tenure of lands: *agomarocyon*, Black Book of Merthen; *ago'* is apparently for **agweth*, W. *agwedd*, condition.

a-gyl, *adv.*, back, in return, *a gul*, P.C. 1562: see **kyl.**

ahanan, *adv.*, away, from here, hence: originally " away from us "; *dun a.*, let 's be off, let us go away; see **a**, *prep.*

aha·s, *adj.*, keen, severe, cruel, dreadful: originally " odious," as W. *achas.*

a-hēs (Late *a heaze*), *adv.*, at full length, from end to end, wholly, altogether, at last: see **hēs.**

aj., aja (*age*), *m. pl.* **-jys**, age: corrected to one syllable, but first written as two, P.C. 1184 (E.).

ajy, see **aswy.**

a-jȳ (*achy* B.M.), *adv.*, in: *a. dhe*², within, inside (of time) in less than; see **chȳ.**

alabauster, *m.*, alabaster, P.C. 3136 (M.E.)

†**alargh** (C. Voc. *elerhc*), *m.*, *pls.* **elergh, elerghy**, swan, *ylfette* Aelfric: replaced by **swan.**

Alban, *f.*, Scotland (Lh.).

Albanek, *adj.*, Scotch, Scottish.

alemma (for *a'n le-ma*, Late *alebma*), *adv.*, from here, from now, away, hence: *a.-rak*, from now on, henceforward; *a. bys gorfen bys*, from now on to the world's end; colloq. *mos 'lemma*, to go hence.

alenna, alena (for *a'n le-na*, Late *aledna*), *adv.*, from there, from then, away, thence: *a.-rak*, thenceforward; in place-names *a.* has sometimes become *aluna* and taken the adjectival meaning "distant," as in Penaluna, Fente'luna; *alemma* similarly seems to mean " near " in " Halabalebba," *hal a-barth alemma.*

a-lēs (Late *'leaze*), *adv.*, apart, abroad, widely.

***Alman**, *m.*, *f.* **-es**, *pl.* **-ow**, German.

Almayn, *f.*, Germany, R.D. 2148.

Almaynek, *adj.*, German; *m.*, German language.

alōes, *m. pl.*, aloes, P.C. 3198 (3 syllables).

alowa, *vb.*, to allow, B.M. 2259 (M.E.).

als (pr. *ōls*), *f.*, *pl.* **-yow**, cliff, shore, strand, C. Voc., *saestrand* Aelfric, Lh.: place and personal names Owles, Olds.

***alsen**, *f.*, *pl.* **-now**, razor (W., B.).

alter (C. Voc. *altor*), *f.*, *pl.* **-yow**, altar, O.M.: *weofod*, Aelfric.

†**altrewan** (C. Voc. *altruan*), *f.*, *pl.* **-neth**, stepmother.

***altrow** (C. Voc. *altrou*), *m.*, *pl.* **-on**, stepfather.

a·lüsen (*alusyon*, *-yen*, B.M.), *f.*, *pl.*, **-ow** (*alesonow* B.M. 1829), alms, charity.

alü·senjy, *m.*, *pl*, **-ow**, almshouse (W., B.)

alü·senor, *m.*, *pl.* **-yon**, almoner (W., B.).

alwhedha (*luhwedha* Lh.), *vb.*, to lock, turn a key on.

alwhedhor, *m.*, *pl.* **-yon**, treasurer (W., B.).

alwheth (*alweth*, C. Voc. *alwed*), *m.*, *pl.* **a·lwhedhow, -whe·ow**, key.

a·lyon (*allyon*), *m.*, *pl.* **-s**, alien (M.E.).

am, *poss. pron.*, my: used after prep. or conj. ending with cons., and as *'m* after vowel; *y'm*, in my, *a'm*, of my, are often *om* in MSS.

am (Late *ab(e)m*), *m.*, *pl.* **-mow**, kiss.

amal, *m.* or *f.*, *pl.* **e·melow** (*emblow*), edge, side, W. *ymyl*: in place-names followed by *gwyn, mur* as masc., *wyn, vur, gres* as fem., sing. Amble, pl., Embla.

amanyn (C. Voc. *amenen, emenin*, Lh. *manyn*), *m.*, butter (A. Boorde).

amanynna, *vb.*, to butter (W., B.).

a·mary, *m.*, *pl.* **-s**, almonry, ambry, Pryce M.S.

amaya, *vb.*, to dismay, distract: p. pt. *amays* (*ameys*, 2 syllables,) distraught, O.M. 193, B.M. 2158. (M.E.).

ambos, *m.*, *pl.* **-ow**, contract, agreement, promise: *yn-dan a. yth-esos*, thou art under an indenture, P.C. 2259.

ambosa, *vb.*, to promise, make a contract.

amendya (Late *'mendya*), *vb.*, to amend, make amends, set right, atone, improve, correct, reform, be of better behaviour, abandon bad ways (M.E.).

amendys, *m. pl.*, amends, atonement, O.M. 2259 (M.E.).

***amēthy**, *vb.*, to till, farm (W.,V.).

amma, *vb.*, to kiss : p. pt. *ymmys* ; 2 s. subj., 3 s. impf. ind., *ymmy* ; usually *a. dhe*[2], but exceptionally without *dhe*, M.C. 231.

amontya (*amowntya*). *vb.*, to count, compute, reckon, M.C. ; (with neg.) avail, be of use, amount to anything, C.W. (M.E.)

†**amser** (C. Voc., miswritten *anser*), *f.*, *pl.* **-ow**, time : replaced by **termyn**, **prȳs**.

amūk, *m.*, defence, protection, prevention (M.W., M.B) : Cos-abmeck, place-name.

amüvya, *vb.*, to perturb, agitate, startle, cause emotion in, B.M. 1311 (M.E. *ameve*) : 3 s. pres.-fut. *amuf.*

***a·myral**, *m.*, *pl.* **s**, admiral (M.E.).

an (C. Voc. *en*, occasionally also in M. Cor.), *art.*, the ; after conj., or prep. ending in vowel, **'n**: *an*[2] before f. sing. nouns and m. pl. nouns denoting persons ; *a'n*, from the, also of one, O.M. 79, from one, B.M. 1267 ; in MSS. occasionally written *a* before consonants, perhaps as a contraction only.

'an, contraction of **agan.** q.v.

an-, see Appendix II.

†**anaf**, *m.*, *pl.* **-avas**, slow-worm, C Voc.

anal, *f.*, breath, B.M. 4093, Lh..

analy, -a, *vb.*, to breathe (W.B.).

anawel, see **enawel.**

†**ancar**, *m.*, *pl.* **-coryon**, anchorite, recluse, C. Voc., *ancra* Aelfric.

†**ancar**, *m.*, *pl.* **-corow**, anchor, C. Voc. : *drehevel, tewlel, a.*, to cast, raise, anchor ; *bos, powes, war a.*, to lie at anchor.

a·ncarjy, *m.*, ermitage (W.).

a·ncarva, *f.*, anchorage (W.).

anclathva, etc., see **enclathva**, etc.

ancō·f, *m.*, forgetfulness, oblivion (W., B.).

a·ncombra, *vb.*, to bother, hamper, impede, embarras, distract, perplex, puzzle, be too much for, encumber, M.C., B.M. (M.E., *encombre*) : 3 s. pres. fut. *ancomber* : p. pt. *-brys.*

a·ncombrynsy, *m.*, botheration, nuisance, embarrasment, puzzlement, perplexity, encumbrance (O.M. 2517, 2542 (M.E. *encombraunce*).

ancorya, *vb.* to anchor (W., B.).

ancoth (*unc(h)ut* C. Voc., *uncouth* Pryce, *onketh* Kerew), *adj.*, unknown, strange, outlandish, uncouth : though this is O.E. *uncuth*, Aelfric has "advena, *utan cuman*" ; see **cothman.**

ancothfos, *m.*, unknown thing, uncouthness, solecism, impropriety, R.D. 2548 (O.E. *uncuth* and *bos*, but assimilated to *an-*, *gothvos*).

ancow (C. Voc. *ancou*), *m.*, death.

†**ancredor mor** (C. Voc. *ancredwur mor*), *m.*, *pl.* **-oryon mor**, viking, pirate, *wicing, flotman* Aelfric : "sea.pagan" seems a likely meaning ; see **crēs.**

ancrēs, *m.*, disquiet, distress, R.D. 208.

androw· (for *an derow·*), *m.*, late afternoon or early evening, time from 3 o'clock to sunset : *dhe a. nans-o marow*, P.C. 3121, He was already dead at 3 o'clock ; the literal meaning is "the beginning (of night)" *an derow(nos)*, W. *dechreu(nos)*, B. *enderv, derou(noz)*, V. *anderù, d'anderù(noz).*

androwyth, *m.*, (late) afternoon-time ; *adv.*, this afternoon, (B).

anē·s (*annes, anneys*), *adj.*, ill at ease, troubled, wearied, O.M. 700, B.M. 2904 ; **m.*, uneasiness (M.B.).

aneth, *m.*, *pl.* **-ow**, marvel, adventure, strange or incredible thing, romance, fable, R.D. 1302, 1512 ; *yn Polsethow y-whylyr anethow*, in the Pool of Arrows shall be seen wonders, prophecy in Glasney Cartulary ; lit. hard to attain or believe, cf. W. *anoeth.*

†**anfü·r**, *adj.*, unwise, imprudent, C. Voc. : *unsnoter* Aelfric.

anfü·s, *f.*, ill-luck, unhappiness, misfortune, misery.

a·nfüsy, -üjy, *m.*, disaster, calamity, undoing, malignity.

anfüsyk, -üjyk, *adj.*, unfortunate, unhappy; *m.*, *pl.* **-ygyon**, unlucky one, wretch.

anger, *m.*, anguish, trouble, vexation (M.E. *angre*).

angra, *vb.*, to anger, annoy, vex, become angry (E.) : p. pt. *engrys* (Gw. **engrez**).

angus, *m.*, anguish (M.E. *anguys*).

anhedhek, *adj.*, easeless, diseased ; *adv.*, without respite, incessantly, B.M. 2630 : see **hedhy.**

anhü·n, *m.*, insomnia (W., B.).

anken, *m.*, *pl.* **-yow**, misery, grief, trouble, distress, pain.

ankenek, *m.*, penance, expiation, means of showing contrition, O.M. 2256.

ankensy, a·nkensy (*-ynsy*), *adj.*, grievous, dolorous, P.C. 1360, M.C. 184.
ankenya, *vb.*, to inflict grief or pain (B.).
ankevy (Late *nakevy*), *vb.*, to forget: 3. s. pret. *ancovas*; see **cōf.**
anla·n, -yth, var. of **aflan, -yth** (W.).
annedhy, *vb.*, to inhabit, house, provide with lodging: p. pt. *annedhys*, housed, living in a house, O.M. 1722; cf. **tryga, regnya.**
***anner,** *f.*, *pl.* **-as,** heifer (W., B.): replaced by **lejek** or **denewes.**
anneth, *f.*, *pl.* **-edhow,** dwelling, habitation, P.C. 705.
***annown,** *m.*, the shades, underworld, abode of the dead (W.,B.).
annȳa, nȳa (Late *nea*), *vb.*, to tire, weary, vex, bother, worry, trouble, annoy (M.E. *anuye, nye*): *ny-th annyaf*, I will not trouble thee, C.W. 1215; *na-whyla agan nya*, seek not to trouble us, C.W. 1277.
an pyth, *rel. pron.*, that which, what, lit. the thing: *an* may be dropped, e.g., *ny won' pyth 'wraf*, I know not what I shall do, R.D. 1592.
ansa·ns, *adj.*, unholy, profane (W.).
ansa·nsoleth, *m.*, impiety, profanity (W.).
a·ntecrȳst, *m.*, antichrist, R.D. 224 (M.E.).
antel (*antell*), *f.*, snaring, inveiglement, treachery, temptation, M.C. 19, lit. poise, tension, balance: Carn Antel, rock-name.
antel, *vb.*, to set a trap, string a bow, stretch, poise ready to fall or spring off (W.,B.).
***a·ntyquary,** *m.*, *pl.* **-ow,** antiquary (Lh.,E.).
antȳthy, *adj.*, incapable, inert, without normal powers or faculties, B.M. 3052: see **tȳthy.**
anva·b, *adj.*, childless (W.,B.).
†**anvabeth** (C. Voc. *anvabat*), *m.*, childlessness, sterility, *unwaestmbaernis* Aelfric: see **map.**
†**anv·ēn** (C. Voc. *anuein*), *adj.*, weak, *unstrang* Aelfric: see **mēn,** *adj.*
anvla·s, *m.*, tastelessness, insipidity (W.).
anvō·th, *m.*, unwillingness, reluctance: *a'y a.*, against his will, M.C. 175; see **bōth.**
anvrȳ·, *m.*, disrespect, dishonour (W.).
anwa·n, *f.*, *pl.* **-wonow,** anvil, Lh.
anwesy, *vb.*, to take cold (W.,B.).
anwesek, *adj.*, chilly, apt to take cold (W.B.).
anwhē·k, *adj.*, harsh, ungentle, rough, unpleasant, unkind.
anwhekter, *m.*, roughness, unkindness.
anwos (*anwys* B.M., *annez* Lh.), *m.*, chill, cold, feeling of chilliness.
anwy·w, *adj.*, unfit, unworthy (W.): see **gwyw.**
†**anya·gh** (C. Voc. *aniach*), *adj.*, unwell, infirm, *untrum* Aelfric.
a-ogas, *prep.*, near at hand, close by.
aparell, *m.*, equipment, gear, apparel, C.W. 1036 (M.E. *aparaile*): *a. a dhyllas*, an outfit of clothing.
apern (*apparn* Lh.), *m.*, *pl.* **-pronyow** (*aprodniow* Kerew), apron (Late, E.).
aper·t, *adj.*, open, obvious, manifest; *adv.*, openly, obviously, clearly (M.E.).
apērya, *vb.*, to impair, harm: *y a. ny-vynnys*, I had no wish to do it harm, B.M. 3793 (M.E. *apeiren, enpeiren*).
a-poynt, *adj.*, punctual; *adv.*, promptly (Fr.): *re a.*, over-promptly, with too much alacrity, P.C. 3032.
appa, *m.*, *pl.* **-pys,** ape, (E.); " monkey," apish person (D.).
appe·n (*a'n pen*), *prep.*, at the end of, B.M. 2882.
apposya, *vb.*, to confront, examine, test by questions (M.E. *appose*): *mar myn ow dyscans servya, genough pan ven apposyes*, if my learning will suffice when I am examined by you, B.M. 525.
appoyntya (*'poyntya*, C.W.), *vb.*, to appoint (M.E.).
aquytya (*aquyttya*), *vb.*, to requite, repay, make return to, acquit, release from further obligation (M.E. *aquyte*).
aquytyans, *m.*, requital, receipt.
ār, *m.*, ploughed land, tilth (W.).
***ār,** *f.*, *pl.* **-ow,** slaughter, battle (W.,O.B.).
ara, *adj.*, slow, Borlase: probably from W. *araf.*
***arva,** *f.*, carnage, battle (W.,O.B.).
A.raby, *f.*, Arabia.
a·radar, see **ardar.**
a·radow, *adj.*, arable (W.).
ara·deror (C. Voc. *araderuur*), *m.*, *pl.* **-yon,** ploughman, *yrdhlingc* Aelfric.
a·rak(g), ara·k(g), *adv.*, *prep.*, before, in the presence of, in front: combines with prons. as **rak(g),** Appendix V.
aral, *adj.*, *pron.*, *pl.* **erel,** other, another: **re erel,** others; used in either sing. or pl. after dual.
aras, *vb.*, to plough (Lh., Gw.).

ara·y, *m.*, order, array, O.M., B.M. (M.E.).
araya, *vb.*, to arrange, set in order, array, B.M. 4474 (M.E.).
archer, *m.*, *pl.* **-s**, archer, B.M., C.W. (M.E.).
arda·k, *m.*, demur, stop, delay : *hep a.*, forthwith, P.C. 1870, cf. W. *atreg.*
ardar, for **a·radar** (C. Voc. *aradar*), *m.*, *pl.* **erder**, **e·reder**, plough, *sulh* Aelfric.
***ardhorn**, *m.*, wrist (W., B.) : replaced by **conna brēgh.**
aredy, see **yredy.**
areth, *f.*, *pl.* **-yow**, declamation, oration, loud or violent speech, P.C. 954.
arethva, *f.*, rostrum, platform (W.).
arethya, *vb.*, to make a speech, harangue, hold forth (W., V.).
arethyor, *m.*, *pl.* **-oryon**, orator, public speaker (W.).
arf, *f.*, *pl.* **arvow**, arm, weapon : *tus arvow*, men-at-arms ; *ens (tennens) pup dh'y arvow*, to arms !
arfeth, *m.*, *pl.* **-edhow**, hire, wages, B.M. 3201 (*arveth*) ; *vb.*, to hire, employ, use the services of, keep in ones service, P.C. 2262.
argel, *f.*, *pl.* **-ow**, sequestered place, retreat : place-names, Argel Wun, Du, Wyn.
argh, *f.*, *pls.*, **-ow**, **erghy**, coffer, chest, strong-box, hutch: *arghow*, treasury; *a.ys*, corn-bin (B.).
argh, see **erghy.**
argh-, see Appendix II.
a·r(gh)adow (*arhadow*, *aradow*), *m.*, command, bidding, commandment.
ar(gh)ans (*arhans*, *arans*), *m.*, silver ; *col.*, money (followed by pl. pron.) : ***a.** *bew*, quicksilver.
ar(gh)anser, **-jer**, *m.*, *pl.* **-oryon**, money-changer (W.).
arghdȳagon, **arghȳagon**, *m.*, *pl.* **-as**, archdeacon (W., B.).
†arghēl (C. Voc. *archail*), *m.*, *pl.* **-eleth** (*arthelath*, C.W. 61), archangel, *heahengel* Aelfric.
†arghenas (C. Voc. *orchinat*), *m.*, footwear, shoes, *gescy* Aelfric.
†arghepscop (C. Voc. *archescop*), *m.*, *pl.* **-obow**, archbishop, *ercebisceop* Aelfric.
arghoferyas, *m.*, *pl.* **-ysy**, chief-priest (W.).
***argoll**, *m.*, danger of loss, perdition (W., B.).
***argovrow**, *m.*, *pl.* **-on**, dowry (W., B.).
a·rgūment, *m.*, argument, reasoning, P.C. 1661 (M.E.).
argya, *vb.*, to argue (M.E.).

arlodhes, **arludhes** (C. Voc. *arludes*), *f.*, *pl.* **-ow**, lady, mistress, *hlaefdige* Aelfric.
arlo·dheseth, *m.*, ladyship (W.).
a·rlottes (*arluth*, *-sys*), *m.*, lordship, jurisdiction, P.C. 1604.
arluth (*arloth*, C. Voc. *arluit*), *m.*, *pl.* **arlydhy**, lord, master, sir, *hlaford* Aelfric.
aro·nd (*a wronnd*, O.M. 1083), *prep.*, around, on all sides (M.E.).
†āros (C. Voc. *airos*), *m.*, *pl.* **-yow**, poop of ship, *steorsetl* Aelfric.
art, *m.*, *pl.*, **-ys**, art (M.E.) : *tebel a.*, black magic, B.M. 2364.
arta, *adv.*, again, once more, on a future occasion: *hag a. pertheugh cof gwell pand' wrellen dheugh comondya*, and another time remember better what I bid you. B.M. 1064.
arth, **ār'**, *m.*, high place : in place-names Trenarth, Ayr.
arva, *vb.*, to arm : p. pt. *ervys (yrvys).*
***arval**, *m.*, grist, toll of flour (W., B.).
arvek, *adj.*, armed ; *m.*, *pl.* **-vogyon**, armed man (W.).
arveth, see **arfeth.**
arvēth (*ar*, *bedha*), *vb.*, to affront, insult, be audacious to, attack, adventure against, R.D. 2407 : 3 s. pret. *arvedhas* ; a special form without inf. ending, see **bedha.**
arvjy, *m.*, *pl.* **-ow**, arsenal (W.).
arvor, *m.*, coastland (W.,B.).
arvorek, *adj.*, of the coast (B.).
***arwedha**, *vb.*, to signal, signify, make a sign (W.,B.).
***arwedhek**, *adj.*, symbolic, emblematic (W.,B.).
***arwedhynsy**, *m.*, token (B.).
***arweth**, *f.*, *pl.* **-edhyow**, sign, symptom, symbol, badge, emblem, banner (W.,B.).
arȳa, **'rȳa** (for *re² Varya*), *interj. of surprise*, by Mary ! : variants, *rya reva! rya rya ! rya, sos !* Lh. (D "areea") ; see **sōs.**
aryēn, *m.*, hoar frost (W.,B.).
as-, see Appendix II.
ascallek, *f.*, thistle-bed, thistly ground.
ascallen (C. Voc. *askellen*), *f.*, *col.* **ascal**, thistle : *a.mogh*, sow-thistle (W.) ; *a. dybry*, artichoke (B.).
ascendya (*assendya*), *vb.*, to ascend (M.E.) : *y rascen thys*, R.D. 175, seems miscopied for *yn-ascendys*, risen.
***asclejen**, *f.*, *col.* **asclas**, chip, splinter (W., B.).
***asclejy**, *vb.*, to chip, splinter (W.,B.).

ascor, *m.*, offspring, yield, produce ; *vb.* to yield (W.) : see **dascor.**

ascorn, *m.*, *pl.* **eskern** (*yscarn*), bone : ***a-scoth***, shoulder-blade, ***corf gyllys yn eskern***, skeleton.

ascornek, *adj.*, bony (Lh.).

ascra (*hascra, nascra*), *f.*, bosom ; fold of clothing forming breast-pocket : ***a.lan dyogel hy ferghen***, secure is he who has a clear conscience (from W. proverb).

***ascryfa,** *vb.*, to ascribe.

ascūsya, *vb.*, to excuse, P.C., B.M. (M.E).

ascūsasyon, *m.*, excuse, defence (M.E.).

asectour (*acectour*), *m.*, *pl.* **-s,** executor, B.M. 3523 (M.E. *seketour*, etc.).

asedha, etc., see **esedha.**

asen (Late *asan*), *f.*, *pl.*, **asow,** rib, barrel-stave, rib of boat, spoke of wheel.

asen, *m. or f.*, *pl.* -**as,** ass, donkey : †*a. gwyls*, onager, wild ass, *wilde asse* Aelfric; *margh-a*, jackass (W.) ; *asenyk*, ass-foal (W.,B.).

aseth, see **eseth.**

askel, *f.*, *pl.* **eskelly,** wing, naker-shell : see **eskelly-grēghyn.**

askellek, *adj.*, winged (W.,B.).

asper, *adj.*, grim, harsh, hardy, stern, O.M. 2203 (M.E.).

aspȳa (C.W. -as), *vb.*, to espy, look out for, search or spy out, observe, watch : 2 s. imp. *aspȳ* (M.E. *aspye*).

aspȳas, *m.*, *pl.* **-esy** ; **aspȳer,** *pl.* **-ȳoryon,** scout, spy.

***assay·,** *m.*, *pl.* **-ys,** attempt, essay, trial (M.E.).

assaya, saya, *vb.*, to try, attempt, essay, test, taste, make trial of: 2 s. imp. ***assay*** ; ***a saya***, to make trial, R.D. 2051 (M.E. ***assay, say***).

ass(a)-[2] (*yss(a)*), ***exclam. verbal particle,*** How...! : for uses see Appendix VII.

assentya, *vb.*, to agree, acquiesce, assent to (E.) : *yn-assentys*, assentingly, C.W. 654; ***henna oll ny a-assent,*** on that we all agree, B.M. 2926 ; ***a. gans***, to take the side of, C.W. 247.

asshew, *m.*, issue (Late, E.).

***assortya, sortya,** *vb.*, to assort (E.).

astel, *vb.*, to make a broken effort, R.D. 395; to interrupt, break off, suspend, stop: ***a-wruk y das dhe a.*** which his father caused to be discontinued, O.M. 2426.

astell, *f.*, *pl.* **estyll,** board, shingle, plank, Lh., Borlase.

astevery, *vb.*,? to pour back, make up for, refill : ***rag a. an coll,*** to repair the loss, B.M. 1590 ; see **devera.**

astra·nj (C.W. ***stranj***), *adj.* strange, foreign (M.E.).

***astronomek,** *adj.*, astronomical.

astro·nymer, *m.*, *pl.* **-s,** astronomer, conjurer, B.M. 3897 (M.E.).

***Asvens,** *m.*, Advent (W.).

†**asver,** see **ȳs-asver.**

asvlas, *m.*, aftertaste (W., B.).

aswels (Late ***ajels***), *m.*, revived pasture, new growth of grass.

aswon (Late *ajan*), *vb.*, to know, recognize, be acquainted with ; p. pt. and 3 s. pret. ***asu·onys:*** used of persons or of abstractions like ***bolungeth, gras ;*** **aswonvos, -fos,** is a variant inf., with 1 s. pret. ***aswonfys,*** P.C. 1412, and not a regular ***bos*** compound.

aswonvos, -fos, *m.*, knowledge, acquaintance, R.D. 769.

aswy, later **ajy,** *f.*, *pl.*, **-ow,** gap, breach, pass, opening : place-names, common.

aswȳa, *vb.*, to breach (W.).

aswȳak, *adj.*, gapped (W.).

atal, *col.*, rubbish, mine-waste (O.E. ***adl***).

ater, see **adar.**

athvejy, *vb.*, to ripen (W., B.).

athves (*arvez* Lh. for ***a'ves***), *adj.*, ripe, mellow.

athvetter, *m.*, ripeness (B.).

atla (*adla, athla*), *m.*, *pl.* **-lȳon,** rogue, rascal, vagabond, outlaw (O.E. ***utlah***).

atta, see **otta.**

atta·l (*as-, tal*), *m.*, repayment.

atta lāst, at last, P.C. 1890 (M.E) ; used for rhyme with **wāst.**

attamya, *vb.*, to broach, venture upon, meddle with, make a first cut or bite into a fruit, loaf, etc., M.C. 153 (M.E. *attame*).

attendya, *vb.*, to notice, observe, attend, pay heed to, consider, understand (M.E.) : ***a cothfes y a.,*** if thou couldst understand it, B.M. 867.

atte·nt, *m.*, attempt, endeavour, trial, experiment, B.M. 2930 (M.E.).

attē·s, *adj.*, at ease, comfortable (M.E. ***at ese***).

***attorny,** *m.*, *pl.* **-s,** attorney (E.).

atty· (Late ***ate***), *m.*, spite, malignity, animosity : ***my a-wra moy dyses rag a. dhyso,*** I will cause more disease for spite to thee, B.M. 2655; ***heb a.,*** without spite, Paul hurling-ball motto ; see **drog-atty.**

attylly, *vb.*, to repay : as **tylly.**

***auctour,** *m.*, ***pl.*-ys,** author (M.E.).

***auctoryta**, *m.*, authority (M.E.).

a-ūgh (Late **'ugh**), *adv.*, *prep.*, above, over : combines with prons. as **yn**, Appendix V : in special adverbial uses *a-ughof(-af)*, *a-ughon*, above me, us, mean overhead; *a-u. y ben*, over his head, *ughel a-u. ghon* in excelsis, on high.

av-, see **an-**.

aval, *m.*, *pl.* **-low**, apple : *a. saben*, fir-cone ; *a. bryansen*, larynx (W.) ; *owraval*, orange (W.) ; *a. -grun*, *grunaval*, pomegranate (W.) ; *a.glawnek*, peach (W.) ; **a.kerensa*, tomato, " love-apple."

avallen (C. Voc. *auallen*),*f.*, *pl.*-**now**, col. **avalwȳth**, apple-tree: *a. woth*, crab-tree.

avallennek,*f.*, *pl.* **-egow**, orchard (B.).

aval-lōn, *m.*, *pl.* **-ow**, orchard (W.).

a-van, **ava·n** (Late *a-vadn*), *adv.*, above, on high, aloft, overhead : see **ban**.

***avanen**, *f.*, *col.* **avan**, raspberry (W.).

a-var, **ava·r**, *adv.*, early : *whath a. prys-soper yu*, supper-time is early yet, P.C. 696 ; see **bar**.

ave·l, **avel** (Late *'vel*), *adv.*, like, as : combines with prons. as **yn**, Appendix V., *l* being doubled in 3rd person.

***aventurya**, *vb.*, to make a venture, speculate (M.E.).

a-vēs, **avē·s**. *adv.*, outside, away : *avēs dhe,*[2] outside of ; *saf a.*, stand off ! *seveugh 'ves a-denewen*, stand aside !

avla·n, **-eth**, see **afla·n**.

avlavar, see **aflavar**.

avlythys, see **aflythys**.

avodya, **avoydya**, *vb.*, to stand off, go away or out (M.E.). : 2 s. imp., 3 s. pres. fut. *avoyd*; *avoydama*, I'll be off (like *oma*, *wrama*) C.W. 1292 ; see **vodya**.

†avon (C. Voc. *auon*), *f.*, *pl.* -**venow**, river, *flod* Aelfric.

avōnd, *interj.*, avaunt ! B.M. 3492 (M.E.).

avonsya, *vb.*, to promote, bring forward, exalt, prefer, advance : 2 s. imp. *avōns* (M.E. *avaunce*) ; *a. a'n kensa benfys*, prefer to the first benefice, O.M. 2612.

***avonsyans**, *m.*, promotion, advancement.

avorow (C. Voc. *auorow* , *adv.*, to-morrow, *to merigen* Aelfric : see **morow**.

avowa (Late *vowa*), *vb.*, to avow, admit and justify, own, acknowledge, confess, allow, vow : *my a-n-avow*, R.D. 2120, *my a-n-vow*, C.W. 480, I declare it (M.E.).

***avowtry**, *m.*, adultery (M.E.).

***avowtyer**, *m.*, *pl.* **-s**, adulterer (M.E.).

avy, *m.*, envy, enmity, jealousy, ill-will, crossness : *perthy a. orth*, to bear malice against (M.E.).

†avy (C. Voc. *auy*), *m.*, liver: *a.-las*, gizzard (W.,B.).

-avȳ·, **-evȳ·**, *suffixed pron.*, me : emphatic form of **-vy**.

avȳ·s, *m.*, advice, opinion, counsel, consideration (M.E.) : *der a.* by the advice of, B.M. 172 ; *saw gwell a.*, better opinion excepted, B.M. 2700.

avȳsya, *vb.*, to observe, mark, consider, mind, counsel : *avysyes of*, I have made up my mind, B.M. 577 ; *a'n beth my re-avysyas*, I have taken note of the grave, R.D. 399 ; *avysyens ef a henna*, that is his look out, B.M. 1031 (M.E.).

avȳsyans, *m.*, notice.

a-wartha, **awartha** (*a*, *gwartha*, pr. "awortha," later "worra "),*adv.*, above, on top, aloft, overhead : *y'n wedhen a.*, up in the tree.

awatta, see **awotta**.

awayl (C. Voc. *(ge)aweil*), *m.*, *pl.* **-ow**, gospel : *a, pregoth an a. gwreugh*, go, preach the Gospel, R.D. 2464.

awayla, *vb.*, to evangelise.

awaylor, *m.*, *pl.*, **-yon**, evangelist.

awel (C. Voc. *auhel*),*f.*, *pl.* **-low**, weather, wind, breeze, gale, *hwidha*, *weder* Aelfric : *hager-a.*, storm.

a-wēl (dhe), *adv.*, in sight of, in presence of, before : *a-w. dheugh*, in your sight ; see **gwēl**.

awell, *m.*, craving, want : *a.bos*, *a.dhe*[2] *vos*, extreme hunger (V. *olbouid*); *a. dowr*, *dyllas*, *arghans*, etc. (B.).

***awen**, *f.*, inspiration, poetic imagination (W.)

***awen**, *f.*, *pl.* **-now**, jaw, mandible (W.,B.)

awhē·r, *m.*, sorrow, distress, chagrin, trouble : *hep a.*, readily, willingly, voluntarily, easily, freely : *yn a.* (adverbially), unhappily (D. " in a pure weer," in great distress) ; see **whēr**.

awhesyth (C. Voc. *ehidit*), *m.*, *pl.* **-ydhas**, skylark, laverock, O.M. 1203, *lauerce* Aelfric.

a-woles, *adv.*, *prep.*, below, at the bottom: see **goles**.

awos, **awo s** (late*'wos*, *'os*, *'us*, *a us*), *conj.*, because of, for the sake of, in order to, in spite of, notwithstanding ; *m.*, see **ous** : *my a-n-gwra a.merwel*, I will do it though I die, C.W. 1099 ; *a . bos claf y* *dhywla*, in spite of his hands being sore, M.C. 158; *a. my dhe gows*, although I should speak, O.M. 1437; *a. Dew*, for God's sake.

a-wosa, *adv.*, after: see **a'y wosa, wosa.**

awotta, awot (vars. *awatta, awetta, ow otta*), *interj.*, behold! lo! see!: lengthened form of **otta**, q.v., preserving probably the interrog. particle of *a-welta?* seest thou? from which it is derived; contracted sometimes before vowels to **awot**; see **ow, ot.**

ay, hay, *interj.*, oh! eh! hi! hey!

aylas, see **ellās.**

a'y ōs, *adv.*, ever (past), lit. of his age, M.C. 135, R.D. 331 (*ahos*, Norris, *ayos, y* obliterated, MS.); see **a'y üs, ōs, yn y ōs.**

ayr, *m.*, air: see **yēr.**

ayrek, *adj.*, airy (W.).

***ayrgelgh**, *m.*, atmosphere (W.).

aysel (*eysel*), *m.*, vinegar, verjuice (M.E. *aysel, eyzil*): replacing **gwȳn fyllys.**

a'y wosa, *adv.*, nevertheless, notwithstanding, afterwards, lit. after it, B.M. 837.

a'y üs (*a'y yus, a us*), *adv.*, ever (past), always hitherto, lit. of his age, M.C. 152, P.C. 786, B.M. 2376, C.W. 1470: see **üs**, *f.*

B (mutations V, P, F)

baban, *m.*, *pl.* **-as**, baby, doll, puppet, B.M. 3405; remains m. in either sex.

babansys, *m.*, infancy (W.).

baby, *m. or f.*, *pl.* **-ow**, baby (E.).

ba·cheler (*bakcheler*), *m.*, *pl.* **-s**, bachelor, celibate, B.M. (M.E.).

bad, *adj.*, bad, wrong, in error (E.); *adv.*, badly, amiss: prefixed in *b. -den*, C.W., *b. -ober*, Lh.

badhya, *vb.*, to bathe; see **bath.**

†**badüs**, *adj.*, moonstruck, lunatic, C. Voc., *monadhseoc* Aelfric: from ***bad**, *m.*, stupor, dizziness (B.).

bagas, *m.*, *pl.* **-ow**, cluster, troop, pack, flock, bush, bunch, Lh., see **penvagas.**

bagh, *f.*, *pl.* **-ow**, cell, dungeon, B.M. 3562.

bagh, *m.*, *pl.* **-ow**, hook, hinge: *baghow an darras*, door-hinges, Lh.

bagha, *vb.* to ensnare, trap, catch with a hook, R.D. 1150.

bagyl (*bagel, -al*, baculus, Pryce MS.), *f.*, *pl.* **-glow**, crosier, pastoral crook, B.M. 3007.

bak, *m.*, *pl.* **-kys**, breakwater (E. "back").

bakken, *m.*, bacon, Gw., Borlase.

†**bal**, *f.*, *pl.* **-ow**, plague, pest, C. Voc., *cwild* Aelfric; nuisance (D.).

***bal**, *m.*, white spot in horse's brow (W., B.).

bal, *m.*, *pl.* **-ow**, mine, tin-workings, Borlase (D. "bal").

***balek**, *adj.*, jutting; *m.*, *pl.* **-logow**, projection (W., B.).

***balgh**, *adj.*, proud, haughty (W., B.).

***balghter**, *m.*, pride (W., B.).

balya, *vb.*, to beat (E.D. "bal").

balyer (*balliar* Lh.), *m.*, *pls.* **-s, -ow**, barrel, hogshead.

ban, *m. or f.*, *pl.* **-now**, height; *adj.*, high: *sa b.* (for *saf yn-ban*), stand up!; in place-names *ben*, f., as Venwyn (Bynwyn 1523); see **a-van, war-van, yn-ban.**

banallen, banathlen, *f.*, *pl.* **-now**, broom-bush; besom, *col.* **banal, ba·nathel**, broom flowers or plants, C. Voc., *brom* Aelfric (D. "bannel").

banallek, banathlek, *f.*, *pls.* **-egow, -egy**, broom-brake, place where broom grows.

baner, *m.*, *pl.* **-ow**, banner (M.E.).

bank, *m.*, *pl.* **-ncow**, bank, sand-hill: place-names.

banken, *f.*, *pl.* **-now**, bank, dyke, weir, dam, Lh.

banna (late *badna*), *m.*, *pl.* **-ow, bannahow** (*h* silent), drop; (of seeing, hearing, sleeping) bit, jot, anything, at all: *bythqueth whath, tebel na mas, ny-wylys gansa b*, never yet, good or bad, have I seen a blink with them, P.C. 398.

bannya, *vb.*, to read banns (E.): *bannys yns-y*, their banns are up, Gw.

†**banow** (C. Voc. *baneu*), *f.*, *pl.* **ba·nowas, by·newy**, sow, pig, *swin* Aelfric: in Breton, a sow with a litter, in other Celtic languages, a young pig.

bans, *m.*, *pl.* **-ow**, high place, height, cliff: place-names, Lh. MS.

baptyst, *m.*, baptiser: ? used as "baptism", B.M. 4128.

bar, *m.*, *pl.* **-ow**, summit, climax, Lh.; *crisis (B): see **a-var.**

bar, *m.*, *pl.* **-ow**, bunch, thickly-branching bough (W., B.): see **baren.**

bar, *m.*, *pl.* **-rys**, tribunal, bar; bolt (E.): *ord'neugh b. dhe esedha, ha my a-wra y jujjya*, arrange a bar (at which) to sit, and I will judge him, P.C. 2225,

bara, *m.* (*no pl.*), bread, *hlaf* Aelfric: **b. cales*, ship-biscuit; †*b. can*, C. Voc., *b. gwyn*, white bread; *b. gwaneth*, wheaten bread; *b. kergh*, oaten bread; *b. sugal*, rye bread; *b. barlys*, barley bread; *b. gwel*, *hep gwel*, leavened, unleavened, bread; *b. an gok*, sorrel, (W.).

barcādo, *m.*, *pl.* **-s**. "bulk" of pilchards in fish-cellar, J. Boson; lit. boatload (Spanish).

bardhek, *adj.*, bardic.

bardhonek, *m.*, *pl.* **-nogow**, poetry, poem (W., B.).

bardho'nÿeth, *m.*, poetry, poesy (W., B.).

baren, *f.*, *pl.* **-now**, small branch, bunch of twigs, besom (D. "barren").

barf (C. Voc. *baref*), *f.*, *pl.* **-rvow**, beard.

barfüs, *adj.*, bearded; *m.*, *pl.* **-y**, cod-fish.

bargen, *m.*, *pl.* **-ys**, bargain: *b. tȳr*, farm, holding of land (Late, E.).

bargenya, *vb.*, to bargain (Late, E.).

bargos (*bargez* Lh.), *m.*, *pl.* **-as**, **-ojas**, buzzard, O.M. 133: Carn Bargus, rock-name.

***barlen**, *f.*, *pl.*-**now**, lap (W., B.).

ba'rlysen, *f.*, barley-corn, *col.* **barlys**, barley: see **hēdhen**.

***barn**, *f.*, judgment: replaced by **brüs**, but †*ber* in **ünver** has the same root (W., B.); *barneriow*, borrowed by Gwavas for "judges," is misunderstood as "barons" in P.

barrek, *adj*, branched, twiggy (B.).

†**barth**, *m.*, *pls.* **byrth**, **berdhyon**, *f.*, **bardhes**, *pl.* **-ow**, bard, of second degree in Gorsedd; entertainer, minstrel, C. Voc., *gligman* Aelfric: †*b. hyrgorn*, trumpeter, C. Voc., *bymere* Aelfric.

barthüsek (*barthesek*), *adj.*, marvellous, amazing, prodigious, R.D. 109, 1177, M.B. *berzudec*.

barvek, *adj.*, bearded (W., B.).

barver, *m.*, *pl.* **-yon**, barber (W., B.).

barya, *vb.*, to bolt, bar: 3 s. pres.-fut. *bar*; *my a-var*, P.C. 3049.

bās, *adj.*, shallow: Dowrow Baze, Penberth.

basdowr (*basdhour* Lh.), *m.*, shallow, ford.

basket, *m.*, *pl.*, **-tys**, basket, Lh.: *b. dorn*, hand-basket (E.).

basnet, *m.*, *pl.* **-tys**, basinet, helmet, R.D. 2581 (M.E.).

bason (? *bathon*, *bazon* M.C. 45), *m.*, *pl.* **-ys**, basin, P.C. 842 (M.E.).

bassya, *vb.*, to grow shallow, become lower; p. pt. *bassys*, O.M; 3 s. pres.-fut. *bās*.

baster, *m.*, shallowness (W.).

bat, *m.*, *pl.* **-tys**, club, cudgel, bat, P.C. 607 (M.E.).

batalyas, *vb.*, to fight a battle (M.E.).

batel (*bateyl*), *f.*, *pl.* **-lys**, battle (M.E.).

bāth (C. Voc. *ba(h)et*), *m.*, *pl.* **badhas**, boar.

†**bath** (C. Voc. *bat*), *m.*, *pl.* **-ow**, coin, piece of money, *mynet* Aelfric.

bath, *m.*, *pl.* **-ys**, bath (M.E.): *gul b. yn.* bathe in, take a bath in, B.M. 1512, 1777.

†**bathor**, *m.*, *pl.* **-yon**, coiner, money-changer, C. Voc., *mynetere* Aelfric.

bathy, *vb.*, to coin money (W.).

batty (*bath, ty*), *m.*, mint, money-house (W.).

bay, *m.*, *pl.* **-ow** (*baiou* Lh.), kiss: see **baya**.

bāy, *m.*, *pl.* **-ys**, bay, indentation of coast (D. "baa").

bay, *m.*, *pl.* **-ys**, bay, branch of bay, P.C. 261.

baya, *vb.* to kiss (M.E. *ba*): used without *dhe*, see **amma**.

bay'wedhen, *f.*, *col.* **-wȳth**, bay-tree (W.).

bē, see **bēgh**.

bean, see **bȳghan**.

bedha, *vb.*, to dare, venture, presume: 2 s. imp., 3 s. pres.-fut. *bēth*; *Saf! Yn-nes na-veth re dont!* Halt! Do not venture near too saucily! B.M. 3470; *ma na-veth y avowa*, so that he dares not own to it, P.C. 1783; *my a-veth y leverel*, I make bold to say it, B.M. 1997; *na ny-vedhaf ... dhe'm tas ow fas dyscudha*, nor dare I show my face to my father, C.W. 1368 (*awos* for *ow fas*); *ny-vedhaf dos yn-mesk*, I dare not come among, P.C. 1429, C.W. 1517.; see **arveth**.

†**bedhewen** (C. Voc. *bedewen*), *f.*, *col.* **bedhow**, birch-tree, *byrc*, Aelfric.

bedhow, see **beth**.

bedhros, *f.*, *pl.*-**ow**, burying-place (W., B.).

bedhy, *vb.*, to bury (Late only).

bedhygla, *vb.*, to bellow, low, roar, Lh., Borlase.

†**bēfer**, *m.*, *pl.* **-s**, beaver, C. Voc., *beofer* Aelfric.

bēgel, *m.*, *pl.* **-yow**, navel; boss, tump.

beggya, *vb.*, to beg.

beggyer, *m.*. *pl.* **-s**, beggar, B.M.; pl. also *beggars*, R.D. (E.).

bēgh, in MS. **bē**, *m.*, *pl.* **-yow**, burden, load, O.M. 1057, 1296, 1299: *b. eythyn*, a burn [load] of furze, Pryce M.S. note;

the final consonant of B. *bec'h*, W. *baich* is kept in **beghya.**

bēghüs, *adj.*, burdensome, oppressive (W.,B.).

beghya, *vb.*, to burden, oppress : 2 s. imp. *bēgh* (*byhgh* O.M. 122, miscopied *bashe* C.W. 402).

bēgy, -a, *vb.*, to bray as an ass, Pryce (W., B.).

bejeth (*bedgeth* Keigwin), *m.*, face, surface : late corruption of **vysach.**

be laver (*-ber*), *adj.*, fair to see, handsome, O.M. 2271 ; Fr. *bel à voir*, term of appreciation, cf. D. "my handsome."

belerek, *f.*, *pl.* **-egy,** cress-bed (B).

beleren, *f.*, col. **†beler,** cress-plant, water-cress, C. Voc., *caerse* Aelfric : see **cas-beler.**

bell, *m.*, war, M.C. 249.

bēn (*been*), *m.*, *pl.* **-ow,** stem, trunk, O.M. : see **gwedhen-vēn.**

bēn, see **hy-bēn.**

bene·dyksyon (*benedycconn*, B.M.), *m.*, benediction (M.E.).

benen, *f.*, *pl.* **-es,** woman, wife, *bryd* Aelfric ; **b. bryas,** bride, Lh. **†** *b. priot.*

benena (*bynena*), *vb.*, to seek women, P.C. 2838 : inf. only.

benenrȳth (C. Voc. *benen rid*), *f.*, female, woman, R.D. 851,875, *wifhades man* Aelfric : see **rȳth.**

benenvā·s, ben'vā·s (Late *bednvas*, C. Voc. *benenvat*), *f.*, goodwife, housewife, *fordhwif* Aelfric : *B. Jowanna*, Goody Joan.

benesek, benejek, *adj.*, blessed.

bene·sykter, bene·jykter, *m.*, blessedness.

benewen, *f.*, *pl.* **-now,** wench, little female.

benfys, be·nefys, *f.*, benefice (M.E.).

benk, *m.*, *pl.* **-ow,** bench, Lh.

bennath (Late *bednath*), *f.*, *pl.* **-nothow,** blessing : *b. sewes !* *benna' sewes !* let a blessing follow ! O.M. 1917, P.C. 2145 ; *bennate·w*, contraction of *b. Dew*, God's blessing ; *govyn b.*, to say grace ; *gasa b.*, to give a parting blessing.

benow, *f. and col.*, female.

benyga, *vb.*, to bless, hallow : p. pt. *benygys*, holy, hallowed, blessed.

bēr, *m.*, *pl.* **-yow,** spit for roasting, C. Voc., Lh.

ber, *f.*, *pl.* **-row,** *d.* **dywver,** shank, leg.

ber, *adj.*, short, brief : *a ver spas*, shortly ; *war ver lavarow*, in short, in few words.

***bera,** *vb.*, to drop (W.,B.).

ber-anal, *m.*, asthma, short breath, Lh.

berder, *m.*, brevity, shortness (W.).

bergam, *adj.*, crookshanked, bandy-legged (D.).

berhē·, *vb.*, to shorten, grow shorter : see TABLE in APPENDIX VIII.

berlewen (Lh. *bur-lūan*), *f.*, Venus, the morning-star : V. *berleüen*, f., but evidently connected with B. *gwerelaouenn* f. morning-star. Probably Venus as star of the West originally, cf. V. *golern*, f., B. *gwalarn*, m., North West, W. *gorllewin*, m., West; possibly *berlewen* is for *bore-worlewen*, morning-Venus.

bern, *m.*, *pl.* **-yow,** heap, rick, stack, C. Voc., Lh., *hreac, hype* Aelfric.

bern, *m.*, care, concern, interest, solicitude : *hep b.*, without minding, willingly.

bern, *def. vb.*, it concerns matters : used with neg., e.g., *travyth ny-vern*, it matters nothing ; *dha salujy ny-vern*, there's no harm in saluting thee.

berna, *vb.*, to heap, stack, pile up (W.,B.).

***berow,** *m.*, boiling (W.B.) : see ***berwel.**

†berry (C. Voc. *berri*, perhaps for *berni*), *m.*, fatness, grossness, *faetnys*, Aelfric : see **bor.**

berryk, *adj.*, fattish, gross, gorbellied, P.

***berth,** *m.*, prosperity, excellence (W.,B.).

†berthūan, *f.*, *pl.* **-as,** ? wren (parrax, *wrenne* Aelfric) : see **gwrannen.**

'berth-yn, see **aberth-yn.**

***berwel,** *vb.*, to boil (W.,B.) : as **merwel;** replaced by **bryjyon.**

berya, *vb*, to run a spit through, transfix : *my a-th-ver*, I'll spit thee, B.M. 2408.

***besont,** *m.*,*pl.* **-ns,** bezant (M.E.).

besow, see **bysow.**

bēst (*beast* C.W.), *m.*, *pl.* **-es, -as,** beast : *b. arlydhy*, the deer, lordly game, B.M. 3465.

best, *m.*, moss: *an men us ow-rullya ny-vyn nefra cuntell b.*, the rolling stone will never gather moss, Lh., Borlase ; ? for ***mūsk**, W. *mwswg*, cf. *belin*, for **melyn.**

betegens, see **bytegens.**

beth, *m.*, *pl.* **-edhow,** grave, sepulchre, tomb.

beth-scryfa, *m.*, epitaph (W.).

betysen, *f.*, *col.* **betys,** beet-plant (W., B., D. "bitts").

bew, *adj.*, alive, lively : *yn*[5]*-few*, living.

bew (C. Voc. *biu*), *m.*, living flesh, the quick, (state of) life, *lif* Aelfric: *b. an lagas*, pupil of the eye, C. Voc., *seo* Aelfric ; *dasserghy dhe*[2] *vew*, to rise again to life,

P.C. 3085; *a'gan b.*, in our living flesh, R.D. 74; *yn y² vew*, while alive (W., B); *treghys, gwenys, bys y'n b.*, cut, pierced, to the quick (B.).

bewa, *vb.* to live: *nyns-us bewa*, there is no (more) living; *orto b.*, to live upon (by eating) it.

bewder, *m.*, liveliness (W., B.).

†**bewdern** (C. Voc. *bindorn* for *biudern*), *m.*, refectory (O.E. *beoddern* Aelfric).

*__bewesen, -jen__, *f.*, pith, pulp, kernel, core (W., B.).

bewhē·, *vb.*, to quicken, enliven (W., B.).

bewles, *m.*, stonecrop (W.).

bewnans, bewnas (Late *bownas*), *m.*, life, livelihood, lifetime: *kelly an b.*, to forfeit ones life; *yn b. da, yn b. glan*, in a state of grace; *dyndyl y² vewnans*, to earn his living; *yn ow b.*, etc., as long as I live, always; *dry dh'y vewnans*, restore to life; *n* is added before *-ans* in this and **mernans**.

bewvyth, *f.*, houseleek (W.).

blām, *m.*, blame, fault (M.E.): *godhvos b. dhe*, to attribute blame to; *my a-wysk hep b.*, there's nothing wrong with my striking, P.C. 2737.

blamya, *vb.*, to blame, censure, find fault with (M.E.).

blas, *m.*, savour, taste, relish, smell, R.D. 2160: see **dyflas**.

blasa, *vb.*, to savour, relish: p. pt. *blesys* (W., B.).

bledhen (C. Voc. *blidhen*), *f.*, *pl.* **-dhynnow**, year, *gear* Aelfric: see **blōth**.

blejan (C. Voc. *blodon*), *m.*, **blejyewen, blejen**, *f.*, *pl.* **-jyow**, flower, bloom, blossom, *blosan* Aelfric.

blejennyk, *m.*, *pl.* **-jyowygow**, floweret (B.).

blejyowa, *vb.*, to blossom, flower (W., B.).

blēs (C. Voc. *blot*, Late *blease*, Lh. *blēz*), *m.*, flour, meal: **b. hesken*, sawdust (B.).

blewen, *f.*, *col.* **blew**, hair: *b. an pen*, hair of head, *b. an lagas*, eye-lash, C. Voc., Lh., *braewas* Aelfric.

blewak, *adj.*, hairy, C.W. 1588.

blōgh, *adj.*, hairless, close-shaven, bald: *pen b.*, tonsured pate, B.M. 3828.

blōghhē·, *vb.*, to make or become bald (B.).

blojon (*-gon*), *m.*, *pl.* **-s**, bludgeon, O.M. 2709 (E.).

blonegek, *adj.*, greasy (W.).

†**blonek** (C. Voc. *blonec*), *m.*, fat, grease, lard, ***rysel*** Aelfric.

blōth, *m.*, year, year of age (with num.).

blothwyth, *f.*, year's time (B.): ?contracted to *blythy'*, B.M. 1537.

blōthyas, *m.*, *pl.* **-ysy**, yearling, year-old person or thing (W., B.).

blou, *adj.*, blue, Lh. (E.).

blüdhya, *vb.*, to soften, weaken, enervate, M.C. 53.

blüth, *adj.*, tender, soft, cf. B. *blizik*.

blȳdhes, *f.*, *pl.* **-ow**, she-wolf.

blȳdhy, see **blȳth**.

*__blȳn__, *adj.*, inactive, tired (W., B.).

blȳn, *m.*, *pl.* **-ow**, top, point, tip.

blȳnya, *vb.*, to sharpen, point; precede, lead (W., B.).

blȳth (C. Voc. *bleit*), *m.*, *pl.* **-ȳdhy**, wolf, *wulf* Aelfric: *bly' (blygh)*, C.W. 1149; in C. Voc. a lynx is described as *kemmysk b. ha ky*, following Aelfric's *gemeneged hund and wulf*, mixed dog and wolf.

blythy, see **blothwyth**.

bō, *conj.*, either, or: see **pō**.

bobba (*boba*), *m.*, *pl.* **-bys**, fool (?M.E.).

*__bobans__, *m.*, pomp (M.E.).

bocler, *m.*, *pl.* **-s**, buckler, M.C. 74 (M.E.).

†**bod**, see **bos**.

bodhar (C. Voc. *bothar*), *adj.*, deaf; *m.*, *pl.* **-yon**, deaf person.

bo·dhara, -hē·, *vb.*, to deafen: inf. *-he·* as **berhē·** (W., B.).

body, *m.*, *pl.* **-s**, person, body (M.E.).: *un b.*, a single person.

bōgh (C. Voc. *boch*), *m.*, *pl.* **-as**, buck, he-goat, *bucca* Aelfric.

bōgh (C. Voc. *en voch*), *f.*, *pl.* **-ow**, *d.* **dywvōgh**, cheek, *ansyn* Aelfric.

bōghek, *adj.*, big-cheeked (W., B.).,

bōghes, *m.*, a little; *adj.*, few little, usually before s. noun, no mutation caused; *adv.*, slightly, little.

bōghes-venough, *adv.*, seldom, rarely, B.M. 4161: see **menough**.

boghosek,-jek (C. Voc. *bochodoc*), *adj.*, poor; *m*, *pl.* **-sogyon, -jogyon**, poor person, pauper, *hafenleas, dhearfa* Aelfric.

bōghvlew, *col.*, whiskers: see **blewen**.

bojek, *f*, *pl.* **-egow**, place covered with bushes (B.); *adj.*, bushy (B.): see **bọs**.

bokē·n, *conj.*, or else: see **bō, kēn**.

bōl *(boell, bool)*, *f.*, *pl.* **-ow**, axe, hatchet.

bol, see **mōl**.

bōld, *adj.*, bold, M.C. 78, B.M. 3480 (E.).

bōlder, *m.*, temerity, presumption, boldness, M.C. 163.

***bolghen**, *f*, *col.* **bolgh**, rounded seed-pod, boll (B.).

bolla, *m.*, *pl.* **-lys**, cup, bowl; playing-bowl, Lh.; *pl.* papal bull, B.M.

bolunjeth (*bolnejeth* B.M., *blonojeth* C.W.), *m.*, will, desire, wish: for *bolunseth*, B. *bolontez*, Lat. *voluntat(em)*; *gwra dha volunjeth*, do as thou wilt.

bolunjethek, *adj.*, willing (coined by Lh.).

bōlyk, *m.*, *pl.* **-ygow**, small hatchet (W.,B.).

bom (*bum*), *m*, *pl.* **-myn**, bang, heavy blow, thump, bump: *b. a dan ha lughes*, stroke of fire and lightning, fire-ball.

bommen, *f.*, *pl.* **-now**, blow, stroke, buffet.

bond-hat, *m.*, hat-band, Lh.

bones, see **bōs**.

bongors, *m. pl.* **-as**, bittern (W.B.): perhaps replaced by **clabyttour**.

bonk (*bunk*, Lh.), *m.*, *pl.* **-ys**, knock, blow, bump.

bonkya, *vb.*, to knock.

bonkyer (*bunkiar* Lh.), *m.*, *pl.* **-yoryon**, cooper: ? mistakenly translated as if from Fr. *coup*, blow.

bonny, *m.*, *pl.* **-es**, cluster, clump, bunch of ore (Borlase, D. "buddy").

bonnyk, *m.*, *pl.* **-ygas**, little bird (?meadow pipit) that accompanies the cuckoo (D. "bodnick").

bony, *f*, *pl.* **-ow**, tool used to cut plank in two, P.C. 2564: one would expect either *hesken* (B.) or *sagha* (M.E.) for "saw," so this is probably "hatchet."

bonȳ'l, bō an ȳl, *conj.*, or else, see **bō, ȳl**.

†bor, *adj.*, fat, C. Voc., *faet* Aelfric.

bora, *m.*, *pl.* **-ys**, domestic boar, Lh. (E.).

†bora (C. Voc. *bore*), *m.*, dawn, morn; replaced in M. Cor. by *myttyn*; "boregweth," Lh., is no doubt like "boynedh," coined by him from Welsh.

bord, *m.*, *pl.* **-ys**, board, table-top, Lh. (E.).

†bo'reles, *m.*, daisy, dawn-plant, C. Voc., *daeges eage*, Aelfric.

***borgh**, *m*, *pl.* **-ow**, burgh, borough, rampart (W., B.).

bōs, bones, *irreg. vb.*, to be, take place, exist, abide; also (with infixed prons., *my a-m-büs*, etc.) to have: in the latter sense *bōs* is not used as an auxiliary verb, incorrect personal inflections are often given to it in MSS., *a-s-bedheugh-why*, etc.; equally anomalous forms were made with inf., *dha vota, ow bosaf*, etc., which are not used in unified Cornish; for parts see TABLES in APPENDIX VIII; *bos* is also used as a suffix with the meaning of "state," "being," see **ponvos, gwylfos**.

bōs, (*boys, bous*, C. Voc. *buit*, Late *boos*, Lh. *bŭz*), *m.*, food, meal, meat in general, bait, *mete* Aelfric: *b. -hyjy*, duckweed (B.); *b. Pask*, feast of Passover; *b. soper*, supper.

bos, *m.*, *pl.* **-ssow**, dwelling-place: used in place-names, often keeps its old form, *bod*: may be *boj* before vowels, and because of its final *s* may be *bos*4, *bo*4 before mutable consonants: see **gwavas, hewas, kynewas**.

bos, *m.*, *pl.* **-ow, bojow**, bush, R.D. 539 and *bosnos* (*b. enos*), O.M. 1397, B. *bod*: see **bojek**.

bōsa (*bŭza*), *vb.*, to feed animals or fire, supply a mill, etc., Lh. (D. "bush the fire").

bōst, *m.*, *pl.* **-ow**, brag, boast (E.).

bōster, *m.*, *pl* **-teryon**, boaster (E.).

bōsty, *m.*, *pl.* **-ow**, restaurant, eating-house (W.).

bōstya, *vb.*, to boast.

***bo'tasen**, *f.*, *col.* **botas**, boot (W., B.).

***botel**, *f.*, *pl.* **-low**, bottle (E.).

bōth, *m.*, will, inclination, consent; *b. y vrys*, purpose of his mind, intention; *dre dha voth*, with thy permission, by thy leave, pray, please; *dens pan vo b. gansa*, let them come when they like; *sewya y voth*, to follow his bent.

both, *f.*, *pl.* **-ow**, nave of wheel, boss, protuberance (W.).

bothak, *adj.*, hump-backed, bossed; *m.*, *pl.* **-thogyon**, hunch-backed (D.); *pl.* **-ogas**, a blind or pout (fish) Lh. MS., (D., V. *bohek*): as fish-name this may be for *boghak* (cf. *gorthell* for *gorhel*, C.W. 2255) *h* in Vannes Breton can represent both *gh* and *th*, and either "bossed" or "blubber cheeked" would refer to the puffed out membranes over the fish's eyes when caught.

bothan, *m.*, *pl.* **-now**, hump, hunch, swelling, Borlase, D.

bothen, *f*, *pl.* **-now**, corn-marigold (D., B. *bozenn*).

bothel, *f.*, *pl.* **-low**, blister (D.).

***boton**, *m.*, *pl.* **-now**, button.

***botonna**, *vb*, to button.

bo'tteler, botler. *m.*, *pl.* **-s**, butler, O.M.; tankard-bearer, Lh. (M.E.).

PASTURE (FODDER)

bownder (C. Voc. *bounder*), *f.*, *pl.* **-yow,** lane; (formerly) leasow, open grazing ground, C. Voc., *laeswe,* Aelfric: always " Vounder," lane, as place-name.

bowjy, *m.*, *pl.* **-ow,** cowhouse, shed, Lh. (D.): *b. deves,* sheep-fold, Lh.

bowyn (*bowin* Lh., *boen* P.), *m.*, beef, B.M. 3224: Park B., Beef Close.

box, *m*, *pl.* **byxyn,** branch of box, P.C. 261; box-tree, C. Voc., *box* Aelfric.

box, *m.*, *pl.* **-ys,** box (receptacle).

box, *m.*, *pl.* **-ow,** box (blow).

boxas, *m*, *pl.* **-esow,** fisticuff, buffet.

bo·xesy (*-xusy*, *-xcusy*), *vb.*, to box, cuff.

boya, *m.*, *pl* **-yes,** boy, page, manservant, C.W. 1395, 1651 (M.E.).

brāf, (*breyf*, C.W. 229), *adj.*, fine, grand; *adv.*, greatly (E.D. "braave," "braa'," "braa'ly").

brāg(k), *m.*, malt, C. Voc., O.M., Gw.

braga, *vb.*, to malt (W.).

†bragas (C. Voc. *bregaud*), *m.*, sweet-drink, mead and ale mixed, "bragget," *beor* Aelfric.

brager, *m. pl.*, **-oryon,** maltster (W.).

bragesy, *vb.*, to sprout, ferment (W., B.).

bragva, *f.*, malthouse (W.).

bragya (*brakgye* R.D. 2018), *vb.*, to talk big, brag of what one will do, threaten idly (M.E.): 2 s. imp., 3 s. pres.-fut. *brak(g)*.

bragyer, *m. pl.* **-oryon,** braggart.

brakty, *m.*, malthouse (W.).

brakys, *m. pl.*, brakes, C.W. 1363 (E.).

bram (*brabm* Lh.) *m.*, *pl.* **bremmyn**. fart: *b. an gath,* fiddlesticks! C.W. 1305.

bramma, *vb.*, to fart.

brān, *f.*, *pl.* **brȳny,** crow: *b. vras,* carrion crow, raven; *b. dre,* rook, Lh.; *b. lus,* hooded or Market-Jew crow; Park Breeny, Zawn Brinny, place-names; see **marghvran, mōrvran.**

branch, *m.*, *pl.* **-ys** branch (E.).

***branel,** *m.*, *pl.*, **-low,** frame for the mould-board of a wooden plough (W., B.).

bras, *m.*, plot, pitfall, ambush, treachery, treason, perfidy: *par may codhas yn ow b.*, so that he fell into my toils, R.D. 2334.

brās (late pr. *brōs*, pl. *brosyon*), *adj.*, great, large, big, comp. *brassa, moy,* superl. *an brassa, moyha*; *m.*, *pl.* **-yon,** the great, heroes, great people: *b.-lavarow,* threats; *ahanas ef a-wra pur vras,* he will make very much of thee.

brās-o·berys, *adj.*, magnificent, Lh. (invented).

braster, *m.*, greatness, size, splendour, majesty, magnificence, pride.

brastereth (*brostereth* Keigwin), majesty.

brasy, *vb.*, to plot, commit treason (W.).

brath, *m.*, *pl.* **-ow,** bite, wound (W.).

brathky, *m.*, *pl.* **brathcün,** savage cur, sheep-worrying or biting dog: used also as a revilement.

brathles, *m.*, pimpernel (W.).

brathy, *vb.*, to bite, wound by biting (W.).

***brawagh,** *m.*, *pl.* **-ow,** terror (W.B.).

†brawd (C. Voc. *bruud*), *m.*, brother: replaced by **broder,** if M. Cor. it would probably have become **brüs.**

***braweghy,** *vb.*, to terrify (W., B.).

brē, *f.*, *pl.* **-ow,** hill: with loss of stress becomes *-bra*, e.g., " Mulfra (*mol vre*)."

breder, see **broder.**

bre·dereth (accent also normal), *m.*, confraternity, brotherhood.

***bregh,** *f.*, small-pox, erruptive disease (W., B.); *m.*, *pl.*, **-ow,** spot, freckle (W).; *adj.*, brindled, freckled (W.).

brēgh (Cor. Voc. *brech*), *f.*, *pl.* **-ow,** *d.* **dywvrēgh** (M.C. *deffregh*), arm, shaft of cart, spoke of wheel, "arm" of mill-sail, sea, etc.

†brēghal (Cor. Voc. *brechol*), *m.*, *pl.* **-ghellow,** sleeve.

brēghas, *f.*, *pl.* **-esow,** armful (W. B.).

brēghek, *adj.*, armed, having arms (B.).

breghy (*brehy*, B.M. 2419), *pl.*, motes, flue, dandruff.

***brēn,** *adj.*, rotten (W., B.).

brennya, *vb.*, to direct, give directions: see **brennyas.**

†brennyas (C. Voc. *brenniat*), *m*, *pl.* **-ysy,** forecastle look-out, mate of ship, stationed at the bow, *ancerman* Aelfric.

bre·nnygen (*bernigan* Lh.), *f.*, *col.* **brennyk,** limpet: dim. of **bron.**

bresel, *m.*, *pl.* **-yow,** war, strife, struggle.

breselek, *adj.*, warlike (B.).

breseler, -yer, *m.*, *pl.* **-loryon,** warrior.

bresely, *vb.*, to war (B.).

breselyas, *m.*, *pl.* **-ysy,** warrior (B.).

brēst, *m.*, breast, O.M. 2717 (E.).

brēst, *m.*, brass, latten (Lh.).

brēstplāt (*brüstplat*),*m.*, breastplate, R.D. 2591 (M.E.).

Breten, *f.*, Britain: *B. Vür,* Great Britain, *B. Vyghan,* Brittany.

Bretennek, *adj.*, British.

Breton, *m.*, *pl.* **-yon,** Breton.

Bretonek, *adj.*, Breton; *m.* Breton language.

Bretones, *f.*, *pl.* **-ow,** Breton woman.
brew, *adj.*, broken, injured, wounded; *m.*, *pl.* **-yon,** break, fragment, cut, wound: see **brewyonen.**
brewlyf, *f.*, grindstone (W., B.).
brewy (Late *browy*), *vb.*, to break, crumble, crush, smash, pound, hurt, wound.
brewyonen, *f.*, *pl.* **brewyon,** crumb, bit, single fragment, *cruma* Aelfric; little fellow (D. "brewyan," "crumb of a cheeld"): see **brew.**
brō, *f.*, *pl.* **-yow,** country, land, region, M.C. 250.
†brōcha (C. Voc. *broche*), *m.*, *pl.* **-ys.** brooch, buckle, clasp, *dolc*, *preon* Aelfric (O. Fr.).
broder (Lh. *bredar*,? for *brodar*, C.W., Gw., but cf. *bruder*, ?*brüder*, P.C. 188), *m.*, *pl.* **breder,** brother: *b.* *-da*, brother-in-law; see **bredereth, sȳra, brawd.**
brōgh (C. Voc. *broch*), *m.*, *pl.* **-as,** badger, *brcc* Aelfric: *mylweth dyghtys ages b. gans nep mylgy*, a thousand times worse treated than a badger by any greyhound, P.C. 2926, cf. B.M. 1280.
brōgha, *vb.*, to fume, fret (W., B.).
bron (*brodn*, Lh.), *f.*, *pl.* **-now,** *d.* **dywvron** (C. Voc. *duivron*, C.W. *devran*, *defran*), breast, udder: *kettep map-pron*, every mother's son, every individual.
bron (Late *burn*), *m.*, *pl.* **-yon, -now,** hill: place-names, Tolvern (*tal vron*), etc.
bronlen, *f.*, *pl* **-now,** bib (W.).
bronna, *vb*, to give the breast (W., B.).
bronnen (C. Voc. *brunnen*, Lh. *brudnan*). *f.*, *col.* **bron** (Lh. *brun*), rush, *resce* Aelfric: *b. mor*, sand-rush; *pen-b.*, feather-pate, scatterbrain.
bronnek, *f.*, *pl.* **-egy,** rush-grown place, marsh, (W., B.).
†brōs, *m*, *pl.* **-ojow,** sting, prick, point of sharp implement or weapon, C. Voc., *sticels* Aelfric.
brōs, *m*, pottage, stew, thick broth, R.D. 142.
brōs, *adj.*, extremely hot; *m.*, great heat (D. "broze").
brōsa, *vb.*, to sting, prick, goad (B.).
brōsya, -jya, *vb.*, to stitch, embroider (W., B., D., "broach").
brottel, *adj.*, frail, inconstant, unlasting, unstable, fickle (M.E.).
†brow (C. Voc. *brou*), *f.*, *pl.* **-yow,** hand-mill, quern, *cwyrnstan* Aelfric.
brows, *col.*, crumbled or fragmentary stuff; *pl.* **browsyon, -jyon,** separate bits, splinters, crumbs; **browsyonen,** *f.*, crumb, fragment, Lh. (D. "browse," "browjans").
browsy, *vb.*, to crumble (D.).
brunyon (*brudnyan* Borlase), *pl.*, groats, oatmeal.
brüs (vowel spelt *ue, eu, ē*), *f.*, *pl,* **-ow,** judgment, sentence, verdict, decision.
brüslys, *f.*, *pl.* **-yow,** assize-court (W.).
brüstplāt, see **brēstplāt.**
brüsy, -jy, *vb.*, to judge, sentence.
brüsyas, *m.*, *pl.* **-ysy,** judge.
†brüsyth (C. Voc. *brodit*), *m.*, *pl.*, **-ydhyon,** judge, *dema* Aelfric.
brȳ, *m.*, account, value, esteem, ado, regard, deference, respect, consideration, worth, honour, importance: *gul vry* (*a*), to make account of, show respect, pay attention, mind, treat with consideration; *vry* here is in permanent mutation, probably from *a²vry*, cf. **'vas.**
***bryallen,** *f.*, *pl.* **-now,** col. **bryally,** primrose (W.): see **†brylūen.**
bryā·nsen, -jen (*briansen* C. Voc., *bryongen* R.D. 1007, *brandzha* Lh.) *f.*, throat, windpipe, gullet, *throta*, Aelfric.
brȳbour, *m.*, *pl.* **-s,** vagabond, pilferer (M.E.).
brȳel, see **brythel.**
brȳf, *f.*, *pl.* **-yvow,** bleating of sheep (W.).
brȳght, *adj.*, bright, O.M., B.M. (M.E.).
brȳhy (*brihi* Borlase), *vb.*, to brew.
brȳja (*bryge*),? *vb.*, to think, contemplate: *ny-wodhough pandr' a-gewseugh, na pandra a vryja 'wreugh*, you know not what you say, nor what in intent you do, P.C. 444; perhaps for *a vrys a-wreugh*, by intent you do, see **brys** (mind).
bryjyon (C. Voc. *bredion*), *m.*, boiling, seething, *gesod*, Aelfric; *vb.*, to boil, seethe (Lh. *brijan*, *brujan*): p. pt. *bryjyes* (*brujiaz* Lh., *brijiez*, P.); 2 s. imp. *brōs*; 3 s. pret. *brojas*; *ymons-y ow-rostya hag ow-pryjyon*, they are roasting and boiling, Lh.; noun and inf. are the same, cf. **wherthyn,** see also **bros, *berwel.**
bryk, *m. and col.*, *pl.* **-kys,** brick, C.W. (E.).
***brykethen,** *f.*, *col.* **bryketh,** apricot (B.).
brylly, see **brȳthel.**

†**brylūen**, *f.*, *pl.*, **-now**, *col.* **brȳlū** Voc. C.) *breilu*), rose : cf. B. *brulu*, foxgloves, W. *briallu*, primroses.

brynk, *m.*, *pl.* **-ow**, gill of fish (D. "brink").

bryntyn, *adj.*, noble, excellent, first-rate ; *m.*, *pl.* **-yon**, nobleman.

brȳny see **brān**.

brȳonjen, see **brȳansen**.

brȳs (*breys*, B.M.), *m.*, womb.

brȳs, (*bres*, *breys*, Lh. *an brēz*), *m.*, *pl.* **-yow**, mind, thought, way of thinking : *ow b. dhym yma ow-ton*, it is borne in upon me, B.M. 2638.

†**brȳth** (C. Voc. *bruit*), *adj.*, streaked, spotted, freckled, mottled, speckled, dappled, variegated, *fah*, Aelfric.

brȳtha, *vb.*, to spot, mottle (W., B.).

brȳthel, **brȳel** (C. Voc. *breithil*), *m.*, *pls.* **-lly**, **brylly**, mackerel, *maecefisc* Aelfric (D. "breeal").

brythen, *f.*, *pl.* **-now**, *col.*, **brȳth**. freckle, spot (B.).

brythennek, *adj.*, freckled (B.).

Brython, *m.*, *pl.* **-yon**, Ancient Briton, Brythonic Celt.

Brythonek, *adj.*, British, Brythonic ; *m.*, Brythonic language (i.e. Cornish, Breton or Welsh).

bryton, *m.*, thrift, sea-pink (D. "brittons"): see **tam ōn**.

bryvya (Lh. *brivia*), *vb.*, to bleat as a sheep.

***büal**, *m.*, *pl.* **-as**, buffalo (W., B.).

büalgorn, *m.*, *pl.* **-gern**, bugle-horn (W., B.).

***büan**, *adj.*, quick, lively (W., B.).

büarth, *m.*, *pl.* **-ow**, cattle-yard (W., B.).

būben, *f.*, *pl.* **-now**, lamp-wick (D. "booban").

bucca, *m.*, *pl.* **bukkyas**, hobgoblin, imp, bogy, scarecrow : *b. nos*, C.W., *b. du* (D.), goblin, bugbear, *b. gwyn*. ghost (D.).

***büdhek**, *adj.*, victorious (W., O.B.) : name of saint, "Budock" in English spelling.

büdhy, *vb.*, to drown, submerge, (of ship) founder, be drowned or sunk : *dh* becomes *th* as final, in subj., and before *s*.

bügel, *m.*, *pl.* **-eth**, herdsman, shepherd, cowherd, pastor, *hyrde* Aelfric : *b. deves*, shepherd ; *b. gever*, goatherd ; *b. mogh*, swineherd; *b. lothnow*, neatherd, etc.

bügelek, *adj.*, pastoral, bucolic (W., B.).

bügeles, *f.*, *pl.* -ow, shepherdess (W., B.).

bügelya, *vb.*, to guard animals (W., B.).

būgh (C. Voc. *buch*, Late *bew*), *f.*, *pl.* **-as**, cow : see **mōrvūgh**.

***būgheth**, *f.*, lifetime (W., B.).

būghyk-Dew, *f.*, ladybird, ladycow (B.).

buk, *m.*, he-goat, Lh. (E.) : see **bōgh**, *m.*

buket, *m.*, *pl.* **tys**, bucket (E.) : *b. godra*, milking-pail Lh.

***būlgh**, *m.*, *pl.* **-ow**, breach, notch, gap, dent, hare-lip (W., B.).

būlgha, *vb.*, to breach, notch (W., B.).

būlho·rn, *m.*, *pl.* **-as**, snail, Lh. (D.).

būlügen, *f.*, *col.* **būlük**, earthworm (*bulligan* Borlase, *beligan* P.MS. ; D. "buliggan," "buluggan").

būlȳen, *f.*, *col.* **būly**, *pl.* **būlȳow**, rounded stone, pebble, boulder (D. "bully").

burjes, *m.*, *pl.* **-jysy**, burgher, burgess, freeman of borough, citizen, townsman, M.C. 214 (M.E.).

burmen, *f.*, *col.* **burm**, portion of barm, yeast, Borlase (O.E. *beorma*, E.D. "burm").

būs, see **bōs**, *m.*

būsel (*būzl* Lh.), *m.*, cattle-dung : *b. vergh*, horse-dung.

būselen, *f.*, *pl.* **-now**, cow-dropping (B.).

būsh (*busch*), *m.*, *pl.* **-ys**, bush, crowd, cluster, flock, mass, B.M., C.W., (D. "bush" of fish), cf. **bagas**.

bussa (*bōs-sēth*) *m.*, large salting-pot (D) : *b. 'manyn*, a pot of butter (*bors a manyn* Gw. MS.).

büthyn (C. Voc. *budin*, P. *vethan*, *vythyn*), *m.*, *pl.* **-yow**, meadow, *maed*, Aelfric : Penbuthiniowe, Tregavethan, etc., place-names.

buyldya, *vb.*, to build, C.W. 2297 (E.).

by', contraction before *n* of **byth**.

***Bȳbel**, *m.*, Bible : **Byblek*, Biblical.

bȳbyn-būbyn (*beeban booban*, Ray, 1612, "beevin bovin" D.), *m.*, *pl.* **-as**, shrimp.

***bȳgel**, **b. nōs**, *m.*, bugbear, hobgoblin (W., B.).

bȳghan, **bȳan** (C. Voc. *boghan*), *adj.*, little, small : late comp. *byghanna*, see **lē**, **lȳha**.

byjyon (*bidzheon* Lh.), *m.*, dunghill.

byken (*byth*, *kēn*), *adv.*, ever : always in mutation after **bys**, see **vyken**.

byketh, *adv.*, perpetually : see **vyketh**.

'byla, see **a-blē**.

bylen (*belan*), *m.*, *pl.* **tüs vylen**, villein, villain ; *adj.*, villainous ; *adv.*, horribly : *an bylen*, the evil one, the devil.

by·lyny, *m.*, villainy, vileness.

by·nary (C.W. *benary*), *adv.*, for ever (follows vb.) : as M.B. *bet nary* ; see **bys**, **vynary.**

byner (*byth, yn, ür,* C.W. *bydnar*), *adv.*, never : used before optative particle **re(s,j)-.**

bynk, see **mynk.**

***byns**, *f.*, vice, gripping instrument (B., W., Carnarvon D.).

bynytha(*benytha*), *adv.*, ever, for evermore; *b. ny-*, never, nevermore : see **vynytha.**

byrla (*byzla* Davies Gilbert), *vb.*, to embrace, hug, P. (Late, perhaps corrupt).

bȳs (*beys, bēs,* C. Voc. *en bit*), *m.*, world : *y'n b.*, at all, *an yl y'n b.*, whichsoever, *keper y'n b. ha, del*, exactly like, as ; *gwyn y vys*, happy his lot, blessed ; *oll an b.*, everybody ; *an b.*, business, affairs in general, P.C. 2411, N. Boson ; *awos an b.* (with neg.), for the world, on any account see **gwynvȳs.**

bȳs (C. Voc. *bis, bes,* Lh. *bēz*), *m.*, *pl.* **besyas**, finger : thumb to 4th finger, *b.-bras, b.-rag, b.-cres, peswera-b.* or *b.-bysow, b.-byghan*; *b.-tros* (C. Voc. *bis truit*), m., pl. *besyas-tros, treys*, toe.

bys (C.W. *bez*), *prep.*, *conj.*, until, as far as, up to, even to : *b. worfen* (or *gorfen*) *bys*, till the end of the world ; *b. Loundres*, up to London ; *b. dhyn*, to us ; *-vynytha, -vynary, -nefra*, evermore, for ever ; *b. voy*, any more ; *b. dy* (or *ty*), thither, to her ; *b.-yn*, unto, all the way to ; *b.-y 'th*, until thy ; *b.-pan*², *b.-may*⁵, (before vb.) until ; causes second mutation in following *b, g, gw, m.* : *c, k, p* are unchanged ; *d* mostly becomes *t* ; this and radical *t* may cause the *s* to become *t*, see **byteweth.**

bysken, *f.*, *pl.* **-now**, finger-stall, thimble, lit. finger-skin : *b. mes*, acorn-cup (B.).

bysmēr, *m.*, infamy, ignominy, reproach, scandal, contempt, disgrace, besmirching (M.E. *bysmare*) ; *rag gul dhyn-ny b.*, to scandalize us, bring us into disgrace.

bysna, *m.*, warning or example to evil-doers (M.E. *bysne*) : *ma 'n-jeffo pup-oll b. ow-myras orto*, that all may have warning when seeing him, P.C. 2092.

bysow (C. Voc. *bisou*, Lh. *bezo*), *m.*, *pl.* **besewow**, finger-ring, ring, *hringc* Aelfric ; *lagasow b.*, wall-eyes in horses, Lh. M.S.

bystel (C. Voc. *bistel*), *f.*, gall, bile, *gealla* Aelfric.

bysy, *adj.*, busy, occupied, diligent, employed, attentive, requisite, important, called for, taken up, insistent, fussy (M.E.): *dhyso ef a-vyth b.*, it shall be in full use for thee, O.M. 405 ; *b. a-vyth dhedha*, it will be of import to them, O.M. 335 ; *b. vyth*, it will take, O.M. 398 ; *b. vya oll an blu*, it would require the whole parish, R.D. 2106 (D. "busy all"); *b. yu dheugh bones war*, you must be careful, P.C. 999 ; *b· vya dhys gothvos*, thou woulds't have to know, P.C. 1672.

bȳsya, *vb.*, to finger (W.).

bysydhya, -jydhya, *vb.*, to baptize : 3 s. pres.-fut. *bysyth.*

bysydhyans, *m.*, baptism.

bysydhyer, *m.*, *pl.* **-yoryon**, baptist (W.).

bysyth, *m.*, baptism : *tas, mam, flogh, b.*, godfather, godmother, godchild (W., B.).

bysythven, *m.*, font (W., from E. fontstone).

bysqueth, see **bythqueth.**

***by·takyl**, *m.*, *pl.* **-clys**, binnacle (E.).

bytege·ns (*bytygyns*, M.C. *betegyns*, for *byth dhe gens*), *adv.*, nevertheless, yet, however.

byteweth (*bys, deweth*), *adv.*, to the end or extremity, in fine, after all, B.M.

byth, *adv.*, ever, always, any, not any, no : usually with neg. ; *b. well*, (not) ever a better, *b. moy*, (not) any more ; *b. pan*², whenever, as soon as ever ; mutations as for **bys**, except in *byth4queth, b. moy ;* see **-vyth.**

byth, etc., see **bōs**, Table in Appendix VIII.

bytheth, see **bytteth.**

byth-onen, *pron.*, any one, ever a one, P.C. 772.

bythqueth, bysqueth (Late *bisca(th)*), *adv.*, ever (of past, with positive or neg).

bytteth (*byttyth, bythyth*, for *byth deth*), *adv.*, ever, any day, any more (of future, with neg.).

byxyn, see **box.**

C (mutations G, H, and of Ch, J)

N.B. With vowel change of *a, o, to e, y, c* becomes *k* ; *c* is always hard except before *e, y.*

cabel, *m.*, blame, censure, slander, accusation, proof of guilt, O.M. 2673.

cabester, *m.*, *pl.* **-trow**, halter, noose, loop, attachment of fish-hook to lead (D.).

cablüs, *adj.*, culpable, blameworthy (B.).

cably, *vb.*, to blame, censure, calumniate,

accuse, defame, incriminate, inculpate, find guilty: p. pt. *cablys*.

Cablys, de-Yow[3] **Hablys**, *m.*, Maundy Thursday (Lat. *Capitilavium*, Palm Sunday): a var. is *Camlys*, *de-Yow Hamlys* (*-os*, for rhyme), P.C. 654, as M.B. *dez Yaou Hamblit*.

cabūlen, *f.*, *pl.* **-now**, stone tied to rope and splashed into the water to drive pilchards back into the seine (D. "caboolen").

cabūler, *m.*, *pl.* **-loryon**, stirrer, one who bestirs himself (D. "cabooler").

cabūly, *vb.*, to stir, mix, dabble, splash (D. "cabooly-stone," "cabble," W. *cyboli*, V. *kabouilhein*).

caca (*kaka* P.), *vb.*, to void excrement (E.D.).

cacha, *m.*, *pl.* **-chys**, latch of door (D. "catch").

cachya (var. *chachya*), *vb.*, to catch, seize, snatch, entrap (in argument), hitch, make fast (M.E. *cache*, *chache*): p. pt. *kychys*, 2 pl. imp. *kycheugh*; *yn ow ros...y gachya*, catch him in my net, P.C. 55.

cadar, *f.*, *pl.* **-eryow**, chair: place-names Chapel an Gadar, Cadar Myghal; *c. vreghek*, armchair (B.).

caderya, *vb.*, to take the chair (W.).

caderyer, *m.*, *pl.* **-yoryon**, chairman (W.).

***cadōn**, *f.*, bond, chain, trace (W., B.).

caf, *m.*, *pl.* **-avyow**, cave, B.M.

cafalek, see **cavylek**.

cafans, *m.*,? take, person or thing to be taken, M.C. 67: unless for *cafsen*.

†cafas (C. Voc. *cafat*) *m.*, cup, vase, vessel, *faet* Aelfric.

***cafor**, *m.*, chafer, beetle, C. Voc. (O.E.), *ceafor* Aelfric.

cafos, cavos, cawas, *vb.*, to have, get, find, discover, find out by study, provide (for), invent: 3 s. pres.-fut., *kyf*, 3 pl. *kefons*: 3 s. impf. ind. *kefy*, impf. subj. *caffa*, p. pt. *kefys*; *a-gyf bos lour*, that will furnish (M.E. *fynde*) food enough, O.M. 1060: *ty-a-vyn y gafos ledhys*, thou wishest to get him slain, P.C. 2455; *ny-vyth kefys gowak*, he will not be found out to be a liar, C.W. 2366.

cagal, *m.*, dung of sheep, goats, etc.; clotted filth on fleece or clothing, Borlase: *c. deves*, sheep-dung, Lh. MS.

cagh, see **caugh**.

cagla, *vb.*, to bedaggle fleece with sheep-dung or spatter clothing with mud (D. "caggle").

caja, *f.*, daisy: *c. vras*, ox-eye daisy (*gajah broaz*, Borlase, D. "gadgavraws,"); Park Catcher, field-name.

cāken, *f.*, *pl.* **-kys**, cake, Lh. (E.).

†cal, *adj.*, cunning, sly, C. Voc., *paetig* Aelfric.

cal (*kal*), *m.*, penis, Lh.. Gw.

cala (C. Voc. *kala*), *col.*, straw, *s.* **gwelengala**: *c. gwely*, straw bedding, *beddingc* Aelfric; once *calav*, but as in B. *kolo*, the *v*, representing *m* of *calam(us)*, is lost.

calamajȳna (?*cala* for *carlyth*), *m.*, cuckoo-ray, fish (D. "callamajeena").

Calan, *m.*, Calend, 1st of month: *C. Genver*, *de-Halan Genver*, New Year's Day; *nos-C. Gwaf*, Hallowe'en; *C. Gwaf*, All Hallowtide, *de-Halan Gwaf*, Nov. 1, All Hallows; *Cala' Me*, *de-Hala' Me*, May Day; *C. Hedra*, Oct. 1st, etc.; *de-Whalan* is a less correct spelling of *de-Halan*.

calcar, *m.*, *pl.* **-cras**, weever-fish (D.): see **calken**.

calcor, *m.*, *pl.* **-yon**, calculator, mathematician, B.M. 1735.

cales, *adj.*, hard, severe, difficult; comp. *calessa* (*calassa* C.W. later *calacha*, *calatsha* Lh.); *gwȳthys c.*, hard worked; *cales-paynys*, harsh torments.

***calesen, -jen**, *f.*, *pl.* **-now**, callosity, corn: **c. kȳk*, tumour (W., B.).

calesy, caleshē·, *vb.*, to harden (W., B.): *caleshe* as **berhē**.

caletter, *m.*, difficulty, hardness.

calken, *f.*, *pl.* **-now**, father-lasher, fish (D.); cf. Ir. *calg*, prickle, sting.

calkya, *vb.*, to caulk a ship (E.); *my a-galk*, I will caulk, C.W. 2286.

call (*gal*, rust, P.), *m.*, tungstate of iron (D.), B. *kailh houarn*, iron-ore.

callen, *f.*, *pl.* **-now**, layer of iron-ochre on face of rock (D.).

***ca·llester**, *m.*, flint (W., B.); replaced by **mēn flynt**.

ca·lmynsy (*calmindzy* Lh. MS.), *m.*, stillness, tranquillity, calm, serenity.

cals, calj, *m.*, heap, pile, many, plenty, a full supply, an abundance: *anedha kyn y-th-fe c.*, though thou hast store of them, B.M. 2046; *c. meyn*, a heap of stones, M.C. 11, P.C. 62.

†caltor, *f.*, *pl.* **-yow**, cauldron, crock, open kettle, C. Voc., *cytel* Aelfric: see **caudarn**.

Ca·lvary, *m.*, Calvary.

cam (Late *cabm*), *adj.*, crooked, wry, distorted, †squinting, C. Voc., *scelgegede* Aelfric; *prefix*, wrong, mis- ; *m.*, wicked person, rogue, *pl.* **-mow**, crime, fault, injustice, bend, curve, arc, arch : *gans c.*, unjustly; Lhuyd in his *camgarrek*, bowlegged, *camlagajek*, squinting, *camscodhak*, crooked-shouldered, used *cam-*, prefix, as "crooked"; this does not agree with its general use and these seem to be inventions based on **camhensek**.

cam, see **cammen**.

cam, *m.*, *pl.* **-mow**, step, pace, gait : *mos, gweskel, whetha*, etc., *war gam*, go, strike, blow, etc., gently, moderately, steadily; *ke war dha gam* ! *eugh war agas c. why* ! *eugh why war gam* ! go easy! don't be hasty! don't exaggerate! hold on! steady! cf. B. *it war ho tres* ! with same meaning; *cam* may also have been used as meaning "track," see **camdhavas**.

camdhavas (*cabmdhavas* P.), *m.*, lit. "sheepstep" (?"track"), but used latterly in place of **camneves**.

camder, *m.*, crookedness (W.).

camdremena, *vb.*, to transgress, trespass.

camdyby, *vb.*, to err in thought, R.D. 996.

camdybyans, *m.*, error.

camgarrek, see **cam**.

camgemeres, *vb.*, to mistake: replaced latterly by **myskemeres**.

camgryjyans, *m.*, heresy.

†**camhensek** (C. Voc. *camhinsic*), *adj.*, unjust, unrighteous, malignant, of evil ways, *teonful* Aelfric; ? M. Cor. *cam y hens*.

camhenwel, *vb.*, to misname: 3 s. pret. *-wys* (W., B.).

camlagajek, see **cam**.

camleverel, *vb.*, to mispronounce.

camleveryans, *m.*, mispronunciation.

Camlys, see **Cablys**.

camma, *vb.*, to bend, curve, crook, writhe, distort: *c myn, ganow*, to grimace; p. pt. *cammys* (Late *cabmes*).

***cammek**, *f.*, felloe of wheel (W., B.)

cammen, *adv.* (used to enforce negative), in (no) way, (not) in any wise, (not) at all: before *n*, may be shortened to *cam*; *na(g)*- is used after it, but *ny(ns)*- before it, unless in relative; M.B. *camhet*, pace (B. *kammed*), is used similarly, *ne... camhet* answering to Fr. *ne...pas*; Cor. *cammen*, f., a single pace, is probably a noun also, though not found as such.

camneves (P. *cabmdhavas*, C. Voc. *camnivet*), *f.*, rainbow, *renboga* Aelfric: lit. heavenly arch; see **camdhavas**.

camomdhōn, *vb.*, to misconduct oneself.

campolla (*kem-*, *polla*, Late *compla*, W. *cymhwyllo*), *vb.*, to mention, B.M.; to reason (W.), see **pōll**.

campyer, *m.*, *pl.* **-yoryon**, champion, Lh. (from Welsh).

†**cams**, *f.*, *pl* **-ow**, alb, surplice, *albe* Aelfric.

camscodhek, see **cam**.

camva, *f.*, stile (W.).

camvrüsy, *vb.*, to misjudge.

camwonys, *vb. and m.*, to blunder, bungle.

camwo·rtheby, *vb*, to reply impertinently.

camworthyp, *m.*, impertinence.

camwül, *vb.*, to do ill, trespass.

camwyth, *m.*, misdeed, misdoing.

camwythres, *m.*, ill-deed, wrongdoing (W.).

cān, *f.*, *pl.* **-ow**, song, poem.

can, *m.*, glory, splendour, brightness, whiteness, shine, O.M. 2640, R.D. 515; fluor-spar (D.): *c. tyr*, quartz (D. "carn tyer"); see **lōrgan**, **stērgan**.

†**can**, *adj.*, very white (of bread): *bara c.*, C. Voc.

cana, *vb.*, to sing; (of musical instruments) to sound: p. pt. *kenys*, etc., as **cara** in Appendix VIII.

cancar, see **canker**.

canel, *m.*, *pl.* **-lys**, spigot, Borlase (E.D.).

canel, *f.*, *pl.* **-nolyow**, **-low**, channel: place-names, The Gannel, Venton Gannel.

caner, **-ör**, *m.*, *pl.* **-oryon**, singer (W., B.): see †**kenyas**.

ca·njeon (*cangeon*), *m. or f.*, *pl.* **-s**, changeling, wretch (M.E. and O. Fr. *cangeon*): misread *caugeon* Norris, Williams, Stokes.

canker (C. Voc. *canc(h)er*, Lh. *kankar*), *m.*, *pl* **kencras**, crab (D. "canker," harbour-crab); *no pl.*, canker, corrosion, cancer, corn rust.

canmēl, *vb.*, to laud, praise highly (W., B.).

†**canna** (C. Voc. *kanna*), *m.*, *pl.* **-nys**, flagon, can, water-pot, *buc* Aelfric.

canna, *vb.*, to bleach, whiten (W., B.).

cannas, *f.*, *pl.* **-ow**, messenger, deputy, envoy, legate, missionary, ambassador; message: represented by m. pron.

cannaty, *m.*, *pl.* **-ow**, mission-house (W.).

†**canores**, *f.*, *pl.* **-ow**, songstress, C. Voc, *sangystre* Aelfric.

canquyth (*cans gwyth*), *adv.*, a hundred

times : *dek c.* ten hundred times, P.C. 574.

cans, *card. num.* ; *m.*, *pl.* **-ow**, hundred : final *s* is lost in *pencangour*, *canquyth* cf. *pym woly* (W. *can*, *pum* before nouns).

†cans, obsolete C. Voc. form of **gans.**

***cans**, *m.*, *pl.* **-ow**, rim of circle, sieve, etc. (W., B.).

cansbledhen, *f.*, *pl.* **-dhynnow**, century, hundred years, Lh.

cansblōth, *m.*, hundred years of age.

canscolm, *m.*, knotgrass (W.) : see **mylgolm, colm.**

cansplēk, *adj.*, hundredfold.

canspōs, *m.*, hundredweight, 112 lbs, J. Boson.

canspüns, *m.*, hundred-pound weight P.C. 3144.

canstel, *f.*, *pl.* **-low**, basket, P. : as B. *kanistell*, from Med. Lat. *canistellum*, dim. of *canistra*.

cansves, *ord. num.*, hundredth.

cansvyl, *adj.*, *m.*, *pl.* **-yow**, hundred thousand, O.M. 1614.

canter, *m.*, *pl.* **-trow**, frame for fishing-line (D.).

†cantol (C. Voc. *cantuil*), *f.*, *pl.* **-yow**, candle : *c. gor, sof*, wax-, tallow-, candle, *sem–c.*, candlegrease.

†ca·ntolbren (C. Voc. *cantulbren*) *m.*, *pl.* **-nyer**, candlestick, *candelstaef* Aelfric : see **chownler.**

ca·ntolor, *m.*, *pl.* **-yow**, chandelier ; *pl.* **-yon**, chandler (W., B.).

***canon**, *m.*, *pl.* **-ys**, cannon (E.).

†capa, *f.*, *pl.* **-pyow**, cope, cape, cloak, C. Voc., *caeppe* Aelfric ; see **cōp.**

cappa, *m.*, *pl.* **-pys**, Lh. (M.E. *cappe*).

***capten**, *m.*, *pl.* **-ow**, captain.

capyas (*capios*), *m.*, writ of arrest, capias, P.C. 2266, misread *carios* Norris, Williams.

car (*kār* Lh.), *m.*, *pl.* **kerens**, friend ; kinsman ; father : *†c. ogas*, near relative ; C. Voc., *sibling* Aelfric : *pur ogas c.*, very near kinsman, B.M.

car, *m.*, *pl.* **kerry**, car, cart : **c.-tan*, motor (B.) : *c.-slynkya*, sledge.

car, see **kēr.**

cara, *vb.*, to love, like, care for; as auxiliary, like or care to : *ny-garsen orto metya*, we should not care to encounter him ; *byth ny-garaf*, I shall never care (to do so), for parts see TABLE in APPENDIX VIII.

cara·dewder (*-dowder*), *m.*, lovableness, amiability.

ca·radow, *adj.*, beloved, loving : *m.* or *f.*, *pl.* **-yon**, dear one.

carbons, *m.*, *pl.* **-ow**, cart-bridge: Carbens, Carbis, place-name.

cardeyl, *m.*, manure (W., B.).

cardhen, *f.*, brake, thicket (W.) : place-names.

cardynal, *m.*, *pl.* **-as**, cardinal (W., B.) : *c. -trylost*, var. of *carlyth-trylost* ; see **carlyth.**

cares, *f.*, *pl.* **-ow**, friend, lover, f. (W., B.).

care·tysen, *f.*, *col.* **caretys**, carrot, Lh.

***carg**, *m.*, *pl.* **-ow**, load, burden, cargo (B.).

***carga**, *vb.*, to load, charge (B.).

carghar (*carhar*), *m.*, *pl.* **-ow**, fetter, shackle, (in pl.) stocks, B.M. 3686: ***c. horn***, gyves, *c. pren*, stocks, Lh. MS. ; see **stok,**

carghara (*car'a* M.C. 75), *vb.*, to fetter, shackle, pillory, put in stocks, B.M. 3573.

carhens, *m.*, *pl.* **-y**, cart-road (B.).

carjy, *m.*, *pl.* **-ow**, cart-shed (B.).

carlyth, (*karlath*, Lh., ? for ***cawr-lȳth***), *f.*, *pl.* **-ow**, Lh. M.S., smooth ray, skate : *c. trylost*, skate, Borlase.

carn, *m.*, *pl.* **-ow**, rock-pile.

carn, *m.*, *pl.* **-ow**, hoof : ***c. collan***, knife-handle, Lh. (probably from W.).

carnak, *adj.*, rocky (W., B.).

carnak, *adj.*, hoofed (W., B.).

carnal, *adj.*, carnal, C.W. 1315 (E.).

carneth, **carna**, *f.*, *pl.* **-nedhow**, heap of rocks : *th* prevents mutation of following *c k, t, d*, turning *gw* to *qu* in place-name Carnaquidden.

†carol (C. Voc. *karol*), *m.*, *pl.* **-yow**, choir, *chor* Aelfric.

caroly, *vb.*, to sing in concert, carol (W.).

carow (C. Voc. *caruu*), *m.*, *pl.* **kerewy**, stag, hart.

ca·rpenter, *m.*, *pls.* **-toryon**, **-s**, carpenter, O.M. 2410, 2557.

***carrak**. *m.*, *pl.* **-ys**, carrack, medieval ship (M.E.).

carregek, *adj.*, rocky (W., B.).

carrek, *f.*, *pl.* **ca·rrygy**, rock mass, huge rock : *c. sans*, rock altar used in ordeal.

***carten**, *f.*, *pl.* **-now**, card (B.).

***carth**, *m.*, *pl.* **-yon**, tow, oakum, offscourings (W., B.).

***cartha**, **-y**, *vb.*, to scour, clean out (W., B.).

***carthpren**, *m.*, plough-staff (W., B.).

carvȳl, *m.*, *pl.* **-as**, carthorse (W.).

carya (*cariah* P.), *vb.*, to cart ; 3 s. pres.-fut. *car* ; p. pt. *caryes* (*kerrys* C.W. 2076 = *kerghys*).

*__caryach__, *m.*, *pl.* __-ajys__, carriage (M.E.).
__caryn__, *m.*, *pl.* __-yas__, carcase, carrion (M.E. *careyn*).
__cās__, *f.*, *pl.* __-ow__, war, battle, fight.
__cās__, *m.*, cause, case, matter, affair, event, business, hap, incident (M.E.): *na-dhowt a'n c.*, have no doubt of it; *my a lever an c. dhys*, I'll tell thee what.
__cas__, *m.*, hatred, hate, enmity, trouble, disaster, misery; *adj.*, hateful, displeasing: *c. yu genej*, I dislike; *mur a gas vya genef*, I should be very reluctant.
__casa__, *vb.*, to hate: p. pt. *kesys*; 3 s. pres.-fut. *cās*, R.D. 1889.
__casa·dewder__, *m.*, hatefulness: formed after __caradewder__.
__ca·sadow__, *adj.*, hateful, detestable, repulsive, vile; *m. or f.*, *pl.* __-yon__, wretch, villain: *an gasadow*, f., O.M. 2691.
__casal__, *f.*, *pl.* __-selyow__, *d.* __dywgasal__, arm-pit: *yn-dan y gasal*, under his arm; *c. ha c.*, arm-in-arm (B.); *c. mordhos*, the groin (W.).
__cas-beler__, *m.*, winter-cress (D. "cassabully").
__cascorn__, *m.*, *pl.* __-skern__, horn of battle (W.).
__casek__ (C. Voc. *cassec*), *f.*, *pl.* __ca·sygy__, mare: *c.-cos*, woodpecker, lit. "woodmare" (B.).
__caskergh__, *m.*, *pl.* __-ow__, campaign (W.).
__caslan__, *f.*, *pl.* __-now__, battlefield (W.).
__caslys__ (†*cadlys*), *f.*, *pl.* __-yow__, head-quarters, entrenchment: place-name, Gadlys.
†__casor__, __cajor__ (C. Voc. *cadwur*), *m.*, *pl.* __-yon__, warrior, *cempa* Aelfric.
__caspows__, *f.*, *pl.* __-yow__, coat of mail (W.).
__cast__, *m.*, *pl.* __-ys__, trick, dodge (M.E.).
__castel__, *m.*, *pl.* __-tylly__ (Scawen), castle: var. *kestel* in place-names; anciently pl.
__castel__, *m.*, *pl.* __-lys__, village (M.E. from *castellum* in Vulgate).
*__caster__, *m.*, male organ of animal (W., B.).
__castya__, *vb.*, to trick (W.).
__castȳga__, *vb.*, to thrash, flog.
__castȳk(g)__·, *m.*, flogging (D. "casteeg").
__casvargh__, *m.*, *pl.* __-vērgh__, war-horse, charger (W.).
__caswyth__, __cajwyth__, *m.*, thicket: Tregaswith, Cadgwith, place-names.
__casyer__ (*kazher* Lh.), *m.*, a large sieve (E.D. "casier," "cayer").
__cath__ (C. Voc. *kat*), *f.*, *pl.* __-as__, cat: *c. helyk*, willow catkin (B.); see __gourcath__.

__cathecū·mynys__ (pr. *-um'nys*), *m.*, catechumen(us), B.M. 1818 (Lat.).
__cathes__, *f.*, *pl.* __-ow__, she-cat (W., B.).
__cathyk__, *m.*, *pls.* __-ygow__, __-thasygow__, kitten (B.).
__caudarn__, *m.*, *pl.* __-s__, cauldron, Lh., (M.E. *cawdryn*).
__caugh__ (*kāwh* Lh.), *m.*, filth; excrement, dung, ordure: *c.-dyllo*, to defecate (D. "cockdollar").
__caugha__, *vb.*, to void excrement (W., B.).
__caughty__, *m.*, privy (W.).
__caughwas__, *m.*, *pl.* __-weryon__, faint-hearted, mean-spirited, careless, slack, or sluggish fellow.
*__caun__, *m.*, *pl.* __-ow__, trough, gutter, hollowed half of tree (W., B.).
__cauns__, *m.*, *pl.* __-ys__, paved or cobbled way (E.D.), Pednycawnce (*pen an c.*) place-name.
__caunsya__, *vb.*, to pave (E.D.).
__causer__, *m.*, *pl.* __-s__, cause (person who causes), B.M. 4001 (E.).
__cavanscüs__, __-skys__, *m.*, escape, subterfuge, evasion (cf. W. *cyfan*, entire and __skēs__, __scüs__), M.C. 151.
__cavanscüsa__, *vb.*, to escape, get off, evade, O.M. 321.
__cavach__, *col.*, cabbage, Lh. (E.).
__cavos__, see __cafos__.
__cavow__, *m.*, *pl. used as abst. s.*, grief, sorrow: sing., *caf*, B. *kanv*, is disused.
__ca·vylek__ (*cafalek*), *adv.*, contentious, cavilsome: *del yua pyth c.*, as it is a cause of wrangling, a bone of contention, O.M. 2784.
__cawas__, see __cafos__.
__cawlen__, *f.*, *col.* __cawl__ (C. Voc. *caul*, Lh. *kaol*), cabbage, kale, *caul* Aelfric.
†__cawr__ (C. Voc. *caur*), *m.*, *pl.* __kewry__, giant.
__cawres__, *f.*, *pl.* __-ow__, giantess (W.).
__cawrvargh__ (C. Voc. *caur march*), *m.*, *pl.* __-vērgh__, camel, *olfend* Aelfric.
*__cāy__, *m.*, quay (E.).
__cendal__, see __sendal__.
__cercot__, see __surcot__.
__certan__, *adv.*, certainly; *adj.*, a certain, B.M. 4426; *pron.*, certain people, C.W. 2231 (M.E.).
__certüs__, *adv.*, certes, verily, O.M. 2122 (M.E.).
__challa__, __chal__, *m.*, *pl.* __-lys__, jowl, jaw-bone (M.E. *chawle*).
__chalynj__, __-nch__, *m.*, claim, challenge, B.M. 2371 (M.E. *chalange*).

chalynjya, *vb.*, to demand as a right, challenge (M.E.).
chambour, (*tshombar* Lh.), *m.*, *pl.* **-s**, bedroom, chamber (M.E.).
Chanel, *m.*, British Channel, B.M. 1089 (E.).
chanjya, *vb.*, to change, alter (E.).
***chansel**, *m.*, *pl.* **-s**, chancel (E.).
***chansler**, *m.*. *pl.* **-s**, chancellor (E.).
chapel (*Tshappal* Lh.), *m.*, *pl.*-**yow**, chapel (E.).
chaplen, *m.*, *pl.* **-s**, chaplain, B.M. 4034 (E.).
chappon (*tshappon* Lh.), *m.*, *pl.* **-s**, capon, O.M. 1206 (E.).
chaptra, *m.*, *pl.* **-trys**, chapter (Late, E.).
charj, **charych**, *m.*, *pl.* **-ys**, charge, care, account, responsibility, order, duty (E.).
charjya, *vb.*, to charge, exhort, bid, order, C.W. (E.).
chartour (*chartur*), *m.*, *pl.* **-s**, charter, deed of freehold, O.M. (M.E.).
charych, see **charj**.
chast, *adj.*, chaste, C.W. 1314 (E.).
chastÿa, *vb.*, to chastise, reprove: 3 s. pres.-fut. *chasty* (M.E.).
chassya, *vb.*, to chase; drive, hunt (M.E.): *gans ow whyp my a-n-chas may kertho garwa y gam*, with my whip I'll drive him so that he may walk with a more uneven gait, P.C. 1196.
chattel (*chattal* C.W., *-tel* Gw., *shattal* Lh.), *col.*, cattle (M.E.).
chayn (*chēn*), *m.*, *pl.* **-ys**, chain (E.).
chaynya (*chēnya*), *vb.*, to chain (E.).
chayr (*cheyr*, *cheer*), *m.*, *pl.*, **-ys**, chair: *c. epscop*, bishop's throne, B.M. 3002 (M.E. *chayre*).
chēk, *m.*, *pl.* **-kys**. pot, crock, cauldron, R.D. 139 (O.E. *ceac*, vessel).
chekker (*tshekkar* Lh.), *m.*, *pl.* **checcras**, stonechat (D. "chacker"), or wheatear (D. "chicker"): *c.-eythyn*, furzechat, Lh. MS.
chenon, *m.*, *pl.* **-s** (B.M. 2812), canon (M.E.).
che·nonry, *m.*, canonry (M.E.): *c. an clos*, c. of the close, O.M. 2772.
***chēny**, *m.*, china-ware (E.D.).
chēr, *m.*, mien, aspect, demeanour, cheer, state of mind (M.E.): *gwellha dha jer! byth da dha jer!* cheer up! *drok agan c.*, etc., in misery, in a cheerless state.
che·rubyn, *m.*, cherub (M.E.): pl. used as sing.
cherya, *vb.*, to cherish, care for, B.M. 3193 (M.E., Fr. *chérir*).
che·ryta, *m.*, charity (M.E.).
chēson (*cheyson*), see **achēson**.
chet, *m.*, *pl.* **-ttys**, fellow, chit, captive, caitiff (M.E.).
che·valry, *m.*, knighthood, order of knights, distinction in warfare, chivalry (M.E.): *pen an c.*, head of the knightly order, B.M. 174.
chōca, **chōk** (*tshawk*, *-a*, Lh.), *m.*, *pl.* **-ōkys**, jackdaw, chough (E.D. "chawk").
chofar, *m.*, *pl* **-s**, chafing-dish, Lh. (E.).
chōgha (*tshauha* P.), *m.* *pl.* **-ghys**, jackdaw, chough (D. "chaw").
chōns, *m.*, chance, O.M. 2822: see **goda chōns**.
chōrl, *m.*, *pl.* **-s**, churl (M.E.).
chownler (*tshownler* Lh.), *m.*, *pl.* **-s**, candlestick, chandelier (M.E. *chaundelere*).
***churra-nōs**, *m.*, nightjar.
chȳ (older *tȳ*, C. Voc. *ti*, latest *chei*, *tshyi* Lh.), *m.*, *pls.* **-ow**, **treven**, house, building, family: as suffix becomes *-jy* or after sharp consonant *-ty*; *c.-anneth*, dwelling-house; *c. -cok*, cookshop; *c. -forn*, bakehouse; *c. -gwary*, gaming-house; *c. -marghas*, markethouse; *c. -pobas*, bakehouse; *c. -whel*, workshop; *c. -whetha*, blowing-house, blast-furnace; as unstressed first element in compound names *chy* is usually pronounced **sha**, *Chypons*, as "Shapons," etc.; *y'n chymma* (*chy-ma*), in this house; see **a-jȳ**, **tȳ**, **yn-chȳ**.
chycok (*tshikuk* Lh.), *f.*, *pl.* **-as**, swallow: ?swift, see **gwennol**, **cōk**, *f.*
chȳf, *adj.*, chief (M.E.): *c. -cyta*, capital, *c. -gwythor*, foreman, *c. pryva-gwythyas*, chief of bodyguard, *c. warden*, chief keeper.
chyffar, *m.*, bargain, chaffer, M.C. 40 (M.E.).
chȳften, *m.*, *pl.* **-s**, chieftain (M.E.).
chȳl, *m. or f.*, child (Late, E.): *c. vyghan*, little child, endearment (D. "cheel veean"); *c. yn jughan!* poor little thing! (D. "cheel en jewan"), see **dū(gh)an**.
chylla, *m.*, *pl.* **-lys**, lamp for burning train-oil (D.E. "chill").
chymbla (*tshimbla* Lh.) *m.*, *pl.* **-blys**, chimney (E.D. "chimbly").
***chyru·rjery**, *m.*, surgery (M.E.).
***chyrurjyen**, *m.*, *pl.* **-s**, surgeon (M.E.).
cla·byttour (*clabitter* P.), *m.*, *pl.* **-s**, bittern (M.E. *clawe*, *bitore*): Sir Humphrey Davey records that the bittern's claw was in use as a shooting-mascot; see **bongors**.

clāf, *adj.*, sick, ill, sore, leprous, *adlig*, Aelfric; *m.*, *pl.* **clevyon**, sick person, especially leper: *c. -dyberthys*, separated leper; *ow holon res-eth yn c., gallas ow holon c.*, my heart has gone sick, P.C. 1027 2610.

clamder, *m.*, swoon, faint, numbness, unconsciousness, P.C. 2593: cf. D. "clammed," "clamoured," often ill, Polwhele, suggesting **clāf**; "clam" is also used for "qualm."

cla·mdera, *vb.*, to swoon, faint, become unconscious, stupefied, or numb: 3 s. pret. ending *-ys* or *-as*; *yth-esof ow- c.*, I am getting numb (with cold), P.C. 1224.

clap, *m.*, chatter, prate: *syns dha glap*! hold thy tongue! (M.E.).

clappya, *vb.*, to chatter, gabble, jabber, talk (M.E.).

***clask**, **caskel**, *m.*, collection; *vb.*, to beg, gather (W., B.): replaced by **beggya**.

***class**, *m.*, *p.* **-ys**, class (E.).

***classya**, *vb.*, to classify (E.).

clattra, *vb.*, to tattle, talk noisily, B.M. 861 (M.E.).

clavjy, **clojy**, *m.*, lazar-house, hospital: place-name Clodgy.

clavor, *m.*, leprosy, scurf: see **clavorek**.

†**cla·vorek**, **clavrek** (C. Voc. *claf(h)orec*), *adj.*, leprous, *hreoflig*, *licdhrowere* Aelfric; *m.*, *pl.* **-egyon**, *leper*.

†**clawster** (*clauster*, C.Voc.), *m.*, *pl.* **-trow**, cloister, *clauster* Aelfric; see **cloyster**.

cledha (for †*cledhef*), *m.*, *pl.* **-dhevyow** (always incorrectly *-dhedhyow*, *-dhydhow*, Late *dhyow*), sword: *c. 'dan*, sword of fire (*a* omitted), C.W. 965; *c. byghan*, poniard; *c. mur*, two-handed sword, claymore; *cledha* was evidently thought to stand for *cledheth*, hence the pl. used.

cledhek, *adj.*, left-handed (Lh.).

cledhevas, *m.*, *pl.* **-esow**, sword-stroke (W.).

cledhevyas, *m.*, *pl.* **-ysy**, swordsman (B.).

clēdhya, **clüdhya**, *vb.*, to dig a trench, excavate (W., B.).

cledhya, **cledhevya**, *vb.*, to wield a sword (W., B.).

cledhyas, *m.*, *pl.* **-ysy**, left-handed man (B.).

cledhyer, **cledhevor**, *m.*, *pl.* **-yoryon**, **-oryon**, swordsman (W., B.).

clegar, *m.*, *pl.* **-grow**, cliff, precipice: place-names Clicker, Cligga.

clēgh, see **clōgh**.

clēghȳ· (Lh. *glihi*, P. *clehe*, B.M. *clehy* for *clēgh-yȳ*), *m.*, ice: lit. icicles, 'ice-bells,' W. *clych ia*; see **clōgh**, **yey**.

†**clēghyk** (C. Voc. *clechic*), *m.*, *pl.* **-ygow**, small handbell, *litel belle* Aelfric.

clēghtour, †**clēghty** (C. Voc. *clechti*), *m.*, belfry, steeple, *belhus* Aelfric; (D. "cleeta," as fishermen's taboo-name).

cleja, see **clesa**.

clejor, *m.*, shelter (W., B.).

clēm, *m.*, *pl.* **-ys**, defence, counterclaim, R.D. 625 (M.E. *claime*).

clēr, *adj.*, clear, bright, comp. *clerra*; *adv.*, completely: *c. passyes*, quite past, C.W. (M.E. *clere*).

clērder, *m.*, clearness, clarity (W.).

clērhē·, *vb.*, to clear, brighten (W.): as **berhē**.

clerjy, *m.*, learning, erudition; the learned (M.E.).

cle·rÿon, *m.*, *pl.* **-s**, clarion; c.-player, B.M. 276 (M.E.).

cles, *adj.*, sheltering, warm, snug, cosy (W., B.).

clesa, **-ja**, *vb.*, to shelter, make snug (W., B.).

***clēsen**, *f.*, *pl.* **-now**, scar, cicatrice (W., B.).

cleswedhen, **-jwedhen**, *f.*, *col.* **cleswȳth**, **-jwȳth**, sheltering tree: in Treglidgwith.

clēth, **clüth**, *m.*, *pl.* **-edhyow**, trench, ditch, excavation.

clēth, *adj.*, left; *m.*, †North: *a'n barth c.*, *a-gleth*, on the left; *a'y luf gleth*, with his left hand; *a-gleth dhodho*, on his left; *c. ha dyghow*, to the left and to the right, on all sides.

cleves (C. Voc. *clewet* for *clevet*), *m.*, *pl.* **-vejow**, illness, sickness, malady, leprosy, *adl* Aelfric; *c. an myghtern*, king's evil; *c.-bras*, *-mur*, leprosy; *c. seson*, ague.

clew, *m.*, sense of hearing (W., B.).

clewans (Late *clowans* P.), *m.*, hearing.

clewes (Late *clowas*), *vb.*, to hear, hearken, smell, feel sensation: originally *clewvos*, this is still partly declined as **bōs**; 3 s. fut. *clewvyth*; 3 s. subj. *clewfo*; 3 s. imperf. *clewo*; the 2 pl. imp. is usually made *clewyeugh*, with added *y*; this was evidently used as a noun also, as in D. "cutting a bra' *clewyew* about it," i.e., making a great "hark ye" about it, letting all the town know of it; see **oyeth**.

cleys, *f.*, *pl.* **-eysow**, **-jow**, trench, ditch: place-names, *Clyja*, *Meneth Clysow*, etc., as W. *clais*.

†**clof**, *adj.*, lame, C. Voc., *healt* Aelfric.

cloffy, *vb.*, to limp, go lame (W.).
clofny, *m.*, lameness (W).
clog, *f.*, *pl.* **-ow,** crag, cliff: Carn Clog, place-name.
clōgh (C. Voc. *cloch*), *m.*, *pl.* **clēgh,** bell: †*c. mur*, church-bell, C. Voc., *mycel belle* Aelfric; *c. an marow*, death-knell (B.); *den an c.*, bell-ringer, sexton, (Borlase); †*c.-dybry*. refectory bell, dinner-bell, C. Voc., *cimbal* Aelfric; see **clēghy.**
cloghprennyer, *m.*, gallows, Lh., B.M.: lit. " bell beams " as in Eng. D.
clojy, clojya, see **clavjy, closya.**
clōk, *m.*, *pl.* **-ys,** cloak, P.C. 2682 (E.).
***clok,** *m.*, *pl.* **-kys,** clock (E.).
clomyer, see **colomyer.**
clopen, *m.*, noddle, knob, skull, numskull (W.B.).
cloppek, *adj.*, limping, lame, Lh.
cloppya, *vb.*, to limp, hobble Gw., (E.D., cf. Fr. *éclcper*).
clōr (*clour*), *adj.*, mild, meek, temperate, cool, gentle, moderate; (adverbially), quietly, stealthily, gently, etc., R.D. 392, B.M. 4332.
clōrder, *m.*, mildness, meekness, gentleness, lukewarmness, indifference (W., B.).
†**clōrek** (C. Voc. *cloireg*), *m.*, *pl.* **-egas,** clerk, cleric, clergyman, *preost*, *cleric* Aelfric.
clōs (C. Voc. *cluit*), *f.*, *pl.***-ojow,** hurdle, wattle, crate, framework, gate, harrow, *hyrdel* Aelfric: †*c. dywvron*, breast, C. Voc.; *c. chy*, frame of roof (W.).
clōs, *m.*, glory, bliss and splendour of heaven, Ord.; fame, renown (W., B.).
clōs, *m.*, *pl.* **ys,** enclosure (M.E.).
clōs, *adj.*, close, enclosed, fastened, shut; *adv.*, closely.
closya, clojya, *vb.*, to harrow: see **clōs,** *f.*
clot (*clotte*, one syllable, P.C. 1399), *m.*, *pl.* **-ttys,** clot (E.).
clot-boffen, *f.*, tripe, Gw. Borlase.
clowd, *m.*, *pl.* **-ys,** cloud, C.W. (E.).
clowt, (*clout*, Lh. *clut*), *m.*, *pl.* **-tys,** clout, patch; blow: *c. -lystry*, dishclout (E.).
clowtya, *vb.*, to patch, R.D. 1509; to strike, C.W. 220 (M.E. *clout*).
†**cloyster** (C. Voc. *cloister*), *m.*, *pl*, **-trow,** cloister: see **clawster.**
***clūgyar,** *f.*, *pl.* **-yēr,** partridge: replaced by **grūgyar,** in W. " grouse " (W., B.).
***clūgh,** *m.*, *pl.* **-ghas,** crag (W.).
clūn, *f.*, *pl.* **-yow** (*clenniaw* Borlase), *d.* *dywglūn* (C. Voc. *duiglun*, B.M. *duklyn*), hip, haunch, loins, *hype*, *lendena* Aelfric.
†**clūn,** *m.*, *pl.* **-now,** pasture, browsing-ground: Clun Ewic, Domesday Book; see **ewyk.**
cluttya, *vb.*, to roost as a hen (D., B.).
clūth, see **clēth.**
clyjjy, *m.*, toffee (D. "clidgy").
***clyket,** *m.*, *pl.* **-tys,** latch (M.E., W., B., all from Fr. *clicquette*).
clyn (C. Voc. *clin*, *penclin*), *m.*, *d.* **deuglyn** (*dewgleyn*), knee, *cneow* Aelfric: variant of **glyn.**
cobba, *m.*, *pl.* **-ys,** simpleton (D., cf. Eng. "cob," gull).
†**cober,** *m.*, copper, C. Voc.
***cōcha,** *m.*, *pl.* **-ys,** coach (E.).
codha, *vb.*, to fall, happen: 3 s. pres.-fut. *coth*; 3 s. subj. *cotho*; 3 s. plupf. *cothsa*; *c. war*, *worth*, befall to; *gasa dhe godha*, to drop, let fall.
cōf, *m.*, *pl.* **-covyon,** memory, recollection: *perthy c.*, to remember, Late 2 s. imp. *per' co'*.
***cofes,** *m.*, *pl.* **-yow,** confession (W., B.).
***coff,** *m.*, belly (B.).
coffen, *f.*, *pl.***-now,** open mine-working (D.).
***coffy,** *m.*, coffee.
coflyver, *m.*, register (W.).
coflyverva, *f.*, registry (W.).
cofro, *m.*, keepsake (W.).
cofryn, *m.*, *pl.* **-now,** casket (W.).
cofscryfa, *vb.*, to register (W.).
cofscryfer, *m.*, *pl.* **-oryon,** registrar (W.).
cofhē˙, *vb.*, to remember: 3 s. fut. *cofha* (*cofua*) P.C. 827 (correcting *pysough* to *pesquyth*); as **berhē˙.**
cofva, *f.*, remembrance, memory: so understood by scribe, P.C. 827; see **cofhē.**
cofyr, *m.*, *pl.* **-frow,** coffer, strong-box, chest, Lh., B.M. (E.).
cōg, see **cōk(g).**
***cogen,** *f.*, *pl.* **-now,** wooden bowl (W., B.).
coges, *f.*, *pl.* **-ow,** woman-cook.
***cogga,** *m.*, *pl.* **-ys,** cog, medieval ship (M.E.).
coggas, *m.*, *pl.* **-ers,** priest, minister, Gw.
***cok(g),** *m.*, *pl.* **-gyon,** grandfather, ancester: kept only in **hengok(g), dӯhok(g), gorhok(g)**: see **hendas,** replacing it.
cōk(g), *f.*, *pl.* **-gas,** cuckoo (Lh.): *arluth an gok*, ?lord of the cuckoo, P.C. 2890, is used contemptuously.
cōk, *m.*, *pl.* **cūcow,** sailing fishing-boat, square-sailed ancestor of Cornish lugger, Lh., Gw.

cōk (C. Voc. *kog*), *m.*, *pl.* **cogow**, man-cook, *coc* Aelfric.

cok-Gyny, *m.*, *pl.* **-kys-G.**, turkey-cock, "Guinea-cock" in old sense, Lh.: see **yar.**

cōk (C. Voc. *cuic*), *adj.*, empty, vain, worthless, one-eyed, *anegede* Aelfric; *m.*, *pl.* **kegyon**, worthless person or thing (D. "kegyons," "kegs").

†cōklynasen, *f.*, *col.* **-lynas** (C. Voc. *coiclinhat*), yellow dead-nettle, *blindnetel* Aelfric.

col, colgh, *m.*, *pl.* **-ow** (*kulhu* Lh.), point, peak; awn or beard of corn: see **†culyn.**

cōl, *f.*, divination, omen; belief, trust (W.).

cola, *vb.*, to trust, believe, credit, give ear, hearken; lend, entrust: takes *orth* as prep. "to," "in"; (*dha*) *bysy, col orthyf-vy*, pray lend me ("paji kulaa tu vee," Tradition).

coler, *m.*, rage, Gw. (M.E. *colre*).

***colghes**, *f.*, *pl.* -**ow**, quilt, mattress (W.,B.): Lat. *culcita*; see **kewlet.**

coljy, *m.*, *pl.* **-ow**, college, B.M. 2688: ? for *collej-jy*, college-house, or Lat. *collegi(um)*.

coll (Late *cul*), *m.*, loss, damage, perdition: *gasa dhe goll*, neglect, waste, leave derelict; *mos dhe goll*, be lost, neglected, go into oblivion; *ass-yu hemma mur a goll!* What a great loss this is! B.M. 4467.

collan, *f.*, *pl.* **-ow**, large sheath-knife, R.D. 2042—69.

collas, etc., see **kelly.**

†collel, *f.*, *pl.* **kellyl, kellylly**, knife, *sex* Aelfric; cuttle-fish (*call*, Ray, "cole" D.): **†c.** *gravya*, scribe's scraping-knife, chasing-tool, scalpel; *c. gam*, curved knife (W.); *c.-lesa*, octopus (D. "goluzzow," "guzzalezza").

collenky (*cowl lenky*), *vb.*, to swallow down: as **lenky** (later *clonca, klunka*, Borlase, D. "clunk").

collenwel (*cowl lenwel*), *vb.*, to fulfil, fill, complete, (with *both*) satisfy, accomplish: as **lenwel.**

†colles (C. Voc. *collet*), *m.*, *pl.* -**ow**, loss, *lyre* Aelfric.

coll-lōn, *m.*, *pl.* **-ow**, hazel-grove.

co·llwedhen (C. Voc. *colwiden*), *f.*, *col.* **-wȳth**, hazel-tree, *haesel* Aelfric.

colm, *m.*, *pl.* **-ow**, knot, tie, bond: *yn c.*, in bonds; *c.-re*, hangman's knot, slip-knot, P.C. 1525: see **kelmy, rē.**

colmek, *adj.*, knotty (W., B.).

colmen, *f.*, *pl.* **-now**, knot, bond, tie, fastening: *yn un golmen*, in one bond, tied up together, P.C. 177.

colmor, *m.*, *pl.* **-yon** (*colmurian*, Pryce), binder, sheaf-binder.

†colodhyonen (C. Voc. *culurionen*, *r* written for character "thorn"), *f.*, *pl.* **colodhyon**, bowel, *innodh* Aelfric; as W. *coluddionyn*.

colom (*colam*, C.W.), *f.*, *pls.* **-as, -lmas**, dove, pigeon, O.M., C. Voc., *culfre* Aelfric; *c. cos*, wood-pigeon, Lh.

colomyer, clomyer, (*klomiar* Lh.), *m.*, *pl.* **-s**, pigeon-house, dove-cote: field-names, Clumyer (Lat. *columbarium*).

colon (Late var. *collan*), *f.*, *pl.* **-now**, heart: used in sing. and pl. as endearment; *gans c. dha*, with a will; *gans dha golan*, with (all) thy heart.

colon (C. Voc. *talon*, venter, for *calon*), *m.*, *pl.* **-yow**, (*koloneiou* P.), gut, entrail, bowel, belly: accepted anatomy of mermaids seems to require this in P.C. 1743, it also fits O.M. 365, *ow holon gwak*.

colonen, *f.*, *pl.* **-now**, core, of apple, etc. (B.).

colonnek (*kolannak, kulednak*, Lh.), *adj.*, hearty, bold, good-hearted, stout-hearted.

***coloven**, *f.*, *pl.* **-now**, column (W.).

colpes, *m.*, *pl.* **-ow**, lever, fulcrum (E.D. "colpice," "coupress").

†colter, *m.*, *pl.* **-trow**, coulter of plough, C. Voc., *culter* Aelfric.

†cōlyak (C. Voc. *c(h)uillioc*), *m.*, *pl.* **-yogyon**, soothsayer, diviner, augur, *wiglere* Aelfric.

†colyn (C. Voc. *coloin*), *m.*, *pl.* **kelyn**, puppy, whelp, cub.

cōlyn (*kolan*, Lh.), *m.*, *pl.* **cōlys**, coal of fire: *c. bew*, live coal; *c. leskys*, firebrand; *c. marow*, cinder.

***colyta**. *m.*, *pl.* **-tys**, acolyte (M.E. *colyte*).

†colyoges (C. Voc. *cuillioges*), *f.*, *pl.* **-ow**, divineress, witch, *wycce* Aelfric.

com-, see **ke-**, Appendix II.

comendya. *vb.*, to entrust or commit to the care of; to commend, B.M., A. Boorde (M.E.).

comen voys, *m.*, general acclaim, *vox populi*, B.M. 2710 (M.E.).

comner, *m.*, *pl.* **-s**, commoner, P.C. 2470 (M.E.).

comolen, *f.*, *pl.* **comolow**, *col*, **comol**, cloud (W., B.).

comolek, *adj.*, cloudy (Lh.).

comōndment, *m.*, *pl.* **-ns**, commandment, order (M.E.).
comōndya, *vb.*, to command, order, bid (M.E. *comaunde*).
co·mpany, compny, *m.*, company (M.E.).
comparya, *vb.*, to compare : *c. gans*, vie with, claim equality with, C.W. 216 (M.E.).
compas, *m.*, compass, extent : *worth c.* completely, C.W. 19 (E.).
compes, *adj.*, even, straight, smooth, level, right, accurate, proper, fit : comp. *compossa* ; *my a-vyth c. ganso*, I'll be even with him, C.W. 492 ; adverbially, *c. yntre deu*, right in two, O.M. 2536.
composa, *vb.*, to straighten, smooth, make right, verify, fit, Gw. : p. pt. *composys*.
composter, *m*, evenness, accuracy, propriety, fitness, Keigwin, N. Boson (D. "ally compooster").
comprehendya, *vb.*, to comprise, include, C.W. 11 (E.).
compressa, *vb.*, to oppress, overburden, keep down, O.M. 1424 (M.E.).
comptya, *vb.*, to count, C.W. (M.E.) : see **acontya**.
Comūn Sans, *m.*, Holy Communion (W.).
comūnya, *vb.*, to commune, take the Sacrament : p. pt. *-yes*, houseled, B.M. 4272.
comūnyans, *m.*, communion.
con-, see **ke-**.
cōn (*coyn*), *f.*, *pl.* **-yow**, supper, late dinner.
cona, *vb.*, to sup : *es conys dheugh* ? Have you supped ? Lh.
concevya, *vb.*, to conceive, B.M. 846, Davies Creed (E.).
conclūdya, *vb.*, to defeat or silence in argument, refute, bring to a conclusion, nonplus, settle, decide, P.C. (M.E.).
conduyk (*conduyke* C.W. 86), *m.*, conduct, direction, management (M.E. *conduycte*).
condysyon (*conduconn*, B.M.), *m.*, position, condition (M.E.).
confort, *m.*, comfort, support, help, encouragement (M.E.).
confortya, *vb.*, to console, comfort, strengthen, back up, encourage, fortify one, reinforce, help (M.E. *conforte*).
confundya, *vb.*, to confound, overthrow, B.M. 2033 (M.E.).
conjorya, *vb.*, to conjure, beseech, adjure, P.C. 1321 (M.E.).
conna (Late *codna*), *m.*, neck, *swyre* Aelfric ; *c. bregh*, d. *deugonna b.*, wrist ; **c. tros*, instep : *codna* was corruptly used in Late Cor. for *corn* in *c. whylen*, *c. tal*, Lh. Gw.
conna-gwyn, *m.*, *pl.* **-as**, weasel, whitneck, stcat, Lh. : see **†lovennan**.
connar, *f.*, fury, rabies, hydrophobia, Borlase : see **†conneryak**.
connek (Late *cudnick*), *adj.*, clever, adroit ; *m.*, skill, wit, C.W. 1406 (*conycke*).
†conneryak (C. Voc. *conerioc*), *adj.*, rabid, furious, *gemyndleas* Aelfric.
connyng (*-yngh*), *m.*, cleverness, adroitness, P.C. 1458 (M.E.).
co·nquerrour, *m.*, *pl.*, **-s**, conqueror, B.M. (M.E.).
conquerrya, *vb.*, to conquer, O.M. 909 (M.E.).
conquest, *m.*, conquest, R.D. 2629 (M.E.).
cons, *f.*, vagina.
consay·t (*conseyt*), *m.*, idea, notion, concept (M.E. *consayte*) : *nyns yu worshyp dhe'th eghen dha g.*, thy fancy does no credit to thy family, B.M. 361.
conscyans (*concyans*), *m.*, conscience, P.C. 1979 (M.E.) : *war ow honscyans !* on my conscience ! C.W. 2408.
consecraytya, *vb.*, to consecrate, B.M. 2984 (M.E.).
consel, *m.*, *pl.* **-s**, council (M.C.) : see **consler**.
consler, co·nseler (first *e* silent), *m.*, *pl.* **-s**, councillor (M.E.).
constrȳna, *vb.*, to constrain, P.C. 1512 (M.E.).
consūmya, *vb.*, to consume, destroy, C.W. 2537 (M.E.).
consylya, *vb.*, to plan, counsel, Lh. (M.E.).
contentya, *vb.*, to content, satisfy : *contentys gans*, well-pleased with, C.W. 668 (M.E.).
co·nternot, *m.*, counternote, counter-tenor, alto part in plain-song, O.M, 561 (M.E.).
conteth, *m.*, earldom, county, B.M. 512.
contra·dÿa, *vb.*, to gainsay, contradict, P.C. 2426 : p. pt. *-dyes* (M.E., Fr. *contredire*).
co·ntrary, *m.*, opposer, adversary, M.C. 146 (M.E.) ; *adv.*, otherwise, C.W. 630.
contraryus, *adj.*, opposed, opposite, P.C. 1731 (M.E. *contrarious*).
contrewaytya, *vb.*, to ambush, lie in wait against, P.C. 2299 (M.E. *countrewaite*).
controlya, *vb.*, to control, coerce, order about, C.W. 1680 (M.E.).
†contronen, *f.*, *col.* **contron**, maggot, C. Voc., *madhu* Aelfric.
contronek, *adj.*, maggoty (B.).
contronno, etc., see **kentreny**.

convedhes, *vb*., to understand, recognize, apprehend, perceive.

conversasyon (*-ascon*), *m*., manner of life, mode of thought or existing, deportment, demeanour, behaviour (M.E.).

conveyour, *m*., passage in *plen an gwary* through which actors made concealed entrances, C.W. stage-directions (M.E.).

convyctya, *vb*., to convict, M.C. 18 (M.E.).

conyn (*kunin* Lh.), *m*., *pl*. **-as**, rabbit, coney: Park Connin, field-name.

conynessa, *vb*., to go rabbitting (W., B.): inf. only.

cōp, *m*., *pl*. **-ys**, cope, *Hayl, Syr Epscop, esos y'th c. owth esedha*, Hail, Sir Bishop, who art sitting in thy cope, P.C. 931 (M.E.).

copel, *m*., *pl*. **-plow**, couple, pair, O.M. 1024: as pl., arrangement of two hooks one over another (D. "cuplaw").

***copy**, *m*., *pl*. **-yow**, copy (E.).

***co·pўa**, *vb*., to copy.

†cor, *m*., *pl*. **-as**, dwarf, C. Voc., *dweorf* Aelfric.

cōr, *m*., way, manner, style, sort; used only in *war nep c*., in some, or any, way (?O.E. *cer, cyr*, turn, time).

cōr, (C. Voc. *coir*), *m*., wax: *mayth ystynno avel c*., that it may stretch like wax, P.C. 2723.

cor', see **coref**.

***Corawys**, *m*., Lent (W., B.): from Lat. Quadragesima.

corbel, *m*., *pl*. **-blys**, corbel, bracket, O.M. 2446 (M.E.).

corden, *f*., *pl*. **kerdyn**, string, cord, string of instrument, C. Voc.: pl. M.C. 131.

coref, cor' (C. Voc. *coruf*), *m*., ale, beer: *c. gwella*, best-drink, strong ale, Gw.

coren, *f*., *pl*. **-now**, cake of wax (W., B.).

***cores**, *f*., *pl*. **-ow**, dam, weir (W., B.): Nancorras, place-name.

corf, *m*., *pl*. **-ow**, body, person: *c. da*, powerful man; *lyes c*., many people; *c. eglos*, nave; *c. eskern*, skeleton; *c. ha pen, treys ha dywla*, all over ones body.

corfak, *adj*., corpulent (W., B.).

corflan, corlan (*korhlan*), *f*., *pl*. **-now**, churchyard, Lh.

corlan, *f*., *pl*. **-now**, sheepfold,: *cor* is an old word meaning "sheep," Ir. *caor*; the *n* is now usually lost in place-name Roscorla, but kept in Gorland, Gurlyn.

corn, *m*., *pl*. **kern, kernow**, horn of animal, trumpet: *c. eva*, drinking-horn; *c.-tan*, horn tinder-box (B.).

corn, *m*., *pl*. **kernow**, corner, projection, nook: *c dowr*, creek; *c. tal*, forehead; *c. y dal*, his brow; *c. an olas*, chimney-corner (B.); *c. cunys*, wood-corner (B.).

cornel (*kornal* Lh), *f*., *pl*. **-ly, -low**, corner, nook.

cornwhylen (*kodnahwilan* Lh.), *f*., *pl*. **-las**, lapwing, peewit (D. "corniwillen").

cornya, *vb*., to horn, butt (W.).

***corol**, *m*., *pl*. **-low**, dance (B.).

***corolly**, *vb*., to dance, Lh. (but from B.).

corres, *f*., *pl*. **-ow**, female dwarf, Lh.

cors, *f*., *pl*. **-ow**, fen, reed-covered bog: Pencorse, Goss Moor, place-names.

cors (for *cours*), *m*., *pl*. **-ow**, time, turn, spell, course, moment, *poweseugh un c*., rest awhile, P.C. 2146 (M.E.).

corsen (C. Voc. *koisen* for *korsen*), *f*., *pl*. **-now**, *col*. **kers, cors**, reed plant or stem, *hreod* Aelfric: *c. mor*, sand-rush (B.); see **kersek**.

cort (*curte* B.M.), *f*., *pl*. **-ys**, court, Gw. (M.E.).

cortes, *adj*., courteous, polite (M.E. *curteys*).

co·rtesy (*-eysy*), *m*., courtesy, generosity, B.M. 299 (M.E.).

corvarfus, *m*., *pl*. **-y**, haddock (W.).

corwheth, *m*., *pl*. **-ow**, spiral eddy of wind (B.).

corwyns, *m*., whirlwind (W., B.).

coryar, *f*., *pl*. **-yēr**, partridge (W., B.).

coryk, *m*., *pl*. **-ygow, -esygow**, little dwarf, elf (W., B.).

cos, *f*., itching, tickling (W.).

cōs (*coys*, C. Voc. *cuit*, Late *coos*, Lh. *kūz*), *m*., *pl*. **-ow, -ojow**, wood, forest.

cosa, *vb*., to itch, tickle, scratch, (figuratively) be sore from beating: 3 s. subj. *cosso*, P.C. 2084.

cōsak, *adj*., woody (W., B.).

coscar (C. Voc. *coscor, goscor*), *col*., household, retinue, dependants, people, lads, *incniht* Aelfric, sing.; see **maw**.

coscas, etc., see **kesky**, **cusca**.

cosel (*kuzal* Lh.), *adj*., soft, quiet, slow, restful, smooth-mannered; *adv*., softly, O.M. 2074 (D. "cuzzle").

coselhē·, *vb*., to quieten, pacify, free from disturbance, lull, soothe, soften: as **berhē**.

co·soleth (*kesoleth*, Lh. *kuzaleth*), *m*., quiet, rest, tranquillity, patience, P.C. 719.

cosva, *f*., itching, thrashing (W.): see **cosa**.

cost, *m*., *pl*. **-ys**, cost, charge, expense (M.E.): *nyns-eth yn c*., thou shalt not be put to expense, B.M. 2823.

cōst, *m.*, *pl.* **-ys**, region, clime, part or side of a country (M.E.).

†**costa** (C. Voc. *coste*), *m.*, zedoary, putchook, an ingredient of incense, *cost* Aelfric (Arabic *koost*).

costen (*kostan* Lh.), *f.*, *pl.* **-now**, buckler, targe, archery-target, Lh.; flat target-like basket, of straw-rope interwoven with bramble-slivers (D. "costan").

costya, *vb.*, to cost, C.W. 2445 (M.E.).

costyans, *m.*, expense, cost.

cosva, *f.*, itching, tickling (W.).

†**cōsyorgh** (C. Voc. *kytiorch*), *m.*, *pl.* **-as**, wild buck, *rahdeor* Aelfric.

cot (C.W. *cut*), *adj.*, short, brief, (adverbially) suddenly, abruptly: comp. *cotta*; *my a-wra pur got y wyns*, I will make his breath full short, B.M. 2253; *yn cot-termyn*, shortly, at once, C.W.

cōta, *m.*, *pl.* **-tys**, coat; coat-of-arms, Lh., N. Boson (E.).

cōth, *adj.*, old, ancient, of age, C.W. 1152: comp. *cotha* is used as "senior."

cōth, *def. vb.*, to behove, be due, suitable or fitting: used in 3 sing. only; has forms compounded with *bos*, as well as regular forms; pres.-fut. *coth*; impf. ind. *cotho*; impf. subj. *cothfa*, *cotha*; pres.-fut. subj. *cothfo*, *cotho*; plupf. *cothfya*, *coffya*, *cossa* (for *cothsa*), *my a-gossa*, I ought, P.C. 2216, but usually *y cothfya dhym*, etc.

cōth, *m.*, fall (W., B.): see **codha**.

cōth (*cooth*), *adj.*, known, familiar, C.W. 603 (O.E. *cuth*); possibly a contraction of **coweth**, but cf. **ancoth**, **ancothfos**, **cothman**.

cothan, *m.*, bed-rock (D.).

cōthhē·, *vb.*, to grow old (B.): as **berhē**.

cothman, *m.*, *pl.* **-mens**, acquaintance, friend, comrade (O.E. *cuth man*): in pl., kith and kin, B.M. 1951.

cōthwas, *m.*, *pl.* **-wesyon**, old fellow, gaffer; *an c.-gof*, the old smith fellow, P.C. 1695.

***cōthny**, *m.*, old-age (B.).

cotthē·, *vb.*, to shorten, abbreviate: as **berhē**.

cough, *adj.*, blood red, scarlet: *pennow c.*, broken pates, P.C. 2326.

courser, *m.*, *pl*, **-s**, charger (M.E.): *an c. melen*, the tawny war-horse, O.M. 1965.

covath, *m.*, remembrance, memory, memorial, keepsake, record: *gasa an c.*, leave off remembering, lose the recollection, O.M. 1283, 1359.

covathor, *m.*, *pl.* **-yon**, recorder (W.).

co·vaytys (*-eytys*), *m.*, covetousness, greed (M.E. *coveitise*).

co·vetya (*covityah* Kerew), *vb.*, covet.

covva (*cova*, for *cüdhva*), *f.*, hiding-place, concealment, C.W., Gw.: *dhe govva*, in hiding, C.W. 1848, into hiding, J. Tonkin.

covya, *vb.*, to hatch, brood, cherish as a hen its chicks, B.M. 1355 (M.E. *covey*).

covyon, see **cof**.

cow, *m.*, *pl.* **-yow**, hollow, excavation; *adj.*, hollow (W., B.).

cowa, *vb.*, to hollow (W., B.).: see **cowans**.

cowal, *adv.*, completely, wholly, fully, entirely; *adj.*, complete, entire, utter, whole: as prefix usually **cowl-**.

***cowan**, *f.*, *pl.* **-as**, owl (W., B.).

cowans, *m.*, excavation; long shallow pit for washing fine tin-stuff (D. "gounce").

coward, *m.*, coward, O.M. 2157 (M.E., O. Fr. *coart*).

co·wardy, *m.*, cowardice, O.M. 2161 (M.E.).

cowas, *f.*, *pl.* **-wosow**, sudden shower, rain-storm, *scur* Aelfric; blast, attack of illness (B., cf. **shora**); *c. gwyns*, gust, squall (B.); *c. newl*, thick mist (W.); *hager-gowas*, downpour, cloudburst, O.M. 1080.

cowbren, *m.*, hollow tree (W.).

cowel, *m.*, *pls.* **-low**, **kewel**, basket; pannier; cradle (W., B.): *c. gwenyn*, bee-hive (B.); *c. edhen*, bird-cage (B.).

coweras, see **kewyras**.

cowesek, *adj.*, showery (W., B.).

coweth, *m.*, *col.* **-a**, (for **-eth**), companion, mate, match, associate, fellow peer, equal, comrade: in col., fellowship, company, etc.; *c. dhym yu tanow, ow howetha yu tanow*, I have few equals, B.M. 514, C.W. 121; *ha 'y gowetha*, and those like him, who do as he did, C.W. 2056—62.

cowethas, *f.*, *pl.* **-ow**, company, society, group, association.

cowethes, *f.*, *pl.* **-ow**, helpmate, female companion.

†**cow·ethlyver** (C. Voc. *coweidliuer*), *m.*, *pl.* **-lyvrow**, manual, handbook, portable church service-book, *handboc* Aelfric.

cowethya, *vb.*, to associate, consort, keep company, M.C. 41.

cowethyans, *m.*, fellowship, association, communion, intercourse, Gw.

cowethyas, *m.*, *pl.* **-ysy,** colleague, partner, associate (W.).
***cowgans,** *adj.*, certain, sure (W., B.); replaced by **certan.**
cowl (*coul*), *m.*, broth, soup, pottage: *vynytha ny-evyth c.*, thou shalt nevermore sup broth (thou shalt live no longer), O.M. 2701; cf. P·C. 1620.
cowl-, see **cowal.**
cowl, *m.*, *pl.* **-ow,** maw, fish-gut; rennet; curd (D.).
cowla, *vb.*, to curdle, coagulate: *leth cowlys*, sour, curdled, milk, Lh.
cowldhrehevel, *vb.*, to finish building.
cowlegneth, *m.*, gluttony: see **cowlek.**
cowlek, *adj.*, gluttonous; *m.*, *pl.* **-legyon,** glutton (D. "cowlack").
cowlen, see **cawl.**
cowles, *m.*, curd, coagulation, jelly: *morgowles*, jelly-fish (D. "Malagowla," "murgils," etc.).
cowlwül, *vb.*, to finish, perfect, complete: p. pt. *cowlwres*, *-wrys*.
cows, *m.*, *pl.* **-ow,** speech, talk, discourse.
cows, *vb.*, to speak, say: 3 s. pres.-fut. *cows*; pret. *cowsas*, etc., conjugated regularly; see **kewsel.**
cowsys, *m.*, *pl. and abst.* **cow·sesow,** B.M.**cow·jejyow,** opinion, inward thought, mind, conscience, heart, bosom; (originally) cavity, hollow: see **cow.**
coynt, *adj.*, strange, extraordinary, odd, curious, unexpected, shifty, wily, quaint (M.E.).
coyntys, *m.*, unusual thing, pecularity, shift, wile, ruse (M.E.).
crāf, *m.*, *pl.* **-ow,** big stitch, tacking (W.,B.).
craf, *m.*, *pl.* **-vow,** clasp, grip, grasp, clutch (W.,B.).
†craf, *adj.*, tenacious, covetous, avaricious; *m.*, miser, C. Voc., *gytsere*, Aelfric.
crafa, *vb.*, to grip, secure, hold together, stitch roughly, tack, baste: 2 s. imp. *crāf* (D. "crafe").
cragh, *m.*, *pl.* **creghy** (*crehy*, B.M. 2418), scurf, scab; *adj.*, scurvy, scabby, petty: *c. varth*, poetaster; *c. vedhow*, half-drunk; *c. vedhek*, quack; *c. denjentyl*, squireen, etc. (W., B.); *pen creghy*, scurfy pate.
crak, *m.*, *pl.* **-kys,** clap, pop, crack, snap; *adv.*, *interj.* bang! snap! (M.E.): *my a-der, c.! ow honna*, I'll break my neck, snap! O.M. 2184. *y ben, c.! my a-dorsa*, I would break his head, crack! R.D. 397.
crakkya, *vb.*, to break, snap, crack (M.E.).
crakkya-conna, *adj.*, breakneck, steep.
crambla, *vb.*, to climb, creep, scramble, Lh. (M.E. *crambil*).
***cramen,** *f.*, *pl.* **-now,** scab over sore (W., B.).
crampetha, *vb.*, to go begging pancakes (B.): inf. only.
crampethen, *f.*, *pl.* **-now,** *col.* **crampeth,** pancake, Lh.
cramyas, *vb.*, to creep, crawl (D.E. "crame"): 3 s. pres.-fut. *crām*.
crāna, *m.*, *pl.* **-ys,** crane, Lh. (E.).
***crap,** *m.*, grip (W., B.).
***crapya,** *vb.*, to grip, grapple (W., B.).
***cras,** *adj.*, toasted, parched (W., B.).
***crasa.** *vb.*, to parch, toast: p. pt. *cresys* (W., B.).
***crasen,** *f.*, *pl.* **-now,** *col.* **cras,** toast (W., B.).
***craster,** *m.*, aridity (W., B.).
cravas, *vb.*, to scrape, scratch; *m.*, scratch, scrape (W., B.): Cravas Satan, place-name.
***cravell,** *f.*, *pl.* **-ow,** scraper, hoe (W., B.).
***cravellas,** *vb.*, to scrape, hoe (W., B.).
†crēador, *m.*, creator, C. Voc., *scyppend* Aelfric.
crēasyon (*creacon*), *m.*, creation, C.W. 2535 (M.E.): see **gwrȳans,** substituted for this in Keigwin's title, *An Gwreans a'n Bys*.
crēatūr (*creater*), *m.*, *pl.* **-toryon,** creature, being.
crēatya, *vb.*, to create, C.W. 150 (E.).
crebogh, *adj.*, wrinkled, withered (W., D. "cribbage-faced").
crēf (*creÿf*, *crȳf*, C. Voc. *crif*), *adj.*, strong, mighty, vigorous, lusty, robust.
crefder. **-ter** (Lh. *krevder*), *m.*, strength, might.
crefhē·, *vb.*, to make or grow stronger, N. Boson: as **berhē.**
crafny, **f.*, avarice, B. *krezni*; *adj.*, greedy, grasping, avaricious: *ny-vynnaf bos mar grefny*, I won't be so greedy, C.W. 682; the noun seems to have replaced **†craf** as adj.
creft, *f.*, *pl.* **-ow,** craft, art, O.M. C. Voc., *craeft* Aelfric (O.E.).
†creftor, *m.*, *pl.* **-yon,** craftsman, artificer, C. Voc.
†crek(g), *adj.*, indistinct of speech, hoarse; *m.*, stammerer, C. Voc., *stamur* Aelfric.
creger, *m.*, *pl.* **-goryon,** hangman, hanger (B.).
crēghy, see **cragh.**

crēghyn, see **croghen.**
cregy, *vb.*, to hang: 2 s. imp. *crok*, 3 s. pres.-fut. *crēk*; 3 s. pret. *crogas*; *dhe'th c.*, hang you! *gasa y ben dhe gregy*, to let his head droop.
cregyn, see **crogen.**
cregynnek, *adj.*, shelled; *m., pl.* **-nogyon,** testaceous animal (W.).
crehylly, see **cryghylly.**
crejy, see **crysy.**
crejys, *m.*, credit, trust, confidence, reliance, credence, belief: *dhe well y-th-fyth c.*, the better shalt thou have credit; *tam vyth ny 'fyth c. dhe'th cusulyow,* not a jot shalt thou have trust for thy advice, C.W. 569, 626, as W. *credyd*, B. *kreted.*
crellas, *m.*, rough hut, remains of ancient dwelling (D.): possibly for *cryghyllyas*, applied to a shaky building.
cren (Late *kern*), *m., pl.* **-now,** shake, quake: *c. an leghow,* ague fit, Lh. MS.; see **yn-cren.**
cren (*kren, kern* Lh.), *adj.*, round, circular.
crender, *m.*, roundness (W., B.).
crenna (Late *kerna*), *vb.*, to tremble, quake, shiver: *c. a'y varf*, to shake in his beard (with fear).
crenner, *m., pl.* **-oryon,** trembler, Quaker (W).
***crēr**, *m., pl.* **-yow,** relic of saint (W., B.).
***crērva**, *f.*, reliquary, shrine (W.).
crēs (var. *creyth*), *f.*, faith, belief.
crēs (*creys, crȳs*, Late *creas*), *m.*, middle, centre, midst; mid-section of buddle (D.); *adj.*, middle: *yn ewn-gres anodho,* right in the middle of it: *Mor C.*, Mediterranean; *Kernewek-C.*, Middle Cornish; Gew Graze, Kimyell Craze, etc., place-names.
crēs (*creys, crȳs*, Late *creez, creege*), *m.*, peace: *gas dhym c*! let me be! *c. Dew aberth-yn anneth, chymma*! God's peace in the dwelling, house! P.C. 667, 705 (said on entering).
cressya, *vb.*, to increase, multiply, C.W.: variant of **encressya** (M.E., *cressyn*).
***cresten**, *f., pl.* **-now,** crust, scurf, coating (W., B.).
***crestenna,** *vb.*, to form a crust, gather scurf (W., B.).
cresy, crejy, see **crysy.**
creven, *f*, *pl.* **-now,** crust, scab, Lh. (D. "crevan").
crō, *adj.*, fresh, W. *croyw* (Crankan rhyme).
†**crōadur**, creature, C. Voc., *gesceaft* Aelfric: replaced by **crēatūr.**
crōch (*croych* B.M. 4183), *m., pl.* **-ys,** crutch (M.E.): in dual *ma's orth deu-groch, ny-gerdhaf,* I walk only on crutches, B.M. 4183.
crōder (C. Voc. *croider*), *m., pl.* **-drow,** coarse, corn-sieve, riddle, *sife* Aelfric: *c. cron,* sieve-rim with sheepskin bottom, used as corn-measure, tambourine, and common receptacle (D. "crowdy-crawn").
crodra (*kroddre*),. *vb.*, to sift, riddle, winnow, P.C. 882.
croffolas, see **crothvolas.**
croft, *m., pl.* **-ow,** uncultivated holding (E.): place-names, common.
crogen, *f., pl.* **cregyn,** shell, carapace, skull; limpet-shell (D.): *c. an pen,* skull; *c. an glyn,* knee-pan.
crogennek, *adj.*, having a shell (W., B.).
crōghen (*crohen*, C. Voc. *croin*), *f., pl.* **crēghyn,** skin, hide: *c. an lagas,* eyelid (B.); *c. lewen,* louse-skin (P.).
crogla, (*lē*), *m. or f.*, gibbet, hanging-place (B.): Grogley Downs, Pengrugla, place-names.
***croglath,** *f., pl.* **-ow,** noose, springe (W., B.).
croglen, *f., pl.* **-now,** curtain, hanging (W.).
crogor, *m., pl.* **-yon,** hangman (W.).
crōk, *f., pl.* **-ogow,** hanging, suspension, gallows; tweak or tug (D. "grock"): *settya c. yn,* to tweak, twitch; *re-n-jeffo c.*, may he hang!
crokken (*crockan* Gw.), *f., pl.* **-now,** springe, snare, noose.
crokpren, *m. or f., pl.* **-nyer,** gallows (W., B.): see **cloghprenyer.**
crom (Late *crum, crubm*), *adj.*, crooked, bent, curved, rounded, cylindrical, crumpled, (of fingers) cramped, numb with cold (D. "crum").
***crombyl,** *f., pl.* **-yow,** bird's crop (W., B.).
cromlegh, *f., pl.* **-yow,** cromlech, dolmen, megalithic tomb-chamber; Grumbla, place-name.
cromma, *vb.*, to bend, curve, go numb with cold (W., B.).
cromman (*crobman* Lh.), *m., pl.* **-ow,** reap-hook, sickle: *c. -eythyn,* furze-hook, Gw.
crommen, *f., pl.* **-now,** small bream (D. "grobman").
cromnen, *m.*, vaulted ceiling (W.): see †**nen.**
crōn, *m., pl.* **-ow,** thong, strap: found in

pl. only, this seems a specialized form of **croghen.**

cronek (C. Voc. *croinoc,* lit. " thick-skinned," " skinny "), *m., pl.* **cronogow, -ogas,** toad, *tadie* Aelfric : *c. du,* dark toad ; *c. melen,* light toad ; *c. -ervys,* tortoise (B.) ; *c. -e. mor,* turtle ; see **mōrgronek.**

cro'nekyn, *m.,* little toad : *c. hager du,* ugly little black toad, used as term of abuse by Dolly Pentreath (Tradition).

cronkya (*crunckia* Borlase), *vb.,* to beat, thrash.

cronogas (*cranagas*), *vb.,* to hop like a toad (P.).

cronor, *m., pl.* **-yon,** skinner, fellmonger, currier (W.).

cropya (*cruppya*), *vb.,* to penetrate, probe, stab, crush in, force into, M.C. 134, C.W. 917 : 3 s. pres.-fut. *crop* (*a-grup* P.C. 2120) ; (M.E. *grope* with **c** for *g*).

cropyl, *m., pl.* **-s,** cripple, B.M. 4205 (M.E.).

***cros,** *m., dim.* **crojyn,** *f.,* **-en,** little child (W. *crot,* B. *krot*).

crosser (var. *crossyer*), *m., pl.* **-s,** crozier-bearer (M.E.).

crothak, *adj.,* ? grumbling, fault-finding, C.W. 1105, cf. B. *krozus.*

crothak, *adj.,* big-bellied (W.,D. " gruthick ").

crothval, *m.,* murmur, complaint : *gul c. war,* to murmur against, O.M. 1837.

cro'thvolas, cro'ffolas, *vb.,* to make complaint, murmur, grumble ; *geseugh dhe-ves c.,*leave off complaining,O.M. 1662.

crow, *m.,* gore, bloodshed, death, M.C. 74, 131.

crow, *m., pl.* **-yow,** shed, hut, sty, hovel, cot : *c. mogh,* pig-sty (D. " pig's-crow ").

crow, *m.,* hole, perforation : *c. arf,* helve socket (W.).

crowd, *m., pl.* **-ys,** fiddle, violin, O.M. 1997 (M.E.).

crowder, *m., pl.* **-s,** fiddler, P. (D.E.).

crowdra, *vb.,* to loiter, idle (D. " crowder," " crowdle ").

crowjy, *m., pl.* **-ow,** cot-house, cabin, one-roomed cottage : place-names.

crow-nasweth, *m.,* eye of needle : misprinted *trov,* B.M. 468 (W. *crau,* B. *krao*).

crows (C. Voc. *crois*), *f., pl.* **-ow,** cross, rood : *c. eglos,* transept (W., B.) ; (*A*) *Grows Cryst ben'dycyta !* a pious ejaculation, B.M. 3677.

crowsa, crowsya, *vb.,* to crucify.

crowsek, *adj.,* cross-shaped ; cross-tempered (D. " crowzack ").

crowsforth, *f., pl.* **-rdhow, crowshens,** *f. or m., pl.* **-y,** cross-road (W., B.).

crowspren, *f. or m.,* cross, crucifix.

crowst (*croust*), *m., pl.* **-ys,** noon-meat, meal taken to work-place, picnic lunch, O.M. 1901, D. (M.E., O. Fr. *crouste,* crust).

crowsyk, *f., pl.* **-ygow,** little cross (W., B.).

crūel, *adj.,* cruel, B.M. (M.E.).

crügell *f., pl.* **-low,** little mound : Carn Creagle, rock-name, as B. *krugell.*

crügya, *vb.,* to pile, heap (W.).

crügyn, *m., pl.* **-now,** small heap (W.).

crük(g) (C. Voc. *cruc*), *m., pl.* **-ügyow,** mound, barrow, *hyl, beorh* Aelfric ; mow of corn (D.) : *c. muryon,* ant hill, Creeg Murrian, field-name.

crullya, *vb.,* to curl (M.E. *crull*) : *blew crullyes,* curly hair, Lh.

crün, crēn, *m., pl.* **-yow,** artificial pool, reservoir, collection, gathering (of liquids especially): *c.-melyn,* millpond, Lh. MS.

crüny, *vb.,* to dam, accumulate, gather, collect (of liquids especially), M.C. 224 : 3 s. pret. *crunys.*

cruppya, *vb.,* to creep, C.W. (O.E. *creopan*).

crūth, *f.,* bird's crop, belly (D. " grooth," W. *crwth*).

crȳ (Late *crei*), *m., pl.* **-ow,** cry, call, clamour (M.E.).

crȳa (*creya,* Late *creia*), *vb.,* to cry, call, call out for, shout, bark (M.E.) : *c. war,* call to, call on ; in Late Cor. used as " to name " also, following English " call."

crȳb, *f., pl.* **-ow,** comb, crest, ridge or reef of rocks : *c. an chy,* ridge of the roof, Lh.; Pengreep, Greeb, place-names.

crȳba, crȳbas, *vb.,* to comb, Lh.

crybba, *vb.,* to notch (D. to " crib " a flint, W. *crip.*).

crybell, *f., pl.* **-ow,** cock's comb, crest, tuft, topknot, tassell (W., B.).

crybella, *vb.,* to fray or tease out rope, etc., to tuft, crest (D. " cribble ").

crȳben, *f., pl.* **-now,** crest : *c. mel,* honeycomb ; *c. culyek,* cock's comb, Lh.

crȳbya, *vb.,* to card wool, Lh.

crȳbyn, *f., pl.* **-now,** wool-card (B.).

crȳbyon, *pl.,* combings (W.).

crȳf, (*kriv,* Lh.), *adj.,* raw, crude, green,

unripe, uncooked (D. " creeved ").
crȳgell, *f.*, *pl.* **-ow**, cricket (insect); spider-crab (D. " creagle ").
***crȳgh**, *m.*, wrinkle, rumple, ripple; *adj.*, wrinkled, crumpled, rippled, (W.).
cryghlam, *m.*, somersault (D. " crickmal ").
cryghlemmel, *vb.*, to turn head over heels.
***crȳghy**, *vb.*, to ruffle, rumple, ripple, shrivel (W.).
cryghylly (*krehylly*), *vb.*, to jar, jolt, rattle, shake: *mayth yu cryghyllys ow dyns*, so that my teeth are made to chatter, P.C. 1218.
cryjy, see **crysy**.
cryjyk, *adj.*, believing, religious; *m.*, *pl.* **-ygyon**, believer: see **dyscryjyk.**
crȳk(g), *m.*, *pl.* **-ygow**, crack, fissure (D. " creag ").
crȳn, *adj.*, dry, brittle; niggardly: *m.*, *pl.* **-yon**, barley-bran (D. " crinion ").
crȳna, *vb.*, to become dry or brittle (D. " creen," W., B.).
crynder, *m.*, dryness, avarice (W., B.).
crȳor, *m.*, *pl.* **-yon**, crier (W., B.).
crȳs, *m.*, vigour, vehemency, force, speed: in phrase *gans mur-grys*, *mur a grys*, forcibly, hastily, etc.
†**crȳs** (C. Voc. *kreis*) *m.*, *pl.* **-yow**, shirt, shift, chemise.
crȳs, *m.*, *pl.* **-yow**, shake, shiver, quake: see **dorgrȳs.**
crys-hōk (*kryssat* Lh.), *m.*, *pl.* **-ys**, kestrel, " cress-hawk " (E.D.).
***crȳspows**, *f.*, waistcoat: *c. oferyas*, cassock (W.).
crystyon, *m.*, *pl.* **-stonyon**, **-stenyon**, Christian.
crysy, **-jy** (*cresy*, *jy*), *vb.*, to believe, have faith in: takes *dhe*, *crys dhym.* believe me; 3 s. pret. *crysys*; in MSS. *e* may be substituted for *y* anywhere, but there is no vowel-change in sympathy with vowel of endings; the same applies to *pysy* and *synsy*.
crȳsya, *vb*, shiver, shake (W., B.).
crysyans, **cryjyans** (*crejyans*), *f.*, belief, faith, sect, religious body.
***crȳthen**, *f.*, *pl.* **-now**, scar (W.).
cūcū, *f.*, cuckoo; blue wrasse (D.): *blejen an gucu*, bluebell (D. " Guckow ").
***cüdell**, *m.*, *pl.* **-as**, sparrow-hawk (W., B.).
***cüden**, *f.*, *pl.* **-now**, skein (W., B.).
cüdha, *vb.*, to cover, hide, blindfold, conceal: 3 s. subj. *cutho*; 3 s. plupf. *cuthsa*; 3 s. pres.-fut. *cuth*.
cüdhan, see **cüdon.**
cüdhans, *m.*, covering, concealment: see **cüdha.**
cüdhen, *f.*, soft layer on face of hard granite (D. " keathan ").
cüdhlen, *f.*, *pl.* **-now**, veil (W.).
cüdhy, *vb.*, to grieve, make sorry: p. pt. *cudhys*, O.M. 1336, R.D. 766, 2326.
cüdhyjyk, *adj.*, sorry, contrite, repentant.
cüdhyjygeth, *m.*, contrition (B.).
cüdhygykhē·, *vb.*, to cause to repent (B.): as **berhē.**
†**cüdon**, **cüdhan**, *f.*, *pl.* **-as**, wood-pigeon, C. Voc., *wuduculfre* Aelfric.
cüdyn (C. Voc. *cudin*), *m.*, *pl.* **-now**, lock of hair, *loc* Aelfric: John Ergudyn (*ergh*, *cudyn*), Snowlock, B.M. p. 106.
cüf, *adj.*, dear, beloved, loving, amiable, kind, friendly; expensive (D. " keef "); *m.*, *pl.* **-yon**, dear one, friend: *c.-colon*, dear heart, beloved one, dearly beloved.
cüfter, **-der**, *m.*, kindness.
†**cūgol**, *m.*, *pl.* **-low**, cowl, monk's hood, C. Voc., *cugle* Aelfric.
cūgh, *m.*, head-covering, crown of hat, cover of hive: see **pengūgh.**
cuhüdha, **-as**, *vb.*, to accuse, denounce, impeach, tell tales about: 3 s. pres.-fut. *cuhuth.*
cuhüdhans, *m.*, *pl.* **-ow**, charge, accusation.
cuhüdhor, *m.*, *pl.* **-oryon**; **-dhyas**, *m.*, *pl.* **-ysy**, accuser (W.).
†**cuhüdhojak** (C. Voc. *cuhudhudioc*), *m.*, *pl.* **-jogyon**, accuser, prosecutor, *wregere* Aelfric.
cül, *adj.*, narrow, slender, slim, lean, Lh., N. Boson, C. Voc., *hlaene* Aelfric.
***cūlbren**, *m.*, bludgeon, knob-stick (W.): see **gulbredengu**, Appendix I.
cülder, *m.*, narrowness, slenderness (W.).
cüldyr, *m.*, *pl.* **-yow**, isthmus (W.).
cülforth, *f.*, *pl.* **-fordhow**, pass, defile (W.).
cülvor, *m.*, strait (W.).
culyak, *m.*, worthless person (D. "culliack").
cülyek, (C. Voc. *chelioc*), *m. pl.* **-yogas**, cock, male bird, *coc* Aelfric; *c.-kenys*, cock-crow; †*c.-goth*, *-godhow*, gander, *ganra* Aelfric; *c.-Gyny*, turkey-cock; *c.-hos*, *-hyjy*, drake, Lh.; †*c.-redan*, grasshopper, *gaerstapa* Aelfric; *c. r. askellek* locust; *c.-gwyns*, weathercock (W.).
†**culyn** (C. Voc. *culin*), *m.*, chaff: possibly for *culiu* (*colyow*), another pl. of **col.**

cūm, *m.*, *pl.* **-mow**, small valley, dingle: place-names, Coombe, Boscubm, etc.

cümyas (*cummyas*, Lh. *kibmiaz*), *m.*, leave, license, permission: *ry c. a wul*, to give permission to do; *omma gas dha gumyas*, take thy leave of this place, B.M. 2969.

†**cün**, *m.*, *pl.* **-ysy**, chief, lord: in ancient personal names.

cün, see **ky**.

cun-, see **ke-**.

cüna, *vb.*, to light (D. "kenner," a pipe-lighting, W. *cynneu*).

cünda, see **kynda**.

cünjy, *m.*, *pl.* **-ow**, kennel for hounds.

cuntell, *vb.*, to gather, assemble, aggregate, collect; *m.*, gathering, collection, meeting, Gw. (*centle*).

†**cuntelles** (C. Voc. *cuntellet*), *f.*, *pl.* **-ow**, congregation, assembly, *gegaderung* Aelfric.

cuntellyans, *m.*, *pl.* **-ow**, gathering, collection, meeting, congress, Gw.

cünyjek, *f.*, place for gathering or storing fuel; *adj.*, abounding in fuel: Kenidjack, place-name.

cünyjen, *f.*, *pl.* **-now**, billet, block, *col.* **cünys** (*kinnis*, Lh.), fuel, firewood.

cünyssa, *vb.*, to gather fuel (W., B.): inf. only.

cūr, *m.*, *pl.* **-ow**, limit, extent, border of country, Lh.

cūr, *m.*, *pl.* **-ys**, ? court, B.M. 2011 (Fr. *cour*): see **remōsyon**.

cür, *m.*, care, keeping, cure of souls; cure, remedy, M.C. 191: in *bommyn dres keyn, mar pyth-e yeyn, ny-dhe dhe gur*, a wrongwise stroke, if once it is cold, won't come accurate, P.C. 2730, *dhe gur* seems to mean "careful," "exact," as Lat. *accuratus*; cf. *dos dhe squyr*.

cür, *m.*, *pl.* **-yow**, choir, R.D. 1899.

cürgan, *f.*, *pl.* **-ow**, chant, choral song (W.).

curun, **curyn**, *f.*, *pl.* **-now**, crown: †*c. ruy*, diadem, C. Voc., *cynehealm* Aelfric.

curuna, *vb.*, to crown.

curyak, *m.*, *pl.* **-ÿogas**, pimple, red speckle or face-spot, Lh.

cüs, see **kēs**.

cusca (*cosca*), *vb.*, to sleep; to dry rot, go mouldy, decay (D.): 3 s. pres.-fut., 2 s. imp. *cusk*; *my re-guscas pos*, I have slept heavily, R.D. 511; *cusk war dha dor*, sleep face downwards, O.M. 2070; *k* would presumably be lost before *s* as in **dysky**.

cuscajor (C. Voc. *cuscadur desimpit*), *m.*, *pl.* **-yon**, sleeper: †*c. desempys*, lethargic person, one who falls into torpor or is sleepy unseasonably, *ungelimplic slapol*, Aelfric.

cuscas, *m.*, sleep, doze (W., B.).

cusk (*cosk*), *m.*, sleep; rot in timber, mould, corrosion (D.).

†**cuskty** (C. Voc., *cuski* for *cuscti*), *m.*, *pl.* **-ow**, dormitory, *slaepearn*, Aelfric.

cussya, *vb.*, to curse, C.W. 788 (D.E. "cuss"): p. pt. *cussyes* (*cushez* Gw.).

†**cüssyn** (C. Voc. *cussin*), *m.*, *pl.* **-now**, kiss (O.E. *cyss*, *cos* Aelfric, with dim. *-yn*).

cusül, *f.*, *pl.* **-yow**, advice, opinion, counsel, plan or method to adopt, way of proceeding, resolution, *raed* Aelfric: *pyth yu dhym c. orth an dra-ma dhe wruthyl?* What is my best course in dealing with this? P.C. 1432: *my a-wor c. dha dhym dhe wruthyl*, I know a good plan for me to carry out, O.M. 2802.

cusülya, *vb.*, to advise, counsel, plot: *omgusulya*, to take counsel together.

cusülyans, *m.*, consultation.

†**cusülyador** (C. Voc. *cusulioder*), *m.*, *pl.* **-yon**, counsellor, *raedbora* Aelfric.

cüth, *m.*, sorrow, grief, trouble, travail: *c. ny-gan-gas*, we shall not cease from sorrow, R.D. 2456, lit. sorrow will not leave us; see **cüdhy**.

cüth, *adj.*, concealed, secret; *m.*, hiding-place (W., B.).

cüth, see **cüdha**, **cüdhy**.

cūth, *f.*, *pl.* **-ow**, husk, pod, Lh.: *c.-faf*, bean-pod; *c.-pys*, peascod; *cuthow*, chaff (D. "cutha", dregs, perhaps confused with **godhas**).

cüva, *m.*, *pl.* **-vys**, tub (D. "keeve," O.E. *cyf* or Fr. *cuve*).

cüy, *vb.*, to foal ("to geey" D., Borlase).

cȳder, *m.*, cider, B.M. 1969 (M.E.).

cymbal, *m.*, *pl.* **-s**, cymbal, O.M. 1999 (M.E.).

cyta (*cyte*), *f.*, *pl.* **-tys** (*-tes*), city (M.E.).

cythol, *m.*, *pl.* **-s**, dulcimer, citole, O.M. 1997 (M.E.).

D (mutations Dh, T)

d', see **dhe**[2].

-d-[5], *infixed pron.*, thee : occasional var. of **-th-**[5].

da, *m.*, good, good thing, possession ; *adj.*, good, goodly, valid, of full measure ; (adverbially) well, irreg. comp. *gwell*, superl. *an gwella* : with *bos* and *gans*, expresses satisfaction, *kyn na-ve d. genes*, though thou mightst not be pleased ; *pur dha yth-hevel y vos*, it seems very clear that he is ; *tryhans kevelyn d.*, 300 full cubits ; *na-wra vry, rak puptra-oll a-vyth d.*, never mind, for everything will be all right, O.M. 534 : see **magata, yn-ta.**

da[2], see **dha**[2].

†**da**, *m.*, fallow-deer, doe, C. Voc. (O.E.), *da* Aelfric.

dader (*dadder*), *m.*, goodness, good, bounty, favour, benefit, profit, edification, profitable knowledge or talk : *ow-profya dodho d.* (for) offering him a kindness, B.M. 485 ; *dysky d.*, to learn that which is good for us, B.M.

dafar (*daffar*, D. " daffer "), *m.*, means, provision, preparation, materials, furniture, receptacle, table-ware (D.), straw pad to protect pack-horse's back (D.) : *d. lathva*, munitions, Keigwin.

dafar (*daphar*, Borlase), *vb.*, to provide, furnish, prepare.

daffola, see **deffola.**

dager, *m. and col.*, *pl.* **-grow**, tear, drop : found in pl. only, with col. sense, **dagren** may be used as sing.

dagren, *f.*, *separative pl.* **-now**, *col.* **dager**, teardrop, small drop.

dagrewy, dagry, *vb.*, to shed tears (W.,B.).

dagyer, *m.*, *pl.* -s, dagger, Lh. (E.).

dagyow, *pl.*, dried cod-fish (D. " daggyow ").

dala, see **dathla.**

dalgh, *m.*, hold (B. *dalc'h*, W. *dalo*) : unused root of **dalghen, -na.**

dalghen (*dalhen*), *f.*, *pl.* **-now**, hold, grasp, grip : *set d. ynno* ! pl. *settyeugh dalghennow ynno* ! lay hold of him !

dalghenna (*dalhenna. dalg(h)enna*), *vb.*, to grasp, seize, take hold.

dall (C. Voc. *dal*), *adj.*, blind ; *m.*, *pl.* **dellyon**, blind man : *hens dall*, blind alley (B.).

dalla', see **dalleth.**

dalla, *vb.*, to blind : *namna 'gan-dallas golou*, light almost blinded us, R.D. 302.

dalles, *f.*, *pl.* **-ow**, blind woman (W., B.).

dalleth (C.W. *dallath*, Late *dallah*), *m.*, beginning, commencement, start.

dalleth (*dallath*, Late *dalla*), *vb.*, to begin, start, commence, inaugurate, originate, set going : 3 s. subj. *dallatho* ; 3 s. pret. *dallathas* ; 3 s. plupf. *dallathsa*.

dallethfos (C.W. *dallathvas*; *dalle h,bos*), *m.*, beginning, genesis, origin.

dalva, da'thelva, *f.*, quarrel, dispute, row (D. " dalva ") : see **dathel, omdhal.**

dama, *f.*, *pl.* **-myow** (Late *dameeowe*), dame, mother (M.E.) : *d. -dha*, mother-in-law (see **sӯra**) ; *d.-wyn*, beldame, grandmother, Lh. ; *d.-kyogh*, jacksnipe (D. " dameku ") ; *d. 'n hern*, allis shad (D. " damon herring ") ; *my a-lever dhys, d.*, I tell thee, mother, C.W. 1283.

damach, *m.*, damage, harm, disaster, B.M. 1077 (M.E.).

dampnasyon (*-ascon* B.M.), *m.*, damnation (M.E. *dampnacioun*).

dampnya (*dampna, damnya*), *vb.*, to condemn, damn (M.E.).

damsel, *f.*, *pl.* **-s**, damsel, O.M. 2105 (M.E.).

dan[2], *prep.*, under, beneath : used with *a-*, *yn-* ; see **a-dhan**[2], **yn-dan**[2].

danjer, *m.*, jurisdiction, disposal, dominion, control, power ; (with *perthy, hep*) objection, reluctance, demur, grudging, scruple, hesitation, difficulty : *perthy d*, hesitate, make a difficulty, O.M. 168.; *cafos yn d.*, hold in thrall, get into one's power, Chart. Endors. ; *gul d. dhe*, pay feudal service to, B.M. 3483 (M.E. *daunger*, O. Fr. *dangier*).

dans, *m.*, *pls.* **dyns**, †**danneth** (C. Voc. *dannet*), tooth : *den hep dyns*, toothless man, Lh. ; *d. a-rak*, front tooth ; *d. a-dhelergh*, back tooth ; *d. harraw*, harrow-tine (Late) ; *d.-lew*, dandelion (W.) : *yn despyt wor' dha dhyns*, in the teeth of thy opposition.

danvon (*danfon, danon*), *vb.*, to send, dispatch, report, have word taken, send to say : the *v* is dropped M.C. 123 and usually in Late Cor., though Kerew writes 3 s. pret. *davanas* with first *n* dropped ; *o* becomes *e* before *e, y*, e.g., p. pt. *danvenys* ; *d.warlergh*, to sent for, send to fetch.

danvo'nadow, *m.*, message, report or instructions sent, P.C. 998.

da-ober, *m.*, *pl.* **-ow**, good work or deed, R.D. 2599.

†**dar**, *m.*, *pls.* **dery**, **derow** (used as *col.*), oak, C. Voc.: see **derowen.**
dar, *prep.*, *adv.*, ? beyond, extremely, M.C. 135, O.M. 2719.
dar, *interj.* (of surprised inquiry), what? why? eh?: used before *ny-* without interr. particle *a-*, ***Ay! Ay! Ay! Dar, ny-wreugh vry?*** Hi! Hi! Hi! What, do you show no regard? B.M. 953, but ***Ow! Dar, budhy a-vynta?*** Ho! What, dost want to be drowned? C.W. 2441.
dar-, see Appendix II.
darbar, *m.*, preparation, contrivance (D. "darber," a cord-spinning device).
darbarer, *m.*, *pl.* **-roryon**, workman's assistant, provider (W., B.).
darbary, *vb.*, to prepare, make ready, provide, furnish, equip, supply, appoint, grant, vouchsafe: *Dew re-dharbarro*, may God grant; *Mahum darber hardygras dhe...!* Mahound deal vengeance on...!
darfos, *m.*, event; *vb.*, to happen: *bos* compound; 3 s. pret. and impf. subj. *darfa*; p. pt. *darfedhys.*
dargan, *f.*, prediction (W., O.B.).
dargana, *vb.*, to predict (W., O.B.): as **cana.**
darleverel, *vb.*, to foretell (O.B.): as **leverel.**
darn, *m.*, *pl.* **-ow**, fragment, piece, part, portion; *pron.*, some: *d. ow fobel, d. y bobel*, some of my, his, people, B.M. 2489, 2496.
***daromres**, *vb.*, to frequent, haunt, come and go; *m.*, movement to and fro (W., B.).
†**darrajor** (C. Voc. *darador*), *m.*, *pl.* **-yon**, doorkeeper.
darras (C. Voc. *darat*), *m.*, *pl.* **da'rrajow**, **da'r'jow** (Late *darjeu*, *derggawe*), door: *d. a-rak*, front-door; *d. a-dhelergh*, back-door, Lh.
darwa'r, *def. vb.*, 2 s. imp. only, be forewarned! or, be very cautious! Chart. Endors.
darȳvas, see **derȳvas.**
das, *f.*, *pl.* **deys**, stack, rick: see **goldheys.**
das-, see Appendix II.
dasa, *vb.*, to stack (W.).
dascafos, *vb.*, to refind, re-discover: p. pt. *daskefys*: as **cafos.**
dascodha, *vb.*, to fall back, relapse: as **codha.**
dascor (*de-ascor*), *vb.*, to yield, give up, return, resign, p. pt. *daskerys*; *m.*, yield, return, restitution (B.): see **ascor, hepcor.**
dasformya, *vb.*, to reorganise: as **formya.**
daskemeres, *vb.*, to retake, regain, Lh.
daskene'sygeth, *m.*, rebirth.
daskenethly, *vb.*, to regenerate (W.).
daskenys, *p. pt.*, reborn.
***daskylyas**, *vb.*, to ruminate, chew cud (B., cf. W. *cil*, cud).
daslenky (Lh. *dadlunky*), *vb.*, to swallow down.
dasleverel, *vb.*, to repeat, say again: as **leverel.**
dasprē'n, *m.*, redemption, ransom (W., B.).
dasprena (*dysprena*), *vb.*, to redeem, ransom, buy back: as **prena.**
dasprenyas, (*dysprynnyas*), *m.*, *pl.* **-ysy**, redeemer, re-buyer.
daspryntya, *vb.*, to reprint: as **pryntya.**
dasscry'f (*skref*) *m.*, *pl.* **-yvow**, copy, Lh.
dasscryfa, *vb.*, to copy, write again: as **scryfa.**
dasseny *vb.*, to resound, echo, reverberate: 3 s. pret. *dassonas* (W., B.).
dasserghy (*dasserhy*, *dasserry*, *datherghy*, *dathery*), *vb.*, to rise again: 2 s. imp. *dassorgh*; 3 s. pres.-fut. *dassergh*; 3 s. pret. *dassorghas.*
dasserghyans, *m.*, resurrection, revival.
dasso'n, *m.*, echo, reverberation (B.).
dastenythy, *vb.*, to regenerate: as **denythy.**
dastenythyans, *m.*, regeneration.
dastrehevel, *vb.*, to rebuild, raise again: as **drehevel**
dastewynya, *vb.*, to reflect, shine back: as **dewynya.**
dasvewa, *vb.*, to live again, revive: as **bewa**; *dasvewys yu ow spyrys*, my spirits are revived, B.M. 3762.
dasvewnans, *m.*, revival, reanimation.
daswül, *vb.*, to remake, restore: as **gül.**
dathel, **dal**, *f.*, *pl.* **dathlow**, **dalow**, debate, discussion, argument, case (W.,B.).
†**da'thelor**, **dalor** (C. Voc. *datheluur*), *m.*, *pl.* **-yon**, orator, debater, advocate, *gemotman* Aelfric.
dathelva, see **dalva.**
datherghy, **dathery**, see **dasserghy.**
dathla, **dala**, *vb.*, to discuss, debate, plead, argue (W.): see **omdhal.**
***daun**, *m.*, *pl.* **-ow**, drop (W.).
davas (C. Voc. *dauat*), *f.*, *pl.* **dēves**, *separative pl.* **devysyow**, **-yjyow**, sheep: there seem to be traces of a nasal mutation after *an* in place-names and in the

corruption of *camneves* to *camdhavas* by way presumably of *cam an navas*, cf. V. *en avad*; for *en navad*, the sheep.
davasyk, *f.*, *pl.* **deve·sygow**, little sheep.
dayly (*deyly*), *adv.*, daily, B.M. 3697 (E.).
dē (C. Voc. *doy*), *m. and adv.*, yesterday.
de[2], *prep.*, see **dhe**[2], the usual form.
de-[2], see Appendix II.
dē-, **dū-**, **dew-**, *m.*, day: vars. of **dēth**, used as prefix to name of day or in compounds like **dēgol**; the *th* may be kept before the *y* of *Yow*; *de*[3], *du*[3] before *Calan* only: *de-*, *du* is omitted if the article is used, *war an Sul*, etc; *du* is like W. *duw*, *dyw*.
dē, see **dü**.
***dēaghüby**, **deüby**, *vb.*, to deliver, free (W., B.): replaced by **delyfra**.
deantel (*dyantell*), *adj.*, hazardous, unsteady, ready to fall, insecurely poised; *as adv.*, precariously (D. "dantels"): see **antel**
debātya, *vb.*, to dispute, wrangle, combat, B.M. 3476 (M.E.).
debonē·r, *adj.*, gentle, kind, gracious, complaisant (M.E.).
debrenna, *vb.*, to itch, tickle.
debron, *m.*, itching, tickling, strong desire: ***yma d. dhe'm dywvregh mar bell bos hep y wul***, my arms itch at being so long without doing it, B.M. 1187, 3432.
debry, see **dybry**.
dēca, see **dēga**.
decernya, *vb.*, to discern, distinguish a difference (M.E.): *gothvos d. ynter*, to be able to differentiate between, B.M. 28.
dedevy, *vb.*, to sprout, spring up (B.).
dedhe·wadow, *m.*, promise, O.M. 1624, 1871.
dedhewy, *vb.*, to promise: 2 s. imp., 3 s. pres.-fut. *dedhow*; p. pt. and 3 s. pret. *dedhewys*.
dedhewys, *f.*, promise, M.C. 83.
***dedhwy**, *vb.*, to lay eggs (W. B.): 3 s. pres.-fut. *dedhow*; 3 s. pret. *dodhwas*.
dēdhwyth, **dȳdhwyth**, *m.*, *pl.* **-yow**, day's time, P.C. 388; *adv.*, to-day, by day, this day (past), in the daytime.
dēdhyow, see **dēth**.
dedh'ȳ, stressed form of **dhedha-ȳ**, B.M. 3122.
dēf, see **düf**.
defendya, *vb.*, to erase, expunge, delete, prohibit, annul, M.C. 188 (M.E.).
defe·ns, *m.*, defence (M.E.): *dhe wul d. a-rak tus*, to resist an attack (make a defence) in public, P.C. 2306.
deffola (*daff-*, *daf-*), *vb.*, to outrage, violate, defile, shame, crush, injure, wound, lit. trample on, P.C. 1398, R.D. 492 (M.E. *diffoile*, *defoil*, *defoulen*, O. Fr. *deffouler*).
defow·t (*dyfout*), *m.*, default, blemish, M.C. 192 (M.E. *defaute*).
defnyth, *m.*, *pl.* **-yow**, material, stuff, makings, subject-matter, usable substance: *gul defnyth a*, to make use of, P.C. 2548.
defrȳ·, *adv.*, indeed, verily, seriously: put first, it gives greater force to what follows, *d. benygys ty yu!* blessed *indeed* art thou! otherwise it is a mere expletive; *yn pur defry*, most certainly; *re Synt Defry*, by St. Verily, oath, C.W. 606.
defȳa, *vb.*, defy, despise, B.M. (M.E.): 3 s. pres.-fut, *defȳ*.
dēga (Late var. *dēka*), *m.*, tithe: *deka, deka!* was cried on the arrival of fishing-boats with a catch, on which the proctors or their agents came to receive the tithe.
degēa, **-as**, *vb.*, to shut, close, enclose: p. pt. *degēs*.
degemeres (*dy-*), *vb.*, to accept, admit, receive, B.M. 433, 2573; take possession of, seize, P.C. 124: *den a-vyth degemerys yn-ban yn-mesk arlydhy*, a man will be welcomed to a higher position among lords; p. pt. is here made *dege·merys* in verse.
degenow, see **degensow**.
dēgensetē (*degensytte*, B.M. 3417, *degenzhete* Lh.; *de genziate*, Lh. M.S., *dēth kens es dē*), *m.*, day before yesterday; *adv.*, on the day before yesterday.
degensewa (*-sywe*), *vb.*, to impend, threaten, draw near: *ow-tegensewa*, imminent, just coming, O.M. 1079.
degensow (*degenow*, R.D. 2561), *adv.*, recently, just now.
degevy, *vb.*, to tithe, pay tithe, C.W. 1071
deghesy (*dehesy*), *vb.*, to fling, let fly, throw or strike violently, dash, hurl, O.M. 2703: 3 s. pres.-fut. *deghes*, P.C. 1515; *degheseugh dhedha, warnedhy!* have at them, it! B.M. 3534, 3948.
deglena, *vb.*, to shake, quiver, shiver, tremble, shudder (? for *de-*, *crenna*, W. *dygrynu*): *yma ow threys ha'm dywla dyworthyf ow-teglena*, my feet and hands are shaking off me (with cold), P.C. 1217; 3 s. pres.-fut. *degly·n*, P.C. 3047, C.W. 485.

dēgol, dūgol (*dē*, *gōl*), *m.*, *pl.* **-yow,** holiday (D. "duggle"): *d. Stul,* Twelfth Day; *d. Myghal,* Michaelmas; *d. deys,* harvest-home (D. "diggle-dize").

degō·th (*dogoth*), *def. vb.*, it behoves, is due: as **cōth,** of which it is a strengthened form.

degrē·, -gra· (*dygre, dycre*), *m.*, rank, station, class, step in direct descent (M.E.): *arluth why yu a dhygra* (rhyme *dh'y gwysca*), you are a lord in rank, R.D. 1923: *a Gaym, map Adam, yth-of sevys, a'n seythves d.*, from Cain, son of Adam, am I descended, in the seventh generation (including Adam), C.W. 1437.

degves, *ord. num,* tenth.

degwyth, *adv.*, ten times.

dēgwȳth, *m.*, weekday, workday.

degy, see **dōn.**

dehelghya, dehellya, *vb.*, to chase along, hurry (D. "jale").

dēhen, *m.*, cream, Gw.

dehenjy, *m.*, *pl.* **-ow,** creamery (B.).

dehenna, *vb.*, to form cream (B.).

dehennek, *adj.*, creamy (B.).

dehesy, see **deghesy.**

dēk, *card. num.*, *pl.* **dēgow,** ten.

dēkplēk, *adj.*, tenfold.

del[2] (Late corruptions *der, tr', try,* etc.), *adv.*, so, as, how: mutation of following *d* is often prevented; used directly before vb. unless with infixed pron., *mar scon dhedha d. ymmy,* as soon as thou kissest them, but *del y-m-kyrry,* as thou love me; *kepar d.*, just as; *d. y-s-brewaf... d. vyth...,* so will I strike her...as that shall be...O.M. 2712.

del, *m.*, form, likeness, manner: kept only in compounds, **fatel, kettel, yndella, yndelma.**

†delē, *f.*, *pl.* **-lēyow,** yard of sail, C. Voc., *segelgyrd* Aelfric.

delen, *f.*, *pl.* **delyow** (Late *delkyow*), *col.* **dēl** (*deyl, deel*), leaf.

delergh (later *deller,* Lh. *delhar*) *m.*, rear, hinder part, stern of ship: *wor' tu d.*, towards the rear, aft: see **a-dhelergh, war-dhelergh.**

deleth, *def. vb.*, it behoves, is fitting, suitable, meet, proper: 3 s. pres. only found; *deu vylygys, y-teleth warbarth aga bos gorrys,* a cursed pair, it is meet they should be put together, P.C. 2553: see **delys.**

***delevy,** *vb.*, to yawn (W., B.).

†delk (C. Voc., *delc*), *m.*, *pl.* **-lcow,** brooch, clasp, necklet (O.E. *dolc, dalc*), *myne, swurbeah* Aelfric.

dellny, *m.*, *blindness* (W.).

***delow,** *f.*, *pl.* **-ow,** idol, image, statue (W.).

dēlya, *vb.*,to put forth leaves (W., B.).

delycyous, *adj.*, delicious, C.W. (M.E.).

delyfra, dely·frya, *vb.*, to deliver, release, allow to go, set free: 2 s. imp., 3 s. pres.-fut. *delyrf, delyr'* (*vy*): 3 s. plupf., *delyrfsa; ef a-s-delyrf genough,* he will let you take them, P.C. 184; *d. orth, dyworth,* to deliver from.

***delynya,** *vb.*, to delineate, draw, picture, portray (E.).

***delynyans,** *m.*, drawing, picture.

delys, *m.*, *pl.* **-yjow,** merit (B.); *vb.*, inf. (if used) of **deleth:** p. pt. (if used) **deledhys**; cf. **gonys.**

delȳt (*dylyt*), *m.*, delight (M.E.): *yma dheugh mur a dhelyt a omknoukya,* you take great delight in hitting one another, P.C. 2323.

demandya, *vb.*, to demand, Lh. (E.).

demedhy (*domedhy, demydhy*), *vb.*, to marry, be married, espouse: 3 s. pres.-fut. *demeth*; 3 s. subj. *demetho*; 3 s. plupf. *demethsa.*

demma (*dymma*), *m.*, *pl.* **-mys,** half-penny (M.E. *dyme,* tenth part).

dēn (*dean,* Lh.), *m.*, *pl.* **tüs,** man, person, one, *d.* **deu-dhēn,** two men, pair, man and woman: *†d.-coscar,* retainer (C. Voc.); *†d. ancoth* (*unchut*), stranger, C. Voc., *utan cuman* Aelfric; *d. noweth,* bridegroom; *d. mor,* sailor; *d. Dew,* saint; *d. an clogh,* bell-ringer: *d. y'n bys* (with neg.), nobody at all.

dēna, *vb.*, to suck.

deneren, *f.*, *pl.*, **-now,** penny-piece, single penny; see **dynar.**

denewes (C. Voc. *deneuoit, denowes* Bilbao MS.), *m.*, *pl.* **-wys,** young ox or heifer, *styrc* Aelfric.

denewy, *vb.*, to pour, flow, shed: 3 s. pres.-fut. *dynwa*; see **denow.**

dēn-jentyl, *m.*, *pl.* **tüs-j.,** gentleman: Wheal Tis Gentle, mine-name.

dēnlath, *m.*, homicide, manslaughter, murder, M.C. 124; manslayer, murderer, O.M. 2335.

denow, *m.*, outpouring, effusion (W., B.): see **denewy.**

dēn-rȳal, *m.*, pl. **tüs-r.,** nobleman, R.D. 1907, B.M. 436.

densa (for *dēnda*, *denja*), *m.*, good man, saintly person, kind man; familiarly, my good man; cf. **dremās.**
densak, *adj.*, having a tooth: see **dynsak**.
dēnseth (pr. *densa* M.C. 223), *m.*, humanity, human feeling: ? for **dēnüseth**, see **dēnüs.**
Densher, pow-D., *f.*, Devonshire, N. Boson (D.E.): see **Dewnans.**
dēnsys, *m*, manhood, humanity, human kind, state or time of human life: *yn ow d.*, while I live; in several places R.D. misread as *deusys*; see **dewsys.**
dēnty, *adj.*, dainty, fastidious, C.W. 1456 (M.E.): *tam d.*, tit-bit, as field-name.
dēnüs, *adj.*, human: suggested by **dēnseth**
denvyth (Late colloq. *denneth*), *m.*, *pron.*, anybody, anyone: used with *awos*, or with neg. or *hep*, as "nobody"; as "any man," *den-vyth* is used.
dēnyk, *m.*, *pl.* **tüsygow**, dwarf, manikin, gnome (B.).
dēn-yowynk, -yonk, *m.*, *pl.* **tüs-y.**, young man, stripling, R.D. 1639: *d. whek*, gentle youth.
dēnüs, *adj.*, human: suggested by **dēnseth.**
denys (*-es*), ? reared, begot, B.M. 251, 295: 3 s. pret. of a vb. like W. *deifnio* (? inf. *denel*), or less probably a cut-down form of *denythys*.
denythy, *vb.*, to give birth to, beget, bring forth, generate: p. pt. and 3 s. pret. *denythys*.
denythyans, *m.*, generation, birth, Keigwin.
der, see **drē**[2].
deragla, *vb.*, to chide, scold, rail, brawl, Lh.
dera·k(g), *prep.*, before, in presence of: combines with pronouns as **rak(g)**, Appendix V.: see **a-dherak**.
deray·, *m.*, *pl.* **-ys**, disarray, tumult, disorder, disturbance, confusion, (M.E. *desray*, D. "derry"); *gul d.* break enemy's ranks, O.M. 2224; *ef re-wruk mur a dheray*, he has caused a great deal of disorder, P.C. 380.
***deres**, *m.*, *pl.* **-yow**, step, stair (W., B.).
derevel, see **drehevel.**
dernyk, *m.*, *pls.* **-ygow, darnowygow**, little bit (B.).
derow·, *m.*, beginning (W., B.): replaced by **dalleth**, but kept in **androw·**, q.v.
de·rowek, *f.*, *pls.* **-egow, -egy**, oak-grove (B.).
de·rowen, *f.*, *pl.* **-now**, *col.* **dar, derow**, oak-tree: *pren derow*, oak timber.
derowennek, *f.*, *pls.* **-egy**, place where oak-trees grow (B.).
dervy·n, *vb.*, to ask, need (to be), call for, demand, require, expect: 3 s. pret. *dervynnys*, *-as*; 3 s. plupf. *dervensa*; *y-tervyn y enora*, he must needs be honoured.
derȳ·vadow, *m.*, account, reporting: see **derȳvas.**
derȳvas (*daryvas*), *m.*, account, report, statement; *vb.*, to recount, tell, state, declare: 3 s. pres.-fut., 2 s. imp. *derȳf*; 3 s. pret. *deryvys*.
descendya (*desendya*), *vb.*, to descend (M.E.).
***descryfa**, *vb.*, to describe.
***descryvyans**, *m.*, description.
desedha, *vb.*, to set, put in place, dispose, arrange, fit, be fitting, suit: 3 s. pres.-fut. *deseth*.
desēgha, *vb.*, to dry up, dessicate: as **sēgha.**
desempys (C. Voc. *desimpit*), *adj. and adv.*, sudden, immediately: see **a-dhesempys.**
desef, *m.*, *pl.* **-evyow**, supposition, thought, expectation (M.B.).
desevos, *vb.*, to presume, expect, suppose, imagine, think, fancy: 3 s. pres.-fut. *desef*; *na-dheseven*, 1 pl. impf. subj., is spelt *na thesan* C.W. 631.
deskerny (*de-*, *eskern*, *-y*), *vb.*, to grin, snarl, M.C. 96.
desmygy (*dysmegy*, Late *dismiggia*), *vb.*, to guess, find out, imagine, invent, divine, discover: as W. *dychmygu*.
desmyk, *m.*, invention, riddle, discovery: as W. *dychymyg*, *dy-*, prefix, *cymyg*, fancy.
despȳt (*dyspyt*), *m.*, spite, despite, defiance, scorn, contempt, insult: *yn d. dhe*, in spite of (M.E.).
despȳtya, *vb.*, to spite, insult, vex, worry (M.E.).
desta (*dysta*), *vb.*, to witness, testify: var. of *testa*, O.M. 2543, 2789; cf. **dustuny**; followed by *na-* in neg.
destewel, *vb.*, to silence, calm, quieten (W., B.).
destna, de·styna, *vb.*, to destine (M.E.); p. pt. *destnys*, R.D. 2336.
desȳr, *m.*, wish, will, request, desire, supplication (M.E.): *dyworth Cryst y-whruk pysy certan d.*, from Christ he besought a certain petition, B.M. 4426.

desyrya, *vb.*, to desire, request: 3 s. pres.-fut. *desÿr* (M.E.).
determya, *vb.*, to determine, decide, conclude: p. pt. *determys,* C.W. 236 (M.E. *determyd*).
dēth, dȳth, after *n*, **jēth** (*deyth,* C. Voc. *det*), *m.*, *pl.* **-dhyow,** day, date: *ef re-ros dhyn d. hyr lowr,* he has given us long enough credit (a sufficiently distant date, B.M. 1930.; *yn y dhedhyow, yn ow dedhyow,* etc., always, all his (my) life long, at all times, consistently, perpetually; *yn jeth nag yn nos,* (not) at any time, at all; *y'n j. hedhyu,* to-day (pres. and fut.); *hedhyu yn j.*, to-day (past); *dyworth an j.*, at daybreak; *d. brus,* (on) doomsday; see **dē-.**
dettor, *m.*, *pl.* **-s,** creditor: M.E. *dettour,* debtor, but reversed in meaning, P.C. 503; see **kendoner.**
deu[2] (*dew, dyw*), *card num.*; *m.*, two: both suffers and causes mutation, *an*[2] *dheu*[2] *dhēn*[2] *vās,* the good couple; *d. ha d.*, by couples, two at a time, in pairs; *an dheu,* both; *agas deu,* both of you; see **dowdhek, dyw**[7].
deu-[2], *dual prefix,* before masc. nouns naming paired parts of body: the texts confuse **deu-,** m. with **dyw-**[2], f.
deublēk, *adj.*, twofold, double: see **plēk.**
deudhegves, *ord. num.*, twelfth.
deudhek (*dowdhek*), *card num.*, twelve: *den a'n d.*, juryman.
deugansves, *ord. num.*, fortieth.
deu ügans, deugans, *card. num.*, two-score, forty.
***deuny,** *vb.*, to trickle (W. *defnu,* B. *denedeo,* m. pl.): see ***daun.**
devar (*düfer,* B.M.), *m.*, duty, what is due, thing incumbent, 2528 (M.E. *devar*).
devedhyans, *m.*, lineage, origin, descent, B.M. 439, Lh.: formed from **dōs.**
†**dever,** *m.*, *pls.* **deverow, defryon,** ancient variant of **dowr**: Ardeverow, place-name.
devera (*dyvere*), *vb.*, to drop, drip, water, trickle, pour, shower, shed, bleed: 3 s. pres.-fut. *dever,* 3 s. subj. *deffro,* 3 s. pret. *devras.*
deveren, *f.*, *pl.* **-now,** drop of water (B.).
dēves, see **davas.**
devones, see **dōs.**
devorya, *vb.*, to devour, B.M. 4178 (M.E.).
devōs, see **dōs.**
***devos,** *f.*, *pl.* **-ow,** rite, custom (W.,O.B.).
devrak, *adj.*, watery; boggy (Lh.).

devȳja, devȳsa. *vb.*, to hunt sheep: inf. only.
devȳjor (*deveeder*), *m.*, *pl.* **-yon,** sheep-worrying dog: *neb na-gar y gy a-n-gwra d.*, he who loves not his dog will make him a choke-sheep, proverb, Scawen.
devyn (*dyvyn*), *m.*, *pl.* **-now,** quotation, citation, extract, B.M. 78.
devynny, *vb.*, to quote, recite (W.)
devȳs, *m.*, *pl.* **-ys,** device, fancy, will (M.E.): *a-dhevys,* complete, at point device, every inch; *dhe'm d.*, just as much as I like; *henna yu pyth a-dhevys,* that's just the thing, ideal; see **a-dhevȳs.**
devȳsya, *vb.*, to devise, plan: see **devȳs.**
devysyow, see **davas.**
Dew (C. Voc. *Du, Duy*), *m.*, *pl.* **-ow,** God: *D. genough-why,* goodbye; *mar myn D.*, God willing; *D. dyfen!* God forbid!: see **durdala, -datha. -sona.**
dew-, see **dē-.**
dewana (*dy-*), *vb.*, to penetrate: p. pt. *dewenys,* O.M. 783: see **gwana.**
dewas (C. Voc. *diot*), *m.*, *pl.* **-wosow,** liquor, drink, draught, potion: *d. coth,* stale liquor; *d. cref,* strong drink; *d. -vrag,* malt-liquor; *d. an darras,* stirrup-cup, probably adapted from Ir. *deoch an dorrus* (P., D. " dash an darras ").
dewaslester, *m.*, *pl.* **-lystry,** drink-pot (W.).
dewedha, *vb.*, to end, finish; 3 s. pres.-fut. *deweth*; 3 s. subj. *dewetho*; 3 s. plupf. *dewethsa.*
dewedhes, *adj.*, *adv.*, late: *a-dhewedhes,* of recent times, latterly, N. Boson.? translating E. " of late."
dewenys, see **dewana.**
dewes (*dues*), *f.*, *pl.* **-ow,** goddess; *kepar y'n bys ha d.*, for all the world like a goddess, O. M. 155.
deweth (*dua* Gw.), *m.*, end, finish, conclusion, termination (in point of time): *deth d.*, the day of judgment.
dewetha, *comp. adj.*, later; *an d.*, superl., last; latest: formed from **deweth,** *m.*, but **dewedhes** is used as positive.
dewethva, -fa (*dowethva* C.W. 2), *f.*, ending, end, R.D. 41.
Dew-gweres, *m.*, " God-speed " or " criss-cross," cross at head of old horn-book alphabet, usually in red: ✠ **abc...,** read *D.*, *a, b c,* B.M. 99, cf. *gweres...ow fysadow,* speed my prayer, O.M. 1829.

dewha·ns (*dy-*, *du-*, *dyhons*), *m.*, inclination, propensity, eagerness (W.); *adv.*, eagerly, incontinently, immediately, quickly: *pur-dhewhans*, right fast, M.C. 222: see **a-dhewhans.**

dewhelans, dewhylyans, *m.*, remission, atonement, forgiveness.

dewheles, *vb.*, to return, come back, atone, remit: 3 s. pres.-fut. *dewhel*; 3 s. pret. *dewhelys*; *byner re dhewhylly, genes my a-wra pysy*, that thou mayst never return, shall I pray for thee, O.M. 2196; *byner re-dhewyllyn, menough y-wrer y bysy gans agan kerens nessa*, that we may never return, often will one be caused to beseech it on behalf of our nearest relatives, B.M. 3439.

dewl, see **dyawl.**

dewlüjy, -yjy (*deulugy* for *dyewlysy*), *m.*, devilry, wickedness, diabolical influence or power.

Dewnans (*Deunanz*, Lh.), *f.*, Devon.

dewnos (*deunos*, P.C. 20, for *dewynas*, or possibly a vb., B. *divinout*), *m.*, witchery, supernatural insight, magic, divination: see **dewyn** (pl. **-yon**).

dewolow, see **dyawl.**

dewotty (*dewas*, *ty*), *m.*, *pl.* **-ow**, drink-shop, ale-house (W.).

dewraga, *vb.*, to flow, gush, inundate, O.M. 1084: see **dowrak.**

dewsys, dewjys, *m.*, divinity, godhead, deity.

dewyn, *m.*, *pl.* **-now**, shine, ray, beam, W. *tywyn*: see **dewynya.**

dewyn, *m.*, *pl.* **-yon**, diviner (W.): see **dewnos.**

dewynya (*dywh-*), *vb.*, to shine, R.D. 2533, M.C. 243.

dewynya, *vb.*, to divine (W.): see **dewnos.**

dewynÿeth, *f.*, art of divination (W.).

dewys (*dywys*), *vb.*, to choose, make choice, select: p. pt. *dewysys*.

dewys, *m.*, choice (W., B.).

dēyn, *m.*, *pl.* **-ow**, dean: *syr d.*, Sir Dean; by scansion given one syllable, but representing W. *deon*, B. *dean* with two.

dēynjy, *m.*, *pl.* **-ow**, deanery, house (W.).

dēynÿeth, *f.*, deanery, office, etc. (W., B.).

deys, see **das.**

dha[2], (usual softening of **da**[2]), *poss. pron.*, thy: corruptly *dheth*, C.W.; *d.-honen*, thyself; *d. gows d.-honen*, thy own speech.

dhanna, *conj.*, then, Lh. (E. "then"): *doroy an golow, d.*, bring the light, then, Jowan Chy an Horth, 41.

dhe[2], before vowel **d', dh'** (usual softening of **de**[2]), *prep.*, to, for, at: combines with prons., Appendix V., but is occasionally used uncombined with those of 1st and 2nd persons, *dhe vy*, *dhe jy*, *dhy(n) ny*, *dhy why*; *dhym*, *dhymmo*, for me, is used to express impatience in *taw dhymmo!* hush! *pyma dhym?* wherever is it? etc.; *dhe'th voth*, *dh'agan desyr*, etc., according to thy will, our desire; *dhe wyth*, on a weekday, *dhe Sul*, on a Sunday; *de-Mergher dhe nos*, on Wednesday night; before comp. adj., *dhe well*, the better, *dhe weth, lacca*, the worse, *dhe gens*, the sooner, *dhe voy*, the more, etc.; with *bos*, *yma dhodho*, he has, etc.; required after certain verbs that need no prep. in English, *amma*, *crysy*, *grassa*, *plekya*; an ejaculatory optative is made with *dhe* before poss. pron. and an inf., as *Dew dhe'm sylwel!* God save me! *dhe'th cregy!* be hanged! *dhe be yma ow wajys*, my wages are to pay, P.C. 2257, *nyns-yu dhe grysy dhodho*, there is no believing in him, he is not to be credited; *ef yu mur dhe vlamya*, he is greatly to be blamed.

dhe-denewen, *adv.*, sidelong, C.W. 1553.

dhe-drē, *adv.*, home, back; as interj., home with you!

dhe-hēs, *adv.*, at length, at last, M.C. 109.

dhejȳ, see **dhesȳ.**

dhe-ēs, *adj.*, profitable, advantageous, useful, R.D. 876.

dherak(g), see **a-dherak(g).**

-dhesȳ·, -dhejȳ·, *suffixed pron.*, thou, thee, doubled emphatic form of *-sy*, *-jy*: used unsuffixed also, *kergh y dhejy*, fetch them thyself, P.C. 2282; *my a-vyn dhejy, a-dro*, I will (do so to) thee, all round, P.C. 2313: see **-tesȳ.**

dhe-vēs, *adv.*, off, away: *gasa d.*, leave off; *dysky d.*, take off (of clothing); see **mēs.**

dhe-wary, *adj., and adv.*, at liberty, free: see **gwary.**

dhe-woles, *adv.*, to the bottom, down below, R.D. 2196.

dhe-wȳr, *adv.*, in truth, verily.

dhy, see **dy.**

dhynny, see **dhe**[2].

dhywa·r[2] (for *a-dhywa·r*), *prep.*, off from, R.D. 404: see **dywar**[2].

dhywar-lür, *adv.*, up from the ground, B.M. 4227; see **a-dhywar**[2], **war-lür.**

dhyworth, see **a-dhyworth**.
dhywhy, see **dhe**[2].
doctour, *m.*, *pl.* **-s**, doctor.
***dodhwas**, etc., see **dedhwy**.
dōf, dō', *adj.*, tame, gentle : *gwyls ha d.*, wild and domestic animals, B.M. 7.
dofhē', *vb.*, to tame : as **berhē**.
do'hajēth (*doghajeth*, P.C., *dohajeth*, *dohojyth*, Lh.), *m.*, latter half of day, noon to sunset ; *adv.*, this afternoon or evening: *kens es hanter-d.*, before mid-afternoon, P.C. 2912 ; contracted from *dyworth ewha an jeth* : see **ewha**, **kensewha**.
dojel, *m.*, *pl.* **-as**, young pollack (D. "dudgel").
dōl, *f.*, *pl.* **-ow**, dale, meadow with stream : place-names, e.g., Doleer, *d. hyr*.
dōl, *m.*, *pl.* **-ys**, share, dole, Borlase, P.(E.).
dolō's, *vb.*, to pretend, give out falsely, M.C. 250 (Lat. *agere dolose*, to act fraudulently, *dolus*, fraud).
dōm, *m.*, doom, judgment, B.M. 4007.
do'mhel (*de-*, *o'mwheles*), *vb.*, to upset, overthrow, subvert, ruin, counteract against, B.M. 2652 : special inf. without added ending, as W. *dymchwel* ; 3 s. pret. *do'mhelys*.
domynasyon, *m.*, dominations, order of angels, C.W. 56 : pl. *-s* was omitted probably because *-yon* already suggested Cor pl. ending.
dōn (Late *degy*), *irreg. vb.*, to bear, carry, carry off, bring, take, convey : *d. dyworto*, take away from him ; *d. ganso*, bring off, take with him ; *d. dustuny*, bear witness ; for parts see TABLE in APPENDIX VIII.
dones, see **dōs**.
dōns (Late *downs*, *daunce*), *m.*, *pl.* **-yow**, dance (M.E. *daunce*) : *d. meyn*, megalithic circle, said to be of dancers turned to stone.
donsya (*downsya* C.W.) ; *vb.*, to dance (M.E. *dauncen*).
donsyer, *m.*, *pl.* **-yoryon**, dancer.
donsyores, *f.*, *pl.* **-ow**, dancer, danseuse.
dōr (C. Voc. *doer*), *m.*, *pl.* **-ow**, earth, soil, ground : with old nasal mutation, *an nor*, or compounded with *bys* as *an norvys*, the earth, the world ; *an dor*, without mutation, the ground ; *nor* is often treated as a distinct word, used without a written *an*, e.g., *nor ha nef*, *nef ha nor*, *mor*, *nor*, *ha'n nef*, etc., but always means "the world" until the latest period, when it was used of ground also ; *dorvys* is never found in its radical form ; *d. ysel*, *yseldor*, bedrock, bottom (C,W., Lh.) ; adverbially *dhe'n d.*, down; *yn-dan d.*, underground ; *gorra y'n d.*, to bury, B.M.
dorgē, *m.*, *pl.* **-ow**, earthen hedge, earthwork (D. "durgy").
dorgell, *f.*, *pl.* **-ow**, vault, cellar (W.).
dorgrȳs (*dorgys* M.C. 200, 209), *m.*, earthquake, P.C. 3086 : the second *r* is lost in M.C., cf. **gorgȳs**,
dorgȳ, *m.*, *pl.* **-gün**, terrier (W.).
dorgȳs, see **dorgrȳs**.
dorn, *m.*, *pl.* **-ow**, *d.* **deudhorn**, fist, hand, handle : *d. dyghow*, right hand ; *d. cleth*, left hand (*glikin*, Lh., is D.E. "click-hand") ; *d. ardar*, plough-tail ; *mes a dhorn*, out of hand, at once (Late, from E.) : *yn ow d.*, led by me, P.C. 2528, cf. *in manu ejus*, Lat. stage-direction p. 393.
dorna, *vb.*, to thump, thrash (W., B.).
dornas, *m.*, *pl.* **-esow**, thump ; handful (W., B.).
dornla (*lē*), *m.*, handle, handhold, Lh.
dornscryfa, *vb.*, to write by hand, Lh. ; *m.*, manuscript.
dornva, **-veth**, *f.*, *pl.* **-vedhy**, hand-breadth, span (W.) : see **mesva**.
dorrep (*dowr*, *ryp*), *m.*, waterside : Trethorep, place-name, cf. **morrep**.
dōs, **dones**, **devōs**, **devones**, *irreg. vb.*, to come, be derived : the longer inf. forms are used for euphony or slight emphasis ; 1 pl. imp. *dun*, is commonly used as "let us go" ; *d. gans*, to carry off ; *d. ha*, before inf., to come to, happen to ; *d. dre gans*, to pierce or run through with, R.D. 2587, B.M. 1266 ; for parts see TABLE in APPENDIX VIII.
dōth, *adj.*, prudent, discreet, tactful, wise, well-behaved, sage, demure, Chart. Endors. ; comp. *dotha*, B.M. 2944 ; *m.*, *pl.* **-yon**, sage (W.).
dothter, *m.*, prudence, tact (W.).
dōtya, *vb.*, to dote, act like a fool, become witless, B.M. 346 : p. pt. *dotyes*, doating, gone mad, B.M. 462 (M.E. *doten*).
dour (pr. *dūr*), *adv.*, with care, punctitiously, scrupulously, stringently, exactly, completely ; *m.*, care, anxiety, R.D. 1327.
dour, see **dowr**.
dout, see **dowt**.
dova, *vb.*, to tame, break in, Lh. ; 3 s.

pres.-fut., 3 s. imp. *dōf*, *dō*.

doveth, *m.*, tameness (W.).

do way, *interj.*, give up, put away, lay aside, have done with! let be! O.M. 485 (M.E. *do wey*).

dowdhek, var. of **deudhek**, keeping older form, *dow*, of *deu*, M.C., Gw.

down (*doun*), *adj.*, deep, profound, low; (adverbially) deeply, far in.

downder, *m.*, profundity, depth, Lh.

downhē·, *vb.*, to deepen: as **berhē.**

downvor, *m.*, deep sea (W., B.).

dowr, dour (C. Voc. *douer, dofer, dour, dur*, Late *dower*), *m.*, *pl.* **-ow**, water, fresh water (as opposed to **hyly, mōr**), urine: *d. son*, holy water (W.); *d. tom*, ardent spirits: *d. t. Frynk*, brandy; *d. t. lollas*, rum; **d. t. Ywerdhon, Alban*, Irish, Scotch, whisky; in compounds *dowr* tends to keep its ancient sound as *dur*; see **dever.**

dowra (Lh. *douria*), *vb.*, to water, give water to drink.

dowrak, *adj.*, watery; *m.*, watery place: Dowrack, place-name; see **dewraga.**

dowrargh, *m.*, *pl.* **-ow**, water-tank, cistern (W.).

dowrbons, *m.*, *pl.* **-ow**, aqueduct (B.).

dowren, *f.*, *pl.* **-now.** water-place: Dowren, place-name.

dowrērgh, *m.*, sleet, lit. water-snow (B.).

dowrfals, *m.*, *pl.* **-ljow**, leak: see **fals.**

dowrgy (C. Voc. *doferghi*), *m.*, *pl.* **dowrgün**, otter, lit. water-dog.

dowrhē· (Lh. *dourhi*), *vb.*, to water plants, etc.: as **berhē.**

dowrhens, †**deverhens**, *m.*, *pl.* **-y**, watercourse, (W.).

dowrla (*dowr, lē*), *m.*, watering-place for cattle, watery ground: Durla, place-name.

dowrlam, *m.*, waterfall (W.).

dowrlan, *f.*, waterside (W.).

dowrva, *f.*, watering-place for cattle: Durva, field-name.

dowrvargh, *m.*, *pl.* **vērgh**, hippopotamus (W.).

dowryar, *f.*, *pl.* **-yēr**, coot (W., B.).

dowst (Late *douste*), *m.*, dust, chaff, M.C. 195, Kerew (D.E.).

dowt (*dout*), *m.*, doubt, fear; *conj.* lest, for fear of, that (M..E): *yma d. dhym ef dh'y wul*, I fear he may do it; *ym ι d. dhym nag-yua vas*, I fear it is not good.

dowtya (*doutya*), *vb.*, to fear, dread, mistrust, doubt (M.E.).

drabba, for **drubba**, see **drȳ.**

draffa, see **drehevel.**

draggya, *vb.*, to drag: p. pt. *dreggys*, Borlase *dregas* (E.).

drăght, *m.*, *pl.*-**ys**, draught, O.M. 2627 (E.).

dragon (*dragun*, Lh.), *f.*, *pl.* **-as**, dragon, B.M.: see **drȳk.**

dral, *m.*, *pl.* **-yow**, bit, scrap, piece: in O.M. 2782, *ha, tewleugh e d. ha d. yn Besseda pur-gowal*, go, cast it bit and bit into Bethsaida quite wholly, the sense is evidently not "bit by bit", as the timber is in one piece, but probably "(every) bit and scrap"; an alternative is to read *drayl ha drayl*, "drag by drag," but though the vb. *tenna* is used of the log, it is actually carried.

dralya, *vb.*, to break into bits (W., B.).

dram, *m.*, *pl.* **-mow**, swathe of cut corn (D.).

drayl, *m.*, a drag: see **dral, draylya.**

draylya, *vb.*, to drag, trail along the ground, B.M. 1352 (M.E. *drailen*).

draylyer, *m.*, *pl.* **-yoryon**, person or thing that trails behind (D. "draalyer").

drē[2] (*der*), *prep.*, through, by means of, by way of: combines with prons., see Appendix V.; as prefix, thoroughly, see Appendix II; *der* is a variant already common in B.M., and found once, *dyr*, in M.C. 35, but not in Ord.; *d. hun, d. gusk*, in one's sleep; *d. nos*, by night; *ytho, d. henna yth-yu dha vos*, that means, then, that thou art, P.C. 2015; *dos d.*, see **dōs.**

drē, *adv.*, home: var. of **trē.**

dredhy (*dre, hy*), *adv.*, thereby, M.C. 152: cf. **gensy, dȳ.**

drefen, *conj.*, because, on account of: used with nouns or with inf. of vbs. except in neg., when *na* follows it; *d. an vertu*, because of the power, M.C. 61; *d. ow bos*, because I am, on account of my being; *d. ty dhe'm servya*, because thou servest me; *d. na-vynnyth crysy*, because thou wilt not believe.

dregyn, *f.*, mischief, injury, harm, B.M., Chart. Endors: see **drōk.**

drehedhes, *vb.*, to reach, completely attain, P.C. 2758: as **hedhes.**

drehevel, derevel (late *drevel, deraffa, draffa*), *vb.*, to raise, build, lift up, rise, rear up: 3. pres.-fut. *drehaf*, *dreha*, *deref*; 2 s. imp. *drehaf, drefa*; 3 s. pret.

drehevys, *derevys*; 3 s. subj. *drehaffo*; 3 s. plupf. *drehafsa*.

drehevyans, derevyans, *m.*, uprising, raising, building, construction: *d. an dowr*, spring (Lh.).

drēm, *m.*, keening, lament (M.E. *dreme*, sound, song): *na-wreugh d. warnaf-vy*, make no lament over me, P.C. 2640.

dremā's, *m.*, saint, thoroughly good man; (familiarly) goodman, husband: cf. **densa.**

drēn (C. Voc. *drain*), *m.*, *pl.* **dreyn, drӯn** (C. Voc. *drein*), thorn, prickle, spine, fish-bone.

drenak (*dranick* Ray), *adj.*, thorny; *m.*, *pl.* **-ogas**, spur-dogfish; *f.*, *pls.* **-egow, -egy**, thornbrake.

drenen, *f.*, *pl.* **-now**, *col.* **dreyn**, thorn-bush.

drēs (*drys*, *dreys*), *prep.*, beyond, over, above, past, besides, except: combines with prons., see Appendix V; *d. eghen, d. kynda*, extraordinary; *d. nos*, overnight; *d. an mor*, across the sea; *d. an vledhen*, all the year round; *d. an bys*, beyond everything; *d. an vro, an bys-oll*, all over the country, the whole world; *d. ken*, perverse, contrary, in the wrong direction, thwartwise; *gul d. dyfen, gorhemmyn*, act against the prohibition, command; *kemer queth dresos*, take upon thee a garment, B.M. 3076; *d. henna*, also, moreover; *ny-yl bos splanna golow es henna, d. an howl y-honen*, there can be no brighter light than that, except the sun itself: *nyns-us arluth dresto-ef*, there is no lord but he.

drewyth, *m.*, *pl.* **-yon**, druid, of first degree in Gorsedd (W., B.).

dreyn, see **drēn.**

dreynek, *f.*, *pls.* **-egow, -egy**, thorn-brake; *adj.*, thorny, barbed.

dreysek, *f.*, *pls.* **-egow, -egy**, briar-brake.

dreysen, *f.*, *pl.* **now**, *col.* **dreys, drӯs** (C. Voc. *dreis*), bramble, briar.

dro'coleth (*drokkuleth*, *drokeleth*), *m.*, harm, injury, wrong.

drōg, see **drōk.**

drōga (Lh. *droaga*), *vb.*, to hurt (W.).

drogatty (*druggatye* Gw.), *m.*, fits, obsession by an evil spirit: see **atty**, and context to B.M. 2655.

drogeth, *m.*, vice, evil, malice (W., B.).

drog-gras, *m.*, revenge, harsh requital: lit. "evil grace," from M.E.; see **yfla gras, hardygras.**

drōk (C. Voc. *drog*), *m.*, *pl.* **-ogow**, evil, harm, ill, illness, malady, wickedness.

drōk(g), drok(g)-, *adj.*, bad, ill, evil, wicked, naughty, hurtful: usually prefixed; excl. *drocca*, *droga*, irreg., comps. *lacca*, *gwēth*, superl. and equat., *gwetha*; with *bos* and *gans* expresses dissatisfaction, *d. yu genef*, I am sorry, (as exclamation) alas!

drokbrederys, *adj.*, malicious (Lh.).

drok-bryson, *m.*, dungeon, R.D. 2002: see **pryson.**

drokdavasek, *adj.*, ill-tongued (Lh.).

drok-dewedha, *vb.*, to come to a bad end, P.C. 1828.

drokdheweth, *m.*, miserable end, R.D. 2086.

drokdyby, *vb.*, to suspect (W.).

drok-genesek, -ejek, *m.*, one born bad, R.D. 2186.

drok-gēr (C. Voc. *drocger*), *m.*, infamy, ill-report, notoriety, *unhlisa* Aelfric.

drok-gerya, *vb.*, to report ill of: p. pt. *d.-geryes* (*drocgeriit*, C. Voc.), *unhlisful* Aelfric.

drok-lam, droglam, *m.*, *pl.* **-mow**, mishap, misadventure.

drok-ober, *m.*, *pl.*, **-ow**, ill-deed.

drok-oberor (C. Voc. *droc(h)oberor*), *m.*, *pl.* **-yon**, ill-doer, criminal, *yfeldaede* Aelfric.

drok-pollat, *m.*, *pl.* **-ys**, rascal, bad fellow, C.W. 769.

drok-pӯs, *p. pt.*, ill-pleased (translating M.E. *ill apaid*): see **pē.**

drokter, *m.*, wickedness, evil, harm, Keigwin.

droktra, *m.*, wickedness, evil, P.C., R.D.: cf. **trūethtra, ūthektra.**

drok-trō, *m.*, ill turn, P.C. 3066.

drok-ūra, *vb.*, to besmear, besmutter: see **ūra.**

drok-vrūs, *f.*, bad judgment, ill-will, spite, grudge, Lh.

drokwas, *m.*, *pl.* **-wesyon**, bad fellow, rogue, knave: *an jowl d.*, the evil one.

drokwhans, *m.*, *pl.* **-ow**, lust, evil desire (B.).

drolla (*daralla* Lh.), *m.*, *pl.* **-lys**, tale, story (D.E. "droll").

droppya, *vb.*, to drop, M.C. (M.E.): see **pendroppya.**

drushya (*drushen* Lh., ? for *drushea*), *vb.*, to thresh (E.D.).

drushyer, *m.*, *pl.* **-yoryon**, thresher, Lh.

drüth (*druyth*), *adj.*, valued, dear, precious, O.M. 1621, R.D. 2492.

drȳ (*drey*), *irreg. vb.*, to bring, take with one, persuade, (with *yn-mes*) put, reach, (with *dhe*, *yntra dywla*, etc.) give: *drubba*, late contraction of *doroy omma*, bring here; *doro dhym dha vay*, give me a (lit. thy) kiss; see **rȳ**, Table in Appendix VIII.

†drȳk (C. Voc. *druic*), *f.*, *pl.* **-ygow**, dragon: replaced by *dragon*.

drylsy, -jy, *m.*, monotonous, tiresome noise (D. "drilsy, -jy").

drynk, *m.*, medicinal draught, potion, B.M. 1462 (M.E.).

dryppyn (*-pan*), *m.*, little drop, Borlase.

dū-, see **dē-**.

dü, dē (*due*), *adj.*, ended, finished, spent, done (M.E. *do*).

dū (C. Voc. *duw*, Lh. *diw*), *adj.*, black, sombre, dark; *m.*, blacking, black colour or pigment: *mys D.*, *mys D. ken Nadelek*, P., November; the latter is possibly from Lhuyd's Welsh, p. 100, but may be Cor., though *mys D.*, B. *miz du*, is usual.

dūa, *vb.*, to blacken, smut (W.).

dūan, see **dū(gh)an**.

***duches**, *f.*, *pl.* **-ow**, duchess (M.E.).

***ducheth**, *m.*, duchy: as **conteth**.

dūder, *m.*, blackness, gloom (W., B.).

düf, dēf (C. Voc. *dof*), *m.*, *pl.* **devyon**, son-in-law, P.C., *adhum* Aelfric.

düfer, see **devar**.

dufydhy, see **dyfüdhy**.

dū(gh)an (*duon*, *duwhan*, *dewhan*), *m.*, grief, trouble, sorrow.

dū(gh)anhē· (*duwenhe*, *dewhanhe*), *vb.*, to grieve: as **berhē**.

dugol, see **dēgol**.

dūhē·, *vb.*, to blacken: as **berhē** (B.).

dük, later **dūk** (C.W. *duke*), *m.*, *pl.* **-ys**, duke (M.E.): rhymes *gwrük* B.M. 2264, *Belsebuk* P.C. 1926.

dūlās, *adj. and m.*, deep blue or green (W.).

dun, see **dyn**.

dür, *m.*, steel (W., B.).

dūr, *adj.*, bold, brave: Sloggett motto *bedheugh d.* (as W. *dewr* or M.E. *dure*, hard).

dür (*duer*, *dēr*), *def. vb.*, it concerns, matters, is of interest: *ny-m-dur man*, *ny-m-d. travyth*, *a henna*, that is nothing to me, I don't mind or care a bit, at all, for that: *clew, mara 'th tur*, listen, if thou carest, R.D. 845.

durdadha-why (contraction of *Dew roy deth da dheugh-why*, *dar day dew a why*, A. Boorde), *interj.*, good day to you, Carew: see **rȳ**.

durdala dywhy (contraction of *Dew re-dallo dywhy*, *dar dalo de why*, A. Boorde), *interj.*, thank you, lit. God repay to you, Carew, P.: see **tylly**.

durnostadha (contraction of *Dew roy nos da dheugh*, *ternestatha*, Carew), *interj.*, good night to you.

dursona (contraction of *Dew re-sonno*, *dar zona*, A. Boorde), *interj.*, blessings! lit. God bless: also probably for *Dew re-sowenno*, God speed; it is followed by *dys*, *dywy*, B.M. 587, 4194, probably in imitation of *durdala*.

dürya (Late *dirria*), *vb.*, to last, endure (M.E. *dure*).

dustüny (C. Voc. *tistum* for *tistuni*, C.W. *destynye*), *m.*, *pl.* **-ünȳow**, witness, testimony, evidence: *gewitnys*, *gecydhnys* Aelfric; *Dew (dhe'm) d.*, God (for my) witness; the word has acquired a permanent mutation.

dustü·nȳa, *vb.*, to bear witness, testify.

dūta, *m.*, duty, B.M. 3198 (M.E. *dueté*).

dūwhan, see **dū(gh)an**.

dworennō·s, see **dyworth**.

dȳ, dhȳ (*de*, *hy*), *adv.*, thither, (of movement), there to that place; *bys-d.*, *bys-ty*, right to it, as far as that; *hy* here is used as "it," as in **gensy**; see **motty**.

dy-[2], see Appendix II.

dyagha (*dyaha*), *m.*, tranquillity, freedom from fear; *adj.*, unalarmed (M.E. *aghe*, O.E. *ege*, awe, fear): *cuskyn-ny gans d.*, let us sleep with ease of mind, R.D. 402.

dyagon (C. Voc. *diagon*), *m.*, *pl.*, **-as**, deacon, levite, *diacon* Aelfric.

dyagones, *f.*, *pl.* **-ow**, deaconess (W.).

dyagonȳeth, *m.*, diaconate (W.).

dyaha, see **dyagha**.

dȳal, *m.*, revenge, retribution, vengeance: *tylly* or *kemeres d. war*, to wreak vengeance on: *trom-dhyal*, *dyal uskys*, a sudden vengeance.

dyala. *vb.*, to be avenged on, be vindictive towards, inflict punishment on, torment, execute.

dyalar (*dealer*), without pain or grief, B.M. 3086 : see **galar.**
dyallos, *adj.*, powerless, impotent (W.).
dyalor, *m.*, *pl.* **-yon,** avenger (W.).
dyalwhedha, *vb.*, to unlock.
dyalwhedhyk, *m.*, *pl.* **whe·dhygow,** small-key : *nyns-us d. a-m-gwyth,* there are no trifling keys that shall prevent me ! B.M. 3690.
dyalwheth (C. Voc. *dialhwet*), *m. pl.*, **-edhow,** key ; *adj.*, unlocked.
dyanel, *adj.*, breathless (W., B.).
dyanwesy, *vb.*, to get oneself warm (B.).
dya·nk, *m.*, to escape ; *vb.*, to escape, run away : 3. s. pres.-fut. *dyank* ; p. pt. and 3 s. pret. *dyenkys* ; (D. pronunciation "jank.")
dyanken, *adj.*, untroubled (B.).
dyannedhy, *vb.*, to move goods, remove from a dwelling (W.,B.).
dyanneth, *adj.*, uninhabited (B.).
dyanowy, *vb.*, to yawn, gape (B.).
dyantell, see **deantel.**
dya·rf, *adj.*, unarmed (W.).
dyarghen, -as, *adj.*, barefoot, shoeless (W.) : see **arghenas.**
dyarva, *vb.*, to disarm (W.).
dyaw·l, jawl, dewl (*deaul, joul, jowle,* C. Voc. *diavol*), *m.*, *pl.* **dewolow, jawlow,** devil : usually spelt with *j* in sing. after *n*, but *an dewolow* (C.W. *dhewolow*) in pl. ; *pyle an j.* where the dickens ?
dyawlak, *adj.*, devilish (W., B.).
dyawles, *f.*, *pl.* **-ow,** she-devil : spelt *jawles* after *n.*
dyba·ls, *adj.*, infrequent, rare, scattered (B.); see **pals.**
dybarow (*debarowe*), *adj.*, distinct, unmatched, unlike others, odd ; *adv.*, separately, one by one, C.W. 404.
dyba·rth, *f.*, separation, division, parting, segregation.
dybē·gh, *adj.*, sinless (W., B.).
dybe·n, *adj.*, headless, endless (W. B.).
dybenna, *vb.*, to behead, lop, crop : p. pt. *dybynnys,* B.M. 1351.
dȳber (C. Voc. *diber,* Symonds, *deeber*), *m.*, *pl.* **-brow,** saddle.
dybe·rth (*-barth*), *vb.*, to separate, isolate, segregate, distinguish, discriminate, divide, scatter, disperse, part, depart : 2 s. imp., 3 s. pres. -fut. *dyba·rth* ; *d. yntra,* to intervene, separate combatants ; *den, claf, dyberthys,* leper ; *dyber'-dowr,* broad-brimmed hat, lit. shed-water.
dyberthyans, *adj.*, impatient : see **perthyans.**
dyberthva, *f.*, separation, distinction, isolation, C.W. 84.
dybla·ns, *adj.*, distinct, separate, clear, unblemished, precise, *adv.*, separately, distinctly.
dyblü·f, *adj.*, unfledged, featherless (W.,B.).
dyblüva, *vb.*, to pluck feathers (W., B.) : see **plüven.**
dyblysca, *vb.*, to shell eggs, nuts, etc. W., B.) : see **plysken.**
dybly·sk, *adj.*, shell-less (W., B.).
dybō·s, *adj.*, weightless, unimportant (W., B.).
dybowes. *adj.*, restless, unceasing (B.).
dȳbra, *vb.*, to saddle (W., B.),
dybreder, *adj.*, heedless, thoughtless (B.).
dybrenna, *vb.*, to unbar, unbolt (B.).
dȳbror, *m. pl.* **-yon.** saddler (W., B.).
dybry (*debry,* C. Voc. *diberi*), *vb.*, to eat ; to tickle : stem-vowel *e* except before *y* ; 3 s. pres. fut. *deber* ; 3 s. subj. *deppro* ; 3 s. plupl. *dep'sa* ; p. pt. and 3 s. pret. *dybrys* ; *kens es d.*, very shortly ; *nefra na-wrello d.*, so that she may never eat (i.e. live no longer) O M. 2706.
dybrȳas, *adj.*, unmarried (W.).
dybrȳ·s, *adj.*, without value (W.).
dybystyk, *adj.*, unhurt (B.).
dybyta, *adj.*, pitiless.
dyclō·s (*dyckles*). *adj.*, joyless, hapless, inglorious, C.W. 1031 : no mutation of *cl* ; rhyme-word is *boos* (*bōs*).
dycrē, see **degrē.**
†**dycre·ft** (C. Voc. *dicreft*), *adj-*, inert, stupid : *craeftleas* Aelfric ; no mutation of *cr.*
*__dyderghy__, *vb.*, to uncoil : 3 s. pret. *dydorghas* (W.).
dydha·n, *adj.*, amusing, pleasing (W.).
dydhana, *vb.*, to amuse, charm, comfort, rejoice.
dydhēhenna, *vb.*, to skim milk (B.).
dydhē·l, *adj.*, leafless.
dydhemedhy, *vb.*, to divorce (B.).
dydhemeth, *adj.*, unmarried, celibate (B.).
dydhēna, *vb.*, to wean (W., B.).
dydhew·, *adj.*, atheistic, godless (W., B.).
dydhȳbra, *vb.*, to unsaddle (B.).
dydhy·ns, *adj.*, toothless (W., B.).
dydhy·sk, *adj.*, unlearned, untaught (W., B.).
dydrō·s, *adj.*, noiseless, silent (W., B.).

dydrüeth, *adj.*, merciless (W., B.).
dydrȳg·h, *adj.*, unconquered (B.).
dyegrys (for *deegrys*), *adj.*, *or p. pt.* terrified, shocked, trembling, B.M. 3667 (cf. W. *egr(yd)*).
dyegy, *m.*, laziness, sloth, idleness (W,, B.).
dȳek (C. Voc. *dioc*), *adj.*, lazy, slothful, idle : *sleac* Aelfric.
dyekter, *m.*, idleness.
dȳen, *adj.*, whole, entire, perfect : *oll yntyen*, completely, utterly.
dyena, *vb.*, to pant, be out of breath, gasp, P.C. 2511.
dyenef, dyena, *adj.*, soulless, inanimate (W., B.).
dyerbyn, dyerbyna (for *de-*, *erbyn*), *vb.*, to meet, encounter : see **erbyn.**
dyeskynna. dyskynna (*deysk-*, *dyysk-*, B.M. *skynnya*, C.W. *skydnya*), *vb.*, to descend, come down, dismount (of vengeance, etc.), fall : *hap drok orthough a-skyn*, ill-luck will fall on you, B.M. 1285 ; see **wharth, yskynna.**
dyeskynyans, *m.*, descent.
dyeskys, -yjyow, *adj.*, shoeless (W.).
dȳeth, dȳheth (*dygheth*), *m.*, grievous thing, cause for regret, as W. *dyhedd* : *d. yu*, it is a pity ; *anodho d. vya*, it would be a pity for him ; *d. yu dhym gul yndella*, I am loath to do so.
dyfasya, *vb.*, to deface, alter the appearance of, C.W. 477 (M.E. *difface*).
dyfeleby, see **dyheveleby.**
dyfe·n (*defen*), *m.*, ban, interdict, prohibition, forbidding ; *vb.*, to forbid, debar, prohibit ; †defend, see **†dyfennor:** takes *na-* with subj. in following vb., and *orth* or *dyworth* (late) as prep. *Dew dyfen!* God forbid ! ; *dyfennys orthyn*, forbidden to us.
dyfe·nnadow, *m.*, prohibition, O.M. 238.
†dyfennor (C. Voc. *diffennor*), *m.*, *pl.* **-yon**, defendant, *beladigend* Aelfric.
dyffra, *vb,*, to differ : 3 s. pres.-fut. *dyffer* ; see **dyffrans.**
dyffrans, *adj.*, different ; *m.*, difference (C.W.).
dyffre·s (*dyffras*), *vb.*, to relieve, protect, save : 3 s. pres.-fut. *dyffres* ; takes *a*[2] as prep., from.
dyffresyas, *m.*, *pl.* **-ysy**, protector, one who relieves (W.).
dyfla·m, (*deflam*) *adj.*, blameless, M.C. 32: **blam.**
dyfla·s, *adj.*, shameful, disgraceful, distasteful, disgusting : see **blas.**
dyflasa, *vb.*, to turn away from, be ashamed of or offended with, be disgusted with, P.C. 901 : p. pt. *dyflesys*.
dyflassys, *m.*, disgust, distastefulness (W.).
dyformya, *vb.*, unmake, C.W. 174.
dyfow·t (*defout*), *m.*, *pl.* **-ow**, defect, blemish, M.C. 192.
dyfrē·th (*deffryth* C.W.), *adj.*, feeble, powerless, lacking in vigour.
dyfrethter, *m.*, feebleness : see **dyfrēth.**
dyfüdhy (*dufydhy*), *vb.*, to quench or extinguish flame, put out fire, O.M. 2637 : 3 s. pres.-fut. *dyfu·th*.
dyfüdher, *m.*, extinguisher (W.).
dyfüdhyans, *m.*, extinction, quenching (W.).
dyfü·n (*dy-*, *hün*), *adj.*, sleepless, awake.
dyfüna (*devina* Lh.), *vb.*, to awake, awaken.
dyfüna (for *dyfüneth*), *m.*, waking state, sleeplessness : see **a-dhyfüna.**
dyfygya, *vb.*, to .fail, cease, grow less, be defective, become exhausted : 3 s. pres-fut. *dyfy·k*.
dyfygyans, *m.*, decline, failure (W.).
dyfy·k, *m.*, *pl.* **-ygyow**, lack, defect, failure : **d. an howl* eclipse (W.).
dyfȳ·th, dyvȳth (*deveyth*, C. Voc. *difeid*), *m.*, wilderness, waste ; *adj.*, waste, desert, lonely: *mor d.*, main or open sea, C. Voc., *wid sae* Aelfric.
dyfȳthya, *vb.*, to lay waste (W.).
dygēa, -as, *vb.*, to unclose, unfence, open, O.M. 964 : p. pt. *dygē·s* ; opposite to **degēa.**
dygelmy, *vb.*, to untie, unknot : as **kelmy.**
***dygemysky**, *vb.*, to separate things mixed (W.).
dygereth, *adj.*, unrebuked, excused (W., B.).
dygesso·n, *adj.*, unharmonious (W.).
dygevelsy (*dygavelsy*), *vb.*, to disjoint, P.C. 3179 : var. of **dyskevelsy.**
dȳgheth, see **dȳeth.**
dȳ(gh)ow (*dyhow*), *adj.*, right (hand): *m.*, †South : *a-dh. dhe*, on the right hand of.
dȳ(gh)owbarth, *f.*, right hand ; *m.*, †South Country : *a dh-*, on the right hand ; see **parth.**
†dy(gh)owles (C. Voc. *dehoules*), *f.*, southernwood.
dy(gh)owyas, *m.*, *pl.* **-ysy**, right-handed person (B.).
dȳghtya, *vb.*, to use, serve, treat, prepare, order, construct, provide (M.E. *dyghte*) : read *may fo dyghtys an vreder*, so that the

brethren may be served, P.C. 692.
dygnā·s, *adj.*, unnatural, uukindly, perverse, monstrous.
dygolon, dyg'lon, *f.*, faint-heartedness, discouragement; *adj.*, faint-hearted: *na-gemer d.*, don't be downhearted! B.M. 3674.
dygo·ll, *adj.*, *adv.*, without loss (W., B.).
dygomol, *adj.*, cloudless (W.).
dygompes, *adi.*, uneven, incorrect (B.).
dygomposter, *m.*, inequality, incorrectness (B.).
dygonfortya, *vb.*, to discomfort, discourage: var. of **dysconfortya**.
dygoweth, *adj.*, companionless, solitary (B.).
dygrōghen, *adj.*, skinless, flayed (W.).
dygroghenna, *vb.*, to flay, skin (W.).
dygrȳbys, *p. pt.*, unkempt, dishevelled: see **crȳba**.
dygü·f, *adj.*, unkind (M.B.).
dygu·sk, *adj.*, sleepless (W., B.).
dygü·th (*degueth*), *adj.*, care-free, merry, B.M. 3228: see **cüth**.
dygü·th, *adj.*, unconcealed (W.,B.).
dyhanow, *adj.*, anonymous, nameless (W., B.).
dyharas (*deharas*), *vb.*. to apologize, B.M. 3344.
dyheveleby, dyfeleby (*defaleby* C.W.), *vb.*, to alter, deform, make unlike.
dyhevelep, *adj.*, unlike, altered.
†dȳhok(g) (C. Voc. *diw(h)og*), *m.*, *pl.* **-ogyon**, great-great-grandfather; ancestor, *feortha faeder*, Aelfric: see **cok(g)**.
dyho·rn, *adj.*, unshod (of horse): see **horn**.
dyjyn, *m.*, *pl.* **-now**, doit, little piece (D. "didgan") cf. **myjyn**.
dylātya (*delledzha* Lh.), *vb.*, to defer, put off, postpone, delay (M.E. *dylate*): *ef a-dhylatyas an termyn*, he span out the time, *Jowan Chy an Horth*.
dylē·, *adj.*, without place (W., B.).
dylēa, *vb.*, to remove, abolish (W., B.).
dylēs, *adj.*, profitless, useless (W.).
dylē·th, *adj.*, milkless, dry (W.).
dyllajy, *vb.*, to clothe (W.,B.).
dyllans, *m.*, discharge, issue: see **dyllo**.
dyllas (C. Voc. *dillat*), *m.*, *pl.* **-ajow**, clothing, clothes, dress, apparel: *d. gwely*, bedclothes, *eal bedreaf* Aelfric; sing. is used of all clothes worn by one person at one time.
dyller, *m.*, *pl.* **-loryon**, sender forth, editor: see **dyllo**.
dyllo (*duello*), *irreg. vb.*, to discharge, explode, let go, set free, issue, unleash, send forth: *d. gwyns*, to belch; *d. gos*, to let blood; for parts see Table of **rȳ**, Appendix VIII.
dyly·m, *adj.*, blunt, unsharpened: see **lym**.
dȳn, *m.*, *pl.* **-yon**, hill-fort: ancient place-names, Dynmiliek, Domeliock, Dingerein, Pendeen, Dunmear, etc.
dynagha, *vb.*, to deny, retract, reject: as **nagha**.
dyna·m, *adj.*, flawless, spotless, immaculate (W.B.): see **nam**.
dynar (C. Voc. *dinair*), *m.*; *pl.* **-nerow**, penny; *feoh* Aelfric; see **deneren**.
dynargh, *m.*, greeting, P.C. 2195.
dynas, *m.*, *pl.* **-ow**, hill-fort, entrenched camp: place-names, Castel an Dynas; Pendennis, etc.
dynā·s, *adj.*, unkindly, unnatural, M.C. 87: see **nās**.
dynatur (*denatar*, M.C. 139), *adj.*, unnatural.
dyndyl (Late *dendel*), *vb.*, to deserve, win, earn, gain, get as reward.
dynerghy (*denerghy*), *vb.*, to greet, hail, salute: as **erghy**.
dyne·rth, *adj.*, powerless (W., B.).
dynew·l, *adj.*, free from mist.
dyns, see **dans**.
dynsak, dynjak (C. Voc. *dens(h)oc*, Borlase *denjack*, D. "tinsack"), *adj.*, toothed, long-toothed, *m.*, *pl.* **-sogas**, hake; **d. dowr**, pike, C. Voc., *hacod* Aelfric.
dynsel, dynjel (*dendzhall* Borlase), *vb.*, to bite, chew: 3 s. pret. *dynsys*.
dynya (*dynnya*, B.M. 2883), *vb.*, to entice, allure, coax.
dy·nyta, *m.*, dignity, rank, worth, stateliness, propriety, correct attitude: *d. an gos ryal yu pur dhyogel*, what is incumbent on the blood royal is quite certain, B.M. 1627.
dynyver, *adj.*, innumerable (B.).
†dyo·dhenes (C. Voc. *diothenes*, M.B. *dieznez*), *f.*, want, lack, misery, *hyndh* Aelfric; the first *e* merely separates *dh* from *n*; if still used in M. Cor., *dyones* would be a likely form, as B. *dienez*.
dȳogel (*dyougel*, C. Voc. *diogel*), *adj.*, certain, indisputable, sure, secure, safe, *orsoth* Aelfric; used adverbially with or without *yn*[5]-, certainly: *my a-vyn y examna h'a'y dus h'a'y dyscas whare*,

prag nag-usons dyogel, I will examine him anon both of his people and of his teaching, why they are not reliable, P.C. 1212.

dyogeleth, *m.*, security, safety (W.).

dyogelhē·, *vb.*, to make sure (B.): as **berhē.**

dyogely, *vb.*, to secure, insure (W., B.).

dyow, see **dyghow.**

dyppa, *m.*, *pl.* **-pys,** small pit or hollow (D. "dippa," E.).

dyrā·s, *adj.*, graceless, profane (W., B.).

dyredenna, *vb.*, to clear ground from bracken (B.).

dyrew·l, *adj.*, turbulent, unruly (W.).

dyrüsca, *vb.*, to peel, scrape off skin, bark, abrade: see **rüsken.**

dys-, see Appendix II.

dysacra, *vb*,, to desecrate, profane (B.).

dysawor, *adj.*, unsavoury, B.M. 4135.

dyscador, -jor, *m.*, *pl.* **-yon,** teacher, instructor, professor (Lh).

dyscans, *m.*, education, knowledge, learning, B.M., Lh.: *cafos d.*, to get an education B.M. 85; *ow megyans yu, bos gorrys dhe dhyscans,* it is vital to me to be educated, B.M. 26.

dyscant. *m.*, descant, second part in plain-song, O.M. 562.

dyscarga, *vb.*, to unload, discharge, empty, pour out (B.).

dyscarthy, *vb.*, to scour out (W.).

dyscas, *m.*, teaching, lesson, doctrine, moral.

dyscavylsy, see **dyskevelsy.**

dyscle·r, *adj.*, blurred, foggy, dim (B.).

dysclērya, *vb.*, to blur, befog (B.).

dysclōsya, *vb.*, to disclose, reveal, C.W. 2120, 2357 (E.).

†**dysclӯen** (C. Voc. *disclien*), *f.*, *pl.* **-now,** scribe's wooden parchment-smoother, splint; *spelc* Aelfric.

dysco·lm, *adj.*, knotless (B.).

dysconfort, *m.*, discomfort, discouragement, grief (M.E.).

dysconfortya, *vb.*, to discomfort, discourage, grieve (M.E.): see **dygonfortya.**

dyscora, *vb.*, to lop trees (B): see **scoren.**

dyscrassyes (*dyscrasiis* B.M. 1405), *adj.*, afflicted, out of grace (M.E. *disgrace,* misfortune, *graceles,* out of God's favour, Med. Lat. *disgraciatus,* unfortunate): see **grassyes.**

dyscrōghen, *adj.*, skinless (B.).

dyscroghenna, *vb.*, to flay (B.).

dyscryjyans, *m.*, unbelief.

dyscryjyk, *adj.*, unbelieving; *m.*, *pl.* **-jygyon,** infidel, unbeliever, sceptic.

dyscrysy, -cryjy, *vb.*, to disbelieve.

dyscüdha, *vb.*, to uncover, disclose, unblindfold, open the hand, etc.: as **cüdha**; *lemmyn dyscuth, ha lavar p'yu an pren a-bew an bows,* now open up, and say which is the lot that shall get the coat, P.C. 2852.

dysda·yn, *m.*, disdain (M.E.): *my a-n-kemer yn d.*, I shall think it unworthy of me, C.W. 1448.

dysēgha, *vb.*, to quench thirst, refresh: see **desēgha** with opposite meaning.

dysenor (*-onor*), *m.*, dishonour, O.M. 2792.

dyse·nora, *vb.*, to dishonour: see **enora.**

dyserry, *vb.*, to be appeased, relent, cease to be angry or troubled; appease, remove anger: as **serry**; *may tysorra an Tas whek,* so the sweet Father might be appeased, O.M. 2258.

dysert, *m.*, desert, B.M. 4030, 4138 (M.E.).

dysē·s, *m.*, misery, disquiet, disease (M.E. *dysese*).

dysēsya, *vb.*, to disquiet, trouble, deprive of ease (M.E.).

dysevel, *vb.*, to upset, trip up, cause to fall, M.C. 5, 14.

dyskelmy, *vb.*, to untie, disentangle (B.).

dyskevelsy (*dyscavylsy*), *vb.*, to dislocate, unjoint: 3 s. pret. *dyskevalsas*: see **kevals, dygevelsy.**

dyske·vera (*deskyvra*), *vb.*, to expose, betray, C.W. 577-8 (M.E.).

dysky, *vb.*, to learn, teach, educate, direct, instruct: *k* lost before *s* in pret. and pluperf. (P.C. 2002, M.C. 78); the difference between "teach" and "learn" is shown by preps. *dhe, gans*; *rag d. dhedha tountya,* to teach them (not) to be cheeky, B.M. 3300; *may hyllyn genes dysky,* that I could learn from thee.

dy'sky, *vb.*, to doff, put off; strip, undress: replacing *dywysca,* cf. W. *diosg* for *diwisco*; *d. dhe-ves,* to take off.

dyskӯans (C. Voc. *diskient*), *adj.*, witless, ignorant, *unwis* Aelfric.

dyskybel (C. Voc. *discebel*), *m.*, *pls.* **-blon, blyon,** disciple, adherent, follower, *leorning cniht* Aelfric: the *y* consonant of the pl. *-yon,* tends to disappear, though occasionally sounded.

dyskynna, see **dyeskynna.**

dyslē·n (C. Voc. *dislaian*), *adj.*, disloyal, unfaithful, faithless, *ungetreowe* Aelfric : see **lēn.**

dysly·w (C. Voc. *disliu*), *adj.*, discoloured, of mixed colours, pale, colourless, vague, formless, *hiwleas* Aelfric: see **lyw.**

dyslywa, *vb.*, to discolour, stain, fade, smear colours (W., B.).

dysmaylya, *vb.*, to unwrap, unswathe : see **maylya.**

dyso·n, *adv.*, forthwith, anon, without another word : see **son.**

dyspē·r, *m.*, despair, B.M. 2712 (M.E. *dispeire*).

dysplegya, *vb.*, to unfold, develop (B.).

dysplesour, *m.*, displeasure, C.W. (E.).

dysplēsya, *vb.*, to displease, B.M. (M.E.) : *ha na-veugh-why dysplesyes,* so as to avoid offending you, B.M. 119, 322.

dysplētya, *vb.*, to unfold, unfurl, display : ? made from the M.E. p. pt. *dyspleyed.*

dysplewyas (*dysplevyas,* P.C. 2832), *vb.*, to spread out, splay, stretch apart (M.E. *dysplaye,* O. Fr. *desployer*) : var. of **dysplētya.**

dysprena, -nyas, see **dasprena -nyas.**

dysprēsya, *vb.*, to despise, decry, spurn, misprize (M.E. *dispraisen*).

dysprēsyans, *m.*, contempt, neglect.

dysprevy, *vb.*, to disprove (W.).

dyspūtya, *vb.*, to debate, argue; discuss : 3 s. pres. -fut. *dyspūt* ; *d. cas orth*, wrangle with (M.E.).

dyspuyssant, dyspüsant, *adj.*, powerless, B.M. 2283 (M.E.).

dyspȳt, see **despȳt.**

dysquedhes, *vb.*, to show, exhibit, appear, be apparent or obvious, disclose, discover, teach, make a revelation, reveal : 2 s. imp. *dysqua*, or usually before vowel *dysqueth* ; this vb. is occasionally used in reflexive sense, "appear, show oneself," etc., without the prefix *om*, e.g. O.M. 1439, P.C. 978 : see var. **dyswedhes.**

dysquedhyans, *m.*, revelation, declaration, show, manifestation, lesson, demonstration, exhibition, indication, evidence, token.

dysquytha, *vb.*, to repose, relax, rest (B.): see **squytha.**

dyssa·yt (*dyssēt*), m., deceit, deception, B.M. 4045 (M.E. *deceite*).

dyssaytya, *vb.*, to deceive, outwit, M.C. 194 : vb. from **dyssayt.**

dystaga, *vb.*, to untether, detach (B.).

dysta·k, *adj.*, untethered, independant (B.): see **stak.**

dystakkya, *vb.*, to unfasten : see **takkya**

dystempra, *vb.*, to ruffle, vex, upset, B.M. 2937 (M.E.).

***dyste·r,** *adj.*, insignificant, of no account (W., B.) : see ***ster.**

dystō·, *adj.*, roofless (B.).

dystough, *adv.*, immediately, directly, quite soon, suddenly : see **a-dhȳstough.**

dystrewy, *vb.*, to destroy, undo, ruin, murder (M.E. *distruye*) : later forms were *dystruya* B.M., *destrya* C.W., Lh.

dystructyon (*dis-*), *m.*, destruction, C.W. (M.E.).

dystryppya, *vb.*, to strip, P.C., M.C. (M.E.) : see **stryppya.**

dystȳ·, *vb.*, unroof (B.).

***dystyllya,** *vb.*, to distil (W. from E.) ; 3 s. pres. fut. *dystyl.*

dyswā·r, *adj.*, unwary, rash, inadvertent, heedless, B.M. 3238 : see **wār.**

dyswedhes, *vb.*, var. of **dysquedhes :** 2 s. imp. *dyswa*, or before vowel *dysweth*,

dyswül, dyswüthyl, dyswrüthyl, *vb.*, to destroy, unmake, undo, spoil ; see Table of **gül** in Appendix VIII.

dyth, *m.*, *pl.* **-ys,** saying, recitation, dictum: *py d. munys kewseugh-why*, or tell a little piece, B.M. 96.

dȳth, see **dēth.**

dyvagha, *vb.*, to unhook, unhinge (W.).

dyvagly, *vb.*, to disentangle, release from a trap (W.).

dyva·rf, *adj.*, beardless (W., B.).

dyvarow, *adj.*, deathless, undying, immortal (W.).

dyvarra, *vb.*, to prune, disbranch (B.).

dyvarva, *vb.*, to shave, take off the beard (W., B.).

dyvedhow, *adj.*, sober, not drunk (B.).

dȳvers, *adj.*, divers, different, B.M. 4483 (M.E.).

dyve·th, *adj.*, shameless, unabashed.

dyvewnans, *adj*,, torpid, lifeless (W.).

dyveyna, *vb.*, to clear ground of rocks and stones (B.).

dyvo·s, *adj.*, foodless, in want (W.).

dyvotter (*dyvos, -der*), *m.*, want, starvation, O.M. 365.

dyvrē·s (C. Voc. *diures*), *m.*, *pl.* **-ow,** exile, outlaw, expatriated or banished person, *utlaga* Aelfric : see **dyvrōa.**

dyvrō·, *adj.*, exiled (W., B.).

dyvrōa, *vb.*, to emigrate, expatriate : p. pt. *dyvrēs*, used as noun.
dyvrōeth, *m.*, exile (W.).
dyvusür, *adj.*, immeasurable (W.).
dyvyn, *m.*. *pl.* **-yon**, fragment, morsel (W.).
dyvynya (*devenya*, *dufunya*, B.M.), *vb.*, to chop, mince, hack, cut up, dissect.
dyvynÿeth, *f.*, anatomy dissection (W.).
dyvȳth, see **dyfȳth**.
dyw[2] *card num.*, two, used with f. nouns: *an*[2] *dhyw*[2] *venen*[2] *goth*, the two old women.
dyw-[2] (*du*, *de*, C. Voc. *dui*), *prefix*, forming dual of f. noun naming paired parts of the body : see **deu-**[2].
dÿwa·ll, *adj.*, without mishap or deficiency (W., B.) : see **gwall**.
dÿwalla, *vb.*, to protect from accident, supply a defect (W., B.).
dÿwa·r[2], *prep.*, off from, from on top of : combines with prons. as **war**, see Appendix V.
dÿwe·l, *adj.*, invisible (B.).
dywen, see **gen**.
dÿweres, *adj.*, helpless : see **gweres**
dÿwe·rn, *adj.*, mastless, dismasted (B.).
dÿwernya, *vb*, to dismast (B.).
dÿwethyn, *adj.*, unyielding, stiff (B.).
dywglün, see **clün**.
dÿwha·ns, see **dewhans**.
dÿwha·rth, *adj.*, serious, unsmiling (B.).
dÿwhȳ· (*dywy*, *dhywy*), var. of **dheugh-why** to you.
dywla, **dywlüf**, see **lüf**.
dÿwoles, *adj.*, bottomless (W.).
†**dÿwolewyth** (C. Voc. *diwuleuuit*), *m.*, crown of head, pate, *knol* Aelfric.
dÿwo·rth (Late *durt*), *prep.*, from: combines with prons. as **(w)orth**, Appendix V ; with *gorra*, *dysky*, off, away ; with *dedhewy*, *grontya*, *rewardya*, by ; *d. an nos*, contracted to **dwo·rennōs**, at nightfall, by night, at night-time ; *d. an myttyn*, in the morning early, *seyth ur d. an m.*, 7 o'clock in the morning, etc. (B.) ; see **dohajeth**.
dÿwosa, **-ja**, *vb.*, to bleed, draw blood from.
dÿwoskes, *adj.*, bleak, unsheltered (W.).
dÿwō·th, *adj.*, docile, not wild : see **gōth**.
dÿwrȳ·, *adj.*, seamless (W.).
dÿwrȳas, *vb.*, to unstitch (B.).
dÿwrȳdhya, *vb.*, to uproot, eradicate (W., B.).
dywscōth, **dywscovarn**, see **scōth**, **scovarn**.
dywvrēgh, **dywvron**, see **brēgh**, **bron**.
dywwyth, *adv.*, twice.
dywy (*dewy*), *vb.*, to burn, kindle, light up, blaze, flame, flare : *an bos 'nos dywy awra*, *saw nyns-usy ow-lesky*, yonder bush flames, but it is not burning away, O.M. 1397, *otta an tan ow-tewy*, see how the fire is blazing, P.C. 693.
dÿwyryon, *adj.*, insincere (B.).
dywys, *m.*, *pl.* **-yon**, adherent, follower (W.).
dÿwy sk, *adj.*, unclad (W., B.).
dÿwysygneth, *m.*, perseverance, devotion : see **dywysyk**.
dÿwysyk, *adj.*, earnest, zealous, assiduous, persevering, faithful, conscientious, devout.
dÿwysykter, *m.*, zeal, application, earnestness : see **dywysyk**
dÿwȳ·th, *adj.*, workless, unemployed (W.).
dÿwȳ·th, *adj.*, without guard, defenceless : see **gwȳth**.
dÿwyver, *adj.* wireless (W.).

E

-e, **e**, *pron.*, suffixed to verb or as object to imp., he, him, it(m.) : becomes **-va**, **va** (*fe*), after vowel, and **a** as suffixed to *yu*.
ēa, see **ȳa**.
†**ēal** (C. Voc. *e(h)al*), *m.*, head of cattle, beast, yoke-ox, *nyten* Aelfric : cf. Ir. *eallach*.
***eben**, *m.*, ebony (M.E.).
Ebbrow, *f.*, Israel, in phrase *Fleghes Ebbrow*, Hebrew children (M.E., *childir of Ebbrowe*) ; *m.*, Hebrew language ; *adj.*, Hebrew.
eber, *m.*, *pl.* **ebrow**, sky, atmosphere, vapour (W., B.) : see **ebron**.
ebol (*ebel*, *ebal*), *m.*, *pls.* **-ylyon**, **ebylly**, colt, foal : *e. asen*, ass-foal ; *drok-e.* (figuratively), stubborn, intractable person, C.W. 2398 ; Ebble, rock-name ; also a small mow, made of corn or hay left over, D. " ibble."
eboles, *f. pl.* **-ow**. filly (W., B.).
Ebrel, **mȳs-E.**, *m.*, April, Lh.
ebren, **ebron** (C. Voc. *(h)uibren*, C.W. *ybbren*, *yborn*, Late *ebbarn*), *f.*, sky, firmament, welkin, *wolcn* Aelfric.
†**eby**, *vb.*, to say ; †**eb**, **yp**, *m.*, utterance (W.). : kept only in **gortheby**, **-yp**.
ebyl (C. Voc. *ebil*), *m.*, *pl.* **-yow**, **-yon**, peg, nail, treenail, *naegl* Aelfric : *e. pren* wooden pin, dowel, Lh. ; †*e. horn*, iron

nail, bolt (C. Voc.).

ebylya, *vb.*, to peg or pin together (W., B.).

edhen, *f.*, *pl.* **ydhyn, edhyn** (C. Voc. *(h)ethen*), bird, wild fowl: *tebel-e.*, evil bird, bad angel, O.M. 223; Carrack an Eathin, rock-name, suggests pl. *ȳdhyn*.

Edhow, see **Yedhow**.

edrega (for *edregeth*), *m.*, repentance, remorse, regret, contrition, chagrin: *ny a-gan-byth e.*, we shall be sorry; *codha yn e.*, repent, be remorseful.

edrek, *m.*, regret, sorrow, repentance, compunction.

edyak, *m.*, simpleton, idiot, P., Borlase (D. "edjack"),

ëe·f, (C.W. *yef*), *pron.*, he, him: emphatic form of **-ef**, usually suffixed; the first *e* is obscure, the second stressed.

ēf (C.W. *eve*), *pron.*, he, him, it (m.); as suffixed, **-ef**, him, of him.

efan, *adj.*, large, ample, wide, broad, commodious, spacious, plain, vast; *adv.*, evidently, at large, amply: *e. may hyl cafos y es hep danjer*, so roomy that he may have accommodation without difficulty, P.C. 676: see **e(f)-** Appendix II.

efander, *m.*, space, breadth, latitude (W.).

efany, *vb.*, to expand, enlarge (W.).

efanyans, *m.*, expansion, enlargement (W.).

efreth, etc., see **evreth**.

eger, eger-Dew (*egr* Lh.), *m.*, *pl.* **-ow, -ow-D.**, daisy: **e.-jarn**, garden daisy; apparently from its opening (*egery*) with day; see **boreles, caja**.

egery, (*egyry, ygyry*), *vb.*, to open, explain, disclose, expound: 3 s. pret. *agoras*; 2 s. imp. *ago·r*; 3 s. pres.-fut *ege·r* (both in MSS. indifferently *uger, ygor*).

ēghā·n (*eyghan, eyhan*), *interj.*, alas! as Ir. and Gaelic *ochōn*, W. *ochan*.

ēghel, *f.*, *pl.* **-yow**, axle (W., B.).

ēghen (*heghen, ehen*), *f.*, sort, kind, species, manner, tribe, family, kindred, kin, anything, any sort, utmost: *pen oll y e.*, chief of all his clan, *pup e.*, every kind, everything; *awos e.*, at all costs, for all sakes; *dres e.*, beyond everything; *yn pup e.*, utterly; *yn dyspyt oll dh'y e.*, in spite of his utmost; *e. a*, any sort of: see **agh**.

eglos (Lh. *egliz*), *f.*, *pl.* **eglosyow** (*eglusyow*, P.C. 1175 *eglesow* Kerew), church: *s* prevents mutation of following *c, k, d, p, t*.

ēgwal, *adj.*, equal, *adv.*, equally, or *m.*, copy, specimen, C.W. 2198.

***egyn**, *m.*, *pl.* **-now**, germ, shoot, sprout, (W., B.).

***egyna**, *vb.*, to sprout, germinate (W., B.).

ēja, see **üja**.

el, *f.*, *pl.* **-yow**, jut, brow, sharp edge: in **elek, el-esker** and **elgeth** (W. *ael*).

ēl (C. Voc. *ail*), *m.*, *pl.* **-eleth**, angel, *engel* Aelfric.

elek, *m*, *pl*, **-egas**, red garnard (D.); *adj.*, big-browed (W.).

elergh, see **alargh**.

ēles (*elez*), *f.*, *pl.* **-ow**, angel (Gw.).

†**el-esker** (C. Voc. *elesc(h)er*), *f.*, shin, shin-bone, *scyne. scinban* Aelfric.

†**elestren**, *f.*, *col*, **elester**. yellow iris, flag (D. "laister,") other tall, blade-leafed plant, sedge, bent *segc* Aelfric: †*stray e.*, matting of woven marram-grass or "sand-spire," "Perran broadcloth"; a similar confusion of meaning is found in Lat. *acorus*, sedge, *iris pseudo-acorus*, flag, and in dialect Eng. "spire," iris, sedge, bent, etc., "seg" sedge, bulrush, iris, etc.

elewek, *f.*, *pl.* **-egow, -egy**, elm-grove.

elf, see **ȳfla**.

elgeth (C. Voc. *elgeht*), *f.*, *pl.* **-yow, -y**, chin, *cin* Aelfric.

elgethek, *adj.*, big-chinned (B.).

ellā·s (M.C. *elhas*, C.W. *aylas*), *interj.* of grief, alas! (M.E., O. Fr. *ha las!*): *e. mar pedhen shamys!* alack, if we should be put to shame! B.M. 420; *e., ow map, bythqueth dhe'th gorra dhe scol!* alas, my son, that ever thou wert sent to school! B.M. 363.

elowen, *f.*, *col.* **elow** (Lh. *elaw*, P. *ulow*), elm-tree.

†**els**, *m*. *pl.* **-yon**, step-son, C. Voc., *steopsunu* Aelfric.

†**elses**, *f.*, *pl.* **-ow**, step-daughter, C. Voc., *steopdohter* Aelfric.

elven, *f.*, *pl.* **-now**, spark, atom, element (W., B.) *men-e.*, porphyritic rock (D. "elvan").

elvenny, *vb.*, to sparkle (B.).

ely, see **yly**.

elyk, *m.*, *pl.* **ele·thygow**, little angel, cherub (B.).

elyn (C. Voc. *elin*), *m.*, *pl.* **-now**, *d.* **deuelyn**, elbow, *eleboga* Aelfric; angle, corner: see **kevelyn, penelyn**.

e·melow (*emblow*), see **amal**.

e·merōd, *m.*, *pl.* **-rōs**, emerald (M.E,

emeraude).

†e·mperes, -pres (C. Voc. *emperiz*), *f.*, *pl.* **-ow,** empress, *thes caseres cwen* Aelfric.

emperoreth, *m.*, empire (B.).

e·mperour, emprour (C. Voc. *emperur*), *m.*, *pl.* **-yon,** emperor, *casere* Aelfric.

emske·munya, 'ske·munya (*ym* , *om*-, B.M. *scumunya*, C.W. *skemyna*), *vb.*, to excommunicate, curse, ban : p. pt. *emskemunys* (*emscumunys*, *'skemynys*, C.W. *'skym'nys*) ; used also as *m.*, accursed person or thing ; the *m.* of *em*- is intrusive, imitating *om*-, *ym*- and often so spelt, cf. B. *eskuminiga*, W. *ysgymuno*, Med. Lat. *excommunicare*.

en, see **an.**

ēn, ēnas, see **ōn.**

ena (C.W. *nena*, Lh. *nenna*, *enna*), *adv.*, there, then, at that place or time : Later Cor. *nena* is perhaps affected by *yn ur·na*: see **-na.**

ena, see **enef.**

†enawel (C. Voc. *anauhel*), *f.*, tempest, *storm* Aelfric.

enclathva (*anclathva*), *f.*, burial ; burying-place, cemetery, P.C. 1545.

encledhyas, *m.*, burial.

encledhyes (*ancledhyas*), *vb.*, to bury, inter : 3 s. pres.-fut., 2 s. imp. *enclath*.

encressya, *vb.*, to increase, O.M. 48 (M.E. *encresse*) : see **cressya.**

eneby, *vb.*, to set one's face to, face, oppose (W., B.).

enef, ena, *m.*, *pl.* **-evow, e·nefow,** soul, *sawul* Aelfric : *warlergh Cryst enef dhe ry*, after Christ's giving up the ghost, M.C. 199.

enep (C. Voc. *eneb*), *m.*, *pl.* **-ebow,** face ; page of book, surface, *tramet* Aelfric ; though found in no M. Cor. MS. this was still common in Late Cor., *prag nag-esough-why ow-colghy agas e.?* why don't you wash your face ? Borlase MS.

e·nepwerth, *f.*, dowry (W., B.).

Enes, *m.*, Shrovetide, Lat. *Initium*, Lh.

enesek, *adj.*, insular ; *m.*, *pl.* **-sogyon,** islander ; *f.*, *pl.* **-egy,** archipelago (B.).

enesyk, *f.*, *pl.* **-ygow,** islet (B.).

†enetheren (C. Voc. *enederen*), *f.*, *col.* **enether,** entrail, *dhearmas* Aelfric : as O. Ir. *inathar*, Greek *enteron*.

eneval, *m.*, *pl.* **-les,** animal, beast, P.C. 205.

enewores, 'newores, *m.*, the point of death, B.M. 4350 : lit. "soul-yielding," see **ena, gores.**

engrys, see **angra.**

†enke·nethel, ankenel (C. Voc. *enc(h)inethel*), *m.*, *pl.* **-ethlow,** giant, monster, *ent* Aelfric ; *adj.*, not of human race : cf. M.B. *enquelezr*, giant, B. *an keler*, Will o' the Wisp, W. *anghenedl*, foreign race, *anghyngel*, monster.

†enkys (C. Voc. *encois*), *m.*, frankincense, incense, *stor* Aelfric ; *†e.lester*, thurible, censer, *storcyl* Aelfric.

†enledan, see **henledan.**

***enlu·myna,** *vb.*, to illuminate (M.E.).

eno, *adv.*, in or at that place, there (without motion), yonder, distant and not necessarily visible.

enor (*enour*), *m.*, *pl.* **-ys, -s,** honour : see **onour.**

enora, *vb.*, to honour : see **onoura.**

enos, 'nos, *adv.*, over there (without motion) yonder, distant but visible : used after *ot*, *gweles*, B.M. ; ***an** bos 'nos*, yonder bush, O.M. 1397.

ensa, ensy, see **otta.**

ente·nt, *m.*, purpose, intention, C.W. 496 (E.).

entra (*yntra*), *vb.*, to enter (M.E. *entren*).

envy, *m. and pl.*, enemy, enemies, B.M. 1012, 1069.

envy, *m.*, ill-will, enmity, grudge, envy (M.E.) : used of a madman's spite against mankind, B.M. 3837.

e·nvÿes, *adj.*, malicious, spiteful, grudging, envious (M.E.). : *e. of er-y-byn*, I have a grudge against him, C.W. 440.

enwedhen, *f.*, *col.* **enwȳth,** ash-tree, Lh. : see **onnen.**

enys, *f.*, *pl.* **enesow** (*enezo* Lh.), island ; peninsula ; land insulated by streams or roads : final *s* is usually made hard in place-names, Ennis, Ince, Ninnis, etc.

†ēok (Cor. Voc. *e(h)oc*), *m.*, *pl.* **ēogas,** salmon, *lex* Aelfric : replaced by **sowman.**

***ēos,** *f.*, *pl*, **-ow,** dim. **ēosyk,** nightingale (W., B.).

epscobeth, *m.*, bishopric (W., B.).

epscop (C. Voc. *escop*, Late *ispak*, *especk*), *m.*, *pl.* **-cobow,** bishop : pl. usually accented *e·pscobow* in verse.

***epystol,** *m.*, *pl.* **-ow,** epistle (W.) : see **lyther** (W., B.).

ēqual, *adj.*, equal, C.W. 604 : see **ēgwal.**

ēr, *m.*, defiance, refusal to believe, stubbornness, challenge; insistence : ***an e.***

bras, the great heresy, R.D. 1525.
ēr, see **ür**, **ērgh**.
†er, *m. pl.*, **-yow** (C. Voc. *erieu*), temple (of head), *thunwencge* Aelfric.
ēr (C. Voc. *er*), *m.*, *pl.* **-as** (Late *-yow*), eagle, *earn* Aelfric: *e. benow*, she-eagle (W.).
ēr, *m.*, *pl.* **-ys**, heir, B.M. 372 (M.E.).
ēr, *adj.*, fresh, raw, green, sappy, juicy, Lh.
er-, see Appendix II.
er, *prep.*, for, for the sake of, on account of, by, to: no instance of compounding with prons. as in Welsh; *er bones* .., for being in; *er an ascal*, by the wing; *er ow fyth*, by my faith, *er y wew*, to his woe, worse luck for him; see **erbyn**.
erba, *m.*, *pl.* **-bys**, herb (M.E. *erbe*).
***e·rberjour**, *m.*, *pl.* **-s**, harbinger (M.E.).
e·rberow, *m.*, *pl.* **-ys**, shelter, lodging, place of safety (M.E. *herberow.*).
erbyer, *m.*, *pl.* **-s**, kitchen-garden (M.E. *herber*, Lat. *herbarium*): Erbyer Gwarra, field-name.
erbyn (*er*, *pen*, Late *warbyn*, *-bidn*, *'beddn*), *prep.*, against, in readiness for, by the time that: *e. agan bos gansa*, by the time we are with them; *e. bos henna gwres*, by the time that was done; *dos e.*, *mos e.*, to meet; poss. prons. inserted, *er-ow-fyn*, against me, *er-y-byn*, against him, etc.; also encountering, greeting, coming to meet him, as *mur joy us er-y-byn-ef*, R.D. 2490, *my a-glew hager noys...er-y-byn*, R.D., 2297, there is great joy, I hear a horrible noise, at his arrival; *gul e*, to oppose.
erbȳs, *m.*, economy, thrift (B.).
erbysy, *vb.*, to save, spare, economize, be thrifty (W., B.).
erbyser, *m.*, *pl.* **oryon**, economizer.
†erbysyas (C. Voc. *(h)e(n)bidiat*), *m.*, *pl.* **-ysy**, thrifty person, miser, *spaerhende* Aelfric.
ērder, *m.*, freshness, greenness, juiciness (W.).
erder, see **ardar**.
eredy, see **yredy**.
erel, see **aral**.
ēres, *f.*, *pl.* **-ow**, heiress (M.E.): as **ēr**.
erewyk, *m.*, *pl.* **-ygow**, small plot of ground (W., B.).
ergh, **yrgh** (C. Voc. *irch*, Lh. *er*, *err*), *m.*, snow: *yma ow-cul e.*, it snows, Borlase.
erghek, *adj.*, snowy (B.).
erghlaw, *m.*, sleet (W.).
erghy, **yrghy**, *vb.*, to command, enjoin): 2 s. imp. *argh*; 1 s. pres.-fut. *arghaf*; 3 s. *ergh*; 2 s. subj., 3 s. impf. ind. *erghy*; 3 s. pret., p. pt. *erghys*; vars. *yrgh*, etc.
ermyt, see **hermyt**.
erna²(g), *conj.*, until, till: used directly before *vb.* as **na²(g)**, adds *g* before vowels in *bos* and *mos*: following infixed *-th-*, is lost in *erna' fo*, until thou mayest have, etc., *erna 'n-prenna*, until he expiates it, O.M. 2152.
ernōth, *adj.*, ill-clad, half bare, M.C. 50.
erow (C. Voc. *erw*), *f.*, *pl.* **erewy**, acre, *aecer* Aelfric; (in names) field, e.g. Erowidden like E. "Whittaker."
erowhēs, *m.*, furlong (long measure); or else pole, as W. *erwyd*.
errya, *vb.*, see **ērya**.
ertach, **e·rytach** (*ertech*), *m.*, *pl.* **-ajys**, heritage, portion, birthright, O.M. 354 (M.E. *(h)erytage*).
ertons, **e·rytons** (*hertons*), *m.*, inheritance, heritage, B.M. 2452 (M.E. *(h)erytaunce*).
***ervynen**, *f.*, *col.* **ervyn**, turnip (W., B.).
ervyra (*yrvyra*), *vb.*, to decide, intend, fix, settle, resolve, plan, determine, strictly enjoin, form a firm opinion, be convinced: 3 s. pres.-fut. *ervyr*; *ervyrys of*, my mind is made up.
ervys, see **arva**.
ērya, *vb.*, to defy, challenge, insist, dare, stand out against, C.W. 1162: *owth-erya*, ? defiant, B.M. 968 (*W. herio*, *haeru*), unless for *errya*, to stray, rove, wander (M.E. *erren*).
erys, etc., see **aras**.
e·ryta, *vb.*, to inherit (M.E.): see **ertons**.
ēs (*eys*), *m.*, ease, comfort, convenience, accommodation; *adj.*, comp. *esya*, easy: *cafos y e.*, take his ease, have plenty of room; *yn e.*, in comfort, at ease, free from care (M.E.); see **anēs**, **dysēs**, **attēs**.
es (*ys*, *eys*), *conj.*, than: shorter form of **ages**; combines with prons. as **yn**, see Appendix V., *s* being doubled in 3rd person.
escar, *m.*, *pl.* **yskerens**, enemy, foe.
†escop, see **epscop**.
esedha, **sedha**, (*ysedha*, *asedha*), *vb.*, to sit: contracted forms, 1 s. fut. *yth-se'f* for *esedhaf*; 3 s. fut., 2 s. imp. *esa* for *eseth*; 3 s. subj. *esetho*; 3 s. plupf. *esethsa*; inf. *sedha* is found from B.M. onwards.
ēsel, *m.*, *pl.* **ysyly** (*esely*, in verse *y·syly*) limb, arm or leg;

member of society (B.) : ***e.*** *dhe'n tebel-el*, a limb of satan, B.M. 969.

ēseleth, *m.*, membership : see **ēsel.**

eseth (*aseth*, *yseth*), *f.*, *pl.* **edhow**, seat, throne or abiding-place (M.C. 52) ; sitting posture : with *a* and poss. pron., *a'y eseth*, etc. sitting down, M.C. 244.

esethva (*asethva* M.C. 143, *ysetva* M.C. 13), *f.*, sitting-place, seat.

esethvos, *m.*, *pl.* **-ow**, eisteddfod, session (W.).

***esew**, *adj.*, in want (W., B.).

***esewes**, *m.*, privation, want (W., B.).

ēshē·, *vb.*, to facilitate, accommodate, make easy : as **berhē.**

eskelly-grēghyn (*skerligrehan* Lh.), *m.*, bat : lit. skinwings, see **askel**, **crōghen.**

†esker, *f.*, *pl.* **-yow**, *d.* **dywesker**, shank, leg; (ship-building) knee (B.)

eskern, see **ascorn.**

eskernek, *adj.*, bony, full of bones (W., B.).

eskys, *f.*, *pl.* **eskyjyow**, **'skyjyow** (C. Voc. *eskidieu*), shoe : *dwyskeugh* ***an*** *genter -ma yn ow e.-vy*, knock this nail into my shoe, Lh.

Est, **mȳs E.** (*e* long), *m.*, August.

Est, see **Yst.**

†estren, *f.*, *col.* **ester**, oyster, C. Voc., *ostre* Aelfric.

***estren**, *m.*, *pl.* **-yon**, foreigner, stranger (W., B.).

***estrenes**, *f.*, *pl.* **-ow**, foreign or strange woman.

***estrennek**, *adj.*, strange.

estyll, see **astell.**

estyllen, **styllen** (*astyllen* Lh.), *f.*, *pl.* **-now**. *col.* **estyll**, plank, board, shelf (W., B.) : *stillen* (mining), P., is E.D. " stilling " : see **styll.**

ēsya, *vb.*, to ease, make easy or comfortable, faciliate, accommodate, refresh, relieve (M.E. *ese*).

ētegves, *ord. num.*, eighteenth.

ētek, *card num.*, eighteen.

†etew (C. Voc. *it(h)eu*), *m.*, *pl.* **-y**, firebrand, block, billet, log (for burning) : *e. Nadelek*, Yule-log (B.).

ēth (C. Voc. *awuit*), *m.*, *pl.* **-ow**, odour, scent, fragrance, exhalation, effluvium, vapour ; in C. Voc. air, atmosphere, *lyft* Aelfric.

eth, *m.*, *pl.* **-ys**, hearth, P.C. 1244 (E.D. "eth," "yeth") : see **olas.**

ēth, *card num.*, eight.

ēthen, *f.*, *pl.* **-now**, vapour, zephyr (B.).

ēthenna, *vb.*, to exhale (B.).

ēthes, see **ēthves.**

†ēthlen (C. Voc. *adlen*), *f.*, *col.* **ēthel**, poplar-tree, aspen, *aeps*, Aelfric.

ethlek, *f.*, *pl.* **-egy**, poplar-grove (B.).

ethom, (*othom*), *m.*, *pl. and* **abst. -mow**, want, need, necessity : *pyth yu an e.?* what need is there ? *ny-n jeves e. golghy*, he has no need of washing.

ethomek (*othomek*), *adj.*, needy, in urgent want ; *m.*, *pl.* **-omogyon**, person in want.

ēthves, **ēthes**, *ord. num.*, eighth.

ēthwyth, *adv.*, eight times.

eva, *vb.*, to drink, imbibe : 2 s. imp. *ȳf* ; 2 s. subj. *yffy* ; 3 s. subj. *effo* ; 3 s. plupf. *efsa*.

evredhy, **efredhy**, *vb.*, to maim, cripple, disable.

evreth, **efreth**, **evredhek**, *adj.*, crippled, maimed, mutilated, disabled ; *m.*, *pls.* **-edhyon**, **-edhygyon**, cripple : the spelling with *f* before *r* is characteristic, though optional.

-evȳ, see **-avȳ.**

†ewen (C. Voc. *(h)ivin*), *f.*, *col.* **ew**, yew-tree.

ewer, *m.*, evening, as W. *ucher* : in **gorthewer** only.

ewha (for *ewheth*, W. *echwydd*), *m.*, time from noon to nightfall, afternoon, evening : *ajy dhe e. an jeth*, ere night, R.D. 275 ; originally " noon," " mid-day rest," as B. *ec'hoaz*, V. *ahoé* : see **kensewha**, **doghajēth.**

ewhyas, **ewyas**, *vb.*. to ride, make a cavalry raid, B.M. 3453, as W. *echwa*.

ewn, *adj.*, right, just, correct, proper, regular, exact, straight, very ; *m.*, the right : usually prefixed to nouns and vbs. : *yn e.-gres a*, in the very middle of; *e.-gara*, to love.

ewna (*owna* Kerew), *vb.*, to make right, set in order, mend, adjust, fit, arrange, justify.

ewnder, *m.*, equity, justice, exactness, rightness (W., B.).

†ewnhensek (C. Voc. *eunhinsic*), *adj.*, upright, just : *ewn y forth* would be likely to replace this in M. Cor.

ewn-hēs (*hys*), *adj.*, of the proper length, O.M. 2525, 2563.

ewnter (C. Voc. *euiter*, ?for *euinter* or *eunter*, Lh. *ownter*), *m.*, *pl.* **-tras**, uncle : C. Voc. *euiter* resembles W. *ewythr*, but neither B. *eontr* nor Late Cor. *ownter*,

***ewonek**, *adj.*, foamy (W., B.).
***ewonen**, *f.*, foam-flake, *col.* **ewon**, foam, spume (W., B.).
***ewony**, *vb.*, to foam, spume (W., B.).
†ewrē (*?ewregh*, C. Voc. *eure*), *m.*, *pl.* **-as**, goldsmith: the change of *owr* to *ewr-* in composition, W. *aur*, *eur-*, is lost elsewhere, *eure*, as spelt should mean "gold-seeker," and *eurech*, W. *eurych* may be intended.
ewyas, see **ewhyas**.
ewyk, (C. Voc. *eu(h)ic*), *f.*, *pl.* **-ygas**, hind, deer: *yweges*. O.M. 126, is used with *gavar*, *carow*, etc., as if sing.; it may be a doubled fem. form.
ewyn (C. Voc. *euuin*), *m.*, *pl.* **-as** (*'winaz* Lh.), nail of finger or toe; talon of bird; claw of bird or animal; clove of garlic or shallot).
†ewyncarn (C. Voc. *ewincarn*), *m.*, *pl.* **-ow**, hoof, claw.
†ewynek (C. Voc. *euynoc*), *adj.*, having nails or claws: see **kenynen.**
ewynrew (*windraw* Lh.), *m.*, numbness of fingers or toes from cold, lit. nail-frost (D. "Wenders").
exaltya, *vb.*, to exalt, elevate, raise in position, extol, educate for a high position, B.M., C.W. (M.E.).
examnasyon, *m.*, examination: from **examnya**
examnya (for *examynya*), *vb.*, to examine, question, interrogate, P.C. C.W. (M.E. *examyne*): no *p* is developed between *m* and *n* as in *dampnya*, *solempnyta*, because of the silenced M.E. *y*.
experyans, *m.*, trial, proof, demonstration; experiment, B.M. 4391 (M.E.).
exylya, *vb.*, to exile, O.M, 1576 (M.E.).
eyles, *m.*, liver-fluke in sheep; also sundew, its supposed cause (D. "iles").
eyn, see **yēyn.**
Eynda, *f.*, Ind, India, R.D. 2457 (misread *Cynde* Norris): *as colour, indigo blue (M.E.).
eysel, see **aysel.**
eythen, *f.*, *pl.* **-now**, prickle (W.).
eythynek, *f.*, *pl.*-**egy**, furze-brake (W.).
eythynen (C. Voc. *eythinen*), *f.*, furze-bush, *col.* **eythyn**, furze: *e. Frynk*, common or great furze; *bagas e*, furze-bush; *crommen-e.*, furze-hook; *begh e.*, burden of furze-fuel; *bern e.*, furze-rick.

F

fā, see **faven.**
faborden, *m.*, bass in singing, lit. false burden (M.E. *faburden*, Fr. *faux bourdon*).
facya, *vb.*, to give a face to, put a good face on, dissemble, pretend, boast, brag, P.C. 1680, 2065: *facyes*, faced, C.W. 499 (*fashes*): see **fās.**
fāf, see **faven.**
fagosen, *f.*, *pl.* **-now**, *col.* **fagas**, faggot (W., B.).
fakel, *f.*, *pl.* **-clow**, flame, inflammation (D. "fackle"); torch, Lat. *facula*.
faklen, *f.*, *pl.* **-now**, torch (W.).
fakly, *vb.*, to flame, inflame (W.).
falgh (*filh* Lh. from *pl.*), *f.*, *pl.* **fylghyow**, scythe.
falghas, *vb.*, to cut with a scythe (B.).
†falghun (C. Voc. *falbun* for *falhun*), *m.*, *pl.* **-as**, falcon, *hwealhafoc* Aelfric.
falja, see **falsa.**
fall, *m.*, fail, fault, deficiency, used only in *hep f.*, without fail, certainly, translating M.E. *sauns faile* or *wythowte fal* as P.C. 2523: see **fyllel.**
falladow, *m.*, failure: used only in *hep f.*, undoubtedly; see **fall.**
fals (pr. *fōls*, *vowlz*, Lh.), *f.*, *pl*, **-fylsyow**, sickle.
fals, falj (pr. *fōls*, *foulz*, Lh.) *adj.*, false, treacherous, deceitful (usually prefixed, causing no mutation in following noun or vb.); *m.*, falsity, false or disloyal person (M.E.).
fals (pr. *fōls*), *m.*, *pl.* **-ljow**, cleft, split, rift (B.).
falsa, falja, Late **falya** (*feldzha*, ? from p. pt., *fallia*, Lh.), *vb.*, to split, cleave, rive: p. pt *felsys*; 3 s. pres. -fut. *fels, felj*; 2 s. imp. *fals, falj*.
falslych, *adv.*, falsely, treacherously, unjustly (M.E.).
fa'lsury, *m.*, falseness, falsehood, insincerity, injustice: *quarel a f.*, unjust demand; *gul f.*, cheat, commit fraud.
falya, see **falsa.**
fancy, *m.*, pleasure, delight, fancy, C.W. (E.).
fangya (*fanja*, Gw.), *vb.*, to get (D.E. "fang").
fannya, *vb.*, to fan, blow into flame, P.C. 1271 (E.).
fara, *m.*, behaviour, ado; *vb.*, (also *farya*) to behave, fare (M.E. *faren*): *tebel -f.*,

drok-f., to fare ill, come off badly; 3 s. pres. fut. *far*; 3 s. plupf *farsa*.

fardel, -dhel, *m., pl.* **-low,** bundle, package, as pl. luggage (M.E.): exceptionally this has not pl. *-lys*; cf. **garlont.**

farwe·l, *interj.*, farewell (M.E.): *genes f., genough f.*, Goodbye! *gasa f.* to take leave.

faryng, *m.*, conduct, goings-on, P.C. 374 (M.E.).

fās (*face*), *m., pl. and abst.* **-ow,** face, countenance, appearance (M.E.); pretence, boast, brag: *yn f. ...*, into the presence of..., B. M. 3215; *gallas* (MS. *gallaf*) *fasow!* bragging is all over! C.W. 326: see **facya.**

***fask,** *f., pl.* **-scow,** faggot, tie (W.).

***faskel,** *m., pl.* **-low,** bond, strop (W., B.).

***fasky,** *vb.*, to bind a faggot or bundle: p.pt. *feskys* (W.).

fast, *adj.*, fast, firm, tight, strict, quick; *adv.*, fast, firmly, tightly, quickly (M.E.).

fasthē·, *vb.*, to make firm, confirm, R.D. 1163: as **berhē.**

fastya, fasta, *vb.*, to tie, fasten together, tighten, make firm, establish: 3 s. pres.-fut., 2 s. imp. *fast*; 3 s. subj. *fastyo, fasto*; 3 s. plupf. *fastsa*.

fasya, see **facya,**

fat, *adj.*, fat, O.M. 1192 (E.).

fatel[2] (*fetel*), *adv.*, how: for uses see **del**[2]; *fatlagenawy* (*fatlaghan a why*, Carew), contraction of *f. yu genough-why?* how are you?; *f. vyth lemmyn?* what now? (cry of despair); *f. vyth dyn?* what will become of us?; *fatel* is not used twice in one sentence; *dyskys* fatel *dons* .., *ha* del *vydhaf hembronkys*, taught *how* they shall come, and *how* I shall be led, M.C. 61; see **fatla.**

fāth, var. of **fās.**

fatla, *adv.*, how: form of **fatel** used without a following vb., *ny-won f.*, I know not how; the final *a* probably represents *yu*, it is, cf. **praga, pyla.**

faucun, *m., pl.* **-ys,** falcon, Lh. (M.E. *faucon*): see **falghun.**

fauns, *m.*, a fall in wrestling, Borlase (? Fr. *enfoncer*).

faven, *f., pl.* **-now,** *col.* **fāf, fā,** bean: *cuthow- fa'*, bean-pods; *my ny-synsaf a'th geryow bold un faven gok*, I care not one worthless bean for thy bold words, B.M. 3481; *my a-n-syns nebes a'n fa'*, I value it at a few beans, B.M. 2616.

fa·vera, *vb.*, to favour, treat generously; resemble (M.E.): *favereugh ny*, let us off! B.M. 3349, pr. *favreugh*.

favour, *m.*, favour; appearance, countenance, aspect, C.W. (M.E.).

***fawek,** *f., pls.* **-egow, -egy,** beech-grove (B.).

***fawen,** *f., pl.* **-now,** *col.* **faw,** beech (W., B.).

***faw-wedhen,** *f., pl.* **faw-wȳth,** beech-tree (W., B.).

fay (*fey*), *m.*, faith (M.E.).

faynt (*feynt*), *adj.*, faint, feeble, B.M. 683 (M.E.).

fayntys (*feyntys*), *m.*, feigning, pretence, P.C. 1478 (M.E.).

faytour (*feytour*), *m, pl.* **-s,** vagabond, swindler, impostor, B.M. 3436 (M.E.).

fe, see **va.**

febȳr, see **fevȳr.**

fēcla, *vb.*, to fawn, flatter, feign, M.C. 40: 3 s. pres.-fut. *fekyl*; 3 s. subj. *fecclo*; 3 s. plupf. *fekylsa*.

fekyl, *adj.*, false, flattering, perfidious, treacherous: *f. cher*, feigning demeanour, M.C. 65 (M.E.).

fēl (*feyl*), *adj.*, subtle, wily, crafty, clever, cunning; *adv.*, cunningly, etc.

felder, *m.*, cunning (W.).

felj, see **falsa.**

fell, *adj.*, cruel, fierce, terrible, destructive, deadly (M.E.).

felon, *m., pl.* **-s,** felon, P.C. 1983 (M.E.).

fels, see **falsa.**

felshyp, *m*, company, fellowship, crew, gang, B.M. 2155 (M.E. *felaweshipe*).

felsys, etc., see **falsa.**

felyon, see **fol.**

fe·nester, *f., pl.*–**ne·stry,** window, C. Voc., *ehdhyrl* Aelfric: Lh. writes *der an veistir* for *dre an f.*, either for *fen·ster* or a late form with *n* dropped.

fenestrek, *adj.*, windowed (W.).

fenestry, *vb.*, to make windows (W.).

fenna (Late *fedna*), *vb.*, to overflow, spread, as B. *fenna*: place-name Fenton Fedna.

†fe·nokel (C. Voc. *fenoc(h)el*), *m.*, fennel, *fenol* Aelfric: Pryce has *funil*, suggesting *fenyl* as a variant; *f. cun*, scentless mayweed (B.); *f. mor*, samphire (W.).

fenten (*fynten*, C. Voc. *funten*), *f., pl.* **-tynyow** (Late *-tidniow*), spring, fountain, surface well: in place-names usually E. Cornwall 'fenter,' W. Cornwall 'venton'; the distinction between *fenton* and *pyth*

is still kept, though " well " covers both.
fer, *f*., **-ow**, shank, leg, C. Voc., *sceanca* Aelfric: *fer-noth*, bare-legged, M.C. 50.
fēr (*feer* B.M.), *m*., *pl*. **-yow**, fair, market: see **tre-**; W. *ffair*, B. *foar* are f., but *henna* refers to *fer*, B.M. 2201; in B.M. *feer* is rhymed with *sür*, *desȳr*, suggesting E.D. " feer."
*__ferdhyn__, *m*., *pl*. **-now**, farthing.
ferdhyn-tȳr (*ferthen teere*), *m*., land-farthing, 30 English acres, quarter of Cornish acre: Carew, 1599, in Hearne's *Curious Discourses* (M.E. *f*‹*e*›*rthynge*.).
*__ferf__, *adj*., firm, steadfast (W., B.).
fergh, see **forgh**.
ferror, *m*., *pl*. **-yon**, farrier, blacksmith, P.C. 2669 (M.E.).
*__fervder__, *m*., firmness (W., B.).
fesont, *m*., *pl*. **-ons**, pheasant, O.M. 1192 (M.E. *fesaunt*).
fest, *adv*., very, extremely, indeed, right (M.E. *faste*, O.E. *faest*): used before or after adj. or adv., e.g., *f. lowenek*, *f. yn-cref*, *gallosek f*.
*__fest__, *f*., *pl*. **-ow**, feast, banquet (W., B.): not B.M. 277, which is the previous word.
festyna, see **fystyna**.
fēsya, *vb*., to drive away, put to flight, Gw. (O.E. *fesian* E.D. " veaze.").
fēth, *adj*., overcome, beaten (B.).
fēth, var. of **fās**.
fetha, *vb*., to defeat, conquer, vanquish, overcome, subdue, tire out: *fethys adhyworto*, beaten off from him, repulsed by him, P.C. 146.
fether, *m*., *pl*. **-thoryon**, conqueror: see **fetha**.
fevȳr (*febyr*), *m*., *pl*. **-s**, fever, B.M. 693 (M.E. *fevire*).
feyntys, see **fayntys**.
feytour see **faytour**.
flam, *m*., *pl*. **-mow**, flame, *lig* Aelfric: see **noweth**.
flamgōs, *m*., spurge (W., B.).
flattor, *m*., *pl*. **-yon**, deceiver, wheedler, cosener, R.D. 1511 (M.E).
flattores, *f*., *pl*. **-ow**, wheedling woman, cajoleress, R.D. 1067.
flattra, **-rya**, *vb*., to wheedle, cajole, beguile, talk flowery nonsense, delude, inveigle (M.E. *flatre*).
flēghes, see **flōgh**.
flēghyk, *m*.,*pls*. **fleghesygow**, **fleghygow**, little child: see **flōgh**.
flent, see **flynt**.
flēr, (C. Voc. *flair*), *m*., stench, stink, fetor, bad smell, P.C. 1547, *braeth* Aelfric (O. Fr., from Lat. *flagrare* for *fragrare*).
flērya, *vb*., to stink.
flērynsy, **-ynjy**, *m*., fetidness, foulness of odour, R.D. 2133.
flērys, **-ēryüs** (*-yys*), *adj*., stinking, fetid: *m*., stinkard, R.D. 1890.
flōgh, *m*., *pl*. **flēghes** (C. Voc. *flechet*), *separative pl*. **flēghysyow**, **-yjyow** (Late *fle'jyow*), child, boy, young person, *cnapa* Aelfric: *f. wyn*, grandchild, Lh.; *f. byghan*, baby; *f. -bysyth*, godchild (W., B.).: see **flēghyk**.
flogholeth, *m*., infancy; *col*., children, O.M. 2838 (in addressing assembly).
flōghva, *f*., nursery: see **flōgh**.
flok, *m*., *pl*. **-kys**, flock, P.C. 895 (E.).
floren, *f*., fine mealy tin (D. " floran ").
floren (Lh. *fluran*), *f*., *pl*. **-now**, lock: *f. crok*, padlock.
flous, see **flows**.
flownen (*-nan* Gw.), *f*., *pl*. **-now**, pert girl, hussy: cf. B. *flaoñ*, *flaouenn*.
flowr, **flour**, *f*., *pl*. **-ys**, flower, finest specimen; *adj*., perfect, unequalled, surpassing, eminent: as adj. rhymes with *emperour* (M.E.).
flows (*flous*), *m*., trifling, idle talk (M.E. (*wythout*) *flous*, P.C. 1346): *hep f*., truly; *gas dha f*., drop thy nonsense.
flüken, *f*., soft ground interrupting a lode (D. " flookan ").
†**flür-rak(g)** (C. Voc. *flurrag*), *m*., forestage, forecastle, *thaer se ancerman sit* Aelfric (O.E. *flor*, floor): see **brennyas**.
flynt, *m*., flint, O.M. 1860 (E.).
fo, in M.E., oaths, *by my fo! by Goddys fo!* var. of *fot*, foot (Skeat).
fō, *m*., flight, retreat: *mos*, *fya*, *dhe'n f*., to run away, flee, take to flight, retreat; *gorra dhe'n f*. to put to flight.
†**fōesyk** (C. Voc. *fadic*, ? for *foedic*), *m*., fugitive, runaway, *flyma* Aelfric.
fōgo, **fougo**, *f*., *pl*. **-gevyow**, cave, underground chamber (D. " foogo "): see **ōgo**.
fōk(g), *f*., *pl*. **fogow**, hearth, forge, furnace, blowing-house, focus.
fol, *adj*., foolish, crazy; *m*., *pl*. **felyon**, fool, madman, *stunt* Aelfric: †*f. tergusca* (C. Voc. *f.-terguske*), raving madman, one who goes mad from want of sleep, *se the thurh sleapleaste awet* Aelfric; *avel pyth, tus, fol*, impetuously, like mad.

foles, *f.*, *pl.* **-ow**, foolish woman, mad woman (W.).
folneth, *m.*, folly, foolishness, R.D. 961.
folwherthyn, *vb.*, to giggle: see **wherthyn**.
foly, *m.*, folly (M.E.).
foly, *vb.*, to grow foolish (W., B.).
***fōn**, *m.*, new-mown hay (W., B.).
***fonek** *f.*, *pl.* **-egow**, **-egy**, hayfield (W., B.).
fonen, *f.*, *pl.* **-now**, hay-band (W.); small rush, used to make sheep-spans (D. "fun").
for', see **forth**.
forest, *m.*, *pl.* **-ys**, forest, C.W. 1468 (M.E.).
forgh (*forh*, *an vorh* Lh.), *f.*, *pl.* **fergh**, **ferghy**, fork, prong: *f. tyrforgh*, 3-pronged fork (*triforh* Lh.); *f. arghans*, table fork.
forghdrōs, **-dreys**, *adj.*, cloven-hoofed (W.).
***forlya**, *vb.*, to whirl (*forling*, as M.E., B.M. p. 220).
form, *m.*, *pl.* **-ys**, bench, form (M.E., D. "furm").
form, *f.*, *pl.* **-ow**, form, shape, B.M. 3683.
formya, *vb.*, to form, create, fashion, frame, make.
formyas, *m.*, *pl.* **-ysy**, creator, maker.
formyer, *m.*, *pl.* **-yor**, **-yon**, former, creator.
forn, *f.*, *pl.* **-ow**. oven, furnace, kiln, kitchen stove, C. Voc., Lh., P.: *f. lym*, lime-kiln; *f. meyn-pry*, brick-kiln, *f. lystry pry*. potters' kiln; see **gelforn**.
forner, *m.*, *pl.* **-noryon**, one who tends a kiln or furnace (B.).
fornys, *f.*, *pl.* **-yow**, furnace (W., B.),
fors, *m.*, power, energy, force: *na-vo re f. ow natur*, so that the vigour of my constitution may not be too much, B.M. 1973; matter, care, concern, heed, regard, consideration (M.E. *force*): *ny-rof* (*wraf*) *f.*, I don't care (M.E. *I give, or make, no force*); *ny-rēs* (*dhyn*) *f.*, *nyns-us f.*, *na f.*, no matter (M.E, *no force*).
forsakya, *vb.*, to forsake, B.M., Lh. (E.).
forsōth, *adv.*, indeed, forsooth, C.W. (E.).
forth, **for'** (C. Voc. *ford*), *f.*, *pl.* **fordhow** (late *forrow*), road, way, manner, style: *f. dybarth*, fork or parting of roads; *dres y'n f. da*, brought into the way of Salvation; *war*, *y'n*, *f.*, on the way; *a'n f. -na*, by that way; *for'-eglos*, *fr'eglos*, *fryglos*, church-way path; *f.-vur*, high road; *henfor'*, abandoned road; *f.-horn*, railway; *f. lan*, thoroughfare, free way; *y'th f. gwra mos*, go thy ways; *yn-mes a bup f.*, beyond all bounds; *y'n for'-ma*, *-na*, thus, so; *th* prevents mutation of following c, *k*, *d*, *t*; owing to the unwritten mutation of *f*, which in place-names is written, this word is more familiar in these as "vor," in "Henvor," "Trevorrow," etc.
fortyn. *m.*, fortune, chance, luck, B.M.: *f. Dew*, the favour of God,
fortynya (*fortidnia*, N. Boson), chance, favour, betide, make successful (M.E.).
fōs, *f.*, *pl.* **-ow**. house-wall, wall, rampart, dike (anciently, dike in sense of trench): *f.-chy*, wall of house; *fosow da gans lym ha pry ha pen cref warnedha-y gwreugh drehevel*, build good walls with lime and clay and a strong top on them, O.M. 2450. The "strong top" is a course of solid stone-work without clay; *s* prevents mutation of following *c*, *k*, *d*, *p*, *t*; in place-names commonly "vose."
foul (pr. *fūl*), *m.*, *pl.* **-ys**, fool (M.E.).
fout, see **fowt**.
fow, *f.*, *pl.* **-ys**, cave, den, P.C. 336 (D. "vow").
fowt (*fout*), *m.*, *pl.* **-ow**, lack, defect, fault (M.E.); *conj.*, for want of, in default of.
***fram**, *m.*, frame, framework (W., B.).
***framma**, *vb.*, to frame, join woodwork (W., B.).
Francas, see **Frynk**.
***franchys**, *m.*, freedom, franchise (E.)
frank, *adj.*, free, frank, at liberty: *f. ha lel ota-sy*, free and loyal art thou, Godolphin motto.
fra'nkyncens (*frokensense*, Kerew), *m.*, frankincense (E.).
frantyk, *adj.*, frantic, Kerew (E.).
frappya, *vb.*, to beat, rap, knock, B.M. 961 (M.E. *frappe*).
fraus, *m.*, fraud: *hep f.*, verily, R.D. 1293 (Latin, for rhyme to *Emmaus*).
frēga, *vb.*, to tear up, tatter: p. pt. *fregys* used as *m.*, tatterdemalion (D. "fraygus").
Frenk, **-ek**, see **Frynk**, **ek**.
frenna, *vb.*, to fret, Gw.: possibly for **fromma**.
***fresk**, *adj.*, fresh (W., B.).
frēth, **freth**, *adj.*, eager, eloquent, fluent, unrestrained, forthright, vigorous, energetic: all rhymes suggest a short *e*, but W. *fraeth*,

B. *fraez*, imply a long one.
frethter, *m.*, promptness, fluency, etc.
***fromma** (cf. *frenna* Gw.), *vb.*, to be agitated, fret, fume (W., B.).
fron (Late *frodin*, Symonds, 1644, *frudn*), *f.*, *pl.* **-now**, bridle, restraint; *brake (B.): *f. dhall*, bridle with blinkers (W.).
***frōn**, *f.*, *pl.* **-ow**, nostril: replaced by **fryk(g)** (W., B.).
frona, *vb*., to curb, restrain (W., B.).
***frony**, *vb.*, to sniff, snort (W., B.): see ***frōn**.
frōs (C. Voc. *frot*), *m.*, *pl.* **-ow**, stream, current, tide race (D. "froze"): *f. tredanek*, electric current (W.).
frōs, *m.*, row, tumult, disturbance (D. "froze").
frōsa, *vb.*, to stream, gush, rush (W., B.).
frōth, *m*, tumult, brawl, stir, fuss, Lh.: cf. Eng. D. "frawth," Suffolk, unless a var. of **trōs**.
früdha, *vb.*, to fray out, unravel, tatter, separate threads of fabric (D. "freathe," cf. **früth**).
frūt, *m.*, *pl.* **-ys**, fruit (E.): see **†frūyth**.
***früth**, *m.*, damage, harm, tear (W., B.).
†frūyth (C. Voc. *fruit*), *m.*, *pl.* **-ow**, fruit, *waestm* Aelfric: replaced in M. Cor. by **frūt**.
frȳa (*fria* Lh.), *vb.*, to set free (E.).
frȳa (*fria* Lh.), *vb.*, to fry (E.).
fryglos, see **forth**.
frȳk(g) (C. Voc. *fruc* or *friic*, C.W. *frieg*, *freyge*), *m.*, *pl.* **-ygow**, *d.* **deufryk**, nostril, in pl., nostrils; and also nose.
Frynk, *f.*, France; *m. pl.* **-yon**, **Francas**, Frenchman.
Frynkek, *adj.*, French; *m.*, French language.
Frynkes, *f.*, *pl.* **-ow**, Frenchwoman.
fū, see **vū**.
†fūelen (C. Voc. *fuelein*), *f.*, wormwood, *wermod* Aelfric.
fūg, *f.*, cavity in rock (D. "vug").
fūgen, *f.*, *pl.* **-now**, **-gas**, pastry, dinner-cake (D. "fuggan"): see **hogen**, **whȳogen**.
fük(g), *m.*, *pl.* **-yow**, feint, sham; *adj.*, fictitious: *f. hanow*, pseudonym (W.).
fükya, *vb.*, to feign, play unfairly (D. "feak").
fumado, *m.*, *pl.* **-s**, salted (originally smoked) pilchard, D. "fermaid" (Late, Spanish).
fundya, *vb.*, to found, lay foundations, B.M. 1150 (M.E. *founde*).
fundyer, *m.*, *pl.* **-yoryon**, founder.
fundyans, *m.*, institution, founding.
fünen, *f.*, *pl.* **-now**, band, fillet, Lh.
für (Late *fir*, *feer*), *adj.*, wise, cautious, careful, clever, *snoter*, *maenigtiwe* Aelfric: *bedheugh-why f.*. take care! *bedheugh-why furra nessa*, be wiser next time!
***fürf**, *f.*, *pl.* **-vyow**, form, shape, C. Voc., *hiw* Aelfric: replaced by **form**.
fürneth, *m.*, wisdom (B.).
füs, *f.*, fortune, prosperity: see **anfüs**.
†füsek (C. Voc. *fodic*), *adj.*, fortunate, *gesaelig* Aelfric: see **anfüsek**.
füst, *f.*, *pl.* **-ow**, club, bludgeon, flail, P.C. 1172.
füsta, *vb.*, to thresh, to give one a thrashing, Lh.
fȳ, *interj.*, fie! (M.E.): *f. dhyso!* out upon thee!
fȳa, *vb.*, to flee: 3 s. pres.-fut., 2 s. imp. *fy*; *f. dhe'n fo*, to take to flight.
fȳa, *vb.*, to despise, scorn, cry fie on: *da yth-omlath a-fyys*, well he fights whom I despised, B.M. 2491: *hag a-fy dhe gafos hy both*, who scorns to have her own way, Chart. Endors.; *pan fyyth*, when thou scornest, B.M. 429; see **fȳ**.
fydhya, *vb.*, to trust, hope, rely (on), confide (in): takes *yn*; *del fydhyaf*, as I trust or hope; 3 s. pres.-fut. *fȳth*; *th* also in 3 s. subj. and before *s*.
fyenasow (*fyanasow*), *abstract pl.*, grief, anxiety, harassment, solicitude, care.
fygūr, (*fegure*, C.W. 487), *m.*, figure, shape (M.E.).
fygesen, *f.*, *col.* **fyges**, fig, dried fruit: *f. ledan*, broad-fig, flat dried fig; *f. an howl*, raisin; **f. Corynt*, currant; **f. Malyk*, (malaga) raisin; **f. ryal* date.
†fykbren (C. Voc. *ficbren*), *m.*, fig-tree, *fictreow*, Aelfric.
fyl (*fylh*), *m.*, *pl.* **-lys**, viol, fiddle, O.M. 1997: see **fyllores**.
fylgeth, see **hylgeth**.
fyllel, *vb.*, to fail, lack, come short, go wrong, be found wanting: 3 s. pres.-fut. *fyll*, 1 s. *fallaf*; 3 s. pret. *fyllys*; 3 s. subj. *fallo*; *gwyn-fyllys*, vinegar; *tra ny-fyll dhyso*, thou shalt want for nothing; *ny-fyll a'y borpos genef*, he shall not fall short of his aim through me: see **fall**.
fyllor, *m.*, *pl.* **-yon**, fiddler, violinist (W.): see **†harfellor**.
†fyllores (C. Voc. *fellores*), *f. pl.* **-ow**, woman violinist; see **fyl**.

fylta (*fyltya*), *m.*, vileness, filth, M.C. (M.E. *filthe*, Wessex D. "filt").
fȳn (*fyne*), *m.*, *pl.* **-ys.** fine, C.W. 250.
fȳn, *f.*, *pl.* **-yow**, end, limit: *deth f.*, the last day; *hep f.*, endlessly.
fȳn, *adj.*, fine, delicate, keen, astute, smart; as *adv.*, finely, perfectly, extremely; *f. gonedhys*, faultlessly wrought; *cales f.*, excessively hard, M.C. 196 (*feyn*); *f. ervys*, armed cap-a-pie.
fy·negel, *f.*, *pl.* **-glow**, furrow (W.).
fynegler, *m.*, *pl.* **-ow**, furrower, launce-crook for catching sand-eels (D. "fingler").
fynegly, *vb.*, to plough lightly, turn the soil as swine, use a lance-crook (D., W., B.).
fynny, *f.*, bent, coarse grass: *f. vür*, tussock-grass (D. "vidny veor"); Rosevidney, place-name.
fynsya (for *fy·nysya*), *vb.*, to finish, bring an affair to a successful conclusion, B.M. 3525 (E.): cf. **punsya, rafsya**, etc.
fynweth, *f.*, end, cessation, M.C. 212.
†fȳol (C. Voc. *fiol*), *f.*, *pl.* **-ow**, vial, cup.
***fȳonen** *f.*, *col.* **fȳon**, narcissus (B.).
†fy·rmament (C. Voc. *firmament*), *m.*, firmament, *roder* Aelfric.
fysek, *f.*, medical science, physic: *lyver a f.*, book of medicine, B.M. 1418, is followed by *dok hy, f.*, though *lyver* is *m.*
fysk, *adj.*, hasty, impetuous; *m.*, haste (W.).
fysky (*fesky*), *vb.*, to hasten, hurry, rush, O.M. 1685: as **dysky**; *pandr 'yu an f. es genes*? What's all your hurry? B.M. 2099.
fyslak, *m.*, pesterer, nuisance, fidget, Borlase (?D. "fussle," to fuss).
fysmant, *m.*, *pl.* **-mens**, countenance, appearance, complexion, C.W. 527, pl., B.M. 1205 (M.E. *visement*).
fystyna, festyna (*festinna* Lh.), *vb.*, to hasten.
fysycyen (*fecycyen*), *m.*, *pl.* **-s**, physician, B. M. 1421 (M.E. *fysicien*).
fyt, *m.*, *pl.* **-tys**, match, turn, bout, B.M. 3380 (M.E. *fit*): *gul f. a*, make a match with, try a bout with.
fȳth (*feyth, fēth*), *f.*, faith, trust, reliance.
fȳth, *adj.*, fertile, cultivated (W.): see **dyfȳth.**
†fȳthüs (C. Voc. *faidus*), *adj.*, beautiful, well-formed, richly adorned, luxuriant, *wel gewliteyod* Aelfric.
fyttya, *vb.*, to prepare, make fit or ready (E.D. "fit," as in "fit mait," prepare meals): *fyttyeugh dhe vos*, prepare to go, Gw.

G (mutations -, W, C, K, H, and of Gw, W, Qu, W, Wh)

'ga, see **aga, maga**, conj.
gadlyng, *m.*, *pl.* **-s**, vagabond, P.C. 2691 (M.E.).
gaf, see **gava.**
†gahen, *f.*, henbane, C. Voc., *hennebelle* Aelfric: cf. Ir. *gafenn.*
gāja (*gage*), *m.*, *pl.* **-jys**, forfeit, pledge, pawn: *gasa yn g.*, P.C. 1186, to forfeit.
gaja, see **caja, gasa.**
gal, *m.*, *pl.* **-ow**, villain, outcast, criminal, rascal (O.E. *gal*, wanton, wicked); *map g.*, *myrgh g.*, disreputable, gutter-bred person.
galar, *m.*, *pl. and abstract* **-ow**, grief, sorrow, affliction, pain.
galarek, *adj.*, doleful (B.).
galargan, *f.*, *pl.* **-ow**, dirge (W.).
galaror, *m.*, *pl.* **-yon**, mourner (W.).
galarwysk, *m.*, *pl.* **-as**, mourning dress (W.).
galary, *vb.*, to bewail, lament, mourn, sorrow (W., B.).
gallas, etc., see **mōs** in TABLE, APPENDIX VIII.
gallos (*-us*), *m.* (*verbal noun*), power, might, ability, authority, control; *irregular vb.*, to be able, be able to do; for parts see TABLE, APPENDIX VIII (inf. is found only as verbal noun; Lhuyd supplies *gally* from Welsh *gallu* as he does *menni*, W. *mynnu*, for *mynnes*, but in W. *gallu* is the noun also; B. *gallout* is similarly noun and vb., and W. *-u*, B. *-out*, are properly inf. -endings, as *-os* is in Cornish); *oll dhe'm g.*, as far as I am able; *ny-sef henna y'th hallos*, that is not possible for thee; *warnedha kemer g.*, assume authority over them; *dre dha allos dha-honen*, unaided.
gallosek, -ojek, *adj.*, powerful, mighty, puissant, potent.
***gallȳna**, *m.*, *pl.* **-ys**, guinea-fowl (Lat. *gallina Africana*, E.D. "gleeny"): *yar Gyny* is a turkey-hen.
galow, *m.*, call, invitation.

galsa, galsof, etc., see **mōs,** TABLE, APPENDIX VIII.
galwans, *m.*, calling, vocation (W.).
gām (*game*), *m.*, game, play; hunted wild animals, B.M., C.W. (M.E.).
'gan, see **agan.**
-gan-, *infixed pron.*, us, see **agan, -n-.**
ganow (C. Voc. *genau*), *m.*, mouth: *war anow,* by word of mouth, through the mouth; *kewsel orth y anow,* have direct speech with him; *g. cam,* anchovy, lit. crooked-mouth (B.); see **gen.**
ganowas, *m.*, *pl.* **-esow,** mouthful (B.).
ganowek, *adj.*, big-mouthed, gaping (B.).
gans (Late *gen*), *prep.*, with, by; (with, *clewes, dysky*) from; (with *gul noys, kewsel, pysy, eva*) on behalf of, in favour of, for the good of: combines with prons., see TABLE, APPENDIX V.; *gallas ganso,* he has got it, he is done for; *dun ganso,* let us go off with him, let us take it away; *an vyctory eth genef,* I won the victory; *drok yu genef gul,* I am sorry to have made; *cas vya genef gul henna,* I should hate to do that; *da yu genef,* I am glad, I like it; *mar dha yu genef,* I would as soon; *gwell yu genef,* I would rather; *yma genef,* I have; *ass-yu joy genef gothvos,* how rejoiced I am to know.
gans-hemma, *adv.*, moreover, herewith, -upon, -by, besides this, too, withal, as well.
gans-henna (*genz hedna* Lh.), *adv.*, moreover, therewith, -upon, -by, besides that, too, withal, as well, B.M. 4282, C.W. 1604.
gar, *f.*, *pl.* **-row,** *d.* **dywar,** leg (including thigh); stem of flower, stalk of plant.
†garan, *f.*, *pl.* **-as,** crane, C. Voc.
garek (*garrek* Lh.), *adj.*, legged, leggy.
garen, *f.*, *pl.* **-now,** shank, stem, stalk. *pen ha g.*, all head and stalk, without body, lean (D. "pednygarren," undersized fish).
gargam (*gargabm* Lh.), *adj.*, bow-legged, bandy-legged.
gargasen (*gargesen*), *f.*, *pl.* **-now,** gullet (B.); *m.*, guzzler, glutton (term of abuse), B.M. 2423, 3322.
garget, *m.*, *pl.* **-tow,** garter, Lh.: *kelmeugh agas gargettow!* fasten your garters! Borlase MS.
garlont, *f.*, *pl.* **-ow,** ? **-ons,** garland, wreath, metal band, circle (M.E.): exceptionally this is given a Celtic pl., perhaps only for rhyme, O.M. 2549. but cf. **baby, baner, fardel, maner,** all with pl. **-ow.**
garlythen, *f.*, *col.* **garlȳth,** sole, kind of flat-fish (B.): see **lȳth.**
garm, *f.*, *pl.* **-ow,** outcry, shout.
garma, *vb.*, to shout, cry out: *g. war,* to cry to, M.C. 37, as D. "garm upon."
garow, *adj.*, rough, rugged, violent, coarse, uneven, rude, harsh, cruel, unkindly, formidable, terrible: comp. *garwa, may kertho garwa y gam,* that he may walk at a rougher pace, P.C. 1197.
ga'rowder, *m.*, roughness, harshness (B.).
garth, *m. or f.*, *pl.* **-ow, -dhow,** enclosure, garden.
garth, *f.*, *pl.* **-ow,** hill, promontory: see **penarth.**
gartha, *vb.*, to make a garden or enclosure (W., B.).
garthen, *f.*, *pl.* **-now,** enclosure.
†garthow (C. Voc. *garthou,* wrongly *arho* Lh.), *m.*, *pl.* **-yow,** ox-goad.
'gas, see **agas.**
-gas-, *infixed pron.*, you.
gasa, gaja (Late *gara*), *vb.*, to leave, leave off, cease, abandon, desert, quit; allow, let, permit: p. pt. *gesys*; 3 s. pres.-fut. 2 s. imp. *gās, g. cres dhym,* let me alone, leave me in peace, *geseugh cres!* peace! B.M. 1312; *g. vy dhe weles,* let me see; *g. ny dhe vos alemma,* let us go hence; *g. dhym dhe ombrena,* leave it to me to redeem myself; *g. e,* give him up; *g. covath,* lose remembrance; *g. cumyas,* take leave; *g. spas dhym,* make way for me; *g. dhe-ves strevya,* leave off wrangling; *g. dha wow,* cease thy lying; *dhe gerdhes g. an welen!* let the switch keep going! 2 s. pret. *gyssys,* with suffixed pron., *gysta*; *a-gysseugh genef,* which you let me have, R.D. 38.
gāst (*gēst* Lh.), *f.*, *pl.* **gȳsty,** bitch; woman of bad character.
gava (*gafa*), *vb.*, to forgive, remit, pardon: used with *dhe* when transitive; p. pt. *gyvys, gefys*; 3 s. pres-fut., 2 s. imp. *gaf*; 3 s. plupf. *gafsa*; *my a th-pys dhym a ava,* pray forgive me (O.E. *(for)gifan*).
gavar, *f.*, *pl.* **gēver,** goat: *g.-hal,* snipe (D. "gaverhale," from its bleating sound); *g.-mor,* crayfish; spider-crab (D. "gayver", from their "horns).''
gavel, *f.*, *pl.* **-yow,** grasp, hold, capacity, ability to hold, M.C. 237.
***gavel** or ***gawl,** *f.*, *pl.* **-gavlow,** fork,

furcation, stride (W., B.).
***gavlak**, *adj*., forked, straddling (W., B.).
***gavlya**, *vb*., to straddle (W., B.).
gavrewyk, *f*., *pl*. **-wygas**, antelope, gazelle (W.).
gay, *adj*., splendid, noble, fine (M.E.): comp. and exclam. *gaya; 'tomma gaya aval dhys*! look what a magnificent apple for thee! C.W. 737.
gedya, *vb*., to guide, direct, show the way: 2 pl. imp. *gedyeugh*; 3 s. pres.-fut. *gȳd* (M.E. *gyde*).
†**gēl** (C. Voc. *g(h)el*), *f*., *pl*. **-as**, leech; bloodsucker: *g. margh*, horseleech.
geler. *f*., *pl*. **-ow**, coffin, R.D. 2320; bier, B.M. 4487 (W., B.).
gelerlen, *f*. pall (W.).
gelforn (for *govelforn*), *f*., *pl*. **-ow**, blacksmith's forge (D. " roar like gelvern").
***gell**, *adj*., light brown, bay, fawn-coloured, tawny (W., B.): **gellruth*, auburn, tawny; **g. kesten*, chestnut, roan (B.).
***gellder**, *m*., tawniness, brownness.
†**gelvyn** (C. Voc. *gelvin*), *m*., *pl*. **-as** beak, bill.
gelvynak (*gulvinak*, Lh.), *adj*., long-billed; *m*., *pl*. **-ogas**, curlew.
gelwel, **gylwel**, *vb*, to call, name, invite: 3 s. pres.-fut. *gelow*, 2 *galwaf*; 2 s. imp. *galwy* (P.C. 3056, B.M. 2432); 3 s. pluperf. *gawlsa* for *galwsa*; p. pt. *gylwys*; 3 s. pret. *ge(y)lwys*; *y-m-gylwyr*, I am named; the curious 2 s. imp. ending *-wy* may be the regular one for all Cor. vbs. with inf. *-wel*, but *galwy* is the only example.
gelwesygeth, *f*., calling, profession (W., B.).
gelwesyk, *adj*., called, nominated (W.).
†**gem** (*g* hard), *m*., *pl*. **-mow**, gem (O.C. Gloss).
gen (Lh. *gēn*), *f*., chin; *pl*. **ganow**, mouth; *d*. **dywen**. jaws, chaps.
gen (*gedn* Lh.), *m*. *pl*. **-ow**, chisel; stone-chisel, O.M. 2317; iron wedge.
gen, **genef**, etc., see **gans**.
genesygeth, *f*., time of birth, birth, B.M. 4387: *a'y enesygeth*, from birth onwards.
genesygla, *m*., birthplace: see **lē**.
genesygva, **-jygva**, *f*., birth, manner of birth, B.M. 850.
genesyk, **genyjyk**, *adj*., native, born, natural; *m*., *pl*. **-ygyon**, aborigine, native: *drok, tebel, g*., one naturally evil, or ill-born, R.D. 2186, B.M. 2287.

genna, *vb*., to chisel, gouge, wedge (W.,B.).
gensy, *adv*., therewith, lit. with it: *ha g. oll, hagens'oll* (*hagenzol*, Lh.), and also; furthermore, likewise, therewithal, lit. and with it all; *ha g. doth*, and well-behaved moreover, Chart. Endors.; see **gans**, **hȳ**.
genva, *f*., *pl*. **-ow**, horse's bit (W.).
Genver, **mȳs-G.**, *m*., January, Lh.
genys, *p*. *pt*., born; well-born, of high lineage, B.M. 358: only part of verb in use apparently; see **denythy**.
gēr (B.M. *geer*, C.W. *gere*, Late *gear*), *m*., *pl*. **-yow**, word, saying, report, *verb: †*drok-ger*, infamy, C. Voc.; *kewsel g. 'vas gans*, speak a word in favour of; *kettoth ha'n g*., on the word, *fystyn gans an g*., hasten with the message.
†**gērda**, *m*., fame, reputation, C. Voc., *hlisa* Aelfric: not found as M. Cor.
geren, *f*., *pl*. **-now**, single word: pl. verbiage, twaddle, (mere) words, B.M. 2964.
gērlyver (*-lever* P.), *m*., *pl*. **-vrow**, **-fryow**, dictionary, lexicon.
gērlyvryn (*-levren* Lh.), *m*., glossary, abridged dictionary (W.).
gerrak (*girak* Lh.), *m*., *pl*. **-ogas**, gar-fish (D.E. " gerrock," dim. of " gar "): see **mōrnasweth**.
gērva, *f*., glossary, vocabulary (W.).
gērya, *vb*., to be verbose, to pronounce on (D. " garey "): *geryes* (C. Voc. *geriit*) *da*, well-reported, famous, renowned, *hlisful* Aelfric.
geryador, *m*., dictionary, glossary, vocabulary (W., B.).
geryak, *adj*, verbose (W.).
gēs, (*gays*, C.W. *geas*, Lh. *geaze*), *m*., jeer, mockery, joke, jest, satire: as M.B. *gaes*; *g. a-wrussons anodho*, they made a mock of it, C.W. 2428.
gēsya (*geysya*), *vb*., to jeer, mock, jest, M.C. 137: *bos gesyes*, to be made fun of, mocked, B.M. 401.
gesys, etc., see **gasa**.
gevel, *f*., *pl*. **-yow**, tongs, pincers (W., B.): †*g. horn* (C. Voc. *geuel hoern*), snuffers, iron tongs, *isentanga* Aelfric; *g. tan*, fire-tongs (B.); *g. know*, nut-crackers (W.); *g. vyghan*, forceps, pliers.
†**gevel**, *m*., *pl*. **-as**, *f*. **-es**, twin (W., B.).
gevelya, *vb*., to pinch, draw nails (W.).
gēver, see **gavar**.
gē'veryk, **gēvryk**, *m*., *pl*. **-ygow**, goatling;

red gurnard (D. " gaverick "); spider-crab (D. " gaberick ") : see **gavar.**

gew (*gu*), *m., pl. and abst.* **-ow,** woe, grief, misery : *er y wew,* worse luck for him, to his woe ; *y 'fyth gewow,* thou shalt have woe ; see **go-.**

gew, see **gu.**

glan (Late *gladn*), *f., pl.* **-now,** brink, bank, waterside, margin, verge, upright side, edge, *staedh* Aelfric.

glān, *adj.,* clean, clear, innocent, pure, holy; *adv.,* quite, utterly, completely, entirely ; *yn-lan,* cleanly, wholly; *dhe'n glan,* utterly, O.M. 859, may be for *dhe'n lan,* to the utmost (verge), **glan f.**

glān, see **gwlān.**

glander, *m.,* purity, B.M. 533.

glanhē, *vb.,* to clean, clear, P.C. 865 : as **berhē.**

glanyth (*glannith* Lh.), *adj.,* clean, neat, tidy, J. Boson.

glanythther (*glannuthder, glanithder* Lh.), *m.,* cleanliness, neatness.

glās, glascor, see **gwlās, gwlascor.**

glas, *m.,* maw, stomach ; *maga* Aelfric : *venjyans y'th glas ! y 'gas glas !* P.C. *mollatew yn dha las !* Carew, curses ; see **mollath, venjyans.**

glās, *adj.,* blue, green, glaucous, grey, pale, wan, (of fruit) unripe: *glaswer,* blue-green (W.), *glasruth,* purple, violet (W., B.) ; *glaswyn,* blue-grey (W., B.) ; *blew g.,* grey hair.

glasa, *vb.,* to flourish, grow green, blue, pale, etc.; put forth leaves, sprout, O.M. 584.

glāsen, *f.,* green place, verdure : Chylason, place-name.

glasneth, *m.,* verdure, greenness : place-name Glasney(th).

†glastanen, *f., col.* **glastan,** holm-oak, ilex, evergreen oak, C. Voc., *ac* Aelfric.

glaster, *m.,* greenness, blueness (W., B.).

glaswedhen, *f., col.* **-wȳth,** sapling (W.).

glaswels, *m.,* growing grass, pasture (W.).

glasyjyon, *m.,* grass-plot, green, O.M. 2036.

***glavor,** *m.,* drivel, slaver (W., B.).

***glavorya,** *vb.,* to slaver (W., B.).

glaw (C. Voc. *glau*), *m.,* rain : *gul g.,* to rain, Lh.

glawek, *adj.,* rainy (W., B.).

glawen, *f., pl.* **-now,** rain-drop (B.).

glawlen, *f., pl.* **-now,** umbrella (W.).

glawjy, *m., pl.* **-ow,** shed, shelter against rain (D. " glowjy ").

gleb, see **glyp,**

***glēgh,** *m.,* moisture : *gora yn g.,* put to soak (W., B.).

***glēghy,** *vb.,* to soak, steep (W., B.).

gleny, *vb.,* to cling, cleave, adhere, stick : *g. hardlych orth,* stick fast to.

glesyk, *adj.,* greenish, blueish (B.).

glesyn, *m., pl.* **-now,** grass-plot, green, patch of grass-wrack : Glisson, place-name (D. " glizzon ").

†glesyn (C. Voc. *glesin*), *m.,* woad, blue dye : see **glās.**

glēth, (*glēdh* Lh.), *m.,* chickweed : *g. dowr,* brookweed (B.).

glew (*glu*), *adj.,* bright, clear, transparent, piercing, penetrating, of blows or pain, acute : *aspy ahas ha g.,* keep a keen and clear look-out, O.M. 2062.

***glew,** *adj.,* bold (W., M.B.).

glōry, *m.,* glory, C.W. (M.E.).

glōryes (pr. *glōr·yes*), *adj.,* glorious, B.M., C.W. (M.E.).

glōs, (*gloys*), *f., pl.* **-ow,** pang, anguish, pain, spasm, qualm ; used with *kemeres, na-gemer g.,* don't take a qualm ; *g. a-n-kemeras,* a pang seized him.

glōsa, *vb.,* to hurt (B.).

glōsen, *f., pl.* **-now,** *col.* **glōs,** (C.W. *glose,* P. *gloas*), dried cow-dung fuel, C.W. 1092, 1107 (D. "glaws").

***glossa,** *m., pl.* **-sys,** interpretation, gloss (E.).

***glossya,** *vb.,* to interpret (E.).

glo·teny, glotny, *m.,* gluttony, M.C., P.C. (M.E. *glotony*) : *gul g.,* commit (the sin of) gluttony.

glow, *col.,* charcoal ; coal : *g. -dor, -pol,* pit-coal (for distinction) : see **cōlyn.**

glüjek, *adj.,* sticky, viscous (W., B.).

glüs (C. Voc. *glut*), *m.,* glue, bird-lime, paste, *lim* Aelfric.

glüsa, glüja, *vb.,* to stick (W., B.) ; ?make a paste or pulp of, B.M. 2398.

glūth, *m.,* dew, Lh.

glūtha, *vb.,* to dew (W., B.).

glūthek, *adj.,* dewy (W., B.).

glūthen, *f., pl.* **-now,** dewdrop (B.).

glūthenna, *vb.,* to gather into rain (D. " gluthen up ").

glūthvelwen, *f., pl.* **-wes,** small slug, " dew snail " (W.).

†glybor (C. Voc. *glibor*), *m.* wetness, wet, moisture, fluid, *waeta* Aelfric.

glybya (*glebya* B.M.), *vb.,* to wet, moisten: 3 s. pres.-fut. *glyp,* subj. *glyppo,* **plupf.** *glypsa* ; *dun-ny, glybyn agan myn,* **come, let's wet our whistles ! B.M. 3276.**

glyn, *m.*, *pl.* **-now**, deep valley : place-name.

glyn (*gleyn*), *m.*, *pl.* **-yow**, *d.* **deulyn** (*dowlyn* M.C.), knee : *penglyn*, d. *pendeulyn*, point of knee; *mos war ben glyn*, to kneel on one knee ; *war bendeulyn*, on both knees ; *pen y dheulyn*, his knees: see **clyn**.

glyngam, *adj.*, knock-kneed (W.).

glyp(b) (Late *gleb*), *adj.*, wet, damp, moist, liquid ; comp. *glyppa*.

glyttra (*o klittra*, pres.-pt. Borlase), *vb.*, to glitter, sparkle, gleam (E.).

glyvedhas, see **gwelyvedhes**.

gnās, *f.*, nature, quality : *drok y gn.*, ill-natured, P.C. 1142, 2969 ; W. *gnaws* : see **dygnās**, **nās**.

go-, see Appendix II.

go-, form of **gew**, woe, as compounded with suffixed prons. (form 2, Table, Appendix IV) in interjs., *govy·!* woe 's me ! etc. : *göef·!* woe betide him ! woe worth the wight ! is sometimes contracted into *gwef!*

gōans, *m.*, digestion (B.).

gobans, *m.*, *pl.* **-ow**, small hollow or dingle : Gobbens, place-name.

gobenner, *m.*, *pl.* **-yow**, bolster (W., B.).

gober, *m.*, *pl.* **-brow**, reward, recompense, remuneration, fee, wages, payment : *gallas hy g. gensy*, she has got her deserts, O.M. 2764.

goberna (*go , prena*), *vb.*, to hire, Pryce ; to deserve, merit (W.).

gobra, *vb.*, to reward, hire (W., B.).

goccor, see **gwycor**.

goda-chōns (misread *thous* Norris), *m.*, good-luck, O.M. 2822 (M.E. *gode chaunce*) ; *g. re-th-fo*, good luck to you ! (meant invertedly).

godegh, *m.*, lurking-place, cover for game, holt : *g. conyn*, rabbit-warren, place-name " Goodakinnin " : see **teghy**.

goderry, *vb.*, to interrupt, break the force of (W., B.) : see **terry**.

godhaf, **godhevel**, *vb.*, to suffer, endure, tolerate, bear, brook, experience, permit, acquiesce, allow : 3 s. pret. *godhevys* ; 3 s. subj. *godhaffo* ; 3 s. plupf. *godhafsa* ; *dowt na-vedha namoy godhevys dheugh*, lest no more should be allowed you, Lh.

Godhal, see **Gwydhal**.

godhas·, **go 'dhōr**, see **gōth**.

godhas (C. Voc. *guthot*), *m* , *pl.* **-dhojyon**, sediment, grounds, lees, dregs, *drosna* Aelfric ; in C. Voc. the Latin *fer* is miswritten for *faex* : *godhow* (*godho*, Lh., P.) is a late corruption of this, perhaps confused with **cūth**, **-ow**.

godhevel, see **godhaf**.

godhessa, *vb.*, to catch moles (W., B.) : inf. only.

godhevel, see **godhaf**.

godhevyans, *m.*, sufferance, long-suffering, endurance (W.).

godhow, see **godhas**, **gōth**.

godhvos, see **gothvos**.

godhyk, *m.*, *pl.* **-ygow**, gosling (B.).

godhyvas (*gudhivaz* Lh. in Borlase), *vb.*, to brim as a sow : ?late var of **godhevel**.

godolgh, *dim.* **godolghyn**, *m.*, *pls.* **-ow**, **-now**, slight rise of ground, tump : Godolghan, place-name : see **tolgh**.

godor, *m.*, break, interruption, shelter (W., B.).

godra (*gudra* Lh.), *vb.*, to milk : inf. only.

godrak (*guedrak*, Borlase), *m.*, cow's first milk.

godra·m (*gudrabm*), *m.*, cramp, Borlase (D. " godrabm ").

godref, **-ra**, *f.*, *pl.* **-evy**, small farm or hamlet, lodgment : ?place-name Godrevy.

godrer, *m.*, *pl.* **-oryon**, milker (W., B.).

godrōs (*go-*, *trōs*), *vb.*, to menace, threaten, scold, R.D. 2408 ; *m.*, *pl.* **-ow**, threat, menace (B).

God-spēda, *interj.*, God-speed (M.E.).

Godys cors, *m.*, God's curse, B.M. 2090 (M.E.).

gof (M.C. *goff*, Lh. *gōv*), *m.*, *pl.* **goves**, **-vyon**, smith : Angove, Trengove, -goff, personal and place names : *g. du*, blacksmith, Lh. : see **map-gōf**, **govel**.

gogell (*ogall* Gw.), *f.*, *pl.* **-ow**, pulpit, lit. little cell or chamber : *yma 'n pronter y'n ogell ow-pregoth*, Gw., the parson is preaching in the pulpit : see **purcat**.

gogo, *f.*, *pl.* **gogevyow**, cave.

gohel, *m.*, avoidance (W.).

goheles (R.D. *gowheles*, *go³-*, *keles*), *vb.*, to shun, escape, avoid, be shy of, B.M.

gohelüs, *adj.*, shy, retiring (W.).

gojogen, see **gosogen**.

goky (*gokky*, C.W. *gucky*), *adj.*, foolish, comp. *gokÿa* ; *m. pl.* **-ÿes**, fool (M.E. *goky*, D. " gucky ").

gokyneth (in verse *go·kyneth*), *m.*, folly, absurdity, foolishness.

gōl (*goyl*, C. Voc. *guil*), *m. or f.*, *pl.* **-yow**, sail; arras, wall-hanging, C. Voc., *wahreft* Aelfric ; veil, P.

gōl, *m.*, *pl.* **-yow**, parish feast, revel, wake,

festival, holiday; watch, banquet; vigil: *kefrys g. ha gwyth,* alike on feasts and working days; *G. Myghal,* Michaelmas: see **dēgol, golöwan, golva.**

goldheys, *m.,* harvest-home, lit. ricks festival, like O.E. *hreac-mete,* "rick-meat," harvest feast (D. "gulthize"): vars. are **gol-dey's, gōl an deys, degol-dey's** (D. "guldize," "golandize," "dicklydize," etc.); see **gōl, das.**

goles (Lh. *golaz,* Gw. *gullas*), *m.,* bottom, base, lowest part: *a-woles,* below; *dhe-woles,* at the bottom; *war woles,* towards the bottom; *a-barth a-woles,* on the lower side; *g. tros,* sole of foot, *pl.* **-ow,** *d. deuwoles t.*; a misinterpreted name of the Land's End as "bottom end" was Penwolase, Leland, Pedn an Wollaz, N. Boson, for *Pen an Wlas.*

golesen, *f., pl.* **-now,** under-petticoat (B.).

golesky, *vb.,* to singe, scorch, char (W.).

golewder, golöwder, *m.,* brightness, glory, radiance, lightness.

golgh, *m.,* washing, *pl.* **-yon,** slops, suds (W.).

golghy (*golhy*), *vb.,* to wash: *may hallons bos golghys aga threys,* that they may be with washed feet, P.C. 840, see **gorowra.**

golgheres, *f., pl.* **-ow,** washerwoman (B.).

golghty, *m.,* laundry (W.).

golghva, *f.,* lavatory, bath, laundry, washing-place (W.).

gōljy, *m.,* watch-house (W.).

gōlnōs, *f.,* vigil (W.).

***golo,** *m., pl.* **-yow,** cover, wrapping, shelter, protection (W., B.).

***golöy,** *vb.,* to wrap, cover, protect (W., B.).

golōgh, *m.,* adoration (W.).

gologhas (*gollohas*), *m.,* adoration, worship, praise, laud.

gologhy, *vb.,* to adore, worship (W.).

golok (*an woolak,* Keigwin), *f.,* sight, vision, glance, look, view, presence: *gweskel war an wolok,* to strike across the eyes, P.C. 2100; *myryn orto un wolok,* let's take one peep at him, B.M. 3386.

golokwedrow, *pl.,* spectacles (W.).

golosk, *m.,* charred wood or coal, coke (W.).

golovas, see **gwelyvos.**

golow, *adj.,* light, bright, shining; *m.,* (C. Voc. *golou,* Late *gulow*), *pl.* **-lowys,** light: *g. deth,* daylight; *worth g. nos,* by night's light, in the dark, P.C. 1253.

Golöwan (Late *Golūan*; *gol -Yowan,* older pronunciation of *Jowan,* Late *Jūan*), *m.,* Midsummer: lit. "Vigil or Wake of John," as W. *gwyl Ioan,* B. *gouél Jan.*

golöwbren, *m.,* lamp-post (W.).

golöwder, see **golewder.**

golöwjy, *m., pl.* **-ow,** lighthouse (W.).

golöw-lester (C. Voc. *goloulester*), *m., pl.* **-lystry,** light-vessel, lamp. *leohtfaet* Aelfric.

golöwva, *f., pl.* **-ow,** beacon: ?Carn Galva, place-name, unless **golva.**

golöwy, *vb.,* to give light, lighten, enlighten, illuminate, shine, flare up, B.M., C.W.: *fatel usy ow-colowy,* how it lightens, Lh.

golöwyjyon (*golvygyen*), *m.,* radiance, glory, B.M. 3681: perhaps pl. of **golöwys,** used as abst. sing.

golöwylyon, *pl.,* spangles, sparkling fish-scales on clothing (D. "golowillions").

golöwyn, *m., pl.* **-new,** ray, beam of light (W.).

golöwys (*golowas* Lh.), *m.,* splendour, glory, illumination; lightning, Lh.: *g. an howl,* sunbeam, ray, Lh.; this coincides with *golowys* used as pl. of *golow* O.M. 34, 52.

†gols, *m.,* hair of the head, C. Voc., *fex* Aelfric: *g. an Werghes,* maiden-hair fern (W.).

golsowes, see **goslowes.**

†golüsak (C. Voc. *wuludoc*), *adj.,* wealthy, rich, *welig* Aelfric: replaced by **rych.**

golva (C. Voc. *guillua*), *f.,* night-watch, vigil, *waecce* Aelfric; watching-place, look-out; Penolva, Pednolver, place-name.

golvan (*gulvan* Lh.), *m., pl.* **-as,** sparrow, C. Voc.: *g. -ge,* hedge-sparrow, Lh..

golwyth, *m.,* feastentide (B.).

goly, *m., pl.* **lÿow,** wound, sore.

gōlya, *vb.,* to sail (B.).

gōlya, *vb.,* to feast, celebrate a feast, make holiday, banquet, give a feast to: *ef nefra ny vyth golys,* never shall he be feasted, B.M. 3610.

golÿa, *vb.,* to wound, hurt: *tebelwolyes,* badly wounded, B.M. 2490.

gōlyas, *m.,* vigil, watching, keeping awake; *vb.,* to keep watch, stay awake.

gōlyer, *m., pl.* **-yoryon,** sentinel, watchman (W.).

golÿth (C. Voc. *guleit*), *m., pl.* **-yon,** roast meat, *braede* Aelfric: *g. bowyn,* steak, *g. davas,* chop, *g. mogh,* rasher (W.).

gōn (*goyn*, C. Voc. *guein*), *f.*, *pl.* **-ow**, sheath, scabbard.
gōn (*gūn* Lh.), *m.*, *pl.* **-ow**, gown, monk's habit, robe : *g. hyr.* priest's cassock, B.M. 1902.
gon, *m.*, *pl.* **-nys**, gun (as E., B.M.) : *g. mūr,* cannon.
gonador (*gunnadar* Lh.), *m.*, *pl.* **-yon**, sower.
gonedhaf, etc., see **gonys**
gonesegeth, *f.*, agriculture, culture, service (W., B.).
gonesek (C. Voc. *gonidoc*), *m.*, *pl.* **-sogyon**, serving-man, servant, workman, *then* Aelfric.
gonyow, see **gūn.**
gonys, *m.*, work, service, tillage; mine-working (D. "gunnies").
gonys (Late *gunnes*), *vb.*, to work, serve, till, cultivate : *g. has*, to sow ; *gonedh-* is stem ; 1 s. pres.-fut. *gonedhaf*, 3 s. pres.-fut. *goneth* ; 3 s. subj. *gonetho* ; 3 s. plupf. *gonethsa* ; p. pt. *gonedhys.*
gonysyas (C. Voc. *gunit(h)iat*), *m.*, *pl.* **gonesysy, -yjy** (*-ugy*), workman, labourer, farm-worker : **†***g. erow*, field-worker, *aecerman* Aelfric.
gor-, see Appendix II.
***gōr**, *adj.*, broody (of hen), hatched (of egg); *m.*, suppuration, hatching (W., B.).
gora, gorra (C. Voc. *guyraf*, Lh. *gorha*), *col.*, hay, *hig, gaers* Aelfric.
gora, see **gorra.**
gorar(gh)anja, *vb.*, to silver over (W.).
gorbesky, *vb.*, to overfeed (W.).
†gorbollak (C. Voc. *gurbulloc*), *adj.*, mad, irrational, out of one's senses, *wod* Aelfric; *m.*, *pl.* **-ogyon**, madman (W. *gorffwyllog.*)
gordevy, *vb.*, to overgrow, grow rank (W.) : also **gorthevy.**
gordheweth, *m.*, conclusion ; as *adv.*, at last, finally, definitely, conclusively.
gordhya (rarely *gordhy, gordha*, C.W. *gworthya*, Late *gworria*), *vb.*, to honour, worship, adore, pay respect to (O.E. *wordhian*) : *dh* becomes *th* in 3 s. pres.-fut. *gorth*, 3 s. subj. *gorthyo*, etc., but *th* is lost before *s* ; *dhe voy denvyth ny-m-gor'sa, kyn facyen mur*, nobody would respect me the more, though I were to boast a lot, P.C. 1679 ; *rak na-wor'sys*, because thou didst not honour, O.M. 1867.
gordhyans (Late *gorrians*), *m.*, worship, honour, glory.
gorēr, *m.*, *pl.* **-yow**, adverb (W.).
gores, *m.*, release, giving up, deliverance (W., B.) : same word as **gweres**, but used in sense otherwise lost in Cor. ; see **enewores.**
gorenys, *f.*, *pl.* **-nesow**, peninsula (W.,B.).
gorfals, *adj.*, superabundant (M.B.) : see **gor-, pals.**
gorfalster, *m.*, suberabundance, glut (M.B.).
gorfalsterek, *adj.*, lavish, overabounding (M.B.).
gorfalsterekhē, *vb.*, to overabound (M.B. *gourfauterecat*) : as **berhē.**
gorfen (*gor-, pen*), *m.*, end, conclusion.
gorfenna, *vb.*, to come to an end, make an end of, finish, conclude, O.M. 228, Lh. : miswritten *y worlene*, P.C. 2111.
gorgē (*gor-, kē*), *m.*, *pl.* **-ow**, low or broken-down hedge (D. "gurgy," "gurgo".
gorgūl, *vb.*, to be careful to do strictly or do before everything : 2 s. imp. *gorgwra*, O.M. 987.
gorgȳs, *m.*, distrust, suspicion, R.D. 1499, 1501 : ?for **gorthgrēs** *f.*, cf. **dorgȳs.**
†gorhān (*gor-, cān*), *f.*, *pl.* **-ow**, incantation (W.) : see **gorhenyas.**
†gorhana, *vb.*, to enchant : as **cana.**
gorhel (C. W. *gorthell*, Late *gurroll, goral*, etc.), *m.*, *pl.* **-olyon** (*-ollion*, J. Boson), ship, vessel, ark : ***g.** *tān*, steamer : see **lūf-gorhel.**
gorhēl, *adj.*, lavish, over-generous.
gorhemmyn (C. Voc. *gurhemin, gor-, kemmyn*, Late *gorebmyn, garebma*), *m.*, *pl.* **-ow**, command, edict, bidding, injunction ; pl. also greetings, compliments (B.) ; *vb.*, to command, bid, order ; send greetings, J. Boson: 3 s. pret. *gorhemmynys, ymons-y ow-corhemmyn dheugh-why*, they send remembrances to you.
gorhemmynadow (B.M., C.W. *gormenadow*), *m.*, **commandment,** injunction.
†gorhenyas (C. Voc. *wurcheniat*), *m.*, *pl.* **-ysy**, enchanter.
†gorher (C. Voc. *(en)gurbor* for *gurhor*, Lh. *gorwer*), *m.*, *pl.* **-yow**, cover, lid ; paten, *huseldisc* Aelfric : i.e. *g. an kelegel*, cover of the chalice.
gorheras (*gwarhaz*, roof of mouth, Lh., *gueres*, horse-cloth, Pryce), *m.*, covering.
gorhery, *vb.*, to cover, hide up, put a cover or lid on : 2 pl. imp. *gorhereugh* (*gwarrow*

Lh.), 3 s. pret. *-as* (*goreras* Kerew).

†**gorhok(g)** (C. Voc. *gurhhog*), *m.*, *pl.* **-ogyon,** great-great-great-grandfather, *fifta faeder*, Aelfric: see **dyhok(g)**.

gorholeth (in verse *go·rholeth*), *m.*, requisition, bidding, asking, demand, request, O.M. 675, 2841.

gorholy, *vb.*, to require, ask (W. *gor-*, *holi*).

gorlenky, *vb.*, to gluttonize (W.): as **lenky**.

gorlenwel, *vb.*, to over-fill (W., B.): as **lenwel**.

gorlesky, *vb.*, to over-burn, scorch (W.,B.): as **lesky**.

gorlosten, *f.*, *pl.* **-nas**, earwig (W., B.).

†**gorlewen**, *f.*, the west, Lh.: though from Welsh, this seems likely to have been O. Cor. also: see **berlewen**.

gorlün, *adj.*, over-full (W.).

gorlywa, *vb.*, to over-colour, exaggerate (W.).

***gorm**, *adj.*, brown, dun (W., O.B.).

gormel (no inf. ending), *vb.*, praise, laud, B.M. 1420: miswritten "gornvall" with *nv* for *me* C.W. 711; "gormollow" for *gormeleugh* Gw.; 3 s. pret. *gormolas*.

gormola, for **gormoleth**, *m.*, praise, laudation, triumph, glory, Lh., Gw.

gormoledhüs, *adj.*, triumphant, jubilant; glorious (W.).

gorow, *m.* and *col.*, male.

gorowra, *vb.*, to gild over, cover with gold: *gorowrys y gernygow*, with little gilded horns, B.M. 3396.

gorquytha (*gor-*, *gwytha*), *vb.*, to be very careful or mindful, mind: requires no prep., *gorquyth y gara*, be mindful to love him: see **gorra**, **gwȳth**.

gorra, see **gora**.

gorra, **gora**, *vb.*, to place, put, set, lay, send, take, accompany, induct, lead, drive: *g. dhe dhyscans*, to educate: *g. wyth a*, take care of (M.E. *set keep of*); *g. wyth dhe*, take care to: see **gwȳth**.

gorryth (C. Voc. *gurruid*; *gour*, *rȳth*), *m.*, male, man: *g. wow*, hermaphrodite (D. "gallywow"): see **benenrȳth**.

gorsaf, *m.*, station, standstill, fixed state (W., B.).

gorseth, *f.*, *pl.* **-edhow**, meeting of bards, lit. seat, throne (W.).

gorth, *adj.*, opposed, contrary, stubborn, stiff-necked; *prefix*, adverse, against, see Appendix II.

gortheby (*-yby*, Gw. *gweryby*, *gorryby*), *vb.*, to reply, respond, answer, counter, retaliate: used with or without *dhe*, to; 3 s. pres.-fut. *gorthyp*; 3 s. pret. *gorthebys*; in verse often *go·rtheby*.

gorthenep, *m.*, reverse side (W., B.).

Gortheren, **mȳs-G.** (wrongly *Gorephan* Lh.), *m.*, July, B.M. 2070, 2194.

gorthevy, *vb.*, to overgrow, grow rank (W.): variant **gordevy**.

gorthewer (*gorthuer*, C. Voc. *gurthuwer*, Late *gothewer*, Lh. *gudhihuar*, *dh* for *th*), *m.*, evening; *adj.*, late; *adv.*, this coming evening: *yn-newer g.*, late last night.

gorthewlel, *vb.*, to broadcast grain (B.).

gorthfōs, *f.*, *pl.* **-ow**, bulwark (W. *gwrthglawdd*).

†**gorthfyl** (C. Voc. *gorthfel*; *gorth*, *mȳl*), *m.*, *pl.* **-as**, snake.

gorthgrēs, *f.*, distrust, counter-belief (W.).

gorthter, *m.*, obstinacy, stubbornness.

gorthroghya, *vb.*, bathe, immerse, plunge under water (W., B.).

gorthyp (Late *gorryb*), *m.*, *pl. and abst.* **-thebow**, reply, rejoinder, answer, response.

gortos, *vb.*, to stop, wait, delay, tarry, await, abide the coming of, make a stand against: 2 pl. imp. *gorteugh*; 3 s. pres.-fut, 2 s. imp., 3 s. impf. subj. *gorta*; *gorta, ty dhen, dhym omma!* Stop now, thou man, when I tell thee! B.M. 3840 (*dhym* used as with **tewel**, q.v.); *ny-s-gorta myl den-ervys*, a thousand armed men would not withstand it, B.M. 3947.

gorty (*gour*, *ty*), *m.*, husband, man of the house.

gorūghel (*gorewhal* Lh.), *adj.*, sublime, supreme (W.).

gorvennas, *vb.*, to vie, rival (W., B.): as **mennas**.

gorvyn, *m.*, envy, jealousy, rivalship (W. B.).

gorwedha, see **growedha**.

gorwel, *m.*, horizon (W., B.).

gorweles, *vb.*, to see beyond; *m.*, mental or supernatural vision (W., B.).

gorweth, see **groweth**.

gorwyth, see **gora**, **gwȳth**.

gorwyw, *adj.*, super-excellent (W.).

gory, *vb.*, to brood, hatch eggs (W., B.).

gōs (*goys*, C. Voc. *guit*, C.W. *goos*, Lh. *gūdzh*), *m.*, blood, gore, connection by descent; *gos yu y ben*, his head is (covered in) blood; *ow g. nessa*, my next-of-kin; see **ünwōs**.

gosa, *vb.*, to make bloody: p. pt. *gosys*,

bloodstained, M.C. 219.

gosek, gojek (Late *gooshak*), *adj.*, bloody, sanguine; *m.*, blood-spot: *g.-gwy(th)*, black spot caused by pinch (D. "gwidgy-gwee.")

†**goscor**, retinue, household, *hiwraeden, hired* Aelfric: old var. of **coscar**, q.v., as V. *koskor, goskor*, W. *cosgordd, gosgordd*.

goscotter, *m.*, shelter, shade, O.M. 361: see **goskes**.

goskejwyth, *col.* shade-trees, bower, hedge (W.).

goskes, *m.*, shelter, cover, shade, shadow (W., B,).

goskesek, *adj.*, shady, sheltered, brànchy, bushy (W., B.).

goskesy, *vb.*, to shelter, put under cover, shade, O.M. 1719.

gōsky, *m.*, *pl.* **gōscün**, bloodhound (W., B.).

goslowes, golsowes (Late *gosowas, gorowas*; *gor-* and *selow*, W. *sylwi*, B. *selaou*), *vb.*, to hear, listen to, pay attention, hearken: 2 s. imp. *goslow*, 3 s. imp. *goslewys, golsewys*, 2 pl. imp. *gosloweugh, golsoweugh*; usually takes *orth* as prep., sometimes *dhe*, sometimes no prep.

goslowyas, golsowyas, *m.*, *pl.* -ysy, hearer, pl. auditory, audience (B.).

gosogen, gojogen (*gudzhugen* Lh.), *f.*, *pl.* **-now**, hog's-pudding, black-pudding.

gosrüth, *adj.*, blood-red (W.).

gossen, *f.*, rust, ferruginous earth (D. "gossan").

gostyth (*gustyth*), *adj.*, subject, obedient, submissive.

gōth, *m.*, pride, haughtiness: originally "rage," as W. *gwyth*, but already Lat. *suberbia, modignys* Aelfric, in C. Voc., cf. Lat. *ferocitas* with same dual meanings.

gōth (*goyth*, C. Voc. *guit*), *f.*, *pl.* **godhow**, goose: Polgooth, goosepond; Lower an Gothow, geese-garden, place-names.

gōth, **gō'**, (C. Voc. *god*), *f.*, *pl.* **godhas**, mole, *wandewurpe* Aelfric; in sing. usually *go 'dhor* (Lh. *gūdhăr, gūdh-dhăr*) earth-mole, for distinction.

gōth, gwȳth (C. Voc. *guid*), *f.*, *pl.* **gwȳthy**, vein, *aeddre* Aelfric; conduit, stream, channel: *gwythy bras*, arteries; *lyf-woth*, flood-stream, O.M. 1093 (gender made to follow first word, *lyf*, m.).

gōth, gwȳth (C. Voc. *guit, goit*), *adj.*, wild, fierce; uncultivated, untamed.

gothek, *f.*, *pl.* **-egy**, place abounding in streams (B.).

†**gothen** (C. Voc. *goden*), *f.*, *pl.* **-thnow**, *d.* **dyw-wothen**, sole of foot: †*g.-tros* (*g. truit*), foot-sole, C. Voc., *fotwylm* Aelfric; *g. -eskys*, shoe-sole (W.).

gothfos. see **gothvos**.

†**gōthfyl, gwȳthfyl** (C. Voc. *guitfil*, Late *(g)withel*), *m.*, *pl.* **-as**, wild beast: *wildeor* Aelfric; *g.-lonek*, lion, "wild beast of the bush" or "bushy beast," *withellonack* Borlase.

gōthfys, *col.* honeysuckle, woodbine (W., B.).

gōthkenyn (C. Voc. *goitkenin*), *col.* crow-garlic lit wild leek, *crawan leac* Aelfric.

gothvos, -fos, govos (Lh. *godhaz*, N. Boson *guthvaz*), *irreg. vb.*, to know, have knowledge, know how, be able: *g. a*, be aware of, know about; *g. gras*, to be grateful; in 2 imp. *gothfyth, -fedheugh*, beware, mind (as M.E. *wit thou well*); for parts see Table in Appendix VIII.

gothvos, -fos, *m.*, knowledge, ability: *dhe'm g.*, as far as I know, or can.

gothys, gothüs, *adj.*, proud, haughty.

go to! *interj.*, come! go to! B.M. 961 (M.E.).

goumman (*gūmman, gūbman* Lh), *m.*, seaweed.

gour (*gor*, C. Voc. *gur*, Late *goore*), *m.*, *pl.* **tüs**, man, husband, *wer, waepman* Aelfric: *g. an chy*, master of the house; **g. efan*, yeoman, freeman (W.); *g. pryas*, bridegroom, C. Voc.; *g. yowynk*, youth, adolescent, C. Voc.; *g. gwedhow*, widower.

gourgȳ, *m.*, *pl.* **gourgün**, male dog, man-dog, ? werewolf (D. "mazed as a gurgy).''

gourhēs, *m.*, fathom, 6ft., lit. man's length (W., B.).

gourhēsa, *vb.*, to fathom (W., B.).

gouroleth, *m.*, manliness (W.).

gouryl, *adj.*, virile, manly (W.).

govedhow, *adj.*, tipsy (B.).

govel (C. Voc. *gofail*), *f.*, *pl.* **-yow**, smithy, blacksmith's shop: see **gōf**.

govel-forn, see **gelforn**.

govelya, *vb.*, to forge iron (W., B.).

govenek, *m.*, *pl. and abst.* **-ygyon**, desire, petition, wish, hope, request, O.M. 453, B.M. 2900.

gover (C. Voc. *guuer*), *m. pl.* **-ow**, brook, stream, rivulet, *ridh* Aelfric; *g. -fenten*, well-spring, O.M. 1845.

goverek, *adj.*, abounding in streams.
goverek (*go-*, *merek*), *adj.*, snivelling: Wella G., "snuffling Billy" ("Will the Snob-nose," Tonkin), old nick-name.
goveren, *f.*, *pl.* **-now**, brooklet (W., B.).
go·vernans (*-nens*), *m.*, government, sway, rule, B.M. 256 (M.E. *governaunce*).
go·vernour, *m.*, *pl.* **-s**, governor (M.E.).
governya (*go·verna* C.W.), *vb.*, to govern, rule, regulate, arrange, provide for, control, O.M., P.C. (M.E.).
govery, *vb.*, to drip, run slowly (W.).
goves, see **gōf.**
govyjyon, *m.*, sorrow, care, regret.
govyn, *m.*, question; (*goffen*, *gōfen*, *gophen* Lh., *goofen* Scawen), *vb.*, to ask, demand, require, inquire: takes *orth* as prep. "of"; 3 s. pret. *govynnys*, *-as*; 3 s. plupf. *govensa*; 2 s. pres.-fut. with suffixed pron. (*pandra*) *woventa*; in verse accent is often on the last syllable, but Tonkin's spelling *gophidn* (P.) is misread from Lhuyd's *uar'a go phidn* for *er-aga-fyn*, p. 252.
govynnadow, *m.*, request, question, demand, asking, P.C. 599, in verse *govy·nnadow*.
govys, *m.*, regard, account, behalf: used with *a*, of, and poss. prons.; *a'm g. -vy*, on my account, etc.
gow, *m.*, *pl.* **-yow**, lie, falsehood; *adj.*, false, untrue: *hep wow*, *heb ow*, indeed, lit. without a lie.
†**gowdhan** (C. Voc. *goudhan*), *m.*, *pl.* **-as**, clothes-moth grub, mite, *modhdhe* Aelfric.
gowegneth, *m.*, falsehood, untruth, lying, R.D. 906.
gowek (C. Voc. *gouhoc*) *adj.*, lying: *m.*, *pl.* **-wygyon**, liar, lying flatterer, *leas olecere* Aelfric.
gowleverel, *vb.*, to lie: as **leverel**.
†**gowleveryas** (C. Voc. *gouleveriat*), *m.*, *pl.* **-ysy**, teller of lies, untruthful person, *unsodhsagol* Aelfric.
gow-lȳ, *m.*, *pl.* **-ow**, false oath, perjury.
gow-lȳa, *vb.*, to swear falsely, commit perjury, B.M. 3740.
†**gowyles** (C. Voc. *gouiles*), *col.*, ?field-gentian, Lat. *anadonia*, *feldwyrt*, Aelfric.
***gōy**, *vb.*, to digest (B.).
grabalyas, *vb.*, to grapple, clutch: *prevyon ow-crabalyas*, clinging vermin (*crabaliaz*, translated "worms creeping like crabs," Pryce): see **grabel.**
grabel, *m.*, *pl.* **-blys**, grappling-iron, grapnel, R.D. (D. "grabble," M.E. *graple*).
gradhya, *vb.*, to grade, graduate (W.).
graghell (*grachel* Lh.), *f.*, *pl.* **-low**, pile, heap (D. "grackle").
graghella, *vb.*, to gather into a heap (B.).
grammaryan (*gramarion*, *m.*, *pl.* **-s**, grammarian, B.M. 92 (M.E.).
grammer, *m.*, grammar, B.M. 20 (M.E.).
grās, **grāth** (*grays*, *grayth*, *grac*), *m.*, *pl.* **grassys** (*-yes*. C.W., *gorzehez* Lh.), thanks, gratitude, grace, good opinion, favour, virtue (M.E.): used in sing. and pl. as meaning "thanks" (as M.E. *graces*), *merastawhy*, *merastadu*, late contractions of *mur ras dhywhy*, *mur ras dhe Dhew*, much thanks to you, to God; *aswonvos*, *gothvos*, *g. dhe*, to thank (M.E. *to con thank*), *mur r. a-wodhon nefra dhywhy a 'gas bolunjeth*, we shall always be most grateful to you for your intention, B.M. 309; *dhys y- whon g. rak dha dhesyr*, I thank thee for thy wish, R.D. 869; in mutation it is difficult to distinguish the sing. from **rās**, *pl.* **-ow**, q.v.; see also **drog-gras**, **hardygras**, **yfla gras.**
grassa, *vb.*, to thank, give thanks (M.E. *grace*): takes *dhe*; 2 s. imp. *grassa.*
grassyans (*g o r s e a n s* Keigwin), *m.*, thanksgiving, thanks, grace.
grassyes, **-cyes** (*grassiis*, etc., B.M.), *adj.*, gracious, benign (M.E. *gracyous*): see **dyscrassyes**, **ungrassyes.**
†**grath** (C. Voc. *grat*), *m.*, *pl.* **-adhow**, step, stair; degree, grade: replaced by **degrē**, **grē.**
grāth, variant of **grās.**
grava (for *gravath*, Lh. *gravar*), *m.*, *pl.* **-vathow**, barrow, litter, palanquin; *g. dhywla*, hand-barrow, gurry; *g.-ros*, wheelbarrow; *g.-deuvargh*, horse-borne litter.
gravya (C. Voc. *gravio*), *vb.*, to carve, cut out of stone, engrave, chase, scrape: 2 s. imp. *grāf*; p. pt. *gravyes*, *-ys*.
†**gravyor** (C. Voc. *gravior*), *m.*, *pl.* **-yon**, sculptor, carver, engraver, *grafere* Aelfric.
***grē**, *m.*, regard, favour, liking (M.E. *gree*): *kemeres yn g.*, take in good part.
grē, *f.*, *pl.* **-yow**, flock, herd, stud: see **grēlyn.**
grē, *m.*, status, rank, degree (M.E. *gree*): "degree," C.W. 51, 59, seems for *gre*; *nep a-vo y'n moyha g. a-vyth an brassa hynwys herwyth nep a-vo yn le*, He who

is in the highest rank is called the greatest according to anyone who is in a lesser, P.C. 777.

***gregga**, *vb*., to cackle (W., B.).

Grēca, *m*., Greek language, Greek, N. Boson, see **Grew** ; *m*., *pl*. **-kys**, Greeks.

gref, *m*., *pl*. **-evys**, grief, grudge, complaint, ailment, harm, distress (M.E. *greef*) : *kerdhes hep g. my a-yl*, I can walk easily; *gweres dhyn orth agan g.*, aid us against our illness.

greffya, see **grevya**.

grefons, grevons, *m*., complaint, grievance, illness, B.M. 1000 (M.E. *grevaunce*).

***grek**, *m*., cackling (W., B.).

grēlyn (C. Voc. *grelin*), *m*., horse-pond, cattle-pond, *seadh* Aelfric.

grēont, *m*., *pl*. **-ons**, greyhound, B.M. 3220 (M.E. *grehond*).

grevya (*greffya*, Late *greevia*), *vb*., to grieve, aggrieve, afflict, oppress, distress, make ill, bear or weigh down (M.E. *greve*) : 3 s. pres.-fut. *grēf*; *yma hun orth-ow-g.*, sleep is lying heavy on me, O.M. 1921.

Grew, *m*., Greek language (M.E.): ?mistakenly written for *gwreugh* (rhyme *deu*), R.D. 2464.

grolyak, *adj*., cracked-voiced, craking ; *m*., complaining person (D. "grulliack," B. *groilh*).

grōm (*grome*), *m*., *pl*. **-mys**, groom, B.M. 2548 (M.E.).

***gromyal**, *vb*., growl (W., B.).

gromercy (*grant merci*, Late *gramercy*, *gura-massi*, Lh. MS.), *m*., *interj*., thank you, great thanks, gramercy (M.E. *graunt mercy*).

gron, *m*., mass, bundle, bunch, heap: *gyllys yn g.*, all huddled up, contracted, B.M. 542 (as B. *grounn*, W. *grwn*).

grond, *m*., ground, bottom, ground level, B.M. (M.E.): *g. beaten*, "beat" land (its sward pared and burnt to manure it), Gw.

grondya (*gronndya*), *vb*., to found, lay foundations, ground, base (M.E. *grounde*).

grōnt (*graunt*), *m*., grant, leave, permission (M.E. *graunt*).

grontya, gronta (*grantya*), *vb*., to grant (M.E. *graunten*): 2 s. imp., 3s. pres.-fut. *grōnt*, *a-wrōnt* ; 3 s. plupf. *grontsa*.

grot (*groyt*). *m*., *pl*. **-ys**, groat, B.M. 3326 (M.E.).

grow (C. Voc. *grou*), *col*., gravel, grit, coarse sand, *sandceosel* Aelfric (D. "graow") ; *f*., pebble-beach (W., B.).

growdyr, *m*., gravelly granite subsoil, scouring-sand (D. "growder").

gröwedha, gorwedha, *vb*., to lie down : *gorwedha* is a late form, but it may have been in continual use, as it agrees with W. and B. ; 3 s. pres.-fut., 2 s. imp. *groweth*, *a-wroweth* ; 3 s. subj. *-tho* ; plupf. *-thsa*.

gröweth, gorweth, *m*., lying posture : with *a* and poss. pron., *a'y wrou eth*, etc., lying down.

gröwethva, *f*., resting-place, couch, lair.

***growsen**, *f*., *col*. **grows**, gooseberry (W.).

growjyon, *m. pl*., dregs, grouts (D. "growjions," "grushions," from E.)

growynek, *adj*., granite, gravelly (W.).

growynen, *f*., pebble, grit; *pl*. **-ynnow**, *col*. **growyn** (O.M. 2756), pebbles, gravel: *men-g.*, granite.

grüf, (*grueff*, B.M.), *m*., face, front of body (M.E. *gruf*, *grof*, whence "grovelling," M.E. *groflyngys*).

grügek, *adj*., heathy; *f*., heath-grown place (W., B.).

grüglon, *m*., *pl*. **-ow**, heather-bush (D. "griglans") : see **lōn**, m.

grügyar (*grigear* Carew), *f*., *pl*. **-yēr**, *dim*. **-yēryk** (*gurgirik* Lh.), partridge, O.M. 1203 : see **grük(g)**, **yar**.

†grügys (C. Voc. *grugis*), *m*., *pl*. **-ow**, girdle, belt : **g. run*, penitential hair-cloth.

grügysa, *vb*., to gird, girdle (W.).

grük(g), *col*., heath, ling.

grünen (C. Voc. *gronen*), *f*., *col*. **grün**, grain, berry, kernel, *cyrnel* Aelfric ; hard roe of fish (D. "grean").

grürgh (*grue(r)gh*), *adj*., ? tiny, innocent, harmless : *fleghes g. ha byghan*, B.M. 1692, *fleghes g.*, 1705, *flogh g.* 1776.

†grüth (C. Voc. *grud*). *f*., *pl*. **-üdhyow**, jaw, cheek, *hleor*, Aelfric.

grüthyl, see **gül**.

gryghyas, goryhyas, *m*., whinnying (*a kruhiaz* Lh. for *ow-cryghyas*) ; *vb*., to neigh, whinny : as M.B. *gouriziat*, B. *gouric'hal*, *grizinka*, W. *gweryru*.

grÿja, *m*., starry ray (fish), D. "greeja".

gryll, *m*., *pl*. **-as**, cricket : *g. -vor*, spider-crab, D. "griggle" (in B., sea cray-fish).

***grÿs**, *m*., *pl*. **-ys**, step, stair (M.E. *grees*, *greces*, pl., W. *grisiau*), see **grath**.

grysla (*grisla* Lh.), *vb*., to grin, show the teeth (D.E. "grizzle").

grysyl (*grisyl*), *adj*., grisly, frightful (M.E.),

gū, gew (*giu, guw,* C. Voc. *guyu*), *m., pl.* **-yow,** lance, javelin, spear: see **gȳa.**

gūccow, see **cūcū.**

***gūdhūgen,** *f., pl.* **-now.** neck-cloth (W., B.).

***gūdhūk,** *m., pl.* **-ūgow,** neck, throat (W., B.).

†gūhȳen (C. Voc. *guhien*), *f., col.* **gūhȳ,** wasp.

†gūhyth (C. Voc. *guhit*), *f. pl.* **-hydhow,** daughter-in-law, *snoru* Aelfric.

gül, güthyl, gwrüthyl (*grüthyl,* Late *gwythel, gwȳl*), *irreg. vb.,* to do, make, commit, accomplish, compose, cause, make into: *g. dhe dhen g.,* cause a man to do; *g. dhe wul,* have done, cause to be made; *my ny-wodhyen gul dodho,* I could not cope with him, C.W. 1017; *an jyst yu gwrys crows,* the beam that is made into a cross, P.C. 2583; *gul dhym aswonvos,* to give me to understand; *my a-wra,* I will (do so), can be used in reference to an unnamed vb.; *pand 'wrama ganso-ef,* what have I to do with him?; for parts see Table In Appendix VIII.

güllа, *m., pl.* **-lys,** gull: *ny a-wruk gweles an carnow mayth usy an gullys ha'n ydhyn-mor erel ow-cul aga nythow,* we saw the rocks where the gulls and other sea-birds make their nests (Lh.); from E.D. "gooll," see **gwylan.**

gül wȳs (*gweel weez*), *m.,* make-believe, pretence; **gül wȳs,** *vb.,* to make believe, pretend, N. Boson (Late, from D.E. "makewise").

gūn, gōn, *f., pl.* **gonyow,** down, plain, unenclosed land, *feld* Aelfric.

gūnblüf, *col.,* cotton-grass (W.).

gūnran, *f., pl.* **-now,** moorland part of a parish or property; see **morrep.**

gurys, see **gwrȳs.**

gūsen (C. Voc. *guiden,* Lh. *gūzen*), *f., pl.* **-now,** faggot-bind of withy, *widhdhe* Aelfric.

gustel, *m., pl.* **-tlow,** riot, tumult (W.).

gustla, *vb.,* to riot, revolt, raise a tumult, M.C. 249.

gūsygen (*guzigan* Lh.), *f., pl.* **-now,** bladder, blister (*D.* "goosygen").

güthyl, see **gül.**

†gutrēl (C. Voc. *gut(re)hel*), *m., pl.* **-trolow,** furniture, *yddisc* Aelfric: O.B. *(ti)gutrel.*

Gwāf (C. Voc. *goyf*), *m., pl.* **gwavow** (Late *-vyow* Gw.), Winter.

gwagel (*wagel* Ray), *f., pl.* **-as,** great skua.

gwagla (*gwak, lē*), *m.,* vacancy, void, hiatus, vacuum (W.).

gwagva, *f.,* vacuum (W.).

gwāk(g), *adj.,* empty, void, vacant, hungry, weak, ineffective, vain; *m., pl.* **-agyon,** vacuum, void, empty space.

gwakhē', *vb.,* to empty, make void: as **berhē.**

gwakter, *m.,* emptiness, vacancy, vanity (W., B.).

gwal, *m., pl.* **-low,** wall, rampart: usually replaced by **fōs,** but kept in place-names.

gwalgh (pr. *gwolh*), *m.,* satiety, repletion (W., B., D. "wolla," a bunch of rich ore).

gwalgha, *vb.,* satiate, cloy, stuff with food (B.).

gwall, *m., pl.* **-ow,** mischance, accident, lack, neglect, defect: *dre wall,* accidentally, P.C. 1180.

gwan, *f., pl.* **-ow,** stab, sting, prick, piercing: *g. spern* (miswritten *spyr*), pricking of thorns, M.C. 205.

gwan (C. Voc. *guan,* Late *gwadn*), *adj.,* weak, feeble, lowly, mean, poor; as prefix to nouns, bad: **†***g. a skyans,* mind-sick, insane, C. Voc., *gewitseoc* Aelfric.

gwana, *vb.,* to stab, sting, prick, pierce, gore, transfix, spike, spear: p. pt. *gwenys.*

gwander, *m.,* weakness, debility, infirmity.

gwandra (pr. *gwon-*), *vb.,* to wander, stroll, stray, ramble, walk about (E.): *saf, ha gas cavow dhe wandra,* give over, and let sorrow slide, lit. go roaming, C.W. 1243.

gwan-dȳak, *m., pl.* **-ȳogow,** bad manager, lit. poor farmer, C.W. 920.

***gwanek,** *f., pl.* **gwenyk,** wave (W.).

gwanethen (pr. *gwon-*), *f.,* wheat-grain, *col.* **gwaneth,** wheat: *g. Frynk,* buckwheat (Lh. MS.); see **bara.**

gwanhē', *vb.,* to weaken, enfeeble: as **berhē.**

gwan-ober, *m.,* crime, ill-deed, C.W.

gwan-worty, *m.,* adulterer, bad husband.

gwan-wrē'ty (*guadngurti* Lh.), *f.,* adulteress, bad wife.

gwan-wycor, *m., pl.* **-yon,** sorry dealer, bad trader, M.C. 40.

gwar, *adj.,* see **whar.**

†gwar (C. Voc. *guar*) *f., pl.* **-row,** neck, nape, bend of neck: *serth y war,* stiffnecked.

gwara (C. Voc. *waroe*), *col.,* ware, goods, merchandize for sale (O.E.), *waru* Aelfric: *w* in C. Voc. often stands for *gw,* but *waroe* may come straight from O.E., though *gwara* is the M. Cor. form, P.C. 318.

gwarak (C. Voc. *guarac*), *f.*, *pl.* **-regow,** bow, arch; †folded document, diploma, *boga* Aelfric: *g. an glaw*, rainbow, *ow g.*, my (rain)bow, O.M. 1244; see **camneves.**

gwaregor, *m.*, *pl.* **-yon,** archer, bowman (B.): see **sēthor.**

gwarhas, see **gorhas.**

gwarnya (pr. *gwōr-*), *vb.*, to warn, notify, caution, inform, admonish (M.E. *warne*).

gwarnyans, *m.*, warning.

gwartha (pr. *gwortha*, for *gwarthaf*, Late *gwarra*), *m.*, *pl.* **-avyon,** top, summit; *adj.*, upper: see **a-wartha.**

gwarthek (Late *gwarrek*, *gwarrhog*, Lh.), *col.*, horned cattle: *g. godra*, milch-kine.

gwarthevya, *vb.*, to dominate, rule as paramount.

gwarthevyades, *f.*, *pl.* **-ow,** suzeraine, lady paramount.

gwarthevyas, *m.*, *pl.* **-ysy,** overlord, suzerain, lord paramount, B.M. 7.

***gwarthowl,** *f.*, *pl.* **-ow,** stirrup (W.).

gwary (*gware* Lh.)., *m.*, *pl.* **ÿow,** play, game, pastime, fun, sport, dramatic show: prefixed as *g.-kylys*, skittles, *g.-pelyow*, bowling, etc.; Lhuyd's *hwary* (*whary*) is not a Cornish form, though like W., B.).

gwary, *vb.*, to play, act: p. pt. *gwarÿes*: 2 s. imp., 3 s. pres.-fut. *gwary*.

gwarya, *vb.*, to stoop, bend, fold (W., B.).

gwary-cān, *m.*, *pl.* **gwarÿow-c.,** opera, (B.).

gwary-dons (*guare dauns*, Borlase), *m.*, *pl.* **gwarÿow-d.,** ball, dance.

gwarÿer, *m.*, *pl.*, **-ÿoryon,** player, actor.

gwary-jy, *m.*, *pl.* **-ow,** play-house, theatre.

gwary-mȳr (*guirremear* Scawen), *m.*, spectacle, pageant, miracle-play lit. play-sight.

gwary-myrkel, *m.*, miracle-play (M.E. *pley of miracle*).

gwaryva, *f.*, *pl.* **-ow,** theatre (W., B.).

gwas (C. Voc. *guas*), *m.*, *pl.* **-gwesyon,** youth, servant, man, fellow: prefixed or suffixed, as in **gwas-gof, cothwas;** *pup g.*, *yn kettep g.*, down to the last man, everyone of them; *an gwella g.*, the best man; †*g.-bathor*, minter, coiner, C. Voc.; by a muddle in C. Voc. Aelfric's *mynetere*, coiner, and *maenigtiwe*, clever, are translated together as *guas bathor fur*.

***gwasarn,** *m.*, litter for beasts to lie on (W., B.).

gwasca (*gwasga* Lh. from B.), *vb.*, to squeeze, nip, press (W., B.): see **gweskel,** with changed meaning.

gwasek, *adj.*, slavish; *m.*, *pl.* **-sogyon,** servile person (W.).

gwas-gof, *m.*, *pl.* **gwesÿon-gof** or **-goves,** smith's servant, smith-fellow, P.C. 2479.

gwask, *f.*, press, pressure (W., B.).

gwasonÿeth, *f.*, homage, service feudal servitude (B.): *gwasanaeth*, bondage, Gw., P., is Welsh.

gwastas, *adj.*, level, smooth: Noon Wastas, *an un wastas*, place-name.

gwas-whēl (Colloq. *gossel* Kerew), *m.*, workman, servant.

gwavas (*gwaf*, *bos*), *m.*, winter abode, permanent farmstead: as opposed to **hewas, kynewas.**

gwavwels, *m.*, winter pasture: Wavells, field-name.

gwavy, *vb.*, to pass the winter, hibernate (W., B.): see **havy.**

gwaya, *vb.*, to move, stir: *alemma ny-m-bus g.*, I can't get away, B.M. 4098.

gwayn, *m.*, gain, profit, advantage (M.E. *gayne*).

Gwaynten (C. Voc. *guaintoin*), *m.*, Spring(time), *lengcten* Aelfric.

gwaytya, *vb.*, to wait, expect, hope, mind, attend, be on the watch, take care (M.E. *wayten*); *gwayt pell na-vyth hep dos dhyn!* mind not to be long in coming back! B.M. 3275.

gwaytyans, *m.*, hope, expectation, wait.

gwaytyer, *m.*, *pl.* **-yoryon,** waiter.

gwēder, *m.*, *pl.* **-drow,** glass, glass vessel: *g. glas*, blue glass urinal, B.M. 1445; **g.-aspya*, spy-glass; **g.-myras*, looking-glass.

gwedhen (C. Voc. *guiden*), *f.*, *col.* **gwȳth** (*gweyth*, *gwēth*), tree: *g.-know*, hazel-bush; *g.-avallow*, apple-tree; **g.-gwerthyjow*, spindle-tree, etc.

gwedhennek, *f.*, *pl.* **-egow, -egy,** grove, tree-grown place; place-names, Trewithennick, becoming Trannack, etc.

gwedhen-vēn, *m. or f.*, tree-trunk, C.W. 759: *an w.*, *f.*, following gender of first word; see **bēn,** *m.*

gwedhow (C. Voc. *guedeu*), *adj.*, widowed, bereft of husband or wife; †*f.*, widow, C. Voc.

gwe'dhöwsys, *m.*, widowhood (W).

gwedhra, *vb.*, to wither, Lh.; 3 s. pres.-fut.

gwedher; *dh* becomes *th* in subj., *dhr* becomes *th* before *s*.

gwedra, *vb.*, to glaze (W., B.).

gwedrek, *adj.*, glassy, glazed (W., B.).

gwedren, *f.*, *pl.* **-now**, tumbler, drinking-glass, Lh.: *g. a wyn*, glass(ful) of wine.

†gwedresyf (C. Voc. *wedresif*), *f.*, *pl.* **-yvas**, newt, lizard, *efeta* Aelfric.

gwedror, *m.*, *pl.* **-yon**, glazier (W., B.).

gwef, see **göef**, **gwyw**.

gwek(g), *col. pl.* **-egas**, bindweed, vetch, climbing plant (D. "weggas," as B. *gweg*, W. *gwyg*).

gwēl (*gweall* C.W.), *m. or f.*, *pl.* **-ow**, sight, prospect, view: made f. O.M. 753, *Dew, tecca wel yu homma!* What a lovely sight this is! perhaps a slip for *hemma*; *gwel* is m. in B.: see **a-wēl**.

gwēl, *m.*, barm, yeast, leaven: *bara heb g.*, unleavened bread, Borlase.

gwēl, see **gwelen**.

gwēl (*gweyl*, *gwȳl*), *m.*, *pl.* **-yow**, open arable field, field of battle: *yn g. nag yn pras*, (not) anywhere at all; *synsy g.*, hold the field; *dhe wel* (*guel*) into battle, B.M. 2318, 2340.

gwelen (C. Voc. *guaylen*), *f.*, *pl.* **-lyny**, *col.* **gwēl**, rod, yard (long measure), long handle, shaft, pole, switch, stem: *g.-car*, pole of ox-cart, shaft; *g.-gala*, straw; *g.-gol*, yard of sail; *g.-hyk*, *-hygen*, hook-rod for catching cuttle-fish (D. "gulaneeg," "goolniggan"); *g. ryal*, *g.revaneth*, C. Voc., sceptre; *anodho ny-settyaf gwel-gala*, I don't care a rap for him.

gweles, *vb.*, to see, behold: 2 s. imp., 3 s. pres.-fut. *gwel*; vowel usually becomes *y* in sympathy with endings, but may remain *e* before *-y* in impf. ind., *-ys*, and *-yth*; contracted forms *a-wylsta* (*gwylsys, ta*), hast thou seen? *a-welta* (*welyth, ta*,), seest thou?

gweles, *m.*, ability to see, sight, vision, Lh. (W., B.): usually seems replaced by **golok** or **syght**, but probable in C.W. 1670.

gwelesygeth, *f.*, vision, apparition (W., B.).

gwelf (*gwelv* Lh., for *gwevel*), *f.*, *pl.* **-lvow** (*-vans* Lh.), *d.* **dyw-welf**, lip, muzzle: in W., *gwefl*, used chiefly of animals; see **gwelven**, **†gwēus**,

gwelhevyn (C. Voc. *guesbeuin*, for *guelheuin*), *m. and col.*, chief, ruler, head-man, C. Voc; leading people, nobles (B.M.); formed from **gwelhaf**, an obsolete form of superlative **gwella**.

gwell, *adj.*, *irreg. comp.* of **da**, **mās**, better: *g. yu dhym*, it is better for me; *g. yu genef*, I prefer; *pandr' yu g. orthyf dhe vos gwrys?* what had better be done for me?; prefixed to vb., *gwellblekya*, to please better, O.M. 2108; *ny-won den byth well*, I know no better man; *mas dhe well y-m-gortheby*, unless thou answer me (the) better.

gwella, *adj.*, *irreg. superl.* of **da**, **mās**, best; (after noun) excellent, surpassing; also *equative*, *g. gallaf*, as well as I can; *an g.-oll y'n bys*, the very best in the world; *a'n g.*, of the best (sort); *ow marghak g.*, my best of knights; *y'n g. prys*, most happily or fortunately.

gwella, *vb.*, to make better, R.D. 2242.

gwellhē·, *vb.*, to make better, improve, amend, speed: as **berhē**.

gwelsen, *f.*, *pl.* **-now**, grass-blade, *col.*, **gwels**, grass: *gwels gora*, grass left for hay.

gwelsek, **-jek**, *f.*, *pls.* **-egow**, **-egy**, grass-grown place; *adj.*, grassy (W., B.).

gwelsow, **-jow** (for *gwelsef*), *m.*, *pl.* **-sevyow**, shears, clippers: **g. byghan*, scissors.

gwelvek, *adj.*, blubber-lipped, Lh.

gwelven, *f.*, *pl.* **-now** (*guelawennow*, P.), lip: see **gwelf**, **†gwēus**.

gwely (*guyly*, C. Voc. *gueli*), *m.*, *pl.* **-ȳow**, bed, layer, stratum, (anciently) tribe, family: *g.-cala*, straw-mattress, paillasse; *g.-pluf*, feather-bed; **g. deth*, day-bed, sofa; *y'n gwely*, in bed ("in the bed" D.); *den y'n g. ow-croweth*, bedlier, bedridden person (P. *gueli-croweth*).

gwelyny, see **gwelen**.

gwelyvedhes, **benen-g.** (*glyvedhas* Lh.), *f.*, *pl.* **-ow**, midwife: "*Germogh o myghtern, Breg o gwelyvedhes*" (*Germow mathern, Breage lavethas*), old saying, "Germoe was a King, Breage was a midwife, Borlase.

gwelyvos (*golovas* Lh.), *m.*, lying-in: *benen yn g.*, woman in childbed.

***gwēn**, *f.*, *pl.* **-ow**, smile (W., B.).

gwen, *m.*, anus, R.D. (?M.E. *grenne*).

***gwena**, *vb.*, to smile (W.).

gwenel, *vb.*, to struggle, kick, writhe, wriggle (W. *gwingo*, B. *gwinkal*, cf. *yn*, narrow, W. *ing*, B. *enk*); 3 s. pret. *gwenys*: see **o·mwen**.

gwenen, *f.*, *pl.* **-now**, blister, wen, sore, Lh.

gwenenek, *adj.*, pock-marked, spotty (B.).
gwenenen (C. Voc. *guenenen*), *f.*, *col.* **gwenyn**, bee : *g. uyls*, bumble-bee (W.).
Gwener, *f.*, Venus, **dē-**, **dū-**, **G.**, *m.*, day of Venus, Friday : *de-G. an Grows*, Good Friday.
gwennol (C. Voc. *guennol*), *f.*, *pl.* **-nyly**, swallow ; weaver's shuttle (W.) : *g. dhu*, swift (W.) ; see **morwennol.**
gwenogen (*gwednhogian* Lh.), *f.*, *pl.* **-now**, wart.
***gwenwharth**, *m.*, smiling, smile (B.).
***gwenwherthyn**, *vb.*, to smile (B.).
gwenwhys (C. Voc. *guenwuit* ; *gwenhez*, N. Boson), *adj.*, clever, wise, skilled, *gleaw* Aelfric : the word seems the same in C. Voc. and *Nebes Geryow*, but is unexplained.
†**gwenyn** (C. Voc. *guenoin*), *m.*, poison, venom : †*g.-ryas*, poisoner, C. Voc., *unlybwyrhta* Aelfric.
gwenyn, see **gwenenen.**
gwenyna, *vb.*, to poison, envenom (W.).
gwenynek, *adj.*, venomous, poisonous (W.).
gwenys, see **gwana.**
gwēr, †**gwyrth** (C. Voc. *guirt*), *adj.*, green : *maga wher avel an gwels*, as green as grass, Lh.
gweras (*gwyrras*, C. Voc. *gueret*), *m.*, *pl.* **-ow**, ground, soil, earth, mould, C.W. 2081—4.
gweres, *m.*, help, aid, succour, remedy, relief, healing, cure ; *vb.*, to help, aid, assist, speed, relieve, heal, cure : 3 s. pres.-fut. *gweres* ; p. pt. *gweresys* ; used with *dhe*, B.M. 4536, *gweres dhym, Syr Yarl, yn-len*, help me, Sir Earl, loyally ; *gweres ow cul*, etc., help to make, etc. (lit. in making,) : see **Dew-gweres.**
gwereser, **-or**, *m.*, *pl.* **-oryon**, helper (W., B.).
gwergh, *adj.*, maiden, virginal, pure (B.).
gwerghes (*gwyrghes*, *gwerhas*), *f.*. *pl.* **-ow**, **-y**, virgin, maid : *s* prevents mutation in *a Werghes Ker Marya*, R.D. 1200.
gwerghsys, *f.*, virginity (B.).
gwern, *f.*, *pls.* **-ow**, **-y**, marsh, swamp.
gwern, *f.*, *pl.* **-ow**, mast of ship or boat : *gorhel tyr g.*, three-master ; *g. a-rak*, foremast : *g. vras*, mainmast ; *g. a-dhelergh*, mizen.
gwernak, *adj.*, marshy, swampy.
gwernen (C. Voc. *guernen*), *f.*, *col.* **gwern**, alder-tree, *alr* Aelfric.
gwernek, *f.*, *pl.* **-egow**, **-egy**, alder-grove.
gwerrya (*guerrya*), *vb.*, to make war, B.M. 3454 (M.E. *guerre*, *werrey*).
gwers, *f.*, *pl.* **-yow**, verse ; *an wers... y-s-leverys*, the verse...he said (it), B.M. 4435, Gw.
gwerth, *f.*, sale, value, price (W., B.).
gwertha (Late *gwerra*, *guerha*), *vb.*, to sell, (of commodities) to find a purchaser, J. Boson : *g. a dry funs*, to sell for £3.
gwerthjy, *m.*, *pl.* **-ow**, shop.
gwerthys (C. Voc. *gur(h)thit*), *f.*, *pl.* **-yjow**, spindle.
gwerwels, *m.*, pasture, growing grass, Lh.
gweskel (*gwyskel*), *vb.*, to strike, beat, knock : 3 s. pres.-fut. *gwysk*, 1 s. *gwascaf* ; 3 s. subj. *gwasco* ; 2 s. imp. *gwask* ; p. pt. and 1 s. pret. *gwyskys* ; 3 s. pret. *gwe(y)skys* ; *k* would be dropped before *s*, 2 s. pret. *gwyssys*, etc.
gwesper, *m.*, *pl.* **-ow**, evening service, evensong, vespers : *prys g.*, eventide, M.C. 230.
gwest, *f.*, lodging, entertainment, O.M. 356, 361.
gwesta, *vb.*, to seek entertainment : inf. only (W.).
gwestē·, *m.*, *pl.* **-tyon**, guest (W.).
gwestva, *f.*, hospitality ; guest-room (W.).
gwesty, *m.*, *pl.* **-ow**, guest-house, lodging-house, inn (W.).
gwesty, *vb.*, to entertain (W.).
gwesyk, *m.*, *pl.* **-ygyon**, **-yonygow**, little fellow : dim. of **gwas.**
gwesyon, see **gwas.**
gweth, *f.*, *pl.* **-edhow**, aspect, form (W.) : found only as **-weth**, suffix.
gwēth, *adj.*, *irreg. comp.* of **drōk**, worse.
gwetha, *adj.*, *irreg. superl.* of **drōk**, worst ; also *equative*, *g. godhya*, as badly as he could : see **gwella.**
gwetha, *vb.*, ? to grow worse, O.M. 689 ; perhaps for **gwȳtha.**
gwethhē·, *vb.*, to make worse, prey upon one's spirit, damage, deteriorate: as **berhē.**
gwethneth, *m.*, suppleness, elasticity (W.).
gwethter (*gwethder* Lh.), *m.*, deterioration, worseness.
gwethyn, *adj.*, pliable, flexible, supple, tough, elastic, M.C. 131 : comp. *gwethna*.
gwe·thynder, *m.*, suppleness, flexibility (W., B.).
gwethynhē·, *vb.*, to toughen, make supple : as **berhē** (W., B.).
†**gwēus** (C. Voc. *gueus*), *f.*, *pl.* **-ow**, *d.* **dyw-weūs**, human lip.

gwēusek, *adj.*, thick-lipped, labiate, labial (W., B.).
gwevya, *vb.*, to flee, wander, become a vagrant, M.C. 247.
gwewen (*an*), *f.*, heel, Lh., Kerew : ?late form of **gyewen**, used for tendon Achilles.
gwlān, glān (C. Voc. *gluan*, Late *gloan*, *glawn*), *col.*, wool : with *gluan* cf. C. Voc. *gruah*, etc., with *gru* for *gwr-*.
gwlanek, *adj.*, wooly (W., B.).
gwlanen, *f.*, flannel (W.).
gwlas (C. Voc. *gulat*, *glas*, Late *glaze*, *gwalazt*), *f.*, *pl.* **-ow**, country, nation, kingdom, *aethel* Aelfric : *s* prevents mutation of following *c*, *k*, *d*, *p*, *t*; *Pen an Wlas*, the Land's End ; *G. an Haf*, Somerset (W.).
gwlascarer, *m.*, *pl.* **-roryon**, patriot (W.).
gwlasegeth, *m*, politics (W.).
gwlasek, *adj.*, political, national (W.).
gwlascor (*glascor*, Late *guelasca*, *gulasketh*, etc.), *f.*, *pl.* **-ow**, kingdom.
gwlaskerensa *f.*, patriotism (W.).
gwra, etc., see **gül**.
gwrageth, see **gwrēk**.
gwrāgh (C. Voc. *gruah*). *f.*, *pl.* **-as**, old woman, hag, witch, *eald wif* Aelfric ; wrasse (D.) ; *wood-louse (W., B.).
gwraghya, *vb.*, to grow old and hag-like (W., B.).
gwrannen (*gwradnan* Lh.), *f.*, *pl.* **-as**, wren : see **†berthūan**.
gwredhen (C. Voc. *grueiten*), *f.*, *pl.* **-now**, **gwrydhyow** (C. W. *-dhow*), *col.* **gwrȳth**, root, *wyrt ruma* Aelfric.
gwrēk (*grueg*, *greg*), *f.*, *pl.* **gwrageth**, wife, matron, woman, *wif* Aelfric : *g. wedhow*, widow ; *?gwrē' da*, goodwife (*gwra da* Andrew Boorde), possibly as distinguished from *g. dha*, a good wife: see **gwrē'ty**.
gwrek (*gurek*, Borlase), *m.*, *pl.*-**kys**, wreck (E.).
***gwrem**, *m.*, *pl.* **-yow**, hem (W., B.).
gwrēs, *f.*, heat, ardour, Lh.
gwrēsek (W.), **gwrēsüs** (B.)., *adj.*, ardent, fervent, warm.
gwrē'ty (O.M., C.W. *gwreghty*, C.W. *gwrethty*, Chart. End. *gwreg(h) ty*), *f.*, housewife: *k* lost before *t*, cf. **muscotter**.
gwrüthyl, see **gül**.
gwrȳ, *m.*, *pl.* **-ȳow**, seam, stitching, R.D. 1921 ; thin seam of ore, D. "grie".
gwrȳador, *m.*, *pl.* **-yon**, stitcher.
gwrȳadores, *f.*, *pl.* **-ow**, seamstress.
gwrȳans, *m.*, action, making, doing : *y wryans- ef yu hemma*, this is his doing, B.M. 3959.
gwrȳas (Late *guriaz*), *vb* , to sew, stitch : in Borlase MS. *gwreugh-why gwryas*, "sow you," is next to *gwyns an barlys*, as if the meanings of Eng. "sew" and "sow" were confused ; a word *?gwregha* or *gwryghas*, to cultivate, is doubtfully suggested by *a-wreghaf*, O.M. 521 : see **wregha**, Appendix I.
gwrȳdhya, *vb.*, to root, take root.
gwrȳdhyow, see **gwredhen**.
gwrȳer (*gwrear*, C.W.), *m.* *pl.* **-ȳoryon**, creator, maker (Late).
gwrȳghonen, *f.*, *col.* **gwrȳghon**, spark, P.C. 2101, 2717.
gwrynya (*gwridnia* Lh.); *vb.*, to grip, hug, squeeze, wrestle, grapple, P.C. 1887 : 3 s. pres.-fut. *gwryn*, P.C. 1132.
gwrynyer, *m.*, *pl.* **-yoryon**, wrestler, grappler (B.).
gwrȳs (*gurys*, *grueys*), *m.*, crystal : *gwyn avel g.*, white as crystal, P.C. 1790, B.M. 1288 ; cf. *g. avel crystal*, B.M. 1521.
gwrȳth (*guryth*), *f.*, ? service, action, performance, deeds, R.D. 850, 876, P.C. 2024.
gwȳa (*gwia*, Lh.), *vb.*, to weave, knit, twine, twist : *omwya a-dro dhe*, to twine around, as a climbing plant (B.).
gwȳador (*gweader*, *gwiader* Lh.), *m.*, *pl.* **-doryon**, weaver.
gwȳadores, *f.*, *pl.* **-ow**, woman weaver ; convolvulus, bindweed (B.).
†gwȳas (C. Voc. *guiat*), *m.*, web, woven cloth, texture, fabric : **g. kefnysen*, spider's web.
gwyber, *m.*, poor-cod, "power," kind of fish (D. "gwibber").
gwyban, *f.*, *pl.* **-as**, fly, Lh.
gwybesen (C. Voc. *guibeden*), *f.*, *col.* **gwybes**, gnat, midge, mosquito : in the proverb *an wybesen a-ladha margh—a calla*, the midge would slay a horse—if it could, B.M. 2421, the gnat is compared with a dragon-fly, once thought to kill horses : see **nader-margh**.
gwybessa, *vb.*, to catch gnats, waste time (W.) : inf. only.
gwybya, *vb.*, to dart, flit (W.).
gwyca, *vb.*, to peddle, hawk, cry wares (W.).
gwycor (colloq. *goccor*, C. Voc. *guicgur*), *m.*, *pl.* **-yon**, trader, peddler, hawker, *mangere* Aelfric ; *gwan-wycor*, bad

bargainer, M.C. 40.

gwydhal, *m.*, *pl.*, **-dhyly**, thicket: Wheal Gothilly mine and Goon an Gothal seem to represent this, W. *gwyddeli*, pl., rather than "Irishman," for which *-as* is a likelier pl.

Gwydhal, Godhal, *m.*, *pl.* **-as** (*dhyly* Lh.), Gael, Irishman, Lh.: *G. Alban*, Highlander.

Gwydhalek, *adj.*, Irish, Gaelic; *m.*, Irish or Gaelic language.

Gwydhales, *f.*, *pl.* **-ow**, Irishwoman.

gwydhek, *f.*, *pls.* **-egow**, **-egy**, tree-grown place; *adj.*, wooded (B.).

***gwydhyf**, *m.*, *pl.*, **-yvow**, hedging-bill (W., O.B.).

***gwydyla**, *vb.*, to take a devious course, waddle, wriggle (B.).

gwyf, see **gwyw**.

***gwȳgh**, *m.*, squeak, shrill, piping cry (W., B.).

†**gwȳghal**, *vb.*, to squeak, cry shrilly (W., B.).

gwȳghen, *f.*, *col.* **gwȳgh**, periwinkle, winkle (D. "gweean").

gwȳk(g), *f.*, *pl.* **-ygow**, wood, grove: see **kellywyk.**

gwȳk, *f.*, *pl.* **-ygow**, church-town, village (Lat. *vicus*): place-names.

gwylan (C. Voc. *guilan*), *f. pl.* **-as**, gull, sea-mew, *maew* Aelfric: see **gulla.**

†**gwyles** (C. Voc. *guyles*), *col.*, lovage (herb), *lufestice* Aelfric.

gwylfos, *m.*, wilderness, forest-land, B.M.

gwyll (*gwilleiw*, as sg. Lh.), *m.*, *pl.* **-yow**, beggar, vagrant, robber (W., B.).

gwyls, *adj.*, wild, savage, uncultivated.

†**gwylskyn** (C. Voc. *guilsc(h)in*), *m*, *pl.* **-as**, frog: cf. *quylkyn* and also B. *gwesklen*, *glesker*, etc.

†**gwylter** (C. Voc. *guilter*), *m.*, *pl.* **-tras**, **-trow**, hunting dog, large greyhound, "velter," *rydhdha* Aelfric (Lat. *vertragus*, *veltris*, from Gaulish).

gwȳn (C. Voc. *guin*, *win*), *m.*, wine: *g. marow*, palled wine (Lh.).

gwyn (C. Voc. *guyn*, Late *gwidn*), *adj.*, white, pale faced, fair, pleasant, splendid; (in mutation with names of relationship) grand-, *syra-wyn*, *flogh-wyn*; (with names of Saints or day) holy, blessed; *Marya Wyn*, blessed Mary, *de-Yow Wyn*, Thursday a clear week before Christmas; *gwyn ow bys!* Happy I! lit. fair my world or affairs.

gwyn, *m.*, white colour or clothing: *g. an lagas*, white of the eye; *g. oy*, white of egg; *gwyskys yn g.*, dressed in white.

†**gwȳnbren**, *m.*, *pl.* **-yer**, vine, C. Voc., *wintreow* Aelfric.

gwynder. *m.*, whiteness, brightness, B.M. 3667: *g. an lagas*, white of the eye (B.).

†**gwȳn-fyllys** (C. Voc. *guinfellet*), *m.*, vinegar, lit. spoilt wine; see **fyllel.**

Gwyngala (*Gwedn gala* Lh.), **mȳs-G.**, *m.*, September. B.M.

gwynhē·, *vb.*, to whiten; as **berhē**.

***gwynkya**, *vb.*, to wink (E.).

gwȳnlan, *f.*, *pl.* **-now**, vineyard (W.).

gwynna, *vb.*, to make white or fair (W., B.).

gwynnak (*gwydnak* Lh.), *m.*, *pl.* **-egas**, whiting (fish).

gwynnyk (*gwidnak* Gw.), *adj.*, whitish, light in colour.

gwynrew, *m.*, numbness of fingers from cold: variant of **ewynrew** (D. "gwenders," W. *gwynrew*).

gwȳnrünen, *f.*, *pl.* **-now**, *col.* **gwȳnrün**, grape (W.).

gwynrüth, *adj.*, pink (W.).

gwyns, *f.*, windlass, winch, winze.

gwyns (C. Voc. *guins*), *m.*, *pl.* **-ow**, wind, breath: **g. a-dro*, whirlwind, cyclone; *mos gans an g.*, be borne away by the wind, R.D. 2292.

gwynsa, *vb.*, to winnow: *gwyns an barlys*, winnow the barley, Borlase MS.

gwynsak, *adj.*, windy.

gwynsell (Lh. *guinzal*), *f.*, *pl.* **-ow**, winnowing-fan.

gwynsella, *vb.*, to fan, winnow (W.).

gwynvȳs, *m.*, felicity, bliss, lit. fair world; *adj.*, happy, fortunate.

gwynvysyk, *adj.*, blessed, happy (W., B.).

gwȳnwedhen, *f.*, *pl.* **-wȳth**, vine (W.): see **gwȳnbren.**

gwȳnwedren, *f.*, wine-glass.

***gwynyolen**, *f.*, *col.* **gwynyol**, maple-tree (W.).

gwȳr (C. Voc. *guir*), *m.*, truth, right, justice, fact; *adj.*, true, real, right, genuine, actual: *dhe wyr*, in truth; *yn-w(h)yr*, truly; often prefixed, as *g.-dhega*, true tithe; *g.-Dhew*, *g.-sans*, etc.

gwyras, *f.*, *pl.* **-rosow**, drink, liquor, ardent spirits, P.C. 2975.

gwȳrder, *m.*, truth, O.M. 1752.

gwȳrhevelep, *adj.*, plausible, Lh. (invented).

gwȳrhevelepter, *m.*, plausibility, verisimilitude, Lh. (invented).

†**gwȳrleveryas** (C. Voc. *guirleveriat*), *m.*, *pl.* **-ȳsy**, truth-teller, *sodhsagol* Aelfric.

GWYN
GWEN
VENUS / GWENER
QUEEN
GWENDOLINE
GUINEVERE

gwyrotty, *m.*, *pl.*-**ow**, dram-shop (W.).
†**gwyrth**, see **gwēr**.
gwȳryon, var. **gwȳr'on** (C. Voc. *guirion*), *adj.*, righteous, just, innocent, true, sincere, *sodhfaest* Aelfric.
gwȳryoneth, vars. **gwȳry'oneth**, **gwrȳ'oneth** (C.W. *gwreanathe*), *m.*, truth, sincerity, reality, righteousness.
gwȳryonsys, *m.*, innocence.
gwȳs (C. Voc. *guis*), *f.*, *pl.* **-y**, sow, kept for breeding.
gwysca (*gwesca*), *vb.*, to dress, clothe, wear, put on, don : *c* becomes *k* before *e*, *y*, and is lost before *s*; *a-s-gwyskens a-dro dhodho*, let him put it round him, P.C. 1788; *mars us dhys duan g. an corn, roy e tre arta*, if to wear the horn thou find thyself aggrieved give it back again, *Image of Idlenesse*,c. 1570.
gwyscas (*gueskas*, P.), *m.*, *pl.* **-cosow**, clothing, covering, coating, layer: wrongly given as pl. of **gwysk** (*guesk*) P.
gwysen, see **gūsen**.
†**gwysk** (C. Voc. *guisc*), *m.*, *pl*, **-scow**, dress, vesture, clothing, *reaf* Aelfric : the meanings "husk," "pod," "bark" (Lh., P.) are evidently misrenderings of *indumentum* in Cor. Voc., see **üs**, **cūth**, **plysken**, **rüsken**.
†**gwyskty** (C. Voc. *guiscti*), *m.*, vestry, *raegelhus*, Aelfric.
gwystel (C. Voc. *guistel*), *m.*, *pl.* **-tlow**, pledge, pawn, surety, hostage, wager, *gysel* Aelfric.
gwystla, *vb.*, to wager, become surety, engage, pawn, pledge (W., B.).
gwystlor, *m.*, *pl.* **-yon**, pledger (W.).
gwysygen, see **gūsygen**.
gwȳth (C. Voc. *gueid*), *m.*, *pl.* **-yow**, act, work : *gol ha g.*, feast and work-day, *nanyl dhe wyth na dhe Sul*, neither on a week-day nor on a Sunday.
gwȳth, see **gwedhen**, **gōth**.
gwyth, *m.*, *pl.* **-yow**, time, occasion : commonly suffixed to numerals or to advs. of number; see **dēdhwyth**, **nōswyth**, **trawythyow**.
gwȳth, *m.*, keeping, guard, ward, defence, protection, care : *gor wyth*, *kemer wyth*, "set keep," take care, mind, followed by prep.—*a'y enef*, of his soul, *dh'y dhampnya*, to condemn him ; the unusual mutation in *wyth* may result from regarding *gor gwyth* as *gorwyth*, a supposed or real var. of *gorquyth*, and passing this on to *kemer wyth*.
gwytha, *vb.*, to keep, guard, protect, prevent, (with neg.) ensure : *g. dhe*, keep to ; *g. war*, watch over : *g. worth*, prevent, guard against ; *g. rak*, protect from ; *g. erbyn*, keep until ; *gwyth'-tejy*, contraction of *gwythsys-tejy*, B.M. 1050.
gwȳtha, *vb.*, to work, set working, exploit, O.M. 1502-15.
†**gwȳthor** (C. Voc. *gueiduur*), *m.*, *pl.* **-yon**, worker, workman: *g. arghans*, silversmith; *g. chy* (C. Voc. *g. ti*), architect, foreman builder, *yldest wyrhta* Aelfric : *g. cober*, coppersmith ; *g pry*, potter ; *g. plom*, plumber, etc.
gwȳthres, *m.*, deed, act, action, work.
gwythva, **gwyffa**, *f.*, store-place (D. "wippa," net-room in boat).
gwȳthva, *f.*, work-place, factory (W.).
gwythvosen, *f*, *col.*, **gwythvōs**, **gwyfōs**, honeysuckle, woodbine (W., B.).
gwȳthy, see **gōth**.
gwythyans, *m.*, preservation, Lh.
gwythyas (C. Voc. *guidthiat*), *m.*, *pl.* **-ysy**, guardian, keeper, warden, guard : *hyrde* Aelfric; *pryva-g*, body-guard, O.M. 2397.
gwȳthyek, *adj.*, bloodshot, veined.
gwȳthyen, *f.*, *pls.* **-now**, **gwȳthy**, vein, blood-vessel.
***gwyver**, *m.*, *pl.* **-vrow**, wire (W.).
gwyw, **gwyf**, **gwef** (*gyw*), *adj.*, fit, worthy, proper, meet, deserving, comp. *gweffa* : *del yua g.*, as he deserves ; *a pes-sy g. ow metya*, wert thou worthy of meeting me, B.M. 2420.
***gwywer**, *m.*, *pl.* **-as**, squirrel (W., B.).
gȳa, *vb.*, to spear, lance, transfix with a spear : 3 s. pres.-fut. *gy*, P.C. 2234; see **gū**.
gyewen (C. Voc. *goiuen*, Lh. *geion*), *col.* **gyew** (*ieyw*), sinew, tendon, nerve, P.C. 2681 : see **gwewen**.
gyglot (*giglot*), *m. and f.*, *pl.* **-s**, wanton person, P.C 1183, in Eng. line (M.E.).
gyk, *m.*, least sound (with neg.), C.W. 534, as M.B. *guic* ; see **myk**.
***gȳky**, *vb.*, to peep (E.D. "geek").
gȳl (*geyl*), *m.*, guile, deceit, trickery (E.) : *hep g.*, indeed.
gȳla, see **kȳla**, **y-gȳla**.
gyllys, see **gallos**, also **mōs**, Tables in Appendix VIII.
gylwys, see **gelwel**.
Gyny (*Gini* Lh.), *f.*, Guinea : *yar.-g.*,

turkey-hen ; *culyek-g.*, *cok-g.*, turkey-cock ; the name "guinea-cock" was often so used c. 1700.

gyrr (*an girr* Lh.), *m.*, gripes, Borlase.

gȳs (*geys*), *m.*, *pl.* **-yow**: fashion, manner, guise, C.W. 2548 (M.E. *gyse*).

gysty, see **gast**.

gyth, *m.*, *pl.* **-yon**, complaint, R.D. 852 : cf. W. *gyth*, murmur ; *pyjyth*, the alternative reading to *py gyth*, makes bad sense.

gyttern, **gyttren**, *m.*, *pl.* **-s**, guitar, cithern, zither, O.M. 1998 (M.E.).

gyvyans (*gefyans*), *m.*, *pl.* **-ow**, forgiveness, remission, pardon : *my a-vyn pysy g. bos mar dhyek y'th kever.* I will beg pardon *for* being so remiss to thee, B.M. 3359 ; (as exclamation) *Arluth, g. dyworthys !* Pardon, Lord ! R.D. 1570 ; see **gava.**

H

ha(g) *conj.*, and ; as ; *prep.*, with ; also translates so, and so, therefore, yet, then, when, even, while, both, accordingly, for, moreover, etc. : before vowels *hag* (but *h'a* for *hag a*, and if, R.D. 2105, and *ha'w* for *hag ow-*, and my) ; combines with *an* and poss. prons. as *ha'n*, *ha'm*, etc. ; *ha'y* may stand for "and his (her)" or "and of his (her)" (*ha a'y*), etc. ; idiomatic uses are--*devedhys warbarth ha'n kensa galow*, come simultaneously *with* the first call ; *kepar ha pan ve*, just *as* if he were ; *wor' tu ha*, towards ; *kemmys* (*kenyver*) *ha*, as much (many) *as* ; *kettoth ha'n ger*, as quick *as* the word ; *ha...ha* .., *both*...and... ; *gwedhen ha serpont ynny*, a tree *with* a serpent in it ; *yndella gwra, ha mar ny-wreth*, do so, *for* if thou dost not ; *nyns-yu marth cuth kyn y-m-bo ow-mos, ha ny-m-byth gober*, no wonder I am vexed at going, *when* I shall get no reward ; *ha my ow-mos*, *as* I went ; *hag ef yn-ten*, *while* he was outstretched ; *mar te ha codha*, if it comes to fall ; *deu ha deu*, two *by* two ; *ogas ha bledhen*, nearly a year ; *mur gowak hag a-lever gow*, a great liar who tells untruth. After *otta*, *myr* and before adjs. *ha* has the force of "how," *myr h. stordy yu an gwas*, see *how* obstinate the fellow is ; *mar ahas ha dre spyt ef dhe verwel*, so keen *that* through spite he shall die ; *ha bedhens*, *then* so be it ; *gordhya (dynagha) ha my a-*, (do but) worship (deny) and I will, B.M. 893, 941; in a string of nouns or vbs., with or without preps., *ha* is commonly omitted, e.g., *aysel, bystel kemyskys* ; *yn cuth*, *yn moreth* ; *dhe'm kemeres*, *dhe'm shyndya.dhe'm paynya; gwerthys,ledhys*, etc. ; *Dew tal dyal warnough, ha tus ungrassyes*, God wreak vengeance on you, and (all such) graceless folk, B.M. 1596 (cf. similar use of **na**).

ha, **a**, see **mōs**.

Hablys, see **Cablys**.

haccra, see **hager**

Hāf, *m.*, *pl.* **havow**, (Late *-vyow*, Gw.), Summer : *Gwlas an H.*, Somerset (W.).

hag, see **ha.**

hagens'oll, see **gensȳ**.

hager, *adj.*, ugly, hideous, foul, threatening, rough, cruel, fierce, comp. *haccra* : *h. awel*, stormy weather, tempest ; *h. gowas*, downpour of rain, cloudburst.

hagry, *vb.*, to make ugly or foul, Keigwin : p. pt. *hagrys*, so altered by him from *flayrys*, C.W. 2248.

hakkya (*hakya*), *vb.*, to hack, hew, O.M. 2228 (E.).

hakney, *m.*, *pl.* **-s**, ambling nag, O. M.1966 (M.E. *hakeney*).

hakter, *m.*, ugliness, danger, cruelty, C.W. 289 : *dre h.*, by harsh means or force, opposite to *dre dekter*, cf. B. *dre gaer pe dre heg*, willy-nilly ; see **tekter**.

hāl, *f.*, *pl.* **-low**, moor, down ; stream-work for tin : *bew-h.*, a layer rich in tin, Borlase.

halan, see **calan**,

***halow**, *m.*, saliva, spittle (W., B.).

halya, *vb.*, to heave, hoist, haul (E.) : 2 s. imp. (or interj. from E.) *hala*; *hala dhys!* heave in ! 3 s. or pl. imp. *halyens* ; *hala ! op as shal !* heave ! up as (high as it) will (go) ! P.C. 2830 (M.E.).

Hamlys, see **Cablys**.

†**hanaf** (*hanath* Lh.), *m.*, *pl.* **-avow**, drinking-cup, beaker, C. Voc., *hnaep* Aelfric, Lat. *hanapus*.

hanaja, **-asa**, *vb.*, to sigh, murmur, Lh.

hanajen, **asen**, *f.*, *pl.* **-now**, sigh, murmur, Lh.

hanas, *m.*, *pl.* **-ow**, sigh, murmur, whisper; *vb.*, to murmur, speak under one's breath, M.C. 79.

handla, *vb.*, to feel, stroke, pat, handle, manipulate, treat (O.E. *handlian*) : p. pt, *hyndlys*; 2 s. imp., 3 s. pres. -fut. *handel*, before vowel, *handl*.

haneth, *adv.*, to-night, this evening (pres., fut. or past): *yn nos h.* (pres.), or *h. yn nos* (pres. and past), this (very) night; *kens h. dhe nos* (fut.), before this coming night, ere night comes on.

hangya, *vb.*, to execute by hanging, B.M. 1245 (E.).

hanna, see **hedhes.**

hanow, *m.*, *pl.* **hynwyn**, name, noun: **h. gwan*, adjective (W.); *py h. yua?* what is he called? *gelwel den mes a'y h.*, to miscall, call a person names (D. " out of his name "): *h. da*, reputation, fame, *gwyth dha h. d.*, preserve thy reputation, B.M. 339, *y-fyn ry h. da dhe'n mowysy-oll*, it will earn all the girls a good character, J. Boson.

hans, *adv.*, yonder, over there, C.W. 1547 (? for **yn-hans**, metre requires another syllable): usually **yn-hans** and not found suffixed as B. *-hont*, but Hunds, field-name, suggests *an park(yn)-hans*.

hansel (*honthsel*, Late *haunsell*), *m.*, first meal, early breakfast (O.E. *handselen*, given into the hands).

hanter, *m.*, *adj.*, half: *h.-cans*, fifty; *h. hogh*, flitch of bacon; *h. da ragtho*, half good enough for it; *try deth ha hanter*, three days and a half.

hantera, *vb.*, to halve (W., B.).

hanterdēth, *m.*, mid-day.

***hantergelgh**, *m.*, semicircle (W., B.).

hanternōs, *f.*, midnight (W., B.): see **nōs.**

hanterür, *f.*, half-hour.

***hanvos**, *m.*, existence, state of being; *vb.*, to exist, be derived, come from (W., M.B.): see **henath.**

hap, *m.*, chance, fortune, luck, B.M. 1285 (M.E.).

hapya, *vb.*, to chance, happen (M.E. *happe*): *yth-hapyas dhym gul foly*, it chanced to me to commit a folly, P.C. 1438.

harber, *m.*, *pl.* **-ys**, refuge, shelter, lodging, abode, harbour (M.E.): *y'n h.*, in, under cover, housed.

hardlych, har'lych, *adv.*, with precision, strictly, exactly; (with *gleny*) closely, hard, fast (O.E. *heardlice*): see **harth.**

ha·rdygras (*-th*), *m.*, vengeance, severity. ill-will (M.E. *hardegrace*).

†harfel, *m.*, *pl.* **-low**, fiddle, viol, C. Voc.: replaced by **fyl.**

†harfellor, *m.*, *pl.* **-yon**, fiddler, viol-player, C. Voc.: see **fyllores.**

harlot, *m.*, *pl.* **-los** (var. *-loth*), rogue, villain, rascal (M.E.).

ha·rlotry (*harlutry*, C.W. 91), *m.*, vileness, rascality, contamination, filth (M.E.).

ha·rlotwas, harlot-gwas, *m.*, *pl.* **-wesyon**, rascally fellow, R.D., P.C.

harlych, see **hardlych.**

harow, *interj.*, Alack! Help! R.D., B.M. (M.E., O. Fr. *haro*).

harp, *m.*, *pl.* **-ys** (*harpes*, O.M. 1996), harp; harpist (in orchestra): see **telen.**

***harpour**, *m.*, *pl.* **-s**, harper (M.E.).

harrow (*harau* Lh.), *m.*, *pl.* **-s**, harrow (Late, E.): see **clōs, *oges.**

harth (*hard*), *adj.*, able, competent, hardy, bold, strict, precise, exact: comp. *har'ha*; *nyns-o harth dhe*, he dared not, was not strong or bold enough to: this seems to be for **hether* (W. *hydr*, M.B. *hezr*) affected perhaps by O.E. *heard*; see **hardlych.**

harth, *m.*, *pl.* **-ow**, bark (of dog), (W., B.).

hartha (Late *harra*), *vb*, to bark (Lh.).

hās, see **hasen.**

hasa, *vb.*, to seed, run to seed, Borlase.

hasek (*hazick* P.), *adj.*, seedy, seeded.

hasen, *f.*, *pl.* **-now**, single seed, *col.* **hās**, seed, progeny, semen, *pl.* **-ow**, kinds of seed: *has-lyn*, linseed.

haser, *m.*, *pl.* **-soryon**, sower (B.).

hast, *m.*, haste, hurry (M.E.): *war, yn, gans, h.*, speedily, hurriedly.

***hastyf**, *adj.*, hasty (M.E. *hastif*): as **jolyf.**

hat, *m.*, *pl.* **-tys**, hat, Lh. (E.).

hātya, *vb.*, to hate (E.): *yth-esof-vy owth-hatya den yu boghojek ha prowt*, I hate a man who is poor and proud, Borlase MS.

haun (*hean*, P.), *m.*, *pl.* **-ys**, haven, Borlase (D.E. " hawn ").

hautyn, houtyn, *adj.*, haughty, overbearing, O.M. 2069 (M.E. *hauteyn*).

haval, *adj.*, like, similar, resembling: takes *dhe* or *orth*: *h. dhys, na-yl den bos havalla*, (so) like thee, that no man can be more like, C.W. 1325.

havalder, *m.*, *pl.* **-drow**, likeness, Gw., P.: see **hevelep.**

havalla, see **hevelles.**

havar, *m.*, fallow (W.): see **Hāf, ār.**

havas, *m.*, period, duration, or season of summer: *ef a-wruk mos y'm cok-vy lyes h. dhe gemeres puscas*, he went in my boat many summers to catch fish, Gw. MS.; cf. V. *hañuad.*

†**havos**, see **hewas.**
havrak, *f.*, *pl.* **-regow**, **-regy**, (summer) fallowground: field-name; see **havar.**
Havren, *f.*, Severn (W.).
havy (*have*, N. Boson), *vb.*, to take a summer excursion or holiday: *H. an Arlodhes Kernow*, The Duchess of Cornwall's Progress.
havyas, *m.*, *pl.* **-ysy; havyor**, *m.*, *pl.* **-yon**, *f.*, **-es**, *pl.* **-ow**, Summer visitor, holiday-maker, tripper: see **havy.**
hay, see **ay.**
hayl (*haal*, *heyl*), *m.*, estuary; *lys h.*, estuary mud, O.M. 2708; Hayle, place-names.
hayl (*heyl*), *interj.*, hail! (E.).
haylya (*heylya*), *vb.*, to cry hail! P.C. 2833.
†**hē**, *m.*, skin, C. Voc., *hyd* Aelfric.
he²-, see APPENDIX II.
heb, see **hep.**
hebasca (for *hebasketh*), *f.*, easement, relief, calming, comfort, solace: *h. dheugh-why*, be comforted, B.M. 3753.
hebask, *adj.*, easy, calm, suave, patient (B.).
hebaskhē', *vb.*, to ease, calm, mollify, soothe (B.): as **berhē.**
heblēk, *adj.*, bendable, foldable, flexible (W., B.).
heblēth, *adj.*, easily interwoven (W.).
heblyth (*hyblyth*), *adj.*, pliant, flexible, supple, lithe, limber, lissom, M.C. 131: see **plyth.**
heborth, *adj.*, portable, bearable (W.).
Hebra, see **Ebbrow.**
heby-hors, *m.*, hobby-horse: *an h. ha'y gowetha*, the hobby-horse and his "pare," B.M. 1061 (E.).
hedhas, see ***hēth.**
***hēdhek**, *f.*, barley-field (W., B.).
***hedhel, hēl**, *f.*, *pl.* **-y**, plough-handle (W., B.): replaced by **dornardar.**
***hēdhen**, *f.*, *col.* **hēth**, barley-corn, barley (W., B.): replaced by **barlys.**
hēdhes, *f.*, *pl.* **-ow**, hind roe; see **hēth** (W., B.).
hedhes (Late *headhes*), *vb.*, to reach, extend, fetch, attain to, hand to another: 2 s. imp., 3 s. pres.-fut. *hēth*; 2 s. subj. *hetho*; 3 s. plupf. *hethsa*; *h. bys-yn*, extend as far as; *hanna!* late colloq. for *heth ena!* fetch there! *hedheugh e genough!* fetch it along! cry to oxen, D. "hedok ha genna."
hedhy, *vb.*, to stop, pause, rest, desist, cease: as **hedhes**; *hedheugh!* halt! hold! B.M. 3235; *kens es h.*, before resting, straightway, right off, without stopping.
hedhysk, *adj.*, teachable, well-read, learned (W.).
hedhyū, hedhew (*hydhyw*, C. Voc. *hed(h)eu*), *adv.*, to-day: *y'n jeth h.*, this day (pres. or fut.); *h. y'n jeth*, this day (pres. or past); *h. -vyttyn*, this morning.
hedor, *adj.*, fragile, breakable (W., B.).
Hedra, mȳs-H., *m.*, October, Lh., Gw.
hedra², *conj.*, while, whilst, as long as: used directly before vb.; in C.W. *h. ven*, is spelt *ha drevon* or *drevon*; *nefra ena h. vo*, as long as ever it is there.
hedrō, *adj.*, changeable, fickle (B.).
hedrogh (*hydruk*, Borlase), *adj.*, brittle, easily cut.
heforth, *adj.*, passable; easy; skilled (W.).
hegar, *adj.*, amiable, kindly, lovable, affectionate, M.C. 40.
hegas, *adj.*, hateful, unamiable (W., B.).
heglew, *adj.*, resonant, audible (W., B).
hegōf, *adj.*, memorable (W.).
hegōl (*hogul*), *adj.*, credulous, trustful, credible, O.M. 627.
hegoleth, *m.*, credulity, superstition (W.).
hegoll, *adj.*, easily lost (W., B.)
hegos, *adj.*, easily tickled, ticklish (W.).
hegyn, see **hogan.**
hel, see **helgh.**
hēl, *m.*, *pl.* **-ow**, hall, parlour, Ord., C. Voc. *heal* Aelfric, D. "hale".
†**hēl** (*hail* C. Voc.), *adj.*, generous, bountiful liberal, hospitable, *cystig* Aelfric.
helavar, *adj.*, eloquent, fluent (B.).
hēlder, *m.*, liberality (W.B.).
helergh (*holergh*), *adj.*, in the rear, behind hand, late: *pan o pur h. an jeth*, when the day was well advanced, quite past its dawning, M.C. 244.
helgh, hel, *m.*, hunt; Brehelgh, place-name.
helghor (C. Voc. *helhur*), *m.*, *pl.* **-yon**, huntsman, *hunta* Aelfric: see **honter.**
helghya, hellya (*helfia* Lh.), *vb.*, to hunt, chase, pursue, drive.
†**helghyas, hellyas** (C. Voc. *helhiat*), *m.*, *pl.* **-ysy**, hunter, pursuer, persecutor, *ehtere* Aelfric.
helghyer, hellyer (*hellier* P.), *m.*, *pl.* **-yoryon**, hunter, driver.
helgorn, *m.*, *pl.* **-gern**, hunting-horn (W.).
helgȳ, *m.*, *pl.* **-gün**, hounds (W.).

helgȳk, *m.*, game (W.).
hell (*hel.* O.M. 461, *hyl*, B.M. 3331), *adj.*, tardy, reluctant, slow, behindhand.
hellerghy (*-yrghy*), *vb.*, to trace, track, detect, follow a clue, O.M. 2118.
hellerghyas, *m.*, *pl.* **-ysy**, detective, sleuth, tracker.
hellya, see **helghya.**
hellys (for *hen lys*), *f.*, old court : place-names ; see **hēn.**
helma, see **hemma.**
***helosk**, *adj.*, combustible.
hēlsys, *f.*, generosity (B.).
helva, *f.*, hunting (W.).
helvargh, *m.*, *pl.* **-vergh**, hunting-horse (W.).
helwysk, *m.*, hunting-dress (W.).
helygen (C. Voc.*heligen*), *f.*, *col.* **helyk**, *pls.* **helygy**, **-gennow**, willow-tree, withy : *dos tre pen-helygen*, to return home without success, is suggested by D. " come back penny-liggan " and B. *halegenn*, adj., unsuccessful, bootless, baulked, cf. " wear the willow."
helygles, *m.*, willow-herb (W.).
helyglöwarth, *m.*, withy-bed, willow-garden : Halgoluir, Halagalower, place-names.
hem, *dem. pron.*, this ; used instead of *hemma* before *yu*, *o* in *bos*, unless pron. is emphasized.
hembronk, **hembronkya** (*hombronk*) *vb.*, to lead, conduct, bring : 3 s. pret. *hembroncas*, *-kyas*, p. pt. *hembronkys*, *-brynkys* ; 3 s. impf. ind. *hembronky*, *-brynky.*
hembrynkyas (C. Voc. *hebrenc(h)iat*), *m.*, *pl.* **-ysy**, leader, conductor : **†*h.*** *-lu*, *-luyth*, captain, general, duke, *heoratoga*, *lateow* Aelfric ; **†*h.*** *plu*, parish priest, *maessepreost* Aelfric.
hemma (vars. *henma*, P.C. 1327, *helma*, B.M., C.W., *hebma*,C.W.) *dem. pron. m.*, this, this time, this one, this thing, this man, see **hem**, **homma.**
hēn, *adj.*, old, ancient, antique, archaic, obsolete, comp. *hena* : used in place-names, as prefix, and in phrases *tus h.* elders, *yowynk ha h.* young and old ; the *n* is lost before *l* in *Helles* (Helston) for *Henlys*, old court ; see **cōth.**
hen, *dem. pron.*, that : used instead of *henna* before *yu*, *o* in *bos* unless pron. is emphasized, and before *ny-*, *na-* ; **hen* in *hemma* (*hen(om)ma*), *henna* (*hen(e)na*) originally meant " this."
hēnath (*heeneth*), *m.*, succeeding generation, descendants, posterity, Gw., P. : root is found in ***hanvos.**
henavak (?*empack*, N. Boson), *adj.*, *m.*, *pl.* **-vegyon**, senior, ancient, as W. *hynafol*,*henefydd*, etc.
hendas (C. Voc. *hendat*), *m.*, *pl.* **-ow**, grandfather, *ealda faeder*, Aelfric ; more loosely, forefather,ancestor, C.W.
hender, *m.*, antiquity, age (W.).
hendra (*hen*, *tre*), *pl.* **-drevy**, **-vow**, *f.*, fixed habitation: place-names, see **gwavas**, **hewas**, **kynewas.**
hendra (*hen*, *tra*), *f.*, *pl.* **-ow**, antique, antiquity (B.).
henforth, **henfor'**, *f.*, *pl.* **-rdhow**, **r'ow**, old and superseded road : Henvor, place-name.
hengof, *m.*, *pl.* **-ovyon**, tradition (W., B.).
hengok(g) (C. Voc. *hengog*, C.W. *hengyke*), *m.*, *pl.* **-ogyon**, great-grandfather, *thridde faeder*, Aelfric; more loosely, ancestor, forefather, C.W. 1702: see **dyhok(g).**
†henledan (C. Voc. *enlidan*, for *hens. ledan*), *m.*, plantain, way-bread : literally " way-broad," *wegbraede* Aelfric ; see **hens**, **ledan**, the *s* (older *t*) is lost before *l* as in B. *heledan*, W. *henllydan.*
henma, see **hemma.**
henna (Late *hedna*, *hedda*), *dem. pron. m.*, that, that time, that one, that thing, that man : see **hen**, **honna.**
henor, see **enor.**
hens (C. Voc. *hins*), *m.*, *pls.* **-y**, **-yow**, **henjy**, way, road, journey, course : *h. dall*, *hentall*, blind alley (B.) ; *mos yn h.*, to set out.
hensa, see **hynsa.**
hensys, *f.*, antiquity (B.).
henvam, *f.*, *pl.*- **mow**, grandmother, ancestress (W.) : see **hendas.**
henwel, *vb.*, to name, utter name of, nominate, denominate, call, repute : 3 s. pret. *he(y)nwys*, 1 s. pres.-fut. *henow* ; p. pt. *hynwys* is used also as meaning " set apart," " sacred " ; with fut. of *bos* in habitual-present sense, *a-vyth henwys*, is called.
hen-whethel, *m.*, *pl.* **-thlow**, legend.
henyēth, *f.*, *pl.* **-ow**, traditional language (W.)
henys, *m.*, old age : *a newyth hag a h.*, in youth and age, B.M. 167.

hep(b)², *prep.*. without, lacking, minus, not counting, besides: combines with prons. see APPENDIX V.; mutation affects only *d*, in *danjer*, *deweth*, *dowt*, and *g* in *gorfen*, *gow*, and these optionally, apparently as survivals, *hep*4 in **hepcor** only.
hepcor, *vb.*, to renounce, give up, forfeit, yield, forego, spare, dispense with, lay aside; **m.*, what can be foregone (W.).
hepcoryans, *m.*, renunciation (W.).
hep-forth (C. Voc. *hebford*), *adj.*, trackless, impassible, *butan wege* Aelfric.
hep-mar, *adv.*, doubtless: Lh. gives a late colloquial contraction *hemmar*.
hep nam, see **nam**.
hep-par, **hep-parow**, *adj.*, unequalled, incomparable.
hep-wow, see **gow**.
herberow, see **erberow**.
herdhas, see **horth**.
herdhya, *vb.*, to ram, thrust, shove, push, butt; *h. dhe-ves* (of boat), launch; 2 s. imp. *horth*, 3 s. pres.-fut. *herth*, 1 s. *hordhyaf*; 3 s. pret. *hordhas*; see **horth**.
herdhyans, *m.*, thrusting, impetus.
hermyt (C. Voc. *ermit*), *m.*, *pl.* **-ys**, hermit, B.M. 1948, *westen setla* Aelfric.
hern, see **horn**.
hernen, *f.*, *col.* **hērn** (C. Voc. †*hering*, *haerinc* Aelfric, Late *hearn*), pilchard Gw., Lh.; **h.-wyn**, *col.* **hērn-gwyn**, herring, Lh.: *dama 'n hern*, allice shad (D. "damon herring"); Lat. *allec*, C. Voc., actually comprises salted or smoked herrings, pilchards, sardines and anchovies.
hernes, *m.*, armour, trappings, harness (M.E. *herneys*).
hernessya, *vb.*, to put on armour, harness or equipment, B.M. 3221 (M.E.).
hernya (*hernia*, P.), *vb.*, to shoe a horse: 2 s. imp. *horn*, 3 s. pres.-fut. *hern*.
hernyor (C. Voc. *heirnior*), *m.*, *pl.* **-yon**, farrier, shoe-smith, *isenwyrhta* Aelfric: see **hernya**.
hertach, see **ertach**.
hertons, see **ertons**.
herwyth, *prep.*, according to, in accordance with, on the authority of; used with *yn* it has the force of a noun implying close connection, e.g., *yn dha h.*, with thee, on thy person, in thy company, etc.; *yn h. chy Marya*, in association with, or the vicinity of, the building of Mary, B.M. 640.
hēs (*heys*, *hȳs*), *m.*, length, extent: *a-hes*, at full length, outstretched, entirely; *dhe-hes*, at last, at length; *kemer hy deu h.*, take twice its length; *h. oll ow croghen scorjyes*, scourged to the whole extent of my skin; see **hēs-ha-hēs**.
hēs (O.C. *hēd*), *f.*, *pl.* **-ow**, swarm of bees, flight of birds, school of fish: *tewlel h.*, to swarm (B.); see **hevva**.
hēs-ha-hēs (*hyssëas*, M.C. 45), *adv.*, from end to end, entirely, all along, as V. *hed ha hed*.
hesk, *adj.*, dry, milkless, sterile (W., B.).
***hesken**, *f.*, *pl.* **-now**, saw (B.).
†**hesken** (C. Voc. *hesc(h)en*), *f.*, *col.* **hesk**, sedge: in C. Voc. wrongly made "reed," as *hreod*, Aelfric, Lat. *canna*, *arundo*.
***heskenna**, *vb.*, to saw (B.).
hesky, *vb.*, to go dry, lose its milk: *bugh heskys*, a cow gone dry, Borlase.
heson, *adj.*, sounding easily or well (W., B.).
†**hesp**, *m.*, *pl.* **-ow**, lock, hasp, C. Voc., *haepse*, *hespe* Aelfric (O.E.).
hēsya, *vb.*, to swarm, throng, flock together, form a school of fish (W.).
hēth, *m.*, *pl.* **-dhas**, stag, red-deer: place-name *Cruk Heyth*, cf. *Crug Carow* (W., B.).
hēth, see **hēdhen**, **hedhes**, **hedhy**.
hēthken, m., deerskin (W.).
heveleby, *v.*, to liken, make similiar: see **dyheveleby**.
hevelep, *m.*, *pl.* **-ebow**, likeness, resemblance, portrait, image; *adj.*, like, similar, equal: *yn-hevelep*, apparently, seemingly, in semblance.
hevelepter, *m.*, likeness, image, similarity, equality.
hevelles, **havalla** (inf. not found), *vb.*, to seem, appear to be: 3 s. plupf. *havalsa* (*'falsa*, C.W. 1918); 3 s. pret. *havallas*; 3 s. impf. ind. *hevelly* (*'fylly*, C.W. 784); *yth-hevel genef*, it seems to me; *h. orth*, compare with; see **haval**.
***hevleny**, *adv.*, this year (W., B.).
hevva (O.C. *hēd,-va*), *f.*, swarming, flocking or shoaling of bees, birds or fish: (D. "hevva," cry raised when pilchards are seen); see **covva**, **scovva**, **hēs**.
hevys (C. Voc. *heuis*), *m.*, *pl.* **-yow**, shirt, smock, *syric* Aelfric: *h. run*, cilice, penitential hair-shirt, B.M. 4443.
***hewar**, *adj.*, manageable, docile (W.).
hewas, older **havos** (*hāf*, *bos*), *m.*, summer-dwelling, dairy-farm: Hewas, place-names; Huish, Hawesse, personal name.
hewel, *adj.*, visible (W., B.).

heweres, *adj.*, helpful, ready to aid, B.M. 3133: see **gweres.**
hewerth, *adj.*, saleable (W., B.).
†**hewōl** (C.V. *hewuil*), *adj.*, vigilant, *wacol* Aelfric.
heyjy, see **hōs.**
heyjyk, hȳjyk, *m.*, *pl.* **-ygow.** duckling.
ho, *interj.*, ho !
hobba, *m.*, *pl.* **-bys**, riding-horse, hobby: place-name, Stable H.
ho·berjon, -son, *m.*, *pl.* **-s**, habergeon, hauberk, sleeveless coat of chain-mail, R.D. 2536 (M.E. *habergeoun*).
hogan, *m.*, *pl.* **hegyn**, haw, hawthorn-berry (D. "hoggan").
hogen (*hogan*), *adv.*, ? still. yet, in time to come, O.M. 272, C.W. 99: cf. W. *hagen*, but, yet, however, B.*hogen*, but.
hogen. *f.*, *pl.* **-gas**, dinner-cake, baked pastry cake (D. "hoggan" and corruptly "hobbin"): this and **fūgen** are both later vars. of **whȳogen.**
hōgh (C. Voc. *hoch*), *m.*, *pl.* **-as, mōgh**, pig, hog, swine: *hanter h.*, flitch, Lh.
†**hōghwū** (C. Voc. *hochwuyu*), *m.*, *pl.* **-ow**, boar-spear: see **gū.**
hogūl, see **hegōl**.
hōk, *m.*, *pl.* **-ys**, hawk, : *maga fery avel h.*, as merry as a hawk, B.M. 1901.
hokkya (*hokya*), *vb.*, to hesitate, shilly-shally, stammer, put off, postpone: *hep h.* forthwith.
hōl, *m.*, *pl.* **-yow**, following, succession, sequel (B.): see **holya.**
hōl (*hole*), *adj.*, whole, B.M., Gw. (E.).
holan (C. Voc. *haloin, -ein*), *m.*, salt, Lh., J. Boson.
holanek, *adj.*, salt, saline (W., B.): replaced by **sal.**
†**holaner** (C. Voc. *haloiner*), *m.*, *pl.* **-oryon**, salter, salt-maker.
holany, *vb.*, to salt (W., B.): replaced by **salla.**
holergh, see **helergh.**
holm(a), see **hom(ma).**
holya, *vb.*, to follow, go or come after: 3 s. pres. -fut., 2 s. imp. *hōl.*
holyer, *m.*, *pl.* **-yoryon**, follower.
hom (*holm* B.M.), *dem. pron. f.*, this: used before vowels in *bos*, unless pron. is emphasized.
hombronk, see **hembronk.**
homma (*holma* B.M., C.W.), *dem. pron. f.*, this, this one, this woman: *holma* s like *helma*, see **hemma**,

hon, *dem. pron. f.*, that; used before vowels in *bōs* unless pron. is emphasized.
hond, *m.*, *pl.* **hons**, hound (M.E.): term of abuse B.M. 2414.
honen (Late var. *hunnan*), *m.*, self, selves: used with all poss. prons., e.g., *ow-h.*, myself, adverbially, by myself; *my ow-h.*, I myself, *ow... ow-h.*, my own...; *ow-h. oll*, all by myself, all alone; with preps. *dhe'm h.*, to myself, etc.
honna (Late *hodna, hodda*), *dem. pron. f.*, that, that one, that woman: used with reference to all f., nouns, as e.g., named places in B.M. 2285, 2289.
honter, *m.*, *pl.* **-s**, hunter, B.M. 3161 (M.E.).
honthsel, see **hansel.**
***hopysen**, *f.*, hop-plant, *col.* **-hopys**, hops (W., B.).
***hopysek**, *f.*, *pl.* **-egow, -egy**, hop-garden (B.).
hora (*whorra* Carew), *f.*, *pl.* **-ys**, whore, O.M., Lh. (M.E. hore).
horben (*horth, pen*), *m.*, *pl.* **-now**, hand-rammer, used to make a firm foundation, lit. "ramhead," O.M. 2322.
horn (C. Voc. *hoern*), *m.*, *pl.* **hern**, iron: *h. margh*, horse-shoe.
hornak, *f.*, iron-bearing ground.
hornek, *adj.*, like iron.
horsen, *m.*, *pl.* **-s**, whoreson (as insult), (M.E.).
horth', hor', *m.*, *pl.* **hordhas** (Late *horras, hurroz* Lh.) ram, male sheep: see **herdhya.**
hōs (C. Voc. *hoet*), *m.*, *pl.* **hȳjy, heyjy** (*heidzhe* Borlase), duck, *ened* Aelfric: Polhigey, place-name.
hōs, *adj.*, hoarse, Lh. (E.D. "hoaze").
†**hosan**, *f. pl.* **-ow** (C. Voc. *fosaneu* for *hosaneu*), *col.* **hōs** (C. Voc.), hose, stocking, long hose, *hosa*, Aelfric.
hosket, *m.*,**-tys,-tow**, hogshead, Gw. (E.D. "osgit").
hōst, etc., see **ōst.**
hōsy, *vb.*, to speak hoarsely (E.D.): see **hōs.**
hōsyas (*hoiziaz* Lh.), *m.*, hoarseness: see **hōs.**
†**hot** (*hout*, O.M. 2598), *m.*, *pl.* **-tys**, headgear, hood, hat, C. Voc., *haet*, Aelfric (O.E.).
***hōthel, hōl**, *m.*, *pl.* **-thlow**, lifetime (W., B.).
hothfy, *vb.*, to swell, blister, puff up, rise

in **bubbles**, B.M. 4458 : see **whethfy.**
houl, see howl.
houtȳn, see **hautȳn.**
how (*hou*), *interj.*, calling attention, ho! hullo! (M.E.): *H.! dus yn-rak!* Hi! Come on out! R.D. 1989.
howl, houl (C. Voc. *heuul*, C.W. *howle*), *m.*, sun, (without *an*) sunlight: *avel h. dre weder a,* like sunshine that goes through glass, B.M. 853.
howldrehevel, howldrevel (*houldreval* Lh.), *m.*, sunrise, *East.
howlsedhas (*houlzedhas* Lh.), *m.*, sunset, West: see **sedhas.**
***hūa,** *vb.*, to hoot, raise a cry (W., B.).
***hüal.** *m.*, *pl.* **-ow,** fetter: replaced by **carghar-horn** (W., B.).
hūb, ūb, *m.*, hubbub, noise, W. *wb.*
hubbadrylsy, *m.*, great noise (D. " uppadriljy "): see **drylsy.**
hubbadullya, *m.*, riotous noise (D. " obbadillia," " hubbadullia "): cf. B. *Kabaduilh*, W. *cabidwl*, medley, row.
hüda, *vb.*, to charm, enchant, work magic (W., B.).
hüder, *m.*, *pl.* **-oryon,** enchanter, magician, deceiver, Ord.
hudhes (*hotheys*), *f. or col.*, covering, rugs, blankets, B.M. 4446: cf. W. *(en)hudded.*
***hü·dhygel, hüdhyl,** *m.*, soot, grime: see **hylgeth** (W.B.).
hüdhyk, *adj.*, joyful, gleeful, happy, glad: *h. y golon,* merry-hearted, O.M. 2818; (adverbially) gleefully, R.D. 2304: see **hüth.**
†**hüdol,** *m.*, *pl.* **-yon,** sorcerer, magician, C. Voc., *dry,* Aelfric: see **hüder.**
hujes (*hugez* Kerew), *adv.*, exceedingly, hugeous (E.).
hük (*hugk*), *f.*, *pl.* **-ys, hücow,** riding-hood, hooded cloak, P.C., R.D.: (M.E. *huke,* O. Fr. *hucque,* Med. Lat. *huca.*
hūla, see ūla.
hūla (*hoola,* Gw., *hoalea* Lh.), *vb.*, to cry, lament, bewail, weep: perhaps for **ōla,** but cf. M.E. *houlen* to howl.
hülla, see **hünlef.**
hün, *m*, sleep, slumber: †*h. desempys,* lethargy, sudden sleepiness, coma, C. Voc. *ungelimplic slapolnys* Aelfric.
hüna, *vb.*, to sleep (W., B.).
hünes (*huenneys*), *m.*, sleeping, action of sleep, slumbering, B.M. 4448.
hüngan, *f.*, *pl.* **-ow,** lullaby (W.).
hünjy, *m.*, dormitory (W.): see **cuskly.**
hünlef, hülla, *m.*, nightmare (D. " hilla ").
hünros (*-rus, henros,* Late *hendres*), *m.*, *pl.* **-ow,** dream, vision; *vb.*, to dream.
hüny, *pron.*, one: found used only after *lyes, pup,* to which might be added *boghes, lower.*
hurlya. *vb.*, to play at hurling, formerly the Cornish national ball-game, Lh., Borlase.
hurlyas, *m.*, *pl.* **-ysy, -yjy** (*hurlegey* Gw.), hurler.
hurtya (*hertia* Lh.), *vb.*, to hurt.
hüs (O.C. *hüd*), *m.*, magic, charm, illusion, jugglery, P.C., B.M.: see **hüder.**
huth, *m.*, covert, shade (W. *hudd*): Huthnance, place-name; see **hudhes.**
hüth, *adj.*, joyful, happy, at ease, M.C. 225.
hüthhē·, *vb.*, to make happy, comfort, ease, R.D. 1877: as **berhē.**
hüthter, *m.*, joyfulness, happiness, comfort: see **hüth,**
hüvel (C. Voc. *huuel,* B.M. *üfel,* C.W. *evall*), *adj*, humble, lowly, modest, obedient, accessible, unassuming, without haughtiness, *eadmod* Aelfric.
hüvelder (B.M. *üvelder*), *m.*, humility, friendliness, accessibility, R.D. 425.
hüvelhē·, *vb.*, to make humble, humiliate.
†**hüvelsys** (C. Voc. *huueldot*), *f.*, humility, modesty, *eadmodnys* Aelfric.
hüvla, *vb.*, to be humble, obey, Lh.
hy-, see **he-,** Appendix II.
hȳ (Late *hei*), *pron.*, she, her, (of weather, time, circumstances, condition or f. nouns) it: *nebes esen ow-tyby y-fedha-hy y'n for'-ma,* little were we thinking it would be like this, B.M. 3351; *hy yu dhe well,* it is (all) the better, O.M. 1628; *yndella hy a-besyas,* so it continued; *yth-yu-hy dewedhes,* it is late; *kens hy bos nos,* ere nightfall, etc.; also combined with preps., *glaw yu ynny,* it promises rain, *dy,* thither, *gensy,* withal, etc; when " it " represents an unmentioned m. noun or pron. or inf. of vb., however, *y, -n-,* are used, not *hy, -s-*; *y'th hallos y vos gorrys,* that it is put into thy power, *my a-n-gwra,* I'll do it, etc., and even as "it" of condition *hy* is never replaced by *honna,* e.g., *Dar! dufa-hy dhe henna?* What! has it come to that? B.M. 3287; the m. pronominal prep. is always used also, *na-gemer marth anodho,* be not surprised at it, C.W. 560.
hȳ³, *poss. pron.*, her, its.
hy-bē·n, y-bē·n, *pron. f.*, the other one of

two, lit. her (or its) fellow : properly the fem. equivalent (*ben*, root of *benen*, *below*) to *kyla* in **y-gȳla**, but in M. Cor. used also less correctly as masc. ; *an yl hy-ben*, one another.

***hybyow**, *adv.*, by, past, with vbs. of motion (W., B.) : seems replaced by **drēs**, with noun or pron.

***hycas**, *vb.*, to hiccup : see **hyk**.

hyga, *vb.*, to play tricks, tease, cheat, Gw., P. : 3 s. pres.-fut. *hyk* ; subj. *hycco*.

hygen, *f.*, *pl.* **-now**, fish-hook : see **gwelen**.

hygenna, *vb.*, to hook, catch with rod and line (B.).

hyhȳ·, **-yhȳ·**, *pron.* (emphatic), she, her, herself.

hȳjy, see **hōs**.

hȳk(g) (C. Voc. *hyc*, Lh. *hig*, *yg*), *m.*, *pl.* **-gow**, fish-hook, *angel* Aelfric : *h. horn*, iron hook, Lh. ; see **gwelen**.

hyk, *f.*, *pl.* **-ygyon**, trick, cheat (B.).

***hyk**, *m.*, *pl.* **hycow**, hiccup (W., B.).

hylgeth, *m.*, soot : ?metathesis of **hüdhygel**, like W. *helgaeth* ; Lhuyd writes "filgeth," but probably confusing written capital H and F, as in "Hloh" for *Flogh*.

hyly, *m.*, brine, salt water, sea-water : *yn dowr nag yn h.*, in fresh water nor in salt, R.D. 2318.

hylȳen, *f.*, pickle of brine (B.).

hylȳenna, *vb.*, to pickle in brine (B.).

***hympna**, *m.*, *pl.* **-nys**, hymn (M.E. *hympne*, M.B. *hympn*) : cf. **solempnyta**, **dampnya**.

hyndlys, etc., see **handla**,

hynsa (*hensa* for *henseth*), *m.*, fellow being, others, fellows, peers, associates, neighbours, O.M. 2136, B.M. 2925, as B. *hente(z)*.

hynwyn, **-wys**, see **hanow**, **henwel**.

hynwys, *adj.*, sacred, sanctified, holy, hallowed, dedicated to sacred purpose, set apart, O.M. 144, P.C. 1951, M.C. 217, B.M. 2455 : see **henwel**.

hȳr (C. Voc. *hir*), *adj.*, long, lengthy, tall, tedious, prolix : *hep na hyrra lavarow*, without further discussion, B.M. 2920.

hȳrbenys, *m.*, long penance ; *vb.*, to fast long: *kynth-eses owth- h.*, though thou wast long fasting, B.M. 3885.

hȳrder, *m.*, length, tediousness (W., B.).

hȳreth (Late *heerath*), *m.*, longing, yearning, nostalgia, loneliness, homesickness.

hȳrethek (*herethek*)) *adj.*, longing, yearnful, nostalgic, lonely, homesick, B.M. 4314, 4526.

***hȳrgelgh**, *m.*, oval, ellipse (W.).

hȳrgernyas, *m.*, *pl.* **-ysy**, trumpeter : see **kernyas**.

†**hȳrgorn** (C. Voc. *hirgorn*), *m.*, *pl.* **-gern**, trumpet, lit. "long horn," *byma* Aelfric.

hȳrgren, *adj.*, oval, cylindrical (W.).

hȳrhē·, *vb.*, to lengthen : as **berhē**.

hȳrneth (*hyr(e)nath*, C.W. 1729), *f.*, a tediously long time : *h. bew of y'n bys-ma*, I have been living irksomely long in this world.

hȳrōs, *m.*, longevity, great age (W., B.).

hȳryk, *adj.*, longish, somewhat long (B.).

hyssëas, see **hēs-ha-hēs**.

J

-ja, see **-sa**.

jag, *m.*, *pl.* **-gys**, jolt, jar, jog, P.C. 2817 (M.E.).

***jam**, *m.*, jam (E.).

jammes, *adv.*, ever, always (Anglo-Fr.).

jarden. **jarn** (*dzharn*, Lh.), *m.*, garden, C.W. 1801 (Anglo-Fr.).

jaudyn, **joudyn** (*jawdyn*, C.W.), *m.*, *pl.* **-s**, fellow, rascal, knave (M.E. *jaudewyn*).

jawl (*jaul*), var. of **dyawl**, following *n*.

jayler (*geyler*), *m.*, *pl.* **-s**, gaoler (M.E.).

Jentyl, *m.*,*pl.* **-lys** (*Gentelles*,Gw.), Gentile.

jentyl (*gentyl*), *adj.*, gentle, polite, pleasing, well-born; *adv.*, finely, elegantly, (M.E. *gentil*) : see **dēnjentyl**.

je·ntylys, *m.*, courtesy, politeness, grace, gentleness, prettiness (M.E. *gentillesse*).

jerkyn, *m.*, short coat, Lh. (M.E.).

jēt (*jeit*), *m.*, jot, iota : rhymes with "strayte" C.W. 659.

jēth, var. of **dēth**, following *n*.

jevan (*gevan*), *m.*, demon, fiend, P.C., R.D.

jevody·, **jevojȳ·** (*jevuje* B.M. 1589), *interj.*, I tell you (M.E. *jeo vos dy*, etc., for F. *je vous dis*).

jolyf, *adj.*, lively, sprightly, frisky, alert, cheerful, jolly, R.D. 2013 (M.E. *jolif*).

jorna (*dzhurna*, Lh.), *m.*, *pls.* **-nys**, **-nyow**, day : *an j. -ma war seythen*, to-day week, Lh. (Late, but from M.E. *journee*, *jorne*. day's work.

joudyn, see **jaudyn**,

j'ouē (*del jouē·*), (as) I have heard, M.C. 227 (M.E. from Fr. *j 'ai ouï*).

Jovyn, *m.*, Jove, Jupiter, god of heathens.
jöwal, *m.*, *pl.* **-elys**, **-ys**, jewel (Late, M.E. *jowel.*)
jö·weller, *m.*, *pl.* **-s**, jeweller (M.E.): see **jowal.**
jowl, see **jawl.**
joy, *m.*, *pl.* **-ës**, joy (M.E.): in many places R.D. for Norris *joy* read MS. *roy.*
juglour (*jugleer*), *m.*, *pl.* **-s**, juggler, conjurer, B.M. 921 (M.E.).
junnya, **yunnya**, *vb.*, to join, put together with others, add, adjoin, O.M. 2658 (M.E. *joyne*): *a-vynnough-why j. agas whednar?* will you club your sixpence? Borlase MS.
junnyans, *m.*, joint adjunct, addition.
junt (*junct*), *m.*, *pl.* **-tys**, joint, member, part of body, M.C., B.M. (M.E. *joynt*).
juj, *m.*, *pl.* **-jys**, judge (M.E. *juge*).
jujja, **-ya**, **yujja**. **-ya** (*iugge, yuggye*), *vb.*, to judge, intend, think fit, form an opinion (M.E.).
jūst, *m.*, *pl.* **-ys**, joust, tourney (M.E.).
just, *adj.*, just (M.E.).
juster (*iucter* for *just(ys)er*), *m.*, *pl.* **-s**, judge, justiciary, M.C. (M.E. *justicere*).
jūstya, *vb.*, to joust, tilt, B.M. 2317 (M.E. *juste*).
justys, *m.*, *pl.* **-yow**, justice, magistrate (M.E.).
jȳ, see **sȳ**, **ynsȳ.**
-jy, see **chȳ.**
jȳant (*gean* Pryce MS), *m.*, *pl.* **-ns**, giant (M.E. *geant*).
jyn (*gyn*), *m.*, *pl.* **-nys**, contrivance, gin, apparatus, mechanism, engine: **j. -scryfa*, type-writer; **j-tan*, steam-engine, etc. (M.E. *gyn*); see **ynjyn.**
***jynjy**, *m.*, *pl.* **-ow**, engine-house.
***jynwȳth**, *m.*, machinery.
jȳst (*gist*), *m.*, *pl.* **-ys** (*gystys*), beam, joist, prop, shore (M.E. *gyste*, O. Fr. *giste*).

K (mutations G, H).

N.B. With vowel change of *e*, *y* to *a*, *o*, *k* becomes **c**.

***kay**, *m.*, *pl.* -ys, quay.
kē, *m.*, *pl.* **-ow**, hedge, low wall of earth and stone, fence: (*gesys*) *war an k.*, (left) unclaimed, for anyone to pick up, ownerless, B.M. 1253, 1896.
kē, see **mōs.**
ke-, etc., see Appendix II.
kēas, (*keaz*, Lh., Borlase), *vb.*, to hedge, fence, enclose, shut up: p. pt., *kēs*, *kēys*; *m.*, *pl.* **-ow**, cover, lid (W.): 2 pl. imp. *kēeugh* (*keauh*, Borlase MS.); Noon Gays (*an un ges*), place-name.
†**keber**, *f.*, *pl.* **-bryow**, beam, rafter, joist, (heraldry) chevron, C. Voc., *raefter* Aelfric: replaced by **jȳst.**
***kedhow**, *m.*, mustard (W.).
kedry·n, *f.*, trouble, quarrel, disputation (D. "cudridn").
kedrynya, *vb.*, to dispute, quarrel: see **trynya.**
kēer, *m.*, *pl.* **-ēoryon**, hedger, closer, shutter (W., B.).
kef, *m.*, *pl.* **-yon**, stump, tree-trunk, log (W., B.).
keflesca, *vb.*, to set swinging or moving (B.): see **lesk.**
kefnysen, **-nyjen**, *f.*, *col.*, **kefnys**, spider (B., cf. D. "cuffan," spider-crab).
kefrȳs, in verse usually **kefrȳ·s** (*kyffrys*, *kefreys*), *adv.*, also, as well, likewise, too, moveover, alike, together, at the same time: *k. ha*, as well as.
kefrȳsy, **-ȳjy**, *vb.*, to associate, confederate (B.).
kefrȳsyans, *m.*, federation.
kefrȳsyas, *m.*, *pl.* **-ysy**, confederate, ally, (B.).
kefys, see **cafos.**
keger, *col.*, hemlock (W., D. "keggar"): see **kegysen.**
kegyn (C. Voc. *keg(h)in*), *f.*, *pl.* **-ow**, kitchen: *mollath Dew yn gegyn!* God's curse in the kitchen! jocular oath.
***kegyn**, *f.*, *pl.* **-as**, jay (B.): cf. W. *cegid*, green-woodpecker.
kegyner, *m.*, *pl.* **-oryon**, cook (B.).
kegyn-vyrgh, *f. pl.* **-es**, kitchen-maid.
kegyn-wrēk, *f.*, *pl.* **-wrageth**, cook.
kegyon, see **cōk**, *adj.*
kegẏsen, *f.*, *col.* **kegys**, hemlock, umbelliferous plant: *k. dowr*, water-hemlock; *gwelen-gegys*, hemlock-stalk, kex.
kehaval, *adj.*, equal, similar, corresponding; *adv.*, alike, C.W. 2201.
kehavalhē·, *vb.*, to compare, liken: as **berhē.**
keheja, see **keheseth.**
keher (*c(h)eher*, pulpa, miscopied *cheber*, vulva, C. Voc.), *m.*, *pl.* **-ow**, flesh, muscle, B.M. 3291, *lira* Aelfric,

keherek, *adj.*, muscular, brawny (W.).
keheryn, *m.*, *pl.* **-now**, piece of flesh, muscle (W.).
kehēs, *adj.*, of equal length (W.); *k. ha*, as long as.
keheseth, keheja (*kehedzhe* Lh.), *m.*, *pl.* **-ethow**, extent, measure, (of syllable) quantity (W.); expansion, reaching or stretching of the body, full stretch, Lh.; *equator, equinox (W., B.); equivalent (W.): *k. deth ha nos*, equinox (W., B.), *k. Merth* vernal equinox, *k. Gwengala*, autumnal equinox (B.).
kehēsnōs, equinox (W.).
kehēsy, -jy, *vb.*, to equalize, proportion (W.).
kekefrys, in verse usually **-frȳ's**, *adv.*, also alike, withal, at the same time, together, as well: *k. ha nos ha deth*, as well by night as by day.
kekemmys, *pron.*, all, whoever, whatever, lit. as many (as): *k. us ynna gwres*, everything that is created in them, O.M. 54.
kēl, *m.*, *pl.* **-ow**, hiding, shelter, bower; *adj.*, hidden, secret (W.): ? place-names Castel Kel (Cayle), Ker Gel (now Crill); see **argel, keles.**
keladow, *m.*, concealment, secrecy subterfuge, O.M. 2117.
†**kelegel**, *m.*, *pl.* **-glow**, chalice, C. Voc., *calic* Aelfric; see **gorher.**
keleren, *f.*, *col.* **keler**, earth-nut, pig-nut (D. pl. "kellas," "killy(mores)").
keles, *vb.*, to hide, conceal, keep secret: 2 s. imp., 3 s. pres.-fut. *kēl.*
***kelf**, *m.*, *pl.* **-yow**, stock, stem, pillar (W., B.).
***kelgh**, *m.*, *pl.* **-ow**, circle, round (W., B.).
***kelghen**, *f.*, *pl.* **-now**, circlet, necklace (B.).
***kelghtro,-dro**, *m.*, revolution, circuit, orbit (W.).
***kelghy**, *vb.*, to encircle (W., B.).
***kell**, *f.*, *pl.* **-ow**, cell (W., B.).
***kell**, *f.*, *pl.* **-yow**, *d.* **dywgell**, testicle (W., B.).
***kellek**, *adj.*, entire, uncastrated (W., B.): ?replaced by **lawen**.
kelly (C. Voc. *kelli*), *f.*, *pl.* **-ÿow**, grove, copse, *holt* Aelfric.
kelly, *vb.*, to lose, forfeit: p. pt. *kellys*, *kyllys*; 3 s. pres.-fut. *kyll*; 3 s. subj. *collo*; 3 s. pret. *collas.*
kellyl, -y, see †**collel**,
kellyllyk (C. Voc. *kellillic*), *m.*, *pl.* **-ygow**, penknife, *cnif* Aelfric: dim. of **collel**; see **kyllygen.**
kellyn (*kelin*, Borlase, *ken*, *lyn*), *m.*, weed that coats standing pools, duckweed, floating scum: *n* lost before *l*, cf. **hünlef, hellys.**
†**kelly-wyk** (O.C. *celliwic*), *f.*, *pl.* **-ygow**, wood, grove.
kelmy (*kylmy*), *vb.*, to bind, tie, lash, knot, oblige: 3 s. pres.-fut. *kelm*; 2 s. imp. *colm*; 3 s. pret. *colmas*; p. pt. *kelmys*, bound, obliged; *k dhe*, bound for, on the way to, B.M. 4185, 4372.
kelorn, *m.*, *pl.* **-ow**, bucket, pail (W., B.).
***Kelt**, *m.*, *pl.* **-yon**, Celt.
***Keltek**, *adj.*, Celtic.
***kelvyth**, *adj.*, artificial, artistic (W.).
kelyn, see **colyn, kelynen.**
kelyna, *vb.*, to whelp (B.).
kelynek, *f.*, *pl.* **-egy**, holly-grove: place-names,
kelynen, *f.*, holly-tree; *col.* **kelyn** (C. Voc. *kelin*), holly, *holen* Aelfric.
kelynyk, *m.*, *pl.* **-ygow**, little puppy.
kelyonen (C. Voc. *kelionen*), *f.*, *col.* **kelyon**, fly: *k. kyk*, bluebottle-fly.
kelyonek, *adj.*, full of, or covered with flies.
kem-, see **ke-.**
kember, see **kemper.**
Kembrek, *adj.*, Welsh; *m.*, Welsh language, Gw.
Kembres, *f.*, *pl.* **-ow**, Welshwoman.
Kembrō, *m.*, *pl.* **-brÿon**, Welshman, Lh.
Kembry (*Kimbra*, Lh.), *f.*, Wales.
***kemena, *comyna**, *vb.*, to cut, cut out, hew, chop (W., B.): see **scomyn.**
Kemerer, *m.*, *pl.* **-roryon**, one who takes, tenant (W., B.).
kemeres, *vb.*, to take, receive, accept: 2 s. imp., 3 s. pres.-fut., *kemer* (Late *kebmer*); *dhys kemer e, kemereugh e dheugh* (with *dhe*), take it; *k. gallos*, to assume power; *k. yn-ban*, to rise and leave the table, B.M. 456; the old 3 s. pret. ending *-t*, (now *-th* in Welsh *kemerth*) is found only in *pan gemert kyg*, M.C. 3.
kemeryans, *m.*, acceptance: *k. da*, favourable reception, Keigwin.
kemmyn, *m.*, *pl.* **-ow**, bequest, commendation.
kemmynna (C.W. *comena*), *vb.*, bequeath, leave by will, commit or commend to another's care: 3 s. pret. *kemmynnys.*
kemmynnadow, *m.*, bequest.
kemmyneth, *m.*, *pl.* **-edhow** (*comenetha* Gw.), commendation.

kemmys (*kymmys*, C.W. *kebmys*; *ke-, myns*), *adj.*, so or as many, so or as much, so or as great (used with sing. or pl.); (as quasi noun) as many people (as), all such (as), all those (who): with numerals, *deu-gemmys, pymp-k*, twice, five times, as many, etc.; *k. ha*, as much as; *k. vyth an ponvotter*, the misery will be so great (no particle), P.C. 2656; *gwynvys k. a-n-gwrello*, happy all who do it (particle), O.M. 605.

***kempen**, *adj.*, neat, tidy, orderly, concise (W., B.).

***kempenna**, *vb.*, to tidy, set in order (W., B.).

kemper, kember, *m.*, *pl.* **-prow, -brow,** junction of waters (W., B.): place-names Tregember for Tredhegember, Trev(h)emper.

kemusür, *m.*, symmetry; *adj.*, symmetrical (W.).

kemyn, *adj.*, common; *m.*, *pl.* **-yon**, commoner; *f.*, commons, commonalty: *brosyon ha k.*, great ones and ordinary folk, B.M. 3215, *Chy an Gemyn*, House of Commons.

kemysk (C. Voc. *commisc*), *m.*, mixture, blend, concoction: see **blȳth,**

kemyskrȳth, *adj.*, mongrel, hybrid (W.).

kemysky, *vb.*, to mix, blend, stir, mingle: *yn-kemyskys*, in a mingled condition.

kemyskyans. *m.*, admixture.

kēn, see **keyn**.

kēn (C. Voc. *c(h)en*), *m.*, cause, law-case, reason, occasion, *intinga* Aelfric: *hep k.*, groundlessly, without cause.

ken, *m.*, *no pl.*, skin, hide, scale, peel, rind, coating, scum, scoria: see **kellyn, kenna.**

ken, kyn, *conj.*, *prep.*, ere, before (of time): used without particle before inflected parts of vbs. and before infs. or nouns; *k. of los*, ere I go grey-headed; *k. mos*, before going; *k. kescar, dybarth*, before separating; *k. penseythen*, before the week is out; see **kens, kynyaf.**

kēn, *adj.*, other, different, more, else, another, (anything) more; *adv.*, or else, otherwise, any more: *k. es, ages*, other than, anything else but; *k. re*, others; *k. tra*, something more, O.M. 794; *k. maner*, or else, otherwise; *my ny-won k.*, that's all *I* know.

ken-, see **ke-**.

kenak, *f.*, *pl.* **-negy**, in Kenegy, Tregenegy, Leskinnick, this may mean reed-bed; W. *cawn*, reeds, should be *kēn, cün*, in Cornish.

kenak (*kunac* Lh.), *m*, *pl.* **-ogas**, worm, ring-worm, lug-worm; rush-light; (endearment) tender one, cf. D. endearment "poor worm": Kennack Sands, place-name.

kenas, *adj.*, skinny, scaly, scummy (W.).

kencras, see **canker.**

ke'nderow (Lh. *canderu*), *m.*, *pl.* **-dyrewy**, cousin.

kendevryon, *pl*, meeting of waters: old name of Helford Haven; see **dever.**

kendon (Lh. *kundan*), *f.*, debt: *ny-vyn-e nefra dos mes a gendon*, he will never be out of debt, Lh.

kendoner, *m.*, *pl.* **-oryon**, debtor, P.C. 502.

ke'nethel, kenel (C. Voc. *kenethel*), *f.*, *pls.* **-thlow, -ow**, generation, race, nation, *cynren* Aelfric.

kene(th)legeth, *m.*, nationality.

kene(th)legy, *vb.*, to nationalize.

kene(th)lek, *adj.*, national, racial (W.).

***kengel**, *f.*, *pl.* **-glow**, band, girth, girdle (W.).

kenj, see **kens.**

kenkya, *vb.*, to contend, Lh.

kenna (Late *kedna*), *vb.*, to coat with dirt, etc. (D. "keddened").

kennen (†*cennen*, O.C. gloss), *f.*, *pl.* **-now**, thin skin, film, pellicle; cataract on eye (D. "kennin," "kennel"): *k. oy*, membrane of egg; *men-k.* small polished stone, believed to cure cataract, the Welsh *maen magl* (D. "kennin' stone").

kennerth, *m.*, encouragement (B): see **nerth.**

kens, kenj, kyns (Late *kenz*), *comp. adj.*, former; *prep.*, *conj.*, ere, before (of time); *adv.*, formerly, sooner, rather, aforetime, once upon a time: sometimes *kenj* before *es*; *k. es dos...*, *k. dos...*, ere the coming of ..., before ...comes; *k. (es)ef dhe dhos*, before he comes; *k. es hemma, henna* (Late *kens'enna*), ere now, ere then; before inflected part of vb. takes *del*; *k. del vy*, rather than that thou wert; *dhe gens*, the sooner; *na hens*, not before; *keper ha k.*. just as it used to be; *k. lemmyn*, ere now, hitherto, before; *k. oll*, especially, chiefly, first of all; *k. (es) vyttyn*, before morning; *k. penseythen*, before the week is out; *k. bos prys-bos*, *k. es hedhy, dyberth, dybry*, before knocking off work, without a break, right off; *y dyller k.*, its former place; *k. nep-pell*, ere long, see **ken**, *conj.*, *prep.*

kensa, *superl. adj.* (*kynsa*, Late *kenza*) first, foremost; *adv.*, rather, sooner, at first: *k. my a-scul dha wos*, I will more likely shed thy blood, B.M. 2389.

kensewha (later *kenjowha*, *kenzhoha* Lh.), *m.*, forenoon, morning from 9 to noon, as V. *kentahoé*: see **kens**, **ewha**.

kenshēs, *f.*, first swarm of bees (W., B.).

kens-lemmyn, *adv.*, ere now, hitherto, P.C. 1194.

kensow, *adv.*, recently: found in **(a)gensow**, **(de)gensew(a)**, **(də)gensow**, as B. *kentaou*, W. *cynneu*.

kens-scryf, *m.*, first writing, original; preface, Lh. (W., B.).

kensynsy, **-synjy** (*gan zyngy*, Tonkin, Borlase), *vb.*, hold on, keep hold of, Fishermen's Catch, Tonkin MS.

kenter, *f.*, *pl.* **-trow**, nail, spike: *k.-horn*, iron spike, pl. *kentrow-hern*, P.C. 2938, perhaps distorted for rhyme, but cf. **eskelly-grēghyn**, apparently with same pl. of material: **k. tro*, screw.

kentra, *vb.*, to nail, with one nail; to spike: 2 s. imp. *kenter*, but before vowels, *kentr*, cf. **handla**.

kentreny (*-treyny*), *vb.*, to become maggotty, R.D. 74: 3 s. pres.-fut. *kentren*; 3 s. pret. *contronas*; see **contronen**.

kentrevak (Late *contrevak*), *adj.*, neighbouring; *m.*, *pl.* **-vogyon**. neighbour.

kentrevoges, *f.*, *pl.* **-ow**, female neighbour, gossip, B.M. 1551.

kentrewy, **kentrowa**, *vb.*, to nail, with many nails: p. pt. *kentrewys*; 3 s. subj. *kentrowo*.

kentryn (*kentron*, Carew), *m.*, *pl.* **-now**, spur, dim. of **kenter**: *ry k. dhe*, to spur on.

kentrynna, *vb.*, to spur, stimulate, urge onward.

kenwerth, *m.*, commerce, trade (B.).

kenyas (C. Voc. *c(h)eniat*), *m.*, *pl.* **-ysy**, singer, chanter, *sangere* Aelfric.

kenynek, *f.*, *pls.* **-egow**, **egy**, leek-garden.

kenynen, *f.*, *col.* **kenyn** (C. Voc. *kenin*, *kinin* Lh.), leek-plant: †*k. ewynek*, garlic, C. Voc.; *goth-k.*, crow-garlic, C. Voc.; *ewyn k.*, a clove of garlic (V,).

kenys, etc., see **cana**.

kenys, *m.*, *pl.* **-nesow**, singing, crowing (of cock): *kens es bos culyek-k.*, ere cock-crow, P.C. 903, altered to "kyns bos then kullyek kenys," in which *then* seems likely to be *dhe'n*, at the.

***keny·therow**, *f.*, *pl.* **-thyrewy**, female cousin (W., B.).

kenyver, **-fer** (*kynyfer*, Late var. *kenifra*), *adj.*, every, so many: *k. ha*, as many as, *y a-vya a bederow k. hag a olyow*, they would be of paternosters the same number as of wounds, M.C. 228; usual accent in verse is *ke·nyver*.

kepar, **kepa·r** (*ke-*, *par*, late metathesis *pocar*, *'car*), *adv.*, as, in the same way, like, alike, equally, like as, even, as, just like: *k. ef del devas, yndella an bows a-wre*, even as he grew, so did the coat, M.C. 161; *oll a'n da ha'n drok k.*, for all the good and the evil equally, M.C. 24; *k. y'n bys*, exactly as; *k. ha* (Late *carra*) before nouns and prons., *k. del*[2] or *k. ha del*[2] before inflected parts of vbs.

kēr, *f.*, *pl.* **-row**, fort, city: in ancient place-names usually *car*, with mutation sometimes resembling 3rd, in others "Gear," for *an*[2]*gēr*.

kēr (*kere*, *kear* C.W., *kēr* Lh.), *adj.*, dear, beloved, cherished, costly, expensive, comp. *kerra*: *pur-ger ty a-vyth gwythys*, most preciously shalt thou be cared for, B.M. 3640.

CHER

kerdhes (Late *kerras*), *vb.*, to walk, go, move along, (as verbal noun) ability to walk or way of walking, progress: 3 s. pres.-fut. *kerth*; 3 s. subj. *kertho*; 3 s. plupf. *kerthsa*; *ke dhe gerdhes!* be off! get out! *gas e dhe gerdhes!* keep it going! *scantlowr y-hallaf k.*, I can scarcely get along, B.M. 543, spoken by a *cul de jatte*, M. Lat. *kalus*, who cannot walk.

kerdhesyas (Late *?kerrējas*), *m.*, *pl.* **-esow**, step, pace, "go," as W. *cerddediad* (D. "kerrayjes," used of swinging).

kerdhynen, *f.*, *col.* **kerdhyn**, mountain-ash berry; rowan, quicken-tree (W., B., D. "care").

kerdyn, see **corden**.

keredhy, *vb.*, to chastise, rebuke, correct, B.M. 3250: 3 s. pres.-fut. *kereth*.

kerens, see **car**.

kerensa, **kerenja** (for *kerenseth*, Late *carenza*, *carenja*, *crenja*), *f.*, love, charity, friendship, affection, sake: *rak k. orthys*, for love of thee; *rag dha gerensa*,

for thy sake.
***keresyk**, *adj.*, dear ; *m. or f.*, *pl.* **-sygyon**, dear one (W., B.).
Kere·sk, *f.*, Exeter, Lh.
***keresen**, *f.*, *col.* **keres**, cherry, cherry-tree (W., B.) : **keresen vorel*, morello cherry.
kereth, *f.*, correction, reproach, chastisement, blame : see **keredhy**.
kergh, *m.*, way : used only in **yn-kergh**, and as root of **kerghes**.
kerghek, *f.*, *pl.* **-egy**, oat-field (B.).
kerghen, *f.*, *col.* **kērgh** (C. Voc. *keirch*, *kerth*, C.W. 1066, *keer*, Bilbao MS.), oat, oats.
kergher, *m.*, *pl.* **-oryon**, fetcher, carrier, bringer (B.).
kerghes (*kerhes*, *kyrghes*), *vb.*, to fetch, bring, carry, get : with dropped *gh*, 2 pl. imp. may be *ker'eugh* : p. pt. *ker'ys* (C.W. *kerrys*) ; *dun dh'y gerghes*, let's go and get it ; with *gans*, cause to be brought by, *kergh dhys ow ena gans el*, cause my soul to be fetched to thee by an angel, P.C. 429.
kerghwels, *m.*, oat-grass (W.).
kerghyn, *m.*, immediate environment : used only in **yn-kerghyn**.
kerghyth, **keryth** (C. Voc. *c(h)erhit*), *f.*, *pl.* **-ydhas**, heron, *hragra* Aelfric : Polkerth, place-name, for *pol k.*
***Kergront**, *f.*, Cambridge (**W.**).
kern, see **corn**.
kerna, see **crenna**.
kernek, *adj.*, horned.
kērneth, *m.*, dearness, expensiveness, dearth (B.).
Kernewek (Late *Cornoack*, etc.), *adj.*, Cornish ; *m.*, Cornish language.
Kernewekhē·, *vb.*, to put into Cornish, Cornicise : as **berhē**.
Kernewes, *f.*, *pl.* **-ow**, Cornishwoman.
Kernow (Late *Curnow*, etc.), *f.*, Cornwall (also Cornouaille in Brittany, B., *Kerne*, B.M.) ; *m.*, *pl.* **-yon**, Cornishman.
†**kernyas** (C. Voc. *c(h)erniat*), *m.*, *pl.* **-ysy**, **-yjy**, horn-blower, trumpeter, *horn blawere* Aelfric.
kernyk, *m.*, *pl.* **-ygow**, little horn, B.M. 3396 ; little corner, ? Porthkernick, place-name.
kerra, see **kēr**.
kers, see **corsen**.
kersek, *f.*, *pls.* **-egow**, **-egy**, fen, reed-swamp : Pengersick, place-name.
kersya (for *kesürya*), *vb.*, to comfort, set at ease, console : 3 s. pres.-fut., 2 s. imp. *kers* or *kesür* ; *o·mgersyeugh !* be of good cheer ! make yourselves at home! B.M. 296.
kert, *m.*, *pl.* **-ys**, chariot, cart, R.D. 236 (M.E.).
kerth (C. Voc. *kerd*, Late *ker'*), *m.*, walking, ability to walk ; walk, expedition, journey, *sidhfaet* Aelfric ; *ro dhym ow herth*, give me my power of walking, P.C. 401 ; *ow herth omma gullas dhe goll*, my journey hither is thrown away, B.M. 478 ; see **yn-kerth**.
kerthva, *f.*, walking-place, walk, promenade, foot-path (W.).
kervya, *vb.*, to carve (W.) : 3 s. pres.-fut., *kerf*.
kēry, *vb* , to wall, fortify (W.).
kerÿa, *vb.*, to make or mend shoes (B.) : see **kerÿor**.
keryas, *m.*, *pl.* **-ysy**, *f.* **-yades**, lover, sweetheart (W., B.).
†**keryn** (C. Voc. *keroin*), *f.*, *pl.* **-y**, tun, barrel, tub, B.M. 3226.
†**kerÿor** (C. Voc. *c(h)ereor*), *m.*, *pl.* **-yon**, cobbler, shoemaker, cordwainer, *sutere* Aelfric.
kerys, etc., see **cara**.
kēs, **cüs** (Cor. Voc. *caus*, *cōs*, P. *keas*), *m. and col.*, cheese, *cyse* Aelfric : *k glas*, unripe cheese, Borlase.
kes-, see Appendix II.
kesen (*kezan* Lh.), *f.* *pl.* **kesow** (P.), turf of peat, cut for fuel: for pl. cf. **asen**, rib.
keser (*cezzar*, *kesser* Lh. MS.), *m.*, *pl.* **-ow**, hollow stem of umbelliferous plant, kex.
kesēr, *m.*, *pl.* **-ys**, co-heir (B.).
***keseren**, *f.*, hailstone, *col.* **keser** (*kezzar* Lh.), hail, C. Voc.
kescāja *m.*, sweepstake : see **gāja**.
kescar, *m.*, dispersion, separation ; *adj.*, scattered ; *vb.*, to disperse, scatter, part : *ken k.*, ere we leave one another : see **scar**.
kescodhaf, *vb.*, to sympathise, condole ; *m.*, sympathy (W.).
kescodhevyans, *m.*, sympathy (W.).
kescolon, *adv.*, with one accord, in concord, single-heartedly, unanimously, P.C., B.M.
kescorra (*ketgora* Lh.), *vb.*, to collate.
kescoweth, *m.* (**kescowetha**, *f.*, company, used as *pl.*), companion, associate, M.C. 110.
kescryfa *vb.*, to exchange correspondence.
keskerdhes, *vb.*, to walk together, go in a procession (W.).

keskerth, *m.*, procession.
keskewsel, *vb.*, to converse.
kesky, *vb.*, to advise, exhort, admonish: as **lesky**; *col-jy dhym, men dha gesky*, hearken to me, able to advise thee, C.W. 650.
keskȳans (*ke-, skyans*), *m.*, conscience, Pryce: ?a late invention.
keslowenhē', *vb.*, to congratulate: as **berhē**.
kesoberyans, *m.*, co-operation, collaboration.
kesoleth, see **cosoleth**.
†**kespar** (C. Voc. *c(h)espar*), *m. and f., pl.* **-ow**, spouse, married person, *gemecca* Aelfric.
kesregnya, -raynya, *vb.*, to reign together, C.W. 7, 1961: p. pt. *kesregnyes*, used as "reigning," cf. **annedhy, tryga**.
kesresek, *vb.*, to run together: as **resek**.
kesscryfa, *vb.*, to correspond, write together.
kesseny, *vb.*, harmonize. sound together.
kessenyans, *m.*, harmony, agreement; (of bells) peal, Lh.
kesson, *adj.*, harmonious (W.): *m., pl.* **-yow**, consonant (Lh. from W.).
kesstrevya, *vb.*, compete (B.).
kesstrȳf, *m.*, competition (B.).
kessydhya, *vb.*, to punish, chastise.
kessydhyans (*cossythyans*), *m.*, infliction, punishment: *sur-gessydhyans*, certain retribution, C.W. 1122.
kessynsy, -jy (*gusendzhi*, Borlase), *vb.*, to lay a wager, bet, lit. hold simultaneously.
kest, *f., pl.* **-ow**, narrow-mouthed basket made of straw-rope (W., B.).
kestalkya (*l* sounded), *vb.*, to converse, chat, B.M. 236: see **talkya**.
kestenen, *f., col.* **kesten**, chestnut; chestnut-tree (W., B.).
kesünya, *vb.*, to unite (W.).
kesünyans, *m.*, union.
kesür, *m.*, comfort, consolation, solace (W.): see **kersya**.
†**kesva, kevva** (C. Voc. *c(h)etua*), *f.*, assembly, meeting, *gemetingc* Aelfric.
kesvewa, *vb.*, to live together, cohabit, C.W. 1314.
kesvewnans, *m.*, living together, married state.
kēsvȳth (*kēs, mȳth*), *m.*, cheese-whey (W., M.B.).
kesyewa, *vb.*, to yoke together, conjugate (W.).
kesys, etc., see **casa**.
ketella, ketelma, see **yn-ketella, yn-ketelma**.
kēth (C. Voc. *caid*), †*m., pl.* **-yon**, slave, serf. bondman, *theowa* Aelfric; *adj.*, caitiff, servile, subject, dependent, vassal, low-born, common: †*k.-prenys* (C. Voc. *caid prinid*), bought slave, *geboht theowa* Aelfric; *marghogyon k.*, liege knights; *tus k.*, minions, vassals, retainers.
keth, *adj.*, identical, same, only used after *an*: mutations as after *an*, but (with exception of *jeth*), *d, t, c, k*, are not affected; *keth* itself is not affected by *an*; *y'n k. vaner-ma*, just like this, in this very way.
kethel, *f., pl.* **-ly**, sheath-knife, C. Voc., *sex* Aelfric.
†**kēther, kē'r** (C. Voc. *carder* for *caider*, M.B. *cazr*, B. *kaer*), *adj.*, fair, handsome, beautiful, *wlitig* Aelfric: replaced by **tēk**, perhaps because of confusion with **kēr**, dear.
†**kēthes** (C. Voc. *caites*), *f., pl.* **-ow**, bondmaid, bondwoman, female slave.
kēthneth, *m.*, slavery (B.).
kethor, *m.*, hair on body (W., B.).
ke'thorva (*ketorva* Lh.) *f.*, pubes, groin.
ketherȳeth, *f.*, puberty (B.).
kēthwas, *m., pl.* **-wesyon**, slave (W.).
kettel[2] (for *kettottel, kettoth del*), *adv.*, as soon as: used as **del**[2], *k. dersys an bara*, as soon as the bread had been broken, R.D. 1318; *k. y'n jeffo a-n-bay*, as soon as he has him who will kiss him, P.C. 986.
kettep (*kes-, pup*), *adj.*, each, every: used before *-onen, pen, pol* (? or *oll*), *tam, dynar, map -pron, chet*, etc., *yn k. gwas*, to the last man; as adv., *yndella kettep-onen*, so in every detail, exactly so, just so, P.C. 2801.
kettermyn (*kes-* or *keth, termyn*), *m.*, interim, same time, Lh.: *yn k.-na*, at the same time; perhaps invented.
kettoth (*kes-, tōth*), *adv.*, as soon as, used with *ha* before noun, *k ha'n ger*, upon the word, instantly: see **kettel**.
keugh, see **mōs**.
kev-, see **ke-**, Appendix II.
kevals (C. Voc. *c(h)efals*), *m., pl.* **-yow**, joint, articulation, *lidh* Aelfric: see **dygevelsy, dyskevelsy**.
kevambos, *m., pl.* **-ow**, covenant (W.).
kevannedhy, *vb.*, to settle, dwell, inhabit,

occupy premises (W.B.).
kevar, *m.*, joint ploughing of land held in common (W., B.).
kevaras, *vb.*, to plough together (W., B.).
Kevardhū·, **mȳs-K.**, *m.*, December, Lh., Gw.
kevarwedha, *vb.*, to direct, guide, indicate: 2 s. imp. *kevarweth* (*-wouth*, P.C. 1043).
kevarwedhor, **-dhyas**, *m.*, *pls.* **-yon**, **-ysy**, director, guide (W.).
kevarwedhyans, *m.*, direction, guidance (W.).
kevarweth, *m.*, information (W.).
kevelecca, *vb.*, to shoot woodcock (W.): inf. only.
kevelek, *m.*, *pl.* **-ogas**, woodcock, Lh.
kevelyn, *m.*, *pl.* **-now**, cubit, half-yard: *re hyr yu a gevelyn*, it's half a yard too long, too long by a cubit.
kever, *m.*, regard, respect, direction, connection, relationship: found only as used with *yn*; *yn-kever hemma*, with regard to this; *y'm kever*, about me, to me, towards me (of abstract ideas).
ke·verang, **ke·veren** (for *kevran*, *kev-ran*), *f.*, *pl.* **-ow**, hundred of county, canton: metre demands *kevrang* as pronunciation B.M. 2217, and Borlase has (*an*) *gevren*, but pl. is *keverangow* as place-name; *nebes an geveren* is translated "little of public affairs" (Scawen).
kevesedha, *vb.*, to sit down (W., B.).
keveseth, *m.*, seat, posterior (W., B.): see **eseth**, which seems to replace this.
kevōs, *adj.*, contemporary, coeval (W., B.): *k. gans*, of the same age as.
†**kevōth**, *m.*, *pl.* **-ow**, power, wealth (W.).
†**kevōthak** (C. Voc. *c(h)efuidoc*), *adj.*, powerful, almighty, *aelmihtig* Aelfric; wealthy (W.).
kevran, *f.*, *pl.* **-now**, share, portion, dividend (W., B.): see **keverang**.
kevranna, *vb.*, to divide, share (W., B.): see **ranna**.
kevrannek, *adj.*, participating, associated; *m.*, *pl.* **-nogyon**, sharer, shareholder (W., B.).
kevrannor, *m.*, *pl.* **-yon**, participator, shareholder (W., B.).
kevren, *f.*, *pl.* **-yon**, fastening, bond; conjunction; flail-joint (D. "kevern," "keveran").
***kevrȳn**, *m.*, mystery (W., B.).
***kevrynek**, *adj.*, mystic, mysterious (W., B.).

kevy, *vb.*, to remember: as **ankevy**, but generally replaced by *perthy cof*.
kevyewa, *vb.*, to yoke oxen together (W.).
†**kevyl**, *m.*, *pl.* **-ow**, horse: Nankevil, Nankivell, place-name.
kew, *f.*, *pl.* **-yow**, enclosure, close, field: Kewe Vyan, etc., as field-name, but most commonly found as "the Gew" (*an gew*).
kewar, *adj.*, correct, exact, accurate, orderly, M.C. 138, as W. *cywir*, *cywair*.
kewarghek, *f.*, *pl.* **-egow**, **-egy**, hemp-field (B.).
kewarghen, *f.*, hemp-plant, *col.* **kewargh** (*kūer* Lh.), hemp.
kewel, see **cowel**.
kewer (Lh. *kewar*), *f.*, weather, storm.
kewera, *vb.*, to fit, fulfil, keep a promise.
keweras (*coweras* M.C. 83), *m.*, fulfilment, perfection.
kewerder, *m.*, **kewereth**, *m.*, accuracy, precision, correctness (W.).
kewlet (*kyulat* Lh.), *m.*, coverlet, counterpane, bedspread, quilt (M.E. *coylte*, Lat. *culcita*): see ***colghes**.
kewny, *col.*, moss, liverwort, lichen, mildew, green scum, grass-wrack (D. "cuney," as B. *kivni*).
kewnȳen, *f.*, *pl.* **-now**, fragment of moss, etc. (B.).
kewnȳa, *vb.*, to become moss-grown, etc. (B).
kewnȳek, *adj.*, mossy, etc.; *f.*, *pl.* **-egy**, **-egow**, place covered with moss, etc.
kewry, see **cawr**.
kewsel, *vb.*, to speak, talk, converse, say: takes *orth* as prep. "to"; *k. gans*, to speak in favour of, defend; 3 s. pres.-fut. *kews*; 3 s. pret. *kewsys*; 2 s. imp. *cows*; *awos an dew a-gewsyth*, in spite of the god thou mentionest, O.M. 1513; see **cows**.
kēwȳth, *col.*, hedging, brushwood (B.).
keybal, **kȳbal**, *m.*, ferry-boat (W. *ceubal*, O.B. *caubal*, Lat. *caupulus*).
keybalhens, **kȳbalhens**, *m.*, *pl.* **-y**, ferry-boat way, ferry (O.B. *caubalhint*): ?Kybyllys, Kebellyes Passage, old name of King Harry Passage.
keyn, **kȳn** (C. Voc. *c(h)ein*, Lh. *kein*, Late *kine*), *m.*, *pl.* -ow, back, ship's keel, ridge, *hryc* Aelfric: *k. to*, *chy*, ridge of roof; *k. dorn*, back of hand; *war geyn margh*, on horseback; *dres k.*, in the opposite direction, all wrong.

keynak (Lh. *keinac*), *m.*, *pl.* **-nogas,** shad (fish).

keynans, kȳnans, *m*, *pl.* **-ow,** ravine, gorge: as W. *ceunant*, Kynance, place-name.

†keynrēs (C. Voc. *c(h)a(h)enrit*), *m.*, torrent, brook: cf. W. *cefnllif, cenllif* and **rēs,** root of **resek.**

keynvor, *m.*, main sea, ocean (W., B.).

keyva, kȳva, *f.*, cavity (W.).

knak, *m.*, *interj.*, snap, crack; *adv.*, immediately: *k. omma*, this instant, right here, B.M. 1644, 1652.

knava (*kunava* Lh., *k* sounded), *m.*, *pl.* **-vys,** rascal, rogue, knave (M.E.).

knēsen (*k* sounded), *f.*, *col.* **knēs, knüs,** skin: meaning as Ir. *cnēs*, not as W. *cnawd*, flesh.

knofen (*knufan* Lh., *k* sounded), *f. col.* **know,** nut, hazel-nut: *k. Frynk*, walnut; **k. muscat*, nutmeg; **k. faw*, beech-mast; *gwedhen-k.*, hazel-tree.

***knōgh** (*k* sounded), *m*, mound, boss, hillock (W., O.B.).

knouk (*k* sounded), *m.*, *pl.* **-kys,** knock, blow, rap (M.E.).

knoukya, (*k* sounded), *vb.*, to knock, hit, strike (M.E.).

know, see **knofen,**

knowa, *vb.*, to gather nuts: inf. only.

knowek, *adj.*, abounding in nuts, nutty: Kelly Knowek, Kellygnowek, nut-grove, place-name.

knyghyas, -ghas (*kunihiaz, -haz,* Lh., *k* sounded), *m.*, neighing, whinny.

knysken (*kniskan* Borlase, *k* sounded), *f.*, *pl.* **-now,** flagon, tankard.

knyvvyas (*kuniviaz* Lh., *k* sounded), *vb.*, to shear.

kȳ (C. Voc. *ki, c(h)i*), *m.*, *pl.* **cün** (*cuen*), dog, hound: *k. stak*, ban-dog, dog kept on chain (B); *k. hyr*, greyhound, long-dog, P.: in abuse, *gweth os es k.!* thou art worse than a dog! R.D. 2026; *dhyso cryjy my ny-vynnaf moy es k.*, I will not believe thee any more than a dog, 2360, etc.

ky-, see **ke-.**

kyb, *f.*, *pl.* **-ow,** cup (W., B.).

kybel, *f.*, *pl.* **-low,** tub, mine-bucket (D. "kibble").

kȳbya, *vb.*, to snatch (D. "keeb," W. *cipio*).

kycca. *vb.*, to hunt or beg for meat (W., B.): inf. only.

kychys, see **cachya.**

***kydel,** *m.*, *pl.* **-lys,** stake-net (M.E.).

kyf, etc.; see **cafos.**

kyfvewy (*kyffnywy, n* for *u*), *m.*, *pl.* **-ow,** feast, *col.*, guests, convivials, feasting company, B.M. 293, as B. *kouvi*, M.B. *couvy, couffy*, Lat. *convivium.*

kyfvewya, *vb.*, to invite to a feast, feast together (B.).

kyfvewyas, *m.*, *pl.* **-ysy,** feaster (B.).

kyfya, *vb.*, to confide in, rely on, trust: *mara mynta ow hyfya*, if thou wilt trust me, C.W. 574.

kyfyans (*kefyans*), *m.*, confidence, reliance, trust: *ny-s-tevyth fowt a gyfyans*, shall have no lack of trust, O.M. 1805; *rak dyndyl dhyso k.*, to win for thyself trust, O.M. 1808.

***kyfyth,** *m.*, *pl.* **-yow,** pickle, preserve, jam, confection (W., B.).

***kyfythya.** *vb.*, to preserve, pickle (W., B.).

kȳga, *vb.*, to become fleshy (W., B.).

kȳgek, *adj.*, fleshy (W., B.).

kygel (C. Voc. *kigel*), *f.*, *pl.* **-yow,** distaff (D. "kiggal").

kȳger, *m.*, *pl.* **-goryon,** butcher (W., B.).

kygereth, *f.*, *pl.* **-ow,** butcher's shop, butchery (B.).

kȳglyw, *adj.*, flesh-coloured (W.).

†kȳgver (C. Voc. *kiguer*), *m.*, *pl.* **-yow,** flesh-hook, flesh-fork, *awel* Aelfric.

kȳjy, *m.*, *pls.* **-ow, cünjyow,** kennel.

kyjya, *vb.*, to join, stick fast, unite (D. "kidge").

kȳk(g) (C. Voc. *kig, c(h)ic*), *m.*, *pl.* **-gow,** flesh, flesh-meat: *k. gwyls*, game; *k. sal*, salt meat; *k. -mogh*, bacon; *k. -bowyn*, beef; *k. -selsyk*, sausage-meat; *k. -carow, -ewyk*, venison; *k. -davas*, mutton; *k. -lugh*, veal, etc.; *k. yn knes*, "flesh and fell," entirely, in bodily form.

***kȳkbren,** *m.*, *pl.* **-yer,** skewer.

kykesow, *pl.*, Cornish heath (D. "kekezza").

kȳl, *m.*, *pl.* **-ys,** skittle, ninepin (E.D. "keels," Fr. *quilles*): *gwary-kylys*, (*keelez* Gw.) game of skittles; *keal*, shin, Pryce MS., suggests that, as in Breton, this may have been used in jest for "leg."

kyl (C. Voc. *c(h)il*), *m.*, *pl.* **-yow, -yer,** recess, nook, reverse, back, cud, nape, *hnecca* Aelfric: *k. an dorn*, back of the hand (B.); **see a-gyl, daskylyas, pol-**

kyl; pl. *-yer* is suggested by place-names Killiers, Kilyur, applied to rough, overgrown mounds.

kӯla, see **y-gӯla.**

kyla, *vb.*, to draw back, recede (W., B.).

kylben, *m.*, occiput, back of the head: *mellow k.*, cervical vertebrae; *omwheles dh'y gylben,* to fall right backwards, C.W. 1114; cf. **pol-kyl.**

kylden, *m.*, pull backwards, withdrawal, recoil, retreat, set-back, reverse, drag; *a'n bys yu cales k.* ? from the world that is a hard struggle, R.D. 244; *adj.*, obstinate, stubborn, dragging against one (W.).

kyldenna, *vb.*, to draw, pull or drag backwards, retire, recoil, R.D. 2082.

kyldhans, *m.*, *pl.* **-dhyns,** back tooth, wisdom-tooth (W., B.).

kyldrō, *f.*, *pl.* **-yow,** backward turn, ruse (W., B,).

kylgӯ, *m.*, *pl.* **-gün,** coward, sneak (W.).

kyllas, *col.*, clay slate (D. "killas").

kyllygen (for *kellyllygen*), *f.*, *pls.* **-ygy, -ygys,** *col.* **kyllyk,** razor-shell and fish, solen (P., D. "cleg," etc.): Lh. makes *kylygi* sing., "cockle" apparently a mistake, though *kyllyk* may have been loosely used of all shell-fish living in sand: see **kellyllyk.**

kyllys, see **kelly.**

kymmys, see **kemmys.**

kyn, see **ken.**

kyn[5](th) (*ken(th)* and less correctly *kyn(s)*), *conj.*, though: *-th* added before vowels and silenced *h*, as *kynth 'evelly,* B.M. 3708; followed by *na(g)-* in neg.; idiomatic uses are, *kyn fo mar vras,* however big it may be; *mynny-jy k. na-vynny,* whether thou wilt or no; *nyns-yu marth cuth k. y-m-bo ow-ton an pren a-dhe-dro, ha...,* It's no wonder that I'm troubled at carrying the log about when..., O.M. 2819; *kyn y-n-* may contract to *kyn,* and in C.W. *kynth* becomes *ke'th*; *kyn* is there misused for *pan,* conj., cf. B. *kenevé* for *panevé.*

kyn-, see **ken-,** Appendix II.

kynbogh (Lh. *kinbuk*), *m.*, *pl.* **-as,** wether goat.

kynda (*cünda, kenda*), *m.*, nature, kind, species (M.E. *kinde*): *k. mapden,* the human race, O.M. 1950; *a bup eghen a gynda,* of all manner of living species, C.W. 2270; *dres k.*, extraordinary; *awos k.*, on any account.

kynewas, older **kynyavos,** *m.*, autumn dwelling: place-name, see **kynyaf.**

kynewel, see **kynyewel.**

kyng, *m.*, *pl.* **-ys,** king, B.M. (E.).

***kynnyk(g),** *m.*, *pl.* **-ygow,** offer, proposal; *vb.*, to propose, offer: 3 s. pret. *kynnygas* (W., B., from Lat. *condico*); replaced by **profya.**

kyns, kynth, see **kyn[5](th).**

kӯnvan, *m.*, mourning, lamentation (W., B.).

kӯnvanüs, *adj.*, lamentable (W., B.).

kynweres, *m.*, succour, help, assistance, aid, B.M. 544.

kӯny, *vb.*, to lament, mourn, wail, whine, C.W. 919, 1016.

kynyaf (C. Voc. *kyniaf, kyn-, gwaf*), *m.*, Autumn, *herfest* Aelfric: lit. "before winter," perhaps this may also mean "harvest" as in W. and O.E.; see **kynewas.**

kynyavos, see **kynewas.**

kynyewel, *vb.*, to dine: 2 s. imp. *kynyow*; 3 s pres.-fut. *kynyew*; 3 s. pret. *kynyewys*; 3 s. subj. *kynyowo.*

kynyfer, see **kenyver.**

kynyow (*kidnio* Lh.), *m.*, *pl.* **-yewow,** dinner, O.M. 1140.

kyōgh (*kio* Lh.), *f.*, *pl.* **-as,** snipe: see **dama.**

kyst, *f.*, *pl.* **-yow,** chest, box: *k. ven,* stone coffin; burial chamber in tumulus, Borlase (from W.).

kysten (*kistan*), *f.*, *pl.* **-now,** small box or chest, Borlase (from W.).

kӯsya, *vb.*, to damage, destroy, capsize, make an end of, do for (D. "keaze," W. *cisio*).

kywhethel, *m.*, *pl.* **-thlow,** tale (D. "kywhiddle," W. *cychwedl*).

L

***labedha,** *vb.*, to throw stones at, stone to death (W., B.): 2 s. imp. *labeth.*

labol, ?*adj.*, brindled, striped: dog's name, B.M. 3228.

laca (*lakka,* Lh.), *m.*, *pl.* **lakkys,** small stream, runlet, spring (E.D. "lake").

lacca, *irreg. comp. adj.*, worse: positive, *lak,* worthless, P.; slack, loose, lax (W.), is not found in MSS.

lacye (*lacie*), see **lathya,**

lader, *m.*, *pl.* **ladron,** thief, brigand, robber, *sceath* Aelfric; *l. cleves*, pestilent disease, B.M. 679.

ladha, *vb.*, to kill, slay, put to death, put out (a light): p. pt. *ledhys*; *dh* becomes *th* as final, in subj., and before *s*.

ladra, *vb.*, to steal, rob, thieve: p. pt. *ledrys*; 3 s. pres.-fut., 2 s. imp. *lader*; *d* becomes *tt* in 2 and 3 s. subj. and *t* before *s*, *r* here dropping out, e.g., *lyttry, lattro, lattra, latsa*.

ladrans, *m.*, theft.

ladres, *f.*, *pl.* **-ow,** female thief (B.).

lafür (*lavur*, C.W. *lavyer*), *m.*, labour, toil, work, travail, pangs of childbirth.

lafürüs, *adj.*, toilsome, laborious (W., B.).

lafürya (*lavyrrya* C.W., *laviria* Lh.), *vb.*, to labour, toil, work; travel, make a tiresome journey, proceed: *p. pt. lafuryes*, worn out with toil or travel, O.M., B.M.; *rag ef dhym dhe l.*, because of his trudging to me, P.C. 1786.

lafüryans, *m.*, travelling, B.M. 480; labouring, toil.

lāfyl, *adj.*, lawful, permissable, B.M. 4301 (M.E. *leful*).

lagas (C. Voc. *lagat*), *m.*, *pl.* **-ajow, -ow,** *d.* **deulagas,** eye; patch of blue in clouded sky (D. "laggas"): old pl. *legys* (C. Voc. *legeit*) seems lost; *l. awel*, weather-dog, fragmentary rainbow, Borlase; *l. molys*, blear-eye (of horse), Lh. MS.; *l. bysow*, wall-eye (horse), Lh. MS.; †*l. davas*, limpet (out of shell), Gw.; *yn. l. an howl*, in full sunlight, in open day (B.).

lagasek, lagajek (*lagadzhek* Lh.), *adj.*, full of eyes, big-eyed, quick of sight, Lh.; *m.*, gazer, starer, gaper, goggler, B.M. 3813; wary, sharp-sighted person, B.M. 1018.

lagata, *vb.*, to stare, goggle: see **lagater.**

lagater, *m.*, blind or bib (fish), lit. goggler (D. "lagatta").

†**lagen,** *f. pl.* **-now,** pond, puddle, slough, C. Voc.

lagenna, *vb.*, splash, bespatter (B.).

lagha (*laha*), *m.*, *pl.* **-ghys,** law, religion, system of laws or doctrines (M.E. *laghe*).

lagya, *vb.*, to splash (E. D. "lag," "laggen in dower," splashing in the water): see also **lagenna.**

lagyar, *f.*, *pl.* **-yēr,** moorhen (D.): see **lagen, yar.**

lam, *m.*, *pl.* **-mow,** leap, hop, jump, bound, stride; little time or space; hap, chance: *droklam*, mishap; *Lam Goëmagot*, "Gogmagog's Leap" on Plymouth Hoe; *ny-lettys saw un l.*, I only stopped a moment; *war (yn) un l.*, at once, in a trice; **bledhen l.*, leap-year.

lamma, *vb.*, to leap, hop, jump, bound, stride; 3 s. pres.-fut. *lam*; 3 s. pret. *lammas*; see var. **lemmel.**

lamva, *f.*, stile, stepping-place (W.).

lan (Late *ladn*), *f.*, *pl.* **-now, -yow,** monastic enclosure; as suffix, enclosure: in place-names the *n* may disappear, e.g., Roscorla, Lafrowda, Lavansa, Lavyhale, Lavabe, Lamana, or become *l*, as Lelant for Lananta; the late inserted *d* is seen in Laddenvean for Lanvyghan and the old mutation of *k* to *h* in Lanhevern.

lanergh (C. Voc. *lan(h)erch*), *m.*, *pl.* **-y,** glade, clearing in wood, open space: *holt*, Aelfric, takes ***saltus*** in the other sense of "grove."

lanow, *m.*, fullness, high tide (W., B.): see **lenwel.**

lantern, later **launtyer,** *m.*, *pl.* **-s,** lantern (M.E.).

lanwes, *m.*, abundance; flow; flowing tide, O.M. 1430.

lappa, *m.*, *pl.* **-pys,** lappet, flap, lap, front of skirt of long garment, P.C. 1244 (O.E. *lappa*).

lappya, *vb.*, to leap, jump, frisk, perform tumbling tricks (O.E. ***hleapan***).

lappyor (C. Voc. *lappior*), *m.*, *pl.* **-ryon,** acrobat, vaulter, leaper, tumbler, *hleapere* Aelfric; (mining), dresser of refuse ore (D.).

lappyores (*lappiores*), *f.*, *pl.* **-ow,** female acrobat or tumbler, *hleapstre* Aelfric.

lapya, *vb.*, to lap, lick clean: *Lap Keryn,*? "Lick Tub," dog's name, B.M. 3226 (O.E. *lapian*).

larch, larj (*lardzh* Lh.), *adj.*, large, great, liberal, extensive: comp. *larchya, -jya*, B.M. 2352 (M.E. *large*); *lærgya*, is used as positive C.W. 2176, though perhaps as comparative 780.

larjes, -jes, *m.*, liberality, bounty, bestowal, O.M. (M.E. *largesse*).

***lās,** *m.*, *pl.* **-ys,** lace (E.).

†**las** (C. Voc. *lad*), *m.*, *pl.* **-ow,** liquor, a gift of drink, *waeta* Aelfric: *l.-vyth* (C. Voc. *laduit*), nothing, lit. no reward of drink, as W. *llad*.

lash (*lasche*), *m.*, slash, lash, stroke, M.C. 138 (E.).

last, *m.*, nastiness, noisomeness, loathsomeness, M.C. 202.
lastethes, *m.*, filth, scum, vermin, weeds, etc. (B. *lastez*): like **mostethes, plosethes.**
lasya, see **lathya.**
lath, *m.*, slaughter, killing: see **dēnlath.**
lath, *f.*, *pl.* **-ow**, yard-measure, yard: *hyga a'n l.*, play tricks with the yard-stick, Gw., misprinted *cath*, P.
latha, **lasa**, *m.*, *pl.* **-thys**, **-sys**, lath or strut (E.).
lathva, *f.*, murder, slaughter (Keigwin).
lathya, **lasya** (*lacya*), *vb.*, to fasten, fix, sieze together.
***la·tymer**, *m.*, *pl.* **ys**, teacher of Latin, interpreter (M.E.).
Latyn (*Latten* N. Boson), **-ynek**, *adj.*, Latin; *m.*, Latin language.
laudya, *vb.*, to praise, laud, C.W. 57 (M.E.).
laun, *m.*, *pl.* -ow, blade, flake, plate (D. "lawn," W., B.).
laun, *m.*, *pl.* -ow, clearing, open working of mine (D. "lawn").
launtyer, see **lantern.**
launya, *vb.*, to fix a blade to; sliver, flake; plate, veneer (W., B.).
lauta, see **louta.**
lavar, *m.*, *pl. and abst.* **-ow**, speech, saying, utterance, spoken word, proverb, motto, *spraec* Aelfric: *war nebes (ver) lavarow*, in short, briefly.
lavasos, *vb.*, to venture, presume, dare, R.D. 1835, 1892; allow oneself, submit, B.M. 1115; claim as a due, O.M. 496; permit, allow, let, suffer, deign, P.C. 1226, R.D. 873: 2 s. imp. *lavas*; 3 s. pres.-fut. *leves*; 3 s. subj. *lavasso*; *my a-th-pys a l.*, pray let me; the apparently opposite meanings are found also in W. on one hand and in M.B. on the other.
lavrak (C. Voc. *lafroc*), *m.*, *pl.* **lavregow**, pair of breeches; *m. or f.*, sloven, draggle-tail, slut (D.): **†***l. pan*, cloth breeches, *waedbraec* Aelfric; ***l.** *hyr*, long trousers.
lavyn, *pl.* -yon (*lavidnian*, Act of Parliament, 1605), sand-eel, launce; lit. blade, as W. *llafn*, (D. "vidnans," Borlase "visnans" (*s* for *d*) with pl, *-s* as in "muryons"); var of **laun.**
†law, see **lüf.**
lawa, *m.*, laud, praise, worship; *vb.*, to laud: used only in pious ejaculation *dh'y lawa!* praise Him! may He be praised! (M.E. *loue*).
lawan, see **lawethan.**
lawen, *adj.*, entire, uncastrated (of animals): *l. cath*, tom-cat, B.M. 3413.
lawethan, **lawan**, ? *m.*, devil, or *pl.*, imps, fiends, R.D., C.W.: cf. W. *llywethan*, leviathan, which might possibly be used as a name for a devil, R.D. 128; Keigwin translates *drog-lawan*, which seems the same word, as "bad brat," sing., C.W. 1721; *Ha my! canjeon-l.*, R.D. 139, may be "A moi! changeling-imps!"
lawns, **lawnj**, *m.*, *pl.* **-yow**, lawn, sward: Lounge Meadow, place-name, W. *llawnt.*
lay, *m.*, *pl.* **-s**, religious law, creed, belief, P.C. 936, B.M. 1865 (M.E.).
lē, **-la**, *m.*, *pl.* **-ow**, **-yow**, place, spot, situation: *yn y le*, instead of him; *adv.* (*yn*) *le(may)*, *le(na-)*, (in a place) where, wherever; as unstressed, pronounced *la*, and as final word of compound, so spelt, e.g., *yn pup*, *nep*, *lower*, *lyes*, *le* (pr. *la*), and *dowrla*; cf. **trē.**
lē, *adj.*, irreg. comp. of *byghan*, *boghes*, less, lesser, smaller: as quasi noun, a less quantity; *adv.*, to smaller extent (not used to qualify adj. or p. pt.): *dhe l. nefra my a-n-car*, the less ever shall I love him, B.M. 481.
lecyans (*lesc-*, *less-*), *m.*, leave, permission, licence, B.M. (M.E. *lycence*).
ledan, *adj.*, broad, wide.
ledanen, *f.*, *pl.* **-now**, plantain, Borlase.
ledan-les, *m.*, *pl.* **-losow**, plantain, Lh.: see **†henledan.**
leder, *f.*, *pl.* **-drow**, **-dry**, steep slope, cliff, declivity, P.: Chair Ladder (*chayr l.*), rock-name.
ledrek, *adj.*, sloping (W.).
ledry, *vb.*, to slope (W.).
ledrys, etc., see **ladra.**
lēdya (C.W. *leadya*), *vb.*, to lead, conduct, guide: 3 s. pres.-fut. *lēd* (M.E. *lede*).
lēdyor (*lӯder* Lh.), *m.*, *pl.* **-yon**, leader.
ledhys, see **ladha.**
lēf, *m.*, *pl.* **-levow**, voice, utterance, cry, entreaty.
lēf, see **lüf**.
lēfa, *vb.*, to cry out, shout: *?ty a-lefas*, thou hast shouted, O.M. 2434, unless this is 3 s. pres.-fut. of **lavasos.**
lefans (**†***lefant*), *m.*, *pl.* **lefyns**, **-fanjas** frog, toad, hopping thing: place-name Polyphant (O. Cor. *pol lefant*, as W. *llyffant*): see **cronak, gwylskyn.**

legessa, *vb.*, to catch mice : inf. only.
legessa, †-sē, *m.*, *pl.* **-syon**, mouse-catcher, mouser, B.M. 3414.
legest (*-gast* Lh.), *m.*, *pl.* **-gesty** (*-ti* Lh.), lobster, C. Voc., *loppestre* Aelfric : from Lat. *locusta*, but translating *polypus* in C. Voc., as " lobster " does in Aelfric's and other old vocabularies ; D. " long-oyster," cray-fish, is from Fr. *langouste* or Sp. *langosta*, not *legest*.
lēgh, *f.*, *pl.* **-ow**, flat rock, ledge, slab, tablet : Lay, etc., place-names (D.) : see **cromlegh.**
leghen (*lehen* Lh.), *f.*, *pl.* **-now**, slate, shale, thin flat stone.
lēghow (*lēauh* Lh.), *pl.*, rickets, ague (B. *lec'h* sing., W. *llechau* pl.) : *cren an l.*, ague, shivers, Lh. MS. (with *sern* for *cern*).
lēghven, *m.*, *pl.* **-veyn**, flagstone, slab (W.).
***legry**, *vb.*, to corrupt, decompose : *legria* Lh., from W. *llygru*, cf. B. *liñkra* to go stale.
lēhē·, *vb.*, to lessen : as **berhē.**
lejek, *f.*, *pls.* **-egas, -egow**, heifer, Lh. : ? in place-name, Poljigga for *pol lejegow*.
lejer, ?leja (Lh. *letshar*), *m.*, frying-pan : cf. D. " latchet," cake made in frying-pan, and W. *lletwad*, ladle; this may properly be *leja* for *lesweth*, cf. Lh. *gravar* for *grave(th)*.
lējyon, see **lȳjyon.**
lēk (C. Voc. *leic*), *adj.*, lay, non-clerical, illiterate, unlearned ; *m.*, *pl.* **lēgyon**, layman, *laewede man* Aelfric.
lēksys, *m.*, laity (B.).
lēl, *adj.*, true, just, proper, correct, leal, loyal, faithful (M.E. *leale, layal*) : comp. *lella* ; usually prefixed to nouns and vbs. ; *aga gorra y'n l.-forth*, to set them on the right road, B.M. 2331.
lelder, *m.*, loyalty, truth, justice.
lemen (*lemmyn*), *adv.*, *conj.* only, save, but : *nyns-yu l. ky*, it's only a dog ; *nag-us arluth·l. ef*, there is no lord save he ; *my a-th-pyssa a lavasos l. amma unwyth dhe'th tros*, I would beseech thee, to give permission but to kiss thy foot only, R.D. 874.
lemma, *vb.*, to sharpen, whet, strop : see **lym.**
'lemma, see **alemma.**
lemmel (Late *lebmal*), *vb.*, to leap, hop, bound, jump, stride : 2 s. imp. *lam*; 3 s. pres.-fut. *lem* ; 3 s. pret. *lemmys* ; 3 s. plupf. *lamsa* ; see **lamma, terlemmel.**
lemmyk, *m.*, *pl.* **-ygow**, sup, little drop, B.M. 3313 : dim. of **lom.**
lemmyn (C. Voc. *luman*, Late *lebmen, lebben*), *adv.*, now, at present : *fatel vyth l.?* what now ? what next ? (in dismay).
len, *f.*, *pl.* **-now** (Late *lednow*), cloth, blanket, whittle, P., C. Voc., *hwitel* Aelfric.
lēn (C. Voc. *laian*), faithful, trusty, true, honest, *getreowe*, *geleafful* Aelfric (Frankish, cf. Ger. *lehen*).
***len**, *vb.*, to read : borrowed by Lh. from B., but already replaced by **rēdya**, C. Voc.
le·ndury, *m.*, good faith, sincerity, honesty, loyalty : *lēn*, with added *d* before suffix *-ury*, as in **traytury, falsury** ; *aquytya gans l.*, pay back scrupulously, B.M. 3490.
lēnes (C. Voc. *laines*), *f.*, *pl.* **-ow**, nun, C. Voc. : ling (fish), O.M. 138.
***lēnjy**, *m.*, nunnery (W., B.).
***lenkeren**, *f.*, *col.* **lenker**, mawworm (W., B.).
lenky, *vb.*, to swallow : 3 s. pres.-fut. *lenk*; 2 s. imp. *lonk* ; 3 s. pret. *loncas*.
***lenner**, *m.*, *pl.* **-yow**, reader : Lh. from Breton, used in avoidance of **rēdyor.**
lent, *adj.*, slow, remiss, tardy, B.M. 3245 (M.E.).
lenter, *adj.*, shining, gleaming, polished, bright (B.).
lentry, *vb.*, to shine. polish (B.) : see **terlentry.**
lenwel (late *lenall*), *vb.*, to fill, replenish : p. pt. *lynwys* ; 3 s. pret. *le(y)nwys*; 3 s. subj. *lanwo* ; 3 s. pres.-fut. *lenow* ; 2 s. imp. *lanow* ; *l. a*, to fill with ; *morlenwel*, time of high water.
leper, *m.*, *pl.* **-s**, leper, B.M. 1359 (E.).
lēr, see **lür.**
lergh, *m.*, trace, track, path: used with *war* and with inserted poss. prons. as meaning " after " ; see **†trūlergh, warlergh.**
lēs, *m.*, breadth, width ; landyard of 18 feet square, D. " lace " : *trelles* (*tryllеs*), three times the width O.M. 393 ; *l. tyr*, (*lace teere*), a " lace " of ground (Carew MS., 1599, Hearne's *Curious Discourses*).
les, see **lys.**
lēs, *m.*, profit, advantage, behoof, interest, use, good, benefit, *hydh* Aelfric ; to serve, be of use (of things) : *nyns-yu dhe l.*, it is of no use ; *myr dh'y l.*, watch over his interests ; *oll rag agan l.* for the good of

us all; **les-kemyn*, commonwealth; *ef a-drel dhyso dhe-l.*, it will turn out profitable for thee; C.W. 739.

†les, -les, *m.*, plant, -wort (in old compounds): see **losowen**, made from pl., **losow**.

***les-**, *prefix*, half, step-, substitute (W., B): see Appendix II.

lēs, *m.*, lie (M.E): used only in *wythout l.*, Eng. in P.C. 1879.

lēsa, *vb.*, to spread, unfold, expand, open wide, P.C. 221.

lēsans, *m.*, expansion, spreading, opening out.

†les-an-gōk (C. Voc. *lesengoc*), *m.*, marigold, *solsaece* Aelfric, lit. "cuckoo-flower"; see **cōk**,

lesca, lüsca, *vb.*, to rock, swing, push off, give or take impetus (B.); see **lesk.**

†les-derth (C. Voc. *lesdeith* for *-derth*), *m.*, feverfew: see **terthen.**

†les-dosak (C. Voc. *lesdus(h)oc*), *m.*, betony, *se laesse bisceopwyrt* Aelfric: see **tosak.**

***lesflōgh**, *m.*, *pl.* **-flēghes**, step-child.

***leshanow**, *m.*, *pl.* **-hynwyn**, nickname, nom-de-plume (W., B.).

leshenwel, *vb.*, to nickname (W., B.).

lēshya (*lescia*), *vb.*, to leash hounds, B.M. 3220 (M.E.).

lesk, lüsk, *m.*, *pl.* **-scow**, oscillation, rocking (B. *lusk*); cradle, Lh., ? for *cowel-lüsk*, "rocking-basket."

lesky (*leysky, lysky*), *vb.*, to burn, consume or be consumed by fire; to smart: 3 s. pres.-fut. *lesk*; 2 s. imp. *losk*; 3 s. subj. *losco*, 3 s. pret. *loscas*; 3 s. plupf. *lossa*, *k* lost before *s*.

†les-lōs (C. Voc. *lesluit*), *m.*, horehound: see **†lōsles.**

†les-serghak (C. Voc. *lesserchoc*), *m.*, burdock, *late, clyfwyrt* Aelfric: **l. byghan*, goose-grass, cleavers; see **serghak.**

lesta, *vb.*, to hinder, prevent, as W. *llestair*: *my a-gas-lest rak dysky drok dhym kewsel*, I will stop you from learning to speak evil to me, B.M. 3751.

***lestās**, *m.*, *pl.* **-ow**, stepfather (W., B.).

lester, *m.*, *pl.* **lystry** (C. Voc. *listri*), vessel (utensil or ship).

lester-cōk (*lestercock* Carew), *m.*, float with mast and sail, used to carry fishing-tackle out from shore: meaning seems "empty vessel," "unmanned ship" rather than "ship-boat," see **cōk**, adj.

***lesvap(b)**, *m.*, *pl.* **-vebyon**, stepson (W., B.).

***lesvam**, *f.*, *pl.* **-mow**, stepmother (W., B.).

***lesvrōder**, *m.*, *pl.* **-vreder**, stepbrother, (W., B.).

***lesvyrgh**, *f.*, *pl.* **-es**, stepdaughter (W., B.).

***leswhōr**, *f.*, *pl.* **-wheryth**, stepsister (W., B.).

let, *m.*, hindrance, opposition, obstacle, obstruction, check, delay (M.E.): *hep l. na strech*, without stop or stay; *hep namoy l.*, without any more delay, immediately.

letany, *f.*, litany (W., B.).

lēth (*leyth*, C. Voc. *lait*), *m.*, milk: ***l.** cowlys*, curds; *l. cryf* (*creeve*), raw milk; *l. cudhys* (*kithez*), scald milk, Gw.; see **levryth.**

lēthan, *m*, milt, soft roe of fish (W., B.).

lēthek, *adj.*, milky (W., B.).

***lether**, *m.*, leather (as W., B., Ir.).

lēthwrēk, *f.*, *pl.* **-wrageth**, milk-woman, milkmaid.

lettrys, *adj.*, learned, literate, lettered (M.E. *letred*): *pynak vo, l. py lek, a weles an chy ny-m-dur*, (by) whomsoever it be, lettered or lay, I don't mind the house being seen, P.C, 681.

lettya, *vb.*, to hinder, prevent, delay, put off, balk, baffle, pause, stop (M.E. *lette*): *hep l.*, immediately; *l. a*[2], keep one from, make one late for; *ny-lettys saw un lam*, I only stopped a moment.

lēty (*lēth, ty*), *m. pl.* **-ow**, dairy, milk-house: Laity, place-name.

letysen, *f.*, *col.* **letys**, lettuce (W., B.).

leven, *adj.*, smooth, even, level.

levenhē·, *vb.*, to make smooth: as **berhē.**

leverel (*laverel, laol* Lh., *lawle* Gw.), *vb.*, to tell, say, relate: takes preps. *dhe*, to, *a*, about; 3 s. pres.-fut. *lever*; 2 s. imp. *lavar*; p. pt., 3 s. pret. *leverys*; *an beth leverys*, the said (already mentioned) tomb, M.C. 252; see **ragleverel.**

leveryans, *m.*, *pl.* **-ow** (*laverianzo*, Lh.), pronunciation.

†leveryas (C. Voc. *leveriat*), *m.*, *pl.* **-ysy**, speaker, teller, talker.

levesyn, etc., see **lavasos.**

levna, *vb.*, to smooth, make even: Le·vvenas (*levnys*), a level part of Lelant Towans; see **leven.**

†levryth (C. Voc. *leverid*), *m.*, sweet milk, fresh milk; *adj.*, new, of milk (B., V.).

lew (C. Voc. *leu*), *m.*, *pl.* **-yow**, rudder,

helm, *steorscofol* Aelfric.
lew (C. Voc. *leu*), *m.*, *pl.* **-as**, lion, *leo* Aelfric.
lewa, *vb.*, to devour, gobble, as a lion his prey (W.).
lewen (C. Voc. *lowen, lewen*), *f.*, *col.* **low**, louse: †*l. ky*, dog-louse; **l. losow*, greenfly; *crakkya-l.*, "crack-louse," name of thumb in finger-play, B. Victor Tradition.
lewes (*leues* Pryce), *f.*, *pl.* **-ow**, lioness.
lewgh, *m.*, fog, fine mist rising from water (D. "lew").
lewpart, *m.*, *pl.* **-as**, leopard (W.).
lewta, see **louta**.
lewyader, *m.*, *pl.* **-doryon**, steersman, pilot (P. from W.)
lewyas, *vb.*, to steer, guide, direct.
lewyer, *m.*, *pl.* **-oryon**, steersman, conductor.
lewyk, *m.*, *pls.* **lewygow**, **lewowygow**, lion's whelp (B.).
†**lewyth** (C. Voc. *leuuit*), *m.*, steersman, director, governor: cf. Leuiut, personal name, Camborne inscribed altar-stone.
lō, *f.*, *pl.* **-yow** (late contraction *lew* Lh.), spoon, ladle: **l. mason*, mason's trowel; **l. balas*, garden trowel.
lōas, *m-*, *pl.* **-ow**, spoonful (W., B.).
lobba, *m.*, *pl.* **-bys**, lout, lubber (E.D.).
loder, *m.*, *pl.* **-drow**, stocking, C. Voc., Lh.
†**loē·**, *m.*, *pl.* **-ow**, ruler, ruling-stick, straight-edge, C. Voc., *reogolsticca* Aelfric: cf. **lewyas**.
logel, *f.*, *pl.* **-low**, sepulchre, sarcophagus, M.C. 233; coffin, R.D. 2179; chest, C. Voc., *cyst, mederce* Aelfric (Lat. *loculus*).
lōgh, *f.*, *pl.* **-ow**, lake, inlet of water: place-names, Looe, Loe Bar, etc.
lōgh, *adj.*, lax, remiss, wanting in respect, negligent, B.M. 3798.
logosen (C. Voc. *logoden*), *f.*, *col.* **logas**, mouse: *l. vras*, rat; †*l. fer*, calf of leg, *spaerlira* Aelfric.
lōk, *m.*, presence, P.C. 2329, B.M. 3375: *y'm lok, dhe'm lok*, before me (?M.E. *loke*, look).
lok, *f.*, *pl.* **-gow**, monastic cell (B. *log*, Loc-, W. *(mynach)log*, Lat. *locus*): in place-name Luxulyan, Lok-Sulyen.
lollas (in *dowr-tom l.*, rum, Borlase), ? for *dowr tom molas(ses)*, Fr. *mélasse*, rather than "America," "West Indies," for which no Cornish name is likely.
lom, *m.*, *pl.* **-mow**, drop (B.): see **lommen**, **lemmyk**.
lom (Late *lobm*), *adj.*, bare, naked: Top Lobm, sand-hill name, St. Ives.
lomder, *m.*, bareness (W.).
lomhē·, *vb.*, to make bare, strip: as **berhē**.
lommas (*lobmaz*, Lh.), *m.*, *pl.* **-ow**, small bream, "chad" (fish).
lommen, *f.*, *pl.* **-now**, sup, mess of food: *l. cowl*, mess of pottage, P.
lom-nōth, *adj.*, stark naked (W., Gael).
lon, **lothen** (C.W. *lodn*), *m.*, *pls.* **lonnow**, **lothnow** (Late *lodnow*), young ox, bullock, steer; animal, brute, beast; brutal or beastly person: *l.-gwarak*, yoke-ox, P.; *l.-davas*, wether sheep, Lh.; *l.-bowyn*, steer, *pymp l.-b. dyvynys y a-dhep'sa yn deu dheth*, in two days they would devour five cut-up beeves, B.M. 3224; *l. a'n par-ma*, such a brute, Lh.
***lōn**, *f.*, loin (W.).
lōn (*loin* P.), *m.*, *pl.* **-ow**, grove, bush.
lonak, *adj.*, bushy: *gothfyl l.* (*withellonack*), lion, Borlase; cf. W. *llwynog*, fox; see **gōthfyl**.
lonek, *f.*, *pls.* **-egow**, **-egy**, bushy place.
loneth, *f.*, *pl.* **-y**, kidney, Lh. (D. "linuth").
long, *def. vb.*, belongs: *a-long*, that belongs, C.W. 2253 (M.E. *longen*).
lonk, *m.*, gullet, throat, action of swallowing (W., B.): see **lenky**.
lonklyn, *m.*, vortex, whirlpool (W.).
lonktrēth, *m.*, quicksand (B.).
lōr (C. Voc. *luir*, M.C., C.W. *loer*, Lh. *lūr*), *f.*, moon.
lorden, *m.*, *pl.* **-s**, clown, clumsy lout, blockhead (M.E. *lurdayne*, O. Fr. *lourdon*).
lordya, *vb.*, to rule, domineer, lord it, play the lord, O.M. 901, C.W. 456 (M.E. *lorde*).
lorel, *m.*, *pl.* **-s**, vagrant, rascal (M.E.).
lōrgan, *m.*, moonshine, moonlight (W., B.): see **can**, m.
lorgh (C. Voc. *lorch*, Lh. *lor*) *m.*, *pl.* **-ow**, pilgrim's staff, walking-stick, pole; Cornish rod of land, 9 feet sq., half lace (Carew, see **lēs**): *l. bras*, stout staff, club (Lh. *l. vras*, as if f.); in *nep a-n jeffo l. gorrens y scryp dyworto*, let him who has a staff take from it its scrip, P.C. 920, *l.* is m., as W. *llwrw*.
***lōrwedhen**, *f.*, *col.* **-wȳth**, laurel-tree (W.).
***lōrya**, *vb.*, to crown with laurel (B.).
los, *m.*, loss, B.M. 2256 (E.).
lōs (*loys*, C. Voc. *lōt*, *luit*, Lh. *lūz*), *adj.*,

grey, hoary ; mouldy, mildewed, lichened : *yowynk ha l.*, young and old ; *ken of l.*, before I am grey (i.e., go grey-headed while waiting).

lōs, *adj.*, vile, soiled, squalid, foul, B.M. 1967, as B. *lous*.

losel, *m.*, *pl.* **-s**, vagabond, idler (M.E.).

losel-was, *m.*, *pl.* **-wesyon**, ne'er do well, idle fellow, P.C. 2718.

losk (C. Voc. *losc*), *m.*, burning, combustion; inflammation ; corn-smut, Lh : see **lesky**.

loskvan (*loscvan*), *m.*, burning, R.D. 1249.

loskvēn, *m.*, brimstone (W.).

loskveneth, *m.*, *pl.* **-edhyow**, volcano (W.).

†lōsles (C. Voc. *lotles*), *m.*, mugwort.

losöwa, *vb.*, to collect plants, gather simples (W., B.) : inf. only.

losöwek, *f.*, *pls.* **-egow**, **-egy**, kitchen-garden, herbary ; *adj.*, herbal, botanical (B.) ; herbacious (W.).

losöwen (Lh. *luzūan*), *f.*, *col.* **losow**, *pl.* **losowys**, plant, herb, vegetable ; remedy, medicine, B.M. 1483 : Lhuyd in his quotation (see *plēth*), evidently from N. Boson, makes *losowen* m., like W. *llysieuyn*, with pron. and mutations to correspond—*an luzūan bian gen i 'ar nedhez*, but in Cor., as in B., it is f. ; pl. is used of different species of plant, O.M., col. being used of one species or many of one kind, e.g., *losow-mogh*, hogweed (D. "lizzamoo"), and sing. of each individual specimen ; see **†les**.

losöwer, *m.*, *pl.* **-woryon**, botanist, herbalist (W., B.).

losöweryeth, *f.*, botany (B.).

losöwjy, *m.*, *pl.* **-ow**, conservatory, greenhouse (W.).

lōsrew, *m.*, hoar-frost (W.).

lost, *m.*, *pl.* **-ow**, Late **-yow** (*loisa*), tail, tail-end ; tail of buddle, tailings of tin-slime (D.) ; bait cut from mackerel's tail, (D.) ; *l. lovan*, rope's end ; tail of adit ; *prag ythesough-why ow-sedha war agas l. oll an jeth ?* why do you sit stuck there all day long ? Borlase MS ; *un pysk bras vaw y lostyow*, one great nine-tailed fish, Tonkin MS.

lostek, *adj.*, long-tailed ; *m.*, *pl.* **-togas**, reynard, fox, Lh. : see **löwarn**.

losten, *f.*, *pl.* **-now**, train of dress, skirt of gown, tail of shirt (B.).

†lostledan, *m.*, *pl.* **-as**, beaver, lit. broad-tail (W.) ; replaced already C. Voc. by **bēfer**.

lōsy, *vb.*, to go grey or mouldy (W., B.).

lōsyk, *adj.*, greyish.

lothen, see **lon**.

Loundres (*Londres*, A. Boorde), *f.*, London, Gw.

lour, see **lowr**.

lous, see **lows**.

louta, **lewta** (*leauta*, *lauta*, C.W. *lowta*), *m.*, loyalty, probity, equity (M.E. *lewte*, Fr. *loyauté*).

lovan, *f.*, *pl.* **-vonow**, rope, stout cord : *lovonow pup eghen*, cordage of all sorts, C.W. 2291.

lovanen, *f.*, *pl.* **-now**, string, fine rope, Lh.

†loven, *f.*, *pl.* **-now**, bed, couch, Lh., as obsolete : perhaps from W. *llwyfan*, platform.

†lovennan (C. Voc. *louennan*), *f.*, *pl.* **-as**, weasel, *wesle* Aelfric : see **conna-gwyn**.

lover, *adj.*, leprous ; *m.*, *pl.* **-vryon**, leper (B.).

lovrek, *adj.*, leprous, mangy (B.).

lovry, *vb.*, to become a leper (B).

lovryjyon, *m.*, leprosy, B.M. 1356 : **l. cun*, mange (W.).

low, see **lewen**.

löwarn (C. Voc. *louern*, B.M. *lowern*, P. *lorne*), *m.*, *pl.* **lewern**, fox, O.M. 895.

löwarth (Late *looar*), *m.*, *pl.* **-ow**, garden (may be f. also, as in W., B.).

löwartha, *vb.*, to garden (B.).

löwarther, *m.*, *pl.* **-thoryon**, gardener (B.).

†löwarth-gwȳth (C. Voc. *luworchguit*), *m.*, orchard, fruit-garden, plantation : *virgultum* is taken in its other sense of "shoot," *telgra*, by Aelfric.

lowek, *adj.*, lousy (W., B.).

löwen (C. Voc. *lauen*, late *loan*, *looan*), *adj.*, glad, joyful, happy, blithe : comp. *lowenna*.

löwena (for *loweneth*), *f.*, joy : *l. dhys*, joy to thee, equivalent to "what cheer !" or "hail to thee !" as a common greeting.

löwender, *m.*, joy, happiness, mirth, jollity, C.W. 1428.

löwenek, *adj.*, merry, glad, joyful.

löwenhē·, *vb.*, to make glad, rejoice, be glad : as **berhē**.

lower, *m.*, *adj.*, many, much : *l. a ys*, much (of) corn ; used before sing. or abst. noun, causing no mutation, *l. gow*, many lies ; see **lowr**.

löwernes, *f.*, pl. **-ow**, vixen, she-fox.

lowr, **lour**, **lōr** (*loer*, C.W. *lower*, Lh.

lawr), *adj.*, *m.*, enough; *adv.*, sufficiently, in plenty: as adj. usually follows pl. or abst. noun, but *l. pegans dhe vewa*, enough to live on, B.M. 4292; *hen yu l. dhyn*, that's enough for us; as adv., may either follow or precede adj. or vb., *hyr l.*, *l. hyr*, long enough; *gon l.*, I know (well) enough; *ny-a yl l. y leverel*, we may well say it; in Late Cor. *lowr* and *lower* are confused, and the latter seems to have affected the pronunciation, though *lōr* still holds in B.M.; see **scantlowr.**

lows (*lous*), *adj.*, lax, careless, negligent, slack, flabby, loose, R.D. 2379 (M.E. *laus*, *lous*).

lows, *m.*, ?shoot, growth, sprout: Crankan rhyme "Trelowza," *try l. a*; cf. W. (*gweir*)*lawd.*

lowsel (*louzall* Lh.), *vb.*, to slacken, relax: 3 s. pret. *lowsys.*

lowsethes, *m.*, slackness.

lowt, *m.*, *pl.* **-ys**, lout, C.W. 1504 (E.).

***lōyas,** *f.*, *pl.* **-yesow**, spoonful (W., B.).

lū (C. Voc. *luu*), *m.*, *pl.* **-yow**, multitude, crowd, host, army, M.C. 163: *l. lystry*, fleet, C. Voc.

lūb, *m.*, slime (D. "loob").

lūba, *vb.*, to make slimy: see **trelūba.**

lüf (*leyf*, *lēf*, C. Voc. *lau*, *lof*), *f.*,*pl.* **-yow**, *d.* **dywlüf**, **dywla** (*dula*, C. Voc. *duilof*), hand: *l. dhyghow*, right hand; *l. gleth*, left hand; *dh'y dhywla*, for (each of) his hands, P.C. 2740.

lüf (*leuf*), *adj.*, dear; *adv.*, dearly, prefixed B.M. 65 (M.E. *lefe*, O.E. *leof*).

lüfban, *m.*, felt (W.): see **pan.**

lüfvedhek, *m.*, *pl.* **-ygyon**, surgeon (W.).

†lüfworhel, (C. Voc. *lofgurhchel*), *m.*, implements, *andluman* Aelfric: *lofgutrehel* may be meant; see **†gutrēl.**

†lugarn, *m.*, *pl.* **lugern**, lamp, C. Voc., *blacern* Aelfric.

lugarn-lȳth, late contractions **lugar'-lȳth, luga'-lȳ'** (*lug aleth* Ray), *f.*, *pl.* **-as**, brill, fish (D. "lugaleaf," "lugalay," lit. lantern flat-fish): see **lȳth.**

lūgh (*loch* C. Voc., *leaw* Bilbao MS.), *m.*, *pl*, **-y**, calf: *l. ogo* (*leuirgo*, Borlase, "Lugo Rock," Falmouth Harbour), seal, cave-calf; *l.-ewyk*, hind-calf, C. Voc.; Park Lee, Loy, Lawy, etc. field-names.

lūgh, *m.*, flash, gleam (W., B.).

lūghesen, *f.*, lightning-flash, gleam, *col.* **lūghes** (C. Voc. *luhet*, Lh. *lowas*), lightning, *leget* Aelfric: *l. gam*, forked lightning (B.).

lūghesy, *vb.*, to flash, gleam, lighten (W., B.)

lūghgen, *m.*, calf-skin, vellum (B.).

lūghty, *m.*, *pl.* **-ow**, calf-house: Lutey, place-name.

luk, *adj.*, enough (after noun); *m.*, luck (Late, E.): *cales l.*, hard lines, rough luck; *puscas l.*, fish in plenty.

lulla, *vb.*, to lull (Late, E.): *lull ha lay*, sing "lullay," lullaby, P.

lün (*luen*, Late *lēn*), *adj.*, full, replete, loaded, abundant, complete: often prefixed, as *l.-dregereth*, abounding mercy, etc.

Lün, dē-, dū-, L., *m.*, day of Luna, Monday.

lün-a-rās, *adj.*, full of grace: *ow thas whek*, *l.*, *da*, my good, gentle, gracious father, P.C. 1031.

lünder, *m.*, fullness, completeness: see **lün.**

lün-gallosek, *adj.*, of power unlimited, plenipotentiary, O.M. 2089.

lür (*lēr*, *luer*, C. Voc. *lor*), *m.*, ground, floor, (as coupled with *nef*) earth: *dhe'n l.*, down, on the ground; *dun dh'y gemeres dhe'n l.*, let us go and take it down, P.C. 3141; *war l.*, on, along, the ground.

lürlen, *f.*, *pl.* **-now**, carpet (W.).

***lusen,** *f.*, *col.* **lūs**, whortle-berry, "hurt" (W., B.).

lüsewek, *adj.*, ashy.

lüsewen, *f.*, *col.* **lüsow, lüjow** (*lidzhū* Lh.), ash, ember.

lüst (*luyst*),*m.*, *pl.* **-ys**, lust, list, desire, inclination, pleasure, B.M. 427, 1824 (M.E.).

***lüsyk,** *adj.*, in heat (of sow) (W., B.).

†lüyth (C. Voc. *luid*, and *luir* for *luit*), *m.*, battle-array, army, *fyrdinge* Aelfric.

lȳ, lȳf, *f.*, *pl.* **lȳfyow**, breakfast, lunch, noon-meat.

lȳ, *m.*, *pl.* **-ow**, oath (W., B.).

lȳa, *vb.*, to take an oath, swear; see **gowlȳa.**

lȳbel, *m.*, written summary of charge against prisoner, M.C. 189 (M.E.).

lȳch (*lich*), *adj.* and *m.*, *pl.* **-ys, -jys**, liege, B.M. (M.E. *lige*): *ow arluth l.*, my liege lord; *ow l. wordhy*, my worshipful liege; *l. ryal*, sovereign liege.

lycour, *m.*, liquor, M.C. 202 (M.E.).

lȳder, see **ledyor.**

lȳen, *m.*, learning, literature, scholarship: see **maplȳen.**

lȳen (C. Voc. *lien*), *m.*, *pl.* **-enyow**, linen

cloth, sheet, kerchief: *l.-dywlüf*, towel, napkin, C. Voc.; *l.-gwely*, sheet, C. Voc.; *l.-dorn*, handkerchief; *l. conna*, neck-cloth; see **scodhlȳen.**

lȳennor, *m., pl.* **-yon,** linen-draper (W., B.).

lȳes (*lüas*, M.C. *leas*, Lh. *liaz*), *adj. and indef. pron.*, many, many people: precedes nouns in sing; *gans l.*, by many (people); (with neg.) *nep l.*, no great number.

lȳes-gwyth, *adv.*, often, frequently, many times, P.C. 884: *lyesquyth* is a likely var., cf. **pesquyth.**

lyeshē˙, *vb.*, to multiply (B.): as **berhē.**

lȳes-hüny, *pron.*, many, many a one: see **hüny.**

lȳes-lyw, *adj.*, many-coloured, motley (B.).

lȳes-plēk, *adj.*, manifold.

lȳes-scryfa, *m. and vb.*, multigraph (B.).

lyes-tū, *adj.*, many-sided.

lȳf (*lyw(e)* C.W.), *m., pl.* **lȳfow** (*-vyow* C.W.), flood, deluge: *lyf-woth*, flood-stream, O.M. 2093.

***lyf,** *m., pl.* **-yvyow,** file (W.).

lyfrēson, *m.*, liberation, setting at liberty, R.D. 1676 (M.E.).

lyfryk, *m., pl.* **-ygow, -frowygow,** pamphlet, booklet (B.).

lyfryn, *m., pl.* **-now,** booklet (Lh. *levran* from W.).

lyfryow, see **lyver.**

lyfya, *vb.*, to lunch, dine at noon: see **ly,** f.

lȳha, *adj.*, irreg. superl. of *byghan, boghes*, least, as quasi noun, (the) least in importance or quantity: *dhe'n l.*, at least.

lȳjyon, *m., pl.* **-s,** legion, M.C. 72 (M.E.).

lyk(g), *adj.*, obscene (B.); *m., pl.* **lygyon,** privy members; *scaf a'y lygyon*, person careless of decency, wild arum (D. "scavaligion").

lykkya, *vb.*, to lick (E.): see **soras.**

lyklōd, *m.*, likelihood, N. Boson (D.E.).

***lyl,** *f., pl.* **-as,** goat (W.).

†**lylȳen** (C. Voc. *lilie*), *f., pl.* **-now,** *col.* **lyly** (B.), lily: C. Voc. may imitate O.E. *lilie, lilige* Aelfric.

lȳm, *m.*, lime, O.M. (E.).

lym, *adj*, sharp, keen, acute, penetrating.

***lȳmaval, aval-lȳm,** *m., pl.* **-low,** lemon, lime-fruit.

lymbo, *m.*, limbo, C.W.

lymder, *m.*, sharpness, acuteness, keenness (W., B.).

***lymner,** *m., pl.* **-s,** painter, artist (M.E.).

lympya (*lempia*, Borlase), *vb.*, to limp (Late, E.).

lyn, *m.*, fluid, liquid, water, lymph, serum, blood: *scullya l.*, shed blood, B.M. 3504.

lyn (C. Voc. *lin*, Late *lidn*), *f., pl.* **-now,** lake, pool; (in sea) anchorage: Lidden, place-names; see **grēlyn, pysklyn.**

lyn (C. Voc. *lin*), *m.*, flax, linen: *towal a l.*, linen towel, P.C. 836; *has l.*, linseed.

lȳn (*lyne*), *m., pl.* **-ow,** line, race, B.M.

lȳn, *f., pl.* **-yow,** slip, slang or stitch of land: Lean, field-names.

lynaja, *m.*, lineage, in Eng. line, P.C. 1183, line afterwards corrected to fit pr. *lynaj* (M.E. *lynage*).

lynak, *adj.*, full of pools; watery, purulent (W., B.).

†**lynasen** (C. Voc. *lin(h)aden*), *f., col.* **lynas** (Lh. *linaz*), nettle.

lynbysk, *m., pl.* **-buscas,** carp (W.).

***lyndaga,** *vb.*, to strangle (W., B.).

***lyndak,** *m.*, strangle, snare (W., B.).

lynen, *f., pl.* **-now,** line, stripe (W., B.).

lynen, *f.*, flax-plant (W., B.): see **lyn,** flax.

lynek, *f., pl.* **-egy,** flax-field (B.).

***lynek.** *m., pl.* **-egas,** linnet (B.).

***lynenna,** *vb.*, to draw, sketch in outline.

lynos, *col.*, duckweed (W., B.).

lyn-vūgh, *m.*, cow-pond: Lidny View, field-name.

lynyeth, lyneth (*lydnyathe* C.W.), *f.*, lineage, stock, ancestry or progeny: *l. mapden*, human race; *a'y l. yth-of*, I belong to the same family as he.

†**lynyn** (C. Voc. *linen*), *m., pl.* **-now,** string, twine, thread; line, Lh.

lȳon, *m., pl.* **-s,** lion, M.C. 21 (M.E.): see **lew.**

***lȳones,** *f., pl.* **-ow,** lioness.

lys, les (†*lis*), *f., pl.* **-yow,** court, hall, palace: *s* prevents mutation of following *c, k, d, p, t*: place-names (*an*) Gadlys, Liskeard, Lestewdar, etc.

lȳs, *m.*, mud, mire, slime, P.C. 838.

lysak, lyjak, *adj.*, muddy, slimy.

lȳsek, *f.*, muddy place, mire.

lyst, *m., pl.* **-ys,** palisade around tilt-yard, list for jousting, R.D. 223 (M.E.).

lysten, *f., pl.* **-now,** swaddling-band, bandage, selvedge, list, fillet (M.E. *list* or Fr. *liston*).

lystry, see **lester.**

lystryer, *m., pl.* **-yow,** dresser, plate-rack (B.).

lysyow, lyjyow, *m.*, wood-ash, lye (W.,B.).

lȳth, *f.*, *pl.* **-as**, flounder, flatfish: see **carlyth**, **lugarn-l.**, cf. W. *llythien*, pl. *llythi*, B. *lizenn*, pl. *lized*.
lyth (*leyth*), *m.*, *pl.* **yow** (C.W. 2280), limb, member, joint (O. and M.E. *lith*): *ha'm corf dhe weth, ascorn ha l.*, and my body the worse (for it) bone and limb, i.e. all over, R.D. 848.
†lȳth (C. Voc. *leid*), *m.*, *pl.* **-ow**, progeny, tribe, *maegth* Aelfric.
***lȳth**, *adj.*, soft, tender, feeble; humid, moist (W.): see **aflythys.**
***lȳtha**, *vb.*, to rot with damp, moisten; soften (W., B.).
lyther, *m.*, *pl.* **-ow**, letter, *Awaylow ha Lytherow*, Gospels and Epistles; *l. kemyn*, will (W.); pl. would be used also as M.E. *lettres*, of one missive.
lyther-doll, *m.*, postage (W.).
lytheren (C. Voc. *litheren*), *f.*, *pl.* **-now**, letter of alphabet, *staef* Aelfric.
lytherenna, *vb.*, to spell (B.).
lytherenȳeth, *f.*, spelling, orthography (W.).
lytherva, *f.*, **-jy**, *m.*, *pl.* **-ow**, post-office (W.).
lytherwas, *m.*, *pl.* **-wesyon**, postman (W.).
lyttry, see **ladra.**
lyu, see **lyw.**
lȳva, *vb.*, to flood, submerge, inundate (W., B.).
lȳven (*livan* Lh.), *f.*, *pl.* **-now**, leaf of book, page (E. "leaf").
lyver (C. Voc. *liver*), *m.*, *pls.* **lyfrow**, **lyfryow** (2 syllables), later **lyvrow**, book, volume: *an Lyver*, the Bible; *an Lyfryow*, the Scriptures; *l. a fysek*, medical book; **l. termyn*, periodical; **l. dedhyow*, calendar.
ly·verjy, *m.*, *pl.* **-ow**, library (W).
ly·verva, *f.*, *pl.* **-ow**, library (Lh. *Levarva Cotten*, Cottonian Library, from W.); bookcase (W.).
***lyvvya**, *vb.*, to file (W., B.).
***lyvyon**, *pl.*, filings (W.).
lyw (*lyv*, C. Voc. *liu*, C.W. *lew*), *m.*, *pl.* **-yow**, colour, hue, appearance, aspect, semblance, complexion, (of sun) brightness, *bleoh* Aelfric: *gwell l. dhymmo-vy may fe*, so that I might have a better appearance, R.D. 2201 (written *guel yv*).
lyw, see **lyf.**
lywa, *vb.*, to colour, paint, depict, P.C. 697.
lywans, *m.*, painting, colouring, coloration.
lywles, *m.*, woad (W.).
lywor (C. Voc. *liuor*), *m.*, *pl.* **-yon**, colourist, painter, *metere* Aelfric; dyer.

M (mutations V, F or V)

'm, see **am**, *poss. pron.*
-m-, *infixed pron.*, me.
†ma, *f.*, place; used only as suffix *va*, *-fa*, see Appendix III.
-ma, *suffixed pron.*, I, me: causes loss of *f*, as in *byma* (*byf*, *ma*), *wrama* (*wraf*, *ma*), found also suffixed to *genef* in *genama*, M.C. 193; in Late Cor. *-ma* or *-ama* was abusively used as a suffix turning 3 sing. into 2 sing., e.g., *ni orama* (*wor-ama*) for *ny-won*, *aljama* for *alsen*, etc.
'ma, see **bōs**, Table in Appendix.
-ma, *suffix* (for **omma**, *adv.*, here), with *an* takes the place of demonstrative prons. "this," "these": *an re-ma*, these; *an den-ma*, this man; occasionally joined to noun, *y'n dremma*, *y'n chymma*, in this town, house; see **alemma**, **yndelma**, **y'n ur-ma.**
ma, see **mar**[4]**(s)**, **may**[5]**(th).**
māb, see **māp.**
mabyar, *m. and f.*, *pl.* **-yēr**, young fowl, pullet, chicken (D. "mabyer"): see **map(b)**, **yar.**
mad, *adj.*, mad, O.M. 489 (E.).
madama, *f.*, madam (M.E.): *m. vras*, great lady, P.C. 1935.
†ma·derē, *m.*, groundsel, C. Voc., *grundeswelige*, Aelfric, as B. *madre*: *m. bras*, ragwort; in C. Voc. Lat. *sinitia* is for *senecio*.
maga[5] (Late *'ga*; Borlase MS. *gu*), *conj.*, as: *m. ta del o*, as good as it was; *m. fur drok*, as great an evil; *m. ta avel an owr*, as good as gold, *m. wher avel an gwels*, as green as grass, etc., *an* is used before following col. or quasi col. nouns, but not before sing., *m. fuscok avel tarow*, as mad as a bull, Borlase MS.; Lh. mistook the contraction *'ga* for W. *ky(n)*, B. *ken*, which is lost in Cornish.
maga, *vb.*, to feed, nourish, rear, raise up: p. pt. *megys*; 3 s. pres.-fut. *mak*; *ha Kernow genys ha Kernow megys*, a Cornishman born and bred.
magata·, *adv.*, too, also, as well.
magel, *f.*, *pl.* **-glow**, entanglement, mesh of net, stitch of knitting (W.).
mageres, *f.*, *pl.* **-ow**, nurse (B.).
magereth, *m.*, breeding, nurture (W., B.).

maghteth (C. Voc. *maht(h)eid*, Boorde *mathtath*, C.W. *mayteth*), *f.*, *pl.* **meghtythyon**, maid, virgin ; maidservant, handmaiden : *m. glan*, pure maiden.

maglen, *f.*, *pl.* **-now,** trap, snare, C. Voc., *gryn* Aelfric ; mesh, grating, grid ; long-handled grid for washing pilchards (D.).

magly, *vb.*, to trap, entangle (W.).

māgor, *f.*, *pl.* **-yow,** wall, especially of old ruins; ruin : Magor, place-name, from Roman remains there.

magorya, *vb.*, to wall, enclose (W., B.).

Mahom, *m.*, Mahomet, Mahound, regarded as the god of Saracens and Infidels (M.E.).

māker, *m.*, creator : *dha vaker*, C.W. 156.

mākya, mēkya, *vb*, to make, set oneself to, pretend, make a show of (M.E. *make*) : *sconya dhys ny-vēk*, she will not offer to refuse thee, Chart Endors..

mal, *m.*, readiness, will, urgency, eagerness : used only in expressions such as *m yu genef*, I am fain, willing ; *gans m.*, *gans bones m.*, with a will ; *dhym assa-vya m.*, how glad I should be ; *agan cregy-ny yu m.*, all is in favour of hanging us ; *cows ganso genen o m.*, we were delighted to talk with him ; *an prys m. yu genef*, the time is welcome to me.

māl, (*mayl*), *interj.*, blast ! the devil ! : *M. ! Myshyf re-gas-doggo !* Pest ! Harm sieze you ! B.M. 3746.

mala, later **melyas** (Lh. *meliaz*), *vb.*, to grind (W., B.) : p. pt. *melys*.

malan, *m.*, devil : *re Synt Malan !* by St. Belial ! *pysk m.*, fishing-frog, devil-fish (*pesk mollan* Ray, 1662) ; *pryf m.*, pipe-fish, "a small fish," Lh. MS. (D. "praave ").

mal bew², **m. ba**² (*be*), *interj.*; *adv.*, plague take,devil a (B.M., C.W.) : *m. dam, onen, vanna*, never a scrap, one drop ; *ny-vyes m. serrys*, thou wouldst not be vexed at all, C.W. 813 ; *m. edrek es dhymmo*, deuce take the repentence I have, C.W. 1290 ; this is not the ordinary optative form with 2 s. imp., or it would be *mal pew* ; the mutation suggests an original *y*² in *mal(a-)be(w) (y)dam*, plague shall own the bit of it ; see **māl**, **pew**.

mallart, *m.*, *pl.* **-ars,** drake, O.M. 1199 (M.E., D. "mollard").

malor, *m.*, *pl.* **-yon,** grinder (W., B.).

†**malōwen,** *f.*, *col.* **malow** (C. Voc. *malou*), mallow, *hocleaf* Aelfric : ***m.** *lowarth*, hollyhock.

mam (Late *mabm*), *f.*, *pl.* **-mow,** mother ; *an vam* (*vabm*, Lh. MS.), the milt or spleen : *m.-bysyth* godmother (W., B.) ; *m. gwenyn*, stock of bees (P.).

mamdra (*trē*), *f.*, *pl.*, **-drevow,** chief town, metropolis (W.).

mameglos, *f.*, *pl.* **-glosyow,** mother-church (W., B.).

mammeth (for *mamveth*, C. Voc. *mamaid*), *f.*, *pl.* **-ow,** nursing-mother, B.M. 1675 ; fostermother, wet-nurse : see †**mēth**, †**tasveth**.

mammyk, *f.*, mammy (B.).

mamscryf, *m.*, original text (B.).

†**mam-tȳlū** (miswritten C. Voc. *manteilu*), *f.*, materfamilias, lady of the house, *hyredes moder*, *h. hlaefdige* Aelfric.

mamvrō, *f.*, *pl.* **-yow,** motherland (W., B.).

***mamyēth,** *f.*, *pl.* **-ow,** mother-tongue (W.).

man, *m.*, (with neg. only) anything ; *adv.*, in the least, in any degree, at all : *ny-s-teva m. dh'y be*, they had naught to pay him, P.C. 508 ; *ny-dal, amont, m.*, it is of no use at all ; *nys-o m.*, it was by no means so, not so at all, M.C. 6 ; *nyns-yu henna m.*, that is not so at all, P.C. 2399.

man-, *prefix*, small (W., B.) ; see **manylyon.**

managh (C. Voc. *manach*, Lh. *manah*), *m.*, *pl.* **menegh,** monk.

managhek, *adj.*, monkish, monastic.

†**managhes** (C. Voc. *manaes*), *f.*, *pl.* **-ow,** nun, *mynecenu* Aelfric.

managhty, *m.*, *pl.* **-ow,** monastery (W., B.).

manal, *f.*, *pl.* **-low,** sheaf ; rectorial tithes : *m. ys*, sheaf of corn (P.); place-name Skyber an Vanal, tithe-barn, i.e., barn for the "sheaf," Med. Lat. *garba decimae*.

manala, *vb.*, to put (corn) into sheaves, to heap up : p. pt. *menelys*.

manblūf, *col.*, down, fluff, small feathers (W., B.).

manek (*manak* Lh), *f.*, *pl.* **-egow,** glove ; *m. plat*, steel gauntlet : *y-fu ow manegow plat spygys bras dre ow dywla*, my gauntlets of plate (armour) were great spikes through my hands, R.D. 2589 ; see **plāt.**

maner, *f.*, *pl.* **-ow,** manner, way, respect, custom, way of life (M.E.).

maner, *m.*, *pl.* **-noryow,** manor (W., B.).

ma'nerlych, *adv.*, becomingly, worthily, fittingly, O.M. 2200 (M.E. *manerly*) : see **hardlych.**

manhot, *m.*, manhood, B.M. 3174 (M.E.).

manly, *adv.*, manfully, B.M. 2344 (M.E.).
mans, *adj.*, maimed, crippled in, or lacking, one or both hands, feet, or both, B.M.; *m.*, *pl.* **-yon**, cripple, C. Voc., *anhenda* Aelfric: *m. ow ysyly a-hes*, (with) my limbs completely crippled, B.M. 4182.
mansӯon, *m.*, *pl.* **-s**, abiding-place, C.W. 2020 (M.E. *mansioun*).
mantel, *f.*, *pl.* **mentylly**, mantle, cloak, C. Voc., P.C.
manteth, *m.*, stone (disease): *cleves an m.* (*klevaz y mantedh*), stone sickness, Lh.
mantol, *f.*, *pl.* **-yow**, balance, scales (W.): field-name Tormental, *?torn mantol*, turn scale.
mantolly, *vb.*, to weigh with scales (W.).
manvlew, *col.*, down, fine hair (B.).
manylyon, *pl.*, small particles; inferior tin (D. " manillion ").
māp(b) (C.W. *mabe*, but vowel shortens unless stressed), *m.*, *pl.* **mebyon**, son, male child: *Map an Den*, the Son of Man; *m. aflavar*, infant, C. Voc.; *m.-gal*, rascal; *m.-lagas*, pupil of eye (W., B.); *m.-pron (bron)*, O.M. 1983, *m.-vam*, O.M. 235, individual, mother's son; *m. y dhama*, *m. y vam*, himself, what's-his-name, *m. dha vam*, *dhama*, thyself (disrespectfully); *m. an jevan*, *m. an pla*, *m. dewl*, imp's spawn, devil's kin; see **meppyk.**
map-dēn, **mabden**, *m.*, *and col.*, human being, mankind: *kynda m.*, the human race, O.M. 1950.
map-gōf, **mabgof**, *m.*, *pl.* **mebyon-goves**, blacksmith's apprentice, P.C. 2724.
maplӯen, *m.*, *pl.* **mebyon-lӯen**, cleric, clergyman; clerk: *M. ow Sel Pryva*, my Clerk of the Privy Seal, O.M. 2600.
map-mēthryn (C. Voc. *mab meidrin*), *m.*, *pl.* **mebyon-m.**, foster-son.
map-mollothow, *m.*, one cursed by his parents, C.W. 1516.
***mappa**, *m.*, *pl.* **-pys**, map.
map-pron, see **map.**
mar, *m.*, doubt: used in *hep m.*, *hep nep m.*, doubtless; elsewhere replaced by **dowt.**
mar[4](s), **mara[4](s)**, *conj.*, if (of likely or possible events); (after *gweles*, *danvon*, *prevy*, etc.) if so be, in case, in the hope that, lest, to see whether, so that; (in exclamatory sentences) what if, if only, if but: *ellas, m. pedhen... !* alas, what if I were to be... ! B.M. 2159; *m. calla wharfos !* if only it might be! R.D. 2439: *m. pedhaf kelmys lemmyn !* if only I were bound now! O.M. 1349; takes *s* before vowels in *bos* and *mos*; used directly before vb., commonly in indicative mood; sometimes written *ma* before *ny-*[2]; statement or request with *mar* requires *na(g)-* in neg. reply.
mar,[2] *adv.*, so, such a, as: *kyn fe m. vras*, though it were (ever) so great, however big it might be; (with *ha*) *payn m. ahas ha dre spyt ef dhe verwel*, pain so dreadful that through despite he shall die, R.D. 2050; (with *del*), *m. dha del res*, as well as need be; (with *avel*) *mar bos avel men*, as heavy as a stone.
mara[4](s), see **mar[4](s).**
marbel, *m.*, marble, C.W. 2183 (M.E.).
ma·rchondӯs, *m.*, merchandise (M.E.): see **marchont.**
marchont, *m.*, *pl.* **-ons**, merchant, B.M. 1890 (M.E. *marchaunt*): Late *merchant*, pl. *-s*, J. Boson, Lh.
marder, **ma·roder**, *m.*, deadness, stagnation, numbness (W.).
margh (C. Voc. *march*, Late *mar*), *m.*, *pl.* **mergh**, (of group) **merghas**, **marghas**, horse, stallion: in compounds *gh* prevents mutation of following *c*, *k*, *d*, *t*; *m.-asen*, he-ass, jackass; *an*[2] *vergh*, *-as*, the horses (exceptional mutation) place-names Noon Veres, Croft an Vergh; **m.-horn*, bicycle, **m.-tan*, locomotive (B.).
mar(gh)ak, in MSS. **marıak**, **-ek**, *m.*, *pl.* **-ghogyon**, **marregyon**, knight, horse-soldier, cavalier: *m. Dew*, monk, as Lat. *eques Christi*; see **ago-marghogyon.**
marghajor, *m.*, *pl.* **-yon**, marketer, merchant (B.).
marghajores, *f.*, *pl.* **-ow**, market-woman (B,).
marghas (*marhas*, Late *maras*), *f.*, *pl.* **-ow**, **-ajow**, market, P.C.: *s* prevents mutation of following, *c*, *k*, *d*, *t*.
marghasa, *vb.*, to market, trade (W., B.): inf. only.
marghbol (*pol*), *m.*, horsepond: field-name Park Marble.
marghken, *m.*, horsehide (W., B.).
mar(gh)oger, *m.*, *pl.* **-goryon**, horseman, rider (W., B.).
mar(gh)oges, *f.*, *pl.* **-ow**, horsewoman (W., B.).
mar(gh)ogeth, in MSS. **marogeth**, *vb.*, to ride: 3 s. pres.-fut. *marghak*; 3 s. subj.

marghocco; 3 s. pret. *marghogas*, 1 s. pret. *marghegys*.
mar(gh)ogeth, *m.*, horsemanship (W., B.).
mar(gh)oglu, *m.*, cavalry (W.).
mar(gh)ogor, *m.*, *pl.* **-yon**, rider (W., B.).
mar(gh)ogÿeth, *f.*, knighthood, chivalry (W., B.).
marghreden, *col.*, polypody fern (W.).
marghredyk, *m.*, horse-radish (W.).
marghty, *m.*, stable (W.): see **stābel.**
marghvēn, *m.*, *pl.* **-veyn**, horse-block, mounting-stock (W.).
marghvran (C. Voc. *marburan* for *marhvran*), *f.*, *pl.* **-vrȳny**, raven, O.M. 1106.
mark, see **merk(ya).**
***marnas, ma'ronas**, *m.*, *pl*, **-ow**, elegy (W.).
marnas, mar's, ma's (C.W. *menas, me's*), *conj.*, *prep.*, unless, except, save, only, exclusive of: used with impersonal conjugation, and set directly before the noun or pron. unless an adverbial phrase intervenes, *m. ty a-vo*, unless thou art, but *m. dhe well y-m-gorthebeugh*, unless you reply better to me, R.D. 47.
marner (for *maryner*), *m.*, *pl.* **-s**, sailor, mariner, B.M. 502 (M.E.).
marogeth, see **mar(gh)ogeth.**
marou (*marū*, Lh.), *m.*, marrow (E.): see ***mēr.**
marow, *adj.*, dead, lifeless, deceased, (of fire) out, (of drink) flat: *Dew, dhym assa-vya mal a pena m. a'n bys!* Oh, how welcome it would be to me if I were dead out of the world! B.M. 686.
marrak, see **mar(gh)ak.**
mars, see **mar(s), marnas.**
martesen, -tejen, *adv.*, perhaps, possibly, perchance.
marth, *m.*, *pl.* **-ow**, wonder, astonishment, amaze(ment), miracle, prodigy, marvel: *yma m. dhym ahanas ty dhe vynnes*, I am surprised that thou art willing; *m. a-m-bus a'th lavarow*, thy words surprise me; *mur a varth bras*, much of a great wonder, R.D. 1232, M.C. 157.
marthüs, -ys, *m*, *pl. and abst.* **-ow**, marvel, miracle, portent, prodigy: *dhym yma henna m. bras*, that is a great marvel to me; *adj.*, wonderful, Keigwin; *adv.*, wonderfully, surprisingly, marvellously: *m. gwan*, astonishingly weak; *m. yn-fras*, wondrous greatly; *m. ef yu den bras*, he is an amazingly big man; *hon yu m. cusul fur*, that is wonderfully wise advice; *m. kerys*, wonderfully loved.
marthüsy, üjy, *m.*, *pl. and abst.* **-thojyon, -thejyon** (C.W. *marudjyon*, s., *-odgyan*, pl., P. *marudgyan*, pl.), wonder, portent, miracle, marvel: *yma dhym murvarthejyon*, I am greatly wondering, lit. there is to me great wonder (abst.,) P.C. 770; *y-whelys deffrans marthojyon*, I saw divers marvels (pl.) C.W. 1898; *an marthojyon aga thermyn*, the wonders of their time, P.; whether *-ejyon*, is properly pl. is doubtful, it may be a var. of *-yjyon*, *-ojyon* only being pl., cf. **golowyjyon, lovryjyon**, etc.
marvor (*marow, mor*), *m.*, neap-tide (B.).
marwyl, †-wol, *adj.*, mortal (W., B.).
marya, *vb.*, to marry, B.M. 312 (M.E.): see **demedhy.**
maryach, -aj, *m.*, *pl.* **-ajys**, marriage, B.M. 177, 332 (M.E.).
mās, *adj.*, good; irreg. comp. *gwell*, superl. *gwella*; *m.*, good one(s): *an drok ha'n m*, the bad and the good; see **'vās, yn-fās.**
ma's, see **marnas.**
maskel, *f.*, *pl.* **-sclow**, husk, pod, skin, refuse of fruit or vegetables (W., B.).
masken (for *marscaun*, *marow-†scaven*), *m.*, *pl.* **-yow**, bier: *war y vasken*, upon his bier, B.M. 4358, as B. *marskaon*, V. *marù-skan*, W. *marw-ysgafn*, lit. dead-bench; see **scaun.**
masoberor, *m.*, *pl.* **-yon**, well-doer, Lh.
mason, *m.*, *pl.* **-s, -ys**. mason, O.M.
māta, *m.*, *pl.* **-tys**, mate, comrade, B.M. (M.E.): *matys da*, boon companions, good fellows, A. Boorde.
mater, *m.*, *pl.* **-s** (*-ow* Keigwin), matter, subject, P.C., C.W. (M.E.).
-mavȳ', *suffixed pron.* (emphatic), I, me.
maw (*mao* Symonds), *m.*, **mebyon** or **coscar** *used as pl.*, lad, son, youth, servant, disciple: see **mowes.**
may[5](th) (*ma*, *y[5](th)-*), *conj.*, that, as; (of time) when; (of place) where; at, on, in, with, for, from or by which or whom; whence, whither, whereby: becomes *ma* before *m* or *n* (*ma'm-bo, ma na-*, etc.) and infixed *'gan, 'gas;* takes *th* before vowels and silent *h*; in Late Cor. survived only with *gallos*, to which it was joined, as *mal, mallo, malja* for *may hyl, may hallo, may halsa.*
mayJes, *interj.*, help me! P.C. 362 (Anglo-

Fr. *m' aydez,* for Fr. *aidez moi*) : cf. *se deu ma eyd,* O.M. 2680.

mayla, maylya, *vb.,* to wrap in a cloth, swathe, bind, bandage, swaddle (M.E. *mayle*).

mayn (*meen,* B.M. 1406), *m.,* medium, way, means, mediation ; mediator, M.C. 8 (M.E. *meyn*).

maystry (*meystry*), *m.,* mastery, superhuman or irresistible power, ascendancy, master-stroke, miracle, prowess, swagger, bluster, force (M.E.) ; *vb.,* to master, dominate, rule, bluster, O.M. 409, P.C. 363 (M.E. *maistrie*) : *gul m.,* to domineer, act with assertion or defiance, swagger, hector, O.M. 2144, P.C. 377.

Mē, mȳs-M., *m.,* May.

me, see **mȳ**.

meawl, var. of **mewl.**

mebyl, *col.,* goods, personal property, B.M. 1688 (M.E., Fr. *meuble*).

mebyon, see **map.**

medel, later var. of **medhel.**

medhegy, *vb.,* to doctor, give medicine (W., B.).

medhek (C. Voc. *med(h)ec*), *m., pl.* **-ygyon,** doctor, physician, leech : *bos m. dhe,* treat medically.

medheklyn, *m.,* hydromel, metheglin (W.).

medhekneth (C. Voc. *med(h)ecnaid,* Gw. *methacknath*), *m.,* physic, medicine, *laecedom* Aelfric.

medhel (B.M., C.W., Lh. *medel, -al*), *adj.,* soft, slack, tender, delicate, weak, O.M. 928 : a change not unlike that of *medhel* to *medel* is that of *whethel* to D. " whiddle " and of *whethlow* to *whetlow.*

medhelder (*medalder* Lh.), *m.,* softness, tenderness, delicacy, effeminacy.

medhelhē· (*medhelhe* Lh.), *vb.,* to soften, weaken, enervate, mollify : as **berhē.**

medhes, *def. vb.,* to speak, say : *medhaf,* I say ; *yn-meth(-ef)* (Late *ameth, meth*), he said, quoth he ; *yn-meth(-hy)* (*ynmethy*), she said, quoth she ; *ynmedhans(-y)*, quoth they (present of narration) ; this use of *yn-* as particle is pecular to *medhes,* cf. M.B. *e mez,* etc.

medhew (*metheu* P.C. 698, as *methen* Norris), *adj.,* soft, W. *meddf.*

medhow, *adj.,* drunken, drunk, intoxicated, Lh.

me·dhöwsys, *m.,* intoxication (W.).

me·dhöwy, *vb.,* to intoxicate: *omvedhowy,* to get drunk (W., B.).

medhōwynsy, *f.,* drunkenness (B.).

medhygȳeth, *f.,* remedy, cure, medicine, P.C. 2713, B.M. 1487.

medra (Late *madra*), *vb.,* to ken, take sight, aim, C.W. 1552; attain to, emulate, P. : 2 s. imp. and 3 s. pres.-fut. *meder.*

†medynor (C. Voc. *medinor*), *f., pl.* **-ow,** hinge, *hearre* Aelfric.

meghtythyon, see **maghteth.**

megva, *f.,* suffocation ; asthma (W.).

megy, *vb.,* to smoke, smother, stifle, suffocate, quell, silence, extinguish, eclipse, put out fire or light : 2 s. imp. *mōk* ; 3 s. pres.-fut. *mēk* ; 3 s. pret. *mogas* ; p. pt. *mygys, megys.*

megyans (*mygyans*), *m..* nourishment, nutriment, sustenance, vital need, refreshment; nurture, training, upbringing, culture, O.M. 131, B.M. 25, etc. : *m. dhe'n ena,* food for the soul ; see **maga.**

megynnow (*mygenow,* Lh. *meginou,* Borlase *'gynnow*), *pl.,* bellows : the old sing. *megyn, f.,* is lost, cf. O.E. (*blast*) *baelg,* sing., now pl. only.

megys, etc., see **maga, megy.**

†mehyn (C. Voc. *mehin*), *m.,* lard, baconfat, bacon, *spic* Aelfric.

mejy, mejwas, see **myjy, myjwas.**

mēk, see **mākya.**

mel, *m., pl.* **-low,** joint, articulation : *m. keyn,* vertebra, *mellow y geyn,* the joints of his back, P.C. 1619 ; *m. chayn,* link (B.).

mēl, *m.,* honey : *whecca es m.,* sweeter than honey, R.D. 144; *cryben m.,* honeycomb, Lh.

mela, *vb.,* to gather honey : inf. only (W.).

***mēl, mül,** *m.,* praise (W., B.) ; the root of **gormel,** W. *moli,* B. *meuli.*

melder, *m.,* deliciousness, honey-sweetness : (as endearment) *ow m.,* my honey, delight, darling.

melek, *adj.,* honeyed, honey-yielding (W., B.).

melen, *m., and adj.,* yellow, (of horse or hound) tawny, bay : *ruthvelen,* deep yellow, orange-tawny, Lh. ; *m. cor,* wax-yellow (B.) ; *m. oy,* egg-yolk, Lh.

melender, *m.,* yellowness.

melenek, *m., pl.* -egas, green linnet (W., B.).

melenyk, *adj.,* yellowish (B.).

†meles (C. Voc. *melet*), *m.,* vermilion, red-lead : *lyw m.,* red-lead paint, C. Voc., *teafor* Aelfric.

melgowas (*mēl, cowas*), *f.*, *pl.* **-osow**, honeydew (W.).
mellya, *vb.*, to meddle, interfere, be concerned, B.M., C.W. (M.E. *mell*) : takes *orth* and *gans* ; *gansa ny-vynnaf m.*, I'll have nothing to do with them.
mellyans, *m.*, interference.
***melody**, *m.*, *pl.* **-s**, melody (E).
***melodyes**, *adj.*, melodious (E.).
mels, see **mols.**
†**melwhen** (C. Voc. *melyen*, ? *y* for *w*), *f.*, slug or snail, *snegel* Aelfric.
melwhesen, -whejen (*molhuidzhan*, etc., Lh., " melwidgeon " D.), *f.*, *col.* **melwhes**, slug, dewsnail: *m. velen*, large, spotted slug ; *m. dhu*, black slug.
melwhessa, *vb.*, to catch snails (B.) : inf. only.
†**melwhyoges** (C. Voc. *melwioges*), *f.*, *pl.* **-ow**, snail with shell, as distinct from slug; *se the haefdh hus*, " that [snail] which hath a house," Aelfric.
melyas, see **mala.**
†**melyen**, see **melwhen,**
melyn (C. Voc. *melin*, Lh. *belin*), *f.*, *pl.* **-yow**, mill : *m. -dhowr*, water-mill ; *m.-droghya* (later *drokkya*), tucking-mill, fulling-mill ; in place-names usually Vellan, the late corruption with *b* for *m* was not general.
melynjy (Late *belinjy*), *m.*, *pl.* **-ow**, mill-house : place-names Melingey, Bolingey, Velingey, Valency, etc.
melynor (Late *melydner*, *belender* Lh.), *m.*, *pl.*, **yon**, miller.
†**melyonen** (C. Voc. *mel(h)yonen*, Lat. *vigila*, for *viola*), *f.*, *col.* **melyon**. violet; ?also clover (see **mullyonen**) or other fragrant flower, *claefre* Aelfric.
melys, -üs, *adj.*, honeyed, sweet (W., B.) ; sweetish, insipid (D. " milsy," used of flour).
mēn (*mean* Lh.), *m.*, *pls.* **meyn, mȳn** (*myyn*), Late, of stones or stone-weights, **mēnow** or **meynow** (*meanow* Kerew, *minow* J. Boson), isolated rock, stone, fruit-stone : *m.-amber*, logan-rock ; *m. -beth*, tombstone; *m.-lur*, foundation stone; *m.-melyn*, mill-stone ; *m.-ten*, lodestone (B.) ; *m-olas*, hearthstone; *m.-pobas*, bakestone, griddle ; *m.-plumen*, plum-stone ; **m.-pry*, brick (see **bryk**) ; *an² veyn*, the stones (exceptional mutation) ; see **elven, flynt, growyn, kyllas.**
mēn, *adj.*, strong, powerful, able, eager, strenuous : *col-jy dhym, m. dha gesky*, hearken to me, capable of advising thee, C.W. 650 ; *toth m.*, at great speed ; see **yn-fēn.**
menas, see **marnas, myn.**
mēndarth, *m.*, saxifrage (B.).
'mendya, see **amendya.**
menedhek, *adj.*, hilly, mountainous : Trevenithick, place-name.
menedhor, *m.*, *pl.* **-yon**, mountaineer (W.).
menedhyas, *m.*, *pl.* **-ysy**, mountaineer (B.).
menedhyk, *m.*, *pl.* **-ygow**, hillock (B.).
menegh, see **managh.**
menēghek, *adj.*, monastic ; *m.*, monastic land : Meneage, Treveneague, Lesneague, place-names.
menēghy, *m.*, *pl.* **-yow**, sanctuary, place of asylum or refuge : Mennay, place-name.
***menegy**, *vb.*, to point out, mention, report, declare (W., B.).
***menek**, *m.*, *pl.* **-egow**, mention, indication (W., B.).
mēnek, *adj.*, stony, stone-like.
***me·nestral**, *m.*, *pl.* **-s**, minstrel (M.E.).
me·nestrouthy, *m.*, instrumental music, minstrelsy O.M. 770 (M.E. *mynstralcye*, O. Fr. *menestralsie*, with changes *als*, *ous*, *outh*).
meneth (C. Voc. *menit*), *m.*, *pl.* **-nydhyow** hill, mountain, *dun* Aelfric : in place-names often *mena*, *mener*, with silent *th*, e.g., Polmenna for *pen m.*
menglēth, glüth, *m.*, *pl.* **-edhyow**, stone-quarry : place-names Mungluth, Mongleath, Mungla(r), Trungle (for Trevengleth) ; hardly distinguished from **munglēth**, see **mēn, clēth.**
menhy·r, *m.*, *pl.* **-yon**, longstone, monolith, standing stone : Meneare, Tremenheere, Menherion, etc., place-names.
menkek, *m.*, *pl.* **-egow**, ling, heather (W. *myncog*, D. " nekegga", for pl.).
mennas, see **mynnes.**
menough, *adv.*, often, repeatedly, again and again ; *adj.*, frequent, repeated : see **bōghes -venough, namenough.**
menoughy, *vb.*, to repeat, reiterate, frequent (W.).
menowes (*benewes*, Lh.), *m.*, *pl.* **-ow**, awl.
mens, see **myns.**
menstrel (C.W. *mynstrel*), *m.*, *pl.* **-s**, minstrel (M.E.).
†**menta** (C. Voc. *mente*), *f.*, mint, *minte* Aelfric.

mentēna (*-teyna*), *vb.*, to stand by, uphold, aid and abet, maintain, B.M. (M.E. *maynteyne*) : 3 s. pres. *mentēn*.

mentēnour, *m.*, *pl.* **-s**, supporter : *m. fay* defender of the faith, B.M. 3023 (M.E. *maynteynour*.).

mentons (for *mentenons*) *m.*, maintenance, B.M. 3518 (M.E. *mayntenaunce*).

mentylly, see **mantel.**

mēnwȳth, *m.*, masonry, stonework.

mēny (*meyny*, C.W. *mayny*), *m.*, household, family, retinue, troop, inmates (M.E. *meynee*, O. Fr. *maisnee*).

mēnya (*menia*), *vb.*, to mean, Gw. (E.).

***me'nyster**, *m.*, *pl.* **-trys**, minister (E.).

menystra, *vb.*, to administer the sacraments, serve, B.M. 999 (M.E.).

†menystror (C. Voc. *menistror*), *m.*, *pl.* **-yon**, butler, cup-bearer, one who administers, *byrle* Aelfric.

meppyk, *m.*, *pls.* **-ygow**, **mebyonygow**, little boy.

mēr (C. Voc. *mair*, *maer*), *m.*, *pl.* **-as**, chief, mayor, *gerefa*, *prafost* Aelfric: **†m.-*bos*** (C. Voc. *maerbuit*), steward, food-master, *dihtnere* Aelfric.

***mēr**, *m.*, marrow (W., B.) : see **marou.**

mercy, *m.*, mercy (M.E.) : *ahanaf kemer m.*, have mercy on me ; *pysy m.*, to pray (for) mercy.

me'rcȳabyl, *adj.*, compassionate, merciful, R.D., B.M. (M.E. *merciabyl*).

merek, *adj.*, snivelly, snuffly : *m.*, *pl.* **-rogyon** sniveller (D. "murrick) ; see **goverek.**

***me'rewen**, *f.*, *col.* **merew**, juniper (W.).

mergh, see **margh.**

Mergher (*Merher* B.M., *Marhar* Lh.), **dē**, **dū**, **M.**, *m.*, day of Mercury, Wednesday : *de-M. Lusow*, Ash-Wednesday ; *kens es du-M. dhe nos*, before Wednesday night, B.M. 2254.

merk (*mark* B.M.), *m.*, *pl.* **-ys** (*markyz* Lh.), mark (M.E. *merk*).

merkyl (*mirkl* Lh.), *m.*, *pl.* **-rclys**, miracle, O.M., B.M. (M.E. *miracle*) : see **gwary-merkyl.**

merkya (*markia* Lh.), *vb.*, to mark, notice, put a mark on : 2 s. imp. *mark !* B.M. 3953 ; 3 s. pret. *marcas* (M.E. *merken*.).

mernans, **mernas** (*marow*, *-(n)ans*), *m.*, death : *gorra dhe'n m.*, put to death ; *gul m. dhe*, give a (sort of) death to ; *pan vernans a-n-jeva-ef*, what (sort of) death he had, O.M. 2219 ; see **bewnans.**

Mērth (Lh. *Merh*), **dē-**, **-dū-**, **M.**, day of Mars, Tuesday ; **mȳs-M.**, *m.*, month of Mars, March : *de-M. Enes*, Shrove Tuesday ; *an kensa M.*, the first Tuesday in March.

merther, *m.*, *pl.*, **-yon**, martyr ; (place-names) church consecrated to martyr.

mertheres, *f.*, *pl.* **-ow**, martyr (B.).

mertherya (*-ürya*), *vb.*, to martyrize.

mertherynsy, *f.*, martyrdom (B.).

merwel (*myrwel*), *vb*, to die, expire, (of flame) go out : 3 s. subj. *marwo* ; 3 s. pret. *merwys* ; 3 s.-pres.-fut. *merow* ; *marow*, adj., is used as p. pt.

mery, *vb.*, to drop, snivel (W.) : see **merek.**

mery, *adj.*, merry, pleasant, O.M., B.M. (M.E.) : *maga fery avel hok*, as merrily as a hawk, B.M. 1901.

***merys**, *m.*, *pl.* **-yow**, medlar (W.).

***merwedhen**, *col.* **-wyth**, medlar-tree (W.).

mēs, *m.*, *pl.* **-ow**, thumb : kept in *mesva*, but otherwise replaced by **bȳs brās.**

mēs, see **mesen.**

mēs (*meys*), *m.*, *pl.* **-yow**, field : rare apart from use in advbs. *a-ves*, outside ; *dhe-ves*, off, away; *yn-mes*, *mes*, out ; *mes a*, *yn-mes a*, away from, out of ; *mes a jy*, *mes a'n chy*, *yn-mes a'n chy*, out of doors, outside ; *yn-mes alemma*, out of this place.

mes (*mas*, Late *buz*), *conj.*, but.

mesclen (C. Voc. *mesclen*, Lh. *beslen*), *f.*, *col.* **meskel**, mussel.

†mesen, *f.*, *col.* **mēs**, acorn, C. Voc.

mesk, see **mysk.**

messa, *vb.*, to gather acorns (W., B.) : inf. only.

***messach**, *m.*, *pl.* **-jys**, message (M.E.).

me'ssejer (*masejer* B.M.), *m.*, *pl.* **-s**, **-ys**, messenger (M.E. *messegere*).

messe'nt, *adj.*, ill-scented, musty, B.M. 3398 (M.E. *mausent*).

mēstra (*tre*), *f*, suburb, outskirts of town (W.).

mēster (C. Voc. *maister*), *m.*, *pl.* **mestrysy**, **-yjy**, master : pl. ending, *-ysy*, is assimilated to that of *-yas* ; *m. a grammer*, Latin master ; **†m.** *mebyon*, schoolmaster, C. Voc., *cildrehyrda* Aelfric: *mest'r ha maw*, every individual, master and man, C.W. 294 (*m^r^* MS., expanded as *myrgh* Stokes).

mēstres (*meystres*), *f.*, *pl.* **-ow**, mistress, Chart. Endors. 36., Lh.

mēstry, see **maystry.**
mestrynsys, -jys (*mesternges*), *m.*, power, dominion, M.C. 102: from **maystry**, with *n* inserted before suffix *-sys.*
mesva, -veth, *f.*, *pl.* **-vedhy**, inch (*misue* Carew MS., 1599).
meth, *f.*, shame, bashfulness, shyness: *fy dheugh rak m.!* fie for shame! *taw-dhejy rak m.!* hush for shame!
†mēth (*maid, mat*), *m.*, fosterage, nursing, C. Voc.: see **mammeth, †mēthryn, †tasveth.**
meth, *m.*, *pl. and abst.* **mothow**, failure, loss, miss, miscarriage, break-down, fiasco: *py ny a-gan-byth m.*, or we shall have loss, O.M. 1078; *agan whel a-vyth mothow*, our work will be a failure, O.M. 1226.
meth, see **medhes.**
mēth, *m.*, mead, metheglyn, O.M, 2294, 2434: *gwyn py m.*, wine or mead; C. Voc.*medu, meddou* seem O.E. *meodu* as in Aelfric.
mēth, *adj.*, tender, soft; comp. *medha* (B.): see **medhew.**
methek, *adj.*, ashamed, shy (B.).
Metheven, mȳs-M., *m.*, June, B.M. 4303: Lh. *mis Efin*, month of June, is a misunderstanding, cf. B. *miz Even* for *miz Mezeven*, actually *meth* represents an old word for "middle," and *even* one for "of summer," Ir. *medōn*, W. *hefin.*
†mēthor (C. Voc. *maidor*), *m.*, *pl.* **-yon**, tapster, victualler, sutler, *taeppere* Aelfric.
†mēthryn (C. Voc. *meidrin*), *vb.*, to nurture, foster: see **map m., myrgh m.**
methüs, methys, *adj.*, shameful (B.).
metol, *m.*, steel, Lh.
mēthy (*methia* Lh.), *vb.*, to supply with food or drink; to nurse, Lh.: see **mēthor.**
metya, *vb.*, to meet (M.E. *mete*): *m. orth*, meet with; *m. gans*, encounter.
meugh, *m.*, *pl.* **-yow**, bail, surety, guarantee, security: *ny-n-jevyth m.*, he shall have no bail, P.C. 1118; found also as *mygh-* in **myghtern**, anciently *machtiern.*
meughya, *vb.*, to be bail, guarantee (W.).
mevya, see **müvya.**
mewl (*meul*, for rhyme *meawl*), *m.*, mischief, disgrace, reproach, harm: *re-th-fo, re-gas-bo, m.!* bad luck to thee, you! P.C. 2048, R.D. 79.
†mewyonen (C. Voc. *menwionen*, *n* for *u*), *f.*, *pl.* **mewyon**, ant: may be for *meurionen* in C. Voc., though like W. *mywionen*; see **muryonen.**
†mēyl (C. Voc. *me(h)il*, Lh. *mehal*), *m.*, *pl.* **-ylly**, mullet, *heardra* Aelfric: *m. ruth*, red mullet (B.).
mēylessa, *vb.*, to catch mullet (B.): inf. only.
meyn, see **mēn.**
meynek, *adj.*, stony, full of stones; *f.*, *pls.* **-egow, -egy**, stony ground: Dorminack, Carvinack, Carveynec, etc., place-names.
mō, *m.*, dark, murk: in phrase *m. ha myttyn*, by dark and by day, murk and morn, B.M. 2738.
†modrewy (C. Voc. *moderuy*), *f.*, *pl.* **-ow**, bracelet, circlet, ring, *beah* Aelfric.
modryp (C. Voc. *modereb*, Lh. *modrab*), *f.*, *pl.* **modrebeth**, aunt, *moddrige* Aelfric: *m. abarth mam*, maternal aunt; *m. abarth tas*, paternal aunt, C. Voc.
mōgh (Late *mow*), *col.*, pigs, swine: no sing. used apparently, see **porghel, hōgh.**
mogh ?*adj.*, vain, fruitless, or mis-spelt var. of **meth, mothow**, B.M. 955: *pan yu m. oll ow dughan*, since all my trouble is for nothing.
mōgha, moygha, see **moyha.**
mōghhē·, *vb.*, to greaten, increase, magnify, enhance, enlarge: *may foghaho hy huth-hy*, that her travail may be increased, O.M. 297; as **berhē**; formed from *mogh*, an obsolete form of **moy.**
mōk (C.W. *mooge*), *m.*, smoke, fume, reek.
mōl, *m.*, viscid substance, clot, agglutination of hardened blood, gum, etc., as W. *mol*, R.D. 2537, for *dar bol* read *dre vol*: see **mōly.**
mōl (as prefix pr. *mul*), *adj.*, bald, callow, bare, round-topped, hornless: place-name Mulfra, see **brē**; D. "brummal (*bar m.*) mow", a domed corn-mow.
mola, see **mōlgh.**
mōlder, *m.*, baldness (W., B.).
moldra, *vb.*, to murder; ***m.**, murder (M.E. *mordre*).
moldrer, *m.*, *pl.* **-oryon**, murderer.
mōlgh (Late *mola*, C. Voc. *moelh*), *f.*, *pl.* **-as**, ousel, throstle: *m. las*, fieldfare, "bluebird"; *m. dhu*, blackbird; *m. los*, thrush, "greybird"; the *a* of *mola* represents an obscure vowel inserted in pronunciation between *l* and *gh.*
mōlhē·, *vb.*, to make or become bold: as **berhē.**
mollath, *f.*, *pl.* **-othow**, curse, imprecation;

mollatew (contraction of *m. Dew*), God's curse ; *m. Dew war a'-th-trelyas*, God's curse on him who converted thee.

mollethy (*moleythy*), *vb.*, to curse: 3 s. pret. *mollythys*, C.W. 1357 ; 3 s. subj. *mollotho*.

mollethyans, *m.*, cursing, malediction, Lh.

mollothek, *adj.*, accursed, M.C., B.M.

mols (*molz, moulz*, Lh.), *m.*, *pl.* **mels**, wether sheep, C. Voc., O.M. 1384: the Mouls, rock-name.

molsken, *m.*, basan or basil leather (B.).

mōly, *vb.*, to coagulate, harden like gum, (of eyes) become bleared or "sanded" with sleep: *lagajow molys* (*lygadzhio mwlez* Lh. MS.), horse's blear eyes ; see **mōl**, *m.*

mon, *m.*, dung, manure: fish-offal (D. "mun").

mōn (C. Voc. *muin*), *adj.*, slender, fine, thin, O.M. 2443, *smael* Aelfric.

mona (Late *munna*), *m. and col.*, *pl.* **-nÿes**, money: col. and followed by pl. pron., unless a single coin is meant; see **arghans**.

mong, *m.*, *pl.* **-ow** ; **mongen**, *f.*, *pl.* **-now**, mane (W., B.).

mongar (*mungar* Lh.), *f.*, *pl.* **-gēr** ; **mongaren**, *f.*, *pl.* **-now**, horse-collar (D. "munger," "mungern," one of straw).

mones, see **mōs**.

mont (*mount, mownt*), *m.*, mount (M.E.) : *M. Calvarya, M. a Galvary*, Calvary.

mōr, see **moren**.

mōr, *m.*, *pl.* **-ow**, sea : †*m. dyfyth*, open sea ; *m. bras*, ocean ; †*spaven m.*, calm sea ; *hager m.*, rough sea ; *dhe'n m.*, *dhe 'mor*, to sea ; *yma 'n m. ow-tos, mos*, the tide is rising, falling ; in several compounds as traditionally known *mor-* has become D. "mul-", cf. W. *morfran, mulfran*, cormorant.

mōra, *vb.*, to go blackberrying (W., B.) : inf. only.

mōra, *vb.*, to put to sea, launch, sail (W., B.).

mōrast, *f.*, *pl.* **-rysty**, blue shark (B.) : see **gāst**.

mōrben, *m.*, *pl.* **-now**, wooden mallet, O.M. 2704: if not *mur, mor* may be for *morth*, Lat. *martus*, as *morthol* for *martiolus*, *martellus*, cf. **horben**.

†**mōrbren** (C. Voc. *moyrbren*), *m.*, *pl.* **-nyer**, mulberry tree, *morbeam* Aelfric ; see **moren**.

mōrcath, see **mōrgath**.

mōrdan, *m.*, phosphorescence (W., B.).

mōrdarth, *m.*, surf, breakers.

mōrdhos (C. Voc. *morboit* for *mordoit*, Lh. *morraz*), *f.*, *pl.* **-ow**, **-ojow**, d. **dywvōrdhos**, thigh: *m. hogh*, ham.

mōrdon, *f.*, *pl.* **-now**, sea-wave (W.).

mōrdrōs, *m.*, sound of surf (W., B.).

mōrdryg, *m.*, low tide, ebb (W.) : see **tryg**.

morek, *adj.*, maritime, nautical, naval (B.).

morel, *adj.*, deep glossy black (M.E., O. Fr., Fr. *cheval moreau*) : *pyma dhym ow margh m.?* wherever has my jet-black steed got to ? B.M. 2111.

moren (*moran* Lh.), *f.*, *col.* **mōr** (C. Voc. *moyr*), mulberry, blackberry, berry, drupel: *m.-dhu*, pl. *mor-du*, blackberry ; **m.-ruth*, raspberry ; *m.-cala*, garden-strawberry, Lh. ; see **syvÿen**.

moren (C.Voc. *moroin*), *f.*, *pl.* **moronyon**, maid, girl, young woman, wench: used rather as "chit", Ord. ; see **mōrvoren**.

mōrēr, *m.*, *pl.* **-as**, sea-eagle, erne (W.).

moreth, *m.*, regret, grief, sorrow or pining for loss or absence: *gans m. yth-of lynwys war-dha-lergh*, I am full of yearning for thee, O.M. 2194.

morethek, *adj.*, grieved, sorry, homesick, regretful, pining, yearning, remorseful, melancholy.

mōrgath (*morcath* Pryce), *f.*, *pl.* **-as**, skate (fish) : see **cath**.

mōrgelyn, *col.*, sea-holly, eryngo (W.) ; see **kelyn**.

mōrgowl, **mōrgowles** (*mulgouly* Ray, *morgoulis* Borlase), *m.*, medusa, jelly-fish, "sea-curd" (D. "malagowla," "murgil," etc.) : see **cowl**, **-es**.

mōrgronek (*mulgronek*), *m.*, *pl.* **-nogas**, blenny, fish (D. "mullygranick," "bulgranit," etc.) : see **cronek**.

mōrgy (*murgy*), *m.*, *pl.* **morgün**, spotted dogfish, row-hound, "sea-dog" (D. "murgy") : see **kȳ**.

mōrhesk, *col.*, sea-sedge, marram-grass (W.).

†**mōrhōgh** (C. Voc. *mor hoch*), *m.*, *pls.* **-as**, **mōrvōgh**, porpoise, "sea-hog," *mereswin* Aelfric.

mōrlader, *m.*, *pl.* **-dron**, pirate, sea-rover (W., B.).

mōrlanow, *m.*, high tide (W.).

mōrlenwel (*morlenol* Lh.), *vb.*, to rise, flow ; as vb. noun, rising of tide.

†**mōrnader**, *f.*, *pl.* **-drys**, lamprey, "sea-adder," C. Voc., *myrenaeddre* Aelfric.

mōrnasweth, -najeth, *f., pl.* **-edhyow,** needle-fish, pipe-fish, lit. sea-needle (W., B.) : see **nasweth, pryf-malan.**

mōrnya (*murnya*), *vb.*, to mourn, lament, C.W. (M.E.).

mọrnyng, *m.*, mourning, R.D 438 (M.E.).

morow, *f.*, morrow : *an vorow*, (on) the morrow, B.M., ; cf. W. *mory, y fory,* Gaelic *an màiraech* : see **avorow.**

morrep (*mor, ryp*), *m.*, coastland, seaboard: Morrop, Morrab, Merreps,place-names; see **gūnran, dorrep.**

mōrsarf, *f., pl.* **-syrf,** sea-serpent (W.).

mōrter, *m.*, socket, mortise, P.C. 2815 : perhaps miswritten for *mortes*, M.E. *mortas*, Fr. *mortaise*.

mōrthelek, *adj.*, hammer-marked, rough-beaten, dinted, P.C. 2731.

mōrthol, *m., pl.* **-ow,** hammer, O.M. 1002.

mōrtholya, *vb.*, to hammer (W., B.).

mōrtholyk-ancow, *m., pl.* **-ygow-a.,** death-watch beetle (B.).

mōr-tȳd (*teed*), *m.*, tide (P.).

mōrva, *f.*, sea-brink, shore, seaside: Morvah, place-name.

mōrvanagh (*mulvanagh*), *m., pl.*-**venegh,** monk-fish, "sea-monk (D. " mulvaanah").

mōrvargh, *m., pl.* **-vergh,** sea-horse (W., B.).

mōrlvȳth, *m., pl.* **-ȳdhy,** shark, lit. sea-wolf (W., B.) : see **sharca.**

mōrvoren (-*on*), *f., pl.*-**ronyon,** mermaid, P.C. 172, 2403 : see **moren.**

mōrvran, *f., pl.* **-rȳny,** cormorant, lit. sea-crow (W.; B.).

mōrvūgh, *f., pl.* **-as,** walrus, lit. sea cow (W.).

†mōrvȳl (C. Voc. *moruil*), *m., pl.* **-as,** whale, lit. sea beast : Carn Morvel, Scilly ; see **mȳl.**

mōrwas, *m., pl.* **-wesyon,** seaman.

mōrwels, *col.* grass-wrack.

mōrwennol, *f., pl.* **-nyly,** tern, sea-swallow (W.) : see **gwennol.**

mōrwhannen, *f., col.* **-whyn,** sandhopper, lit. sea-flea (W., B.).

mōs (*moys*, C. Voc. *muis*), *f., pl.* **-ow,** table, *beod, myse* Aelfric ; *onen a'y vos* one who sat at his table, a commensal of his, R.D. 860 ; *wor' ow mos* (*war ow bos* MS), at my table, P.C. 813, Luke XXII, 30.

mōs, mones, *irreg. vb.*, to go, proceed (with *claf, coth, squyth*, etc.), get, become: *m. gans*, to be taken, won or gained by, go off with, etc. ; *m. dhe wul*, to go (so far as) to do ; *m. rag*, to vouch for ; *a gans dha whethlow*, be off with thy nonsense ; the def. vb. **gallas,** etc., p. pt. *gyllys* is used instead of perf. and plupf., *dun* as 1 pl. imp. and *ke, keugh* as 2 imp.; *deu ur gyllys*, two hours since, Borlase MS. ; see Table in Appendix VIII.

most, *m., pl.* **-yon,** filth : *dour a vostyon*, dirty water (*vistian* Lh. MS.).

mostethes, *m.*, filth, dirt, defilement.

mostya, *vb.*, to befoul, soil, become defiled, B.M. 3863.

mothow, see **meth,** m.

motta, *m., pl.* **-tys,** ? mote : *avel mottys*,? as (thick as) motes B.M. 1275.

motty, contraction of *mos dy*, C.W. 1303.

Moufras, *m.*, Mauferas, a medieval devil-name : misprinted Monfras B.M.

mousak (*mosek*, B.M., *mowzack* Carew, *mouzak*, Borlase, *musac*, Pryce), *adj.*, stinking, ill-smelling, fetid.

mousas, -sa, *vb.*, to smell, sniff (B.).

mousegy, *vb.*, to stink, R.D. 171.

mowa, *m., pl.* **-wys,** grimace, mow (M.E. *mowe*).

mowes (C.W. *moos*, Lh. *mōz*), *f., pl.* **-wysy** (Late *muzzy*, Lh. *musy, muzi*), maid, girl, wench, f. of **maw.**

moy (Late *mūi*, N. Boson *mouy*), *adj.*, irreg. comp. of *bras, mur*, more, greater, another, (an) additional; as quasi noun, more (as compared with *cals*) ; *adv.*, more greatly, in addition, henceforth, any more : as adj., usually before sing. or abst. noun as "more," after noun as "another," "additional" : as adv., used before p. pt. and non-Celtic adj., as *m. grassyes,wordhy*, B.M. 192, 4389 (in C.W. only, redundantly before **comp.** adj., as *m. splanna*), and with vb. as *bythqueth ny-gerys m. den*, never loved I more a man ; in *moy podrek a'y ysyly*, B.M. 3048, *moy* is used before a descriptive phrase, in which *podrek* is noun rather than adj. ; *byth m.* (C.W. *bys voy*), any more ; *sul voy ... dhe voy*, the more ... the more ; see **na-moy.**

moyha, mōgha (*moghya*), *adj.*, irreg. superl. of *bras, mur*, most, greatest (in number or quantity) ; as quasi noun, greatest quantity ; *adv.*, (the) most greatly (with or without *an*) ; *mogha* is from an obsolete comp. *mogh*.

moyn (*moin* P.), *m., pl.* **-ow,** mine : *m. sten*, tin-mine.

***mūl,** *m., pl.* **-as,** mule (W.) : D.E. *moyl*

may have been used for this, pl. *-ys*.

*__mūles__, *f*., *pl*. __-ow__, she-mule (W.).

__mullyonen__, *f*., *col*. __mullyon__, clover, trefoil: Dor Mullyon, Rosemullion, place-names; cf. __melyonen__.

__munak__, *f*., mineral-bearing ground: Monek, place-name.

__mūn__, *m*., ore, mineral.

__munglēth__, __-glüth__, *m*., *pl*. __-edhyow__, open mine-working: as place-name may be confused with __menglēth__, q.v.

__münys__, *adj*., small, minute.

__mür__, *f*., *pl*. __-yow__, wall (W., B.): replaced by __fōs__.

__mür__ (*mēr*, *meyr*, *mear*, C. Voc. *maur*), *adj*., great, large, big, many, (*adverbially*) much, greatly; *m*., much: *m. a*, before p. pt. or adj., extremely, B.M. 658, 2904; before noun, much, many; *a'n keth den-na gwres yu m*., that man is made much of, B.M. 808 (in C.W. and later Cor. *mur* is used before comp. adj., as *m. lacca*, *m. le*, etc., much worse, much less, etc.): see __moy__, __moyha__.

__müreth__, *m*., greatness, grandeur, majesty, pomp (W.).

__mürhē__, *vb*., to magnify, make great: as __berhē__.

__muryonen__, *f*., *pl*. __muryon__, ant (D. "muryons"): see †__mewyonen__.

__mūs__, *m*., moss (D. "mooss").

__müs__, *adj*., mad, R.D. 971: in derivatives the *ü* becomes obscure *u*.

__muscogen__, *f*., *pl*.__-now__, fool.

__muscok__ (? *müs*, *cok*), *adj*., mad, distracted, amazed; *m*., *pl*. __-cogyon__, crazy person: *cok* in this may be the adj., but *cok*, "cuckoo," seems also to include "foolish person," as "gowk" does, see Eng. Dial. Dict.

__muscotter__ (for *muscokter*, Lh. *meskatter*), *m*., madness, folly.

__muskegy__, *vb*., to become or drive mad, craze, distract, bemuse: 3 s. pret. *-cogas*; p. pt. *muskegys*, *-kygys* (*muscügys* B.M., *meskeeges* N. Boson).

__musür__, *m*., *pl*. __-ow__, measure.

__musüra__ (*mysere*), *vb*., to measure.

__musüronӯeth__, *f*., mathematics (W.).

*__mūsyk__, *m*., music (M.E.).

*__mūsy·cӯen__, *m*., *pl*. __-s__, musician (M.E.).

__müter__, see __mӯtour__,

*__mūtya__, *vb*., to moult, sulk alone (D. "mooty," M.E. *mouten*).

__müvya__, __mevya__, *vb*., to move, stir, incite, perturb; propose, B.M. 260 (M.E. *meve*): 3 s. pres.-fut. *müf*, *mēf*; see __amüvya__, __remüvya__.

__müvyans__, __mevyans__, *m*., movement.

__mӯ__, *f*., *pl*. __-ow__, field: Mudgeon (*m. ojyon*), Mee, Mea, field-names (W. *mai*).

__mӯ__ (*me*, Late *mee*), *pron*., I, me: *my owhonen*, myself.

__mygenow__, see __megynnow__.

__Myghā·l__ (*Myhal*, C.W. *Myghale*, *Mehall*), *m*., Michael (M.E. *Myghel*): *dugol-M*., *gol-M*., Michaelmas: used as common invocation of surprise, *M*., *syr*, *dheugh gramercy!* Indeed sir, many thanks to you! C.W. 593.

__myghte·rn__ (*mytern*, Late *matearn*, *metearn*), *m*., *pl*. __-yow__, __-ow__, king, monarch, sovereign; originally "surety monarch," viceroy, regent (see __meugh__, *__tern__): accent is variable in verse, but may remain on *-tern*, as late spellings suggest, because this was formerly *tӯern*, *tigern*, and may change on adding a proper name, as *My·ghtern Margh*, *My·ghtern Caswelyn*, B.M. 2464.

__myghternas__, *f*., *pl*. __-osow__, kingdom, M.C. 102.

__myghternes__ (Late *metearnas*), *f*., *pl*. __-ow__, queen.

__myghterneth__, *m*., sovereignty, royalty, kingship.

__myghternyth__ (*maternath* Keigwin, cf. W. *teyrnaidd*), *adj*., royal.

__mygla__, *vb*., to cool, grow lukewarm or indifferent (W., B.).

__mygyans__, see __megyans__.

__mygyl__, *adj*., slightly warm, lukewarm, tepid, not zealous, indifferent, half-hearted (D. "miggle").

__mygylder__ (*mugilder* Lh.), *m*., lukewarmness, tepidity, indifference, lack of ardour.

__mygys__, see __megy__.

__myjer__ (Lh. *midzhar*), *m*., *pl*. __-oryon__, __myjwas__, *m*., *pl*. __-wesyon__ (*megouzion* (P.), reaper.

__myjy__, __mejy__ (Lh. *midzhi*, P. *mege*), *vb*., to reap.

†__myjyl__ (C. Voc. *midil*), *m*., *pl*. __-ow__, reaper.

__myjyn__, *m*., *pl*. __-now__, mite, tiny bit (D. "midgan"): cf. __dyjyn__.

__myk__, *m*.; a least possible sound: used with neg. C.W. 534, as B. *mik*; see __gyk__.

__myken__ (*mikan* Lh.), *f*., spite, animosity, malice.

mȳl (C. Voc. *mil*), *m.*, *pl.* **-as** (Late *-yow*), animal, wild beast, living creature.
mȳl[2] (*myell* C.W., *meele* Bilbao MS.), *card. num.*; *f.*, *pl.* **-yow**, thousand: *tyr myl* contracts to *tremmyl*.
mylast, *f.*, *pl.* **-lysty**, greyhound bitch (W.): see **mylgy**, **gast**.
mylblēk, *adj.*, *adv.*, thousandfold, O.M. 523.
myldrōs, *m.*, millepede (W.).
myldȳ·r (*moldeer* N. Boson, *myle dere* A. Boorde), *m. pl.* **-yow**, mile.
mylgolm, *m.*, knotgrass (B.): see **canscolm**.
mylgy, *m.*, *pl.* **-gün**, greyhound, coursing hound, gaze hound, lit. wild-beast hound.
***mylhenta·ll** (*myl hens dall*), *m.*, labyrinth, lit. 1,000 blind alleys (B.): *Kerdroya*, Troy Town, is a more probable Cor. name.
†**myll** (C. Voc. *mill*), *f.*, *pl.* **-as**, poppy: possibly an error, cf. W. *nill*, poppy, *mill*, violet.
myl-pryf (Lh. *mil-prēv*), *m.*, *pl.* **-prevyon**, snake-stone, druidical glass-bead charm: (D. "millproo").
mylüs, **-ys**, *adj.*, beastly, brutal; *m.*, *pl.* **-yon**, brute, B.M. 3805.
mylva, *f.*, menagerie, zoo (W.).
mylves, *ord. num.*, thousandth.
mylvledhen, *f.*, *pl.* **-dhynnow**, millennium, thousand years.
mylvlōth, *m.*, thousand years of age.
mylvyl[2], *card. num.*, *f.*, *pl.* **-yow**, million.
mylwell, *comp. adj.*, thousand times better.
mylweth, *comp. adj.*, thousand times worse.
mylwyth, *adv.*, thousand times.
mylyga, *vb.*, to curse, ban, execrate: 3 s. pres.-fut. *mylyk*; 3 s. subj. *mylycco*; p. pt. *mylygys*, accursed; as m., accursed person or thing, *deu v lygys*, two lying under a curse, a banned pair, P.C. 2553.
mylyon, *m.*, million.
myn (C. Voc. *min*), *m.*, *pl.* **menas** (Bilbao MS.), kid, young goat, *ticcen* Aelfric (D. "minny").
mȳn (*myyn*, Late *min*, *meen*, Lh. *mein*), *m.*, *pl.* **-yon**, edge, point, brink, lip, mouth, muzzle, face: *taw, syns dha vyn!* or *taw-sy dha vyn!* shut up! R.D. 995; *drefa dha vyn*, raise thy face, B.M. 1450; *whylen m.-hogh*, weevil, *logosen m.-hogh*, shrewmouse (B.); *pen ha m.*, heads and points, pin game (D. "pednymean"); *yma men bras dres oll an m.*, there is a great stone over the whole orifice, R.D. 401; *pur wow a-lever dha vyn*, thy mouth speaks utter falsehood, P.C. 2679.
mynchya, *vb.*, to play truant (D.E. "minchy").
mȳndū (*myendu* Leland, 1542), *adj.*, black-muzzled, used as personal name.
mynek, *adj.*, long-muzzled, pointed; *m.*, *pl.* **-nogas**, long-nosed skate (D. "minnick").
mynen (Lh. *mynan*), *f.*, kid: dim. of **myn**.
†**mynfel** (C. Voc. *minfel*), *m.*, yarrow, milfoil.
mȳnga·m, *adj.*, crook-mouthed (W., B.).
mȳngow·, *adj.*, false-mouthed, lying; *m.*, liar, B.M.
mynk, *f.*, *pl.* **-ncow**, ?platform or scaffold, *an vynk* P.C. 2868: cf. B. *menk*, m., platform outside a building, approached by steps, W. *mainc*, f., bench; or if *bynk* cf. W. *bainc*, f., M.E. *bynk*, bench.
mynnas, *m.*, wish, will, purpose, intention, desire.
mynnes (*mennas*, Lh. (wrongly) *menni*), *vb.*, to wish, want, will, purpose, like to, be minded or willing to: *mynnaf* (later *mannaf*) *dhe derry*, I wish to break; (as auxiliary) *mar myn ow dyscans servya*, if my learning will serve; *ny-vynnaf orth el namoy dos dhe'n stat-ma*, I do not want an angel to arrive at this state any more, C.W. 134; *my a-vyn* (Late *vedn*), I will (do so): for parts see TABLE in APPENDIX VIII.
mȳnrew· (*-reyv*, B.M. 2385), *adj.*, *m.*, ?"frosty-chops," greybeard.
myns (*mens*), *m.*, magnitude, size, quantity, amount, extent, number; *adj.*, as much or as many as: *worth an m.*, according to the amount, M.C. 117; *oll m. o*, all that there was; *m. na-wra*, all that do not; *pup den-oll degens ganso y byth a'n m. a-allo*, let everyone carry with him his property to the amount that he is able, O.M. 1592; *an sansesow, m. del yns*, the saints (f.), as many as they are, B.M. 579; see **kemmys**, in which the *n* of *myns* is lost.
mynsonȳeth, *f.*, geometry (W.).
mȳnvlew, *col.* moustache, cat's whiskers.
mȳnwharth, *m.*, smile (B.).
mȳnwherthyn, *vb.*, to smile (B.).
mȳnya, *vb.*, to nuzzle, rub noses together (D. "meen").
mynyk, *m.*, *pls.* **-ygow**, **menasygow**, little kid: rock-name Minnick.
***mynysen**, *f.*, *col.* **mynys**, minute.

mȳowal, *vb*., to mew as a cat: 3 s. pres.-fut., *myow* (W., B.).
mȳr, *m*., appearance, look, expression, face, show, R.D. 855, Gw.: *mar codhes m. Cryst*, if thou knowest what Christ looks like: see **gwary-mȳr, tarowvȳr.**
myr (*mer*), *m*., myrrh, P.C. 3143.
mȳras (*-es*), *vb*., to look, see, behold, consider, B.M. 2690; visit, B.M. 1981, R.D. 1536: takes *orth* as prep. "at," otherwise none; *myreugh agas lyfrow*, con over your (lesson-)books, B.M. 95; *pan vyrys*, when one saw me, P.C. 1257; *m. dhe*, see to, look after, B.M. 3656; *m. war*, oversee; *m. war-van*, look up; 3 s. pres.-fut., 2 s. imp., *mȳr*; see **mȳr.**
myrgh (C. Voc.*much* ? for *mirch*, Late *merh*), *f*., *pl*. **-es**, daughter, girl, young woman: *m. gal*, low wench; *m. hy dama*, *m. dha dhama*, her (thy) self, see **map.**
myrghesa, *vb*., to run after girls (W., B.): inf. only.
myrghyk, *f*., *pl*. **myrghesygow**, little girl, small girl.
myrour, *m*., *pl*. **-s**, mirror (M.E.).
myrtwedhen, *f*., *col*. **-wȳth**, myrtle (W., B.).
mȳs (C. Voc. *mis*, Late *meese*), *m*., *pl*. **-yow**, month: prefixed to name of month, *m.-Genver*, etc., as suffixed in D. "January-month," etc.
mȳsek, *adj*., monthly (B.).
myshevya, *vb*., to injure, ruin, cause disaster (M.E. *myscheve*).
myshȳf (*myschēf*, C.W. *myshew*), *m*., *pl*. **-evys**, injury, ruin, disaster (M.E. *mischeve*).
mysk, mesk, *m*., middle, midst (replaced by **crēs** except in **yn-mysk.** q.v.); *prep*., among, contraction of *yn-m*.: see **kemysk.**
myskemeres, myjkemeres, *vb*., to mistake, Lh. (D. "midgegomorrows," etc.): a late word, *mis-* from Eng.
mȳsky, *vb*., to mix, mingle, blend (W., B.): see **kemysky.**
mȳsquyth, *m*., month's time (W., B.).
myster, *m*., craft, guild, mystery (M.E. *mystir*., M. Lat. *misterium*).
my·sterden, *m*., *pl*. **-s, -dyns**, member of guild, craftsman (M.E. *mystirman*): Cor. *dēn* is here given an English pl.
my·stery, *m*., mystery, C.W. 2119 (M.E.).
mystrest (*-rust* C.W.), *m*., mistrust, C.W. 1744 (M.E.).
mystrestya (*-trustya* C.W.), *vb*., to mistrust (M.E. *mystryste*): see **trestya.**
***mȳta**. *m*., *pl*. **-tys**, half-farthing, mite (M.E. *myte*.)
mȳth (*meith*, Lh.), *m*., whey.
mȳtour (*müter*, B.M. 3010), *m*., *pl*. **-s**, mitre, O.M. 2615 (M.E.).
myttyn (C. Voc. *metin*, Late *mettén*), *m*.. *pl*. **-ow**, morning, *adv*., in the morning: *hedhyu m*., to-day at morn; *hedhyu vyttyn*, this morning; *de vyttyn*, yesterday morning; *ternos vyttyn*, to-morrow morning; *kens es vyttyn*, before morning; *de-Gwener vyttyn*, on Friday morning; *de-Pask vyttyn*, Easter morn; *myttynwyth*, the morning time (B.).

N

'n, see **an.**
-n-. *infixed pron*., him, it; us.
-na (for **ena**, there), *suffix*, with **an** takes the place of demonstrative prons. that, those: *an re-na*, those; *an den-na*, that man; occasionally joined directly to noun, *y'n forna*, in that way; see **alena, yndella, y'n ur-na.**
na-[3] (for *nep*), *adv*., no, (not) any: used with neg. before comp. adjs. and **kēn**; see **nahēn**; *ny-m-bus bewa na fella*, I have no longer to live.
nā, *adv*., *interj*., no, nay: used only in C.W. 2014 and Late Cor.; in M. Cor. the verb of question is repeated in negative, *Yu gwyr?* Is it true?—*Nag-yu*, It is not, No.
na[2] **(g)-**, *relative neg. and imp. neg. verbal particle*, that not, (were it) not that; not; with *rak* especially, lest: *rak, na-wrella dasserghy, nefra ny-gan-bya joy*, for were he *not* to rise again, we should never have joy, R.D. 1028; but *rak na-vy-jy yn awher*, lest thou be in trouble, R.D. 474; for other uses see APPENDIX VII.
na(g), *conj*., nor, neither, or; (rarely) and: *na...na...*, neither...nor...; adds *g* before all vowels; combines with article and poss. prons. as **ha(g)**; *emperour, na myghtern gwlas, na sodon...a-fyl a'ga remua*, an emperor, or a king of a country, or a sultan, shall fail to remove them, O.M. 2055; *ty nag ongrassyes del os*, thou, nor (any other such) graceless one as thou art, B.M. 3498, 3517; *drok gwayt na-wrylly..., na byth moy na-dhewhylly*, take care not to do harm, *and* not to come back any more (joining two negatives), B.M. 4146; *My*

ny-won.... *Na my*, I don't know.... Nor (do) I, P.C. 2537.

na(ns)-, na(nj)-, naw(nj)-, new(nj)-, *definite verbal particle of time*, by or at this, or that, particular time, at present, now, then, already, at this moment: used only before vowels in *bos*, when it adds *ns*; for uses see APPENDIX VII.

Nadelek, dē-N. (*Nadelik, Nedelack*), *m.*, Navitity, Christmas Day, Lh., P.: see **dū.**

nader, *f.*, *pl.* **-dron**, viper, adder, *naeddre* Aelfric: *n.-margh*, dragon-fly, Lh. MS., from E.D. "horse-adder" (var. "horse-stinger"), the dragon-fly being popularly believed dangerous to horses; see **mornader.**

na fors, *interj.*, no matter! (M.E. *no force*).

nag, see **na(g).**

nagh, *m.*, denial, refusal: *mar nyns-eth a'y n.*, if thou wilt not give up refusing it, lit. depart from its refusal, B.M. 3561.

nagha, *vb.*, to deny, refuse, disavow, recant, withdraw, renounce, forswear; stem vowel changes with ending, p. pt. *neghys*; 1 pl. pres.-fut. *neghyn*; *nagh y*, deny them, B.M. 919.

nagonen, *pron.*, not one, not any, never a one, none at all, not a single one: used with neg. vb., e.g., *ny-glewys drok n. ef dhe wul*, I have not heard of his committing a single crime, P.C. 2435; *dall na bodhar ny-asa, nag aflavar n.*, he left no blind or deaf man, nor ever a dumb one, M.C. 25,

nahēn (*nep, kēn*), *adj.*, any other, any more, otherwise: used with neg., occasionly implied only: *tra n.*, naught else, *nyns-us n.!* there's nothing else for it! B.M. 3623; see **na-**[3].

najeth, see **nasweth.**

nāker ,*m.*, *pl.* **nācrys**, kettle-drum, O.M. 1998 (M.E., O. Fr. *nacaire*, from Arabic *nakkarah*).

nam, *m.*, defect, blemish, flaw, imperfection, default, exception: used only with *hep*, giving force of adj. or adv., *hep n.*, perfect, positive, regular, arrant, downright; completely, utterly, positively, perfectly, entirely.

namenough (*nep menough*), *adv.*, (with neg.), rarely, seldom, B.M.

namma, *vb.*, to blemish, to spoil; to except (W., B.).

namna(g) (*nam, na(g)*), *adv.*, almost, nearly, well nigh, just about, all but, lit. a defect that not: used directly before vb. as *na(g)-*, adding *g* before vowels in *bos* and *mos*.

namnyge·n. *adv.*, just now, just before: *nos tewl yth-o n.*, it was but now dark night, B.M. 3680.

namo·y (*nep moy*), *adj.*; *adv.*, (not) any more, (not) again (with neg. or *hep*): see **na-**[3].

namür (*nep mür*), *adj.*; *adv.*, not many, not much; (with neg.) hardly, scarcely: requires *a*[2] before noun, *n. a dorn da ny-wraf*, I don't do many kindnesses; *ny-welys n.*, I have hardly seen; *ny-m-aswon n. a dus*, few people know me; *n. my ny-m-bus*, I have not much; *ny-gar n. y wul*, few like to do it.

nans (anciently *nant*), *m.*, *pl.* **-ow** (*nanssow* M.C. 170), valley, dale, *dene* Aelfric; may be *nanj* before vowels and in place-names is often *nans*[4], *nan*[4], *na*[4], e.g., *nans*[4] *pyghan*, Nepean, *nans b* becoming *namb*, *namp*, etc.; Lant- may replace Nant- in E. Cor.; see **war-nans, yn-nans.**

nans-, nanj-, see **na(ns)-.**

nansȳ· (*nansye*), ?Anglo-Fr. *non si*, not so, O.M. 485, in a line of English.

nany·l (for *na'n ӯl*, Late *noniel*), *pron.*; *conj.*, neither, (not) either: *nep na-n-jeves n.*, he who has neither; *n. yn nos nag yn jeth*, neither by night nor by day; *n. ogas nag yn-pell, ny-s-gwelaf*, neither near nor far do I see it, O.M. 1141; *ny-re n. dhyn bos na dewas*, he gives us neither meat nor drink, O.M. 1810; N. Boson uses this also to enforce a preceding negative as in Eng., *na nag-yu an bobel goth dhe vos scodhyes war(nedha), n.*, nor are the old folk to be depènded on, neither; but this is doubtful Cornish.

napell, see **nep-pell.**

nappa, *m.*, *pl.* **-pys**, nap: see **nappya.**

nappya (*napya*), *vb.*, to take a nap, B.M. 958 (M.E.).

nās, *f.*, nature, disposition, character: var. of **gnās**, as W. *naws*, B. *neuz*, occurring in **dynās**, and, as a correction, P.C. 1142.

nascra, see **ascra.**

nasweth, najeth (Late *naja, nadzhedh* Lh.) *f.*, *pl.* **-wedhow, -jedhow**, needle: see **crow-nasweth.**

nāsya, *vb.*, to affect, modify the nature or dispositson of (W., B.).

nasyon, (*nasconn, nascyon*), *m.*; *pl.* **-s,**

nation, B.M. (M.E. *nacioun*).

nath, *m.*, *pl.*, **-as**, puffin (D.): Carrick Nath, rock-name.

natur (*-ter*, *-tar*, *-ttur*), *f.*, nature, constitution, character, M.C., B.M., Lh.: *erbyn n.*, unnatural, -ly.

natureth, *m.*, natural affection, human nature, M.C. 223.

naturor, *m.*, *pl.* **-yon**, naturalist (B.).

na-vē, **na-vȳa**, *conjs.*, but for, were it not, or had it not been for: used before noun, pron. or *bos* with adj. or p. pt.

navyth.? *adv.*, not at all, R.D. 1020: possibly *na-vyth*, it is not, habit. pres.

naw, *card. num.*. nine: *dreugh y dhymmo, ha my a-s-ygor, an darrasow aga n.*, give them to me, and I will open all nine of the doors, lit. the doors their nine, R.D. 639.

nawes, see **nawves**.

na-whāth (*na huăth*, Lh.), *adv.*, *conj.*, nevertheless, notwithstanding, as V. *nahoah*, John of Chyanhorth 24: see **whāth**.

nawnj-, see **nans-**.

nawnjegves, *ord. num.*, nineteenth.

nawnjek, *card. num.*, nineteen.

nawves, **nawes**, *ord. num.*, ninth.

neb, see **nep**: in Late Cor. also used for *y'n le may*, as contracted to *lebba*; see **tereba**.

nebes, *m.*, *adj.*, *adv.*, some, a little, something, little, few, somewhat: as adj. followed by pl. or abstract noun, without mutation.

neb-lȳes, *adv.*, (with neg.) in any great number, at all many, B.M. 740, 3054.

nebonen, see **nep-onen**.

neb-ür, *m.*, any hour; *adv.*, at any time, ever, B.M. 52.

nedha, *vb.*, to spin, twist,: 3 s. pres.-fut. *nēth*; 3 s. subj. *netho*.

***nedha**, **nedhef**, *m.*, *pl.* **-evyow**, adze (W., B.).

nedhen, *f.*, *col.* **nēth**, nit, Lh.

nedher, *m.*, *f.* **-ores**, *pls.* **-oryon**, **-ow**, spinner: see **nedha**.

nēf, *m. or f.*, *pl.* **nevow**, heaven, sky, climate: often *an nef*; *gwlas(cor) n.*, the kingdom of heaven; *ynny*, f., refers to *nef* C.W. 25; *an n. da*, B.M. 461, makes *nef* m.

nefra, *adv.*, ever (future), for ever; (with neg.) never (O.E. *(ne)aefre*): note contraction *nefr'ow-*, B.M. 4461.

negedhek, *adj.*, negative (W.)

negedhys, *adj. and m.*, *pl.* **-yjyon**, recusant, apostate: term of abuse.

negesa, *vb.*, to go on an errand (W.): inf. only.

negeth, *m.*, negative; refuser, denier (W.).

***negh**, *m.*, pining, fret, vexation (W., B.).

***neghy**, *vb.*, to pine, fret, vex (W., B.).

nēghys, etc., see **nagha**.

negys, *m.*, *abst. and pl.* **-sow**, **-syow**, business, affair, commission, errand, message: *spedya n.*, bring an affair to a successful conclusion; *mones n.*, to go an errand; *gwellhës yu agas n.*, your business is bettered, B.M. 3316; *us n. dheugh orthyf-vy ?* have you business with me ? B.M. 3126.

nell, *m.*, might, power, force, strength.

†**nēn**, *m.*, *pl.* **-now**, roof, ceiling: in **nenbren**.

nena, see **ena**.

†**nenbren**, *m.*, *pl.* **-nyer**, roof-tree, ridge-beam, (loosely) roof, C. Voc., *fyrst* Aelfric.

nenlen, *f.*, canopy (W.).

nep, before vowels usually **neb**, *adj.*, any, some, (with nums.) about, approximately, (with neg) no, not any; *rel. pron.*, who, he who, one who, any who, whoever, whosoever, (after preps.) whom; as pron., *nep* is usually sing. and used of persons only, but also represents pl., e.g., P.C. 788, 3092, R.D. 158, where it is followed by pl. vb. and by *-s-*; as adj. it occasionally means no matter what, as *dun yn-kerth, cowetha, dhe n. hensy rag cudha*, let us get away, comrades, to hide in no matter what direction, lit. ways, B.M. 1307.

nep-dēn, *m.*, anybody, someone, anyone, (with neg.) nobody, no-one.

nep-lē, *m.*, some place; *adv.*, anywhere.

nep-onen (*nebonen* Lh.), *pron.*, someone, anyone, somebody, R.D. 1403.

nep-part (*na part*), *m.*, some portion or part; *adv.*, anywhere, C.W. 939.

nep-pell (*na pel*), *adv.*, (with neg.) any distance or way, any length of time, at all far or long: *nyns-yu n.*, not long since; *kens n.*, ere long; *ny-vyn mos n.*, he does not wish to go far.

nep-plas, *m.*, some place; *adv.*, anywhere.

nep-pow, *m.*, any country; *adv.*, anywhere, Lh.

nep-prȳs, *adv.*, some time, (with neg.) at any time, ever, at all, O.M. 1222.

neppyth (*napyth*), *m.*, something, (not) anything; *adv.*, somewhat: *n. a*, some (adj.); *n. re dom*, somewhat too hot;

ny-wra awos n., don't on any account; see **travyth**.

†**nep-tra, nebtra** (C. Voc. *nebtra*, Chart. End. *neb tra*). *m.*, aught, anything, something, commonly replaced by **neppyth**; see **travyth**.

nep-tū, *m.*, *adv.*, anywhere, on any side, B.M. 1915, C.W. 1045: *rak na-n-gwelaf dhym a n.*, because I do not see him anywhere about me, R.D. 865.

nerth, *m.*, *pl.* **-ow**, strength, energy, might, power, force, body of armed men: *y-cusulyaf leverel dos n. warnan ha'y dhon dhe-ves*, I advise that we say that an armed force fell upon us and carried him off, R.D. 570.

nertha, *vb.*, to fortify, strengthen (W., B.).

nerthek, *adj.*, powerful, potent (W., B.).

nēs, *adj.*, irreg. comp. of *ogas*, closer, nearer; *adv.*, (with neg.) any more, ever, at all, indeed: *dos n.*, to draw nigh, approach, come near; *nebes n.*, a little closer; *ny-vedhaf..., na-vedhaf n.!* I dare not..., no, I never dare! or I dare not indeed! B.M. 771; *ny-vynsen..., na-vynsen n.*, I would not..., no, that I would not, B.M. 1044; *ny-dowtsen..., na-wrussen n.*, I should not fear, no, that I should not, B.M. 2590; *den a-vo marow ny-dhasvew n.*, a man that is dead will not revive any more, R.D. 949; *na-doch vy n.!* do not touch me at all! R.D. 875; *termyn-vyth n.*, at any time at all, O.M. 1360: see **yn-nēs**.

nēshē·, *vb.*, to come or bring nearer (W., B.): as **berhē**.

neshevyn, nessevyn (C. Voc. *nesheuin*), *m. and col.*, kinsman, neighbour, next-of-kin, C. Voc., *maeg* Aelfric; relatives, B.M.; from *neshaf*, ancient form of superlative **nessa**; cf. **gwelhevyn**.

nessa, *adj.*, irreg. superl. of **ogas**, nearest, next; *adv.*, next time; *m. and pl.*, next-of-kin, relatives: *yn y n.*, next his skin; *y bows n.*, his undermost dress; *bedheugh-why furra n.*, be wiser next time.

nessa, *vb.*, to draw near, approach: 3 s. pres.-fut., 2 s. imp. *nēs*.

nēth, see **nedhen**.

nevek, *adj.*, heavenly, celestial (B.).

***new**, *f.*, *pl.* **-yow**, trough (W., B.): *n. tos*, kneading-trough (B.).

newer, see **nyhewer**.

newl (*niwl* Lh.), *m.*, *pl.* **-ow**, fog, mist, haze, Gw.

newlek, *adj.*, misty, foggy, hazy (W.).

newlen, *f.*, *pl.* **-now**, mist-cloud: *n. rew*, hoar-frost (W., B.).

newnj-, see **nans-**.

newodhow, see **noweth**.

newores, see **enewores**.

newyth, *m.*, immaturity, childhood: in phrase *a n. hag a henys*, in youth and age, B.M. 167.

nobyl, *adj.*, noble, O.M., C.W.; *m.*, *pl.* **-blys**, noble (coin), "gold penny," one third of a pound, B.M. 3338 (M.E.): see **rosa-noblen**.

nomber (*numbyr*), *m.*, number, O.M., B.M., C.W. (M.E.).

nōr, *m.*, the world; **an norvȳs·**, *m.*, the terrestrial world, all the earth; see **dōr**.

norter, *m.*, breeding, nurture, B.M. 287 (M.E. *norture*).

Nōrth, Nōr', *m., and adj.*, North, B.M. 3427: *N.-Yst*, B.M. 664 (*Noor East*, J. Boson), North-East, etc. (E.).

nos, *m.*, *pl.* **-ow**, mark, token, Lh.

nosa, noja, *vb.*, to mark; replaced by **merkya**.

nōs, *f.*, *pl.* **-ow**, night, time after sunset, eve of feast: *s* prevents mutation of following *c, k, d, p, t.*; *n. tewal (du) yu*, it is pitch dark; *n. da dheugh*, good night,, good evening! (on parting); *pup n. ha deth*, continually; see **dhe, drē, drēs, dyworth, yn-nōs**.

'nos, see **enos**.

nōswyth, *adv.*, in the night-time, this night, B.M. 1785; *f.*, *pl.* **-yow**, night-time, vigil, eve of feast: no mutation in following *c, k, d, p, t*; *N. Nadelek*, Christmas Eve, etc; *n. vas dheugh*, good evening (on meeting, B.).

nōth (*noyth, noeth*), *adj.*, naked, bare: after vb. other than *bos, gallas*, etc. in *mos* usually *yn-noth*; *n. glan*, stark naked; *mar n. genys del vya*, as bare as he had been born.

nōtha (for *notheth*), *f.*, nakedness, C.W. 969.

nōthben, *adj.*, bareheaded (W.).

nothlen, *f.*, *pl.* **-now**, winnowing-sheet, P.C. 881.

nōthtrōs, *adj.*, barefoot (B.).

nothya, *vb.*, to winnow, fan corn (W., B.).

nothyer, *m.*, *pl.* **-yoryon**, winnower (W., B.).

nōtya, *vb.*, to make known, announce,

report; ? remark, note, observe, P.C. 434 (M.E.).

now, *adv. and interj.*, now: note *n. lemmyn* used together, B.M. 3426 (E.).

nowedher, *m., pl.* **-oryon,** innovator (W.).

nowedhy, *vb.*, to renew, renovate, innovate (W., B.).

nowedhyans, *m.*, innovation, renewal.

nowedhynsy, *m.*, novelty (B.).

noweth (*nowyth*, older *newyth*), *adj.*, new, fresh, novel; *adv.*, newly, freshly, just; *m., pl.* **newodhow** and in C.W. **nowethys,** news, tidings: *newodhow n.*, fresh tidings; *n. flam*, brand-new, "flam-new" (D., W., B.); *den, benen, tus n.*, bridegroom, bride, bridal pair (B.); see **newyth.**

nowethhē·, *vb.*, to renovate (B.): as **berhē.**

nown (C. Voc. *naun*), *m.*, hunger, starvation O.M. 400: *yma n. bras dhym*, I am very hungry.

nownek, *adj.*, hungry, famishing; *m., pl.* **-negyon**, starveling (W., B.).

***nowyjyans** (*nowejans* Lh.), *m.*, alteration, change (from W. *newidiant*).

***nowys,** *vb.*, to change, alter; *m.*, change (W.): not found as Cor. or B.; see **chanjya.**

†**noy** (C. Voc. *noi*), *m., pl.* **-ens,** nephew, *neua* Aelfric.

noys, *m.*, clamour, din, R.D., B.M. (M.E. *noyis*): *gul n. gans*, to raise a clamour in favour of, B.M. 2711; *hager n.*, hideous outcry.

***nüf,** *m.*, swimming (W., B.): replaced by **nyj.**

nüja, *vb.*, to fray out, fringe (B.).

†**nüjen** (C. Voc. *noden*), *f., pl.* **now,** *col.* **nüs, nēs,** thread.

nüjenna, *vb.*, to thread, embroider with thread (B.).

numbyr, see **nomber.**

nüs, see **nüjen.**

***nüvya,** *vb.*, to swim (W., B.): replaced by **nȳjya.**

nȳ (Late *nei, nye*), *pron.*, we, us.

nȳa, see **annya.**

nȳ·cyta (*nyscyta*), *m.*, ignorance, nescience, folly, (in old sense) nicety, M.C. 127, 185 (M.E. *nycete*).

ny[2] **(ns)-,** *neg. verbal particle*, not: *nyns-us scappya dhyn-nyny!* there is no getting away for us! *nyns-yu dhe dhenvyth gwertha gras Dew*, it is not for anyone to sell God's grace; *y vewnans nyns-us gwytha*, his life is not to be saved; *nyns-yu crysy dhedha*, there is no believing them, etc.; for uses see APPENDIX VII.

nyhewer, newer (*nehuer* Lh., for *nythewer*), *adv.*, last night, yesterday evening: *bys-yn newer gorthewer*, until quite late last night, B.M. 103.

nȳj, *m.*, flight, flying; floating; swimming.

nȳja, nyjya (C.W. *nyedga*, Lh. *nyidzha*), *vb.*, to swim; float; fly: 3. s. pret. *nyjyas*; 2 pl. imp. *nyjyeugh*; p. pt. *nyjys, -yes* (*nighies* Gw.), used as "afloat," "floating," cf. **tryga.**

nȳl, see **ȳl.**

nyns, see **ny(ns).**

nynȳ·, *pron.* (emphatic), we, us, ourselves.

nȳth (C. Voc. *neid*), *m., pl.* **-ow** (*neitho* Lh.), nest: *n. hep oy otomma!* here's an eggless nest! the place is empty! the bird has flown! B.M. 3302.

†**nȳth** (C. Voc. *noit*), *f., pl.* **-ow,** niece, *bewimmen* Aelfric.

nȳthowa, *vb.*, to go birds'-nesting (B.): inf. only.

nȳthva, *f.*, nesting-place (W.).

nȳthy, -ya, *vb.*, to nest, build a nest (W., B.).

nyver, *m., pl.* **-ow,** number: *tremmyl orth n.*, 3000 in number.

nyvera, *vb.*, to count, reckon, number: p. pt. *nyvyrys.*

nyveryans, *m.*, enumeration: see **nyvera.**

O

Ō, *interj.*, O, oh, R.D. 887 (M.E.).

ō, see **bōs.**

obaya, *vb.*, to yield, submit, surrender, comply, obey (M.E. *obeien(to)*): takes *dhe, dhe Yedhow sur o. nefra ny-vynnaf orthough*, I shall certainly never want you to give in to a Jew, B.M. 3535.

ober, *m., pl.* **-ow,** work, act, deed, fact: *yn o.*, in fact, actually, M.C. 65.

obereth, *m.*, performance, life-work, works, deeds, M.C. 259, O.M. 604.

oberor, *m., pl.* **-yon,** worker, doer, wright, craftsman, C. Voc.

oberwas (*obèrwaz*), *m., pl.* **-wesyon,** workman, Lh.: see **gwas.**

obery, *vb.*, to work, spend work about, carry to perfection, do, perform: p. pt. *oberys*, wrought, done.

oblāsyon (*oblacon*), *m.*, oblation, sacrifice, C.W. (M.E. *oblacioun*).

occāsyon, *m.*, occasion, C.W. 2332—4 (M.E.).

occūpȳa, *vb.*, occupy, C.W. 256 (M.E.).

***ōdhüs**, *adj.*, jealous (B) : see **ōth**.

ōdor, *m.*, odour, R.D. 144 (M.E.).

oel, see **oyl**.

of, see **ow**.

oferen, *f.*, *pl.* **-now**, service, mass : *o.-brys*, high mass (B.) : *o.-vyttyn*, low mass (B.).

oferenny, *vb.*, to celebrate mass (W., B.).

†**ofer-gūgol**, *m.*, chasuble, C. Voc., *maessehacele* Aelfric ; see **cūgol**.

oferyades, *f.*, *pl.* **-ow**, priestess (W.).

†**oferyas** (C. Voc. *oferiat*), *m.*, *pl.* **-ysy**, priest, *maessepreost* Aelfric.

offendya, *vb.*, to resist, kick or strive against, offend (M.E.).

offens, *m.*, resistance, opposition, offence, O.M. 1350 (M.E.).

offryn, *m.*, *pl.* **-now**, offering.

offrynna, **-nya**, *vb.*, to offer up, sacrifice.

***offys**, *m.*, *pl.* **-ys**, office (E.).

***o'ffyser**, *m.*, *pl.* **-s**, officer (E.).

ogas (Lh. *ogaz*), *adj.*, near, close ; *adv.*, nearly, almost ; *m.*, near position, vicinity: used before noun. and adj. ; see **nēs**, **nessa** ; *o. dy*, later *ogasty*, *ogatty*, near to it, nearly so, almost ; *yn ow o.*, near me ; *o. dhym*, close to me ; *omma yn o.*, close at hand ; *o. ha bledhen*, nearly a year ; *o. dall*, almost blind ; see **a-ogas**.

***oges**, *f.*, *pl.* **-ow**, harrow : replaced by **clōs**, **harrow** (W., B.).

***ogesy**, *vb.*, to harrow : replaced by **closya**.

ōgh (Lh. *ōh*), *interj.*, of grief or dismay, oh ! ah ! alas !, Ord. (D. "awgh").

ōghen, see **ojyon**.

ōgo, *f.*, *pl.* **ogevyow**, cave (D. "ogo") : see **fōgo**.

ojyon (C. Voc. *odion*, Lh. *udzheon*, Bilbao MS. *odgan*), *m.*, *pl.* **ōghen** (*ohan* P.), ox.

***ōker**, *m.*, usury (M.E.).

***ō'kerer**, *m.*, *pl.* **-s**, moneylender (M.E.).

ōl (*ooll* C.W.), *m.*, *pl.* **-ow**, trace, mark, print, impression, track ; (figuratively) indication, sign, token : **o. ros*, cart-rut ; *olow* (*oleow*), printer's type, Keigwin ; *a skyans* (*dhader*), *prest* (*byth*) *nyns-us o. ty dhe dhysky*, of sense (profit), there is never a sign that thou hast learnt, B.M. 266, 380.

ōla (*wōla* M.C.), *vb.*, to weep, cry, lament, bewail : *ty a-n-ol*, thou wilt repent it.

olas (C. Voc. *oilet*), *f.*, *pl.* **-ow**, hearth, fireplace, cooking-place ; (with extended meaning) home: *hyrstyngc* Aelfric (frying) is a more correct translation of *frixorium*.

olcan, *m.*, metal, tin (W. *alcan*) ; Wheal Olcan or Olgan, Sancreed, Gw. MS.

†**o'leker** (C. Voc. *wilecur*, O.E. *(leas) olecere*, Aelfric), *m.*, *pl.* **-s**, parasite, flatterer.

†**olew** (C. Voc. *oleu*), *m.*, olive-oil, *ele* Aelfric : *grunen-olew*, olive(berry).

†**olewbren** (C. Voc. *oleubren*), *m.*, *pl.* **-nyer**, olive-tree, *elebeam* Aelfric.

***olew-wedhen**, *f.*, *col.* **-wyth**, olive-tree (W., B.).

olewy, *vb.*, to anele, anoint with holy oil (B.) : see **ungya**, **untya**.

oll (*ol*, Late *ul*), *adj.* ; *adv.*, all, (the) whole, every ; wholly, entirely, (with *byth*) at all : prefixed only to *gallos* ; *pup-o.*, all, everyone ; *noth-o.*, quite bare ; *an bys-o.*, the whole world ; *o. an bys*, all the world ; *pup tra-o.*, *o. puptra*, everything ; *o. myns trespas a-wrug-e*, the whole offence that he has committed, P.C. 1814 ; *yn o. Kernow*, in the whole of Cornwall ; *o. why a-ra*, you shall all ; *travyth-o.*, *tra-vytholl*, nothing at all ; as "all" always precedes preps., *cres o. dheugh-why*, peace unto you all ; *o. y'n pow*, in all the country ; *o. dhe'm gallos*, to the extent of my ability.

ollgallos, *m.*, omnipotence (B).

ollgallosek (late *-jek*), *adj.*, almighty, omnipotent : see **kevōthak**.

ollgallosekter, *m.*, omnipotence, almightiness : Keigwin's *olgalluster* must be for *ollgallosetter*, cf. **muscotter**.

ōlva, *f.*, lamentation, weeping, wailing, M.C. 4.

olyf, *m. and col.*, olive: *Meneth O.*, Mount of Olives ; *Meneth Olyved*, Mt. Olivet ; see **olew**.

olyfans (C. Voc. *oliphans*), *m.*, *pl.* **-as**, elephant, *ylp* Aelfric : *dans o.*, ivory, Lh.; *nt* (so misprinted Norris) has become *ns* here although *oliphant* is O. Fr.

om-[2], **ym-**[2], (*em-*, Late *ham-*, *hum-*), *reflexive, mutual or reciprocal prefix to vb.* : in MSS. mutation is often ignored ; *y-honen*, etc., is sometimes added ; special meanings are sometimes given to *vbs.* with **om-**, often by stressing the normally unstressed prefix ; for ordinary meanings

see the vbs. without prefix.
om, see **am.**
omach, *m.*, homage: see **omajer.**
o·majer, *m.*, *pl.* **-s**, vassal, retainer, B.M. 3482 (M.E. *omager*).
ombarüsy, *vb.*, to get ready, wait in readiness, be prepared, B.M. 3244.
omblegya, *vb.*, to submit.
o·mbredery, *vb.*, to bethink oneself, recollect, consider, B.M. 2857.
ombrevy, *vb.*, to show one's character, prove oneself, C.W. 920.
o·mdenna (*ombdina* Carew), *vb.*, to withdraw, draw back, revoke, refrain, retract, contract, shrink, M.C., B.M.
omdesy, *vb.*, to bask (W.).
omdewlel (*umdowla* Lh.) *vb.*, to wrestle, throw one another: 3 s. pret. *omdewlys.*
omdhevas, *adj.*, destitute, bereft, orphan, B.M. 1827; *m.*, *pl.* **-ow**, *f.* **-ades**, orphan.
omdhevasy, *vb.*, to orphan, bereave of parents (B.): p. pt. **-vesys.**
omdhevatty, *m.*, *pl.* **-ow**, orphanage (W., B.).
o·mdhon (Late *humthan*), *vb.*, to conceive; **omdhōn**, to demean or conduct oneself, behave: this reverses the distinguishing accents in Welsh *ymddwyn.*
omdhysevel, *vb.*, to trip and fall, overbalance, M.C. 14.
omdhysquedhes, *vb.*, to appear, let oneself be seen: *o. ny-vynna*, he would not show himself, R.D. 1496.
omdow·l, *m.*, *pl.* **-ow**, wrestling, contest, conflict, Keigwin.
omdowlor, *m.*, *pl.* **-yon**, wrestler, Lh.
omdroghya (*hambrokkya*, Lh., for *omdrokkya*), *vb.*, to wash, bathe: see **trokkya.**
omgamma, *vb.*, to distort oneself: *o. myn*, to make a wry mouth, M.C. 196.
o·mgemeres, *vb.*, to undertake: *o. rak*, make oneself responsible for, B.M. 1882.
o·mgersya, *vb.*, to make oneself comfortable, be at ease, B.M. 296.
omgemeryans, *m.*, undertaking.
o·mglewes, *vb.*, to feel (in health): *fatel omgleweugh omma?* how do you feel now? B.M. 709.
omgonfortya, *vb.*, to take courage, be of good cheer, B.M. 3080.
omgows, *m.*, *pl.* **-ow**, conversation.
omgrowsa, *vb.*, to cross oneself (W., B.).
omgüdha (**-gwetha**), *vb.*, to hide, C.W. 1519, see stage-direction, p. 120.
o·mgwen, see **o·mwen.**
omgwetha, *vb.*, to dress, put on clothing, C.W. 858: see **omgüdha**, with which this seems confused, and **quetha.**
omhowla, *vb.*, to bask in the sun (W.).
omhenwel, *vb.*, to style oneself.
o·mlath (*e·mbloth*, *e·mloth*, Late *o·mbla*), *vb.*, to fight, special form of *omladha*, without inf. ending; *m.*, *pl.* **-adhow**, fight.
omlowenhē·, *vb.*, to rejoice: as **berhē.**
omma (Late *umma*, *ubma*, *ubba*), *adv.*, here, at this point, on the spot, now: a late contraction of *doroy omma* is *drubba*, *drabba*; see **-ma.**
omrȳ, *vb.*, to surrender; (with *dhe*) devote oneself, B.M. 326, 2127.
o·msynsy, *vb.*, to feel, hold, think or esteem oneself, O.M. 2222: *my a-omsyns* (*vinsens* MS.) *certan a-ugh pup myns a-ve bythqueth whath formys*, I consider myself above all that were ever yet created, C.W. 280.
omwe·l, *m.*, *pl.* **-yow**, visit (W., B.).
omweler, *m.*, *pl.* **-loryon**, visitor (W., B.).
omweles, *vb.*, to interview, visit: unless instransitive, this requires *an yl y gyla*, etc. (W., B.).
o·mwen, **o·mgwen** (*ymguen*, R.D. 2097), *vb.*, to stir, wriggle, wince, struggle, special form of ***omwenel**, without inf. ending; see **gwenel.**
o·mweres, **o·meres** (*omm eres*), *vb.*, to take care of oneself, manage without help, O.M., B.M.: *ny-m-bus o.*, I am incapacitated, helpless; *omwe·res* is presumably to help one another.
o·mwethhē·, *vb.*, to pine, R.D. 1170.
o·mwheles, **o·mheles**, **o·mmeles**, *vb.*, to upset, overthrow, overset, overturn, fall, tumble down: 3 s. pret. *omwhelys*; 3 s. subj., *mayth ommello*, is miswritten *may ron mayle*, R.D. 388; see **do·mhel.**
omwolghy, **omolghy**, *vb.*, to wash (W., B.).
o·mwül, **-wrüthyl**, *vb.*, to pretend to be, appear, seem, turn oneself into: *ganso omwra ow herth omma gallas dhe goll*, through him it seems that my journey here has been wasted, B.M. 477.
ōn (C. Voc. *oin*, Bilbao MS. *oane*), *m.*, *pls.* **ēn** (*ean*), **ēnas**, lamb: *o. Pask*, Paschal lamb; *maga dof avel o.*, as tame as a lamb; *kepar hag o.*, like a lamb, O.M. 894, B.M. 1121, etc.

on, see **onnen.**

ōna, *vb.*, to lamb, yean (W., B.).

onen, (Late *wonnen*), *m. and f., pron.*, one, single person or thing : follows gender of noun, *fest o. dek*, a very fine one (f.) ; *pup-o.*, everyone ; *ken o.*, another one, someone else, M.C. 145 ; *o y'n bys*, a single one ; **re** is used as pl. ; see **nagonen, nebonen.**

ōnes, *f.*, *pl.* **-ow**, ewe-lamb (W., B.).

onest, *adj.*, proper, suitable, decent, fitting, seemly, R.D. 1946 (M.E.).

o'nester, *m.*, propriety, decency, seemliness, B.M. 487 ; fitting thing, B.M. 3027.

ongel, *m.*, colewort, cabbage, Borlase : *yu canstel da rag gorra agas o. y'n seth?* is a basket good to put your cabbage in the pot? Scawen, proverb.

ōngen, *m.*, lambskin (B.).

only, *adv.*, only, C.W., B.M. (E.).

onnek, *f.*, ash-grove (B.).

onnen, *f.*, *col.* **on**, ash-tree : *my a-s-pe yn-dan o.*, I'll pay them under an ash (with the stick), B.M. 3289 ; see **enwedhen.**

onour, *m.*, *pl.* **-s**, honour (M.E.): see **enor.**

o'noura, *vb.*, to honour : see **enora.**

ōnyk, *m.*, *pl.* **ēnygow**, lambkin (W., B.).

o'nyment, *m.*, *pl.* **-mens**, ointment, unguent, P.C. (M.E.).

***onyonen**, *f.*, *col.* **onyon**, onion (W., B.).

opery, *vb.*, to act, operate, get to work, go about doing a thing, B.M. 2613 : probably a var. of **obery.**

ōpya (*opea*), *vb.*, to throw open, make vacant, C.W. 240 (E.).

opyn, *adj.*, *and adv.*, open,-ly, B.M. (M.E., cf D. "oppm," *o* short).

†ōr (C. Voc. *oir*), *adj.*, excessively cold, frigid.

or, *f.*, *pl.* **-yon** (Lh. *urrian*), border, edge, brink, margin, boundary.

o'ratry, *m.*, *pl.* **-s**, oratory chapel, B.M.

ord, see **orth.**

o'rdena, ordna, or'na, *vb.*, to order, put in order, give orders, appoint, ordain, arrange, regulate, direct, provide (M.E. *ordeyne*) : *or'neugh ragtha pup y bows*, give all their jackets a dusting, B.M. 3311 ; *my a-s-or'nas yn-few tre*, I ordered them (to be sent) home alive, B.M. 1784.

o'rdenal, *m.*, *pl.* **-ys**, order of service ; prompt-copy of miracle-play (M.E. from M. Lat. *ordinale*).

o'rdenans, ordnans, *m.*, ordinance, O.M. 1893 (M.E.).

o'rdenary, *m.*, *pl.* **-s**, miracle-play stage-manager and prompter, Carew ; official directing religious ceremonies (M.E.).

ordna, see **ordena.**

ordyr, *m.*, *pl.* **-drys**, order of knighthood, rank, command, condition, O.M., C.W. (M.E.).

ordys, *pl.*, holy orders, B.M. 521, 529 : *ry o. dhe*, to ordain ; ? for *ordrys*, second *r* lost as in **dorgys, gorgys**, or pl. made direct from Lat. *ordo* ; see ***ürth.**

orēmus, *m.*, prayer, "let us pray," R D. 648 (Lat.).

***orfrays**, *m.*, gold embroidered border on garment (M.E.).

organ, *m.*, *pl.* **-s**, organ, O.M. 1999.

organyth, *m.*, *pl.* **-ydhyon**, organist (W.) : as **†pȳbyth.**

or'na, see **ordena.**

†ōrny, *m*, chilliness (W.) : see **ōr.**

orren, *f.*, *pl.* **-now**, bundle of thatching-reed (D. "orran").

†ors, *m.*, *pl.* **-as**, bear, C. Voc.

orses, *f.*, *pl.* **-ow**, she-bear (B.).

orth, worth, contractions **ort, ord, wor', ot-, wos-**, *prep.*, at, by : with *kewsel, cola, goslowes, ry cusul, dyfen, deryvas, takkya, gleny, bos da*, etc., to ; with *myras, scrynkya*, at, upon; with *serry*, at, with ; with *govyn, gothfos*, of, from ; with *mynnes, gweres, bos gweres, cusul, sawment, yly*, etc., for (*ny-vynnaf orta bos*, I do not wish for them to be) ; with *bewa*, by, on ; with *gwytha, herdhya, settya, gweres, bos gweres, sevel*, against ; with *codha*, on, upon ; replaces particle *ow(th)-* with inserted poss. prons., *ow-tysky*, teaching, *orth-*, or *worth-*, *aga-dysky*, teaching them, *my a-th-wheres orth-y-dhon*, I will help thee to carry him off, O.M. 893 ; combines with prons., see Appendix V. ; the initial *w* is used or omitted indifferently, but is preferable after a vowel and is almost always used when the final *th* is silent, as in many expressions (where *wor'* is invariably spelt *war* in MSS., though causing no mutation), e.g. *wor' deweth, squych, tan, ton, troshes, tu ha*; *prena wor' an saw*, buy by the horse-load ; *ort, ord* are used chiefly before *an* ; *ot-, wos-* are used only as prefixed to *deweth, dalleth*, which become *oteweth, wosteweth* (vars. *wor', ow, tyweth*) and *wostalleth* ; Lhuyd records the late colloquial pronunciation of *yth-esof-vy worth-agas-pysy*, I beg you, as *thera vȳ*

war uz pyzy.
ōrwȳns, *m.*, freezing blast (W.).
ōs, *m.*, *pl.* **-ow,** age, time, period, epoch: as W. *oed*; *hyr o.*, great age; *Osow Cres*, Middle Ages; *a'y o.*, ever (in past, as W. *erioed*); *yn y o.*, etc., ever (in past, present or future), *yn ow o.*, ever, B.M. 1867; *byth ny-s teffa gwell bugel yn aga o.*, never could they have a better pastor at any time, B.M. 2786; see **üs,** f.
ōst, *m.*, *pl.* **-ys,** host. army, O.M., B.M. (M.E.).
ōst, *m.*, *pl.* **-ys,** host, innkeeper, Lh. (M.E.).
ostel, *f.*, *pl.* **-yow,** mansion, hostel, hotel, O.M. 1710 (M.E.).
ostes, *f.*, *pl* **-ow,** hostess, A. Boorde, Lh. (M.E.).
***o'stlery** *m.*, hostelry (M.E.).
ostya, *vb.*, to lodge at an inn, Lh.
ostyas, *m.*, *pl.* **-ysy,** lodger, guest: see **ostya.**
ōswyth, *m.*, *pl.* **-yow,** era, age (B.).
ot, see **otta,**
oteweth, worteweth, wosteweth (*orth, deweth*), *adv.*, at last, in the end: a very late contraction is *'tewa'*, Borlase; with *wos* for *wo(r)th* cf. *bys* for *byth*; the *s* or *th* cause following *d* to become *t*
***ōth,** *m.*, jealousy (B.); zeal, zest (W.).
othom, -ek, see **ethom.**
otta, ot (vars. *atta, at,* C.W. *yta*), *interj.*, lo! behold! see! here (there) is (are): *ot* is a contraction used only before vowels and not compulsory even there, e.g., *ot an* or *otta an,* see the, *ot omma* or *otta omma,* see here, here is; the latter is usually contracted to *otomma,* and *otta vy, vy, va, hy, to ottavy, ottava, ottahy*; *otta* also combines in *ottensa,* see him or it, m., *ottensy,* see her or it, f., with the otherwise unused prons. *ensa, ensy,* answering to the Welsh conjunctive prons. *yntau, hithau*; as pl. *ottensy,* see them, similarly seems to have *ensy,* as W. *hwyntau,* rather than *ynsy,* as W. *hwynthwy*; *ot ena, otta ena,* see there, there is, and *otta ty, ny, why,* are commonly written separately, but *otta y* is not found; forms in C.W. are "tomma" for *otomma,* "ytowns y" or "ytowns" for *ottensy* or *ot ynsy,* "ytama" for *ottavy,* "yta ef" for *ottava* or *ot eef*; *ottava ow-crowedha,* there it lies, lit. see it lying; *otta ny genough,* here we are, lit. see us with you; see **awotta.**
our, see **owr.**
ous (contraction of *awos*) *m.*, cause: *a nep o.*, on any account, R.D. 1368.
oū'tlayer, *m.*, *pl.* **-s,** outlaw, B.M. (M.E.).
over-, *prefix,* over- (E.): *a overbyn,* from overhead, C.W. 2288; *over-sottal,* too subtle, C.W. 615; *overdevy,* to overgrow, C.W. 1507, etc., *o* as in D. "awver," "ovver."
overcummya, *vb.*, to overcome, B.M. 4012 (E.).
ovyth, *m.*, *pl.* **-ydhyon,** ovate, of third degree in Gorsedd (W.): taken from Lat. *vates,* soothsayer.
ow[4]**(th)-,** *pres. participle verbal particle,* -ing: for uses see Appendix VII.
ow[3], *poss. pron.*, my: after prep. or conj. ending in vowel, *'w*; *ow chy ow-honen,* my own house; see **am.**
ow, *interj.*, ho! hullo!: sometimes prefixed to *ot, otta,* as a var. of **awot, awotta.**
öwn (C.W. *owne*), *adj.*, own (E.): *y o. dywla,* his own hands, *dhe'th o. vroder,* to thy own brother, C.W. 1531, 1300.
own, *m.*, fear, dread: *perthy o.*, to dread; *byth na-borth o. a henna,* never be afraid of that; *kemeres o.*, to take fright, be alarmed; *o. a-m-bus, o. dhym yma,* I am afraid; *rag o.* for fear, lest, e.g., *rag o. ty dhe'm ladha,* for fear of thy slaying me.
owna, (*ouna*), *vb.*, to fear, Gw., Lh.: probably from W,; see **own, perthy.**
ownek, *adj.*, afraid, timorous; *m.*, *pl.* **-negyon,** coward.
ownekhē' (p. pt. *ownakes,* P.), *vb.*, to frighten: as **berhē.**
ownter, see **ewnter.**
owr, our (Lh. *ower*), *m.*, *pl.* **-ys,** hour, in reckoning time (M.E.): *a-jy dhe o.*, within an hour, C.W. 2389: *nep try o.*, some three hours, R.D. 2555: see **ür.**
owr, our (C.W. *ower*), *m.*, gold: see **†ewrē.**
owra, *vb.*, to gild: see **gorowra.**
owraval, *m.*, *pl.* **-low,** orange (W.).
owrbysk, *m.*, *pl.* **-buscas,** goldfish (W.).
owrdynk, *m.*, *pl.* **-ncas,** goldfinch: see **tynk,** also **melenek,** Addenda.
owrek, *adj.*, golden, gold-bearing; *f.*, *pl.* **-egy,** gold-mine (B.).
owrlyn (*ourlyn*), *m*, silk, O.M. 1752.
owror, *m.*, *pl.* **-yon,** goldsmith (B.): see **†ewrē.**
owrwernen, *f.*, lime-tree, linden (W.).
owt (*out*), *interj.*, (of dismay or dislike), oh!;

o. warnas ! out upon thee! (M.E.).
owth, see **ow**[4] **(th)**.
oy (C. Voc. *uy*), *m.*, *pl.* **-ow**, egg : *ny-rof o.*, I care not a fig ; *ny·dal o.*, it's not worth a straw ; see **gwyn**, **kennen**, **melen**, **plysken**.
oyeth (*th* for *s* misread *o yech* by Lh.), *interj.*, hear ! o yes ! : *o. sy !* hear here ! (O. Fr. *oyez ci*) ; *o. or !* hear now ! (O. Fr. *oyez or*) ; the following Cornish is always *glewyeugh !* in mutation, see **clewes**.
oyl (*oel*), *m.*, *pl.* **-ys**, oil (M.E.).
oynment, var. of **onyment**, M.C., P.C. (M.E. *oynement*).

P (mutations B, F)

Pa', see **pan**.
pabeth, *m.*, papacy (W.).
padel, *f.*, *pls.* **-llow**, **-lly**, pan, deep dish : ***p.-dorn**, saucepan ; *p.-ynk*, ink-pot, *p.-ynkyn*, cuttle-fish ; changeable person (D. "padelinken") ; *p.-tomma*, warming-pan, Lh. MS ; *p. horn*, iron pan, "baker," C. Voc., *isenpanna* Aelfric ; *p. penglyn*, knee-pan (W.).
padelyk, *m.*, *pl.* **-ygow**, little pan or dish, knee-pan, saucer (W.).
pader, *m.*, *pl.* **pederow**, the Lord's Prayer, pater ; bead, unit of rosary.
padera, *vb.*, to say prayers, patter (W., B.).
paderen, *f.*, *pl.* **-now**, bead, single or small (B.).
pagan, *m.*, *pl.* **-ys**, heathen, pagan, B.M. 2242.
paganÿeth, *f.*, heathendom, paganism (W.).
pahan, see **pan**.
paja, **pajya**, *m.*, *pl.* **-jys**, page, serving-lad (M.E.) : *p.-mergh*, ostler, stable-boy, groom, B.M. 2393 ; see **boya**.
pajer, see **peswar**.
pajya, see **paja**.
pāl, *f.*, *pl.* **-yow**, shovel, O.M., Lh., D. : *p. bren*, wooden shovel (B.) ; *p. forn*, baker's peel (B.) ; *p. ros*, water-board of mill-wheel (B.)
pal, *m.*, *pl.* **-ys**, mantle, pall, P.C. 2128.
palas, *vb.*, to dig, excavate.
***pa·lather**, **palar**, *m.*, *pl.* **pe·lether**, **peler**, beam, plough-tail, shaft : *p.-bregh*, upper-arm bone (W., B.).
†**palf**, *f.*, *pl.* **-vow**, palm of hand, C. Voc., *handbred* Aelfric.
palfray, *m.*, *pl.* **-s**, palfrey, O.M. 1969 (M.E.).
paljy, *m.*, *pl.* **-on**, palsy ; palsied person, B.M. 4483 (M.E. *palasye*).
paljya (*palgea* Kerew), *vb.*, to paralyze.
pallen, *f.*, *pl.*, **-now**, coverlet : *p.-vargh*, horse-cloth ; *p.-wely*, bedspread (B.) ; see **pal**.
palm, *m.*, *pl.* **-ys**, palm branch or tree, P.C., M.C. (M.E.).
palmor, *m.*, *pl.* **-yon**, pilgrim, palmer, R.D. 1477.
palor, *m.*, *pl.* **-yon**, digger, shoveller, excavator : see **pāl**.
†**palores**, *f.*, *pl.* **-ow**, chough ; lit., she-digger, C. Voc. : translated "chough or daw" Lh., "Cornish daw or chough" Pryce ; in Aelfric, *hroc* (rook), but *graculus* is usually "daw" ; see **brān**, **chōca**.
pals (pr. *pōls*), *adj.*, plentiful, numerous, thick, M.C. 165 : used after pl. noun.
palshē·, *vb.*, to abound, multiply (B.) : as **berhē**.
palster, *m.*, plenty (B.).
palvala, *vb.*, to grope, feel one's way (W., B.).
paly, *m.*, velvet, brocade, glossy silk fabric, P.C. 1784 (Med. Lat. *palla*, O. Fr. *palie*): *cath baly*, ermine (W.) ; see **pen-paly**.
palys, *m.*, *pl.* **-ys**, palace, B.M., 4159 (M.E. *paleys*).
pan (late *padn*), *m.*, *pl.* **-now**, cloth, woven fabric : *p.-bows squerdys ny-vyth 'vas*, the torn cloth of a coat will be of no use, P.C. 2848 ; *purpur pannow fyn*, fine purple, B.M. 1966 ; *p.-sagh*, sacking, sackcloth.
pan[2], **pa'**, *adv.*, when (relative), at the time that ; *conj.*, since, seeing that, inasmuch as, (after interj. *owt*, *ellas*, *govy*, etc.) that ever : used directly before vb. except in neg. (when *na*[2]- follows it) or with infixed pron., *pan y-n-*, etc.; *d* is usually excepted from mutation after *pan* ; *pa'* is used before *n* ; as conj., *pan* is mistakenly replaced by *kyn* in C.W., and in Late Cor. anomalous forms like *poth* before vowels in *bos or mos*, *pe* before *gul* and *dos*, e.g., *potheu*, *potho*, *pereeg*, *peteffa*, are used for *pan yu*, *o*, *wruk*, *deffo* ; *kepar ha p. ve*, just as though he were ; see **p'ür**.
pan[2], **pahan**[2], **pana**[2], *pron.*, what, *interj.*, what a ; following *d* or *p* usually resists mutation ; *pana* is somewhat rarely made to cause mutation, perhaps because it

represents *pan yu*.

pandra (*pendra*), *pron.*, *interj.*, what (lit. what thing); loses final *a* before vowels in *bos* (*pandr' yu*, etc.) and forms occasional contractions with *gul*, e.g., *pand'ruk* for *pand(ra a-w)ruk*, *pand 'ra'vy* for *pand(ra a-w)raf-vy*, etc.

panesen, **panen** (Lh. *panan*), *f.*, *col.*, **panes** (Lh. *panez*), parsnip : *panen* may be from D.E. "pane."

pannor, *m.*, *pl.* **-yon**, draper, cloth-dealer : from **pan**.

pans, *m.*, *pl.* **-ow**, hollow, dip, dingle, low ground : Pans Hallow, place-name.

pap, *m.*, *pl.* **pabow**, pope, B.M.

paper (*papar*), *m.*, *pl.* **-yow**, paper, Lh.

par, *prep.*, by (Fr.) : used in M.E. expressions *parhap*, *parde*, etc., and also (?corruptly) in M.C. 1, *par lavarow*.

par, *m.*, *pl. and abst.* **-ow**, equal, mate, match, peer ; sort, kind : *hep par*, *hep parow*, matchless ; *a'n par-ma*, *-na*, like this, that ; *nyns-us denvyth a'y barow*, *nyns-us y bar*, *ny-n-jeves p.*, he is unmatched ; *ny-m bus p.*, *sur*, *ow-pewa*, I surely have no equal alive, C.W. 1439 ; *nag-us hy far a'n barth-ma dhe Bons Tamar*, that there is no equal to her on this side Tamar Bridge, Chart. Endors.

par, *adv.*, as, so: *p. may*[5], so that (with subj.) ; *p. del*[2], since, inasmuch (with indic.).

para (*parah*), *m.*, *pl.* **-rys**, flock, drove, gang, Gw. : as W. *parri*.

para, *vb.*, to prepare, J. Boson : probably an inf. formed from *parys* taken as a p. pt.

***parabolen**, *f.*, *pl.* **-now**, parable (B.).

pa·radys, **pa·radhys** (*paradice* C.W., *paraves* Gw.), *f.*,paradise, O.M.

paragh (pr. *pargh*), *vb.*, to forbear, endure, hold out, last, B.M. 1885, 1475, 2488 : inf. used with *gallos* or *mynnes* ; this seems a var. of *parhē·*, as W. *para* of *parhau·*.

paramour, *adv.*, for love's sake, in kindness: cf. Cor. *del y-m-kyrry* : *Lyghtfoude, cannas*, *p.*, Lightfoot, messenger, of your kindness, P.C. 1632 (M.E.).

parcel, *m.*, number, band, squad, party, B.M. (M.E.).

pa·rchemyn (C. Voc. *parchemin*), *m.*, parchment, vellum (O. Fr.), *bocfel* Aelfric.

parchemynek (Lh. *parshmennek*), *adj.*, made of parchment or vellum.

parchemynen (Lh. *parshmennen*), *f.*, *pl.* **-now**, sheet of parchment.

pardē·, *inter.*, pardie, by God, P.C. 1111 (M.E. *pardee*).

pardona (*parduna* Lh.), *vb.*, to pardon (E.) : *my a-vyn agas p.-why*, I'll forgive you.

parfay·, *interj.*, in faith, P.C. 564 (M.E. *parfey*).

parhap, *adv.*, perhaps, perchance (M.E.).

parhē·, see **paragh**.

park, *m.*, *pl.* **-rcow**, field, close, enclosure: in field-names the *k* alone may survive, e.g., Canodgeon for *p. an ojyon*.

parkya, *vb.*, to enclose ; to put in a field, park (W., B.).

parkyn, *m.*, quillet, little field : this may sometimes explain the *an*, meaningless or not causing correct mutations, after *park* in field-names.

parlet, see **perlet**.

parleth (*-edh*), *m.*, parlour, Lh.

parow, see **par**.

part, *m.*, *pl.* **-ys**, share, part ; *adv.*, in part, B.M., C.W. (M.E.) : *dhy'm p.-vy*, for my part, B.M. 1562.

parth (*perth*, Late *par*), *f.*, *pl.* **-ow**, part, (right or left) hand, side : *th* prevents mutation of following *c*, *k*, *d*, *t*, but *parth* is f. in Cor., though m. in Welsh and Breton, *an*[2] *barth*[2] *wyr*, P.C. 2025; *a bup parth*, all round, on all sides, R.D. 2558 ; *a'n barth dyghow*, on the right ; see **a-barth**.

party, *m.*, party, side, set of opponents, B.M. 3477 (M.E.).

parüssa, see **parys**.

parüsy, *vb.*, to cook, prepare, make ready.

†**parwys** (C. Voc. *poruit*), *m.*, *pl.* **-y**, wall, party wall, *wah* Aelfric.

parya, *vb.*, to pair, couple : as **comparya**.

parys (C. Voc. *parot*), *adj.*, ready, apt, prepared, willing ; cooked, *gesoden*, *gebacen* Aelfric: comp. *parüssa*; *lemmyn gwreugh p.!* make ready now ! *gwra dhymmo p.*, be prepared for me, C.W. 2419, 1992 ; *aga bos a-vyth p.*, their meal will be cooked, P.C. 695 ; *parussa of-vy dhedha-y* (*dedh'y*), I am more ready for them, B.M. 3122.

pās, *m.*, *pl.* **-ys**, pace (M.E. *passe*) : used as lineal measure, probably a thousandth part of a mile, B.M.

pās, *m.*, *pl.* **-ow**, cough, Lh. : *p. garm*, *-tāk*, whooping-cough (W.).

Pask, **Pasch**, **dē-**, **dū- P.**, *m.*, Easter; *de-P*, *vyttyn*, Easter Morning; *an P. byghan*, Low Sunday (W.); ***Pasch*** is a M.E. spelling.

pask, *m.*, feeding, nourishment (W.B.): see **pesky**.

passa, *vb.*, to cough (B.).

passya, *vb.*, to pass, surpass, Gw., Lh. (M.E.): ***abashe***, C.W. 149, for ***a-bas***, that surpasses.

passyon (***pascon, passon, pascyon***, etc.), *m.*, passion (M.E.).

pastel, *f.*, *pl.* **-llow**, morsel, scrap, B.M. 2450 (M.E., O.Fr.): *p-dyr*, quillet, small plot of ground; *p.-vro*, region, district (B.)

pasty, *m.*, *pl.* **-s**, pasty, D. (M.E. ***pastee***).

pat, *m.*, pate (M.E.): *re'm p.*, oath, P.C. 1385.

***patāta**, *m.*, *pl.* **-tys**, potato.

pater, *m.*, the Lord's Prayer, M.C. (Lat.): see **pader**.

patron, *m.*, pattern, example (M.E., D. "pattron").

patrȳargh, *m.*, *pl.* **-ȳergh**, patriarch (W.).

paw, *m.*, *pl.* **-yow**, *d.* **deubaw**, foot, paw; claw of crab, crook of grapnel, fluke of anchor (D.): see **peswar-paw**.

pawa, *vb.*, to paw (B.).

paw-brān, *m.*, buttercup, crowfoot (B.).

pawgam, *adj.*, club-footed (B.)

†**pawgen** (C. Voc. *paugen*), *m.*, *pl.* **-now**, leather sock, low shoe, brogue, ***meon*** Aelfric, pl. of *meo*, shoe.

payment (*pemont*), *m.*, *pl.* **-mens**, payment, M.C., B.M. (M.E.).

payn (*peyn*), *m.*, *pl.* **-ys** (***penys***), pain, torment, anguish, torture, punishment: ***war bayn merwel***, on pain of death (M.E. *payne, peyne*).

payna,-ya (*peyna*), *vb.*, to torture (M.E.).

paynes, *f.*, *pl.* **-ow**, pea-hen, Lh.

payon (C. Voc. *paun*), *m.*, *pl.* **-as**, peacock, O.M. 132, *pawa* Aelfric.

pē, *vb.*, to pay: in only parts found, the root vowel merges with that of the ending, absorbing vowels other than *y*; vowel endings would probably resist this, as *pēa, pēy, pēo,* as would the *s* in *pēsa*, etc.; p. pt. *pȳs*, *pys da*, contented, appeased, satisfied, delighted (M.E. *wel apayd*,); *drok-pys*, displeased, discontented, dissatisfied, distressed (M.E. *yvel apayd*); 3 s. pret. *pēs*, 2 pl. imp. *pēgh*; *hep p.*, unpaid, ***dhe*** *be*, (still) to pay; *pe dhe*, pay out, punish, B.M. 975, 1061.

peb, see **pup**.

peber, *m.*, *pl.* **-oryon**, baker, C. Voc., ***baecestre*** Aelfric.

peberyn, *m.*, *pl.* **-now**, harbour-crab, "baker crab" (D. "peperan").

pebores, *f.*, *pl.* **-ow**, female baker.

pebys, see **pobas**.

pechya, *vb.*, to pierce, stab, pitch (M.E. *picche*): p. pt. may be *pȳghtys* (M.E. *pyghte*); *y a-yrghys...an gu lym ef a bechya*, they bade that he should thrust the sharp spear, M.C. 218.

peder, *card. num.*, four, used with f. nouns: see **peswar**.

pederewa, *vb.*, to say prayers, patter (W.).

pedergwyth, *adv.*, four times.

pederow -pronter (*pedri praunter*), *pl.*, knapweed, lit. priest's beads, from the likeness of its dark, scaly involucres to the beads of a chaplet, P. Mundy MS.: see **pader**.

pedrak, *adj.*, square, angular (D. "pedrack mow").

pedren (? Late *pejern*, whence *patshan* Lh.), *f.*, *pl.* **-now**, *d.* **dywbedren**, haunch, hind-quarter, buttock, crupper, P.C. 2094.

pedrevanas, *vb.*, to creep on all fours, B.M. 4218.

pedreven (*-an*), *f.*, *pl.* **-now**, lizard: *p. an dowr*, newt, evet, salamander, Lh.; *pedrevor* Lh. seems a misprint for this.

pedry, *vb.*, to rot, decay, putrify: 3 s. pres, -fut. *peder*; 2 s. imp. *poder*; 3 s. pret. *podras*; 3 s. subj. *potro*; 3 s. plupf. *potsa*; see **poder**.

pega'ns (*py, gans*), *m.*, wherewithal, livelihood, means, utensils, provisions, B.M., C.W., Lh.: B.M. 4292, ***ha lowr p. dhe*** *vewa*, not *p. lowr*, shows adverbial origin as *py gans* "with which"; preps. once followed *py* regularly, see **prak(g)**.

pēgh (*peg(h)*, Lh. *pēh*), *m.*, *no pl.*, sin: *den-vytholl na- dhowtyens pegh*, let no-one at all dread sin, P.C. 1182; ***gaf*** *dhym ow fegh*, forgive me my sin, O.M. 2726; ***gul*** *p.*, to commit sin.

pēgha (*peha*), *vb.*, to sin.

peghador (*pehadur*), *m.*, *pl.* **-yon**, sinner.

peghadores (*pehadures*), *f.*, *pl.* **-ow**, sinning woman.

peghadow, *m.*, sinning, transgression.

pēghas (*pehas*), *m.*, *pl.* **peghosow** (*-asow*), sin, offence.

peglen, *f.*, *pl.* **-now**, tarpaulin (W.): see

pēk.
pējya, see **pēsya.**
pēk (*peyk* C.W.), *m.*, pitch.
pēl (*pelle*, T. Boson), *f.*, *pl.* **-yow**, globe, sphere, ball, playing-bowl : *p. arghans*, silver-coated ball used in hurling, see **hurlya** ; * *pel-dros*, football.
***pelgens**, *m.*, Christmas-Eve midnight service; dawn (W., B.).
pell, *adj.*, *adv.*, far, distant, long, for a long time : *gwayt p. na-vyth hep dos dhyn*, don't be long in coming to us, mind ! B.M. 3275.
pella, *comp. adj.*, farther, longer ; *adv.*, furthermore, besides : *na*[3] *fella*, (with neg.) any longer.
pellder, *m.*, distance, great way, long time ; *adv.*, afar : *yn p. dyworth*, far away from, C.W. 1361 ; *p. adro y'n bys*, afar about the world, C.W. 1384.
pellen, *f.*, *pl.* **-now**, ball, clew, dumpling, round body, C. Voc., *cliwen* Aelfric : *an belle-'ma*, this ball, N. Boson ; *p. whel*, ball of yarn or thread.
pellenna, *vb.*, to roll into a ball (W.B.).
pellgewsel, *vb.*, to telephone (B.).
pellgows, *m.*, telephony, **-er**, telephone (B.).
peller, *m.*, *pl.* **-oryon**, white-witch, charmer (D.) see **pellhē.**
pellhē·, *vb.*, to send far, drive away, expel, eject, banish, B.M. 2083 : as **berhē**.
pellscryfa, *vb.*, to telegraph (B.).
pellscryven, *f.*, *pl.* **-now**, telegram (B.).
pellweler, *m.*, telescope (W.); see **gweder** (*aspya*).
***pellyst -gour** (C. Voc. *pellistgur*), *m.*, *pl.* **-ow -tüs**, (man's) sheepskin cloak, *pylece* Aelfric; †*p. ken* (C. Voc. *ker*), (woman's) fur cloak or skin garment, *crusene*, *deorfellen roc* Aelfric: pilch, pelisse, in original meaning of Lat. *pellicia.*
pēmont, see **payment.**
pen (Late *pedn*), *m.*, *pl.* **-now**, head, chief, chapter, beginning, end, top : *p. an darras*, lintel, Lh. MS. ; *p. kenter*, head of a nail ; *p. ha tyn*, head and tail, reversed side by side (D.) ; *p. war woles ha goles war-van*, topsy-turvy ; *p. kensa*, beginning, *p. dewetha*, end (for distinction); *p. ha garen*, head and shank, without body (D.) ; *p. goles*, bottom end, base ; see **erbyn.**
pen, *adj.*, *prefix*, head, chief, principal : superl. *an penna.*
penans, *m.*, penance, M.C 10, 60.
pena·rth, penā·r' (*pen, garth*), *f.*, promontory : in place-names Penare, Nare; if *pen arth* this would be m., but W. *penardd, penarth, peniarth* are all made f., as from *garth.*
pen-barfüs, *m.*, *pl.* **-y.** three-bearded rockling, fish (D. " pedn borbas ").
pen-blōgh, *m.*, *pl.* **-now, b.**, shaven pate, tonsured crown, B.M. 3828.
pen-blōth, *m.*, anniversary, birthday (W.).
pen-brās, *m.*, *pl.* **-now -b.**, thickhead, fool, C.W. 1340: *p., a-vynnough-why bos cregys ?* Do you want to be hanged, fathead ? R. Brome, *Northern Lass*, 1632 ; *Hycca P.*, Dick the Jolthead, nickname, Tonkin.
pen-bronnen, *pl.* **-now-bron**, *m.*, " rush-head," fool, R.D. 2096.
pen-cales, *m.*, *pl.* **-now -c.**, stubborn person ; *adj.* hard-headed, obstinate (W., B.).
†pencangour (C. Voc. *pencanguer*), *m.*, centurion, chief of a hundred-court, *hundredes ealdar* Aelfric : see **cans.**
Penca·st, *m.*, Whitsuntide, Pentecost, Lh. : Saundry Pencaste, name at St. Ives, 1605.
pen-cōk, *m.*, *pl.* **-now-c.**, empty head, or cuckoo-pate, gawk-head, one not worth listening to.
pen-cough, *m.*, *pl.* **-now-c.**, broken, lit. red, pate, P.C. 2326.
pen-crēghy, *m.*, *pl.* **-now-c.**, scabby-head, B.M. 2418, C.W. 2326 : see **cragh.**
penclün, *f.*, *pl.* **-yow**, *d.* **pen dywglün**, hip, haunch, C. Voc.
†penclyn, see **clÿn.**
pen-dall, *m.*, blindman's buff (B.).
pendeulyn, see **glyn.**
pendra, pender (*pen, tre*), *f.*, village, hamlet : place-names, Penderleath, etc.
pendra, see **pandra.**
pendrō, *f.*, giddiness, vertigo (W.).
pendroppya (Lh. *pendruppia*), *vb.*, to nod, droop : see **droppya.**
pen-dū, *m.*, *pl.* **-now-d.**, boil, " black-head " ; tadpole, Lh.
pendūen (*pendiwen* Lh.), *f.*, *col.* **pendū**, bullrush.
peneglos, *f.*, *pl.* **-lysyow**, cathedral (B.).
penelyn, *m.*, *d.* **deubenelyn**, point of the elbow.
penfenten, *m.*, *pl.* **-tynyow**, headspring, source : place-names Bolventor, Penventinnie, etc.
***penfester**, *m.*, *pl.* **-trow**, halter, head-stall

(W., M.B.).
penfol, *adj.*, silly, dizzy (W., B.).
pengam, *adj.*, wrong-headed, wrynecked (W., B.); *m.*, wryneck, bird (B.).
pengarn, *m.*, *pl.* **-as**, gurnard, C.W. 410 : *p. glas*, grey gurnard, Lh. MS.
pengasen, *f.*, paunch-end, B.M. 3927.
Pen-glās, *m.*, horse-skull carried on pole as hobby-horse (D. "penglaze"); scabious flower (W., B.).
penglow, *m.*, *pl.* **-as**, titmouse (W., B.).
penglyn, see **glyn**.
†**pengūgh(-gwrēk)**, *m.*, (woman's) hooded cloak of fur, C. Voc., *crusene, deorfellen roc* Aelfric, see **pellyst** (*ken*).
pen-gwyn (late *pedn gwidn*), *adj.*, white-headed, Gw.
pen-ha-mȳn, *m.*, a game played with pins, "head-and-tip" (D. "pednamean").
penhens, *m.*, way's end, terminus (B.).
pen-lōs, *adj.*, grey-headed (W.).
pen-medhow, *m.*, *pl.* **-now-m.**, drunkard (W., B.).
pen-mōl, *adj.*, bald-headed (W., B.).
pennek, *adj.*, big-headed (B.): personal name Penneck.
pennōth, *adj.*, bare-headed : *ef a-dryk p. yn-hans*, he will stand aloof, cap in hand, B.M. 440.
penōlva, *f.*, fishermen's look-out point : Pednolver, place-names : see **gōlva**.
pen-paly, *m.*, *pl.* **-as**, blue tit (D. "pednpaly") : see **paly**.
penplas, *m.*, headquarters, chief seat, B.M. 2268.
penpral, *m.*, skull of animal, Lh. : perhaps connected with **pral**, clog : see **spral**.
pen-puso·rn, *m.*, "chief burden" in plain-song, R.D. 2353.
pen-pylys (*pedn pylles*), *m.*, plucked-head, scurvy fellow, C.W. 2318.
pen-pyst, *m.*, fool, O.M., B.M. : cf. E.D. Dic. "pist fool."
pen-rewler, *m.*, *pl.* **-oryon**, president, chief ruler.
penrȳ·n, *m.*, *pl.* **-yow**, promontory, headland : as place-name pr. Pe'ryn, Preen, with *n* lost.
pensagh, *m.*, mumps, goitre (W., B.).
***pensak**, *col.*, hops, the hop-plant (W.).
penscaf, *adj.*, giddy, dizzy, heedless (W., B.).
penscryfa, *m.*, superscription.
pensevyges, *f.*, *pl.* **-ow**, noblewoman (W.).
pensevygeth, *f.*, principality (W.).
pensevygyans (*pednzhivikianz*, Lh.), *m.*, nobility : ? invented.
pensevyk (C. Voc. *pendeuig*), *m.*, *pl.* **-ygyon** (*pednzivigian* Lh.), prince, nobleman, B.M., C.W., *ealdorman* Aelfric : *p. an wlas*, King.
penseythen, *m.*, week's end, end of a week, R.D. 30, B.M. 595 : used only in *ken(s) p.*, before a week is up, out, over ; see **seythen**.
pensōgh, stupid, slow-witted (B.).
pensyon (*pencon*), *m.*, pension, fund, M.C. 38.
pentan, *m.*, back-log, firebrand (W., B.).
pentern, *m.*, *pl.* **-ow**, chief ruler (W.) : see **tern**.
penty, *m.*, farm-house, cottage (W., B.).
***pēntya**, *vb.*, to paint (M.E. *peynte*).
†**pen-tylū** (C. Voc. *penteilu*), *m.*, head of family, paterfamilias, householder, *hyredes hlaford* Aelfric.
pentȳ·r, *m.*, *pl.* **-yow**, headland : place-name Pentire.
penvagas (Late *pednvagas*), *adj.*, bush-headed, shock-headed, tufted; *m.*, three-bearded rockling (D. "pettyfox"); sea-anemone (D. "piddifogger"), see **bagas**.
penvledhen, *m.*, year's-end, end of a year, R.D. 72 : used as **penseythen**, see **bledhen**.
penvyghterneth, *m.*, dominion, chief sovereignty, R.D. 991.
penvȳs, *m.*, month's-end, end of a month, P.C. 1646 : used as **penseythen**; see **mȳs**.
penwely, *m.*, bolster (B.) : see **gwely**.
pen-wlas, *f.*, chief country, used of heaven, R.D. 2530.
penwyth, *m.*, extreme point, very end : place-name, Pe·nwith, cf. **fynweth**.
pen-yar, *m.*, the "neck," last-cut bunch of corn, used in harvest-ceremony, lit. "hen's head" (D. "pedna-yar").
penyn, *m.*, *pl.* **-now**, little end left over (D. "pednans"); head of buddle (*pednan*, Pryce); tadpole : Pol Penenna, *pol penynnow*, tadpole pond, place-name.
penys (*pynys*), *m.*, penance, fasting; *vb.*, to do penance, fast : see **hȳrbenys**.
pen-ȳs, *m.*, *pl.* **pennow-ȳs**, ear of corn, P.
penytty, *m.*, hermitage, place of penitence, anchorite's cell (B.).
pep, see **pup**.
pēr, *m.*, *pl.* **-row**, cauldron, crock, boiler. C. Voc., *hwyr* Aelfric : *towl perrow*, "Lent-crocking" ceremony, lit. crock-

throwing (D. "colperra").

pēr, see **peren**, and **peravy**, Appendix I.

†**pērbren**, *m.*, *pl.* **-nyer**, pear-tree, C. Voc., *pirige* Aelfric.

peren, *f.*, *pl.* **-now**, *col.* **pēr**, pear (W.,B.).

perfyt, *adj.*, perfect (satirically), C.W. 2353 (M.E. *parfyt*).

perfyth (*pyr-*), *adj.*, perfect, complete, entire; (adverbially) completely, etc.

per(gh)en (*perhen, peren*, Gw. MS.), *m.*, *pls.* **-nas**, **-now**, owner, landowner, master, one who is responsible for another: *foul y berghen*, lit. "a fool his master", i.e., worthless vagrant, whom none but a fool would claim, P.C. 2112, 2752.

per(gh)enegy, *vb.*, to appropriate, lay claim to (W.).

per(gh)enek (*perhennek*), *m.*, *pl.* **-ogyon**, possessor, proprietor, owner, B.M. 16.

per(gh)enna, *vb.*, to possess, own (B.).

per(gh)enogeth, **per(gh)enȳeth**, *m.*, proprietorship, possession, ownership (W., B.).

per(gh)yryn, **prȳeryn** (C. Voc. *pirgirin*), *m.*, *pl.* **-as**, pilgrim, foreigner, stranger, R.D. 1261, *aeltheodig* Aelfric.

per(gh)yrynsys, *f.*, pilgrimage (W., B.).

***perl**, *m.*, *pl.* **-ys**, pearl (E.).

pērlan, *f.*, *pl.* **-now**, pear-orchard (W.).

perlet (for *prelat*), *m.*, *pl.* **-ys**, prelate, B.M. 515 (M.E.): *parlet* Norris, but in MS. same contraction is used for *par* and *per*.

perna, see **prena**.

***pers**, *adj. and m.*, light (Persian) blue (M.E.).

†**pēr-sēth** (C. Voc. *perseit*), *m.*, two-handled pot or crock, *sester* Aelfric: see **pēr**, m., **sēth**, m.

person, *m.*, *pl.* **-s**, person: *try Ferson an Drynsys*, the three Persons of the Trinity; *un Dew os ha Persons try*, one God art thou and three Persons, O.M. 110 (M.E.).

perth, *f.*, *pl.* **-y**, bush: no mutation in following *c, k, d, p, t*.

perthejes (*pertheges*), *vb.*, ? to break loose or become violent, P.C. 1009, R.D. 598.

perthy (Late *perry*), *vb.*, to bear, carry, endure, tolerate, brook, undergo, sustain, persist, hold out, withstand: used as "have" with *avy, awher, cof* (late co'), *danjer, dowt, meth, own*; 3 s. pres. -fut. *perth*; 2 s. imp. *porth*: 3 s. pret. *porthas*; *p. orth*, hold out against, put up with, B.M. 2635.

perthyans, *m.*, endurance, toleration, patience, Keigwin, King Charles' Letter.

***perthyn**, *vb.*, to belong (W.).

pervers (*purvers*), *m.*, overthrow, turning upside-down, reverse, turn of events (M.E., Lat. *perversum*).

perveth, *m.*, interior, middle: occurs only in **a-berveth**.

peryl (*perel*, C.W. *perill*), *m.*, *pl.* **-yow**, danger, risk, peril: *rak p.*, in spite of, B.M. 924; *yn ow feryl-vy*, at my own risk, O.M. 197.

peryllya, *vb.*, to incur risk, run into danger, be endangered, B.M. 615.

pēs (*peys, pays*), *interj.*, peace! the conventional call for silence of miracle-players, B.M., C.W. (M.E. *pays*, O. Fr. *pais*).

pēs, see **pē**.

pes, *adv.*, how many: followed by sing. noun, *p. myldyr*, how many miles? A. Boorde; see **pesquyth**.

pesak, *adj.*, rotten, decayed; *m.*, *pl.* **-ogyon**, rotten thing (D. "pezzack").

pesky, *vb.*, to feed, graze, fatten: 3 s. pres. -fut. *pesk*; 2 s. imp. *pask*; subj. *pasco*; pret. *pascas*; *k* is lost before *s*; Park Pisky, field-name.

pesquyth (*pes, gwyth*), *adv.*, as many times, as often (as), whenever: followed by *may(th)*; *p. may's-gwelaf-vy hy remembra ahananough-why my a-wra*, whenever I see it I will remember you, C.W. 2502 (restored); *why a-m-cofha-vy ...pesquyth may feva evys*, you shall remember me...whenever it is drunk, P.C. 828 (MS. *pysough*).

peswar (Late *pajer*), *card num.*, four: used with m. nouns; see **peder**, f.

peswardhek, *card num.*, fourteen.

peswardhegves, *ord. num.*, fourteenth.

peswar-paw (Late and D. *pajerpow*), *m.*, *pl.* **-as**, newt; lizard; ranatra (water insect); lit. "four-feet."

peswera (*peswore* M.C. 247, Late *peswarra*, corruptly *peswartha*), *ord. num.*, fourth.

pesy, see **pysy**,

pēsya, **-jya** (*pyjya* C.W.), *vb.*, to last, abide, continue, keep on; tolerate, stand, endure: 3 s. pres.-fut. *pȳs*; *yn joy a-bys*, in lasting joy, B.M. 4348; *hy a-bejyas*, it lasted, M.C. 201; *ny-bejyaf*, I won't endure, C.W. 1364, 1509, 1670.

pethyk, *m.*, smart blow (D. "pethick").

***petygrew**, *m.*, *pl.* **-s**, pedigree (M.E.).

petysyon (*petyconn*), *m.*, petition, B.M. 4300 (M.E.).

pew, pewy (*pewi* Borlase), *def. vb.*, to own, possess, win, be entitled to, have a right to: *ty a-bew ow gras nefra*, thou shalt ever have my favour, O.M. 974; see parts in APPENDIX VIII.

pewas (M.C. 117 *peuas*, Late *powas*, Hutchens Memorial, Paul, *poes*), *m*, reward, recompense, award.

peyn,-a, see **payn,-a.**

pla, *m.*, *pl.* **-ow**, plague, pest, devil: *aberth an p.*, in the devil's name; *map an p.*, devil's spawn; *jag an p.*, the deuce of a jolt, the devil's own jog, P.C. 2817.

plāg, *m.*, *pl.* **-ys**, plague, C.W. (E.).

plāgya, *vb.*, to plague, C.W. (E.).

planet (*-at*), *m.*, *pl.* **-tys**, planet, C.W. (E.).

plank, *m.*, *pl.* **-ys** (*-cos, -es*), plank (E.): as used, *plankys* seems only another pl. of **plynken**, q.v., and *plank* is not found, but carpenters may well have used *plank,-ys*, as "plank," *plynken,-now*, as "board"; in Breton *plenk* is col., *plankenn* sing., and *plankennou*, pl.

plans, *m.*, *pl.* **-ow**, plant (B.).

plansa, *vb.*, to plant: p. pt. *plynsys*, O.M.

plas, *m.*, *pl.* **-yow**, plate, place at table (D., W., B.).

plās (*plāth*), *m.*, *pl.* **-ow**, mansion; place: *y'n p.*, on the spot, P.C. 2303.

***plaster**, *m.*, plaster (W., B.).

***plastra**, *vb.*, to plaster (W., B.).

plāt, *m.*, *pl.* **-yow**, plate; plate armour (M.E.): see **brēstplāt, manek.**

plat, *adj.*, flat, splayed (M.E.); *tros-plat*, splay-footed, Lh. (E.D. "plat-footed"); see **plattya.**

plāth, var. of **plās.**

plattya, *vb.*, to crouch, squat, C.W. 1547 (M.E. *platte*); to flatten out, (of hair) make smooth (D. "platty"): see **plat**, adj.

playn, *adj.*, full, complete, C.W. 1893 (M.E. *pleyn*).

playn, *m.*, *pl.* **-ys**, carpenter's plane (M.E.).

playnya, *vb.*, to plane, O.M., C.W. (M.E.).

plē[5] **(th)** (contraction of *py lē y*[5] *(th)-*), *adv.*, where, whither: used directly before vb., unless with infixed pron.; adds the *th* of *y(th)-* before vowels in *bos* and *mos*; *ple yma* becomes *plema*; see **a-blē, pyla.**

***plēdya**, *vb.*, to plead, advocate (E.).

***plēdyer**, *m.*, *pl.* **-yoryon**, advocate (E.).

plegadow, *m.*, inclination, bent, leaning, disposition, acceptance, compliance; *adj.*, inclined, disposed, agreeable, acceptable, compliant, conformable.

plegya (*plekgya*), *vb.*, to bend, fold, furl, stoop, blow, incline, tend, yield, comply: 3 s. pres.-fut. *plēk*; 3 s. subj. *plecco*; *dhym gwruk p.*, he caused me to give way, R.D. 1849; *p. y'n dor*, to bow down.

plegyans, *m.*, inclination, tendency, bent.

plēk, *m.*, *pl.* **-egow**, bend, fold, used also as suffix to numerals or adjs. of number, *seythplek*, sevenfold, *tryflek*, threefold, *deublek*, twofold, *lyesplek*, manifold, etc.: *p. hens*, corner, bend in road (W., B.); *p. mor*, creek, bay (B.).

plēkya, *vb.*, to please: requires *dhe*; *ty a blek dhe'n arlydhy*, thou wilt please the lords; *ny-blek dhym an re-na*, I don't like those.

plemmyk, *m.*, *pl.* **-ygow**, plummet, dim. of **plom**: *leverel dhe blemmyk*, tell bluntly, flatly, say out plump, B.M. 3314.

plēn, *m.*, *pl.* **-ys**, plain, arena, open area of playing-place, O.M., B.M., (M.E. *pleyn*, *p. place*): *p. an gwary*, playing-place, circular open-air theatre, Plain an Gwarry, place-name.

plenta (*plente*, C.W. *plenty*), *m.*, plenty (M.E. *plente*).

plēnta, *m.*, *pl.* **-tys**, plaint (M.E. *pleinte*).

plēntya, *vb.*, to act as plaintiff, set forth an accusation, M.C. 33 (M.E. *pleinten*).

plēsour, *m.*, *pl.* **-ys**, pleasure, B.M., C.W. (M.E.).

plēsya, *vb.*, to please (M.E. *plesen*): does not require *dhe* as *plēkya* does; *my a-gas-pys, mara peugh-why plesyes*, I ask of you, if you please, B.M. 194; *yma genef dhe'th p.*, I have what thou wilt like, C.W. 728.

plēth, *f.*, *pl.* **-ow**, *d.* **dywblēth**, plait of hair, R.D. 854; ridge of corn-mow (D. "plaith"): *an losowen vyghan ha gensy gar nedhys, es ow-tevy yn agan hallow-ny, es cryes pleth-Marya*, the little plant with a twisted stem, that grows on our moors, which is called Lady's-tresses, Lh.

plēth, see **plē(th).**

plethen, *f.*, *pl.* **-now**, fine plait, braid (D. "plethan").

plethenna, plēthy, -a, *vbs.*, to plait, braid, wattle (D. "plethan up").

plom (*plobm* Lh), *m.*, lead: *p. ruth*, red-lead, Lh.; see **plemmyk.**
plontya, *vb.*, to disseminate, spread abroad, plant, propagate: *p. whethlow*, to spread lying reports, R.D. 1355 (M.E. *plaunten*).
plontyans, *m.*, propaganda.
plos, *adj.*, dirty, filthy, foul, wretched, worthless; *m.*, *pl.* **-syon** (*plussyon*), foul, worthless person or thing: *dhe blossyon avellough-why*, to common folk like you, R.D. 1497.
plosegy, *vb.*, to get dirty: as **mousegy.**
plosek, *m.*, *pl.* **-sygyon**, filthy or worthless fellow.
plosethes, *m.*, foulness, filth, rubbish, B.M. 3527.
ploswas, *m.*, *pl.* **-wesyon**, dirty fellow: see **gwas.**
plottya, *vb.*, to plot, Gw. (E.).
plū (*plew*, C. Voc. *plui*), *f.*, *pl.* **-yow**, parish.
plūak, *m.*, *pl.* **-ogyon**, parishioner (W.).
plüf, see **plüven.**
†**plumbren**, *m.*, *pl.* **-nyer**, plum-tree, C. Voc., *plumtreow*, Aelfric.
plumen, *f.*, *pl.* **-now**, plum: *men p.*, plum-stone; *gwedhen-p.*, plum-tree, Lh.
plumsugan, *m.*, **plumsugesen** (written *planozhiagezan*, Lh. MS.), *f.*, *pl.* **plumsugas**, three-bearded rockling, fish (D. "plumzuggan").
***plüstren**, *f.*, *pl.* **-now**, mole on skin (B.).
†**plüvak** (C. Voc. *plufoc*), *f.*, *pl.* **-vogow**, feather-pillow; *adj.*, feathered (W., B.).
plüven, *f.*, *pl.* **-now**, *col.* **plüf**, feather, quill-pen, C. Voc., Lh.: *p. ergh*, snow-flake (B.); *p. munys*, **manbluf* (W.), down, fluff; *scryfa p.*, penmanship, B.M. 71; *gwely-pluf*, feather-bed.
plüvya, *vb.*, to plume, fledge, grow feathers (W.B.).
plüvyn, *m.*, *pl.* **-now**, little or undeveloped feather (D. "pleven").
plȳght (*plygth*), *m.* pledge, promise, R.D. 620 (M.E. *plighte*).
plȳghtya, *vb.*, to pledge.
plynch, *m.*, *pl.* **-ys**, start, blink, blench, wince, shrinking (M.E. *blench*): *wor' un p.*, with a sudden start, P.C. 1004.
plynchya, *vb.*, to blench, flinch, blink, wink, wince, squirm, move suddenly to avoid injury, M.C. 130 (M.E. *blenche*).
plynken (*plyenkyn*, Lh. *plankan*), *f.*, *pl.* **-now**, piece of squared timber, board: pl. is used of shingles apparently O.M. 2475, though sing. refers to heavy timber P.C. 2517; see **plank.**
plynsys, see **plansa.**
plysca, *vb.*, to shell, husk (W., B.).
plysken, *f.*, *pl.* **-now**, *col.* **plysk**, husk, shell of egg or nut, Lh. (D. "pliscan").
plȳt (*pleyt*), *m.*, plight, predicament, condition (M.E. *plyt*): *pan p. ymava*, (in) what state he is, RD. 2053—8.
plyth, *adj.*, flexible, limber, pliant: see **heblyth.**
pō, **bō**, var. **pȳ** (C. Voc. *pi*), *conj.*, or, either, whether: *po .. po...*, either... or (else)...; *po Dew dyfen!* interj., God forbid it should be otherwise! (as M.E. *elles God forbede*), C.W. 685; *py* is usually restricted to "or"; see **bō, bokēn, bonȳl, pykēn, pynȳl.**
pob, var. of **pup.**
pobas, *vb.*, to bake; 3 s. pres. -fut. *pep*; p. pt. *pebys*: *b* becomes *pp* in 2 and 3 s. subj. and *p* before *s*; *men-p.*, bakestone, girdlestone; *horn-p.*, iron griddle, "baking-ire"; see **peber.**
pobel (C. Voc. *pobel*, *popel*), *f.*, *pl.* **-blow**, folk, people: treated as f. sing. after *an*², *un*². and as affecting adjs., but is replaced by pl. pron. and followed by pl. vb. except in impersonal conjugation; †*p. tyogow*, rustics, C. Voc., *ceorlfolc* Aelfric; *mollothow mur a bobel*, the curses of many people, B.M. 1579.
pobla, *vb.*, to populate: p. pt. *peblys* (W., B.).
pocar, late metathesis of **kepar.**
poder, *adj.*, rotten, decayed, corrupt, worthless, Lh.; *m.*, mundic, worthless stuff (D.): see **pedry.**
podras, etc., see **pedry.**
podrek, *adj.*, corrupted, decayed, full of sores; *m.*, *pl.* **-ogyon**, corrupt or depraved person, sorcerer, N. Boson: *my ny-welys namenough moy p. a'y ysyly*, I have rarely myself seen one more unsound in his limbs, B.M. 3048.
podrethek, *adj.*, corrupt, rotten, putrid, gangrenous, purulent, covered with sores, B.M. 541, 3061.
podrethes, *m.*, corruption, putridity, rotten part, sore, bruised condition, O.M. 2714.
podryn (*podren*), *m.*, worthless fellow, "rotter", B.M. 2290, 3323.
podyk, *m.*, *pl.* **-ygow**, jug, lit. small pot (D. "paddick").

†pog(k) (C. Voc. ***impog*** for ***un pog***), ***m.***, kiss: in C. Voc. ***en***, the, and ***ym*** for ***un***, one, a, are similarly prefixed to other words, cf. W. *poc*, B. *pok*; this seems replaced in M. Cor. by **am, bay.**

pojer, ***m.***, small round earthen dish (D. "podger").

pok, ***m.***, *pl.* **-kyow**, push, shove, poke (D. "pock").

pokēn, see **pykēn.**

poket (***pokkat*** Lh.), ***m.***, *pl.* **-tys**, pocket, Lh. (E.).

pokkya, (Lh., ***pokkia***), ***vb.***, to push, poke, thrust (D. "pock").

†pokkȳl (C. Voc. *poccuil*), ***m.***, kiss: replaced by **bay.**

pokkys, ***pl.***, pox; ***sing.*** **pocca**, ***m.***, pock-mark: ***p. Frynk***, French disease; ***p. munys***, small-pox, Lh.

pol, ***m.***, *pl.* **-low**, pool, pond; mud, mire, anchorage; pit, *pyt* Aelfric: *p. bogh*, dimple (B.); *p. lagas*, eye-socket (B.); *p. pur*, clear pool; *p. strong*, dirty pool; in place-names Pol- is sometimes a corruption of Pen- or Pons-.

pol, ***m.***, poll, head (E.): used only in *(yn)kettep p.*, every person, possibly for *kettep oll.*

CROAK **pol-cronogow**, ***m.***, toad-pool: place-name, Pol Kernoggoe.

pol-down, ***m.***, abyss, deep pit, Lh.

pol-glow, ***m.***, coal-mine.

pol-gōth, ***m.***, goose-pond: Polgooth, place-name.

pol-growyn, ***m.***, gravel-pit.

pol-grün, ***m.***, dammed-up pond: Polgrean, place-name.

pol-holan, ***m.***, salt-pan, salt-pond (B.).

pol-hȳjy, **-heyjy**, ***m.***, duck-pond: Polhijy, place-name.

pol-hyly, ***m.***, brine-pit (W.),

pol-kyl, ***m.***, occiput, nape: *codha war bol hy hyl, y gyl*, etc., to fall right backwards; cf. **kylben.**

†poll, ***m.***, reason (W., B.); replaced by **skȳans**, etc., see **†gorbollak.**

†polla, ***vb.***, to think, consider (W., B.): see **campolla.**

pollat (***polat, pullat***), ***m.***, ***pl.*** **-ys**, fellow, lad, C.W. (Anglo-Fr. *poulot*, boy, youth, lit. chick, cf. "pullet," "pult," E.D. Dic.): *drok-p.*, rascal; *p. bras*, fine fellow, smart lad.

pollen (Lh. ***pollan***, D. "pullan"), ***f.***, *pl.* **-now**, little pool, sea-pool, puddle: *p. -troyllya*, whirlpool (W. *llyn tro* Lh.).

pol-lon, plon (*pludn*, Borlase), ***m.***, cattle-pond.

pol-margh, -mērgh, ***m.***, horse-pond: place-name Polmarth.

pol-penynnow, ***m.***, tadpole-pond: Pol Penenna, place-name.

pol-prȳ, ***m.***, clay-pit: Pol Pry, place-name.

pol-rōs, ***m.***, wheel-pit of water-mill (D. "pulrose").

pols, polj., ***m.***, moment, instant, short while or space, lit. push, pulse, heart-beat: *p. da, polta* (Lh. *pulta*), a good while or deal; *p. byghan*, a little time or way, as B. *poulzig* (O. Fr. *pouls*).

pol-stēn, ***m.***, tin-pit, mine, Lh.

polta, see **pols.**

polter**, ***m., powder, dust (W., B.).

pol-trō, ***m.***, whirlpool (W., B.): see **pollen.**

poltrygas, ***m.***, ? ***pl.***, **-gosow**, gaiters (buskins), spatterdashes, Borlase: probably lit. "stop mud", see **pol, trygas**, but cf. Fr. *triquehouse*, cloth gaiters of countrymen, whence B. *trikheuzou.*

polvelyn, ***m.***, mill-pool: Polvellan, place-name.

pompyon**, ***m., *pl.* **-s**, pumpkin, gourd (W., M.E.).

pon (Late ***podn***), ***m.***, light flying dust (D. "podn").

ponow, *pl.* used as ***abst. s.***, pain of spirit: sing. **pōn** (W. *poen*, B *poan*), ***m.***, is replaced by **payn** except in **ponvos**, etc.

pons, ***m.***, *pl.* **-ow, -onjow**, bridge: in place-names may be *ponj* before vowels and, owing to the final *s*, *pons*⁴, *pon*⁴; keeps in E. Cor. its ancient (pre-C. Voc.) form *pont*, e.g., Penpont is in W. Cor. Penponds; *p. -forth*, viaduct (W.): *p. an scoth*, collar-bone (W.).

ponsyk, ***m.***, *pl.* **-ygow**, little bridge (B.).

ponsyn, ***m.***, *pl.* **-now**, little foot-bridge: ? *p.* in place-names, Ponsengath, Ponsendane rather than *pons an.*

ponvos, -fos, ***m.***, trouble, vexation, misery: *yth-yu sur mur a bonvos*, it is indeed a very painful matter, B.M. 1606; see **ponow.**

ponvosyk, -fosyk, *adj.*, troubled, vexed, miserable, R.D. 1256.

ponvotter (*sd* become *tt*), ***m.***, state of trouble, misery, wretchedness.

ponya (Lh. ***punnia***), ***vb.***, to run, trot: used only of living creatures; see **resek.**

pōpa, *m.*, *pl.* **-ys**, puffin (D. "pope").
†**popty** (C. Voc. *popei* for *popti*), *m.*, bake-house, *baecern* Aelfric; see **chy-pobas.**
***po·pynjay**, *m.*, *pl.* **-s**, parrot (M.E.).
pōr, *m.*, pasture: Poor, field-names.
poran (? *pur ewn*), *adv.*, quite, right, just, exactly, straight.
porgh, *m.*, *pl.* **-ow**, pig, swine.
porgh-bügel, *m.*, bottle-nosed shark (D. "porbeagle").
porghel (D. "porl," Lh. *porhal*, C. Voc. *porchel*), *m.*, *pl.* **porghelly**, porker, vear, young pig, *fearh* Aelfric.
porghelly, *vb.*, to bring forth pigs: *porghellys yu an wys*, the sow has farrowed (W., B.).
porghellyk, *m.*, *pl.* **-ygow**, sucking-pig.
porpos, *m.*, *pl.* **-pesow**, plaice, Lh.
porpos (*purpas*), *m.*, purpose, design, intent, B.M., C.W. (M.E.): *a borpos dhe*, on purpose to; *dhe'm p.*, by my intention: *spedyes dour dhe borpos*, carried out exactly to plan; *dhe'n p.-na ymons ow-cows*, they are speaking to that intent, C.W. 2161 (*toos* for *cows*).
***porren** (*porran*), *f.*, *col.* **pōr**, leek, P., ? from Breton *pourren* Lh.: see **kenynen.**
porrēs, po·rres (*porrys*, *pür*, *rēs*, obscure *ü* as *o*, *purryes* C.W.), *adv.*, of necessity, urgently: *res yu p.*, it is most necessary.
pors, *m.*, *pl.* **-ys**, purse, B.M. (M.E. *purs*).
port, *m.*, *pl.* **-ys**, port-hole, entry-port, cargo-port, O.M. 962, C.W. 2267 (M.E.).
portal, *m.*, *pl.* **-ys**, porch, vestibule, entry; *p. an eglos*, church-porch, Lh. (M.E.).
porth, *m.*, *pl.* **-ow**, doorway, gateway, defile between hills, entrance, gate, *geat* Aelfric: *p. horn*, outer entrance with portcullis; Porth Horn, St. Michael's Mount, Tintagel.
porth, por', *m.*, *pl.* **-ow, perth**, port, harbour, cove, landing-place: in place-names, owing to final *th*, often *porth*[4], *por'*, e.g., Porthquin (*porth*, *gwyn*), and sometimes contracted before vowels or *h* to *pr'*, e.g., Priest, *porth Ust*, St. Just's landing-place, and before *l* to *pe* or *p*, e.g., Pelistry, Towan Blistra, *p. lystry*, harbour of ships: see **lester, scath.**
porthas, etc., see **perthy.**
porther, *m.*, *pl.* **-thoryon**, porter, door-keeper, janitor, P.
portheres (by scansion, *po·rtheres*), *f.*, *pl.* **-ow**, porteress, P.C. 1225.
***portraya**, *vb.*, to depict, pourtray, paint (M.E. *portreye*).
***portrayans**, *m.*, portrait, picture.
***Po·rtyngal**, *f.*, Portugal (M.E.).
porva, *f.*, pasture, grazing-place: Bosparva, place-name; see **pōr.**
porven, *f.*, *pl.* **-now**, *col.* **porf**, rush, rush-wick (D. "purvan"): col. used as "rush-grown place," cf. **corsen.**
pory, *vb.*, to graze, browse (W., B.): see **pōr.**
pōs, *m.*, *pl.* **-ow**, weight, pressure; pound-weight: see **canspōs.**
pōs (*poys*, Lh. *pūz*), *adj.*, heavy, grievous, overpowering, oppressive, sultry, close: comp. *possa*; *anal bos*, fetid breath, B.M. 4094: *p. yu genef*, I am most reluctant, B.M. 1633.
posa (*puza* Lh.), *vb.*, to lean, rest one's weight, weigh, press, droop: *p. war-nans*, *war-dhelergh*, *war-rak*, *a'n yl tenewan*, to lean downwards, backwards, forwards, to one side, M.C. 205–6.
posnya, -na, *vb.*, to poison: p. pt. *posnys*, O.M. 1559 (M.E. *poyson*).
possessyon (*poscessyon*), *m.*, possession, feudal holding, property, B.M. 2400 (M.E.).
po·ssybyl, *adj.*, possible, P.C. 1032 (M.E.).
post, *m.*, *pl.* **-ow**, column, pillar, post, C. Voc., Ord., *swer* Aelfric.
poster (*puster* Lh.), *m.*, heaviness, sultriness (D. "poster," thunder-cloud).
posyjyon, *m.*, heaviness, drowsiness, sadness oppression, O.M. 526, 1906.
pot, (*poyt*), *m.*, *pl.* **-tow**, pot, B.M. 3325: *p. pry*, *horn*, earthen, iron, pot; *p. gwyn*, bag-pudding, "whit-pot," hasty-pudding, Lh.; *p. mesen*, acorn-cup (B.).
pōt, pūt, *m.*, *pl.* **-ow**, kick (D. "poot").
potestas (for *potestates*), powers, order of angels, C.W. 55 (Lat.).
pōth, *m.*, sheep-rot, B.M. 3066: as W. *pwd*, B. *peud*.
pōth, *adj.*, hot, scorching (W., B.).
potha, *vb.*, to heat (W., B.).
pothter, *m.*, heat (W., B.).
potor, *m.*, *pl.* **-yon**, potter (W., B.).
pottro, see **pedry.**
pottya, *vb.*, to put: *p. quarel dhe*, lay a claim against, B.M. 3486 (M.E.).
pottys, *pl.*, entrails, B.M. 1272, Lh.MS. (E.).
potvan (*pōth*, *-van*), *m.*, scorching, heat, hotness: clearly written *potvan* R.D. 2343 (but *pocvan*, with *c* for *t*, R.D. 2341), this is *powan* (? for *povvan*) C.W. 460.
pōtya (*pottya*), *vb.*, to kick, spurn (M.E.

put, D. " poot ") : *yn-dan drey may fo potyes*, that it may be spurned under foot, O.M. 2807.

pow (C. Voc. *poli* for *pou*), *m.*, *pl.* **-yow**, country, county, shire, province, region, land, countryside : *den p.*, countryman ; *p. Kernow*, Cornwall ; *p. Densher*, Devon (Late) ; *p. Saws*, *p. an Sawson*, England ; *p. Ysel*, Netherlands, etc.

power (*poher*, Keigwin, Kerew, *pour*, Borlase), *m.*, power (E.).

powes, *m.*, rest, quiet, repose, truce, pause.

powes, *vb.*, to rest, be still, halt : 3 s. pres.-fut., 2 s. imp. *powes*.

powesva, *f.*, rest, place or state of rest : *deth a bowesva*, day of rest, O.M. 145, C.W. 416.

pows (C. Voc. *peis*, *peus*), *f.*, *pl.* **-yow**, coat, gown, tunic, knight's surcoat : *p. croghen*, coat of skin, Kerew ; *p. gwrek*, woman's outer garment, C. Voc., *roc* Aelfric.

poynt, *m.*, point, least amount, item, particular, bodily condition (M.E.) : *yn p. da*, *p. ta*, R.D. 1756, in good health, well ; *ny-synsaf p.*, I shall not mind at all, C.W. 1138 ; *yn nep*, *pup*, *p.*, in any, every, respect ; *p. a skyans*, adage, maxim, Lh. ; *p. a falsury*, treacherous turn, M.C. 83 ; see **a-poynt**.

poyntya, see **appoyntya**.

praga, **pyraga**, *adv.*, why, wherefore ; *interj.*, why, what for ; *m.*, cause of it, reason why : as adv. these are emphatic forms of **prak(g)**, the final *a* probably represents *yu*, is it, it is, cf. **fatla**, **pȳla** ; as interj. *praga* is followed by *pandra*, B.M. 2099, C.W. 2329.

prak(g), *adv.*, why, wherefore ; *m.*, reason why : originally *py rak*, for what ; as adv. followed by particles y^5*(th)-* in positive, na^2*(g)*-in negative.

pral, **-la**, see **spral**, **-la**.

prās, *m.*, *pl.* **-ow**, meadow, common pasture : *yn gwel nag yn p.*, anywhere at all.

prat, *m.*, *pl.* **-tys**, trick, wile, cunning device (M.E. ; O.E. *praet*, craft).

pray, *m.*, prey, M.C. 21 (M.E.) : see ***prēth**.

praydha (vars. *y pray the*, *in preytha*, *y praytha*), I prithee (M.E.).

praysya (*preysa*), *vb.*, to praise (E.) : *ny-vynnaf pell ombraysya*, I won't sing my own praises long, P.C. 1677.

precyous, *adj.*, precious, precise, beautiful, finely wrought ; *adv.*, precisely, carefully, exactly (M.E. *precius*).

preder, *m.*, *pl. and abst.* **-ow** (*pryderow*), thought, care, worry, anxiety, melancholy, dejection (as M.E. *thoghte*) : *gyllys of yn prederow*, I have become uneasy, R.D. 16.

†**prederüs**, **-ys** (C. Voc. *priderys*), *adj.*, careful, solicitous, anxious.

predery (*prydyry*, Late *pedery*), *vb.*, to think, reflect, meditate, consider : p. pt., 1 and 3 s. pret. and 3 s. imp. *prederys*, 3 s. subj. *prederro*.

prederyans (*pederyans* Keigwin), *m.*, opinion, Lh.

***prēdhya**, ***prēdha**, *vb.*, to prey on, live by prey, capture : 3 s. pres. -fut. *prēth* (W., B.).

pref, see **prevy**, **pryf**.

pregoth (Late *progath*, *proga'*, Lh. *porogga*), *m.*, *pl.* **-gowthow**, sermon, preaching ; *vb.*, to preach : with added syllable, *o* becomes *ow*, which changes to *ew* in sympathy with *y* endings.

pregowther (C.W. *progowther*), *m.*, *pl.* **-thoryon**, preacher.

pren (Late *predn*), *m.*, *pl.* **-yer**, **prynner**, tree, log, hewn timber, beam, wood, bar, stick, piece of wood ; lot, cut : *tewlel p.*, to cast lots, and thence to draw straws or cuts, P.C. 2847 ; *p. -gwely*, bedstead (W).; in Late Cor., Lhuyd says, the meaning " tree " was lost.

prēn, *m.*, purchased (W., B.).

prena, **perna**, *vb.*, to buy, redeem, be redeemed, expiate, pay for, purchase, merit : p. pt. *prenys*, *pernys* (C. Voc. *prinid*) ; 3 s. pres. -fut. *pren* ; *gwerthens y huk dhe brena anedhy cledha*, let him sell his cloak to buy with it a sword, P.C. 922 ; *an pyth a-wruk dhe brena*, that which he caused to be redeemed, B.M. 2746 (cf. **sylwel**) ; special fut. *why a-n-prenvyth*, you shall pay for it, B.M. 3750.

prena (for *preneth*), *m.*, expiation, M.C. 234.

prener, *m.*, *pl.* **-noryon**, buyer (W., B.).

prenna, *vb.*, to bar, bolt, P.C. 3039.

presens, *m.*, presence, C.W. 2029 (M.E.).

***presep**, *m.*, *pl.* **-ebow**, crib, manger (W. B.).

presont, **-ent**, *m.*, *pl.* **-ons**, present, gift. B.M. (M.E.).

prest, *adv.*, readily, quickly. continually,

incessantly, always, ever, still, now, at once (M.E.).

***prēth**, *m.*, prey, spoil: replaced by, or re-spelt as, **pray** (W., B.).

preven, *f.*, *pl.* **-now**, moth grub, small worm, Lh.: see **prȳf.**

preventya. *vb.*, to forestall (M.E.): *my a-n-prevent*, I'll be beforehand with him, C.W. 493.

prevy, *vb.*, to prove, try, test, experience: 3 s. pres.-fut. *prēf*; 3 s. subj. *proffo*; 2 s. pret. *prefsys*; 3 s. pret. *provas.*

processyon, *m.*, procession, B.M. (M.E.).

prōf, *m.*, proof, trial, test: *yn p.*, as proof, in fact, indeed, forsooth, moreover.

profüs (*profes*, *profeth*, C. Voc. *profuit*), *m.*, *pl.* **-füsy**, **-üjy**, **-yjy**, prophet, *witege* Aelfric.

profüsa, **-üja**, **-yja**, *vb.*, to prophesy (W., B.).

profüsans, *m.*, prophesy (W., B.).

profüsek, **-füsüs**, *adjs.*, prophetic (B.).

profüses, **-fejes**, *f.*, *pl.* **-ow**, prophetess (W., B.).

profya, *vb.*, to offer, tender for acceptance, proffer, try, essay: *mar mynner dhym y brofya*, if anyone wants to offer it to me, B.M. 2880.

promys (*-mes*), *m.*, *pl.* **-mesys**, promise, B.M., C.W. (M.E.).

promysya, *vb.*, to promise, C.W. 889 (M.E).

pronter (C. Voc. *prounder*), *m.*, *pl.* **-yon**, parson, clergyman, beneficed priest, *sacerd* Aelfric (Med. Lat. *provendarius*).

pronterjy, *m.*, *pl.* **-ow**, parsonage, rectory, vicarage.

provochya (*provucha*, Borlase, misprinted *provueha* Lh), *vb.*, to provoke: ?Anglo-Fr. *provocher* from Lat. *provocare.*

provy, **-vya** (*pruvia* Lh.), *vb.*, to procure, purvey, provide, B.M. 1870, C.W. 2290 (M.E. *purveie*).

prow, *m.*, gain, advantage, profit (M.E. *prowe*, O. Fr. *prou*, Med. Lat. *produm* from *prodeste*): *anedha ty ny'fyth p.*, thou wilt get no good of them, P.C. 2658.

prowt (*prout*), *adj.*, proud, puffed up, pleased (M.E.).

prȳ, *m.*, clay, earth, mould: *p.-gwyn*, china-clay; *mos, bos gorrys, yn p.*, to be buried, R.D.; *chy p.*, cob-walled cottage (W., B.); *lym ha p.*, mortar of lime and clay mixed, as traditionally used in Cornwall, O.M. 2450; see **pol**, **pyt.**

prȳas (C. Voc. *priot*), *adj.*, married; *m. and f.*, *pl.* **-yosow**, spouse, husband, wife: *s* prevents mutation of following *c*, *k*, *d*, *t*, when f.

prydydhek, *adj.*, poetic (W.).

prydydhes, *f.*, *pl.* **-ow**, poetess (W,).

prydydhy, *vb.*, to compose poetry (W.).

prydydhȳeth, *m.*, poetry (W.).

†prydyth (C. Voc. *pridit*), *m.*, *pl.* **-ydhyon**, poet, *sceop*, *leothwyrhta* Aelfric.

prȳek, *f.*, *pl.* **-egow**, place abounding in clay (B.).

prȳen, *f.*, clayey ground (D. "pryan").

prȳeryn, see **perghyryn.**

prȳf (C. Voc. *prif*, Lh. *prēf*), *m.*, *pls.* **pryves**, **prevyon**, worm, vermin, reptile, creeping thing, wretch: *p. blewek*, hairy caterpillar; *p.-dor*, leatherjacket; *p.-golow*, glow worm; *p.-cawl*, green caterpillar; *p. pren*, tree caterpillar (C. Voc.); *p.-malan*, pipe-fish, lit. devil's worm (Lh. MS.); *p. -mor*, sea-worm, nereis (D. "praav").

prȳgwyth, see **prȳjwyth.**

prȳjwyth (*prys*, *gwyth*; *prygwyth*, *priueth* in MS.), *m.*, moment, instant, short space of time, O.M. 860, P.C. 1055.

pryk, *m.*, *pl.* **-kys**, point, degree, pitch, mark, *dos dhe'n p. -na*, attain that pitch, C.W. 785: (M.E.).

pryl, *m.*, *pl.* **-yon**, small solid mass; sheep-dropping; tin-stone (D. "prill").

pryleghen, *f.*, *pl.* **-now**, tile (W.).

prynces, *f.*, *pl.* **-ow**, princess (M.E.).

pry'ncypal, *adj.*, principal, B.M. 253 (M.E.).

pryncy'pata, *m.*, *pl.* **-tys**, principality, princedom, C.W. 53 (M.E.).

pryns, *m.*, *pl.* **-cys**, prince (M.E.).

prynt, *m.*, *pl.* **-ys**, print, C.W. 1750.

***pryntjy**, *m.*, *pl.* **-ow**, printing-office.

***pryntya**, *vb.*, to print, impress (E.).

***prȳor**, *m.*, *pl.* **-s**, prior (E.).

***prȳores**, *f.*, *pl.* **-ow**, prioress (E.).

prȳosol, *adj.*, bridal, matrimonial (W., B.).

prȳs, *m.*, *pl.* **-yow**, **-ȳjyow**, price, value, eminence, worth: *a brys*, worthy, valuable.

prȳs (*preys*, *prēs*, C. Voc. *prit*), *m. pl.* **-yow**, **-yjyow**, time, while, season, tide, meal-time, meal, repast; credit, time in which to pay: *yn gwetha p.*, most unfortunately, unhappily. unluckily; *yn gwella p.*, most happily, fortunately, opportunely, luckily; *p.-bos*, meal-time;

p.-ly, breakfast(-time); *p.-soper* supper (-time); *p.-gwesper*, vespers, eventide; *p. mos alemma*, time to leave; *un p.*, for a moment; *un p. kens nos*, a while ere nightfall; *a-vedha p. bys deth-brus?* is there to be credit till Doomsday? B.M. 1925; see **a-brӯs**.
prysclowek, *f.*, scrub, shubbery, place covered with bushes: place-name.
prysclowwyth, *col.*, scrubby, stunted trees: place-name.
pryskcōs, *m.*, *pl.* **-ow**, thicket (W.).
pryskel, *m.*, *pl.* **-sclow**, brushwood, thicket, copse: Levine Prisklo, place-name.
prysken, *f.*, *col.* **prysk**, bush, brushwood.
pryskwӯth, *col.*, copse (W.).
prysner (*presner*), *m.*, *pl.* **-s**, prisoner (M.E.).
pryson (*preson*), *m.*, *pl.* **-yow**, prison (M.E.): *drok-p.*, dungeon, R.D. 2002.
prysonya, *vb.*, to imprison (M.E. *prisone*).
prӯva, *adj.*, private, privy, personal; *adv.*, privily (M.E. *prive*): *taclow p.*, hidden matters, private affairs; *p.-ywythysy*, body-guard.
pryvesek, *adj.*, worm-eaten, verminous (W.).
pryvessa, *vb.*, to hunt vermin (W.); inf. only.
pryvesy, *vb.*, to become verminous (W.).
pryveta (*prevetta*), *m.*, *pl.* **-tys**, privity, C.W. 859 (M.E. *prevete*, *privite*).
pryveth, *adj.*, secret, privy, private; *adv.*, privately, in secrecy: *bos p. ganso*, to be in his confidence, share his secrets, R.D. 1092.
pryvetter, *m.*, privacy: see **pryveth**.
prӯwӯth, *m.*, pottery (W.).
psalmus, see **salmus**.
pub, see **pup**.
***püber**, *m.*, pepper (W., B.).
pül, *m.*, *pl.* **-yow**, stake, post, pile, column, steeple: Carn Pele, place-name; *p.-yet*, *p.-clos*, gatepost (B.).
püns (*penz* Lh., *pens* C.W.), *m.*, *pl.* **-ow**, pound, sovereign; pound-weight.
punsya (for *punysya*), *vb.*, to punish (M.E. *punshe*): cf **fynsya**.
***punyon**, *m.*, *pl.* **-s**, gable (M.E., D., Fr. *pignon*).
pup, **pub** (*pop*, *peb*), *m.*, *pron.*, *adj.*, all, every, each: as adj. is followed by sing. noun, causing no mutation: *fya p. a'y du*, to flee each his own way; *whyla dhyn p. y welen*, seek a rod for each of us; *a bup tu*, *a bup parth*, on either side, on all sides; *a bup tu dhedha*, on each side of them; *golsowens p.!* let everyone hearken!: *p. oll*, *p. den oll*, all, everybody, emphatic.
pup-dhewheles, *vb.*, to atone for all: *den yu dhe bup-dhewheles* he is man for all-atoning, P.C. 56.
pup-hüny, *pron.*, everyone: see **hüny**.
pupnos, *f.*, *adj.*, *adv.*, every night, nightly (W.): *p.-oll*, emphatic.
pup-plas, *adv.*, everywhere.
pupprӯs, *adv.*, always, at all times.
puppyna·k(g), *pron.*, whoever, whatever; where or whenever: a stronger word than **pypynak(g)**; *p.-oll*, emphatic, whoever at all, etc.
pupteth (*dēth*), *m.*, *adj.*, *adv.*, every day, always, daily: *p.-oll*, emphatic, every single day.
puptra, *pron.*, everything: *p.-oll*, *pup tr'oll* (*trawle* B.M. 4473), emphatic.
pup-tu, *adv.*, on all sides, everywhere, C.W. 1256: usually *a bup tu*.
pup-ur(-oll), *adv.*, always, at all times.
pūr, *m.*, snivel, nasal mucus, Lh.
pür, *adj.*, pure, clean, unalloyed, unmitigated, sheer, absolute, very, comp. *pürra* (*pyrra* C.W.); *adv.*, right, thoroughly, full, very, quite: *dour p.*, clean water; *myghternes p.*, a very queen; *an purra ladron*, the veriest thieves; *p. wyr*, right truly; see **poran**, **porres**.
p'ur[5], **py ür**[5], *adv.*, at what time, when: used directly before vb., as *p. fuf-vy*, when was I, O.M. 576, unless with infixed pron., as *p. y-n-gwelaf*, when I shall see him, R.D. 725; the *th* of *yth-* is not added, however, before vowels in *bos* and *mos*, e.g., *py ur a tus*, when will men go, P.C. 603; this may be explained as for *py ur (yu) a*, as also may *p'ur a-wylsta*, when hast thou seen, B.M. 1253, 1896, instead of the expected *p'ur whylsta*.
püra, *vb.*, to cleanse, scour, furbish (W., B.).
purcat, *m.*, pulpit, preaching-place, Lh. (Lat. *(cathedra) praedicatorii*).
purek. *adj.*, snivelling, snotty (Pryce).
purjya (*purdzha*, Lh.), *vb.*, to purge.
purpur, *m. and adj.*, purple (M.E.): set before noun in *p. pannow*, *pal*, purple cloths, pall.
pürra, see **pür**.
pür-rēs, see **porres**.
purvers, see **pervers**.

puscas, -kes, see **pysk.**
pusorn, *m., pl.* **-sernow,** bundle, bale, R.D: *pen p.*, burden or refrain of song.
pusornas (*pozzorrez* Lh.), *vb.*, to bundle together; to sing the burden of a song: p. pt. *pusernys.*
py, *interr. pron.*, who, which, what: formerly preceded preps., as still in **prak, pegans,** and *py gansa*, by whom; *py* (*a*²) is suggested by *py hanow*, of what name, *py*² *doll* (*an jawl*), by what hole, see **toll,** and *py* (*yn*) by *py cost, le, plas, plas, tyller*, where; before *yu, le, rak*, *py* may contract to *p*, see **pyū, py'ū, plē(th), prak(g)**; *py lyes, py-sul*, how many.
py⁵(th) (*py, y(th)*), *adv.*, where, whither: used directly before vb., unless with infixed pron; takes the *th* of *yth-* before vowels in *bos* and *mos*; combines with *yma* as *pyma*, and *pymava* (*py yma -va*); *byth war pyth ylly*, mind where thou goest, B.M. 1103.
pȳ (C. Voc. *pi*), *conj.*, or, see **pō,**
pȳasen, *f.*, *col.*, **pȳas,** magpie: Park Pyas, field-name.
pyb (C. Voc. *pib*, possibly *wib*), *f., pl.* **-ow,** pipe (in all senses).
pȳba (*peba* C.W.), *vb.*, to pipe.
pȳben (*piban* Lh.), *f., pl.* **-now,** little pipe, tube.
pȳber (Late *peeber*), *m., pl.* **-boryon.** piper, flute-player.
†pȳbyth (C. Voc. *pip(h)it*, written *wip(h)it*), *m., pl.* **-ydhyon,** piper.
pycher, *m., pl.* **-s,** pitcher, pot with handle (E.): *p. pysa*, urinal, chamber-pot, Lh.; *p. dowr glan*, a pitcher(ful) of clean water, P.C. 629.
pyffya, *vb.*, to puff (D. "piffer," porpoise).
pyga, *vb.*, to prick, sting, stimulate, goad, Lh.
pygal, *f., pl.* **-golow,** pick, mattock, hoe, Lh. (D. "piggal").
pyg-bȳghan (*pig bihan* Lh.); **pyg-gwyn** (D. "piggywidn"), *m.*, smallest pig of litter.
pygemmys. *adv.*, how much, how great, how many, how greatly; *p. hes*, how long, O.M. 2104; see **py, kemmys.**
pyger, *m., pl.* **-goryon,** goader, stimulant.
pyg-gwyn, see **pyg-byghan.**
pyjy, see **pysy.**
***pȳk,** *m., pl.* **-ygow,** point (W., B.): *pl.* **-ys, pike,** weapon (E.).
pykē·n, pokē·n. *conj.*, or else, otherwise, before *bo*, either (on the one hand): *p. certan bynary why a-vyth avel fleghes, bo yn-assentys ty a-glew*, either you wlll certainly always be like children, or thou wilt hearken assentingly, C.W. 652; see **pō, pȳ.**
***pykern,** *m., pl.* **-ow,** cone, peak, pointed mass (W., B.).
pyl, *m., pl.* **-yon,** peel, stripping; (pl.) slag tin (D. "pillion").
pȳl (*pil* Lh.), *m., pl.* **-yow,** hillock, mound, heap, (of sea-birds) flock, pile (D. "pill"): *p.-go' dhor* (*pil gudhar*, Lh.), mole-hill; *p. -teyl*, muck-heap, dung-pile, Lh.; *a'n corfow ny a-wra pyl*, of the bodies we will make a heap, B.M. 1621.
pȳl (*peyl*), *m., pl.* **-ys,** head or "pile" of arrow, C.W. 1560 (M.E.).
pȳla (*py yn lē*), *adv.*, where, whither: form of **plē(th)** used without a following verb, *my yu ow-pos gorrys ny-won p.*, I am being taken I know not whither, C.W. 2126; this may have originated as *py le yu*, cf. **fatla, a-bȳla.**
pylas, *m.*, naked or bald oats, *avena nuda* (D. "pillas", B. *pilad*).
pylla (*pyla*), *vb.*, to plunder, spoil, rob, pillage, B.M. 1268, 3423 (M.E. *pille*).
pyllar (*pillar* C.W.), *m., pl.* **-s,** pillar, column (E.).
†pyllen (C. Voc. *pillen*), *f., pl.* **-now,** fringe, rag, frayed cloth, *snaed* Aelfric.
pyllenek, *adj.*, ragged (B.).
pyltya, *vb.*, to pelt, push, harass, M.C. 112 (E.D. "pelt").
pylya, *vb.*, to strip, skin, peel, make bare: p. pt. *pylys* (*pilez* Lh.), bald, scant of locks, bare; *pen pylys*, hairless head (M.E. *piled pate*), C.W. 2318.
pylyak, *adj.*, scurvy, paltry; *m., pl.* **-yogyon,** incapable, useless or indigent person; spider-crab, as being worthless (D. "pilliack").
pym', see **pymp.**
pȳment, *m.*, sweet, spiced wine, O.M. 1915 (M.E.).
pymp (Late *pemp*), *card num.*; *m., pl.* **-ow,** five: final *p* is omitted in *pym-woly Cryst*, the Five Wounds of Christ, and in **pymthegves, pymthek,** as in B. *pemzek*, but not regularly before nouns as in W. *pum.*
pymp-bȳs, pympȳs, *m.*, starfish, lit. five-fingers, as D.E.; cinquefoil (B.).

pympdelen, *f.*, cinquefoil (W., B.).
pympes, *ord. num.*, fifth.
pymthegves, *ord. num.*, fifteenth: see **pymp.**
pymthek, *card num.*, fifteen: see **pymp.**
pyn (Late *pidn*), *m.*, *pl.* **-nys**, peg, pin (E.).
pȳn, *m.*, pain, punishment, suffering, "pine" (M.E. *pyne*).
pyna·k(g), *pron.*, whosoever, whatsoever: *p.·oll*, emphatic; following *a-*[2] may be omitted, e.g., *p. vo* or *p. a-vo*, also *p. may fo*.
py·nakyl(*pinakyll* M.C.), *m.*, *pl.* **-s**, **-aclys**, pinnacle, P.C. 84 (M.E. *pynakill*).
†pȳnbren (C. Voc. *pinbren*), *m.*, pine-tree, *pintreow* Aelfric.
***pyncel**, *m.*, *pl.* **-s**, artist's brush, pencil (M.E.); *p.-plom*, lead-pencil; *p. men*, slate-pencil.
pynna, *vb.*, to peg or pin together, fasten tree-nails, O.M. 963 (E.).
pynsor, *m.*, *pl.* **-s**, pair of pincers, P.C. 3149—51 (M.E. *pinsours*).
pynȳ·l (*py a'n ȳl*), *pron.*, which (of two), *p. pynag-oll*, whichsoever; *adv.* (*py y'n yl*), whither, to which (of two places): *p. ellen fors ny-wraf*, it's no odds to me to which I go, B.M. 1257; see **bonȳl.**
pypyna·k(g), *pron.*, whoever, whatever; *adv.*, whenever: *p.-o·ll*, emphatic; used as **pynak(g).**
†pypyth, see **pybyth.**
pȳs (*s* sharp, *pice* C.W., *pis* Lh.), *m.*, *pl.* **-ys**, piece (E.).
pȳs, see **pē**, **pēsya**, **pȳsen.**
pȳsa (*piza* Lh.), *vb.*, to make water.
pysador, *m.*, *pl.* **-yon**, suppliant.
pysadow, **-jadow**, **-yadow**, *m.*, prayer, supplication, praying.
pysas (*pizaz* Lh.), *m.*, urine, stale.
pyscador, **pyscajor** (C. Voc. *piscadur*, Lh. *pusgadur*), *m.*, *pl.* **-yon**, fisherman: *p. an myghtern*, kingfisher, Lh.
pysen, **-jen**, *f.*, *pl.* **now**, prayer (W., B.): replaced by **pysadow.**
pȳsen, *f.*, *pl.* **-now**, *col.* **pȳs** (Lh. *pēs*), pea, pea-plant: Dor Pease, *dor p.*, field-name.
pysk (C. Voc. *pisc*), *m.*, *pl.* **-puskes**, **-cas**, fish: *p. sal*, salted fish, Lh.; *p. malan*, devil-fish, fishing-frog (*pesk mollan*, Ray, 1674, D. "devil").
pyskessa (*pusgetsha* Lh.), *vb.*, to go fishing, catch fish: inf. only.
†pysklyn (C Voc. *pisclin*), *f.*, *pl.* **-now**, fish-pond, *fiscpol* Aelfric.
pyst, see **pen-pyst.**
pystry, *m.*, sorcery, witchcraft, magic, P.C. 1764.
pystrȳa, *vb.*, to work magic.
pystrȳor, *m.*, *pl.* **-yon**, wizard, sorcerer, magician, P.C., R.D.
pystrȳores, *f.*, *pl.* **-ow**, witch, sorceress, O.M. 2668.
pystyga, *vb.*, to hurt, harm, P.C. 98, M.C. 197: 3 s. pres.-fut. *pystyk*.
pystyk, *m.*, *pl.* **-ygow**, hurt, injury, harm, R.D. 2305.
***pystyl**, *m.*, *pl.* **-low**, spout, fall of water (W., cf. D. "pizzil").
py-sül (*pezealla* Lh., for *p.-s. a-*, or *ha*), *pron.*, how many, how much, whatever, as much or many as: *govyn p.-s. a-vynnyth*, ask as much as thou wilt, P.C. 592.
pysy, **-jy** (*pesy*, *-jy*), *vb.*, to pray, beg, entreat, supplicate: following inf. takes prep. *a*, as "to"; *p. gans*, to intercede for; 3 s. pret. *pysys*; *dha bysy*, prithee, O.M. 1607, R.D. 1649; see **crysy.**
***pysȳn**, *m.*, *pl.* **-ow**, piscina (B.).
pyt, *m.*, *pl.* **-tys**, pit (O.E. *pytt*): *y'n p. ysella*, in the deepest dungeon, R.D. 2010; *p. yffarn*, the pit of hell, C.W. 421; *p.-pry*, clay-pit, Pit Pry, place-name.
pyta, *m.*, pity (M.E. *pite*): *kemeres p. a*, take pity on.
pyteth (*pytet*), *m.*, compassion, M.C. 164, 177, 223.
pytethüs, **-ys**, (*-ays* for rhyme B.M. 1678), *adj.*, compassionate, pitiful.
pȳth, *m.*, *pl.* **-ow**, pit, shaft, stone-lined sunk well, C.W. 329 (D. "peeth").
pyth (*peyth*, *peth*), *m.*, *pl.* **-ow**, **taclow**, thing, article, property; substance, pl. *pythow* is used as meaning riches, possessions, sing. *p. an bys*, worldly wealth; *p. pronter*, a priest's goods or estate, N. Boson; *avel p. fol*, like a mad thing, M.C. 182, P.C. 2765; *orthyf na-whyla p. es*, seek not of me anything whatever, lit. a thing that there is, B.M. 918; see **an pyth**
pȳth, *adj.*, avaricious, stingy, reluctant to give, R.D. 1958, as B. *piz*: *kyn fy mar byth*, though thou be (ever) so grudging.
pyth, *interrog. and rel. pron.* what: contraction of *py pyth*, what thing; *a-* is usually omitted after it, as *p. wraf*, *p. vo*; as rel. used especially after **gothvos.**
pyth, see **py[5](th).**

†**pȳthyonen** (C. Voc. *ymbithionen* for *un b.*), *f.*, *pl.* **pȳthon,** sheet of paper, etc., leaf or open page of book, *ymele* Aelfric: cf. W. *peithyn*, sheet, page.

pyū, p'yū, pyw (*pu*), *interrog. pron.*, who: though formed from *py yu*, *p'yu*, and used also as meaning "who (or what) is?" this can also be followed by *yu*, as in M.C. 69; when the vb. is intended it is usual to insert an apostrophe; see **pȳ.**

p'yūa (*pewa, py, yu, e*), *interj,*, what? who? lit. what (who) is it? C.W. 1601, Lh.; also at end of sentence, *ny-wraf vry erbyn p.*, I mind not against whom it is, C.W. 434; Lh. was probably wrong in writing, even as Late Cor., *p'yua yu an den-na?* who is that man? but his *p'yua es ena?* who is (it that is) there? seems possible.

pyū-pyna·k(g), *pron.*, whoever: *p.-p.-o·ll*, emphatic form; see **pynak(g).**

py ür, see **pür.**

Q (mutations of Qu Gw, Wh)

quallok, *m.*, hulking fellow, O.M. 2068: cf. "whallock," "wallocking," "hullock," "hulk," E.D. Dic.

***quarel,** *m.*, *pl.* **-s,** pane of glass (D.E. "quarle").

quarel, *m.*, claim, demand, quarrel, warlike enterprise (M.E.): *synsy q.*, to maintain a claim, sustain a cause, B.M. 2588; see **pottya.**

quart, *m.*, *pl.*, **-ys,** quart, A. Boorde.

quarten, *f.*, *pl.* **-now,** quart, quarter, Lh., Gw.

quarter, *m.*, *pl.* **-trys,** quarter: *my ny-allaf predery pana gwarter yth-ama*, I have no idea in what direction I shall go, C.W. 1741.

quartron, *m.*, *pl.* **-ys,** quarter, region, district, point, compass direction (M.E. *quarteron*, O. Fr. *quartron*): *aspyens pup a'y gwartron*, let each search in his own locality, B.M. 980.

quartrona, *vb.*, to cut in quarters, B.M. 1918, 3608 (M.E.).

questyon, *m.*, *pl.* **-s,** inquiry, question, P.C., B.M. (M.E.).

queth, *f.*, *pl.* **-ow,** garment, clout, Ord., B.M., C.W.; breast-hook of boat (D., with var. prs. "queth", "quaith", "gwaith").

quetha, *vb.*, to clothe; cover with a cloth, M.C. 96, C.W. 978.

quoff, *m.*, distention, repletion, as M.Breton *coeff* (D. "quaff").

quoffy, *vb.*, to swell, overeat (D.): cf. **hothfy** and M.B. *coezfiff*, now *koenvi.*

quyk. *adj.*, quick, alive; *adv.*, speedily, quickly (M.E.): *mar gwyk*, so soon C.W. 2383.

quylkyn (*kwilken* Lh.), *m.*, *pl.* **-now,** frog (D. "quilkin", "wilky"): see older form **gwylskyn.**

quyllen (*kuillan* Lh.), *f.*, *pl.* **-now,** quill (E.).

quyt (*quyth* M.C.), *adv.*, without hindrance, free, quit, on even terms, justly (M.E. *quit, quyte*): *q.-jujjys*, deservedly sentenced, P C. 2901.

quȳt, *adv.*, quite, P.C., C.W. (M.E.).

quyttya, *vb.*, to quit: 2 s. imp. *quyt*; *scon yn-mes q. a'm golok*, get out of my sight quickly, O.M. 1530 (miswritten *quyk*, corrected to *voyd*).

R

rabmen, *m.*, granite gravel, Borlase (D. "rab").

racan (*rakkan* Lh.)., *m.*, *pl.* **-ow,** garden rake: see ***rastel.**

racanna, *vb.*, to rake (W.): see **racan.**

racca, *m.*, comedy: mealtime entertainment given by minstrels, C. Voc. (O.E.), *racu* Aelfric.

rach, *m.*, heed, care reck (M.E. *recche*): *gans mur a r.*, with a great deal of care, P.C. 2722.

***raf,** *f.*, *pl.* **-fow,** cord, band (W., B.).

rafna (for *ravynya*), *vb.*, to plunder, ravage, raven, B.M. 2091 (M.E *ravyne*).

rafner, *m.*, *pl.* **-oryon,** marauder: see **rafna.**

rafsya (for *ravysya*), *vb.*, to ravish, transport: p. pt. *rafsys*, rapt, carried away, R.D. 198.

rafsyans, *m.*, transport, rapture: see **rafsya.**

rag-, *prefix*, fore-, pre-: see **rak(g).**

ra·gomōgh (*ragama* Symonds), *m.*, hog (Fr. *ragot*, young boar, and **mōgh**).

ragdas, see **raktas.**

ragenys, *f.*, *pl.* **-nesow,** near island (W., B.).

rag-ēr, *m.*, *pl.* **-yow,** preposition; lit. foreword (W.).

rag-gorra, *vb.*, to set before, prefix, Lh,

rag-hanow, *m.*, *pl.* **-hynwyn**, pronoun (W).
rag-henna, **rag henna**, *adv.*, therefore.
rag-henwel, *vb.*, to name before : p. pt. *-hynwys*, aforesaid, already named, Lh.
raglavar, *m.*, *pl.* **-ow**, preface, prologue (W., B.).
raglen, *f.*, *pl.* **-now**, fisherman's apron; in later meaning, petticoat-trousers, but lit. "fore-cloth" (D.).
ragleverel, *vb.*, to say before: p. pt. *ragleverys*, already mentioned, M.C. 224.
ragown, *m.*, foreboding, presentiment (W.).
ragresek, *vb.*, to run before, proceed (W., B.).
ragresor, **-segyth**, *m.*, *pls.* **-yon**, **-ydhyon**, forerunner, precursor (W., B.).
ragvlas, *m.*, foretaste (W., B.).
ragvrüs, *f.*, prejudice (W.).
ragwel, *m.*, foresight (W., B.).
ragweles, *vb.*, to foresee (W., B.).
rahaya, *vb.*, to sneeze, Borlase (imitative) : see **strewy**.
rajel, *m.*, ground covered with loose rocks (D. "radgell"); Radell, place-name, Zennor bounds, 1613.
rak(g), *prep.*, for, to, in order to, for the purpose of, because of (with *gwytha*, *cudha*, *scusy*, *lesta*, etc.), against, from, (with neg. *na(g)-*) lest, (with *may*) in order that, so that; *conj.*, for; *prefix*, fore-, pre- : combines with prons., see APPENDIX V.; *r. na-vy*, lest thou be; *r. may hyllyf*, so that I may; *r. ty dhe weles*, because thou sawest; *dus r.!* (to opponent) come on!; *r. dodho*, any further, onward, on, M.C. 173 (cf. W. *myned rhagddo*, to go on); see **a-rak(g)**, **dherak(g)**, **a-dherak(g)**.
rakpreder, *m.*, forethought (W., B.).
rakpren, *m.*, subscription (B.).
rakprena, **-perna**, *vb.*, to subscribe (B.).
rakscryf (Lh. *ragscref*), *m.*, *pl.* **-ow**, preface.
raktas (*ragdas* Lh.), *m.*, *pl.* **-ow**, forefather: see **hendas**.
rambla, *vb*,, to straddle, stand or walk with feet wide apart, or with knees bowed outwards, Lh., cf B. *ramblein*.
ran (C.W. *radn*), *f.*, *pl.* **-now**, part, lot, portion, specimen, share, division, fortune, fate; *as pron.*, some, some persons, someone: *r. a-yl*, *r. aral ny-yllons*, some can, others can't; *kemerens pup r. a'y du*, let each appropriate his share, P.C. 2859; *ry r. dhe*, to give some to; *dhe r. a'n re-na*, to some of those, C.W. 2356; *res yu dhe r. cafos cur*, somebody has to take charge, B.M. 2977; *squattyes ynter dyw r.*, broken in two, C.W. 1708; *cales r.*, a hard fate, R.D. 2260; *dyswa r. a'th vaystry*, show an example of thy power, P.C. 2869.
randra (*tre*), *f.*, suburb, ward of borough (W.).
randȳr, *f.*, *pl.* **-yow**, region (W., B.).
ranjy, *f.*, *pl.* **-ow**, apartment in house (W., B.).
ranna (Lh. *radna*), *vb.*, to part, divide, separate, share, deal, distribute, allot, apportion, (of heart, etc.) burst or break itself into parts: p. pt. *rynnys*; *termyn a-dhe ef a-ran yntredhon an gwyr*, in time to come he will deal justice between us, B.M. 1922.
ranvrō, *f.*, *pl.* **yow**, region (B.).
ranyēth, *f.*, *pl.* **-ow**, dialect (B.).
rās, *m.*, *pl. and abst.* **-ow**, grace, blessing, favour, virtue, worth, value, as W. *rhad*: *gans mur a r.*, *dhe r.*, excellently; clearly distinguished from **grās**, q.v., in *ras o ganso*, Chart. Endors., *ha ras*, B.M. 4380, *a gemmys ras*, M.C. 235, *ow ras*, R.D. 1584, *map ras*, dearly beloved or favourite son, R.D. 510, B.M. 486, *mur ow rasow*, B.M. 3917.
***rasca**, *vb.*, to plane (B.) : replaced by **playnya**.
***rask**, *f.*, *pl.* **-scow**, plane (B.) : replaced probably by **playn**.
***raskel**, *f.*, *pl.* **-sclow**, spoke-shave (W.).
***rastel**, *f.*, *pls.* **-lly**, **restel**, hay-rake, rack, grid (W., B., Med. Lat. *rastellum*) : see **racan**.
***ratha**, *vb.*, to scrape, rake, rasp (W., B.).
raunson (C.W. *rawnson*), *m.*, ransom (M.E.).
raynya, see **regnya**.
rē (Late *ry(ma)*, *ri(na)*), *pron.*, some, ones, persons: *ken r.*, *r. erel*, others; *an r.-ma*, these, rarely contracted to *re-m'* before *yu*; B.M. 3544; *an r.-na*, those; *an keth re-na*, those same people; *r. munys*, little ones; *an r. cotha*, the older ones; *re a'n dus-ma*, some of these people; *gans re.*, by some people; *an re munys ow-tenna*, the little sucklings, unweaned infants, lit. those sucking, P.C. 438, B.M. 1509.

rē, *adj.*, running, free, loose: found only in *colm r.*, slip-knot, P.C. 1525.

rē²(n), *prep.*, by (in oaths): adds *n* before vowels; combines with *an* and poss. prons., *re'n, re'm (rum), re'th*; *re Synt Jovyn!* by Jove! *ren ow thas!* bedad! *re'm pen, tros*, etc., by my head, foot, etc.; *re Varya (refarya)*, marry come up! lit. by Mary! see **arȳa**; *re Dhew a'm ros!* by God who made me! *re Synt Deffry!* by St. Verily!

rē², *adv.*, too, excessively, over- (before adj. or vb.); *m.*, too much, an excess or superfluity: *r. nebes*, too little; *r. re-dhyscryssys*, thou hast been too incredulous, R.D. 1040; *ny-yllyr r. dha wordhya*, it is impossible to venerate Thee too much, O.M. 1852; *na-wreugh eva r.*, don't drink too much, P.; *r. a un dra ny-dal travyth*, too much of one thing is worth nothing, P.

re² (s,j)-, *optative and perfect verbal particle*, for uses see APPENDIX VII.

rē, see **rȳ**, APPENDIX VIII.

rēa, see **arȳa**.

reb, see **ryp(b)**.

rebel, *m.*, *pl.* **-s**, rebel (M.E.).

rebellya, *vb.*, to rebel (M.E.).

rebellyans, *m.*, rebellion, rebellion, C.W. 293 (M.E. *rebelling*): see **rebellya**.

rebükya, *vb.*, to rebuke, M.C. (M.E.): p. pt. is spelt *rebekis* M.C. 2, suggesting *ü* elsewhere; scansion suggests pr. *re·bükya*.

receva, resseva (*resceva*), *vb.*, to receive, admit (M.E.): 3 s. pres.-fut., 2 s. imp. *recef*: requires *dhe*, *recef e dhys*, take it, *r. dhys*, take, *ef a-n-recevas dodho-ef*, he received him, cf. *kemer e dhys* and D. "take 'n to 'ee"; scansion suggests pr. *re·ceva*.

rech, *m.*, *pl.* **-ys**, scent-hound, running hound, B.M. 3166 (M.E.): the *rech* or *rach* was the hound proper, as distinguished from the *lymer*, kept on a leash, or the *grehond*, used for coursing or hunting by sight.

record, *m.*, *pl.* **-ys**, record, witness, register, O.M., C.W. (M.E.).

recorda, *m.*, *pl.*, **-dys**, recorder, flûte anglaise, musical instrument, O.M. 2000 (M.E.).

recordya, *vb.*, to record, witness, B.M. 1629 (M.E.).

redempsyon (*-cyon, -con*), *m.*, redemption, C.W. 286, 2543 (M.E.).

redenek, *f.*, *pls.* **-egow, -egy**, fern-brake; *adj.*, ferny; place-name Redennick.

redenen, *f.*, *col.* **reden**, fern, bracken, C. Voc., *fearn* Aelfric: *r. ruth*, bracken turned red, Lh.; *r.-derow*, *r. gwyth*, oak-fern, polypody (B.); ***r.** *an myghtern*, royal fern; Splat an Redan (fern plot), place-name.

redy, *adv.*, readily (M.E.): see **sür-redy, yredy**.

rēdya (Borlase MS. *riddia*), *vb.*, to read (O.E. *raedan*): 3 s. subj. *retyo*; this early replaced **len**, see **rēdyor**.

†redyk (C. Voc. *redic*), *m.*, *pl.* **-ygow**, radish, *raedic* Aelfric (O.E.).

†rēdyor (C. Voc. *redior*), *m.*, *pl.* **-yon**, reader, *raedere* Aelfric (O.E.).

†rēdyores (C. Voc. *rediores*), *f.*, *pl.* **-ow**, reading woman, *raedistere* Aelfric.

rēf (C. Voc. *ruif*. Lh. *rēv*), *f.*, *pl.* **revow**, shovel, Lh.; oar, C. Voc., *rodher* Aelfric: *r.-tan*, fire-shovel, Lh.

†rēf, see **†ruy**.

ref (*reff*), *m.*, presumption, assumption, as W. *rhyf*: *ny th-whelaf, kyn cowsaf orthys dre r.*, I see thee not, though I speak to thee at a venture, lit. by presumption, B.M. 2555.

rēgnya, raynya, *vb.*, to reign, B.M., C.W. (M.E. *regne*): p. pt. *regnyes* is used as meaning "reigning," B.M. 760, cf. **annedhy, nyja, tryga**; see **kesrēgnya**.

***regy**, *vb.*, to tear: 3 s. pret. *rogas*; 2 s. imp. *rōk* (W., B.): replaced by **squardya**.

†regythen (C. Voc. *regi(h)ten*), *f.*, *col.* **regyth** (as B *regez*), live coal, glowing charcoal, ember, gleed, *glēd* Aelfric.

rejoycya (*regoyssya*), *vb.*, to rejoice, C.W. (M.E.).

reken, *m.*, *pl.* **-knys**, bill, account, reckoning, B.M. 2836, A. Boorde (M.E.).

rekna, *vb.*, to reckon, count, number, cast up accounts, B.M., C.W. (M.E. *rekne*): *r. gans*, settle a difference with, B.M. 799.

***rem**, *m.*, rheumatism (B.).

remaynya, *vb.*, to remain, abide, stay, C.W. 2074 (M.E.).

remedy, *m.*, cure, help, remission, remedy, C.W. 425 (M.E.).

remembra, *vb.*, to remember, B.M., C.W. (M.E.).

remembrans, *m.*, remembrance: see **remembra**.

re·menant (*remenat* Lh.), *m.*, *pl.* **-ys**, remnant, remainder, B.M. 2503 (M.E.):

with *remenat* cf. *ramenet* in St. Columb Green Book.

remōsyon (*-moconn*), *m.*, removal, promotion (M.E. *remocyon*): in B.M. 2011, *r. dhe'n cur*, preferment at the court, is a mistranslation of *curarum remocio*, removal of cares, in *Vita Mereadoci*.

remüvya; **remūa** (*remmvve*), *vbs.*, to remove, change place, move, shift, stir, fidget (M.E. *remeve*, O. Fr. *remouvoir*, and M.E. *remuwe*, *-mewe*, Fr. *remuer*): as in M.E., the vbs. are somewhat mixed, p. pt. of *remua* seems *remuys* (*remmvys*) O.M. 2045, but *remufa* (*remvfe*), R.D. 396, is not *remu-fe*, fut., and must be imperf. subj. of *remuvya*; see **amüvya**, **müvya**.

***renk**, *m.*, *pl.* **-yow**, rank, row (W., B.).

renky (Lh. *renki,-a*), *vb.*, to snore, snort, croak, gurgle,

***renkya**, *vb.*, to rank in order (W., B.).

renkyas, *m.*, snorting, snoring, croak, rattle in throat, Lh.; pl. **-ysy**, snorer, snorter.

†**rennyas** (C. Voc. *renniat*), *m.*, *pl.* **-ysy**, carver, steward, seneschal, divider, distributor, *discthegn* Aelfric: see **ranna**.

rent, *m.*, *pl.* **-ys**, revenue, annual income, rent, B.M. 3264 (M.E.).

rē'outa, *m.*, dignity, regard, respect, honour, lit. royalty (M.E. *reauté*, *ryalté*).

repentya, *vb.*, to repent, C.W. (M.E.).

repre'f (*-eff*), *m.*, reproof, rebuke, blame, B.M. 1770 (M.E.).

reprefa, **repryfa**, *vb.*, to reprove, censure, reproach, reprobate, O.M., B.M. (M.E. *repreve*): 3 s. pres.-fut., 2 s. imp. *repref*.

requyrya, *vb.*, to require, request, call on, entreat, demand. P.C., C.W. (M.E. *requeren*).

rēs, **rȳs** (*reys*), *m.*, need, necessity, occasion: *r. yu dhym*, I must; *pan vo r.*, when there is occasion; see **porres**.

rēs, *def. vb.*, it is necessary, it behoves, 3. s. pres. only: *mar dha del r.*, as well as need be; *ny-r. dhys*, thou needst not, etc. (in Late Cor. only, *my a-r.*, I must, etc.).

†**rēs** (C. Voc. *c(h)a(h)en rit*), *m.*, course, race, running of water.

res (C. Voc. *rid*, O.E. Charters *hraet, hryd*), *f.*, *pl.* **-yow**, ford: place-names give mutations as after **rōs**, heathland; both of these words may be corrupted to Tres- or **Les-** and they are often confused in spelling.

rēs, *f.*, *pl.* **-yow**, row (W., B.).

rēsa, *vb.*, to set in line, arrange (W., B.): E.D. "race" coincides with this.

resegyth, *m.*, *pl.* **-ydhyon**, racer, runner (W.).

resek, *vb.*, to run: 3 s. pres. -fut. *rēs*; used of water, roots, vehicles, etc., as well as of living creatures.

†**resekva** (C. Voc. *redegva*), *f.*, *pl.* **-ow**, course, race, career, orbit of heavenly body, *ryne* Aelfric.

reseva, see **receva**.

resna (for *resona*), *vb.*, to reason, C.W. 2395 (M.E.).

Resōghen, *f.*, Oxford (W.): Lh. makes this *Red Ousk*.

rēson, *m.*, *pl.* **-s**, reason, argument (M.E. *resoun*): *mes a r.*, unreasonable.

resor, *m.*, *pl.* **-yon**, runner, courier, racer (W., B.).

resortya, *vb.*, to resort (M.E.); *r. dhe*, rally round, B.M. 2269.

rester, *f.*, *pl.* **-try**, arrangement (W.): see **restry**.

restorya, *vb.*, to restore, return, give back, B.M. (M.E.).

resto'ryta, *m.*, restitution, restoration (M.E.): *gul r. dhe*, make amends to, compensate, indemnify, B.M. 2178.

restrer, *m.*, comb (D. "ruster," "rustring-comb").

restry, *vb.*, to arrange, make tidy: 3 s. pres. -fut. *rester* (D. "ruster," to comb hair).

restya, *vb.*, to rest, remain fixed (M.E. *reste*): *synsy gu dhe r.*, to couch a spear in rest, R.D. 2586.

restys, see **rostya**.

***rēth**, *f.*, *pl.* **-yow**, right, law, order (W., B.)

***rēthya**, *vb.*, to regulate, fix a law (B.).

†**revador**, **-jor** (C. Voc. *ruifadur*), *m.*, *pl.* **-yon**, rower, oarsman, seaman in oared vessel, galley-slave, *redhra* Aelfric.

†**revaneth** (C. Voc. *ruifanaid*), *m.*, kingdom, *rice* Aelfric.

†**revanes** (C. Voc. *ruifanes*), *f.*, *pl.* **-ow**, queen: see †**ruy**.

rever, *m.*, *pl.* **-vrow**, fundament, rump, anus (W., B.).

***reverthy**, *m.*, *pl.* **-ow**, flood, inundation, overflow, high tide, torrent (W., B.).

reveth, **reva** (Lh. *revedh*), *adj.*, strange, astounding, surprising: ***nebes agan tyr, agan treveth, ha byghan r.,*** loosely translated "a little heritage of homely race", N. Boson, suggests *reveth* as a noun also; see **arȳa.**

revrek, *adj.*, big-rumped (W., B.).

revrond, *adj.*, reverend (M.E.).

revrons (*reverons*, 2 syllables, C.W. *refrance*), *m.*, respect, reverence (M.E.): **saw r.*, **saw dha r.*, save reverence, expression of apology for mentioning anything offensive (M.E.): *r. dhyso*, respect to thee (a greeting), R.D. 495.

revya, reva, *vb.*, to row, paddle (W., B.).

revyans, *m.*, rowing: see **revya.**

rew (C. Voc. *reu*), *m.*, frost, ice, C.W., Lh.

rew, *m.*, row, succession, line: *yn r.*, *yn un r.*, one after another, in line, file, or procession, in close succession, without intermission (M.E. *upon a row, on a rewe, by rewe*, etc.).

†**rew,** see **ruy.**

rewardya, *vb.*, to reward, Ord., B.M. (M.E.).

***rewhans,** *m.*, span, measure (W., B.).

***rewhansa,** *vb.*, to measure by spanning, span (W., B.).

rewl (Late *rowl*), *m.*, *pl.* **-ys,** rule, order, regulation, management, direction: *kemer dha r. dha-honen*, be thy own guide, have thy own way, B.M. 504.

rewler (Late *rowler*), *m.*, *pl.* **-loryon,** ruler.

rewlya (Late *rowlya*), *vb.*, to rule, regulate, guide, decide, set in order.

rewy, *vb.*, to freeze, B.M. 3057.

rō, *m.*, *pl.* **-ow, -how,** gift, present, donation, endowment: see **rȳ.**

robbya, *vb.*, to plunder, rob, B.M., Lh. (M.E.).

robbyor (C. Voc. *robbior*), *m.*, *pls.* **-yon, -s,** brigand, robber, *reafere* Aelfric (O. Fr. *robeour*, from Frankish).

†**rōcha** (C. Voc. *roche*), *m.*, *pl.* **-chys,** thornback, roker, *reohche* Aelfric (O.E.): see **carlyth, morgath, talver.**

***rōgh,** *m.*, *pl.* **-ow,** grunt (W., B.).

***rōgha,** *vb.*, to grunt like a pig (W., B.).

***rōk,** *m.*, *pl.* **rogow,** rent, tear (W., B.): replaced by **squard**; see ***regy.**

rōl, *f.*, *pl.* **-yow,** roll, list, P.C., B.M. (M.E.): **r.-scryfa*, scroll.

rolbren, *m.*, *pl.* **-nyer,** roller (W.).

rollo, etc., see **rȳ.**

rolven, *m.*, *pl.* **-veyn,** stone-roller.

rōlya, *vb.*, to enrol (B.).

rolya, rulya (Lh. *rhullio*), *vb.*, to roll, trundle, wheel a barrow (D. "rully"): 3 s. pres.-fut. *rol.*

rōm, *m.*, *pl.* **-ys,** room, division in a boat, O.M., C.W., D. (M.E. *roum*).

Rōm, *f.*, Rome, B.M. 2514: *Reven*, Lh., is from W.

rond (*round* Lh.), *adj.*, round, B.M. 3408 (M.E.).

ronk, *adj.*, hoarse, croaking, hollow-voiced, D. "runky"; *m.*, snort, croak, snore, gurgle, rattle in throat: see **renky.**

rōs, *f.*, *pl.* **-yow,** heathland, moor; promontory, isthmus, peninsula, as Ir. and Gael. *ros*, in Roseland, Eglos Rose; ?hill (B.): in place-names often *ros*[4]; *s.* prevents mutation of following *c, k, d, p, t.*

rōs (C. Voc. *ruid*, Lh. *rūz*), *f.*, *pl.* **-ow,** net: *towl r.!* cast net! (D. "cowl rooze," "tola rooze").

rōs, *f.*, *pl.* **-ow,** wheel, Lh.; circle, circuit (W.): *r. dynsak*, cog-wheel (B.); *s* prevents mutation of following *c, k, d, p, t.*

rōs, see **rȳ.**

rōsa-noblen, *f.*, *pl.* **-now,** rose-noble, gold coin, value 6/8, B.M. 2881 (M.E.).

***rosella,** *vb.*, to whirl, spin round; 3 s. pres.-fut. *rosel* (B.).

rosen, *f.*, *pl.* **-now,** *col.* **rōs,** rose: *r.-ky*, dog-rose; *r.-mogh*, poppy (W., B.).

rōsla, *m.*, *pl.* **-lēyow,** cart-rut, wheel-track (B.).

rostya, *vb.*, to roast, Lh.: p. pt. *restys*, P.C. 698, later *rostyes*, Lh.

rōsya, *vb.*, to stroll about, promenade, walk around (D.).

rōsyas, *m.*, walk, stroll (W.).

rōsyer, *m.*, *pl.* **-yoryon,** stroller, rambler (D. "rousy-vounder"): see **bounder,**

rōsyk-kenter, *m.*, rowel of spur (B.).

rōsyn (Late *rūzan*), *m.*, *pl.* **-now.** small net: Mean Ruzen, rock-name.

rōth (*roath*, Keigwin), *m.*, order, form: cf. W. *rhith* and vowel-change in **toth, nothlen, strotha,** B. *tiz, niza, striza*, W. *tuth, nithlen.*

rounsyn (*rounsan, rozan*), *m.*, *pl.* **-as,** nag (M.E. *rouncy*, Anglo-Fr. *runcin*, Ital. *ronzino*); in Late Cor. rendered as "ass" in versions of Commandment X., and in interpretation of Goon Rounsan, place-name, Gw.

rōw, *m.*, *pl.* **-ys,** row of houses, P.C. 2668 (M.E.).

row, *f.*, *pl.* **-ow,** bond, strop (D., B. *raou*).

roweth, *m.*, importance, prestige, personal consequence, dignity, high state or position, O.M. 884, B.M. 4539 : *r. an bys*, worldly rank, B.M. 357.

rowl, see **rewl.**

rowtor, *m.*, *pl.* **-s**, ruler, dominant, influential or controlling person, M.C. 100 (Fr. *routier*, guide, one who knows the way).

rowtya, *vb.*, to rule, direct, control, bear sway, domineer, B.M. 2368, 2453, C.W. 607, Kerew ; lit. to direct, from Fr. *route*: see **rowtor**.

roy, see **rȳ**.

rüdhak, *m.*, *pl.* **-dhogas**, robin (W.) : D. "ruddock," P., is E.

rüdhlas, *adj.*, purple (W.).

rüdhya, *vb.*, to redden, blush (W., B.).

rüdhyk, *adj.*, reddish, Lh.

rulya, see **rolya**.

rün, **-en**, see **rȳn**, **-en**.

rün (*ruen*, *royne*), *m.*, *pl* **-as**, seal, sea-calf: an Garrek Run, O.M. 2463, Caregroyne, Leland, the Black Rock, "Seal Rock," in Carrack Roads, Falmouth Harbour ; O. Cor. would be *rōn*, as Ir. and Gael. *rōn*, Manx *raun*, W. (*moel*) *rhon*, B. *reun(ig)*, seal.

rünen, *f.*, *col*, **rün** (*ruen*, Lh. *rēn*, *rean*), coarse hair, especially of mane or tail : *r. margh*, horsehair, Lh. MS. ; *r. mogh*, bristles ; *hevys r.*, cilice, hair-shirt, B.M. 1968.

rüsken, *f.*, *col.* **rüsk** (C. Voc. *rusc*), bark, rind, peel, *rinde* Aelfric (D. "risk").

rüskek, *adj.*, having bark, or peel, rough-barked.

†rūta (C. Voc. *rute*), *m.*, rue, the herb, *rude* Aelfric, Lat. *ruta*.

rūth, *f.*, *pl.* **-ow**, crowd, rout, troop, band, throng ; *r. vur*, a great multitude, M.C. 108, Kerew (?M.E. *route*).

rüth (*ruyth*, C. Voc. *rud*, Lh. *rydh*), *adj.*, red, scarlet, Ord.

rüthvelen, *adj.*, orange, tawny (W.).

rūthy, *vb.*, to relent, have ruth, take pity, B.M. 908 (M.E. *rewthe*, *routh*, pity).

ruttya (Lh. *rhuttia*), *vb.*, to rub down, apply friction to (D. "rut").

†truy(f) (C. Voc. *ruy*, *ruif*), *m.*, *pl.* **-vaneth** (M.B. *rouanez*)) ruler, king : replaced by **myghtern** ; if M. Cor., *ruy* might have become *rew*, and *ruif* have become *rēf*, cf. vowel-change in *Dew*, *plu* (*plew*), O. Cor. *Duy*, *plui*, B. *Doue*, *ploue*, *roue*, and *rēf*, oar.

rȳ (*rey*, Late *rei*), *irreg. vb.*, to give, grant, deliver, accord, bestow : for parts see Appendix VIII : *pandra* (*pyth a-*) *vynnough dhym dhe r. ha* (*my-a-wra*, etc.), what are you willing to give me if (I do, etc.), M.C. 39, P.C. 586, B.M. 1458 ; 3 s. pret. is used as "made" in *re Dhew a-m-ros*, by God that made me, B.M., C.W. ; *Dew re-th-ros flowr hy hynsa*, God has created thee most perfect of thy (lit. her) kind, O.M. 2136, *re'n Arluth dhe'n bys a m-ros*, B.M. 2252, shows how "gave to the world" is implied elsewhere ; *roy* alone is used for *re-roy*, may he grant, and as 2 s. imp. before vowels, *roy e* (printed *rog ha*) seems an accepted var. of *ro va* in *Image of Idlenesse* sentence, c. 1570.

rȳal (*-el*, C.W. *reall*), *adj.*, royal, kingly, regal, noble, supreme, splendid, magnificent: probably from Lat. as W. *rhial*, B. *real*, but coinciding with M.E. *riall*, *real*, see **rēouta**.

†rȳas (C. Voc. *reiat*), *m.*, *pl.* **ryesy**, giver, one who administers (medicine, poison, etc.).

rȳans, *m.*, act of giving : see **rȳ**.

ryb, see **ryp(b)**,

rybon, *adv.*, close by, near at hand, lit. by us, P.C. 460,

***rybyn**, *m.*, streak, line (W., B.).

rych, *adj.*, rich, sumptuous, M.C., Ord., B.M. (M.E.) : replaces **†golüsak.**

rychys, **rychyth**, *m.*, wealth, riches, B.M. (M.E. *richesse*) : with *rychyth* cf. **fath**, **oyeth**, etc.

rydel, *m.*, *pl.* **-low**, coarse sieve, riddle (W., B., D.).

ryder (Lh. *ridar*), *m.*, *pl.* **-drow**, sieve, riddle : see **crōder.**

rydra, *vb.*, to sift, as grain from chaff : see **crodra.**

rȳelder (*reelder*), *m.*, splendour, pomp, magnificence, B.M. 2942.

***rȳf**, *m.*, *pl.* **rȳvow**, number (W.) : kept in **derȳvas**, cf. Fr. *conter* from Lat. *computare*, Eng. "tell," "account."

***rygol**, *m.*, groove, trench (W., B.).

***rygolya**, *vb.*, to trench (W., B.).

rygthy, see **rak(g)**,

ryll, *m.*, *pl.* **-yow**, cleft, furrow, sloping side of heap (D.).) : Rill, place-name.

rȳm (*rim* N. Boson), *m.*, *pl.* **-ys**, rhyme, rhymed verse (M.E. *rym*).

rȳmya, *vb.*, to rhyme (M.E.) : see **rȳm.**

ryn, rün, *m.*, *pl.* **-yow**, promontory, projecting ground, hill, hill-side, slope: Bodrean, Treen, Penryn, place-names; the meaning "hill," as in W., B. and P.C. 2654, seems very rare in place-names.
***ryn**, *m.*, *pl.* **-yow**, secret, mystery (W., B.); see ***kevryn**.
†rynen, rünen, *f.*, *pl.* **-now**, hillock, burrow, C. Voc., *hyl* or *beorh* Aelfric.
†rynk (C. Voc. *rinc*), *f.*, *pl.* **ryncas**, quail, "arish-hen," *ersc hen* Aelfric.
rynny, *vb.*, ? to shiver with cold or to puff smoke, blow off steam, R.D. 2343: W. *rhynnu* has either meaning and the mediaeval hell was a place of extreme cold alternating with fire, but a volcano seems likely to be described.
rynnys, see **ranna**.
ryp(b) (Late *reb*), *prep.*, beside, by, hard by, close to, combines with prons., see APPENDIX V.; *m.*, (in compounds) bank, side: see **dorrep, morrep**.
ryth (C. Voc, *ruid, rid*), *f.*, kind, sex: used as suffix, see **gorryth, benenryth**.
ryth, *adj.*, clear, free, open, plain: Goon Reeth, Wheal Reath, place-names.
rythsys, *m.*, freedom, liberty, openness (W.).
ryver, *m.*, *pl.* **-s**, river, stream, B.M. 1141 (M.E.).

S

-s-, *infixed prons.*, her, it(f.); you (contraction of *-gas-*), them.
-sa, -ja, *suffixed pron.*, thou: softened form of **-ta**, used only with *os*, the *s* of which then disappears.
sa', see **sevel**.
saben (*zaban* Lh.), *f.*, *col.* **sap**, fir-tree, pine: *aval s.*, fir-cone; *plankys s.*, deal bords; *nasweth-s.*, *najeth-s*, pine-needle; see **sybwedhen, pynbren**.
Sabot (*-bout*), *m.*, Sabbath, P.C. (M.E.).
sacra, *vb.*, to consecrate, ordain as priest (M.E. *sacren*): *dhe epscop gwraf dha s.*, I consecrate thee as a bishop, O.M. 2614 (*dhe* is optional, cf. B.M. 2952, 3021).
sacrement, *m.*, *pls.* **-mens, -s**, sacrament (M.E): *an sacrements seyth*, the seven sacraments, B.M. 997.
sacry·fya (*sacrefie*), *vb.*, to sacrifice, P.C. 626 (M.E. *sacryfye*): 3 s. pres.-fut. *sacryfy*.
sa·cryfys (*-fyth*, B.M. *sakyrfeys*), *m.*, *pl.* **-ys**, sacrifice (M.E.).
sacry·fysa (*sacrifice*), *vb.*, to sacrifice, C.W. 2487: later var. of **sacryfya**.
***sacrylych**, *m.*, sacrilege (M.E.).
sad (*sadt*), *adj.*, sober, grave, staid, steadfast, firm, fixed, steady, constant, serious (M.E.): *ow husul yu s.*, my advice is unwavering, R.D. 1593; *torment s.*, unfailing torment, O.M. 491.
Sadorn, de-, du-S., *m.*, day of Saturn, Saturday.
saf, *m.*, stand, erect posture, stance: with *a* and poss. pron., *a'y s.*, *a'm s.*, etc., straight, erect, upright, up, on end, standing.
saf, saffo, etc., see **sevel**.
***safron, safern**, *m.*, saffron (E.): *s. an jawl*, dodder (D. "devil's saffron", cf B. *bleo-diaoul*, "devil's hair").
safla (*le*), *m.*, *pl.* **-ow**, position (W.).
sagh (C. Voc. *sach*, *zah* Lh.), *m.*, *pl.* **-ow**, sack, bag: *s. dorn*, hand-bag; *†s. dyawl*, demoniac, lit. devil-sack, *deofolseoc* Aelfric (?O.E. *seoc*, sick, mistranslated as *saec*, sack; B. *sac'h-diaoul*, like W. *sach diawl* is from C. Voc. *sach diauol*); *s. eskern*, thin person (B.); *s. wheth*, wind-bag, wordy speaker (B.); *s. bos*, stomach (B.).
sagha, *vb.*, to put in a bag (W., B.).
saghlen, *m.*, *pl.* **-now; saghlyen**, *f.*, *pl.* **-nyow**, sackcloth (W.).
saghwysk, *f.*, sackcloth garments (W.).
sal (*zal*), *adj.*, salted, salt: *pysk s.*, salt fish; *dowr s.* brine (Lh., J. Boson).
salla (*zalla* Lh.), *vb.*, to salt: p. pt. *sellys* Lh., *sallys* J. Boson),
***salm**, *m.*, *pl.* **-ow**, psalm (W., B.).
salmus, *m.*, *pl.* **-ys** (*psalmus*, O.M. 1998), shawm, oboe-like instrument (M.E. *shalmus*, var. of *shalme*, O. Fr. *chalemie*).
salow, *adj.*, sound, healthy, whole, out of danger, B.M. 1513, 1710: see **sylwel**.
salujy, -usy, *vb.*, to salute, P.C., C.W.: 3 s. pres.-fut. *salus* (M.E. *saluse*).
salvador (?*v* for *w*), *m.*, saviour, C.W. 1865: see **sylwador**.
salvasyon (*-vasconn*), *m.*, salvation, B.M. 1248 (M.E.).
***salyour**, *m.*, *pl.* **-s**, salt-box, salt-cellar (M.E.).
sampel (*sompel*, N. Boson, *sampl* Lh.), example, instance, precedent (M.E. *ensampel, essample*): *rag s.*, for instance, Lh.; *oll an s.* the whole matter, N. Boson.
sampla, *vb.*, to sample (E.).

sandal, *m.*, *pl.* **-ys**, sandal (E.).

***sans** (*zanz* Lh.), *m.*, *pl.* **syns**, holy man, saint (not as title, see **Sen, Synt**); *adj.*, holy, sacred: final *s* has become hard in place-name Penzance as in Trenance, etc., see **nans**.

sanses, *f.*, *pl.* **-ow**, holy woman, saint (not as title, see **Synta**), B.M. 579.

sansoleth, *m.*, holiness, sanctity, saintliness, B.M. 137.

sansour, *m.*, *pl.* **-s**, censer (M.E. in stage-direction B.M. p. 256).

sansyl, **†-ol**, saintly (W., B.): see **sansoleth**.

†sant, *m.*, dish, course, meal, mess, lit. what is "sent" (as "mess" from Med. Lat. *missum*), C. Voc. (O.E.), *sand* Aelfric.

sarf, *f.*, *pl.* **syrf**, **sarfy**, serpent, O.M. 286, 797.

***sarn**, *f.*, *pl.* **-ow**, causeway, stepping-stones (W.): ? in place-name Rejarn if *res s.*; see **causn**.

Sarsyn, *m.*, *pl.* **-s**, Saracen, Moor, Moslem, Mahometan, P.C. 2027 (M.E.): see **Mahom**.

Sarsynek, *adj.*, Saracenic, Moorish, Moslem, Mahometan, Mohammedan.

Satnas, Sattenas, Satan, *m.*, Satan (M.E. *Satanas*).

Saun (*sawn* Lh. MS., "*zawn*" D.), *f.*, *pl.* **-yow**, deep gorge in cliffs, extending below sea-level: lit. mouth, as W. *safn*, cf. B. *saon(enn)*, valley.

***sautour**, *m.*, *pl.* **-s**, psalter (M.E.).

sautry, *m.*, *pl.* **-s**, psaltery, zither-like instrument, O.M. 1997 (M.E.).

Sāvyour (*Savyur*), *m.*, *pl.* **-s**, Saviour, Redeemer, B.M. 4226 (M.E.).

saw (Late *save*, ? for *sawgh* as W. *sawch*), *m.*, back load, horseload, Ord., P.: *ny-dal tus perna cunys wor an s.*, folk ought not to buy fuel by the horseload, Gw.

saw (later *sow*, *sowe*), *adj.*, safe, sound, whole, hale, healed, well; *adv.*, *conj.*, save, except, unless, only, but (M.E. *sauf*); *s. oll on nyny a'gan dyses*, we are all cured of our afflictions, O.M. 2024; *ny-lettys s. un lam*, I only stopped a moment, O.M. 470; *dha lef y-glewaf, s. dha fas my ny-welaf*, I hear thy voice, but I cannot see thy face, O.M. 588; *s. gwell avys*, with deference to better opinion, B.M. 2700; *s. dha revrons, s. agas gras*, with apologies (for mention or contradiction (M.E. *sauf reverance, sauf your grace*).

sawder, *m.*, safety, preservation, Keigwin, King Chas. Letter: late var. of **sawment**.

sawment, *m.*, *pl.* **-mens**, preservation, security, safety, safe-keeping, C.W. 2184; salve, remedy, B.M. 1373 (M.E.).

sawor (*sawer*, B.M., C.W.), *m.*, *pl.* **-yow**, fragrance, savour, flavour, odour, taste, O.M, 1740, 1991.

sa'woren (Lh. *sawarn*), *f.*, *pl.* **-now**, odour, taste.

sa'worek, *adj.*, savoury, fragrant (B.).

sa'wory, *vb.*, to savour, taste (W., B.): *saworys mas*, well flavoured (B.).

Saws (*Sows*), *m.*, *pl.***-on** (*an Zawson* Lh.), Saxon, Englishman: *Bro Saws, Pow Saws, Pow an Sawson*, England. Lh., Gw.

Sawses, *f.*, *pl.* **-ow**, Englishwoman (W., B.).

Sawsnek (Late *Sowsnack*, Lh. *Zowznak*), *adj.* English, Saxon; *m.*, English language.

sawthan, *m.*, surprize, amazement, bewilderment (B.).

sawthanas (*sowthanas*), *vb.*, to surprise, startle, mislead, take unawares, bewilder, stupefy, err, lead or go astray, P.C. 610, 2417: p. pt. *sawthenys*, 3 s. pres.-fut. *sawthan*; *s. yn-mes a bup for'*, to wander entirely from the point or lead others entirely off the track, become extravagantly misled.

sawya (Late *sowia*), *vb.*, to save, preserve, heal, cure, salve, anoint with healing ointment, M.C. 37; be healed, recover, O.M. 1762 (M.E. *sawen*): *s. a*, to save from, cure of; cf. **sylwel**.

sawys, *m.*, health, soundness: *may 's-teffo lun yeghes ... ha s. a bup cleves*, that they may have complete health ... and soundness from every sickness, B.M. 4289.

saya, *m.*, light fine serge, say; *vb.*, to bolt flour, sift through say (M.E. *saye*, Med. Lat. *sagium*): place-name Melyn Saya, Vellan Sajia, sifting-mill, bolting-mill.

saya, see **assaya**.

saym (*seym* O.M., *saim* J. Boson), *m.*, train-oil, pilchard-oil, O.M. 2708 (M.E. *sayme*, O. Fr. *saing*, Med. Lat. *saginum*).

scaf (B.M. *schaff*, CW. *skave*), *adj.*, light, nimble, swift, quick; *adv.*, lightly, easily, quickly: *s. y ben*, featherheaded (B.); *s. y dros*, light-footed, swift, cf. M.E. Lyght of Fout, Lyghtfoude, a messenger, P,C. 1532, R.D. 1606, and Lyghtfote, messenger

in Townely Plays.
scafhē·, *vb.*, to lighten : as **berhē**.
scafter, -der (Lh. *scavder*), *m.*, lightness.
scajyn, *m.*, *pl.* **-now**, a vagabond (D. "scadgan") : ? from **cas**.
scala, *m.*, *pl*- **-ys**, shallow bowl or dish, saucer, C. Voc. (Frankish, O. Fr. *escale*), *bledu* Aelfric.
scaldya (*sk-*, *scl-* for *sch-*), *vb.*, to burn, inflame, scald, B.M. 2107, 3059 (M.E.).
scant (*sch-*), *adj.*, scarce, scanty ; *adv.*, hardly, scarcely (M.E.) : *mur a s.*, extremely scarce, B.M. 658 ; with neg., *s. ny-welaf un banna*, I hardly see a bit, C.W. 1461.
***scanten**, *f.*, *pl.* **-now**, *col.*, **scant**, scale of fish or reptile, flake, lamina (B.).
***scantek**, *adj.*, scaly, flaky (B.).
scantlowr, *adv.*, hardly, scarcely, barely, lit. scarce enough: used without neg., *s. y-hallaf*, *s. y-hylly*, I can, he could scarcely; *my a-wruk s. clewes*, I hardly heard, Wm. Bodener.
scantlyn, *m.*, *pl.* **-s.** foot-rule, measure, pattern, scantling, O.M. 2510 (M.E. *scantilon*, Anglo-Fr. *escauntilon*).
scapya (B.M. *schappya*), *vb.*, to escape (M.E. *scapen*, *aschape*, O. Fr. *eschaper*, *escaper*).
scar, *m.*, separation ; *vb.*, to separate (W., B.) : kept only in **kescar**.
scarf, *m.*, *pl.* **-ys**, scarf, long joint in timber, O.M. 2530 (M.E.).
scarfa, *vb.*, to scarf timber, O.M. 2523 (M.E.).
***scartha**, *vb.*, to clear, clean, scour (W., B.): see **cartha**.
scat, -tya, see **squat, -tya**.
scath, *f.*, *pl.* **-ow**, boat : *s.-hyr*, longboat ; *s.-ros*, seine-boat, Lh. ; *s.-clos*, raft ; Carn Scath, Porth Scathow, place-names.
scattra, *vb.*, to scatter, Borlase MS. (E.) : *yma scattrys* (Lh. *sgattrez*) *gans an gwyns mar vur pluf*, so many feathers are scattered by the wind.
scaun, -sken (†*scaven*), *m.*, *pl.* **-yow**, bench (Lat. *scamnum*) : kept only in **masken**.
scavel (C. Voc. *scauel*), *f.*, *pl.* **-low**, bench, stool, *sceamul* Aelfric : *s. -dros*, footstool, C.W. 20 ; *s. an gow*, scandal-party, gossip (D.) ; *s.-cronek*, mushroom, toadstool (B.).
scawen, *f.*, *col.* **scaw** (D. "scow"), elder-tree ; *s. dor*, *s. benygys* (W.), *s. byghan* (B.), dwarf elder ; *s. gwragh*, maple (B.) ; *s. dowr*, figwort ; *s. cough*, belladonna ; *s. du*, hemp-agrimony (D. ; place-names, Boscawen, Tresco, Trescaw, Inis Schawe (*enys scaw*), Leland.
scawennek, *f.*, *pl.* **-egy**, **-egow**, elder-grove (B.).
sch-, see **sc-**, **sk-**, **sh-**.
sclander, *m.*, scandal, slander (M.E.).
sclandra, *vb*, to accuse, reproach, scandalize, offend, slander (M.E. *sclaundre*, O. Fr. *esclandre*, Lat. *scandalum*).
sclew, *m.*, defence, shelter.
sclewy, *vb.*, to shelter : p. pt. *sclewys*, field-name Sclewes.
scoch-forth, *f.*, *pl.* **-ordhow**, short-cut, alley, passage between buildings : cf. E. Dial. Dic. "scotch," to curtail, cut short "scotch," "scutchell," "twitch," "twitchel", narrow opening, passage, short-cut.
***scochon**, *m.*, *pl.* **-s**, escutcheon, blazoned shield, coat-of-arms (M.E.).
scodhak, *adj.*, broad-shouldered (W., B.).
†**scodhlȳen** (C. Voc. *scuidlien*), *m.*, *pl.* **-now**, priest's amice, *sculdorhraegl* Aelfric : see **scōth, lȳen**.
scōdhya, scoudhya, *vb.*, to lean a shoulder on, put a shoulder to ; support (Keigwin) ; depend on (N. Boson) : 3 s. pres. -fut. *scōth*; *th* also in 2 and 3 subj. and before *s*.
scogyn (*scoggan*, Borlase), *m.*, *pl.* **-now**, fool ; boiled mackerel's head (D. "scoggan") ; possibly for **müscogyn**, but cf. W. *ysgogyn*, fop.
scōl, *f.*, *pl.* **-yow**, school, C. Voc., B.M.
scoler (*skolar* Lh.), *m.*, *pl.* **-loryon, -yow**, (*-io* Lh.), scholar, schoolboy.
scolhygȳeth, *f.*, scholarship, scholarliness (W.).
†**scolhȳk** (C. Voc. *scolheic*), *m.*, *pl.* **-ygyon**, scholar, schoolman, student, *scolman* Aelfric.
scolhyksys, *m.*, scholarship (W.).
scoljy, *m.*, *pl.* **-ow**, school-house (W.).
scolk, *m.*, *pl.* **-ys**, sneak (D.E.).
scolkya (*-chya*), *vb.*, to skulk, sneak, slink, stalk, be furtive, keep oneself hidden, lurk, M.C. 74, P.C. 1002 (M.E.) : *scolkyeugh dhy yn-dan-dava*, approach him stealthily, continually feeling your way ; *why a-dheth dhym ... yn-un-s.*, you have come slinking up to me, approached me clandestinely, surreptitiously.
scollya, see **scullya**,

scommyn (*scobman* Borlase), *m.*, *pl.* **scommow** (D. "scubma"), chip, splinter; pl. matchwood, kindlings, wreckage: as W. *(go)sgymon*, see ***kemena**.

scon, *adj.*, quick; *adv.*, quickly, forthwith, at once, soon: *yn-s.*, with all speed: *marthus s.*, suddenly; *dhe sconna*, the sooner (N. Boson.).

sconya, *vb.*, to refuse, deny, withold, reject, object, object to, decline to comply with shun (O.E. *scunian*).

scoren (C. Voc. *scorren*), *f.*, *pl.* **-now**, *col.* **scōr**, main branch, bough; bowed stick, used by butchers to hang carcase on; see **skyren**.

scorja, scorjya, *m.*, *pls.* **-ys, -yes**, scourge, whip used to chastise (M.E. *scorge*).

scorjya, *vb.*, to scourge (M.E.).

scorn, *m.*, mockery, affront, P.C. 349, B.M. 368 (M.E.): *s. oll a'n pow* the laughing-stock of all the county.

scornya, *vb.*, to mock, jest at, make a laughing-stock of, trifle with, affront (M.E.).

scorrek, *adj.*, branched (B.).

scōs, *m.*, *pl.* **-ojow**, shield, buckler; (figuratively) protection, defence, as W. *ysgwyd*, B. *skoed*: *mercy yu s. dhe nep a-n-pys*, mercy is a shield for him who asks it, P.C. 22 (printed *stos*, but clearly *scos* in MS.).

scōswas, *m.*, *pl.* **-wesyon**, shield-bearer, esquire (W.).

scot, *m.*, *pl.* **-tys**, tavern-reckoning, shot, B.M. 3340 (M.E.)

scōth, scouth (C. Voc. *scuid*, Late *scūth*, *skooth*), *f.*, *pl.* **-odhow**, *d.* **dywscōth** (*duscouth*), shoulder: *ryp dha s.*, close beside thee, B.M. 1244: no mutation in following *c, k, d, p, t*.

scout, see **scowt**.

scovarn (C. Voc. *scouarn*), *f.*, *pl.* **-ow**, *d.* **dywscovarn**, ear, handle of jar, pitcher, wheelbarrow, etc.: *ry agan gwella s. dodho*, pay him our best attention to him, J. Tonkin, Gw.

scovarnak (C. Voc. *scovarnoc*), *adj.*, long-eared, handled; *f.*, *pl.* **-nogas**, hare (D. "scavernick"): *s. vyghan*, leveret.

scovva (for O.C. *scodva*, see **skēs, goscotter**), *f.*, shelter, shade, refuge; tabernacle, tent, booth, O.M. 1717: cf. **covva, hevva**.

scowl (C. Voc. *scoul*), *m.*, *pl.* **-as**, kite, *glida* Aelfric.

scowt (*scout*), *f.*, *pl.* **-ys**, skit, hoyden, wanton girl (M.E. *scowte*).

scravynyas (*skrivinas* Lh.), *vb.*, to scratch, claw.

scraw, *m.*, *pl.* **-as**, black-headed gull (W., B.).

scrawyk, *m.*, *pl.* **-ygow, -esygow**, tern; black-headed gull (D. "scarraweet").

***screw**, *m.*, *pl.* **-ys**, screw (E.).

scrogyn, *m.*, *pl.* **-now**, gallows-bird (D. "scroggan"): see **crōk**.

scrüth, *m.*, *pl.* **-ow**, shiver, shudder, trembling, horror, shrug: *s. own mur a-s-kemeras*, they were seized with a great shudder of terror, M.C. 254; *s. yu y glewes*, it is horrible to hear (B.).

scrütha, *vb.*, to shiver, shudder, tremble, shrug (W., B.): see **scrȳja**.

scrüthüs, -ys, *adj.*, horrible (B.).

scryf, *m.*, *pl.* **-yvow**, writing, bill, document, article (W., B.).

scryfa (Late *skreefa*, Lh. *skrepha*), *vb.*, to write: 3 s. pres.-fut. *scrȳf*; *men scryfys*, inscribed stone.

scryfa, scryva (for *scryveth*, C. Voc. *scriuit*), *m.*, *pl.* **-vadhow**, writing, writ: *s. pluven*, handwriting, penmanship, B.M. 71; *s.-composter*, orthography, N. Boson.

scryfer, *m.*, *pl.* **-foryon**, writer, scribe (W., B.).

scry·flyver, *m.*, *pl.* **-yfrow**, manuscript book, Lh.

scryfwas, *m.*, *pl.* **-wesyon**, clerk, quill-driver (W.).

scryfyas (*skrefiaz* Lh.), *m.*, *pl.* **-ysy**, writer.

scrȳja, *vb.*, ?to shriek, screech: 2 s. imp. *scryg*, R.D. 853, is *scryj*, rhymed with *treys* (for *dreyj*), and is not M.E. *skryke*; it may mean "tremble" cf. W. *ysgrydu* (var. of *ysgrythu*), B. *skrija*, suggesting possible Cor. *scrüsa* var. of **scrütha**.

scrymba, see **scrȳnva**.

scrynkya, *vb.*, to grin, snarl, grimace, show or gnash the teeth, O.M. 570, D. "skrink".

scrȳnva, *f.*, gnashing of teeth, R.D. 2344, as B. *skrign*: MS. has *skrȳva* with contraction-sign for either *m* or *n* over the *y*, read by Norris as "skrymba."

scryp, *m.*, *pl.* **-pys**, scrip, wallet attached to pilgrim's staff, P.C. 914 (M.E.).

Scryptor, *m.*, *pl.* **-s**, the Scriptures (M.E.): *an S. Benygys*, P.C., *S. Sans*, Lh., Holy Writ.

scryrya, *vb.*, to explain, interpret, describe,

M.C. 201 (M.E. *scry*, *scryve*, *descryve*, O. Fr. *descrire*).
***scryvell**, *f.*, *pl.* **-y**, curry-comb (W., B.): already replaced C. Voc. by **strȳl.**
scryven (C. Voc. *scriuen*), *f.*, *pl.* **-now**, writing: **†*s.*** *danvon*, note, missive, letter, *aerend gewrit* Aelfric; *s.-beth*, epitaph (W).
†scryvynyas (C. Voc. *scriuiniat*), *m.*, *pl.* **-ysy**, writer, scribe, secretary.
scüb, *m.*, sweeping; broom (W., B.).
scüba, *vb.*, to sweep, brush (W., B.).
scübel, *f.*, *pl.* **-bylly**, **-low**, besom, birch-broom (W.).
†scübylen (C. Voc. *scubilen*), *f.*, *pl.* **-now**, birchrod, scourge, *swipa* Aelfric; small brush or mop (B.); *s. forn*, malkin, baker's oven mop (B.).
scübyon, *pl.* sweepings (W., B.).
scüdel, **scūdel** (*skidal skūdel* Lh.), *f.*, *pls.* **-low**, **-ly**, dish, porringer, C. Voc., M.C. 43, D. "scuddle": *s. dowr*, water-lily (B.).
***scül**, **skēl**, *f.*, *pl.* **-yow**, ladder (W., B.).
scūl. **scōl**. *m.*, waste, neglect, carelessness: *tewlel dhe s.*, carelessly cast aside, treat wantonly; Keigwin.
scullya, **scollya**, *vb.*, to waste, shed, scatter, spill, pour: 3 s. pres. -fut. *scūl*, *scōl*.
scullyak, **scollyak**, *adj.*, wasteful; *m.*, *pl.* **-yogyon**, spendthrift, scapegrace (D. "scullyak").
scullyon, *pl.*, slops, scattered waste material (D. "scullion").
***scülya**, **skēlya**, *vb.*, to scale a wall, climb a ladder (B.).
scumbla, *vb.*, to evacuate (of animals or birds), to make a filthy mess, B.M. 3952 (M.E. and D. *scumber*).
scurel-wyrly, *adj.*, squirly-whirly, scampering and whirling about, dog's name, B.M. 3227: cf D.E. "squirl" Devon, "skerry-werry" Cor., *E. Dial. Dic.*
***scūrya**, *vb.*, to scour, cleanse (W., B.).
scüs, see **skēs**.
***scūsāsyon**, *m.*, excuse (M.E.).
scüsy, **skēsy**, *vb.*, to get away quickly, evade, frisk about, refuse to be caught (E.D. "skeeze"), or to take fright, start away, shy, see **skēs**: *pysk ragof ny-wra s.*, no fish shall escape from or elude me, O.M. 139; see **cavanscüsa.**
scüth, *m.*, misfortune, damage, loss, hurt, harm, injury, scathe, R.D. 2519, 2570 (O.E. *sceath*): perhaps *skēth* so spelt to rhyme with *rüth*.
scüthen (*skithen* Borlase MS.), *f.*, *pl.* **-as**, Manx shearwater, "pilchard-bird" (D. "skidden"): cf W. *ysguthan*, wood-pigeon.
sē, *m.*, *pl.* **-ys**. throne, seat (M.E.): *s. epscop*, bishop's throne, see in original sense; see **trygsa**.
sē', see **sēth**,
seban, *m.*, soap (Scawen, Borlase).
sebony, *vb.*, to soap, lather.
secu·nd (*second* C.W.), *ord. num.*, second, O.M. 17 (M.E. *secou·nde*).
sedca, see **esedha**.
sedhas, *m.*, sinking, setting (of sun): unless a late inf. replacing **sedhy**; see **howlsedhas.**
sedhek, *adj.*, sedentary (W.); *m.*, ? sitting-place, session, or tribunal, M.C. 77.
sedhor, *m.*, *pl.* **-yon**, diver, plunger (W.)
sedhy, *vb.*, to immerse, submerge, bathe, dip, sink, dive or plunge into water, founder: (of sun) set, sink below sea horizon: 3 s. pres. -fut. *sēth*; *saw y dreys na-vons sedhys*, except his feet that may not be bathed, P.C. 863.
sēf, see **sevel**,
sefryn, see **sovran**.
sēg, see **sēk(g)**.
sēgh (*seygh*, *sygh*, Lh. *zēh*), *adj.*, dry, parched, dessicated, withered, barred, arid.
sēgha (*seha* Lh.), *vb.*, to dry, wipe: p. pt. *seghys*, *syghys*; 2 s. pret. *syghsys*, R.D. 854.
sēghen, *f.*, *pl.* **-dow**, dry place, opposite to **dowren**; dead tree (B.): Bosseghen, Bronseghen, place-names.
sēghes (*zehaz* Lh.), *m.*, thirst: *s. dhym yma*, I am thirsty, I thirst.
sēghla (*lē*), *m.*, barren or waterless place: ? Zelah, Trezelah, place-names.
†sēghor (C. Voc. *sichor*), *m.*, drought, dryness, aridity, Lh.
sēghter, *m.*, dryness, aridity, Lh.
sēghtyr, *m.*, *pl.* **-yow**, dry land (W.).
sēgy, *vb.*, to steep, soak (W.): see **sēk(g)**.
***se·kerder**, *m.*, security, Lh. from W. *sicr*.
sēk(g) (*zeag*), *m.*, brewer's grains, draff, P.
†sēl, *f.*, *pl.* **-yow**, base, foundation, C. Voc., *grundweal* Aelfric.
sel, *f.*, *pl.* **-yow**, seal, impression: *s. pryva*, privy-seal, O.M. 2600.
selder (*selda* Lh.), *m.*, cellar: more probably E.D. "cellder," for "cellar,"

than **(y)selder** so used.

***sell**, *m.*, gaze, view (W., B.).

***sellos**, *vb.*, to look, view, as B. *sellout*: replaced by **mȳras**; *sylly*, Williams, W. *syllu*, is based on an old misreading of C.W. 784 (see **heveles**) and on *sylvyth*, O.M. 744, which should be read *nag esel-vyth nahen*, nor any other limb whatever.

selow, *vb.*, to attend, listen, hearken (W., B.): replaced by **goslowes**.

***selsygen**, *f.*, *pl.* **-now**, *col.* **selsyk**, sausage (W., B.): *kyk-s.*, sausage-meat (B.).

sēlven, *m.*, *pl.* **-veyn**, foundation-stone (W.): see **mēn** (*-lür*).

selwel, see **sylwel**.

selya, *vb.*, to seal (W., B.).

sēlya, *vb.*, to found (W.).

semlant, *m.*, *pl.* **-ans**, semblance, countenance, appearance, R.D. 2060 (M.E.).

semly (*sembly*, *semely*), *adj.*, *adv.*, seemly, comely; becomingly, C.W. 438, 1909.

sempel (*sympell*), *adj.*, simple, foolish, ordinary, plain, mere, insignificant, B.M., C.W. (M.E.).

sempelhē·, *vb.*, to simplify: as **berhē**.

Sen, *m.*, Saint, as title (M.E.): see **sans**, **Synt**.

sendal (*cendel* Ord., *sendall* M.C.), *m.*, fine linen (M.E. from M. Lat. *sindonum*).

†seneth (C. Voc. *sened*), *m.*, *pl.* **-edhow**, synod, ecclesiastical council, *sinodh* Aelfric; senate, parliament (W.).

senedhor, *m.*, *pl.* **-yon** (wrongly *-ezerrio* Lh.), member of synod; senator (W.).

sensy, see **synsy**.

Sent, see **Synt**.

sentry, *m.*, sanctuary, glebe-land (M.E.): place-names.

se·ntury (*centurie*), *m.*, centurion, M.C. 208, P.C. 3119.

seny, *vb.*, to sound, ring (W., B.): 2 s. imp, *son*; 3 s. pres.-fut. *sen*; subj. *sonno*; pret. *sonas*; plupf. *sonsa*; p. pt. *senys*.

†sēr (C. Voc. *sair*), *m.*, *pl.* **-y**, artificer: **†s.** *pren*, carpenter, woodworker, *treowwyrhta* Aelfric.

se·rafyn (*-phyn*), *m.*, seraph, O.M., C.W. (M.E., pl. as sing.).

***serfel**, *m.*, chervil (W., B.): see **†coifinel**, Appendix I.

sergh, *m.*, affection, attachment, over-fondness (W., B.).

sergha, *vb.*, to cling, cleave, adhere, attach oneself, be over-fond: *sergh war glegar*, lizard, lit. cliff-clinger (D. "sharagliggo").

†serghak (C. Voc. *(les) serchoc*), *adj.*, clinging, attached, over-loving.

serghegen, **seregen**, *f.*, *pl.* **-now**, goose-grass, cleavers; burdock (B.): may be distinguished as *s. vyghan*, *s. vras* respectively; see **†les-serghak**.

serghy, **serry**, *vb.*, to rise: kept only in **dasserghy**.

***serjont**, *m.*, *pl.* **-ns**, sergeant (M.E.).

serpont, *m.*, *pl.* **-ns** (C.W. *serpentys*, but old rhyme *-ans*), serpent (M.E.).

serry, *vb.*, to anger, vex, offend, provoke, discompose; to be angry or agitated: as **terry**; requires *orth* as prep. "with"; *ef re-sorras*, he has become angry.

serth, **ser'**, *adj.*, straight on end, erect, steep, upright, sheer, perpendicular, scarped, stiff, rigid, P.C. 2140: Penzer (*pen s.*), cliff-name.

serthals, *f.*, *pl.* **-yow**, precipice, sheer cliff (W.).

serthter, *m.*, steepness, stiffness (B.).

serthy, *vb.*, to rise steeply, stand straight up, stiffen (W.).

servont, *m.*, *pl.* **-ns** (*-nth*), servant (M.E.).

servya, *vb.*, to serve, do service, wait at table, suffice, serve the purpose, suit, do, prove adequate: 2 s. imp., 3 s. pres.-fut. *serf*, 3 s. subj. *servyo*; plupf. *serfsa*; *mar myn ow dyscans s. genough pan ven apposyes*, if my instruction will suffice when I am examined by you, B.M. 524.

servyas, *m.*, *pl.* **-ysy**, **-yjy**, server, servant, disciple.

***servyour**, *m.*, *pl.* **-s.**, server, tray (M.E.): see **tallyour**.

servys, *m.*, *pl.* **-ys**, service; apprenticeship; church-service, O.M. 2622 (M.E.): *gul dha s. ty a-wra*, thou shalt serve out thy time, P.C. 2261.

sēson, *m.*, *pl.* **-s**, season, period: *cleves s.*, intermittent fever, ague, B.M. 680 (M.E.).

sēssa (*seyssa*), *vb.*, to take seizin of a freeehold, O.M. 2768 (M.E. *sese*).

sessya, **cessya** (*sescyas* MS. P.C. 523), *vb.*, to cease, stop (M.E. *sesse*, *cesse*).

sēsya, *vb.*, to lay hold of, seize (M.E. *saise*).

sēth (C. Voc. *seit*, Lh. *zeath*), *m.*, *pl.* **-ow**, pot, jar, crock, *crocca* Aelfric: see **bussa**, **pēr-sēth**.

sēth, **sē'** (C. Voc. *sait(hor)*, C.W. *segh* for *se'* Lh. *zea*), *f.*, *pl.* **-ow**, arrow, M.C.,

C.W.: *otta an s. compes, ten hy yn-ban bys y'n pyl*, here is the arrow level, draw it right up to the head, C.W. 1560.

sēth, *m.*, *pl.* **sedhow**, *m.*, depth, sinking, plunge: as W. *sawdd*; see **sēdhy**; an old form of pl., *sodhow*, may be kept in place-name Dansotha, anciently Dofen Sodho (? *down sodhow*).

seth, see **esedha**.

sethen (*zethan* Lh.), *f.*, *pl.* **-now**, small arrow; *ray of light (B.).

sethor (C. Voc. *saithor*, Lh. *zethar*), *m.*, *pl.* **-oryon**, archer, shooter, Lh.; *pl.* **-as**, gannet, solan-goose, Lh. MS., *scealfra* Aelfric: in the latter sense *sedhor*, diver, W. *soddwr*, would fit, but the spellings are against it, and the gannet's resemblance in flight to a bow and in diving to a arrow, make **sethor** a perfect name.

settya, *vb.*, to set, put, place, appoint, fix, value, account, esteem (M.E. *sette*): p. pt. *settyes*, *-ys*, *syttys*; 3 s. plupf. *setsa*, *s. orth*, *dhe*, *erbyn*, oppose; *s. war*, set upon, attack; *s. carow*, bring stag to bay, B.M. 3168; *s. chy*, let a house (D. "set"); *anodho ny-settyaf gwelen-gala*, of him I set not a straw, from M.E.

sevel (*syvel*, Lh. *zeval*, *saval*), *vb.*, to stand, rise, stay, remain, stop, desist; raise up, make stand: p. pt., 3 s. pret. *sevys*; 3 s. subj. *saffo*; 2 s. imp. *saf*, *sa'*; 3 s. impf. indic. *syvy*; 3 s. impf. subj. *saffa*, 3 s. plupf. *safsa*; 3 s. pres.-fut. *sēf*; *saf yn-ban! sa' ban!* rise up! *sa', sa'!* let be! (D.); *s. (w)orth*, resist, abstain from, *da yu s. orth un prys*, it is well to do without one meal, B.M. 121; *worthyn ny-sef*, he shall not resist us, R.D. 1790; p. pt. is used as meaning derived, descended, sprung, B.M., C.W.

sevellak, *m.*, *pl.* **-legas**, redwing, bird (D. "swellack," "shewollock," cf. B. *savelleg*, landrail).

sevür, *adj.*, severe, serious (M.E.).

sevüreth, *m.*, gravity, seriousness, B.M. 938.

sevy, see **syvyen**.

sevyans, *m.*, standing, uprising, Hals. Creed: the authority is worthless, but it may be a genuine word.

sevylyak, *adj.*, standing, fixed; *m.*, *pl.* **-yogyon**, bystander, one kept standing in one place: *ha my s. omma*, and I stuck here, C.W. 458.

sew (*ziw* Lh.), *m.*, *pl.* **-yon**, bream, gilthead, fish, C.W. 410.

†**sewa**, **-wya**, *vb.*, to sew (O.E. *suwan*, *siwian* or Lat. *suere*): see **sewyas**.

sewājya, *vb.*, to assuage, relieve, mitigate, allay, B.M. 1004 (M.E. *swage*, O. Fr. *souager*).

sewen, see **sowyn**.

sewt, *m.*, colour or kind of dress (M.E. *suyte*, *sute*): in R.D. 2551 read *dyllas a'n s.-na*, a garment of that colour, as M.E. *of oo sute*, *of the same suyte*, miswritten (with contractions expanded) *a sevrth-na*.

sewya, **sewa** (*sywe*), *vb.*, to follow, result, come after, ensue, pursue (M.E. *sewe*): *bennath sewes*, may a blessing ensue, O.M., P.C.; *na-as y voth hep sewya*, leave not his will unobeyed, lit. unfollowed, M.C. 116.

†**sewyas** (C. Voc. *seuyad*), *m.*, *pl.* **-ysy**, stitcher, sewer, *seamere* Aelfric.

sewyades. *f.*, *pl.* **-ow**, seamstress: f. of **sewyas**.

seyssa, see **sēssa**.

seytegves, *ord. num.*, seventeenth.

seytek (Lh. *seitag*), *card. num.*, seventeen.

seyth (*syth*, late *seith*, *zith*), *card. num.*, seven.

seythen (*sȳthen*, C. Voc. *seithum*, *m* for *n*, Bilbao MS. *sithen*, Lh. *zeithan*), *f.*, *pl.* **-now**, week: *an jorna-ma war s.*, a week to-day, this day sennight, Lh.

seythves, **seythes** (*sythvas* C.W., *seithaz* Lh.), *ord. num.*, seventh: *may fe s. deth hynwys; hen yu, deth a bowesva*, so that there should be a holy seventh day; that is, a day of rest, O.M. 144.

shafta, *m.*, *pl.* **-tys**, mine shaft (E.): place-names.

shagga, *m.*, *pl.* **-gys**, shag, crested cormorant, Lh. (E.).

shakya (*sackye* M.C., *schakya*, B.M., *shakiah*, P.), *vb.*, to shake, wag (E.).

shām (*scham*), *m.*, shame, disgrace, Ord., B.M. (M.E.): *govy rak s.!* alack for shame! B.M. 797.

shamya (*sch-*), *vb.*, to put to shame, disgrace, humiliate, B.M. 420.

shanel (*-ol* Lh.), *m.*, gutter, kennel, channel (E.).

shāp (*shape*), *m.*, *pl.* **-ys**, shape, C.W. 476 (E.).

shapya (*sch-*), *vb.*, to form, fashion, model, bring to required pattern, shape, O.M. 2562, C.W. 2524 (E.): p. pt. *shapys*, *-yes*.

shara, *m.*, *pl.* **-rys**, share, lot, portion, C.W. (E.) : *my a·vyn keas ow s. -vy*, I'll fence off my plot, Borlase MS.
sharca, *m.*, *pl.* **-rkys**, shark (E.): *sharkeaz*, pl. in Lh. MS., is made *sharkeas*, sing., in Arch. Brit. : see **mōrvlȳth.**
sheft, *m.*, *pl.* **-ys**, shaft of spear, arrow, etc. (O.E. *sceaft*) : *compes avel s.*, as straight as a spear-shaft, O.M. 2494.
sherewa (*sch-*), *m.*, *pl.* **-wys**, rogue, rascal, villain, wicked man (M.E. *scherewe*, *shrewe*).
sherewneth (*sch-*), *m.*, wickedness, M.C. 19, 52.
sherewynsy (*scherwynsy* B.M.), *m.*, wickedness, O.M., C.W.
shērp (*scherp*, *scharp*), *adj*,, *adv.*, sharp (O.E. *scearp*) ; sharply, smartly, Ord., C.W.
shoppa, *m.*, *pl.* **-pys**, shop, workshop (E.): place-names.
shora (*sch-*), *m.*, *pl.* **-ys**, assault, onset, seizure, fit, lit. shower, B.M. (M.E. *shour*) ; see **cowas.**
showr, *m.*, a great quantity, C.W. 1189, 2445 (E.D.) : later form of **shora.**
shöwya (*shoyah*), *vb.*, to show, Kerew, (E.) : p. pt. *shewys* probably.
shyndya (*sch-*, *sy-*), *vb.*, to injure, ruin, disgrace, undo, reprimand, put to shame (M.E. *shende*, O.E. *scaendan*): 3 s. pres. -fut. *shynt*.
skemunya, see **emskemunya**.
skenna, *m.*, *pl.*, **-nys**, sinew, M.C. 183,; *dim.* **skennyn**, *m.*, *pl.* **-now**, tough bit of meat (D. "skednan").
skentoleth, **skȳentoleth** (*-eleth*, *-uleth*), *m.*, knowledge, wisdom : in verse *ske·ntoleth*, which would account for obscure penultimate, spelt *e*, *u*, *o*.
skentyl for **skȳentyl** (*skyntyll*), *adj.*, learned, wise, knowing, crafty, M.C.
skēs, **scüs** (C. Voc. *scod*), *m*, *pl.* **-ow** shade, shadow ; umbrage, uneasy feeling, dread, suspicion, B.M. 3233 : see **goscotter**, **scovva**, keeping the older vowel, and **cavanscüs.**
skēsek, **-jek**, *adj.*, shady, sheltered, shadowy; (of horse) apt to shy at shadows; (of person) ready to take umbrage, suspicions (W., B.).
skeswedhen, **-jwedhen**, *f.*, *col.* **-wȳth**, privet, lit. shade-tree (D. "skedgwith", "skedge").
skēsy, see **scüsy.**
sket, *adv.*, at once, like a shot, straightway, headlong, P.C. 1639 (M.E.).
skēth, see **scüth.**
sketh, *m.*, *pl.* **-ow**, strip, tatter, long piece, long way (D. "sketh").
skethen, *f.*, *pl.* **-now**, slice, long strip or rag (D. "skethan").
skethenna, *vb.*, to slice, tatter.
skethennek, *adj*, ragged, tattered.
skether, *m.*, *pl.* **-thryow**, chop, lop, splinter (W., B.).
skethrak, *adj.*, splintered, sharp-pointed (W.) ; *m.*, splintered thing (? D. "shedrack").
skethren, *f.*, splinter, lopping, billet of wood (B.).
skethry, *vb.*, to chop, lop, prune, splinter (W., B.).
skethryk, *m.*, *pl.* **-ygow**, **-rowygow**, little splinter ; *pl.* smithereens.
skevens (C. Voc. *sceuens*), lungs, lights, *lungena*, Aelfric : see **scaf.**
skew, *f.*, *pl.* **-yow**, shelter, screen (W.).
skewya, *vb.*, to shelter : p. pt. Skewys, place-name.
skȳans (C. Voc. *skient*), *m.* *pl.* **-ow**, knowledge, science, sense, wisdom, understanding, wits: *s. prenys*, experience; *dhym re-dhros ow s.*, he has brought me to my senses, lit. my sense to me, B.M. 3848, but also *dhe'm s. pan oma dres*, since I am brought to my senses, 4130 ; see **skentyl.**
skȳansek, **-ensek** (C. Voc. *skientoe*), *adj.*, wise, prudent, intelligent : *my a·grys nag-ota re s.*, I think thou art not over-sensible, B.M. 377.
skyber *f.*, *pl.* **-yow**, barn ; *s. efan*, the "large upper room" of Scripture, referred to also as *chy* P.C. 674—83, as if a separate building ; see **manal.**
skȳentyl, **-oleth**, see **skentyl**, **skentoleth.**
'skyjyow, see **eskys.**
skyl, *m.*, *pl.* **-yow**, nook, recess : place-names, Skillywadn, Skill Vean (as if f.) ; cf. *kyl*, m., W. *cil*, *ysgil*, m.
skȳl, see **skyllen.**
skyla, *m.*, *pl.* **-ys**, reason, cause, M.C. 142, 187 (M.E. *skylle.*).
skyla, *def. vb.*, to be a reason or cause (M.E. *it skills*) : used without particle ; 3 s. pres.-fut. *skyla*, is a cause, M.C. 211, there is reason, M.C. 125.
skyllen, *f.*, *col.* **skȳl**, sprout, shoot, eye of potato, cutting, as W. *ysgewyll* : *mar*

vunys avel skyl-brag, as small as malt-sprouts, O.M. 2720; see **brāg**.

skylwyn (*sch-*), *adj.*, whitish, B.M. 3391: see **skyl-**, Appendix II., **gwyn**.

***skȳn**, *m.*, sprinkling, scattering (W., B.).

†skynen (C. Voc. *scinen*), *f.*, *pl.* **-now**, earring, *earpreon* Aelfric.

skynnya (*skydnya*), see **dyeskynna.**

***skȳnya**, *vb.*, to sprinkle, scatter (W., B.).

skyren, *f.*, *pl.* **-now**, ? butcher's gambrel, as B. *skourr*, B.M. 3403: Lh. writes *skiran*, pl. *skiraw*, as a var. of **scoren.**

skyryonen, *f.*, *pl.* **skyryon**, splinter (W., B.).

***skȳt**, *m.*, *pl.* **-ys**, squirt, skeet; diarrhoea (E.D.): in last meaning cf. B. *skid*.

skytlen (*skitlan*), *f.*, *pl.* **-now**, bull's pizzle, Lh. MS.

***skȳtya**, *vb.*, to squirt, syringe (E.D.).

***skyvel**, *m.*, *pl.* **-vlow**, talon, fang (W., B.).

***skyvly**, *vb.*, to snatch, claw, devour (W., B.).

slakya, *vb.*, to slacken, grow less, cease, C.W. 2470 (M.E. *slake*).

sley, *adj.*, clever (M.E. *sleigh*): see **sleyneth.**

sleyneth (*-ueth* Stokes), *m.*, skill, cleverness, adroitness, sleight (M.E. *sleighte*).

slodya, *m.*, *pl.* **-yes**, sledge-hammer, O.M. 2318 (M.E. *slegge*): ?*dy* representing *j*.

slȳm (*sleme*), *m.*, slime, C.W. (E.).

slynk, *m.*, slide; *adj.*, slippery (E.): Slinkydeen, name of rock used as a sitting slide, see **tȳn**.

slynkya (*sklynkya*), *vb.*, to slide, glide, drag oneself along, creep, crawl as a snake, C.W., B.M. (O.E. *slincan*, M.E. *slynk*, *sklynk*, D. "slink").

slyppya (*sleppia*), *vb.*, to slip, Lh. (E.).

smāt, *adj.*, hardy, rough, stout, stalwart; *m.*, *pl.* **-tys**, unfeeling, hard-bitten fellow, stout lad (O.E. *smaete*, *smeat*, smitten, beaten): *dre ow threys y-tuth un s.*, a ruffian ran my feet through, R.D. 2587.

smōth, *adj.*, *adv*,. smooth, smoothly, C.W. (E.).

smyllyng, *m.*, smell, scent, O.M. 1743 (M.E.).

snel, *adj.*, quick, active, speedy, B.M., R.D. (O.E., M.E.).

†snod, *m.*, *pl.* **-ys**, fillet, ribbon, C. Voc. (O.E.), *snod* Aelfric.

sobmen, see **summen.**

socor (*sokyr*), *m.*, succour, aid, reinforcement (M.E.).

socra (Late *succra*), *vb.*, to succour, give aid to, relieve (M.E. *socoure*): p. pt. *socrys*, 3 s. pres.-fut. *socor*.

***sōder**, *m.*, solder (E. "sawder").

sodha, *vb.*, to serve, take office, be employed: 2 s. imp. *sōth*, M.C. 175; see **sōth.**

sodhak, *m.*, *pl.* **-dhogyon**, officer, one who discharges a function (W.).

sōdon, *m.*, *pl.* **-ys**, soldan, sultan, Saracen prince, O.M. 2056 (M.E. *saudan*).

***sōdra**, *vb.*, to solder (E.).

†sōf, sō (C. Voc. *suif*), *m.*, tallow, suet, as B. *soa(v)*, *ungel* Aelfric.

sōgh (C. Voc. *soch*, Lh. *zōh*), *m.*, *pl.* **-yow**, ploughshare.

†sōgh (C. Voc. *soch*), *adj.*, blunt, dull, as B. *souc'h*: see **†talsōgh, pensōgh.**

sojeta (C.W. *subject*), *m.*, *pl.* **-tys**, subject, liege (M.E. *sojet*): sing. is used as col. M.C. 211; *s. ancow*, mortal, one liable to die, C.W. 379.

sol, *m.*, *pl.* **-yow**, foundation, base, O. Cor. gloss; sole of foot (B.): see **yn-sol.**

solabry's (*solla-*, ? for *sül a² brȳs*), *adv.*, already, just now, erewhile, formerly.

soladhē'th (*solla-*, ? for *sül a² dhēth*), *adv.*, long since, for a long time past, since long ago.

***solas**, *m.*, solace, pleasure, amusement (M.E.).

solempna, *adj.*, solemn, M.E.

sole'mpnyta, -ty, *m.*, *pl.* **-tys**, gravity, impressiveness, solemnity, ceremony, celebration, C.W. 2082 (M.E.).

†soler, *m.*, *pl.* **-yow**, loft, upper floor, C. Voc., *upflor* Aelfric; (mining) stage, platform (D. "soller").

sols (*sowls* Kerew, *zowlz* Lh.), *m.*, *pl.* **-ow**, shilling: in C. Voc. *sols* mistranslates *pecunia*, cattle, money, as *dinair* does *nummus*, coin; *feoh* Aelfric, covers all the actual meanings; see **dynar.**

Soly, *m.*, Sol, heathen sun-god, B.M.: see **Sül.**

†sommys (C. Voc. *sommet*), *vb.*, to move about, flit, as W. *symud*, no inf. ending: see ***ūgh-sommys.**

***somons**, *m.*, summons (M.E.).

sompē'r, *adj.*, unequalled, peerless, P.C. B.M. (M.E. *saumpere*, Fr. *sans pair*).

***sompna**, *vb.*, to summon (M.E. *sompne*, *somne*).

***sompnour**, *m.*, *pl.* **-s**, summoner (M.E.).

son, *m.*, *pl.* **-yow**, sound, noise, rumour, report, murmur, clamour: *gas dha s.!*

leave off thy noise, say no more! R.D. 1010.

son, see **seny.**

sōn, *m., pl.* **-ow**, charm, blessing, healing spell (D. "soon").

sona (*zona* Lh.), *vb.*, to bless, hallow, sanctify, charm: *my a-gas-son a'n barth cleth*, I'll give you a left-hand blessing, i.e., a curse, B.M. 3420: see **dursona.**

soper, *m., pls.* **-s, -ow**, supper (M.E.): *prys-s.*, supper-time; *bos s.*, evening meal.

sopya (*-ppya*), *vb.*, to sup, P.C., M.C. (M.E. *sopye*).

sōr, *m.*, anger, wrath, grudge, vexation, trouble: see **serry.**

sordya (*surjya*, P.), *vb.*, to arouse, stir up; arise, spring up, be raised, of strife, etc., M.C. (M.E. *sorde*, *sourde*, Fr. *sourdre*).

sorn, *m., pl.* **sernow**, small place, nook, cranny: *a bup s.*, from every hole and corner, P.C. 3056.

sorras, etc., see **serry.**

sort (*zart* Lh.), *m., pl.* **-as**, hedgehog, C. Voc., *il* Aelfric; sea-urchin (*short* Ray, "zart" D.): **s. mur*, porcupine; final *t* suggests non-Celtic origin, cf. Fr. and B. *sourd*, deaf person; salamander.

sort, *m., pl.* **-ow**, sort, kind, B.M., C.W. (M.E.).

***sortya**, see ***assortya.**

sōs (*sûaz* Lh.), *m.*, friend, friends, associates, "soce," Lat. *socius*, used in addressing a company: *'rya s.!* (*rea suaz!* Lh., "arrea soce!" D.), what next! see **arȳa.**

sosten (*susten* B.M., C.W.), *m.*, sustenance, nourishment, food (M.E. *susten*).

sostena (*sustone*), *vb.*, to sustain, supply with food, O.M. (M.E. *sustene*).

sotel (*suttall* C.W.), *adj.*, crafty, clever, subtle (M.E.).

sōth (*soyth* B.M. 2292, *sooth* Scawen), *m.*, *adj.*, south: *S.-West*, South-West, etc. (M.E.).

sōth, *f., pl.* **sodhow**, service, office, employment: *del farsyn yn-ta menough yn agas s.*, as often we have behaved well in your employ, R.D. 1881; see **sodha.**

sothva, *f., pl.* **-ow**, place of employment, state of service, office (W.).

sotla, *vb.*, to subtilize, disguise, use artifice about, Gw.: see **strechya.**

sotry, *m.*, craft, subtlety, cunning, M.C. 21 (? M.E., cf. Med. Lat. *subtella*, astuteness).

soudor, *m., pls.* **-yon, -drys**, soldier (M.E. *soudyour*).

sovran (*sefryn* O.M., *soveran* B.M.), *m., pl.* **-s**, sovereign (M.E.).

sowena (for *soweneth*), *f.*, prosperity, success, well-being, P.: written *sewen* (cf. *karens* for *kerensa*) in toast, *Yeghes ha S. whath dheso-jy ha dhe'th Henath*, Health and Prosperity to thee and thy Posterity, Ustick, see **sowyn, -y.**

soweth, *interj.*, alas! unhappily! more's the pity! worse luck! lit. which is worse, *usy gweth*, as W. *ysywaeth*, B. *siouaz*: *yn-s.*, sadly, dreadfully; M.C. 120.

sowl, *m.*, soul: in oath *re'm s.!* by my soul! (E.).

sowlen, *f., col.* **sowl** (*zowl* Lh.), stubble, thatching-reed: Park Sowle, field-name; *chy s.*, thatched cottage (B.).

sowlek, *adj.*, stubbly; *f., pl.* **-egow, -egy**, stubble-field (B.).

sowlwōth, *f., pl.* **-odhow**, stubble-goose (W., B.).

sowman, *m., pl.* **mens**, salmon; O.M. 136, Gw. (M.E. *sauman*).

sows (*saws* Lh. MS.), *m., pl.* **-ow**, sauce.

sowyn, *adj.*, prosperous, thriving, successful, flourishing, as B. *seven*: see **sowena.**

sowyny (B.M., C.W. *sew-*), *vb.*, to prosper, succeed, thrive, flourish, (of soil) be fertile, bear vegetation: 2 pl. imp. *soweneugh!* your health! P.; 3 s. subj. *sowenno*; 3 s. pres.-fut. *sowen*; *ny-sewenaffa*, C.W. 1285, for *ny-sowynaf-vy*; see **dursona.**

sowynyans (*sawynyans*, Keigwin), *m.*, prosperity, success, thrivingness.

***spadhy**, *vb.*, to geld: 2 s. imp. *spath* (W. B.).

spāl, *m., pl.* **-yow**, fine, forfeiture (D. "spale").

spāla, *vb.*, to fine (D. "spale").

***Spanyer**, *m., pl.* **-s**, Spaniard (D.E.).

sparbyl, *m., pl.* **-blys**, sparable (E.): Park Sparbles, field-name.

sparya, *vb.*, to spare, abstain, refrain from, desist, stint (M.E. *spare*).

spās (*spāth*), *m.*, space, room, way, scope, interval of time, chance, opportunity, license (M.E. *space*); *adv.*, as long as, whilst; *gas dhym s.*, make room or way; *grant an s.*, grant the concession; *spas en-vy ena*, while I was there, Borlase MS. cf. **termyn**, *adv.*; see **spȳs.**

***spath**, *adj.*, gelded (W., B.).

spaven, span (C. Voc. *spauen*), *m.*,

quiet interval, stopping of storm, lull, stillness: *s. mor*, calm, C. Voc.
spa·venhē·, **spanhē·**, *vb.*, to quieten, lull, still (of weather): as **berhē** (B.).
spavnell, **spanell**, *f.*, *pl.* **-ow**, little calm spot or moment: D. "spannel," calm side of rock around which tide is running; dim. of **spa(ve)n**, cf. **crügell**, **graghell**.
Spayn, *f.*, Spain, R.D. 2147.
Spaynek, *adj.*, Spanish language.
specyal, *adj.*, *adv.*, special, -ly: *s. bras*, to a most unusual degree, M.C. 110 (M.E.).
specyly, **spesly**, *adv.*, especially, B.M. (M.E.).
spēda, *f.*, success, prosperity, help: *god s. dhys!* good speed! *s. dek*, fair speed, good going (O.E. *spede*, *f.*).
spedhesen, *f.*, *col.* **spedhes** (C.W. *speras*), briars, brambles.
spēdya, *vb.*, to succeed, progress, make speed, hasten, cause to prosper, bring about, accomplish: 3 s. pres. -fut. *spēt* (M.E.).
spekyar (*spekkiar* Lh.), *adj.*, speckled; ? "speck" **-yar**, used of hen; cf. **spletyar**.
***spellya**, *vb.*, to spell (E.).
spēna (*speyna*), *vb.*, to spend, use up, expend (M.E. *spene*, *spende*): 3 s. pret. *spenas*, M.C. 10; *s. gwyns*, to waste breath; a var. *spendya* is not found before C.W., Borlase has *spenjys*, its p. pt., for *spendyes*.
spencer, *m.*, *pl.* **-s**, butler, P.C., B.M. (M.E.).
spens, *m.*, *pl.* **-ys**, larder, buttery, spence (M.E., D.).
spēra, *m.*, *pl.* **-rys**, spear, C.W. 1994 (M.E. *spere*).
spe·rnabyl, *adj.*, meek, submissive, forbearing, "spurnable" (M.E.).
spernek (C. Voc. miswritten *sernic*), *f.*, thorn-brake: place-name Sparnick.
spernen, *f.*, *col.* **spern**, thorn-bush, thorn, *dhyfel* Aelfric: *s. du*, blackthorn; *s. melen*, buckthorn (B.); *s. gwyn*, hawthorn; *curun s.*, crown of thorns.
splan (Late *spladn*), *adj.*, bright, shining, clear, evident, open, splendid, illustrious, glorious, brilliant, lucid, resplendant; *adv.*, clearly, brightly, etc.: *y'n jeth splan*, in broad daylight, R.D. 1503.
splander, *m.*, brightness, splendour, glory, clearness, lustre, lucidity, C.W., Lh.
splanhē·, *vb.*, to make bright or clear: as **berhē**.
splanna, *vb.*, to shine, glitter, be bright, Lh.
splanyjyon, *m.*, brightness, splendour (B.): cf. **golowyjyon**.
splat, *m.*, *pl.* **-tys**, plot of ground (D.E.): place-name, Splattenridden (*s. an* or dim. *splatyn redan*), fern-plot.
spletyar (*splettiar* Lh. MS.), *adj.*, spotted, dappled: ? "splat"**-yar**, used of hen, E.D. "splatty," spotted; cf. **spekyar**.
spong, *m.*, *pl.* **-ow**, sponge, M.C. 202, as W. *ysbwng*.
sport, *m.*, *pl.* **-ys**, sport, game, B.M. 1056 (M.E.).
sportya, *vb.*, to sport, go hunting, B.M. 3204-14 (M.E.).
spral, **pral**, *m.*, *pl.* **-low**, fetter, impediment, clog for animal, sheep-span, hobble (B.).
spralla, **pralla**, *vb.*, to fetter, hamper, impede, clog, hobble, span, tail-pipe (D. "spral," "pral").
sprallyer, *m.*, hobble, sheep-span (D.).
***sprūs**, **gwedhen s.**, *f.*, spruce (E.).
sprūsen, **spūsen**, *f. pl.* **-now**, *col.* **sprūs**, **spūs**, kernel, pip (*sprusen* f., col. *spruse* C.W.): *spus* is less correctly used as m. and f. sing. in O.M.; cf. M.B. *splusenn*, *spusenn*, f.
sprūsek, **spūsek**, *adj.*, full of pips; *f.*, *pl.* **egow**, **-egy**, seed-bed (B.).
spȳcer, *m.*, *pl.* **-s**, grocer (M.E.): see **spȳsa**.
spȳcys, see **spȳsa**.
spȳk, *f.*, *pl.* **-ys**, **-ygys**, spike-nail (M.E.).
***spȳknard**, *m.*, spikenard (M.E.).
spylgarn, *m.*, *pl.* **-as**, cormorant, shag (D. "spilgarn"); ? "dangle-shank," cf. B. *a-ispilh*, dangling, and **garen**.
spyrys (*sperys*, C. Voc. *spirit*), *m.*, *pl.* **-yon**, **-yjyon** (*spriggian* Borlase), spirit, ghost, goblin, sprite, fairy, *gast* Aelfric.
spyrysegȳeth, *f.*, spiritualism (W.).
spyrysek, *adj.*, spiritual (B.).
spyryseth, *f.*, inspiration (W.).
spȳs, *m.*, period of time, intermission, concession: *a ver s.*, shortly; *ny' fyth s.*, thou shalt have no concession; though used much like **spās**, this is a distinct word, as W. *ysbaid*.
spȳsa, *m.*, *pl.* **spȳcys**, spice, M.C. 234 (M.E. *spyce*, O. Fr. *espice*).
spȳt (C.W. *spyta*), *m.*, spite, malice, virulence (M.E.): *dre s.*, through despite, R.D. 2050.
spyty, *m.*, hospice, hospital, as W. *ysbyty*;

? in Nanspeyty, place-name.

spȳtya, *vb.*, to spite, vex.

spȳtys, *adj.*, malicious, malignant, spiteful, virulent, M.C. 112 (M.E. *spytus*).

squard, squerd, *m.*, *pl.* **-yow**, break, tear, rent (D.).

squardya, squerdya, *vb.*, to break, tear, rend, lacerate, become torn or broken, M.C., Ord.: p. pt. *squerdys*, *-yes* (D. "squarded").

squat, **scat** (*skuat*), *m.*, *pl.* **-tow**, blow, buffet, knock, slap, break, Lh., D.; *adv.*, with a bang, smash, crash, P.C. 2816 (D.E.).

squattya, scattya (*squatchia* J. Boson, *skwatsha* Borlase MS.), *vb.*, to hit, knock, break, C.W., Lh.; (of a mine) abandon, D.: cf. "squot," "swat," Cor. "scat," E.D. Dic.; *s. yn-ban*, (of pilchards) to break out of bulk; *eskyjyow coth squattyes* (*skitchow coth skwatchez*), old broken shoes, Gw.

squych (*skwych*), *m.*, *pl.* **-ys**, snatch, twitch, spasm (M.E., "D. "squitch"): *war s.*, with a jerk, R.D. 2595.

squychya, *vb.*, to jerk, make spasmodic movements, twitch, switch (D. "squitchy" M.E. *quycchyn*); see **squych**.

squȳer, *m.*, *pl.* **-yon** (Lh. *skwerrion*), esquire, squire, O.M. 2004, 1640 (M.E.): see **scōswas**.

squȳr, *m.*, *pl.* **-ys**, standard, pattern, carpenter's set-square, O.M.: *dhe s.*, square, exact, correct, *dos dhe s.*, to come true to measurements (M.E. *by squyre*), O.M. 2544.

squȳth, *adj.*, tired, weary, fatigued: *s. of dre vur lafurya*, I am weary from much journeying, O.M. 2049.

squytha, *vb.*, to tire, weary, fatigue, O.M. 737.

squythans (*-ens*), *m.*, fatigue, weariness, P.C. 477.

squythder, *m.*, tiredness, weariness, Keigwin: *perthyans hep s.*, indefatigable prosecution, King Charles' Letter.

stābel, *m.*, *pls.* **-blyow, -blys**, stable: S. Hobba, Park an S., place-names.

staga, *vb.*, to tether, fix to one place (B.): see **stak**.

stagell, *f.*, *pl.* **-ow**, tie, attachment, bond (B.): *s. an tavas*, tongue-string, *s. an frygow*, separation of nostrils (B.).

stagen, *f.*, *pl.* **-now**, lake, pool, Lh.: ? for "stang," M.E. *stank*, O. Fr. *estanc*, or direct from Lat. *stagnum*.

stak(g), *m.*, *pl.* **-agow**, tether; scope of tethered animal (B.); nightmare with sensation of being unable to move (D. "stag"); *adj.*, fastened, fixed; *adv.*, without moving, on the very spot: *merwel stak omma*, die here right on the spot, B.M. 1368; *ky s.*, chained dog, (B.).

stalla, *m.*, *pl.* -lys, stall (M.E.).

stallasyon (*-ascon*), *m.*, installation: *tus nobyl yn s. dhe'th gorra yu devedhys*, noblemen have come to induct thee into installation, B.M. 3017 (M.E.).

stampa, *m.*, *pl.* **-pys**, stamp; in pl. tin stamping-mill, "stamps" (E.): Park an Stampis, place-name.

stampya, *vb.*, to stamp (E.).

stanch, *adj.*, staunch, watertight, C.W. 2289 (M.E. *stanche*).

stanch-üra, *vb.*, to pay a ship's hull with pitch, tar, tallow, etc., O.M. 954: see **üra**.

stank, *m.*, heavy tread (D.).

stankya, *vb.*, to trample heavily on or into (D. "stank"): W. *sangu*, B. *sanka* suggest an intrusive *t*, perhaps imitating E. "stamp".

stap, *m.*, *pl.* **-pys**, step, pace (O.E. *staep*), *ny-vynnons un s. lafurya*, they won't travel a single step, B.M. 3286.

stark, *adv.*, fixedly (M.E.): *kyn fyren warnas mar s.*, however hard I might stare at thee, C.W. 1626: in MS. *start*, but though like B. *start*, with similar meaning, this does not rhyme.

***starn**, *f.*, *pl.* **-yow**, harness, frame, framework (W., B.): *s. gwyader*, loom (B.).

***stasyon**, *m.*, station (E.).

stāt, *m.*, *pl.* **-ys**, state, estate, rank, B.M., C.W (M.E.).

stātly, *adj.*, stately, splendid, C.W. (M.E.).

stāt-ūghel, *m.*, the peerage, lofty station, B.M. 437.

stātya, *vb.*, to convey an estate, B.M. 413 (M.E.).

***stayr**, *m.*, *pl.* **-ys**, stair (M.E. *steyre*).

stēda, *m.*, *pl.* **-dys**, steed, horse, O.M. 1964 (M.E. *stede*, O.E. *steda*).

stedfast, *adj.*, steadfast, P.C. (M.E.).

†ste'fenyk, stevnyk (C. Voc. *stefenic*, Lh. *stevnig*), *f.*, palate, roof of mouth, *goma* Aelfric.

stella, *adv.*, still, yet, N. Boson, Lh. Gw. (M.E. *stille*).

stēn (*stean* Lh.), *m.*, tin: *whel s.*, tin-pit P.; *s. du*, unsmelted, *s. gwyn*, smelted, tin.

stēn, *m.*, *pl.* **-ys**, earthenware jar (E.D. "stain"): "milk pail," Lh., must be a slip, following W. *ystēn*.

stenak, *f.*, tin-bearing ground, tin streamwork: Stennack Wyn, S. Las. etc., place-names.

stenor (*stener, stunnar* Lh.), *m.*, *pl.* **-yon**, tinner, tin-miner, tin-dresser; water-wagtail, "dish-washer" (from its waterside habits, as if vanning tin).

stēnys, -üs, *adj.*, stannous, containing tin: *stoff s.*, tin-stuff, P.

***ster**, *m.*, *pl.* **-yow**, signification, sense, meaning, importance, purport (W., B.).

steren (*sterran* Lh.), *f.*, *pl.* **-now**, *col.* **stēr** (*steyr*), star: *s. codha*, falling star; *s. gwandra*, planet, Lh.; *s. lesky*, comet, Lh.; **s. stak*, fixed star; *ster golowys*, constellation, Lh. MS.; *an steren*, the pole-star (B.); *degol an Steren*, Epiphany (B., see **Stūl**).

sterennek, *adj.*, starry, spangled (W., B.).

sterenny, *vb.*, to sparkle, spangle (W., B.).

sterennyk, *m.*, *pl.* **-ygow, -nowygow**, asterisk, little star (W., B.).

stērgan, *m.*, starlight, starshine, the stars, O.M. 36: see **can**, m.

stergannek, *adj.*, starlit, bright with stars (V.).

sterlyn, *m.*, *pl.* **-s**, coin of full weight; *adj.*, sterling (M.E. *sterlinge*): *dek warn ugans s.*, thirty pieces of money of standard weight, P.C. 1554.

stervya, see **storvya**.

†stevel (C. Voc. **steuel**), *f.*, *pl.* **-yow**, room, chamber, dining-room, *bur* Aelfric: apparently replaced in M. Cor. by **rōm**.

stēvya, *vb.*, to hasten, hurry, dash, rush (E.D. "stave"): 3 s. pres.-fut. *stē^f^*; *yn-un-s. oll y eth*, they all went speeding, M.C. 239.

stewan (Lh. *stiran*,? for *stiuan*), *m.*, *pl.* **-now**, blow, slap, drubbing (D. "stuan").

stewanny, *vb*, to belabour (W.).

†stlaf, *adj.*, lisping, mumbling, indistinct of speech; *m.*, *pl.* **-levyon**, lisper, mumbler, C. Voc., *wlips*, Aelfric.

†stlaveth, *m.*, lisping, mumbling (B.).

†stlevy, *vb.*, to lisp, speak indistinctly: 3 s. pres.-fut. *stlaf*.

stoff (*stuff* P.), *m.*, goods, substance, stuff, stock, store, supply, plenty, means (M.E. *stuffe*): *s. a-jy*, household store, B.M. 1869; see **stēnys**.

stoffya, *vb.*, to stuff, furnish, stock (W., M.E.).

stok (C. Voc. *stoc*), *m.*, *pl.* **-kys**, stock, block, stump, stub (O.E. *stoc*), *styb* Aelfric: *y'n stokkys*, in the stocks, B.M. 3554.

†stōl, *f.*, *pl.* **-yow**, stole, C. Voc. (O.E.), *stole* Aelfric.

†stōl-lüf (*s. lof* C. Voc.), *f.*, priest's maniple, lit. hand-stole, *handlin* Aelfric.

stons, *m.*, stance, fixed position, stand, posture of defence taken by a warrior, R.D. 2579 (O. Fr. *estance*, M.E. *staunce*).

stoppya (*stopya*), *vb.*, to stop, B.M. 1423, Gw. (M.E. *stoppen*).

stōpya, *vb.*, to bend down, bring lower, stoop, cause to stoop, O.M. 201 (M.E.).

stordy, *adj.*, sturdy, obstinate, heedless, bold, P.C. 2271 (M.E. *stourdie*, O. Fr. *estourdi*).

†stork (C. Voc. *storc*), *m.*, *pl.* **-ys**, stork (O.E.), *storc* Aelfric: see **whybon**.

storvya (? for *stervya*), *vb*, to kill or perish with cold or hunger (M.E. *sterve*, O.E. *steorfan*, p. pt. *storfen*): p. pt. *storvys*, M.C. 177, 3 s. pret. *storvas*, 3 s. pres.-fut. *storf*; apparently taken from O.E. p. pt. unless the *o* is for *e*.

stōs, see **scōs**.

stowt, stout, *adj.*, proud, strong, powerful, stubborn, unyielding, Ord., C.W. (M.E.).

straft, *adv.*, straightway, Gw. (D.E. with *f* for *gh* as in "boft," "dafter," "slafter"): see **strayt**.

stranj, see **astranj**.

stranjnes, *m.*, strangeness, C.W. 1800 (M.E.).

strās, *m.*, *pl.* **-ow**, bottom, low ground, bilge of ship, bottom of boat: place-names Penstraze, Penstrassow, Trestraise, D. "straits" of boat.

†strayl (C. Voc. *strail*), *m.*, *pl.* **-yow**, matting, tapestry thrown over seat, etc. (O.E.), *strael*, *setraegel*, Aelfric: **†s.** *elester*, mat of sand-rushes, *meatte* Aelfric.

strayt, *adj.*, straight, C.W. (E.).

straytly, *adv.*, straightly, C.W. (E.).

strech, *m.*, *pl.* **-ys**, tarrying, stay, delay: *hep let na s.*, without stop or stay, R.D. 117.

strechya, -cha, *vb.*, to lengthen out time, tarry, loiter, linger, delay; stretch, extend; adapt or adjust to what is greater (M.E.

strecche) : *ow* (MS. *tur*) *lythyow...my a-vyn dalleth s.*, I'll begin to stretch my limbs, C.W. 2281 ; *ymons-y menough ow-sotla ha s. aga-honen*, they often disguise and accommodate themselves, Gw., Tonkin.

strekys, *m.*, *pl. and abst.* **-kesow** (*-cusow*), stroke, (as abst.) beating (M.E. *stryk*) : var. of **strocas.**

strēm, *m.*, *pl.* **-ys**, stream, O.M. 1083 (M.E. *streem*, O.E. *stream*).

strepya, see **stryppya.**

strēt, *m.*, *pl.* **-ys**, street (O.E. *straet*) : *S. an Oghen, S. an Pol, S. an Don* (**dodn**), *S. Myghal*, street-names at Newlyn, St. Ives, Penzance, Helston ; W. *ystrȳd*, B. *stread* would as Cor. have final *s* and be f., pl. *-ow*.

strēth (C. Voc., *stret*), *f.*, *pl.* **-ow**, stream, brook, *burna, broc* Aelfric, M.C. 219, O.M. 772.

strētyn, *m.*, *pl.* **-now**, little street, lane ; ? confused with *stret an* in Street an Garow, St. Ives ; cf. **parkyn.**

strevya, *vb.*, to strive, contend, dispute, argue, make an effort, M.C. (M.E. *stryve*): 3 s. pres.-fut. *strȳf* ; see **strȳf.**

strevyans, *m.*, effort, contention.

strew (*strihwe* Lh.), *m.*, *pl.* **-yow**, sneeze.

strewles, *m.*, sneezewort (W.).

strewy (*striwhi* Lh.), *vb.*, to sneeze.

strocas, -yas, *m.*, *pl.* **-cosow**, blow, stroke, buffet, weal (M.E. *strook*) : see **strekys.**

strōll, *m.*, mess, litter (D., as B. *strouilh*).

strolla, *vb.*, to make dirty (B.).

strollek, *adj.*, muddy, dirty (B.).

strong, *adj.*, dirty (of liquid) ; *m.*, filth (as B. *stronk*) : Pulstrong, place-name.

stronga, *vb.*, to befoul a liquid (B.).

strōth, *adj.*, tight, strict, squeezed in (B. *striz*, cf. **tōth**, B. *tiz*).

strotha, *vb.*, to bind about the middle, gird, squeeze, wring, tighten, restrict, O.M., R.D.

***strüs**, *m.*, *pl.* **-yow**, ostrich (W. *estrys*).

strȳf, *m.*, strife, wrangling, P.C. 30 (M.E., O. Fr. *estrif* from Frankish) : *bos yn s.*, to quarrel, Lh.

strȳfor (C. Voc. *strifor*), *m.*, *pl.* **-yon**, wrangler, contentious person, *geflitful* Aelfric : see **strȳf.**

strȳk (*strīk* Lh.), *adj.*, active, nimble, swift (E.D. "strick," M.E. *streke*).

†strȳl (C. Voc, *streil*), *f.*, *pl.* **-yow**, curry-comb, *horscamb* Aelfric (Med. Lat. *strilla*, Lat. *strigilis*).

strylla, *vb.*, to curry a horse : see **strȳl.**

†strȳng (C. Voc. *streing*), *m.*, clasp, buckle, *oferfengc* Aelfric.

stryppya (*strepya*), *vb.*, to strip, B.M. 1929—33 (M.E.) : see **dystryppya.**

studhya (*stedhya*), *vb.*, to study, investigate, apply oneself to learning, B.M. 1490—5 (M.E. *stodye*).

Stūl, dēgol-S., dūgol-S., Twelfth-Day, Epiphany, Lh. : perhaps from W. *dydd Ystwyll*, Lat. *Stellae Festum* ; see **steren.**

stūl, *m.*, frame of timber in mine (Late, from German *stuhl*).

stüm, *m.*, *pl.* **-mow**, turn, bend, leaning, tendency, inclination : place-names, Stimcodda (*s. cosow*), Stencoose, St. Coose (*s. cos*), Stengilly (*s. an gelly*).

stümma, -ya, *vb.*, to turn, bend, lean, tend, incline (W., B.).

***stüs, stēs**, *f.*, *pl.* **-ow**, course, series, range, file (W., B.).

†stūt, *m.*, *pl.* **-tys**, gnat, gad-fly, warble-fly, any stinging fly, C. Voc., *stut* Aelfric : cf. "stout," etc., E. D. Dic. ; see **gwybesen, sudronen.**

***stüven**, *f.*, *pl.* **-now**, warp (W., B.).).

***stüvy**, *vb.*, to warp yarn (W., B.).

styf, *f.*, *pl.* **-yvow**, jet, squirt (B.).

styfak (*stiphak* Lh.), *m.*, *pl.* **-fogas**, squid as B. *stif(ell)eg, sifoc'h.*

styken (*stikedn* Lh.), *f.*, *pl.* **-now** (*stukednaw* Borlase), pale, post, stake, stick.

stykenna, *vb.*, to stake, set posts or paling.

styll (*stil* Lh.), *m.*, *pl.* **-yow**, ? tie beam or rafter, O.M. (Med. Lat. *stillus*) : this is quite distinct in meaning from either **astell** or **estyllen**, which are used of a small, flat board, a shingle, or a shelf, and none of these words is connected with the mining terms "stull" and "stilling," neither of which is Celtic ; in O.M. 2441-6 the bulk of a tree is used for *styllyow* ; *tennow, lathys* and *corblys* being made from its boughs and the slender part of its stem ; a similar apportionment of sizes is given again O.M. 2471—5, but it is difficult to fix the exact meaning of the terms.

styllen, see **estyllen.**

stȳth, *adj.*, pliant, flexible, ready to bow or bend, as W. *ystwyth* : see **gostyth.**

styward (*-art*), *m.*, *pl.* **-s**, steward, B.M. 2363 (M.E.).

sūba, *vb.*, to steep, saturate, soak bread: see **sūben**.

†**sūben**, *f.*, *pl.* **-now**, morsel, sop, C. Voc., *snaed* Aelfric, D. "subban".

subject, see **sojeta**.

substans, *m.*, substance, essence, being, B.M. 1318; means, property, C.W. 2235 (M.E.).

†**sudronen**, *f.*, *pl.* **-now**, *col.* **sudron**, drone, C. Voc., *draen* Aelfric; drone-fly, horse-fly (B.).

sudronenny, *vb.*, to buzz, drone (B.)

sugalen, *f.*, *col.* **sugal** (*sogal* Bilbao MS.), rye-plant, rye, Lh.

sugaldyr, *m.*, rye-land: Segoulder, St. Golder, Chygolder, field-names.

sugalek, *f.*, *pl.* **-egow**, **-egy**, rye-field, P.

sugan, *m.*, juice, sap, essence, Lh., D. "zuggans," essential parts: see **plumsugan**.

sugna, *vb.*, to suck: 3 s. pres.-fut. *sugen* (W., B.).

sugnek, *adj.*, juicy, sappy (W., B.).

***sugra**, *m.*, sugar; *vb.*, to sweeten with sugar (M.E. *sugre*, D. "shugger").

***sül**, **süthel**, *m.*, *pl.* **-yow**, heel (W., B.).

Sül, **dē-S.**, **dū-S.** (Zeel, Ziel Gw. MS.), *m.*, *pl.* **-yow** (*Zelio* P.), day of Sol, Sunday: *an S.*, the Sabbath, (on) Sunday; *an gol ha'n S.*, feast-days and Sundays; *nanyl dhe wyth na dhe S.*, (with neg.) neither on a working day nor on a Sunday, not at all, never, R.D. 1833, 2250; *S. Gwyn*, Whit Sunday; *de-S. Blejyow*, Palm Sunday, Flowering Sunday, M.C. 27; see **Soly**.

sül[2] (*seyl* C.W.), *pron.*, such, he that, that, those, who, all those who, whoever, as much or many as: *s. voy ancow a-wrellough, dhe larchya-praysys y-fydheugh commendys wosa-hemma*, the more deaths you cause, the more generously-praised will you be commended hereafter, B.M. 2351; *s. a-vynno bos sylwys*, all who wish to be saved, M.C. 2; *s. a*, as many as are going, R.D. 136; see **py-sül**.

Sülwyth (*Zylvath* Gw. MS., *Zeeleva* Kerew, *Zilgweth* Lh.), *m.*, Sunday(-time); *adv.*, on a Sunday: *an S.*, the Sabbath.

sum, *m.*, *pl.* **-mys**, sum, whole amount, total (E.): *py-sul yu s. a'n fleghes?* how much is the total number of the children? B.M. 1604; *al an sum*, P.C. 1352, however, is M.E. *all and some*, one and all.

summen (*sobmen*), *f.*, *pl.* **-now**, sum, Gen. I., 21, in Davies Gilbert's M.C.

sump, *m.*, water-pit in mine (Late, from German *sumpf*.

supposya (*seposia*, *soposya* B.M.), *vb.*, to suppose, infer, B.M.; to substitute, impute falsely, palm off, forge, counterfeit, Lh. (M.E., as Fr. *supposer*).

sür (Late *seer*), *adj.*, *adv.*, sure, -ly (M.E. *seur*).

surcot (*cercot*), *f.*, *pl.* **-tys**, surcoat, loose garment, as worn over armour, P.C. 1784, 2074 (M.E. *surcote*).

sürlȳ', *adv.*, surely, B.M. 1141, 3600 (M.E.).

sür-redy, *adv.*, most surely: see **redy**.

susten, see **sosten**.

***süthel**, see **sül**.

swan, *m.*, *pl.* **-nys**, swan, O.M. 133 (M.E.): see **alargh**.

***swaysya**, **swayjya**, *vb.*, to swing the arms (D.E. "swaize," M.E. pres. pt. *suagynk*, B.M. p. 220).

swynnen (*suidnan* Lh.), *f.*, *pl.* **-now**, draught, sup.

***sy**, *m.*, buzz, hiss (W.): cf. **drylsy**.

sȳ, **jȳ**, *pron.*, suffixed or object of imp., thou, thee: a softened form of **tȳ**.

sȳ, *vb.*, to hanker, itch, take a whim or fancy, as W. *ysu*: see **sȳans**.

sȳa, *vb.*, to buzz, hiss (W.).

sȳans (*seeanz*, N. Boson, *sceanz*, P.), *m.*, whim, hankering, fancy: *fleghes hep skyans a-vyn gul aga s.*, senseless children will carry out their whimsies, Jenkins of Alverton.

†**sybwedhen**, *f.*, *col.* **sybwȳth** (C. Voc. *sibuit*), fir-tree, *aeps* (? for *saep*) Aelfric: see **saben**.

sȳder, *m.*, cider, B.M. 4451 (M.E.).

syg, *f.*, *pl.* **-yow**, trace (harness), leash, tie, attachment, chain, bond (W., B.): see **sygen**.

***syga**, *vb.*, to shatter, bruise, sprain (W.).

sygen, *f.*, *pl.* **-now**, attachment, fastening cord, loop, as on lead of fishing-line (D. "siggen").

syger (*sēgur*, *zigur*, etc., Lh.), *adj.*, sluggish, lazy, leaky, slow, idle.

sygera, *vb.*, to ooze, drain away, leak slowly, smoulder, simmer, idle, dawdle, D. "sigger": p. pt. *sygerys* (*sigeris*), drained, emptied, Lh.

sygerneth (*segernath*), *m.*, laziness, sluggishness, indifference, sloth ; *why a-dal gasa s.*, you must shun idleness, Borlase MS. ; also wrongly as adj., lazy, dull, Gw. MS., Borlase.

sȳgh, see **sēgh**.

sȳght (*sygth*), *m.*, sight, thing seen, sense of vision, R.D. 619, B.M. (E.) : *yn s. dhyn-ny*, in our sight ; usually replaces **gweles** as noun.

***syjan**, *m.*, silk (W., B.) : see **owrlyn**.

†syker (C. Voc. *sicer*), *m.*, any strong drink, wine excepted, as Aelfric (Med. Lat. *sicera*).

***syllaben**, *f.*, *pl.* **-now**, syllable (W., B.).

***syllaby**, *vb.*, to spell (W.).

Syllan (*Sillan*, N. Boson, *Zillan* Lh. MS.), *f.*, Scilly, the Scilly Isles.

sylly (C. Voc. *selli*), *f.*, *pl.* **-yas**, eel, conger, O.M. 136, C.W. 410 : *s. dowrer*, fresh-water eel, Lh. ; *s. whek*, sun-dried conger, "conger douce," young conger (D. "silliwig") ; B. *sili* is col. with sing. *silien*.

Sylwador, *m.*, *pl.* **-yon**, Saviour, Redeemer.

sylwans, -was, see **sylwyans, -wyas**.

sylwel, selwel, *vb.*, to save, be saved (of souls) : as **gelwel** ; *gul dhe bup den-oll s.*, cause every man to be saved, R.D. 975.

sylwyans, sylwans, *m.*, salvation : the *y* is not sounded after *w* preceded by a consonant, cf. W. *ceidwad* for *ceidwiad*.

Sylwyas, Sylwas, *m.*, *pl.* **-wysy**, Saviour : *y* silent as in **sylwyans**.

†sym (C. Voc. *sim*), *m.*, *pl.* **-as**, ape, monkey.

sy·mphony, *m.*, *pl.* **-s**, mediaeval guitar-shaped hurdy-gurdy, O.M. 2000 (M.E.).

sȳn, *m.*, *pl.* **-ys** (Late *seenez*), sign, distinguishing mark, token, symbol (M.E. *signe*) : *s. an grows*, processional cross, lit. sign of the cross, B.M. 4066 ; *na-vo hyrra es am s.*, that it be no longer than my mark, O.M. 2511.

sȳna, *vb.*, to sign, mark (B.).

syn·aga, *m.*, *pl.* **-gys**, synagogue : "synagogue" and "temple", sing. John XVIII, 20, are made pl. P.C. 1255—7.

syns, see **sans**.

synsy, -jy) (*sensy, -jy*), *vb.*, to hold, grasp, seize, keep, observe, maintain, sustain, esteem, value, estimate, feel, consider : *synsys dhe*, beholden to, under an obligation to : *s. fer*, to hold a fair ; *dhe soth ny a-vyn s.*, we will keep to the southward, B.M. 2292 ; *wor' tu ha'y vam a-n-pewo, y ben a-vynnas s.*, towards his mother whose he was, his head he wished to hold, M.C. 207 ; *ny-synsaf-vy a'th crefter un faven gok*, I don't value thy might at one infertile bean, B.M. 2406 ; 3 s. pret. *synsys* ; 2 s. imp. *syns*, 3 s. subj. *synso*, no vowel change, though *e* is alternatively used in MSS.: see **kensynsy**.

synsyans, *m.*, obligation, estimation, etc. : see **synsy**.

†synsyas (C. Voc. *sinsiat*), *m.*, *pl.* **-ysy**, close-fisted person, grasper, *faest hafod*, *uncystig* Aelfric : see **synsy**.

Synt, *m.*, **Synta**, *f.*, *pl.* **-tys**, Saint, as title (M.E.) : see **sans, -es, Sen**.

Sȳr, syr, syrra (*syour*, B.M. *ser*, P. *sarra*), *m.*, *pl.* **serys**, Sir, sir, title and vocative of respect ; may be prefixed to other titles, *S. Arluth*, *S. Emperour*, *S. Justys*, etc., and in pl. *Syr Doctours*, etc. (M.E. *syre*, *Syr Lord*).

sȳra (C.W. *sera*, Gw. *seera*), *m.*, *pl.* **sȳrys**, sire, father (M.E.) : *s.-da*, father-in-law, P.C. 570 ; *s.-wyn*, grandfather (Lh. *sira widn*) ; see **tās, †whygeran, gwyn**.

syrf, see **sarf**.

***sythel**, *m.*, *pl.* **-thlow**, strainer, colander, filter (W., B.).

***sythla**, *vb.*, to strain, filter (W., B.).

syttys, etc., see **settya**.

syvȳa, *vb.*, to gather strawberries (W., B.) : inf. only.

syvȳen, *f.*, *col.* **syvy** (*sevi* Lh., P.), strawberry : see **moren** (*-cala*).

T (mutations D, Th)

-ta, *suffixed pron.*, thou : joined to vb. ending in *th* or *s*, which may be lost in contraction, as *ota* for *os ta*, *wreta* for *wreth-ta*, *gwythta* for *gwythsys-ta*, etc.

tābel, *m.*, *pl.* **-blys**, table (Late) : Table Main (*t. men*), place-name.

***ta·bernakyl**, *m.*, *pl.* **-aclys**, tabernacle (E.): as **pynakyl**.

tabour, *m.*, *pl.* **-s**, drum, tabor, O.M. 1995 (M.E.).

tacla, *vb.*, to trim, deck, array, furnish : 3 s. pres.-fut. *takyl* ; p. pt. *taclys*, B.M. 3004 (*teklys* Keigwin); *taclyys*, P.C. 2164, Norris, is for *tackyys* in MS., see **takkya**.

taclow (*taklow*), *pl.*, things, living creatures, matters, affairs, gear, tackle (M.E. *takyl*) : *t. pryva*, private matters ; *an t. es ow-*

quaya gans bewnans, the creatures that are moving with life, Gen. I., 20; sing. seems unused, *pyth* or *tra* replacing it.

taga, *vb.*, to choke, stifle, strangle, throttle: p. pt. *tegys*, 3 s. pres.-fut. *tāk*, 3 s. subj. *tacco*.

tag-ardar, *m.*, rest-harrow (W.).

tagell, *f.*, *pl.* **-ow**, noose (B.); double-chin (W.); both lit. choker, see **taga**.

tag-hȳr (*taghir*), *m.*, cuttlebone, Borlase (D. "gear," "shegee").

tāk(g), *m.*, choking (W., B.).

tāk, *m.*, *pl.* **taccow**, clap of hands (B.): see **takya**.

takkya (*tackya*), *vb.*, to nail, secure, fasten, affix: 3 s. pres.-fut. **tak**; *ynny-hy bedhens takkyes* (*tackyys* MS.), on it let him be nailed, P.C. 2164.

takya, *vb.*, to clap hands (D. "tack"): see **tāk**.

tāl (*taal*), *m.*, *pl.* **-yow**, brow, forehead, C. Voc., Ord., C.W.; front, end, top, Gw.; gable, garret (D. "tallyow"): *t. an chy*, gable of the house, Lh.; *t. goles*, bottom end, Gw.; *corn t.*, forehead; in place-names often Tol-; see **a-dal**.

tāl, see **tylly**.

tala (*tallah*), *m.*, *pl.* **-lȳs**, tale; speaking, voice, Kerew, Gen. III., 17: an alternative is to suppose *tallah* written for *dal* or *dala*; see **dathel, dathla**.

talar, *m.*, headland in ploughed field, O.Cor. gloss to Smaragdus, as W., B.: see **ar**.

talek (C. Voc. *tal(h)oc*), *adj.*, big-browed, large-fronted; † *m.*, *pl.* **-ogas**, roach, dace, chub, skelly, *scealga* Aelfric.

talfat, see **talyk**.

†**tagel**, *f.*, pantry, buttery, store-cellar, C. Voc., *hyddern* Aelfric: in C. Voc. *sigillum* is not translated, this being *cellarium* only.

†**talgh** (C. Voc. *talch*), *m.*, bran, *gretta* Aelfric.

talgüdyn, *m.*, forelock (W.): see **cüdyn**.

talkya (*l* sounded), *vb.*, to talk, converse, O.M. 150, C.W. 544 (M.E. *talken*): see **kestalkya**.

tallyour (*talhiar* Lh.), *m.*, *pl.* **-s**, trencher, serving-dish, P.C. 745 (M.E. *tailloir*): *t. pren*, wooden dish or platter (D. "tolyer predn").

talpen, *m.*, *pl.* **-now**, knob (W., B.).

†**talsōgh** (C. Voc. *talsoch*), *adj.*, stupid, dull, blunt-witted, *dwaes* Aelfric: see **tāl, sōgh**.

talver, *m.*, *pl.* **-as**, skate, fish, lit. short-browed (D. "three-tail talver").

talvedhys (*talvez* Lh.), *p.*, *pt.*, worth, valued: see **talvos**.

talvesa, -eja, *vb.*, to reward, value, Keigwin: ? made from *talvez* for **talvedhys** or var. of **talvos**.

talvōl, *adj.*, bald-browed (W.).

talvos (*talves* N. Boson), *vb.*, to value, price: see **tylly**, the only M. Cor. inf. actually found, though both may have existed together.

talyk (*tallack, tallic* P.), *m.*, *pl.* **-ygow**, garret: this resembles E.D. "tallet," loft, in W. Cornwall "talfat," but is probably a dim. of **tāl**, whereas "tallet," "talfat" are from Lat. *tabulatum*; "talfat" is curiously like W. *taflod* with *fl* reversed, but in M. Cor. this should have become *towlas*, and an ancient Celtic loan-word to O.E. would hardly be expected to survive in W. Cornwall alone.

tam (Late *tabm*), *m.*, *pl.* **tymmyn**, morsel, bit, piece, scrap, particle, whit, jot, (of earth) clod, (of food) bite, (of sleep) wink, etc.: *malbew dam*, never a bit; *t. denty*, tit-bit; *ha gwytha t. na-guskens*, and to take care that they slept not a wink, M.C. 241.

tam-ōn, *m.*, thrift, sea-pink (D. "tabm awn").

tān (*tane* P.), *m.*, *pl.* **-ow**, fire: *gans t.*, ablaze, alight, on fire, afire, B.M. 2093, 3712; *wor' tan*, at or by the fire, P.C. 833; *gorra t. yn*, set fire to, set alight, O.M. 1387.

tan, *def. vb.*, 2 imp. sing. *tan*, take thou! here! pl. *tanneugh*, take ye! (in offering something): *t.*, *syns y'th torn an gu-na!* here, hold that spear in thy hand! P.C. 3010; *a'n aval ty kemer, t.!* take thou of the apple, here it is! M.C. 6 (MS. *tam*, not rhyming); *t. dhys dewes ha bos!* take (to thee) drink and food! B.M. 4243; *tanneugh hansel kens sevel!* here's breakfast in bed for you! B.M. 960; *ha tanha y*, Chart. Endors. 9, seems for *a, tan hyhy*, go, take her.

tan, *prep.*, under, by: var. of **dan**, used only in *t. ow fyth*, my faith on it, M.C. 49, O.M. 2534; cf. *war ow fyth, re'm fyth*, on, by, my faith.

tana, *vb.*, to set on fire (W., B.): replaced apparently by *gorra tan yn*.

tanbellen, *f.*, *pl.* **-now**, bomb-shell, cannonball (W.).

tanbren, *m.*, *pl.* **-nyer**, match, match-stick: see **pren.**

tanek, *adj.*, fiery, igneous (B.).

tanflam, *m.*, *pl.* **-mow**, flame of fire, flare (W., B.).

tanflamma, *vb.*, to flare up, burst into flame (W., B.).

tān-gwall, *m.*, conflagration, accidental fire (B.).

tannen, *f.*, *pl.* **-now**, spark of fire (W.).

tān-nōs, *m.*, Will o' the wisp (B.).

tanow, *adj.*, thin, slim, slender, lean ; few, rare, scarce (D. "canno," *c* for *t*) : *ow howetha yu t.*, my equals are few, C.W. 121.

tanöwder, *m.*, thinness, fineness of texture ; scantiness, scarcity, Lh.

tanöwhē·, *vb.*, to attenuate, make slim or scarce : as **berhē.**

tansys, **-jys**, *m.*, *pl.* **-ow**, blaze, bonfire, conflagration.

†**tanter**, *m.*, *pl.* **-toryon**, wooer, suitor, C. Voc., *wogere* Aelfric.

tanvaglen, *f.*, *pl.* **-now**, fire-grate : see **maglen.**

tap, *m.*, *pl.* **-pys**, wooden tap of barrel : *t. an canel*, the pipe and its peg, Borlase, is "tap an(d) cannell" (Fr. *canelle*), stopcock, spigot and faucet.

†**taper**, *m.*, *pl.* **-prys**, **-prow**. wax-candle, C. Voc. (O.E.), *tapor* Aelfric.

taran, *f.*, *pl* **-rennow** (*-ednow* P.), thunder: *crak-t.*, thunder-clap, R.D. 294 ; *men-t.*, "thunderbolt," stone-axe (B.) ; see **tarenna.**

taranek, *adj.*, thunderous, thundery (W.).

***taraw**, *vb.*, to strike, beat ; *m.*, beating (W., B.) : replaced by **gweskel, cronkya, frappya**, etc.

tardar, for **ta·radar**, *m.*, *pl.* **terder**, for **te·reder**, auger, gimlet, O.M. 1002 : *t. tro*, bit and brace (B.).

tardha, *vb.*, to burst, explode, break forth, issue, (of day) dawn, break : 3 s. pres. fut. *tarth*, etc., as **ladha.**

tardhek, see **tredhek.**

tardhell, *f.*, *pl.* **-ow**, embrasure, loop-hole, vent (B.).

tardra, for **ta·radra**, *vb.*, to bore, pierce, drill, tap a barrel (W.) : see **tarder.**

tarenna (Lh. *trenna*, *tredna*), *vb.*, to thunder, roar, boom, explode, detonate, fulminate : *fatel usy ow-colowy ha t.*, how it lightens and thunders, Lh. ; 3 s. pres. fut., 2 s. imp. *taran.*

tarenner, *m.*, *pl.* **-noryon**, thunderer (W.).

tarosvan, **-fan** (C. Voc. *taruutuan*), *m.*, *pl.* **-now**. phantom, fantasy, phantasm, illusion, delusion, apparition, spectre, ghost, *gedwimor* Aelfric, Ord., B.M. : in verse *ta·rosvan.*

tarosvanüs, **-ys**, *adj.*, illusory, fantastic, unreal : see **tarosvan.**

tarow (Lh. *taro*), *m.*, *pl.* **te·rewy**, bull : *maga fuscok avel t.*, as mad as a bull, Borlase MS.

ta·rowvȳr, *m.*, bull-baiting show, bull-ring, bull-fight : Taroveor, place-name ; see **mȳr.**

tarth, **tar'**, *m.*, *pl.* **-rdhow**, burst, break, explosion : *deth-t.*, daybreak, P. ; *t. mor* breaker, surge (B.) ; see **tardha.**

tarya, *vb.*, to tarry, R.D. 445 (M.E. *tary*) : in inf., as in **marya, varya**, the *y* is made a consonant, perhaps imitating **carya**, from **car.**, but 3 s. pres. -fut. would be *tary.*

tās (C. Voc. *tat*, Late *taze*), *m.*, *pl.* **-ow**, father : *an tasow*, P., J. Boson, Keigwin, without mutation, may be correct, cf. B. *an tadou* ; *t.-gwyn*, grandfather, Lh. ; *t.-bysyth*, godfather (W., B.) ; see **sȳra.**

tas, *m.*, *pl.* **-ow**, heap, bundle (D. "tash").

tasek, *adj.*, paternal, patronal ; *m.*, *pl.* **-sygyon**, spiritual father, priest, patron, B.M. 2852.

tasorn (*tasurn* P.), *m.*, *pl.* **-sernow**, wood-pile : cf. **pusorn** and W. *daswrn.*

Tassens (*tās, sans*), *m.*, Holy Father, Pope : *agas, agan, T. a'n Barth North*, heathen devil-god, identified with *Jovyn, Jubyter, Mahum, Moufras*, B.M. 2328, 3427, cf. **sona** ***a'n barth cleth*** ; in the *plen an gwary*, hell was placed at the North of the circle, hence "our Pope of the North."

tāstya, *vb.*, to taste, feel, experience, O.M., C.W. (M.E.).

†**tasveth** (C. Voc. *tatvat*), *m.*, *pl.* **-ow**, foster-father : see †**mēth, mammeth.**

tasyk, *m.*, daddy (B.).

tava, *vb.*, to feel, grope, touch, stroke, pat, be in light contact with : *yn-dan dava*, keeping perpetually just in touch, P.C. 1002 ; 3 s. pres.-fut. *tava*, *my a-dava aga gruf*, I'll stroke their faces (ironical), B.M. 2367.

tavas (C. Voc. *tauot*), *m.*, *pl.* **-ow**, tongue ; language ; *t. -nader*, adder's-tongue fern, Lh. ; *t. clogh*, bell-clapper (B.) ; *t.-carow*, hart's-tongue fern (W., B.); *t.-ojyon*, bugloss (B.); *t.-ky*, borage (B.); as "language" this replaces ***yēth**.

tavasa, -vaja, *vb.*, to tattle, berate, scold (W., B.).

tavasek, *adj.*, verbose, loquacious, talkative, long-tongued, scolding, Lh., Gw.; *m.*, *pl.* **-sogyon**, chatterbox (D. "tavasock"): *drok-davasek*, ill-tongued, Borlase.

tavaseth, *m.*, language, idiom, Lh.: ? imitating W. *tafodiaith*.

tavern (Lh. *-varn*), *m.*, *pl.* **-yow**, inn, tavern, B.M. 3308: *pl.*, **-s**, from M.E., may have been used.

tavernor, *m.*, *pl.* **-yon**, innkeeper (W.,B.): **ta'vernour**, *pl.* **-s**, from M.E., may have been used.

tavethly, *vb.*, to spread, broadcast, show forth, fame, make known, exhibit, display, advertize, report, P.C. 551: p. pt. *tavethlys*; 3 s. pres.-fut. *tevyl* (pr. *tev'l* before vowels); the *th* would probably be lost before *s* in *tavelsa*, *tevylsys*, etc.; *hag a-devyl aga gwara*, who spread out their goods, P.C. 318.

tavethlyans, *m.*, publication, broadcast, display, spread.

†**tavolen**, *f.*, *col.* **tavol**, dock, C. Voc.: *t.-wherow*, sorrel, soursops; *del-tavol*, dock-leaves.

taw, *m.*, silence (W., B.).

tawesek, *adj.*, silent (W., B.).

***tē**, *m.*, tea (formerly pronounced as in D., "tay").

tē. see **tȳ**.

tebel, *adj.* (usually prefixed), evil, wicked; *m.*, *pl.* **-es**, wicked person: *bythqueth whath, t. na mas, ny-welys gansa banna*, never yet, bad or good, have I seen a blink with them, P.C. 397; probably "weak" originally, Lat. *debilis*, cf. **gwan** as prefix.

tebel-art, *m.*, necromancy, black-art, magic, B.M. 2364.

tebel-dewedha, *vb.*, to come to a bad end: *Ay, re-debel-dewethy!* Hi, bad cess to thee! C.W. 520.

tebel-edhen, *f.*, *pl.* **t.-ydhyn**, bird of an ill feather, devil, O.M. 223.

tebel-fara, *vb.*, to come off badly, fare ill, B.M. 2281: see **fara**.

tebel-genesek, *m.*, *pl.* **-sygyon**, ill-born fellow, B.M. 2287.

tebelwas, *m.*, *pl.* **-wesyon**, wicked fellow, P.C., M.C.

tebelwrȳans, *m.*, evildoing, wicked action, B.M. 3502.

tedha, *vb.*, to melt, smelt, found, thaw, dissolve, become melted, Lh.: 3 s. pres.-fut. *tēth*.

tedher, *m.*, *pl.* **-oryon**, melter, founder, smelter (W., B.).

teffo, see **tevy**, also **bōs** as "to have," Appendix VIII.

tegen, *f.*, **-gyn**, *m.*, *pl.* **-now**, pretty little thing, jewel, trinket, ornament with precious stone: probably used of persons also, cf. **whegyn**; *degy-t.*, bear-jewel, nickname of ring-finger ("ticky-tegen," B. Victor): see **tykky-dew**.

tegh, *m.*, lurking, flight, retreat (W., B.): see **godegh**.

teghy, *vb.*, to lurk, sculk, retreat (W., B.).

tegyn, see **tegen**.

tegys, see **taga**.

-tejy, see **-tesy**.

tēk(g) (C. Voc. and Late *teg*), *adj.*, fair, beautiful, pretty, handsome, nice, agreeable, fine, pleasant, without blemish: comp. and excl. *tecca*; *y-fya t.*, *henna a-vya t.*, it, that, would be fine.

teken, *f.*, *pl.* **-now**, little time, moment, Lh.; little bit, scrap (B.): *rak t.*, for a little while, Lh.

tēkhē', *vb.*, to beautify: as **berhē**.

tekter, *m.*, beauty, delight, pleasure, bliss: *dre dekter*, by gentle means, without harshness, without being obliged, willingly, B.M. 408, 2935; see **hakter**.

telghyon, see **talgh**.

tell, see **toll**.

tellek, *adj.*, holey, riddled, porous: *m.*, *pl.* **-lygyon**, pockfretten person or ragamuffin, term of abuse: *avond, t., dhe'th crejy!* begone, holey rascal, hang thee! B.M. 3492.

teller, see **tyller**.

telly, *vb.*, to bore, drill, make a hole through: p. pt. *tellys*; 3 s. pres. -fut. *tell*, 2 s. imp. *toll*; 3 s. impf. ind. *telly*, *tylly*; 3 s. pret. *tollas*; 3 s. subj. *tollo*, 3 s. plupf. *tollsa*.

tellyk, *m.*, *pl.* **-ygow**, little hole, puncture: *t. whes*, pore (B.).

†**telyn** (C. Voc. *telein*), *f.*, *pl.* **-now**, harp: seems replaced by **harp**.

†**telynya**, *vb.*, to harp: see **telynyor**,

†**telynyor, -yer** (C. Voc. *teleinior*), *m.*, *pl.* **-yoryon**, *f.* **-es**, *pl.* **-ow**, harpist, harper.

temmyk, *m.*, *pls.* **-ygow**, Lh., **tymmynygow**, little bit, fragment, atom,

templa, tempel, *m., pl.* **-plys,** temple (M.E.): **tempel** may be a more Celtic form, with pl. **-plow** (W., B).

tempra, *vb.*, to tame, subdue, moderate, control, temper, tone down, P.C.. B.M. (M.E. *tempre*): 3 s. pres.-fut. *temper*; see **dystempra.**

temprer, *m., pl.* **-roryon,** trainer of animals: see **tempra.**

temptasyon (*-acyon*, etc.), *m.*, temptation (M.E.).

temptya, -ta (*temtya*), *vb.*, to tempt (M.E.).

ten, *m., pl.* **-now,** pull, pulling, tug, drag, draught stretch, gunshot; indrawing of breath; drink, act of drinking; drawing, plan, sketch; (carpentry) beam, stretcher: *dre an t.* (wrongly *cen* Norris), by dint of the dragging, P.C. 2138, 2141; *gul tennow orth,* to gainsay, dispute or contend with, B.M. 2965; see **yn-ten.**

tender, *adj.*, youthful, tender (M.E): *t. yn os,* of tender age, immature, B.M. 115: a probable older form would be ***tener** (W., B.).

tenewan (*-on, -en,* Lh. *ternehwan,* N. Boson *treneuhan,* J. Tonkin *ternuan*), *m., pl.* **tenwennow,** side, flank: *gorra seth dhe-denewan,* to set an arrow beside (the bow), C.W. 1553; *poran ryb ow thenewan,* close beside me, C.W. 194; *a'n yl t.*, on one side, aside, sideways, from his side, beside me, etc.; *dun dredha gans cledhevyow a'n* (*a'un*) *t. dh'y gyla,* let's run swords through them from one side to the other, B.M. 1267.

***tenky,** *vb.*, to pledge, bargain, destine: 3 s. pret. *toncas* (W., B.).

***tenkys,** *f.*, fate, destiny (W., B.).

ten-lester, *m., pl.* **-lystry,** tugboat: see **lester.**

tenna (Late *tedna*), *vb.*, to pull, pluck, take (off), haul, drag, draw, extract; sketch, translate (W., B.); prevail on, induce, seduce; shoot; stretch, strain: vowel-change to *y* in stem before *e* and still more before *y* is common in Ord., but not elsewhere; p. pt. *tennys, tynnys;* 2 pl. imp. *tennyn, tynnyn*; *t. dhe,* to shoot at; *t. yn-kerth,* (of bulked fish) to remove; *t. seth, gwarak, gon,* to shoot; *t. cledha,* to draw sword; *pup-oll tennens dh'y arvow,* let everyone take to his weapons, to arms, each one! B.M. 3449; see **omdenna.**

†tenow, †tnow, *m., pl.* **-newyow,** dale, low ground, O. Cor. in charter, as O.W., O.B. *tnou,* now W. *tyno,* plat, B. *traou(n),* bottom, *traonienn,* valley, with *n* become *r* as in *kraouenn,* Cor. **knofen.**

tenros, *f., pl.* **-ow,** drawnet (W.).

tenvargh, *m., pl.* **-vergh,** draught-horse (W.).

tenven, *m., pl.* **-veyn,** magnet, lodestone (W.).

ter-[2], see APPENDIX II.

***tēr,** *adj.*, eager, pressing, urgent, fervent, vehement, impetuous (W., B.).

'ter, late contraction of **ynter.**

tereba, treba, trelebba, lebma, *conj.*, until, even to: these late contractions probably represent *ynter hemma ha* or *ynter an le-ma ha*; cf. B. *trema ha, etrese(g), entrese ha.*

***terebentyn,** *m.*, turpentine.

terewy, see **tarow.**

***terghy,** *vb.*, to coil, wreathe: 3 s. pret. *torghas* (W.); see **torgh,** f.

terghya, -gha, *vb.*, to turn over the soil, dig with the snout (W., B.): 3 s. pret. *torghyas*; see **torgh,** m.

†tergusca, *vb.*, to sleep intermittently, be wakeful, C. Voc.: see **fōl.**

tergwyth, *adv.*, three times: see **tȳr,** num.

terlemmel, *vb.*, to jump about, frisk, skip, palpitate, B.M. 2100: as **lemmel.**

terlenky, *vb.*, to gulp, swallow with difficulty (W., B.): as **lenky.**

terlentry, *vb.*, to glitter, glisten, twinkle, sparkle, shine, C.W. 129, 168: 3 s. pres.-fut. *terlenter.*

termyn, *m., pl.* **-yow,** time, season, term, period; *adv.*, at the time when: *a ver dermyn, a dermyn ber,* quickly, speedily; *yn t. da,* in a good hour, happily; *t. a-dhe,* hereafter, in time to come, in the future, B.M. 1921, 2024; *t. my a-ve maw,* when I was a boy, W. Bodener; *erbyn agan bos gansa, t. vyth dhyn-ny sopya,* by the time we are with them, it will be time for us to have supper, PC. 703.

termynak, *adj.*, dawdling, dilatory, time-wasting; *m., pl.* **-nogyon,** dawdler (D. "tarmenack").

†tern (anciently *tigern*), *m., pl.* **-ow,** sovereign, prince, king (W., B.); kept only in **myghtern.**

ternans, see **tȳr-nans.**

ternestatha, see **durnostadha.**

ternos (*tra-, an nōs*), *adv.*, on the morrow,

next day, lit. over the night: *t. vyttyn*, to-morrow morning, on the following morning; see **trenja.**

terroja (*teroge*, ? for *terroseth*), *m.*, ? havoc, finish (of a chase), R.D. 2303.

terros (*-rus*), *m.*, *pl. and abst.*, **terryjy**, ? ruin, perdition, disaster, destruction, downfall, O.M. 360, 554, P.C. 43, 112, 1532.

terry, *vb.*, to break, destroy, become broken, break into or out of, tear down (house), break in (horse), pick, gather, pluck (fruit, seed, or flowers): 3 s. pret. *torras*; 2 pl. impf. subj. *torren*, 3 s. pres.-fut. *ter*; 2 s. imp. *tor*; 3 s. plupf. *torsa*; plupf. impers. pass. *tersys*, R.D. 1318; *t. dhe'n dor an templa*, to pull down the temple; Lh. in *Jowan Chy-an-Horth*, 46, has *dzhei a dorhaz* (W. *a dorras*) *an dezan* (*y a-dorras an desen*), but the original would have had *a-droghas*, had the meaning "to cut" been intended.

terthen, *f.*, *pl.* **-now** (*tarthennou* B.M. 1423), *col.* **terth**, tertian ague, intermittent fever: see **lesderth.**

tervans (*-vyns*), *m.*, turmoil, din, tumult, R.D. 2576, cf. W. *tyrfu*, *tyrfain*.

tervy, *vb.*, to make a din or tumult (W.).

***tēry**, *vb.*, to be impetuous or eager, take up a cause eagerly, argue vehemently (W., B.).

†tes, *m.*, heat, warmth, C. Voc.: see **†trethes.**

tesen (*tezan*), *f.*, *pl.* **-now**, cake, Lh.: *t. gales*, biscuit (W.).

tesak, *adj.*, sunny, hot, sultry (W.).

test (C. Voc. *tist*), *m.*, *pl.* **-ow**, witness, *gewita* Aelfric; *text (B.): *Dew yn t.!* God (as) witness!

testa, *vb.*, to bear witness (misread *dhe desca*, Norris, R.D. 2115): see **desta.**

***te·stament**, *m.*, testament (W., B.).

***testen**, *f.*, *pl.* **-now**, text, subject (W.).

-tesȳ·, -tejȳ·, *pron.* (emphatic), thou, thee: form of *-desy* preferred after *s*, *th* and as lengthened form of *-ta*; elsewhere it always becomes *-dhesy*, *-dhejy*.

tesy, *vb.*, to warm in the sun (W., B.).

tety-valy, *interj.* (of contempt or impatience), tush! pshaw! pish! tut-tut! tilly-vally! C.W. 1305.

tēth, *adj.*, molten, melted; *m.*, melting: see **tedha.**

tēth, *f.*, *pl.* **-ow**. teat (W., B.).

tethen, *f.*, *pl.* **-now**, teat, Lh.: dim. of **tēth**,

tethla, tethty, *m.*, **tethva**, *f.*, foundry (W., B.).

tethlester, *m.*, *pl.* **-lystry**, crucible (W., B.).

tevy (*tyvy*), *vb.*, to grow, germinate, spring up, shoot, grow together, coalesce, stick fast: 3 s. pres. -fut. *tȳf*; 3 s. pret. *tevys*; *v* becomes *ff* in 2 and 3 s. subj., *f* before *s*; *tevys dhe dhen*, grown up; *ow hoberson, a-ve gwres t. dre vol hes-oll ow croghen scorjyes*, my habergeon, that was caused to cleave by clotted blood all along my scourged skin, R.D. 2537.

tevyl, see **tavethly**,

tew, *adj.*, thick, fat, impenetrable, foggy, O.M. 546, Lh.

tewal, etc., see **tewl.**

***tewas** (Lh. *†tumos* from W.), *col.*, sand (W.): see ***tewesyn.**

tewder, *m.*, thickness, fatness, Lh.

tewedhak, *adj.*, weather-beaten, bearing signs of exposure (D. "towethack," used of complexion): see **teweth.**

tewel, *vb.*, to be silent, cease speaking, hush, hold one's peace: 2 s. imp. *taw*, 3 s. pres. -fut. *tew*, 1 s. *tawaf*; 3 s. pret. *tewys*; 3 s. subj. *tawo*; *taw dhymmo-vy!* hush when I tell thee! *taw gans dha whethlow!* stop with your nonsense! *taw dha vyn!* hold thy tongue!

tewennek, *adj.*, consisting of sand-hills (W., B.).

tewennow, see **towan.**

***tewesek**, *adj.*, sandy (W.).

***tewessa**, *vb.*, to gather sand (W.): inf. only.

***tewesyn**, *m.*, *pl.* **-now**, grain of sand (W.).

teweth, *m.*, storm, weather (W.): see **tewedhak.**

tewhē·, *vb.*, to thicken, fatten: as **berhē.**

tewl, tewal (*teule*), *adj.*, dark, gloomy, murky, blind: *tewal* (like W., B.) is Lhuyd's restoration; in R.D. 539, 1274, B.M. 3680, we have *tewl*; see **tewolgow.**

tewlder, *m.*, darkness, Keigwin, Gen. I.

tewlel (Late *towlal*, *towla*), *vb.*, to throw, toss, cast; intend, contrive, mean (to do), destine: 2 s. imp. *towl*, 3 s. pres. fut. *tewl*; 3 s. pret. *tewlys*: *t. warnodho bos*, accuse him of being; *t. paw*, set foot; *t. deu-dhorn war*, lay hands on eagerly or roughly; *t. pren*, cast lot; *t. towl*, make a plan; *t. ros*, shoot a net.

tewlhē·, tewalhē·, *vb.*, to darken: as **berhē.**

tewlwolow, tewalwolow, *m.*, half-light,

twilight, lit. "darklight" (D. "tulla lulla").

tewlyjyon, tewaljyon, *m.*, darkness, obscurity (B.): cf. **golowyjon.**

tewolgow, tew·olgow, tewlgow (C. Voc. *tiwuigou*, *i* for *l*, Lh. *tūlgū*, Kerew, *tolgo*, D. "tulgy"), *abst. pl.*, darkness, the dark.

teyl, tӯl (*teil* Lh., *tyle* Gw.), *m.*, manure, dung: *pyl t.*, dunghill, Lh.

teyla, *vb.*, to manure (W., B.).

teylek, tylek, *f.*, *pl.* **-egy,** manure-heap (B.): Park an Dillick, field-name.

-th[5]**-,** *infixed pron.*, thee: often drops out before *f* in **bōs** as "to have," e.g., *na 'fe*, etc.

'th[5], *poss. pron.*, thy (after prep. or conj. ending in vowel): *b*, *m*. become *v*, not *f*, after it.

thrōn, see **trōn.**

†tnow, see **†tenow.**

†To-[2], anciently an honorific prefix to saints' names, as Towednack (*To- Gwennoc*), etc., usually found in mutation as *de*, *do* after *Lan* in place-names, Landewednack, Landoho, etc.; an archaic form of the 2 s. poss. pron. so prefixed.

tō, *m.*, **-ow, -how,** roof, thatch, *thaecen*, *rof* Aelfric.

tobacco (*tubakko* Lh.), *m.*, tobacco.

toch, -ya, see **tuch, -ya.**

***tōk,** *m.*, *pl.* **-ogow,** cap (W., B.).

tōkyn (C.W. *-ken*), *m.*, *pl.* **tōknys,** sign, symbol, emblem, token, evidence; *ticket (M.E.): P.C. 338 should be restored as *pan dokyn us a vertu a-dhysquedhysta dhyn-ny*, what token is there of power that thou wast showing to us, replied to l. 343, *tokyn dheugh mar ny-dhyswa*, if no token is apparent to you.

†tolcorn, *m.*, *pl.* **tolkern, -ow,** clarion, trumpet, cornet, C. Voc. *trudhhorn*, *sarga* Aelfric.

tolgh, *m.*, *pl.* **-ow,** hillock, as W. *twlch*: see **godolghyn.**

toll, *m.*, *pl.* **tell,** hole, pit: *py doll an jawl yth-ama, yth-eth-e?* wherever shall I, did he, go? B.M. 794, 1028; *t. lowarn*, *brogh*, etc., den, burrow; *t. ke*, ditch beside a hedge, C.W. 1128; *t. colom*, pigeon-hole; *t. cath*, cat-hole in door (B.); see **tellek, telly, tellyk.**

toll, *f.*, *pl.* **-ow,** toll, tax, customs, duty (W.) see **tollor.**

toll, *adj.*, perforated, holed, hollow, pierced: Gark Tull (*an garrek t.*), rock-name.

toll, -a, see **tull, -a.**

tollborth, *m.*, toll-gate (W.).

tollek, *adj.*, punctured, perforated, hollow, Lh.: see **tellek,** from pl.

tolljy, *m.*, *pl.* **-ow,** toll-house, custom house (W.).

†tollor, *m.*, *pl.* **-yon,** tax-gatherer, toll-collector, customs officer, C. Voc., *tollere* Aelfric.

tollva, *f.*, toll-place (W.).

tollven, *m.*, *pl.* **-veyn, -venow,** holed stone: Tolven, Tolvenou, place-names.

tolly, *vb.*, to take toll, tax, levy a duty (W.): see **tollor.**

tom (C. Voc. *toim*, B.M. *tum*, Lh. *tubm*), *adj.*, hot, warm, ardent: *dowr t.*, ardent spirits; *park t.*, sunny or arable field; *gast dom*, bitch in heat, Lh.

tomals, *m.*, ample quantity, plenty, Lh. (D. "tummals," lots, heaps): the *s* seems an added E. pl., cf. W. *talm*, Ir. *tamal*, space, while, amount.

tomder (C. Voc. *tunder* for *tumder*, Borlase *tombder* for *tobmder*), *m.*, heat, warmth.

tomen (*tuban* Lh. for *tubmen*, *tubben*), *f.*, *pl.* **-now,** earth bank, dam, dyke, mound.

tomhē·, *vb.*, to make hot: as **berhē.**

tomma (Lh., P. *tubma*), *vb.*, to heat, warm: p. pt. *tommys*; 3 s. and pl. *tommens*.

tomyjyon, *m.*, warmth (B.).

ton, *f.*, *pl.* **-now,** wave, billow, Lh.

ton (Late *todn*), *m. or f.*, *pl.* **-yow,** unploughed land, lay, greensward, grass-land, turf, surface: *wor' (war) t.*, on the ground or grass, B.M. 3505; to the surface, D. "up to grass," R.D. 2281; *wor'*, not *war*, is seen in place-names Chywarton, Chiverton, Chivvytodden, without mutation; in W., *ton*, lay, is m., *ton*, surface, is f., in Cor. gender seems varied, Street an Dodden (f.), but Toddencoath (m.).

***tōn,** *m.*, *pl.* **-yow,** tune, melody, accent, tone, intonation (W., B.).

tonek, *m.*, flock, crowd, M.C. 257: ?an epithet from **ton,** turf, with reference to sheep; the translation is Keigwin's.

tonnek, *adj.*, wavy, turbulent, rough (W.).

†tonnel, *f.*, *pl.* **-low,** cask, tun, keeve, C. Voc., *cyfe* Aelfric.

tonnen (Late *todnen*), *f.*, *pl.* **-now,** patch of greensward, growing turf; skin (W., B.): Enys Dodnan, rock-name.

tōnt, tount, *adj.*, impudent, saucy, pert, B.M. (M.E., and D., *taunt*).

tōntya, tountya, *vb.*, to be cheeky, B.M. 3300.
***tōnya,** *vb.*, to intone, accentuate (W., B.).
top, *m.*, *pl.* **-yow,** top, summit, peak, C.W.: *t. an pen*, crown of the head, Lh.; Top Teeb, Top Lobm, place-names.
top, *m.*, *pl.* **-pys,** round-top of ship, B.M. 599 (M.E.).
topyn, *m.*, *pl.* **-now,** tip, pointed top: Carn Topna (*topynnow*), rock-name.
tor, *f.*, *pl.* **-row,** belly, womb: *t. an dorn*, palm of the hand, Lh., or probably ball of thumb (D. "belly of the hand"); in place-names Tor, rock-pile, is O.E.; Torpen, a devil's name, C.W., suggests a mediaeval devil with a second face, "belly-head," rather than B. *torr-penn*, din, bother.
tor, *m.*, *pl.* **-yow,** break, breach, fracture, rupture (W., B.): see **terry.**
tor', see **torn, torth.**
toras, *m.*, (of pigs, etc.), litter (W., B.).
torchen, *f.*, *pl.* **-now,** torch, flare, Lh. (wrongly spelt as if *torghen*).
torek, *adj.*, big-bellied (W., B.).
***torgengel,** *f.*, *pl.* **-glow,** horse's belly-band (W.): see ***kengel.**
†**torgh** (C. Voc. *torch*), *m.*, *pl.* **-as,** hog, barrow-pig, *bearh* Aelfric: *t. cos*, wild boar (W.); see **terghya.**
***torgh,** *f.*, *pl.* **tergh,** wreath, neck-chain, torque, coil (W.).
torleveryas, *m.*, *pl.* **-ysy,** ventriloquist (O.B.): see **tor** f., †**leveryas.**
tor-mēn, *m.*, saxifrage (W., B.).
torment (*-mont*), *m.*, *pl.* **-ns,** torment (M.E.).
tormentor, *m.*, *pl.* **-s, -ys,** officer of the law, executioner, torturer (M.E. *tormentour*).
tormentya (*-montya*, C.W. *tormountya*), *vb.*, to torment, put to torture (M.E.).
torn, tor', *m.*, *pl.* **-ow,** turn, turning, time (M.E.): *tebel dorn*, malicious act; *t. da*, good turn, benevolent act, *namur a dorn da ny-wraf*, not many kind deeds do I perform, C.W. 1442; *war y dorn*, in his turn; *n* dropped before *-ma*, *yn tor'-ma* (C.W. *torn-ma*), at this time; *peswar t.*, cross-roads; *t. an forth*, place where roads meet.
torogen, *f.*, *col.* **torak** (O. Cor. gloss *toroc*), tick, parasitic insect.
torras, etc., see **terry.**
torth, tor' (*torh* Lh.), *f.*, *pl.* **-ow,** loaf: *t. vara*, *t. a vara*, loaf of bread, R.D. 1490, 1314, but Tor' Bara, rock-name; *t. cor*, cake of wax (B.).
***tōs,** *m.*, dough (W., B.).
tos, *m.*, drinking-cup, B.M. 80 (M.E. *tass*, Fr. *tasse*).
tos, *m.*, *pl.* **-ow,** tuft, bunch, tassel (D. "tosh").
tōs, see **tȳ,** irreg. vb.
***tosa,** *vb.*, to knead bread (W., B.).
†**tosak,** *adj.*, tufted: see **lesdosak, tos.**
tosen, *f.*, *pl.* **-now,** *col.* **tōs,** ear of corn (W., B.).
tōth (*tovth*), *m.*, haste, hurry: adverbially *t. bras*, *t. da* or *ta*, *t. men*, *gans mur a doth*, very quickly: see **kettoth, totta.**
tothya, *vb.*, to hasten: 2 s. imp. *tōth*, P.C. 1041.
totta (*toth, da*), *adv.*, quickly, with speed.
toul (M.C. *towyll*, C.W. *tool*), *m.*, *pl.* **-ys,** tool, implement, P.C. (M.E.).
tount, -ya, see **tōnt, -ya.**
tour, *m.*, *pl.* **-ys,** small erection in the *plen an gwary*, used by one playing the part of a king, etc. (M.E. *tour*).
tour, tūr (C. Voc. *tur*, Lh. MS. *tūr*), *m.*, *pl.* **-ow,** steeple, tower: T. Babylon (tower of Babel), rock-name; see **clēghtour.**
***tournay,** *m.*, *pl.* **-s,** tournament (M.E.).
touryk, *m.*, *pl.* **-ygow, -rowygow,** turret (B.).
towal, *m.*, *pl.* **-wellow,** towel, P.C. 836.
towan (? older *tewyn*), *m.*, *pl.* **tewennow,** sand-hill, dune, hillock (D. "towans"): place-names Tewington, Pentewan, Porth Towan, Towan Blistra.
towarghek, *f.*, *pl.* **-egy, -egow,** peat-bog, turbary (B.); turfy place: Park an Turk, field-name.
towarghen, *f.*, *col.* **towargh,** sod, turf, peat for burning (D. "toor"): Tredowargh, place-name.
towl (*toul*), *m.*, *pl.* **-ow,** throw, stroke, cast, plan, project, plot, design, aim, fall in wrestling: *tewlel t.*, to scheme, devise a plan; *t. howl*, sunstroke (B.); *yma war agan t. knoukya*, we intend to strike, O.M. 2698; *ef a-ros t. dhodho*, he threw him, in wrestling.
towla, see **tewlel.**
tra (C. Voc. *tro*, *o* for **a**), *neuter*, *pl.* **-ow** (pl. replaced by **taclow**), thing, affair, business, matter, substance, fact, estate; f. after **an**[2], **un**[2], and as affecting adjs., but preceded by m. numeral and replaced by m.

pron.: *gensy y'fyth t. dek*, with her thou shalt have a fine dowry, B.M. 304; *an dra*, the thing, or more emphatically *un dra*, a certain thing, is used as "this," "that," "what" with vbs. of telling or knowing, *un dra a-won, a-n-gothfes*, what I know, if thou knewest it, O.M. 151, C.W. 545, *my a-th-warn prest a un dra*, I now tell thee this, B.M. 3580, *a ny-wodhough-why un dra?* do ye not know this? R.D. 2445; *ny-dhowtyaf t. y'n bys*, I don't doubt in the least; *ha t. nahen*, and nothing else: see **travyth.**

tra-, see Appendix II.

tragesort (*tragezaut* Ray), *m.*, *pl.* **-as**, spider-crab (D. "'gezza'-crab"): cf. **sort.**

tramōr (*tremor* Lh.), *adj.*, oversea, from over seas.

tranjyak, *m.*, dream, ecstacy, difficulty, Borlase (D. "tranyak"): ? *transyak* from "trance" in old meanings.

trank, *m.*, period; used in expression *t. hep worfen*, time without end, for eternity, for ever and ever.

transformya, *vb.*, to transform, transfer, convey, translate (to heaven), C.W. 2112 (M.E.).

trap, *m.*, *pl.* **-pys**, step-stile (M.E.): field-name Park an Trap.

***traskel**, *m.*, *pl.* **tryskly**, missel-thrush, as B. *draskl*, see ***tresklen.**

travalya (Lh. *travalia*, Borlase *travla*), *vb.*, to walk far, trudge, travel (M.E. *travailen*, D. "travel," to walk).

travel, *m.*, *pl.* **-lys**, walk, trudge, travel, distance walked (D. "travel").

travyth (*trevyth*, *tra*, *-vyth*), *pron.*, *f.*, anything: used only with neg., *hep*, *fyllel*, *awos*, or suggestion of doubt, then replacing **neppyth**, **nep-tra.**

trawythys (*tra-*, *gwyth*, *-ŭs*), *adj.*, rare, scarce, occasional, Lh.

trawythyow (*tra-*, *gwythyow*, B.M. *trewythyow*, Gw. *terwithyaw*), *adv.*, occasionally, sometimes, now and then, lit. over times.

traylya, see **trēlya.**

trayson, trēson (*treyson*), *m.*, treason, treachery, treacherous behaviour (M.E. *traisoun*).

trayta, *vb.*, to betray, M.C. 145: inf. made from *traytor*, M.E. inf. is *trayse*.

traytor (*treytour*, etc.), *m.*, *pl.* **-s**, traitor, betrayer (M.E.).

tray·tury (*tretury*, *treytury*), *m.*, treachery, M.C. 194 (M.E. *traitorye*).

tre-, see **ter-**, **tra-**, Appendix II.

tre-, var. of **try, tyr** in certain compounds, *tredde·n*, *tredde·th*, *treffe·r*, *trelle·s*, *tremmy·l*, *tremmy·s*, see **dēn, dēth, fēr, lēs, mȳl, mȳs.**

tre(f), *f.*, *pls.* **treven, trevy** (houses), **trevow** (towns, villages, hamlets, farms, holdings), dwelling-place, home, home-stead, farm; village, town; †clan, tribe; *adv.*, back, home: *ry t.*, to give back; *mos t.*, to go home; *a-dre*, from home; *dhe-dre*, home, as interj., home with you! *tu ha t.*, homewards; *yn-tre*, at home; *a'n dre*, from the town; *dhe'n dre*, to town; *tu ha'n dre*, townwards; *y'n dre*, in the town, in town; *an dremma*, this town: *tref*, *trev*, occurs before vowels, as *treveglos*; *tre*, like **kēr** (*car*) and **lan**, sometimes causes in place-names a mutation resembling 3rd; rhymes suggest that when unstressed and in adverbial expressions *tra* is the usual pronunciation, as last word of compound place-names this is the spelling also, as Hendra; in place-names *tre an* becomes Tren- and before *b* Trem-, e.g. Trendrine, Trembethow (*an dreyn, an bedhow*); see **drē.**

trebeth (C. Voc. *tribet*, Lh. *trebath*), *m.*, *pl.* **-edhow**, trivet, brandis, tripod, *brandisen* Aelfric.

trebüchya (*trebytchya*), *vb.*, to trip, tumble, stumble, turn upside down, reverse, revert, return, recoil, spring back like a trebuchet, C.W. 270, 1582 (M.E., Fr. *trebucher*).

trebyl, *m.*, *adj.*, treble, soprano, third part in plain-song, R.D. 2360 (M.E.).

***tredan**, *m.*, electricity (W., B.).

***tredanek**, *adj.*, electric (W., B.).

tredhek (Late var. *tardhak*), *card. num.*, thirteen.

tref, see **tre(f).**

treftas (Lh. *trevdas*, invented), *m.*, *pl.* **-ow**, patriarch: see **ugheldas.**

tregereth (*trugar*, *-eth*), *f.*, *pl.* **-ow**, compassion, pity, mercy, sympathy: *kemeres t. war*, to take pity on: *warnas t.!* on thee (I cry) mercy!

tregerethüs, -ys, *adj.*, compassionate, merciful (B.).

†trēgh (C. Voc. *trech*, Lat. *truncus* and *frustum*, miscopied *fructus*), *m.*, *pl.* **-ow**, stump, log, stock, *stoc*, Aelfric; slice, chop, steak, cut, section, *stycce* Aelfric: *t. a vara*, slice of bread; *t. bowyn*, beefsteak, etc.

trēgher, *m.*, *pl.* **-ghoryon**, tailor, cutter, Gw.: Trayer, Trahair, personal name.

treghury, *m.*, treachery, R.D. 90 (M.E. *trecherye*): see **traytury**, the *gh* may be a slip for *ch*.

trēghy, *vb.*, to cut, cut down, chop, slice: 3 s. pret. *trōghas*; 2 s. imp. *trōgh*; 3 s. pres.-fut. *trēgh*, and vowel becoming *e* elsewhere in sympathy with *e* and *y* of endings.

trēghyas, *m.*, *pl.* **-ysy**, cutter, carver: *t. meyn*, stone-cutter, O.M. 2411.

***treky**, *vb.* to exchange (B.): see **trok.**

trelūba, *vb.*, to keep stirring tin-slime (D., "treloobing"); see **lūb.**

trēlya, traylya, trēla (C.W. *trey-*, *try-*, Lh. *tray-*, *trai-*), *vb.*, to turn, wind, twist, change, cause mutation, convert, recant, translate, return, revert: *t. dhe-ves*, turn away; *t. yn-mes a*, pervert from; *t. a-dro dhe*, wind round; *t. wor' tu-ma*, turn this way.

trēlyans (*trayllyanz* Lh.), *m.*, *pl.* **-ow**, translation, turning, changing, mutation.

trem, *f.*, sight, look (W.; B. *dremm*); see **tremyn.**

tremadhēves (*trematheeves* Borlase), *m.*, dance or game in which players form a ring: ? for *tremen a dheves*, passing of sheep, cf. French form of "Oranges and Lemons," *Ramene tes Moutons*.

tremen, *m.*, *pl.* **-yow.** act of passing, migration (B.).

tremena, *vb.*, to pass, surpass, exceed, cross, pass over, pass away, go by, elapse, die, suffer spiritual death: see **camdremena.**

tremenva, *f.*, gangway, passage, crossing, dying, passing (B.).

tremenyans, *m.*, passing, intercourse, Lh.

tremenyas, *m.*, *pl.* **-ysy**, passer-by, traveller (B.).

tremyn, *m.*, appearance, look, aspect, face: *may whothfen t. y'n bys yntredho ha'y gowetha*, that I should recognize a single face amongst him and his companions, P.C. 1287.

trenja (*trendzha* Lh., *tra an jeth*), *adv.*, on the day after to-morrow, two days hence, lit. over the day, as W. *trennydd*: see **ternos.**

trenk (*trink*, Gw.), *adj.*, sour, acid, astringent, sharp, Lh.

trenkles, *m.*, rhubarb: see **†les.**

trenkhē., *vb.*, to make or become sour (B.): as **berhē.**

trenkter, *m.*, sourness (B.).

trēnya, see **trȳnya.**

trenyja (*ter-*, *nyja*, Lh. *tarneidzha*), *vb.*, to flutter, flit, O.M. 1142: describes flapping flight of dove, as V. *treneijal*, to flutter.

trēs, *m.*, *pl.* **-ow**, way, track: *t. aral*, another way, opposed to *an yl torn*, one time, O.M. 2549, as B. *d'un tres arall* (M.E., Fr. *trace*).

***tresklen**, *f.*, *col.* **treskel**, missel-thrush (W.).: see **traskel.**

trēson, see **trayson.**

trēsor (*treasur*), *m.*, treasure, B.M., Gw. (M.E. *tresour*).

tresorya, *vb.*, to treasure (M.E.).

trespas (*-pys*), *m.*, trespass, offence against law or right, transgession (M.E.).

trespassya (*-pascya*), *vb.*, to trespass, transgress, P.C. 1441 (M.E.).

tressa, tryssa, tryja (*tredzha, tridzha*, Lh.), *ord. num.*, third.

trest, see **tryst.**

trest, *m.*, trust, confidence, expectation, hope, assurance, reliance (M.E.): *t. a-m-bus*, I trust, I feel sure, B.M. 301; *oll ow threst warnas yma*, all my trust is in thee, B.M. 3195.

trest. *adj.*, trusty, P.C. 948: possibly for *tryst* used as M.E. *sad*.

trēster, trüster (C. Voc. *troster*), *m.*, *pl.* **-s, -trow**, beam, cross-bar, as W. *trostr*, but given an E. pl. O.M. 963.

trestya (*try-*), *vb.*, to trust, hope, expect confidently: *t. dhe, yn*, to trust to, rely or depend on; *trest dhymmo*, take my word for it; *na-drestyn-ny dhe henna*, let us not rely upon that; *gwreugh-why t. yn y ras*, trust in his grace.

trēth (C. Voc. *trait*), *m.*, *pl.* **-ow**, sand-beach, strand, sea-shore, *sandceosel* Aelfric: *t. lenky*, quicksand, Lh.

trēth, *m.*, *pl.* **-yow**, ferry, passage over water, as B. *treiz*: there was a ferry at Treath, now removed to Helford; Tredreath is probably "ferry-town" at Lelant; Tywardreath named a house on the ancient ferry across to Landreath, ferry enclosure.

trētha, *vb.*, to ferry, cross by a ferry (B.).

trethek, *adj.*, sandy (B.).

trethen, *f.*, *pl.* **-now**, small sand patch (D. "drethan"); grain of sand (B.): **t. vew*, quicksand.

†trethes (*tre-*, *tes*, C. Voc. *en tredes*, *d* as *th*), *m.*, extreme heat, *swalodh* Aelfric.

trēthor, *m.*, *pl.* **-yon**, ferryman (B.).

trēthyas, *m.*, *pl.* **-ysy**, **-yjy**, passenger by ferry (B.)

trettya, *vb.*, to tread, stamp, trample (M.E. *tret*, treads) : *mos yn-un-drettya*, to go tramping, take short high steps, a miracle-player's convention representing great speed and distance of travel, B.M. 1393 ; *t. yn-dan dreys*, to trample underfoot B.M. 2030.

trētury, see **traytury.**

trevas, *f.*, *pl.* **-ow**, **-vajow**, tillage, crop, produce, harvest, O.M. 425.

treven, see **tre(f)**, **chy.**

treveglos, *f.*, churchtown, village or hamlet with parish church : place-names, var. Treneglos with *an*.

trevesygeth, *m.*, settlement, colony (W.).

trevesyk (C. Voc. *trevedic*), *m.*, *pl.* **-ygyon**, **-ejygyon**, husbandman, *tilia* Aelfric ; countryman, rustic, *aecerceorl* Aelfric : † *t. dor*, indigenous inhabitant, native of soil, *inlendisc* Aelfric.

treveth, *f.*, ? tillage ; domicile, homestead, N. Boson.

treveth (*-feth*), *m.*, time, occasion : *lyes t.*, on many occasions, P.C. 1724 ; *tressa t.*, the third time, O.M. 799.

trew, *m.*, saliva, spittle : see **trewa.**

trewa (*trua*, Lh. *treffia*), *vb.*, to spit, expectorate : 3 s. pret. *trewys* ; 3 s. pres.-fut. *trew*.

trewyas (Lh. *trifiaz*), *m.*, spittle.

trewythyow, see **trawythyow**.

treyla, **-ya**, see **trēlya.**

treynya, see **trȳnya.**

trēys, see **trōs**,

tro, *f.*, *pl.* **-yow**, turn, twist, circuit, occasion, vicissitude, opportunity : *a-dro*, about ; *a-dhe-dro*, *a-dre-dro*, round about, all round ; *war nep t.*, at any time ; *drok t.*, ill-turn ; in words from W. and B., **kenter t.*, **lyn t.*, **pol t.*, *tro* has the force of an adj. ; see **trōha(g)**.

trobel (*trubell*), *m.*, trouble, C.W. 1256 (M.E.).

trobla, see **tropla.**

troen, *f.*, *pl.* **-now**, whirl, turn (W., B.) ; caunter lode, mining (D. "trone").

trogel, *m.*, body, as abode of soul : *yn t.*, in earthly life, in the flesh, B.M. 1926, 4367.

trōgh, *adj.*, cut, cracked, broken, scarred, blemished ; *m.*, *pl.* **-ow**, **treghyon**, furrow, groove, cut, section, gash (D. "droke") : *dre wul ow gorhemmyn t.*, through making my commandment void, lit. broken, O.M. 298 : see **trēghy.**

trōgher, *m.*, *pl.* **-yow**, coulter of plough, P.

troghya, *vb.*, to dip, plunge, bathe, steep, full cloth : place-name Melyndroghya, tucking-mill ; see **trokkya**, **omdroghya.**

troghyer, *m.*, *pl.* **-yoryon**, fuller, tucker : see **trokkyer.**

trōha(g) (*tro ha(g)*, B.M. *troha ha*, Ord. *trogha*), *adv.*, towards : combines with poss. prons., etc., as **ha(g)** ; does not take *wor'* as *tu ha* does.

trojen, see **†trōs.**

***trok**, *m.*, exchange (B., as Fr. *troc*, E. "truck").

trok, *m.*, *pl.* **-kys**, **-egys**, box, large chest, coffin, trough (O.E. *trog*) : *t. a horn*, iron chest, R.D. 2135.

trokkya, **trokkyer** (Lh. *trukkiar*), late vars. of **troghya**, **troghyer**, cf. **omdroghya** corrupted to *hambrokkya* : Vellandrukkia, etc., in place-names, possibly from confusion with **trok**, cf. B. *komm*, trough, fulling-mill, but this does not explain *hambrokkya*, see **hedhes** ("hedok").

trom, *adj.*, sudden, unexpected, prompt, immediate : *t. dyal*, retribution without warning ; cf. B. *maro trumm*, sudden death.

tromder, *m.*, suddenness, promptitude (B.).

trompa, *m.*, *pl.* **-pys**, trumpet ; trumpet-player (M.E.) : *trompys*, *cleryons*, *whetheugh-why lemmyn dhyn fest lowenek*, trumpet and clarion-players, blow now for us right merrily, B.M. 276.

trompour, *m.*, *pl*, **-s**, trumpeter, O.M. 1996 (M.E.).

trōn (C. Voc. *trein*), *m.*, *pl.* **-ow**, nose, *nosu* Aelfric ; snout, trunk, nozzle, point of land (W.).

trōn (*thrōn*), **t.-esedha** (C.W. *t.-sedha*), *m.*, *pl.* **-ys**, throne (M.E. *trone*).

trongornvyl, *m.*, *pl.* **-as**, rhinoceros (W.) : see **üncorn.**

tropla, **trobla**, *vb.*, to trouble, vex (M.E.): 3 s. pres.-fut. *trobel* ; p. pt. *troplys* (C.W. *trobles*) ; *p*, *f* are often preferred to *b*, *v* before *l*.

trōs, *m.*, *pl.* **-ow**, noise, clamour, sound, tumult ; sound of surge or of school of fish breaking the surface (D. "troze").

trōs (*troys*, C. Voc. *truit*, Lh. *trūz*), *m.*, *pl.* *pl.* **treȳs** (*trȳs*, C.W. *tryes*), *d.* **deudrōs**, foot; leg of inanimate object, hilt, handle; foot-measure: pl. generally replaces d.; *t.* *-ebol*, *t.* *-margh*, coltsfoot (W., B.); *treys mogh*, barnacles (B.).; *t.* *-plat*, splay-foot (Lh. *trūzblat*); *re'm t.*, by my foot (M.E. *by my fo !*).

†**trōs** (C. Voc, *troet*, Lat. wrongly *turtur* for *turdus*), *m.*, *pl.* **trȳjy**, **treyjy**; **trosen**, **-jen** (Lh. *trodzhan*), *f*,, *pl.* **-nas**, starling, *staer* Aelfric.

trosak, **trojak**, *adj.*, footed, large-footed; *m.*, *pl.* **-sogyon**, person with big feet (W., B.).

tros-hē·s (*troishys*, *tresheys*), *m.*, foot, lineal measure: *ny-dhe dhe'n toll wor' t.*, it won't come to the hole by a foot-length, P.C. 2757; *y-fylly moy es t.*, it was lacking more than a foot, M.C. 180.

trosken (*trosgan* Lh.), scab, itch.

trōsla (*lē*), *m.*, *pl.* **-ow**, treadle, pedal, foothold)W.).

trōsya, **trōjya**, *vb.*, to trudge, plod, pace, hawk or peddle afoot (D. "troach").

trōsya, **-jyer**, *m.*, *pl.* **-yoryon**, peddler (D. "troacher").

***trōth**, *m.*, urine, lye (W., B.).

trōvya, **trouvya**, *vb.*, to discover, find, P., Tonkin MS. (M.E. *trove*).

trōyll, *f.*, *pl.* **-yow**, circuit, spiral, spin, turn (D. "troyl"); lathe (W.).

trōyllek, *adj.*, winding, spiral (W.).

trōyller. *m.*, *pl.* **-loryon**, turner; nightjar (W.).

troyllya (Lh. *troillia*), *vb.*, to twist, twirl, whirl, spin round; turn on lathe: 3 s. pres. -fut. *trōyll*; see **pollen**.

trū (*trew*), *interj.*, alas! sad! woe! pity!

trūan, *adj.*, miserable, poor, wretched; *adv.*, miserably: *ola t.*, weep sadly, name of little finger or toe in finger-play, B. Victor.

trübyt, *m.*, tribute, P.C. 1575; (mining) share of ore (M.E. *tribut*, D. "tribbut").

***trübytor**, *m.*, *pl.* **-yon**, miner working on tribute system (D. "tribbuter").

trūesy (*trewysy*), *adj.*, sad, serious: in verse always *tru·esy*.

trūeth (*treweth*, Late *trua*), *m.*, pity, compassion, distressing or pitiful state of affairs: *kemeres t. a*, to take pity on; *t. mur yu ahanas*, it is a great pity for you, B.M. 1992; *t. bras*, a calamity, P.C., C.W.; *t. vya y vones dyswres*, it would be a pity that he should be killed, P.C. 2437.

trūethek (*trewethek*, Lh. *triwadhak*), *adj.*, pitiful, compassionate, plaintive, exciting pity, piteous; (adverbially), piteously, B.M.

trūethtra (*trewath tra*), *m.*, pitiful affair, calamity, C.W. 838: ? for *truethektra*, cf. **droktra**, **üthektra**.

trüfyl, *adj.*, idle, trifling, R.D. 1055 (O. F.., M.E. *trufle*); *m.*, *pl.* **-flys** trifle.

trüfla, *vb.*, to trifle (B.).

trugar, *adj.*, pitiful (W.): seems lost, apart from its derivative **tregereth**.

†**trūlergh** (*trōs*, *lergh*), *m.*, *pl.* **-ow**, footpath, C. Voc., *paedh* Aelfric.

trüm, *m.*, *pl.* **-yow**, back, ridge (W.): see **trüstrüm**.

trümach (*-mech*), *m.*, passage over sea, crossing by water, O.M: 1650, B.M. 1075 (? M.E. *trimage*, Fr. *trimer*, to go to and fro).

trüs (*trēs*), *adj.*, cross, thwart, adverse, perverse, wrong, transverse, wicked, arrant; *adv.*, perversely, etc.; prefix, trans-: *ladron drus*, incorrigible thieves; see **a-drüs**.

trüsplansa, *vb.*, to transplant (W., B.): as **plansa**.

trüspren, *m.*, *pl.* **-nyer**, cross-timber, crosspiece, P.C. 2562.

trussa, *vb.*, to pack, truss, go packing, take oneself off bag and baggage, begone in haste, M.C., B.M. (M.E. *trusse*).

trüst, **trēst**, *m.*, *m.*, *pl.* **-ow**, cross-beam (W., B.); see **trēster**.

trüstüm, *m.*, fish cut small as bait, lit. across the back (D. "trestram").

trüsy, *vb.*, to pass over, by or through (W., B.); to dawdle (D. "treeze away the time, as W. *trosi*).

***trüth**, *m.*, flattery, cajolery (W., B.).

†**truth** (C. Voc. *trud*), *m.*, *pl.* **-as**, trout, *truht* Aelfric: B. *dluz*, V. *dluh* (for *truth*, Lat. *tructa*) is col: with sing. *dluzenn*, cf. **sylly**,

***trüthow** (wrongly *trūzū* Lh., ?from B. *treuzou*), *m.*, threshold (W., B.).

***trüthya**, *vb.*, to flatter, cajole (W., B.).

trȳ[3], *card. num.*, three: in MSS. anomalous mutations are sometimes made after *an*, e.g., *an*[2] *dry*, *an*[2] *dyr*, *an*[3] *thyr*; see **tre-**, **tȳr** (f.).

***trȳ**, *vb.* to turn, revolve (W., B.): as **rȳ**, but replaced by **trēlya**.

try, tra, tro, tr', very late corruptions, through *der*, of **del**, *del o*, etc., also replacing **may**.

trȳa (*trea*), *vb.*, to try, show by trial, put to the test (M.E.).

***trȳakel**, *m.*, treacle, balm (M.E.).

trȳal (Late *treall*), *m.*, *pl.* **-s**, trial (M.E.).

trȳelyn, *adj.*, three-cornered, triangular: *m.*, triangle.

trȳflēk, *adj.*, threefold, triple, treble (W., B.).

trybeth (*tribba* Gw.), *m.*, *pl.* **-edhow** (*trebedho* Lh. MS.), trumpet, post-horn: Lh. gives pl. as if sing.; *Toby Tribba*, Tom Trumpeter, Gw. MS.

tryg (Lh. *trig*), *m.*, ebb of sea: *mos dhe dryg*, to go gathering shellfish at low tide; *bos t.*, shore-gathered shellfish (D. "trigmeat"); *t. yu*, the tide is out.

tryga (Gw. *treegaz*, N. Boson *trigaz*), *vb.*, to stop, stay, tarry, sojourn, remain, abide, dwell, lodge, inhabit: p. pt. *trygys* is used intransitively as "settled," "dwelling," cf. **annedhy, nyja, rēgnya**; 3 s. pres.-fut. *tryk*; subj. *trycco*; plupf. *tryksa*.

trygas, *m.*, stay, stop: see **poltrygas**.

tryger, *m.*, *pl.* **-goryon**, dweller, lodger, inhabitant, Lh.; *trigger.

trȳgh, *adj.*, superior, conquering, supreme, victorious, triumphant (W., B.).

trȳgher (*tryher*), *m.*, *pl.* **-ghoryon**, conqueror, victor, despot, superior: *ambosow orth t. gwres, anedha nyns-us lagha*, promises made by a victor, there is no law as to them, O.M. 1235, cf. "the grete holde no lawe," *Gesta Romanorum.*

trȳghy, *vb.*, to conquer, be victorious, vanquish, excel, surmount, surpass, triumph (W., B.).

trygla (*lē*), *m.*, abiding-place (W.).

trygsa (*sē*), *m.*, mansion, country seat, B.M. 2215.

trygva, *f.*, *pl.* **-ow**, dwelling, habitation, sojourn, lodgment, place of abode.

trȳhans, *card. num.*, three hundred, O.M., M.C.: also occasionally *try cans*, perhaps giving greater emphasis to number.

trȳhansvyl, *card. num.*, three hundred thousand.

tryhemmys, *adv.*, three times as much.

tryhorn, *m.*, triangle (B).

tryhornek, *adj.*, three-cornered, triangular (B.).

tryja, see **tressa.**

tryk(g), *m.*, fixed position, stance, stay (W., D. "I'll stand my trig").

trȳla, trȳlya, see **trēlya.**

trȳlost, *adj.*, three-tailed: see **carlath, talver.**

trȳlyw, *adj.*, three-coloured, tricolor.

tryn, *f.*, trouble, fuss, quarrel (W.): see **kedryn.**

Trynsys, -jys, *f.*, Trinity.

trȳnya, trēnya (*treynya*), *vb.*, to hang back, lag, be reluctant or averse, R.D. 73, 1797; to draw or stretch out, D. "trainygoat" (*tren y gota*), spread his coat, nickname for a shag: cf. W. *treinio*, to delay, linger, spread abroad, and Fr. *trainer*, Med. Lat. *traginare.*

Try·nyta, *f.*, Trinity, O.M. 58 (M.E.)

tryst (*trest*, C. Voc. *trist*), *adj.*, sad, pensive, mournful, gloomy, cheerless, *unrot* Aelfric; ? sober, serious, also, see **trest.**

trystans (*-yns*), *m.*, sadness, sorrow.

trysthē, *vb.*, to sadden, grieve (W., B.): as **berhē.**

trystya, see **trestya.**

trystys, sadness, sorrow.

trȳthrō, *adj.*, thrice turned or twisted (W.).

trȳthrōs, *adj.*, three-footed: *scavel drythros*, three-legged stool (W.).

tryügans, *card. num.*, threescore, sixty: *onen ha t.*, sixty-one, *dek ha t.*, seventy, etc.

tū (C.W. *tew*), *m.*, *pl.* **-yow**, side, direction: *nep t.*, in any direction; *a bup t.*, in all directions, on every side; *a'n yl t.*, aside, apart; *mos a'n yl t.*, to withdraw from company; *wor' t. delergh*, on the after or hinder side, abaft; *t. ha(g), wor' t. ha(g)*, in the direction of, towards; *wor' t. ha'm*, towards my, etc.; *wor' t. ha tre, wor' t. tre*, homewards; *pup a'y du*, helter-skelter, each his own way, all in different directions; *kemerens pup ran a'y du*, let each appropriate his share, P.C. 2859.

tūbba-rüth, *m.*, *pl.* **-tūbbys-r.**, red gurnard, Lh. MS. (E.D. "tub").

tuch (M.C. *toch*), *m.*, touch, moment, instant, small space (M.E.): *na-wreugh un t. -vyth lettya*, don't delay for a single moment, P.C. 1714; *prag y-m-gyssys t. dhyworthys?* Why hast thou for an instant forsaken me? P.C. 2957.

tuchya, -a (M.C. *tochya*, C.W. *towchya*, Kerew *totchya*), *vb.*, to touch, strike accidentally, dash, P.C., B.M. (M.E.): *tuchys gans mernans (ancow)*, stricken with death, B.M. 4258, 4423.

tūlgow, see tewolgow.

tull (*tol*), *m.*, deceit, fraud: *hep t. na gyl*, frankly, faithfully, undoubtedly, O.M., C.W.

tulla (*tolla*), *vb.*, to deceive, cheat, beguile, betray, disappoint: 2 s. pret. *tullsta* for *tullsys-ta*; special fut. *a-m-tullvyth*, who will betray me, P.C. 739 (MS. *tolvyth*, Norris *cowyth*).

†tullor, *m.*, *pl.* **-yon**, deceiver, cheat, C. Voc., *leas* Aelfric.

tullwysk, *m.*, disguise, masquerade dress (W.).

***tu'lyfant**, *m.*, turban (M.E.): *blejen-t*, tulip.

tummas, *m.*, *pl.* **-ow**, thump, blow, M.C. 138: cf. **boxas, strocas.**

tūr, see **tour.**

†tūren, *f.*, *pl.* **-now**, turtle-dove, C. Voc., *turtle* Aelfric.

turnypen (*turnupan* Lh.), *f.*, *col.* **turnyp**, a turnip (E.).

türont, *m.*, *pl.* **-rons**, tyrant, usurping ruler, despot (M.E. *tyraunt*).

türya, *vb.*, to delve, burrow, rootle, turn up soil as swine or moles (W., B.): see **terghya.**

tüs (Late *tees*, *teaze*, Lh. *tīz*), *f.*, people, folk, men, relatives: though used as pl. of **dēn** or **gour**, this is treated as f. sing. after *an*, *un*, and as affecting adjs., but is replaced by pl. pron., followed by *erel*, pl., and has pl. vb. except in impersonal conjugation; *s* prevents mutation of following *c*, *k*, *d*, *p*, *t*: *t.-arvow*, men-at-arms; *t.-porth*, haveners, collectors of fish-tithe; *t.-jentyl*, gentlemen; *t. hen*, senators; *t.-da*, relatives by marriage, as **sȳra** (*-da*); *ow thus ha my*, my family and I (me).

tuttyn (*-ton*), *m.*, *pl.* **-now**, little stool or seat, hassock, N. Boson (D.E. "tut" with Cor. dim).

tȳ (C. Voc. *ti*), *m.*, *pl.* **-ow**, house; older form of **chȳ**, kept as suffix in **gorty, gwrē'ty, lūghty**, etc., as prefix in **†tȳlū**, and in place-names Tywarnhayle, Tywardreath, Tybesta, Tucoys (anciently Ticoit).

tȳ, *m.*, oath, imprecation: *ef a-dos maga town t. del wodhya*, he swore as profound an oath as he could, M.C. 85; *leverel hep t.-vyth na gowlya*, to say without making any bones about it, speak in plain words, B.M. 3740; this looks like an inf. taking the place of a noun **†*to***, as B. *tou*, oath, *toui* to swear.

tȳ (Lh. wrongly *tiah* for C.W. *tye*, *ty*, one syllable), *irreg. vb.*, to swear, take an oath: *leverel heb y dy*, to say outspokenly, without more ado, in plain language, C.W. 1629; for parts see **rȳ**, Appendix VIII., and note.

tȳ, see **dȳ, dhȳ.**

tȳ (*te*, Late *tee*, *chee*), *pron.*, thou: in vocative *ty²*, *ty dhen*, thou man, etc.

tȳ, *vb.*, to roof, cover (from rain), thatch, slate, lay tiles: although the root is **tō**, roof, the vowel is *ȳ* throughout; p. pt. *tȳes*; 3 s. pres. -fut., 2 s. imp. *tȳ*; *ty, py ny a-gan-byth meth*, put a cover over, or we shall have loss, O.M. 1078.

tȳak, *m.*, *pl.* **-ȳogyon, -ȳogow** (C. Voc. *tiogou*), husbandman, farmer, economist, manager, householder: *gwan-dyek*, a bad manager, C.W. 920; *chy t.*, farm-house, Lh.; Tyack, Teeack, personal name; see **pobel.**

tyby (B.M. *teby*, P. *tibiaz*, *tebyaz*), *vb.*, to think, fancy, imagine, conjecture, suspect, suppose: 3 s. pres. -fut. *typ*; subj. *typpo*; plupf. *typsa*; *ty a gamdyp warnodho-ef*, thou art mistaken about him, R.D. 996.

tybyans, *m.*, thought, opinion, supposition: *dhym t.*, in my opinion, R.D. 1213.

tȳd (*teed* P.), *m.*, *pl.* **-ys**, tide of sea (E.).

tȳeges, *f.*, *pl.* **-ow**, farmer's wife, country-woman, housewife, frugal woman: ? field-name Forty Acres for *for' tyeges*.

tȳegeth, *m.*, *pl.* **-ow**, household, family (B.).

tygen (*tigan* Borlase), *f.*, *pl.* **-now**, wallet, sack.

***tȳger**, *m.*, *pl.* **-gras**, tiger.

***tȳgres**, *f.*, *pl.* **-ow**, tigress.

tygry, ty'kery, *m.*, *pl.* **-as**, kestrel (D. "tigry," "tickaree").

tykky-dew (Lh. *tikki Deu*, ? for *tegen Dew*), *m.*, *pl.* **-as**, butterfly.

tykly, *adj.*, uncertain, unstable, difficult, delicate, nice, ticklish, critical (M.E.): *mater t.*, an affair needing careful handling, B.M. 1455.

tȳl, see **teyl.**

tylda, *m.*, *pl.* **-dys**, tilt, cloth covering, tent: see **tyldya.**

tyldya, *vb.*, to cover with a tilt, tent or cloth, to erect a tent, O.M. 1073 (M.E.

telden).

tylek, see **teylek.**

tyller (*teller*), *m.*, *pl.* **-yow**, place, spot: *t. -marghas,* market-place, Lh.; *py t.?* where?

tylly, *vb.*, to owe, deserve, pay, be worth, avail, requite, repay, recompense: 3 s. pres.-fut., 2 s. imp. *tāl*; 2 pl. imp. *teleugh*; p. pt. and 3 s. pret. *tylys*; *Dew tal dyal warnough!* God wreak vengeance on you! *Dew re-n-tallo dhys,* may God repay thee for it; parallel forms of this vb. are composed with **bōs**; inf. *talvos*; p. pt. *talvys* (*talvez*) for *talvedhys*; *nyns-us travyth a-dal talvos* (*talves*), *y'n bys,* there is nothing worth valuing in the world, N. Boson; see **durdala.**

†tȳlū (C. Voc. *teilu*), *m.*, family, household, *hiwraeden, hired* Aelfric: seems replaced by **mēny.**

tȳm, *m.*, thyme, Lh.

tymber (*tümbyr*), *m.*, timber, O.M.. C.W. (M.E. *tymbur*).

tymmyn, see **tam.**

tȳn (Late *teen*), *f.*, *pl.* **-yon**, bottom, tail-end, tail, breech, posterior, rump, end of anything: adverbially, *pen ha t.,* reversed side-by-side; **t. ha t.,* tail to tail; **t. dres pen,* topsyturvy.

tyn (Late *tidn*), *adj.*, tight, firm, rigid, taut; keen, cruel, painful, tender to touch, sharp, intense (D. "tidden," painful, "crying dagger tiddn," *dagrow t.* as O.M. 402): *yn-t.,* firmly, tightly, P.C. 1131, 1887, painfully, R.D. 1204; see **ten.**

tynder, *m.*, tension, tightness (W., B.).

tȳngough, *m.*, *pl.* **-as**, redstart (W.).

tȳngwyn, *m.*, *pl.* **-as**, wheatear, bird (W.).

tynhē·, *vb.*, to tighten: as **berhē.**

***tynk,** *m.*, *pl.* **-ncas**, finch (D.E "tink").

***tynkyal,** *vb.*, to tinkle (W.).

tȳor, *m.*, *pl.* **-yon**, roofer, thatcher, slater, tiler, O.M.

tȳr (C. Voc. *tir*), *m.*, *pl.* **-yow** (B.M. *teryou*), land, earth, ground: *t. mur,* mainland, R.D. 2328; *t. segh,* dry land, O.M. 1137: *t. devrak,* boggy land, Lh.; *dek puns t.,* land producing ten pounds in annual rent or half a knight's fee, B.M. 2592; *an T. a Dhedhewadow,* the Land of Promise, O.M. 1871; see **myldȳr.**

tȳr^{3} ((*teyr, tyyr,* C.W. *tayre,* Lh. *tair*), *card. num.*, three: used with f. nouns; see **trȳ, tergwyth.**

tȳra (Late *teera,* Carew *teyre*), *vb.*, to land, go or come ashore, B.M. 2243: *Y a-wra t. war an Men Merlyn, a-wra lesky Paul, Pensans ha Newlyn,* They shall land on the Rock of Merlin, who shall burn Paul, Penzance and Newlyn, prophecy attributed to Merlin, fulfilled 1595.

tȳrdelen, *adj.*, three-leaved; *f.*, trefoil (W.).

tȳreth (*-rath, -reyth,* B.M. *tereth,* C.W. *terathe*), *m.*, *pl.* **-ow**, country, land, earth: *an T. Ughel,* the High Country, N. Cornwall, B.M. 2212; *devedhys of yn t.,* I have come ashore, B.M. 632; *an T. a Dhedhewadow,* the Land of Promise, O.M. 1624.

tȳrforgh (Lh. *triforh*), *adj.*, three-pronged.

tȳr-nans (*ternans*), *m.*, valley-land, B.M. 3933.

tȳror, *m.*, *pl.* **-yon**, landsman (W.).

tys-ha-tas, *adv.*, blow for blow, tit for tat, tick-tack, thwickthwack, tiss-toss, P.C.: imitative, cf. Lat. *tuxtax.*

tysca, *vb.*, to gather (W.).

tyscas, *m.*, collection, gleaning (W., B.).

tysk, *m. or f.*, *pl.* **-scow**, mass, quantity (W.); handful, bundle (B.).

tysken, *f.*, *pl.* **-now**, gleaner's sheaf (W., B., D. "tiscan").

tyskenna, *vb.*, to glean (B.).

tyskennor, *m.*, *pl.* **-yon**, *f.*, **-es**, *pl.* **-ow**, gleaner (B.).

tȳtel, *m.*, *pl.* **-tlys**, title, legal right, claim, B.M. 2371 (M.E.).

tȳthy (*tey-*), *col. and abst.*, attributes, inherent faculties, ability, characteristics, belongings, place where one belongs: *tyller t.,* rightful place, anciently estate to which a villein was attached; see **tȳthyak, antȳthy.**

tythya (*tithia* Lh.), *vb.*, to hiss, seethe, sizzle (D. "tethan," pres. pt., hissing as a snake).

†tȳthyak (C. Voc. *teithioc*), *adj.*, native, home-born, indigenous, rightful, vernacular; *m.*, *pl.* **-yogyon**, villein, labourer attached to the soil, serf born on estate, *inbyrdlinc* Aelfric.

tȳyas, *m.*, *pl.* **-ysy**, one who swears, witness on oath, juror: *na-wra-sy bos fals-t. (faulz teaze) erbyn dha gentrevak,* be thou not a false witness against thy neighbour, Kerew, Commandment IX.

U

üfer, *adj.*, vain, futile, frivolous, idle, insipid, B.M. 3001.

üfera, *vb.*, to waste (W.).

†üfern (C. Voc. *lifern, li* for *u*), *m., pl.* **-yow,** *d.* **deu-üfern,** ankle: re-formed from an ancient dual (W. *uffarnau*) of **fer,** anciently meaning "ankle," as W. *ffer*; in O. Cor. and B. this is already forgotten.

üfereth (*evereth*), *m.*, vanity, futility, insipidity, R.D.

üganquyth (*ügans, gwyth*), *adv.*, twenty times.

ügans, *card. num.*, twenty; *m., pl.* **-ow,** score: *onen warn ü.*, twenty-one, etc; see **warn.**

ügansplek, *adj.*, twentyfold.

ügansves, *ord. num.*, twentieth.

†ūgh-, *prefix*, super-, high-: see **a-ūgh, ūghel, ūgh-hewōl, ū.-sommys.**

ūghel (*uhel*, Lh. *yuhal*), *adj.*, high, lofty, (of sound) loud, (of persons) exalted, of high rank, supreme: comp. *ughella*; obsolete comp. and superl. **†***ugh*, **†***ugha.*

†ūgheldas (C. Voc. *huheltat*), *m., pl.* **-ow,** patriarch, *heahfaeder* Aelfric.

ūghelder, *m.*, height, loftiness.

ūgheldyr (*tȳr*), *m., pl.* **-yow,** highland, upland (W.): *an Ugheldyryow*, the Highlands; Welter Gwens (*u. gwyns*), field-name.

ūghelhē·, *vb.*, to exalt, heighten; (Late) make holy, cf. B. *uhelaat*: as **berhē**; *ughelehas* Keigwin, Commandment IV, P., seems for *ughelha·s*, though he writes the p. pt. *ughelles* as if for *ughellys* in Commandment I.; see **ūghellas.**

ūghellas (*yūhellaz* Lh.), *vb.*, to ascend: more properly to make high, heighten; an older inf. may be **ūghella,** like W. *uchelu.*

†ūghelor (C. Voc. *huhelwur*), *m., pl.* **-yon,** nobleman, prince, *aethelingc* Aelfric.

ūghelvar, *m.*, mistletoe (W., B.).

†ūghelvēr (C. Voc. *huheluair*), *m., pl.* **-as,** under-governor of county, high-sheriff, *ealdorman, gerefa* Aelfric.

ūghelvōr, *m.*, high water (B.).

†ūgh-hewōl (C. Voc. *hichhewuil*), *adj.*, extremely vigilant, wide-awake, alert, *thurhwacol* Aelfric: see **†ūgh-.**

†ūghos (C. Voc. *huchot*), *adv.*, upward, up: apparently obsolete in M. Cor., this originally meant "above thee," cf. **a-ūghon, †ysos.**

†ūgh-sommys (C. Voc. *hihsommet*), *m.*, bat, reremouse, lit. high-flitting; see **†sommys, eskelly-grēghyn.**

üja, üsa (*ega* C.W. 1309), *vb.*, to scream, hoot, yell, howl, shriek aloud, give a horse-laugh, (of animals) bellow, roar, bray, neigh, whinny, screech, etc. (D. "eedge," "heedge," W. *udo*, B. *yudal*, V. *hudein*: see **üs.**

üjer, *m., pl.* **-joryon,** hooter, howler.

ūla (C. Voc. *hule*), *m., pl.* **-lys,** owl (O.E.), *ula* Aelfric.

ūllya, *vb.*, to howl, bark, cry, Lh.

ūllyans, *m.*, howling.

ulow, see **elowen.**

ün (Late *idn*), *num. adj.*, one, only, sole; a certain, one particular, a single, a; *prefix*, one, same: mutations as after **an** (but exceptionally *y un*² *vap, vaw*, his only-begotten son); *an u.*, the same, *y'n u. forth*, in the same direction; *y'n u. golmen*, in the same bond; *u. dra*, one particular or important fact; see **y'n-ün-.**

†üncorn, *m., pl.* **-kern,** unicorn, one-horned beast, rhinoceros, C. Voc., *anhyrned deor* Aelfric (who describes at length the elephant-fighting *monoceros*, not the heraldic unicorn).

unctya, see **untya.**

†uncuth, see **ancoth.**

ündas, *adj.*, of the same father (W.).

ündon. *adj.*, monotonous (W., B.).

ungrassyes, -cyes (*on-*), *adj.*, ungracious, graceless, unregenerate, impious, without God's grace, B.M., C.W. (M.E. *ungracyous*): see **dyscrassyes.**

ungya, *vb.*, to anoint, anele, B.M. 4282 (Lat. *ungo*): see **untya.**

unkynda, *adj.*, unnatural, ungrateful, C.W. (M.E.): see **kynda.**

ünlēf, *adj.*, of one voice, in unison (W.).

ünlyw (C. Voc. *unliu*), *adj.*, of one colour, self-coloured, *anes bleos* Aelfric.

ünmēnek, *adj.*, monolithic.

ünnegves, *ord. num.*, eleventh.

ünnek (Late *idnak, ednak*), *card. num.*, eleven: *agan u.*, the eleven of us, R.D. 2395; as in Breton, nasal mutation has affected *d* of **dek.**

unpo·ssybyl (*-ble*), *adj.*, impossible, C.W. 2384 (M.E.).

***ūns,** *m., pl.* **-yow,** ounce (W.).

ünsel (*-sol*), *adv.*, only, alone, O.M. 971,

1031: used after **saw**, *saw u. ow thus ha my*, excepting only my family and myself, *saw u. ty ha'th fleghes*, save only thee and thy children.

ünsys, *m.*, unity, unit (W.),

untya, unctya, *vb.*, to anoint, anele, administer extreme unction, M.C. 35, B.M. 4272 (Lat. *unctus*): see var. **ungya.**

untyans, unctyans, *m.*, unction, anointing: *m. dewetha*, extreme unction.

ünvam, *adj.*, of the same mother (W.).

ünver, *adj.*, of one mind, unanimous, agreed, M.C. 39.

ünverhē·, *vb.*, to agree, come to one opinion, B.M. 2982: as **berhē.**

ünwōs, *adj.*, of the same blood, akin, B.M. 235.

ünwyth (Late *eneth* for *ün'yth*), *adv.*, once, at all, only, just: *drefen u. dha henwel*, just for naming thee, O.M. 2724; *u. a caffen*, if only I might have, B.M. 110.

ünya, -a, *vb.*, to unite, join in one, amalgamate (W.): see **junnya.**

ünyans, *m.*, union, amalgamation (W.).

unyent (*unnient*), *m.*, *pl.* **-ns**, unguent, ointment, M.C. 234.

ünyk (*idnak* Gw. MS., *ednak* Lh.), *adj.*, sole, only, unique solitary, single, singular: *yn-u*, only, merely, Lh. (?from W.).

ünykter, *m.*, solitariness, singularity.

unyve·rsyta, *m.*, *pl.* **-tys.** university, B.M. 78.

ür (*ēr*), *f.*, *pl.* **-yow**, hour, time: *mar tuth an u.*, if the (appointed) time has come, B.M. 746; the vowel tends to become obscure in the adverbial phrases *y'n ur-ma* (Lh. *enurma*), now, *y'n ur-na*, then, *nep ur*, at any time, *pup ur*, always, *py ur*, *p'ur*, when, but rhymes with *mür*, *lür* elsewhere, as R.D. 881; see **owr**, *m.*, preferred in clock-time.

üra (*ira* Lh.), *vb.*, to anoint, grease, lubricate, besmear, bedaub: *stanch-u.*, to pay over, O.M. 954.

üras (C. Voc. *urat*), *m.*, *pl.* **-resow**, ointment, salve, unguent, lubricant, *smyrels*, *sealfe* Aelfric.

***ürdha**, *vb.*, to ordain, admit to an order (W., B.).

urnel, *m.*, urinal (M.E. in B.M. p. 80): see **gwēder** (*glas*).

***ürth**, *f.*, *pl.* **-dhow**, sacred, knightly or bardic order, rank (W., B.): replaced by **ordys.**

ürweder, *m.*, *pl.* **-drow**, hour-glass (W.).

ürwyth, *f.*, *pl.* **-yow**, hour's time (B.).

urȳn, *m.*, urine, B.M. 1444 (M.E.).

üryor, *m.*, *pl.* **-ow**, watch (W.).

ūs (pr. *ewz*), *m.*, usage, habit, practice, custom, P.C. 2034: see **ūsya.**

üs, üj, *m.*, yell, howl, trumpet blast (W., B.): see **üja.**

üs, see **üsyn.**

üs (C. Voc. *(h)uis*), *f.*, *pl.* **-ow**, age, lifetime, as W. *oes* f. (*ōs*, W. *oed*, is m.): *a'y u.*, ever, keeps the original meaning of W. *eisioes*, now "already," "yet," "nevertheless."

üs, üsy, etc., see **bōs**, Appendix VIII.

üsa, see **üja.**

ūsadow (pr. *ewz-*), *m.*, usage, custom, practice, B.M. 135: in verse *u·sadow*.

üsak, *adj.*, chaffy, full of husks (W.).

üscana, *vb.*, to sound a trumpet-blast (W.).

üscorn, *m.*, *pl.* **-kern**, trumpet (W.).

üskys (Lh. *yskyz*), *adj.*, quick, nimble; *adv.*, quickly, swiftly.

ūsya (pr. *ewz-*, Lh. *yūzia*), *vb.*, to use, be accustomed to, habitually wear, take to eat or drink, wear out, perform, practise; p. pt. *usyes*, used, usual, wonted, customary, worn, worn out, worse for wear.

üsyn, *m.*, *col.* **üs**, *pl.* **üsyon** (C. Voc. *usion*), chaff, corn-husk, D. "ishans," "ushans."

üth (*euth*), *m.*, horror, fright, dread, terror, awe: *u. y glewes*, horrible to hear, lit. a horror to hear it, R.D. 2128.

üthek (*uthyk*, *ethuk*, Late *ithik*, *eithick*), *adj.*, frightful, terrible, awful, awe-inspiring: in Late Cor. used adverbially as "extremely," *gwrek u. da*, as D.E. "a ter'ble good wife," P.; see **üthektra.**

üthekter, *m.*, terror, dread, frightfulness, horror, P.C. 2653.

üthektra (*ithek tra* Lh.), *adv.*, greatly, very much; *m.*, frightful affair: Lh. seems to equate *tra* in this with W. *tra* or B. *tre*, extremely, but **droktra, trūethtra** suggest **üthektra** as a noun.

üthfȳl (*mȳl*), *m.*, *pl.* **-as**, monster, frightful beast (B.).

üvel, -der, see **hüvel, -der.**

üvva, *f.*, outcry, yelling, howling, as W. *udfa*, see **üja** and cf. **hevva, scovva.**

V

va (*ve, fe*), *pron.*, suffixed or object of imp., he, him, it (m.): replaces *e, ef,* after vowels except the *u* (*w*) of *yu*, and apparently, as vars. of *ro va, dro va,* the *y* of *roy, doroy*; often joined to vb., *del ova*, as he was, etc.

väe·f, *pron.*, suffixed or object of imp., he, him, it (m.), emphatic form of **-va**: replaces **ëef** after vowels; *awotta v.*, behold him, P.C. 2155.

valy, *m.*, valley (E.): *Valy Ebron*, the Valley of Ebron, CW. 340.

vārya (*y* consonant), *vb.*, to alter, change, derange, change one's nature or mentality: 3 s. pres.-fut. *vary*, p. pt. *varyes*, insane, B.M. 1006 (M.E. *varyed* in special sense).

vās (for *a*[2] *vās*), *adj.*, of use, (not) any good, of service, suitable: *bythqueth ny-ve v. y'n pow*, it has never been well in the country, B.M. 3968; *nyns-us jyst-vytholl v. dhe dravyth ragtho saw* ..., there is no joist at all of any use whatever for it save..., O.M. 2497.

vayl (*veyll*), *m.*, *pl.* **-ys**, veil, M.C. 209 (M.E.).

'vel, see **avel**: in Late Cor. this is substituted for **ages, es**.

venjya, *vb.*, to avenge (M.E. *venge*).

venjyans, venyons, *m.*, vengeance (M.E., D. "venyence"): *myl v. warnas-sy*, a thousand vengeances on thee, Carew.

venym, *m.*, venom, poison, O.M. 1779 (M.E.).

venymya (*vynymmya*), *vb.*, to envenom, poison, O.M. 1757.

venyons, see **venjyans.**

ve·rement, *adv.*, truly, verily, B.M. 2927 (M.E.).

***vermay·l**, *adj.*, *m.*, vermilion (M.E.).

***vernsya**, *vb.*, to varnish (M.E.): cf. **fynsya.**

vertū, *m.*, virtue, power (M.E. *vertue*).

vertūtys, *pl.*, virtues, order of angels, C.W. 64 (Lat. *virtutes*).

***vervȳn**, *f.*, vervain, verbena (W.).

very (*veary*), *adv.*, very, C.W. (E.).

'vēs, contraction of **a-vēs** after vowel or *gh*, B.M. 3113.

vessyl (*vecyl*), *m.*, *pl.* **-s**, vessel, receptacle, B.M. 1519 (M.E.).

vesyon (*besyon*), *m.*, vision, B.M. 984 (M.E.).

vexya, *vb.*, to vex, pester, trouble, annoy, B.M. 2630 (M.E.).

vodya (C.W. *voydya*), *vb.*, to depart, expel, avoid, go away, evade (M.E. *voyden*): *voyd alemma!* begone! away with you! see **avodya.**

volaveth (*-ueth*), *interj.*, ? exact meaning: used by servants in ready reply to a call, P.C. 953, 1351, 2049, this is not Celtic, as it is used in English lines, neither is it a title; *welaway!* a cry of distress, is not apt, see **welawo**; Fr. *vous l'avez*, if meaning "you have what you called for," would fit use and spelling.

vossawya, or **vosya saw**, *vb.*, to vouchsafe, bestow freely, deign to grant: *my a-n-vossaw*, or *vos saw*, I vouchsafe it, or I vouch it safe, P.C. 1793 (M.E. *vousalf, vouch sauf*, etc., O. Fr. *vocher sauf*): see **saw.**

***vōtya**, *vb.*, to vote (E.).

vowa, see **avowa.**

vöward, *m.*, vanguard, battle-front, O.M. 2156 (M.E. *vaward*).

voyd, *adj.*, empty, void, C.W. 242 (M.E.).

voys, *m.*, *pl.* **-ys, -ycys**, voice, Ord., B.M., C.W. (M.E.).

vrȳ, see **brȳ.**

vū, fū (*fvu*), *m.*, view, sight, appearance, P.C., R.D. (M.E. *veue*).

vȳ, *pron.*, suffixed or object of imp., I, me: a softened form of **mȳ.**

vȳaj, -ach, *m.*, *pl.* **-ys, -jys**, voyage, expedition, venture, concern, undertaking, affair, enterprise (M.E. *viage*).

vȳajya (*vaggya* C.W. 1335), *vb.*, to voyage, make a journey, travel (M.E.).

vy·ctory, *m.*, victory (E.): *an v. eth genef*, I won the victory, R.D. 2521.

vyctōryes, *adj.*, victorious: cf. **glōryes.**

vyken (*a*[2], *byth, kēn*), *adv.*, ever, evermore: see **byken, bys.**

vyketh (*a*[2], *byth, keth*), *adv.*, eternally, always the same, B.M. 892.

vȳl (*veyll*), *adj.*, vile, dreadful (M.E.): *v.-dyghtys*, shockingly treated; *v.-despyt*, horrible abuse; comp. *vylla* is used adverbially M.C. 176, *vylla es del o dyskys*, more horribly unclad than he was.

vylen (*velen*), *m.*, villain, churl (M.E. *vileyn*); *adj.*, villainous, churlish, shameful, opprobrious: see **bylen**, an older form, as W. *bilain*, B. *bilen.*

vy·lyny (*-eny*), *m.*, villainy, reproach, vulgarity, discourtesy, vile treatment, ignominy (M.E. *vileinye*): see *bylyny.*

vy·nary (*a^2*, *bynary*), *adv.*, for ever : see **bys.**

vynym, see **venym.**

vynytha (*a^2*, *bynytha*), *adv.*, for ever, evermore, (with neg.) nevermore : *v. na-effo cowl, v. na-dheppro bos*, so that he shall never sup broth, eat food, any more (i.e., live to do so), P.C. 1620, R.D. 541 : see *bys.*

vyrjyn (*-gyn*) *-f. pl.* -ys, virgin, C.W. (E.).

vysach, *m.*, *pl.* **-ajys**, face, countenance (M.E. *vysage*) : see **bejeth.**

vȳsour, *m.*, *pl.* **-ys**, mask (M.E.) : in E. stage-direction, B.M. p. 76.

vytel (C.W. *vyctuall*), *m.*, victuals, viands (M.E. *vitaille*).

vyth, **-vyth** (form of *byth*), *adj.*, *adv.*, (not) any, e'er a, whatever, at all, ever : used only with neg., *hep*, or implied lack, *dafer-v. why ny-dhekseugh*, you carried no receptacle at all (purse or scrip), M.C. 50 ; *v. mar*, ever so (before adj.) ; *kyn fe v. mar vras*, though he were ever so great ; *ny-won v. pyth af*, I know not at all where I shall go, O.M. 355 ; see **denvyth, travyth.**

-vytholl, **vyth-oll**, *adj.*, (not) any at all : suffixed ; see **vyth, oll.**

'w, see **ow.**

wāja (*wage*), *m.*, *pl. -jys*, wages, salary, perquisite, executioner's vails, P.C. 1187 (M.E. *wage*).

war[2] (pr. *wor*), *prep.*, on, upon ; (with *ynny*, *gul crothval*) against : combines with prons., see Appendix V., see also **warn** ; from mutations found, the expressions *w. dharras*, by way of door, *w. anow*, by word of mouth, in his own words, M.C. 170, *w. nebes geryow*, *w. ver lavarow*, in few words, in short, *w. hast*, in haste, evidently contain *war*[2], but in other expressions *war* is frequently written for *wor(th)* ; see **orth.**

wār, **waryeugh**, *def. vb.*, beware, mind, take care (M.E.) : used in 2 s. and pl. imp. only, *bos war* used as inf.

wār, *adj.*, aware, wary, cautious, heedful (M.E.) : *byth, bedheugh, w. !* beware !

warba·rth, **war-barth** (*war, parth*), *adv.*, together, altogether, completely, collectively, jointly, all of you : *w. ha*, simultaneously with, P.C. 2051 ; *un mys seythen, vledhen, w.*, for a month, week, year, on end, J. Boson, W. Bodener ; *oll w.*, simultaneously, with one voice, all in company.

warbyn (*warbidn, 'bidn*), *prep.*, against : form of **erbyn** used in C.W. and later, *war-y-byn* is found as earlier var. M.C. 171 : *Jowan a-dheth war-aga-fyn (phidn)*, John met them, Jowan Chy-an-Horth, 29.

warden, *m.*, *pl.* **-s**, keeper, guardian, warden, C.W. (M.E. *wardain*) : *chyf-w. war*, supreme custodian of, C.W. 999.

war-dhelergh, *adv.*, back, backwards, to the rear : *mos w.*, to retreat, back away, retire, B.M. 4092.

ware, see **whare.**

war-for' (*forth*), *adv.*, on the way, while going or coming, P.C. 1135.

war-gam, see **cam.**

***warleny**, *adv.*, last year (W., B.).

warle·rgh, **war-lergh**, *prep.*, *adv.*, after (of place or time), behind, following, (as cause of sorrow) yearning or longing for, according to : poss. prons. inserted, **war-y-lergh**, after him, etc. ; requires inf. of vb., *w. mapden dhe begha*, after mankind sinned ; *w. dha vones dhe-dre*, after thou goest home ; *gul w.*, to imitate, follow the example or instructions of.

war-lür, *adv.*, down, on the ground.

warn (*war an*), in compound numerals used only directly before *ugans* as *ha* is elsewhere : *deu w. ugans*, 22, lit. two upon the score, but *dek ha try ugans*, 70, etc.

war-nans. *adv*,, down, downwards, in a downward direction, M.C. 205.

war-not, *adv.*, simultaneously, all in concord, all at once (M.E. *by note*).

war-nuk, *adv.*, immediately, lit. on the notch, B.M. 2409 (M.E. *nok*).

war-rak(g), *adv.*, forwards, as one is facing, M.C. 206.

***warrant**, *m.*, warrant, guarantee (E.).

***warrantya**, *vb.*, to warrant, guarantee (E.).

war-ürow (*ar ūrow*), *adv.*, now and then, sometimes, Lh. : perhaps invented.

war-van, *adv.*, up, upwards, B.M. : *drefa w. !* lift up thy head ! *myr w. !* look up !

war-woles, *adv.*, below, at the bottom : *w. pan vyras*, when I looked right down to the bottom, O.M. 781.

war-yew, *interj.*, (to rouse oxen) on the yoke ! (D. "waroo") : see **hedhes.**

wassel, *m.*, wassail, P.C. 2978 (O.E. *was*

hael, be hale !).
wāst, *m.*, waist, P.C. 1889 (M.E.).
wast, *adj.*, idle, unemployed, (of land) vacant, uncultivated, waste, R.D. 2155 (M.E.) : Teer Wast (*tyr w.*), place-name.
wastya, *vb.*, to waste, squander, B.M., C.W. (M.E.).
wat, see **what**.
wel, *interj.*, well ! B.M. 3340 (M.E.).
we·lawō ! *interj.* of grief, welaway ! R.D. 2044 (M.E. *wellawey*, O.E. *walawa*).
welcum, see **wolcum**.
we·ryson, *m.*, reward, guerdon, R.D. 1677 (M.E. *warysoun*).
West (*weyst* B.M. 784), *adj.*, *m.*, **west**, West (M.E.).
whaf, *m.*, *pl.* **-fys**, heavy blow, whack, whop, O.M. (?var. of M.E. *whappe* or cf. "waff," flap, stroke, E. D. Dic.).
***whaly**, *vb.*, to scatter, spill, strew (W., V.): replaced by **scullya**.
whannen (C.Voc. *hwannen*, Lh. *hwadnan*), *f.*, *col.* **whyn** (*whidden* P.), flea : *w.-vor*, *-treth*, *morwhannen*, sand-hopper.
whans, *m.*, *pl.* **-ow**, desire, longing, wish : *dhyn yma w batalyas*, we long to combat, B.M. 2473 ; takes preps. **a** or **dhe** or none as "for" ; *dhe wherthyn ny-s-teva w.*, she had no longing to laugh, M.C. 222, *ny-gan bo w. gwaryow*, we had no wish for games, R.D. 1330, both express anguish.
whansa, *vb.*, to long or yearn for (W., B.).
whansek, *adj.*, desirous, longing, wishful, yearning : *w. dhe*, (with noun) wishful for, desirous of, C.W. 1794 ; (with inf.) longing to, P.C. 37 ; *w. a*, Keigwin (in Davies Gilbert's C.W.), should also be correct.
whar (*war*), *adj.*, meek, humble, gentle, placid, submissive, mild : a permanent mutation of ***gwar** (W. *gwar*, M.B. *goar*), following that in *yn-whar*.
wharē·, **warē·**, **whara** (*wharre*, *warre*), *adv.*, at once, presently, soon, anon : usually rhymed as if pr. "wharra," but not so spelt even in C.W., and often rhyming also with *ē* ; in tradition *taw w. !* became "tai baree !"
wharfos, *vb.*, to happen, befall, take place, come to pass, occur : **bōs** compound used in 3 s. only, and including only the tenses with initial *b*; fut. *whyrfyth*; subj. *wharfo*; pret. *wharfa* ; p. pt. *wharfedhys* ; also inflected as a regular vb. in some tenses, plupf. *wharsa* (unless for *wharfa*), M.C. 132 ; p. pt. *whyrys* (*werys*), B.M. 1412 and *whyrfys*, O.M. 1415 ; impf. ind. impers. passive *whyrys*, R.D. 1190.
wharhē·, *vb.*, to make gentler, civilize, humanize : as **berhē**.
wharth, *m.*, laughter : *bos dyeskynnys yn w.*, to be overcome with laughter, fall a-laughing, C.W. 2306.
wharthüs, **-ys**, *adj.*, laughable, comic, ridiculous (B.).
what, **wat**, *m.*, *pl.* **-tys**, blow, slap, whack, smack (D. "wod," ?var. of M.E. *whappe*, W. *chwap*) : see **whaf**.
whāth (*whēth*, Late *whaeth*, Lh. *hwāth*), *adv.*, still, yet, again, once more, yet another time, furthermore : *w.-oll bewa y a-wra*, while they shall yet live, O.M. 1877 ; *w. bythqueth*, always hitherto, all along so far, B.M. 337.
wheddyth (*whēgh*, *dēth*), *m.*, six days, O.M. 142, C.W. 413.
whedhy (*hwedhy* Lh.), *vb.*, to swell, puff up : p. pt. *whedhys* (*hwedhyz* Lh.) ; ? from Welsh, see **hothfy**, **quoffy**, **whethfy**.
whednar (*whēgh*, *dynar*), *m.*, sixpence, Borlase MS. : see **junnya**.
wheffes (*hweffaz* Lh., for *whēghves*), **whēghes** (B.M. *wehes*), *ord. num.*, sixth.
†**wheger** (C. Voc. *hweger*), *f.*, *pl.* **-grow**, mother-in-law : probably replaced by *dama-dha*, like *syra da* ; see **sȳra**.
whēgh (*whē*, Lh. *hwih*), *card. num.*, six.
whēghes, **whēghves**, see **wheffes**.
whēgoll, **whēk·oll** (Lh. *hwēgol*), *adj.*, entirely sweet, kind, gentle, etc., charming, darling, dearest, sweetest, M.C., O.M.
whegyn, *m.*, **-gen**, *f.*, *pl.* **-now**, sweet or dear little one, sweeting, bantling, B.M. 1565.
wheja (Lh. *hwedzha*), *vb.*, to vomit, spew.
whejalen, *f.*, *pl.* **-now**, blister, boil (W., B.).
whēk, later **whēg** (Lh. *hwēg*), *adj.*, sweet, pleasant, kind, gentle, nice, comp. and exclam. *whecca* ; *m.*, *pl.* **-egow**, darling : *A w. whegow agas mam !* O sweet darlings of your mothers ! B.M. 1653 ; D. "whacca", sweetmeats, may be for *whegow*, sweets, or perhaps for *wheketh*, sweetness, as in "as sweet as whacca."
whekter, *m.*, sweetness, pleasantness, kindness, O.M. 359.
whēl (*wheyl*, *-ȳl*, Late *-eal*, Lh. *hwēl*), *m.*,

and f., pl. **-yow**, work, mine-working: *w. -sten*, tin-mine; *w. -glow*, coal-mine; *w. Yedhewon*, ancient tin-work, lit. Jew's work; *kens gasa w.*, before the job is done, before the finish; *mur a w. dhe wul yma war...*, there is much ado about ..., B.M. 2873; place-names, Wheal-, common title of mines, as Wheal-Rose (*w. ros*), etc.

whēl. *f.*, course, turn (W.).

***whelder** (for *whe·lyder*), *m.*, mouldboard of plough, as W. *chwelydr*, V. *ulid*: cf. **ardar.**

wheles, *vb.*, to turn (W.): apparently kept only in **dewheles, domhel, omwheles.**

whēlva, *f.*, orbit (W.).

***when,** see **whennen.**

***whennek,** *adj.*, weedy (W., B.).

***whennen.** *f., pl.* **-now**, *col.* **when,** weed (W., B.).

***whenner,** *m., pl.* **-noryon,** *f.* **-nores,** *pl.* **-ow,** weeder (W., B.).

***whenny,** *vb.*, to weed (W., B.).

***whe·nogel,** *f., pl.* **-glow,** hoe (W., B.).

whēr (for *awhēr*), *def., vb.*, it ails, pains, grieves, troubles, distresses: *yndella dhymmo y-wher*, I am similarly troubled, R.D. 709; *pandr' a-u·her dhys?* what is the matter with thee?

wherow (Lh. *hwero*), *adj.*, bitter, sharp, harsh, R.D. 2601: comp. and excl. *wherwa* (*hwerwa'* Lh.).

whe·rowder, *m.*, bitterness, harshness (W., B.)

wherthyn (C. Voc. *hwerthin*), *vb.*, to laugh; *m.*, laughter: 3 s. pres.-fut, *wharth*, 2 s. *wherthyth*; 3 s. pret. *wharthas.*

wheryth, see **whōr.**

whēs, whȳs (*wes, wheys*, Lh. *hwēz*), *m.*, sweat, perspiration: *w, yu y dal*, his brow is (covered with) sweat; *w. pup goth-oll ha lyth*, sweat (-covered) every vein and limb, P.C. 2512.

whēsa (*wesa*, Lh. *hweza*), *vb.*, to sweat, perspire.

whe·sygel, *f., pl.* **-glow, whesygen,** *f., pl.* **-now,** blister, bladder, vesicle (W., B.).

whesygenna, *vb.*, to blister, form a bladder (W., B.).

whetgeves, *ord. num.*, sixteenth.

whetek (P. *whettak*, Lh. *hwettag*), *card. num.*, sixteen.

wheth (Lh. *hwedh*), *m.*, swelling: see **whedhy.**

wheth (Lh. *hweth*, C.W. *whath*), *m., pl.* **-ow,** puff blast, breath.

whetha (*whytha*), *vb.*, to blow, puff, breathe, blast; *w. corn*, to blow a horn, trumpet it about, O.M. 207, P.C. 1358; *wheth war gam!* blow easy! P.C. 2716.

whethel, whelth (Lh. *hwitel*), *m., pl.* **-thlow, -etlow,** story, tale, false report, fabrication, nonsense, tattle, gossip (D. "whiddles"): *plontya whethlow*, to spread groundless reports or rumours; *hep w.*, truly, really, indeed; *a gans dha w.!* get out with thy twaddle!

whether, *m., pl.* **-thoryon,** blower.

whethfy, *vb.*, to swell, bubble: var. of **hothfy.**

whethfyans (Lh. *hwethvians*), *m.*, swelling: *w. an dowr*, bubble.

whethla, whethlowa, *vbs.*, to gossip, fable, tell stories (W.): 3 s. pres.-fut. *whethel.*

whethlor, *m., pl.* **-yon,** *f.* **-es,** *pl.* **-ow,** fabler, tattler, teller of romances.

Whevrer, Whevrel (Lh. *huevral, herval*), **mȳs-W,** *m.*, February: the late forms with final *l* for *r*, as W. *Chwefrol* for *Chwefror*, are the only ones actually found.

whōr, whoer (C. Voc. *wuir*, C.W., N. Boson *hoer*, Carew *whoore*, Lh. *hōr*), *f., pl.* **wheryth,** sister: *w. da*, sister-in-law; see **sȳra.**

whȳ (*whee*, Brome, *Northern Lass*, 1632, later *whei*, Lh. *hwei*), *pron.*, you, ye.

†whyb (C. Voc. *wib*, possibly *pib*), *f., pl.* **-ow,** pipe, whistle, tube, *pipe, hwistle* Aelfric.

whyban, *m.*, whistle, with mouth (W., B.).

whybana, *vb.*, to whistle, hiss, sizzle, wheeze, whiz (W., B.).

†whybanor (C. Voc. *wibanor*), *m.*, whistler, hisser; slipper, shoe below the ankles, *swyftlere* Aelfric.

***whybon,** *f., pl.* **-as,** stork (W., B.): C. Voc. copies *storc* from Aelfric.

†whybonol (C. Voc. *wibonoul*), *f., pl.* **-ow,** whistle.

whybya, *vb.*, to quaver, trill (W.).

whyflyn, *adj.*, roaring, blustering, of fire or wind, R.D. 2311 (D.E. "whiffling," "huffling"): cf. *faryng, smyllyng*, with *g* kept.

whygen (Lh. *huigan*), *f.*, soft part of bread, crumb of loaf: *Dybry W.*, nick-name of third finger, B. Victor.

†**why·geran** (C.Voc. *hwigeren*), *m.*, father-in-law, *sweor* Aelfric: apparently replaced by *syra-da*; see **sȳra.**

whyjyon (*whiggian*), *pl.*, naked oats, "pillas, a seed," Borlase: see **pylas**, and cf. Borlase's *spriggian* for *spyryjyon*.

whyl, *m.*, *pl.* **-as**, chafer, beetle: *w. derow*, cockchafer, oakweb (W., B.).

whylas (*hwillaz* Lh.), *vb.*, to seek, search for, examine: 3 s. pres.-fut., 3 s. impf. subj., 2 s. imp. *whyla; y nagha byth na-whyla!* never seek to deny it! P.C. 1407.

whylen (C. Voc. *hwilen*), *f.*, *pl.* **whylas**, beetle, dung-beetle, *scearn wibba* Aelfric: *w. du*, blackbeetle (D. "willen," "jew").

whylessa, *vb.*, to catch beetles (W., B.): inf. only.

whym, *m.*, horse-capstan for winding up kibble in mine-shaft (E.).

whym-wham, *adv.*, capriciously, whimsically, slapdash, unsteadily, this way and that, P.C. 2734 (D.E. "whim-wham").

whyn, see **whannen.**

whynna, *vb.*, to catch fleas (W.): inf. only.

whynnek, *adj.*, flea-ridden, flea-bitten, freckled (W., B.).

whyogen, *f.*, *pl.* **-gas**, dinner cake of pastry (W.): see **fūgen, hogen**; in B. *c'houistoc'henn*.

whyp (*wyp*), *m.*, *pl.* **-pys**, whip (M.E.): *W. a'n Tyn*, "Whip Behind," a jailor's apprentice in P.C., R.D., has probably the common nickname of a hack, drudge or fag, as B. *foet-lost*, lit. "whip-tail."

whyppya, *vb.*, to whip, P.C. 2100 (M.E.).

whyrnor, *m.*, *pl.* **-yon**, hummer (W.).

†**whyrnores** (C. Voc. *huirnores*), *f.*, *pl.* **-ow**, she-hummer; *pl.* **-as**, hornet.

whyrny, *vb.*, to hum, buzz, boom, whiz, whir, snore (W.).

whȳs, see **whēs.**

whyst (*huist* Lh.), *interj.*, hush! (E.).

***whystel, whystlen**, *f.*, *pl.* **whystlas**, shrewmouse (W.).

whystra, *vb.*, to whisper, P.C. 1254 (O.E. *hwaestrian*, E.D. "whister"): 2 s. imp. *whyster*, before vowels *whystr*.

***whythell**, *f.*, *pl.* **-ow**, whistle: *w.-gala*, straw-pipe; *w.-gors*, reed-pipe (W., B.).

***whythella**, *vb.*, to blow a whistle, pipe on a straw or reed (W., B.).

***whythgorn**, *m.*, *pl.* **-gern**, cornet (W.).

whythra, *vb.*, to look or gaze at, behold, observe, scrutinize, examine, investigate, pry into: 2 s. imp., 3 s. pres.-fut. *whythyr*, before vowels *whythr*.

whywhȳ·, *pron.* (emphatic), ye, you, yourselves.

wod, see **woud.**

woja, see **wosa.**

wola, see **ola.**

wolcum (B.M. *welcum*), *adj.*, welcome (M.E.), comp. *wolcumma*: *w. yn-tre!* welcome home! B.M. 216; *eugh po trygeugh, w. vydheugh*, go or stay, you will be welcome, B.M. 4567.

wolcumma (*welcomma* C.W., *welcumba* Gw.), *vb.*, to welcome, make welcome (M.E.).

†**woleker** (C. Voc. *wilecur*), *m.*, flatterer (O.E.): *leas olecere*, false flatterer, Aelfric, is made " liar or flatterer " in C. Voc.

wondrys, *adv.*, wonderfully, wondrously, C.W. (M.E. *wonders*).

wor', see **orth.**

Wordhan, see **Ywerdhon.**

wordhy. *adj.*, worshipful, meritorious, deserving, worthy, honourable, reputable, estimable, distinguished (M.E. *worthy*, O.E. *wurdhig*): see **gordhya**, an older burrowing with added *g*.

worshyp, *m.*, respect, deference, honour, dignity, prestige, prestige, repute, esteem, distinction (M:E.): *gul w. dhe'th nessa*, bring honour to thy kinsfolk, B.M. 2040; *ny-s-bya w. y'n cas*, respect would be wanting to you in the circumstances, R.D. 1943.

worteweth, see **oteweth.**

worth, see **orth.**

wosa, woja (Late *ouga*, Lh. *ūdzha*), *prep.*, after (of time): permanent mutation of **gwosa** (W. *gwedi*. B. *goude*), as contracted from **a-wosa**: *w. hemma* (Late *ujemma*), hereafter; *w. henna* (Late *ujenna*), thereafter; requires inf. of vb., *w. my dhys dh'y dhyfen*, after I forbade it to thee, O.M. 280, *w.ow mos*, after I go; *w. merwel*, after dying; see **a'y wosa.**

wostalleth (*worth, dalleth*), *adv.*, at first, in the beginning, to begin with, at the start: cf. **oteweth**, etc.

wosteweth. see **oteweth,**

woud (*wod*), *adj.*, mad, furious (M.E. *wood*).

wrynch, *m.*, trick, deceit, stratagem (M.E.

wrenche, O.E. *wrence*).

wȳly (*wylly*), *adj*., wily, crafty, C.W. 816 (E.).

wȳs, see **gül-wȳs**,

Y

ȳ, *pron*., they, they, them: in latest **Cor.** quite replaced by *jy*, *anjye*; see **ynsy**.

y, *pron*., she, her, it (f): suffixed unstressed form of **hy**; may be joined to vb., as *yn-medhy* for *yn-meth-hy*.

ȳ², *poss. pron*., his, its (m,).

'**ȳ**³, *poss. pron*., her, its (f.): see **hȳ**³.

y⁵ **(th)-**, *indef. verbal particle*, for uses see Appendix VII.

y', *prep*., in: contraction of **yn**, made especially before poss. prons. and **an**, **ün**, very rarely before a place-name, *y' Bethlem*, *y Paradys*, or before *ban*, *dan*, *weth*, also a rare contraction of **yn**⁵**-** before adjs., *y'-tek*, fairly, *y'-ta*, well (cf. B. *eta*).

yā (B.M. *ëa*, C.W. *yëa*. Lh. *iā*, P., M.S. note to Lh., *eea*), *interj*., giving assent, sometimes derisively, yea, yes (M.E., see var. **yē**): this does not replace the usual affirmative, made by repeating the vb. of the question, as *Yu henna gwyr?* Is that true? *Yu*. (Yes) it is, etc.

yagh (C. Voc. *iach*, Lh. *yăch*), *adj*., well, sound, healthy, vigorous, hale, hearty: *gront dhedha sevel yn-y*., grant to them to rise up sound, B.M. 4121; cf. *yn-few* **(bew)**.

yaghhē·. *vb*., to make or become well, cure, recover: sa **berhē**.

yaghüs, **-ys**, *adj*., healful, health-giving (W.. B.).

yar (Lh. *yăr*, *iăr*), *f*., *pl*. **yēr**, hen, C. Voc., O.M.: *y*. *-Gyny* (*iăr- Gini* Lh.), turkey-hen" P. Mundy); see **mabyar**, **pen-yar**.

yarjy, *m*., *pl*. **-ow**, hen-house, fowl-house (W.).

y-bēn, see **hy-bēn**.

†ydhna, *vb*., to go fowling: inf. only.

†ydhnē, **-na** (C. Voc. *idne*), *m*., *pl*. **-nўon**, fowler, bird-catcher, *fugelaere* Aelfric: pt. of *edhen* with suffix *-ē* (W. *-ai*, *-hai*), seeker.

†ydhnyk (C. Voc. *ydnic*), *m*., *pl*. **-ygow**, chick, chicken, young bird, *cicen*, *brid* Aelfric: dim. of **edhen**.

***ydhyl**, *adj*., feeble, frail, slight, puny, weak (W., B.).

ȳdhyn, see **edhen**.

ydhynor (*edhanor* Lh.), *m*., *pl*. **-yon**, fowler: see **† ydhnē**.

ȳdhyowek, *adj*., ivy-clad (B.); *f*., *pl*. **-egy**, **-egow**, ivy-covered place (B.).

ȳdhyowen, *f*., *col*. **ȳdhyow** (*idhio* Lh.), ivy-bush, ivy.

yē, *interj*., calling attention, Hi! Ho there! P.C. 2663.

yē, *interj*., affirmative, repetitive or derisive, Yea! forsooth! Oh, indeed! see var. **yā**: in Ord. *ye*, and in B.M. *ëa*, is used in both ways; in C.W. *yëa* is affirmative or derisive only.

Yedhow, M.C. **Edhow**, *m*., *pl*. **-ewon** (*Hudhewon*), Jew, Israelite.

Yedhowek, *adj*., Jewish, Hebraic; *m*., Yiddish (W., B.): see **Ebbrow**.

Yedhowes, *f*., *pl*. **-ow**, Jewess (W., B.).

yēghes (*yehes*, Late *ēhaz*), *m*., health: *y a-wra dhys y*., they will give health to thee, O.M. 1794; *'ma 'gan y.-ny dhyn*, we are well, lit. have our health, Lh.; *y. da dheugh!* your health! see **yagh**.

yeman, *m*., yeoman, B.M. 3303 (M.E.): pl. may be **-s**, cf. **cothman**.

yēn, see **yeyn**.

yenes, see **yeunes**.

yēr, see **yar**.

yēr, var. of **ayr**, P.C. 1333.

yēs (*yeys*), *vb*., to confess one's sins, B.M. 607: inf. is made from p. pt. *yessē·s* (*yesseys* B.M.), shriven, O.E. *ge-saed*, *i-sed*, M.E: *y-sayd*, told, said.

yet, *m*., *pl*. **-tys**, gate, Ord., C.W. (M.E., D.): Park an Yet (or Jet), field-name; see **clōs**.

***yēth**, *f*., *pl*. **-ow**, language, idiom, way of speaking: replaced apparently by **tavas** (W., B.).

***yēthador**, *m*., grammar (W.): see **grammer**.

***yēthor**, *m*., *pl*. **-yon** (W., B.), ***yēthyth**, *m*., *pl*. **-ydhyon** (W.), linguist, philologist, grammarian.

yeunadow (*ewnadow* B.M.), *m*., desire, wish, craving, B.M. 30.

yeunes (*yenes*, wrongly *yeues* Norris), *m*., *pl*. **-ow**, desire, yearning, longing, O.M. 2125, P.C. 1046.

yeuny (*yeny*), *vb*., to desire, wish, yearn, long, crave, want: 3 s. pret. *yeunys*, P.C. 1701; 3 s. plupf. *yeunsa* (*unsa* M.C. 21): *ken agesough ny-yeunsen*, I should desire no other than yourself, O.M. 2358;

yeunsen ow bones marow, I should long that I were dead, P.C. 3167.

yew (C. Voc. *ieu*), *f.*, *pl.* **-ow**, yoke, *geoc* Aelfric.

yewa, *vb.*, to yoke (W., B.).

†yewgen (C. Voc. *yeugen*), *f.*, *pl.* -as, polecat, fitchew, foumart, ferret; marten, *maerdh* Aelfric.

†yey, yȳ (C. Voc. *iey*), *m.*, ice, frost, *is* Aelfric: see **clēghy.**

yeyn, yēn, yȳn (vars. *eyn*, *yne*, C. Voc. *iein*, Late *ine*), *adj.*, cold, chill, biter, dismal; (of land) not arable: *powty.*, bleak, wild, windswept country, P.; *garm y.*, lamentable cry, MC. 207; *y. newodhow*, sad tidings, C.W. 1262, cf. W. *oernad*, *oerchwedl.*

yeynder, *m.*, coldness, cool, chill, Lh., Gw.

yeynhē˙, *vb.*, to cool, chill: as **berhē.**

ȳf, see **eva.**

yffarn (*yfern*, C.W. *effarn*), *m.*, hell, *pl.* **-ow**, infernal regions: accent in verse is thrown on either syllable, but is properly on the first, as in place-name Halsa·phron Cliff, *als yffarn.*

yffarnak, *adj.*, infernal (W., B,).

ȳfla-grās, *m.*, revenge, spite (M.E. *yvel* (evil) *grace*): cf. M.E. expressions *yfl (elf) at es*, ill at ease, R.D. 574, *yfl mot thow thee*, ill mayest thou thrive, P.C. 2736.

ȳg, see **hȳk.**

ygery, egery (*-gyry*), *vb.*, to open, disclose, explain, expound: 2 s. imp., 3 s. pres.-fut. *ȳgor* (*üger*); 3 s. pret. *ygoras* (*agores*); p. pt. *ygerys* (*gerres* Kerew); the first vowel is obscure except in *ȳgor*, as M.B. *igor*, inf. *igueriff.*

ȳgor, *adj.*, open; *m.*, opening (B. *(d)igor*).

y-gȳla (*gela*), *pron.*, the other, the second of two: lit. his (or its) fellow, *kyla*, m., otherwise unused; *an yl y-g.*, one another; *pup-onen-oll dh'y-g.*, mutually, reciprocally; *an g.* is used B.M. 2072 as the second of three, incorrectly for *y.g.*; see **hy-bēn.**

-yhȳ, *pron.* (emphatic), she, her, it (f.): form of **hyhȳ**, compounded, or almost so, with vb., *mar pe drok a-oberys, trogh y. gans dha gledha*, if it was evil that I did, slash *it* with thy sword, O.M. 292.

ȳl (*nyl*, *neyl*), *adj.*, *pron.*, the one, the other, one of two: in MSS. usually *an nyl*, as W. *neill*, the *n* of *an* having become fixed to *yl*, but where *an* is not present or implied, MSS. have *yl*, *a'y yl* (*eyl*); it seems preferable therefore to follow B. *an eil*, writing *an yl*; *an y. a-vynnaf y'n bys*, whichever I prefer, P.C. 2186; *nyns- a na'n y. na'y-gyla*, neither of the two will go; *my a-vyn dhe why 'poyntya servys dhe 'n y. ha 'y-gyla*, I will appoint you a service for each one of you (with *teag* for *neal*), C.W. 1063; *my a-grys y-kemersa whath an y. kens es merwel*, I believe he should take yet the other (direction) before dying (with *uyl* misprinted for *nyl*), P.C. 324; *y'n y.*, in one or the other, C.W. 2203; *an y. tu*, aside; *marnas an y. party ny-wharth*, only one of the two parties will laugh, B-M. 3477; see **y-gȳla, pynȳl, nanȳl.**

ȳla, -ya, *vb.*, to second (W., B.); to compose music (W.).

***ȳlewyth**, *m.*, *pl.* **-ydhyon**, musician (W.).

***ȳlow**, *m.*, music, tune, melody (W. *alaw*, *eilon*).

yly (*ely* B.M.), *m.*, *pl. and abst.* **ylȳow** (*elyou* B.M.), salve, ointment, cure, remedy.

ylȳa. *vb.*, to anoint with salve: p. pt. *ylȳes*, (*elys* B.M. 3416).

ylyn (C.W. *elyn*), *adj.*, clean, clear, bright, *adv.*, clearly, fairly, unimpeded, clean off: *omma yth-esof parys rag lafurya pur-y. alemma yn dha negys*, here I am ready to travel quite clear away on thy errand, B.M. 1388.

ym-[2], see **om-**[2], of which this is the regular *Ordinalia* spelling.

yma˙, ymo˙ns, see **bōs**, Appendix VIII.

ymach (C.W. *ymadge*), *m.*, *pl.* **-ajys**, image, B.M. (M.E. *ymage*).

ymajer, *m.*, *pl.* **-s**, sculptor, wood-carver (M.E.).

y˙majery, *m.*, *pl.* **-s**, sculpture, carving (M.E.).

***ymp**, *m.*, *pl.* **-ys**, scion, graft (M.E.).

***ympya**, *vb.*, to shoot, graft (M.E.).

ympynyon (C. Voc. *impinian*, B.M. *ompynyon*, C.W. *apyd(g)nyan*, Lh. *'pidnian*), *pl.*, brains, P.C., R.D.

yn (*idden* N. Boson, *edn* Lh.), *adj.*, narrow, strait, close, confined: *darras y.*, a narrow door, O.M. 961.

yn (Late *en*, *ed*, *et*, *it*), *prep.*, in, within, to, unto, into; on, for, as, as a; as prefix to noun, used much as E. "a-" in "abed," "afoot," "atrip," etc.; used before noun of time with poss. pron. as "during all," *y. ow os, bewnans, dedhyow*, etc. ; combines with prons., see Appendix V. ; contracts with poss. prons. (except 3 person sing.), and with **an, ün** ; *y. henna y-fuf genys*, unto that (end) I was born, P.C. 2021 ; *dalghen y.*, lay hold on, take hold of ; *y. ro, tokyn*, as a gift, sign ; *y. sur Dhew*, as very God, M.C. 93 ; with dual or *deu, dyw*, **yn** is replaced by **ynter**; the late corruptions *ed, et, it* are found chiefly before poss. prons., imitating *itna, edna* for *ynno*, etc. ; see **y, y'n**.

y'n, contraction of *yn an*, in the.

yn-[5], *adverbial particle*, used before adjs., e.g., *da*, good, *yn-ta*, well, and before p. pts. to denote state or condition, e.g., *yn-kemyskys*, mingled, M.C. 58, 219, *yn-kelmys*, bound, P.C. 1569, *yn-tasserghys*, risen again, R.D. 1146, *yn-assentys*, consentingly, C.W. 654 ; adjs. can also be used adverbially without this particle.

yn-ban, y'-ban, 'ban (C.W. *in badn*, Late *aman, man*), *adv.*, up (in late usage only, this is made to translate E. "up" after "break," "lay," "give," "make") : *y. ughel worth scoren*, high up upon a bough, O.M. 805 ; see **sevel**.

yn by-and-by, *adv.*, immediately, C.W. 613 (E.).

y'n-bȳs, see **bȳs**.

***yncens**, *m.*, incense (M.E.) : see **†enkys, frankyncens**.

yn-chȳ, y'-chȳ (Late *'chy, tshyi* Lh.), *adv.*, at home, home, in, within-doors, lit. in the house : *ny a-gergh vytel y.*, we we will bring in food, B.M. 275 ; *ha 'ga don genef y.*, and carry them away home, O.M. 1737 ; *esough-why y.*, are you in ? P. ; see **chȳ, yn-trē**.

ynclynya (*inclenya*), *vb.*, to bow down, make obeisance, stoop, incline, B.M. (M.E.) ; 2 s. imp. *ynclȳn*.

yn-crēn, *adj.*, in a trembling state, M.C. 57 : see **crēn**, m.

yn-cusk (*in coske*), *adj.*, asleep, B.M. 3770.

yn-dan[2], **y'dan**[2] (Late *dadn*), *prep.*, under, below, used also as present-participle particle, see Appendix VII. : combines with prons., see Appendix V. ; *y. seyth bloth*, under seven years (of age) : *y. dros*, under foot : *y'-dan* occurs only P.C. 251, but is like B. *didan* for *dindan*, and would lead naturally to *dadn*.

·yndella (Lh. *andella*, for *y'n del-na*), *adv.*, in that way, after that manner, similarly, so : the late *an delna, an dellana*, Lh., seems a restoration ; *y. re-bo*, so be it, Amen ; *y. dhymmo y-wher*, I am similarly troubled, R.D. 709 ; *pan vyn-e yndella*, since such is his will ; with *keth* inserted, *y'n keth della*, in that same way, is usually made **yn-ketella**.

yndelma (for *y'n del-ma*), *adv.*, in this way, after this manner, similarly, thus, on this wise : see **yn-ketelma**.

ynder, *m.*, narrowness, straitness (W.).

yn-fās, *adv.*, well ; (with neg.) hardly, even, scarcely : *a ny-woffes y. un pryjwyth genef golyas ?* coulds't thou not even keep watch with me for one moment ? P.C. 1054 (*wolsys* for *woffes*) ; see **mās**.

yn-fēn, *adv.*, strongly, eagerly, vigorously, impetuously, firmly : see **mēn**.

y'n for'-ma ; y'n for'-na, *advs.*, in this way, thus ; in that way, so : see **forth**.

yn-gron, *adj.*, contracted, in a bundle, bunch or mass, as B. *grounn*, B.M. 542.

yn-hans, *adv.*, yonder, over there, away, aside, aloof, apart, O.M. 1780 (*haus* Norris), B.M. 440, 3919, C.W. 1743 (here possibly for *an hens*, Stokes) : *y. dhe*, beyond, on the further side of, is suggested by *hunt tho*, N. Boson, *ondes*, Crankan Rhyme : see **hans**.

yn-herwyth, *prep.*, in company with: poss. prons. inserted, *y 'gan h.*, with us, etc.

yn-jēth, yn-j.-hedhyū, *adv.*, to-day (pres. and fut.).

ynjyn (*injyn*), *m.*, *pl.* **-nys**, device, trick, stratagem, wile, contrivance, engine, B.M. 3376 (M.E. *engyn*) ; *adj.*, ingenious, adroit, clever, wily, crafty, P.C. 1886 : see **jyn, ynjynor**.

†ynjynor (C. Voc. *inguinor*), *m. pl.*, **-yon**, engineer, wright, craftsman (O. Fr.), *craeftca* Aelfric.

ynk, *m.*, ink (E.) : see **padel**.

y'n-kensewha, see **kensewha**.

yn-kergh, *adv.*, away : see **kergh**.

yn-kerghyn, *prep.*, all round, on all sides of, around, encompassing, encircling, enveloping, surrounding, close about : poss. prons. inserted, *y 'ga herghyn*, round about them, *dhe wysca kemer dyllas y'th k.*, take clothes about thyself to wear, B.M. 4242.

yn-kerth (Late *yn-ker, a-car, car*), *adv.*, away : see **kerth**.

yn-ketella (for *y'n keth del-na*), *adv.*, in

that same way, even so, just so, just like that: see **yndella.**

yn-ketelma (for *y'n keth del-ma*), *adv.*, in this same way, just like this: see **yndelma.**

yn-kever, *prep.*, about, towards, to, in respect of, with regard to: poss. prons. inserted, *yn y gever*, towards him, etc.: see **kever.**

yn-lē, *prep.*, instead of, in place of: poss. prons. inserted, *yn y le*, in his place, etc.; see **lē.**

yn-mēs (*a meas* Lh.), *adv.*, out: see **mēs.**

yn-meth, see **medhes.**

yn-mysk, yn-mesk (Late *amesk*), *prep.*, among(st), amid(st): pl. poss. prons. inserted, *y 'ga mysk*, among them etc. (in Late Cor. incorrectly *meskanjy*, with pron. suffixed); in *gwas pur uskys y. naw*, a right speedy fellow out of nine (such), B.M. 3258, *sherewa yu y. myl*, he's a rogue in a thousand, B.M. 3280, *yn-mysk* with numeral is used to express rarity or excellence; see **mysk.**

yn-nans, *adv.*, down: see **nans.**

yn-nēs, *adv.*, nigh, near(er), closer: *saf! y. na-veth re dont!* Halt! Don't venture near too saucily! B.M. 3470; see **nēs.**

yn-newer, *adv.*, last night: see **nyhewer.**

yn-nōs, *adv.*, by night, to-night: *y. haneth* (fut.), *haneth y.* (past), to-night, this very night; see **nōs.**

yn-nōth, *adj.*, in a naked state, bare: used in preference to **nōth** alone after verbs other than *bos* and *gallas*, etc., in *mos*; *kynth ellen-vy prest y.*, though I were always to go bare myself, B.M. 3064.

ynny, *m.*, pressure, urging, force, constraint: *hep y.*, readily, voluntarily, of one's own free will.

ynnȳa, *vb.*, to urge, incite, force, constrain, importune, press: 3 s. pres. fut., 2 s. imp. *ynny*; *y. war*, press on, urge against; the second *y* is unexpectedly made a consonant by scansion in *y·nnyas*, *y·nnyough*, M.C. 84, 99, 201.

ynnȳadow, *m.*, urging, pressure: *hep y.*, unconstrained, of one's own accord, O.M. 999.

y·nocent, *adj.*, innocent; *m.*, *pl.* **-cens,** innocent person, B.M. 1708 (M.E.).

yn-pell, *adv.*, afar, far off: *nanyl oges nag y.*, neither close at hand nor far away, O.M. 1141.

yn-prōf, see **prōf.**

yn-sol, *interj.*, up! arise! B.M. 2747; ? *adv.*, standing upright, on one's feet, lit. on sole or base: see **sol.**

ynsȳ·, ynjy· (Late *an gy(e)*, *gy(e)*, Lh. *an dzheī*), *pron.* (emphatic), they, themselves: as M. Cor. found, if at all, only with **ot,** q.v., but inferable from W., B. and the other emphatic Cor. forms and in latest Cor. entirely replacing **ȳ,** a contributing cause of which may perhaps have been the wrong division of *yn-medhans-y* as *yn-meth-anjy*, etc.

yn-ta, *adv.*, as well, also, too, lit. well: *a-ves hag a-jy y.*, outside and inside too, O.M. 953; *yn-whyr y.*, right truly, C.W. 473; *moy y.*, more too, yet more, B.M. 2821; *y'-ta*, R.D. 863, *eta*, A. Boorde, *'ta*, Gw. are contractions like B. *eta*, *'ta*.

yn-tefrȳ·, *adv.*, really, verily, indeed, certainly, to be sure: see **defrȳ.**

yn-tēk, y'-tēk, *adv.*, fairly; completely, in unbroken number: *whegh cans flogh ynwheth y.*, fully six hundred children, too, B.M. 1574.

yn-ten, *adj.*, in an outstretched state, taut, tight, tense, strained, racked, M.C. 205, P.C. 2516, R.D. 2583: see **ten.**

y·nterlüt (*antarlick* Lh.), *m.*, *pl.* **-üdys,** interlude, comedy (M.E.): with *antarlick* cf. Late Cor. *edyak* for "idiot."

yntertaynment, *m.*, *pl.* **-mens,** entertainment, reception (M.E.).

yntertaynya, *vb.*, to entertain, receive hospitably, welcome, accept, C.W. 525 (M.E.).

yntra, ynter (*yntre*, *inter*, Late *'ter*), *prep.*, between, among, (with dual or *deu*, *dyw*), in, into: combines with prons. as **drē,** Appendix V.; *yntredho ha'y gowetha*, between him and his companions, used also uncombined with prons., in 1st and 2nd. persons especially, *y. my ha lynyeth den*, between me and the human race, O.M. 1241; *treghy y. deu*, to cut in two; *y. dha dhywla*, into thy hands; *yntredha aga fymp*, among the five of them, etc.; *ynter* is usual in B.M. and C.W., *yntra* in M.C. and Ord.; in Late Cor. *etre gy* is used for *yntredha*.

yn-trē, *adv.*, at home, within-doors: *pyu us y.?* Who is in? B.M. 3301, lit. who is there at home?

yn-tȳen, *adv.*, wholly, completely: see **dȳen.**

yn-tȳr, *adv.*, ashore, on land, B.M. 627.

yn-ün[2]**-,** *adverbial pres.-participle particle,*

for use see Appendix VII.

y'n ür-ma (*enurma* Lh.); **y'n ür-na,** see **ür.**

yn ȳ ōs, *adv.*, ever (not limited to past), lit. in his age: used also with *aga* and other poss. prons.; see **ōs.**

ynweth, ynwē·th (*-weyth,* C.W. *in wethe,* Late *a weeth,* Lh. *a wēdh*), *adv.*, also, besides, likewise, what is more, too, as well, and also, and...too: *y-leverys-ef y.*, he himself said moreover, R.D. 4; the variant *y weth,* P.C. 609, R.D. 837, may come of scribal errors, but the *n* was not sounded in Late Cor., and is not in B. *ivez.*

yn-whȳr, *adv.*, indeed, truly, verily.

yonk, see **yowynk.**

yorgh (C. Voc. *yorch*), *m., pl.* **-as,** roebuck, *raege* Aelfric: Carn Yorth, The Yaw, rock-names: see **†cōsyorgh.**

yorghes (*iorches* Lh.), *f., pl.* **-ow,** roe.

yorghyk, *m., pl.* **-ghesygow,** roe-deer fawn (B.).

†yōs, yōj (C. Voc. *iot*), *m.*, pap, hasty-pudding (? D. "jowds"): *y. kergh,* porridge, gruel (W., B.).

Yow, dë-, dū- Y., dēth-Y., *m.*, day of Jove, Thursday: *de-Y. Bask,* Ascension Day; *de-Y. Hablys,* Maundy Thursday; *de-Y. Wyn* (*Yew Whidden* Tonkin), "Holy Thursday," a miner's feast, held on the Thursday a clear week before Christmas Day (D. "Chewidden"); Marghas-Yow, Marghas deth-Yow, Marajyow, etc., old names of Marazion; see **Jovyn.**

yowynk, yonk (C. Voc. *iouenc, youonc*), *adj.*, young, single, unmarried (Lat. *juvencus*); comp. *-nca*: *den y.*, fiancé; *benen, myrgh y.*, fiancée (B.).

yowynkes, *m.*, youth, youthfulness; (of persons) the young, children, P.C. 433: cf. **henys.**

yowynkhē·, *vb.*, to make young, rejuvenate (B.): as **berhē.**

yowynkneth, *m.*, youth (time or state), youthfulness, P.C. 434.

yowynksys, *m.*, youth, minority (W., B.).

y praya, y praydha (*in preytha*), I pray thee, prithee, B.M., C.W. (M.E. *I preye thee*).

yredy (*eredy,* C.W. *aredy*), *adv.*, surely, verily, quickly, readily (M.E.).

yrgh, see **ergh.**

yrghys, etc., see **erghy.**

yrvyra, see **ervyra.**

***yrynen,** *f., col.* **ȳryn,** sloe, bullace (W., B.).

†ys, *comp. adj.*, lower; *prefix,* below, under-: in place-names only; see **ysel, ysa, ysos, yslonk**; a very dubious instance of *ys* for *a-ys,* adv., below, occurs, R.D. 979, *moy ys na-ve*; Trevisquite, Tresquite, place-names, represent O. Cor. *tref is cuit* (*ys cos*), homestead below the wood.

ȳs (*eys,* C. Voc. *yd,* Late *ise,* Lh. *is*), *col.*, corn; *pl.* **ysow** (*esow*), sorts or supplies of corn; *sing.*, **ysen,** *pl.* **-now,** grain of corn: *y. ow sevel* (*is saval* Lh.), standing corn; *y. du,* whortleberries, Lh.; *pen y.*, ear of corn; *y. bara,* bread corn, P.

ysa, yja, *superl. adj.*, lowest: only in place-names Trevisa, Trevegia, Boregia, etc.: see **ys, ysel.**

ysak, -ek, *f., pl.* **-segow, -segy,** cornfield; *adj.*, rich in corn.

†ȳs-asver (C. Voc. *(h)it aduer*), *m.*, harvest, *gerip* Aelfric: lit. corn-yielding, as W. *adfer, edfrid,* to restore, yield again.

ysedha, see **esedha.**

ysel, *adj.*, low, lowly, modest, unpretending, humble, abject, mean, vulgar; *adv.*, humbly, in lowly manner, basely, meanly, comp. *ysella,* obsolete comp. and superl. *ys, ysa*: *rag ysow galsof y.*, I have run low in corn supplies, O.M. 373; *y. y-fydhons gwythys,* abjectly they shall be set to work, O.M. 1515; place-names Nanjisal, *nans y.*, Chy Ysella, etc.

yselder (*eselder,* Lh. *iseldor*), *m.*, lowness, depth, humility, abasement: *dres dhe y.*, humbled, humiliated, brought low, C.W. 447; *dre y. payn ha mewl,* through the depths of suffering and shame, B.M. 1166.

yseldȳr, *m., pl.* **-yow,** lowland (W., B.): *an Yseldyryow,* the Netherlands.

yselhē·, *vb.*, to lower, degrade, abase, diminish: as **berhē.**

yselvōr, *m.*, low water, neap tide (W., B.)

ȳsen, see **ȳs.**

yskel (C. Voc. *iskel,* Lh. *isgal*), *m.*, broth, soup, pottage.

yskerens, see **escar.**

yskynlür, *m.*, platform (W.).

yskynna (Lh. *eskynna*), *vb.*, to ascend, mount, Ord. only: everywhere else *y.* is replaced by *sevel, drehevel* or *ascendya* and (perhaps because of the apparent repetition of *dhe* in *dhe dhyeskynna*) *skynnya,* B.M., *skydnya, yskydnya,* C.W., take on the directly opposite meaning of "descend"; yet the older *deskydrya* survives in some Late Cor. versions of the Creed, though it was no doubt from Lhuyd's re-spelt M. Cor. that Tonkin took his suggestion of *eskynyas* in another version as a better rendering of "arose" ; similarly M.B. *disquenn* has no corresponding *isquenn* ; *men-y.*, horse-block, mounting or upping-stock (W.).

yskynyans, *m.*, rising, ascension (W.).

ȳsla (*lē*), *m.*, granary, corn-loft (W.).

ȳslan, *f.*, cornyard (W.).

yslonk, *m.*, abyss (B) : ? Izzack an Pucca, Scilly, for *y. an bucca.*

†**ysos**(C. Voc. *isot*), *adv.*, below, downwards : apparently obsolete in M. Cor., this is *ys* combined with 2 s. pron., lit. "below thee" ; cf. **ūghos** and with 1 pl. pron. similarly used, **ahanan, a-ūghon, rybon.**

yss(a)-², see **ass(a)-²**.

yssew (C.W. *ayshew, asshew*), *m.*, issue, progeny (M.E.).

ȳst (C.W. *Yēst*, late *East*), *m.*, *adj.*, east, B.M. 664.

***y'story, ystry**, *m.*, *pl.* **-ow**, history (W.).

***ysto'rȳor**, *m.*, *pl* **-yon**, historian (W., B.).

ystynna (*-tenna*), *vb.*, to reach, (with *dhe*) put within another's reach, extend, (of sail) set, stretch out, (of hand or foot) put forth, (of glass, etc.) pass to another : 3 s. pres.-fut., 2 s. imp. *ystyn* ; *mayth ystynno avel cor*, so that it will draw out like wax, P.C. 2723.

ystynyans, *m.*, extension.

ysyly, see **esel.**

ysylȳek, *adj.*, large limbed (B.).

yth, see **y⁵(th).**

ythō', *conj.*, then, well then, in that case, so, this or that being so : used with reference to previous statement or condition ; *y., dre henna*, according to that, then, P.C. 1489, 2015.

yū, see **bos**, APPENDIX VIII.

yujja, see **jujja.**

yunker (*junkar* Lh.), *m.*, *pl.* **-s**, young man (E. "younker," Dutch *jonker*, not for *yowynkour*, **yowynk, gour**).

yunnya, see **junnya.**

yurl, *m.*, *pl.* **-ys**, earl, governor of shire, C. Voc., B.M. (O.E. *eorl*), *ealdorman, gerefa* Aelfric.

yüs, see **a'y üs.**

yweges, see **ewyges.**

Ywerdhon, Werdhon (Gw. *Worthen*, Lh. *Wordhun*), *f.*, Ireland : the *y* is obscure, but need not be lost, cf. W. *Ywerddon*, M.B. *Yverdon*, B. *Iwerzon.*

Ywerdhonek, *adj.*, Irish ; *m.*, Irish language.

ywys (*yn wys*), *adv.*, certainly, indeed (M.E. *y wis*) : var. *yn wys* has the same intrusive *n* as in *yn praydha.*

yȳ, see **yey.**

Addenda

s.v. **a**, *prep.*, after *cusulya*:—add *pysy*.

after **ago-marghogyon**, add: —**agrowsen**, *f.*, *col.* **agrows**, hip, berry of dog-rose (W., B.).

after **antel**, add: —***antem**, *m.*, *pl.* **-ys**, anthem (M.E.).

s.v. **banna**, after sleeping, add: — speaking.

after **baya**, add: —**bayol** (C. Voc. *baiol*), *f.*, *pl.* -yow, shallow tub, half-tub, mess-kid, as B. *beol*, W. *baeol*, Fr. *baille*, M. Lat. *bajula* (water-vessel): in C. Voc. and Aelfric Lat. *enula* is probably for *gemmula*, translated *paerl* in another version of Aelfric and apparently a burnishing implement used by scribes, but misread and translated as if M. Lat. *gemella*, Fr. *gamelle*, mess-tub.

s.v. **blewen**, add:—*b. dowr*, water-crowfoot (B.).

after **cardynal**, add:—**carer**, *m.*, *pl.* **-roryon**, *f.* **-rores**, *pl.* **-ow**, lover, admirer, amateur (W., B.).

after **certüs**, add:—**cessya**, see **sessya**.

after **chekker**, add:—**chekkya**, *vb.*, to check, rebuke: Late Cor. *lez e tha jeckya*, **lest** he reprove thee, Gw., for *na-ve ef dhe'th chekkya*,

s.v. **coref**, add:—(B.M. *corff*).

s.v. **cragh**, add:—(*krehy*, C.W. 2326).

s.v. **crenna**, add:—*may crenno pur wyr y dhyns*, so that his teeth indeed will chatter, B.M. 2257.

after **crȳspows**, add:—**crystal** (*-tel*), *m.*, crystal: *yth-eugh gwyn avel c.*, you will become white like crystal, B.M. 1521; **see gwrȳs.**

after **demedhy**, add:—**demedhyans**, *m.*, marriage, espousal: see **maryach.**

after **dygnas**, add:—**dygolm**, **-en**, *adj.*, knotless, unknotted [preferable to **dyscolm**].

s.v. **eno**, add: – R.D. 159, 2332.

s.v. **erghy**, add:—when transitive requires *dhe, my a-ergh dhys*, etc.

after **gōn**, add:—**gona**, *vb.*, to sheathe (W., B.).

s.v. **gorthfyl**, add:—in Late Cor. probably means "conger," represented by *withel* in the traditional *pedn bokser*, *lost withel*, describing a boat with a bluff entrance but a fine run, in Eng. "cod's head and conger tail"; cf. also (*an*) Nor Wethel? the conger ground, Scilly; *bokser* may be for *bogh-serth*, "stiff-cheek," and name some sort of gurnard, Pedn Boxer is a headland, cf. Gurnard's Head.

after **gorthfyl**, add:—**gorthgrēs**, *f.*, distrust, counter-belief (W.).

after **gwal**, add:—**†gwa·lather**, *m.*, *pl.* **gwe·lyther**, ruler, leader, as W. *gwaladr*: in name of Saint Branwalather.

s.v. **gwergh**, add:—(*grue(r)gh* B.M. 1692, 1705, 1776), and add to definition, unspotted, undefiled, untainted: cf. B.M. 4247 with similar mis-spelling *grurhes*, for *gwerghes*; delete (B.).

after **kerth**, *m.*, etc., add:—**kerth**, *m.*, *or f.*, right, as M.W. *kerth*, *m.* right, B. *kerz*, f., property, M.B. *querz*, adv., certainly, indeed, Lat. *certus*, *certe*: *pandr' yu dha gerth y'n pow-ma?* what is thy right in this province? B.M. 2370, is more apt than "what is thy journey?"

s.v. **ladha**, add:—; final *dh* may occur when pron. *e* or *y* is practically joined to to the vb. in pronunciation, as suggested by M.C. spelling *laze* (*ladha*) not *lath e*, *z* usually representing *dh* in M.C.

after **lonak**, add:—**londya**, *vb.*, to land, B.M. 1093 (M.F.).

s.v. **medhes**, for (*yn-methy*) read (*yn-medhy*, M.C. *mezy*), and after *yn-meth* (*-ef*) add (*yn-medha*, M.C. *meza*, *meze*), cf. **ladha.**

s.v. **melenek**, add:—; ? also goldfinch (P. *molenek.*).

after **stryng**, add: —**stryppen**, *f.*, *pl.* **-now**, strip (E.): Wheal Stryppen, mine-name.

after **†tollor**, etc., add:—**tollor**, *m.*, *pl.* **-yon**, one who renews tin-bounds, by cutting a turf from a hole (D. "tollur"): **see toll.**

Corrigenda

Failing conclusive evidence (and in one or two cases because of misprints), the turned point (·) should be deleted from the following words. Welsh precedent would allow it in those here given an asterisk: **abatty, -tyr, abestely, -eleth, aflan, agor, alusen, -jy, -or, alwhedhow, ancarjy, -va, ancof, ancombra, -brynsy, anes, anfur, -fus, -fusy, anhun, anlan, ansans, -oleth, anvab, -ven, -vlas, -voth, -vry, anwan, -whek, -wyw, anyagh, aradow, ardak, ar(gh)adow, arlodheseth, arlottes, attal, avlan, barlysen, baywedhen, benedyksyon, benesykter, bodhara, boreles, botasen, boxesy, bras-oberys, bredereth, brennygen, bryansen, calmynsy, camwortheby, cantolbren, cantolor, caradewder, caradow, caretysen, carrygy, casadewder, casadow casygy, clamdera, collwedhen, cosoleth, cowethlyver, cowsesow, -jejyow, crothvolas, croffolas, danvonadow, darrajow, darwar, dedhewadow, degoth, dervyn, deryvadow, drocoleth, *dyarf, *dybals, *-barth, *-begh, *-ben, *-berth, *-blans, *-bluf, *-blysk, *-bos, *brys, *dyclos, *-creft, dydhan, *-dhel, *-dhew, *-dhyns, *-dhysk, *-dros, *-drygh, dyfen, -nadow, dyffres, *dyflam, *-flas, -freth, *dyfun, *-fyk, -fyth, *dygesson, *-gnas, *-goll, -guf, *-gusk, *-guth, *dyhorn, *dyle, *-leth, -lym, *-nam, *-nas, *-nerth, *-newl, *dyras, *-rewl, dyscler, dyscolm, dylen, *-lyw, *-son, *-ster, dyswar, *dyvarf, *-veth, *-vos, -vres, *-vro, *dywall, *-wel, *-wern, *wysk, *-wyth, enepwerth, godhas.**

for **agor**, m., and **agor**, see **egery**, read :– **agor, -as**, see **ygery, ygor**.

for **angus**, read :– **angūs.**

ber, f., rests only on **dywver**, which might equally be dual of **fer** as pronounced.

for **cably**, read :– **cabla** (inf. suggested by 3 s. imperf. indic. **cabla**).

transpose **cok-Gyny**, etc., and **cok**, *adj.*, etc.

s.v. **cosoleth**, for 719, read :– 715.

for **cren**, *m.*, read :– **crēn.**

for **delȳt**, read :– **delȳ·t.**

for **egery**, etc., read :– **egery**, see **ygery.**

s.v. **faven**, before *ny-synsaf* delete *my.*

s.v. **gelwel**, read :– 1 *galwaf.*

s.v. **goly**, read :– *pl.* **-lȳow.**

s.v. **grurgh** (*grue(r)gh*), delete all that follows and add :– see **gwergh.**

for **gwary-myrkel**, read :– **gwary-merkyl.**

transpose **gwyban** and **gwyber.**

s.v. **gwȳryoneth**, for **gwȳry'oneth**, read :– **gwyr'oneth.**

for **hevelles**, read :– **heveles**, delete *havalla* and superfluous *l* of *havalas, hevely*; correct w.f. letter *a* in *'falsa*.

s.v. **hubbadullya**, read :– B. *kabaduilh.*

for **Kemerer**, read :– **kemerer.**

s.v. **kervya**, for (W.) read :– (M.E. *kerve*).

for **kesregnya**, read :– **kesrēgnya.**

for **sedca**, read :– **sedha.**

s.v. **squych**, read :– (M.E., D. "squitch").

Appendix I.: Dubious Words

As explained in the Introduction, words that have been traced back to misreadings or misunderstandings are omitted altogether; so also are those which seem as yet too uncertainly suggested by place-names or dialect. The following are words, mainly from the Old-Cornish Vocabulary, of which the form or the meaning, or both, seem doubtful.

†antromet, sex (sexus, *werhad odhdhe wifhad*, Aelfric) : ? *an dra meth, tra* is written *tro* elsewhere.

†auain, image (imago vel agalma, *anlycnyss*, Aelfric) : ? *avain* from Lat. *imagine* (Norris) or for *ailun*, as W. *eilun*.

besse, B.M. 1475 : metre requires *bes* as pronunciation, and as a corruption of *bytteth* this is impossible, perhaps *bys*, finger, is meant.

†bidnethein, hawk (accipiter, *heafoc*, Aelfric : ? for *bodu* (W. *boda*) *edhein* (*ydhyn*), hawk of birds; *n* for *u*, *w* for *th* are common slips in C. Voc. MS.

†bruha, livelihood, living, food (victus, *bigleofa* Aelfric: †*brughan* (W. *brwchan*), caudle, flummery, seems too limited in meaning to fit.

†coifinel (serpillum, *fille*, Aelfric) : O. and M.E. *fille* is chervil (*chaerophyllum*), not wild thyme (*serpyllum*) ; *cerfiuel* might be Fr. *cerfeuil*, chervil, but *coit* and O.E. *finel*, "wood-fennel," is quite apt, or *corfinel*, "dwarf fennel" might name chervil, though "fennel" in C. Voc. is *fenochel* ; see **fenokel.**

†discoruunait, madness (rabies, *wodnys*, Aelfric) : *dys-* and *-neth* alone seem clear.

†tenniou, clout, seam (commisura, *clut*, Aelfric) : *en* may be the article, with *niou* possibly for *(g)wryow*.

†ferhiat, thief (fur, *theof*, Aelfric) : ? *feryas*, from vb. *ferya*, from Lat. *fur*.

†guaf, chaste (castus, *claene*, Aelfric : ? for *gwef*, var. of **gwyw**, worthy, cf. **squenip** below.

gudreva, third day hence, Lh. : ? for *godreveth* (*go-*, *treveth*), or an attempt at making Cornish of W. *gwrthrennydd*.

†guahalegh, thane, noble (satrapa, *theyn*, Aelfric) : ? as W. *gwalch*, hero.

gubeddern, mallet, or else ankle-bone, *malleolus*, Lh. : *gobedren* (*go-*, *pedren*) hardly fits either meaning.

gulbredengu, pin-bone, projection of hip, Borlase ; ? for *culbre(d)n* (W. *cwlbren*) *gyew*, "knob-stick of sinews."

†keniat cōbricā, trumpeter (liticen, *truth*, Aelfric) : *kenniat*, "singer," may be used as "player," but *kerniat*, trumpeter, seems likely ; *cō* suggests an abbreviation of *corn*, read as *com*, and *corn-bry cam*, "curved horn of honour" is perhaps possible.

†lefiste escop, bishop's throne, see, or ? staff (cathedra, *bisceopstaef*, Aelfric) : the first four letters are dubious, and the Aelfric Glossary slip of *staef*, staff, for *setl* or *stol*, seat (mistakenly copied from the previous word *candelstaef*), may be followed, but W. *llys-eiste*, "court of sitting," may have been written instead of Cor. *lys-eseth*.

†lewilloit, spleen (splen, *milte*, Aelfric) : ? *lethilloit*, *w* for *th* ; cf. W. *lleithon*, milt.

mujoven (*mudzhovan*), yoke, or couple, pair, second meaning of Lat. *jugum*, Lh.

peravy, pleasures, Scawen : root seems W. *per*, delicious.

†primusdoc, blear-eyed (lippus, *suregede*, Aelfric) : this seems a long way from B. *pikouzek*, but may be miswritten.

ranna or **granna,** ? to mock, jeer, M.C. 137 : no meaning of *ranna* from *ran* seems to fit.

†squenip, unchaste (incestus, *unclaene*, Aelfric) : ? for *(di)squeuiw (dysquyw)*, unworthy, cf. **guaf**, above ; *n* for *u*, *p* for *w* are common in C. Voc., but the loss of *di* is unexplained.

tahwa, sea-calf, seal, Lh. : W. *tachwedd*, slaughter, would fit the spelling, but not the sense.

†tairnant, poultice (malagma, *clidha*, Aelfric) : final *nt* suggests a non-Celtic word, as this would otherwise be *ns* ; possibly miswritten for **unyent.**

thefe, O.M. 2434 : ? *dha fe*, thy faith.

†tot, mor t., ocean (oceanum, *garsegc*, Aelfric) : the normal meaning of *garsegc* is "spear-sedge."

tounack, complete, N. Boson (as copied by Ustick) : possibly *scant tounack* for *scant ewnak*, see **ewn.**

treysy, B.M. 2399, seems to refer to something that one crushes underfoot.

†troc, wretched or miserable person (miser, *earmingc*, Aelfric) : ? for *trot*, W. *tlawd*, B. *treud*, likely to have been *trüs* if M. Cor.

tumarrhar, pl **-hurian** (Polwhele), wooer, suitor, Lh. (followed by Tonkin, Borlase, Pryce, Polwhele) : cf. Ir. *toghairmoir*, suitor, Lh., *Arch. Brit.*, 119.

†ulair, web, mantle (tela vel peplum, *web*, Aelfric).

†undamsi, dependent (cliens vel clientus, *incniht*, Aelfric) : ? for *en thanisi* for O.E. *thén-hyse*, client, thane's servant.

wesse, B.M. 1476 : metre requires *wes*: possibly **ōs**, age, so spelt as eye-rhyme to *besse* above.

wreghaf (? inf. *gwregha*), O.M. 521 : ? like W. *gwrychu*, to hedge, and so to cultivate, or cf. W. *rhychu*, B. *rega(t)*, to furrow, W. *rhych*, furrow, B. *reg*, furrow, successional crop, suggesting Cor. *regha* as a possible word.

wy, B.M. 3953 : ? for *oy*, C. Voc. *uy* ; cf. var. late spellings of **moy.**

Appendix II. : Prefixes

This list does not include such prefixes as are used as separate words

---

a-³, intens.: *ahas, ago(-marghogyon)*, cf. W. *agwedd*.

an-², **†en-**², priv. and neg., without, un-, dis-: affects *b, g, gw, m* and becomes *af-, av-* before *l*; *ancres, anven, aflavar, †enkenethel*; less common in M. Cor. than *dy-, dys-*.

ar-², intens.: *arveth*.

argh-, arch-, chief.: *arghel*.

as-², re-, back, again: causes 2nd. state in following *b, g, gw, m*; *c, k, p* are unchanged, *d* becomes *t*, which *t* may cause the previous *s* of *as-* to become *t* also; *aswels, ascor, attal*.

com-, con-, cun-, variants in different words of **ke-**.

dar-² (*de-, ar-*²), intens., pre-, fore-: *darbary, darwar, darfos, *daromres*.

das²**-** (*de-, as-*), stronger form of *as-*, with same mutations: *dasvewa, dasserghy*.

de-², intens.: *degemeres, deantel*; spelt *dy-* before *e, dyerbyn, dyegrys*, and *dyn-* as compounded with **an-* in *dynargh* (*de-*, W. *annerch*); spelt *d-* in *danvon* (*de-*, W. *anfon*) and *domhel* (*de-, om-, whel*).

deu-², m., **dyw-**², f., dual prefix before nouns naming parts of the body: *deulyn, dywen*.

dre-, intens., thoroughly: *drehedhes, dremas*.

dy-², neg. and priv. (in MSS. often confused with **de-**²): *dynam, dybenna,*; *cl, cr* may resist mutation, *dyclos, dycreft*; *bl* may become *fl, dyflas*; an *f* may be inserted, *dyf(h)un*; for *dywysca* we have *dy'sky*; in *†dyhok(g), dy-*³ keeps an old meaning "extreme" and causes an exceptional old mutation as in W. *dichell*.

dy-, dyn-, see **de-**².

dys-, neg. and priv.: *dyslyw, dyscrysy*; following *g, gw* become *c, k, qu* or else *w, dyscrassyes, dysquedhes* (var. *dyswedhes*), *dyswul*.

dyw-², see **deu-**².

e(f)-, neg.: *efan* (*an* for *yn*, narrow, cf. W. *ehang* with *ang* for *ing*, B. *ec'hon* with *on* for *enk*).

en-, in: *encledhyes*.

er-², intens.: *†erbysyas*; also decreasing, partly, in *ernoth*.

es-, ys-, ancient priv.: *escar, yskerens*.

go-²,³, decreasing, rather, somewhat, nearly, slight: usually causes 2nd state, *godolghyn*, but may cause 3rd in *c, k, goheles*.

gor-²,³,⁴, intens., rarely pejorative, as **go-**: mutations irregular, usually causes 2nd state in following *b, d, g, m*, 3rd in *c, k, p*, 2nd or 3rd in *t*, 2nd or 4th in *gw*; *gordheweth, gorfen, gorhemmyn, gorquytha*; exceptional are *gorge, gorgul gormel*.

gorth-², against, contra-: *gortheby, gorthfyl* (for *gorthvyl, th* affecting *v*).

he-² (*hy-, ho-*), easily, readily, -able: *hedrogh, hegol*; vbs. formed by adding inf. ending *-hē, hebaskhe*, nouns by adding suffix *-eth, -a, hebasca* (for *hebasketh*).

ke- (vars. **ky-, kyn-, kem-, ken-, kev-, com-, con-**), com-, con-, with: *kemysky, convedhes, compes*, etc.

kes-², co-, together, joint: mutations as after **as-**²; *kesvewa, kescolon, kettoth*.

kyn-, before, preceding: *kynyaf*, see **ken**.

***les-**², step-, half-, substitute: mutations as after **as-**²; **lesvam*.

mys-, mis-: *mystrystya, myskemeres*.

om-² (*em-, ym-*), reflexive, mutual and reciprocal: *omweres*, etc.; special meanings are given by stressing the prefix, as in *o·mlath*.

por- (*pür-*), very, quite: *porres, poran*.

rag-, rak-, for: mutations irregular; 2nd state in *b, gw, m, t*, no change in *g, p, c, d* seems probable; *ragleverys*.

skyl-, decreasing, rather, more or less, not very, as B. *skil-*: *skylwyn*.

ter-², **tre-**², of intermittent, repeated, or feeble action: *† tergusca, terlemmel, trenyja, treluba*.

tra-³, **tre-**³, excessive, over, beyond: *tramor, † trethes, ternos, trenja*; in O. Cor. gloss, c. 900, Vatican MS. Reg. 49, this is still a preposition, *tra pen*, pro capite.

†ugh- (C. Voc. *hich, hih*), super-, highly.

Appendix III.: Suffixes

This list does not include such suffixes as are used as separate words

---

-a, inf.: *cara*, *gorra*; when denoting seeking, hunting, e.g , *legessa*, the inf. or verb-noun in *-a* for *-ha* is the only part used; the lost *h* has caused hardening and doubling of *s* before it.

-a, adj. in comparison (Appendix VI.).

-a (contraction of **-eth**, pl. **-edhow** if used), abst.: *notha*, *kerensa*.

-a, see **-ē**.

-ador, **-dar**, agent, instrument, *gonador*, *ardar*.

-adow, abst., from vb.: *arghadow*, *pysadow*.

-adow, adj. from vb.: *caradow*, *casadow*, only examples; used as noun also, pl. **-yon**.

-al, inf., var. of **-el**.

-ak (vars. **-es**, **-yak**, **-yk**), adj. from noun: *lysak*, *lowenek*, *dyscryjyk*, such adjs. being in turn used as nouns, *ankenek*, *lavrak*, *marghak*, *Kernewek*, *pensyvyk*, some with pls. **-ogyon**, **-egyon**, **-ygyon**, rarely **-ogow**; **-yak** is used after *l*, as *pylyak*, *scullyak*, † *colyak*; f. **-oges**, **-eges**, **-yges**, pl. **-ow**; in terms of reproach f. remains *-ak*, as in *lavrak*; names of inanimate things with suffix *-ak* are f., as *pluvak*.

-ans, see **-yans**.

-as (vars. **-es**, **-os**, **-yas**, **-ys**), noun from noun., adj., or stem of vb., expressing action, result or stroke, gender following that of first noun: *peghas*, *boxas*, *dyscas*, *trygas*, *gologhas*; *seghes*, *cleves*, *hunes*, *lanwes*, *yeunes*; *dewnos*; *renkyas*, *golyas*; *dedhewys*, *sawys*; pls., if any, (*-as*, *-os*) **-osow**, (*es*, *ys*) **-esow**.

-as, (vars. **-yas**, **-es**), pl.: *cathas*, *besyas*, *enevalles*.

-as, -dom: *myghternas*.

-as, inf.: *myras*; in Late Cor. often replaces older endings, as "trigaz" for *tryga*.

***-as**, -ful, in borrowed or revived words only: *loas*.

-der (*-ter* after *gh*, *k*, *p*, *s*, *t*, *th*), noun, usually abstract, from adj. or noun: *caradewder*, *melder*, *splander*, *tekter*; previous *s* or *k* may also become *t*, *goscotter*, *caletter*, *muscotter*.

†-ē, **-a** (for *hē*), agent: †*ydhnē*, *legessa* (rare); lost *h* hardens and doubles previous *s* as in verb-nouns; see **-a**.

-egy, inf. from adjs. ending in *-ak*: *mousegy*, *muskegy*.

-ek, inf.: *resek* (rare).

-ek, adj.: see **-ak**.

-ek, **-ak**, f., place abundant in some product of the soil, vegetable or mineral: *banallek* *cunyjek*, *dreysek*, *drenak*, *stenak*; pls. **-egy**, **-egow**.

-el, inf., especially associated with stems ending in *f*, *v*, or *w*: *drehevel*, *lenwel*, *sevel*, *sylwel*, etc., but also found in *fyllel*, *leverel*, etc.

-el, dim.: *brythel*, *porghel*, pl. **-elly**.

-ell, instrument: *gwynsell*, *whythell*, pl. **-ow**.

-ell, f., dim.: *crugell*, *graghell*, *spa(v)nell*.

-en, f., pl. **-now**, sing. of col. noun: *gwedhen*, *mesen*.

-en, dim., f. of **-yn**: *benewen*.

-ens, pl.: *kerens* (rare).

-er, **-yer**, agent from vb.: *troghyer*, *formyer*, *caner*, f. **-ores**, pl. **-ow**, as *palores*, *canores*.

†-er, instrument: † *gorher*; pl. **-yow**.

-es, pl., see **-as**.

-es, see **-ves**.

-es, noun, see **-as**.

-es, f., pl. **-ow**, **-y**: *myghternes*, *mowes*, pl. *mowysy*.

-es, inf.: *gweles*, *kerdhes*.

-esyk, adj. and noun, pl. **-ygyon**: *genesyk*.

-eth, **-neth**, abst., and sometimes f., from adj., pl. **-edhow**: *genesygeth*, *folneth*, *sleyneth*, *drocoleth*, *flogholeth*, *skentoleth*.

-eth, abst. or col. from noun, pl. **-ow**: *natureth*, *bredereth*, *tyreth*.

-eth, inf.: *marghogeth* (rare).

-eth, pl.: *gwrageth*, *eleth*.

-ethes, abst. from adj.: *mostethes*, *plosethes*, *podrethes*.

-gow, abst. from adj.: *tewolgow* (rare).

-hē, inf. from adj.: accent of adj. of more than one syllable remains as secondary accent before it, as in *lo·wenhē·*.

-jy (*chy*), house: *bowjy*; becomes *-ty* after *gh*, *k*, *p*, *s*, *t*, *th*, as in *lety*, *lughty*.

-jy, **-jys**, see **-sy**, **-sys**.

-lych (O.E. adv. ending *-lice*), adv.: *hardlych*, *manerlych*.

-ma, suffixed to noun after *an* or to adj. following such noun, this, these: *yndelma*, *an tyller yn-ma*.

-na, used as **-ma**, that, those: *alena (a'n le-na)*, *yndella (y'n del-na)*, *an gwas-gof du-na*.
-neth, see **-eth**.
-ns, pl. of M.E. words ending in *-nt*, *ts* becoming *s*: *servons*, *greons*, *fysmans*.
-ny, abst. from adj.; the one Cor. example, *crefny*, from *craf*, itself became an adj., but *-ny* occurs in some borrowed words, and †*berry* is perhaps for *berny*; see *-y*, abst.
-ol, see **yl**.
-oleth, see **-yl**, **-eth**.
-on, pl.: *Sawson*.
-onÿeth, as **-ÿeth**, in borrowed words only: *bardhonyeth*.
-or, **-yor**, agent from noun or vb.: *dyscajor*, †*gravyor*; pl. **-yon**, f. **-ores**, pl. **-ow**.
-os, inf.: *desevos*, *gallos*.
-ow, **-yow**, pl.: *sansow*, *delyow*; also used as abst. sing.: *parow*, *cavow*, *ylyow*, *marthusow*, followed by sing. pron.; a few M.E. loan-words not ending in *a* have this pl., as *fardellow*, *babyow*, *garlontow*.
-plēk, -fold, times: *lyesplek*, *deublek*, *tryflek*.
-res, abst.: *gwythres* (rare).
-rȳth (C. Voc. *rid*, *ruid*), kind, sex: *gorryth*, *benenryth*.
-s, pl. of some M.E. loan-words, see **-ys**; also substituted for *-ts*: *harlos*.
-seth, abst.: *denseth*, pronounced *densa*, and probably from an adj. *denus*, with suffix **-eth**, rather than a var. of *densys* with *th* for *s*.
-sy, **-jy**, adj. from noun: *ankensy*.
-sys, **-jys**, abst. from noun: *densys*; with added *n*, *mestrynjys*; with *s* (once *d*) become *t* after *th*, *arlottes*, for *arluthsys*; usually m., but *trynsys* is f.
-ter, see **-der**.
-tra, abst.: *droktra*, *truethtra*.
-ty, see **-jy**.
-üjy, **-üsy**, see **-yjy**.
-ury, abst. in M.E. loan-words, as M.E. *-orye*, *-erye*, but used independently: *treghury*, *traytury*, *falsury*, and with added *d* after *n*, *lendury*.
-üs, **-ys**, adj. from noun: *marthus*, *gothys*; when used as noun, pl. is **-ujyon**, **-ejyon**.
-va, **-fa** (*ma*), f., abst. from noun, place, state: *porva*, *cofva*, *golva*; *s*, *th* (older *d*, *dh*) disappear before it, but doubling the *v*, in *covva*, *hevva*, *scovva*; as abst. this is confused with **-van**.

-van (*man*), abst. from noun: *loskvan*, *potvan*.
-ves, **-es**, in ordinal numerals, eth, -th: *degves*, *pympes*, *wheghes*, *wheghves*, var. *wheffes*, etc.
-weth (*gweth*), f., form: *fynweth*, *ynweth*.
-y, pl.: *bryny*, *mowesy*, *carrygy*; often replaces older vowel-change pl.
-y, inf.: *terry*, *tylly*, *erghy*.
-y, abst. from noun: *anfusy*, *pystry*.
-ya, inf.: *lywya*; the common inf. usually chosen for vbs. from M.E., as *formya*.
-yades, see **-yas**, agent.
-yak, see **-ak**.
-yans, **-ans** (vars. *-ens*, *-yns*), abst. from vb., pl. **-ow**: *gyvyans*, *dyscans*; or rarely from adj., *squythans*, *trystans*, and with added *n*, *bewnans*, *mernans*.
-yas, pl., see **-as**.
-yas inf.: *cramyas*.
-yas, noun, see **-as**.
-yas, agent, pl. **-ysy**, f. **-yades**, pl. **-ow**: *kernyas*, †*rennyas*, *sylw(y)as*.
-yer, **-er**, pl.: *prenyer*, *prenner* (rare).
-yer, agent, see **-er**.
-ÿeth, f., abst. from noun, describing art, doctrine, etc.: *medhygyeth* (from *medhek*).
-yjy, **-üjy**, **-üsy**, abst.: *terryjy*, *deulujy*, *marthusy*.
-yjy, see **-yas**, agent.
-yjyon, abst. from adj.: *glasyjyon*, *golowyjyon*, *govyjyon*, *lovryjyon*, ? *marthejyon*, *posyjyon*; though resembling a pl. of *golowys* in *golowyjyon* (and perhaps actually a pl. of *marthus* in *marthejyon*), this seems a distinct suffix, used as V. *-izion*, m., B. *-ijenn*, f., used there of light and dark, heat and cold only.
-yk, see **-ak**.
-yk, dim.: usually causes vowel-change; pl. may be formed from pl. of original noun, as *tam*, pl. *tymmyn*, dim. *temmyk*, pls. *temmygow*, *tymmynygow*; occasionally pejorative, see **dyalwhedhyk**.
-yl, *-**ol**, adj. from noun: *skentyl*; older *-ol* (also *-ul*, *-el*) is kept in some words before **-eth**.
-ylly, inf.: *cryghylly*; this gives a frequentative meaning, as B. *-ella*, *-ellat* in *mac'hella*, *luskellat*, etc., cf. Eng. "le" in "crackle," "-er" in "chatter" etc.
-yn, abst. and inf.: *wherthyn*.
-yn, pl.: *tymmyn*, *bommyn*, *hynwyn*.
-yn, dim.: †*cussyn*, *tegyn*; see **-en**, **dim.**

-ynsy, -ynjy, abst.: *sherewynsy, flerynjy.*

-yon, pl. *mebyon, ownegyon*; see **-yjyon.**

-yon, inf.: *bryjyon*; this seems to denote continuous slow action, as W. *-ian* in *sefyllian*, etc.

-yor, see **-or.**

-yow, see **-ow.**

-ys, pl.: *stokkys, pajys*; the regular pl. of M.E. loan-words ending in *a.*

-ys, inf.: *gonys.*

-ys, adj., see **-üs.**

-ys, noun, see **-as.**

-ys, abst. from adj.: *trystys, sawys, golowys.*

-ysy, see **-yas,** agent.

-ysyow, -yjyow, separative pl. made from pls. in **-es**: *devysyow* from *deves, fleghyjyow* from *fleghes*, used of scattered or separate individuals, as opposed to those of a group.

†-yth, agent, pl. **-ydhyon,** f. **-ydhes**: *†prydyth, †lewyth.*

-yth, adj., *myghternyth* (rare).

Appendix IV.: Personal Pronouns

	1 Simple, *subject* before vb.	2 Auxiliary, or Simple, *stressed*; suffixed to noun, adj., or vb., or *object* after imperative.	3 Auxiliary, *unstressed*, compounded with vb.	4 Doubled, emphatic form of 2, *stressed* on final vowel.	5 Doubled, emphatic form of 3, with 2 added for stress.
S. 1	*mȳ*	*vȳ*	*-ma, -a*	*avȳ, evȳ*	*-mavȳ, -avȳ*
S. 2	*tȳ*	*sȳ, jȳ*	*ta-, (s)a*, (j)a**	*dhesȳ, dhejȳ, tejȳ*	*-tejȳ*
S. 3	m. *ēf*	m. *ef, e, va**	m. *-a, -va*	m. *ëef, väef*	m. *-väef*
	f. *hȳ*	f. *hȳ*	f. *-y*	f. *hyhȳ*	f. *yhȳ*
Pl. 1	*nȳ*	*nȳ*	...	*nynȳ*	...
Pl. 2	*whȳ*	*whȳ*	...	*whywhȳ*	...
Pl. 3	*ȳ*	*ȳ*	...	*ynsȳ, ynjȳ*	...
		* after final vowel of vb.	* with *os* only, *-jy* may be added as form 4.	* after *s*, *th*.	

	6 Infixed, *object* between particle, etc., and vb., or *subject* in *bos*, to have.	7 Possessive, *unstressed*, for stress 2 or 4 is suffixed to noun or inf.	8 Possessive, form of 7 used after preps. *a, dhe, dh', yn, y'*, and conjs. *ha, na.*
S. 1	*-m-*	*ow*[3], *am**	*'w*[3], *'m*
S. 2	*-th-*[5], *-d-*[5]	*dha*[2]	*'th*
S. 3	m. *-n-*	m. *ȳ*[2]	m. *ȳ*[2]
	f. *-s-*	f. *hȳ*[3]	f. *ȳ*[3], *hȳ*[3]
Pl. 1	*-n-, -gan-, -agan*	*agan*	*'gan*
Pl. 2	*-s-, -gas-, -agas-*	*agas*	*'gas*
Pl. 3	*-s-*	*aga*[3]	*'ga*[3]
		* after preps.	

Appendix V. : Pronominal Prepositions

	1st Conjugation, *-af*, etc.		2nd Conjugation, *-of*, etc.			
	*a*², of, etc.	*war*², on	*rak(g)*, for *	*drē*², by	*drēs*, over	*yn*, in
S. 1	*ahanaf*	*warnaf*	*ragof*	*dredhof*	*dresof*	*ynnof*
S. 2	*ahanas*	*warnas*	*ragos*	*dredhos*	*dresos*	*ynnos*
S. 3	m. *anodho* f. *anedhy*	m. *warnodho* f. *warnedhy*	m. *ragtho* f. *rygthy*	m. *dredho* f. *dredhy*	m. *dresto* f. *dresty*	m. *ynno* f. *ynny*
Pl. 1	*ahanan*	*warnan*	*ragon*	*dredhon*	*dreson*	*ynnon*
Pl. 2	*ahanough*	*warnough*	*ragough*	*dredhough*	*dresough*	*ynnough*
Pl. 3	*anedha*	*warnedha*	*ragtha*	*dredha*	*dresta*	*ynna*
			* *k* as var. in 3rd pers.			

	3rd Conjugation, *-ef*, *-yf*, etc.		Irregular
	gans, with,* etc.	*(w)orth*, by,* etc.	*dhe*², *de*², to, for*
S. 1	*genef*	*orthyf*	*dhym(mo)*
S. 2	*genes*	*orthys*	*dhys(o)*
S. 3	m. *ganso* f. *gensy*	m. *orto* f. *orty*	m. *dhodho* f. *dhedhy*
Pl. 1	*genen*	*orthyn*	*dhyn*
Pl. 2	*genough*	*orthough*	*dheugh*
Pl. 3	*gansa*	*orta*	*dhedha*
	* vars. have *y* as first vowel except in 3 s.m. and 3 pl.	* all forms may have initial *w*.	* all forms may have *d* as initial, especially after *s*, *th*.

N.B. : 1st Conjn. : like *war* is *dywar*. 2nd Conjn. : like *rak(g)* are *hep(b)*, *ryp(b)*, *derak(g)*, *a-rak(g)*, *a-dherak(g)* ; like *yn* are *yn-dan*², *a-dhan*², *a-ugh* (found in 1 s. and pl. only, *-af* written for *-of*), and conjs. *avel*, *ages*, *es*. 3rd Conjn. : like *orth* are *dyworth*, *a-dhyworth* ; *-eugh* is found as var. 2 pl. ending in this conjn.

As the pronominal endings are unstressed, suffixed prons. (2 or 4) are added to emphasize the pron. ; *gans* has *genama* as a rare var. of *genef-vy* ; *gena'* alone is more common.

In addition to being irregular, *dhe*, *de* has vars. that stress the pron. in 1 and 2 s. and pl., *dhe vy*, *dhe jy*, *dhe ny* or *dynny*, *dhe why* or *dywhy* and in 3 pl. *dhedh'y* for *dhedha y*. These vars. in Late Cor. tend to replace the other forms, with exception of 3 pl., in which as everywhere else *-ans* is usually substituted for *-a* as 3 pl. ending, imitating verbal ending. The vowel of *dhym*, *dhys*, *dhyn* may be made long when stressed. *Dhym* is used to emphasize an imperative, *dus a-rag dhym*, *taw dhym*, etc.

Some of these forms have become adverbs : *ahanan*, hence, away, *a-ughon*, overhead, on high, *gensy*, therewithal, etc. *Dhe* has a special adverbial form *dhy*, *dy* (*dhe hy*), thither, to it, †*ughos*, †*ysos* (C. Voc. *uchot*, *isot*), old pronominal 2 sings. of *ugh*, *ys*, as adverbs meant "upwards," "downwards."

Prepositions that combine thus with prons., when used uncombined are never followed by *a* or *dhe* : e.g., *ryp an scovarn*, *a-rag arludhy*. In Late Cor. many preps. were re-shaped by cutting off the prons. from these combined forms, hence *gen*, *ort*, *durt*, *dreth*, *et*, for *gans*, *orth*, *dyworth*, *dre*, *yn*, such forms as *warnam* for *warnaf*, *ganjans* for *gansa* also replaced the older ones.

Appendix VI: Comparison of Adjectives

	POSITIVE	EQUATIVE	EXCLAMATIVE	COMPARATIVE	SUPERLATIVE
Regular	*glan*	*glanna*	*glanna*^{2}	*glanna*	*an glanna*
	hager	*haccra*	*haccra*^{2}	*haccra*	*an haccra*
Irregular	*brās, mür*	*brassa, myns (a-, del), kemmys (del, ha)*	*brassa*^{2}	*moy*	(*an*) *moyha, mogha, brassa*
	bȳghan, bȳan, münys	...	*byghanna*^{2}	*lē*	(*an*) *lȳha, byghanna*
	da, mās	*gwella*	...	*gwell*	(*an*) *gwella*
	drōk, tebel	*gwetha*	*drocca*^{2}	*gweth*	(*an*) *gwetha*
	ogas	...	...	*nēs*	(*an*) *nessa*
	...	...	...	*kens*	(*an*) *kensa*

N.B.: *moy, le, gwell, gweth, moyha, lyha, gwella, gwetha* can be used as comp. and superl. of a past participle, but not of an adjective or an adverb, e.g., *mur gerys, moy kerys, an moyha kerys*, but not *moy da*, etc. Note hardening and doubling of consonant as in *haccra*, originally caused by an *h* in equative and superlative ending as kept in *moyha, lyha*, which affected comparative also. Exclamative is often prefaced with *Dew!*

Appendix VII: Verbal Particles

Indefinite: *y*^{5}(*th*)-, used **(a)** when the subject of the vb. is not already expressed, as in the Personal Conjugation, e.g., *y-leverys*, he said; **(b)** instead of the relative particle *a*-^{2} after verbs of telling, seeing, believing, declaring, promising, swearing, thinking, seeming, knowing, hoping, fearing, doubting, e.g., *y-leverys y- to*, he said he was coming, and **(c)** sparingly, with parts of *bos* especially, to emphasize an already expressed subject noun, adj., or p. pt., e.g., *dasserghys yth yu*, he is *risen*; *dyragough noth y-fyen*, I should be *bare* before you; *a-ugh eglos... an esethva yth-esa*, the seat was *above a church*; *an keth gwasma yth-esa gans Jhesu*, this *very* fellow was with Jesus, *Meryasek yth-yu gylwys*, he is called *Meryasek*; *Seth ow map yth-yu hynwys*, my son is called *Seth* (In B.M., and still more in C.W., this use is often carried to excess, so spoiling the effect of emphasis). *Y(th)*- is usually omitted in rejoinders that repeat the vb. of a previous speech, e.g., *A wodhesta?* —*Gon*., Do you know?—Yes (I know), and is often left out elsewhere, especially before 1 s. pres. -fut of *mynnes, gothvos, leverel, gul, ry, pysy* and parts of *bos*, thus emphasizing the vb. It adds *th* before all vowels and silenced *h*: *kyn, may, ple, py* combine with it, adding its *th*.

Definite: *na(ns)*-, *na(nj)*-, *new(nj)*-, used to give precision to time of vb., e.g., *erbyn bones henna gwres nanj-o prys-gwesper y'n wlas*, by the time that was done it was (already, then, at that time) evensong-time in the land, M.C. 230; *nans-yu hy prys... a ry brus war*, it is (now) time to deliver an opinion upon..., P.C. 2471; *nans-yu seythen*, a week ago, lit. it is (now, at this time) a week; *pup deth nans-yu lyes mys*, every day for several months past, B.M. 682; *nans-us dhym whegh ugans flogh*, I have (now, at this time, already) 120 children, B.M. 1554; *nans-on lafuryes ganso*, we are (already, by this time) tired out by it, O.M. 2823; *nans-yu lemmyn tremenys nep deu cans a vledhynnow na-mbuf...*, (at this time) about 200 years are now past since I have..., O.M. 656. This is actually a particle *na-, naw-, new-* (as W. *neu*), which adds *ns* just as the neg. particle *ny*- does, but which happens to be used only before those parts of *bos* that begin with vowels, and never where it might be mistaken for the neg. particle *na*-.

Relative: *a*-^{2}, used **(a)** when the subject of the vb. is already expressed, as in the Impersonal Conjugation, e.g., *my a-vyn*, I will; **(b)** without expressed subject when the object precedes the vb., e.g., *ro a-rof*, I give a present; **(c)** as a relative, e.g., *an ro a-rof*, the present which I give, and **(d)** before an infixed pronoun followed by imperative vb., e.g., ***a-s-drens***, let him bring them. It is omitted before vowels in ***bos*** and ***mos***, and also when following immediately after adjs., p. pts., and sometimes after nouns or *pynag* (the vb., however preserving its mutation, e.g., *da vya*, it would be good) and remains without addition before all other vowels. It often translates relative prons., who, he who, one, that which, e.g., *a-n-jeffo pows*, he who has a coat ; *ny-glewys gans den genys a-wordhya Cryst bythqueth dhe fara yn-fas*, I have not heard from a born person that anyone who worshipped Christ got on well, B.M. 3972.

INTERROGATIVE ; *a-*[2], used in questions, being placed before the particle *ny-*[2] in negative questions, e.g., *a ny-wreta ?* dost thou not ? It is omitted after interjections, as *dar*, *pandra*, unless an inf. intervenes, e.g., *Pandra ! Wreugh... ? Dar ! Ny-wreta ?* but *Dar! Predery a-wreta...* ?, and also before vowels in *bos* and *mos*. It remains (without addition) before all other vowels. Its use is optional after *pur*[5], and it is occasionally omitted before *ny-*[2], especially in a sentence repeated as a query, as P.C. 2755, *Ny-dhe...,– Ny-dhe...?–Na-wra...*, It won't come,–Won't it come ?–No, it won't.

NEGATIVE : 1. *ny*[2]*(ns)-*, used as general negative particle, whether subject of vb. is expressed or not, e.g., *ny-vyn*, he will not, *my ny-vyn*, I will not, *my ny-vynnaf*, I won't, not I, and after vbs. of believing, seeing, etc., e.g., *y crysaf ny-vyn*, I believe he will not. It adds *ns* before vowels in *bos* and *mos*, and remains without addition before all other vowels.

2. *na*[2]*(g)–*, used **(a)** as negative relative particle, e.g., *nep na-vyn*, he who will not, after conjs. *aban*, *cam(men)*, *drefen*, *kyn*, *ma*, *pan*, *prag*, *rag* and in relative clauses introduced by vbs. of bidding, forbidding, promising, warning, being sure, praying, preaching, teaching, etc., e.g., *pregoth ef a-wra nag-us...*, he preaches that there is not..., or where special emphasis is required on "not," after vbs. of saying, etc., e.g., *A na-lavar na-yl !* O say not that he cannot ! ; **(b)** as negative imperative particle, e.g, *na-wra*, do not, and **(c)** in negative rejoinders that repeat the vb. of a previous speech, e.g., *A-vynnough ?–Na-vynnaf.* Will you ?–No (I will not). It adds *g* before vowels in *bos* and *mos* and remains without addition before all other vowels.

PERFECTIVE AND OPTATIVE : *re*[2]*(s)–*, *re*[2]*(j)-*, used **(a)** before preterite to enforce its perfect sense, e.g., *my re-welas*, I have seen, *splan re-welys*, I have clearly seen, and before pluperfect to enforce its indicative sense, e.g., *ef re-bya*, he had been (not "would be"), and **(b)** before pres.-fut. subj. to make an optative, e.g., *re-wrello*, may he (do), *lowena re-gas-bo*, may you have joy ; more doubtfully **(c)** a further use with pres.-fut. indic. to imply probability is suggested by *re-m-kemer*, ? will be likely to seize me, O.M. 366, possibly due to a scribal error. *Bos* is exempt from mutation after *re-*, e.g., *re-bya*, *re-bo* (in MSS. this seems frequently, though less correctly, extended to *dos* also). *Re-* is absorbed into *roy*, which alone means "may he give," *re-roy* not being used. When perfective, it adds an *s*, also softened to *j*, before vowels in *mos* ; when optative (if *rej-ymmy*, R.D. 2355, is correct) it adds this *s*, *j* before all vowels, but this is less certain. As perfective, *re-* may replace either the indefinite or the relative particle ; no other particle can be used before it, neither can *kyn*, *mar*, *a*, *may*, *pan*, though *del* is so used M.C. 86 (as meaning "how" probably, *omdennas* being written for another word). The negative optative is made by putting *byner* before *re-*, e.g., *byner re-bo*, may it never be. As perfective, *re-* is used as a relative, e.g., *an ro re-ressys*, the gift that thou hast given. Exclamative forms of optative are made with *dhe* and inf., e.g., *Dew dhe'm sylwel !* God save me ! *Dhe 'th cregy !* Hang thee ! *An jawl dh' 'agas lesky !* The Devil burn you ! etc., or else with 2 s. imp., e.g., *Dew dyfen!* God forbid !

PRESENT-PARTICIPLE PARTICLE : *ow*[4]*(th)-*, used before infinitive, adding *th* before vowels or silenced *h*, e.g., *ow-tos*, coming, *owth-henwel*, naming. With a pronoun as object this particle returns to its original prepositional form *(w)orth*, the pron. being made possessive and put between particle and inf., e.g., *orth-ow-dysky*, teaching me. After a phrase of acknowledgement, etc., no prep. like Eng. "for," "in," is required before *ow-*, e.g., *benygys re by ow-try dhyn dowr*, blessed be thou (for) bringing us water, neither is a prep. like Eng. "to," "in" required before *ow-* following *gweres*, e.g., *gweres orth-y-dhon*, help to carry him, lit. (in) carrying him, *gweres ow-cul tan*, assist (in) making a fire.

ADVERBIAL PRESENT-PARTICIPLE PARTICLES : 1. *yn-un*[2], used before an infinitive that describes more fully the action named in a previous verb, e.g., *y-teth dhym yn-an-ola*, he came weeping to me.

2. *yn-dan*[2], used of simultaneously continuous action, *scolkyeugh dhy yn-dan-dava*, slink up to the place keeping all the while just in touch, P.C. 1002.

ADVERBIAL PAST-PARTICIPLE PARTICLE: *yn-*[5], used before p. pt. to denote state or condition, e.g., *dha weles yn-tasserghys*, to see thee risen again, *yn-assentys*, assentingly. This is the same particle as that used before an adj. to make it into an adv.

IMPERATIVE: no particle is required in imperative except before an infixed pron., see RELATIVE, use **(d)**, and in negative imperative, see NEGATIVE 2, use **(b)**.

EXCLAMATIVE OR ADMIRATIVE: *assa-*[2], *yssa-*[2] (*ass-*, *yss-* before vowels in *bos* and before *w* as result of mutation in *gul*) is used especially with *bos*, *gul*, *gallos*, e.g., *A Dhew assa-fuf lowen!* O God, how happy I was! *ass-os goky*! how foolish thou art! *ass-vya tek*! how lovely it would be! *ass-wrussough camdremena*! how you did transgress! *assa-yllyn-ny bos lowen*! How happy we can be! *ass-yu hemma trueth bras*! What a calamity this is!

N.B.: certain conjunctions, *may*[5]*(th)*, *kyn*[5]*(th)*, *mar*[4]*(s)*, *mara*[4]*(s)*, *a*[1], *aban*[2], *hedra*[2], *erna*[2]*(g)*, and certain adverbs, *pan*[2], *del*[2], *fatel*[2], *kettel*[2], *py*[5]*(th)*, *ple*[5]*(th)*, *a-ble*[5]*(th)*, *pur*[5], go immediately before the verb, particles intervening only in the negative, or with an infixed pronoun as object, e.g., *pan wra*, but *pan na-wra*, *pan y-n-gwra*.

The *th* of *mayth*, *kynth*, *pyth*, *pleth* shows that these have absorbed *yth-*; *may* becomes *ma* (without the *y* of the particle) before *na-* or *-n-*, and *pleth*, *pur* can alternatively be written *py le yth-*, *py ur*; *re-* can be used after *py le*, *py ur*.

The INFINITIVE, being a verb-noun, has no negative form, and Eng. "not to" has to be otherwise expressed, e.g., "not to sleep is bad" is *drok yu bos hep cusca*, lit. it is bad to be without sleeping; "he told us not to stop long" is *ef a-wruk agan dyfen pell na-wrellen gortos*, lit. he forbade us that we should not stop long, etc.

Appendix VIII.: Verbs

MOODS. Although as a general rule Indicative Mood is used in principal sentences and Subjunctive Mood in dependent clauses, there are exceptions to this. Note especially the use of imperf. indic. as "would," "was going to," after vbs. of telling, etc., in past, and that of impf. subj. to replace impf. indic. Pluperf. subj. in sense of "would" or "should" is used in principal sentences, but pres.-fut. subj., "I may," etc., is not; "may" in indicative being expressed by pres.-fut. of *gallos* with inf.:– *my a-yl cara*, *y-hallaf cara*, *cara a-allaf*, etc. Subjunctive on the other hand is required in a dependent clause where English needs no "may," as "I shall not be happy until I go again," *Ny-vydhaf lowen ernag yllyf* (1 s. pres. fut. subj. of *mos*) *arta*.

REGULAR VERB. The following verb shows the regular endings in each Mood, Tense and Person, and also illustrates vowel-changes such as are frequently made. With *-y* as inf. ending, vowel-change may extend to inf. also, as in *tylly*, etc.; other stems may remain without vowel-change throughout, as in *gorra*, etc. There are several different inf. endings, *-a*, *-y*, *-ya*, *-es*, *-as*, *-el*, *-wel* being the commonest (see APPENDIX III.), while some infs. are without any added ending. In Late Cor. there was a tendency to use *-as* as a general inf. ending.

Inf. and Verb-Noun CARA, to love, like, care to; as vb.-noun, loving: Present Participle *ow-cara*, loving (with pron., *orth-y-gara*, loving him, etc.), Adverbial Present Participle *yn-un-gara*, loving, lovingly; Past Participle *kerys*, loved, Adverbial Past Participle *yn-kerys*, in a beloved state; Verbal Adjective (in *cara* and *casa* only) *caradow*, beloved, loving, lovable. Nouns of agency are also freely formed from vbs. by the addition of the suffixes *-er* or *-yas* to the stem, and abstract nouns by the addition of *-ans*, *-yans* (see APPENDIX III.).

Mood / Tense	Indicative			Ind. & Subj.
	Present-Future: I love, I shall or will love, etc.	Imperfect: I was loving, I always (neg. never) loved, etc.; after vbs. of telling etc., in past, I was going to love, I would love in future, etc.	Preterite, Past & Perfect: I loved, I did love, I have loved, etc.; with *re-*, I have loved, etc.	Pluperfect: I had loved (ind.) I would or should love (subj.), etc.
Singular 1	*caraf, cara'*	*caren*	*kerys*	*carsen*
Singular 2	*keryth*	*cares*	*kersys*	*carses*
Singular 3	*car*	*cara*	*caras*	*carsa*
Plural 1	*keryn*	*caren*	*kersyn*	*carsen*
Plural 2	*kerough*	*careugh*	*carsough*	*carseugh*
Plural 3	*carons*	*carens*	*carsons*	*carsens*
Impersonal Passive: one loves, etc.	*keryr*	*kerys*	*caras*	*carsys*

Mood / Tense	Subjunctive		Imperative
	Present-Future: I may love, etc.; with *re-*, may I love, etc.	Imperfect: I might, could or should love, etc.	Present-Future: love thou, let him love, etc.
Singular 1	*kyr(r)yf*	*car(r)en*	...
Singular 2	*kyrry*	*car(r)es*	*car*
Singular 3	*carro*	*car(r)a*	*cares, carens*
Plural 1	*kyr(r)yn*	*car(r)en*	*keryn*
Plural 2	*kyr(r)eugh*	*car(r)eugh*	*kereugh*
Plural 3	*car(r)ons*	*car(r)ens*	*carens*
Impersonal Passive	*ker(r)er*	*car(r)es*	...

No rule is kept in M. Cor. for the spelling of the ending in 2 pl. pres.-fut. indic. or subj., *-eugh, -ough* being used indifferently. In regular vbs. preference is here given to *o* in indic., *e* in subj.

Imperf. subj. of vbs. with inf. *-a* is usually undistinguished in M. Cor. from imperf. indic., the doubling of its stem-consonant not being strictly observed and its sharpening still less so.

With suffixed pron., 2 s. pres.-fut. contracts to *kerta*.

To *cara* and a few other vbs. a special future, distinct from present, and made by adding the *byth* of *bos* to its stem, is used in impersonal conjugation: *ty a-m-carvyth*, thou wilt love me, etc. See *Bos* Compounds (e).

Verbs with *-ya* inf. drop the *y* in 2 s. imp. and 3 s. pres.-fut., and also before *s* or *y*: *Y* is kept before *a, e, o*, and p. pt. is made indifferently *-ys* or *-yes*. A few vbs. have alternative inf. endings *-a* or *-ya*, e.g., *sew(y)a, nyj(y)a, trel(y)a*; *gordhya* is occasionally *gordhy* also, but in these *y* is usually kept as above [exception *sewes* 3 s. imp.]. When a *y* is part of the stem, to which *-a* is added as the actual inf. ending, this *y* remains throughout, e.g., *golysa, annyy*, etc.

An unusual 2 s. imp. ending is the *y* of *galwy* in *gelwel*: possibly, since no other example of one occurs, this is the regular ending in all vbs. with inf. ending *-wel*. A similar *y* ending is found, before vowels only, in *ry, dry*, which then have *roy, doroy*. The older 3 s. imp. ending *-es (-ys)* is not found in auxiliary or irregular vbs., being replaced in these, and often in other vbs. also, by the 3 pl. form *-ens*.

The verb CARA has illustrated the usual vowel-changes of *a* in the stem in sympathy with inflexional endings, but 3 s. pres. -fut is often unlike 2 s. imp., having *e* instead of *a*, e.g., *sevel* has 2 s. imp. *saf*, 3 s. pres. -fut. *sef*. An *o* in the stem has similar changes to *e*, and *e* to *y*, e.g., *serry, sor, ser*; *dybry, deppro, depsa, deber*. In such vbs. 3 pl. pres. -fut. follows the sing. Such regular vowel-change must not be confused with the arbitrary use in MSS. of *e* or *y* in any part of the vb., as, e.g., *pesy* for *pysy*.

Consonant-changes are caused :–

(a) by the *s* of pret. and pluperf., which hardens a final *b, d, g, v, dh* of the stem to *p, c or k, f, th*,

(b) by a former *h* in subj., now generally lost, which caused these to double as well as to harden, and doubles other simple consonants except *w, y*; not, however, affecting compound ones like *gh, sk*, etc., or those already double.

In vbs. with inf. *-hē* a syllable *-ha-* is similarly added to the stem before a non-final *s* and also in subj., where the old *h* of subj. endings is kept after it, as in 3 s. subj. *moghha·ho, huthha·ho*, the only person actually illustrating this *-ha-* in the texts. Verbs of this class are stressed on the last syllable except when the stressed *-ha·-* is added.

Verb made by adding *-hē* to adj. Inf. BERHĒ·, to shorten : Pres. Part. *ow-perhē·* ; Past Part. *berhē·s, -hȳ·s*.

Mood		Indicative			Ind. & Subj.
Tense		Pres.-Fut.	Impf.	Pret.	Pluperf.
S.	1	*berhaf*	*berhyn*	*berhys*	*berhasen*
	2	*berhyth*	*berhys*	*berhasys*	*berhases*
	3	*berha*	*berhy*	*berhas*	*berhasa*
Pl.	1	*berhyn*	*berhyn*	*berhasyn*	*berhasen*
	2	*berhough*	*berheugh*	*berhasough*	*berhaseugh*
	3	*berhons*	*berhens*	*berhasons*	*berhasens*
Impers. Pass.		*berhyr*	*berhys*	*berhas*	*berhasys*

Mood		Subjunctive		Imperative
Tense		Pres.-Fut.	Impf.	Pres. -Fut.
S.	1	*berhahyf*	*berhahen*	...
	2	*berhahy*	*berhahes*	*berha*
	3	*berhaho*	*berhaha*	*berhes, berhens*
Pl.	1	*berhahyn*	*berhahen*	*berhen*
	2	*berhahough*	*berhaheugh*	*berheugh*
	3	*berhahons*	*berhahens*	*berhens*
Impers. Pass.		*berhaher*	*berhahes*	...

Certain verbs other than those formed like BERHE have *-a* as their 2 s. imp. and 3 s. pres.-fut. ending: of these *-a* endings *dysqua* is for *dysque(th)*, and *fasta* is probably for *fastha*, but others are found in *denewy, gortos, grassa, halya, tava, whylas*.

Regular Verb without vowel-change as in CARA, but with *y* in Imperf. Indic. and 3 s. pret.—Inf. SYNSY, -JY, to hold : Pres. Part. *ow-synsy* ; Past Part. *synsys*.

Mood		Indicative			Ind. & Subj.
Tense		Pres.-Fut.	Imperf.	Pret.	Pluperf.
S.	1	*synsaf*	*synsyn*	*synsys*	*synssen*
	2	*synsyth*	*synsys*	*synssys*	*synsses*
	3	*syns*	*synsy*	*synsys*	*synssa*
Pl.	1	*synsyn*	*synsyn*	*synssyn*	*synssen*
	2	*synsough*	*synseugh*	*synssough*	*synsseugh*
	3	*synsons*	*synsens*	*synssons*	*synssens*
Impers. Pass.		*synsyr*	*synsys*	*synsys*	*synssys*

Mood		Subjunctive		Imperative
Tense		Pres.-Fut.	Imperf.	Pres.-Fut.
S.	1	*synsyf*	*synsen*	...
	2	*synsy*	*synses*	*syns*
	3	*synso*	*synsa*	*synses*, *synsens*
Pl.	1	*synsyn*	*synsen*	*synsyn*
	2	*synseugh*	*synseugh*	*synseugh*
	3	*synsons*	*synsens*	*synsens*
Impers. Pass.		*synser*	*synses*	...

Doubling of *s* in subj. is not usually observed, but the sound would there presumably be *s*, not *z*; where not doubled, *s* may be made *j* between vowels.

Verbs with imperf. indic. as in *synsy* include :–

(a) those which add to the stem the inf. endings *-el*, *-wel*, *-y*, *-os* [except *dos*, *mos*, *bos* and classes a, b and c of *bos* compounds],

(b) most of those with inf. endings *-es*, *-as* [not *dewheles*, *omwheles*, *mynnes*, *golyas*, *myras*],

(c) *ry*, *ty*, *dry*, *dyllo*, *don*, *govyn*, *dervyn*, *hembronk*, *godhaf*.

No M. Cor. vbs. with inf. endings *-a*, *-ya*, *-he* seem actually to have this form of imperf. indic., though the spelling *keryn*, C.W. 1231, would suggest it for *cara*. In B.M. and C.W. *hevely*, 3 s., is the only apparent survival of it. Occasionally the above rules are broken, the subj. form being used even in Ord. instead of the indic. In Late Cor. this became the rule.

Verbs with 3 s. and impers. pass. ending *-ys* as in *synsy* include :–

(a) all vbs. with inf. endings *-el*, *-wel* [not as part of the stem as in *gormel*],

(b) *aswon*, *attylly*, *cruny*, *crysy*, *dedhewy*, *denythy*, *deryvas*, *dewheles*, *domhel*, *dyank*, *dybry*, *dynerghy*, *dyscrysy*, *erghy*, *godhaf*, *gorhemmyn*, *gortheby*, *kemmynna*, *mollethy*, *omwheles*, *pysy*, *predery*, *tevy*, *trewa*, *tylly*, *yeuny*,

(c) *clamdera*, *dervyn*, *gorra*, *govyn*, in which *-as* is a variant ending. The 3 s. pret. ending *-ys* is rarely found with inf. ending *-a* and never with inf. ending *-ya*. In two vbs. with variant infs. both forms are used, e.g., *kewsel*, *cows* have *kewsys*, *cowsas*; *lemmel*, *lamma* have *lemmys*, *lammas*.

Inf. and verbal noun BŌS, BONES, to be: Pres. Part. *ow-pōs,-s*, *ow-pones*; Past Part. (used only in compounds) *bedhys*.

Mood		Indicative			
Tense		Present			Future and Habitual Present
		I. Simple	II. Habitual	III. Time & Place	
S.	1	*ōf*	*esof*	...	*bydhaf*
	2	*ōs*	*esos*	...	*bydhyth*
	3	*yū (yw)*	*es, üs, üsy, üjy*	*yma, 'ma*	*bȳth*
Pl.	1	*ōn*	*eson*	...	*bydhyn*
	2	*ough*	*esough*	...	*bydheugh*
	3	*yns*	*esons*	*ymons, 'mons*	*bydhons*
Impers. Pass.		*ōr*	*eder*	...	*bydher*

Mood		Indicative			
Tense		Imperfect			Preterite
		I. Simple	II. Habitual	III. Time & Place	
S.	1	*ēn*	*bedhen*	*esen, ejen*	*büf, bēf*
	2	*ēs*	*bedhes*	*eses, ejes*	*büs, bēs*
	3	*ō*	*bedha*	*esa, eja*	*bü, bē*
Pl.	1	*ēn*	*bedhen*	*esen, ejen*	*bün, bēn*
	2	*eugh*	*bedheugh*	*eseugh, ejeugh*	*beugh*
	3	*ens*	*bedhens*	*esens, ejens*	*bons*
Impers. Pass.		*ōs*	*bedhes*	*edes*	*büs, bēs*

Mood		Ind. & Subj.	Subjunctive		Imperative
Tense		Pluperf	Pres.-Fut.	Imperf.	Pres.-Fut.
S.	1	*bȳen*	*byf*	*bēn*	...
	2	*bȳes*	*bȳ*	*bēs*	*byth*
	3	*bȳa*	*bō*	*bē*	*bedhens*, (*bedhes*, lost)
Pl.	1	*bȳen*	*ben*	*bēn*	*bedhen*
	2	*bȳeugh*	*beugh*	*beugh*	*bedheugh*
	3	*bȳens*	*bons*	*bens*	*bedhens*
Impers. Pass.		*bȳes*	*bōer*	*bēs*	...

Present II. and imperf. III. are used with present participles and of time or place with prepositions: the vowel of *ēs*, *üs* becomes obscure with loss of stress. Pres. II. is used in 3rd. person in relative, negative and interrogative, or when the subject is named, elsewhere pres. III. is preferred. Pres. III. and impf. III. are never used in impersonal conjugation: in pres. III. *y* is the indefinite particle, but here compounded with the vb. The habitual-present sense of future is not very common unless with *gelwel, henwel*. Imperf. indic. II., "I used to be," is used especially after vbs. of telling, etc., as meaning "I was going to be": as an extension from this it is also used as an imperf. subj. "I were," "I should, or would, be."

Combined with prons. the final *f* is lost in 1 sing. *oma*, *buma*, *byma*, the *n* being kept in *ena*, *bena*; *osa*, *oja* (direct statement or after *del*, *aban*, *pan*, etc.), and *osta* (C.W.); *esos*, *eses* both become *esta*, and *bes* becomes *besta*. In 3 s. pres. I. the *u* is treated, and often in MSS. spelt, as consonant *w*, and not as a vowel, hence *yua (ywa)* as compounded with pron. *-a*, and never with *-va* which follows the vowels in *ymava*, *may fova*, *del vuva*, etc.

In Late Cornish the *s* between vowels of *esof*, *esa*, etc., (but not of *usy*) often became *r*: e.g., "thera vee lawl" was the colloquial pronunciation of *yth-esof-vy ow-leverel*, I say. In Mid. Cor. such an *s* before *e* or *y* (but not before *o*) is frequently made *j* (spelt *g*), as *eja (ege)*: in Late Cor. this *j* was kept in *ujy*, *uj an (igge, ilzh an)*.

The impersonal passive of Pres. II. is found only in *ow-kewsel yth-eder*, it is being said, they are saying, O.M. 2794, and *mayth eder worth-dha-vlamya*, so that thou art being blamed, so that they are blaming thee, O.M. 2797. Impersonal passive of future is found in ***dredha may fydher (fether) dhe well***, in which one will be the better through their means, O.M. 46. The archaic *d* for *s* of *eder* itself suggests that these forms were rarely used. The others are conjectural, being based on Welsh and Breton.

Bos with infixed pronouns, to have: *cafos* is used instead of *bos* as inf.; no participles; no imperative. After *-m-*, *-gan-(-n-)*, *-gas-(-s-)* in 1 s. and 2 pl., a *b* is inserted before vowels. In 3 s. and pl. *je-*, *te-* (*jev-*, *tev-* before vowels) is prefixed to the vb., which then loses the accent. This is a syllable *de-*, the *d* of which is affected in different ways by *-n-* and *-s-* (it seems likely that originally a *b* developed between infixed *-m-* and the vowels of *us, o*, and that a *d* developed similarly between infixed *-n-* and the same vowels, as in B. *am beus*, and *en deus*, and that from these the other tenses became infected until they finally reacted on the whole pres. and imperf. indic. also). Before *f*, the *-th-* which caused this mutation of *b* is usually elided, as *y'fyth*, etc.

Mood		Indicative				
Tense		Present	Future	Imperf. I.	Imperf. II.	Preterite
S.	1	*y-m-büs*	*y-m-bӯth*	*y-m-bō*	*y-m-bedha*	*y-m-bü, bē*
	2	*y-th-üs*	*y(-th-)fӯth*	*y-th-ō*	*y(-th-)fedha*	*y(-th-)fü, fē*
	3 m.	*y-n-jeves*	*y-n-jevyth*	*y-n-jevo*	*y-n-jevedha*	*y-n-jeva*
	f.	*y-s-teves*	*y-s-tevyth*	*y-s-tevo*	*y-s-tevedha*	*y-s-teva*
Pl.	1	*y-gan-(-n-)büs*	*y-gan-(-n-)bӯth*	*y-gan-(-n-)bō*	*y-gan-(-n-)bedha*	*y-gan-(-n-)bü, bē*
	2	*y-gas-(-s-)büs*	*y-gas-(-s-)bӯth*	*y-gas-(-s-)bō*	*y-gas-(-s-)bedha*	*g-gas-(-s-)bü, bē*
	3	*y-s-teves*	*y-s-tevyth*	*y-s-tevo*	*y-s-tevedha*	*y-s-teva*

Mood		Ind. & Subj.	Subjunctive	
Tense		Pluperfect	Pres.-Fut.	Imperf.
S.	1	*y-m-bӯa*	*y-m-bō*	*y-m-bē*
	2	*y(-th-)fӯa*	*y(-th-)fō*	*y(-th-)fē*
	3 m.	*y-n-jevӯa*	*y-n-jeffo*	*y-n-jeffa*
	f.	*y-s-tevӯa*	*y-s-teffo*	*y-s-teffa*
Pl.	1	*y-gan-(-n-)bӯa*	*y-gan-(-n-)bō*	*y-gan-(-n-)bē*
	2	*y-gas-(-s-)bӯa*	*y-gas-(-s-)bō*	*y-gas-(-s-)bē*
	3	*y-s-tevӯa*	*y-s-teffo*	*y-s-teffa*

Imperf. Indic. I. is simple, II. is habitual and conditional.

This verb is used with particles *a-*, *re-*, *ny-*, *na-* also, and most usually with a simple pronoun followed by *a-* or *re-*, *my a-m-bus*, I have, *hy re-s-teva*, she has had, etc. It is never used as an auxiliary vb. *May* (*ma* before *-n-*, *-gan-*, *-gas-*) or *mara*, *a*, are used directly before it, and *kyn y-n-* becomes *kyn'*. Anomalous forms of this vb., given suffixed prons., as *a-m-boma*, or even personal endings, as *a-m-ben*, *may ben-vy*, *a-s-bedheugh*, *ny-s-tufons*, etc., are common in M. Cor. texts, but had not replaced the more correct forms as given above. It will be noticed that the prefixed *je-*, *te-*, while it does not affect the accent of *bya*, causes vowel-shortening of *üs*, *ēs* to *es*, *ō* to *o*, and of *bü*, *bē* to *va*: similar changes occur in *bos* compounds, see below.

Bos without infixed prons. is used with the preps. *gans*, *dhe* in the same sense of "to have," as *yma genef*, *yma dhymmo*, I have, *an pyth es genes*, what thou hast, *us cumyas dyso?* hast thou permission? etc.

Bos Compounds: these may be classified as:–

(a) Regular, or nearly regular, compounds adding parts of *bos* to their roots with slight modification: *gothvos*, *talvos*, *pew* (without *bos* inf.).

(b) Defective compounds used in 3 sing. only: *coth*, *degoth*, *wharfos*, *darfos*; some forms in *coth*, *degoth*, *wharfos* imitate regular vbs., *darfa* is the only inflected part of *darfos* found, but like *wharfos* it would probably reject those parts of *bos* which begin with a vowel; imperf. indic. impersonal passive of *wharfos* is *whyrys* R.D. 1190.

(c) Irregular compounds with *bos* in certain tenses only: *doṣ* or *devos* (*de-*, *bos*), *clewes* (*clew*, *bos*), *mos*, with *galsof*, etc. *Dos* has pret. *düth*, but 3 s. perfect *düfa*, *dēva* is formed with preterite of *bos*, and *bos* appears in most other tenses; *clewes* has present and preterite of regular vbs., but fut., imperf. indic. and pres.-fut. subj. from *bos*.

(d) Regular verbs retaining *bos* in inf. only: *cafos*, *desevos*, *aswonvos* (alternatively *aswon*, 1 s. pret. is anomalously written *aswonfys*, P.C. 1412, but is usually *aswonys*).

(e) Regular verbs which in impersonal conjugation add 3 s. fut. of *bos* to the stem in order to make a clear distinction of fut. from pres.: *cara*, *gweles*, *prena*, *tulla*, and no doubt several others, though inf. with pres.-fut. of *gul* serves as the more general means of forming a distinct future.

Inf. PEW(Y), to own, possess: Pres. Part. *ow-pew* (Late "me a pewi," for *my yu ow-pewy*, Borlase); Past Part. (if used) *pewvedhys*. Parts actually found are 3 s. pres.-fut. and impf. indic., 2 s. pres.-fut. subj.

MOOD		INDICATIVE				
TENSE		PRESENT	FUTURE	IMPERF.	PRET.	PLUPF.
S.	1	*pewof*	*pewvydhaf*	*pewen*	*pewvef*	*pewvȳen*
	2	*pewos*	*pewvydhyth*	*pewes*	*pewves*	*pewvȳes*
	3	*pew*	*pewvyth*	*pewo*	*pewva*	*pewvȳa*
PL.	1	*pewon*	*pewvydhyn*	*pewen*	*pewven*	*pewvȳen*
	2	*pewough*	*pewvydheugh*	*peweugh*	*pewveugh*	*pewvȳeugh*
	3	*pewyns*	*pewvydhons*	*pewens*	*pewvons*	*pewvȳens*

MOOD		SUBJUNCTIVE			IMPERATIVE
TENSE		PRES.-FUT.	IMPERF.	PLUPF.	PRES.-FUT.
S.	1	*pewfyf*	*pewfen*	*pewfȳen*	...
	2	*pewfy*	*pewfes*	*pewfȳes*	*pewvyth*
	3	*pewfo*	*pewfa*	*pewfȳa*	*pewvedhens* (for -*es*)
PL.	1	*pewfen*	*pewfen*	*pewfȳen*	*pewvedhen*
	2	*pewfeugh*	*pewfeugh*	*pewfȳeugh*	*pewvedheugh*
	3	*pewfons*	*pewfens*	*pewfȳens*	*pewvedhens*

The AUXILIARY VERBS, beside *cara* and *bos*, consist of the following four:—

1. Inf. GOTHVOS, GOTHFOS, GOVOS, to know, know how to, be able: Pres. Part. *ow-cothvos*; Past Part. *gothvedhys*. *Ordinalia* MS. lacks distinction between *dh* and *th* or *f* and *v*, M.C. MS., however, usually has *z* for *dh*. In this vb. *z* is there invariably used before vowels and *y* consonant, *th* being used before *f* and *v*, and *thf* in subjunctive mood alone, as here. This *thf* may be pronounced and written as *ff*, especially in late Cor.

MOOD		INDICATIVE				
TENSE		PRESENT	FUTURE	IMPERF.	PRET.	PLUPF.
S.	1	*gōn*	*gothvydhaf*	*godhyen*	*gothvef*	*gothvȳen*
	2	*godhes*	*gothvydhyth*	*godhyes*	*gothves*	*gothvȳes*
	3	*gōr*	*gothvyth, govyth*	*godhya*	*gothva*	*gothvȳa*
PL.	1	*godhon*	*gothvydhyn*	*godhyen*	*gothven*	*gothvȳen*
	2	*godhough*	*gothvydheugh*	*godhyeugh*	*gothveugh*	*gothvȳeugh*
	3	*godhons*	*gothvydhons*	*godhyens*	*gothvons*	*gothvȳens*
IMPERS. PASS.		*godhyr*	...	...	...	...

Mood		Subjunctive			Imperative
Tense		Pres.-Fut.	Imperf.	Plupf.	Pres.-Fut.
S.	1	*gothfyf*	*gothfen*	*gothfȳen*	...
	2	*gothfy*	*gothfes*	*gothfȳes*	*gothvyth*
	3	*gothfo*	*gothfa*	*gothfȳa*	*gothvedhens* (for-*es*)
Pl.	1	*gothfen*	*gothfen*	*gothfȳen*	*gothvedhen*
	2	*gothfeugh*	*gothfeugh*	*gothfȳeugh*	*gothvedheugh*
	3	*gothfons*	*gothfens*	*gothfȳens*	*gothvedhens*
Impers. Pass.		*godher*	...	...	...

With suffixed pron., 2 s. pres. may be *gosta*; *th* is occasionally elided also. Anomalous contractions with *th* for *f* are *ny-wothefaf* for *go'vydhaf*, R.D. 719, *ny-wythen*,? for *wo'fen*, P.C. 1914. In Late Cor. *(a-) wya* represents *godhya* and *wythen* may be for *wodhyen*.

2. Inf. Gül, güthyl, gwethyl, gwrüthyl, to do, make, cause: Pres. Part. *ow-cül*; Past. Part. *gwrēs, gwrȳs (gwreys)*.

Mood		Indicative			Ind. & Subj.
Tense		Pres.-Fut.	Imperf.	Pret.	Pluperf.
S.	1	*gwraf*	*gwren*	*gwrük*	*gwrüssen*
	2	*gwrēth*	*gwrēs*	*gwrüssys*	*gwrüsses*
	3	*gwra*	*gwrē*	*gwrük*	*gwrüssa*
Pl.	1	*gwren*	*gwren*	*gwrüssyn*	*gwrüssen*
	2	*gwreugh*	*gwreugh*	*gwrüssough*	*gwrüsseugh*
	3	*gwrons*	*gwrens*	*gwrüssons*	*gwrüssens*
Impers. Pass.		*gwrēr*	...	...	...

Mood		Subjunctive		Imperative
Tense		Pres.-Fut.	Imperf.	Pres.-Fut.
S.	1	*gwryllyf*	*gwrellen*	...
	2	*gwrylly*	*gwrelles*	*gwra*
	3	*gwrello*	*gwrella*	*gwrens* (for-*es*).
Pl.	1	*gwryllyn*	*gwrellen*	*gwren*
	2	*gwrellough*	*gwrelleugh*	*gwreugh*
	3	*gwrellons*	*gwrellens*	*gwrens*
Impers. Pass.		...	...	...

With suffixed prons., 1 and 2 pres. -fut. become *gwrama, gwrēta,* 1 s. pret. *gwrüga,* and 2 s. pret. and plupf. *gwrüsta*. In Late Cor. 1 s. pret. *gwrüga* is made *gwrügaf*, 3 pl. *gwrügons*, etc., an anomalous *gwreffo* is used for *gwrello*, and *gwrēs*, like B. *greas*, is used for *gwrük* 3 s. pret., 2 s. impf. *gwrēs* is used for 2 s. pres. -fut. *gwreth* in "po rez" for *pan wreth*, P., "chee na raze" for *ty ny-wreth*, Kerew, "na wres" for *na-wreth*, C.W. 218.

3. Inf. Gallos (*galles*, P.C. 3893), to be able, have power to, "can": no Participles, no Imperative.

Mood	Indicative		
Tense	Pres Fut.	Imperf.	Pret.
S. 1	*gallaf*	*gyllyn*	*gyllys*
S. 2	*gyllyth*	*gyllys*	*gylsys*
S. 3	*gȳl*	*gylly*	*gallas*
Pl. 1	*gyllyn*	*gyllyn*	*gylsyn*
Pl. 2	*gyllough*	*gylleugh*	*gylsough*
Pl. 3	*gyllons*	*gyllens*	*galsons*
Impers. Pass.	*gyllyr*	*gyllys*	*gallas*

Mood	Ind. & Subj.	Subjunctive	
Tense	Pluperf.	Pres.-fut.	Imperf.
S. 1	*galsen*	*gyllyf*	*gallen*
S. 2	*galses*	*gylly*	*galles*
S. 3	*galsa*	*gallo*	*galla*
Pl. 1	*galsen*	*gellen*	*gallen*
Pl. 2	*galseugh*	*gallough*	*galleugh*
Pl. 3	*galsens*	*gallons*	*gallens*
Impers. Pass.	ind. *galsys*, subj. *galser*.	*galler*	*galles*

With suffixed pron., 2 s. pres.-fut. *gylta*, plupf. *galsta* (Late). The stem-vowel is often made *e* for *y*, and var. imperf. subj. endings have *-an*, etc.

4. Inf. mynnes, to wish, be willing: Pres. Part. *ow-mynnes*; Past Part. *mynnys* (if used); no imperative. The stem-vowel is often made *e* in all parts.

Mood	Indicative			Ind. & Subj.
Tense	Pres.-Fut.	Imperf.	Pret.	Pluperf.
S. 1	*mynnaf*	*mynnen*	*mynnys*	*mynsen*
S. 2	*mynnyth*	*mynnes*	*mynsys*	*mynses*
S. 3	*myn*	*mynna*	*mynnas*	*mynsa*
Pl. 1	*mynnyn*	*mynnen*	*mynsen*	*mynsyn*
Pl. 2	*mynnough*	*mynneugh*	*mynsough*	*mynseugh*
Pl. 3	*mynnons*	*mynnens*	*mynsons*	*mynsens*
Impers. Pass.	*mynnyr*	*mynnes*	*mynnas*	*mynsys*

Mood	Subjunctive	
Tense	Pres.-Fut.	Imperf.
S. 1	*mynnyf*	*mynnen*
S. 2	*mynny*	*mynnes*
S. 3	*mynno*	*mynna*
Pl. 1	*mynnen*	*mynnen*
Pl. 2	*mynnough*	*mynneugh*
Pl. 3	*mynnons*	*mynnens*
Impers. Pass.	*mynner*	*mynnes*

With suffixed pron., 2 s. pres.-fut. *mynta*, pret. and plupf. *mynsta*. Later form of 1 s. pres.-fut. is *mannaf* (B.M., C.W.) eventually becoming *madnaf*, *maddama* with inserted *d*.

The following are the remaining IRREGULAR VERBS :—

Inf MOS, MONES, to go : Pres. Part. *ow-mo(nes)* ; Past Part. *ēs* (*eys*, P.C. 2137), but commonly *gyllys* ; this and Perfect and Pluperfect (used without particles) are supplied by a defective vb., *galsof*, I have (am) become or gone, *gylsen*, I had (was) become or gone, etc. Imperative has another defective vb. *ke* : *a (ha)*, 2 pl., is borrowed from 2 sing. (M.C. 99, R.D. 2464, B.M. 2022) ; 3 s. imp. is, as in all irreg. vbs. and many others, replaced by 3 pl. ; 1 pl. imp. " let us go " is expressed by *dun* (see *dos*), C.W. 1333 has *gas ny dhe vos*, but *en* seems lost ; similar exchanges of "come" for " go " in Imp. occur in Welsh (2 s.) and in Breton (1 pl.).

MOOD		INDICATIVE				IND. & SUBJ.
TENSE		PRES.-FUT.	IMPERF.	PRET.	PERFECT	PLUPERF.
S.	1	*āf*	*ēn*	*ȳth*	*galsof*	*gylsen*
	2	*ēth*	*ēs*	*ȳthys*	*galsos*	*gylses*
	3	*ā*	*ē*	*ēth*	*gallas, -es*	*galsa*
PL.	1	*ēn*	*ēn*	*ēthen*	*galson*	*gylsen*
	2	*eugh*	*eugh*	*ētheugh*	*galsough*	*gylseugh*
	3	*ans*	*ens*	*ēthons*	*galsons*	*gylsens*

MOOD		SUBJUNCTIVE		IMPERATIVE
TENSE		PRES.-FUT.	IMPERF.	PRES.-FUT.
S.	1	*yllyf*	*ellen*	...
	2	*ylly*	*elles*	*kē, ā*
	3	*ello*	*ella*	*ens* (for *ēs*)
PL.	1	*yllyn*	*ellen*	*dün* (for *ēn*)
	2	*yllough*	*elleugh*	*keugh, eugh, ā*
	3	*ellons*	*ellens*	*ens*

With suffixed prons., 1 and 2 s. pres.-fut. *ama, eta*.

The tense used as perfect, "I have become," etc., looks like a compound of a stem *gal* with the habitual present of *bos* ; *gal esof*, " I am become," etc., which would account for the *-sof, -sos* in 1 and 2 s. and also for the use without particles. The 3 s., *galles* (B.M. 1036), would thus, as *gal, ēs*, be nearer to the original form than *gallas* with its regnlar 3 s. pret. ending *-as*. The tense used as pluperf. "I had or would become," etc., seems similarly formed from *gal* (before *e, gyl*) with the imperf. of time and place of *bos*, " I was become," etc. Of this tense we have only *galsa*, which though resembling a regular 3 s. plnpf., seems to be *gal esa*, and *gylses* (R.D. 1470) which is a contemporary correction of *galsos* (matching *ty a-alsa* above) and seems to be *gyl eses*. The 3 s. forms *gallas, galsa*, coinciding with those of pret. and plupf. in regular vbs., would be apt to fix such a change of tense. The past part. *gyllys* has the regular -vb. ending *-ys*, not the *-vedhys of bos*.

Inf. DŌS, DONES, DEVŌS, DEVONES : Pres. Part. *-ow-tōs*, etc. ; Past Part. *devedhys*.

MOOD		INDICATIVE				IND. & SUBJ.
TENSE		PRES.-FUT.	IMPERF.	PRET.	PERFECT	PLUPERF.
S.	1	*dōf*	*dēn*	*düth*	*düfef*	*dothyen*
	2	*dēth, düth*	*dēs*	*düthys*	*düfes*	*dothyes*
	3	*dē, dü*	*dō*	*düth, dēth*	*düfa*	*dothya*
PL.	1	*dün*	*dēn*	*düthen*	*düfen*	*dothyen*
	2	*deugh*	*deugh*	*dütheugh*	*düfeugh*	*dothyeugh*
	3	*dons*	*dens, dons*	*düthons, dēthons*	*düfons*	*dothyens*
IMPERS. PASS.		*dēer*				

Mood	Imperative		Imperative
Tense	Pres.-Fut.	Imperf.	Pres.-Fut.
S. 1	*dyffyf*	*deffen*	...
S. 2	*dyffy*	*deffes*	*düs*
S. 3	*deffo*	*deffa*	*dens* (for *dēs*)
Pl. 1	*dyffyn*	*deffen*	*dün*
Pl. 2	*dyffough*	*deffeugh*	*deugh*
Pl. 3	*deffons*	*deffens*	*dens*
Impers. Pass.			

With suffixed prons., 2 s. pres.-fut. *düta*, 3 s. *düva*, 2 s. pret. *düthta*.

Imperf. Indic. is found only in M.C., 3 s. *do*, 3 pl. *dons* (? for *dens*) ; what should be 3 s. is written *de*, R.D. 914. The special Perfect is found in 3 s. (also spelt *dēva*) and 3 pl. *dēfons* (*desons* P.C. 1247), and is used without particles but for *re-* and neg. particles, 1 s. pres.-fut. is spelt *duff* B.M. 3365 and *deaf* C.W. 1760.

Inf. Dōn, to bear, carry : Pres. Part. *ow-tōn* ; Past Part. *degys*.

Mood	Indicative			Ind. & Subj.
Tense	Pres.-Fut.	Imperf.	Pret.	Pluperf.
S. 1	*degaf*	*degyn*	*dük*	*deksen*
S. 2	*degeth*	*degys*	*düges*	*dekses*
S. 3	*dēk(g)*	*degy*	*dük*	*deksa*
Pl. 1	*degon*	*degyn*	*dügon*	*deksen*
Pl. 2	*degough*	*degeugh*	*dügough*	*dekseugh*
Pl. 3	*degons*	*degens*	*dügons*	*deksens*

Mood	Subjunctive		Imperative
Tense	Pres.-Fut.	Imperf.	Pres.-Fut.
S. 1	*dygyf*	*degen*	...
S. 2	*dykky, dygy*	*deges*	*dōk*
S. 3	*docco, dogo*	*dega*	*degens* (for *-es*)
Pl. 1	*dygen*	*degen*	*degen*
Pl. 2	*dygough*	*degeugh*	*degeugh*
Pl. 3	*doccons*	*degens*	*degens*

A later inf., *degy*, seems re-formed from Past Part. (*degy*, P.C. 2313 is *dejȳ*, thee).

Inf. Rȳ, to give : Pres. Part. *ow-rȳ* ; Past Part. *rēs*. Drȳ, dyllo, and tȳ, to swear, resemble *rȳ*, their distinctive features being caused by an *o* in their stems.

Mood	Indicative			Ind. & Subj.
Tense	Pres.-Fut.	Imperf.	Pret.	Pluperf.
S. 1	*rōf*	*rēn*	*res*	*rosen*
S. 2	*rēth*	*rēs*	*ressys*	*roses*
S. 3	*rē*	*rȳ*	*rōs*	*rosa*
Pl. 1	*rēn*	*rēn*	*resen*	*rosen*
Pl. 2	*rough*	*reugh*	*resough*	*roseugh*
Pl. 3	*rons*	*rens*	*resons*	*rosens*
Impers. Pass.	*rēr*			

Mood	Subjunctive		Imperative
Tense	Pres.-Fut.	Imperf.	Pres.-Fut.
S. 1	*ryllyf*	*rollen*	...
S. 2	*rylly*	*rolles*	***rō, roy***
S. 3	*rollo, roy*	*rolla*	***rens*** (for ***rēs***)
Pl. 1	*ryllyn*	*rollen*	***rēn***
Pl. 2	*ryllough*	*rolleugh*	***reugh***
Pl. 3	*rollons*	*rollens*	***rens***
Impers. Pass.			

Pres.-fut. subj. *roy* is used only as optative, when *re-* is absorbed into it: as 2 s. imp. *roy* is used only before vowels, as in *an*, the, *y*, his or them, etc., and, as var. of *ro va*, before *e*, him, it.

Drȳ usually has *d* prefixed to *rȳ*, but *do* in 2 s. imp. *doro* (vars. *dro* and before vowels *doroy*) and 3 s. pres.-fut. *dora*, these are often spelt alike in MSS.

Dyllo has p. pt. *dyllys*, 2 s. imp. and 3 s. pres.-fut. *dyllo* (later *dylla*); pret. is *dellēs*, *dellessys*, *dellōs*, etc., as *rȳ*. The only other person found is 2 pl. imp. *dylleugh*, but the rest is presumably like *rȳ*, except that no *ll* could be added in Subjunctive Mood.

Tȳ, to swear, is also found only in Indicative Mood: to avoid confusion with *tylly* and *telly*, subjunctives might well be formed with auxiliary vbs. rather than in imitation of *ry*. The other vb. *tȳ*, to roof, although equally having *o* in the stem (*to*, roof), has become a regular vb., 2 s. imp. *tȳ*, 3 s. pret. *tȳas*, etc.

Further Corrigenda

---

s.v. **a-barth**, delete *a.-dhon*, etc.
s.v. **dēgol**, add meanings, festival, feast.
s.v. **devar**, before 2528 add :– C.W.
s.v. **fynny**, delete Rosevidney, place-name.
after **gwayn**, add :– **gwaynya**, *vb.*, to acquire, gain, get, obtain, win, secure, B.M., Lh., Gw., P.
juj, **jujjya** are misplaced after **junnya**: to **jujjya** add :– *j. dhe'n mernans*, to sentence to death, P.C. 1979.
s.v. **kenyver**, add :– *k. den us y'n wlas*, every man (lit. as many men as there are) in the land; in Late Cor. one even said *k jorna*, every day, etc., without a following verb.
s.v. **mullyonen**, delete Rosemullion.
after **nomber**, add :– **non**, *f.*, *pl.* **-now**, stream; **nonnen**, *f.*, *pl.* **-now**, streamlet: Rosnon, Rosnonnen, place-names.
s.v. **pla**, for *aberth*, read *a-barth*.
s.v. **rak(g)**, add after **a-dherak(g)**, **war-rak(g)**, and (p. 209) **yn-rak(g)**.
after **yn-prōt**, add **yn-rak(g)**, *adv.*, forward, onward, forth; see **rak(g)**.

ADDENDA

A

***abecedary,** *m.,* alphabet.
acontyans, reckoning, estimation, see **acontya.**
acordyans, agreement, see **acordya.**
†aden, *f, pl.* **-now,** also binding board of book, M. L. *folium* thin board.
adhewedhes, *adj.,* late, recent; *adv.,* lately, recently, see **deweth.**
adhya, [2] *prep.,* from, of time or place.
aghscryf, *m., pl.* **-yow** pedigree, genealogy, see **agh.**
agrowsen, *f., col.* **agrows** hip, berry of dog-rose.
***alamand,** *m., pl.* **-ys** almond (O.F. alemande).
alaw *m., pl.* **elew** water lily, E-C dict. W. alaw, possibly in Porthallow.
alejya, *vb.,* to cite, quote, (M.E.).
amary, *m., pl.* **-s** additional meaning, cupboard, locker.
***antempna,** *m., pl.* **-nys**; ***antem** *m., pl.* **-ys** anthem (M.E.).
***anvenough,** *adj.,* infrequent.
appla, *comp. adj.,* more able, see **abel.**
arghansek, *adj.,* silvery; *f., pl.* **-egow,** silver mine.
arghanty, *m., pl.* **-ow** bank, money-house.
arghdrewyth, *m., pl.* **-ydhyon,** archdruid.
***arnew,** *m. pl.* **-yow,** storm-damage; **arnewa,** *vb.,* to damage by weather.
***arsmetryk,** *m.,* arithmetic (O.F.).
arwystel, *m., pl.* **-tlow** pledge, see **gwystel.**
asowen, *f. pl.* **-now** rib, barrel-stave etc. (Tregeare), see **asen,** *pl.* **asow.**
assoylya, *vb.,* to solve, absolve, explain, discharge.
avysment, *m., pl.* **-ns** consideration, deliberation, etc, see **avys.**
aweth, *f., pl.* **-yow** watercourse.
***awgrym,** *m.,* mathematics, numeration; **nyverow awgrym** arabic numerals.

B

***ballek,** *f.,* bow-net.
bannek, *adj.,* peaked, prominent.
***bansya,** *vb.,* to banish.
barrek, *adj.,* twiggy, branched.
bayol, (C. Voc. *baiol*), *f. pl.* **-yow,** shallow tub, half-tub, sailor's mess kid, as B. *beol,* W. *baeol,* F. *baille,* M. Lat. *bajula* (water-vessel).
bēn, *m., pl.* **-ow** additional meanings, foot, base of hill, mouth of river, bottom end, often becoming **pen** in placenames; see **bēn.**
besewen, *f. col.,* **besow,** birch tree, see **bedhewen.**
blew an jowl, dodder; **blew dowr,** water-crowfoot; see **blewen.**
bokyl, *m., pl.* **boclys,** buckle; **bocla** *vb.,* to buckle.
boll, *adj.,* transparent, translucent, diaphanous, gauzy, clear, thin; *tew yn dar boll,* from dense into flimsy.
bownd, *m., pl.* **-ns** tin bound, miner's claim.
brāca, *m., pl.* **bràkys,** thicket, brake. (E).
brafter, *m.,* grandeur, finery, bravery.
brȳn, *m., pl.* **-now** hill; see also **bron, bre**
***bryn,** *adj.,* rotten; **brȳna** *vb.* to rot.
brȳn, *m.,* brine (E.).
büdhygol, *adj.,* victorious; **büdhygoleth** *m.* victory; see **büdhek.**
burjestra, *f., pl.* **-trevow** borough; **burjesty** *m. pl.* **-ow** guildhall, see **burjes.**
butta, *m., pl.* **buttys** butt for archery, shooting, rifle range.

C

cabūl, *m.*; **cabūlva** *f.* mix-up, medley, hotch-potch; see **cabūlen**
camas, *f.,* bend, bay, placenames, Camas Point, The Gabmas; cf O.W. **camas.**
***cantykyl,** *m. pl.* **-tyclys** canticle (E.)
carer, *m., pl.* **-roryon**; **carores** *f. pl.* **-ow** lover, admirer, amateur, see **cara.**
caspōl, *f., pl.* **-ow** battle-axe; see **cas,**; **bōl.**
chalys, *m., pl.* **chalysys** chalice (E.), see **kelegel.**
***chambrour,** *m. pl.* **-s** valet; ***chambroures** *f. pl.* **-ow** chambermaid.
chanj, *m., pl.* **-ys** change, exchange, mutation; see **chanjya.**
chartour, *m., pl.* **-s** charter, deed of freedom, (E.)
chās, *m., pl.* **-ys** chase, open hunting-ground; see **chassya.**
chaunler, *m., pl.* **-s** chandelier, chandler; see **chownler.**
chekkya, *vb.,* to check, rebuke, (Gwavas).
chersya, *vb.,* to cherish, entertain, treat kindly, caress, fondle; (O.F.).
clether, *f., pl.* **clethrow** stave, rail, shingle, etc.
clychya, *vb.,* to stick, clutch; see **clyjjy.**
cōnter, *adj.,* contrary, opposite, cross; *m., pl.* **-s** cross lode.
contrŏversyta, *m., pl.* **-tys** controversy (E.)
cora, *vb.,* to polish with wax; see **cor.**
corvagh, *f., pl.* **-ow** nook.
cowel lesk, *m.,* cradle; see **cowel.**
coyn, *m.,* corner of tin block; **coynach** *m.,* coinage of tin.
crüskyn, *m., pl.* **-now** drinking pot, flagon, beer mug.
crystal, *m.,* crystal: yth-eugh gwyn avel crystal, you will become white like crystal, B.M. 1521; see **gwrȳs.**
Crystyonyeth, *f.,* Christianity; **crystyonya** *vb.* to christen; see **crystyon.**

D

darwesn, -ejen, *f., pl.* **darwes** ringworm, tetter.
dasknyas, *vb.,* to chew cud, ruminate; see **daskylyas.**
demedhyans, *m.,* marriage, espousal; see **maryach.**
devosyon, *m., pl.* **-s** devotion, worship, (E.).
***drewk,** *m.,* darnel, tares.
drüm, *m., pl.* **-yow** back, ridge; see **trüm.**
dygolm, -en, *adj.,* knotless, unknotted (preferable to **dyscolm**).
dylewghya, *vb.,* to sift from fine particles, see **lewgh.**
dystyr, *adj.,* insignificant, of no account, meaningless; see **styr,** in addenda, **ster** in dictionary.

E

ensompel, *m., pl.* **-plys** example, instance; see **sampel.**
s.v. **erghy,** add:– when transitive requires *dhe, my a-ergh dhys,* etc.
ewl, *f., pl.* **-ow** craving, strong desire.

F

famya, *vb.,* to famish.
folen, *f., pl.* **-now,** leaf or page of a book, sheet of paper (weak as a vollan, Dial.)
folya, *vb.,* to follow (E.); see **holya.**
folyer, *m., pl.* **-s** or **-yoryon,** follower (E.).

G

godenow, *m.,* slight depression in the ground; see **tenow.**
godreva, *f.,* the third day from now; see **go-** (Appendix II) and **treveth,** time, occasion.
godroth, *m.,* infushion of yellow bedstraw used as rennet.
godrotha, *vb.,* to curdle milk with bedstraw.
golans, *m., pl.* **-ow** small valley; see **go-** (Appendix II) and **nans** (Golant).
golghyon, *m., pl.* suds, slops, hogwash.
s.v. **gorthfyl** add:– in Late Cor. probably means "conger", represented by *withel* in the traditional - *pedn bokser, lost withiel,* describing a boat with a bluff entrance but a fine run, in Eng. "cod's head and conger tail"; cf. also *an* Nor Wethel (?the conger ground), Scilly; *bokser* may be for *boghserth,* "stiff-cheek", and name some sort of gurnard, Pedn Boxer is a headland, cf. Gurnard's Head.
gona, *vb.,* to sheathe; see **gōn.**
graffya, *v.,* to graft (E.).
gweryn, *f., pl.* **-eth,** populace, folk, common people; from W. *gwerin.*
gwyndon, *f.,* lay land; see **gwyn** and **ton.**

H

howlgan, *m.,* sunlight, sunshine; see **lorgan, stergan, can.**

K

kerth, *f.,* property, possession; as B. *kerz* f. property and M.W. *kerth* m. right; *pandr'yu dha gerth y'n pow-ma?* "what is thy holding in this country?" B.M. 2370.
knegh, *m., pl.* **-yow** (*k* sounded), hillock; see **knogh.**
knew, *m., pl.* **-yow** (*k* sounded), fleece; see **knyvyas.**

L

londya, *vb.,* to land, B.M. 1093, (M.F.); see **tyra.**

M

s.v. **melenek,** add:– also goldfinch (P. *molenek*)
molas, *m.,* molasses, treacle, (E.); **dowr tom molas,** rum.
mygorn, *m., pl.* **-ow,** knuckle (W.); also **mel dorn,** *pl.* **mellow dorn.**

N

non, *f., pl.* **-now**; **nonnen** *f., pl.* **-now,** streamlet, brook.
***nygromans,** *m.,* sorcery (E.); see **pystry.**
nyveren, *f., pl.* **-now,** numeral, digit; see **nyver.**

O

odyt, *m., pl.* **-s,** adit, water channel for a mine, aqueduct. (E.).
omjersya, *vb.,* to make oneself comfortable, be at ease, B.M. 296; see **chersya** in addenda.
outray, *m.,* excess, outrage, violent or outrageous action. (E.).

P

plowghya, *vb.,* to make a great splash.
poblek, *adj.,* public, also populous. See **pobel.**
pomster, *m., pl.* **-trys,** quack doctor.
pomstry, *m.,* quackery, literally, palmistry. (E.).
***portmantel,** *m., pl.* **-tlow,** portmanteau, (E. from F.)
***predheger,** *m., pl.* **-goryon,** ranter.
predheges, *vb.,* to rant, make a noisy speech, shout.
***predhek,** *m., pl.* **-egow,** a rant.
pych, *m., pl.* **-ys,** stab, thrust, piercing stroke, transfixion.
pychya, *vb.,* to pierce, stab, transfix.
pyctur, *m., pl.* **-s,** picture. (E).

R

raw, *f., pl.* **-yow,** bond, strop; see **row.**
raya, *m., pl.* **-yes,** ray, thornback. (E). See **rogha** in Addenda.
rayn, *m., pl.* **-ys,** reign; **raynya** *vb.* to reign; see **regnya.**
relystyon, *pl.* low grade tin.
rogha, *m., pl.* **-ghys,** ray, thornback; see **raya,** in Addenda.
roper, *m., pl.* **-s,** ropemaker, (E.).

S

sarfek, *adj.,* serpentine; **men sarfek,** serpentine rock; see **sarf.**
sawgh, *m., pl.* **-yow,** backload, horseload; see **saw.**
scōf, *m.* rich tin ore; **scoven,** *f.* ground very rich in tin.
scrübel, *col.,* beasts of burden.
sensour, *m., pl.* **-s,** censer, incense-burner, (M.E. from Norm.F.).
serjya, *vb.,* to sift finely.
shuta, *m., pl.* **-tys,** water conduit.
sogen, *f., pl.* **-now,** damp place.
sompel, *m.,* example, instance; see **sampel.**
soras, *coll., sep., pl.* **soresyow,** dregs, leavings.
sowser, *m., pl.* **-s,** saucer (E.).
s.v. **squych,** additional meaning, electric switch, etc.
stryppen, *f., pl.,* **-now,** strip (E.). Wheal Stryppen, mine-name.
stüth, *m., pl.* **-yow,** state, condition, plight, situation.
styr, *m., pl.* **-yow,** meaning, significance, sense; see **ster.**
styrya, *vb.,* to explain, interpret, give the meaning of.

T

tenva, *f.,* drawing (as in execution or in drawing a chicken).
tenvos, *m.* seduction; see **tenna.**
tender, *m., pl.* -doryon, waiter, attendant. (E.).
tēr, *adj.,*clear, pure (of water).
ternōth, *adj.,* ill-clad, half-naked.
tollor, *m., pl.* -yon, one who renews tin-bounds by cutting a turf from a hole; see **toll,** a hole.
trayn, *m., pl.,* **-ys,** artifice, guile, enticement.
tresoryer, *m., pl.,* **-yoryon,** treasurer; see **tresor.**

V

vycar, *m., pl.* **-s,** vicar.
vycarjy, *m., pl.* **-ow,** vicarage.

W

war-jy, *adv.*, inwardly.
war-ves, *adv.*, outwardly; *prep.*, abroad, outside.
war-wartha, *adv.*, on top of, see **war-woles.**

Y

yawn, *m.*, *pl.* **-as,** bass (fish).
ydhyl, *adj.*, feeble, frail, slight, puny, weak.
yn-dar, *conj.*, instead of, from ... to ... etc.
ynyal, *adj.*, wild, desolate; *m.* wasteland, wilderness.
Ytaly, *f.* Italy; **Ytalek,** *adj.* Italian; *m.* Italian language.
ysyurl, *m.*, *pl.* **-ys,** viscount; see **yurl.**
ȳvra, *m.*, darnel, rye-grass, tares, (eaver, Dial.).
yvynyen, *f.*, *pl.* **yvynyas,** sand-launce; see **lavyn, lavynyon.**

A NEW ENGLISH-CORNISH DICTIONARY

INTRODUCTION.

THIS dictionary aims at giving students of Cornish the means of expressing themselves in words which are either part of the Middle Cornish learnt by them in unified form, or where these fail, loans from Welsh and Breton or from Middle English, so spelt as to harmonise with it.

In putting together a first draft of it for us, Mr. Richard Gendall naturally used the smaller *English-Cornish Dictionary* prepared by Mr. A. S. D. Smith and myself in 1934, but this is more than a new edition of that one, as he also laboriously put into reverse order the words in my *Cornish-English Dictionary* of 1939. Revision of the work as he left it has allowed me to make all kinds of additions, corrections and deletions and for its present state I am responsible.

While all previous dictionaries of Cornish have relied on the printed editions of the texts, this one has gone to photostats of the manuscripts themselves and so profited by many more accurate readings of them. John Tregear's Cornish translations of the homilies from Bonner's *Profitable and Necessary Doctrine* of 1555, unknown in 1939, and giving by far the longest run of Cornish prose, have given us fresh words as well as confirming or correcting some conjectural genders, plurals and infinitive endings.

The bulk of the language is fortunately preserved in existing texts, but place-names, as spelt in medieval documents especially, have supplied many needed words, while hundreds more have survived as "dialect," and if no help comes from these, the kindred Breton and Welsh may agree in preserving a word which re-spelt according to rule repairs our loss, or else Middle English may offer a loan-word which will be equally acceptable when added to those with which we are already familiar. Such borrowings are here marked with an asterisk (*). While Middle-Cornish words, however re-spelt, have no distinguishing mark, those respelt from Old Cornish are given a dagger (†) and those respelt from Late Cornish a double dagger (‡) as an indication that they may not be preferred to those unmarked. The *Cornish-English Dictionary* should be consulted for further particulars as to use and meaning.

For ordinary writing, no diacritical signs are used in unified Cornish, but the vowels are here marked as follows:—

ā — the long *aa* of "braave" : *tās* (father) — "taaze."
ē — *ay* in "day" : *dēn* (man) — "dane."
ȳ, *ü* — *ee* in "see" : *prȳs* (time) — "preeze."
ō — *aw* in "raw" : *dōn* (to carry) — "dawn."
ū — *oo* in "moon" : *gūn* (plain) — "goon."

When final or before *gh*, *o* has the sound of "owe" or "oh", and *u* has the sound of "ewe" or "you." The *gh* serves to mark these. A few obvious loan-words, as *ūsya* (to use) give the same sound to *ū*.

The short sounds of *a*, *e*, *y or ü*, *o*, *u*, are like English *a*, *e*, *i*, *o*, *u*.

au — *aw* in "saw."
aw — *ow* in "cow."
ay — *ay* in "say."
ew, *yw*, *eu*, *yu* have the sound of "ewe," "you."
ey — *ey* in "eye."
ou — *oo* in "moon."

Ow in stressed syllables is in some words "aou" or "ayoo," in others (marked *öw* in the Cornish-English dictionary) it is nearer English long *o* in "so." As unstressed, it varies between *o* and *oo; oy* is like *oy* in "boy," but with a tendency to separate the *y*.

In all unstressed syllables vowels tend to shorten or to have the obscure sound of *u*, as the *o's* in "London." Usually only one syllable in a Cornish word takes the stress, so giving its vowel the full sound. A long stem vowel shortens usually when a plural or other ending is added.

The main accent in a Cornish word falls as a rule on the last syllable but one. There are some exceptions, however, and these are marked here with a reversed full-stop (·): thus the infinitive-ending *-hē·*, added to an adj. to make an inf., is so marked, as in *berhē·* (to shorten), and the same mark points out unusual stresses in *ca·rpenter*, *myghte·rn*, *yma·*, etc., and the final stress in the doubled suffixed prons. *-avȳ·*, *-dhejȳ·*, *-ëe·f*, etc. Loan-words from English usually keep their own accent, as in *ordenal*, *vyctory*, etc. In such words an unstressed vowel often drops out, as in *consler*, for "conseler," *glotny* for "glotony," *punsya* for "punyshya," also occasionally in Celtic words, as *tewl* for *tewal*, *tenwennow* for *tenewennow*. These need no mark.

The numerals added to certain words in the dictionary indicate that they cause mutations of following initials as shown in the table:

1	2	3	4	5
b	v	·	p	f,v
c,k	g	h	·	·
ch	j	·	·	·
d	dh	·	t	t
g	-,w	·	c,k	h
gw	w	·	qu	whw
m	v	·	·	f,v
p	b	f	·	·
qu	gw	wh	·	·
t	d	th	·	·
Radical	Soft	Breathed	Hard	Mixed

In soft mutation *go*, *gu* are treated as *gw*, and *gro*, *gru* as *gwro*, *gwru*.

In mixed mutation after *th*, *b*, *m* often become *v*, *g* may remain unchanged, *go* may become *wo*.

Though no change is made in spelling, there is also a regular soft mutation of *f* to *v* and of *s* to *z*, which is observed in speech, and in the Anglicized spelling of place-names.

Gender is shown as usual by adding "m." or "f." to nouns, or to a series of nouns of the same gender, and plurals are marked "pl." If very unlike the singular, plurals are spelt in full, as *dēn*, m., pl. *tüs*, f., but if formed by adding a pl. ending to an unchanged sing., the added ending alone is given, as *dowr*, m., pl. *-ow* (*dowrow*), *pyscador*, m., pl. *-yon* (*pyscadoryon*), *benen*, f., pl. *-es* (*benenes*), *bügel*, m., pl. *-eth* (*bügeleth*). If the sing. has some change also, the given pl. ending includes its last unchanged letter, as *servont*, m., pl. *-ns* (*servons*), *brennyas*, m., pl. *-ysy* (*brennysy*). If the final consonant of a singular is doubled in plural, this is shown in the pl. ending, as *aval*, m., pl. *-low* (*avallow*), *gon*, m., pl. *-nys* (*gonnys*). Some plurals are formed by changing the vowel of the singular only, as *mēn*, m., pl. *meyn*, others by changing the vowel and still adding an ending, as *maghteth*, f., pl. *meghtythyon*. Diminutives formed by adding *-yk* to the sing. (often accompanied by a change of vowel) may add the pl. ending to either sing. or pl., as *tam*, m., pl. *tymmyn*, dim. *temmyk*, pls. *-ygow* (*temmygow*) or *tymmynygow*. Nouns naming places where natural growths, minerals, etc., are found are formed by adding the suffix *-ek*, f., which has *-egow* or *-egy* indifferently as pl. Some nouns are collective and form the sing. by adding the suffix *-en*, f. which has a separative pl. *-now*, as *pēr*, col., pears in general, *peren*, f., a single pear, *perennow*, separate pears. A few names of animals have in addition to the ordinary pl., used in a more collective sense, a special separative pl., as *margh*. m., pl. *mergh*, sep. pl. *marghas* or *merghas; gavar*, f., pl. *gever*, sep. pl. *gefras* or *gyfras; davas*. f., pl. *deves*, sep. pl. *devysyow*.

Nouns borrowed from Middle English (frequently ending in obscure *a*), add the borrowed pl. -*ys* or -*s* to their last consonant, as *shoppa*. m., pl. -*pys*, (*shoppys*), *faytour*, m., pl. -*s* (*faytours*). Some nouns, especially abstract ones, have no plural; others, as *mēny*, *coscar*, *tüs*, have no singular, the want being supplied by another noun, as for these, *maw*, *dēn*. Parts of the body are named in pairs as dual by prefixing *deu*- to a masculine, *dyw*- to a feminine noun, as *trōs*, m., d. *deudros*, *lüf*, f., d. *dywlüf*, *dywla*. A couple, whether two men or man and woman, is similarly *deudhen*, and groups of other numbers are often formed in the same way, as *tredden* (*trȳ dēn*), *whednar* (*whēgh dynar*), *nawmen* (*naw mēn*), the numeral always taking the accent and the vowel of the noun, or both vowels, shortening. In the compounds *cangour*, *pymwoly*, the final consonants of *cans*, *pymp*, are dropped also, but this is a relic of ancient practice and not a general rule.

R. MORTON NANCE.

ABBREVIATIONS.

When the word treated is quoted or mentioned further in the same article, its initial letter followed by a full-stop represents the whole word. Besides this, the following abbreviations are used:—

a., adjective.
abst., abstract.
adv., adverb.
anat., anatomical.
bot., botanical.
col., collective.
comp., comparative.
d., dual.
def. v., defective verb.
dim., diminutive.
eccl., ecclesiastical.
excl., exclamation.
f., feminine.
fut., future.
geog., geographical.
imp., imperative.
impf., imperfect.
indef., indefinite.
inf., infinitive.
int., interjection.
interrog., interrogative.
intr., intransitive.
lit., literally.
m., masculine.
milit., military.
n., noun.
naut., nautical.
neg., negative.
neut., neuter.
opt., optative.
p.p., past participle.
part., particle.
perf., perfect.
pl., plural.
plupf., pluperfect.
poss., possessive.
pr., pronounced.
prep., preposition.
pres.-fut., present-future.
pres. p., present participle.
pret., preterite.
rel., relative.
relig., religious.
sep., separative.
sing., singular.
subj., subjunctive.
suf., suffix.
super., superlative.
trans., transitive.
v., verb.
var., variant.

AN ENGLISH-CORNISH DICTIONARY.

A

a, indef. art. *ün*; usually as meaning "a certain."
abaft, adv. *wor'tu delergh.*
abandon, v. *gasa*; a. a mine, *squattya.*
abase, v. *yselhē·.*
abasement, n. *yselder*, m.
abate, v. *lehē·, bassya.*
abbess, n. *abajes*, f., pl. *-ow.*
abbey, n. *abatty*, m., pl. *-ow*; a. land, *abbattyr* m., pl. *-yow.*
abbot, n. *abas*, m., pls. *-ow, ebes.*
abbreviate, v. *cotthē·, berhē·.*
abdicate, v. *dascor.*
abed, adv. *y'n gwely.*
abhor, v. *casa*: **-rence,** n. *cas.*
abide, v. *tryga, bōs trygys, gortos,remaynya, pēsya, prest bōs*; abiding-place, *trygva*, f., **trygla*, m.
ability, n. *gallos, gothvos*, m., *tythy*, col. and abst., *connek*, m.
abject, a. *ysel, vȳl*: **-ness,** n. *vȳlta*, m.
ablaze, adv., *gans tān.*
able, a. competent, *harth, abel*, comp. *appla*; powerful, *mēn*; to be a., *gothvos, gallos*; a-bodied man, *corf da, body crēf*; as well as I am a., *gwella gallaf, del wōn, oll dhe'm gallos.*
ably, adv. *yn-connek, yn-gallosek.*
abnormal, a. *drēs kynda*; without normal powers, *antȳthy.*
aboard, adv. *war*, or *yn, lester*, or *gorhel.*
abode, n. *harber*, m., pl. *ys, anneth* f., pl. *-edhow, trygva*, f.; in place-names, *bos*; summer a. *hewas* (†*havos*), autumn a. *kynewas* (†*kynyavos*), winter a. *gwavas.*
abolish, v. *gorra dhe-vēs, defendya, *dylēa.*
abominate, v. *casa*: **-ation,** n. *pyth casadow.*
aboriginal, a. *genesyk*; n. *genesyk*, m., pl. *-ygyon.*
abortive, a. *üfer.*
abound, v. *bōs lanwes a*^{2}, *palshē·.*
abounding, a. *pals.*
about, prep., round a., *a-dro dhe*^{2}, *yn-kerghyn*; approximately, *nep, ogas ha*; concerning, *a-dro dhe*^{2}, *yn-kever*; speak a. *kewsel a*^{2}: adv. *a-dro, a-dhe-dro, a-drē-dro*; a. ready, *ogas parys*; it is a. to come, *yma· ow-tegensewa.*
above, prep. *drēs, a-ugh*; a. all, *drēs puptra, d. ēghen*: adv. *a-wartha, -ava·n*; high a. (us), *ughel a-ughon*: a. (overhead), *a-ughof, a-ughon*; from a., *a wartha*; a. mentioned, *kens leverys.*
abrade, v. *dyrüsca.*
abreast, adv. *tenewan orth tenewan, scoth ryp scoth.*
abridge, v. *berhē·.*
abroad, adv., widely, *a-lēs*; out of the country, *drēs an mōr.*
abrogate, v. *gasa, namoy ūsya.*
abrupt, a., sudden, *desempys*; steep, *serth*: **-ly,** adv. *a-dhesempys, cot, yn-serth.*
absence, n. *fowt, dyfyk*; because of his a., *rak nag-esa ena*; in his a., *hep y vōs y'n lē-na.*
absent, a., he was a., *nyns-esa ena, yth-esa dyworta.*
absolute, a., **-ly,** adv. *pür.*
absolve, v. *delyfra, aquytya, dyllo, assoylya.*
absorb, v. *eva, lenky, dēna*; absorbed in his work, *gyllys down yn y ober.*
abstain, v. *sparya, sevel* (*orth*).
abstract, n. *derȳvas cot, devyn*, m., pl. *-now*: v. *kemeres mēs, tenna dyworth.*
absurd, a. *fol, goky*: **-ity,** n. *folneth, gokyneth.*
abundance, n. *lanwes, cals, palster*, m.
abundant, a. *pals, lün.*
abuse, n. *vy·lyny, tebel-dyghtyans*, m.: v. *tebel-dyghtya, deffola*; in words, *drōkhenwel.*
abusive, a. *drōk.*
abyss, n. *yslonk, pol-down*, m.
accent, n. *tōn*, m., pl. *-yow, pōs lēf.*
accentuate, v. *tonya, posa lēf war*^{2}.
accept, v., take, *kemeres, receva*; welcome, *yntertaynya*; admit, *degemeres.*
acceptable, a. *plegadow.*
acceptance, n. *kemeryans, plegadow*, m.,
access, n., of pain, rage, fever, etc., *shora*, m., pl. *-rys*; easy of a., *ēs y nessa*; there is no a., *nyns-üs forth dh'y entra.*
accessibility, n. *hüvelder*, m.
accessible, a. *a-ȳl bōs hedhys, hüvel.*

accession, n., addition, *encressyans,* m.; a. to throne, *dōs dhe'n sē.*
accident, n. *hap*; mishap, *droglam, drōklam,* m. pl. *-mow, gwall* m., pl. *-ow.*
accidentally, adv. *drē wall.*
acclaim, v. *gül noys gans.*
acclamation, n. *comen voys.*
accommodate, v. lodge, *ostya*; facilitate, *ēsya, ēshē·*; adapt, *compossa.*
accommodating, a. *parys dhe blēkya.*
accommodation, n., room, *spās, rōm, efander, ostyans,* m.; ease, *ēs,* m.
accompany, v. *gorra, mōs,*or *dōs, gans.*
accomplice, n. *kescoweth yn tebelwrȳans,* m., pl. *-a y.t.*
accomplish, v. *gül, cowlwül, spēdya.*
accomplished, a. *perfyth, cowlwrēs, collenwys.*
accomplishment, n. *cowlwrȳans,* m.; attainment, *hedhyans,* m.
accord, v., agree, *acordya*; grant, *rȳ, vossawya*: n. *acord*; with one a., *kescolon.*
accordance, n., in a. with, *herwyth.*
according, adv., a. to, *herwyth, warle·rgh*; a. as, *orth,* with v., *kepar del²*.
accordingly, adv. *ytho·, drē henna, ha.*
account, n., report, *deryvadow, derȳvas* m.; reckoning, *reken,* m., pl., *-knys, aco·nt, charj,* m., pls. *-ys*; value, *brȳ,* m.; on my a., *a'm govys-vy*; (not) on any a., *awo·s an bȳs,* or *neptra,* or *travyth,* or *neppyth,* or *kynda, war vyns-oll,* or *nep ous*; of no a., *sempel, ysel*; make a. of, *gül vrȳ a²*; on a. of, *drefen* (governs inf. except in neg.), *er* (governs inf.); by all a.s, *del levery gans pup-oll*: v. esteem, *synsy, settya, acontya*; reckon, *rekna*; settle a.s with, *rekna gans.*
accumulate, v. *crüny, cuntell.*
accumulation, n. *cuntellyans, bern,* m., pl. *-yow*; of water, *crün,* m., pl. *-yow.*
accuracy, n. *kewerder, composter,* m.
accurate, a. *compes, kewar*; make a. *composa.*
accursed, a. *mylygys, emskemünys, mollothek.*
accusation, n. *cuhüdhans,* m., pl. *-ow, cabel, acusasyon,* m.
accuse, v. *cuhüdha, sclandra, acusya, cably*; a. falsely, *camguhüdha*; a. one of being, *tewlel war dhēn y vōs.*
accuser, n. *cuhüdhor* m., pl. *-yon, cuhüdhas,* m., pl. *-ysy, †cuhüdhojak.* m., pl. *-jogyon.*
ache, n. *glōs,* f., pl. *-ow*: v. *pystyga.*
achieve, v. *drehedhes dhe²*; *cowlwül.*
achievement, n. *cowlwrȳans*; a great a. *gwrȳans drēs ēghen.*
acid, n. *dowr trenk,* m.: a. *trenk*: **-ity,** n. *trenkter,* m.
acknowledge, v. *aswon, aswonvos, amyttya, avowa, meneges.*
acolyte, n. *colyta,* m., pl. *-tys.*
acorn, n. *mesen,* f., col. *mēs*; a. cup, *bysken,* f., pl. *-now, pot mēs, m.,* pl. *-tow m.*; gather a.s, *messa.*
acquaintance, n. *cothman,* m., pl. *-mens*; knowledge, *aswonvos, *acoyntans.*
acquainted, a., they are a., *y a-omaswon*; to a. one with, *gül dhe dhēn aswon.*
acquiesce, v. *godhaf, godhevel, assentya, plegya*: **-nce,** n. *assentyans.*
acquire, v. *cafos, dōs ha bōs perghen a²*: **-ment,** *tra üs kefys.*
acquit, v. *aquytya, assoylya, delyfra, gasa dhe vos quyt, dyllo.*
acquittal, n. *delyfrans,* m.
acre, n. *erow,* f., pl. *erewy; *kevēr,* m., pl. *-yow.*
acrobat, n. *lappyor,* m., pl. *-yon,* f. *-es,* pl. *-ow.*
across, adv. *a-drüs, a-drüs dhe², a-drüs keyn*: prep. *a-drüs, drēs.*
act, v. *gül, obery*; on stage, *gwary*: n. *ober,* m., pl. *-ow, gwȳth,* m., pl. *-yow, gwythres,* m., pl. *-ow.*
action, n. *gwrȳans, gwrȳthyans, gwythres,* m, *gwrȳth,* f.; actions, deeds, *obereth,* bring an a., *plēntya.*
active, a. *bew, scaf, jolyf, snell, ‡stryk.*
activity, n. *bewder,* m.
actor, n. *gwarȳer,* m., pl. *-ȳoryon.*
actual, a. *gwȳr*: **-ly,** adv. *yn ober.*
acute, a. *lym*; of pain, *glew, tyn.*
acuteness, n. *lymder, glewder.*
adage, n. *poynt a skȳans, lavar cōth.*
adapt, v. *ewna, compossa.*
add, v. *rekna, gorra dhe², junnya, nyvera, acontya.*
adder, n. *nader,* f., pls. *-dron, nedras*; a.'s -tongue fern, *tavas nader.*
addition, n. *junnyans, encressyans*; in a., *moy.*
additional, a. *moy*; an a. task, *ün ober moy.*
address, n., of letter, *trygva,* f.; speech, *areth,* f. pl. *-yow*: v., speak to, *gül areth dhe², kewsel orth*; a. letter, *scryfa hanow ha trygva war²*; *danvon.*
adduce, v. *drȳ yn-rak.*
adept, a. *connek, skentyl, ynjyn.*
adequate, a. *lowr*; be a., *servya, bōs lowr.*

adhere, v. *glena, sergha* (*orth, war*[2]), *omlena.*
adherent, n. *holyer,* m., pl. *-yoryon, dyskybel,* m., pl. *-blon, -blyon*: a., adhesive, *üs ow-clena,* †*serghak.*
adit, n. *odyt,* m., pl. *-ys.*
adjacent, a. *ogas, nessa dhe*[2]; adjoining, *ow-junnya dhe*[2].
adjective, n., *hanow gwan,* m., pl. *hynwyn g.*
adjoin, v. *junnya.*
adjourn, v. *astel, hokkya.*
adjudicate, v. *brüsy, ry brüs.*
adjudication, n. *brüs,* f.
adjudicator, n. *brüsyas,* m., pl. *-ysy, brüsor,* m., pl. *-yon.*
adjunct, n. *junnyans,* m.
adjure, v. *conjurya.*
adjust, v. *ewna, settya, desedha.*
adjustment, n. *ewnans,* m.
administer, v. *menystra.*
administration, n., body of men, *menystry,* m.; action, *menystrans,* m.
administrator, n. *menystror,* m., pl. *-yon.*
admirable, a. *bryntyn, da drēs ēghen.*
admiral, n. *a·myral,* m., pl. *-s.*
admiralty, n. *Lys Mōr.*
admiration, n. *marth, brüs ughel.*
admire, v. *synsy bos tēk, cara*; I a. it, *marth a-m-büs a'y dekter.*
admirer, n. *carer,* m. pl. *-roryon,* f. *-ores,* pl. *-ow.*
admission, n. *degemeryans, amyttyans,* m., *gwȳr dhe entra.*
admit, v., receive, *degemeres, amyttya, receva, gasa dhe entra*; acknowledge, *avowa, aswon, amyttya*; confess, *meneges.*
admixture, n. *kemysk, kemyskyans,* m.
admonish, v. *kesky, gwarnya.*
admonition, n. *gwarnyans,* **cosk,* m.
ado, n. *tranjyak,* m.; without more a., *hep kewsel namoy geryow, dyson*; much a. about nothing, *mür a drōs a-dro dhe dravyth.*
adolescent, n. *dēn,* or *benen, yowynk,* pl. *tüs y.*: a. *nag-üs whath tevys dhe ōs, yntra flogh ha dēn.*
adopt, v., child, *kemeres yn y flogh y honen, mēthryn*; resolution, *degemeres.*
adoration, n. *gologhas, gordhyans,* m.
adore, v. *gordhya, gologhy*; love greatly, *mür-gara.*
adorn, v. *afȳna, tēkhē·, tacla*; richly adorned, *taclys yn-tēk,* †*fȳthüs.*
adroit, a. *fȳn, ynjyn, sley.*
adroitness, n. *ynjyn, sleyneth,* m.
adult, a. *a ōs, devedhys dhe ōs, tevys dhe dhēn*: n. *dēn,* or *benen, a ōs.*
adulterer, n. *avowtyer,* m., pl. -s; *gwanworty,* m. pl. *-wērty.*
adulteress, n. *gwanwrē'ty,* f., pl. *-wragetty* or *-wrageth-chȳ.*
adultery, n. *avowtry,* m.
advance, v. *mōs yn-rak, avonsya*; a. as argument, *alejya*: n. *avonsyans,* m.
advancement, n. *avonsyans,* m.
advantage, n. *lēs, gwayn, dader, prow,* m.
advantageous, a. *dhe lēs, 'vās.*
Advent, n. **Asvens,* m.; coming, *devedhyans,* m.
adventure, n. *aneth,* m. pl. *-ow*: v. *arveth, vyajya.*
adverb, n. **gorer,* m. pl. *-yow.*
adverse, a. *trüs, gorth*: **-ly,** adv. *trüs*: **-ity,** n. *anken.*
advertise, v. *notya, gül avȳsyans*: **-ment,** n. *notyans, avȳsyans,* m.
advice, n. *cusül,* f., pl. *-yow, avȳs,* m.; ask a., *govyn cusülyow.*
advise, v. *cusülya* (*a*[2]), *kesky.*
adviser, n. *cusülyer,* m., pl. *-yoryon,* †*cusülyador,* m., pl. *-yon.*
advocate, v. *plēdya*: n. *plēdyer,* m., pl. *-yoryon,* †*dathelor, dalor,* m., pl. *-yon.*
advowson, n. **avoweson,* m.
adze, n. *nedha,* m., pl. *-dhevyow.*
aerial, a. *a'n ayr, a'n ebren.*
aeroplane, n. *jyn-nyja,* m., pl. *-nys n., plēn an ayr.*
afar, adv. *a-bell.*
affable, a. *hegar, cüf.*
affair, n. *tra,* neuter, pl. *taclow, negys* m., abst. and pl. *-yow, cās,* m., *vȳaj,* m., pl. *-ys*; affairs, business, *an bȳs.*
affect, v. *chanjya.*
affectation, n. *maner fals, fekyl chēr.*
affected, *fals y vanerow.*
affecting, a. *trüethek, pytethüs.*
affection, n. *kerensa,* f., *natureth,* **sergh,* m.
affectionate, a. *kerensedhek, caradow, hegar,* †*serghak.*
affianced, a. *demedhys.*
affiliate, v. *ünya*: **-tion,** n. *-yans.*
affinity, n. *havalder,* m.; have a., *bōs ünwōs.*
affirm, v. *afȳa, afydhya, testa, dustünȳa*: **-ation,** n. *dustüny.*
affix, v. *takkya.*
afflict, v., *grevya, dughanhē·*: **-ed,** a. *dyscrassyes, ponvosek, cüthys.*

affliction, n., *galar* m., pl. *-ow, govyjyon, cüth, anken,* m.
affluence, n. *rychyth,* m.
affluent, a. *rych,* †*kevothak,*
afford, v. *gallos rȳ*; I can't a. that, *ny-allaf-vy rȳ kemmys ha henna.*
affray, n. *o·mlath,* m., *cās,* f.
affront, n. *despȳt, scorn,* m.: v. *despȳtya, scornya, arveth.*
afield, adv. *yn-mēs.*
afoot, adv. *war drōs, a drōs.*
aforementioned, aforesaid, a. *kens leverys, üs leverys kens, ragleverys.*
afraid, a. *ownek*; be a., *perthy, cafos* or *kemeres own*; I'm not a. of him, *nyns-üs own dhym anodho.*
afresh, adv. *arta, whath, a-noweth.*
aft, adv. *a-dhelergh, wor'tu delergh.*
after, adv. *warle·rgh, a-dhelergh*: prep. *wosa, warle·rgh*; a. him, *war y lergh*; one a. another, *yn rew*; a. all, *byteweth.*
aftergrass, m. *aswels,* m.
aftermath, n. *dastrēgh,* m.
afternoon, n., noon to nightfall, *dohaje·th,* m., *ewha,* m.; late a., *andro·w,* m; good a., *durdadha*!; this a. **androwyth, dhe androw.*
aftertaste, n. *asvlas,* m.
afterthought, n. *preder nessa, dastybyans,* m.
afterwards, adv. *wosa henna, wosa 'n ür-na, a'y wosa.*
again, adv. *arta, whath, a-noweth*: prefix to v. *as-, das-*; not a., *namoy·*, never a., *nefra namoy·*; a. and a., *menough, arta hag arta.*
against, prep. *erby·n*; a. him, *er y byn*; act a., *gül drēs* (*dyfen, mynnas, gorhemmyn*); urge a., *ynnȳa war*[2]; murmur a., *gül crothval war*[2]; guard a., *gwytha worth* or *rak.*
age, n. *ōs,* m., pl. *-ow, *oswyth,* m., pl. *-yow, aja,* m., pl. *-jys, *hender,* m.; years of a., *blōth,* m.; old a., *henys,* m.; great a., *hȳr ōs,* m.; of a., *cōth, devedhys dhe ōs*; of same a. as, **kevōs gans*; the Middle A.s, *an Osow Cres*; my a. is ten, *dēk blōth ōf*: v. *cothhē·.*
aged, a. *pür gōth, hȳr y ōs.*
agency, agent, n. *mayn,* m., pl. *-ys.*
agglutination, n. *mōl, glüs,* m.
aggravate, v. *gwethhē·*; vex, *grevya.*
aggregate, v. *cuntell*: n. *-yans,* m.
aggression, n. *omsettyans,* m.
aggrieve, v. *grevya.*
aghast, a. *dyegrys.*
agile, a. *scaf, bew, üskys.*
agility, n. *scafter, bewder, üskytter,* m.
agitate, v. *amüvya*; be agitated, **fromma.*
ago, adv., a week a., *nans-yu seythen*; a good while a., *nans-yu polta*; not long a., *nyns-üs nep-pell* or *napē·ll*; many years a., *nans-yu,* or *nans-üs tremenys, lȳes bledhen*; long a., *nans-yu pell, solabry·s.*
agog, a. *pür whansek, pür barys*: adv. *ha'y dhywscovarn a-lēs.*
agony, n. *angus, galarow,* m.; last a., *enewores,* m.
agree, v. *assentya*; be of one mind, *acordya, ünverhē·, bōs ünver,* ‡*agrȳa.*
agreeable, a., compliant, *plegadow*; pleasant, *tēk, whēk*; it is a. to me, *da yu genef.*
agreed, a. *ünver.*
agreement, n. *ambos,* m., pl. *-ow, aco·rd, acordyans, kessenyans,* m.; in a., *kescolon, ünver, ünverhē·s.*
agriculture, n. *gonesegeth,* f., *gonys tȳr,* m.
aground, adv. *war dȳr*; of ship, *gyllys war drethen, fast synsys.*
ague, n. *terthen,* f., pl. *-now, lēghow,* pl., *cleves sēson,* m.; fit of a., *crēn an lēghow.*
ah!, int. *aha*! *ha*!; dismay, *ōgh*!; disgust, *agh*!
ahead, adv. *ara·k* (*g*); go a., *mōs yn-rak.*
aid, n. *gweres, kynweres,* m., *socor,* m.: v. *gweres, socra*; a. and abet, *mentēna.*
ail, v. *grevya*; he is ailing, *clāf yu*; what ails (lit. betides) you? *pandr 'a-wher dhys?*
ailment, n. *cleves,* m., pl. *-ejow*: *gref,* m., pl. *-evys.*
aim, n. *towl*; his a. was bad, *ny-vedras ynkewar*: v. *tewlel,* at target, *medra*; a well-aimed blow, *bom pür-gewar desedhys.*
air, n. *ayr, ēth,* m.; appearance, *semlant,* m. pl. *-ns*: v. *rȳ ayr dhe*[2], *sēgha.*
airy, a. *ayrek.*
aisle, n. **casal* (*eglos*), m.
ajar, a. *hanter ygerys.*
akin, a. *ünwos, nēs.*
alabaster, n. *alabauster,* m.
alack! int. *harow*! *ellā·s*! *eghā·n*! *tru*! **a.-a-day!** *soweth an prȳs*!
alacrity, n. *bewder,* m.; with a., *gans mal, toth da*; with too much a., *rē a-poynt.*
alarm, n. *own,* m,; military, *galow yn arvow*: v. *gorra own yn, ownekhē·*; sound an a., *crȳa yn arvow*; be alarmed, *kemeres* or *perthy own*; alarming, *üthek.*
alas! int. *eghā·n*! *ellā·s*! *soweth*! *tru*! *ogh*! *welawo·*! *dhe voy pyta*!
alb, m. *cams,* f., pl. *-ow.*
alder, n. *gwernen,* f., col. *gwern*: **a. grove,** n. *gwernek,* f., pls. *-egy, -egow,*

ale, n. *cor'*, *cor'f*, *coref*, m.; strong a., *cor'gwella*; a. house, *tavern*, m., pl. *-ys*, **dewotty*, m., *-ow*.
alert, a. *dyfün*, *jolyf*, †*ugh-hewol*.
alien, n. *alyon*, m., pl. *-s*, **estren*, m. pl. *-yon*, f. *-es*, pl. *-ow*: a. *alyon*, **estrennek*.
alight, v. *dyeskynna*: a. *gans tān*, *ow-lesky*; of candle, etc., *ow-colowy*, *gans golow*.
alike, a. *haval*, *kehaval*, *hevelep*: adv. *kefrȳ·s*, *kekefrȳ·s*, *kepa·r*.
alive, a. *bew*, *yn-few*, *quyk*; all a. and kicking, *pür vew*.
all, a. *oll*, *pup*, *pup . . . -oll*: n. *pup*, *pup-oll*, *myns*: adv. *oll*; a. those who, *myns* or *sül a-*; a. that is, *oll myns üs*; *kekemmȳ·s üs*; let a. hearken! *gcslowens pup*!; a. the world, *oll an bȳs*; on a. sides, *a bup tu*; a. broken, *squardyes-oll*; a. alone, *y honen-oll*; come here, a., *deugh omma warba·rth*; I don't mind at a., *ny-synsaf poynt*; (none) at a., *-vyth*, *-vytholl*,*-y'n bȳs*; I don't know at a., *ny-wōn vyth*; I have no doubt at a. that it is, *ny-dhowtyaf tra y'n bȳs y-fo*; I should not fear . . ., no not at a., *ny-dhowtsen . . .*, *na-wrüssen nēs*; nothing at a., *tra-vytholl*; it was not so at a., *nyns-o man*; I did not hear, see, sleep, at a., *ny-glewys*, *welys*, *cuskys banna*; before you a., *a wēl oll dheugh*; to a. my power, *oll dhe'm gallos*; he a. but fell, *namna godhas*; a. three of them, *aga thrȳ*; is that a.? *a nyns-üs kēn?*
allay, v. *lehē·*, *sewajya*, *coselhē·*.
allegation, n. *cuhüdhans*, m.
allege, v. *cuhüdha*, *derȳvas*.
allegiance, n. *lēlder*, m.
alleviate, v. *ēsya*, *gül bōs scaffa*.
alley, n. *scochforth*, f., pl. *-rdhow*; blind a., *hens dall*.
All Hallows, n. *dē-Halan Gwāf*; A. H. Eve, *Gōl Calan Gwāf*.
alliance, n. **ünyans*, **kefrȳsyans*, m.
allot, v. *ranna*, *kevranna*, *o·rdena* (*ordna*).
allotment, n. *ran*, f., pl. *-now*; a. garden, *ran a lowarth kemyn*, *kevran lowarth*.
allow, v. *gasa*, *rȳ cümyas* or *spās a*[2], *godhaf*, *godhevel*, *lavasos*, *alowa*; admit, *avowa*.
allowance, n. *gront*, *godhevyans*, *alowans*, m.
alloy, n. *kemysk*, m.
all-powerful, a. *ollgallosek*, *lüngallosek*.
All Saints' Day, n. *dē-Halan Gwāf*.
All Souls' Day, n. *dēth an Enevow*.
allude to, v. *campolla*; with reverence or honour, *kywhethla*.
allure, v. *dynya*, *hüda*.
allurement, n. *hüs*, *tenvos*, m.
ally, v. *ünya*: n. **kefrysyas*, m., pl. *-ysy*, *confortyer*, m., pl. *-yoryon*.
almighty, a. *ollgallosek*, †*kevothak*.
almond, n. **alamand*, m., pl. *-ys*; a. tree, *gwedhen alamandys*.
almoner, n. *alüsenor*, m. pl. *-yon*.
almonry, n. *alüsenva*, f.
almost, adv., before v., *namna*[2](*g*), before noun, *ogas ha*, before a. or adv., *ogas*.
alms, n. *alüsen*, f., pl., *-ow*, *-sonow*; a. house, *alüsenjy*, m.
aloes, n. *alōes*, m.
aloft, adv., overhead, *a-wartha*, *a-ughon*, *a-van*, *y'n ebren*, upward, *yn-ban*.
alone, a. and adv. *y-honen*; save thee a., *saw ünsel ty*.
along, adv. and prep. *a-hēs*, *ryp*; all a., *hēs ha hēs*; come a.! *düs* or *dün yn -rak*!*dün alemma*! run a., *kē dhe gerdhes*.
alongside, adv. *ryp tenewan*; come a.! *düs* or *deugh rybon*!
aloof, adv. *a-denewan*, *yn-hans* or *yn-hons*.
aloud, adv. *ughel*.
alphabet, n. **abecedary*, m.
already, adv. *solabrȳ·s*; it was a. night, *nans-o-hy nōs*; it is a. done, *gwrēs yu y'n ür-ma defrȳ·*.
also, adv. *ynwe·th*, *kefrȳ·s*, *kekefrȳ·s*, *magata·*, *yn-ta*, *drēs henna* or *hemma*.
altar, n. *alter*, f. pl. *-yow*.
alter, v. *chanjya*, *trēlya*, *dyheveleby*, *dyfeleby*, *varya*; deface, *dyfacya*.
alteration, n. *chanjyans*, *varyans*, *chanj*, m. -pl. *-ys*.
alternate, v. *dōs an ȳl wosa y gȳla*, *gül pup war y dorn*: a. *an ȳl warle·rgh y gȳla*.
alternately, adv. *pup ȳl tro*, *kens an ȳl ha wosa henna y gȳla*.
alternative, n. *dewys yntra deu*.
although, conj. *kyn*[5](*th*), with *na*[2](*g*) in negative, *awo·s*, with inf.
altitude, n. *ughelder*, m.
alto, n. *conternot*, m.
altogether, adv. *yn-tȳen*, *a-hēs*, *warba·rth*,
always, adv. *pupprȳs*, *pup ür-oll*, *pupteth-oll*, *prest*, *jammes*, *yn y dhedhyow*, or *vewnans*, or *ōs*; a. hitherto, *a'y üs*, or *ōs*; ever, *byth*.
amalgamate, v. *junnya dhe onen*, *ünya*; of substances, *kemysky*: **-ed,** a. *yn-kemyskys*.
amalgamation, n. *ünyans*, *kemyskys*, m.
amass, v. *cuntell warbarth*.
amateur, n. *carer*, m., pl. *-roryon*, f. *-rores*, pl. *-ow*.

amaze, v. *sawthanas, gorra marth yn*: **-ed,** *marth ganso.*
amazement, n. *sawthan, marth,* m.
amazing, a. *marthys, barthüsek*: **-ly,** adv. *marthys.*
ambassador, n. *cannas, *lyscannas,* f., pl. *-ow.*
ambiguous, a. *nag-yu dyblans.*
ambition, n. *whans a sevel y'n bӯs, mynnas omavonsya, *gorvyn.*
ambitious, a. *ow-medra ughel.*
ambry, n., cupboard, *a·mary,* m., pl. *-s.*
ambulance, n. *car clavjy*; military, *clavjy bresel, car tüs vrew.*
ambush, v. *contrewaytya*: n. *-yans, bras,* m.
ameliorate, v. *gwellhē·.*
amen, int. *amen, ‡yndella re-bo.*
amenable, a. *gostyth, plegadow.*
amenity, n. *whekter,* m.
amend, v. *gwellhē·, amendya, omamendya ewna*: **-ment,** n. *amendyans,* m.
amends, n. *amendys*; make a., *gül restoryta dhe²*; *gül . . . yn amendys.*
amiability, n. *caradewder, cüfter,* m.
amiable, a. *cüf caradow, hegar.*
amice, n. †*scodhlyen,* m., pl. *-now.*
amid(st), prep. *yn-mysk, yn ewn-grēs a².*
amiss, adv. *yn-cam, bad.*
ammunition, n. *dafar lathva,* m.
among(st), prep. *yn-mysk, yntra,* or before vowel *ynter*; a. them, *y'ga mysk, yntredha, yn aga herwyth,* or *nyver.*
amount, n. *sum, myns,* m. **amo·nt,* m. pl. *-ys*: v. *amontya*; a large a., *mür,* small a., *nebes.*
amphitheatre, n. *plēn an gwary.*
ample, a. *efan, ledan, lowr, lün*; a. quantity, *‡tomals.*
amplify, v. *lēsa, moyhē·.*
amply, adv. *lowr, efan.*
amputate, v. *trēghy mēs.*
amputation, n. *troghva,* f.
amuse, v. *dydhana, hüthhē·*; a. oneself, *omdhydhana.*
amusement, n. *solas,* m.
amusing, a. *dydhan.*
an, indef. art., as meaning "a certain," *ün,* but usually not translated.
analyse, v. *dygemysky.*
analysis, n. *dygemysk,* m., pl. *-scow.*
analyst, n. *dygemysker,* m., pl. *-scoryon.*
anarchy, n. *dyrewl, fowt rewl,* m.
anatomy, n. *skӯans an corf,* m.
ancestor, n. *hendas,* m., pl. *-ow, hengok,* †*dӯhok,* m., pl. *-ogyon*; our a.s, *agan tasow.*
ancestress, n. *henvam,* f., pl. *-mow.*
ancestry, n. *lynyeth,* f., *lynaja,* m.
anchor, n. *ancar,* m., pl *-corow*: v. *tewlel ancār, *ancory*; lie at a., *bōs* or *powes war ancar*; weigh a., *drehevel an ancar.*
anchorage, n. *pol,* m., *lyn,* f., *rōda,* m. pl. *-dys.*
anchorite, n. *ancar,* m., pl. *-coryon, hermyt,* m., pl. *-ys.*
anchovy, n. **ganow-cam,* m., pl. *-as.*
ancient, a. *cōth,* as prefix, etc., *hēn*; old folk, *tüs cōth,* elders, *tüs hēn.*
and, conj. *ha(g)*; four a. twenty, *peswar warn ügans*; a. so, *ytho·, rag henna.*
anecdote, n. *whethel ber.*
anele, v. *untya.*
anemone, n. *blejen gwyns,* f.; sea-a., *penvagas,* m.
anew, adv. *arta, a- noweth, whath.*
angel, n. *ēl,* m., pl. *eleth,* f. *eles,* pl. *-ow,* dim. *elyk,* m., pl. *-elethygow.*
angelic, a. *kepa·r hag ēl*; the a. choir, *cür an eleth.*
anger, n. *sōr,* m.: v. *angra, serry*; to appease a., *dyserry.*
angle, n. *elyn,* f., *corn,* m.: v. *pyskessa gans gwelen,* inf. only.
angler, n. *pyscajor,* m., pl. *-yon.*
angry, a. *serrys*; to be a., *serry*; I'm a. with him, *yma· sōr dhym orto*; to cease to be a., *dyserry.*
anguish, n. *angus, anger, anken,* m., *glōs,* f.
angular, a. *pedrak, cornak, kernek, elynek.*
animal, n. *mӯl,* m., pl. *-as, eneval,* m., pl. *-les, lon,* m., pls. *-now, lothnow.*
animate, v. *bewhe·, gorra bewnans yn.*
animated, a., lively, *bew*; made alive, *bewhēs·.*
animation, n. *bewder.*
animosity, n. *cās, atty,* m., *myken,* f.
ankle, n. *üfern,* pl. *-yow,* d. *deu-üfern.*
annex, v. *ünya, kemeres ave·l perghenek*: n. *chӯ a-long dhe onen brassa.*
annihilate, v. *dyswül, drӯ dhe dravyth.*
annihilation, n. *dyswrӯans,* m.
anniversary, n. *dēth* or *gōl pen blōth.*
announce, v. *derӯvas, nōtya.*
announcement, n. *nōtyans, deryvadow,* m.
annoy, v. *serry, annӯa, angra, vexya, despӯtya.*
annoyance, n. *sōr, annӯans,* m.
annual, a. *pup bledhen-oll, *bledhennek.*

annuity, n. *pega·ns,* or *gront, bledhen*; from investment, *rent,* m. pl. *-ys.*
annul, v. *defendya.*
Annunciation, n. *Gōl Marȳa mȳs-Mērth.*
anoint, v. *untya, üra, ylȳa, sawya, *olewy,* ‡*anoyntya.*
anointing, n. *untyans, ungys,* m.
anomalous, a. *dygompes.*
anomaly, n. *ancothvos, dygomposter,* m.
anon, adv. *wharē·, dyson.*
anonymous, a. *dyhanow, hep hanow.*
another, a. *aral, moy,* before n., *kēn*; one after a., *yn ün rew*; one a., *an ȳl y gȳla*; a. time, *arta*: pron. *aral,* pl. *tüs erel, kēn rē.*
answer, v. *gortheby*: n. *gorthyp,* m., pl. *-thebow.*
answerable, to be a., v. *omgemeres* or *mōs rak.*
ant, n. *muryonen,* f., pl. *muryon*; a. hill, *crük muryon,* m., *muryonek,* f.
antagonism, n. *strȳf, envy,* m.
antagonist, n. *strȳfor,* m. pl. *-yon, escar,* m., pl. *yskerens, envy,* m. and pl.
antagonize, v. *sordya strȳf, stryvya erby·n.*
antecedent, a. *kens.*
antediluvian, a. *kens es dȳal Noy, cōth drēs ēghen.*
antelope, n. **gavrewyk,* f., pl. *-ygas.*
anthem, n. **antem,* m. pl. *-ys, *antempna,* m., pl. *-nys.*
antic, n. *prat,* m., pl. *-tys*; grotesque figure, *boban,* m., pl. *-ys.*
antichrist, n. *antecrȳst,* m.
anticipate, v. *bōs, gül, gweles,* or *gwaytya kens.*
anticipation, n. *gwaytyans, *ragvlas,* m.
antipathy, n. *cās,* m.
antiquarian, a. *a'n osow kens.*
antiquary, n. *carer,* or *studhyer, an taclow pür gōth.* ‡*antyquary,* m., pl. *-ow.*
antiquated, a. *gyllys rē-gōth, mēs a'n gȳs, pür gōth.*
antique, a. *pür gōth*: n. *tra gōth,* neut., pl. *taclow cōth.*
antiquity, n. **hensys,* f., *hender,* m., **hendra,* neut., pl. *hendaclow,* ‡*cothenep, *antyquyta,* m.
antler, n. *corn carow,* m., pl. *kern kervys.*
anus, n. *gwen,* m., **rever,* m., pl. *-vrow.*
anvil, n. *anwan,* f., pl. *-wonow.*
anxiety, n. *preder,* m., pl. *-ow, fyenasow,* abst. pl.
anxious, a. *gyllys yn prederow, prederüs*; he became a., *prederow a-n-kemeras*; if you are a. about him, *anodho mar 'th-üs preder*; I am very a., *mür yu ow fyenasow.*
any, a. *nep,* with neg. or *hep, bȳth, -vȳth, -vytholl, y'n bȳs*; a. man, *nep dēn, dēn-vyth, denvyth*; (not) a. more, *byth moy, namoy·, nēs, bytteth*; a. sort, *ēghen*; (not) a. other, *nahē·n*; (not) a. length of time, *nep-pell*: pron., a. who may be, *nep* or *sül a-vo*; a. one of us, *ahanan-ny vyth-onen.*
anybody, n., pron. *nep dēn, nep onen,* m., with neg., *denvyth.*
anyhow, adv., conj., *yn nep cās,* or *forth,* or *maner,* with neg., *cammen-vyth*; all a., *dyrewl.*
anyone, pron., n., *nep dēn, nep onen,* with neg., *denvyth, den y'n bȳs.*
anything, pron., n., *neppyth,* m., *nep-tra, ēghen,* f.; with neg., *travyth, man*; of seeing, hearing, etc., *banna.*
anywhere, adv. *nep lē, yn lē-vyth, nep part, nep plās, nep pow, nep tu*; a. at all, *yn gwēl nag yn prās*; a. you like, *yn lē may fynny.*
apart, adv., aside, *a'n ȳl tu, a-denewan*; asunder, *a-lēs, an ȳl dyworth y gȳla*; yonder, *yn-hans (hons)*; set a., sacred, a. *hynwys*; isolated, *dyberthys.*
apartment, n. *rōm,* m. pl. *-ys, *ranjy,* m., pl. *-ow,* †*stevel,* f., pl. *-yow.*
apathetic, a. *dyfrēth, syger, hep whans*; he is a., *travyth ny-n-dür.*
apathy, n. *fowt whans, dyfrethter, sygerneth,* m.
ape, n. *appa,* m., pl. *-pys, sym,* m., pl. *-as*: v. *gül warlergh aral.*
aperient, n. *medhy·gȳeth ygery,* f.
aperture, n. *toll,* m., pl. *tell.*
apiece, adv., let them take an apple a., *kemerens pup y aval*; they cost 1d. a., *y-costyens pup ün dynar.*
apologise, v. *dyharas, omascusya.*
apology, n. *dyharas, ascusasyon,* m.
apoplexy, n. **towl gōs,* m.
apostate, n. *negedhys,* m., pl. *-yjyon.*
apostatize, v. *trēlya fȳth, nagha fay.*
apostle, n. *abostol,* m., pl. *abestely,* col. *abesteleth.*
apostolic, a. *abostolek.*
apothecary, n. **apo·tecary,* m., pl. *-s.*
appalling, a. *üthek.*
apparatus, n. *darbar, dafar, jyn,* m.
apparel, n. *dyllas, aparell,* m.
apparent, a. *hewel*; it is a., *yth-omdhysqua.*
apparently, adv. *del hevel, yn-hevelep, del yllyr y weles.*

apparition, n. *tarosvan*, m., pl. *-now*, *omdhysquedhyans*, m. pl. *-ow*, **gwelesygeth*, f.

appeal, n. *galow*, *pysadow*: v. *pysy*, *gelwel* (*orth*).

appear, v., show oneself, *omdhysquedhes*, *dōs ha bōs gwelys*, *dysquedhes*; seem, *omwül*, *hevelly*.

appearance, n. *semlant*, *fysmant*, m., pl. *-ns*, *tremyn*, m., *lyw*, m., *pl. -yow*, *mȳr*, *fās*, *favour*, m.; sight, *vu*, m.

appease, v. *dyserry*, *hebaskhē·*, be appeased, *dyserry*.

appetite, n. *ewl* (*awel*), f., *ewl bōs*, or *dhe vōs*, *whans bōs*, or *dybry*.

applaud, v. *gormel*.

applause, n. *gormola*, m.

apple, n. *aval*, pl. *-low*, m.; a. tree, *avallen*, pl. *-now*, col. *avalwyth*, *gwedhen avallow*, col. *gwȳth avallow*, f.; crab a. tree, *avallen woth* or *wyls*; a. of eye, *bew an lagas*; a. orchard, *avallon*, m., *aval-lan*, f., *avalek*, f., pl. *-egy*; to gather a.s, *avallowa*, inf. only.

appliance, n. *dafar*, *jyn*, m., pl. *-ys*.

applicable, a. *a-dheseth*, *gwyw*, *ewn*.

applicant, n. *govynner*, pl. *-noryon*, *pysador*, m., pl. *-yon*.

application, n. *govenek*, m., pl. and abst. *-nygyon*, *pysadow*, m.; diligence, *dywysykter*, m.

apply, v., put, *gorra*; a. for, *govyn*; a. oneself, *omrȳ*.

appoint, v. *appoyntya*, *o·rdena*; furnish, *darbary*, *tacla*.

appointment, n. *appoyntyans*, m.; make an a., *settya dēth*, or *ür*, or *prȳs*, or *lē*; keep an a., *kewera*, *gwytha ambos dōs*, or *mōs*; miss an a., *fyllel bōs dhe'n lē*, *terry ambos*.

apportion, v. *ranna*, *dyberth dhe bup y ran*.

appreciate, v. *synsy*, *ewnvrüsy*; be a.d by, *bōs drüth dhe*^{2}.

appreciation, n. *synsyans*, m., *ewnvrüs*, f.

apprehend, v. *synsy*, *sēsya*, *settya dalghen yn*; understand, *convedhes*.

apprehension, n. *own*, m.; understanding, *convedhes*.

apprehensive, a. *ownek*, *dowt dhodho*.

apprentice, n. *creftwas*, pl. *-wesyon*, *maw*, pl. *coscar*, *servyas*, pl. *-yjy*, **prentys*, m., pl. *-ys*.

apprenticeship, n. *servys*, **prentshyp*, m.

approach, v. *nessa*, *dōs nēs* or *ogas dhe*^{2}: n. *dōs*, *mōs*, *forth bys yn chȳ*.

approbation, n. *comendyans*, m.

appropriate, v. **perghenegy*, *kemeres*: a. *gwyw*, *ewn*.

approval, n. *comendyans*, m.

approve, v. *synsy bōs da*, *comendya*.

approximate, v. *dōs ogas*, *drȳ nēs*: a. *pür ogas*, *ogas lowr*, *lowr ogas*.

approximately, adv. *ogas ha*,; a. 100, *nep cans*.

apricot, n. **brykethen*, f., col. *bryketh*.

April, n. *Ebrel*, *mȳs-E.*, m.

apron, n. *apern*, m., pl. *-pronyow*; fisherman's a., *raglen*, f., pl. *-now*.

apt, a. *parys*, *compes*.

aptitude, n. *gwywder*, *composter* m.

aquarium, n. *pusketty*, m.

aqueduct, n. *dowrbons*, m., pl. *-ow*; channel, *odyt*, m., pl. *-ys*.

Arabia, n. *Araby*, f.; arabic numerals, **nyverow awgrym*.

arable, a. *aradow*.

arbitrary, a. *herwyth sȳans*, *ow-sewya y vōth*.

arbitrate, v. *brüsy* (*yntra deu barty*).

arbitration, n. *mayn*, *brüs drē vayn*.

arbitrator, n. *mayn*, m.

arbour, n. *scovva*, *delyowek*, f., *dēljy*, m.

arc, arch, n. *gwarak*, pl. *-regow*, *cam*, m., pl. *-mow*: v., arch, *camma*, *plegya*.

archaic, a. *a'n osow kensa*.

archangel, n. *arghēl*, m., pl. *-eleth*.

archbishop, n. *arghepscop*, m., pl. *-obow*.

archdeacon, n. †*arghdyagon*, m., pl. *-as*.

archdruid, n. *arghdrewyth*, m., pl. *-ydhyon*.

arched, a. *cammys*.

archer, n. *sethor*, *gwaregor*, m., pl. *-yon*, *archer*, m. pl. *-s*.

archipelago, n. **enesek*, f. pls. *-egy*, *-egow*, **enysvor*, m., pl. *-ow*.

architect, n. †*gwȳthor chȳ*, m., pl. *-yon c.*

architecture, n. *creft drehevyans*.

archives, n. **cofscryvow*. pl.; place, **cofscryfva*, f.

Arctic, a. *pen a-wartha an norvȳ·s*.

ardent, n. *tom*, *gwrēsek*, *gans tān y golon*.

ardour, n. *gwrēs*, f., *tān*, m.

arduous, a. *cales*, *tyn*.

area, n. *lür*, *keheseth*, *efander*, m.

arena, n. *plēn o·mlath*, m.

argue, v. *dysputya*, *stryvya*, *dathla*, *argya*; a. vehemently, *tēry*.

argument, n. *rēson*, m. pl. *-s*, *argument*, m., pl. *-ns*, *dathel*, f., pl. *-thlow*; dispute. *stryvyans*.

arid, a. *sēgh*, *cras*.

aridity, n. *sēghter*, *sēghor*, *craster*, m.

arise, v. *sevel, sordya, omdhrehevel*; ascend, *yskynna*; arise! *yn-sol!*
aristocracy, n. *gwelhevyn*, m. and col., **pensevygeth*, f., *tüs nobyl*, f., *bryntynyon*, pl., *an gōs ughel.*
aristocrat, n. *arluth*, pl. *-lydhy, pensevyk*, pl. *-ygyon, bryntyn*, pl. *-yon, dēn nobyl*, m., pl. *tüs n.*
aristocratic, a. *nobyl, bryntyn, genys an gōs ughel.*
arithmetic, n. **arsmetryk*, m., *skȳans nyverow.*
ark, n. *argh*, f., pl. *-ow*; Noah's A., *gorhel Noy*, m.
arm, n., of body, *brēgh*, f., pl. *-ow*, d. *dywvrēgh*; carried under his a., *kemerys yn-dan y gasal*; weapon, *arf*, f., pl. *-rvow*; men-at-arms, *tüs arvow*; to arms! *yn arvow! ens pup*, or *pup-oll tennens, dh'y arvow!*: v. *arva.*
armchair, n. **cadar vrēghek*, f., pl. *-deryow brēghek.*
armed, a., having arms, *brēghek*; having weapons, *ervys, *arvek*; a. cap a pie, *ervys a'n treys bys y'n dywen, fȳn ervys.*
armful, n. **brēghas*, f., pl. *-esow, lün y vrēgh.*
armless, a. *dyvrēgh.*
armour, n. *hernes, gwysk horn*, m., *arvow*, pl.; plate a., *plāt*, m.; put on a., *hernessya*, clad in a., *hornwyskys.*
armpit, n. *casal*, f., pl. *-selyow*, d. *dywgasal.*
army, n. *lu*, pl. *-yow, ōst*, pl. *-ys, †lūyth*, m., pl. *-ydhow.*
around, adv. *a-dro, a-dro dhe²*, *a-dre-dro·*, *a-dhe-dro·*, *yn-kerghyn*: prep. *a-dro-dhe²*; of persons, *yn-kerghyn*; a. them, *y'ga herghyn*; put it a. you, *kemer e y'th kerghyn.*
arouse, v. *dyfüna, sordya, müvya*; a. him, *gwra gül dhodho sevel.*
arrange, v. *araya, desedha, o·rdena, ewna, governya*; a. in line, *rēsa*; a. a time or place, *settya*; a. one's hair, *restry.*
arrangement, n. *aray·*, m., *ambos*, f., *towl*, m., *cusül*, f.; to make a verbal a., *omgusülya.*
arrant, a. *pür, trüs, hep nam.*
arras, n. *gōl*, m. or f., pl. *-yow.*
array, n. *dyllas*, pl. *-ow, gwyscas*, m., pl. *-cosow*: v. *gwysca, tacla,*
arrears, in a., adv. *hell, a-dhelergh.*
arrest, v. *synsy, dalghenna* or *settya dalghen yn, sēsya*: n. *dalghen, sēsyans*, m.; writ of a. *capyas*, m.
arrival, n. *devedhyans*, m., *dōs, devō·s, devones*; there is great joy at his a., *mür joy üs er y byn.*
arrive, v. *dōs, devō·s, devones*; it has arrived, *düfa dhe-drē.*
arrogance, n. *gōth*, m.
arrogant, a. *hautyn, gothys.*
arrow, n. *sēth*, f., pl. *-ow*, dim. *sethen*, f., pl. *-now.*
arrowhead, n. *pȳl*, m., pl. *-ys.*
arsenal, n. *arvjy*, m., pl. *-ow, gwythva arvow*, f.
art, n. *creft*, f., pl. *-ow, art*, m., pl. *-ys, sotelneth*, m.
artery, n. *gōth vrās*, f., pl. *gwythy brās.*
artful, a. *fēl, connek, sotel, ynjyn.*
artfulness, n. *felder, connyng, sotelneth*, m.
artichoke, n. *ascallen dybry*, f., col. *ascal d.*
article, n., writing, *scryf*, m., pl. *-yvow*; object, *pyth*, m., pl. *-ow, tra* neut., pl. *taclow*; writing or part of speech, **artykyl*, m., pl. *-yclys*: v. *kelmy yn-dan ambos.*
articulation, n. *kevals*, m., pl. *-yow, mel*, m., pl. *-low.*
artifice, n. *sotelneth, jyn*, m., pl. *-nys*; to use a., *sotla.*
artificial, a. *gwrēs gans dornow, fals.*
artisan, n. *sēr*, m., pl. *-y, creftor*, m., pl. *-yon.*
artist, n. **lymner*, m., pl. *-s.*
artistic, a. *skȳansek yn tekter.*
artless, a. *hep gȳl*; she is an a. child, *flogh yu, ha gensy sōth.*
arum, n., wild, *scaf a'y lygyon*, m.
as, adv., with v., *del²*, *kepa·r del²*; with n. or pron., *ave·l*; with a. or adv., *mar²*, *maga⁵*; a. thou lovest me, *del y-m-kyrry*; a. he grew, so did the coat, *kepa·r ef del devys, yndella an bows a-wrē*; a. white a. snow, *mar wyn*, or *maga whyn, ave·l an ērgh*; as well a. I can, *gwella gallaf*; a. if he were kind, *kepa·r ha pan vē hegar*; just a., with v., *kepa·r y'n bȳs del²*; a. soon a., *kettel²*; a. quick a., *kettoth ha*; a. many, a. much, *kemmy·s, myns, sül*: conj. *pan²*, *aba·n²*; a. I was going, *ha my ow-mōs*; a. he is ill, I must take his place, *aba·n yu clāf, rēs yu dhym kemeres y lē*: prep. *yn, ave·l*; a. a gift, *yn ro*; a. very God, *yn sür Dhew.*
ascend, v. *yskynna, mōs yn-ban, ascendya.*
ascendancy, n. *maystry*, m.
ascension, n. *ascensyon*, m.
Ascension Day, n. *dē-Yow Bask.*
ascent, n. *yskynnans*, m.; way up, *forth yskynna*; slope, *leder*, f.

ascertain, v., *desmygy, gothvos dhe-wȳr.*
ascribe, v. *rȳ, *ascryfa*; I cannot a. to it more than is meet, *ny-allaf-vy rȳ dhodho moy es del gothvya dhym.*
ash, n. *lüsewen,* f., col. *lüsow*; A. Wednesday, *dē-Mergher Lüsow*; wood-a., lye, **lysyow,* m.; a. heap, *lüsewek,* f., pls. *-egy, -egow.*
ash-tree, n. *onnen,* f., col. *on, enwedhen,* f., col. *enwyth*; a. grove, *onnek,* f. pls. *-egy, -egow.*
ashamed, a. *methek, meth ganso*; don't be a., *byth na-borth,* or *na-gemer, meth*; to be a. of, *dyflasa, bōs sclandrys a²*, *bōs methek rak,* or *a²*; to be a., *perthy meth.*
ashore, adv. *yn tyreth, yn tȳr*; to come a. *tȳra, londya,* to run a., *resek war an als, mōs war drēth.*
ashy, a. *lüsewek, kepa·r ha lüsow.*
aside, adv. *a-denewan, a'n ȳl tu, yn-hans.*
ask, v. *govyn*; seek, *whylas*; require, *gorholy*; call for, *dervyn.*
askance, askew, adv. *yn-cam.*
asking, n. *gorholeth, govynnadow,* m.
asleep, adv. *yn cusk*: a. *ow-cusca.*
aspect, n. *tremyn, lyw, semlant, chēr, favour,* m.
aspen, n. *†ēthlen,* f., col., *ēthel.*
aspersion, n. *cabel,* m.; cast a.s, *cably, sclandra.*
aspirate, v. *anella, gül dhe'n lyther "h" bos clewys*: n. *sōn "h."*
aspiration, n. *ten anal,* m., *whans,* m., pl. *-ow*
aspire, v. *whylas, bōs whansek a².*
aspiring, a. *whansek, ow-medra yn-ughel.*
ass, n. *asen,* m. and f., pl. *-as*; wild a., *†asen gwyls*; a. colt, *ebol asen, *asenyk.*
assail, v. *settya war², deghesy dhe².*
assailant, n. *omsettyer,* m., pl. *-yoryon.*
assassin, n. *moldrer,* m., pl. *-roryon, denledhyas,* m., pl. *-ysy.*
assassinate, v. *moldra, ladha drē draytury.*
assassination, n. **moldra,* m., *lathva yn-dan gēl,* f.
assault, v. *drokhandla, arveth, omsettya war²*: n. *omsettyans,* m., *shora,* m. pl. *-rys.*
assemble, v. *dōs warbarth, omguntell, kesomguntell.*
assembly, n. *cuntell, cuntelles, cuntellyans,* m. pl. *-ow, cuntellva,* f., *†kesva,* f.
assent, v. *assentya, bōs yn-assentys, bōs ünver, rȳ,* or *grontya, cümyas*: n. *assentyans,* m.
assert, v. *derȳvas, testa*; a. oneself, *gül maystry.*
assertion, n. *derȳvas, dustüny,* m.
assess, v. *settya myns a vona üs dhe bē*; *synsy prȳs.*
assessment, n. *toll üs settyes.*
assessor, n. *brüsyas tollow.*
assets, n. *pyth,* m.
assiduity, n. *dywysykter,* m.
assiduous, a. *dywysyk.*
assign, v. *o·rdena, appoyntya, gorra, settya.*
assignment, n. *gront.*
assist, v. *gweres, scōdhya.*
assistance, n. *gweres, kynweres,* m.
assistant, n. *gwereser, scōdhyer,* m. pl. *-yoryon*; workman's a., *darbarer,* m., pl. *-roryon.*
associate, v. *cowethya*: n. *coweth,* m., col. *-a.*
associated, a. *kevrennek (gans).*
association, n. *cowethas,* f., pl. *-ow.*
assort, v. **assortya, ranna herwyth kynda.*
assorted, a. *gorrys y'ga sortow, rynnys dh'aga hynda, lȳes ēghen.*
assuage, v. *sewajya, ēsya, hebaskhē·, lēhē·.*
assume, v. *desevos, tyby*; take on oneself, *omgemeres.*
assumption, n. *tybyans, ref, omgemeryans,* m.; the A., *Gōl Marȳa Hanter Est.*
assurance, n. **sürhēans*; confidence, *trest,* m., *fȳth,* f.
assure, v. *afydhya, sürhē·, fasthē·*; I a. you, *dhymmo crȳs*; rest assured, *seveugh yn agas cryjyans.*
assuredly, adv. *yn-tyogel, yn-sür.*
aster, n. **blejen steren,* f., pl. *blejyow stēr.*
asterisk, n. *sterennyk,* f., pl. *-ygow, -nowygow.*
astern, adv., in ship, *wor'tu delergh*; behind ship, *warle·rgh, a-dhelergh,* backwards, *war-dhelergh.*
asthma, n. *ber-anal,* m.
asthmatic, a. *ber y anal.*
astonish, v. *sawthanas*; I am astonished at, *yma mür a varth brās dhym a²*; you a. me, *ahanas marth yu genef,* or *a-m-büs.*
astonishing, a. *marthys, reveth.*
astonishingly, adv. *marthys.*
astonishment, n. *marth brās,* m., *sawthan,* m.
astound, v. *sawthanas*; astounded, *dyegrys, sawthenys glan.*
astounding, a. *reveth.*
astray, adv. *yn sawthan, yn, war,* or *dhe, stray*; gone a., *gyllys mēs a'y forth.*
astride, adv. *ow-marghogeth, *gaulak, y arrow a-lēs.*

astronomer, n. *astronymer,* m., pl. *-s.*
astronomical, a. **astronomek, a'n stēr.*
astronomy, n. **astronomy, scȳens an stēr.*
astringent, a. *trenk.*
astute, a. *fēl, connek, fȳn.*
asunder, adv. *yntra deu, yntra dyw ran.*
asylum, n., refuge, *menēghy, teghyjy, meneghyjy,* m., pl. *-ow*; mental a., *foljy,* m., pl. *-ow.*
at, prep. *orth, dhe²,* *yn, a²*; a. all, with neg., *-vyth, -vytholl, nagonen, y'n bȳs, ünwyth, tebel na mās, cammen, man, hep nam*; a. once, *desempys, a-dhesempys, scon, yn-scon*; a. home, *yn-chȳ.*
atheism, n. *dyscryjyans, nagh Dew.*
atheist, n. *dēn dydhew, dyscryjyk,* m., pl. *ygyon.*
atheistic, a. *dyscryjyk, dydhew, ow-nagha bōs Dew.*
athlete, n. *strȳfor yn gwaryow,* m., pl. *-yon y. g.*
athletic, a. *crēf y gorf, frẹ̄th a'y ysyly.*
athwart, adv., prep. *a-drüs, a-drüs dhe², a-drüs keyn*; a. and along, far and wide, *a-drüs hag a-hēs.*
atmosphere, n. *ayr, †ēth,* m., *ebren,* f.
atom, n. *elven,* f., pl. *-now, temmyk,* m., pls. *-ygow, tymmynygow.*
atone, v. *dewheles, amendya, gül amendys.*
atonement, n. *dewhelans* (*-yans*), *amendys,* m.; as an a., *yn dewhelans.*
atrocious, a. *üthek, hager, garow.*
atrocity, n., quality, *garowder, hakter,* m.; deed, *outray,* m., *hager-ober,* m., pl. *-ow.*
attach, v. *takkya, staga, kelmy*; a. oneself to, *glena orth, sergha.*
attached, a., fixed, *stak*; very fond, *†serghak*
attachment, n. *colm,* m., pl. *-ow, kevran,* f., pl. *-now, stagell,* f., pl. *-ow, sygen,* f., pl. *-now, syg,* f., pl. *-yon*; affection, *kerensa,* f., *sergh,* m.
attack, v. *settya war², arveth*: n. *omsettyans*; a. of illness, *shora,* m., pl. *-ys, cowas,* f., pl. *-wosow.*
attain, v. *hedhes, drehedhes, omdhrehevel, dhe², attaynya, dōs dhe², gwaynya*; he will a. his majority, *ef a-dhē ha bos dēn, devedhys vȳth dhe ōs.*
attainment, n. *drehedhyans,* m.; knowledge, *dyscans,* m.
attempt, v. *whylas, profya, assaya*: n. *assay, prōf, atte·nt,* m.
attend, v. *goslowes, rȳ scovarn dhe²*; wait on, *servya*; pay heed to, *attendya, gwaytya, omrȳ dhe²*; be present, *bōs ena,* or *omma,* or *y'n lē.*
attendance, n., service, *servys, gonys,* those present, *cuntelles,* m.
attendant, n. *servyas,* m., pl. *-ysy*: a. *owth-holya, yn y herwyth, ganso.*
attention, n. *attendyans* m.; to pay a., *gül vrȳ, nōtya, attendya.*
attentive, a. *owth-attendya, parys dhe avȳsya*; polite, *cortes.*
attenuate, v. *tanowhē·, lēhē·.*
attest, v. *testa* (*desta*), *dustü·nȳa.*
attestation, n. *dustüny,* m., pl. *-ow.*
attic, n. *tāl chȳ,* m., pl. *-yow treven, talyk,* pl. m., *-ygow.*
attire, n. *dyllas, gwysk,* m.: v. *gwysca.*
attitude, n. *maner omdhō·n,* or *sevel,* etc.; in a lying, or standing, a., *a'y wroweth, a'y saf.*
attorney, n. **attorny, dēn an lagha,* m.
attract, v. *dynya, tenna.*
attraction, n. *tenvos, ten, dynyans,* m.
attractive, a. *üs ow-tynya, whans y weles.*
attribute, v. **ascrȳfa, rȳ*: n. *tȳthy,* abst. and col.
auburn, a. **gellrüth.*
auction, n. **strȳfwerth,* f.: **-eer,** n. *strȳfwerther,* m., pl. *-thoryon.*
audacious, a. *harth, colonnek, bold*; to be a. *arveth.*
audacity, n. *bolder, colonnekter,* m.
audible, a. *heglew.*
audience, n. *cleworyon, goslowysy,* pl., *cuntelles,* m.
auger, n. *tardar,* m., pl. *terder.*
aught, n. *neptra.*
augment, v. *moghhē·.*
augur, n. *†colyok,* m., pl. *-yogyon.*
August, n. *Ēst, mȳs- Ēst,* m.
aunt, n. *modryp,* f., pl. *-rebeth.*
auspicious, a. *sowyn, †füsyk.*
austere, a. *garow, asper, tyn, sempel.*
austerity, n. *asperder, tynder,* m.
authentic, a. *gwȳr.*
authenticity, n. *lendury, gwȳrder, gwyryoneth,* m.
author, n. **auctour,* m., pl. *-ys, scryfer,* m., pl. *-foryon.*
authority, n. *gallos, *aucto·ryta, lecyans,* m.; to assume a. over, *kemeres gallos war²*; on the a. of, *herwyth.*
authorize, v. *rȳ gallos,* or *cümyas, dhe²,* or *a²*, *grontya lecyans* or *gront.*

autocrat, n. *türont,* m., pl. *-ns, myghte·rn a-rewl a'y honen.*

autocratic, a. *ow-rewlya a'y honen,* or *ave·l türont.*

autograph, n. *hanow scryfys, dornscryf an auctour, sӯn dorn.*

automatic, *a-ӯl gonys,* or *kerdhes, a'y honen,* or *drē jyn.*

Autumn, n. *Kynyaf,* m.; a. dwelling, *kynewas,* m.

avail, v. *amontya, tylly, avaylya*; it is of no a., *ny-amont, ny-dāl man.*

available, a. *a-yllyr y gafos.*

avarice, n. *pythneth, crynder,* m., **crefny,* f.

avaricious, a. *pӯth, crӯn, †craf, crefny.*

avaunt,! int. *avond!*

avenge, v. *dyala, venjya*; be a.d on, *tylly, kemeres, tewlel* or *gül dӯal war*^{2}.

avenger, n. **dyalor,* m., pl. *-yon.*

average, n. *an myns,* or *gallos,* etc., *mayn*: a. *ūsyes.*

averse, a. *contraryüs, dyflesys*; he is a. to, or from, *cās yu ganso, dh'y anvoth yu*; to be a., *trӯnya.*

aversion, n. *cās,* m.; that is his pet a., *ef a-gās henna drēs puptra.*

avert, v. *trēlya dhe-vēs.*

aviary, n. *ydhynjy,* m., pl. *-ow.*

avid, a. *pӯth.*

avidity, n. *pythneth,* m.

avoid, v. *goheles, avoydya.*

avoidance, n. *gohel,* m.

avoirdupois, n. * *averdepoy·s,* m.

avow, v. *avowa.*

await, v. *gortos, gwaytya.*

awake, v. *dyfüna*: a. *dyfün, a-dhyfüna, yn-tyfünys*; wide a., *†ugh-hewol.*

awakening, n. *dyfüna.*

award, v. *jujjya dhe*^{2}, *tylly, grontya, rӯ*: n. *pewas, weryson,* m., *brüs,* f.

aware, a. *wār*; be a. of, *bōs avӯsyes a*^{2}, *gothvos.*

away, adv., position, *a-vēs, a-drē*; motion, *dhe-vēs, yn-kerth, yn-kergh, ahanan,* from here, *alemma,* from there, *alenna,* a. from, *dywo·rth, a-dhywo·rth, mēs a*^{2}, *yn-mēs a*^{2}, *adar*; do a. with, *gorra dhe dravyth*; right a., *kens es hedhy, hep let, a-dhesempys.*

awe, n. *üth, agha,* m.; a. inspiring, *üthek, ow-corra own ynnon.*

awful, a. *üthek.*

awfully, adv. *üthek.*

awhile, adv. *pols,ün pols bӯghan.*

awkward, a. *cam* , *cledhek*; difficult, *cales.*

awkwardness, n. *cledhekter,* m.; embarrassment, *ancombrynsy, caletter,* m.

awl, n. *menowes,* m., pl. *-ow.*

awn, n. *col,* m., pl. *-ow.*

awning, n. *tylda,* m., pl. *-dys,* **howl-len,* f., pl. *-now.*

awry, adv. *yn-cam, yn-whӯüs.*

axe, n. *bōl,* f., pl. *-ow.*

axle, n. *ēghel,* f., pl. *-yow.*

azure, n., a. *glās ebren.*

B

babble, n. *clap,* m.: v. *clappya, clattra.*

baboon, n. *boban,* m., pl. *-ys.*

baby, n. *baby,* m. or f., pl. *-ow, flogh bӯghan,* m., pl. *flēghes b.*; b. talk, **mabyēth,* f.

babyhood, n. *flogholeth,* m.

babyish, a. *ave·l,* or *kepa·r ha, flogh.*

bachelor, n. *dēn dydhemeth,* m., pl. *tüs d., bacheler,* m., pl. *-s.*

back, n. *keyn,* m., pl. *-ow, trüm,* m., pl. *-yow*; reverse side, *kyl,* m., pls. *-yow, -yer*: v. *mōs war-dhelergh*; support, *confortya, scodhya, mentēna*: adv. *dhe-drē, trē, war-dhelergh, wor'tu delergh*: prefix. *das-, as-, at-,* e.g., *astevery,* to pour b., *attylly,* pay b., *daskemeres,* take b.

backbone, n. *ascorn,* m., or *mellow,* m. pl., *an keyn.*

back-door, n. *darras a-dhelergh,* m.

background, n. *pellder,* m., *parth a-dryf dhe'n remenant*; he keeps in the b., *ny-wra omherdhya yn-rak.*

backward, a. *hell, lent.*

backwards, adv. *war-dhelergh*; of fall etc., *war bol y gyl, dh'y gylben.*

bacon, n. *kӯk-mogh, bakken,* m.; b. fat, *†mehyn,* m.

bad, a. *drōk, tebel, gwan-, bad*; b. fellow, *sherewa,* m., pl. *-wys, drokwas, tebelwas,* m., pl. *-wesyon, drōk-pollat,* m., pl. *-ys*; b. lot, sort, etc., *tebel edhen,* f., pl. *t. ydhyn*; b. turn, *drōk-tro,* m.

badge, n. **arweth,* f., pl. *-edhyow.*

badger, n. *brogh,* m., pl. *-as.*

badly, adv. *yn-tebel, yn-trōk, bad.*

badness, n. *drokter, sherewneth, sherewynsy,* m.

baffle, v. *lettya, ancombra.*

bag, n. *sagh,* m., pl. *sēghyer*; hand-b., *sagh dorn*; post-b., travelling-b., **mayl,* m., pl. *-ys*; b.-pudding, *pot-gwyn,* m.

bag up, v. *sagha.*
baggage, n. *fardellow,* m. pl.
bagpipes, n. *pȳbow-sagh,* f. pl.
bah! interj. *tety-valy!*
bail, n., legal, *meugh,* m., pl. -*yow*; go b. for, *meughya*: v. *rȳ meugh*; b. boat, *desēgha.*
bailiff, n. *bayly,* m., pl. -*s.*
bait, n., food, *bōs,* m.; for fishing, cut small, *trustrum,* m.; strip, *skethen,* f., *lost,* m.; crumbled, *brows,* col.: v. *bōsa*; provoke, *pȳga, hyga.*
bake, v. *pobas,* **forna.*
baker, n. *peber,* m., pl. -*boryon.*
bakery, n. *chȳ-forn, chȳ-pobas,* †*popty,* m.
bake-stone, n. *mēn pobas,* m., pl. *meyn p.*
baking-pan, n. *padel horn,* f., pls. -*llow h.,* -*lly h.*
balance, n., scales, *mantol,* f., pl. -*yow*; poise, *antel,* f., *composter, kespōs, omborth,* m.: v. *mantolly, antel, omberthy, kesposa.*
bald, a. *mōl, blogh, dyvlew, pylys*; b. of brow, **talvōl*; make or go b., *bloghē·, mōlhē·*; b.-headed, *pen-mōl.*
baldness, n. *molder,* m.
bale, n. *pusorn,* m., pl. -*sernow*: v. *pusornas.*
balk, v., hinder, *lettya*; shirk, *goheles*: n. *plynken,* f., pl. -*now, trester,* m., pl. -*s.*
ball, n., sphere, *pēl,* f., pl. -*yow, pellen,* f., pl. -*now*; dance, *gwary-dōns,* m.: v., roll into b., *pellenna.*
balm, n. *tryakel,* m.; herb, *gwenynles,* col.
ban, n. *dyfennadow, dyfen,* m.: v. *dyfen, emskemünya, mylyga.*
band, n., metal, etc., *garlont,* f., pl. -*ow,* **kengel,* f., pl. -*glow, fünen,* f., pl. -*now, raf,* f., pl. -*fow*; of men, *parcel, nerth, bagas,* m., *rūth,* f., pl. -*ow*; of muscians, *menestrouthy,* m.
bandage, n. *lysten,* f., pl. -*now*: v. *mayla.*
bandit, n. *rafner,* m., pl. -*noryon.*
bandy, a. *cam y dhywar, gargam, bergam,* ‡*camgarrek*: v., b. words, *cows gerennow.*
bang, n. *bom,* m., pl. -*myn, bonk, cronk,* m., pl. -*ys, tarth,* pl. -*rdhow*; as interj. *crak!, squat!*; he broke it with a b., *ef a-n-torras crak*: v. *cronkya, squattya, dehesy*; make a noise, *dyllo trōs.*
banish, v. *pellhē·, dyvrōa,* **bansya.*
banishment, n. *dyvrōeth,* m.
bank, n., financial, *arghantty,* m.; slope, *bank,* m., pl. -*ncow, banken,* f., pl. -*now, tomen,* f., pl. -*now*; of river, *glan,* f., pl. -*now.*
banker, n. *arghanser,* m., pl. -*soryon.*
bankrupt, n. *marchont squattyes,* m., pl. -*ons s.*: a. *gyllys squat*; to become b., *fyllel pē.*
bankruptcy, *fallans,* m.
banner, n. *baner,* m., pl. -*ow,* **arweth,* f., pl. -*edhyow.*
banns, n. *bannys*; to read b., *bannya*; their b. are up, *bannys yns-y.*
banquet, n. *gōl,* m., pl. -*yow*; **fest,* f., pl. -*ow,* ‡*banket,* m., pl. -*tys*: v. *gōlya.*
banter, n. *gēs,* m.: v. *gēsya.*
bantling, n. *whegyn,* m., pl. -*now.*
baptism, n. *bysydhyans, bysyth,* m.
baptist, n. *bysydhyer,* m., pl. -*yoryon, baptyst,* m., pl. -*ys.*
baptize, v. *bysydhya.*
bar, n., rod, *pren,* m., pls. -*yer, prynner*; of door, legal, *bar,* m., pl. -*rys*; of gate, etc., *clethren,* f., pl. -*now,* col. *clether*: v. *prenna, barya.*
barb, n. *drēn,* m., pl. *dreyn*; **gorthfagh,* m., pl. -*ow.*
barbarity, n. *garowder,* m.
barbed, a. *dreynek.*
barber, n. *barver,* m., pl. -*voryon.*
barberry, n. **spernen velen,* f., col. *spern melen,* **kelyn Frynk,* col.
bard, n. *barth,* m., pl. *byrth, bardhes,* f., pl. -*ow*; meeting of b's., *gorseth,* f., pl. -*edhow.*
bardic, a. **bardhek*; b. lore, **bardhas,* f.; b. robe, **barthgōn*; b. hood, **barthcūgol.*
bare, a. *nōth, lom, mōl, pylys, yn-nōth*; half-b., *ternoth*; b. backed, **keynlom*: v. *lomhē·, pylya, nothhē·.*
barefaced, a., shameless, *dyveth, hep methvyth.*
barefoot, a., adv. *trosnoth, nōth y drōs, dyarghen.*
bare-headed, a. *pennoth, penlom, toplom.*
bare-legged, a. *fernoth.*
barely, adv. *scantlowr, scant.*
bareness, n. *lomder, mōlder,* m., *notha,* f.
bargain, n. *bargen,* m., pl. -*ys, chyffar,* m.; agreement, *ambos,* m., pl. -*ow*: v. *bargenya.*
bargainer, n. *gwycor,* m., pl. -*yon*; bad b., *gwan-wycor.*
bark, n., of tree, *rüsken,* f., col. *rüsk*; having b., *rüskek*; of dog, *harth,* m., pl. -*ow*: v., peel, *dyrüsca*; of dog, *hartha, ullya, crȳa.*
barley, n. *barlysen,* f., col. *barlys*; **hēdhen,* f., col. *hēth*; b. bran, *crynyon,* m. pl.; b. field, *barlysek,* **hēdhek,* f., pls. -*egow,* -*egy.*
barm, n. *gwēl,* m., *burmen,* f., col. *burm.*
barmaid, n. *maghteth-tavern,* f., pl. *meghtythyon-t.*

barn, n. *skyber,* f., pl. *-yow, grünjy,* m.; tithe-b., *s. vanal;* b. owl, *ūla,* m., pl. *-lys.*
barnacle, n. *bernakyl,* m., pl. *-aclys,* **trōs mogh,* m. pl., *treys m.;* b. goose, *morwoth,* f., pl. *-odhow.*
barracks, n. *chȳ soudoryon, soudorjy,* m.
barrel, n. *balyer,* m., pls. *-ow, -s;* b. stave, *asen,* f., pl. *asow.*
barren, a., woman, *anvab;* land, *sēgh;* b. place, *sēghla,* m., pl. *lēow.*
barrenness, n. *anvabeth, sēghter,* m.
barricade, n. *kē lesta, kē stykennow,* m.: v. *lesta;* b. door, *berna balyers po mebyl er y byn.*
barrier, n. *let,* m., pl. *-tys.*
barrister, n. *dēn an bar,* m., pl. *tüs a.b.*
barrow, n. *grava,* m., pl. *-vathow;* hand-b., *grava -dhywla;* wheel-b., *grava-rōs;* mound, *crük,* m., pl. *-ügyow.*
barter, v. *chanjya.*
basan, basil, n., leather, *molsken,* m.
base, n. *sōl,* m., *sēl,* f., pl. *-yow, grond,* m., pl. *-ys, goles,* m.; bottom end, *pen goles,* m.: v. *grondya:* a. *ysel.*
basely, adv. *ysel, yn-tyflas, yn-fylen.*
baseness, n. *vy·lyny, vȳlta,* m.
bashful, a. *methek.*
bashfulness, n. *meth,* f.
basin, n. *bason,* m., pl. *-ys.*
basinet, n. *basnet,* m., pl. *-tys.*
basis, n. *sēl,* f., pl. *-yow, grond,* m. pl., *-ys.*
bask, v. *omdesy, omhowla.*
basket, n. *canstel,* f., pl. *-low;* back-b., pannier, *cowel,* m., pls. *-low, kewel;* large, flat open b., *costen,* f., pl. *-now;* hand-b., *basket dorn,* m., pl. *-tys d.;* of straw rope, with narrow mouth, **kest,* f., pl. *-ow.*
bass, n., music, *faborden,* m.
bastard, a. *genys mēs a dhemedhyans.*
baste, v., sew, *crafa;* in cooking, *üra;* beat, *cronkya.*
bat, n., club, *bat,* m., pl. *-tys;* animal, *eskelly-grēghyn,* m., pl. *-as.;* †*ugh-sommys,* m.
bath, n. *golghva,* f., *bath,* m., pl. *-ys.*
bathe, v. *gorthroghya, troghya, omdroghya, sedhy,* **badhya, gül bath (yn);* sun-b., *omhowla.*
battering-ram, n. *horth bresel,* m., pl. *-rdhas b.*
battle, n. *batel,* f., pl. *-lys, cās,* f., pl. *-ow.* **ar,* f., pl. *-ow,* **arva,* f.; to fight a b., *batalyas;* b.-field, *gwēl,* m., **caslan,* f., pl. *-now;* b. front, *voward,* m.; b. axe, **caspōl,* f., pl. *-ow.*
battlement, n. **crenel,* m., pl. *-lys.*
bauble, n. *tegen,* f., *tegyn,* m., pl. *-now.*
baulk: see **balk.**
bawl, v. *garma, üja.*
bay, n., of sea, *bay,* m., pl. *-ys,* **plēk-mor,* pl. *-egow m.;* bot., *bay,* m., pl. *-ys, bay-wedhen,* f., col. *baywyth;* of dogs, *harth,* m., *harthva,* f.; to bring to b., *settya, synsy dhe harthva.;* b. colour, *melen,* **gell.*
bayonet, n. *cledha-gon,* m., pl. *-dhevyow-g.;* **baynet,* m., pl. *-tys.*
be, v. *bōs, bones;* b. off, *avodya;* it was not to b., *nyns-o-yndella destnys;* to b., or not to b., *po bōs, po hepcor bōs.*
beach, n. *trēth,* m., pl. *-ow, porth,* m., pls. *-ow, perth:* v., of boat, *gorra war drēth.*
beacon, n. *golowva,* f., pl. *-ow.*
bead, n. *paderen,* f., pl. *-now, pader,* m., pl. *pederow.*
beak, n. *gelvyn,* m., pl. *-as.*
beaked, a. *gelvynak.*
beaker, n. *hanaf,* m., pl. *-avow.*
beam, n., of light, *dewyn, golowyn,* m., pl. *-now;* timber, *trester,* m., pl. *-s, plynken,* f., pl. *-now, pren,* m., pls. *-yer, prynner, jȳst,* m., pl. *-ys;* †*keber,* f., pl. *-bryow,* **palather,* m., pl. *pelether.*
bean, n. *faven,* f., pl. *-now,* col. *fāf, fā;* b. field, *favek,* f., pl. *-egy;* b. pods, *cūthow-fāf.*
bear, n. *ors,* m., pl. *-as:* v., carry, *dōn;* endure, *perthy, godhaf, godhevel;* b. down, *grevya;* b. on, *posa;* b. child, *denythy;* it is borne in upon me, *ow brüs dhym yma· owtōn;* I can't b. it, *ny-allaf y wodhevel, ny-besyaf henna.*
bearable, a. *a-yllyr y wodhaf,* **heborth.*
beard, n. *barf,* m., pl. *-vow;* b. of corn, *col,* m., pl. *-ow.*
bearded, a. *barvek, barfüs.*
beardless, a. *dyvarf.*
bearing, n. *fara, chēr,* m., *omdhōn,* inf.; in machinery, etc., *deger.*
bearer, n. *deger,* m., pl. *-goryon.*
beast, n. *eneval,* m., pl. *-les, mȳl,* m., pl. *-as, lon,* m., pl. *-now, best,* m., pl. *-as;* cattle only, †*ēal,* m.; wild b., *gothfyl,* m., pl. *-as;* b. of burden, †*scrübel,* col.
beastly, a. *mylüs, plos.*
beat, v. *gweskel, frappya, cronkya, knoukya, balya;* in fighting, *fetha;* of heart, *lemmel:* n. *bom,* m., pl. *-myn;* of heart, *pols, lam,* m.
beaten, a., in contest, *fēth;* hammered, *morthelek.*

beating, n. *strekesow,* pl. and abst., *stewan,* m., pl. *-now.*
beautiful, a. *tēk, precyous, †fȳthüs.*
beautifully, adv. *precyous, yn-tēk.*
beautify, v. *tekhē·.*
beauty, n. *tekter,* m.
beaver, n. **lostledan,* m., pl. *-as, †befer,* m., pl. *-s.*
because, conj. *rak, awo·s* (with inf.), *drefen* (with noun, pron. or inf., and in neg., *na²-* and inflected verb).
beckon, v. *gül sȳn.*
become, v. *mōs,* or *dōs, ha bōs, codha, wharfos;* suit, *desedha;* what will b. of us now? *fatel vȳth dhyn lemmyn?;* he has b. an invalid, *ef res-ēth yn-clāf, gyllys prest clāf yu.*
becoming, a. *gwyw, semly, del dheseth.*
becomingly, adv. *yn-whyw, semly, maner-lych.*
bed, n. *gwely,* m., pl. *-yow;* feather-b., *gwely-plüf;* at the head, foot, of his b., *orth tāl, trōs, y wely.*
bedad! int. *ren ow thās!*
bedaub, v. *üra, mostya.*
bedclothes, n. *dyllas gwely,* m., pl. *-ow g.,* sing. used of those of one bed.
bedding, n. *hüdhes,* f.; of straw, *cala-gwely,* col.; for animals, **gwasarn,* m.
bedfellow, n. *coweth gwely,* m.
bedlinen, n. *lȳen-gwely,* m., pl. *-yow-g.*
bedraggle, v. *draylya yn plosethes, cagla.*
bedridden, a., b.-person, *dēn prest y'n gwely, a'y wroweth,* or *ow-crowedha.*
bedroom, n. *chambour,* m., pl. *-s.*
bedside, n., at the b., *ryp an gwely.*
bedspread, n. *pallen gwely,* f., pl. *-now g.;* ‡*kewlet,* m., pl. *-tys.*
bedstead, n. **pren gwely,* m.
bedstraw, n. *cala gwely;* Our Lady's b., *cala-gwely Marȳa;* as rennet, *godroth,* m.
bee, n. *gwenenen,* f., col. *gwenyn;* bumble-b., *g.wyls;* stock of bees, *mam gwenyn,* f.; beehive, *cowel gwenyn,* m.
beech-tree, n. *fawen,* f., pl. *-now,* col. *faw, faw-wedhen,* f., pl. *faw-wȳth;* b. mast, *know-f.,* col.; b. grove, *fawek,* f., pls. *-egow, -egy.*
beef, n. *kȳk bowyn, bowyn,* m.
beefsteak, n. *golyth bowyn,* m., pl. *-yon b.*
Beelzebub, m. *Belsebuk.*
beer, n. *coref, cor'f, cor',* m.; strong b., *cor' gwella,* m.; b. shop, *chȳ eva; dewotty,* m.
beet, n. *betysen,* f., col. *betys.*
beetle, n. *whȳl,* m., pl. *-as, whylen,* f., pls. *-nas, whylas;* black b., *whȳl du;* dung b., *whȳl caugh;* to catch b's., *whylessa,* inf. only.
befall, v. *wharfos, codha;* befallen us, *warnan codhys, dhyn wherys* or *wharfedhys.*
befog, v. *dysclērya.*
before, prep., position, *dera·k a-dhera·k, a-rak;* time, *kens(es), ken;* sail b. the wind, *mōs gans an gwyns;* adv., position, *a-rak;* time, *kens;* in presence of, *a-wēl dhe²,* *dh'y lɔk.*
beforehand, adv. *kens.*
befoul, v. *mostya, deffola, plosegy, cagla stronga.*
beg, v. *pysy, beggya;* I b. you to, *my a-th-pys a².*
beget, v. *denythy.*
beggar, n. *beggyer,* m., pl. *-s, brȳbour,* m., pl. *-s,* **gwyll,* m., pl. *-yow:* **-ly,** a. *gal, boghosek, ethomek.*
begin, v. *dalleth:* **-ner,** *dallether,* m., pl. *-thoryon:* **-ning,** n. *dalleth,* m., *†derow,* m.; origin, *dallethfos,* m.; in the b., *wostalleth, wortalleth, y'n dalleth.*
begone! int. *avoyd alemma!* pl. *-yeugh a.! kē,* pl. *keugh, dhe gerdhes! trus!* pl. *trusseugh!*
begotten, a. *denythys, denys.*
begrudge, v. *sconya drē envy.*
beguile, v. *tulla, flattra, hüda:* **-ment,** n. *hüs, flattrans,* m.
behalf, n. *govys;* on b. of, *aba·rth* (after *kewsel, pysy) gans;* on my b., *a'm govysvy, rag ow lēs,*
behave, v. *fara, omdhōn.*
behaviour, n. *fara,* m., *rewl,* f., *conversasyon,* m.
behead, v. *dybenna.*
behind, adv., position, *a-dryf, wor'tu delergh;* movement, *a-dryf, a-dhelergh:* prep., after, *warle·rgh;* hidden by, *a-dryf (dhe²);* b. him, *war y lergh;*
behindhand, a. *hele·rgh:* adv. *a-dhelergh, hell, lent.*
behold, v. *myras, gweles, avȳsya, whythra;* b! *awotta! otta! ot!:* **-en,** a. *synsys.*
behoof, n. *lēs, govys,* m.
behove, it b's., def., v., *coth, degoth, deleth, rēs yu;* I ought, *y-cothfya,* or *talvya, dhym, rēs vȳa dhym.*
being, n. *creatur,* m., pl. *-toryon, substans,* f.; human b., *map-dēn, mabden,* m. and col.; condition, *bōs.*
belabour, v. *stewanny, cronkya.*
belch, v. *dyllo gwyns.*

beldame, n. *gwragh*, f., pl. *-as.*
belfry, n. *clēghtour*, m., pl. *-ow.*
Belial, n. *Malan, Lawethan*, m.
belie, v. *contradya, camguhüdha*; b. promise, *fyllel y gewera*
belief, n. *crysyans*, f., *crejys*, m., *cōl*, f.; creed, *lay*, m., pl. *-s, crēs*, f.; trust, *fȳth*, f.
believe, v. *crysy* (*dhe*²), *cola* (*orth*), *fydhya* (*yn*): **-er,** n. *crȳjyk*, m., pl. *-ygyon*: **-ing,** a. *cryjyk.*
bell, n. *clogh*, m., pl. *clēgh*; church b., *clogh mür*; dinner b., *clogh-dybry*; small hand-b., *clēghyk*, m., pl. *-ygow*; b. tower, *clēghtour*, m., *pl. -ow.*
belladonna, n. *scawen gough*, f., pl. *scaw c.*; b. lily, *arlodhes nōth.*
belligerent, n. *breseler, -yer, -yas*, m., pls. *-loryon, -yoryon, -ysy*: a. *breselek.*
bellman, n. *clogher*, m., pl. *-ghoryon, dēn an clogh.*
bellow, v. *bedhygla, üja.*
bellows, n. *megynnow*, pl.
bellringer, n. *dēn an clogh*, m., pl. *tüs an clēgh, clēghor*, m., pl. *-yon.*
belly, n. *tor*, f., pl. *-row, colon*, m., pl. *-yow*, **bolghen*, f., pl. *-now, crūth*, f.; big-bellied, *torek, crothak, berryk*; b. ache, *drōk tor*; b. full, *lünder tor, lün y dor, fest lowr.*
belong, v. *bōs dhe*², ‡*longya*; it belongs to him, *ef a-n-pew, dhodho-ef yma·*; **-ings,** n. *tȳthy*, col.
beloved, a. *caradow, kerys, cüf, kēr*; b. son, *map rās*: n. *caradow*, m. or f., pl. *-yon*; *cüf-colon*, m.
below, prep. *a-woles, a-barth a-woles, yn-dan*², *ysella es* or *ages*; in place-names only, *ys, a-ys*; adv. *a-woles, war-woles, dhe woles, yn-nans.*
belt, n. *grügys*, m., pl. *-ow.*
belvedere, n. **gwelva*, f.
bemire, v. *cagla.*
bemoan, v. *ola, mornya, kȳny* or *omwethhē· warle·rgh.*
bemuse, v. *müskegy.*
bench, n. *scavel*, f., pl. *-low, form*, m., pl. *-ys*, ‡*benk*, m., pl. *-ow.*
bend, v. *cromma, plegya, camma*, **gwarya*, **stümma*; b. down, *stōpya*; I am bent on doing it, *ervȳrys of dh'y wül, y-fynnaf por-res y wül*: n. *stüm*, m., pl. *-mow, cam*, m., pl. *-mow, plēk*, m., pl. *-egow*; in road, *plēk hens*: **-able,** a., *heblēk, heblyth.*
beneath, prep. *yn-dan*², *a-woles, war-woles, yn-nans*; from b. it, *a-dhanno*; b. it, *yn-danno.*
benediction, n. *benedyksyon*, m., *bennath*, m., pl. *-nothow.*
benefactor, n. †*masoberor*, m., pl. *-yon.*
benefice, n. *benfys*, f., pl. *-ys.*
bemificient, a. *ow-cül da.*
beneficial, a. *mür y lēs.*
benefit, n. *dader*, m., *lēs*, m., *prow*: v. *gül da* or *bōs dhe lēs dhe*²; a thing of no b., *tra na-wra lēs.*
benevolence, n. *kerensa*, f., *da-ober*, m., pl. *-ow, dader*, m.
benevolent, a. *da* (*orth*).
bent, a. *crom, cam*: n. *plegyans, plegadow*, m.; coarse grass, *fynny*, f.
benign, a. *grassyes.*
benumb, v. *cromma, marowhē·*: **-ed,** a. *crom, hep clewes-vyth.*
bequeath, v. *kemmynna.*
bequest, n. *kemmyn*, m., pl. *-ow, kemmyna-dow*, m.
berate, v. *tavasa, godros, deraylya.*
bereave, v. *omdhevasy*: **-ment,** n. *coll.* m., *collva*, f.
bereft, a. *omdhevas, gesys yn awhē·r.*
berry, n. *grünen*, f., col. *grün*; multiple b., *moren*, f., col. *mōr.*
beseech, v. *pysy, conjūrya.*
beset, v. *settya orth.*
beside, prep. *ryp, a-barth* (*dhe*²); close b., *ryp tenewan a*²; *ryp scoth a*²; b. the point, *a-drüs*; b. himself, *mēs a'y rewl*; b. the lake, *war lan an logh*: **-s,** adv. *ynwe·th, pella*: prep. *drēs, hep*; b. this, that, *drēs*, or *gans hemma* or *henna.*
besiege, v. *omsettya adro dhe*²: **-r,** n. *omset-tyer*, m., pl. *-yoryon.*
besmear, v. *drōk-üra, mostya.*
besmirching, n. *bysmē·r*, m.
besom, n. *baren*, f., pl. *-now, scübel*, f., pls. *-bylly, -low*; b. of broom, *banallen*, f., pl. *-now.*
bespatter, v. *cagla, lagya.*
bespeak, v. *o·rdena* (*ordna, orna*).
besprinkle, v. *scullya lyn war*².
best, a. *gwella*; of the b., *a'n gwella*; for the b., *y'n gwella prȳs*; the b. of all the . . ., *flowr an* . . .; he does his b., *oll dh'y allos ef a-wra.*
bestow, v. *rȳ*; b. freely, *vossawya*: **-al,** n. *larjes*, m.
bet, v. *kessynsy, kenwystla.*
bethink oneself, v. *ombredery.*

betide, v. *wharfos, hapya, fortynya*; joy b. you! *lowena re-gas-bo*!
betimes, adv. *a-dermyn, a-brȳs.*
betony, n, *les-dosak,* m.
betray, v. *tulla, dyskevera, trayta*: **-al,** n. *traytury,* m.: **-er,** n. *traytour,* m., pl. *-s.*
betroth, v. *demedhy*: **-al,** *demedhyans,* m., *ambos demedhy*: **-ed,** a. *yn-dan ambos demedhy, dedhewys.*
better, a., adv. *gwell*: v. *gwella, gwellhē·*; think b. of it! *gwellha· dha vrȳs*!
between, prep. *yntra,* before vowel, *ynter*; b. ourselves, *yntredhon agan honen, rak leverel yn pryva.*
bevy, n. *bagas,* m., pl. *-ow*; of birds, *hēs,* m.
bewail, v. *ola, kȳny, *galary.*
beware, v. *gorquytha, gorra* or *kemeres wȳth*; in imp., b! *byth,* pl. *bedheugh, war*! *gothvyth*! pl. *gothvedheugh*! *war*! pl. *waryeugh*! (imp. only); *kemer,* pl. *kemereugh, wȳth.*
beweep: see **bewail.**
bewilder, v. *sawthanas, muskegy*: **-ment,** n. *sawthan,* m.
bewitch, v. *hüda, pystrȳa.*
beyond, prep. *drēs, yn-hans dhe²*, *pella es*: adv. *drēs.*
bezant, n. *besont,* m., pl. *-ns.*
bias, v. *trēlya, rakvrüsy*: n. *plegyans,* m.
bib, n. **bronlen,* f., pl. *-now*; fish, *bothak,* m., pl. *-thogas, lagater,* m., pl. *-tras.*
Bible, n. *Bȳbel*; the Scripture, -s, *an Lyver,* m., *an Lyfryow,* pl.
Biblical, a. *Byblek.*
bicker, v. *stryvya, dyspūtya.*
bicycle, n. *margh-horn,* m., pl. *mergh-h*: v. *marghogeth war vargh-h.*
bid, v. *gorhemmyn, comondya, charjya, erghy*; at sale, *profya*: n., offer, *profyans*: **-der,** n., at sale, etc., *profyer,* m., pl. *-yoryon*: **-ding,** n. *gorhemmyn, gorholeth, arghadow,* m.
bide, v. *tryga*; b. one's time, *gortos an prȳs.*
bier, n. *geler,* f., pl. *-ow, masken* (for *marowscaun*), m., pl. *-yow.*
bifurcated, a. *forghek.*
big, a. *brās, mür.*
bigamist, n. *gour dywwrēk,* m.: **-y,** *dywwregȳeth,* f.
bigot, n. *pen-cales,* m., pl. *pennow-c.*: **-ed,** a. *pen-cales, cales y ben.*
bile, n. *bystel.* f.: **-lious,** a. *bystlek*; b. attack, *shora cleves an bystel.*
bilge, n. *strās,* m., pl. *-ow*; b. water, *dowr pedrys.*
bill, n., account, *reken,* m., pl. *-knys, aco·nt,* m., pl. *-ys, scryf,* m., pl., *-yvow*: beak, *gelvyn,* m., pl. *-as*; long-billed, *gelvynak.*
billet, n., wood, *cünyjen,* f., pl. *-now, skethren,* f., pl. *-now, etew,* m., pl. *-y*; lodging, *erberow,* m.
bill-hook, n. **gwydhyf,* m., pl. *-yvow.*
billow, n. *ton, mordon,* f., pl. *-now.*
bin, n. *argh,* f., pls. *-ow, erghy.*
bind, v. *kelmy, strotha, mayla(-lya)*; of sheaves, *manala*; bundle, *fasky*: **-er,** n. *colmor,* m., pl. *-yon*: **-ing,** n. *colmen,* f., pl. *-now*; of book, *gorheryow,* pl.: a. *a-gelm, nag-yu dh'y derry.*
bindweed, n. *gwek,* col., pl. *-egas, gwyadores,* f., pl. *-ow.*
binnacle, n. *bytakyl,* m., pl. *-clys.*
biographer, n. *scryfer bewnans,* m., pl. *-foryon b.*: **-graphy,** n. *bewnans scryfys.*
biped, a. *deudros(ek)*: n. *creatur d.,* m., pl. *-toryon d.*
birch, n., b. tree, *besewen,* f., col. *besow*: v. *frappya, scorjya*; b. rod, *scübylen,* f., pl. *-now.*
bird, n. *edhen,* f., pl. *ydhyn*; young b. *ydhnyk,* m., pl. *-ygow*; to catch b's., *ydhnessa* (inf. only); b. cherry, *rüdhwernen,* f., pl. *-wern*; b. lime, *glüs,* m.; b. cage, *cowel edhen,* m., pl. *-low ydhyn*; the b's. have flown! *nȳth hep oy otta omma*!; b. catcher, n. *ydhnē·,* m., pl. *-nȳon.*
birth, n. *genesygeth,* f., *denythyans,* m.; manner of b., *genesygva,* f.; give b. to, *denythy*: **-day,** n. *pen-blōth,* m.: **-place,** n. *genesygla,* m.: **-right,** *ertach,* m., pl. *-ajys, gwȳr genesyk,* m.
biscuit, n. *tesen gales,* f., pl. *-now cales, bara daspebys, b. cales, *byskyt,* m., pl. *-tys.*
bisect, v. *trēghy yntra deu.*
bishop, n. *epscop,* m., pl. *-obow, tasek,* m., pl. *-sygyon*: **-ric,** n. *epscobeth,* m. or f., pl. *-ow.*
bit, n. *tam,* m., pl. *-tymmyn, dral,* m., pl. *-yow*; of seeing, etc., *banna*; little b., *temmyk,* m., pls. *-ygow, -ynygow, myjyn,* m., pl. *-now, teken,* f., pl. *-now, dernyk,* m., pls. *-ygow, darnowygow, brewyonen,* f., pl. *brewyon*; horse b., *genva,* f., pl. *-ow*; b. and brace, *tardar tro,* m.; not a b. of it! *nyns-yu henna man*!
bitch, n. *gast,* f., pl. *gysty.*
bite, v. *dynsel*; as a dog, *brathy*: n. *brath,* m., pl. *-ow*; of food, *tam,* m., pl. *-tymmyn*; broken food, *crym,* m., pl. *-yon*: **-er,** n., dog, *brathkȳ,* m., pl. *-brathcün.*

biting, a. *a-vrath*; keen, *yeyn, tyn.*
bitter, a. *wherow*; of cold, *yeyn*: **-ness,** n. *wherowder*, m.
bittern, n. *clabyttour*, m., pl. *-s*; **bongors*, m., pl. *-as.*
bivouac, n. **camp*, m., pl. *-ys*: v. **campya.*
black, a., n. *du*; of horse, *morel*: **-en,** v. *duhē, dua*: **-ing,** n. *du-eskyjyow*, m.: **-ness,** *duder*, m.
black-beetle, n. *prȳf du*, m., pl. *-yves d., whylen dhu*, f., *whyl du*, m., pl. *whylas du.*
blackberry, n. *moren*, f., col. *mōr, moren dhu*, f., pl. *mōr du*; to gather b's., *mōra* (inf. only).
blackbird, n. *molgh* (*mola*) *dhu*, f., pl. *-as du.*
blackguard, n. *map gal.*
black pudding, n. *gosogen*, f., pl. *-now.*
blacksmith, n. *ferror*, m., pl. *-yon, gōf*, m., pls. *-oves, -ovyon*; b's. shop, *govel*, f., pl. *-yow*; b's. apprentice, *map gōf*, m., pl. *mebyon g.*
blackthorn, n. *spernen dhu*, f., col. *spern du*; b. brake, *spernek*, **yrynek*, f., pls. *-egow, -egy.*
bladder, n. *gūsygen*, f., pl. *-now*, **whesygel*, f., pl. *-glow*, **whesygen*, f., pl. *-now.*
blade, n., knife, etc., *laun*, m., pl. *-ow*; b. of grass, *gwerwelsen*, f., pl. *-now*; to affix a b. to, *launya.*
blame, n. *cabel, blam, fowt, repref*, m., *kereth*, f.; the b. is ours entirely, *ny yu oll dhe vlamya*: v. *cably, blamya, gothvos blam dhe*[2]: **-less,** a. *dyflam, hep dyfowt*; he is b., *nyns yua dhe vlamya*: **-worthy,** a. *cablüs, dhe vlamya.*
blanc-mange, n. *pot-gwyn cowlys.*
bland, a. *clōr.*
blank, a. *gwak, gwyn*: n. *gwakter*, m.
blanket, n. *len*, f., pl. *-now.*
blaspheme, v. *cably Dew, mollethy*: **-my,** n. **blasfemy, cows ungrassyes*, m.
blast, n. *cowas*, f., pl. *-wosow, wheth*, m., pl. *-ow*; b. furnace, *chȳ-whetha*, m., *fōk*, f., pl. *fogow*: interj. *mal! aba·rth an pla!*: v. *whetha.*
blaze, n. *tansys*, m., pl. *-ow*: v. *dywy, flamya.*
bleach, v. **canna, *gwynna.*
bleak, a. *yeyn, dywoskes.*
blear, v. *dallhē·*; to become b., *moly, dōs ha bōs gwan y dheulagas*; b.-eyes, n. *lagajow molys.*
bleat, v. *bryvya*: **-ing,** n. *brȳf*, f., pl. *-yvow.*
bleed, v. *devera*; let blood, *dywosa, dyllo gōs.*
blemish, v. *namma, deffola*: n. *defowt*, m., pl. *-ow, nam*, m., pl. *-mow*: **-ed,** a. *trogh, nammys, deffolys.*
blench, v. *plynchya*: n. *plynch*, m., pl. *-ys.*
blend, v. *kemysky*: n. *kemysk*, m.: **-ed,** a. *yn-kemyskys.*
blenny, n. *mōrgronek*, m., pl. *-nogas.*
bless, v. *benyga, sona*; b. you! *dursona dhys! Dew re-th-fenyggo!*: **-ed,** a., holy, *benygys, gwyn*; fortunate, **gwynvysyk, gwyn y vȳs*: **-edness,** *benesykter*, m.: **-ing,** *bennath*, f., pl. *-nothow, sōn*, m., pl. *-ow, rās*, m., pl. and abst. *-ow*: **-ings!** *dursona! benedy·cyta!*; give a parting b. to, *gasa bennath gans.*
blight, n. *drokwheth, scaldyans*; insects, n. *low losow*; in corn, *losk*: v. *shyndya, myshevya*: **-ed,** a. *whethys, scaldyes.*
blind, a. *dall, tewl*; b. man, *dall*, m., pl. *-dellyon*; b. woman, *dalles*, f., pl. *-ow*; b. alley, *hens dall*, **hentall*, m., pl. *-sy d.*: v. *dalla, dallhē·*: n., fish, *lagater*, m., pl. *-tras*: **-fold,** v. *cüdha lagasow*: **-man's buff,** *gwary margh-dall*, **pen-dall*: **-ness,** n. *dellny*, m., **dallensa*, f.: **-worm,** n. †*anaf*, m., pl. *-avas.*
blink, v. *plynchya*: n. *plynch*, m., pl. *-ys.*
bliss, n. *lowena*, f., *gwynvȳs, tekter*, m.: **-ful,** a. *gwynvȳs, gwyn y vȳs.*
blister, n. *gūsygen, gwenen*, f., pl. *-now, bothel*, f., pl. *-low*, **whe·sygel*, f., pl. *-glow*, **whesygen*, **whejalen* f., pl. *-now*; blood-b., caused by pinch, *gosek, gosekgwȳth*, m.: v. *hothfy*
blithe, a. *lowen, jolyf.*
bloated, a. *whethys, whethfys*: **-ter,** n. *hernen-wyn mygys*, f.; col. *hern-gwyn m.*
block, n. *stok*, m., pl. *-kys*; for burning, *etew*, m., pl. *-y, cünyjen*, f., pl. *-now*: v. *degēa, lettya*: **-ade,** v. *omsettya adro dhe*[2]; *degēa trē*, or *scons*: n. *degēans*, m.: **-head,** *penbrās, pen-pyst, pensogh*, m., pls. *-now b., p., s., lorden*, m., pl. *-s.*
blood, n. *gōs, lyn*, m.; draw b. *dywosa, scullya lyn*; when his b. is up. *pan dheffo ha mōs fol*: **-hound,** n. *goskȳ*, m., pl. *-scün*: **-less,** a. *dywōs*: **-shed,** n. *crow*, m., *sculva gōs*, f.: **-shot,** a. *gwythyek*: **-stained,** a. *gosys*; his hands are b., *gōs-oll yu y dhywla*: **-sucker,** n. *gel*, f., pl. *-as*: **-vessel,** n. *gwythyen*, f., pls. *-now, gwȳthy*: **-y,** a. *gosek*; to make b., *gosa.*
bloom, n. *blejan*, m., *blejyewen, blejen*, f., pl. *-jyow*; on grape, plum, etc., *kewny*, col.;

plant, tree, in full b., *losowen*, or *gwedhen, yn hy blejyow.*
blossom, n.: see **bloom**: v. *blejyowa.*
blot, n. *dagren ynk*, f., pl. *-now y.*: v. *gül dagren ynk, d. dhu, scullya ynk, mostya*; dry, *desēgha*: **-ting paper,** *paper desēgha*, m.
blow, n. *bommen*, f., pl. *-now, bom*, m., pl. *-myn, strocas*, m., pl. *-cosow, knouk*, m., pl. *-kys, tummas*, m., pl. *-ow, box*, m., pl. *-ow, boxas*, m., pl. *-xesow, bonk, cronk*, m., pl. *-ys, stewan*, m., pl. *-now, squat* (*scat*) m., pl. *-tow, whaf*, m., pl. *-fys, what*, m., pl. *-tys, clowt*, m., pl. *-ys*; rap, ‡*pethyk*, m.; b. for b., *tys-ha-tas*: v. *whetha*; b. whistle, *whythella*; b. pipe, *pȳba*; b. unsteadily, *whyfla*; b. fire, *fannya*; b. up, *tardha*; b. up fire from sparks, *gül dhe dān dasserghy*: **-er,** n. *whether*, m., pl. *-thoryon*; of horn, *kernyas*, m., pl. *-ysy*: **-ing house,** n. *fōk*, f., pl. *fogow*; *chȳ whetha, c. fōk*, m.
blubber, n. *blonek*, m.: **-lipped,** a. *gwelvek.*
bludgeon, n. *cūlbren*, m., pl. *-yer, blojon*, m., pl. *-s.*
blue, a., n. *glās*, ‡*blou*; b.-green, **glaswer*; b.-grey, **glaswyn*; deep b., **dulas*: n. light b., **pers*; indigo b., *glās Eynda*, m.; b. dye, *glesyn*, m.; to go b., *glasa*: **-ish,** a. *glesyk*: **-ness,** n. *glaster*, m.
bluebell, n. *blejen an gōk*, or *an gūcū*, f., pl. *-jyow a.g.*
bluebottle, n. *kelyonen kȳk*, f., col. *kelyon k.*
blue-tit, n. *pen-paly*, m., pl. *-as.*
bluff, n., cliff, *als serth*, f., pl. *-yow s., clegar*, m., pl. *-grow*; boast, *bōst, fās*, m., pl. *-ow, maystry*, m.; the b. is called, *gallas fasow*: v. *bragya, facya, omwül bōs crēf*: a. *frēth, efan y lavarow, frank*; of shore, *serth ha ledan.*
blunder, v. *camgemeres, myskemeres, camwonys*: n. *camwonys*, m.
blunt, a. *dylym, sogh*; of speech, *stordy, cot y lavarow*: v. *sogha, dylemma*: **-ly,** adv., outspokenly, *dhe blemmyk.*
blur, v. *dysclērya*: n. *dysclērder*, m.: **-ed,** a. *dysclēr.*
blurt, v. *leverel yn-tybreder, yn-stordy*, or *dhe blemmyk.*
blush, v. *rüdhya*: **-ing,** a. *rüth, ow-rüdhya.*
bluster, v. *bragya, maystry, gül maystry*; of wind, *whyfla*: n. *maystry*, m., *fasow*, pl.: **-ing,** a., wind, etc., *whyflyn.*
boar, n. *bāth*, m., pl. *-adhas*; ‡*bora*, m., pl. *-ys*; wild b., *torgh cōs*, m., pl. *-as c.*
board, n. *estyllen*, f., pl. *-now, astell*, f., pl. *estyll, plynken*, f., pl. *-now, bord*, m., pl. *-ys*: v., lodge, *ostya*; b. ship, *mōs a-berveth yn*, or *yskynna yn*: **-er,** *ostyas*, m., pl. *-ysy*: **-ing-house,** *ostjy*, m., pl. *-ow*: **-ing-school,** *scōl-ostya*, f., pl. *-yow-o.*
boast, v. *bōstya, omvōstya, facya, bragya*: n. *fās, bōst*, m., pl. *-ow*: **-er,** *bōster*, m., pl. *-toryon*; *bragyer*, m., pl. *-yoryon*: **-ful,** a. *a-gar bōstya*: **-ing,** n. *fasow*, pl.
boat, n., open rowing b., *scath*, f., pl. *-ow*; long b., *scath-hȳr*; seine b., *scath-rōs*; fishing b. with sails, *cok*, m., pl. *-cūcow*: **b.-hook,** n. *hȳk scath*, m., pl. *-gow s.*: **b.-load,** n. *carg*, m., pl. *-ow*: **b.-man,** n. *dēn scath*, m., pl. *tüs s.*: **b.-swain,** n. †*brennyas*, m., pl. *-ysy.*
bob, v. *squychya*; of hair, *cot-trēghy*: n. *squych*, m., pl. *-ys.*
bodily, adv. *yn-tȳen*: a. *a'n corf.*
bodkin, n. *nasweth lās*, f., pl. *-wedhow l.*
body, n. *corf*, m., pl. *-ow*; person, *body*, m., pl. *-s*; as abode of soul, *trogel*, m.; b. of armed men, *nerth*, m., pl. *-ow*: **b.-guard,** n. *pryva-gwythyas*, m., pl. *p.-gwythysy.*
bog, n., with rushes, *porf, pol porf*; peat b., *towarghek*, f., pls. *-egy, egow*; with reeds, *cors*, f., pl. *-ow*; *kenak, kersek*, f., pls. *-egow, -egy*; of sedge, *heskyn*, m.: **-gy,** a. *devrak, gwernak*; b. place, *kenegen*, f., pl. *-now*, with alders, *gwernek*, f., pls. *-egy, -egow.*
boggle, v. *hokkya.*
bogy, n. *bucca*, m., pl. *bukkyas, tarosvan*, m.; pl. *-now.*
boil, v. *bryjyon*, **berwy,*: n. *pen-du* m., pl. *-now d.*; **whejalen*, f., pl. *-now*; disease of b's., *brēgh*, f.: **-er,** n. *pēr*, m., pl. *-now, caltor*, f., pl. *-yow*: **-ing,** n. *bryjyon*, **berow*, m.
boisterous, a. *mür y drōs.*
bold, a. *harth, colonnek, glew, stordy, dūr, bold*: **-ness,** n. *colonnekter, bolder*, m.
bolster, n. *penwely*, m., pl. *-ow*, **gobenner*, m., pl. *-yow*, **trüsplüvak*, f., pl. *-vogow.*
bolt, v., bar, *prenna, barya*; b. together, *ebylya*; b. flour, *saya, serjya*; run away, *dyank*; swallow quickly, *collenky*: n., bar, *bar*, m., pl. *-rys, pren*, m., pls. *-yer, prynner*; iron b., *ebyl horn*, m., pl. *-yow, -yon, h.*
bolting-cloth, n. *yscar*, m.
bomb, v. *tewlel tanbellen* (*war*[2]), *tanbellenna, bombardya*: n. **tanbellen*, f., pl. *-now*: **-ard,** v. **tanbellenna*, **bombardya.*

bombast, n. *predhek,* m., pl. *-egow, cows whethfys,* m.

bond, n. *colmen,* f., pl. *-now, colm,* m., pl. *-ow, kevren,* f., pl. *-yon, *stagell,* f., pl. *-ow, syg,* f., pl. *-yow, *faskel,* f., pl. *-low, raw,* f., pl. *-yow*; in b's., *yn colmow, yn-kelmys*: **-age,** n. *gwaso·nȳeth,* f.: **b.-maid,** n. *kēthes,* f., pl. *-ow*: **b.-man,** *kēth,* m., pl. *-yon, tȳthyak,* m., pl. *-yogyon*: **b.-woman,** n. *kēthes,* f., pl. *-ow, tȳthyoges,* f., pl. *-ow.*

bone, n. *ascorn,* m., pl. *eskern*; fish b., *drēn,* m., pl. *dreyn*; b. of contention, *pyth cavylek,* m.: **-less,** a. *dyascorn, dyeskern*: **-ny,** a. *ascornek*; full of bones, *eskernek.*

bonfire, n. *tansys,* m., pl. *-ow*; Midsummer b., *tansys Golowan.*

bonnet, n. *pengugh,* m., pl. *-ow.*

booby, n. *bobba,* m., pl. *-bys, goky,* m., pl. *-yes.*

book, n. *lyver,* m., pls. *-lyfrow, lyfryow*; b. of words, standard copy, *o·rdenal,* m., pl. *-ys*: v., b. order, etc., *erghy, gorra yn lyver*: **-case,** n. *argh lyfrow, lyverva,* f., pl. *-ow*: **-let,** n. *lyfryk,* m., pls. *-ygow, -frowygow, lyfryn,* m., pl. *-now*: **-seller,** n. *gwerther lyfrow,* m., pl. *-oryon, *lyfror,* m., pl. *-yon*: **-worm,** n. *prȳf lyver,* m., pl. *-pryves l.*

booking-office, n. **tokynva,* f.

book-keeping, n. *gwythans lyfrow acontys.*

book-maker, n. *kessynser,* m., pl. *-soryon.*

boom, v. *tarenna, whyrny*: n., naut., *pren,* m., *gwelen-gōl a-woles,* f.; rise in value, *moghhēans*: **-ing,** of surf, *mōrdrōs,* m.

boon, n. *bennath,* f., pl. *-nothow, da, dader,* m.

boot, n. **botas(en),* f., pl. *-sow.*

booth, n. *scovva,* f., pl. *-ow, tylda,* m., pl. *-dys.*

booty, n. *pray, da pyllys,* m.

borage, n. *tavas-kȳ,* m.

border, n., of land, *amal,* m. or f., pl. *em·low*; *emelow, cür,* m., pl. *-ow, ōr,* f., pl. *-yon*; edge, *myn,* m., pl. *-yon*; gold b. of garment, **orfrays,* m.; of flowers, *gwelyblejyow,* m., pl.*-yow-b.*; b. land, *ōrdyr,* m.

bore, v., drill, *telly, tardra*; tire, *squytha, annȳa, ancombra*: n., plague, *pla,* m., pl. *-ow, ancombrynsy,* m.: **-edom,** n. *squythter,* m., *annȳans*: **-ring,** a. *rē hȳr, owsquytha, owth-annȳa*: n. *toll,* m., pl. *tell.*

born, a. *denythys, denys, genesyk*; high-b., *genys an gōs ughel*; low-b., *ysel y wōs, drōk genesyk, map gal.*

borough, n. **burjestra,* f., pl. *-trevow.*

borrow, v. **chevysya, mōs yn kendon rak, kemeres,* or *govyn, war wystel,* or *rak sēson*: **-ing,** n. **che·vysons,* m.

bosom, n. *ascra,* f., *dywvron,* d.f.: inward feeling, *cowsesow,* abst.

boss, n. *both,* f., pl. *-ow*; hump, *bothan,* m., pl. *-now*; chief, *mēster,* m., pls. *mestrysy, -yjy*: v. *gül maystry, lordya war*^{2}: **-ed,** a. humped, *bothak.*

botany, n. *losowe·rȳeth,* f.: **-nical,** a. *losowek*: **-nist,** n. *losower,* m., pl. *-woryon.*

both, a., pron. *an dheu, aga deu*; b. of you, *agas deu*; b. of those, *an dheu-na*: adv., both . . . and . . ., *ha . . . ha . . .*; *kefry·s . . . ha . . .*

bother, v. *annȳa* (*'nȳa*), *ancombra*; to b. about, *perthy awhē·r a*^{2} or *awo·s*; don't b! *na fors*!: n. *ancombrynsy,* m.

bottle, n. *bottel,* m., pl. *-low.*

bottom, n. *goles,* m.; tail end, *tȳn,* f., pl. *-yon*; low ground, *strās,* m., pl. *-ow*; b. end, *pengoles,* m.; to the b., *dhe-woles*; at the b., *war-woles, a-woles*: **-less,** *hep goles, dywoles.*

bough, n. *scoren,* f., pl. *-now,* col. *scōr, bar,* m., pl. *-ow.*

boulder, n. *būlȳen,* f., pl. *-ȳow,* col. *būly.*

bounce, v. *terlemmel.*

bound, v. *lemmel, lamma*: n. *lam,* m., pl. *-mow*; tin-b., *bownd,* m., pl. *-ys*; beyond all b's., *yn-mēs a bup forth*: a. *kelmys, ynkelmys*; beholden, *synsys*; b. for, *kelmys dhe*^{2}: **-ary,** n. *ōr,* f., pl. *-yon*; b. stone, *mēn ōr, mēn nos, ōrmen,* m.: **-en,** a. *kelmys*: **-less,** a. *hep ōr, dynyver, hep fȳn.*

bountiful, a. *hēl*: **-ty,** n. *dader, larjes, helder,* m.

bout, n. *fyt,* m., pl. *-tys, torn,* m., pl. *-ow*; have a b. with, *gül fyt a*^{2}.

bow, v. *omblegya, ynclynya*; b. down, *plegya y'n dor*: n., inclination, *omblegyans,* m.; weapon, *gwarak,* f., pl. *-regow*; naut., *pen a-rak,* m.; loop, *plēk,* m., pl. *-egow*; b. net, **ballek,* f., pl. *-egow.*

bowel, n. *colon,* m., pl. *-yow, †colodhyonen,* f., pl. *-odhyon*; b's. of the earth, *downder an dōr.*

bower, n. *delyowek,* f., pls. *-egow, -egy*; *goskejwyth,* col., *kēl,* m., pl. *-ow.*

bowl, n., shallow b., *scala,* m., pl. *-ys, *cogen,* f., pl. *-now*; small b., *bolla,* m., pl. *-lys*; playing b., *pēl,* f., pl. *-yow, bolla,* m.: v. *tewlel pēl*; b. along, *dehelghya.*

bow-legged, a. *gargam, camgarrek*; to walk b., *rambla.*
bowling, n. *gwary-pelyow,* m.; b. green, *glesyn,* m., pl. *-now, tȳr glās,* m.
bowman, n. *gwaregor, sethor,* m., pl. *-yon.*
bowsprit, n. **bospryt, pren pen a-rak,* m.
box, n. *trok,* m., pls. *-kys, tregys, kyst,* f., pl. *-yow*; small b., *kysten,* f., pl. *-now, box,* m., pl. *-ys*; blow, *box,* m., pl. *-ow, boxas,* m., pl. *-xesow*: v., fight, *boxesy.*
box-tree, or **branch,** n. *box,* m., pl. *byxyn.*
boy, n. *map,* m., pl. *mebyon, flogh,* m., pl. *flēghes,* separative plural, *fleghysyow*; dim. *meppyk,* m., pls. *-ygow, mebyonygow*; servant, *boya,* m., pl. *-yes, maw,* m., pls. *mebyon, coscar*: **-hood,** *mapsys,* m.: **-ish,** *ave·l maw, yn meppyk.*
brace, v. *crefhē·.*
bracelet, n. *modrewy,* f., pl. *-ow.*
bracing, a. *yagh, a-grefha·.*
bracken, n. *redenen,* f., col. *-reden*; dead b., *reden rüth*; b. brake, *redenek,* f., pls. *-egow, -egy*; to clear away b., *dyredenna.*
bracket, n. *corbel,* m., pl. *-blys.*
bradawl, n. *brōs,* m., pl. *-ojow.*
brag: see **boast,**
braggart, n. *bōster,* m., pl. *-yon, facyer,* m., pl. *-yoryon.*
bragging, n. *fasow,* pl.
braid, v. *plethenna, plēthy*: n. *plēth,* f., pl. *-ow, plethen,* f., pl. *-now*: **-ing,** n. *plēthwȳth,* m.
brains, n. *ympynyon,* pl.
brake, n., thicket, *cardhen,* f., pl. *-now, brăca,* m., pl. *-ākys*; of vehicle, *fron,* f., pl. *-now*: v. *frona.*
bramble, n. *dreysen,* f., pl. *-now,* col. *dreys, spedhesen,* f., col. *spedhes*; b. brake, *dreysek,* f., pls. *-egow, -egy.*
bran, n. *talgh,* m.; of barley, *crynyon,* pl.
branch, n. *scoren,* f., pl. *-now,* col. *scōr, bar,* m., pl. *-ow, branch,* m., pl. *-ys*; small b., *baren,* f., pl. *-now*: v. *scorenna, dyberth*: **-ed,** a. *scorrek, scorennek, barrek*: **-y,** a. *goskesek.*
brand, v. *merkya*: n. *merk,* m., pl. *-ys*; fire-b., *etew,* m., pl. *-y.*
brandis, n. *trebeth,* m., pl. *-edhow.*
brandish, v. *swaysya, *florsya.*
brand-new, a. *noweth flam.*
brandy, n. *dowr tom Frynk.*
brass, n. *brest,* m.: **-work,** n. *gwȳth brest,* m.: **-works,** n. *gwȳthva brest,* f.
brassard, n. **brēghwysk.*

brat, n. *chet,* m., pl. *-tys.*
brave, a. *harth, colonnek, dūr*: **-ry,** n. *colonnekter,* m.
brawl, v. *kedrynya, raylya, deraylya*: n. *deray·,* m., pl. *-ys, kedry·n,* f., *strȳf,* ‡*frōth,* m.: **-er,** n. *strȳfor,* m., pl. *-yon.*
brawn, n. *nerth keherek,* m.; *keherow,* m. pl.; meat, *kȳk keher, kȳk bāth,* m.: **-y,** *keherek, crēf.*
bray, v. *bēgy, üja*; pound, *brewy.*
brazen, a. *a vrest*; b.-faced, *dyveth.*
breach, n., gap, *būlgh,* m., pl. *-ow, aswy* (*ajy*), f., pl. *-ow*; clean b., naut., *clērdhystryppyans,* m.; breaking, **tor,* m., pl. *-yow, torva,* f.: v. *aswȳa, būlgha, terry*: **-ed,** a. *aswȳak, būlghys.*
bread, n. *bara,* m.; white b., *bara gwyn,* †*bara can*; wheaten b., *bara gwaneth*; oat b., *bara kergh*; rye b., *bara sügal*; barley b., *bara barlys, b. *hēth*; leavened b., *bara gwēl*; unleavened b., *bara hep gwēl*; sacramental b., *bara an oferen*; b. and butter, *bara hag amanyn* (*bara'gamanyn*).
breadth, n. *efander, lēs,* m.
break, n. *tor,* m., pl. *-yow, torva,* f., *tarth,* m., pl. *-rdhow, squard,* m., pl. *-yow, brew,* m., pl. *-yon*; without a break, *hep let, kens es hedhy*: v. *ranna, crakkya, squardya, terry, squattya*; b. to bits, *dralya*; b. down, *fyllel*; b. off, stop, *astel*; b. forth, *tardha*; b. loose, *omdhyllo, omdhelyfra*; b. in, tame, *dova*; b. into, b. out of, b. in horse, *terry*; b. force of, **goderry*; to dawn, *tardha*; of cloud, *omderry, omdenna*: **-able,** a. *hedor*: **-age,** n. *torva,* f., *squat,* m., pl. *-tow, squard,* m., pl. *-yow.*
break-down, n. *meth,* m., pl. *mothow.*
breaker, n. *tarth mor,* m., breakers, *mordarth,* m.; house, ship-b., *terrer chȳ* or *lystry,* pl. *terroryon c., l.*
breakfast, n. *lȳ,* f., pl. *lyfyow*; early b., *hansel,* m.; b. time, *prȳs-lȳ,* m.
breakneck, a. *crakkya-conna, crak y gonna.*
breakwater, n. *bak,* m., pl. *-kys.*
bream, n. *sew,* m., pl. *-yon*; small b., *lommas,* m., pl. *-ow, crommen,* f., pl. *-now, takflogh,* m., pl. *-as, cressyer,* m.
breast, n. *bron,* f., pl. *-now, ascra,* f., *clōs dywvron,* f., *brēst,* m.; to give b., *bronna.*
breast-hook, n., naut., *queth,* f., pl. *-ow.*
breastplate, n. *brēstplāt,* m., pl. *-ys.*
breast-pocket, n. *ascra,* f.
breastwork, n. *fōs ysel,* f., *scons ysel,* m.
breath, n. *wheth,* m., *anal,* m. or f., *gwyns,*

m., pls. *-ow*; intake of b., *ten*, m., pl. *-now*; to be out of b., pant, *dyena*: **-less,** a. *dyanal*: **-lessness,** n. *ber-anal, dyfyk a.*, m.
breathe, v. *whetha, anella*; b. in, *tenna anal.*
bred, p.p. *megys.*
breech, n., posterior, *tӯn*, f., pl. *-yon.*
breeches, n. *lavrak*, m., pl. *-regow.*
breed, v., rear, *maga*; generate, *o·mdhon*: n. *megyans*, m.: **-er,** n. *mager*, m., pl. *-goryon*, f. *-es*, pl. *-ow.*: **-ing,** n. *megyans, norter*, **magereth*, m.
breeze, n. *awel clōr*, f., pl. *-low c.*
Breton, n. *Breton*, m., pl. *-yon*, f. *-es*, pl. *-ow*; B. language, *Bretonek*, m.: a. *Bretonek.*
brevity, n. *berder, cotter*, m.
brew, v. *brӯhy*; of storm, *degensewa*: n. *brӯhyans*, m.: **-er,** n. *brӯhyer*, m., pl. *-yoryon*; b's. grains, *sēk*, m.: **-ery,** n. *chӯ-brӯhy*, m., pl. *-ow b.*
briar, n. *dreysen*, f., pl. *-now*, col. *dreys, spedhesen*, f., col. *spedhes*; b. brake, *dreysek, spedhesek*, f., pls. *-egow, -egy.*
bribe, v. *fals-gobra, *brӯbya, prena dēn*: n. *fals-gober*, m., pl. *-brow*: **-ry,** n. **brӯbyans*, m.
brick, n. *bryk*, m., pl. *-kys, mēn-prӯ*, m., pl. *meyn p.*: **-layer,** n. *settyer meyn-prӯ*, m., pl. *-yoryon m.-p.*: **-works,** *gwӯthva brykkys* or *meyn-prӯ*, f.
bridal, a. *prӯosol*; b. pair, n. *tüs noweth, deubrӯas.*
bride, n. *benen brӯas* or *noweth*, f., pl. *-es b.* or *n.*
bridegroom, n. *gour prӯas*, m., pl. *tüs p.*; *dēn noweth*, m., pl. *tüs n.*
bridesmaid, n. *maghteth brӯas*, f., pl. *megh-tythyon prӯas.*
bridge, n. *pons*, m., pl. *-ow*; small, *ponsyk*, m., pl. *-ygow*; foot b., *ponsyn*, m., pl. *-now*; cart b., *carbons*, m., pl. *-ow*; horse b., *marghbons.*
bridle, n. *fron*, f., pl. *-now*; with blinkers, *fron dhall*, f.
brief, a. *ber, cot*: n., legal, *scrӯf kēn*: **-ly,** adv. *a ver spās, yn cot-termyn*; in a few words, *war ver lavarow, war nebes lavarow.*
brigand, n. *lader*, m., pl. *ladron, robbyor*, m., pls. *-yon, -s, rafner*, m., pl. *-noryon.*
bright, a. *splan, glew, clēr, golow, ylyn, brӯght*: **-en,** v. *splanna*, intrans. *golowy*, trans. *clērhē·, splanhē·, gül bōs splan*: **-ness,** n. *splander, gwynder, can, golewder, golowyjyon, *splanyjyon*, m.; of sun, *lyw*, m.
brill, n., fish, *lugarn-lӯth*, f., pl. *-as.*
brilliance: see **brightness.**
brilliant: see **bright.**
brim, n. *mӯn*, m., pl. *-yon*; b.-full, *collenwys*: v., as a sow, *godhyvas.*
brimstone, n. *loskven*, m.
brindle, a. *brēgh, brӯth, labol.*
brine, n. *hyly, dowr sal*, ‡*brӯn*, m.; b. pit, *pol-hyly*, m., pl. *-low-h.*
bring, v. *drӯ, kerghes, hembronk, gorra, dōn*; b. about, *spēdya*; b. forth, *denythy*; b. lower, *stōpya*; b. forward, *avonsya*; b. nearer, *neshē·*: **-er,** n. *kergher*, m., pl. *-ghoryon.*
brink, n. *ōr*, f., pl. *-yon, mӯn*, m., pl. *-yon, glan*, f., pl. *-now*; of sea, *morva*, f., *als*, m., pl. *-yow, glan mōr.*
briny, a. *sal, holanek.*
brisk, a. *bew, scaf, jolyf, *gwysk*; a b. sale, *gwerth bew.*
bristle, n. *rünen*, f., col. *rün*; pig's b's., *rün mogh*: v. *sevel rün, serry*: **-ling,** a. *ha'y rün ow-sevel, sevys y rün*: **-ly,** a. *garow, rünek.*
Britain, n. *Breten*, f.; Great B., *Breten Vür*: **-ish,** a., of Britons, *Brythonek*; Britannic, *Bretennek*: **Briton,** n. *Brython*, m., pl. *-yon, *Bretanyas*, m., pl. *-ysy.*
Brittany, n. *Breten Vӯghan*, f.
brittle, a. *hedrogh, crӯn, brottel*; to become b., *crӯna*: **-ness,** n. *crynder*, m.
broach, v., with spit, *berya*; begin, *attamya*; b. to, naut., *mōs yn lagas an gwyns*: n. *ber*, m., pl. *-yow.*
broad, a. *ledan, efan*: **-en,** v. *ledanhē·.*
broadcast, v. *scullya a-lēs, *ledandewlel*; of rumours, *plontya*; wireless, **ayrgew-sel*; grain, *gonys a-lēs, gorthewlel*: n. *ayr-gows*, m.
broadcloth, n. **pan-ledan.*
brocade, n. *paly*, m.
brochure, n. *lyfryk*, m., pl. *-rygow, -rowy-gow.*
brogue, n., shoe, †*pawgen*, m.; in English speech, *tōn Keltek.*
broken, a. *trogh, brew, terrys*; of head, *cough*; to become b., *terry*: **-hearted,** a. *trogh y golon.*
broker, n. *mayn*, m.: **-age,** n. *gober, mayn*, m.
bronchial, a. *a'n vrӯansen*: **bronchitis,** n. *losk an vrӯansen*, m.
bronze, n. **brons*, m.
brooch, n. *brocha*, m., pl. *-chys*, †*delk*, m., pl. *-lcow.*

brood, v. *covya*, **gory*; to b. over, *ombredery war²*, *omwethhē·*: n. *bagas ydhnygow*, m., pl. *-ow y.*: **-y,** a. **gōr*.
brook, n. *gover*, m., pl. *-ow*, *gwȳth* (*goth*), f., pls. *-thy*, *-thow*, *strēth*, f., pl. *-ow*, *non*, f., pl. *-now*; abounding in b's., *goverek*: v. *godhaf*, *perthy*: **-let,** n. *goveren*, *nonnen*, *gwythen* (*gothen*), f., pl. *-now*: **-weed,** n. *glēth-dowr*, m.
broom, n., brush, *scübel*, f., pls. *-bylly*, *-low*, *scüb*, m.; plant, *banallen*, f., pl. *-now*, col., flowers or plants, *banal*; b.-brake, *banallek*, f., pls. *-egow*, *-egy*; b. maker, *scübelor*, m., pl. *-yon*, f. *-es*, pl. *-ow*; b. stick, *gwelen scübylen*, f., pl. *-lyny s.*
broth, n. *cowl*, *yskel*, m.; thick b., *brōs*, m.
brother, n. *broder*, m., pl. *breder*; b.-in-law, *broder-da*: **-hood,** n. *bredereth*, m.: **-ly,** a. *ave·l broder*; b. love, *kerensa broder*.
brow, n. *tāl*, m., pl. *-yow*, *corn tāl*, m., pl. *kernow t.*, *el*, f., pl. *-yow*; big-browed, *talek*, *elek*.
brown, a., dun, **gorm*; light b., **gell*; russet b., **gellrüth*; chestnut b., **gell kesten*: **-ish,** a. **gellyk*: **-ness,** n. *gellder*, m.
browse, v. *pory*; browsing-ground, †*clün*, m., pl. *-now*.
bruise, v. *brewy*, **syga*: n. *brew*, pl. *-yon*; of fruit, *podrethes*, m.
brush, v. *scüba*: n., small, *scübylen*, f., pl. *-now*; large, *scübel*, f., pls. *-bylly*, *-low*; artist's b., **pyncel*, m., pl. *-s*.
brushwood, n. *prysken*, f., col. *prysk*, *pryskel*, m., pl. *-sclow*, *kēwȳth*, col.
brutal, a. *garow*, *gwyls*, *mylüs*; **-ity,** n. *garowder*, *bylyny*, m.
brute, n. *mȳl*, m., pl. *-as*; of persons, *bylen*, m., pl. *tüs vylen*, *mylüsyon*.
Brythonic, a. *Brythonek*.
bubble, v. *whethfy* (*hothfy*): n. *whethfyans* (*hothfyans*), m.
buck, n., deer, *yorgh*, m., pl. *-as*; he-goat, *bogh*, m., pl. *-as*, *buk*, m., pl. *-kys*; wild b., *cosyorgh*, m., pl. *-as*: v. *terlemmel*.
bucket, n. *buket*, m., pl. *-tys*, **kelorn*, m., pl. *-ow*; mine or well b., *kybel*, f., pl. *-low*.
buckle, n. *bokyl*, m., pl. *boclys*, †*brocha*, m., pl. *-ys*, †*strȳng*, m.: v. *bocla*, *fasta brocha*.
buckler, n. *costen*, f., pl. *-now*, *scōs rond*, m., pl. *-ojow r.*
buckthorn, n. *ravnen*, f., col. *raven*, **spernen velen*, f., col. *spern melen*.
buckwheat, n. *gwaneth Frynk*, col.
bucolic, n. *bügelek*.
bud, n. *egyn*, m., pl. *-now*: v. *egyna*.
budge, v. *omwen*.
budget, n. **bojet*, m., pl. *-tys*.
buff, a. **gell*, *lyw* **büal*.
buffalo, n. **büal*, m., pl. *-as*, *ojyon gwyls*, m., pl. *oghen g.*
buffet, n. *box*, *tummas*, m., pl. *-ow*, *strocas*, m., pl. *-cosow*, *bommen*, f., pl. *-now*, *boxas*, m., pl. *-esow*, *squat*, m., pl. *-tow*, *whaf*, m., pl. *-fys*; cupboard, *buffet*, m: v. *squattya*, *boxesy*, *gweskel*, *cuffya*.
buffoon, n., entertainer, *gwaryer wharthüs*, m., pl. *-yoryon w.*; silly pers., *goky*, m., pl. *-yes*: **-ery,** n. *gwary fol*, m.
bug, n. *prȳf gwely*, m., pl. *-yves g.*
bugbear, n. *bȳgel*, m., pl. *-yon*, *bȳgel nōs*, m., *bucca du*, m., pl. *bukkyas d.*, *bucca nōs*, *tarosvan*, m., pl. *-now*.
bugle, n. **büalgorn*, m., pl. *-gern*: **-r,** n. *kernyas*, m., pl. *-ysy*.
bugloss, n. *tavas-ojyon*, m.
build, v. *drehevel*, *buyldya*; to finish building, *cowldhrehevel*: **-er,** n. *gwȳthor-chȳ*, m., pl. *-yon c.*: **-ing,** n. *drehevyans*, *chȳ*, m., pls. *-ow*, *treven*, *trevow*.
bulb, n., plant, **crenwredhen*, f., pls. *-now*, *gwrȳdhyow cren*, col. *gwrȳth c.*: electric b., *gwēder tredan*, m.
bulge, v. *whethfy* (*hothfy*), *cromma*: n. *whethfyans* (*hothfyans*), m.
bulk, n. *braster*, *myns*, *tewder*, m.: of pilchards, *barcado*, m., pl. *-s*: **-y,** a. *brās*, *tew*.
bulkhead, n. *fōs*, f., pl. *-ow*, *rōm*, m., pl. *-ys*, *dybarth*, f.
bull, n. *tarow*, m., pl. *te·rewy*; papal b., *bollys*, pl.: **-fight,** n. *tarowvȳr*, m., *o·mlath tüs orth te·rewy*: **-ock,** n. *lon*, m., pl. *lonnow*; b. house, *lonjy*, m.: **-ring,** n. *tarowvȳr*, m.
bullace, n. **yrynen vrās*, f., col. *yryn brās*.
bull-dog, n. *kȳ tarow*, m., pl. *cün t.*
bullet, n. *pellen gon*, f., pl. *-now g.*, **būlet*, m., pl. *-tys*.
bully, n. *smat*, m., pl. *-tys*, *quallok*, m., *den garow*, m., pl. *tüs g.*: v. *compressa*, *annȳa*, *deffola*.
bulrush, n. *penduen*, f., col. *pendu*.
bulwark, n. *scons*, m., pl. *-ys*, *gorthfos*, f., pl. *-ow*.
bumble-bee, n. *gwenenen wyls*, f., col. *gwenyn gwyls*.
bump, n. *bom*, m., pl. *-myn*, *cronk*, *bonk*, m. pl. *-ys*: v. *bonkya*, *cronkya*.

bun, n. *torth,* or *tesen, vȳghan,* f., pls. *-thow, -now, bȳghan.*
bunch, n. *tos,* m., pl. *-ow, bar,* m., pl. *-row, gron,* m., *bagas,* m., pl. *-ow*; of twigs, *baren,* f., pl. *-now*; of ore, *bonny,* m., pl. *-es*; of ribbons, *colm*: v. *gorra yn gron, kelmy yn tosow*; bunched up, *yn-gron.*
bundle, n. *pusorn,* m., pl. *-sernow, tas,* m., pl. *-ow, tysk,* m., f., pl. *-scow, gron,* m., *fardel,* m., pl. *-low*: v. *pusornas,* **gronna, gorra yn gron, gül fardel a*[2].
bungle, n. *camwonys,* m.: v. *camwonys*: **-r,** n. *camwonysyas,* m., pl. *-ysy*: **-gling,** a. *boghes coynt.*
buoy, n. *merk-nyja,* m., pl. *-ys-n.*: v. *synsy war don, gül dhe nyja*: **-ancy,** n. *scafter,* m.: **-ant,** a. *scaf,* **henyj.*
burden, n. *bēgh* (*be*), m., pl. *-yow*; of horse, *saw,* m., pl. *-yow*; music, *pen-pusorn,* m.; to sing b., *pusornas*: v. *bēghya*: **-some,** a. *mür y bōs.*
burdock, n. †*les-serghak,* m., **serghegen vrās,* f., pl. *-now brās,* ‡ *tavol amanyn,* col.
burgess, n. *burjes,* m., pl. *-jysy.*
burgh, n. **borgh,* m., pl. *-ow.*
burgher: see **burgess.**
burglar, n. *lader nōs,* m., pl. *ladron n., terrer chȳ,* m., pl. *-oryon c.*: **-y,** n. *torva chȳ,* f.: **-gle,** v. *terry chȳ.*
Burgundy, n. **Burgayn,* f.
burial, n. *encledhyas,* m., *enclathva,* f.; b. ground, b. place, *enclathva,* f.
burlesque, n. *gwary gēs,* m., pl. *-ow g.*
burly, a. *brās y gorf*; b. person, *quallok,* m., pl. *-ys.*
burn, v. *lesky, dywy, scaldya*: n. *losk,* m.; **-ing,** n. *losk,* m., *loskvan,* m.: a. *ow-lesky,* **tanek,*
burnish, v. *gül dhe splanna,* **burnsya*: n. **burnys, splander,* m.
burough, n. **borgh,* m., pl. *-ow.*
burrow, n., rabbit b., *toll conyn,* m., pl. *tell conynas*; mound, *crük,* m., pl. *-ügyow,* †*rȳnen,* f., pl. *-now*; mine refuse, *bern atal,* m., pl. *-yow a.*: v. *türya, telly yn-dan*[2] *dȳr.*
burst, v. *tardha, ranna, squattya*; of leaf-buds, *dēlya*; b. out laughing, *dyeskynna,* or *codha, yn wharth*: n. *tarth,* m., pl. *-dhow.*
bury, v. *encledhyes, gorra yn prȳ* or *dōr,* ‡*bedhy,* **prȳa.*
bush, n. *bos,* m., pl. *-ow, bagas,* m., pl. *-ow, perth,* f., pl. *-y, prysken,* f., col. *prysk, lon,* m., pl. *-ow, bush,* m., pl. *-ys*: **-y,** a. *bojek, lonak*; b. place, *lonek, prysclowek, bojek,* f., pls. *-egow, -egy, pryskwydhal,* m., pls. *-dhlow, -dhyly.*
bushel, n. *bushel,* m., pl. *-lys.*
business, n. *negys,* m., pl. and abst., *-yow cās,* m., *tra,* neut., pl. *taclow*; affairs, *an bȳs,* m.; b.-like, *fȳn, a-wōr y negys*; mind your own b., *gwra mellya orth dha daclow dha honen*; you have no b. to speak so, *nyns-yu dheugh-why yndella leverel*; it is really not my b., *dhym ny-amo ·nt, defry ·.*
bustle, v. *gonys bysy*: n. *ober bysy.*
busy, a. *bysy*; to b. oneself with, *omrȳ dhe*[2]: **-body,** n. *mellyer,* m., pl. *-yoryon.*
but, conj. *mes, saw*; except, *saw, lemen*; it is b., *nyns-yu mes, marnas,* or *lemen*; b. for him, *na-vē ef*; b. rather, *yn dar.*
butcher, n. *kyger,* m., pl. *-goryon*; b's. shop, *kykty,* m., *kygva,* f., *kygereth,* f., pls. *-ow.*: **-y,** n. *kygereth,* f., pl. *-ow.*
butcher's broom, n. **kelyn Frynk,* **k. bȳghan,* col.
butler, n. *spencer,* m., pl. *-s.,* †*menystror,* m., pl. *-yon, botteler, m.,* pl. *-s.*
butt, v. *herdhya,* **melsa*: n., b. end, *pen,* m., pl. *-now*; for water, *balyer-dowr*; for archery, *butta,* m., pl. *-ys.*
butter, n. *amanyn,* m.: v. *amanynna*: **-y,** n. *spens,* m., pl. *-ys,* †*talgell,* f., pl. *-ow.*
buttercup, n. *paw-brān,* m., pl. *blejyow p.*
butterfly, n. *tykky-dew,* m., pl. *-as.*
buttock, n. *pedren,* f., pl. *-now,* d. *dywbedren.*
botton, n. **boton,* m., pl. *-now*: v. **botonna*: **-hole,** n. *toll boton,* m., pl. *tell b.*
buxom, a. *tew ha yagh, plegadow.*
buy, v. *prena*; b. for £9, *prena a naw püns*; b. back, redeem, *dasprena*: **-er,** n. *prener,* m., pl. *-noryon.*
buzz, v. *sudronenny, sȳa, whyrny*: n. *sȳ,* m.
buzzard, n. *bargos,* m., pls. *-as, -ojas.*
by, prep., position, *ryp, ryp scōth a*[2], *ogas dhe*[2]; close b., *a-ogas, orth*; b. the wing, etc., *er an ascal,* etc.; in oaths, *rē*[2] (before vowel, *rēn*), *tan*; agent, *drē, gans*; b. this or that, time, then, now, *nans* (before vowel in *bōs*); b. the time that, *erby ·n*; b. Christmas, *erby ·n Nadelek*; b. whom, *py gansa,* etc.; b. which, whereby, *may*[5]; too long b. half, *rē hȳr a hanter*; b. or near him, *yn y ogas*: adv. *drēs, ogas*; past me, etc., *dresof,* etc.; aside, *yn-hans* (*hons*); b. night, *yn-nōs orth golow nōs*; b. day, *yn golow deth*; pass b., *tremena, mōs drēs*; by-the-by, by the way, *ha ny ow-cows a'n dra, anodho pan gowsyr, aban üs cows anodho.*

by-and-by, adv. *yn nebes prӯs, wharē, yn bӯ an bӯ.*
bygone, a. *üs tremenys* or *passyes.*
bye-law, n. *lagha-trē, l. cowethas,* m., pl. *-ghys t., c.*
by-path, n. *forth a-drüs,* f., pl. *-ordhow a.*
by-play, n. *gwary a-denewan,* m.
by-road, n. *scoch-forth,* f., pl. *-ordhow.*
by-stander, n. *sevylyak,* m., pl. *-yogyon.*
by-street, n. *strēt a-denewan,* m., pl. *-ys.*
byway, n. *scoch-forth, *gohelforth,* f., pl. *-ordhow.*

C

cabbage, n. *cawlen* f., col. *cawl, ‡cavach, ‡ongel,* col.; c. field, garden, *cawlek,* f., pls. *-egy, -egow.*
cabin, n. *crowjy,* m., pl. *-ow, scovva,* f.; of ship, **cabyn,* m., pl. *-s*; c.-boy, **cabynwas,* m., pl. *-wesyon.*
cable, n. *capel gorhel,* m., pl. *-plys g.*
cackle, v. **gregga*: **-ling,** n. **grek,* m.
cadaverous, a. *ave·l corf marow, nag-üs dhodho saw croghen hag eskern.*
cafe, n. *bōsty, coffyjy,* m., pl. *-ow.*
cage, n. *cowel edhen,* m., pl. *-low ydhyn.*
caitiff, n. *chet,* m., pl. *-ttys*: a. *kēth.*
cajole, v. *flattra, fēcla, *trüthya*: **-r,** n. *flattor,* m., pl. *-yon,* f. *-es,* pl. *-ow*: **-ry,** n. *fekyl lavarow,* pl., **trüth,* m.
cake, n. *tesen,* f., pl. *-now, ‡caken,* f., pls. *-now, -kys*; dinner c., *whyogen (fūgen, hogen),* f., pl. *-gas*; c. of soap, wax, etc., *torth,* f., pl. *-ow.*
calamitous, a. *anfüsyk*: **-ity,** n. *trūeth brās,* m., *anfüsy,* m., *droglam, drok-lam,* m., pl. *-mow.*
calculate, v. *rekna, acontya*: **-ion,** n. *acontyans, reken,* m.: **-tor,** n. *calcor,* m., pl. *-yon.*
Calends, n., first day of month, *Calan, Cala', dē Halan,* m.; C. of Winter, *C. Gwaf.*
calendar, n. *lyver dēdhyow,* m., pl. *lyfrow d.*
calf, n. *lugh,* m., pl. *-y*; of leg, *logosen fer,* f., pl. *logas f.*; c.-house, *lughty,* m., pl. *-ow*; c. skin, *lughken,* m.
call, v. *gelwel, crӯa*; to name, *henwel*; c. for, *dervyn*; c. on, demand, *requӯrya*; c. oneself, *omhenwel*; c. out, *crӯa*; c. to, on, upon, *crӯa war*[2]: n. *crӯ,* m., pl. *-ow*; invitation, *galow,* m.: **-ed,** a. *henwys, gelwys, *gelwesyk*; c. for, required, *bysy*; what are you c.? *py hanow os?*; I am c. A., *Ow hanow yu A., A. y-m-gylwyr*: **-ing,** n., vocation, *galow, galwans,* m., **gelwesygeth,* f.
callosity, n. *calesen,* f., pl. *-now.*
callous, a. *aflythys, gyllys cales y golon*; c. person, *aflythys,* m., pl. *-yjyon.*
callow, a. *dyblüf, mōl, lom y groghen.*
calm, a. *hebask, cosel, clōr*: v. *hebaskhē·, *destewel*: n. *spavnell (spanell),* f., pl. *-ow, spaven mōr,* m.: **-ing,** n. *hebasca,* f.: **-ness,** n. *calmynsy, clōrder,* m.
calumniate, v. *cably, sclandra*: **-ny,** n. *cabel,* m.
Cambridge, n. *Kērgront,* f.
camel, n. *†cawrvargh,* m., pl. *-vergh.*
camomile, n. *camyl,* col.
camp, n., milit., *caslys,* f., pl. *-yow*; pleasure, *camp,* m., pl. *-ys*: v. *gül caslys, campya, tryga yn tyldys.*
campaign, n. **caskergh,* m., pl. *-ow*: v. *gül *caskergh.*
can, n. *†canna,* m., pl. *-nys.*
can: see **able.**
canal, n. *dowrglēth,* m., pl. *-edhyow.*
cancel, v. *defendya dhe-vēs*: **-lation,** n. *defendyans,* m.
cancer, n. *canker,* m.
candid, a. *gwyryon, frank, ganso sōth, efan y lavarow*; c. person, *gwӯrleveryas,* m., pl. *-ysy*: **-ly,** adv. *yn-whӯr, yn gwӯrder, hep wow, rak leverel gwyryoneth, hep fayntys na falsury.*
candidate, n. *ombrofyer,* m., pl. *-yoryon, whyler (bōs dewysys),* m., pl. *-loryon (b.d.).*
candle, n. *cantol,* f., pl. *-yow*; wax c., *taper,* m., pls. *-prys, -prow, cantol gōr*; tallow c., *cantol sōf*; c. grease, *saym-cantol,* m.; c. stick, *cantolbren,* m., pls. *-yer, ‡chandeler (chownler),* m., pl. *-s.*
candour, n. *gwyrder, gwyryoneth,* m.
cane: see **stick.**
canker, n. *canker,* m.
cannon, n. *canon,* m., pl. *-ys, gon mür,* **m.,** pl. *-ys,* m.; c. ball, *tanbellen,* f., pl. *-now.*
canoe, n. **canoa,* m., pl. *-s.*
canon, n. *chenon,* m., pl. *-s*: **-ry,** n. *chenonry,* m.
canopy, n. *queth a stāt,* m., **nenlen,* f., pl. *-now.*
canter, v. *ponya.*
canticle, n. **cantykyl,* m., pl. *-yclys.*
canton, n. *keverang,* f., pl. *-ow.*
canvas, n. *kewarghlen,* f., *canfas,* m.
cap, n. *cappa,* m., pl. *-pys, *tok,* m., pl. *-ogow.*

capability, n. *gallos,* m.: **-ble,** a. *gallosek, harth, abel.*
capricious, a. *efan.*
capacity, n., grasp, *gavel,* f., pl. *-yow*; room, *lē, spās, efander,* m.; ability, *gallos,* m.; filled to c., *collenwys glan.*
cape, n. *capa,* f., pl. *-pyow*; land, *penrȳn,* m., pl. *-yow, pentȳr,* m., pl. *-yow.*
caper, v. *cryghlemmel*: n. *cryghlam,* m., pl. *-now, prat,* m., pl. *-tys.*
capias, n., writ, *capyas,* m.
capital, n. *mamdra,* f., pl. *-revow, -reven, pencyta, chȳf-cyta,* f., pl. *-tys*; in building, *pen pyllar,* m., pl. *-now pyllars*; money, *arghans,* col.; c. letter, *lytheren vrās,* f., pl. *-now brās*: a. *bryntyn, rȳal, gay.*
capon, n. *chappon,* m., pl. *-s.*
caprice, n. *sȳans,* m.: **-ciously,** adv. *whym-wham, herwyth sȳans.*
capsize, v. *kȳsya, omwheles, trēlya keyn yn-ban.*
capstan, n. **cabestran,* **capstern,* m., pl. *-ys*; horse c., *whym,* m., pl. *-mys.*
captain, n. *pen,* m., pl. *-now,* †*hembrynkyas-lu,* m., pl. *ysy-l,* **capytayn,* **capten,* m., pls. *-s, -ow.*
captivate, v. *hüda.*
captive, n. *prysner,* m., pl. *-s, caytyf,* m., pl. *-yvys*; make c. *prēdhya.*: a. *prysonys*: **-vity,** n. *gwaso·nȳeth,* f.; *capty·vyta,* m.
capture, v. *kemeres, cachya, settya dalghen-now yn*; c. prey, **prēdhya.*
car, n. *car,* m., pl. *kerry*; motor c., *car tān.*
carapace, n. *crogen,* f., pl. *cregyn.*
caravan, n. *car tylda, chȳ-car,* m.
carcase, n. *caryn,* m., pl. *-yas.*
card, n. *carten,* f., pl. *-now*; wool-c., *crȳbyn,* f., pl. *-now*: v., c. wool, *crȳbya.*
cardinal, n. *cardynal,* m., pl. *-as.*
care, n., worry, *fyenasow,* abst. pl., *govyjyon,* m., *preder,* m., pl and abst. *-ow*; solicitude, *bern,* m.; keeping, *gwȳth,* m.; heed, *rach, fors,* m.; responsibility, *charj,* m., pl. *-ys*; with c., *dour*; free from c., *yn ēs, attē·s*; to take c., *gwaytya*; take c. to, *gorra wyth,* or *gorquyth, dhe*[2]; take c. of, *gwytha*; take c. of oneself, *omweres*; take c.! *bedheugh why für*! *bedheugh wār*!: v., c. to, *mynnes, cara*; c. for, *chersya, cara*; if thou carest, *mara'th-tür*; I don't c., *ny-m-dür, ny-wraf fors, ny-vern dhym, my ny-synsaf poynt*; I don't c. a hang for it! *anodho my ny-settyaf gwelen-gala*! *ny- synsaf anodho ün faven gōk*!: **-free,** a. *dygüth*; **-ful,** a. †*prederüs, für, wār*; to be c., *wār* (*def. v.*), *bōs wār*; be c.! *wār,* pl. *waryeugh*! *bȳth war,* pl. *bedheugh war*!; be c. beforehand! *darwar*!; be more c. next time! *bedheugh-why fürra nessa*!: **-fully,** adv. *precyous, dour*: **-less,** a. *lows, dybreder, dyswar*; c. fellow, *caughwas,* m., pl. *-wesyon.*: **-lessness,** n. *fowt preder, scul,* m., *sculva,* f.: **-worn,** a. *mür y fyena-sow, gyllys yn prederow.*
career, n. *resekva,* f., pl. *-ow, hens,* pl. *-y.*
caress, v. *chersya, handla yn-cosel,* **palva*: n. **palvas kerensa,* m., pl. *-vosow k.*
cargo, n. **carg,* m., pl. *-ow.*
caricature, n. *hevelep gēs,* or **gorlywys,* m., pl. *-ebow g.*
carnage, n. **arva,* f.
carnal, a. *carnal, a'n kȳk.*
carniverous, a. *a-dheber,* or *üs ow-tybry, kȳk.*
carol, n. *cān carol, c. Nadelek*: v. **caroly.*
carp, n. **lynbysk,* m., pl. *-buskes, -scas.*
carpenter, n. *carpenter,* m., pls. *-s, -oryon,* †*sēr pren,* m., pl. *-y p.*: **-try,** n. *sē·rȳeth,* f.
carpet, n. **tapȳ·t,* m., pl. *-ys,* **lürlen,* f., pl. *-now.*
carrack, n. **carrak,* m., pl. *-ys.*
carriage, n., vehicle, **caryach,* m., pl. *-ajys*; transport, ‡*carryans,* m., *dōn,* inf.; by cart, *caryans*; bearing, *omdhō·n,* inf.
carrier, n. *caryer, deger, kergher,* m., pls. *-yoryon, -goryon, -ghoryon.*
carrion, n. *caryn,* m., pl. *-yas*; c. crow, *brān,* f., pl. *brȳny, kȳgvran,* f., pl. *-rȳny.*
carrot, n. *caretysen,* f., col. *caretys.*
carry, v. *dōn, perthy*; in vehicle, *carya*; bring, *kerghes*; c. off, *dōn*; be carried off by, *mōs* or *dōs gans*; c. away, enrapture, *rafsya*; c. out work, *obery.*
cart, n. *car,* m., pl. *kerry, kert,* m., pl. *-ys*; c. bridge, *carbons,* m., pl. *-ow*; c. horse, *carvyl,* m., pl. *-as*; c. shed, *carjy,* m., pl. *-ow*; c. track, *carhens,* m., pl. *-y*; c. load, **carg,* m., pl. *-ow*: v. *carya*: **-er,** n. *caryer,* m., pl. *-yoryon*
cartilage, n. **mygorn,* m.
carve, v. *trēghy*; c. meat, *kervya*; c. stone, etc., *gravya*: **-r,** n. *trēghyas,* m., pl. *-ysy*; decorative c., **ymajer,* m., pl. *-s,* †*gravyor,* m., pl. *-yon*; c. at table, †*rennyas,* m., pl. *-ysy*: **-ving,** n. **ymajery,* m., pl. *-s*: **-ving-dish,** n. *tallyour,* m., pl. *-s.*
cascade, n. **lamfrōs,* m., pl. *-ow.*
case, n. *trok,* m., pls. *-kys, tregys, cofyr,* m., pl. *-frow*; legal, *kēn,* m.; event, *cās,* m.;

argument, *dathel* (*dal*), f., pl. *dathlow*; in c., *mar*[4]; I am in like c., *yndella dhymmo y-wher*; in any c., *yn nep cās*; sorry c., *drōk* or *tebel stüth*; the c. is altered, *yma· kēn ordnys, chanjys yu an rewl.*
cash, n. *arghans parys* or *bathys, mona,* col.: v. **cashya*: **-ier,** n. **cashyer*, m., pl. *-s.*
cask, n. †*tonnel*, f., pl. *-low*, ‡*balyer*, m., pl. *-s.*
casket, n. *cofyr bӯghan*, **cofryn*, m., pl. *-now.*
cassock, n. *gōn hӯr*, m., pl. *-ow h.*, *crӯspows oferyas*, f.
cast, v. *tewlel*; c. lots, *tewlel pren*: n. *towl*, m., pl. *-ow.*
castle, n. *castel*, m., pl. *-tylly.*
casual, a. *dybreder, drē hap*: **-ty,** n. *droglam, coll* (*bresel*), m., pl. *-ow* (*b.*).
cat, n. *cath*, f., pl. *-as*; tom-c., *gourgath*; she-c., **cathes*, f., pl. *-ow*; little-c., kitten, *cathyk*, f., pl. *-ygow, -thasygow.*
catalogue, n. *rōl*, f., pl. *-yow*: v. *gül rōl.*
catapult, n. *jyn-tewlel*, m., pl. *-nys t.*, *trebüchet*, m., pl. *-tys*: v. *tewlel, trebüchya.*
cataract, n. *lam-dowr mür*, m., pl. *lammow-d. m.*; of eye, *kennen*, f., pl. *-now.*
catastrophe, n. *droglam, drōk-lam*, m., pl. *-mow, terros*, m., pl. *-rysy, -ryjy.*
catch, v. *cachya, cafos, kemeres*; of understanding, hearing, seeing, *convedhes, synsy, clewes, gweles*; hook, *hygenna*; hitch, hook, etc., *bagha*; c. fish, *pyskessa*; c. mice, *legessa*; c. beetles, *whylessa*, etc. (inf. only); c. fire, *kemeres*, or *mōs gans, tān.*
catechize, v. **cathekysa*: **-ism,** n. * *cathekys*, m.
catechumen, n. *cathecumynys*, m., pl. *-ow.*
cater, v. *provӯa*: **-er,** n. *provӯer*, m., pl. *-yoryon.*
caterpillar, n. **prӯf dēl*, m., pl. *pryves d.*: hairy c., *prӯf-blewek*; green c., *prӯf-cawl*; tree c., *prӯf-pren.*
cathedral, n. *peneglos*, f., pl. *-yow, -lysyow.*
catkin, n., willow c., *cath-helyk*, f., pl. *-as-h.*; hazel c., *lost ōn*, pl. *lostow ēn.*
cattle, n. *mylas, -es, bestas, -es*, pl., *chattel*, col.; a head of c., †*ēal, mӯl, best*, m.; horned c., *gwarthek*, col.; c. yard, *gwarthegva*, f., *büarth*, m., pl. *-ow*; c. show, *dysquedhyans gwarthek*, m.; c. shed, *bowjy, chӯ-vylas, grējy*, m.,; c. pond *grēlyn*, m.
cauldron, n. *pēr*, m., pl. *-row, chek*, m., pl. *-kys*, †*caltor*, f., pl. *-yow*, ‡*caudarn*, m., pl. *-s.*
cauliflower, n. **cawlvlejen*, f., pl. *-jyow.*
caulk, v. *calkya.*
cause, v. *gül* (*güthyl, gwrüthyl*), *skyla* (def.), *gül bōs, causya*: n. *praga, kēn*, m.; reason, *skyla, acheson*, m., *cās, caus*, m., pls. *-ys*; one who causes, *causer*, m., pl. *-s*; we have c. to rejoice, *ny a-ӯl lowr bōs lowen*; without c., *hep kēn*; for any c., *a nep ous.*
causeway, n. *cauns*, m., pl. *-ys*, **sarn*, f., pl. *-ow.*
caution, n., warning, *gwarnyans*, m.; care, *fürneth*, m.; c!, *darwar*!: v. *gwarnya*: **-ous,** a. *wār, für*: **-ously,** adv. *war gam, gans rach*; go c!, *kē war dha gam!*
cavalier, n. *marghak*, m., pl. *-ghogyon*: **-lry,** n. *marghoglu*, m.: **-lryman,** n. *soudor margh*, m., pl. *-yon mergh*, or *war vergh.*
cave, n. *fogo, gogo, ogo*, f., pl. *-gevyow, fow*, f., pl. *-ys, cāf*, m., pl. *-āvys, -avyow.*
cavity, n. *keyva*, f., *keydoll, cow, cowans*, m.; natural, in rock, *füg*, f.; hollow part, *gwakter*, m.
caw, v. *renky*: n. *ronk*, **crawkya*, **crawkyans*, m., pl. *-ow.*
cease, v. *hedhy, cessya, gasa, dyfygya, powes*; of rain, etc., *slakya.*
ceiling, n. *nen*, m., pl. *-now*; curved or vaulted c, *cromnen*, m.
celandine, n. **losow lagas*, col.
celebrate, v., feast, etc., *gōlya, rejoycya*; honour with rites, *solempnya*; eccl., *oferenny*: **-tion,** n. *solempnyta*, m., pl. *-tys*; eccl., *oferen*, f., pl. *-now*: **-ted,** a. *kywhethlys*, †*geryes da, mür y hanow.*
celebrity, n. *brӯ*, m.; person, *dēn a vrӯ*, m., pl. *tüs a. v.*
celery, n. **kegys whēk*, col.
celestial, a. *a nef*, **nevek.*
celibate, a. *dydhemeth*: n. *bacheler*, m., pl. *-s.*
cell, n., dungeon, *bagh*, f., pl. *-ow*; organism, *kell*, f., pl. *-ow*; monastic, *lok*, f., pl. *-ogow*; of hermit, *penytty, teghyjy*, m.
cellar, n. **dorgell*, f., pl. *-ow*; as store, †*talgell*, f., *celer*, ‡*selder*, m.; salt-c., **salyour*, m., pl. *-s.*
Celt, n. *Kelt*, m., pl. *-yon*; implement, *mēntaran*, m., pl. *meyn-t*: **-ic,** *Keltek.*
cement, n. *cyment*, m.
cemetery, n. *enclathva*, f., **bedhros*, f., pl. *-ow.*
censer, n. *sensour*, m., pl. *-s.*
censor, v., *brüsy*,: n. *brüsyas* m., pl. *-ysy.*
censure, v. *cably, blamya, reprēfa, rebükya*: n. *cabel, blam*, m.
census, n. *nyveryans an bobel*, m.

centenary, n. *pen-cansbloth,* m.
centre, n. *crēs,* m.: a. **-tral,** *crēs, y'n crēs.*
centurion, *century (sentury).* †*pencangour,* m.
century, n. *cansbledhen,* f., pl. *-ynnow;* of age, *cansblōth,* m.
ceremony, -nial, n. *solempnyta,* m., pl. *-tys,* **ceremony,* m., pl. *-s*: **-nious,** a. *cortes drēs ēghen, rē gortes.*
certain, a., sure, *dyogel, sür;* a c., *ün,* ‡*nebün, certan;* c. people, *certan;* I am c., *sür of*: **-ly,** adv. *yn-tyogel, hep nep mar, certan, yn-tefry·, ywy·s*: **-ty,** n., for a c., *yn sür redy, hep fall, yn tyogel.*
certificate, n. *certyfyans,* m., pl. *-ow, test-scryf,* m., pl. *-yvow, scryven testa,* f., pl. *-now*: **-fy,** v. *certyfȳa, testa, scryfa testans.*
cessation, n. *fynweth,* f., *powes,* m.
chad, n., fish, *lommas,* m., pl. *-ow, takflogh,* m., pl. *-as.*
chafe, v. *ruttya;* fret, *serry,*
chafer, n., beetle, *whȳl,* m., pl. *-as,* †*cafor,* m., pl. *-ys.*
chaff, n. *üsyn,* m., col. *üs,* pl. *üsyon, dowst,* m., *cūthow,* pl., †*culyn,* m.; jest, *gēs,* m.: v., jest, *gēsya, scornya.*
chaffer, n., bargain, *chyffar,* m.
chaffinch, n. *tynk,* m., pl. *-ncas,* **kewargher,* m., pl. *-as,* **askel vrȳth.*
chaffy, a. *üsak.*
chafing-dish, n. ‡*chofar,* m., pl. *-s.*
chagrin, n. *edrega, edrek, awhe·r,* m.
chain, n. *chayn,* m., pl. *-ys, syg,* f., pl. *-yow,* **cadon,* f.: v. *chaynya*: **-ed,** a., of dog, *stak.*
chair, n. *cadar,* f., pl. *-oryow, chayr,* m., pl. *-ys;* arm-c., *cadar vrēghek,* pl., *-eryow brēghek;* to take the c., *caderya*: **-man,** n. *caderyer,* m., pl. *-yoryon.*
chalice, n. *kelegel,* m., pl. *-glow, chalys,* m., pl. *-ys.*
chalk, n. *gwyn,* m.
challenge, n. *ēr,* m., pl. *-yow, chalynj,* m., pl. *-ys*: v. *erya, chalynjya*: **-r,** n. *bedhyas,* m., pl. *-ysy, eryor,* m., pl. *-yon.*
chamber, n. *chambour,* m., pl. *-s.,* †*stevel,* m., pl. *-yow;* underground, *fow,* f., pl. *-ys, fogo,* f., pl. *-gevyow;* in tumulus, *kyst vēn,* f., pl. *-yow mēn;* c. maid, **chambrores,* f., pl. *-ow;* c. pot, ‡*pycher-pȳsa,* m.
chamberlain, n. **chamberlyn,* m., pl. *-s.*
chamois, n. *gavar an menydhyow,* f., pl. *gever* or *gyfras a. m.*
champion, n. **campyer,* m., pl. *-yoryon, pen-strȳfer,* m., pl. *-yon*: **-ship,** n. **campyory,* m.
chance, n. *lam, hap, spās, chons, fortyn* m.; by c., *drē hap*: v. *wharfos, darfos, chonsya, hapya, fortynya*: a. *drē hap.*
chancel, n. **chansel,* m., pl. *-s.*
chancellor, n. **chansler,* m., pl. *-s.*
chandelier, n. **cantolor,* m., pl. *-yow, chandeler (chownler),* m., pl. *-s.*
chandler, n. *cantolor,* m., pl. *-yon.*
change, n. *trēlva,* f., *trēlyans,* m., pl. *-ow; chanj* m., pl. *-ys;* small c., *mona münys*: v. *varya, chanjya, trēlya, remüvya;* alter, *dyheveleby, dyfeleby*: **-able,** *hedro, parys dhe janjya, brottel;* c. person, *padel-ynkyn,* f., pls. *-llow-y., -lly-y.*: **-ableness,** n. *brottelder,* m.: **-ging,** n. *trēlyans,* m., pl. *-ow.*
changeling, n. *canjeon,* m. and f., pl. *-s.*
channel, n. *canel,* f., pls. *-nolyow, -nalow,* ‡*shanel,* m.; gutter, *lōnder,* m., pl. *-drys.* the English C., *an Chanel,* m.
chant, n. *cürgan,* f., pl. *-ow*: v. *cana*: **-er,** n. *kenyas,* m., pl. *-ysy.*
chantry, n. *chōntry,* m., pl. *-s.*
chaos, n. *dera·y, fowt rewl,* m.: **-otic,** a. *dyrewl.*
chap, n., fellow, *gwas,* m., pl. *-gwesyon, pollat,* m., pl. *-tys;* of pigs, etc., *bogh,* d. *dywvogh.*
chapel, n. *chapel,* m., pl. *-yow, mynster,* m., pl. *-ow.*
chaplain, n. *chaplen,* m., pl. *-s.*
chaps, n., jaws, *dywen, dywvogh,* d. f.
chapter, n. *pen,* m., pl. *-now;* eccl., *chaptra,* m., pl. *-trys.*
char, v. *golesky*: **-red,** a. *goleskys;* c. wood, coal, etc., **golosk,* m.
charabanc, n. *car skavelek,* m.
character, n. *natur, gnās, nās,* f.; good c., *hanow da,* m.; what is his c.? *py par dēn yua?*: **-istics,** n. *tȳthy,* col. and abst.
charcoal, n. *glow,* col.; fuel, **golosk,* m., *pren goleskys;* glowing c., *regythen,* f., col. *regyth;* wood for c., *glowwȳth,* col.
charge, v., order, *charjya, erghy;* load, *carga;* rush, *resek war*[2]; charge! *dün warnedha!;* money, *govyn;* in court, *cuhüdha*: n., order, *arghadow,* m.; duty, *charj,* m., pl. *-ys, cür;* in court, *lȳbel,* m.; accusation, *cuhüdhans,* m., pl. *-ow;* money, *cost,* m., pl. *-ys;* load, *carg,* m., pl. *-ow.*
charger, n., horse, *courser,* m., pl. *-s,* **cas-*

vargh, m., pl. *-vergh*; dish, *tallyour*, m., pl. *-s*.

chariot, n. *charet*, m., pl. *-tys*, *kert*, m., pl. *-ys*.

charitable, a. *hēl, mür y jeryta*: **-ty,** n. *alüsen*, f., pl. *-ow*, *kerensa*, f., *cheryta*, m.; in c., *pour cheryta*!

charm, v. *hüda, sona, dynya, dydhana*: n. *sōn*, m., pl. *-ow*; abst. *hüs*, m.; bead c., *mylprȳf*, m.: **-er,** n. *peller, hüdor*, m., pl. *-oryon*, f., *-ores*, pl. *-ow*: **-ing,** *whēgoll, hegar*.

charter, n. *chartour*, m., pl. *-s*: v. *gül chartour a*².

chase, v. *helghya, chassya*; c. along, *dehelghya*; engrave, *gravya*: n. *helgh, chās*, m.; wood, *cōs an chās*: **-ing tool,** n. *collelgravya*, f., pls. *kellyl, kellyly, g*.

chasm, n. *yslonk*, m.; in cliff, *saun*, f., pl. *-yow*.

chaste, a. *glan, chast*: **-tity,** n. *glander*, **chastyta*, m.

chasten, v. *kesky*.

chastise, v. *kessydhya, chastȳa, keredhy, castȳga*: **-ment,** n. *kereth*, f., *castȳk*, m.

chasuble, n. †*ofergügol*, m., pl *-low*, **casül*, f., pl. *-yow*.

chat, v. *kestalkya, keskewsel*: n. *cows*, m., pl. *-ow*: **-ter,** v. *clappya, clattra*; of teeth, *cryghylly, crenna*: n. *clap*, m.: **-ter-box,** *tavasek*, m., pl. *-sogyon*.

chattels, n. *pyth, mebyl*, m.

cheap, a. *prenys da, a vargen da, a brȳs ysel*.

cheat, v. *tulla, hyga, gül fa·lsury*: n. *tullor*, m., pl. *-yon*, *falsgwas*, m., pl. *-wesyon*; action of cheating, **hyk*, f., pl. *-ygyon*: **-ing,** n. *tull, fa·lsury*, m.

check, v. *lettya*; admonish, ‡*chekkya, keredhy*: n. *let*, m.: a., of pattern, †*bryth*.

cheek, n. *bogh*, f., pl. *-ow*, d. *dywvogh, grüth*, f., pl. *-üdhyow*; having big c's., *boghek*; impertinence, *ref*, m.: **-y,** a. *tont*; be c., *tontya*.

cheer, v. *garma yn-lowen, gül noys rak*; c. us up, etc., *gwellhē·* or *bōs da agan chēr, omgonfortya*; I am greatly cheered, *ow holon yu mur-hüdhys*: n., mien, *chēr*, m.; be of good c.! *omgonfortyeugh*!: **-ful,** a. *jolyf, lowenek, da y jēr*: **-fulness,** n. *lowender*, m.: **-less,** a. *tryst, drōk agan chēr*, etc., *dygolon* (*dy·glon*): **-lessness,** n. *dygolon*, f.; *drōk chēr, trystys, trystans*, m.

cheese, n. *kēs*, m.; unripe, c. *kēs glās*; c. whey, *kēsvȳth*, m.; c. press, *kēswask*, f., pl. *-scow*.

chemical a. **kymyk*; **-ist,** n. **kymyst*, m., pl. *-ys*: **-istry,** n. **kymystry*, m.

chemise, n. †*crȳs benen*, m., pl. *-yow benenes*.

cheque, n. **chekken*, f., pl. *-now*.

chequered, a. †*bryth*.

cherish, v. *chersya, chērya*; as a hen its chicks, *covȳa*: **-ed,** a. *kēr, drüth, mürgerys*.

cherry, n., fruit or tree, *keresen*, f., col. *keres*; morello c., *keresen vorel*, f., col. *keres morel*; c. tree, *gwedhen keres*, f.; c. orchard, *keresek*, f., pls. *-egow, -egy*.

cherub, n. *elyk*, m., pl. *elethygow, cherubyn*, m., pl. *-s*.

chervil, n. †*serfel*, m.

chess, n. **gwythpoll*, f.; c. board, **chekker*, m., pl. *-s*.

chest, n. *kyst*, f., pl. *-yow, argh*, f., pls. *-ow, erghy, logel*, f., pl. *-low, cofyr*, m., pl. *-frow*; small c., *kysten*, f., pl. *-now*; large c., *trok*, m., pls. *-kys, tregys*; iron c., *trok a horn*; anat., †*clōs dywvron, bryansen*, f.

chestnut, n., tree and nut, *kestenen*, f., col. *kesten*; colour, **gell kesten*; c. grove, *kestenek*, f., pls. *-egy, -egow*.

chevron, n. *keber*, f., pl. *-bryow*.

chew, v. *dynsel, *knȳas*; c. cud, **dasknȳas*.

chick, n. *ydhnyk*, m., pl. *-ygow*: **-en,** n. *mabyar*, m. and f., *-yēr*; hen, *yar*, f., pl. *yēr*.

chicken-pox, n. *pokkys yēr, *bregh yēr*, f.

chickweed, n. *glēth*, m.

chide, v. *deraylya, gērya, keredhy, omdhal*.

chief, n. *pen*, m., pl. *-now, mēr*, m., pl. *-as, gwelhevyn*, m. and col., †*pente·rn*, m., pl. *-ow, pen-rewler*, m., pl. *-oryon, chyften*, m., pl. *-s*; c. priest, *arghoferyas*, m., pl. *-ysy*: a., prefixed, *pen-, chyf-*.

chiefly, adv. *kens oll, drēs puptra*.

chieftain: see **chief.**

chilblain, n. *losk treys*, m.

child, n. *flogh*, m., pl. *fleghēs*, sep. pl. *fleghysyow, map*, m., pl. *mebyon*; little c., *fleghyk*, m., pls. *fleghesygow, fleghygow, meppyk*, m., pls. *-ygow, mebyonygow*; congregation as "children," *flogholeth*, m.: **-bed, -birth,** n. *gwelyvos*, m.: **-hood,** n. *flogholeth*, m.; c. and old age, *newyth ha henys*: **-ish,** a. *kepa·r ha flogh, floghyl*: **-ishness,** n. *flogholeth*, m.: **-less,** a. *anvab*: **-lessness,** n. *anvabeth*, m.

chill, v. *yeynhē·*: n., fatally, *storvya*: n. *yeynder, anwos*, m.: a. *yeyn*, †*ōr*: **-iness,**

n. **orny*, m.: **-y,** a. *anwesek, nebes yeyn*; c. feeling, *anwos*, m.
chime, v. *seny*: n. *senyans clēgh, s. clōk*, m.
chimney, n. *chymbla*, m., pl. *-blys*; c. corner, *corn an olas*, m.; c. breast, *clavel*, f., pl. *-ys*.
chin, a. *elgeth*, f., pl. *-yow, -y*; double c., **tagell*, f., pl. *-ow*; having a big c., *elgethek*.
china-clay, n. *prȳ gwyn*, m.
china-ware, n. *chēny*, m.
chip, v. **asclejy*: n. *scommyn*, m., pl. *scommow*, **asclejen*, f., col. **asclas*.
chirp, v. **tynkyal*, **gryllya*: **-ing,** n. **gryllyans*, m.
chisel, v. *genna*: n. *gen*, m., pl. *-now*.
chit, n. *chet*, m., pl. *-tys*; wench, *moren*, f., pl. *moronyon*.
chivalrous, a. *kepa·r ha marghak*: **-ry,** n. *chevalry*, **margho·gȳeth*, f.
choice, n. *dewys*, m.; to make a c., *dewys*: a. *dewysys, a'n gwella*.
choir, n. *cür*, m., pl. *-yow, carol*, m., pl. *-yow*; c. master, *pen-kenysy*.
choke, v. *taga*; stifle, *megy*: **-king,** n. *tak*, m.
choose, v. *dewys*.
chop, v. *trēghy, dyvynya, *kemena, skethry*; c. across, *trüstryllya*: n., cut, *trēgh*, m., pl. *-ow, skether*, m., pl. *-thryow*; meat, *golyth*, m., pl. *-yon*; blow, *bom bōl*, etc.: **-per,** n., hatchet, *bōl*, f., pl. *-ow*: **-ping block,** n. *trüstryl*, m., pl. *-yow*.
choppy, a. *tonnek, garow*.
choral, a. *a gür*; c. work, *cürgan*, f., pl. -ow.
chord, n., of notes, *acord*, m., pl. *-ys*; of instrument, *lynyn*, m., pl. *-now*.
chorister, n. *kenyas cür*, m., pl. *-ysy c*.
chorus, n. *kescan*, f., pl. *-ow*, †*carol*, m., pl. *-yow*.
chough, n. *palores*, f., pl. *-ow*, ‡*chōca*, m., pl. *-ys, chogha, ch. gar rüth*, m., pl. *-ys*.
Christ, n. *Cryst*: **-endom,** n. *an bȳs Crystyon, agan hynsa Crystyon, Crystyoneth*, f.: **-ian,** n. *Crystyon*, m., pl. *-tonyon*; a. *Cryst--yon*; c. name, *hanow bysyth*, m., pl. *hynwyn b.*; thy fellow-C., *dha gescrystyon*: **-ianity,** n. *Crystyoneth*, f.: **-en,** v. *bysydhya, crystyonya*: **-ening,** n. *bysydhyans, bysyth*, m.
Christmas, n. *Nadelek*, m.; C. day, *dē-N.*; C. box, **calennyk*, m.
chronicle, v. **cronycla*: n. *covath*, m.; **cronykyl*, m. [2] pl. *-yclys*.
chrysalis, n. **whyler*, pl. *-as, prȳf yn y groghen, crysalys*, m.
chrysanthemum, n. **bothen Cathay*, f., pl. *-now C.*
chub, n. *talek*, m., pl. *-ogas*.
chubby, a. *boghek*.
chuck, v. *tewlel, deghesy*.
chuckle, v. *wherthyn y'n vrȳansen*.
chum, n. *kescoweth*, m., pl. *-a*.
church, n. *eglos*, f., pl. *-yow*: **-town,** n. *treveglos*, f., pl. *trevow e., treneglos*, f. (*tre an eglos*): **-warden,** n. *gwythyas eglos*, m., pl. *-ysy e.*: **-way,** n. *freglos* (*forth eglos*), f.: **-yard,** n. *corflan*, f., pl. *-now*, **bedhros*, m., pl. *-ow*.
churl, n. *vylen, chorl*, m., pl. *-ys*, †*trevesyk dōr*, pl. *-ygyon d.*: **-ish,** a. *vylen, anwhēk, kepa·r ha chorl*.
churn, v. **churnya*; c. up, *trelūba*: n. **churna*, m., pl. *-nys*.
cicatrice, n. *crȳthen*, f., pl. *-now*: **-ize,** v. *crȳthya*.
cider, n. *cȳder*, m.
cilice, n. *hevys rün, grügys rün*, m.,pl. *-yow r*.
cinder, n. *cōlyn marow*, m., pl. *cōlys m.*; *lusewen*, f. *lüsow*.
cinema, n. *gwaya-mȳr*, m.
cinnamon, n. **canel*, m.
cinquefoil, n. *pympdelen*, f., *pymp-bȳs, pympȳs*, m.
circle, n. **kelgh*, m., pl. *-ow, rōs*, f., pl. *-ow*, stone c., *dōns meyn*: **-clet,** n. *garlont*, f., *pls., -ow, -ons*, **kelghen*, f., pl. *-now*: **-cuit,** n. *kelghtro*, m., *tro*, f., pl. *-yow, troȳll*, f., pl. *-yow, rōs*, f., pl. *-ow*: **-cuitous,** a. *ow-mōs adro, gwȳüs*: **-cular,** a. *cren, rond*, **kelghek*: **-culate,** v. *mōs, dōs* or *danvon a-dro*; of blood, *mōs ha dōs*: **-culation,** n. *mōs a-dro*, m. of blood, *mōs ha dōs*.
circumcise, v. **enwosa, cyrcumcȳsya*: **-cision,** m. *enwosans, cyrcumcysyans*, m.: **-ference,** n. *compas*, m., *musür a-dro*, **tro kelgh*, f., pl. *-yow k.*: **-flex,** n. **sȳn crom*, m., pl. *-ys c.*: **-scribe,** v. *settya·lȳn*, or *fȳn, a-dro dhe*[2]: **-spect,** a. *dōth, für* : **-stance,** n. *cās*, m., *tra*, neut., *cyrcumstans*, m. pl., *-ow;* in the c's. *y'n cās-na, yndella pan ve, vo*: **-stantial,** a. *perfyth*; there is c. evidence for that, *yma· lyes tra ow-cül dhyn crysy henna*.
cistern, n. *dowrargh*, m., pl. *-ow, cofyr dowr*, m.
cite, v. **devyn, alejya*: **-tation,** n. *devyn*, m., pl. *-now, dyth*, m., pl. *-ys*.
cithern, n. *gyttern*, m., pl. *-s*.

citizen, n. *burjes*, m., pl. *-ysy*, *cytysan*, m., pl. *-s*.
citole, n. *cythol*, m., pl. *-s*.
citron, n. **cytron*, m., pl. *-s*.
city, n. *cyta*, f., pl. *-tys*.
civic, a. *a'n drē*, *-burjes*.
civil, a. *gwlasek*; polite, *cortes*, **cyvyl*: **-ity**, n. *cortesy*, *whekter*, **cyvylta*, m.: **-ization**, n. **cyvylysasyon*, *wharhēans*, m.: **-ize**, v. *wharhē·*, *cyvylȳsya*.
clad, a. *gwyskys*; ill-c. *ternoth*.
claim, v. *govyn*, *perghenegy*; c. as due, *lavasos*; lay c., *synsy quarel*, *pottya quarel dhe*[2]: n. *quarel*, m., *tȳtel*, m., pl. *-tyls*, *chalynj*, *clēm*, *gorholeth*, m.: **-ant**, n. *pysyer*, m., pl. *-yoryon*, *pysador*, m., pl. *-yon*.
clairvoyant, n. †*colyak*, m., pl. *-yogyon*, f., *-oges*, pl. *-ow*.
clamber, v. *crambla*.
clammy, a. *glyp ha yeyn*.
clamour, n. *noys*, *crȳ*, *trōs*, *sōn*, m.: v. *crȳa*; c. in favour of, *gül noys gans*: **-orous**, a. *ow-carma*, *ow-crȳa*.
clamp, n. **byns*, f.: v. *strotha*.
clan, n. *ken·ethel*, f., pl. *-thlow*, *ēghen*, f.
clandestine, a. *cüdhys*, *a-dryf tüs*, *yn-dan güth*: **-ly**, adv. *a-dryf tüs*, *yn-dan gēl*, *worth golow nōs*.
clang, v. **clankya*: **-ing**, n. **clank*, m., pl. *-ys*.
clap, v. *takya dywla*: n. *crak*, m., pl. *-kys*, *tāk*, m., pl. *taccow*; thunder-c., *tarth*, or *crak*, *taran*: **-per**, n. of bell, *tavas clogh*, m., pl. *-ow c.*: **-ping**, n. *takyans*, *tāk*, m.
clarify, v. *glewhē·*.
clarion, n. *cleryon*, m., pl. *-s*, *toll corn*, m., pl. *tollkern*; c. player, *cleryon*, m., pl. *-s*.
clarity, n. *clērder*, *glewder*, m.
clary, n. herb, **owradal*, m.
clash, v. *omscattya*, *omgontradya*: n. *squat*, m., pl. *-tow*, *trōs*, m.: **-ing**, a. *contraryüs*.
clasp, v., hug, *byrla*, *chersya*; grip, *dalghenna*, *settya gavel yn*, *crafa*: n., grip, *gavel*, f., pl. *-yow*, *craf*, m., pl. *-avow*; brooch, *brocha*, m., pl. *-ys*, †*delk*, m., pl. *-cow*, †*stryng*, m.; hasp, **spanga*, m., pl. *-gys*.
class, n. **class*, m., pl. *-ys*, *ēghen*, f.; rank, *grē*, *degrē·*, m.: v. *gorra y'ga classys*, **classya*: **-ification**, n. **classyans*, m.: **-ify**, v. **classya*.
classic, a. **classyk*,: n. *lyver a'n gwella*.
clatter, v. *cryghylly*, *clattra*: n. *cryghyllyans*, *trōs*, m.
clause, n. *ran lavar*, f.
claw, v. *scravynyas*, **skyvly*: n. *ewyn*, m., pl. *-as*: of crab, *paw*, m., pl. *-yow*, d. *deubaw*: **-ed**, a. *ewynek*.
clay, n. *prȳ*, m.; china-c., *prȳ gwyn*; c.-ground, *pryen*, f., *pryek*, *pryenek*, f., pl. *-egy*, *-egow*; c.-pit, *pol-prȳ*, m., pl. *-low-p.*, *pyt-prȳ*, m., pl. *-tys-p*.
claymore, n. *cledha-mür*, m., pl. *-dhevyow-m*.
clean, a. *glan*, *pür*, *ylyn*, *glanyth*; adv. *ylyn*; c.-away, c.-off, *ylyn*, *quyt*: v. *glanhē·*, **scartha*; c. out, **cartha*; c. tin from fine waste particles, *dylewghya*: **-liness**, n. *glanythter*, *ylynder*, m.: **-ly**, adv. *yn-lan*: **-se**, v. *glanhē·*, *püra*, *scūrya*.
clear, a. *pür*, *glan*, *ylyn*, *splan*, *glew*, *tēr*, *clēr*, *boll*; distinct, *dyblans*; open, *rȳth*: v. *scartha*, *clērhē·*, *glanhē·*; make c. *splanhē·*; explain, *styrya*; of weather, **hynony*: **-ing**, n., in wood, *lanergh*, m., pl. *-y*; open place, *laun*, m., pl. *-ow*: **-ly**, adv. *apē·rt*, *ylyn*, *dyblans*, *splan*; evidently, *hep dowt*, *hep mar*, *del hevel*: **-ness**, n. *splander*, *clērder*, *ylynder*, m.: **-sighted**, *lym y lagas*, *lagasek*.
cleave, v., split, *falsa*; cling, *glena*, *sergha*.
cleavers, n., bot., *les-serghak byghan*, m.
cleft, n. *fals*, m., pl. *-ljow*, *ryll*, m., pl. *-yow*; in cliff, *saun*, f., pl. *-yow*: a. *felsys*, *forghek*.
clemency, n. *trueth*, *cüfter*, m.
clergy, n. *mebyon-lȳen*, pl.; benefit of c. *lyfrēson drē glerjy*: **-man**, n. *maplȳen*, m., pl. *mebyon-lȳen*; †*clorek*, m., pl. *-egas*, *pronter*, m., pl. *-yon*, *oferyas*, m., pl. *-ysy*.
cleric, see **clergyman.**
clerical, a. *eglosek*, *an eglos*; c. error, *camscryf*, m.
clerk, n., business, *scryvynyas*, m., pl. *-ysy*, *scryfwas*, m., pl. *-wesyon*; c. in orders, as **clergyman.**
clever, a. *für*, *fēl*, *connek*, *ynjyn*, *gwenwhys*, *sotel*, *sley*: **-ness**, *sleyneth*, *connyng*, m.
clew, n. *pellen*, f., pl. *-now*; naut., *corn goles gōl*.
client, n. *clȳent*, m., pl. *-ens*, *cusülyas*, pl. *-ysy*: **-ele**, n. *cusülysy*.
cliff, n. *leder*, *lamleder*, f., pls. *-drow*, *-dry*, *als*, f., pl. *-yow*, *clegar*, m., pl. *-grow*, *bans*, m., pl. *-ow*, *clog*, f., pl. *-ow*.
climate, n. *nēf*, m. or f., pl. *nevow*.
climax, n. *bar*, m., pl. *-ow*, *pryk ughella*, m.

climb, v. *yskynna, crambla*; by ladder, *scülya*: n. *yskynva*, f.
clime, n. *cōst*, m., pl. *-ys, nēf*, m. or f., pl. *-evow.*
cling, v. *glena, sergha*; c. together, **kes-clena*: **-ing,** a. *serghak*; c. person, *serghyas*, m., pl. *-ysy.*
clip, v. *knyvyas*: **-pers,** n. *gwelsow*, m., pl. *-sevyow*: **-pings,** n. *knyvyon*, pl.
cloak, n. *clōk*, m., pl. *-ys, capa*, f., pl. *-pyow, mantel*, f., pl. *mentylly*; with hood, *hūk*, f., pls. *-ys, hūcow*; woman's hooded c. of fur, *pengūgh*, m.
clock, n. *clok*, m., pl. *-kys*; 3 o'c. *tȳr ür*: **-wise,** adv. *gans an howl.*
clod, n. *tam*, m., pl. *-tymmyn, towarghen*, f., col. *towargh*; term of abuse, *lorden*, m., pl. *-s.*
clod-hopper, n. *talsogh*, m.
clog, n. *spral*, m., pl. *-low*; shoe, *eskys pren*, m., pl. *eskyjow p.*: v. *taga.*
cloister, n. *clawster, cloyster*, m., pl. *-trow.*
close, v. *kēas, degēa*: n. *park*, m., pl. *-rcow, kew*, f., pl. *-yow*: a. *ogas, yn;* stuffy, *pōs*; c. by, *a-ogas, omma rybon*; c. to, *ryp*; c.-fisted, *synsyas*: **-ly,** adv. *clōs*; cling c., *glena hardlych*: **-ness,** n. *ogaster*, m.; stuffiness, *poster, fowt ayr*, m.: **-er,** n. *kēer*, m., pl. *-ēoryon*: comp. a. *nēs*: comp. adv. *yn-nēs*
clot, n. *mōl*, m., *clot*, m., pl. *-tys*; c. of filth, *cagal*, m., pl. *-glow*: v. *cowla.*
cloth, n. *pan*, m., pl. *-now, gwȳas*; of linen, *lȳen*, m., pl. *-enyow*; woollen, *len*, f., pl. *-now*; c. of gold, **syclaton*, m.: **-e,** v. *quetha, gwysca, dyllajy*: **-es,** n. *gwyscas*, m., pl. *-cosow, gwysk*, m.,pl. *-scow, dyllas*, m., pl. *-ajow*: **-ier,** n. *lyennor, dyllajor*, m., pl. *-yon, gwerther dyllas*, m., pl. *thoryon d.*: **-ing,** n. as for **clothes.**
cloud, n. *comolen*, f., pl. *comolow*, col. *comol, newlen*, f. pl. *-now, clowd*, m., pl. *-ys*; smoke or mist, *bush*, m., pl. *-ys.*: **-burst,** n. *hager-gowas*, f., pl. *-wosow*; *newldarth, comol-darth*, m., pl. *-rdhow*: **-less,** *dygomol*: **-y,** a. *comolek.*
clout, v., patch or strike, *clowtya*: n., blow, *clowt*, m., pl. *-tys*; patch, cloth, *clowt, queth*, m., or f., pl. *-ow.*
cloven-hoofed, a. *carngaulek, forghek y gar-now.*
clover, n. *mullyonen*, f., col. *mullyon*; c. field, *mullyonek*, f. pls. *-egy, -egow.*
clown, n. *lorden*, m., pl. *-s*: v. *gwary yn-fol.*
cloy, v. *gwalgha.*
club, n., weapon, *bat*, m., pl. *-tys, füst*, f., pl. *-ow, cūlbren*, m., pl. *-yer*; society, *cowethas*, f., pl. *-ow*: v. *füsta, battya.*
club-footed, a. *pawgam.*
clue, n. *gedyans*, m.
clump, n. *bonny*, m., pl. *-es.*
clumsy, a. *pōs, cam, dycreft*: **-siness,** n. *dygomposter, camwonys, camder*, m.
cluster, n. *bagas*, m., pl. *-ow, bush*, m., pl. *-ys, bonny*, m., pl. *-es*: v. *tevy yn bagasow, dōs warbarth yn bagas*; c. round, *dōs a-dro (dho-dho) yn bagas.*
clutch, v. *grabalyas, dalghenna yn, crafa, settya gavel yn*; hug, *byrla*: n. *craf*, m., pl. *-vow, gavel*, f., pl. *-yow*; c. of eggs, **gor-yans*, m.
coach, n. *cōcha*, m., pl. *-chys*: v. *dysky*: **-man,** *gwas-cōcha*, m., pl. *gwesyon-c.*
coagulate, v. *cowla, moly*: **-tion,** n. *cowl*, m., pl. *-ow, mōl*, m.
coal, n. *colyn*, m., pl. *colys, regythen*, f., col. *regyth*; fuel, *glow*, col.; pit-c., *g-dōr, g-pol*; live-c., *colyn bew*; dead c., *colyn marow*; c.-heaver, *halyer glow*; c. scuttle, *trok glow*, m., pls. *-kys, tregys g.*; c. measures, place of c. or charcoal, *glowek*, f., pls. *-egy, -egow.*
coalesce, v. *tevy warba·rth, dōs ha bōs onen.*
coarse, a. *garow*: **-ness,** n. *garowder*, m.
coast, n. *als*, f., *arvor, morrep*, m., *glan*, f., *cōst*, m.: **-al,** a. **arvorek*: **-guard,** n. *gwy-thyas an alsyow*, m., *-ysy a.a.*: **-land,** n. **arvor*, m.: **-wise,** adv. *ryp an tȳr.*
coat, n. *pows*, f., pl. *-yow, cota*, m., pl. *-tys*; short c., *jerkyn*, m.; c. of arms, *cota arvow*, m., pl. *-tys a., scochen*, m., pl. *-s*: v. *kenna*: **-ing,** n. *gwyscas*, m., pl. *-cosow, ken*, m. (no pl.).
coax, v. *dynya.*
cob, n., for building, *prȳ*, m., *prȳen*, f.; horse, *hobba*; c.-walled house, *chȳ prȳen.*
cobble, v. *clowtya eskyjyow, *kerva*: **-d,** a., c. way, *cauns*, m., pl. *-ys*: **-r,** n. †*kerȳor*, m., pl. *-yon*: **-stone,** n. *mēn-cauns*, m., pl. *meyn-c.*
cobweb, n. *gwȳas kefnysen*, m., pl. *g. kefnys.*
cock, n. *cülyek*, m., pl. *-ogas*: v., of gun, *antel*: **-ed,** of gun, *antellys*: **-s comb,** n. *crȳben cülyek*, f.
cockchafer, n. *whyl derow*, m., pl. *-as d.*
cockcrow, n. *cülyek-kenys*, m.
cockle, n. **cocla*, m., pl. *-lys.*
cockswain, n. *lewyer*, m., pl. *-oryon.*
cod, n. *barfüs*, m., pl. *-y*; dried, **bacalyaw·*, m.; poor-c., *gwybor*, m., pl. *-as.*

co-equal, a *kehaval.*
coerce, v. *controlya, constrȳna*: **-cion,** n. *constrȳnans,* m.
coeval, a. *kevōs*; c. with, *k. ha.*
coffee, n. *coffy,* m.
coffer, n. *argh,* f., pls. *-ow, erghy*: *cofyr,* m., pl. *-frow.*
coffin, n. *geler,* f., pl. *-ow*; of stone, *kyst vēn,* f., pl. *kystyow mēn*; of iron, *trok a horn,* m., pls, *-kys, tregys a h.*
cog, n., machinery, *dans,* m., pl. *dyns*; c. wheel, *rōs dynsak,* f., pl. *-ow d.*; naut. *cogga,* m., pl. *-gys.*
cohabit, v. *kesvewa.*
cohere, v. *kesclena*; **-rent,** a. *ow-kesclena, a-gesclen*: **-rence, -esion,** n. *kesclenyans,* m.
coil, v. *terghy*: n. *torgh,* f., pl. *tergh.*
coin, n. *bath,* m., pl. *-ow*; sterling, *sterlyn,* m., pl. *-s, mona bathys,* m. and col.: v. *bathy*: **-age,** n. *arghans bathys,* col.; c. of tin, **coynach,* m.: **-er,** n. †*gwas-bathor,* m., pl. *gwesyon b.*
coincide, v. **kenwharfos,* **kendarfos*: **-nce,** n. *kenwharfedhyans,* m.
coke, n. **golosk, glow dōr,* m.
colander, n. **sythel,* m., pl. *-thlow.*
cold, a. *yeyn*; bitterly c., *ōr*: n. *yeynder,* m.; illness, *anwos*; to catch c., **anwesy*; apt.to catch c., **anwesek*: **-ness,** n. *yeynder,* m., **yeynyjyon,* m.
colewort, n. *ongel,* m., *cawl,* col.
collaborate, v. *kesobery*: **-tion,** n. *kesober, kesoberyans,* m.: **-tor,** n. *kesoberor,* m., pl. *-yon.*
collapse, v. *codha yn y-honen, fyllel*: n. *collva,* f., *terros,* m.
collar, n. **band,* m., pl. *-ys*; horse c., *mongar,* f., pl. *-ger, mongaren,* f., pl. *-now*: v. *dalghenna, settya dalghen yn.*
collar-bone, n. *pons an scōth,* m., pl. *-ow a, s.*
collate, v. **kescorra.*
collateral, a. **keslynek.*
colleague, n. *cowethyas,* m., pl. *-ysy.*
collect, v. *cuntell*; esp. of liquids, *crüny*: n. *pysadow ber an termyn*: **-ion,** n. *cuntell, cuntellyans,* m., pl. *-ow*; of liquids, *crün, crēn,* m., pl. *-yow*; in church, *offrynyans,* m.: **-ively,** adv. *warba·rth*: **-or,** n. *cunteller,* m., pl. *-loryon.*
college, n. *coljy,* m., pl. *-ow, collej,* m., pl. *-ys*: **-giate,** a. *collejek.*
collide, v. *deghesy warba·rth*; c. with, *omdheghesy erby·n*: **-ision,** n. *omdheghesyans,* m.
collier, n. *palor glow,* m., pl. *-yon g., glowor,* m., pl. *-yon*; ship, *gorghel glow,* m., pl. *-olyon g.*: **-y,** n. *whēl glow,* m. and f., pl. *-yow g., pol g.,* m., pl. *-low g.*
colloquy, n. *kescows,* m.: **-quial,** a. *an yēth kemyn, kescows.*
colonial, a. **colonyek,* **trevesyk*: n. **colonyek,* m., pl. *-yogyon, trevesyk,* m., pl. *-ygyon*: **-ize,** v. **colonȳsa, settya tüs (yn), annedhy yn tȳr aral*: **-y,** n. **trevesygeth,* f., pl. *-ow*; of animals, *bagas,* m., pl. *-ow.*
coloration, n. *lywans,* m.
colossal, a. *brās drēs ēghen, üthek brās.*
colour, n. *lyw,* m., pl. *-yow*; of dress, *sewt,* m.: v. *lywa*: **-ed,** a. *lywys*; three-c., *trȳlyw*; self-c., *ünlyw*; many c., *lȳes lyw*: **-ing** n. *lywans,* m.: **-less,** a. *dyslyw.*
colt, n. *ebol,* m., pls. *-ylyon, ebylly*: **-s-foot,** n. *trōs-ebol,* m., pl. *losow t.-e.*
column, n. *pül,* m., pl. *-yow, pyllar,* m., pl. *-s, post,* m., pl. *-ow,* **coloven,* f., pl. *-now.*
coma, n. †*hün desempys, cleves hün, cusk cleves,* m.: **-tose,** a. *yn cusk drē gleves.*
comb, n. *crȳb,* f., pl. *-ow, restrer,* m.; of cock, *crybell,* f., pl. *-ow, crȳben cülyek,* f., pl. *-now c.*: v. *crȳba, restry*: **-ings,** n. *crybyon,* pl.
combine, v. *kesünya, omguntell*: **-nation,** n. *kesünyans,* m.
combustible, a. *helosk*: **-tion,** n. *loskvan,* m.
come, v. *dōs (dones, devones)*; c. after, *holya, sewya*; c. back, *dewheles*; c. down, *dyeskynna*; c. near, *dōs ogas* or *nēs*; c. nearer, *dōs nes, neshē·*; c. off badly, *tebel-fara, drokfara*; c. to, happen to, *dōs ha*; c. now! go to! *do way*!; c. on!,to comrade, *dün yn-rak*!; to opponent, menial, etc., *düs yn-rak*!
comedian, n. *gwaryer wharthüs,* m.
comedy, n. *ynterlūt,* m., pl. *-udys.*
comely, a. *sēmly, tēk, whekter y weles.*
comet, n. *steren lesky,* f., pl. *-now l.,* col. *stēr l.*
comfort, v. *chērya, hebaskhē·, dydhana, hüthhē·, confortya*: n. *confort, chēr, hebasca,* f., *hüthter, ēs,* m.; in c., *yn-ēs, attē·s*: **-able,** a. *attē·s*; make c., *ēsya*; make self c., *omjersya*: **-er,** n. *confortyer,* m., pl. *-yoryon.*
comic, a. *wharthüs.*
command, v. *gorhemmyn, erghy, comondya*: n. *arghadow,* m., *gorhemmyn,* m., pl. *-ow, ordyr,* m., pl. *-drys*: **-er,** n. *hembrynkyas,* m., pl. *-ysy*: **-ing,** a., position, **gorughel*:

-ment, n. *gorhemmynadow, arghadow,* m.; *comondment,* m., pl. *-ns.*
commemorate, v. *cofhē·.*
commence, v. *dalleth*: **-ment,** n. *dalleth,* m.
commend, v. *kemmynna, comendya*: **-ation,** n. *kemmyn,* m., pl. *-ow, kemmyneth,* m.; pl. *-edhow*; they send you c's, *ymons-y owcorhemmyn dheugh.*
commensurate, a. *kemusür,*
comment, v. *campolla, gül *campoll*: n. **campoll,* m., *brüs,* f.
commerce, n. **kenwerth,* m.: **-cial,** a. **kenwerthek.*
commiserate, v. *dysquedhes,* or *kemeres, tregereth,* or *pyta*: **-tion,** n. *trüeth, pyteth,* m., *tregereth,* f., pl. *-ow.*
commission, n., act, *gwythres, gwrȳans,* m.; payment, *gober,* m., pl. *-brow*; job, *negys,* m., abst. and pls. *-sow, -syow*: **-er,** n. *negesyth,* m., pl. *-ydhyon.*
commissionaire, n. *porther,* m., pl. *-thoryon.*
commit, v. *gül*; commend, *kemmynna, comendya*; the sin he has committed, *an pēgh re-bēghas, an pēghas ganso üs gwrēs.*
commitment, n. *ambos,* m.
committee, n. *cusülyadoryon,* pl. *consel,* m.
commixture, n. *kemysk,* m.
commodious, a. *efan.*
commodity, n. *gwara,* m. and col.
common, a. *kemyn, kēth, sempel, ūsyes, ysel*: n. *prās,* m., pl. *-ow.*: **-alty,** n. *kemyn,* f.: **-er,** n. *kemyn,* m., pl. *-yon, comner,* m., pl. *-s, dēn kemyn,* m., pl. *tüs k.*: **-place,** a. *ūsyes*: **-s,** n. *kemyn,* f.; House of C., *Chy an Gemyn,* m.: **-wealth,** n. *lēs-kemyn*; the C., *Lēs an Gemyn,* m.
commotion, n. *trōs,* m., pl. *-ow, dera·y,* m., pl. *-ys*; make a c., *gül dera·y, mür a dhera·y.*
communicant, n. *nep üs comūnyes.*
communicate, v., speak, *leverel, kewsel*; write, *scryfa*: **-tion,** n. *negys,* m., pls. and abst. *-sow, -syow, †scryven-danvon,* f., pl. *-now-d.*; passage, *hens,* m., pl. *-y, tremenva,* f., **daromres,* m.; by water, *trēth, trümach,* m.: **-tive,** a. *helavar, parys dhe gewsel.*
communion, n. *cowethyans, comūnyans,* m.; Holy C., **Comūn Sans, an Sacryfys,* m.; office of Holy C., *Oferen,* f., pl. *-now.*; to administer C., *comūnya.*
community, n. *cowethas,* f., pl. *-ow, *kemeneth,* f.; the c., *an gemyn, an düs,* f.
compact, a. *tew, war ver lavarow, *kempen*: n. *ambos,* m., pl. *-ow*: **-ness,** n. *tewder, berder, *kempensys,* m.
companion, n. *mata,* m., pl. *-tys, coweth,* m., col. *-a, kescoweth,* m., pl. *-a, cowethes,* f., pl. *-ow*: **-able,** a. *mal ganso cowethya*: **-less,** a. *dygoweth*: **-ship,** n. *cowethyans,* m.
company, n. *cowethas,* f., pl. *-ow, cowetha, kescowetha;* col., *co·mpany, felshyp,* m.; at feast, *kyfvewy,* col.; keep c., *cowethya*; in c. with them, *y'ga herwyth.*
compare, v. *hevelly, kehavalhē·* (*orth*), *comparya* (*gans*); as compared with, *herwyth*: **-rable,** a. *a-yllyr bōs hevellys*: **-rison,** n. *hevelepter,* m.; beyond c., *hep parow*; by c. with, *herwyth, hag ef hevellys orth.*
compartment, n. *ran,* f., pl. *-now*; in boat, *rōm,* m., pl. *-ys.*
compass, n., pair of c's., extent, *compas,* m.
compassion, n. *tregereth,* f., pl. *-ow, trüeth, pyteth, mercy,* m.; take c. on, *kemeres pyta a*[2]: **-ate,** a. *tregerethüs, pytethüs, truethek, me·rcyabyl.*
compatriot, n. *dēn an keth pow.*
compel, v. *constrȳna.*
compendium, n. *derȳvas cot, cotthēans,* m.
compensate, v. *attyly, astevery, gül restoryta dhe*[2]: **-tion,** n. *atta·l,* m.
compete, v. *kesstryvya*: **-tition,** n. *kesstrȳf, kesstryvyans,* m., pl. *-ow*: **-titor,** n. *kesstrȳfor,* m., pl. *-yon.*
competence, n. *gwywder, gallos,* m.; his c., *y vōs harth dhe*[2]: **-ent,** a. *gwyw, harth.*
compile, v. *cuntell, gorra warbarth.*
complacent, a. *pȳs da anodho y honen, a-omblek.*
complain, v. *crothvolas* (*croffolas*); c. against, *gül crothval war*[2]: **-ner,** n, croaker, *grolyak,* m., pl. *-yogyon*: **-nt,** n. *crothval,* m., *gref,* m., pl. *-evys, grefons,* m.; illness, *gref, grefons,* m., *cleves,* m., pl. *-vejow.*
complaisant, a. *plegadow, debonē·r.*
complement, n. *ran a-gollenow, nyver cowal.*
complete, v. *collenwel, cowlwül, dewedha*: a. *lün, playn, cowal, perfyth, a-dhevȳ·s, dȳen*: **-tion,** n. *cowlwrȳans,* m: **-tely,** adv. *yn-tēk, oll yn-tȳen, dour, hep nam, glan, perfyth, cowal, afȳna, warba·rth, cler, worth compas, yn pup ēghen, hēs ha hēs*: **-teness,** n. *lünder, perfythter,* m.
complex, a. *lȳes-plēk*: n. *plegyans,* m.:

-exion, n. *lyw,* m., pl. *-yow, fysmant,* m., pl. *-mens.*

compliance, n. *plegadow, assentyans,* m.: **-ant,** a. *plegadow, parys dhe blegya*; be c., *bōs yn-assentys.*

complicate, v. *kemysky*; make difficult, *caleshē·*: **-d,** *a. lyēs-plēk, yn-kemyskys.*

compliment, n. *cortesy*; give my c's. to, *reugh ow gorhemmynadow dhe*[2]: v. *gormel*: **-tary,** a., gratis, *rȳth, rēs drē gortesy*; flattering, *cortes, jentyl.*

comply, v. *plegya, obaya* (*dhe*[2]).

compose, v. *scryfa, formya, gorra warba·rth, gül*; c. music, **ȳla*; calm, *coselhē·, dyserry*: **-sedly,** a. *yn-cosel, hep sōr*: **-sition,** n. *formyans,* m.; music, etc., *ober,* m., pl. *-ow*: **-sure,** n. *calmynsy,* m.

compound, a. *kemyskys*: n. *kemysk, kemyskyans,* m.

comprehend, v. *convedhes, attendya*: **-sion,** n. *convedhes,* m.

comprehensive, a. *efan, lün.*

compress, v. *gwrynya warba·rth, strotha,* **gwasca*: n. **gwask,* f.

comprise, v. *comprehendya, synsy.*

compromise, v. *peryllya hanow da*: n. *bargen,* m., pl. *-ys.*

compulsory, a. *constrȳnys, drē nerth.*

compunction, n. *edrega, edrek,* m.

compute, v. *amontya, rekna*: **-tation,** n. *reken,* m., pl. *-nys.*

comrade, n. *cothman,* m., pl. *-s, coweth, kescoweth,* m., col. *-a, mata, m., pl. -tys.*

concave, a. *cow.*

conceal, v. *cüdha, keles*: **-ed,** a. *cüth, yn-dan güth, yn-dan gēl*: **-ment,** n. *kēl, keladow, cüth, cüdhans,* m.; place of c., *covva* (for *cüthva*), f.

concede, v. *dascor, hepcor, godhaf, grontya, alowa, lavasos*; in debate, *aswon.*

conceit, n. *tybyans, consay·t, gōth,* m.: **-ted,** a. *gothys,*

conceive, v. *om·dhon, concevya*; understand, *convedhes.*

concentrate, v. *drȳ dhe ün crēs*; c. mind, *predery gans ente·nt*; c. liquids, *crüny*; c. on work, etc., *omrȳ yn-tywysyk dhe*[2], *settya oll an brȳs war*[2]: **-ted,** a. *kescrünys, a'n creffa*: **-tion,** n. *crün*; of mind, *ente·nt,* m.

concept, n. *tybyans, consay·t,* m.

conception, n. *om·dhon,* m.; idea, *tybyans,* m.

concern, def., v. *dür, bern*; I am not concerned, *ny-m-dür, genef ny-vern*: n. *bern, fors,* m.; undertaking, *vȳaj,* m., pl. *-ys*; it is no c. of mine, *genef nyns-yu bern, travyth ny-m-dür, ny-wraf mellya orto*: **-ning,** prep. *yn-kever, a-dro* (*dhe*[2]), *a*[2], *ow-tuchya* (*a*[2], *dhe*[2]).

concert, n. *gōl* **ȳlow,* or **musyk,* m., pl. *-yow y.* or *m.*; *kescan,* f.

concession, n. *spās, spȳs, godhevyans,* m.

conciliate, v. *ünverhē·*: **-ion,** n. *ünverhēans,* m.

concise, a. *cot, ber,* **kempen.*

conclude, v. *gorfenna, dewedha, determya*; c. successfully, *spēdya* (*negys*); bring to decision, *conclūdya*: **-usion,** n. *deweth, gordheweth, gorfen, conclūsyon,* m.: **-usive,** a. *a-wra conclūdya*: **-usively,** adv. *gordheweth.*

concoct, v. *kemysky, devȳsya, bryjyon warba·rth*: **-tion,** n. *kemysk, godroth,* m.

concord, n. *kessenyans,* m.; all in c., *war nōt, kescolon.*

concourse, n. *cuntellyans,* m., *rūth,* f.

concur, v. *bōs ünver, assentya*: **-rent,** a. *ünver, a-gesrēs.*

concussion, n. *cryghyllyans,* m.

condemn, v. *dampnya, blamya, rȳ brüs erby·n*: **-nation,** n. *brüs erby·n,* f., *condempnasyon,* m.

condense, v. *tewhē·*: **-sation,** n. *tewhēans.*

condescend, v. *lavasos, omblegya, hüvelhē·orth*: **-ding,** a. *hüvel*: **-dingly,** adv. *ynhüvel*: **-nsion,** n. *hüvelder,* m.

condign, a. *del dhegoth.*

condition, n. *plȳt, stüth, condysyon,* m.; of body, *chēr, poynt,* m.; stipulation, *ordyr,* m., pl. *-drys, ambos,* m., pl. *-ow*; c. of performing military service, *ago-marghogyon*: **-nal, -nally,** a., adv. *herwyth ambos* or *ordyr.*

condole, v. **kescodhaf,* **kescalary*: **-lence,** n. **kescodhaf,* m.; **kescalarow,* pl., abst.

conduce, v. *lēdya, gedya, hembronk*: **-cive,** a. *a-lēd, a-hembronk, üs ow-corra* (*dhe*[2]).

conduct, v. *lēdya, hembronk*; c. oneself, *omdhōn, gedya y vewnans, fara*: n. *faryng, conduyct* (*conduyk*), m., *rewl,* f.: **-tor,** n. *lewyer,* m., pl. *-oryon, hembrynkyas,* m., pl. *-ysy*; of 'bus, *tokynor,* m., pl. *-oryon.*

conduit, n. *gōth,* f., pl. *gwythy, pystyl,* m., pl. *-low, shutta,* pl. *-tys, tewel,* m., pl. *-ys,* **condyt,* m., pl. *-ys.*

cone, n. **pykern,* m., pl. *-ow*: **-nical,** a. **pykernek.*

coney, n. *conyn,* m., pl. *-as.*

confection, n. **kyfyth,* m., pl. *-yow*; **-ner,** n. **kyfyther,* m., pl. *-oryon*: **-nery,** n. **kyfythyow,* m., pl.; to make c., *kyfythya.*

confederate, v. **kefrȳsy*: n. **kefrȳsyas,* m., pl. *-ysy*: **-tion,** n. **kefrȳsyans,* m., pl. *-ow.*

confer, v. *omgusülya, keskewsel*; bestow, *rȳ*: **-rence,** n. *kescusülyans, kesleveryans,* m., pl. *-ow.*

confess, v. *avowa*; c. sins, *yēs, meneges*: **-ssion,** n. **cofes,* m., pl. *-esyow, yessans,* m., pl. *-ow*: **-ssor,** n. *yesser,* m., pl. *-soryon.*

confide (in), v. *kyfy, fydhya* (*yn*): **-dence,** n. *fydhyans, kyfyans, crejys, trest,* m.; be in c. of, *bōs pryveth gans*: **-dent,** a. *lün a fȳth, dȳown, harth*: **-ntial,** a. *pryva*: **-ntially,** adv. *yn-pryva.*

confine, v. *prysonya, kēthy*; restrict, *strotha*; c. oneself to, *omwytha a-jȳ dhe²*: **-ned,** a. *yn*: **-nement,** n. *prysonyans,* m.; childbed, *gwelyvos,* m.

confirm, v. *afydhya*; fix, *fasthē·*: **-rmed,** a. habitual, *pür*: **-rmation,** n. *fasthēans,* m.

confiscate, v. *dyberghenna, kemeres herwyth lagha.*

conflagration, n. *tansys,* m., pl. *-ow*; **tangwall,* m.

conflict, n. *omdow·l,* m., pl. *-ow, bresel,* m., pl. *-yow*: **-ting,** a. *ow-contradȳa.*

confluence, n., with sea, †*aber,* m., pl. *-ow*; with river, *kemper,* m., pl. *-prow, kendefryon,* pl.

conform, v. *omblegya,* **kesomformya*: **-able,** a. *plegadow.*

confound, v. *ancombra, confundya.*

confraternity, n. **kembredereth,* m.

confront, v. *sevel erby·n*; question, *apposya.*

confuse, v. *kemysky*: **-sedly,** adv. *yn-kemyskys*: **-sion,** n. *dera·y,* m.; embarrassment, *ancombrynsy,* m.

congeal, v. *cowla*; freeze, *rewy.*

congenial, a. *plegadow.*

conger, n. *sylly,* f., pl. *-as*; c. dried in sun, young c., *s. whēk.*

congested, a. *crünys*: **-tion,** n. *crünyans,* m., pl. *-ow.*

congratulate, v. *keslowenhē·* (*gans*): **-tion,** n. *keslowena,* f., c's! *lowen of genough-why*! *kevrennek of y'th lowender*!

congregate, v. *cuntell, dōs warba·rth*: **-tion,** n. *cuntelles,* f., pl. *-ow.*

congress, n. *cuntellyans,* m., pl. *-ow.*

conjecture, v. *tyby, desmygy*: n. *tybyans,* m., pl. *-ow*; *desmyk,* m., pl. *-ygow.*

conjugal, a. **pryosek,* **pryosol, a gesvewnans.*

conjugate, v. *kesyewa*: **-tion,** n. *kesyewans,* m.

conjunction, n. *kevren,* f., pl. *-yon.*

conjure, v., beseech, *conjorya*; work magic, *pystrya*: **-rer,** n. *juglour, astronomer,* m., pl. *-s, pystryor,* m., pl. *-yon*; **-ring-trick,** n. *prat hüs,* m., pl. *-tys h.,poynt a bystry,* m.

connect, v. *ünya, junnya*: **-tion,** n. *ünyans,* m., pl. *-ow*; blood relationship, *gōs,* m.; in c. with, *yn-kever.*

conquer, v. *fetha, trȳghy, conquerrya*: **-ring,** a. *trȳgh*: **-ror,** n. *trȳgher,* m., pl. *-ghoryon*; *fether,* m., pl. *-thoryon, conquerrour,* m., pl. *-s*: **-quest,** n. *trȳghans,* m., pl. *-ow, conquest,* m.

conscience, n. *conscyans,* m., *cowsys,* m., pl. and abst. *cowsesow*; seat of c., *ascra,* f.: **-ntious,** a. *dywysyk.*

conscious, a. *owth-aswon, ow-clewes*; to be c. of, *aswon, clewes*: **-ness,** n. *aswonvos* m.

conscript, v. *kescryfa*: n. *soudar kescryfys,* m., pl. *-doryon k.*: **-ption,** n. *kescryfans,* m.

consecrate, v. *sacra, sona, consecraytya*: **-ion,** n. *sacrans,* m.

consecutive, a. *yn ün rew, yn rew.*

consent, v. *assentya, lavasos*: n. *bōth,* m.; against one's c., *a'y anvoth.*

consequence, n. *an dra a-sew,* or *a-dhē warlergh,* or *üs ow-holya*; importance, *brȳ, prȳs, roweth,* m.; it is of no c., *nyns-üs fors awo·s henna*; in c., *drē henna*: **-ent,** a. *owsewya, owth-holya*: **-tial,** *ow-sewya*; self-important, *omwhethys*: **-tly,** adv. *ytho·, rag henna.*

conservative, a. *erby·n chanj, a-gar gwytha*: n. *mentēnour,* m., pl. *-s.*

conservatory, n. *losowjy,* m., pl. *-ow.*

conserve, v. *gwytha, sawya.*

consider, v. *predery, avȳsya, ragavȳsya, ombredery, synsy, acontya, myras, attendya*: **-able,** a. *mür*; c. time or amount, *pols da*; c. quantity of, *ran vrās a²*: **-ate,** a. *prederüs*: **-ation,** n. *preder,* m., pl. and abst. *-ow, avȳ·s, fors,* m.; respect, *brȳ,* m.; reward, *gober,* m.; treat with c., *gül vrȳ a²*: **-ing,** conj. *pan², a-ban²*; c. how difficult it is, *hag ef,* or *aban yu, mar gales.*

consign, v. *rȳ, danvon, kemmynna, fydhya*: **-ment,** n. *danvonadow,* m.: **-gnee,** n. *nep a-dhegemer.*

consist, v. *bōs*; it c's. of two things, *a dheu dra yu*: **-tency,** n. *acord, kessenyans,* m.;

-tent, a. *kesson*; c. with, *kesson ha, yn acord gans*: **-tently,** adv. *yn-fast*; at all times, *yn y dhedhyow.*
consolation, n., *confort,* **solas,* m.; *hebasca,* f.: **-e,** v. *confortya, chērya, gwellhē· chēr, hüdha,* **dehüdha.*
consolidate, v. *crefhē·, fasthē·.*
consonant, n. *kesson,* m., pl. *-yow.*
consort, v. *cowethya*: n. *prȳas,* m. and f.
conspicuous, a. *hewel.*
conspiracy, n. *bras,* m.: **-rator,** n. *braser,* m., pl. *-oryon*: **-re,** v. *brasy.*
constable, n. *gwythyas crēs,* m., pl. *-ysy* c.: **-bulary,** n. *gwythysy crēs,* pl.
constancy, n. *lēlder,* m.: **-nt,** a. *lēl, lēn*; continual, *hep hedhy, a-bȳs*: **-ntly,** adv. *prest, pup termyn.*
constellation, n. *stēr golowys,* f., col.
consternation, n. *üth,* m.; in c., *dyegrys.*
constipate, v. *kelmy an colonyow*; **-ted,** a. *kelmys y golonyow* or *golodhyon*: **-tion,** n. *caletter an colodhyon* or *colonyow,* pl.
constituency, n. *an dhewysoryon,* pl.: **-nt,** a. *a-dhewys, üs ran*: n. *dewyser,* m., pl. *-soryon*; c. part, *ran,* f., pl. *-now.*
constitute, v. *synsy, o·rdena, gül*; **-tion,** n. *natur, gnās corf,* f.; act of c., *o·rdenans,* m.; political, *corf-laghys an Stāt*: **-tional,** a. *herwyth lagha*; c. walk, n. *tro-kerdhes,* f., pl. *-yow k.*
constrain, v. *ynnȳa, constrȳna*: **-nt,** n. *ynny,* m.
construct, v. *gül, gwrüthyl, drehevel, dȳghtya, formya*: **-tion,** n. *drehevyans, gwrȳans,* m., pl. *-ow.*
consult, v. *omgusülya* (*gans*); **-tation,** n. *cusülyans,* m.
consume, v., eat, *dybry*; destroy, *consūmya*; by fire, *cowl-lesky*; **-mption,** n. *wastyans,* m.; disease, *cleves skevens,* **tysyk,* m.: **-mptive,** a., n. *clāf a'y skevens,* pl. *clevyon a'ga s.*
contact, v. *tava,* inf.; to get into c. with, *tuchya orth*; by letter, *scryfa dhe*^{2}; orally, *kewsel dhe*^{2}: n. *tava,* inf.; in c., *ow-tuchya.*
contagious, a., c. disease, *cleves a-dhē drē dava.*
contain, v. *synsy, contaynya*; nest containing eggs, *nȳth ynno oyow*; I can't c. myself any longer, *ny-allaf-vy paragh na fella*: **-er,** n. *dafar, synser,* m.
contaminate, v. *mostya*: **-tion,** n. *harlotry, mostethes,* m.
contemn, v. *dysprēsya, fȳa,* **contempnya.*
contemplate, v. *myras, predery, hȳrombredery*: **-tion,** n. *preder hȳr, myras hȳr,* m.
contemporary, a. *kevōs, a'n keth termyn*: n. *dēn a'y dermyn-ef.*
contempt, n. *despȳ·t, bysmē·r, scorn, dysprēsyans,* m.; c. of court, *torva dyfen an lȳs*: **-tible,** a. *a-dāl bōs fȳes, a-dāl y scornya*; c. person, *scübelak,* m., pl. *-logyon,* f. *-oges,* pl. *-ow.*: **-tuous,** a. *ow-fyā, ow-scornya.*
contend, v. *stryvya, gül tennow orth, omdewlel, kenkȳa.*
content, v. *contentya*: a. *lowen, attē·s, pȳs da lowr, contentys*: n., to his heart's c., *orth bōth y vrȳs*: **-ted,** a. *pȳs da*: **-tment,** n. *lowender, ēs,* m.
contention, n. *stryvyans, strȳf,* m.: **-tious,** a. *cavylek.*
contents, n. *pup oll üs ynno.*
contest, v. *omdewlel, stryvya*; c. an opinion, *dyspūtya*: n. *omdowl,* m., pl. *-ow, stryvyans,* m.: **-tant,** n. †*dathelor,* m., pl. *-yon.*
continent, n. *tȳr dȳen, brastyr,* m., pl. *-yow*; **-tal,** a. *a'n brastyr.*
continue, v. *pēsya, dürya*: **-ual,** a. *hep hedhy*: **-ally,** adv. *prest, pup ür-oll, pup nōs ha dēth.*
contort, v. *omgamma, cromma*: **-tion,** n. *cam, gwȳans, cromder,* m.
contract, v. *omdenna*; shrink, *berhē·, lehē·*; agree, *ambosa*: n. *ambos,* m., pl. *-ow*; under a c., *yn-dan ambos*; to make a c., *ambosa*: **-ted,** a., drawn together, *yn-gron.*
contradict, v. *contradȳa, kewsel erby·n*: **-tion,** n. *contradȳans, cows a-drüs*: **-tory,** a. *a-drüs.*
contraption, n. *ynjyn, jyn,* m., pl. *-nys.*
contrary, a. *contraryüs, drēs keyn, gorth*: n. *contrary,* m.; on the c., *a'n tu aral, y'n contrary part, y'n lē a henna*: **-rily, -riwise,** adv. *a-drus, yn-contraryüs, yn-dar.*
contrast, v. **contrastya*: n. **contrast,* m.; in c. with, *pür dhyhevelep dhe*^{2}, *ow-*contrastya orth.*
contravene, v. *gül drēs dyfen*: **-ntion,** n. *torva dyfen,* f.
contribute, v. *pē* or *rȳ ran, junnya*: **-tion,** n. *ran, kevran,* f., pl. *-now, shara,* m., pl. *-rys*: **-tory,** a. *a-gevran, kevrennek.*
contrite, a. *cüdhyjyk, dhodho edrek*; c. people, *cüdhyjygyon*: **-tion,** n. *edrega, edrek, cüdhyjygeth,* m.; act of c., *ankenek.*
contrive, v. *tewlel, devȳsya, darbary*; he will c. to do so, *ef a-wra may hallo yndella gül*:

-vance, n. *ynjyn, jyn,* m., pl. *-nys, darbar,* m., *towl,* m., pl. *-ow, devȳ·s,* m., pl. *-ys.*
control, v. *rowtya, rewlya, controlya, governya*: n. *gallos, danjer,* m.; *rewl,* m., pl. *-ys*: **-ler,** n. *rowtor,* m., pl. *-s.*
controversy, n. *controversyta, dyspūtyans, strȳf,* m.: **-vert,** v. *dyspūtya, *controvertya.*
contumely, n. *bysmē·r, despȳ·t,* m.
convene, v. *gelwel warba·rth, cuntell*: **-ner,** n. *cunteller,* m., pl. *-loryon,* f., *-lores,* pl. *-ow.*
convenience, n. *ēs, confort, lēs,* m.: **-ent,** a. *ēs*; handy, *parys*; if c., *yndella mar peugh plēsyes*; *ha na-veugh-why dysplēsyes.*
convent, n. *lenjy,* m., pl. *-ow.*
convention, n. *cuntellyans,* m., pl. *-ow*; agreement, *ambos,* m., pl. *-ow*; conduct, *ūsadow,* m.: **-nal,** a. *herwyth ūsadow.*
converse, v. *kewsel, talkya, keskewsel, omgewsel, kestalkya*: a. *contraryüs*: **-ation,** n. *omgows,* m., pl. *-ow, cows,* m., pl. *-ow, kescows,* m., pl. *-ow*: **-sely,** adv. *a'n tu contraryüs.*
convert, v. *trēlya*: n. *dyskybel,* m., pl. *-blon*: **-rsion,** n. *trēlyans,* m., pl. *-ow.*
convey, v. *gorra, gedya, transformya, dōn*; c. an estate, *statya*: **-ance,** n. *kert,* m., pl. *-ys*; law, *statyans,* m.
convict, v. *convyctya, dampnya*: n. *dēn convyctyes* or *dampnyes,* m., pl. *tüs c.* or *d.*: **-tion,** n. *prōf a gam, convyctyans,* m.; of mind, *cryjyans dyogel,* m.
convince, v. *gül dhe dhēn crysy*: **-ced,** a. *fasthēs· yn y gryjyans, sür*; to be c., *bōs ervȳrys.*
convivial, a. *lowenek*: **-s,** n. *kyfvewy,* col., *kyfvewysy,* pl.
convocation, n. *cuntellva,* f.
convoke, v. *gelwel warba·rth.*
convolvulus, n. *gwek,* col., pl. *-egas*: **gwȳadores,* f., pl. *-ow.*
convoy, n. *bagas lystry,* m.: v. *hembronk ha gwytha.*
convulse, v. *omgamma, deglena, crenna*: **-sion,** n. *shora,* m., pl. *-rys, cren,* m., pl. *-now.*
cook, v. *parüsy, dȳghtya bōs*: n. *cōk,* m., pl. *cogow, *kegyner,* m., pl. *-oryon,* f. *-ores,* pl. *-ow, kegyn-wrēk,* f., pl. *k. -wrageth, coges,* f., pl. *-ow*: **-ed,** a. *parys*: **c.-house,** *chȳ-cōk,* m., pl. *-ow-c.*
cool, a. *clōr, mygyl, nebes yeyn, *goyeyn, fresk*: v. *yeynhē·, mygla*: **-ness,** n. *clorder, yeynder, mygylder,* m.
coombe, n. *cūm,* m., pl. *-mow, nans,* m., pl. *-ow.*
coop, n. *cowel yēr,* m.
cooper, n. *bonkyer,* m., pl. *-yoryon.*
co-operate, v. *kesobery, keslafürya*: **-tion,** n. *kesober, kesoberyans, keslafüryans,* m.
coot, n. *dowryar,* f., pl. *-yēr.*
cope, n. *cōp,* m., pl. *-ys, capa,* f., pl. *-pyow*: c. with, v. *gül dhe*[2], *omdewlel gans*; I could not c. with him, *my ny-wodhyen gül dhodho.*
copious, a. *lün, pals.*
copper, n. *cober,* m.; vessel, *pēr,* m., pl. *-row*: **c.-smith,** n. *gwȳthor cober,* m., pl. *-oryon c.*
coppice, copse, n. *kelly welenek,* f., pl. *-yow gw., gwelenek,* f., pls. *-egy, -egow, pryskel,* m., pl. *-sclow, pryskwyth,* col.
copy, v. *dasscryfa, *copya, gül warle·rgh*: n. *dasscryf,* m., pl. *-yvow, *copy,* m., pl. *-yow, daspryntyans,* m., pl. *-ow, equal,* m., pl. *-s*: **c.-book,** *lyver-dasscryfa,* m., pl. *lyfrow-d.*
copyright, n. *gwȳr pryntya,* m.
coral, **gwylar,* m.
corbel, n. *corbel,* m., pl. *-blys.*
cord, n. *corden,* f., pl. *kerdyn, raf,* f., pl. *-fow, lovan,* f., pl. *-vonow, lovanen,* f., pl. *-now*: **-age,** n. *lovonow,* f., pl.: **-wainer,** n. *keryor,* m., pl. *-yon.*
cordial, a. *colonnek*: n. *dewas a-bȳk an golon.*
core, n. *crēs,* m., *colonen, *bewesen,* f., pl. *-now.*
cork, n. **corkyn,* m., col. *cork*; **c.-screw,** n. *alwheth *corkyn,* m., pl. *alwhedhow c.*
cormorant, n. *morvran,* f., pl. *-vrȳny, spylgarn,* m., pl. *-as.*
corn, n. *ȳs,* col.; grain of c., *ȳsen,* pl. *-now*; sorts or supplies of c., *ȳsow,* pl.; standing c., *ȳs ow-sevel*; ear of c., *pen ȳs*; rich in c., *ȳsak*; c. land, *yttȳr,* m.; c. on feet, *calesen,* f., pl. *-now*: **c.-bin,** n. *argh-ȳs,* f., pl. *-ow-y.*: **c.-crake,** n. *crekyar,* f., pl. *-yēr*: **c.-field,** *ȳsak,* f., pls. *-segow, -segy*: **c.-flower,** n. **glysynen,* f., col. *glysyn*: **c.-marigold,** n. **caja velen,* f.: **c.-rust,** n. *canker,* m.: **c.-smut,** n. *losk,* m.
corner, n. *elyn,* m., pl. *-now, cornel,* f., pls. *-ly, -low, corn,* m., pl. *kernow, coyn,* m., pl. *-ys*; in road, *plēk hens,* m., pl. *-egow h.*; nook, *sorn,* m., pl. *sernow*; of sack, etc., *bogen,* f., pl. *-now*: **c.-stone,** *pen-mēn,* m.: v. *controlya, gwytha rak scüsy.*
cornet, n. *tollcorn,* m., pls. *-ow, tollkern, *whythgorn,* m., pl. *-gern.*

Cornish, a. *Kernewek*; C. language, n. *Kernewek*, m.: **C.-man,** n. *Kernow*, m., pl. *-yon*: **C.-woman,** n. *Kernewes*, f., pl. *-ow*: **-nouaille,** *Kernow Breten Vȳghan*, f.: **-nwall,** n. *Kernow*, f.: **-nicize,** v. *kernewekhē·*.

coronation, n. *curünyans*, m., pl. *-ow*.

coroner, n. *curünor*, m., pl. *-yon*.

coronet, n. *curünyk*, f., pl. *-ygow*.

corporal, a. *corf*, *a'n corf*: n. *corporal*, m., pl. *-s*.

corporation, n. *corf*, m., pl. *-ow*.

corpse, n. *corf marow*, m., pl. *-ow m*.

corpulence, n. *tewder*, m., *braster corf*, m.: **-nt,** a. *corfak*, *tew*, *brās y gorf*.

correct, v. *ewna*, *amendya*; by word, *kesky*; punish, *keredhy*: a. *kewar*, *ewn*, *squȳr*, *lēl*, *gwȳr*: **-tion,** n. *ewnans*, m., pl. *-ow*, *cosk*, m.; chastisement, *kereth*, f.; under c., *saw gwell avȳ·s*: **-ness,** n. *ewnder*, *kewerder*, m.; of attitude, *dy·nyta*, m.

correspond, v., write, *kesscryfa*, *omworth-eby*; be like, *kehevelly*, *omdhesedha an ȳl dh'y gȳla.*: **-dence,** n., written, *lytherow*, pl.; likeness, *hevelepter*, m.: **-dent,** n. *kesscryfer*, m., pl. *-oryon*: **-ding,** a. *kehaval*.

corridor, n. *tremenva*, f., pl. *-ow*.

corrode, v. *cancra*; rust, *gossenna*: **-osion,** n. *canker*, *cusk*, m.; rust, *gossen*, f.

corrupt, v., rot, *pedry*; morals, *shyndya*: a. *poder*, *podrethek*, *dyslēl*: **-ted,** a. *podrek*, *pedrys*: **-tion,** n. *podrethes*, *poder*, m.

cosen, v. *flattrya*, *flattra*: **-ner,** n. *flattor*, m., pl. *-oryon*, f. *-ōres*, pl. *-ow*.

cost, v. *costya*: n. *cost*, *prȳs*, m., pl. *-ys*, *cost-yans*, m.; at all c's., *awo·s ēghen*: **-tly,** a. *kēr*, *cüf*, *mür y gost*.

costume, n. *dyllas*, m., pl. *-ajow*.

cosy, a. *cles*, *yn ēs*, *attē·s*: **-siness,** n. *clesor*, m.

cot, n. *crow*, m., pl. *-yow*, *crowjy*, m., pl. *-ow*, **penty*, m., pl. *-ow*; child's c., *gwely bȳghan*; dove-c., *colomyer*, m.; sheep-c., *crow an deves*, *devetty*, m.

cottage, n. *chȳ bȳghan*; **penty*, m., pl. *-ow*; one-roomed, *crowjy*, m., pl. *-ow*.

cotton, n. **coton*; c. material, *lȳen coton*, **bombas*, m.: **c.-grass,** n. **gūnblüf*, col., **lyn gwern*, m.: **c.-wool,** n. *gwlan coton*, col.

couch, n. *gwely-dēth*, m., pl. *-yow-d.*, *grow-ethva*, f., *loven*, f., pl. *-now*: v. *plattya*; c. a spear in rest, *synsy gu dhe restya*: **c.-grass,** n. **trüswels*, col.

cough, v. *passa*: n. *pas*, m., pl. *-ow*; whooping-c., *pas garm*, m.

coulter, n. *trogher*, *trōer*, m., pl. *-yow*, †*colter*, m., pl. *-trow*.

council, n. *consel*, m., pl. *-s*, *kesva*, f.; eccles., *seneth*, m., pl. *-edhow*: **-lor,** n. *consler*, *co·nseler*, m., pl. *-s*.

counsel, v. *cusülya*, *avȳsya*, ‡*consylya*: n. *cusül*, f., pl. *-yow*, *avȳ·s*, m.: **-lor,** n. †*cusülyador*, m., pl. *-yon*, †*dathellor*, m., pl. *-oryon*.

count, v. *comptya*, *rekna*, *nyvera*, *amontya*, *acontya*; don't c. on it any more, *na-drest ynno namoy*: **-ting,** *nyveryans*, m.; beyond counting, countless, *drēs aga nyvera*, *dynyver*.

counter, v. *gortheby*: n., in shop, **comptyer*, m., pl. *-s*: **-teract,** v. *gonys erby·n*, *domhel*: **-terbalance,** v. **gorthbosa*: n. **gorthbos*, m.: **-ter-belief,** n. *gorthgrēs*, f.: **-ter-claim,** n. *clēm*, m., pl. *-ys*: **-ter-clock-wise,** adv. *erby·n an howl.*: **-terfeit,** n. *gow*, m., pl. *-yow*: a. *gow*, *fals*, **fük*: v. *gül gow*, *falshē·*, *supposya*, *contrefaytya*: **-ter-note,** n. *co·nternōt*, m.: **-terpane,** n. *kew-let*, m.: **-terpart,** n. *ran gehaval*, f., pl. *-now k.*, *parth kehaval*, f.: **-tersign,** n. *gēr pryva*: **-ter-tenor,** n. *co·nternōt*, m.

country, n. *gwlās*, f., pl. *-ow*, *tyreth*, m., pl. *-ow*, *pow*, m., pl. *-yow*; region, *bro*, f., pl. *-yow*; chief c., *pen-wlās*, f., pl. *-ow*: **-trified,** a. *a'n pow*, *tȳthyak*, *herwyth gȳs tyogow*: **c.-man,** n. *trevesyk*, m., pls. *-ygyon*, *-ejygyon*, *dēn pow*, m., pl. *tüs p.*: **c.-side,** n. *pow*, m.; the c., *an pow a-dro*: **c.-woman,** n. *treve-syges*, *tyeges*, f., pl. *-ow*.

county, n. *pow*, m., pl. *-yow*, *conteth*, m., pl. *-ow*: **c.-court,** n. *lȳs conteth*, f., pl. *-yow c.*

couple, v. *copla*, *parya*: n. *copel*, m., pl. *-plow*; the c., persons, *an dheudhen*; wedded c., *deudhen*, *deubrȳas*, †*kesparow*; by c's., *deu ha deu*.

coupon, n. **colpon*, m., pl. *-ys*.

courage, n. *colon dha*, f., *colonnekter*, m.; take c., *omgonfortya*, *bōs gwell y jēr*: **-eous,** a. *colonnek*, *brās y golon*.

courier, n. *rēsor*, m., pl. *-oryon*, *rēswas*, m., pl. *-wesyon*.

course, n. *hens*, m., pl. *-y*; turn, time, *cors*, m., pl. *-ow*, *proces*, m.; series, **stüs*, f., pl. *-ow*; of action, *cusül*, f., pl. *-yow*; c. of meal, †*sant*, m.; water c., *rēs*, *deveran*, m.; race c., career, orbit, *resekva*, f., pl. *-ow*; study, *dyscans*, m., pl. *-ow*; evil c's., *drōkfordhow*;

of c., *hep mar, hep dhowt, del wodher*; in the c. of time, *ha termyn ow-tremena*; *a-jȳ dhe broces a dermyn*: v. *chassya*.

courser, n. *courser*, m., pl. *-s*; coursing hound, *resky*, m., pl. *-scün*.

court, n. *cür*, m., pl. *-ys, cort*, f., pl. *-ys, lȳs*, f., pl. *-yow*; ancient c., *hellys*, f.: v. †*tanta, dysquedhes kerensa orth, ombrofya ave·l prȳas dhe²*: **-tier,** n. **lysor*, m., pl. *-yon*; **-tship,** n. *cara*, m.; **tantans*, m.; **caro·r-ȳeth*, f.

courteous, a. *cortes*: **-tesy,** n. *je·ntylys, co·rtesy*, m.

cousin, n. *ke·nderow*, m., pl. *-dyrewy, keny·-therow*, f., pl. *-thyrewy*.

cove, n. *porth*, m., pls. *-ow, perth*, dim. *porthyn*, m.

covenant, n. *kevambos*, m., pl. *-ow*.

cover, v. *cüdha, quetha, gorhery*; shelter, *goskesy*; c. with a tilt, *tyldya*; c. with roof, *tȳ*: n., lid, *gorher*, m., pl. *-yow*; shelter, *goskes*, m.; hiding, *covva*, f.; for game, *godegh*, m.; under c., *y'n harber, yn-dan gēl* or *güth*: **-ing,** n. *cüdhans*, m., pl. *-ow, gwyscas*, m., pl. *-cosow, gorheras*, m.: **-let,** n. *kewlet*, m., pl. *-tys*, **pallen*, f. ,pl. *-now*: **covert,** n. *hüth, goskes*, m., *cleswyth*, col.

covet, v. *whansa, covetya*: **-tous,** a. *craf, pȳth*: **-tousness,** n. *covaytys, crefny, pȳth-neth*, m.

cow, n. *bugh*, f., pl. *-as*; c. past bearing calves, *b. gawnagh*, f.: **c.-herd,** n. *bügel*, m., pl. *-eth, b. bughas*: **-hide,** n. *bughken*, m.: **c.-house,** n. *bowjy*, m., pl. *-ow*.

coward, n. *ownek*, m., pl. *-negyon, coward*, m.: **-dice,** n. *cowardy*, m.

cower, v. *plynchya, plattya*.

cowl, n. *cūgol*, m., pl. *-low*.

crab, n. *canker*, m., pl. *kencras*; harbour c., *pe·beryn*, m., pl. *-now*; spider c., *crȳgell*, f., pl. *-ow, gevryk*, m., pl. *-ygow, canker hȳr y baw, podrek, pylyak*, m.; c. apple, *aval gwyls, crabba*, m.; c. a. tree, *gwedhen crabbys*, f.

crabbed, a. *dynā·s, asper*.

crack, v. *crakkya, terry, tardha*: n., sound, *crak*, m., pl. *-kys*; fissure, *crȳk*, m., pl. *-ygow*; interj. *crak*! *knak*!: **-ed,** a. *trogh*; of voice, *grolyak*.

cradle, n. *lesk*, m., pl. *-scow*.

craft, n. *creft*, f., pl. *-ow, myster*, m.; cunning, *sotelneth, felder*, m.; **-tsman,** n. *creftor*, m., pl. *-oryon, mysterden*, m., pl. *-s, oberor*, m., pl. *-yon, ynjynor*, m., pl. *-yon*: **-ty,** a. *fēl, connek, ynjyn, wȳly, sotel, skentyl*.

crag, n. *clugh*, m., pl. *-as, clog*, f., pl. *-ow, clegar*, m., pl. *-grow*: **-gy,** a. *clegerek*; c. place, *clegerek*, f., pl. *-egow, -egy*.

craking, a. *grolyak*.

cram, v. *herdhya, gorlenwel, sagha*.

cramp, n. *godra·m*, m., *colm keherow*, m.: v. *omgelmy*; with cold, *cromma*: **-ed,** a. *crom*.

crane, n. *garan*, f., pl. *-as, crana*, m., pl. *-ys*; machine, *jyn-crana*, m., pl. *-nys-c*.

cranny, n. *sorn*, m., pl. *sernow, crȳk*, m., pl. *-ygow*.

crash, v. *crakkya, deghesy warba·rth*: n. *crak*, m., pl. *-kys*; interj. *crak*!, *squat*!

crate, n. *clōs*, f., pl. *-ojow*.

crater, n. *pyt rond*, m., pl. *-tys r., ganow losk-veneth*, m.

crave, v. *yeuny, pysy*: **-ving,** n. *ewl* (*awell*), f.; *yeunadow*, m., *yeunes*, m., pl. *-ow*.

crawl, v. *cramyas, pedrevanas, slynkya, cro-nogas*; c. along on the belly, *slynkya war dōr a-hēs*.

crayfish, n. *gavar-mōr*, f., pl. *gever-m*.

crazy, a. *müscok, fol, clāf y ympynyon*; c. person, *müscok*, m., pl. *-cogyon, fol*, m., pl. *felyon*: **craze,** v., go, drive c., *müskegy*; of glaze, *falsa gwedrans*: **-ziness,** n. *müs-cotter, müscogneth*, m.

creak, v. **gwȳghal*, **gryllya*: n. **gwȳgh*, m.

cream, n. *dēhen*, m.; to form c., *dehenna*: **-ery,** n. *dehenjy*, m., pl. *-ow*: **-y,** a. *dehennek*.

crease, v. *plegya*: n. *plēk*, m., pl. *-egow*.

create, v. *formya, crēatya, gül, gwrüthyl*: **-tion,** n. *gwrȳans, formyans, crēasyon*, m.: **-tive,** a. *ynjyn, ow-tesevos*: **-tor,** n. *formyas*, m., pl. *-ysy, formyer*, m., pl. *-yoryon, creador*, m., pl. *-yon, maker*, m.: **-ture,** n. *creatur*, m., pl. *-toryon, mȳl*, m., pl. *-as*; living things, *taclow bew, t. üs ow-quaya*.

credence, m. *crejys, cryjyans*, m., *fȳth*, f.

credentials, n. *lytherow crēs*, pl.

credible, a. *hegol*, **hegrēs, a-yller y grysy*; it is not c., *nyns-yu dhe grysy*: **-bility,** n. **hegrejeth*, m.

credit, v. *cola orth, crysy dhe²*: n., belief, trust, *crejys*; in business, *prȳs, dēth hȳr*, m.; do c. to, *bōs*, or *gül, worshyp dhe²*: **-able,** a. *da*, or *gwyw, dh'y braysya*: **-itor,** n. *dettor*, m., pl. *-s*; **creancer*, m., pl. *-s*.

credulous, a. *hegol, cryjyk*: **-lity,** n. *hegoleth*, m.

creed, n., faith, *crēs,* f., *lay,* f., pl. *-es*; the Apostles C., *Crēdo an Abesteleth, an Grēdo,* f.
creek, n. *corn dowr,* m., pl. *kernow d., plēk mor,* m., pl. *-egow m., porth,* m., pls. *-ow, perth, kylen,* f., pl. *-now.*
creep, v. *slynkya, cramyas, pedrevanas, cruppya, crambla, *melwhesenas.*
crescent, n. *hanter lōr* f.
cress, n. *beler,* col; c. plant, *beleren,* f.; winter c., *cas-beler,* m.; c.-bed, *belerek,* f., pls. *-egy, -egow.*
crest, n. *crȳben,* f., pl. *-now, crybell,* f., pl. *-ow, crȳb,* f., pl. *-ow*; c. of hill or bank, *mujoven,* f., pl. *-now*: v. *crybella*: **-ed,** a. *crybennys, crȳbys.*
crest-fallen, a. *ysel y grȳben.*
crevice, n. *fals,* m., pl. *-ljow.*
crew, n. *felshyp,* m., *tüs gorhel,* m.. pl., *marners,* m. pl.
crib, n. **presep,* m., pl. *-ebow.*
cricket, n., insect, *crȳgell,* f., pl. *-ow, gryll,* m., pl. *-as.*
crier, n. *crȳor,* m., pl. *-yon.*
crime, n. *cam,* m., pl. *-mow, gwan-ober, drok-ober,* m., pl. *-ow, camwyth,* m.
criminal, a. *drōk*: n. *drōk-oberor,* m., pl. *-yon, drok-dhēn,* m., pl. *d.-düs, gal,* m., pl. *-ow.*
crimp, v. *crȳghy*: n. *crȳgh,* m.
crimson, a. *rüth-du.*
crinkle, v. *crȳghy*: n. *crȳgh,* m.: **-led,** a. *crȳgh, crebogh.*
cripple, v. *evredhy*: n. *evreth,* m., pl. *-edhyon, evredhek,* m., pl. *-ygyon, cropyl,* m., pl. *-s., mans,* m., pl. *-yon*: **-led,** a. *mans, evreth, evredhek, cloppek.*
crisis, n. *bar,* m., pl. *-ow*; of illness, *poynt tykly,* m.
crisp, a. *cras.*
criss-cross, n. *Dew-gweres,* m.
critic, n. *brüsyas,* m., pl. *-ysy, *crytyk,* m., pl. *-ys*: **-al,** a., of crisis, *tykly*; of critic, *a-*grytyk*: **-icise,** v. *brüsy, *crytyca*: **-icism,** n. *brüs,* f.; **crytycans,* m.
croak, v. *renky*: n. *ronk, renkyas,* m.: **-er,** n. *renkyas,* m., pl. *-ysy*: **-ing,** a., *ronk.*
crock, n., metal, *chek,* m., pl. *-kys, †sēth,* m., pl. *-ow*; large salting c., *†pērseth, bussa,* m.; **-ery,** n. *lystry-prȳ,* m. pl., *chēny, dafar,* m.
crocodile, n. **crocodȳl,* pl. *-ys, *cawrbedrevan,* pl. *-as*; c. tears, *dagrow fekyl.*
cromlech, n. *cromlegh,* f., pl. *-yow.*
crook, v. *cromma, camma*: n., shepherd's c., crosier, *bagyl,* f., pl. *-glow*; c. to catch sand-eels, *fenegler,* m.; c. of grapnel, *paw,* m., pl. *-yow*: **-ed,** a. *cam, cammys, crom*: **-edness,** n. *camder, cromder,* m.
crookshanked, a. *bergam.*
crop, v., lop, *dybenna*; shorten, *cot-trēghy*; browse on, *pory orth*; c. a field , *gonys hās yn gwēl*: n. *trevas,* f., pls. *-ow, -ajow*; of bird, *crūth,* f., **crombyl,* f., pl. *-yow*; maw, *glas, cowl,* m., pl. *-ow*; neck and c., *pup goth ha lȳth, kettep tam.*
crow, n. *brān,* f., pl. *brȳny*; hooded c., *b. lōs, b. Marghas Yow*: v. *cana ave·l cülyek.*
crosier, n. *bagyl,* f., pl. *-glow*; c. bearer, *crosser,* m., pl. *-s.*
cross, n. *crows,* f., pl. *-ow, pren crows,* m., *crowspren,* f.; small c., *crowsyk,* f., pl. *-ygow*; processional c., *sȳn an grows*: v. *mōs drēs* or *a-drüs, tremena*; c. water, **trētha*; c. oneself, *omsona, omgrowsa*: a. *trüs, crowsek*; c. shaped, *crowsek*: **-ly,** adv. *yn-trüs, dhodho sōr*: **-ness,** n. *sōr,* m.
cross-bar, n. *trēster,* m., pls. *-s, -trow.*
cross-beam, n. **trüst,* m., pl. *-ow.*
cross-bow, n. **arblast,* m., pl. *-ys, *füstwarak,* f., pl. *-regow.*
cross-bred, a. *kemyskrȳth.*
cross-cut saw, n. **trüs-hesken,* f., pl. *-now.*
cross-examine, v. *apposya glew.*
cross-eyed, a. *cam y lagas.*
crossing, n. *tremenva,* f.; over water, *trēth, trümach,* m.
cross-lode, n. *cōnter,* m.
cross-piece, n. *trüspren,* m., pl. *-yer.*
cross-road, n. *peswar torn, crowshens,* m., pl. *-y, crowsforth,* f., pl. *-rdhow.*
couch, v. *plattya.*
crowbar, n. *lorgh horn,* m., pl. *-ow h.*
crowd, n. *būsh,* m., pl. *-ys, lu,* m., pl. *-yow, rūth,* f., pl. *-ow, tonek,* m.; a great c., *rūth vür, mür a lu, būsh brās*: v. *gwasca, hēsya, dōs,* or *mōs, yn rūth.*
crowfoot, n. *paw-brān,* m.; water c., *blewen dowr,* f.
crow-garlic, n. *†gothkenyn,* col.
crowing, n. *kenys,* m.
crown, n. *curün,* f., pl. *-now*; of head, *top an pen, †dywolewyth,* m.; of hat, *cūgh,* m.: v. *curüna*; with laurels, **lōrya.*
crucible, n. **tethlester,* m., pl. *-lystry.*
crucifix, n. *crowspren,* f., *pren crows,* m., pls. *-yer, -prynner*: **-ion,** n. *crowsans, crowsyans,* m.
cruciform, a. *crowsek, yn form a grows.*

crucify, v. *crowsa, crowsya, gorra yn crowspren,* or *abe·rth yn crows.*
crude, a., unripe, *crȳf,* **anathves*; rude, *garow.*
cruel, a. *fell, tyn, ahas, crūel, hager, garow, dydrūeth*: **-ty,** n. *hakter, garowder, crūelta,* m.
cruet, n. **cruettys*; c. stand, *lester c.,* m., pl. *lystry c.*
cruise, n. *vȳaj,* m., pl. *-ys*: v. *gōlya, vȳajya.*
crumb, n. *brewyonen,* f., pl. *brewyon, browsyonen,* f., pl. *browsyon, -jyon,* col. *brows*; soft part of bread, *whygen,* f.: **crumble,** v. *brewy, browsy*; crumbled stuff, *brows,* col.
crumple, v. *crȳghy, cromma*; **-led,** a. *crȳgh, crom.*
crunch, v. *dynsel,* **dasknȳas.*
crupper, n. *pedren,* f., pl. *-now,* d., *dywbedren.*
crusade, *bresel sans, b. an Grows,* m., pl. *-yow s.*
crush, v. *deffola, brewy, cropya, squattya*: n. *herdhyans, rūth herdhyes warba·rth,* f.
crust, n. *cresten,* f., pl. *-now, creven,* f., pl. *-now*; to form a c., *crestenna, crevenna.*
crutch, n. *croch,* m., pl. *-ys,* d. *deugroch.*
cry, v. *crȳa, ullya, hūla, üja*; weep, *ola*; c. to, *garma war*[2]; c. out, *garma, lēfa*; c. shrilly, *gwȳghal*; c. wares, *gwyca*: n. *crȳ,* m., pl. *-ow, lēf,* m., pl. *-evow, garm,* f., pl. *-ow*; howl, *ullyans,* m., *üs,* m., pl. *üjow*; raise a c., *hūa, gül crȳ.*
crystal, n. *gwrȳs, crystal,* m.: **-lize,** v. *gwrȳsa.*
cub, n. *colyn,* m., pl. *kelyn*; lion c., *lewyk,* m., pls. *-wygow, -wasygow.*
cubit, n. *kevelyn,* m., pl. *-now.*
cuckoo, n. *cōk,* f., pl. *-ogas, cūcū,* f., pl. *-s.*
cuckoo-pint, n. *scaf a'y lygyon,* m.
cuckoo-ray, n. *calamajȳna,* m.
cud, n. *kyl,* m., pls. *-yow, -yer*; chew the c., **dasknȳas.*
cuddle, v. *chersya,* ‡*byrla.*
cudgel, n. *bat,* m., pl. *-tys, cūlbren,* m.: v. *gweskel, frappya gans bat,* **battya.*
cuff, n., blow, *box,* m., pl. *-ow, boxas,* pl. *-xesow*; on sleeve, *ragvrēghal,* m., pl. *-ghellow*: v. *boxesy.*
culminate, v. *dewedha, dōs dh'y ughelder, dhe'n pryk ughella*: **-tion,** n. *deweth, pryk ughella,* m.
culpable, a. *cablüs, cam, dhe vlamya.*
culprit, n. *drokoberor,* m., pl. *-yon.*
cultivate, v. *gonys*; rear, *maga*: **-ted,** a. *fȳth*: **-tion,** n. *gonys,* m.: **-tor,** n. *tȳak,* m., pls. *tyegyon, tyogow, gonysyas,* m., pl. *gonesyjy.*
culture, n. *gonesygeth*; rearing, *megyans, cyvylta,* m.: **-red,** a. *da y vegyans.*
cunning, a. *connek, connyng, fēl, cal*: n., cleverness, *connyng,* m.; craft, *felder, sotylta,* m.: **-ly,** adv. *yn fēl, drē art.*
cup, n. *hanaf* (*hanath*), m., pl. *-avow* †*fȳol,* f., pl. *-ow, bolla,* m., pl. *-lys,* †*cafas,* m., *kyb,* f., pl. *-ow*; tea-c., **cuppa,* m., pl. *-pys.*
cup-bearer, n. *menystror, hanafor,* m., pl. *-yon.*
cupboard, n. *a·mary,* m., pl. *-s,* **lystryer,* m., pl. *-yow, cubert,* m., pl. *-ys.*: corner c., *buffet,* m., pl. *-tys.*
cupidity, n. *pȳthneth,* m.
cur, n. *brathky,* m., pl. *-thcün.*
curate, n. **curat,* m., pl. *-ys.*
curb, v. *frona, chekkya*: n. *fron,* f., pl. *-now,* **genva,* f., pl. *-ow*; c. stone, **amalven.*
curd, n. *cowl,* m., *cowlesen,* f., col. *cowles*; c's., *lēth cowlys,* m.: **-dle,** v. *cowla.*
cure, v. *sawya, yaghē, gweres*: n. *yly,* m., *pl.* and abst. *ylȳow, medhy·gȳeth,* f., *gweres, cür, remedy,* m.; c. of souls, *cür,* m.
curfew, n. **coverfu,* m.
curious, a. *coynt*; rare, *tanow*; enquiring, *a-gar whyles,* or *gothvos*: **-osity,** n. *whans gothvos,* m.; strange object, *coyntys,* m., *tra goynt,* f.
curl, n. *cudyn crullyes,* m., pl. *-now c., crȳghgudyn,* m.: v. *crullya*: **-ly,** a. *crullys.*
curlew, n. *gelvynak,* m., pl *-nogas.*
currant, n. *fygesen Corynt,* f., col. *fyges C.*
currency, n. *mona,* col.; followed by pl. pron.
current, n. *frōs,* m., pl. *-ow*; electric, *frōs,* or *rēs, tredanek,* m.: a. *a'n jēth, a'n termyn -ma, -na,*
currier, n. *cronor,* m., pl. *-yon.*
curry, n. *sant melen Eynda.*
curry-comb, n. †*stryl,* f., pl. *-yow*: v. *strylla.*
curse, n. *mollath,* f., pl. *-othow*: v. *mollethy, rȳ mollath dhe*[2], *mylyga, emskemünya, skemünya,* ‡*cussya*: **-sed,** a. *mollothek, mylygys*; one c. by parents, *map mollothow*: **-sing,** n. *mollethyans,* m.
curtail, v. *berhē·, cotthē·, cot-trēghy*: **-ment,** n. *berhēans,* m.
curtain, n. *len, l. fe·nester, l. darras,* **croglen,* f., pl. *-now.*
curve, n. *cam,* m., pl. *-mow, lȳn crom,* m., pl. *-ow c., stüm.,* m., pl. *-mow*: v. *cromma, camma, stümma*: **-ved,** a. *crom.*

cushion, n. *plüvak,* m., pl. *-vogow.*
custodian, n. *gwythyas,* m., pl. *-ysy,* f. *-yades,* pl. *-ow.*, *warden,* m., pl. *-s*; c. of, *warden war²*: **-ody,** n. *gwȳth,* m.
custom, n. *ūs, ūsadow,* m., *maner,* f., pl. *-ow, gȳs,* m., pl. *-yow,* **devos,* f., pl. *-ow*: **-ary,** a. *ūsyes.*
custom-house, n. *tolljy,* m., pl. *-ow, chȳ-custum,* m.
customs, n. *toll,* f., pl. *-ow*; c. officer, *tollor,* m., pl. *-yon.*
customer, n. *prener,* m., pl. *-noryon, prenyas,* m., pl. *-ysy.*
cut, v. *trēghy,* **kemena*; carve, *gravya*; c. across, *dōs a-drüs*; c. up, *dyvynya*: n., slice, *trēgh,* m., pl. *-ow*; wound, *brew,* m., pl. *-yon*; incision, *trogh,* m., pls. *-ow, trēghyon*: a. *trogh*; easily c., *hedrogh*: **cutter,** n. *trēgher,* m., pl. *-oryon, trēghyas,* m., pl. *-ysy.*
cutler, n. *collelor,* m., pl. *-yon.*
cutlery, n. *dafar lym, gwara collelor,* m.
cutlet, n. *golyth,* m., pl. *-yon.*
cutting, n., from plant, *skyllen,* f., col. *skyl*; for road, etc., **troghva,* f., pl. *-ow, cledh-yans,* m.
cuttlebone, n. *tag-hȳr,* m.
cuttlefish, n. *padel-ynkyn,* f., pls. *-llow, -lly y.*, *collel,* f., pls. *kellyl, kellylly*; squid, *styfak,* m., pl. *-fogas.*
cyclostyle, n. *lyes-scryfer,* m., *plüven rosyk,* f.
cyclone, *gwyns a-dro, trowyns,* m., pl. *-ow a.*: **-onic,** a. *a-dro, trowynsek.*
cylinder, n. *rōl,* f., pl. *-yow*: **-drical,** a. **hȳrgren, crom.*
cymbal, n. *cymbal,* m., pl. *-ys.*
cynic, n. *dyscryjyk,* m., pl. *-jygyon, scrynkyer,* m., pl. *-yoryon*: **-ical,** a. *dyscryjyk, na-vyn crysy namoy·es kȳ, ow-scrynkya.*

D

dab, n., fish, *lȳth,* f., pl. *-as*; touch, *strocas scaf,* m.: v. *tuchya yn-scaf, posa pols bȳghan war².*
dabble, v. *cabūly, lagya.*
dabchick, n. **tȳndrōs,* m.
dace, n. *talek,* m., pl. *-ogas.*
dad, daddy, n. *tasyk,* m.
daffodil, n. **a·fodyl,* m., pl. *-lys,* **lylyen Corawys,* f., col. *lyly-C.*, **kenynen Peder,* f., col. *kenyn P.*
daft, a. *goky.*
dagger, n. *dagyer,* m., pl. *-s.*
daily, a. *pupteth-oll, pup deth-oll*: adv. *pupteth-oll, dayly.*
dainty, a. *dēnty*: n., tit-bit, *tam dēnty,* m., pl. *tymmyn d.*
dairy, n. *lēty,* m., pl. *-ow*; d. farm, *hewas,* m.; d. maid, *lēthvowes,* f., pl. *-y, lēthwrēk,* f., pl. *-wrageth.*
daisy, n. *ygor, ygor Dew,* m., pl. *-ow D.*, *caja,* f., †*boreles,* m.; garden d., *ygor jarn*; ox-eye d., *caja vrās*; corn-marigold, *c. velen.*
dale, n. *dōl,* f., pl. *-ow, nans,* m., pl. *-ow, tenow·* m., pl. *-newyow, dev·eran* (†*deverhent*), m.
dally, v. *strechya, lettya, dylātya.*
dam, n., dyke, *banken,* f., pl. *-now, tomen,* f., pl. *-now*; weir, *cores,* f., pl. *-ow*: v. *crüny.*
damage, v. *gwethhē·, shyndya, apērya, kȳsya*; d. by weather, **arnewa*: n. *damach,* m., pl. *-ajys, collva,* f., *coll,* m., *torva,* f., **früth,* m.; d. by storm, **arnew.*
dame, n. *dama, madama,* f., pl. *-mys, mestres,* f., pl. *-ys.*
damn, v. *dampnya*: **-nable,** a. *dampnys, emskemünys,* **dampnabyl*: **-nation,** n. *dampnasyon,* m.
damp, -pness, n. *glybor*: v. *glybya*: a. *glyp*; d. place, *sogen,* f., pl. *-now.*
damsel, n. *moren,* f., pl. *-ronyon, damsel,* f., pl. *-s.*
dance, v. *donsya, corolly*; step-d., *lappya*: n. *gwary-dōns,* m., pl. *-yow d.*, *corol,* m., pl. *-low, dōns,* m., pl. *-yow*: **-r,** n. *donsyor,* m., pl. *-oryon, donsyores,* f., pl. *-ow*; step-dancer, tumbler, tin-dresser, *lappyor,* m., pl. *-ryon.*
dandelion, n. *dans-lew,* m., pls. *blejyow* or *losow d-l.*
dandruff, n. *brēghy,* m. pl.
danger, n. *peryl,* m., pl. *-yow, hakter,* m.; to run into d., *peryllya*; d. of loss, **argoll,* m.: **-rous,** a. *peryllys, deantel, hager*: **-rously,** adv., precariously, *deantel.*
dappled, a. *brȳth, spletyar.*
dare, v. *lavasos, bedha, bōs harth dhe²*: **-ring,** a. *harth, bold*: n. *bolder,* m.; d. person, **bedhas,* m., pl. *-dhysy.*
dark, a. *tewl, du*; pitch d., *tewl dall*: **-kness,** n. *tewlder,* **tewlyjyon,* m., *tewolgow,* abst. pl., *mo,* m. (in phrase, *m. ha myttyn*); in the d., *worth golow nōs*: **-ken,** v. *tewlhē·*: **-kish,** a. **godewl.*
darling, n. *cüf-colon, melder,* m., *whegyn,* m., pl. *-now, whegen,* f., pl. *-now,* **keresyk,* m. or f., pl. *-sygyon, caradow,* m. or f., pl. *-yon*:

a. *whegoll, caradow, cüf colon, mür gerys, ewngerys.*
darn, v. *crafa, dasquȳa, ewna lodrow*: n. *dasquȳas*, m.
dart, n. *gu*, m., pl. *-yow, sethen*, f., pl. *-now*: v. *gwybya, pychya, setha.*
dash, v. *deghesy, tuchya*; rush, *stēvya, fysky, mōs yn ün stēvya*: n. *fysk*, m.; make a d. for it, *fysky bys dhodho*; d. of pen, *ten plüven.*
dashboard, n. *tāl car, t. kert*, m.
date, v. *settya dēth*: n., calendar d., *dēth, d. an seythen, d. an mȳs*, m., pl. *-dhyow*; fruit, *fygesen rȳal*, f., col. *fyges r.*
daughter, n. *myrgh*, f., pl. *-es*, dim. *myrghyk*, f., pl. *-ghesygow*; d.-in-law, †*gūhyth*, f., pl. *-hydhow.*
daunt, v. *gorra own yn*: **-tless,** a. *dyown, heb own.*
daw: see **jackdaw.**
dawdle, v. *strechya, sygera, trüsy termyn, dylātya, bōs lent, melwhesenas*: **-ler,** n. *termynak*, m., pl. *-nogyon*: **-ling,** a. *termynak, syger, lent*: n. *sygerneth*, m.
dawn, v. *tardha*: n. *dēth-tarth*, m., pl. *tardhow d.*, †*bora*, m.; at d., *dyworth an jēth.*
day, n. *dēth*, m., pl. *-edhyow, jorna*, m., pls. *-nys, -nyow*; as prefix, *dē-*, m.; next d., *ternos*; three d's., *treddyth*; six d's., *wheddyth*, m.; third d. hence, *godreva*, f.; this d., *y'n jēth hedhyu, hedhyu y'n jēth*; d's. time, *dēdhwyth*, m., pl. *-yow*; work by the d., *dēdhwȳth*, m.; by d., to-d., this d., past, *dēdhwyth*; fut., *y'n keth golow*; any d., *bytteth*; the last d., *dēth fȳn*, m.
daybreak, n. *dēth-tarth, tarth an jēth*, m.; at d., *dyworth an jēth.*
day-labourer, n. *dēdhwythor*, m., pl. *-yon.*
daylight, n. *golow dēth*, m.; in broad d., *yn lagas an howl*; by d., *dēdhwyth.*
daytime, n. *dēdhwyth*, m.
daze, v. *müskegy, sawthanas, dōs ha dalla.*
dazzle, v. *hanter dalla.*
deacon, n. †*dyagon*, m., pl. *-as*: **-ness,** n. *dyagones*, f., pl. *-ow.*
dead, a. *marow*; the d., *an düs varow, an re marow*, ‡*an marow*: **-den,** v. *marowhē·*: **-dly,** a. *-mernans, fell*, **marwyl*: **-dness,** n. *marder*, m.
dead-nettle, n.† *coklynasen*, f., col. *coklynas*; yellow, white, red d., *c. velen, wyn, rüth.*
deaf, a. *bodhar*; d. person, *bodhorek*, m., pl. *-egyon, bodhar*, m., pl. *-yon*; d.-mute, *b.-omlavar*; d. nut, *knofen gok*, f.: **-fen,** v. *bodhara, bodharhē·*: **-fness,** n. *bodharder, bodharsys*, m.
deal, v. *ranna, bargenya*; d. in, *prena ha gwertha*; d. with him, *gül dhodho*; d. cards, etc., *ranna*: n., wood, *saben*, f., *pren sap, p. sybwyth*, m.; business, *gwerth*, f.; a good d., *pols da, polta*: **-ler,** n. *gwycor*, m., pl. *-yon, marchont*, m., pl. *-ns*; bad d., *gwan-wycor*; d. of cards, *rennyas*, m., pl. *-ysy*, f. *-yades*, pl. *-ow.*
dean, n. *dēyn*, m., pl. *-ow*; **-nery,** n. *dēy·nȳeth*, f.; d's. house, *dēynjy*, m., pl. *-ow.*
dear, a., beloved or expensive, *kēr, cüf*; expensive, *mür y gost, ughel y brȳs*; valued, *drüth*; d. one, *cüf-colon*, m., *caradow*, m. or f., pl. *-yon, cüf*, m., pl. *-yon, keresyk*, m. or f., pl. *-ygyon*; **-rest,** *kerra, whegoll*: **-rly,** adv. *yn-kēr*; d. beloved, *lüfkerys, ewngerys*; d. bought, *prenys yn-tyn*: **-rness,** n. *kērneth*, m.
dearth, n. *esow, kērneth, dyvotter, fowt pega·ns*, m.
death, n. *mernans, ancow, crow*, m.; at the point of d., *yn enewores*, m.; put to d., *ladha, gorra dhe'n mernans, paynya bys yn crow, gül mernans dhe*[2]; he will be the d. of you, *dha ancow ef a-vyth*; thou shalt die the d., *tȳ a-fȳth marow-vernans*: **-thless,** a. **dyvarow*, **dyvernans, prest a-vew.*
death-watch beetle, n. **mortholyk-ancow*, m., pl. *-ygow-a.*
debar, v. *dyfen, lettya, gwytha* (*na*[2]).
debase, v. *gwethhē·, yselhē·.*
debate, v. *dyspūtya, dathla, stryvya*: n. *dathel* (*dal*), f., pl. *dathlow* (*dalow*), *dalva*, f., *strȳf lavarow*: **-ter,** n. *da·thelor* (*dalor*), m., pl. *-yon.*
debility, n. *gwander*, ‡*gwanegreth*, m.
debt, n. *kendon*, f., **det*, m., pl. *-tys*: **-tor,** n. *kendoner*, m., pl. *-oryon.*
decamp, v. *trussa, mōs quyt.*
decant, v. *denewy gans rach*: **-ter,** n. **costrel*, m., pl. *-s.*
decay, v. *pedry*; decline, *dyfygya*; of timber, etc., *cusca*: n. *podrethes*, m.; of timber, etc., *cusk, dyfygyans*, m.: **-yed,** a. *poder, podrek, podrethek*; of fish, *pesak*; of timber, etc., *cuskys*; d. fish, *pesak*, m.; thing d., *podrek*, m., pl. *-rogyon.*
decease, n. *mernans*, m., *tremenva*, f.: v. *merwel, tremena*: **-sed,** a. *tremenys, marow.*
deceit, n. *tull, gowegneth, dyssayt, wrynch, gyl, falsury, faintys*, m.: **-ful,** a. *fals* (*falj*), *gowek, fekyl*, **dyssayvabyl.*

deceive, v. *dyssaytya, tulla*: **-ver,** n. *tullor*, m., pl. *-yon, hüder*, m., pl. *-doryon, flattor*, m., pl. *-yon*, f. *-ores*, pl. *-ow.*
December, n. *Kevardhu·, mȳs-K.*, m.
decent, a. *onest*: **-ency,** n. *onester*, m.
deception, n. *tull, hüs, dyssaytyans*, m.: **-tive,** a. *hüdol.*
decide, v. *ervȳra, determya, rewlya, conclūdya*: d. between them, *ranna an gwȳr yntredha.*
decipher, v. *desmygy, dyscüdha, styrya, rēdya scryfa cales.*
decision, n. *brüs*, f., pl. *-ow, ervȳrans, conclūsyon*, m.
decisively, adv. *gordheweth.*
deck, v. *tacla, afȳna*: n., naut., *flūr*, m., pl. *-ys.*
declaim, v. *arethya, predheges.*
declamation, n. *areth*, f., pl. *-yow, predhek*, pl. *-egow.*
declare, v. *meneges, derȳvas, avowa*; I d. it, *my a-n-avow, jevodȳ·*: **-ration,** n. *derȳvas, deryvadow, dysquedhyans*, m.
decline, v. *dyfygya*; refuse, *sconya, avodya*; sink, *sedhy*; droop, *pōsa*: n. *dyfyk, dyfygyans*, m.
declivity, n. *leder*, f., pls. *-drow, -dry, clegar*, m., pl. *-grow.*
decoction, n. *bryjyans*, m., pl. *-ow, godroth*, m.
decompose, v. *pedry*: **-sition,** n. *pedrans*, m.
decorate, v. *tacla, afȳna, tekhē·*: **-tion,** n. *afȳnans, decorasyon*, m.
decoy, v. *hüda, dynya, tulla*; n. *hüder, dynyer*, m.
decrease, v. *lehē·, dysencressya*; in length, *berhē·*; in width, *tanowhē·.*
decree, v. *erghy, o·rdena* (*ordna, orna*): n. *arghadow, o·rdenans* (*ordnans*), m.
decrepit, a. *gyllys gwan, ūsyes.*
decry, v. *dysprēsya, fȳa.*
dedicate, v. *sacra, profya*: **-tion,** n. *sacrans*; of book, etc, *profyans*, m.
deduce, v. *tenna, desmygy, cuntell*; I d. from that, *yma henna ow-cül dhym crysy.*
deduct, v. *kemeres mēs, skyla*: **-tion,** n. *skyla*, m., pl. *-lys.*
deed, n. *gwythres, ober*, m., pl. *-ow*; deeds, *gwrȳth*, f., *obereth*, m.; legal, *chartour*, m., pl. *-s*; good d., *da-ober*, m., pl. *-ow*; kind d., *torn da*, m., pl. *-ys d.*
deem, v. *desevos, predery, tyby, synsy.*
deep, a. *down*; of sleep, *pōs*; the d., *an downvor*, m.: **-pen,** v. *downhē·, gül bōs downa*: **-ply,** adv. *yn-town.*
deer, n., stag, hart, *carow*, m., pls. *kervys, kerewy*; red d., *hēth*, m., pl. *hedhas*; hind, *ewyk*, f., pl. *-ygas*; doe, †*da*; in sense of royal game, *best arlydhy*, m., pl. *-as a.*: **d.-park,** n. *kery*, f., pl. *-es*; **d.-skin,** n. *hethken, ca·rowgen*, m.
deface, v. *dyfasya, dyheveleby* (*dyfeleby*).
defame, v. *cably, sclandra*: **-mation,** n. *cabel, sclandrans, vylyny*, m.
default, n. *nam, defowt*, m.; in d. of, *fowt*: **-ter,** n. *nep a-fyll pē.*
defeat, v. *fetha, trȳghy war*[2]; in argument, *conclūdya*: n. *fethans*, m.: **-ted,** *fēth.*
defecate, v. *caca.*
defect, n. *fowt, defowt*, m., pl. *-ow, nam*, m., pl. *-mow, dyfyk*, m., pl. *-ygyow, gwall*, m., pl. *-ow*: **-tive,** a., d. in normal powers, *antȳthy, nag-yu dȳen, a-dhyfyk*: be d., *dyfygya.*
defence, n. *scōs*, m., pl. *-ojow, gwȳth, sclew, defe·ns, *amuk*, m.; argument, etc., *clēm*, m., pl. *-ys*; excuse, *ascusasyon*, m.; make a d., *gül defe·ns*: **-celess,** a. *dywȳth, dydhyfen.*
defend, v. *gwytha, dyfenna*; d. oneself, *omwytha*: **-ant,** n. †*dyfennor*, m., pl. *-yon*: **-er,** n. *mentēnour*, m., pl. *-s.*
defensive, a. *a-wyth, a-dhyfen.*
defer, v. *hokkya, dylātya*; yield, *plegya dhe*[2]: **-ence,** n. *worshyp, brȳ*, m.; with all d. *ha na-veugh-why dysplēsyes, saw gwell avȳs.*
defiance, n. *despȳ·t, ēr, defȳans*, m.; in d. of him, *yn despȳ·t dhodho, yn spȳt dh'y fās*: **-ant,** a. *a-ēr, a-dhefȳ·*; to be d., *gül maystry, ērya.*
deficiency, n. *fall, falladow*, m., *fowt, gwall*, m., pl. *-ow, dyfyk*, m., pl. *-ygyow*; **-ent,** a. to be d., *fyllel*; he is d. in, *yma·dhodho fowt a*[2]: **-icit,** n. *dyfyk*, m., pl. *-ygyow.*
defile, v. *deffola*; d., become d'ed., *mostya*: **-lement,** n. *mostethes, lastethes*, m.
defile, n. *cülforth*, f., pl. *-dhow, būlgh, keynans, porth*, m., *aswy*, f., pl. *-ow.*
define, v. *styrya*: **-nition,** n. *styryans*, m., pl. *-ow*: **-finite,** a. *dyblans*: **-tely,** adv. *gordheweth.*
deform, v. *dyfasya, hagry, dyheveleby* (*dyfeleby*), *camma*: **-med,** a. *cammys, cam.*: **-mity,** n. *dyfasyans, camder*, m., pl. *-ow.*
defraud, v. *tulla, ladra, dolos.*
defray, v. *pē*; d. expenses, *pē an cost.*
deft, a. *ynjyn, connek.*

defunct, a. *marow.*
defy, v. *defȳa, ērya, gül maystry.*
degenerate, a. *drokgenesyk, gwethhē·s, gyllys gweth es kens*: n. *drokgenesyk*, m., pl. *-ygyon*, ‡*hynderlyng*, m. or f.: v. *dylynyeth-y, gwethhē·, dōs ha bōs gweth*: **-tion,** n. *gwethhēans*, m.
degrade, v. *yselhē·, gül bysmē·r dhe²*; d'd. person, *atla*, m., pl. *-lyon*: **-ding,** a. *lōs, vȳl, bylen*: **-dation,** n. *yselder*, m.
degree, n. *myns, pryk*, m.; grade or rank, *degrē·, grē*, m.
deify, v. *gül bōs dew, gordhya yn lē Dew.*
deign, v. *lavasos*; d. to grant, *vossawya, vosya saw.*
deity, n. *dewsys*, m.; the Deity, *an Dewsys.*
dejected, a. *dygolon, tryst*: **-tion,** n. *preder*, m., pl and abst. *-ow, trystys*, m.
delay, v. *strechya, dylātya, gortos, lettya, tarya*: n. *strech*, m., pl. *-ys, let*, m., pl. *-tys, ardak*, m., **dylasyon*, m.; without d., *hep ardak, hep let-vyth, hep strech.*
delectable, a. **delȳtabyl*, **dydhan.*
delegate, v. *danvon yn cannas*; d. power, *kemmynna gallos*: n. *cannas*, f., pl. *-ow*, represented by m. pron.: **-tion,** n. *cannasow*, f., pl.
delete, v. *defendya dhe-vēs*: **-tion,** n. *defendyans*, m.
deliberate, v. *ombredery, omgusülya, avȳsya*: a. *a-borpos*: **-tion,** n. *cusülyans, avȳsyans*, m.: **-tely,** adv. *hep toth, gans rach, wosa predery.*
delicate, a., sensitive, *fȳn*; soft, *medhel*; difficult, *tykly*; weak, *gwan, blüth*, **blüdhek*; slender, *mōn*; palatable, *dēnty*: **-ly,** adv. *fȳn, yn-tēnty.*
delicacy, n. *medhelder*, m.; a d., *tam dēnty*, m., pl. *tymmyn d.*
delicious, a. *delycyous, pür whēk*: **-ness,** n. *melder, whekter*, m.
delight, v. *dydhana, lowenhē·, delȳtya*; we were d'd. to talk with him, *cows ganso genen o mal*; I am d'd.! *gwyn ow bȳs*!: n. *melder, fancy, tekter, delȳ·t*, m., *lowena*, f.; you take a great d. in, *yma dheugh mür a dhelȳ·t a²*: **-ful,** a. *pür whēk, dydhan, delȳ·tabyl.*
delineate, v. *delynya*: **-tion,** n. *delynyans*, m.
delirious, a. *mēs a'y rewl, ow-müskegy*, †*conneryak*: **-rium,** n. *müscogneth*, m.; †*connar*, f.
deliver, v. *delyfra, dely·frya, lyfrya, rȳ, dascor, dyffres*; d. a blow, etc., *dyllo, desedha*: **-ance, -y,** n. *delyfr(y)ans, lyfrēson*, m.: **-er,** n. *delyfryer*, m., pl. *-yoryon.*
dell, n. *pans*, m., pls. *-ow, -njow, godenow·*, m., pl. *-newyon, haun*, f., pl. *-ow.*
delude, v. *flattra, tulla, hüda*: **-lusion,** n. *tull, hüs*, m., *tarosvan*, m., pl. *-now.*
deluge, n. *lȳf*, m., pls. *lȳfow, lyvyow.*
delve, v. *palas, tūrya.*
demand, v. *govyn, demōndya, dervyn, requȳrya*; d. as right, *chalynjya, synsy quarel*: n. *quarel, govynnadow, gorholeth, demōnd*, m.; unjust d., *quarel a falsury.*
demeanour, n. *omdho·n, chēr, fara, conversasyon, semlant*, m., **arweth*, f.
demented, a. *varyes, mēs a'y rewl.*
demesne, n. **demȳ·n*, m.
demi-god, n. *hanter-dew*, m., pl. *-ow.*
demise, n. *mernans*, m.
democracy, n. **gwery·nȳeth*, m., *rewl an düs, stāt an bobel*: **-at,** n. **gwerynor*, m., pl. *-yon*: **-atic,** a. **gwerynek, a'n bobel.*
demolish, v. *dyswül, gül codha dhe'n lür, terry dhe'n dōr*: **-ition,** n. *torva*, f., *dyswrȳans*, m.
demon, n. *jevan*, m., *dyawl*, m., pl. *-ow*: **-iac,** n. *sagh dyawl*, m., pl. *-ow d., dēn vexyes gans tebel-spyrys.*
demonstrate, v. *dysquedhes*: **-tion,** n. *dysquedhyans, experyans*, m., pl. *-ow.*
demoralise, v. *sawthanas, pedry an cowsys, drȳ dyworth an da dhe wül drok.*
demur, v. *hokkya, sconya*: n. *ardak danjer*, m.
demure, a. *dōth, sad, methek.*
den, n. *fow*, f., pl. *-ys, toll*, m., pl. *tell.*
denial, n. *nagh*, m.
denier, n. **negeth*, m., *negedhys*, m., pl. *-yjyon.*
denominate, v. *henwel*: **-tion,** n. *hanwans*, m., pl. *-ow.*
denote, v. *dysquedhes, merkya.*
denounce, v. *cuhüdha, cably*: **-r,** n. *cuhüdhor*, m., pl. *-yon.*
dense, a. *tew*: **-sity,** n. *tewder*, m.
dent, n. *bülgh*, m., pl. *-ow.*
dental, a. *dynsak, a'n dyns*: **-tist,** n. *medhek dyns*, m., pl. *-ygyon d.*; tooth-drawer, *tenner dyns*, m., pl. *-noryon d.*
denunciation, n. *cabel*, m., pl. *-blow, cuhüdhans*, m., pl. *-ow.*
deny, v. *nagha, denagha, sconya.*
depart, v. *vodya, omdenna, dyberth*: **-ure,** n.

omdennans, m., pl. *-ow*, *dybarth*, m.; d. from custom, *gasa ūsadow*.
department, n. *ran*, f., pl. *-now*.
depend, v., lean, *scodhya*; hang, *cregy*, *restya* (*war*²); rely, *trestya*; that d's. on you, *henna a-bowes genough-why*, *why a-bew rewlya henna*: **-able,** a. *dyogel*, *sür*: **-ants,** n. *coscar*, col., *mēny*, m.: **-ent,** a. *kēth*, *yn danjer dēn aral*.
depict, v. *lywa*, **portraya*, **delynya*, **lymna*.
deplete, v. *gwakhē·*.
deplorable, a. *morethek*, *truethek*, *trueth y weles*; it is d., *dyeth mür yu*.
deplore, v. *kȳny rak*, *mornya*.
depopulate, v. *dybobla*.
deport, v. *exylya*; d. oneself, *omdho·n*.
deportment, n. *conversasyon*, m., *omdho·n*, inf.
depose, v., testify, *testa*, *dustünya*; d. a king, *gorra mēs a'y drōn*.
deposit, v. *gorra*; money, *gorra yn arghow*: n. *godhas*, m., pl. *-dhojyon*; money, *arghow*, f., pl.: **-or,** n. *fydhyas*, m., pl. *-ysy*, *gorrer*, m., pl. *-roryon*.
depraved, a. *podrethek*; d. person, *podryn*, m.: **-vity,** n. *podrethes*, *sherewneth*, m.
depreciate, v. *lēhē· prȳs*, *dybrȳsya*, *yselhē·*: **-tion,** n. *dybrȳsyans*, m.
depredator, n. *prēdhor*, m., pl. *-yon*.
depress, v. *yselhē·*, *dygolonhē·*, *lenwel a voreth*: **-ed,** a. *dygolon*, *ysel y spyrys*, *tryst*: **-ion,** *yselder spyrys*, m.; dent, *būlgh*, m., pl. *-ow*; in ground, *pans*, m., pl. *-ow*.
deprivation, n. *anken*, m., pl. *-yow*, *esow*, *dyvotter*, m.: **-ive,** v. *kemeres mēs*; be d'd. of, *bōs hep*.
depth, n. *yselder*, *downder*, m., *sēth*, m., pl. *sedhow*.
deputation, n. *cannasow*, pl.: **-ty,** n. *cannas*, f., pl. *-ow*.
derange, v. *varya*, *kemysky*: **-d,** a., p.p., *varyes*, *mēs a'y rewl*.
derelict, a. *gesys dhe goll*; to leave d., *gasa dhe goll*, *gasa war an kē*: n. *lester gesys*, m.
deride, v. *gēsya*, *gül gēs a*², *wherthyn orth*: **-rision,** n. *gēs*, *wharth*, m.
derivation, n. *devedhyans*, m.: **-ive** v. *tenna*; d'd. from, *devedhys*, or *sevys a*².
descant, n. *dyscant*, m.
descend, v. *dyeskynna* (*dyskynna*), *descendya*; d'd. from, *devedhys*, or *sevys*, *a*²: **-ant,** n. **dyeskynyas*, m., pl. *-ysy*, *flogh*, m., pl. *flēghes*; d's., *henath*, m.; our d's., *agan hēnath*, *an rē-na a-dhē ahanan*, *nep a-dhē ahanan*; **-scent,** n. *devedhyans*, *dyeskynyans*, m.; ancestry, *gōs*, *lynaja*, *lynyeth*, one step in d., *degrē·*, m.
describe, v. **descryfa*: **-iption,** n. **descryvyans*, m., pl. *-ow*.
desecrate, v. *dysacra*, *deffola*: **-ion,** n. *dysacrans*, m.
desert, v. *gasa*, *fȳa*, *forsakya*: n. *dysert*, *dyfȳth*, *dyfythtyr*, *gwylfos*, m., *dyfythva*, f.: a. *dyfȳth*: **-er,** n. *fȳer*, m., pl. *-oryon*, †*fōesyk*, m., pl. *-ygyon*: **-ion,** n. *fȳans*, m.: **-s,** n., *pewas*, m.; he has his d., *gallas y wober ganso*.
deserve, v. *dyndyl*, *goberna*, *tylly*; as they d., *dhedha del dhegoth*: **-vedly,** adv. *quyt*, *del goth*, *dhegoth*, or *dheleth*: **-ving,** a. *gwyw*, *wordhy*.
dessicate, v. *desēgha*: **-d,** a. *sēgh*, *desēghys*, *crȳn*.
design, v. *tewlel*, *ervȳra*; draw, *delynya*: n. *towl*, m., pl. *-ow*, *delynyans*, *ervȳrans*, m., pl. *-ow*; intention, *porpos*, m.; **-er,** n. *delynyer*, m., pl. *-yoryon*.
desire, v., *yeuny*, *desȳrya*, *mynnes*, *bōs whansek dhe*², or *a*², *bōs dhodho whans*: n. *whans*, m., pl. *-ow*, *yeunadow*, m., *yeunes*, m., pl. *-ow*, *mynnas*, m., *govenek*, m., pl. *-ow*, abst. *-ygyon*, *desȳ·r*, m., *lüst*, m., pl. *-ys*; strong d., *debron*, m., *ewl* (*awell*), f.; evil d., *drokwhans*, m., pl. *-ow*: **-irable,** a. *plegadow*, *whans y weles*: **-irous,** a. *whansek*, *whans dhodho*, *desȳryes*.
desist, v. *hedhy*, *sevel*, *sparya*, *powes*; d. from, *astel*.
desk, n. **margh-lyver*, m., pl. *mergh-lyver*; **desk*, m., pl. *-ys*.
desolate, a. *gesys yn awhe·r*, *dygonfort*; homeless, *dyanneth*; orphaned, *omdhevas*; friendless, *hep car y'n bȳs*; of land, *ynyal*, *wast*, *dyfȳth*: **-tion,** n. *dyfȳthter*, m.; circumstances, *awhe·r*, *tebel stüth*, m.
despair, v. *kemeres dygolon*, *dyspērya*, *codha yn dyspē·r*: n. *dygolon*, f., *dyspē·r*, m.: **-ing,** a. *dygolon*, *hep gwaytyans-vyth*.
desperate, a. *pür ethomek*, *codhys yn dyspē·r*, *müscok*, *hep rach*: **-tion,** n. *ethom brās*, *dyspē·r*, m.
despicable, a. *vȳl*, *gal*.
despise, v. *defȳ·a*, *fȳa*, *dysprēsya*, **contempnya*.
despite, n. *despȳ·t*, m.; through d., *drē spȳt*.
despondency, n. *dygolon*, f., *dyspē·r*, m.: **-ent,** a. *dygolon*, *gyllys y wōs yn dowr*.

despot, n. *türont,* m., pl. *-ns, trӯgher,* m., pl. *-ghoryon*: **-ic,** a. *ave·l türont.*
dessert, n. *gorfen-prӯs,* m., *frūtys,* pl.
destination, n. *pen an hens*; his d., *pen y lafüryans.*
destine, v. *de·st(y)na, tewlel,* **tenky*: **-ny,** n. *de·st(y)nans,* m., **tenkys,* f.
destitute, a. *omdhevas, yn esow, boghosek glan*; d. of friends, *hep car-vyth*: **-tion,** n. *esow, yselder a voghosogneth, fowt bōs ha goskes,* m.
destroy, v. *dystrewy, dyswül, kӯsya, terry, consūmya*: **-truction,** n. *dystructyon, dyswrӯans,* m., *terros,* m., pl and abst. *terryjy*: **-tructive,** a. *a-wra dyswül, fell, ow-terry puptra.*
detach, v. *dygelmy, dyberth, dystaga, dysclena*: **-chment,** n. *dybarth,* f.; troops, *bagas,* m., pl. *-ow, ran,* f., pl. *-now.*
detail, n. *tra,* neut., *poynt,* m.; d's., *pythow münys*: v. *gorra dhe dhevar, derӯvas yn pup ēghen.*
detain, v. *lettya, gül dhe wortos.*
detect, v. *hellerghy, gweles drē whythra glew*: **-tion,** n. *hellerghyans,* m.: **-tive,** n. *hellerghyas,* m., pl. *-ysy.*
deteriorate, v. *gwetha, gwethhē·*: **-tion,** n. *gwethter,* m.
determination, n. *mynnas crēf,* m.; because of his d., *awo·s y vōs ervӯrys*: **-ine,** v. *mynnes porres, ervӯra, determya.*
detest, v. *casa*; I d. such folk, *cās yu genef tüs a'n par-na*: **-able,** a. *casadow, hegas, mür y last.*
dethrone, v. *gorra mēs a'y drōn,* or *sē.*
detonate, v. *tarenna, gül dhe dardha*: **-tion,** n. *tarth,* m., pl. *-rdhow.*
detrimental, a. *a-wra drōk,* or *dregyn, owquethhē·.*
devastate, v. *rafna, dyfӯthya, gül dhodho bōs wast*: **-tion,** n., state, *dyfӯth,* m.; act, *rafnans, dyswrӯans,* m.
develop, v. *dysplegya, moghhē·, encressya*: **-ment,** n. *dysplegyans, encressyans,* m.
deviate, v. *gwandra, gwӯa, varya*: **-tion,** n. *gwӯans, varyans,* m.
device, n., trick, *prat,* m., pl. *-tys*; contrivance, *darbar,* m., *ynjyn,* m., pl. *-nys*; fancy, *devӯ·s,* m., pl. *-ys*; armorial, **arweth,* f., pl. *-edhyow.*
devil, n. *dyawl,* m., pl. *dewolow,* f. *dyawles,* pl. *-ow*; d. names, *Lawethan* (Leviathan), *Malan, Belsebuk, Torpen, Tulfryk, Moufras*; the devil, *an jawl, an plā, an bylen, an tebel-edhen, an tebel-ēl, an tebel*; d. take the . . ., *mal bew* . . .; the d!, *mal!*; d. a bit, *mal bew dam, vanna*; in the d's. name, *a-barth an plā*; the d. of a jolt, *jag an plā*: **-ish,** a. *dyawlak*: **-ry,** n. *dewlüjy,* m. or f.
devil-fish, n., angler, *pysk-malan,* m., pl. *puskes-m.*
devise, v. *devӯsya, tewlel towl.*
devoid of, prep. *hep*; prefix, *dy-*[2], *an-*[2].
Devonshire, n. *Dewnans,* ‡*Densher, pow-D.* f.
devour, v. *lenky, collenky, devorya,* **lewa,* **skyvly.*
devote oneself v. *omrӯ* (*dhe*[2]): **-tion,** n. *devōsyon, lēl-wonys,* m.; love, *kerensa,* f.; worship, *gordhyans,* m.; to duty, etc., *dywysygneth,* m.
devout, a. *dywysyk.*
dew, n. *glūth,* m.; to form d., *glūtha*; d.-drop, *glūthen,* f., pl. *-now*: **-y,** a. *glūthek.*
dew-claw, n. **gorewyn,* m., pl. *-as.*
dexterity, n. *ynjyn, coyntys, sleyneth,* m.: **-t(e)rous,** a. *ynjyn, connek, sley.*
diabolic, -al, a. *dyawlak*; d. power, influence, *dewlüjy,* m.
diaconate, n. *dyago·nyeth,* m.
diadem, n. *curün myghte·rn,* or †*c. ruy*; f., pl. *-now m.* or *r.*
dial, n. *fās clok,* m.; sun d., *üryor howl.*
dialect, n. *ranyēth,* f., pl. *-ow, dӯalect,* m., pl. *-ys.*
dialogue, n. *cows, kescows,* m.
diameter, n. *musür a-drüs*: **-trically,** adv. *a-drüs*; d. opposite, *contratryüs yn-tӯen.*
diamond, n. *adamant,* m., pls. *-ans, -tys.*
diarrhoea, n. *skӯt,* m.
diaphanous, a. *boll.*
diary, n. *dēthlyver,* m., pl. *-yfrow.*
dictate, v. *leverel,* or *rēdya, ughel y lēf, dyctatya*: **-tion,** n. *lavar,* or *rēdyans ughel, dyctasyon,* m.; written at his d., *scryfys warlergh y lavar*: **-tor,** n. *türont,* m., pl. *-rons, trӯgher,* m., pl. *-ghoryon.*
dictionary, n. *gērlyver,* m., pl. *-yfrow,* **geryador,* m.; abridged d., *gerlyfryn,* m.
dictum, n. *lavar,* m., pl. *-ow, dӯth,* m., pl. *-ys.*
die, v. *merwel, tremena*; though I d. for it, *awo·s merwel.*
die, n., pl. dice, **dӯs,* m., pl. *-ow.*
diet, v. *rewlya bōs, ūsya megyans strothys*: n. *megyans rewlys,* m.; meeting, *cuntellva,* f.
differ, v. *dyffra, fyllel acordya*: **-ence,** n. *dyffrans,* m.; it makes no d., *byth ny-vern,*

na-fors awo·s henna: **-ent,** a. *kēn, dyhevelep, dyvers, dyffrans*; in d. places, *yn lȳes lē*: **-entiate,** v. *decernya (yntra)*.

difficult, a. *cales, tykly*; d. to deal with, *trüs*: **-y,** n. *caletter, tranjyak, danjer, ancombrynsy*, m.

dig, v. *palas*; d. a ditch, *cledhya*; d. lightly, *gobalas, fynegly*: **-ger,** n. *palor*, m., pl. *-yon, cledhyer*, m., pl. *-yoryon*.

digest, v. *gōy*: **-ion,** n. *gōans*, m.

dignified, a. *stātly, gans dy·nyta*: **-nity,** n. *dy·nyta, roweth, worshyp, rē·outa, brȳ*, m.

dilapidated, a. *codhys y veyn, dyfygyes*.

dilate, v. *ygery a-lēs*: **-tory,** a. *termynak, hell, lent*.

dilemma, n. *tranjyak, mater tykly*, m.

diligence, n. *dywysygneth*, m.: **-nt,** a. *bysy, dywysyk, servabyl*.

dilute, v. *dowrhē·, tanowhē·, gwanhē·, gorra dowr dhe²*: a. *gwanhē·s, dowrhē·s*: **-tion,** n. *dowrhēans*, etc.

dim, a. *tewl (tewal), dyslyw, *dysclēr*: **-ness,** n. *tewlgow (tew·olgow), dysclērder*, m.

dime, n. *demma*, m., pl. *-mys*.

dimension, n. *musür*, m., pl. *-ow, myns, braster*, m.

diminish, v. *lehē·, yselhē·, berhē· gwanhē·, *dysencressya*.

diminutive, a. *pür vünys, bȳghan drēs kynda*.

dimple, n. **pol bogh*, m., pl. *-low b*.

din, n. *trōs, son, noys, *tervans*, m.; to make a d., *gül trōs, *tervy*.

dine, v. *lyfya, kynyewel*; at evening, *cona*: **-ning-room,** n. *†stevel*, f., pl. *-yow, *kynyowva*, f.: **dinner,** n. *kynyow*, m., pl. *-yewyow*; mid-day, *lȳ(f)*, f., pl. *-lyfyow*; evening, *cōn*, f., pl. *-yow*.

dingle, n. *gobans, golans*, m., pl. *-ow, cūm*, m., pl. *-mow*; dim. *cumyn*, m., pl. *-now*.

dint, n. *būlgh, pol*, m.; by d. of, *drē², drē nerth*: v. *gül pollow yn*: **-ed,** a. *ynno pollow pals*; by hammer, *morthelek*.

diocese, n. *epscobeth*, f., pl. *-edhow*: **-san,** a. *epscobedhek*.

dip, v. *ynclȳna*; in water, *troghya, sedhy, golghy*: n., in ground, *pans, gobans*, m., pl. *-ow*; candle, *cantol sōf*, f., pl. *-yow s.*; bathe, *golgh, omwolgh, nyj*, m.

diploma, n. *†gwarak*, f., pl. *-regow*.

diplomacy, n. **lyscannaseth*, m.; shrewdness, *fēlder*, m.: **-atic,** a. **lyscannasek*; shrewd, *fēl*: **-atist,** n. **lyscannas*, f., pl *-ow*.

direct, v. *o·rdena, lewyas, kevarwedha, gedya, †brennya*; d. knowledge, *dysky*: a. *kewar, compes, ewn, dydro*: **-ion,** n. *tu*, m., pl. *-yow, quartron*, m., pl. *-ys*; guidance, *kevarwedhyans*, m., *rewl*, f.; management, *conduyk*, m.; in the wrong d., *drēs keyn*; in the same d., *yn ün forth*; in all d's., *a bup tu*; stage-d's., *ordnansow gwary*: **-ly,** adv. straight, *poran*; at once, *adhystough, dystough, dyson, hep let, adhewha·ns, kens es hedhy*: conj. *kettel²*: **-or,** n. *kevarwedhor*, m., pl. *-yon, lewyth*, m., pl. *-ydhyon*: **-ory,** n. *lyver kevarwedha*, m., pl. *-vrow k*.

dirge, n. *galargan*, f., pl. *-ow, *dyryja*, m., pl. *-jys*.

dirt, n. *mostethes, plosethes, losethes*, m.; removed d., *scarthyon*, pl.: **-y,** a. *plos, strollek, strong(k), mostys*; of water, *dowr a vostyon*; d. person, *plosek*, m., pl. *-egyon, scübelak*, m., pl. *-logyon*, f., *-loges*, pl. *-ow*: v. *strolla, mostya, loshē·*; get d., *plosegy*.

disable, v. *evredhy*: **-d,** a. *evredhek*; d. in hands or feet, *mans*.

disadvantage, n. *coll, anlēs*, m.; it was much to his d., *yth-esa dhodho mür a goll, anodho ny-n-jeva prow-vyth, mür er y byn o*: **-ous,** a. *na-wra, na-drēl dhe² lēs, hep lēs*.

disagree, v. *fyllel bōs ünverhēs*, or *acordys, stryvya, debatya, omdhal*; that would d. with me, *ny-vȳa rag ow lēs henna*: **-eable,** a. *casadow, hegas, a-gar strȳf*: **-eableness,** n. *casadewder*, m.: **-ment,** n. *strȳf, fowt acordyans*, m.

disappear, v. *mōs mēs a wēl tüs, scapya hep bōs gwelys*: **-ance,** n. *dyank, coll*, m.

disappoint, v. *tulla*: **-ed,** a. *drōk-pȳs, tullys*: **-ment,** n. *tull*, m.

disapproval, n. *cās, gēr drōk*, m.; **-ve,** v. *bōs cās gans*.

disarm, v. *dyarva*: **-ament,** n. *dyarvans*, m.: **-ing,** a., through charm, *ow-cül dhe'n rē erel plegya*.

disarray, n. *dera·y*, m., pl. *-ys*.

disaster, n. *myshyf*, m., pl. *-evys, droklam, mewl*, m.; *terros*, m., pl. and abst. *terryjy, cās, anfüsy, damach, meschons*, m.; cause d., *myshevya*: **-trous,** a. *anfüsyk, ow-trȳ myshyf*.

disavow, v. *nagha*.

disbelief, n. *dyscryjyans, ēr*, m.: **-ve,** v. *dyscryjy*.

disbranch, v. **dyvarra, *dyscora, *dyscorenna*.

disburden, v. **dybēghya, *dysagha*.

disburse, v. *pē, ranna*: **-ment,** n. *payment*, m., pl. *-ns*.

discard, v. *tewlel mēs, t. dhe scul, hepcor, sconya.*
discern, v. *decernya, convedhes, gweles*: **-ment,** n. *convedhes, skȳans,* m.
discharge, v. *dyllo, delyfr(y)a dhe wary, assoylya,* **dyscarga*: n. *dyllans, assoylyans,* m.
disciple, n. *dyskybel,* n., pls. *-blon, -blyon, dyscȳpel,* m., pl. *-plys, servyas,* m., pl. *-ysy, maw,* m., pl. *mebyon.*
discipline, n. *rewlyans,* m., *kereth,* f.: v. *kesky.*
disclose, v. *dysquedhes, dyscüdha, ygery, dysclosya*: **-sure,** n. *dysquedhyans, dyscüdhans,* m.
discolour, v. *dyslywa*: **-ation,** n. *dyslywans,* m.: **-ed,** a. *dyslyw.*
discomfit, v. *serry, do·mhel.*
discomfort, n. *dysconfort, govyjyon,* m.: v. *dysconfortya, dygonfortya, serry.*
discompose, disconcert, v. *serry.*
disconsolate, a. *dygonfortys, dygonfort, yn awhe·r.*
discontent, n. *dysēs,* m.: **-ed,** a. *drōk-pȳs, dyscontentys, dysēsyes.*
discontinue, v. *hedhy, gasa dhe-vēs, astel.*
discord, n. *strȳf, ancrēs, hager-noys,* m.: **-ant,** a. **ow-cül son üthyk y glewes.*
discount, n., rebate, **dyscont,* m.: v. **dyscontya*; disbelieve, *dyscrysy yn ran.*
discourage, v. *dysconfortya, dygonfortya, dygolonhē·*; be d'd., *kemeres dygolon*; **-d,** a. *dygolon*: **-ment,** n. *dygolon,* f.; *dysconfort,* m.: **-ging,** a. *a-wanha· colon.*
discourse, v. *kewsel, gül areth*: n. *cows,* m., pl. *-ow, pregoth,* m., pl. *-gowthow, areth,* f., pl. *-yow.*
discourteous, a. **dyscortes, anwhēk*: **-sy,** n. *vylyny, dyscortesy,* m.
discover, v. *cafos, dysquedhes, dyskevra, desmygy, dyscüdha, ‡trovya*: **-y,** n. *desmyk, dyscüdhans, dyskevrans,* m.
discredit, v. *dyscrysy, dysenora*: n. *mothow, bysmē·r, dysenor,* m.: **-able,** a. *dyflas, owtrȳ bysmē·r.*
discreet, a. *für, dōth*: **-retion,** n. *fürneth,* m.
discrepancy, n. *fowt aco·rd,* m., pl. *-ys a.,* **dyskessenyans,* m., pl. *-ow.*
discriminate, v. *decernya, settya dybarth (yntra), dyberth*: **-tion,** n. *dyberthva,* f.; without d., *hep decernya.*
discursive, a. *ow-quandra.*
discuss, v. *kewsel, omgusülya, dyspūtya,* or *dathla (a-dro dhe²)*: **-ion,** n. *dathel,* f., pl. *dathlow, kescows, omgusülyans,* m., pl. *-ow.*
disdain, v. *fȳa, dysprēsya, dysdaynya*: n. *dysprēsyans, dysdayn,* m.
disease, n. *cleves,* m., pl. *-vejow, dysēs,* m., pl. *-ys*: **-d,** a. *clāf, anhedhek, dysēsys.*
disembark, v. *tȳra.*
disembodied, a. *dygorf.*
disenchanted, a. *dyhüs, dydullys, dyhüdys.*
disengage, v. *lowsel*: **-d,** a. *syger, lows.*
disentangle, v. *dygelmy, dyvagly, dyskelmy, dygemysky.*
disestablish, v. *dysfundya*: **-ment,** n. *dysfundyans,* m.
disfigure, v. *hagry, dyfasya, dyheveleby*: **-ment,** n. *dyfasyans, nam,* m.
disgrace, v. *shyndya, shāmya, gül bysmē·r dhe²*: n. *mewl, bysmē·r, shām,* m.: **-ful,** a. *dyflas, vȳl, bylen.*
disguise, v. *trēlya gȳs,* **tullwysca*; use artifice, *sotla*: n. **tullwysk,* m.; artifice, *sotelneth,* m.
disgust, v. *dyflasa*: n. *dyflassys,* m.: **-ed,** v., be d. with, *dyflasa*: **-ing,** a. *dyflas, hegas.*
dish, n. *padel,* f., pls. *-low, -ly,* dim. *-lyk,* f., pl. *-ygow, scüdel,* f., pls. *-low, -ly*; small round d., *pojer,* m., pl. *-ow*; large serving d., *tallyour,* m., pl. *-s*; shallow d., *†scala,* m., pl. *-lys*; food served, *†sant,* m., pl. *-ndys*: v. *servya, gorra yn padel*: **d.-cloth,** n. *clout-lystry,* m., pl. *-tys-l.*: **d.-cover,** n. *gorher scüdel,* m., pl. *-yow s.*
dishearten, v. *dygolonhē·.*
dishevelled, a. *dygrȳbys, garow y vlew.*
dishonest, a. *dyslēl*; d. person, *lader, tuller,* m.: **-y,** n. *dyslēlder, falsury,* m.
dishonour, v. *dysenora*: n. *dysenor,* **anvrȳ,* m.
disillusion, v. *dydulla, dyhüda.*
disinclination, n. *fowt whans, cās,* m.: **-ned,** a., to be d., *bōs cās gans*; I am d., *ny-m-büs whans a².*
disinfect, v. *dyvenymhē·, glanhē·, püra*: **-ant,** n. *fether venym,* m.: **-ion,** n. *glanhēans,* m.
disinherit, v. *dyse·ryta, kemeres ertach mēs, statya ertons dhe dhen aral*: **-ance,** n. **dysertons,* m.
disinter, v. *dysencledhyes.*
disjoint, v. *dyskevelsy, dygevelsy.*
dislike, v. *casa*; I d., *cās yu genef, ny-garaf, nyns-yu da genef*; I d. more, *gweth yu genef*: n. *cās,* m.
dislocate: see **disjoint.**

disloyal, a. *dyslēn, dyslēl*: **-ty,** n. *dyslēlder,* m.
dismal, a. *yeyn, trūesy, trūan, anwhēk*: **-ness,** n. *trūeth,* m.
dismantle, v. *dystryppya, stryppya, *dydacla.*
dismast, v. **dywernya*: **-ed,** a. **dywern, gyllys y wernow.*
dismay, v. *anüvya, amaya*: n.
dismiss, v. *dyllo dhe wary, danvon dhe-vēs*: **-al,** n. *dyllans dhe wary,* m.
dismount, v. *dyeskynna, *dyvargha.*
disobey, v. *terry dyfen, dysobaya*: **-edience,** n. *torva dyfen,* f., *dysobayans,* m.: **-edient,** a. *dywostyth.*
disobliging, a. *anwhēk, gorth, nag-üs dhe blegadow* or *parys.*
disorder, n. *dera·y,* m., pl. *-ys, fowt rewl,* f.: **-ed,** a. *dyrewl*; in mind, *mēs a'y rewl*: **-ly,** a. *dyrewl.*
disorganize, v. *dyrewlya.*
disown, v. *dysavowa, sconya, nagha.*
dispatch, v. *danvon, spēdya*: n. *danvonadow,* m., *spēda,* f.
dispel, v. *scullya, pellhē·.*
dispense with, v., *hepcor, dascor.*
disperse, v. *scullya, pellhē·, kescar, dybarth, *dysparplya*: **-ion,** n. *kescar,* m.
displace, v. *remüvya, settya,* or *gorra, mēs a'y lē, dylēa*: **-d,** a. *dylē, dylēys*: **-ment,** n. *dylēans,* m.
display, v. *dysplētya, dysplewya*: n. *dysplētyans,* m.
displease, v. *dysplēsya*; be d'd., *dyflasa, bōs drōk-pȳs*: **-sing,** a. *dyflas*: **-sure,** n. *sōr, dughan, dysplēsyans, dysplesour,* m.
dispose, v. *dȳghtya, desedha, araya*: d. of, *rȳ, dascor*: **-sal,** n. *danjer, dȳghtyans,* m.: **-sed,** a., ready, *plegadow.*
disposition, n. *dȳghtyans,* m.; nature, *gnās, nās,* f., *plegadow,* m.; to affect or modify d., **nāsya.*
disprove, v. *dysprevy, prevy bōs gow.*
dispute, v. *debātya, kedrynya, gül tennow orth, argya, stryvya*: n. *dalva* (*da·thelva*), f., pl. *-ow, kedry·n,* f., *quarel, debā·t,* m.
disqualify, v. *gül bōs anwyw.*
disquiet, n. *ancrēs, dysē·s,* m.: **-en,** v. *dysēsya.*
disregard, v. *bōs hep attendya* or *hep gül fors* a^2.
disrepute, n. *drōk-gēr, bysmē·r,* m.: **-table,** a. *drokgeryes*; d. person, *map gal,* m., *myrgh g.,* f.
disrespect, n. *vylyny, fowt brȳ, *anvrȳ,* m.: **-ful,** a. *dygortes, logh*; he was d. to him, *ny-wrük vrȳ anodho.*
dissatisfied with, a. *drōk-pȳs* (a^2), *dyscontentys* (*gans*).
dissect, v. *dyvynya*: **-ion,** n. *dyvy·nȳeth,* m.
dissemble, v. *dyssembla, dolos, facya.*
disseminate, v. *plontya, hasa, scullya a-lēs.*
dissent, v. **dyssentya*: n. **dyssent,* m.
dissimilar, a. **dyhaval, dyhevelep.*
dissipation, n. *sculva,* f., *scul, wastyans,* m.
dissolute, a. *lows, scullyak, dyrewl, tebel y vewnans*: **-tion,** n., death, *mernans,* m.; melting, *tedhans,* m.
dissolve, v. *tedha*; d. meeting, *terry, squattya.*
distaff, n. *kygel,* f., pl. *-yow.*
distant, a. *pell*: **-nce,** n. *pellder,* m.; little d., *pols, lam,* m.; it is no great d., *nyns-yu nep-pell.*
distasteful, a. *dyflas*: **-ness,** n. *dyflassys,* m.
distend, v. *quoffy, dystenna, hothfy*: **-ntion,** n. *quoff,* m.
distil, v. **dystyllya, *styllya*: **-lation,** n. *dystyllyans,* m.: **-lery,** n. **styllva,* f., pl. *-ow, dystylljy,* m.
distinct, a. *dyblans, dybarow*: **-ly,** adv. *dyblans, pür glēr*: **-ion,** n. *dyberthva,* f.; honour, *brȳ, worshyp,* m.; d. in war, *chevalry,* m.
distinguish, v. *dyberth, gweles*; d. a difference, *decernya*: **-ed,** a. *wordhy, bryntyn, a vrȳ.*
distort, v. *camma*; d. oneself, *omgamma*: **-ed,** a. *cam, cammys.*
distract, v. *müskegy, trēlya a-denewan,* or *a'y borpos, amaya, ancombra*: **-ed,** a., distraught, *müscok, amay·s.*
distress, v. *grevya, cüdhy*: n. *ancrēs, gref, awhe·r,* m., *anken,* m., pl. *-yow*: **-ed,** a. *cüdhys*: **-ing,** a. *truēthek.*
distribute, v. *ranna, dyberth*: **-tion,** n. *rannans,* m.: **-tor,** n. *rennyas,* m., pl. *-ysy.*
district, n. *pastel-vro,* f., pl. *-llow-bro, quatron,* m., pl. *-ys, randȳr,* f., pl. *-yow.*
distrust, v. *dyscrysy, *gorthgrysy*: n. **gorthgrēs* (*gorgys*), f.: **-ful,** a. *dyscryjyk*; d. pers., *dyscryjyk,* m., pl. *-jygyon.*
disturb, v. *tropla, annȳa, *ancrēsya*: **-ance,** n. *dera·y,* m., pl. *-ys, ancrēs, frōs, trōs,* m., pl. *-ow, kedry·n,* f.
disunion, n. *fowt ünyans,* m.: **-ite,** v. *dygelmy, dysclena, dyberth.*

disuse, v. *settya a denewan, gasa hep y ūsya*: n. *fowt ūs*, m.
ditch, n. *clēth*, m., pl. *-edhyow*; d. by a hedge, *toll kē*, m., pl. *tell kē*: v. *cledhya*.
ditty, n. *dyth*, m., pl. *-ys*, dim., *-yk*, pl. *-ygow*.
dive, v. *omsedhy*, **dȳvya*, *lamma y'n dowr*: n. *seth*, m., pl. *-edhow*, *lam pen yn-rak*, m., pl. *-mow p. y.*: **-r,** n. *sedhor*, m., pl. *-yon*, **dȳvyor*, m., pl. *-yon*.
diverge, v. *dyberth*: **-nce,** n. *dybarth*, f.
divers, a. *lȳes*, *dȳvers*, *dyffrans*.
divert, v. *trēlya*; amuse, *dydhana*: **-sion,** n. *trēlyans*, m., pl. *-ow*; amusement, *dydhanans*, *sport*, m.
divide, v. *dyberth*, *ranna*, *kevranna*: **-r,** n. *rennyas*, m., pl. *-ysy*.
dividend, n. *kevran*, f., pl. *-now*.
divine, v. *desmygy*, **dewynya*: a. *Dew*, *a Dhew*: **-nation,** n. *cōl*, f.; art of d., **dewy·nȳeth*, f.: **-ner,** n. *cōlyak*, m., pl. *-yogyon*, f., *-yoges*, pl. *-ow*, **dewyn*, m., pl. *-yon*: **-nity,** n. *Dewsys*, m.
division, n. *dybarth*, f., *ran*, f., pl. *-now*, *dyberthva*, f., pl. *-ow*; mathematics, *dyvysyon*.
divorce, v. *dydhemedhy*: n. *torva demedhyans*, f.
dizzy, a. **penfol*, **penscaf*, *scaf y ben*: **-ziness,** n. *scafter pen*, **pendro*, m.
do, v. *gül* (*güthyl*, *gwrüthyl*), *obery*; d. very carefully, *gorgül*; d. (fare) badly, *tebel-fara*; suffice, *servya*; d. for, destroy, *kȳsya*; he is done for, *gallas ganso*; d. without, *hepcor*, *sevel orth*; it won't d., *ny-dalvyth man*, *ny-serf henna*: **-er,** n. *oberor*, m., pl. *-yon*, *gwrȳer*, m., pl. *-yoryon*: **-ing,** n. *gwrȳans*, *gwythres*, ‡*gwrythyans*, m.: **-ne,** a., finished, spent, *dü* (*dē*), *gwrēs* (*gwrȳs*).
docile, a. *dywoth*, *hewar*, *dōf*, *temprys*.
dock, n., harbour, *porth*, m., pls. *-ow*, *perth*, *p. lystry*; weed, *tavolen*, f., col. *tavol*; butter-d., burdock, *t. amanyn*; d. leaves, *dēl-tavol*: v. *dōs yn porth*; d. a horse, *cottrēghy lost margh*: **-yard,** n. **lystryva*, f., pl. *-ow*.
doctor, n. *medhek*, m., pl. *-ygyon*, *doctour*, m., pl. *-s*; quack d., *pomster*, m., pl. *-strys*; savant, *dyscajor*, m., pl. *-yon*: v. *medhegy*; quack d., *pomstrya*.
doctrine, n. *lagha*, m., pl. *-ghys*, *dyscas*, m., *lay*, m., pl. *-s*.
document, n. *scryven*, f., pl. *-now*, *scryf*, m., pl. *-yvow*.
dodder, n. *blew an jawl*, col., *safron an j.*, m.: v. *crenna drē wander*.
dodge, v. *goheles*, *dyank*, *plynchya*: n. *cast*, *wrynch*, m., pl. *-ys*, *prat*, m., pl. *-tys*.
doe, n., deer, *ewyk*, f., pl. *-ygas*, †*da*, m. or f.
doff, v. *dy'sky dhe-vēs*.
dog, n. *kȳ*, m., pl. *cün*; hunting d., *rech*, m., pl. *-ys*, *helgy*, m., pl. *-gün*, †*gwylter*, m., pl. *-tras*; male d., *gourgy*, m., pl. *-gün*; long d., *k. hȳr*; d. kept on chain, *k. stak*; savage d., *brathky*: **-biscuit,** n. *bara cün*, m.: **d.-kennel,** n. *kȳjy*, *cünjy*, m., pl. *-ow*.
dogfish, n. *mōrgy*, m., pl. *-gün*.
dogged, a. *gorth*; to be d., *kȳa*.
doggerel, n. *gwers sempel*, f.
dog-rose, n. *rosen-kȳ*, f., pl. *-now-k.*, col. *rōs-k*.
doit, n. *dyjyn*, m., pl. *-now*.
dole, n. *ran*, f., pl. *-now*, *dōl*, m., pl. *-ys*: v. *ranna*, *rȳ dōl*.
doleful, a. *trüesy*, *trüethek*, *morethek*, *galarek*.
doll, n. *jowanna*, f., *popet*, m., pl. *-tys*.
dolmen, n. *cromlēgh*, f., pl. *-yow*.
dolorous, a. *ankensy*, *tryst*.
dolt, n. *pen-cōk*, *pen-pyst*, m., pl. *-now-c.*, *-p*, †*talsogh*, **pensogh*, m.
dome, n. *to crom*, m., pl. *-how c*.
domestic, a. *chȳ*; animals, *dōf*: n. *servyas*, m., pl. *-ysy*, *paja*, m., pl. *-jys*, *maghteth*, f., pl. *meghtythyon*: **-ate,** v., tame, *dofhē·*, *tempra*.
domicile, n. *trygva*, f., *chȳ*, m., pls. *-ow*, *treveth*, f.: v. *annedhy*.
dominate, v. *gwarthevya*, *maystry*, *lordya*: **-ant,** a. *pen*; d. person, *rowtor*, m., pl. *-s*: **-ation,** n. *domynasyon*, m.
domineer, v. *lordya*, *maystry*: **-ing,** a. *hautyn*.
dominion, n. *mestrynsys*, *danjer*, m.; territory, *tyreth*, m.
don, v. *gwysca*, *gorra yn y gerghyn*.
donate, v. *rȳ*: **-tion,** n. *ro*, m., pl. *-how*.
donkey, n. *asen*, m. or f., pl. *-as*; jackass, *margh-asen*; she ass, **casek-asen*.
donor, n. *rȳas*, m., pl. *-rȳesy*.
doom, n. *brüs*, f., pl. *-ow*, *dōm*, m.: v. *brüsy*, *rȳ dōm*: **-sday,** n. *dēth brüs*, m.
door, n. *darras*, m., pl. *-ajow*; entrance, *porth*, m., pls. *-ow*, *perth*; front d., *darras a-rak*; back d., *d. a-dhelergh*: **d.-handle,** n. *dornla darras*, m., pl. *-lēow d.*: **d.-keeper,** n. *porther*, m., pl. *-oryon*, f., *-ores*, pl. *-ow*, *darrajor*, m., pl. *-yon*: **d.-post,** n. *post darras*: **d.-way,** n. *porth*, m., pls., *-ow*, *perth*.

dormant, a. *yn-cusk, yn-cuskys, hep dyfüna.*
dormitory, n. *cuskty, hünjy,* m., pl. *-ow, cuskva,* f., pl. *-ow.*
dormouse, n. **hünegan,* m., pl. *-as.*
dose, n. *medhy·gӯeth,* f., *ran,* f., pl. *-now, ten,* m., pl. *-now:* v. *medhegy;* with quack remedies, *pomstrya.*
dote, v. *dōtya, müskegy:* **-tage,** n. **penwander henys, dotyans,* m.: **-ting,** a. *dōtyes, *penwan, fol.*
double, v. **dobla;* fold, *plegya, deublegya:* a. *deublēk, dobyl;* twice, *dywwyth.*
doubt, n. *dowt,* m., pl. *-ys, mar,* m.; no d. he is, *ny-rēs dowtya tra y-fo:* v. *dowtya;* don't d. it, *na-dhowt a'n cās:* **-ful,** a. *dowtys:* **-less,** adv. *hep mar, hep dowt* (or *dhowt*).
dough, n. **tōs,* m.
dove, n. *colom,* f., pl. *-as, colomen,* f., pl. *-ennow;* ring d., *cüdon,* f., pl. *-as:* **d.-cote,** n. *colomyer,* m., pl. *-s;* **colomjy,* m.
dowdy, a. *drokwyskys.*
dowel, n. *ebyl pren,* m., pls. *-yow, -yon p.*
down, n. *hāl,* f., pl. *-low, gūn,* f., pl. *gonyow;* feathers, *plüf münys, manblüf,* col.; hair, *blewyk,* m., pl. *-ygow, manvlew,* col.: prep. *a-woles:* adv. *a-woles, war-woles, yn-nans, dhe'n lür, dhe'n dōr;* d. below, *aba·rth a-woles, dhe-woles, war-lür, war-nans, war-woles;* d. with him! *dhe'n dōr ganso!* d. proud hearts! *dhe'n dor colonnow prowt!:* **-wards,** adv. *yn-nans, war-nans, war-woles, dhe'n dōr, wor'tu ha'n lür.*
downcast, a. *dyfrēth;* of heart, *dygolon.*
downfall, n. *cothva,* f., *terros,* m., pl. and abst. *terryjy;* greed has been my d., *pythneth re-wrük ow shyndya.*
downhearted, a. *dygolon:* **-ness,** n. *dygolon,* f.
downhill, adv. *yn-nans;* go d., *dyeskynna.*
downpour, n. *hager-gowas,* f., pl. *-wosow.*
dowry, n. *tra,* neut., **argovrow,* f., pl. *-on.*
doze, v. *nappya, cusca yn-scaf,* †*tergusca:* n. *nappa,* m., pl. *-ys, cusk* or *cuscas cot,* m.
dozen, n. *deudhek,* m.
draff, n. *sēk,* m.
draft, n., sketch, **lynennans,* m., pl. *-ow, *lymnans,* m., pl. *-ow;* rough copy, *kensscryf,* m., *towl,* m., pl. *-ow;* troops, *bagas,* m., pl. *-ow.*
drag, v. *draylya, tenna,* ‡*draggya;* d. away, back, *kyldenna, *kyla;* d. self along, *slynkya:* **-ging,** n. *ten,* m., pl. *-now;* by d., *drē denna.*
draggle, v. *draylya yn plosethes;* d.-tailed, *lavrak, caglys hy losten.*
dragon, n. *dragon,* f., pl. *-as,* †*drӯk,* f., pl. *-ӯcow.*
dragon-fly, n. *nader-margh,* f., pls. *nedras-m., *nadron-m.*
drain, v. *desēgha;* d. away, *sygera, *cartha:* n. *dowrglēth,* m., pl. *-edhyow, carthpӯb,* f., pl. *-ow:* **-age,** n., action, *desēghans,* m.; matter, *carthyon, plosethes,* m.: **-ed,** a. *sygerys, desēghys.*
drake, n. *cülyek-hōs,* m., pl. *cülyogas-hōs, mallart,* m., pl. *-ars.*
drama, n. *gwary, gwary-mӯr,* m., pl. *-yow-m.:* **-tic,** a. *-gwary, *dramatek:* **-tics,** n. *gwaryow:* **-tist,** n. *scryfor gwaryow,* m., pl. *-oryon-g.*
dram-shop, n. *gwyrotty, dewotty,* m., pl. *-ow,* ‡*chӯ-dewas,* m.
draper, n. *pannor,* m., pl. *-yon, lyennor,* m., pl. *-yon:* **-y,** n. *lyennyow, pannow,* pl., *panwӯth,* m.
draught, n., air, *wheth,* m., pl. *-ow;* drink, *ten,* m., pl. *-now, dewas,* f., pl. *-wosow, draght,* m., pl. *-ys,* ‡*swynnen,* f., pl. *-now, lemmyk,* m., pl. *-ygow;* of ship, *downder mōr a-rēs dhe lester:* **d.-horse,** n. **tenvargh,* m., pl. *-vergh, margh tenna,* m., pl. *mergh t.* : **-tsman,** n. *lyennor,* m., pl. *-yon.*
draw, v. *tenna;* sketch, *delynya, *lymna, lynenna;* d. near, *dōs nēs, nessa, degensewa;* d. back, away, *omdenna, kyldenna, kyla;* d. out, *ystynna, trӯnya;* d. up a deed, *gül chartour;* d. nails, *gevelya;* a d'n. sword, *cledha nōth:* **-er,** n. *trok-tenna,* m., pls. *-kys, -egys, -t.:* **-ing,** n., pulling, *tenva,* f.; pull, *ten,* m., pl. *-now;* sketch, *delynyans,* m., pl. *-ow, lynennans,* m., pl. *-ow.*
drawers, n. *hosanow,* f., pl.
drawing-room, n. *hēl,* m., pl. *-ow.*
drawl, v. *draylya geryow,* †*stlevy:* n. †*stlaveth,* m.
draw-net, n. **tenros,* f., pl. *-ow.*
dread, v. *perthy own, dowtya, owna:* n. *agha, dowt, own, skēs, üth, üthekter,* m.: **-ful,** a. *üthek, ahas;* bad, *vӯl:* **-fully,** adv. *üthek, yn-soweth.*
dream, n. *hünros,* m., pl. *-ow;* trance, *tranjyak,* m.: v. *hünros, hünrosa.*
dreary, a. *tryst, trūan:* **-riness,** n. *trystys, trystans,* m.
dredge, v. *draylya, cartha;* d. flour, *scullya blēs* (*war*[2]); d.-corn, *kemyskysow, *brythӯs:* **-r,** n. *draylyer, drayl,* m.

dregs, n. *growjyon,* pl., *godhas,* m., pl. *-dhojyon, cūthow, soresyow,* pl.
drench, v. *cowl-glybya.*
dress, v. *gwysca;* d. oneself, *omwysca;* d. food, *parüsy bōs:* n. *dyllas,* m., pl. *-ajow, gwyscas,* m., pl. *-cosow,* †*gwysk,* m., pl. *-scow;* woman's d., *pows gwrēk,* f., pl. *-yow g.:* **-er,** n. *gwyscor,* m., pl. *-yon,* f. *-es,* pl. *-ow;* of tin, *lappyor,* m., pl. *-yon;* for crockery, *lystryer,* m., pl. *-yow:* **-ing-room,** n. *chambour-gwysca,* m., pl. *-s-g.:* **-maker,** n. *gwrȳadores,* f., pl. *-ow.*
dribble, v. *devera.*
drift, v. *mōs gans an dowr ha'n gwyns.*
drill, v. *telly, tardra;* troops, *dysky, prevy:* n., tool, *tardar,* m., pl. *terder;* of troops, *dyscans,* m.
drink, v. *eva;* d. round, *e. a-dro:* n., draught, *ten,* m., pl. *-now,* ‡*swynnen,* f., pl. *-now, draght,* m., pl. *-ys;* liquor, *gwyras,* f., pl. *-rosow, dewas,* f., pl. *-wosow;* d. wine excepted, †*syker,* m.; d. as gift, †*las,* m.: **-ing-horn,** n. *corn-eva,* m., pls. †*kern, kernow, e.:* **-pot,** n. *dewaslester,* m., pl. *-lystry, crüskyn,* m., pl. *-nys.*
drip, v. *govera, devera, droppya:* n. *deverans,* m.
drive, v. *gorra,* ‡*drȳvya;* chase, *helghya, chassya;* d. away, *pellhē·,* ‡*fēsya;* d. cattle, *hembronk;* vehicle, *lewyas;* nail, *gweskel:* **-er,** n. *lewyth,* m., pl. *-ydhyon, lewyer,* m., pl. *-yoryon;* chaser, *helghyer,* m., pl. *-yoryon.*
drivel, n. **glavor,* m.; nonsense, *üfereth fol.*
drizzle, n. **newlglaw, glūthglaw, glaw münys,* m.: v. *gül* **newlglaw,* etc.
drone, n., bee, *sudronen,* f., pl. *-now,* col. *sudron;* d. fly, *gwyban gōth,* m., pl. *-nas g.:* v. *sudronenny.*
droop, v. *posa, droppya, pendroppya:* **-ing,** a., of spirit, *dyfrēth.*
drop, v. *devera, bera, mery, droppya, gasa dhe godha:* n. *deveren,* f., pl. *-now, lom,* m., pl. *-mow,* dim. *lemmyk,* m., pl. *-ygow, banna,* m., pl. *-how, dager,* m., pl. *-grow, dagren,* f., pl. *-now,* col. *dager:* **-ping,** n., sheep, *pryl,* m., pl. *-yon, cagal,* col.
dropsy, n. *cleves dowr,* m.
drought, n. *sēghor, sēghter,* m.
drove, n. *para,* m., pl. *-rys, grē,* f., pl. *-yon, tonek,* m., pl. *-egow:* **-r,** n. *hembrynkyas lonow,* m., pl. *-ysy l.*
drown, v., *büdhy;* quite d'd., *cowlvüdhys.*
drowse, v. †*tergusca, codha yn cusk:* **-siness,** n. *posyjyon,* m.: **-sy,** a. *pōs, hünek.*
drub, v. *stewanny, cronkya, frappya:* **-bing,** n. *stewan,* m., pl. *-now.*
drudge, n. *maw,* m., pl. *mebyon,* col. *coscar, oberwas,* m., pl. *-wesyon, darbarer,* m., pl. *-roryon:* **-ry,** n. *whēl crēf,* m.
drug, n. *medhy·gȳeth,* f.: v. *drok vedhegy:* **-gist,** n. *gwerther medhy·gȳeth,* m., pl. *-oryon m.*
druid, n. **drewyth,* m., pl. *-ydhyon:* **-ical,** a. **drewydhek:* **-ism,** n. **drewy·dhȳeth,* f.
drum, n. *tabour,* m., pl. *-s;* kettle d., *nāker,* m., pl. *nācrys:* **-mer,** n. *tabouror,* m., pl. *-yon:* **-stick,** n. *pren-tabour,* m., pl. *-yer-t.*
drunk, a. *medhow;* half-d., **cragh-vedhow;* to get d., *medhowy:* **-ard,** n. *pen-medhow,* m., pl. *-now-m.:* **-en,** a. *medhow:* **-enness,** n. **medhowynsy,* f., ‡*medhewnep,* m.
drupel, n. *moren,* f., col. *mōr.*
dry, a. *sēgh, crȳn;* milkless, *dylēth, hesk;* d. land, *tȳr sēgh, sēghtyr,* m., pl. *-yow;* d. pond, *sēghpol;* d. valley, *sēghnans, sēghtenow·,* m.; d. place, d. tree, *sēghen, crȳnen,* f., pl. *-now;* d. stuff, *crynyon,* pl.; to become d., *crȳna,* of cow, *hesky:* v. *sēgha;* d. up, *desēgha:* **-ness,** n. *sēghor, sēghter, crynder,* m.
dub, v. *henwel ave·l marghak, gelwel gans hanow noweth;* with grease, *üra.*
dubious, a. *dowtys, a-yllyr y dhowtya.*
duchess, n. *duches,* f., pl. *-ow:* **-chy,** n. *ducheth,* m.
duck, n. *hōs,* m., pl. *heyjy:* v., dodge, *plynchya;* in water, *troghya:* **-ling,** n. *heyjyk,* m., pl. *-ygow:* **-pond,** n. *pol-heyjy,* m., pl. *-low-h.:* **-weed,** n. *bōs-heyjy,* m., **lynos,* col., *kellyn,* m.
duct, n. *pȳbel,* f., pl. *-low.*
due, a. *gwyw, ewn, a-dāl;* as is d., *del yu devar, del dhegoth;* in d. time, *pan vȳth an ür.*
duel, n. *om·lath deudhen,* m., pl. *-adhow d.*
duet, n. *can,* or *gwary, deudhen,* f., pl. *-ow d.; ober üs gwrēs rak deu lēf, fȳl,* etc.
duke, n. *dük,* m., pl. *-ys, hembrynkyas-lu,* m., pl. *-ysy-l.*
dulcimer, n. *cythol,* m., pl. *-s.*
dull, a., of tools, *sogh, dylym;* lazy, *syger;* without energy, insipid, *dyfrēth;* stupid, *talsogh;* not bright, *dyslyw:* **-ness,** n. *sygerneth, dyfrēthter,* m.
duly, adv. *a-dermyn, del goth, del yua devar;* d. baptized, *lēl-vysydhys.*

dumb, a. *omlavar,* †*aflavar,* **dylavar*: **-ness,** n. *omlavarsys,* **aflavareth,* f.
dumbfound, v. *müskegy, sawthanas*; **-ed,** a. *dyegrys.*
dummy, n. *hevelepter fals,* m.
dumpling, n. *pellen,* f., pl. *-now.*
dun, a. **gorm, dyslyw.*
dune, n. *towan,* m., pl. *tewennow.*
dung, n. *būsel, teyl, caugh, mon,* m.; rabbits, sheep or goats, *cagal,* m.; horse, *būsel vergh*; cow d. as fuel, *glōs,* m.: **-heap, -hill,** n. *pȳl-teyl,* m., pl. *-yow-t., byjyon,* m., *teylek,* f., pl. *-egow, -egy.*
dunnock, n. *golvan-gē,* m., pl. *-as-kē.*
dupe, n. *dēn hedull, dēn üs tullys, dēn ēs y dulla*: v. *tulla, hüda.*
duplicate, a. *deublek*: v. *deublekhē·*: **-ation,** n. *deublekhēans,* m.
duplicity, n. *gȳl, tull, fa·lsury,* m.
durable, a. *a-bȳs, crēf, a-dhür.*
duration, n. *düryans, pēsyans,* m.; for the d. *hedra vo bresel.*
during, prep. *drēs, yn termyn*; d. our life, *hedra vēn bew*; d. this week, *drēs an seythen-ma.*
dusk, n. *tewlwolow,* **anwolow,* m.; at d., *d(y)worennos*: **-y,** a. **godewl.*
dust, n. *dowst,* **polter,* m.; light d., *pon,* m., *brēghy,* pl.: v. **dyboltra, dybonekhē*: **-heap,** *ponek,* f., pls. *-egy, -egow*: **-y,** a. *ponek*: **-er,** n. *clowt,* pl. *-ys,* **dowstlen,* f., pl. *-now.*
duty, n. *devar,* m., *dūta,* m., pl. *-tys, charj,* m., pl. *-ys*; customs, *toll,* f., pl. *-ow*: **-tiful,** a. *gostyth, se·rvabyl.*
dwarf, n. *cor,* m., pl. *-as,* **corres,* f., pl. *-ow,* **dēnyk,* m., pl. *tüsygow*; little d., **coryk,* m., pls. *-ygow, -esygow*; d. beans, etc., *fa münys,* etc.: v. *gül bōs münys.*
dwell, v. *tryga*; d. in, *annedhy*; d. together, settle, *kevannedhy*: **-er,** n. *tryger,* m., pl. *-oryon*; d. by the sea, **arvoryas,* m., pl. *-ysy*; d. by the woods, **argosyas,* m., pl. *-ysy*: **-ing,** n. *anneth,* f., pl. *-edhow, tref,* f., pls. *treven, trevy, trygva,* **annethva,* f., pl. *-ow, trygla, annethla,* m., pl. *-lēow*; d. house, *chȳ-anneth, chȳ-tan,* m., pl. *-ow-a., t., trevow trygva*; in place names, *bos,* f., pl. *-sow*; winter-d., autumn-d., summer-d., *gwavas, kynewas, hewas,* f.; permanent d., *hendra,* f., pls. *-revy, -revow*: a., housed, *annedhys, trygys.*
dwindle, v. *lehē·, dōs ha bōs lē.*
dye, n. *lyw,* m., pl. *-yow*: v. *lywa*: **-r,** n. *lywor,* m., pl. *-yon*: **-ing,** n. *lywans,* m.
dying, n. *tremenva,* f., *mernans, enewores,* m.
dyke, n. *tomen, banken,* f., pl. *-now, fōs,* f., pl. *-ow.*

E

each, a. *kettep, pup, kenyver*: pron. *pup*; e. other, *an ȳl y gȳla*; e. of them, *pup onen anedha*; e. one, *kettep onen, pup hüny.*
eager, a. *frēth, mēn, whansek,* **tēr*; to be e., **tēry, bōs ganso,* or *dhodho, mal.*: **-ly,** adv. *yn-fēn, dewha·ns, yn-frēth*: **-ness,** n. *mal, whans,* **dewha·ns,* **tērder,* m.
eagle, n. *ēr,* m., pl. *-as*; she-e., *ēr benow,* f.
ear, n. *scovarn,* f., pl. *-ow,* d. *dywscovarn*; e. of corn, *pen-ȳs,* m., pl. *-now-ȳ.,* **tosen,* f., pl. *-now,* col. *tōs*; long e.ed., *scovarnak*; to give e., *cola (orth), rȳ scovarn (dhe[2])*; to form e.s. of corn, **hosy,* **dehosy*: **-ache,** n. *drōk* or *cleves scovarn.*
earl, n. *yurl,* m., pl. *-ys*: **-dom,** n. *conteth,* m.
early, adv. *a-var, a-brȳs, a-dermyn*; e. and late in life, *a noweth hag a hēnys.*
earn, v. *dyndyl*; e. one's living, *dyndyl y vewnans*: **-ings,** n. *gober,* m., pl. *-brow, arfeth,* m.; livelihood, *pega·ns,* m.
earnest, a. *dywysyk, mēn, sevür*; in e., *yn-tefrȳ·, yn sevüreth*; e. money, *dynar Dew*: **-ness,** n. *dywysykter, sevüreth,* m.
earring, n. †*skynen,* f., pl. *-now.*
earth, n., soil, *gweras,* m., pl. *-ow, prȳ,* m.; ground, *dōr, lür, tȳr, tyreth,* m.; the ground, *an dōr*; the world, *an bȳs, an nōr, an norvȳ·s*: **-en,** a. *prȳ, a brȳ*: **-enware,** n. *lystry prȳ,* pl., *prȳwȳth,* m.: **-ly,** a. *a'n bȳs*; in e. life, *yn trogel*; it's of no e. use, *ny-dāl travyth y'n bȳs.*
earth-nut, n. *keleren,* f., col. *keler.*
earthquake, n. *dorgrȳs,* m., pl. *-yow.*
earthwork, n. *dorgē,* m., pl. *-ow, fōs,* f., pl. *-ow.*
earthworm, n. *būlügen,* f., col. *būlük.*
earwig, n. **gorlosten,* f., pl. *-nas.*
ease, n. *ēs,* m.; e. of mind, *dyagha,* m.; at e., *hüth, yn ēs, attē·s*; set at e., *chersya*; take one's e., *cafos y ēs, omjersya*; ill at e., *anē·s*: v. *hüthhē·, hüdha*; relieve, *ēsya, hēbaskhē·, dyffres, sewajya*: **-less,** a. *anhedhek*: **-ment,** n. *hebasca,* f.
easy, a. *ēs, hebask,* **heforth*; easier, easiest, *ēsya, an ēsya*; to make e., *ēshē·, ēsya*: **-ily,** adv. *yn-ta, yn-scaf, hep awhē·r, hep caletter, hep let.*

East, n., a. *Yst, Howldrehevel,* m.
Easter, n. *Pask,* m.; E. day, *dē-P.*; E. morning, *dē-P. vyttyn.*
eat, v. *dybry*; good eating, *bōs da,* m.
eaves, n. *mӯn to, m. an to,* m.
eavesdrop, v. *clewes a-dryf tüs.*
ebb, n. *tryg, mordryg,* m.: v. *omdenna.*
ebony, n. *eben,* m.
eccentric, a. *coynt*: **-icity,** n. *coyntys,* m.
ecclesiastic, n. *dēn Eglos*: a. *eglosek.*
echo, n. *dasson, daslēf,* m.: v. *dasseny, dascrӯa, daslēfa.*
eclipse, n. *dyfyk an howl,* m., pl. *-ygow a.h.*; of the moon, *d. an lōr*: v. *megy, cüdha.*
economy, n. **erbys,* m.: **-mical,** a. **erbysek*: **-mise,** v. **erbysy, gwytha y byth*: **-miser, -mist,** n. †*erbysyas,* m., pl. *-ysy*:
ecstasy, n. *tranjyak,* m.
eddy, n., of water, *gorthfrōs, pollen troӱllya, frōs a-dro*: n., of wind, *corwheth,* m., pl. *-ow*: v. *mōs a-dro.*
edge, n. *mӯn,* m., pl. *-yon, amal,* m.f., pl. *e·melow, ōr,* f., pl. *-yon*; sharp e., *el,* f., pl. *-yon.*
edible, a. *a-yllyr y dhybry, da dhe vegyans mabden.*
edict, n. *gorhemmyn,* m., pl. *-ow.*
edify, v. *drehevel, dysky dader dhe*[2]: **-fication,** n. *dader,* m.: **-fying,** a. *da, a-dhrehef an brӯs, a-dhysk dader.*
edifice, n. *drehevyans,* m., pl. *-ow.*
edit, v. *parüsy, dyllo*: **-tion,** n. *pryntyans, ympryntyans, dyllans,* m.: **-tor,** n. *dyller,* m., pl. *-loryon*; e. of periodical, *lewyer lyver-termyn,* m., pl. *-yoryon l. t.*
educate, v. *dysky*: **-tion,** n. *dyscans,* m.
eel, n., conger-e., *sylly,* f., pl. *-yas*; freshwater e., *sylly dowr ēr*; sand e., *lavyn,* m., pl. *-yon.*
e'er a one, pron. *byth-onen, vyth-onen.*
efface, v. *defendya dhe-vēs.*
effect, n. *ober, nerth, deweth,* m.; in e., *yn ober*; he spoke to this e., *y-leverys yn ketelma*; e.s., *stoff chӯ, mebyl,* m.: v. *gül, skyla*: **-tive,** a. *sür.*
effeminate, a. *medhel, benenek, blüth, blüdhek*: **-acy,** n. *medhelder,* m.
effervesce, v. *whethfy,* **ewony*: **-ent,** a. *whethfys,* **ewonek.*
efficient, a. *sür, a-serf.*
effigy, n. *ymach,* m., pl. *-ajys.*
effluvium, n. *flērynsy,* m., *ēth,* m., pl. *-ow.*
effort, n. *stryvyans,* m., pl. *-ow, towl,* m., pl. *-ow*; in spite of all his e., *yn despӯ·t oll dh'y ēghen, awo·s a-allo*; to make an e., *stryvya*; to make a broken e., *astel.*
effrontery, n. *bolder dyveth,* m.
effusion, n. **denow,* m.: **-sive,** a. *tavasek.*
eft, n. *peswar-paw,* m., pl. *-as.*
egg, n. *oy,* m., pl. *-ow*; new-laid e., *oy noweth dedhwys*: **e.-cup,** n. *padel-oy,* m., pl. *-low-o.*: **e.-shaped,** a. *formyes ave·l oy*: **e.-shell,** n. *plysken oy,* f., col. *plysk oyow.*
egotism, n. *kerensa y-honen,* f.: **-ist,** n. *omgarer,* pl. *-roryon.*
eh!, excl. *ay*! *hay*!; interrog. *dar*?
eiderdown, n. *plüf-eyder,* col.: **e.-duck,** n. *hōs-eyder,* m., pl. *heyjy-e.*
eight, a., n. *ēth*; e. times, *ēthwyth*: **eighth,** a., n. *ēthves, ēthes*: **eighteen,** a., n. *ētek*: **eighteenth,** a., n. *ētegves*: **eighty,** a., n. *peswar-ügans.*
eisteddfod, n. **esethvos,* m., pl. *-ow.*
either, conj. *po, bo*; e. . . . or . . ., *pykē·n . . . po . . .*; *po . . . po . . .*; on e. side of, *a bup tu dhe*[2]; not e., pron., conj. *nanӯ·l*; e. of them, *an ӯl po y gӯla, an ӯl y'n bӯs anedha*; *onen a'n dheu*; e., adv. after neg., *na byth moy ny*[2], ‡*nanӯ·l*; a . . . or a . . . either; . . . *byth moy . . .*
ejaculate, v. *crӯa, garma*: **-tion,** n. *crӯ, garm,* m., pl. *-ow.*
Egypt, n. *Ejyp,* f.: **-tian,** n. *Ejyptyon,* pl. *-tonyon*: a. *Ejyptek.*
eject, v. *pellhē·, tewlel dhe-vēs, dyllo.*
eke out, v. *ystynna, gül bōs lowr.*
elaborate, a. *gwrēs gans oberyans mür, afӯnys,* **complek*: v. *cowlwül, obery gans mür a rach*: **-tion,** n. *afӯnyans,* m.
elapse, v. *tremena, passya.*
elastic, a. *gwethyn*: n. *fünen ystynna,* f.: **-icity,** n. *gwethneth, gwethynder,* m.
elate, v. *hüthhē·*: **-ted,** a. *lowenek, hüdhyk y golon*: **-tion,** n. *hüthter, hüdhykter, lowender mür,* m.
elbow, n. *elyn,* m., pl. *-now,* d. *deuelyn*; point of the e., *penelyn,* m., d. *deubenelyn*; sharp e'ed, a. *elynek*; to lean on the e., *deuelyna* (*war*[2]), *posa war benelyn*: v. *elyna,* **kylherdhya.*
elder, n. *dēn hēn,* m., pl. *tüs h.*; comp. adj. *cotha.*
elder-tree, n. *scawen,* f., col. *scaw*; dwarf e., *scaw dōr, scaw benygys, scaw bӯghan*; e.-grove, *scawennek, scawek,* f., pls. *-egy, -egow.*
elect, v. *dewys*: **-tion,** n. *dewys, dewysyans,*

m.; general e., *dewysyans gwlasek*, m.: **-tor,** n. *dewysyas*, m., pl. *-ysy*.
electric, a. **tredanek*: **-icity,** n. **tredan*, m.: **-ify,** v. **tredanhē·*.
elegance, n. *jentylys, tekter, *kempensys*, m.: **-nt,** a. *a-dhevȳ·s, *kempen, fȳn, †fȳthüs, jentyl, bryntyn*: **-ntly,** adv. *jentyl, a-dhevȳ·s.*
elegy, n. **galargan, cān galarow, *marnas*, m., pl. *-ow.*
element, n. *elven*, f., pl. *-now, element*, m., pl. *-ns*: **-tary,** a. *elvennek.*
elephant, n. *olyfans*, m., pl. *-as*: **-ine,** a. *maga pōs ave·l olyphans.*
elevate, v. *drehevel, exaltya*: **-tion,** n. *drehevyans*, m.; height, *ughelder*, m.
eleven, card num. *ünnek*: **-th,** ord. num. *ünnegves.*
elf, n. *spyrys*, m., pl. *-yon, coryk*, m., pls. *-ygow, -esygow*: **-in,** a. *kepa·r ha coryk, pür vünys.*
eligible, a. *gwyw, a-dhewysyr.*
ellipse, n. *hȳrgelgh*, m.: **-ptical,** a. *hȳrgelghek.*
elm-tree, n. *elowen*, f., col. *elow*; e. grove, *elowek*, f., pls. *-egow, -egy.*
elocution, n. *skȳans arethya*, m.
elongate, v. *hȳrhē·*: **-tion,** n. *hȳrhēans*, m.
elope, v. *fȳa, dya·nk, gasa trē*; e. with, *gasa trē gans (dēn), ladra (mowes) dyworth hy herens*: **-ment,** n. *dya·nk*, m.
eloquent, a. *frēth, helavar*; **-nce,** n. *frēthter, helavarder*, m.
else, adv. *kēn*; or e., *kēn, kēn maner, bokē·n, pykē·n*; anything e. but, *kēn es, kēn ages*; nothing e., *travyth*, or *tra, nahē·n*: **elsewhere,** adv. *yn kēn lē*, or *tyller.*
elude, v. *goheles, plynchya, scüsy.*
emaciated, a. *tanow, cül, eskernek.*
emancipate, v. *delyfrya, lyfrya, dyllo*: **-tion,** n. *delyfryans, lyfrēson*, m.
embalm, v. *üra, gorra unyent ha spȳcys dhe*[2], *untya.*
embankment, n. *fōs*, f., pl. *-ow, tomen*, f., pl. *-now.*
embark, v. *mōs aberveth yn lester, *lestra, mōra*: **-rcation,** n. *mōs yn lester.*
embarrass, v. *ancombra*: **-ment,** n. *ancombrynsy*, m.
embassy, n. *cannasow, lyscannasow*, f. pl.; building, **cannaty*, m.
embellish, v. *tēkhē·, afȳna*: **-ment,** n. *tēkhēans.*
ember, n. *lüsewen*, f., col. *lüsow, †regythen*, f., col. *regyth*; E. days, **Cotworyow, dēdhyow an C.*, pl.; E. week, *seythen an C.*, f.
embezzle, v. *ladra, camdrēlya mona*: **-ment,** n. *ladrans, camdrēlyans mona*, m.
embitter, v. *wherowhē·.*
emblem, n. *tokyn*, m., pl. *toknys, sȳn*, m., pl. *-ys, *arweth*, f., pl. *-edhyow*: **-atic,** a. **arwedhak.*
embolden, v. *rȳ colon dhe*[2], *colonnekhē·.*
embrace, v. *strotha, chersya, ‡byrla, kemeres yntra dywvrēgh*: n. *strothans, chersyans, ‡byrlans.*
embrasure, n. **tardhell*, f., pl. *-ow, *crenel*, m., pl. *-lys.*
embroider, v. *brōsya, nüjenna*: **-rer,** n. *brōsyer*, m., pl. *-yoryon*, f. *-yores*, pl. *-ow*: **-ry,** n. *gwȳth brōsyes, brōswyth*, m.
emerald, n., a. **e·merod*, m., pl. *-ros, gwērvēn*, m.
emerge, v. *dōs yn-mēs, dyvüdhy, omsevel, sordya*: **-ency,** n. *ethom*, m., pl. and abst. *-mow, tro*, f., pl. *-yow, sordyans*, m.
emigrate, v. *dyvrōa*: **-tion,** n. *dyvroans*, m.: **-nt,** n. *dyvrēs*, m., pl. *-ow.*
eminence, n. *prȳs, ughelder*, m.; geog. *ban*, m. or f., pl. *-now, ugheldyr*, m., pl. *-yow, bans*, m., pl. *-ow*: **-ent,** a. *ughel, flowr, a brȳs.*
emit, v. *dyllo.*
emolument, n. *gober*, m., pl. *-brow, pega·ns*, m.
emotion, n. *müvyans*, m., pl. *-ow*; to cause e. in, *amüvya.*
emperor, n. *e·mperour (emprour)*, m., pl. *-yon.*
emphasis, n. **pōslēf*, m.: **-size,** v. *posa war*[2], *rȳ *pōslēf dhe*[2]: **-atic,** a. *frēth, gans *pōslēf.*
empire, n. *emperoreth*, m., pl. *-ow.*
employ, v. *arfeth, rȳ whēl dhe*[2]; use, *gül defnyth a*[2]: **-ed,** a. *bysy*; to be e., *bōs bysy, *sodha*: **-ee,** n. *servyas*, m., pl. *-ysy, gwȳthor*, m., pl. *-yon*: **-er,** n. *mēster*, m., pl. *mestrysy*: **-ment,** n. *sōth*, f., pl. *sodhow, arfeth*, m., pl. *-edhow, servys*, m.; place of e., **sothva*, f., pl. *-ow.*
empower, v. *rȳ gallos dhe*[2].
empress, n. *e·mperes*, f., pl. *-ow.*
empty, v. *gwakhē·, dyscarga*: a. *gwak, cōk, voyd*; e. space, *gwak*, m., pl. *-agyon*; e. headed, *pen-cōk*; e.-h. person, *pen-cok*, m., pl. *-now-c*: **-tied,** a. *gwakhē·s, sygerys*: **-tiness,** n. *gwakter*, m.

emulate, v. *medra, comparya gans, whylas bōs par dhe*^{2}*, gül warle·rgh*: **-ion,** n. *kes-strÿf, comparyans,* m.
enable, v. *rȳ gallos dhe*^{2}.
enact, v. *o·rdena* (*ordna, orna*).
encamp, v. **campya, tryga yn tyldys*: **-ment,** n., milit. *caslys,* f., pl. *-ow.*
enchant, v. *hüda, †gorhana*: **-er,** n. *hüder,* m., pl. *-oryon, †gorhenyas,* m., pl. *-ysy*: **-ment** n. *hüs,* m., *†gorhan,* f., pl. *-ow.*
encircle, v. *gorra,* or *mōs, a-dro dhe*^{2}, **kelghy*: **-cling,** a. *yn-kerghyn, üs a-dro.*
enclose, v. *kēas, degēa, magorya, gartha*: **-sed,** a. *clōs, kēs, kēek*: **-sure,** n. *clōs,* m., pl. *-ys, park,* m., pl. *-rcow, garth,* m. and f., pl. *-ow, -dhow, kew,* f., pl. *-yow, kēl,* f., pl. *-yow, garthen,* f., pl. *-now*; as suffix, *-lan,* f., pl. *-now, -yow*: to make an e., *gartha.*
encompass, v.: see **encircle.**
encore! int. *arta!*
encounter, v. *metya gans, dyerbyn*: n. *dōs* or *mōs erbyn, metyans,* m.
encourage, v. *confortya, rȳ colon dhe*^{2}, **kennertha*: **-ment,** n. *confort, *kennerth,* m.: **-aging,** a. *ow-rȳ,* or *a-rē, colon*; that is e., *colon a-rēr gans henna.*
encroach, v. *omherdhya, kemeres tyller* (*war*^{2}): **-ment,** n. *omherdhyans,* m.
encumber, v. *ancombra*: **-brance,** n. *ancombrynsy,* m.
end, n. *pen,* m., pl. *-now, deweth,* m., *dewethva,* f., *fȳn,* f., pl. *-yow, fynweth,* f.; very e., *penwyth,* m., *pen dewetha*; e. of road, *penhens,* m.; in the e., *worteweth* (*wosteweth, oteweth*); to the e., *byteweth*; a month on e., *ün mȳs warba·rth*; stand on e., *sevel a'y sāf*; from e. to e., *afȳna, a-hēs, hēs-ha-hēs*; to that e., *dhe'n porpos-na, yn henna*; a bad e., *drōk,* or *tebel, dheweth,* m.; to come to a bad e., *drōk,* or *tebel dewedha*; to make an e. of, *dystrewy, kȳsya*: v. *gorfenna, dewedha, bōs dewēth a*^{2}, **fyn-wedha*: **-ed,** a. *dü* (*dē*), *dewedhys*: **-ing,** n. *dewethva,* f., *pen,* m.: **-less,** a. *hep fȳn, hep worfen, dydheweth, dyben*; e. chain, *chayn nag-üs dhodho na pen na lost, c. hep pen-vyth*: **-lessly,** adv. *hep fȳn, bys vynary, hep hedhy,* or *cessya.*
endanger, v. *peryllya.*
endear, v. *gül bōs kerys, dyndyl y gara*: **-ment,** n. *kerensa,* f., *chersyans,* m.
endeavour, v. *assaya, astel, whylas, stryvya*: n. *stryvyans,* m., pl. *-ow, atte·nt,* m., pl. *-ys.*
endorse, v., cheque, *scryfa hanow war y geyn, keynscryfa, kylscryfa*: **-ment,** n. *keynscryfa,* m., pl. *-vadhow.*
endow, v. *kemmynna da dhe*^{2}; e. with an estate, *stātya*: **-ment,** n. *kemmyn, kemmyn-yans, da kemmynnys,* m., *ro,* m., pl. *-how.*
endue, v. *lenwel* (*gans*), *‡endewya.*
endure, v., last, *pēsya, dürya*; suffer, *godhaf, perthy, paragh*: **-ance,** n. *perthyans, god-hevyans, düryans,* m.
enemy, n. *envy,* m., s. and pl., *escar,* m., pl. *yskerens, escares,* f., pl. *-ow.*
energy, n. *fors, nerth, gallos,* m: **-etic,** a. *frēth, nerthek.*
enervate, v. *blüdhya, medhelhē·.*
enfeeble, v. *gwanhē·*: **-ment,** n. *‡gwane-greth,* m.
enforce, v. *constrȳna*: **-ment,** n. *constrȳ-nans,* m.
engage, v. *gwystla*; promise, *ambosa*; e. the enemy! *dhe wēl!*: **-ment,** n. *ambos,* m., pl. *-ow*; fight, *om·lath*: **-ing,** a. *hegar, caradow.*
engender, v. *denythy.*
engine, n. *jyn,* m., pl. *-nys*; steam-e., *jyn-tān, ynjyn,* m., pl. *-nys*; e. house, *jynjy,* m., pl. *-ow*; e. driver, *lewyas jyn, jynour,* m., pl. *-s*: **-neer,** n. *ynjynor,* m., pl. *-yon*: **-neering,** n. *skȳans jynnys,* m.
England, n. *Pow Saws, P. an Sawson,* m., *Bro Saws,* f.: **-lish,** a. *Sawsnek*; E. lang., *Sawsnek,* m.: **-lishman,** n. *Saws,* m., pl. *-on*: **-lishwoman,** n. *Sawses,* f., pl. *-ow.*
engrave, v. *gravya*: **-ver,** n. *gravyor,* m., pl. *-yon*: **-ving,** n. *gravyans,* m., pl. *-ow*; e. tool, *collel-gravya,* f.
enhance, v. *moghhē·, crefhē·, encressya.*
enjoin, v. *erghy, gorhemmyn, charjya*; e. strictly, *ervȳra.*
enjoy, v. *gül defnyth vās a*^{2}, *ūsya, kemeres plesour drē*^{2}; I e., *da yu genef, my a-gar, yma· dhymmo mür a dhelȳt a*^{2}; e. oneself, *omlowenhē·*: **-able,** a. *da, whēk, tēk, a-rē lowender, dydhan*: **-ment,** n. *tekter, ple-sour, lowender, delȳt,* m.
enlarge, v. *moghhē·, encressya, *efany*: **-ment,** n. *moghhēans,* m.
enlighten, v. *golowy*: **-ment,** n. *golewder, clērhēans,* m.
enlist, v., army, *omrolya*; e. aid, *gwaynya gweres.*
enliven, v. *bewhē·.*
enmity, n. *cās, envy* (*avy*), m.
enormous, a. *üthek brās*: **-mity,** n. *üthekter,* m.

enough, a., adv., m., *lowr*; a., ‡*luk*; that's e. for us, *hen yn lowr dhyn*; well e., *mar dha del rēs.*
enquire, enquiry: see **inquire, inquiry.**
enrage, v. *serry, angra, gorra connar yn.*
enrich, v. *gül bōs rych, *kevothegy.*
enrol, v. *scryfa yn rōl, *rōlya, gorra dhe rōl*; e. oneself, *omrōlya*: **-ment,** n. *rōlyans, omrōlyans,* m.
ensconce oneself, v. *mōs dhe govva, whylas scons.*
ensign, n. *baner,* m., pl. *-ow, arweth,* f., pl. *-wedhyow, sȳn,* m., pl. *-ys.*
ensnare, v. *bagha, *magly.*
ensue, v. *sewya, holya, dōs warle·rgh.*
ensure, v. *gwytha, sürhē, gorra drēs mar y'n bȳs.*
entail, v. *hembronk dhe*[2], *drȳ ganso.*
entangle, v. *magly, kemysk-kelmy*: **-ment,** n. *ancombrynsy,* m., **magel,* f., pl. *-glow.*
enter, v. *entra* (*dhe*[2]), *mōs a-berth yn.*
enterprise, n. *vyaj,* m., pl. *-ys.*
entertain, v. *dydhana, yntertaynya, *gwesty*: **-er,** n. *yntertaynour,* m., pl. *-s,* †*bārth,* m., pl. *byrth, bardhes,* f., pl. *-ow*: **-ment,** n. *yntertaynment,* m., pl. *-mens*; lodging, *gwest,* f.; to seek e., *gwesta* (inf. only).
enthrone, v.: **-ment,** n. *gorra yn sē, trōn, chayr,* or *stallasyon.*
enthusiasm, n. *tān colon,* m.: **-stic,** a. *gans tān y golon.*
entice, v. *dynya, *slokkya.*: **-r,** n. *dynyer,* m., pl. *-yoryon.*
entire, a. *dȳen, perfyth, cowal, hep nam*; of body, *kyk yn knēs*; uncastrated, **kellek*: **-ly,** adv. *a-hēs, hēs-ha-hēs, yn pup ēghen, afȳna, glan, cowal, hep nam, warba·rth*; as prefix or suffix, *oll*; the fault is hers e., *honna yn oll dhe vlamya.*
entitle, v. *rȳ gwȳr*; be e. to, *pew* (def. v.).
entomb, v. *encledhyes, gorra yn beth.*
entomology, n. *prȳvy·dhȳeth,* f.: **-gist,** n. *prȳvyth,* m., pl. *-ydhyon.*
entrail, n. *colon,* m., pl. *-yow,* †*ene·theren,* f., col. *e·nether,* †*colodhyonen,* f., col. *colodhyon.*
entrance, n. *porth,* m., pls. *-ow, perth*; way in, *forth entra,* f.; going in, *mōs a-jȳ, entrans,* m.
entrance, v. *rafsya*: **-cing,** a. *ow-trȳ rafsyans.*
entrap, v. *cachya, *magly*; in argument, *conclūdya.*
entreat, v. *pysy, requȳrya*: **-y,** n. *govenek,* m., pl. abst. *-nygyon, pysadow,* m.; hear our e.! *clew agan lēf*!
entrenchment, n., camp, *dynas,* m., pl. *-ow, kēr,* f., pl. *-row, caslys,* f., pl. *-yow, castel dōr,* m.
entrust, v. *comendya, cola* (*dhe*[2]), *gorra yn charj* (*dhe*[2]).
entry, n. *mōs* or *dōs aberveth*; way in, *porth,* m., pls. *-ow, perth.*
entwine, v. *nedha, gwȳa.*
enumerate, v. *nyvera, rekna, acontya*: **-tion,** n. *nyveryans, reken, aco·nt,* m.
envelop, v. *maylya, cüdha*: **-e,** n. *maylyer,* m., pl. *-s*: **-ing,** a. *yn-kerghyn, üs a-dro dhe*[2].
envenom, v. *gwenyna, venyma.*
environment, n. *pup üs a-dro* (*dhe*[2]).
environs, n. *an pow a-dro* (*dhe*[2]).
envoy, n. *cannas,* f., pl. *-ow.*
envy, n. *envy* (*avy*), **gorvyn,* m.: v. *perthy envy*: **-viable,** *mür dh'y yeuny, gwyn y vȳs*: **-vious,** a. *e·nvyes, *gorvynnek.*
epaulette, n. *colmen scōth,* f., pl. *-now s.*
ephemeral, a. *ün jēth.*
epidemic, n. *cleves-rē,* m.
Epiphany, n. *Stül, dēgol-Stül, dēgol an Steren,* m.
episode, n. *wharfedhyans,* m., pl. *-ow, ran whethel,* f., pl. *-now w.*
epistle, n., Scriptural, **epystol,* m., pl. *-ow;* letter, *lytherow,* pl. (used as sing. also), †*scryven-danvon,* f., pl. *-now-d.*
epitaph, n. *scryven-beth,* f., pl. *-now-b.*; *beth-scryfa,* m.
epoch, n. *ōs,* m., pl. *-ow, termyn,* m., pl. *-yow.*
equal, a. *kehaval, hevelep, ēqual*: n. *par,* m., pl. and abst. *-ow, coweth,* m., pl. *-a*: v. *bōs par dhe*[2], *drehedhes dhe*[2], *comparya gans*: **-ity,** n. *kehavalder, hevelepter,* m.; to claim e. with, *comparya gans*: **-ize,** v. *gül bōs kehaval, kehesy, kesposa*: **-ly,** adv. *equal, kepa·r*; he is e. wise, *maga für yu agessa-y.*
equate, v. *comparya, kesposa*: **-tion,** n. *comparyans,* m., pl. *-ow*: **-tor,** n. *keheseth,* m.
equestrian, a. *marghak*: n. *marghak* (*marrek*), m., pl. *-ghogyon,* f., *marghoges,* pl. *-ow.*
equilibrium, n. *composter, *kespōs, ewnbōs,* m.
equinox, n. *keheseth,* (*keheja*) m., pl. *-edhow, k. dēth ha nōs, *kehēsnōs,* f.: **-noctial,** a. *kehesedhek.*
equip, v. *darbary, hernessya, dȳghtya*:

-ment, n. *aparell, hernes,* m.; to put on e., *hernessya.*

equitable, a. *ewn, tēk, gwyw*: **-ity,** n. *ewnder, lēouta (louta), composter,* m., *gwȳrvrüs,* f.

equivalent, a. *kemmys*; e. to, *k. ha*: n. *keheseth,* m., pl. *-edhow, equal,* m., pl. *-s.*

era, n. *termyn,* m., pl. *-yow, ōs,* m., pl. *-ow, ōswyth,* m., pl. *-yow.*

eradicate, v. *dywrȳdhya.*

erase, v. *defendya*: **-r,** n. *ruttyer* (m.), or *cravell* (f.), *defendya.*

ere, conj. *kens (es), ken*; e. now, *kens-lemmyn*; e. they cross, *kens es y dhe dremena.*

erect, v. *drehevel, sevel*: a. *a'y sāf, serth, sevys*; e. posture, *sāf,* m.: **-tion,** n. *drehevyans,* m., pl. *-ow*: **-tness,** n. *serthter,* m.

ermine, n. **ermyn,* m., **cath baly,* f.

erne, n. *ēr an mōr, mōrēr,* m., pl. *-as.*

erode, v. *ūsya*: **-osion,** n. *ūsyans,* m.

err, v. *sawthanas*; in thought, *camdyby*; in observation, *camweles*; in deed, *camdremena, camwül*; to take amiss, *camgemeres*: **-roneous,** a. *gow, fals, cam-,* ‡*myskemerys*: **-ror,** n. *camdybyans,* m.; fault, *fowt,* m., pl. *-ow*; relig., *tebelgryjyans,* m.; mistake, *sawthan,* ‡*myskemeryans,* m.; chance e., *gwall,* m., pl. *-ow*; in e., *bad.*

erudite, a. *dyskys, gwenwhys*: **-tion,** n. *clerjy,* m., *dyscans down.*

erupt, v. *tardha*: **-tion,** n. *tarth,* m., pl. *-rdhow.*

eryngo, n. *morgelynen,* f., col. *morgelyn.*

erysipelas, n. *tān gwyls,* m.

escape, v. *dyank, fȳa, scappya, scüsy, cavanscüsa, goheles*: n. *dyank, cavanscüs,* m.: **-pade,** n. *prat,* m., pl. *-tys, scüsyans,* m.

eschew, v. *goheles, sevel orth.*

escort, v. *gorra, hembronk, lēdya*: n. *gwythyas,* m., pl. *-ysy, hembrynkyas,* m., pl. *-ysy.*

escutcheon, n. *scōs,* m., pl. *-ow, scochon,* m., pl. *-s, cota arvow,* m., pl. *-tys. a.*

especial, a. *specyal*: **-ly,** a. *kens oll, drēs pup tra, spe·cyly.*

espionage, n. *aspȳans,* m.

espouse, v. *demedhy*: **-sal,** n. *demedhyans,* m., *maryach,* m., pl. *-ajys.*

espy, v. *aspȳa.*

esquire, n. *squȳer,* m., pl. *-yon,* **scoswas,* m., pl. *-wesyon*; Esq., *Sq.*

essay, n. *assa·y,* m., pl. *-ys, atte·nt,* m., pl. *-ys*: v. *prevy, assaya, profya.*

essence, n. *sawor,* m., pl. *-ow, substans,* f., *sūgan,* m., *ēth,* m., pl. *-ow*: **-ntial,** a. *a-rēs, na-yllyr y hepcor*; it is e., *rēs porres yu . . .*; the e's., *an suganow, an taclow a-rēs, nayllyr aga hepcor.*

establish, v. *fastya (fasta), fundya, sevel*: **-ment,** n. *fundyans,* m.

estate, n. *stāt,* m., pl. *-ys*; property, *pyth,* m., pl. *-ow, da,* m., *tra,* neut.

esteem, v. *synsy, gül vrȳ a*[2], *acontya, omsynsy, settya*: n. *worshyp, brȳ,* m.

estimable, a. *wordhy, bryntyn.*

estimate, v. *synsy, nyvera, acontya, rekna*: **-tion,** n. *synsyans, brȳ,* m., *brüs,* f.

estuary, n. *hayl,* m., pl. *-yow.*

eternal, a. *nefra a-bys*: **-ally,** adv. *bynary, bynytha, byketh, vyketh, vynary, vyken, nefra, bys vȳken, b. vynary, b. nefra, b. vynytha*: **-nity,** n. *trank hep worfen,* m.

etymology, n. *skȳans geryow,* m., **gery·dhȳeth,* f.: **-gist,** n. **geryth,* m., pl. *-ydhyon.*

eucharist, n. *Corf Crȳst.*

eulogy, n. **canmola,* m., pl. *-ledhow*: **-gise,** v. **canmel.*

evacuate, v. *trussa a*[2], *gwakhē·*; defecate, *scumbla*: **-tion,** n. *trussans,* m.

evade, v. *scüsy, vodya, cavanscüsa, goheles*: **-asion,** n. *gohel, gohelans, vodyans, cavanscüs,* m.; **-asive,** a. *fēl, gohelüs.*

evangelic, a. *awaylek*: **-ise,** v. *awayla*: **-ist,** n. *awaylor,* m., pl. *-yon.*

evaporate, v. *desēgha,* **ethenna*: **-tion,** n. *desēghans,* m.

eve, n., of feast, etc., *gōl,* m., pl. *-yow, nōs, noswyth,* f., *nōs-gōl.*

even, a. *leven, compes, gwastas*; to make e., *levna*; to be e. with, *bōs compes gans*: adv., prep., e. as, like, *kepa·r ha*; e. as he grew, so did the coat, *kepa·r ef del devys, yndella an bows a-wrē*; coulds't thou not e. keep watch for one moment? *a ny-wothfes yn-fās ün prȳjwyth golyas?*; e. he believes it, *ef a-n-crȳs, ef ynwe·th*; e. though, e. if . . ., yet . . ., *ha kyn*[5]*(th), ha mar*[4]*(s) . . ., whath . . .*; e. to, *bys yn, bys dhe*[2]: **ly,** adv. *yncompes*: **-ness,** n. *composter, levender,* m.

evening, n. *gorthewer,* m.; early e., *androw·,* m.; noon to nightfall, *ewha,* m.; this coming e., *gorthewer*; this pres., fut. or past e., *haneth*; this pres. e., *yn nōs haneth*; this pres. or past e., *haneth yn nōs*; this fut. e., *haneth dhe nōs*; yesterday e., *nyhewer*; until late yesterday e., *bys yn n'ewer gorthewer*; tomorrow e., *avorow dhe nōs.*

evening-star, n. *steren wesper,* f.

evensong, n. *gwesper,* m., pl. *-ow.*

event, n. *wharfos, darfos, cās,* m.; at all e's., *yn nep cās, pyna·k a-wharfo*: **-ful,** a. *lenwys a lȳes wharfos.*
eventide, n. *prȳs gwesper,* m.
eventual, a. *a-dhē yn deweth, a-sew, a-sewyas,* etc.: **-ly,** adv. *worteweth (wosteweth, oteweth).*
ever, adv. *byth, nefra, prest, pupprys, jammes, yn y ōs, neb-ür*; fut. *nefra, b(v)ynary, b(v)ytteth (b(v)ycheth), b(v)yken, b(v)ynytha, yn y ōs*; past, *a'y ōs, a'y üs, b(v)ythqueth (bysqueth)*; for e., *bys vyken, bys vynary, bys vynytha, bys nefra*; not e., *nep-prȳs, nefra, vyth, nēs,* with neg.; e. a better, *byth well*; e. a one, *byth onen*; as soon as e., *byth pan*^{2}, *kettel*^{2}; for e. and e., *trank hep worfen*; e. so great, *vyth mar vrās.*
evergreen, a. *pupprȳs ow-clasa, *bythwer*; e. oak, *glastanen,* f., col. *glastan.*
everlasting, a. *hep deweth,* or *fȳn, nefra a-bȳs.*
evermore, adv. *trank hep worfen, bys-vynary, vyken, bys-vyken, b(v)ynytha, bys-vynytha, bys-nefra.*
every, a. *pup, pup . . . -oll, kenyver*; before *onen, pen, pol, tam, dynar, map, gwas,* etc., *(yn) kettep*; e. day, *pupteth -oll., ‡kenyver jorna*; e. one of them, *yn kettep gwas, pup gwas*; e. man Jack, *mēster ha maw, kettep map bron*; in e. direction, *a bup tu*; e. one, *pup-onen.*
everybody, everyone, pron. *pup, pup-oll, pup-onen, pup dēn-oll, oll an bȳs, pup-hüny*; e. who, *sül a*^{2}, *puppyna·k a*^{2}, *kemmȳ·s a*^{2}.
everything, pron. *puptra, puptra-oll, oll pup tra, pup ēghen*; e. that, *kekemmy·s a*^{2}.
everywhere, adv. *pup-plas, pup-tu, pup tyller, pupla.*
evet, n. *pedrevan an dowr,* f., pl. *-now a.d.*
evict, v. *gorra mēs* or *yn-mēs*: **-tion,** n. *bōs gorrys mēs a'y jȳ, dyberghennans,* m.
evidence, n. *tokyn,* m., pl. *toknys, dustüny,* m., pl. *-yow, dysquedhyans,* m.
evident, a. *splan, efan, ape·rt*; it is quite e., *pür dha yth-hevel, y-hyllyr y- weles*; it is e. from that, that . . . is, *drē henna yth-yu, bōs* . . .: **-ly,** adv. *pür, efan, del hevel, del wylyr.*
evil, a. *tebel, drōk*; (prefix) *cam-, gwan-, hager-*; e. beast or person, *bylen,* m.; the e. one, *an tebel ēl, an jawl drokwas, an bylen,* m.: n. *drokter, droktra,* m., *drōk,* m., pl. *-ogow, *drogeth,* m., *dregyn,* f.; the king's e., *cleves an myghte·rn,* m.; e.-doer. *drokoberor,* m., pl. *-yon*; e.-doing, *tebelwrȳans, camwythres, drokobereth,* m.; e.-minded, *drōk y gnās, tebel y vrȳs.*
evoke, v. *gelwel mēs ,sordya.*
evolve, v. *dysplegya, omdrēlya*: **-lution,** n. *dysplegyans,* m.
ewe, n. *davas,* f., pl. *deves,* sep. pl. *devysyow,* dim. *davasyk,* f., pl. *devesygow*; e. lamb, *ōnes,* f., pl. *-ow.*
ewer, n. *pycher-dowr,* m., pl. *-s d., dowrlester,* m., pl. *-lystry.*
exact, v. *dervyn, govyn, demondya*: a. *harth, kewar, squȳr, ewn, a-dhevy·s, strayt*: **-ing,** a. *a-wovyn mür, bysy ow-covyn*: **-ly,** adv. *hardlych, poran, precyous, dour*; e. as, like, *kepa·r y'n bȳs (del*^{2} with vb., *ha* with n.), *poran del*^{2}, with vb.; e. so, *yndella kettep-onen*: **-ness,** n. *kewerder, composter, ewnder pür,* m.
exaggerate, v. *gorlywa, moghhē·, encressya, ystynna rē*: **-tion,** n. *moghēans,* m.
exalt, v. *avonsya, ughelhē·, exaltya, gormel*: **-ed,** a. *ughel, exaltyes*: **-tation,** n. *exaltyans, gormola,* m.
examine, v., inspect, *whythra, whylas*; in knowledge, *apposya, examnya*: **-nation,** n. *apposyans, examnasyon,* m.
example, n. *ensompel, ‡sampel,* m., pl. *-plys, patron,* m., *ran,* f., pl. *-now*; warning, *bysna,* m.; for e., *yn ensompel, ‡rag sampel.*
exasperate, v. *serry drēs musür, garowhē·, asperhē·*: **-tion,** n. *sōr brās,* m., *connar,* f.
Excalibur, n. **Calespūlgh.*
excavate, v. *palas, cledhya*: **-tion,** n. *clēth (clüth),* pl. *-edhyow,* m., *cow,* m., pls. *-yow, -yer, cowans,* m.: **-tor,** n. *palor,* m., pl. *-yon, cledhyor,* m., pl. *-yon.*
exceed, v. *tremena, mōs drēs, bōs moy age·s*: **-ingly,** adv. *üthek, ‡hūjes*; prefix, *pür-*; after adj., *drēs musür, drēs ēghen.*
excel, v. *trȳghy*; surpass, *tremena*: **-lence,** n. *dader, bryntynsys,* m.: **-lent,** a. *bryntyn, gwella*; supremely e., **gorwyw*: **-lently,** adv. *yn-fryntyn, gans mür a rās, dhe rās.*
except, prep. *saw, adar, drēs, marnas (mars, mas)*: **-tion,** n. *torva rewl,* f., *nam,* m.; without e., *hep nam, hep gasa dēn nagonen na-vo . . .*
excess, n. *rē,* m.; to e., *gans outray,* m.: **-ive,** a. *drēs musür, rē vür*: **-ively,** adv. *rē*; e. hard, *cales fȳn.*
exchange, v. *chanjya*; n. *chanj, chyffar,* m.
exchequer, n. *arghow an Stāt,* pl.
excise, n. *toll,* f., pl. *-ow*; e. officer, *tollor,* n., pl. *-yon.*

excite, v. *müvya*; don't get e'd., *kē war dha gam*: **-table,** a. *ēs y vüvya.*
exclaim, v. *garma, crӯa.*
exclamation, n. *garm,* f., pl. *-ow, crӯ,* m., pl. *-ow.*
exclude, v. *kēas mēs, gwytha na-dheffo aberveth*: **-ding,** prep. *marnas, hep rekna, adar*: **-usive,** a., of clubs, etc., *kēs, yn*; e. of, *hep nyvera.*
excommunicate, v. *emskemünya*: **-tion,** n. *emskemünyans,* m.
excrement, n. *caugh,* m.; to void e., *caugha,* ‡*caca.*
excruciating, a. *pür dyn, tyn drēs ēghen.*
excursion, n. *tro y'n pow,* f., pl. *-yow y'n p.*; to make a summer e., *havy.*
excuse, v. *ascūsya,* **dygeredhy*: n. *ascūsasyon, ascūsyans, ascūs,* m.: **-d,** a. **dygereth, ascūsyes.*
execrate, v. *mylyga, mollethy, emskemünya.*
execute, v., inflict punishment, *gorra dhe'n mernans, dyala*; carry out, *gül, collenwel*: **-tion,** n., hanging, *crok,* f., pl. *-ogow*; beheading, **dybennans,* m.; performance, *gwrӯans,* m.: **-tioner,** n. *tormentor,* m., pls. *-s, -ys,* **dybenner,* m., pl. *-oryon*: **-tive,** a. *-obery*; e. power, *gallos-obery,* m.: n. *cusül-obery,* f.: **-tor,** n. *asectour,* m., pl. *-s.*
exemplary, a. *a-rē patron*; of punishment, *a-vo bysna.*
exemplify, v. *rӯ dysquedhyans a*².
exempt, a. *quyt*: v. *dyllo* or *lyfrya quyt*: **-tion,** n. *delyfryans, lyfryans,* m.
exercise, v. *lafürya, omassaya*: n. *lafür,* m., *assa·y,* m., pl. *-ys*; school e., *ober,* m., pl. *-ow.*
exert, v. *ūsya, gül*; e. oneself, *gül oll dh'y allos*: **-tion,** n. *lafür,* m.
Exeter, n. *Kere·sk,* f.
exhale, v. *ethenna*: **-lation,** n. *ēth,* m., pl. *-ow, ēthen,* f., pl. *-now.*
exhaust, v. *squytha, desēgha, gwakhē·, spēna*: n. *ēth spēnys,* m.: **-ted,** a. *squyth, squythys, lafüryes*; to become e., *dyfygya*: **-tion,** n. *dyfygyans, squythans,* m.
exhibit, v. *dysquedhes, dyscüdha*: n. *tra üs dysquedhes*: **-tion,** n. *dysquedhyans,* m.
exhilarating, a. *a-yaghhā, a-lowenhā·.*
exhort, v. *charjya, kesky, ynnӯa, arethya*: **-tation,** n. *ynny, ynnӯadow, keskyans,* m. *areth,* f., pl. *-yow.*
exhume, v. *dysencledhyes,* **dybrӯa.*
exigency, n. *ethom,* m., pl. and abst. *-mow.*
exile, v. *dyvrōa, exylya*: n. *dyvrōeth,* m.; an e., *dyvrēs,* m., pl. *-ow*; in e., e.d, *dyvro, exylyes.*
exist, v. *bōs* (*bones*), *bewa*: **-tence,** n. *bewnans,* m.; during his e., *hedra vē bew.*
exit, n. *forth ow-mōs mēs*; door, *darras,* m., pl. *darrajow*; to make an e., *omdenna, mōs yn-mēs.*
exorbitant, a., of price, *rē vrās*; of dealer, *ow-covyn rē, rē ughel y brӯsyow.*
exorcise, v. *gorra dyawl dh'y dӯthy, pellhē· tebel spyrys.*
expand, v. *efany, lēsa*: **-nse,** n. *efander, lēs,* m.: **-nsion,** n. *lēsans, efanyans, keheseth, lēs, hēs,* m.
expatriate, v. *dyvrōa, danvon mēs a'n wlās*: **-ted,** a. *dyvro, dyvrēs.*
expect, v. *gwaytya, dervyn, desevos, trestya*: **-tation,** n. *gwaytyans,* m., **desef,* m., pl. *-evyow, govenek,* m., pl. and abst. *-nygyon.*
expectorate, v. *trewa.*
expedience, n. *lēs,* m.: **-ncy,** n. *forth a-vo gwell*: **-nt,** a. *dhe lēs*: n. *towl, cast, wrynch,* m.
expedite, v. *spēdya*: **-ition,** n., despatch, *spēdyans,* m., pl. *-ow*; military, etc., *vӯaj,* m., pl. *-ys, kerth,* m., pl. *-rdhow, caskergh,* m., pl. *-ow*; to make an e. on horseback, *ewhyas.*
expel, v. *pellhē·, vodya, danvon* or *gorra dhe-vēs, tewlel mēs*: **-pulsion,** n. *pellhēans,* m.
expend, v. *spēna*: **-iture,** n. *costys,* pl., *mona spēnys,* col.
expense, n. *costyans,* m., *cost,* m., pl. *-ys*; be at an e., *mōs yn cost*: **-sive,** a. *kēr, cüf*: **-siveness,** n. *kērneth, cüfter,* m.
experience, v. *prevy, godhaf, godhevel, tastya*: n. *prevyans, skӯans pernys,* m.; observation, *experyans,* m.
experiment, v. *assaya, prevy*: n. *atte·nt,* m., pl. *-ys, experyans,* m., pl. *-ow, assa·y,* m., pl. *-ys, prof,* m.: **-tal,** a. *rak assaya.*
expert, a. *connek, ynjyn*: n. *dēn connek,* m.
expiate, v. *prena*: **-tion,** n. *ankenek, prena,* m.
expire, v. *merwel, dascor y enef* or *spyrys*: **-ation,** n. *fӯn, deweth,* m.
explain, v. *styrya, egery, clērhē·*: **-lanation,** n. *styryans,* m.
explicit, a. *clēr, efan.*
exploit, n. *towl fӯn,* m., pl. *-ow, f., gwrӯans mür*: v. *trēlya dh'y lēs y honen.*
explode, v. *tardha, dyllo ten, tarenna*:

-osion, n. *tarth,* m., pl. *-dhow*: **-osive,** a. *hedarth, tardhek*: n. *defnyth tardha,* m.
explore, v. *aspȳa glew, whythra tyryow noweth*: **-ration,** n. *whythrans, vȳaj yn tȳr nag-üs gothvedhys*: **-rer,** n. *whythrer,* m., pl. *-roryon.*
export, v. *gwertha mēs a'n pow*: n. *gwerth mēs a'n pow,* f.
expose, v. *dyscüdha, nōthhē·, dysquedhes, dyskevra*; crime, guilt, *cuhüdha(s)*: **-sition,** n. *dysquedhyans, *exposysyon,* m.: **-sure,** n. *dyscüdhans, nōtha, fowt goscotter,* m.
expostulate, v. *crothvolas, gül crothval*: **-tion,** n. *crothval,* m.
expound, v. *egery, styrya, *expownya.*
express, v. *derȳvas, meneges*: n. *an pyth üs ow-mōs* or *danvenys pür üskys*: **-ion,** n., on face, *mȳr, chēr,* m.; saying, *lavar,* m., pl. *-ow*; opinion, *derȳvas,* m., *cusül,* f.: **-ly,** adv. *yn-efan*; say e., *kewsel geryow efan.*
expulsion, n.: see **expel.**
expunge, v. *defendya (dhe-vēs).*
exquisite, a. *afȳnys.*
extant, a. *üs whath y'n bȳs.*
extempore, a. *hep y studhya*: **-rize,** v. *kewsel, scryfa* or *gül hep darbary.*
extend, v. *ystynna, strechya, hedhes*: **-ed,** a. *a-lēs*; of aims, *lēsys, ystynnys*: **-nsion,** n. *ystynyans,* m., *keheseth,* m., pl. *-edhow*: **-nsive,** a. *efan, larch*: **-nt,** n. *keheseth,* m., pl. *-edhow, hēs, myns, compas, cūr, efander, lēs,* m.; grant of land, *ysty·n,* m.
extenuating, a. *a-wra ascūsya.*
exterior, a. *a-vēs, war-vēs*: n. *tu a-vēs, tu war-vēs,* m.
exterminate, v. *dyswül, dyswrȳdhya*: **-ion,** n. *dyswrȳans,* m.
external, a. *a-vēs, war-vēs.*
extinguish, v. *dyfüdhy, megy*: **-er,** n. *dyfüdher,* m., pl. *-oryon*: **-tinct,** a. *marow, kellys a'n bȳs*: **-ction,** n. *dyswrȳans,* m.; of fire, *dyfüdhyans,* m.
extirpate, v. *dywrȳdhya.*
extol, v. *gormel, exaltya.*
extort, v. *cafos drē nerth, tenna* or *kemeres drē hakter, gwrynya mēs*: **-ion,** n. *an pyth üs kemerys,* or *kemeryans, drē nerth.*
extra, a., adv. *drēs henna, moy.*
extract, v. *tenna, dewys*: n., quotation, *devyn,* m., pl. *-now*; preparation, *godroth crēf*: **-ion,** n. *tennans,* m.; descent, *lynyeth,* f., *devedhyans,* m.
extraordinary, a. *drēs kynda, drēs ēghen, coynt.*
extravagance, n. *scul,* m., *sculva,* f., pl. *-ow*: **-nt, -ntly,** a., adv. *orth y scullya, mēs a (bup) forth, scullyak*; e. person, *scullyak,* m., pl. *-yogyon.*
extreme, a. *pella, dewetha*: n. *pen pella,* m., pl. *-now p., fynweth, f.*: **-ly,** adv. *drēs ēghen, drēs musür, fest, fȳn, rē, mür, marthys, ‡üthek*: **-mis,** n., in e., *yn enewores, owtascor y enef*: **-mity,** n. *pen,* m., pl. *-now, penwyth,* m., *fynweth,* f.; to e., *gans outray.*
extricate, v. *dyvagly, tenna mēs.*
exuberance, n. *gordevyans, lanwes, rē,* m.: **-nt,** a. *ow-kewsel rē, ow-corlenwel, ow-cordevy.*
exult, v. *bōs fest hüdhyk, omlowenhē· yn-frās*: **-ant,** a. *gormoledhek (-edhüs), hüdhyk fest.*
eye, n. *lagas,* m., pls. *-ow, -ajow*; d. *deulagas*; of needle, *crow-nasweth,* m.; of potato, *skyllen,* f., col. *skyl*; sharp e.d., large e.d., *lagasek*; to hit across the e.s., *gweskel war an wolok*: v. *lagata, whythra glew*: **e.-ball,** n. *aval an lagas,* m.: **e.-brow,** n. *abrans,* m., pls. *-ow, -njow*: d. *deuabrans*; bushy browed, *abransek*: **e.-glass,** n. *gwederlagas,* m., pl. *-drow-l.*: **e.-lash,** n. *blewen an lagas,* f., col. *blew an l.*: **e.-lid,** n. *croghen an lagas,* f., pl. *crēghyn an lagasow* or *dheulagas*: **e.-sight,** *golok,* f., *gweles,* m.: **e.-sore,** n. *hakter,* m., *tra cās* or *glōs y weles, defow·t yn-mysk tekter.*

F

fable, n. *whethel,* m., pl. *-thlow, aneth,* m., pl. *-ow.*
fabric, n. *gwȳas,* m.: **-ate,** v. *devȳsya.*
fabulous, a. *anethek, marthys.*
face, n. *fās,* m., pl. and abst. *-ow, tremyn,* m., *mȳn,* m., pl. *-yon, enep,* f., pl. *-ebow, mȳr,* m., *vysach (‡bejeth),* m., pl. *-ajys, grüf,* m.; grimace, *mowa,* m., pl. *-wys*; soft f. on hard granite, *cüdhen,* f.; right in his f., *ynter y dheulagas*: v. *sevel adhera·k fās a*[2]; give f. to, put f. on, *facya*; fair-faced, *facyes yn-tēk.*
facilitate, v. *ēshē·, ēsya.*
facing, adv. *a-dāl*; f. one another, *an ȳl a-dal y gȳla.*
facsimile, n. *equal, hevelep,* m.
fact, n. *tra,* neut., pl. *taclow, ober,* m., pl. *-ow, gwȳr,* m.; in f., *yn ober, yn-tefrȳ·, yn-whȳr, yn prōf, hep wow*: **-ual,** a. *gwȳr, a wyryoneth.*

factory, n. **gwȳthva*, f., pl. *-ow*.
faculties, n. *tȳthy*, col.; without one's proper f., *antȳthy*.
fade, v. *dyslywa, gwedhra, *gwewy*: **-d,** a. *gwedhrys, *gwew, kellys y lyw*.
faggot, n. *bēgh cünys*, m., pl. *-yow c.*, **fagosen*, f., pl. *-now*, col. *fagas*, **fask*, f., pl. *-scow*.
fail, v. *fyllel, dyfygya, drokfara*; without f., *hep falladow, hep fall*: **-ing,** n. *dyfyk*, m., pl. *-ygyow*: prep. *fowt, hep*: **-ure,** n. *meth*, m., pl. and abst. *mothow, dyfyk*, m., pl. *-ygyow, dyfygyans*, m.
fain, v., I am f., *mal yu genef*; I would f., *mensen a*[4].
faint, v. *clamdera*: n. *clamder*, m.: a. *faynt, gwan, clăf*: **-ness,** n. *clamder*, m.: **f.-hearted,** a. *dygolon, gwan y golon*; f. *-h.* fellow, *caughwas*, m., pl. *-wesyon*: **f.-heartedness,** n. *dygolon*, f.
fair, n. *fēr*, m., pl. *-yow*; f. ground, **fērla*, m.: a. *tēk, gwyn, glan, ylyn*; just, *ewn*; to make f., *gwynna*; f. haired, *pen melen*: **-ly,** adv. *yn-tēk, ylyn, yn-ewn*; it is f. good, *da yn ran yu*: **-ness,** n., beauty, *tekter*, m.; justice, *ewnder*, m.
fairy, n. *spyrys*, m., pl. *-yjyon*; the f's., *an bobel vȳghan*.
faith, n. *fȳth*, f.; *fay*, m.; belief, *crēs, crysyans* (*cryjyans*), f.; good f., *lendury*, m.; to have f. in, *cryjy dhe*[2]; f.! *parfay*! *re'm fay*!: **-ful,** a. *lēn, lēl, dywysyk*: **-fulness,** n. *lendury, lelder, leldury, dywsykter, dywysygneth, lēouta*, m.: **-fully,** adv. *hep tull, yn-lēl*; yours f., *dheugh-why yn-lēl*; f. pray, serve, believe, *lēl-* (or *lēn-*) *bysy, -wonys, -grysy*, etc.: **-less,** a. *dyslēn, fals, fekyl*,; relig. *dyscryjyk*.
falcon, n. *falghun*, m., pl. *-as, faucun*, m., pl. *-ys*: **-er,** n. *falghunor*, pl. *-yon*: **-ry,** n. *falghuno·rȳeth*, m.
fall, v. *codha*; fail, *fyllel*; f. back, *dascodha*; f. backwards, *omwheles dh'y gylben*; let f., *gasa dhe godha*; f. down, *omwheles*; vengeance, of luck, etc., *dyeskynna, codha*; to make f., *dysevel*; of water level, *bassya*: n. *coth*, m.; in wrestling, *towl, fauns*, m., pl. *-ow*.
fallow, n. *ton*, m. or f., pl. *-yow*; summer f., *havrak*, f., pls. *-egow, -egy*.
fallow-deer, n. *ewyk lōs*, f., pl. *-ygas l.*
false, a. *fals, gow*; of character, *fekyl*; f. person(s), *fals*, m.; make f. statement, *dolō·s*: **-ehood,** n. *gow*, m., pl. *-yow, gowegneth, falsury*, m.: **-ely,** adv. *yn-fals, falslych*: **-eness,** n. *gow, falsury*, m.: **-ity,** n. *fals*, m.
falter, v. *hokkya*.
fame, n. *brȳ, hanow da, *clōs, †gerda*, m.: **-mous,** a. *a vrȳ, mür y hanow, †geryes da*; to make f., *kywhethla*.
familiar, n., f. spirit, *dyawl cōth*: a. *cōth, gothvedhys, ūsyes, aswonys*.
family, n. *tȳlu*, m., pl. *-yow, kerens*, pl.; household, *tüs chȳ, mēny*, m., **tyegeth*, m., pl. *-ow*; race, *lynyeth, ēghen*, f.
famine, n. *dyvotter, esow*, m.
famish, v. *famya, merwel drē*, or *clamdera rak, nown*: **-ed,** a. *nownek, ogas marow drē nown, storvys, gyllys ysel rag esow*: **-ing,** a. *nownek, dhodho ewl vrās dhe vōs*.
fan, v. *fannya*; f. corn, *gwynsella*: n. *gwynsell*, f., pl. *-ow*.
fanatic, n. *fol drē grysyans, dēn a-grȳs drēs rēson*, m.: **-al,** a. *tom y ben*.
fancy, v., imagine, *tyby, desevos*; to take a whim, *sȳ*: n. *sȳans*, m., pl. *-ow, consay·t, devȳ·s*, m., pl. *-ys, fa·ntasy*, (‡*fancy*) m.; f. dress, **tullwysk*, m.
fang, n. *skyvel*, m., pl. *-vlow, dans hȳr ha lym*.
fantastic, a. *tarosvanüs, pür goynt*: **-asy,** n. *tarosvan*, m., pl. *-now, fa·ntasy*, m., pl. *-s*.
far, a., adv. *pell*, comp. *pella*, super. *an pella*; it is not f., *nyns-yu nep-pell*; f. in, *down*; as f. as, *bys dhe*[2]; as f. as I can, *oll dhe'm gallos, mar vür del wōn*; f.-off, *a-bell*; f. and wide, *ogas ha pell, a-drüs hag a-hēs*; f. away from, *yn pellder dyworth*; from f. away, *adhywo·rth pellder*; not any farther, *na fella*; f. fetched, *coynt, kerghys a-bell*; f. gone, *gyllys ysel*.
farce, n. *gwary fol, g. gēs*, m., pl. *-yow f., g.*
fare, v. *fara*; f. badly, *drōk-f., tebel-f.*: n., food, *bōs, megyans*, m.; for journey, *gober vyajya*, m., pl. *-brow v.*; for ferry, *dynar trēth*, d. *trümach*.
farewell, n. *cümyas*, m.: interj. *farwel*! *Dew genough-why*! *genough farwel*!; bid f., *kemeres cümyas tēk, gasa cümyas gans*.
farm, n. *trē(f)*, f., pl. *trevow, bargen tȳr*, m., pl. *-ys t.*; small f., *godref*, f., pl. *-evy*; dairy f., *hewas*, m.; f. house, *chȳ-tȳak*, m., pls. *-ow, treven, t.*: v. *gonys tȳr*, **amēthy*: **-er,** n. *tȳak*, m., pls. *-yogyon, -yogow*; f's. wife, *tyeges*, f., pl. *-ow*: **f.-stead,** n. (winter), permanent f., *gwavas*; (summer), dairy f., *hewas* (*havos*), m.: **f.-yard,** n. *garth*, m. or f., **büarth*, m. or f., pl. *-ow*.

farrier, n. *hernyor,* m., pl. *-yon, ferror,* m., pl. *-yon.*
farrow, v. *porghelly.*
fart, v. *bramma*: n. *bram,* m., pl. *bremmyn.*
farthing, n. *hanter-demma, ferdhyn,* m., pl. *-now*; land f., 30 acres, *ferdhyn tȳr.*
fascinate, v. *hüda, sona, dynya*: **-ting,** a. *hüdol*: **-tion,** *hüs,* m.
fashion, n. *gȳs,* m., pl. *-yow, maner,* f., pl. *-ow, facyon,* m., pl. *-s*: v. *shapya, formya*: **-able,** a. *herwyth an gȳs.*
fast, v. *penys, sevel orth bōs, orth ün prȳs*; for long time, *hȳrbenys*: a., adv. *üskys, fast, tōth brās, tōth da* or *ta, totta·, gans mür a dōth, mēn, yn-fēn, pür dhewha·ns, *büan*; cling f., *glena hardlych*; tight, firm, *fast, stak, tyn, yn-kelmys*; make f., *cachya, fasthē·, fastya*: **-en,** v. *takkya, fastya, lathya, kelmy*; f. in one place, *staga*; bolt, *prenna, barya*: **-ened,** a. *stak, clōs, kelmys, yn-kelmys, takkyes*: **-ening,** n. *kevren,* f., pl. *-yon, colm,* m., pl. *-ow, colmen,* f., pl. *-now, sygen,* f., pl. *-now, *ēry,* m., pl. *-ow*: **-ing,** n. *penys,* m.
fastidious, a. *precyous, ēs y dhyflasa.*
fat, a. *tew, kȳgek, †bor, ‡berryk, fat*; greasy, *blonegek*; to grow f., *kȳga*: n. *blonek,* m.: **-ness,** n. *tewder, ‡berry,* m.: **-ten,** v. *tewhē·, pesky.*
fatal, a. *-mernans, -ancow, *marwyl*: **-ity,** n. *mernans, ancow, *marwoleth,* m.
fate, n. *destnans,* m., *ran,* f., pl. *-now, *tenkys,* f.; chance, *hap,* m.; ill-f.d, *anfüsek.*
father, n. *tās,* m., pl. *-ow, sȳra,* m., pl. *sȳryow, car,* m.; f. in God, *tasek,* m., pl. *-ygyon*; having same f., *ündas*; f.-in-law, *sȳra-da,* m., pl. *sȳrys-da, †whygeran,* m.; in a fatherly manner, *ave·l t., kepar· ha t.*
father-lasher, n., fish, *calken,* f., pl. *-now.*
fathom, n. *gourhēs,* m.: v. *gourhēsa.*
fatigue, v. *squytha, lafürya*: n. *squythans, squythter,* m.: **-d,** a. *squyth, squythys, lafüryes.*
fault, n. *fowt, defow·t,* m., pl. *-ow, cam, blām,* m.; to lay the f. on, *gothvos blam dhe*[2]; to find f. with, *blamya, keredhy*; it is not my f., *nyns-oma-vy dhe vlamya*; f.-finding, *crothak, ow-whylas fowtow, a-gar cably*: **-less,** a. *hep fowt, dynam, dyflam*: **-lessly,** adv. *hep fowt*; f. wrought, *fȳn-gonedhys.*
favour, n. *dader,* m., *rās,* m., pl. and abst. *-ow, grē,* m., *grās,* m., pl. *-ys, fortyn,* m., *favour,* m.; speak in f. of, *kewsel gans, k. gēr da rak*; I am in f. of that, *da yu genef henna*: v. *fortynya, favera*: **-rable,** a. *da, 'vās, dhe lēs*: **-rite,** a. *drüth, moyha kerys, cüf*; f. son, *mab-rās*: n. *cüf,* m., pl. *-yon*; my f. flower, *an-vlejen üs genef an gwella-oll.*
fawn, v. *fecla.*
fawn, n. *yorghyk,* m., pl. *-ghesygow, †lugh ewyk,* m.: **f.-coloured,** a. *gell.*
fealty, n. **fēouta,* m.
fear, v. *owna, perthy own, bōs own dhe*[2], *dowtya*; I f., *yma· dowt dhym, own a-m-büs*; I f. he will do it, *yma· dowt dhym ef dh'y wül*: n. *dowt, own,* m.; for f. that, *rag own*: **-ful,** a. *üthek*; afraid, *ownek*: **-less,** a. *dyown, hep(b) own, colonnek, harth*: **-lessness,** n. *colonnekter,* m.
feasible, a. *a-ȳl bōs gwrēs, a-yllyr y wül, *hewül.*
feast, v. *gōlya*; f. together, *kyfvewa*: n. *kyfvewy,* m., pl. *-ow, *fest,* f., pl. *-ow*; parish f., *fery,* m.; celebrate, give f., *gōlya*: **f.-day,** n. *dēgōl,* m., pl. *-yow*: **feastentide,** n. *gōlwyth,* m.: **feaster,** n. *kyfvewyas,* m., pls. *-ysy, kyfvewyow.*
feather, n. *plüven,* f., pl. *-now,* col. *plüf*; small or undeveloped f., *plüvyn,* m., pl. *-now*; small f's., down, **manblüf,* col.: v. *gorra plüf (dhe nȳth)*: **f.-bed,** n. *gwely-plüf,* m., pl. *-yow-p.*: **-ed,** a. *plüvak*; **f.-less,** a. *dyblüf, lom, mōl*; **f.-pillow,** n. *plüvak,* f., pl. *-vogow.*
feature, n. *tremyn,* m., *tra,* neut., pl. *taclow*; attributes, *tȳthy,* col.
February, n. *Whevrer, mȳs-Wh.,* m.
federation, n. *ünyans,* m., pl. *-ow.*
fee, n. *gober,* m., pl. *-brow*; fief., *fē,* m.
feeble, a. *dyfrēth, lȳth, gwan, faynt, *ydhyl*: **-ness,** n. *dyfrethter, gwander, ‡gwanegreth,* m.
feed, v. *maga*; of cattle, *pory, pesky*; of animals, mill, etc., *bosa*: **-ing,** n. *pask, megyans,* m.
feel, v., by touch, *handla, tava*; of senses, *tastya, clewes*; of health, *omglewes*; emotion, *kemeres, perthy, prevy*; be of opinion, *synsy*; f. oneself, *omsynsy*; f. the way, *mōs yn ün dava, *palvala*: **-ing,** n. *colon, pyteth, denseth, natureth,* m.
feign, v. *fükya, fecla, faynya, omwül, ‡dyssembla*: **-ed,** a. *fekyl, faynys*: **-ing,** a. *fekyl*; f. demeanour, *fekyl chēr,* m.: n. *fayntys, falsury,* m.
feint, n. *fayntys, *fük,* m., pl. *fügyon.*
felicity, n. *gwynvȳs, *fely·cyta,* m.
fell, v. *gül dhe godha, trēghy dhe'n dōr.*

fellmonger, n. *cronor*, m., pl. *-yon*.

felloe, n. **cammek*, f., pl. *-egow*.

fellow, n. *gwas*, m., pl. *gwesyon*, dim. *gwesyk*, m., pls. *-ygow*, *-yonygow*, *coweth*, m., col. *-a*, *mata*, *pollat*, *chet*, m., pl. *-tys*; with poss. pron., *hynsa*, m. and pl.; abusively, *jaudyn*, m., pl. *-s*; fine f., *pollat brās*; match, *par*, m., pl. and abst. *-ow*; as prefix, *kes-*, *ken-*, etc., e.g., f.-Christian, *kescrystyon*; f.-member, *kenēsel*, m., pl. *-nysyly*; f.-creature, with poss. pron., *hynsa*, m. and pl.: **-ship,** n. *felshyp*, *cowetha*, *cowethyans*, m., *cowethas*, f., pl. *-ow*.

felon, n. *felon*, m., pl. *-s*, *drok-oberor*, m., pl. *-yon*: **-y,** n. *camwyth*. m., *drok-ober* m. pl. *ow*.

felt, n. **lüfban*, m.

female, n. *benenrȳth*, *benow*, f. and col.

feminine, a. **gwrēgyl*, *gwrēgek*; prefix, *benen-*: **-nity,** n. *gwregoleth*, m.

fen, n. *kersek*, f., pls. *-egow*, *-egy*, *cors*, f., pls. *-ow*, *kersy*, *kenak*, f., pls. *-negow*, *-negy* *kenegen*, f., pl. *-now*, *heskyn*, m., pl. *-now*, *gwern*, f., pls. *-ow*, *-y*.

fence, v., with swords, **skyrmya*, *gwary gans cledha*, *omgledhevya*; enclose, *kēas*: n. *kē*, m. pl. *-ow*, *payl*, m., pl. *-ys*: **-cing,** n. *gwary cledha*, *defnyth kē*. m.

fender, n. *kē-olas*, m., pl. *-ow-o*.

fennel, n. †*fenokel*, m.

ferment, v. *brogesy*, *gwȳtha*: n. *tervans*, *burm*, m.: **-ation,** n. *gwȳth*, m.

fern, n. *redenen*, f., col. *reden*; oak-f., *redenderow*, *reden-gwȳth*; royal f., *reden an myghte·rn*: **f.-brake,** n. *redenek*, f., pls. *-egow*, *-egy*: **f.-covered,** a. *redenek*.

ferocious, a. *gwyls*, *garow*: **-ity,** n. *hakter*, f., *garowder*, m.

ferret, n. *conna-gwyn dof*, m., pl. *-nas d.*, †*yewgen*, f., pl. *-as*.

ferruginous earth, n. *gossen*, f.

ferry, n. *trēth*, m., pl. *-yow*; f. boat, *keybal*, *scath-trēth*, m.; f. way, *keybalhens*, m., pl. *-y*; f. man, *trēthor*, m., pl. *-yon*: v. *trētha*.

fertile, a. *fȳth*, *rych*, *da*; to be f., *sowyny*: f. ground, *gwrēsen*, f., pl. *-now*: **-ility,** n. †*gwalsowas*, **fȳthter*, m.

fervour, n. *gwrēs*, f., *frethter*, *tān colon*, m.: **-vent,** a. *gwrēsek*, **tēr*, *frēth*.

fester, v. *crüny*, **gory*, *pedry*: **-ing,** a. *podrethek*: n. *podrethes*, **gōr*, m.

festival, n. *gōl*, *degol*, m., pl. *-yow*.

festive, a. *lowen*: **-vity,** n. *lowender*, m.

fetch, v. *hedhes*, *kerghes*; f. a good price, *hedhes dhe brȳs da*.

fetid, a. *mousak*, *flērys*, *flēryüs*; of breath, *pōs*: **-ness,** n. *flēr*, *flērynsy*, m.

fetter, n. *carghar*, m., pl. *-ow*; of animal, *spral*, m., pl. *-low*: v. *carghara*; of animals, *spralla*.

feud, n. *cās*, **corrosy*, m.

feudal, a. *kēth*; f. tenure, *agomarghogyon*; f. estate, *fē*, m.; f. service, *gwaso·nȳeth*, f.; to pay f. service to, *gül danjer dhe*².

fever, n. *fevyr*, m., pl. *-s*; tertian ague, *terthen*, f., pl. *-now*; ague, *cleves-sēson*, m., pl. *-vejow-s*.

feverfew, n. †*les-derth*, m.

few, a. *nebes*, *tanow*, *boghes*: n. *boghes*, m.

fib, n. *gow*, m., pl. *-yow*, *whethel*, m., pl. *-thlow*: v. *leverel gow*.

fiancé, n. *dēn yowynk*, m., *myrgh yowynk*, f.

fiasco, n. *meth*, m., pl. and abst. *mothow*.

fickle, a. *brottel*, **hedro*; f. person, fig., *padel-ynken*, f., pls. *-llow*, *-lly y*.

fiction, n. *fayntys*, *whethel desmygys*, m.: **-itious,** a. **fük*, *fals*.

fiddle, n. †*fyl*, m., pl. *-lys*, *crowd*, m., pl. *-ys*, †*harfel*, m., pl. *-low*: v. *gwary fyl* or *crowd*: **-r,** n. *crowder*, m., pl. *-s*, †*fyllor*, m., pl. *-yon*, f., †*fyllores*, pl. *-ow*, †*harfellor*, m., pl. *-yon*.

fiddlesticks! int. *tety-valy*!; impolitely, *bram an gath*!

fidelity, n. *lendury*, *lēlder*, *lēldury*, m.

fidget, v. *remüvya*, *omwe·n*, *fysla*: n. *fyslak*, m.

fie! int. *agh*! *fȳ*! *fȳ dhyso*!; to cry f. upon, *fȳa*.

fief, n. *fē*, m., pl. *-ys*.

field, n. *park*, m., pl. *-rcow*, *mȳ*, f., pl. *-ow*; enclosure, *kew*, f., pl. *-yow*; open, arable, or battle f., *gwēl*, m., pl. *-yow*; meadow, *prās*, m., pl. *-ow*; stitch, *lȳn*, f., pl. *-yon*.

fieldfare, n. *molgh lās*, f., pl. *-as l.*

field-marshal, n. *lewyth gwēl*, m., pl. *-ydhyon g.*

fiend, n. *jevan*, m., *dyawl*, m., pl. *dewolow*: **-ish,** a. *dyawlak*: **-ishness,** n. *dewlüjy*, m.

fierce, a. *fell*, *hager*, *gōth*, *gwyls*, *garow*: **-ness,** n. *garowder*, *fellder*, m.

fiery, a. *tanek*, *a dān*.

fife, n. *tollcorn*, m., pl. *tollkern*.

fifteen, n., a. *pymthek*: **-th,** a. *pymthegves*.

fifth, n., a. *pympes*.

fifty, n., a. *hantercans*, *dēk ha deugans*: **-tieth,** n., a. *degves ha deugans*.

fig, n. *fygesen,* f., col. *fyges*; dried f., *fygesen ledan*; f. tree, *gwedhen fyges,* f., †*fykbren,* m.; I don't care a f. for him, *anodho my ny-rōf oy, my ny-synsaf anodho ün faven gōk, anodho my ny-settyaf gwelen-gala.*
fight, v. *o·mlath*; f. a battle, *batēlyas*; f. with fists, etc., *omknoukya*: n. *cās,* f., pl. *-ow, o·mlath,* m., pl. *-adhow, batēl,* f., pls. *-lys, -yow.*
figure, n. *fygūr,* m., †*furf,* f., pl. *-vyow*; numeral, *nvveren,* f., **awgrym,* m.: v. *fygūra, nyvera.*
figwort, n. *scaw-dowr,* col.
filbert, n. *knofen lowarth,* f., col. *know l.*
file, n. *lȳf,* m., pl. *-yvyow*; line, *rēs,* f., pl. *-yow, stüs,* f., pl. *-ow*; in f., *yn ün rew*: v. *lyvya*: **-lings,** n. *lyvyon,* pl.
fill, v. *lenwel, collenwel*; f. with, *lenwel a*[2].
fillet, n. *fünen, lysten,* f., pl. *-now,* †*snod,* m., pl. *-ys*; of meat, *golyth,* m., pl. *-yon*; of fish, *skēthen,* f., pl. *-now.*
filly, n. *eboles,* f., pl. *-ow.*
film, n. *kennen,* f., pl. *-now.*
filter, n. **sythel,* m., pl. *-thlow*: v. *sygera, *sythla.*
filth, n. *most, last,* m., pl. *-yon*; *mostethes, plosethes, lastethes, caugh, vȳlta, harlotry,* m.; on sheep's wool, clothes, etc., *cagal,* m.: **-y,** a. *plos, lōs, mostys,* ‡*mostethüs*; f. person, *plosek,* m., pl. *-ygyon, ploswas,* m., pl. *-wesyon*; f. person or thing, *plos,* m., pl. *-syon*; to get f., *omvostya, omgagla.*
fin, n. *askel pysk,* f., pl. *eskelly p.*
final, a. *dewetha*: **-ly,** adv. *gordheweth, oteweth.*
finance, n. *arghanso·rȳeth,* f., **fyna·ns,* m., *skȳans,* or *gallos, arghans,* m.: v. *provya arghans rak*: **-cial,** n. *arghansek, *fynancyal*: **-cier,** n. *arghanser,* m., pl. *-yon.*
finch, n. **tynk,* m., pl. *-ncas.*
find, v. *cafos,* ‡*trovya*; f. out, *desmygy*; f. by study, provide, *cafos*: n. **desmyk,* m., *an pyth üs kefys.*
fine, v. *spala*: n. *spāl,* m., pl. *-yow, amendys,* pl. *fȳn,* m., pl. *-ys*: a. *precyous, gay, tēk, bryntyn, brāf*; delicate, slender, *mōn*; clear, refined, *fȳn, tēr, pür*; to make f., *afȳna, tēkhē·*; f. fellow, *smat, pollat,* m., pl. *-tys*; f. weather, **hynon,* f.; to become f., **hynony*: **-ly,** adv. *fȳn, precyous, jentyl*: **-ness,** n. *tanowder, terder,* m.: **-nery,** n. *tekter, dyllas brāf,* m.
finger, n. *bȳs,* m., pl. *besyas*; thumb, *bȳs-brās*; 1st f., *bȳs a-rag*; 2nd f., *bȳs-crēs*; 3rd f., *peswera bȳs, bȳs-bysow*; 4th f., *bȳs-bȳghan*; nicknames, thumb, *crakkya-lewen*; 1st f., *lykkya-soresyow*; 2nd f., *dybry-whygen*; 3rd f., *degy-tegen*; little f., *ola-trūan*: v. *bȳsya*: **f.-ring,** n. *bysow,* m., pl. *-sewow*: **f.-stall,** n. *bysgon (bysken),* f., pl. *-now.*
finish, v. *dewedha, gorfenna, cowlwül, fynsya*: n. *deweth, fynweth, gorfen, pen,* m.; of a chase, *terroja,* m.; before the f., *kens gasa whēl, kens tremena*: **-ed,** a., over, *dü, dē*; complete, *cowlwrēs*; he is f.! *gallas ganso*!
fir, n. *sybwedhen,* f., col. *sybwyth, saben,* f., col. *sap*; f. cone, *aval saben,* pl. *-low s.*
fire, n. *tān,* m., pl. *-ow*; conflagration, *tansys,* m., pl. *-ow, *tan-gwall,* m.; set f. to, *gorra tān yn*; on f., *gans tān*; at, by, near the f., *wor'tan, ryp an olas*: v. *gorra tān yn*; f. a gun, *tenna, dyllo*: **f.-arms,** n. *arvow-tān,* pl.: **f.-brand,** n. *pentan,* m., †*etew,* m., pl. *-y, colyn leskys,* m., pl. *-colys l.*: **f.-engine,** n. *jyn dyfüdhy,* m., pl. *-now d.*: **f.-escape,** n. *dyank a dān,* m.: **f.-irons,** n. *hern tān,* pl.: **f.-place,** n. *olas,* f., pl. *-ow*: **f.-ship,** n. **tanlester,* m., pl. *-lystry*: **f.-shovel,** n. *rēf-tān,* f., pl. *revow-t.*: **f.-wood,** n. *cünys,* col.; place for gathering or storing f., *cünyjek,* f., pls. *-egy, -egow*; to gather f., *cünyssa* (inf. only); abounding in f., *cünyjek*: **f.-works,** *tanow-creft, tegynnow-tān,* pl. *tanwȳth,* m.
firm, a. *fast, tyn, sad, crēf, *ferf*; to make f., *fasthē·, fastya*: **-ly,** adv. *fast, yn-fēn, tyn*: **-ness,** n. *crefter, ferfter,* m.
firmament, n. *ebren,* †*fyrmament,* m.
first, a., n. *kensa*; 1st of month, *Calan* (before *m, Cala*), *dē-Halan,* m.: adv., at f., *wostalleth, kensa*; f. of all, *kens oll*: **-ly,** adv. *yn-kensa*; in the f. place, *y'n kensa lē*: **f.-rate,** a. *bryntyn, rȳal.*
fish, n. *pysk,* m., pl. *puskes* (*puscas*); f.-bone, *drēn,* m., pl. *dreyn*; f.-hook, *hȳk,* m., pl. *hygow, hygen,* f., pl. *-now*; f.-scarer (stone splashed in water), *cabūlen,* f., pl. *-now*; f.-pond, *pysklyn,* f., pl. *-now*; f.-gut, *cowl,* m., pl. *-ow*; f. market, *marghas puskes,* f., pl. *-ow, -ajow, p.*: v. *pyskessa,* inf. only: **-erman,** n. *pyscador, -ajor, dēn an puskes*: **-ing-boat,** n., sailing, *cok,* m., pl. *cūcow*; rowing, *scath-rōs,* f., pl. *-ow r.*: **-ing-frog,** n. *pysk-malan,* m., pl. *puskes-m.*: **-ing-rod,** n. *gwelen pyskessa,* f., pl. *-lysy p.*; hook-rod for cuttle, *gwelen-hȳk*: **-ing tackle,** n. *taclow-pyskessa,* pl.: **f.-monger,** n. *gwer-*

ther puskes, m., pl. *-oryon p.*: **f.-wife,** n. *gwrēk an puskes, gwerthores puskes.*
fissure, n. *crўk*, m., pl. *-ygow, fals*, m., pl. *-ljow*; deep f. in cliffs, *saun*, pl. *-yow.*
fist, n. *dorn*, m., pl. *-ow*, d. *deudhorn.*
fisticuff, n. *boxas*, m., pl. *-esow, tummas*, m., pl. *-ow.*
fit, v. *desedha, kewera, ewna*; match, *fyttya*: n. *shōra*, m., pl. *-ys*; f.s., *drogatty*, m.: a. *ewn, gwyw, compes*; to make f., *ewna, composa, fyttya*; think f., *jujja*: if you think f., *yndella mar peugh plēsyes*: **-ness,** n. *composter, gwywsys, gwywder*, m.: **-ting,** a. *onest, ewn, gwyw*; what is f., *onester*, m.; to be f., *desedha*; it is f., (def. vbs.) *y-coth, y-tegoth, y-teseth*: **-tingly,** adv. *manerlych.*
five, n., a. *pymp*, m., pl. *-ow* (before *woly, -thek, -thegves, pym*): see **fifteen, fifth, fifty.**
fix, v. *settya, lathya, takkya*; decide, *ervўra*: n. *tranjyak*, m.: **-ed,** a. *sad, sevylyak, stak*: **-edly,** adv. *stark.*
flabby, a. *lows, medhel, dyfrēth, *lўth.*
flag, n. *baner*, m., pl. *-ow*; iris, *elestren*, f., col. *elester*; f. marsh, *elestrek*, f., pls. *-egy, -egow*: v. *gwedhra.*
flagon, n. *crüskyn, canna*, m., pl. *-nys.*
flagrant, a. *dyflas, ape·rt.*
flag-ship, n. *gorhel-baner*, m., pl. *-olyon-b.*
flag-stone, n. *lēghven*, m., pl. *-veyn.*
flail, n. *füst*, f., pl. *-ow.*
flake, v. *launya*: n. *laun*, m., pl. *-ow, *scanten*, f., pl. *-now*, col. *scant*; snow-f., *plüven ērgh*, f., pl. *plüf ē.*; foam-f., *ewonen*, f., col. *ewon*: **-ky,** a. *launek, *scantek.*
flame, n. *flam*, m., pl. *-now, *tanflam*, m., pl. *-mow, fakel*, f., pl. *faclow*: v. *dywy, fakly, flāmya, flamma*; burst into f., **tanflamya.*
flank, n. *tenewan*, m., pl. *tenwennow.*
flannel, n. *gwlanen*, f.
flap, v. *trenjya, *flyccra, *flappya*: n. *lappa*, m., pl. *-pys.*
flare, v. *lughesy, dywy*; f. up, *golowy, dewynya, *tanflamya*: n. *torchen*, f., pl. *-now, *tanflam*, m., pl. *-mow, tansys*, m.
flash, v. *lughesy, dewynya*: n., lightning, *lughesen*, f., col. *lughes, *lugh*, m.
flask, n. **costrel*, m., pl. *-s.*
flat, a. *leven, compes, gwastas, plat*; of drink, *marow*: n. *parth chў, ranjy*, f.; mud-f., *lysek*, f., pls. *-egy, -egow.*
flatfish, n. *lўth*, f., pl. *-as.*
flatten, v. *plattya, levenhē·.*
flatter, v. *fēcla, flattra*: **-er,** n. *lo·senjer*, m., pl. *-s*; insincere person, *flattor*, m., pl. *-yon*, f., pl. *-ow, dēn fekyl y jēr, gowek*, m., pl. *-wygyon*: **-ing,** a. *fekyl*: **-y,** n. *fekyl chēr, f. lavarow*, m.
flaunt, v. *dysplētya.*
flautist, n. *pўber*, m., pl. *-oryon.*
flavour, n. *blas*, m., pl. *-ow, sawor*, m., pl. *-yow*; having a good f., *saworek, saworys* or *blesys mās, da y vlas*: v. *blasa, sawory*: **-ing,** n. *saworans*, m.
flaw, n. *nam*, m., pl. *-mow, fowt*, m., pl. *-ow*: **-less,** a. *dynam, hep nam, hep fowt, hep defow·t.*
flax, n. *lyn*, m.; f. plant, *lynen*, f.; f. land, *lyndyr*, m., pl. *-yow*; f. field, *lynek*, f., pl. *-egy.*
flay, v. *dygroghenna, dyscroghenna*: **-ed,** a. *dygroghen, -nys.*
flea, n. *whannen*, f., col. *whyn*; sand f., *whannen-mōr, w.-trēth, morwhannen*; to catch f.s., *whynna* (inf. only): **f.-bitten,** a. *whynnek.*
fledge, v. *plüvya*: **-ling,** n. *ydhnyk*, m., pl. *-ygow.*
flee, v. *gwevya, tēghy, fўa, mōs* or *fўa dhe'n fo.*
fleece, n. *knew*, m., pl. *-yow, k. gwlan*: v. *knyvyas*; fig., *pylla.*
fleet, n. *lu-lystry*, m., pl. *-yow-l*: a. *scaf y drōs, üskys*: **-ing,** a. *scon, a-dremen, üs scaf ow-tremena, nep-pell na-bўs.*
flesh, n. *keher*, m., pl. *-ow, kўk*, m., pl. *-ygow*; piece of f., *keheryn*, m., pl. *-now*; in the f., *yn trogel, kўk yn knēs*: **-y,** a. *keherek, kygek*; to become f., *kўga*: **f.-coloured,** a. *lyw kўk, *kyglyw*: **f.-fork, f.-hook,** n. †*kygver*, m., pl. *-yow.*
flexibility, n. *gwe·thynder*, m.: **-ble,** a. *gwethyn, heblēk, heblyth, plyth.*
flicker, v. *crenna, dascrenna, flamya yn-wan, *flyccra*: n.
flight, n., on wings, *nyj*, m.; escape, *fo, tēgh*, m.; take to f., *mōs* or *fўa dhe'n fo*; put to f., *gorra dhe'n fo, fēsya*; a f. of birds, *hēs*, f., pl. *-ow.*
flimsy, a. *tanow, scaf, brottel*; of textile, *boll.*
flinch, v. *plynchya.*
fling, v. *deghesy, tewlel.*
flint, n. *flynt, mēn-flynt*, m., pl. *meyn f.*, **ca·llester*, m.; strike-a-light, *mēn-tān.*
flippancy, n. *scafter cows*, m.: **-ant,** a. *scaf y davas.*
flit, v. *trenyja*, †*sommys, *gwybya.*

flitch, n. *hanter hogh,* m.
float, v. *nyja*: n. *corkyn*; with sail, to carry fishing tackle out from shore, *lester-cok*: **-ing,** a. *nyjys, üs ow-nyja*: n. *nyj,* m.
flock, n. *para,* m., pl. *-rys, flok,* m., pl. *-kys, tonek,* m., pl. *-egow, bagas,* m., pl. *-ow, bush,* m., pl. *-ys, grē,* f., pl. *-yow*; of birds, *hēs,* f., pl. *-ow*; of sea-birds over fish, *pyl,* m., pl. *-yow*: v., birds, *hēsya*; people, *stēvya*: **-ing,** n. *hevva,* f.
flog, v. *castȳga, scorjya*: **-ging,** n. *castȳk, scorjyans,* m.
flood, n. *lȳf* (*lȳw*), m., pl. *-ow* (*-yvow*); f.-tide, *morlenwel,* inf., *lanwes, lanow,* m.; inundation, *büdhyans, *reverthy,* m., pl. *-ow*: v. *lȳva, büdhy*: **f.-gate,** n. **flosyet,* m., pl. *-tys*: **f.-stream,** n. *lȳf-wōth,* m.
floor, n. *lür,* m.; on the f., along the f., *war lür.*
flounder, v. *lagya, stankya, omdewlel*: n., fish, *lȳth,* f., pl. *-as.*
flour, n. *blēs,* m.: **-y,** a. *blēsek.*
flourish, v. *sowyny, *florsya*; of trees, etc., *glasa*; of sword, *gwevya, shakya*: **-ing,** a. *sowyn, yn poynt da*; of plant, *gwēr, tevys yn-ta, ow-clasa.*
flow, v. *dewraga, denewy, resek*; of tide, *morlenwel*; f. quickly, *frōsa*: n. *lanwes, frōs,* m., pl. *-ow*: **-ing,** a., of tide, *ow-tōs, ow-lenwel*; of hair or garment, *hȳr ha lows.*
flower, n. *blejan,* m., *blejyewen,* f., pl. *-jyow, blejen,* f., pl. *-now, flowr,* f., pl. *-ys,* ‡*flowren,* f., pl. *-now*; choice, prime, *flowr*; f. bed, *blejyowek,* f., pls. *-egy, -egow*: v. *blejyowa*: **-et, floret,** n. *blejennyk,* m., pl. *-jyowygow*: **-ing,** a. *blewjyowek*; a f. tree, *gwedhen yn hy blejyow.*
flue, n., fluff, *brēghy,* pl.; for smoke, **tuel chymbla,* m.
fluency, n. *frēthter,* m.: **-nt,** a. *frēth, helavar, ow-resek.*
fluff, n. *manblüf, plüf münys,* col., *brēghy,* pl.
fluid, a. *devrak*: n. *lyn, glybor,* m.
fluke, n. *hap*; of anchor, *paw,* m., pl. *-yow*; liver f., *eyles,* m.
flunkey, n. †*dēn coscar,* m., pl. *tüs c.*
fluor-spar, n. *can,* m.
fluster, v. *serry.*
flute, n. †*whybonol,* f., pl. *-ow*; f. anglaise, *recorda,* m., pl. *-dys.*
flutter, v. *trenyja*: n., in a f., *amay·s.*
fly, v. *nyja*; let f., *deghesy, dyllo*: n. *kelyonen,* f., col. *kelyon*; small f., *gwyban,* f., pl. *-as*; bluebottle f., *kelyonen kȳk*; full of f's., *kelyonek*: **f.-paper,** **dygelyoner*: **f.-blown,** a. *kentrenys*: **-ing,** n. *nyj,* m.
foal, n. *ebol,* m., pls. *-ylyon, ebylly*: v. *cüy.*
foam, n. *ewon,* f.; f. flake, *ewonen,* f.: v. *ewony*: **-ing, -y,** a. *ewonek.*
focus, n. *fōk,* f., pl. *fogow*: v. *drȳ dhe ewn fōk.*
fodder, n. *bōs lonnow, megyans bestes,* m.
foe, n. *escar,* m., pl. *yskerens, envy,* m. and pl.
fog, n. *newl,* m., pl. *-ow*; rising from water, *lewgh,* m.; f. bank, *newlen,* f., pl. *-now*: **-gy,** a. *newlek, tew, lewghek.*
foil, v. *lettya.*
fold, n. *plēk,* m., pl. *-egow*; for sheep, *corlan,* f., pl. *-now*: v. *plegya, *gwarya*; f.ed paper, †*gwarak,* f., pl. *-yegow*: **-able,** a. *heblek, heblyth.*
foliage, n. *dēl,* col., *glasans, glasneth,* m.
folk, n. *pobel,* f., pl. *-blow, tüs,* f., used as pl. of *dēn*: **-lore,** n. *dyscans ha hengovyon an bobel.*
follow, v. *sewya, holya, mōs* or *dōs warle·rgh,* ‡*folya*; f. example of, *gül warle·rgh*; f. clue, *hellerghy*: **-er,** n. *holyer,* m., pl. *-yoryon, sewyer,* m., pl. *-yoryon, sewyas,* m., pl. *-ysy*; disciple, *dyskybel,* m., *-blon, -blyon, dyscypel,* m., pl. *-plys, *dywys,* m., pl. *-yon*; courting, *draylyer,* m., pl. *-yoryon*: **-ing,** n., persons, *mēny,* m., *coscar,* col.: a. *warle·rgh, a-sew, üs ow-sewya.*
folly, n. *folneth, müscotter, gokyneth, foly, nȳ·cyta,* m.
foment, v. *tomma, golghy gans yly tom*; instigate, *sordya.*
fond, a. *cryjyk yn-fol, dōtyes*; loving, *caradow*; be f. of, *dōtya war*[2], *cara*; he is f. of swimming, *da* or *mal yu ganso nyja*: **-ness,** n. *kerensa,* f., *dōtyans,* m.
fondle, v. *chersya,* ‡*byrla, *dorlosa.*
font, n. *bysythven,* m., pl. *-veyn.*
food, n. *bōs, sosten, megyans,* m.: **-less,** a. *dyvōs, yn dyvotter, hep sosten.*
fool, n. *fol,* m., pl. *felyon,* f. *-es,* pl. *-ow, pen-brās, pen-bronnen, pen-pyst,* m., pls. *-now-b., -bron, -p., foul,* m., pl. *-ys, müscok,* m., pl. *-cogyon, müscogen,* f., pl. *-now, scogyn,* m., pl. *-now, bobba,* m., pl. *-bys*; act like a f., *dōtya*: **-ish,** a. *fol, sempel, goky*; grow f., *foly*: **-ishness,**: see **folly.**
foot, n. *trōs,* m., pl. *treys,* d., *deudrōs*; of animal, *paw,* m., pl. *-yow,* d. *deubaw*; measure, *trōs-hēs,* m.; f. rule, *scantlyn,* m., pl. *-s*; foot-sole, *gothen,* f., pl. *-thnow,* d. *dywwothen*; person with big feet, *trosak,* m., pl. *-sogyon*: **f.-ball,** n. *pēl-drōs,* f. pl.,

-yow-trōs: **-ed,** a., large f., *trosak*; three f., *trythrōs*: **f.-fall,** n. *son trōs,* m., pl. *-yow treys*: **f.-hold,** n. *trosla,* m., pl. *-ow*: **f.-path,** n. *kerthva,* f., pl. *-ow,* †*trūlergh,* m., pl. *-ow*: **f.-print,** n. *ōl trōs,* m., pl. *-ow treys*: **f.-step,** n. *ōl* or *son trōs,* m.: **f.-stool,** n. *scavel-drōs,* f., pl. *-low-treys*: **f.-wear,** n. †*arghenas,* m.

for, prep. *rak(g), dhe²*; f. being . . ., *er bones* . . .; f. that end, *yn henna*; mourn f., etc., *kyny,* etc., *warle·rgh*; f. ever, *bys vyken, vynary*: f. one month, *drēs ün mȳs*; (he acts) f. him, *yn y lē*; fie f. shame! *fȳ dhys rak meth!*: conj., *rak, awo·s.*

forbear, v. *godhaf, godhevel, perthy, pa·r(a)gh*: **-ance,** n. *godhevyans, perthyans,* m.: **-ing,** a. *ow-codhaf mür, pell ow-perthy.*

forbid, v. *dyfen*: **-ding,** a. *hegas*: n. *dyfen, dyfennadow,* m.

force, n. *nerth, nell, crȳs, maystry, fors,* m.; armed f., *nerth,* m., pl. *-ow*; f. of speech, document, etc., *vertu,* m.; by f., *drē nerth, drē hakter*: v. *ynny, constrȳna*; f. way into, *cropya, herdhya*: **-cibly,** adv. *drē hakter, drē nerth, gans mür-grȳs* or *mür a grȳs.*

forceps, n. *gevel vȳghan,* f., pl. *-yow b., pynsor,* m., pl. *-s.*

ford, n. *res,* f., pl. *-yow, basdowr,* m., pl. *-ow,* **rojyth* (*roswyth*), m., pl. *-wydhow.*

fore, a., adv. and prefix, *rak(g)*; prefix, *dar-.*

foreboding, n. **ragown,* m., **darogan,* f.

forecast, v. *ragleverel, ragweles,* **darleverel,* **darogana*: n. *darogan,* f., *raglavar,* m., pls. *-ow.*

forecastle, n. †*flūr-rak, castel a-rak,* m.

forefather, n. *hendas,* m., pl. *-ow, hengok,* m., pl. *-ogyon.*

forefinger, n. *bȳs a-rak* (*b. rag*), m., pl. *besyas a.*

forego, v. *mōs* or *bōs kens*: **-ing,** a. *üs gorrys kens*: **-gone,** a., f. conclusion, *tra a-ȳl bōs ervȳrys hep dustüny*: see **forgo.**

forehead, n. *tāl,* m., pl. *-yow*; top of f., *corn tāl,* m.; having a large f., *talek.*

foreign, a. *tramor, estrennek, astra·nj*: **-er,** n. *estren,* m., pl. *-yon,* f., *-ēs,* pl. *-ow, perghyryn,* m., pl. *-as, alyon,* m., pl. *-s.*

foreman, n. *chȳf-gwȳthor,* m., pl. *-yon.*

foremast, n. *gwern a-rak,* f., pl. *-ow a.*

foremost, a. *kensa.*

forenoon, n. *kensewha,* m.

forerunner, n. **ragrēsor,* m., pl. *-yon,* **ragresegyth,* m., pl. *-ydhyon, e·rberjour,* m., pl. *-s.*

foresee, v. **ragweles*: **-sight,** n. **ragwēl, provȳans,* m.

forest, n. *cōs,* m., pl. *-ow, coswyk,* f., pl. *-ygow, forest,* m., pl. *-ys*; f. land, *gwylfos, dyfȳthcos,* m.: **-er,** n. **forstor,* m., pl. *-yon.*

forestage, n., naut., †*flūr-rak,* m.

forestall, v. *preventya, lettya.*

foretaste, n. *ragvlas,* m.

foretell, v. *profüsa,* **darogan,* **darleverel,* **ragarwedha.*

forethought, n. *rakpreder,* m.

forewarned, a., be f.! *darwar!*; f. is forearmed, *dēn üs gwarnyes a-omhernes.*

forfeit, v. *gasa yn gaja, kelly, hepcor*: n. *gaja,* m., pl. *-jys, spāl,* m., pl. *-yow.*

forge, v. *govelya*; falsify, *supposya, gül falsury*: n. *gelforn,* f., pl. *-ow, fōk,* f., pl. *-ogow, tanjy,* m., pl. *-ow*: **-ry,** n. *fük, falsury, scryfa gow,* m.

forget, v. *ankevy, gasa a'n covath, g. a'y gōf*: **-ful,** a. *gwan y gōf, dygof*: **-fulness,** n. *ancōf,* m., *ancofva,* f.: f.-me-not, n. **scorpyonles,* **porth-cōf-ahanaf-vy.*

forgive, v. *gava* (*dhe²*), ‡*pardona*: **-ness,** n. *gyvyans,* m.: **-ing,** a. *parys dhe ava.*

forgo, v. *hepcor.*

fork, n. *forgh,* f., pls. *fergh(y)*; tree, etc., **gaul,* f., pl. *-ow*; 3-pronged f., *forgh tȳrforgh*; table f., *forgh arghans*; of roads, *forth dybarth,* f., pl. *-dhow d.*: v. *dyberth, falsa*: **-ed,** a. *forghek,* **gaulak, felsys.*

forlorn, a. *omdhevas, gesys, kellys.*

form, n., shape, *form,* f., pl. *-ow,* ‡*gwra,* m., ‡*shāp,* m., pl. *-ys,* †*furf,* f., pl. *-vyow*; order, *composter,* ‡*rōth,* m.; bench, *form,* m., pl. *-ys*; f. of hare, *growethva f.*: v. *formya, shapya, gül*: **-ation,** n. *formyans,* m., pl. *-ow*: **-ed,** a., well-f., *gwrēs yn-tēk, fythüs*: **-er,** n., maker, *formyer,* m., pls. *-yoryon*: **-less,** a. *dyslyw,* ‡*hep rōth.*

former, a. *kens*: **-ly,** adv. *kens, solabrȳ·s.*

formidable, a. *garow, üthek.*

forsake, v. *gasa, forsakya.*

forsooth! interj. *yn prōf! dhe wȳr! forsōth!*

forswear, v. *nagha, hepcor*; f. oneself, *gowlȳa.*

fort, n. *kēr,* f., pl. *-row*; hill-f., *dyn,* m., pl. *-yon, dynas,* m., pl. *-ow*: **-tification,** n. **kērwyth,* m.: **-tified,** a. *kērek, kērys*: **-tify,** v. *crefhē·, nertha, kēry*; f. spirits, *confortya.*

forth, adv. *yn-rak*; out, *yn-mēs, mēs.*

forthright, a. *frēth, ewn yn-rak.*

forthwith, adv. *dyson, hep ardak, hep hokkya, desempys, a-dhesempys.*

fortitude, n. *colonnekter, perthyans,* m.

fortnight, n. *dyw seythen,* f.

fortune, n. *fortyn,* m., *ran,* **füs,* f.: **-nate,** a. *gwynvȳs, gwyn ow bȳs,* etc., †*füsyk*: **-nately,** adv. *yn gwella prȳs, drē hep da.*

forty, a., n. *deugans*: **-tieth,** a., n. *deugansves.*

forward, adv., direction, *war-rak*; motion, *yn-rak*: v. *spēdya, danvon pella.*

fossil, -ized, a. *trēlyes yn mēn*: n. *tra kens esa yn-few, ha lemmyn üs gyllys yn mēn.*

foster, v. *maga,* †*mēthryn*: f. daughter, *myrgh-mēthryn,* f., pl. *-es-m.*; f. father, †*tasveth,* m., pl. *-ow*; f. mother, *mammeth,* f., pl. *-ow*; f. son, *map-mēthryn,* m., pl. *mebyon-m.*: **-ing,** n. *mēth,* m.

foul, a. *plos, lōs, hager, mostys*; of wool, etc., *caglys*; by f. means, *drē hakter*: v. *mostya, hagry,* **stronga*; naut. *resek erby·n*; f. anchor, *ancar camgelmys,* m.: **-ness,** n. *plos(ethes), most(ethes), last(ethes), vylta, harlotry, caugh,* m.; on wool, etc., *cagal,* m.; fetidness, *flerynsy,* m.

found, v., lay foundations, *grondya, fundya, sēlya*; metal, *tedha*; **-ation,** n. *sol,* m., *sēl,* f., pls. *-yow, grond, fundasyon,* m.; f. stone, **selven,* m., pl. *-veyn, men lür,* m., pl. *meyn lür*; of institution, *fundyans,* **sēlyans,* m.: **-er,** v. *büdhy, sedhy*: n. *fundyer,* m., pl. *-yoryon*; of metal, *tedher,* m., pl. *-oryon*: **-ing,** n., of institution, *fundyans,* m.: **-ling,** n. *flogh kefys*: **-ry,** n. *tethla, tethty,* m.; *tethva,* f.

fountain, n. *fenten,* f., pl. *-tynyow*; f. pen, *plüven-fenten,* f., pl. *-now-f.*

four, a., n. *peswar,* f. *peder*; f. times, *pedergwyth*: **f.-fold,** a. *peswarplēk*: **f.-footed,** a. *peswarpaw,* ‡*peswartrosek*: **f.-score,** a., n. *peswarügans*: **-th,** a., n. *peswera.*

fourteen, a., n. *peswardhek*: **-th,** a., n. *peswardhegves.*

fowl, n., domestic, *yar,* f., pl. *yēr*; wild f., *edhen wyls,* f., pl. *ydhyn gwyls*; f. house, *yarjy,* m., pl. *-ow*: **-er,** n. *ydhynor,* m., pl. *-yon,* †*ydhnē,* m., pl. *-nȳon*: **-ing,** n., to go f., †*ydhna* (inf. only).

fox, n. *lowarn,* m., pl. *lewern, lostek,* m., pl. *-togas*; f. hole, *toll lowarn,* m., pl. *tell lewern.*

foxglove, n. ‡*manek lowarn,* ‡*manek rüth,* **manegow an spyrysyon,* pl.

fraction, n. *ran,* f., pl. *-now, darn,* m., pl. *-ow.*

fracture, n. *torva,* f., **tor,* m., pl. *-yow*: v. *terry.*

fragile, a. *hedor, hedrogh.*

fragment, n. *brewyonen,* f., pl. *brewyon, tam,* m., pl. *tymmyn,* dim. *temmyk,* m., pls. *-ygow, tymmynygow, browsyonen,* f., pl. *browsyon,* col. *brows, darn,* m., pl. *-ow,* dim. **dernyk,* m., pls. *-ygow, darnowygow*; cut up f., *dyvyn,* m., pl. *-yon*; f. of wood, chip, *scommyn,* pl. *scommow.*

fragrance, n. *sawor,* m., pl. *-yow, ēth,* m., pl. *-ow*: **-ant,** a. *saworek, whēk ȳ glewes.*

frail, a. *brottel, gwan,* **ȳdhyl*: **-ty,** n. *gwander,* ‡*gwanegreth,* m.

frame, n. *frām,* m., pl. *-ys,* **starn,* f., pl. *-yow*; for fishing line, *canter,* m., pl. *-trow*; mining, ‡*stūl,* m., pl. *-ys*; for mould-board of plough, **branel,* m., pl. *-low*: v. *frāmya, formya*: **f.-work,** n. *clōs,* f., pl. *-ojow, frām,* m.

France, n. *Frynk,* f.

franchise, n. *franchȳs,* m.

frank, a. *frank*; to be f., *leverel dhe blemmyk*: **-ly,** adv. *hep tull na gȳl, heb y dȳ, hep tȳ-vyth na gowlȳa.*

frankincense, n. †*enkys, frankyncens,* m.

frantic, a. *mēs a'y rewl, conneryak, maga füscok ave·l tarow.*

fraternal, a. *-broder, -breder,* **broderek, a vroder*: **-nity,** n. *bredereth,* m.

fraternise, v. *kescowethya.*

fraud, n. *tull, fraus,* m.; he's a f., *falsgwas yu*: **-ulent,** a. *drē dull, fals, gow.*

fray, v. *üsya, früdha, nüja, crybella*: n. *bresel,* m., pl. *-yow, omlath,* m., pl. *-adhow*: **-ed,** a. *üsyes*; f. edge of cloth, *pyllen,* f.

freak, n. *coyntys, ancothfos,* m.; person, *dēn coynt,* m., pl. *tüs c.*: **-ish,** a. *coynt, ancoth.*

freckle, n. *brythen,* f., pl. *-now,* col. *brȳth, brēgh,* m., pl. *-ow*: **-d,** a. *brȳth, brēgh, brythennek.*

free, a. *rȳth, quyt, frank, dygabester, dyspral, hep cost, dhe wary*; to go f., *mōs dhe wary*: v. *delyfrya, lyfrya,* ‡*frȳa, dyllo dhe wary*: **-dom,** n. **franchys,* **franketh,* **rȳthsys,* m.: **-ly,** adv. *hep awhe·r, hep ardak, rak travyth.*

freehold, n. *gront trank hep worfen*: **-er,** **franklyn,* m.

freeman, n. *burjes,* m., pl. *-jysy,* **gour-efan,* m., pl. *tüs-e.*

freeze, v. *rewy.*

freight, n. *carg,* m., pl. *-ow.*

French, a. *Frynkek*; F. language, *Frynkek*, m.: **F.-man,** n. *Frynk*, m., pls. *Francas*, *Frynkyon*: **F.-woman,** n. *Frynkes*, f., pl. *-ow.*

frenzy, n. *connar*, f., *müscotter*, m.

frequent, a. *menough*: v. **menoughy*, **darom-res*: **-ly,** adv. *menough*, *yn-fenough*, *lȳes-gwyth.*

fresh, a. *noweth*, *ēr*, **fresk*, ‡*cro*; of weather, *clōr*: **-en,** v. *erhē·*, **nowedhy*: **-ly,** adv. *noweth*, *a-noweth*: **-ness,** n. *ērder*, m.

fret, v. *serry*, ‡*frenna*, **fromma*, **brogha*, **nēghy*: **-ting,** n. *fyenasow*, **nēgh*, m.

friable, a. *hevrew.*

friar, n. *managh*, m., pl. *menegh*, *broder*, m., pl. *breder*, col. *bredereth.*

friction, n. *ruttyans*, *rūt*, m.

Friday, n. *dē* or *du Gwener*, f.; Good F., *de G. an Grows.*

friend, n. *cothman*, m., pl. *-mens*, *coweth*, m., col. *-a*, f. *-es*, pl. *-ow*, *cüf*, m., pl. *-yon*, *car*, m., pl. *kerens*, f. *cares*, pl. *-ow*; addressing a group, ‡*sōs*, m. and pl.: **-liness,** n. *hüvelder*, *colonnekter*, m.: **-ly,** a. *cüf*, *whēk*, *ave·l car*, *hegar*: **-ship,** n. *kerensa*, f.

fright, n. *üth*, *own*, m.; take f., *scüsy*: **-en,** v. *gorra own yn*, *gül üth dhe*^{2}, *ownekhē·*: **-ened,** a. *ownek*, *ownekhēs·*: **-ful,** a. *grysyl*, *üthek*; f. affair, or thing, *üthektra*, m.: **-fully,** adv. *üthek*: **-fulness,** *üthekter*, m.

frigid, a. *ōr*, *pür* or *fest yeyn*: **-ity,** n. *yeynder crēf.*

fringe, n. *pyllen*, f., pl. *-now*; on the f. of, *ryp*, *war oryon a*^{2}: v. *nüja.*

frisk, v. *terlemmel*, *lappya*, *scüsy*: **-y,** a. *jolyf*, *bew.*

fritter, n. *crampedhen*, f., col. *crampeth.*

frivolous, a. *üfer*, *scaf.*

frock, n. *pows gwrēk*, f., pl. *-yow g.*

frog, n. *gwylskyn*, m., pl. *-as*, ‡*quylkyn*, m., pl. *-now*, †*lefans*, m., pl. *lefyns*, *-fanjas.*

frolic, v. *terlemmel*, *hyga*, *gwary*: **-some,** a. *gwarȳek*, *lowenek.*

from, prep. *a*^{2}, *mēs a*^{2}, *dywo·rth*, *a-dhy-wo·rth*, ‡*dhȳa*^{2}, ‡*a-dhȳa*^{2}; cause, *drē*^{2}; with *govyn*, *gothvos*, *orth*; with *gwy·tha*, *scüsy*, *cüdha*, *lesta*, *rak*; f. over, off, *dywa·r*, *a-dhywa·r*; f. under, beneath, *a-dhan*^{2}; f. here, *ahanan*; f. here or now, *alemma*; f. now on, *alemma rak*; f. there or then, *alenna*; f. end to end, *a-hes*, *afȳna*; f. one thing to its opposite, *yn-dar*, e.g., f. wild to mild, *gwyls yn-dar clōr*; f. that it seems, then . . ., *dre henna yth-hevel*, *ytho·* . . .; forth, out, away f., *mēs a*^{2}.

front, n., forehead, f. of house, brow of hill, etc., *tāl*, m., pl. *-yow*; of body, *grüf*, m.; of battle, *voward*, m.; of garment, *lappa*, m., pl. *-pys*; in f., *a-rak*, *a-dhera·k*: a. *a-rak*; f. door, *darras a-rak*, *d. 'rak*: **-ing,** adv. *a-dāl.*

frontier, n., m. *ōr*, f., pl. *-yon.*

frost, n. *rew*, †*yey*, m.: **f.-bite,** n., of fingers, *ewyn-rew*, m.: **f.-bitten,** a. *rewys.*

froth, n. *ewon*, f.: v. *ewony*: **-y,** a. *ewonek.*

frown, n. *plēk tāl*, m.: v. *plegya tāl.*

frowzy, a. *flērys*, *plos-flērys.*

frugal, a. *tanow*, *scant*, *boghes y eva ha dybry*: **-ity,** n. *preder na-vo rē na sculva.*

fruit, n. *frūt*, m. and col., pl. *-ys*; dried f. in general, *fyges*, col.: **-ful,** a. *rych*, †*kevothak*, **fȳth*: **-fulness,** n. †*gwalsowas*, **fȳthter*, m.: **-less,** a. *hep frūt-vyth*; useless, *mogh*, *üfer.*

frustrate, v. *ancombra*, *drȳ dhe goll* or *dhe dravyth*, *lettya*, *lesta*: **-ation,** n. *ancom-brynsy*, *let*, m.

fry, v. *frȳa*: n. *puskesygow*, *puskes byghan*, pl. : **-ing pan,** n. ‡*lejer*, m., pl. *-ow*, *padel-frȳa*, f., pl. *-ly-f.*

fuel, n. *cünyjen*, f., col. *cünys*; of dried cow-dung, *glosen*, f., pl. *-now*, col. *glōs*; place for storing or gathering f., *cünyjek*, f.; to gather f., *cünyssa* (inf. only); abounding in f., *cünyjek.*

fugitive, n. ‡*foesyk*, m.: a. *üs ow-fȳa*; of colour, etc., *brottel.*

fulcrum, n. *colpes*, m., pls. *-ys*, *-ow.*

fulfil, v. *collenwel*, *kewera*: **-ment,** n. *keweras*, m.

full, a. *lün*, *cowal*: adv. *pür*: v. *troghya*: **-er,** n. *troghyer*, m., pl. *-oryon*: **-ing-mill,** n. *melyndroghya* (*-drokkya*), f.: **-ly,** adv. *yn-tȳen*, *yn-tēk*, *cowal*; of time, *playn*: **-ness,** n. *lanwes*, **lanow*, *lünder*, m.

fulminate, v. *tarenna*, *dyllo crak taran*, *bragya*: **-ation,** n. *tarth taran*, *bragyans brās*, m.

fume, v. *megy*, **fromma*, **brogha*: n. *mōk*, m.: **-mitory,** n. *mōk dōr*, m.

fun, n. *gwary*, m.; make f. of, *gēsya*, *gül gēs a*^{2}; what f! *ass-yu hemma gwary tēk*!: **-ny,** a. *wharthüs.*

function, n. *gwythres*, m., pl. *-ow*; it is my f. to do so, *my a-bew*, *ow devar yu*, or *y-long dhym*, *gül yndella.*

fund, n. *pensyon*, m., pl. *-s*; f.s., *arghow.*

fundament, n. *gwen,* m., **rever,* m., pl. *-vrow*: **-al,** a. **selvenek.*
funeral, n. *encledhyas,* m.
furbish, v. *glanhē·, püra, *furpsya.*
fur, n. *ken mȳl,* m., pl. *k. mylas, *pelour,* m.; f. coat, †*pellyst ken.*
furious, a. †*conneryak, mēs a'y rewl, serrys üthek, sōr brās dhodho*: **-ly,** adv. *gans outray.*
furl, v. *plegya, *fardella, kelmy war an delēyow.*
furlong, n. *erowhēs,* m., pl. *-ow.*
furnace, n. *forn,* f., pl. *-ow, fornys,* f., pl. *-yow, fōk,* f., pl. *-ogow.*
furnish, v. *provya, tacla, darbary, dafar, cafos, stoffya*: **-iture,** n. *pyth-chȳ, stoff, dafar,* m., *mebyl,* col., †*gutrēl,* m., pl. *-trolow.*
furrow, n. *trogh,* m., pls. *-ow, trēghyon, fynegel,* f., pl. *-glow, ryll,* m., pl. *-ys*: v. *fynegly*: **-er,** n. *fynegler,* m.
further, adv. *pella*; (not) any f., *na fella*; any f. onward, *rak dodho*: v. *spēdya, avonsya, gweres*: **f.more,** adv. *drēs henna, pella, whath, (ha) gensy.*
furtive, a. *ave·l lader, yn-dan gēl* or *güth*; to be f., *skolkya.*
fury, n. *connar,* f., *sōr brās,* m.
furze, n. *eythynen,* f., col. *eythyn*; common or great f., *eythyn Frynk*; dwarf f., *ethyn dōf*; f. bush, *bagas eythyn,* m., pl. *-ow e.*; f.-hook, *cromman-eythyn,* m., pl. *-ow-e.*; f.-brake, *eythynek,* f., pls. *-egy, -egow*; f.-chat, *chekker-eythyn,* m., pl. *checcras-e.*
fuss, v. *gül son, fysla*; stop f.ing! *gās dha son!*: n. *son,* m., pl. *-yow, frōth,* m., **tryn,* f.; making a f., *ow-cül "clewyeugh" brās*: **-y,** a. *bysy*; f. person, *fyslak,* m., pl. *-logyon.*
futile, a. *üfer, trüfyl, na-dāl oy*: **-ity,** n. *üfereth,* m.
future, n. *termyn a-dhē,* m.; in f., *alemma rak, wosa hemma*: a. *a-dhē, a-sew, üs ow-tōs, a-vȳth wosa hemma.*

G

gabble, v. *clappya, clattra,* †*stlevy*: n. *clap,* m.
gable, n. *tāl (chȳ),* m., pl. *-yow (c.), punyon,* m., pl. *-s.*
gad-fly, n. *kelyonen margh,* col. *kelyon m.,* †*stut,* m., pl. *tys.*
Gael, n. *Gwydhal,* m., pl. *-as*; Scottish, Irish G., *Gwydhal Alban, G. Ywerdhon*: **-ic,** a. *Gwydhalek*; G. lang., *Gwydhalek,* m.
gaff, n., for fish, *gwelen-hȳk, g.-hygen,* f., pl. *-lyny-h.*
gaffer, n. *cothwas,* m., pl. *-wesyon.*
gaiety, n. *lowender, *jo·lyfta,* m.
gain, v. *dyndyl, gwaynya*; he g.ed the day, *an vyctory eth ganso*: n. *gwayn, prow, lēs,* m.
gainsay, v. *contradya, gül tennow orth, cows a-drüs, kewsel erby·n.*
gait, n. *cam.* m., pl. *-mow, kerdhes,* m., *forth k.,* f.
gaiters, n. *poltrygas,* m., pl. *-gosow.*
galaxy, n. *Hens Sen Jamys,* m., *Scül Jacob,* f.
gale, n. *awel,* f., pl. *-low, gwyns crēf,* m., pl. *-ow c.*
gall, n. *bystel,* f.
gallant, a. *gay, cortes*: n. *pollat,* m., pl. *-ys.*
galley, n., naut., *galy,* m., pl. *-s*; kitchen, *kegyn gorhel,* f.; g. slave, *revador kēth,* m., pl. *-yon k.*
gallop, v. *ponya*: n. *ponyans,* m., *ponya,* inf.
gallows, n. *cloghprennyer,* m., *crōk,* f., pl. *-ogow, crokpren, crogbren,* m. and f., pl. *-yer*; place, *crogla,* m.; g. bird, *scrogyn,* m., pl. *-now.*
gamble, v. *gwary erby·n hap* or *chōns, kessynsy*: **-ing,** n. **hapwary,* m.
gambol, v. *terlemmel, cryghlemmel*: n. *terlam, cryghlam,* m.
gambrel, n. *skyren,* f., pl. *-now.*
game, n. *gwary,* m., pl. *-ow, sport,* m., pl. *-ys, gām,* m., pl. *-ys*; wild g., *gām, *helgyk, kȳk gwyls,* m.; royal g., *best arlydhy,* f., pl. *-as a.*: **g.-keeper,** n. *gwythyas an gām,* m., pl. *-ysy an g.*
gaming-house, n. *chȳ-gwary, c.-hapwary,* m., pl. *-ow-g., h.*
gander, n. *cülyek-gōth,* m., pl. *-yogas g.*
gang, n. *felshyp,* m., pl. *-s, para,* m., pl. *-ys, bagas,* m., pl. *-ow.*
gangrene, n. *podrethes,* m.: **-nous,** a. *podrethek.*
gangway, n. *tremenva,* f., pl. *-ow*; of ship, *plynken tȳra,* f., pl. *-now t.*
gannet, n. *sethor,* m., pl. *-as.*
gaol, n. *pryson,* m., pl. *-yow, jayl,* m., pl. *-ys*: **-er,** n. *jayler,* m., pl. *-s.*
gap, n. *aswy (ajy),* f., pl. *-ow, būlgh,* m., pl. *-ow*: **-ped,** a. *aswȳak (ajȳak), būlghys.*
gape, v. **dyanowy*; stare, *lagata*: **-r,** n. *ganowek,* m., pl. *-wogyon*; starer, *lagasek,* m., pl. *-sogyon*: **-ping,** a. **ganowek*; staring, *lagasek.*
garage, n. *carjy,* m., pl. *-ow.*

garb, n. *gwysk, dyllas,* m., *quethow,* pl.: v. *gwysca.*

garden, n. *lowarth,* m., pl. *-ow, jarden* (*jarn*), m., pls. *-dnys* (*-nys*), *garth,* m. or f., pls. *-ow, -dhow, gerdhyer*; kitchen g., *losowek*; flower g., *blejyowek,* f., pls. *-egow, -egy*; to make a g., *gartha*: v. *lowartha*: **-er,** n. *lowarther,* m., pl. *-thoryon*: **-ing,** n. *whēl* or *gonys an lowarth,* m.

gar-fish, n. *gerrak,* m., pl. *-ogas.*

garland, n. *garlont,* f., pls. *-ow, -ons.*

garlic, n. *kenynen ewynek,* f., col. *kenyn e.*; clove of g., *ewyn kenyn,* m., pl. *-as k.*; wild g., ramsons, *coskenyn,* col.; crow g., *goth-kenyn,* col.

garment, n. *queth,* m. or f., pl. *-ow, pows,* f., pl. *-yow, gwysk,* m., pl. *-scow.*

garnish, v. **garnsya, tacla.*

garret, n. *talyk,* m., pl. *-ygow, talyow.*

garrison, n. *gwythysy,* m. pl., **ga·rnyson,* m.

garrulous, a. *tavasek.*

garter, n. *garget,* m., pl. *-tow.*

gas, n. **gas,* m., *ēthen,* f.

gash, v. *trēghy, falsa*: n. *trogh,* m., pls. *-ow, trēghyon*; of sword, *cledhevas,* m., pl. *-ow.*

gasp, v. *dyena, anella* or *tenna anal yn-cales*: n. *ten anal cot,* m., pl. *-now a. c.*

gate, n. *yet,* f., pl. *-tys, porth,* m., pl. *-ow*; hurdle, *clōs,* f., pl. *-ojow*: **g.-keeper,** n. *porther,* m., pl. *-oryon,* f. *-ores,* pl. *-ow*: **g.-post,** n. *pül-yet, pül-clōs,* m., pl. *-yow-y., -c.*: **g.way,** n. *porth,* m., pl. *-ow.*

gather, v. *cuntell*; fruit, flowers, *terry*; corn, *tysca*; liquids, *crüny*; into heap, *graghella*; fuel, *cünyssa*; shell fish, *mōs dhe dryk*(*g*); apples, *avallowa*; acorns, *messa,* nuts, *knowa,* etc.; of people, *kesomguntell*: **-er,** n. *cunteller,* m., pl. *-loryon*: **-ering,** n. *cuntell,* m., *cuntelles,* f., pl. *-ow, cuntellyans, omguntellyans,* m., pl. *-ow*; of liquids, *crün,* m., pl. *-yow*; sore, *pen du,* m., pl. *-now du.*

gaudy, a. *gorlywys, rē splan*; g. dress, *gwysk Cala-Mē,* m.

gaunt, a. *tanow, ascornek, trüeth y weles*; g. person, *scalyak,* m., pl. *-yogyon.*

gauntlet, n. *manek plāt,* f., pl. *-egow p.*

gauze, n. *pan boll, *newlwȳas,* m.

gay, a. *lowenak, jolyf, gay.*

gaze, v. *whythra, lagata, myras glew* (*orth*): n. *golok,* f., *mȳr,* m.

gazelle, n. *gavrewyk,* f., pl. *-wygas.*

gazer, n. *lagasek,* m., pl. *-sogyon.*

gear, n., tackle, *aparell,* m., *taclow,* pl. *dafar,* m., col. *pythow,* pl.

geld, v. **spatha*: **-ed,** a. **spath*: **-ing,** n. *eneval spathys.*

gem, n. *gem,* m., pl. *-mow* (*g.* hard).

gender, n. *rȳth,* f.

genealogist, n. **aghscryfer,* m., pl. *-foryon*: **-gy,** n. **aghow,* f., pl. **aghscryf,* m., pl. *-yvow.*

general, a. *ūsyes, kemyn*: n. *hembrynkyas-lu,* m., pl. *-ysy-l.*; pen, m., pl. *-now*: **-ly,** adv. *del yu ūsyes, herwyth ūsadow.*

generate, v. *denythy*: **-tion,** n. *denythyans, degrē·,* m., *ke·nethel,* f., pls. *-thlow*; succeeding g., *hēnath,* m.

generosity, n. *helsys,* f., *cortesy,* m.; Oh, what g.!, *Ha, larjes!*: **-ous,** a. *hēl.*

genesis, n. *dallethfos,* m.

genial, a. *colonnek, lowenek.*

genius, n. **awen,* f., pl. *-ow*; person, *dēn ynjyn, *awenyth,* m., pl. *-ydhyon.*

gentian, n., field g., †*gowyles,* col.

Gentile, n. *Jentȳl,* m., pl. *-lys.*

gentility, n. *jentylys,* m.

gentle, a. *jentyl, whar, whegoll, whēk, debo-nē·r, dōf* (*do*), *clōr*: **-ness,** n. *jentylys, clorder, wharder, whekter,* m.

gentleman, n. *dēn-jentyl,* m., pl. *tüs-j.*

gentlewoman, n. *benen-jentyl,* f., pl. *-es-j.*

gently, adv. *clōr, drē dekter*; go g., *kē war dha gam,* etc.

gentry, n. *gwelhevyn,* col., *tüs jentyl,* pl.

genuine, a. *gwȳr, lēl, gwyryon*: **-ness,** n. *lendury,* m.

geographer, n. **doryth,* m., pl. *-ydhyon*: **-phy,** n. *skȳans an nōr,* m., *dory·dhȳeth,* f.

geologist, n. **doror,* m., pl. *-yon*: **-gy,** n. **doro·rȳeth,* f.

geometry, n. **mynso·nyeth,* f., **jȳo·metry,* m.: **-rical,** a. **mynsonek.*

germ, n. *egyn,* m., pl. *-now.*

German, a. *Almaynek*; G. lang., *Almaynek,* m.; person, *Alman,* m., pl. *-as,* f. *-es,* pl. *-ow.*: **-y,** n. *Almayn,* f.

germinate, v. *tevy, *egyna.*

gesticulate, v. *kewsel drē sȳnys*: **-tion, gesture,** n. *sȳn,* m., pl. *-ys.*

get, v., obtain, *cafos, kerghes,* ‡*fangya*; g. ready, *ombarüsy*; g. to work, *dalleth ober*; g. away, g. off, *cavanscüsa, dyank, scüsy*; g. along, *kerdhes*; g. away! *kē dhe gerdhes!*; g. away with you!, in disbelief, *a gans dha whethow!*; to become, *mōs* or *dōs ha bōs*; g. on, *spēdya, sowyny*; he's got it, *gallas*

ganso; I have got, *yma· dhymmo, my a-m-büs*; g. up, *sevel*; earn, *gwaynya*.
ghastly, a. *dyslyw, gwyn, üthek, grysyl.*
ghost, n. *bucca gwyn*, m., pl. *-bukkyas wyn, tarosvan*, m., pl. *-now, spyrys*, m., pl. *-yon, skēs dēn marow*, pl. *skesow tüs varow*; the Holy G., *an Spyrys Sans*: **-ly,** a. *ave·l spyrys, tarosvanüs*; appertaining to the spirit, *spyrysek.*
giant, n. *jȳant*, m., pl. *-ns*, †*cawr*, m., pl. *kewry*, †*enke·nethel*, m., pl. *-ethlow*: **-ess,** n. **cawres*, f., pl. *-ow.*
gibber, v. *clattra*: **-ish,** n. *cows hep stȳr*, m. †*stlaveth*, m.
gibbet: see **gallows.**
gibe, n. *gēs*, m.: v. *scornya, gül gēs, gēsya.*
giddy, a. *penscaf, scaf y ben*: **-diness,** n. **pendro*, f., *scafter pen*, m.
gift, n. *ro*, m., pl. *-how (-ow), presont*, m., pl. *-ons.*
gigantic, a. *fest brās*; prefix. †*cawr-*.
giggle, v. **folwherthyn.*
gild, v. *owra, gorowra.*
gill, n., of fish, *brynk*, m., pl. *-ow.*
gilt, a. *gorowrys*: n. *gorowrans*, m.
gimlet, n. *tardar bȳghan*, m., pl. *terder b.*
gin, n., trap, *maglen*, f., pl. *-now, jyn*, m., pl. *-nys*; spirits, **jenevra.*
gipsy, n. *Ejyptyon*, m., pl. *-tonyon*, f. *-es*, pl. *-ow.*
gird, v. *strotha, grügysa*: **-le,** n. *grügys*, m., pl. *-ow, kengel*, f., pl. *-glow.*
girdlestone, n. *mēn-pobas*, m., pl. *meyn-p.*
girl, n. *mowes*, f., pl. *-wysy, myrgh*, f., pl. *-es, moren*, f., pl. *moronyon*; to run after g's., *myrghessa* (inf. only).
girth, n., harness, **torgengel*, f., pl. *-glow.*
give, v. *rȳ*; g. up, *hepcor, dascor*; with *dhe*², *yntra dywla*, etc., *drȳ*; g. up! *sa! sa!*, *gās hy dhe-vēs! do way!*; g. back, *restorya, rȳ trē*; g. way, *plegya, plynchya*; g. oneself away, *ombrevy bōs kēn es del omwra*: **-r,** n. *rȳas*, m., pl. *rȳesy, nep a-rē*: **-ving,** n., act of g., *rȳans*, m.,
gizzard, n. **avy-lās*, m.
glad, a. *lowen, lowenek, hüdhyk*; make g., be g., *lowenhē·*; I am g., *da yu genef*: **-den,** v. *lowenhē·, hüthhē·*: **-ness,** n. *lowena*, f., *lowender, hüdhykter*, m.
glade, n. *lanergh*, m., pl. *-y.*
glance, n. *golok*, f., *mȳr üskys, towl lagas*, m.: v., g. at, *myras üskys*, or *ün wolok, orth.*
glare, n. *golow crēf*, m.: v. *golowy, lagata yn-whoth* or *sōr dhodho.*
glass, n., substance or vessel, *gwēder*, m., pl. *-drow*; tumbler, *gwedren*, f., pl. *-now*; spy-g., *gwēder-aspȳa*; looking-g., *myrour*, m., pl. *-s, gwēder-myras*; wine-g., *gwedren-gwȳn*; g. of wine, *gwedren a wȳn*: **-sy,** a. *gwedrek.*
glaucous, a. *glās*, **gwērlōs.*
glaze, v. *gwedra*: n. *ken gwedrek*: **-d,** a. *gwedrek, gwedrys*: **-zier,** n. *gwedror*, m., pl. *-yon.*
gleam, n. *dewyn*, m., pl. *-now, lugh*, m., f. *-esen*, col. *-es*: v. *glyttra, lughesy, dewynya*: **-ing,** a. **lenter, ow-tewynya.*
glean, n. *tyskenna*: **-er,** n. *tyskennor*, m., pl. *-yon*, f. *-es*, pl. *-ow*: **-ing,** n. *tyscas*, m.
glebe, n. *sentry*, m., pl. *-s.*
glee, n. *lowena*, f., *lowender*, m.; song, *cān tredden*, f., pl. *-ow t., canyk*, f., pl. *-ygow, kescan*, f., pl. *-now*: **-ful,** a. *hüth, hüdhyk*: **-fully,** adv. *yn-hüdhyk.*
glen, n. *glyn*, m., pl. *-now.*
glide, v. *slynkya*: n. *slynk*, m.
glimmer, n. *golow gwan*, m., pl. *-lowys g.*: v. *gwanwolowy*, **flyccra, golowy yn-whan.*
glimpse, n. *vu*, m., *golok*, f.
glisten, glitter, v. *terlentry, dewynya, splanna*, ‡*glyttra*: **-ing,** a. *ow-terlentry*, **dewynek.*
globe, n. *pēl*, f., pl. *-yow*: **-bal,** a. *a'n norvȳ·s yn-tȳen*: **-bule,** n. *pellen*, f., pl. *-now*: **-bular,** a. *cren.*
gloom, n. *duder, tewlder*, m., *tewolgow*, abst. pl.; of spirits, *moreth, trystys, trystans*, m.: **-y,** a. *tryst*; dark, *tewl.*
glory, n. *gordhyans, golowys, golowyjyon, golewder, clōs, splander, glory*, m.: **-rify,** v. *gordhya*: **-rious,** a. *splan, gwyn, golow, gloryes.*
gloss, n. *splander*, **burnys*; explanation, *styryans*: v. **burnsya*; explain, *styrya.*
glossary, n. *geryador, gerlyvryn*, m., *gerva*, f., pl. *-ow.*
glove, n. *manek*, f., pl. *-egow*: **-r,** n. *manegor*, m., pl. *-yon.*
glow, n. *golow*, m., pl. *-lowys*: v. *golowy*: **g.-worm,** n. *prȳf-golow*, m., pl. *pryves-g.*
glue, n. *glüs*, m.: v. *glüsa.*
glut, n. *gwalgh, gorlanwes*, **gorfalster*, m.
glutton, n. *cowlek*, m., pl. *-egyon, gargasen*, f., pl. *-now, gloton*, m., pl. *-s*: **-ize,** v. *gorlenky*: **-ous,** a. *cowlek, gargasennek*; to be g., *gül glo·teny*: **-y,** n. *glo·teny* (*glotny*), *cowlegneth*, m.

gnash, v. *deskerny, scrynkya*: **-ing,** n. *scrȳnva*, f.

gnat, n. *gwybesen*, f., col. *gwybes*; stinging g., *stut*, m., pl. *-tys*; to catch g.'s, *gwybessa* (inf. only).

gnaw, v. *dynsel*, **knȳas*.

gnome, n. *denyk*, m., pl. *tüsygow, knokker*, m., pl. *-s*.

go, v. *mōs, mones, kerdhes*; g. by, *tremena*; g. after, *holya, sewya*; g. off with, *mōs gans*; g. to! *do way! go to!*; g. away, out, *mōs dhe-vēs, yn-mēs, avodya*; g. so far as to do, *mōs dhe wül*; g. easy, *kē war dha gam*; I am going to . . ., *my a-wra . . .*; he said he was going to be, *y-leverys y-fedha*; let's g., *dün alemma*; g. up, *yskynna*; g. down, *dyeskynna*; g. out, of flame, *merwel*; g. wrong, *drokfara*; he is going on for 100, *yma·ow-nessa y gans bloth*; keep it going! *gas e dhe gerdhes!*: **-ing,** n. *spēda*, f; while the g. is good, *hedra vo gesys dhyn spas*; goings on, *fara, faryng*.

goad, n. *garthow*, m., pl. *-yow, pȳger*, m., pl. *-goryon*: v. *pȳga, brosa*.

goat, n. *gavar*, f., pls. *gever, gyfras, lyl*, f., pl. *-as*; he g., *bogh*, m., pl. *-as*, ‡*buk*, m., pl. *-kys*; young g., *myn*, m., pl. *menas, ge·veryk, gevryk*, f., pl. *-ygow*: **g. herd,** n. *bügel-gever*, m., pl. *-eth-g.*: **g. skin,** n. *gavargen*, m.

goblin, n. *bucca nōs*, m., pl. *bukkyas n., spyrys*, m., pls. *-yon, -yjyon*.

God, n. *Dew*, m.; G. speed! *Dew-gweres!, dursona! God speda dhys!*; by G., *rē Dhew! pardē!*; G. willing, *mar myn D.*; G. forbid, *D. dyfen!*; heathen g., *dew*, m., pl. *-ow*: **-dess,** n. *dewes*, f., pl. *-ow*: **-head,** n. *dewsys*, m.: **-less,** a. *dydhew*: **-ly,** a. *ewnhensek, da, dywysyk*.

godchild, n. *flogh-bysyth*, m., pl. *fleghes-bysyth*.

godfather, n. *tās-bysyth*, m., pl. *-ow-b*.

godmother, n. *mam-bysyth*, f., pl. *-mow-b*.

goggle, v. *lagata*: **-r,** n. *lagasek*, m., pl. *-sogyon, lagater*, m., pl. *-toryon*: **-ling,** a. *lagasek, ow-lagata*.

goitre, n. *pensagh*, m.

gold, n. *owr*, m.; g. mine, *owrek*, f., pl. *-egy, pol-owr*, m.: **-en, g.-bearing,** a. *owrek, owr*, n.: **g.smith,** n. *owror*, m., pl. *-yon*, †*ewrē*, m., pl. *-as*.

goldfinch, n. **owrdynk*, m., pl. *-ncas*.

goldfish, n. *owrbysk*, m., pl. *-buskes*; g. bowl, *gweder o.*, m.

good, a. *da, mās*; any g., *'vās*; g. thing, *da*, m.; it's no g., *ny-amont man, ny-dhē lēs anodho, nyns-yu 'vās*: n. *dader, lēs, prow*, m.; speak, pray, etc., for the g. of, *gans*: **-ly,** a. *da, bryntyn*: **-ness,** n. *dader*, m.: **g.-for-nothing,** n. *lo·selwas*, m., pl. *-wesyon*: a. *nag-üs 'vās dhe dravyth, na-dāl man*: **g.-bye!** int. *Dew genough-why! genes (genough) farwel!*: **g.-day,** int. *Dew roy dēth da dheugh-why (durdadha-why)!*: **G. Friday,** n. *De-Gwener an Grows*, m.: **g. luck,** n. *hap da, goda-chons*, m.: **g. man,** n. *dremā·s, densa, demmā·s (dēn mās)*, m.; goodman, husband, householder, *gorty*, m., pl. *gwērty*: **g.-natured,** a. *da y gnās*: **g.-night!,** int. *Dew roy nōs da dheugh (durnostadha)!, Dew roy dhys nōs da!*: **goods,** n. *stuff*, m., *substans*, f., *gwara, mebyl*, col., *pyth*, m., pl. *-ow*: **g. wife, goody,** n. *ben'vā·s (benen vās)*, f., *gwrē'ty (gwrēk ty)*, f.

goose, n. *gōth*, f., pl. *godhow*; g.-green, n. *prās-gōth, p.-godhow*; **gosling,** *godhyk*, m., pl. *-ygow*: **g.-grass,** n. *serghegen vȳghan*, f., pl. *-now bȳghan, les-serghak bȳghan*, m.

gooseberry, n. **growsen*, f., col. *grows*.

gore, v. *gwana*: n. *gōs, crow*, m.; insertion, *darn tryhornek y'n pows*.

gorge, v. *gorlenky*: n. *keynans*, m., pl. *-ow, bülgh*, m., pl. *-ow, haun*, f., pl. *-ow*; in cliff, *saun*, f., pl. *-yow*.

gorgeous, a. *lȳes lyw, splan*.

gorse, n. *eythyn*, col.; g.-bush, *eythynen*, f.

gospel, n. *away·l*, m., pl. *-ow*.

gossamer, n. **gwün*, m.

gossip, v. *whethla, kesclappya yn ün sclandra*: n. *whethel üfer*, m., pl. *-thlow u., scavel an gow*, f.; person, *whethlor*, m., pl. *-yon*, f. *-es*, pl. *-ow*; in kindly sense, *kentrevoges*, f., pl. *-ow*.

gouge, n. *gen, cow*, m., pl. *-ow*; v. *genna, cowa*.

gourd, n. **pompyon*, m., pl. *-s*.

govern, v. *rewlya, rowtya, governya*: **-ment,** n. *rewl*, m., pl. *-ys, governans*, m.; body of people, *rewloryon*, m., pl.: **-or,** n. *rewler*, m., pl. *-loryon, rowtor*, m., pl. *-s, lewyth*, m., *governour*, m., pl. *-s*.

gown, n. *pows*, f., pl. *-yow, gōn*, m., pl. *-ow*.

grab, v. *settya dalghen yn*.

grace, n., thanks, *grās*, m., pls. *-sow, -sys, rās*, m., pl. and abst. *-ow, grassyans*, m.; as quality, *je·ntylys*, m.; out of g., *dysgrassyes*; full of g., *lün a rās*; in a state of g., *yn* *bewnams da, glan*; to say g., ‡*leverel grās, govyn bennath, grassa dhe Dhew agan bōs*: **-ful,** a. *tēk hy form, jentyl*: **-less,** a. *dyrās, ungrassyes*: **-cious,** a. *grassyes, debonē·r, lün a rās.*

grade, n. **grath,* m., pl. *-adhow*: v. *gradhya*: **-dually,** adv. *tam ha tam, nebes ha nebes*: **-duate,** v. **gradhya.*

graft, v. *graffya,* **ympya*: n. *graf,* m., pl. *-fys,* **ymp,* m., pl. *-ys.*

grain, n. *grünen,* f., col. *grün*; of corn, *ȳsen,* f., pl. *-now,* col. *ȳs*; sorts or supplies of g., *ȳsow,* pl.; g.-bearing, *ȳsak*; brewer's g's., *sēk,* m.; to form g. in the ear, *grünya*: **granary,** n. *ȳsla,* m.

gramercy!, int. *gromercy!*

grammar, n. *grammer,* m.; book, **yēthador,* m.: **-ian,** n. **yēthor,* m., pl. *-yon, yēthyth,* m., pl. *-ydhyon, grammaryan,* m., pl. *-s.*: **-atical,** a. *gramasek.*

gramophone, n. *jyn-kewsel,* m., pl. *-nys-k.*; g. record, *record,* m., pl. *-ys.*

grand, a. *mür, ughel, rȳal, gay, brāf*: **-eur,** n. *müreth,* m.: **g.child,** n. *flogh-wyn,* pl. *flēghes-gwyn*: **g.son,** n. *map-wyn,* pl. *mebyon-gwyn*: **g.daughter,** n. *myrgh-wyn,* f., pl. *-es-gwyn*: **g.father,** n. *syra-wyn,* m., pl. *syrys-gwyn, tās-gwyn,* m., pl. *-ow-gwyn, hendas,* m., pl. *-ow*; great-g., *hengok,* m., pl. *-ogyon*; great-great-g., †*dyhok,* m., pl. *-ogyon*; great-great-great-g., †*gorhok,* m., pl. *-ogyon*: **g.mother,** n. *dama-wyn,* f., *henvam,* f., pl. *-mow*: **g.-uncle,** n. **gorewnter,* m., pl. *-tras*: **g.-aunt,** n. **gorvodryp,* pl. *-rebeth.*

grange, n. *grünjy,* m.

granite, n. *mēn-growyn*; g. gravel, *rabmen,* m.; soft face on hard g., *cüdhen,* f.: a. *growynek.*

granny-knot, n. **camgolm,* m., pl. *-ow.*

grant, v. *rȳ, grontya, darbary, vossawya*: n. *gront,* m., pl. *-ys, ro,* m., pls. *-how, -ow*; of land, *ystyn,* m., pl. *-now.*

grape, n. *grappa,* m., pl. *-pys,* **gwȳnrünen,* f., pl. *-now,* col. **gwȳnrün*: **g.-vine,** n. ‡*gwedhen grappys,* †*gwȳnbren,* m.

graphic, a. *bew, delynyes yn-splan.*

grapnel, n. *grabel,* m., pl. *-blys.*

grapple, v. *gwrynya, grabalyas,* **crapya*; g. with, *dalghenna yn*: **-r,** n. *gwrynyer,* m., pl. *-yoryon*: **-ling-iron,** n. *grabel,* m., pl. *-blys.*

grasp, v. *dalghenna, synsy, settya dalghen yn, camma besyas war*[2]: n. *dalghen,* f., pl. *-now, gavel,* f., pl. *-yow, craf,* m., pl. *-avow,* **crap,* m.: **-er,** n. *synsyas,* m., pl. *-ysy*: **-ing,** a. *crefny, pȳth.*

grass, n. *gwels,* col.; g.-blade, *gwelsen,* f., pl. *-now*; g. left for hay, *gwels gora*; fresh g., *erwels, gwerwels, glaswels*; cotton-g., *gün-blüf,* col.; bent or coarse g., *fynny,* f.; tussock-g., *fynny vür*: **-hopper,** n. *cülyek-reden,* m., pl. *-yogas-r.*: **g.-land,** n. *glas-wels,* m., *porva,* f., *ton,* m. or f., pl. *-yow, gwerwels,* m.; **g.-plot,** n. *glasyjyon,* m., *glesyn,* m., pl. *-now*: **g.-wrack,** n. *kewny, k. mor,* col., *morwels,* col.; patch of g.w., *glesyn,* m., pl. *-now*: **-y,** a. *gwelsek*; g. place, *gwelsek,* f., pls. *-egow, -egy.*

grate, v. *cravas,* **rathella*: n. *tanvaglen,* f., pl. *-now.*

grateful, a., to be g., *gothvos* or *aswon grās*; I am g., *gōn, y-whōn, mür rās* (*dhe*[2]).

gratify, v. *plēkya* (*dhe*[2]): **-ing,** a. *plegadow.*

grating, n. *maglen,* f., pl. *-now.*

grating, a. *garow.*

gratitude, n. *grās, grassyans,* m.

grave, n. *bēth,* m., pl. *-edhow*: **g.-digger,** n. *palor bedhow,* m., pl. *-oryon b.*: **g.-stone,** n. *mēn-bēth,* m., pl. *meyn-b.*

grave, a. *trüesy, solempna, sevür, sad*: **-vity,** n. *sevüreth,* m.; specific g., *poster,* m.; solemnity, *solempnyta,* m.

gravel, n. *rabmen,* m., *grow, growyn,* col.; g. subsoil, *growdyr, growyndyr,* m.; g. heap or place, *growynek,* f., pls. *-nogow, -negy*; g. pit, *pol-growyn,* m., pl. *rabmen,* m., *growglēth,* m., pl. *-edhyon, growek,* f.: **-ly,** a. *growynek, growek.*

gravy, n. *sows, sūgan kȳk,* m.

graze, v., feed, *pesky, pory*; wound, *dyrüsca, cravas*: n., wound, *cravas,* m.: **-zing ground,** n. *porva,* f., *clün,* m., pl. *-now.*

grease, n. *blonek, saym, üras,* m.: v. *üra*: **-sy,** a. *blonegek, droküry s.*

great, a. *mür, brās, larch*; make g., *mürhē·*; so g., as g. (as), *kemmy·s ha*; how g. a length *pygemmys hēs*; the g., *an brāsyon,* m., pl.; g. in relationship, see **grand-**: **-er,** a. *moy*: **-est,** a. *moyha* (*mogha*): **-ly,** adv. *mür-, yn-für, yn-frās, fest,* ‡*braf*; more g., *moy*; most g., *moyha*; how g.? *pygemmys?*: **-ness,** n. *braster, müreth,* m.

greed, n. *crefny,* f., *pythneth, covaytys,* m.; **-y,** a. *pȳth, crefny,* †*craf*; g. person, *synsyas,* m., pl. *-ysy.*

Greek, a. *Grēca*: n., G. lang., *Grēca, Grew,* m.; G. person, *Grēca,* m., pl. *-kys.*

green, a. *glās, gwēr, ēr*; raw, *crȳf*; deep g., **dulas*; light g., **gwervelen*; blue-g., **glaswer*, **gwerlas*; grow g., *glasa*: n. *glasyjyon*, m., *glasen*, f., *glesyn*, m., pl. *-now, ton*, m. or f., pl. *-yow*: **-ish,** a. *glesyk*: **-ness,** n. *glasneth, glasny, glaster, ērder*, m.: **-s,** n. *cawl*, col., *losow jarn*, pl.: **g.finch,** n. *melenek*, m., pl. *-egas*: **g.fly,** n. *lewen losow*, f., col. *low l.*: **g.house,** n. *losowjy*, m., pl. *-ow, chy gwēder*, m.: **g.-lane,** n. *forthlas* (*forlas*), f.: **g.sward,** n. *ton, glaston*, m. or f., pl. *-yow*.

greet, v. *dynerghy*; send g.ings, *gorhemmyn*: **-ing,** n. *dynargh*, m.; g.s., *gorhemmynadow*, m.

grey, a. *lōs*; blue-g., *glaswyn*; of hair, *glās, lōs*; go g., *lōsy*: **g.beard,** n. *mȳn-rew*, m.: **g.-haired,** a. *pen-lōs, pen-glās*: **-ish,** a. *losyk, nebes lōs*: **-ness,** n. *losny, loseth*, m.

greyhound, n. *mylgy*, m., pl. *-gün, kȳ hȳr*, m., pl. *cün hȳr, greont*, m., pl. *-ns*; large g., †*gwylter*, m., pls. *-tras, -trow*; g. bitch, *mylast*, f., pl. *-lysty*.

grid, n. *maglen*, f., pl. *-now*, **rastel*, f., pls. *-lly, restel*.

griddle, n. *horn-pobas*, m., pl. *hern-p.*; bakestone, *mēn-pobas*, m., pl. *meyn-p.*: v. *pobas war vēn py horn*.

grief, n. *moreth, cüth*, m., *anken*, m., pl. *-yow, gew*, m., pl. and abst. *-ow, cavow, fyenasow*, pl. and abst. *trystys, trystans, dughan*, m., *galar*, m., pl. and abst. *-ow, gref*, m., pl. *-evys*; without g., *dyalar*; to inflict g., *ankenya*: **-ievance,** n. *grefons*, m., *grēf*, m., pl. *-evys*: **-ieve,** v. a., *trysthē·, dughanhē·, cüdhy, dysconfortya, grevya*, **galary*: **-ieved,** a. *morethek*; I am g., *cüth a-m-büs, yma·cüth y'm colon*: **-ievous,** a. *pōs, ankensy*; g. thing, *dȳeth*, m.

grim, a. *asper, garow*: **-ness,** n. *aspe·ryta, garowder*, m.

grimace, v. *scrynkya, camma* or *omgamma mȳn* or *ganow, gül mowys*: n. *mowa*, m., pl. *-wys*.

grime, n. *hylgeth*, **hüdhygel* *(*hüdhyl*), m.

grin, v. *scrynkya, deskerny, grysla*: n. *scrynk*, m., pl. *-ys*.

grind, v. *mala*, ‡*melyas*: **-er,** n. *malor*, m., pl. *-yon*: **g.stone,** n. **brewlyf*, f.

grip, v. *dalghenna, gwrynya, crafa*, **crapya*: n. *dalghen*, f., pl. *-now, craf*, m., pl. *-avow, gavel*, f., pl. *-yow*.

gripes, n. ‡*gyrr*, m.

grisly, a. *üthek, grysyl*.

grist, n. †*talgh*, m., pl. *telghyon*, **arval*, m.

grit, n. *growynen*, f., pl. *-now*, col. *growyn*; fig. *perthyans*, m., *colon dha*, f.: **-ty,** *growynek*.

groan, v. *hanaja, kȳny, lēfa, üja*: n. *hanajen*, f., pl. *-now*.

groat, n. *grōt*, m., pl. *-ys*.

groats, n. *brunyon*, pl.

grocer, n. *spȳcer*, m., pl. *-s*.

groin, n. *casal mordhos*, f., pl. *-selyow m., kethorva*, f.

groom, n. *paja-mergh*, m., pl. *-jys-m., grōm*, m., pl. *-mys*: v. *servya, ruttya* or *strylla margh*.

groove, n. *trogh*, m., pls. *-ow, trēghyon*, **rygol*, m.

grope, v. *tava*, **palvala*: **-ing,** adv. *yn-dan dava*.

gross, a. *tew, garow*, ‡*berryk*: **-ness,** n. *tewder, garowder*, †*berry*, m.

grotesque, n. *boba·n*, m., pl. *-ys*.

ground, n. *dōr*, m., pl. *-ow, gweras*, m., pl. *-ow, grond, lür*, m., *tȳr*, m., pl. *-yow*; to the g., on the g., down, *dhe'n lür*; on the g., along the g., *war lür*; g. level, *grond*, m.; mining, soft g., *flūken*, f.; clay g., *prȳen*, f.; g. rich in tin, *scoven*, f.; rusty g., *gossen*, f.: v. *grondya, fundya*: **g.-floor,** n. *lür a-woles*, m.: **-less,** a. *hep kēn, hep rēson*: **-lessly,** adv. *hep kēn*.

ground-ivy, n. *ydhyowen- dōr*, f., col. *ydhyow-d*, m.

grounds, n., reason, *praga, kēn*, m., *skyla*, m., pl. *-ys*; g. for trial, *acheson*, m., pl. *-ys*; park, *tyryow, lowarthow*, pl.; dregs, *godhas*, m., pl. *-dhojyon*.

groundsel, n. †*maderē*, m.

group, n. *bagas*, m., pl. *-ow, cowethas*, f., pl. *-ow*; v. *gorra yn bagas* (*-ow*).

grouse, v.: see **grumble.**

grouse, n. **cülyek gwyls*, m., pl. *-yogas g.*; hen g., **yar wyls*, f., pl. *yēr gwyls*.

grouts, n. *growjyon*, pl.

grove, n. *kelly*, f., pl. *-ow, lōn*, m., pl. *-ow, gwȳk, kelly-wyk*, f., pl. *-ygow*.

grovel, v. *cramyas, codha war y rüf, war dor a-hēs*.

grow, v. *tevy, encressya*: **-th,** n. *tevyans*; shoot, *lows*, m.; disease, *canker*, m.

growl, v. *crothvolas*, **gromyal*: n. *crothval*, **rogh*, m.

grub, n., larva, *prȳf*, m., pl. *pryves, preven*, f., pl. *-now*; clothes moth g., *gowdhan*, m., pl. *-as*; maggot, *contronen*, f., col. *contron*.

grudge, v. *serry, perthy grefons* or *avy*: n. *sōr*, m., *drokvrüs*, f., pl. *-ow, grēf*, m., pl. *-evys*: I have a g., *e·nvȳes ōf, yma· grefons dhym*: **-ing,** a. *e·nvȳes*; ungenerous, *pȳth*: n., demur, *danjer, ardak*, m.
gruel, n. *yōs kērgh*, m.
gruff, a. *garow, ronk*: **-ness,** n. *garowder, renkyas*, m.
grumble, v. *crothvolas* (*croffolas*), **gromyal*; g. at, *gül crothval war*[2]: n. *crothval*, m.: **-ling,** a. *crothak, prest ow-crothvolas.*
grunt, v. *renky*, **rogha*: n. **rogh*, m., pl. *-ow.*
guarantee, v. *mōs rak, meughya, warrantya*: n. *meugh*, m., pl. *-yow, warrant*, m., pl. *-ys.*
guard, n. *gwȳth*, m.; person, *gwythyas*, m., pl. *-ysy*: v. *gwytha*; g. against, *gwytha orth*; g. oneself from, *omwytha rak*: **-ian,** n. *gwythyas*, m., pl. *-ysy, warden*, m., pl. *-s.*: **-less,** a. *dywyth.*
guess, v. *desmygy*: n. *desmyk*, m.; by g., *drē ref.*
guerdon, n. *weryson*, m.
guest, n. *ostyas*, m., pl. *-ysy*, **gwestē·*, m., pl. *-tyon*; to a meal, *kyfvewyas*, col. *kyfvewy*; to be a g., *ostya*; to entertain g's., *gwesty*: **g.-house,** n. *gwesty*, m., pl. *-ow, ostel*, m., pl. *-ys*: **g.-room,** n. *gwestva*, f., pl. *-ow.*
guide, v. *kevarwedha, lewyas, gedya, ledya, rewlya*: n. *kevarwedhor*, m., pl. *-yon, kevarwedhas*, m., pl. *-ysy, ledyor*, m., pl. *-yon, fordhor*, m., pl. *-yon, gȳd*, m., pl. *-ys*: **-dance,** n. *kevarwedhyans*, m.
guild, n. *myster*, m., pl. *-s*; g.-hall, *lysty*, m., pl. *-ow.*
guile, n. *gȳl, tull*, **sotylta, sotelneth*, m.; without g., *hep tull na gȳl.*
guilt, n. *cam, pēgh, camwyth*, m.; proof of g., *cabel*, m.; to find or prove g., *cably*: **-y,** n. *cablüs*; not g., *dybēgh.*
Guinea, n. *Gyny*, f.: g. coin, *gyny, püns owr Gyny*, m., pl. *-ow o. G.*: **g.-fowl,** n. *gallȳna*, m., pl. *-ys*: see **turkey**: **g.-pig,** n. *hogh gyny*, m., pls. *-as, mogh g.*
guise, n. *gȳs*, m., pl. *-yow.*
guitar, n. *gyttern*, m., pl. *-s.*
gulf, n. *plēk mōr*, m., pl. *-egow m.*
gull, n. *gwylan*, f., pl. *-as, gulla*, m., pl. *-lys*; black-headed g., *scraw*, m., pl. *-as, scrawyk*, m., pls. *-ygow, -esygow*: see **tern.**
gullet, n. *brȳansen, gargasen*, f., pl. *-now, lonk*, m.
gulp, v. *terlenky.*
gum, n. *glüs*, m.; g's. of mouth, *kȳk an dyns*, m.
gun, n. *gon*, m., pl. *-nys*: **g.boat,** n. *lester gonnys*, m., pl. *lystry g.*: **g.-carriage,** n. *kert gon*, m., pl. *-ys g.*: **g.powder,** n. **polter gon*, m.: **g.shot,** n. *ten gon*, m., pl. *-now-g.*: **g.smith,** n. *gōf gon*, m., pls. *goves, -vyon, g.*
gurgle, v. *renky*: n. *renkyas*, m., pl. *-yosow.*
gurnard, n. *pengarn*, m., pl. *-as*; grey g., *pengarn glās*; red g., *elek*, m., pl. *-egas, tubba-rüth*, m., pl. *tubbys-r.*
gurry, n. *grava dywla*, m., pl. *-vathow d.*
gush, v. *dewraga, frōsa, tardha*; in speech, *fēcla*: n. *denow, frōs*, m., *tarth*, m., pl. *-dhow*; speech, *fekyl lavarow.*
gust, n. *cowas*, f., pl. *-wosow, whaf gwyns*, m., pl. *-fys g.*
gut, n. *colon*, m., pl. *-yow*; fish-g., *cowl*, m., pl. *-ow*: v. *gwakhē·, dygowla puskes.*
gutter, n. *shanel*, m., *caun*, m., pl. *-ow*; of roof, etc., *lōnder*, m., pl. *-drys*: **g.snipe,** n. *map gal*, m., pl. *mebyon g., myrgh gal*, f., pl. *-es g.*
guzzle, v. *dybry* or *eva rē*: **-r,** n. *gargasen*, m., pl. *-now.*
gyves, n. *cargharow-horn*, m., pl.

H

habergeon, n. *hoberjon*, m., pl. *-s.*
habit, n. *ūs, ūsadow*, m.: **-ual,** a. *ūsyes.*
habitation, n. *trygva*, f., pl. *-ow, anneth*, f., pl. *-edhow.*
hack, v. *hakkya*; h. up, *dyvynya, hakkya dhe dymmyn.*
haddock, n. **corvarfus*, m., pl. *-y,*
haft, n. *dorn*, m., pl. *-ow.*
hag, n. *gwragh*, f., pl. *-as.*
haggard, a. *tewedhak, tennys y fās, lafüryes.*
haggle, v. *hokkya.*
hail, v. *dynerghy, haylya*: int. *hayl!*
hail, n. *keser*, col.: v. *gül keser*; h.-stone, *keseren*, f.
hair, n. *blewen*, f., col. *blew*; of head, *gols*, m.; fine h., *manvlew*, col.; coarse h. of animals, *rünen*, f., col. *rün*; h. on body, *kethor*, m.; penitential h.-cloth, *grügys rün*, m., pl. *-ow r.*; h. shirt, *hevys rün*, m., pl. *-yow r.*: **h.dresser,** n. *barver*, m., pl. *-yon, dȳghtyer blew*, m., pl. *-yoryon b.*: **-less,** a. *blogh, pen-pylys, mōl, dyvlew*: **-y,** a. *blewak, kethorek.*
hake, n. *dynsak*, m., pl. *-sogas.*

hale, a. *yagh, saw, crēf.*
half, a., n. *hanter,* m.; as prefix, **les-*; h. good enough for, *hanter da rak*; to h. kill him, *hanter y ladha*: **h.-breed,** a. *kemyskrȳth*: **h.-brother,** n. *hanter-broder,* m., pl. *-breder*: **h.-clad,** a. *ternoth*: **h.-hearted,** a. *mygyl*; to grow h., *mygla*: **h.-heartedness,** n. *mygylder,* m.: **h.-hour,** n. *hanterür,* f.: **h.penny,** n. *demma,* m., pl. *-mys*: **h.-sister,** *hanter-whōr,* f., pl. *-wheryth*: **h.-way,** n. *dhe hanter an hens*: **h.-way house,** *tavarn an hanterhens.*
hall, n., room, *hēl,* m., pl. *-ow*; building, *lys,* f., pl. *-yow.*
hallo, halloo, int. *how*!: v. *crȳa, garma.*
hallow, v. *sona, benyga*: n. All H.s Tide, *Calan Gwāf, *Gōl Pup Sans,* m.; All H.s Day (Nov. 1), *dē-* or *dü-Halan Gwāf,* m.; H. e'en, *nōs-Calan Gwāf,* f., *Gōl C. G.,* m.: **-ed,** a. *benygys, hynwys.*
halt, v. *powes, sevel, gortos, hedhy*: int. *ho*! *heth*! *hedheugh*! *saf*! *seveugh*! *gorta*! *gorteugh*!: n. *powesva,* f., *safla,* m., pl. *-lēow.*
halter, n. *cabester,* m., pl. *-trow, *penfester,* m., pl. *-trow.*
halve, v. *ranna* or *trēghy yntra deu, hantera, *deuhantera.*
halyard, n. *rōp,* m., pl. *-ys.*
ham, n. *mordhos hogh,* f., pls. *-ow, -ojow h.*
hamlet, n. *godref, pendra,* f., pl. *-revy.*
hammer, n. *morthol,* m., pl. *-ow*: v. *mortholya*: **-ed,** a. *morthelek.*
hammock, n. *gwely crōk* or *lesk,* m., pl. *yow c.* or *l.*
hamper, v. *ancombra, lettya, spralla*: n. *basket brās,* m., pl. *tys-b., *ha·nafer,* m., pl. *-s.*
hand, n. *lüf,* f., pl. *-yow,* d., *dywlüf, dywla, dorn,* m., pl. *-ow,* d., *deudhorn*; right h., *dorn dȳghow, lüf dhȳghow*; left h., *dorn clēth, lüf glēth*; direction, *parth,* f., *tu,* m.; all h.s., *mēster ha maw*; on every h., *a bup tu*; on the other h., *yn forth aral*; close at h., *rybon*; large h.ed., *dornek*: v. *ystynna, hedhes*; h. over, *dascor*; h.-bag, *sagh dorn,* m., pl. *-ow d.*; h.-barrow, *grava-dywla,* m., pl. *-vathow d.*; h.-bell, *clēghyk,* m., pl. *-ygow*; h.-book, *cowethlyver,* m., pl. *-vrow*; h.-breadth, *lēslüf,* m., **dornva,* f., pl. *-vedhy*; h.-cart, *kert dywla,* m., pl. *-ys d.*; h.ful, *lün y dhorn* (*a*[2]), *tysk,* m. or f., pl. *-scow, *dornas,* m., pl. *-esow*; h. hold, *dornla,* m., pl. *-lēow.*
handicap, v. *lettya*: n. *let,* m., pl. *-tys.*
handicraft, n. *creft,* f., pl. *-ow.*
handkerchief, n. *lȳen-dorn,* m., pl. *-enyow-d.*
handle, v. *tava, dȳghtya, handla*: n. *dornla,* m., pl. *-lēow, dorn,* m., pl. *-ow, trōs,* m., pl. *treys*; of knife, *carn,* m., pl. *-ow*; of plough or wheelbarrow, *dorn,* m.; of vessel, etc., *scovarn,* f., pl. *-ow,* d. *dywscovarn*; having a h., *scovarnek, dornek*; without a h., *dydhorn, dyscovarn.*
handmaiden, n. *maghteth,* f., pl. *meghtythyon.*
handsaw, n. **hesken,* f., pl. *-now, *lȳf,* m., pl. *-yvyow.*
handsome, a. *tēk, bryntyn*; Noah, my h., *Noy tēk.*
handwriting, n. *scryfa plüven,* m., *dornscryfa, dornscryf,* m., pl. *-yvow.*
handy, a. *parys.*
hang, v. *cregy*; execute, *hangya*; h. back, *trȳnya*: **-er, -man,** n. *creger, *crogor,* m., pl. *-oryon*: **-ing,** n., suspension, *crōk,* f., pl. *-ogow*; curtain, etc., *croglen,* f., pl. *-now, gōl,* m. or f., pl. *-yow*; **-ing up,** a. *yn crōk*; I don't care a h., *ny-rōf oy.*
hank, n. **kengel,* f., pl. *-glow.*
hanker after, v. *whansa, bōs whansek, cafos whans* or *sȳ a*[2]: **-ing,** n. *sȳans, whans,* m., pl. *-ow.*
hap, n. *hap,* m., pl. *-pys, chōns,* m., pl. *-ys*; mishap, *droklam, hap drōk, meschō·ns*: **-hazard,** a. *whym-wham, drē hap, par del wharfo*: **-less,** a. *anfüsyk.*
happen, v. *wharfos, darfos, codha, hapya, chōnsya*; to h. to, *dōs ha*; what has h.ed. to thee? *pandr' a-wher dhys*?: **-ing,** n. *cās, chōns, darfos, wharfos,* m.
happy, a. *lowen, lowenek, hüdhyk, gwynvȳs, gwynvȳsyk, hüth*; make h., *hüthhē·, lowenhē·*; h. my lot! *gwyn ow bȳs*!: **-pily,** adv. *yn termyn da*; most h., *yn gwella prȳs*: **-piness,** n. *lowena,* f., *lowender, hüthter, gwynvȳs,* m.
harangue, v. *arethya, predheges*: n. *areth,* f., pl. *-yow, predhek,* m., pl. *-egow.*
harass, v. *pyltya, ancombra*: **-ment,** n. *fyenasow,* pl. and abst., *ancombrynsy,* m.
harbinger, n. *e·rberjour,* m., pl. *-s*; **ragresor,* m., pl. *-yon.*
harbour, n., for shipping, *porth,* m., pls. *-ow, perth*; shelter, *harber,* m., pl. *-ys, e·rberow,* m., pl. *-ys*: v. *skewya, rȳ e·rberow dhe*[2].

hard, a. *cales*; h. of hearing, *pōs y glewes*: adv., closely, *fast, hardlych*; h. by, *ogas, rybon*; h. work, *whēl crēf*; difficult work, *whēl cales*; h. cash, *arghans bathys*; h. by, adv., prep., *pür ogas*: **-bitten,** a. *smat, aflythys*: **-en,** v. *calesy, caleshē*; as gum; etc., *moly*: **-ened,** a. *aflythys*; h. person, *aflythys*, m., pl. *-yjyon*: **-headed,** a. *pen-cales*: **-hearted,** a. *cales y golon, gyllys y golon pür gales*: **-ly,** adv. *scant, scantlowr, (ny-)namür, scant (ny-)*: **-ness,** n. *caletter*, m.: **-ship,** n. *cales ran*; injustice, *cam*, m., pl. *-mow*; severity, *anwhekter, anken*, m.: **-ware,** n. *dafar horn*, m.; **-worked,** a. *gwȳthys cales*: **-working,** a. *dywysyk*: **-y,** a. *smat, harth, asper, crēf.*
hare, n. *scovarnak*, f., pl. *-nogas.*
harebells, n. **clēgh an ēos*, pl.
hark, int. *goslow, -eugh*! *clew, -yeugh*!; h. to what I say! *goslow dhym a-gowsaf*! *clew-sy ow geryow*!
harm, n. *pystyk*, m., pl. *-ygow, drōk*, m., pl. *-ogow gref*, m., pl. *-evys, drocoleth, drokter, dregyn, damach, anfüsy, mewl*, m.; no h. will come of it, *nȳ-dhē drōk-vȳth anodho*: v. *apērya, pystyga, shyndya, myshevya*: **-ful,** a. *drōk*: **-less,** a. *hep drōk, dyflam.*
harmony, n. *aco·rd, kessenyans, composter*, m.: **-nious,** a. *kesson*: **-ize,** v. *kesseny, acordya.*
harness, n. *hernes*, m., **starn*, f., pl. *-yow*: v. *hernessya.*
harp, n. †*telyn*, f., pl. *-now, harp*, m., pl. *-ys*: v. †*telynya*: **-er, harpist,** *harpour*, m., pl. *-s*; as member of orchestra, *harp*, m., pl. *-ys*, †*telynyor*, m., pl. *-yoryon*, f., *-yores*, pl. *-ow.*
harrow, n. *clōs*, f., pl. *-ojow, harrow*, m., pl. *-s*, **oges*, f., pl. *-ow*; h.-tine, *dans-harrow*, m., pl. *dyns-h.*: v. *clōsya*, **ogesy.*
harsh, a. *anwhēk, asper, garow, cales, wherow*: **-ness,** *wherowder, garowder*, m.
harum-scarum, a. *scaf y ben, dybreder.*
hart, n. *carow*, m., pls. *kervys*, **kerewy*: **-'s tongue,** n. *tavas-carow*, m.
harvest, n. *trevas*, f., pl. *-ow, -ajow*; h. home, *goldheys, degol-deys*, †*ȳs-asver*, m.: v. *myjy, dōn trē*: **-er,** n. *myjer*, m., pl. *-joryon, myjwas*, m., pl. *-wesyon.*
hash, n. *bōs dyvynys*, **brewgyk*, m.: v. *dyvynya.*
hasp, n. †*hesp*, m., pl. *-ow*, **spanga*, m., pl. *-gys*, **clyket*, m., pl. *-tys.*
hassock, n. *tuttyn*, m., pl. *-now.*
haste, n. *tōth, fysk, hāst*, ‡*hastenep*, m.; in h., hastily, *war, yn* or *gans h., tōth brās, t. da, t. ta, totta·, t. mēn, gans mür a dōth*: **-ten,** v. *spēdya, stēvya, fysky, fystyna*: **-ty,** a. *fysk*, **hastyf*; thoughtless, *dybreder.*
hasty-pudding, n. *yōs, pot-gwyn*, m.
hat, n. *hot, hat*, m., pl. *-tys*; broad-brimmed, *dyber'-dowr*, m.: **-band,** n. *bond-hat*, m.
hatch, n. **hach*, m., pl. *-ys.*
hatch, v. *covÿa*, **gory*: **-ed,** a. **gōr*: **-ing,** n. **gor*, m.
hatchet, n. *bōl*, f., pl. *-ow*; small h., *bolyk*, m., pl. *-ygow.*
hate, v. *casa, bōs cās gans, hātya*: n., hatred, *cās, envy (avy), attȳ·*, m.: **-ful,** a. *cās, casadow, hegas*: **-fulness,** n. *casadewder*, m.
hauberk, n. *ho·berjon*, m., pl. *-s.*
haughty, a. *gothys, ughel y ben, hautyn*, **balgh*: **-tiness,** n. *gōth*, m.
haul, v. *halya, tenna*; drag, *draylya*: n. *ten*, m., pl. *-now*: **-ier,** n. *halyer*, m., pl. *-yoryon.*
haunch, n. *clün*, f., pl. *-yow*; d., *dywglün, pedren*, f., pl. *-now*, d. *dywbedren, penclün*, f., pl. *-yow*, d. *pen dywglün.*
haunt, v. **daromres*; of ghost, *tropla*: n., place, *tyller ūsyes*, m.
have, v. *cafos*; own, *pew*; I h., *my a-m-büs, yma· dhym, yma· genef, my a-bew*; to h. to go, etc., *bōs rēs* or *bysy dhe vōs*, etc.; h. done! *gās e*! *do way*! *havydo·*!
haven, n. *porth*, m., pl. *-ow, harber*, m., pl. *-ys*, ‡*haun*, m., pl. *-ys.*
havoc, n. *terros, terroja, dystrewyans, dys-wrȳans*, m.
haw, n. *hogan*, m., pl. *hegyn.*
hawk, v., wares, *gwyca, trōsya*; hunt, **fal-ghuna*, †*ydhna*: n. †*falghun*, m., pl. *-as, hōk*, m., pl. *-ys*: **-er,** n., dealer, *gwycor*, m., pl. *-yon, trōsyer*, m., pl. *-yoryon*; falconer, *falghunor*, m., pl. *-yon*: **-ing,** n. *falghun-o·rȳeth*, f.
hawser, n. *capel gorhel*, m., pl. *-plys g.*
hawthorn, n. *spernen wyn*, f., col. *spern gwyn.*
hay, n. *gora*, col; new-mown, *fōn*, m.; h. loft, *talyk gora*, m., pl. *-ygow g.*; h. rick, *das gora*, f., pl. *deys g.*; h. band, *fonen*, f., pl. *-now*; h. field, *fonek*, f., pls. *-egow, -egy*; h. fever, *cleves strewy.*
hazard, n. *peryl*, m., pl. *-yow, chōns*, m., pl. *-ys*: v. *peryllya*: **-ous,** a. *deantel.*
haze, n. *newl*, m., pl. *-ow, lewgh*, m.: **-zy,** a. *newlek.*

hazel, n. *gwedhen know,* f., col. *gwȳth k., knowwedhen, collwedhen,* f. col. *-wȳth, collen,* f., col. *coll*; h. grove, *coll-lōn,* m., pl. *-ow, kellygnow, -ek, -wȳth, collwydhek,* f.

he, pron. *ef*; suffixed or object of imp., *e, -a, -va*; stressed, *ee·f, -vāe·f*; that person, *henna*; this person, *hemma.*

head, n. *pen,* m., pl. *-now*; top, *blȳn,* m., pl. *-ow*; of arrow, *pȳl,* m., pl. *-ys*; of nail, *pen kenter*; h. to tail, *pen ha tȳn, pen ha lost*; it's all h. and shank, *nyns-yu mes pen ha garen*; h. first, *trōs warle·rgh pen*; back of h., *kylben,* m.; a h. of cattle, †*eal,* m.; big h.ed., *pennek*; h. and point game, *pen ha mȳn*; to turn h. over heels, *cryghlemmel*: a., as prefixes, *pen-, chyf-*: **h.ache,** n. *drōk pen,* m.: **h.gear,** n. *cugh,* m., pl. *-as, hot,* m., pl. *tys, dyllas pen,* m.: **h.man,** *gwelhevyn,* m. and col.: **h.spring,** n. *penfenten,* m., pl. *-tynyow, pengover,* m., pl. *-ow*: **h.stall,** n. **penfester,* m., pl. *-trow*: **h.-wind,** n. **gorthwyns,* m., pl. *-ow.*

heading, n. *penscryfa,* m., pl. *-vadhow.*

headland, n. *pentȳr, penryn,* m., pl. *-yow, penarth,* f., *trōn,* m., pl. *-ow*; in ploughed field, *talar,* m.

headlong, adv. *sket war y ben, y-ben yn-rak, dyswa·r*: a. *serth, crakkya-conna.*

headquarters, n. *caslys,* f., pl. *-yow, penplas,* m., pl. *-ow.*

headstrong, a. *gorth, stowt, stordy.*

headway, n., to make h., *mōs yn-rak.*

heal, v. *sawya, yaghhē·, gweres, ylȳa*: **-ed,** a. *saw*; to be h., *sawya*: **-ing,** n. *sawment, sawys,* m.: a. *yaghüs, a-saw*: **-th,** n. *yēghes, sawys,* m.; your h! *soweneugh! yēghes da dheugh-why!*; we are in good h., *yma·'gan yēghes-ny dhyn*; to give h. to, *gül yēghes dhe*[2]: **-th-giving,** a. *yaghüs, ow-rȳ yēghes*: **-thy,** a. *yagh, yn-yagh, salow, saw.*

heap, n. *graghell,* f., pl. *-low, gron,* m., *bern, pȳl,* m., pl. *-yow, tas,* m., pl. *-ow*; little h., *crügell,* f., pl. *-low, crügyn,* m., pl. *-now*; mound, *crük,* m., pl. *-ügyow*; abundance, *cals,* m.: v. *berna, graghella, crügya.*

hear, v. *clewes, goslowes*; h. about, *clewes a*[2]; hear! hear! *clew! clew! clewyeugh!*; h! (O yes!), *oyeth!*: **-er,** n. *goslowyas,* m., pl. *-ysy*: **-ing,** n. *clewes, clewans,* m.; sense of h. **clew,* m. **:-ken,** v. *goslowes, clewes, cola* (*orth*).

hearse, n. *masken* (for *marow -scaun*), f., pl. *-yow.*

heart, n. *colon,* f., pl. *-now*; fig., *cowsys,* m., pls. *cowsesow, -jejow*; h. beat, *lam colon,* m., pl. *-mow c.*; to take h., *omconfortya*; learn by h., *dysky drē gōf*: **-breaking,** a. *dhe derry* or *ranna colon*: **-broken,** a. *trogh y golon*: **-ily,** adv. *colonnek, a lün golon*: **-less,** a. *dybyta*: **-y,** a. *colonnek, yagh, saw.*

hearth, n. *olas,* f., pl. *-ow, eth,* m., pl. *-ys*; furnace, *fōk,* f., pl. *fogow*; h. rug, *len-olas,* f., pl. *-now-o.*; h. stone, *men-olas,* m., pl. *meyn-o.*

heat, n. *tomder,* **pothter,* †*tes,* m.; ardour, *gwrēs,* f.; extreme h., *brōs,* †*trethes,* m.; in h., of animals, *tom,* **lüsyk,* ‡*godhevek.*

heath, n., plant, *grük,* col.; Cornish h., *kykesow,* col.; a h., *grügek,* f., pls. *-egy, -egow*; h.-land, *rōs,* f., pl. *-yow*: **-er,** n., bush, *grüglon,* m., pl. *-ow*; ling, *menkek,* m., pl. *-egow*: **-y,** a. *grügek.*

heathen, a. *pagan, dyscryjyk*: n. *pagan,* m., pl. *-ys, dyscryjyk,* m., pl. *-ygyon*: **-dom,** n. *paga·nȳeth,* f.

heave, v. *halya, tenna*; h. up, *drehevel.*

heaven, n. *nēf,* m. or f., pl. *-vow*; the Kingdom of H., *Gwlās*(*cor*) *Nēf,* f.: **-ly,** a. (*a*)*nef,* **nevek.*

heavy, a. *pōs*: **-viness,** n. *poster,* m.; of spirits, etc., *posyjyon,* m.

Hebrew, a. *Yedhow*: **-braic,** a. *Ebbrow,* m., pl. *-as*; H. lang., *Ebbrow,* m.

hedge, n. *kē,* m., pl. *-ow*; earth h., *dōrgē,* m., pl. *-ow*; low, broken down h., *gorgē*; growing h., **goskejwyth,* col.; outer h., bank, **argē*: v. *kēas*; fig., *omwytha a bup tu rak coll, sconya leverel dhe blemmyk*: **-d,** a. *kēs, kēek*: **h.-hog,** n. *sort,* m., pl. *-as*: **-ging-bill,** n. **gwydhyf,* m., pl. *-yvyow*: **-r,** n. *kēer,* m., pl. *-ēoryon*: **-ing,** n. **kewȳth,* col.

heed, v. *attendya, goslowes, gül vrȳ* or *fors, bōs avȳsyes, bōs wār, rȳ scovarn, gwaytya*: n. *fors, rach, preder,* m.; take h., *kemeres wȳth, gorquytha, darwa·r*; take h. lest, *gwaytya na*[2]: **-ful,** a. *wār, prederüs, avȳsyes*: **-less,** a. *stordy, penscaf, dybreder.*

heel, n. *gwewen,* f., **sül,* m., pl. *-yow.*

heifer, n. *lejek,* f., pls. *-egas, -egow*; young h., *denewes,* m., pl. *-wys.*

height, n. *ughelder,* m.; geog., *bans,* m., pl. *-ow, ban,* m. or f., pl. *-now, arth,* m.: **-en,** v. *ughelhē·,* ‡*ughellas*; increase, *moghhē·, encressya.*

heinous, a. *hegas, drōk drēs ēghen.*

heir, n. *ēr*, m., pl. *-ys*, *-yon*; co-h., *kesēr*, m., pl. *-ys*: **-ess,** n. *ēres*, f., pl. *-ow*: **h.loom,** n. *pyth erytys* or *kemmynnys*, m., pls. *-ow*, *taclow*, *e.*, *k.*
hell, n. *yffarn*, m., pl. *-ow*: **-ish,** a. *yffarnak.*
helm, n. *lew*, m., pl. *-yow*: **-sman,** n. *lewyader*, m., pl. *-doryon*, *lewyer*, m., pl. *-yoryon.*
helmet, n. *basnet*, m., pl. *-tys*, **helm*, m., pl. *-ys.*
help, v. *gweres*, *kynweres*, *confortya*, *dyffres*, *spēda*, *scodhya*, *socra*; God h. me, *Dew re-m-gweresso*, *Dew gweres*!; as far as I might h. it, *myns may hallen omwytha*: n. *gweres*, *remedy*, *confort*, *socor*, m.: int. *A*, *gweres vy*! *How*, *gwereseugh*! *haro·w*! *maydes*!: **-er,** n. *gwereser*, m., pl. *-soryon*: **-ful,** a. *heweres*, *dhe lēs*: **-less,** a. *dyweres*, *antȳthy*; I am h., *ny-m-büs omweres*: **-mate,** n. *cowethes*, f., pl. *-ow.*
helter-skelter, adv. *pup a'y du.*
helve-socket, n. *crow arf*, m., pl. *-ow arvow.*
hem, n. **gwrem*, m., pl. *-yow*: v. **gwremya.*
hemisphere, n. *hanter an norvȳ·s*, *m.*
hemlock, n. *kegysen*, f., col. *kegys*, *keger*; water-h., *kegys dowr*; h. stalk, *gwelen-gegys*, f., pl. *gwel-g.*; dry, *keser*, m., pl. *-ow*; place overgrown with h., *kegysek*, *keserek*, f., pls. *-egow*, *-egy.*
hemp, n. *kewarghen*, f., col. *kewargh*; h. field, *kewarghek*, f., pls. *-egow*, *-egy*, *canabyer*, m., pl. *-s*; h. land, *kewarghtyr*, m.
hemp-agrimony, n. *scawen dhu*, f., col. *scaw d.*
hen, n. *yar*, f., pl. *yēr*; h. house, *yarjy*, m., pl. *-ow.*
henbane, n. †*gahen*, f.
hence, adv. *ahanan*, *alemma*; therefore, *ytho·*, *drē henna*: **-forth, -forward,** adv. *alemma-rak.*
her, pron., poss. and object, *hy*³, *'y*³; suffixed, *-hȳ*, *-ȳ*; infixed, *-s-*; emphatic, *-hyhȳ·*, *-yhȳ·*; with prep., *dhedhy*, *anedhy*, etc.: **-s,** pron. *dhedhy-hȳ*; it is h., *hy a-n-pew*, *dhedhy-hȳ yth-yu*: **-self,** p. *hy honen*; jocular, *myrgh hy dama* or *mam.*
herald, n. *herōt*, m., pl. *-rōs*: **-ic,** a. *herwyth arvow*: **-ry,** n. *lagha arvow.*
herb, n. *losowen*, f., col. *losow*, pl. *losowys*, †*lēs*, m., *erba*, m., pl. *-bys*: **-acious,** a. *losowek*: **-al,** a. *losowek*; book, *lyver losow*, m.: **-alist,** n. *losower*, m., pl. *-woryon*: **h.-garden,** n. *losowek*, f., pls. *-egy*, *-egow.*
herd, n. *grē*, f., pl. *-ow*: **-sman,** n. *bügel*, m., pl. *-eth(-a).*
here, adv. *omma*, *y'n lē-ma*; right h., *knak omma*; h! (take!), *tan*!; from h., *ahanan*, *alemma*; h. is, h. are, before vowel, *ot*, *awot*, before cons. *otta*, *awotta*, *otomma*, *awotomma*; h. he is, etc., *(aw)otta -vae·f*, etc.; h. is the man, *ot an dēn*: **-abouts,** adv. *a-dro dhe'n tyller-ma*: **-after,** adv. *wosa hemma*, *alemma rak*: n. *termyn a-dhē*: **-by,** adv. *gans* or *drē hemma*: **-in,** adv. *y'n tyller-ma*, *yn hemma*: **-tofore,** adv. *kens*, *k. (ag)es hemma*: **-upon, -with,** adv. *gans-hemma.*
heresy, n. *camgryjyans*, *tebelgryjyans*, m., *ēr*, ‡*e·rysy*, m., pl. *-s*: **-etic,** n. *camgryjyk*, m., pl. *-jygyon*, ‡*ertyk* (*e·rytyk*), m., pl. *-ys*: **-etical,** a. *camgryjyk*, **ery·tycal.*
heritage, n. *ertach*, m., pl. *-ajys*, *ertons*, m.
hermaphrodite, n. *gorryth wow*, m.
hermit, n. *ancar*, m., pl. *-coryon*, *hermyt*, m., pl. *-ys*: **-age,** n. *ancarjy*, *penytty*, *teghyjy*, *hermytty*, m., pl. *-ow*, *hermytach*, m., pl. *ajys.*
hero, n. *dēn brās y golon*, m., pl. *tüs brās aga holon*, *brasyon*: **-ic,** a. *brās y golon*, *colonnek drēs ēghen*: **-ine,** n. *myrgh* or *benen brās hy holon*, f., pl. *myrghes* or *benenes brās aga h.*: **-ism,** n. *colonnekter drēs ēghen*, m.
heron, n. *kerghyth*, f., pl. *-ydhas*: **-ry,** n. *kerghythva*, f.
herring, n. *hernen wyn*, f., col. *hern gwyn*; red h., *hernen rüth.*
hesitate, v. *hokkya*, *perthy danjer*; don't h. to eat it, *y dhybry byth na-borth danjer*: **-tingly,** adv. *yn ün hokkya*: **-ation,** n. *hokkyans*, m., (with *perthy*, *hep*) *danjer*, m.
hew, v. *trēghy*, *falsa*, **kemena*, *hakkya.*
hey! hi!, int., as call for attention, *ay*!, *hay*!, *ȳa*!, *how*!; call to stop, *ho*!
hiatus, n. *gwakter*, **gwagla*, m.
hibernate, v. *gwavy*, *cusca drēs an gwāf*: **-ation,** n. *cusk gwāf*, m.
hiccup, v. **hycas*: n. **hyk*, m., pl. *hycow.*
hide, n. *croghen*, f., pl. *crēghyn*; strip of h., *crōn*, m., pl. *-ow.*
hide, v. *keles*, *cüdha*; h. oneself, *omgeles*, *omgüdha*; h. up, *gorhery*; h. away, *gorra yn-ban dhe govva*: **-den,** a. *cüth*, *kēl*, *prȳva*: **-ing,** n., in(to) h., *dhe govva*, *yn dan gēl*, *y. d. güth*: **-ing-place,** n. *covva* (from *cüth-va*), f., *kēl*, m., pl. *-ow*, *cüth*, m.
hideous, a. *hager*, *üthek*; to make h., *hagry*: **-ness,** n. *hakter*, *üthekter*, m.

high, a. *ughel*; as old prefix, †*ugh-*; on h., *a-van, a-ughon, yn ughelder*; h. place, *arth, bans*, m., pl. *-ow, ban*, m. or f., pl. *-now*; h. tide, **lanow*, **gorlanow*, m.; the h. seas, *dyfȳthvor*: **-land,** n. *ugheldyr*, m., pl. *-yow*: **-er,** n. *Gwydhal Alban*, m., pl. *-as A.*: **the H's.,** n. *an Ugheldyryow*: **-ness,** n. *ughelder*, m.

highway, n. *forth-vür*, f., pl. *-dhow-mür*: **-man,** n. *lader an forth-vür*, m., pl. *ladron a. f. v.*

hiker, n. *gwandryas*, m., pl. *-ysy*.

hilarity, n. *lowender, wharth*, m.: **-ious,** a. *lowenek, codhys* or *dyeskynnys yn wharth, mery bys yn folneth*.

hill, n. *meneth*, m., pl. *-nydhyow, bron*, m. or f., pls. *-yon, -now, bryn*, m., pl. *-yow, brē*, f., pl. *-ow* (as suffix, *-bra, -vra, -fra*), *rȳn*, m., pl. *-yow, garth*, f., pl. *-ow*: **-ock,** n. *menedhyk*, m., pl. *-ygow, knogh, knēgh*, m. pl. *-yow, pȳl*, m., pls. *-yer, -yow, tolgh*, m., pl. *-ow*; small h., *godolgh*, m., pl. *-ow*: dim. *godolghyn*, m., pl. *-now*; h. of sand, *towan*, m., pl. *tewennow*; h. or mound, *rȳnen*, f., pl. *-now*; round-topped h., *meneth crom*, m., *molfra*, f.: **-side,** n. *rȳn*, m., pl. *-yow*; very steep h., *leder*, f., pl. *-drow*: **h.-top,** n. *pen meneth, mujoven*, f., pl. *-now*: **-y,** a. *menedhek*.

hillo! int. *how*!

hilt, n. *trōs*, m., pl. *treys, dorn*, m., pl. *-ow*.

him, pron. *ef, e*; suffixed, *-va*; emphatic, *-ee·f, -vae·f*; infixed, *-n-*; of, to, h., etc., *anodho, dhodho*, etc.: **-self,** pron. *y honen*; jocular, *map y dhama, m. y vam*; all by h., *y honen-oll*.

hind, n. *ewyk*, f., pl. *-ygas*; h. roe, *hedhes*, f., pl. *-ow*.

hind, n., on farm, *gwas tȳak*, m., pl. *gwesyon t.*

hind, -er, a. *a-dhelergh*: **-er part,** n. *delergh, tu d.*, m.: **-ermost,** a. *an dewetha, an moyha warle·rgh*: **h.-quarters,** n. *pedren*, f., pl. *-now, d. dybedren*.

hinder, v. *lettya, lesta*: **-drance,** n. *let*, m., pl. *-tys*.

hinge, n. *bagh*, m., pl. *-ow*, †*medynor*, f., pl. *-ow*.

hint, v. *leverel yn-dan gēl, rȳ neppyth a aswonvos*, **hyntya*: n. *tokyn*, m., pl. *-knys*, **hynt*, m., pl. *-ys*.

hip, n. *clün*, f., pl. *-yow*, d. *dywglün, penclün*, f., pl. *-yow*, d. *pen dywglün*: h. bone, *cūlbren gȳew*, m.

hip, n., of rose, **agrowsen*, f., col. **agrows*.

hippopotamus, n. *dowrvargh*, m., pl. *-vergh*.

hire, v. *arfeth, gobrena*; pay wage to, **gobra*: n. *arfeth*, m., pl. *-edhow*: **-ling,** n. **goberwas*, m., pl. *-wesyon, servont gober*, m., pl. *-vons g*.

his, pron. *y*²; it is h., *ef a-n-pew, dhodho-ef yth-yu*.

hiss, v. *tythya, whybana*, **sȳ*, **sȳa*: **-er,** n. *whybanor*, m., pl. *-oryon*: **-ing,** n. **sȳa*: inf. *tythyans*, m.

history, n. *y·story*, m., pls. *-ow, -s*: **-rian,** n. *ystoryor*, m., pl. *-yon*: **-ric,** a. *ystorek*.

hit, v. *squattya* (*scattya*), *knoukya, cronkya*: n. *squat* (*scat*), m., pl. *-tow, what*, m., pl. *-tys, bommen*, f., pl. *-now*; h. or miss, *cam py compes*.

hitch, v. *cachya*; fasten, *kelmy*: n. *colm*, m., pl. *-ow, colmen*, f., pl. *-now*.

hither, adv. *omma, wor' tu-ma, bys omma*; come h! *düs nēs*!: **-to,** adv. *whath, kens* (*es*) *lemmyn, a'y üs, bys y'n ür-ma, bys y'n jēth hedhyu*.

hive, n. *cowel gwenyn*, m., pls. *-low g., kewel-g*.

ho! int. *how*! *ow*!; hold! stop! *ho*!

hoard, v. *gwytha clōs, gorra yn-ban dhe govva, cuntell, gwytha*: n. *frūt gwythys*, m. *arghans cuntellys*, col.; place, *covva*, f., **armerth*, m., pl. *-ow*.

hoar-frost, n. *rew gwyn, newlen rew*, f.; **losrew*, m.

hoarse, a. *hōs*, †*crek, ronk*: **-ly,** adv., to speak h., *hōsy, renky*: **-ness,** n. *hosyas, renkyas*, m.

hoary, a. *lōs, gwyn*.

hoax, n. *tull, dyssayt*, m.: v. *tulla, dyssaytya*.

hobble, v. *cloppya*; h. an animal, *spralla*: n. *cam cloppek*, m.; of animal, *spral*, m., pl. *-low, sprallyer*, m., pl. *-s*.

hobby, n. *hobba*, m., pl. *-bys*; h. horse (May Day), *hoby-hors*, m.; the h.h. and his "pare," *an hoby-hors ha'y gowetha*; Christmas h.h., *Pen-glās*, m.

hobgoblin, n. *bucca, b.-nōs*, m., pl. *bukkyas*, **bygel, b. nōs*, m.

hobnail, n. *kenter eskys*, f., pl. *-trow e*.

hoe, n. *pygal*, f., pl. *-golow*, **whenogel*, f., pl. *-glow*, **cravell*, f., pl. *-ow*: v. *pygellas, cravellas*.

hog, n. *hogh, torgh*, m., pl. *-as*, col. *mogh*; young, *ragomogh*, m.: **h.'s.-pudding,** n. *gosogen*, f., pl. *-now*: **h.-weed,** n. *losowmogh*, col.

hogshead, n. *balyer,* m., pls. *-s, -ow, hosket,* m., pls. *-tys, -tow.*
hoist, v. *halya, tenna yn-ban*: n. *halyer,* m.
hold, v. *synsy*; contain, *contaynya*; h. on, *dalghenna, kensynsy*; h. out, endure, *paragh, perthy*; h. or esteem oneself, *omsynsy*; h. the field, *synsy gwēl*; h. together with stitches, *crafa*; **h**. on! h. hard! *hedheugh*! *ho*! *kē war dha gam*!; h. forth, *arethya, predheges*: n. *dalghen,* f., pl. *-now, gavel,* f., pl. *-yow, dornla,* m.; of ship, *strās,* m., pl. *-ow*; keep h. of, *kensynsy*; lay h. of, *sēsya, settya dalghen(now) yn*; take h., *dalghenna*; imperative, *tan*! *tanneugh*!: **-ing,** n., farm, *bargen* (*tȳr*), m., pl. *-ys t., tre(f),* f., pl. *trevow*; small h., *godre*(f), f., pl. *-evy*; uncultivated h., *croft,* m., pl. *-ow.*
hole, n. *toll,* m., pl. *tell*; perforation, socket, *crow,* m., pl. *-ow*; small, *sorn,* m., pl. *sernow, tellyk,* m.. pl. *-ygow*: **-d,** a., punctured, perforated, etc., *tellys, polys, toll*; with one h., *tollek*; full of h's., *tellek.*
holiday, n. *dēgol, gōl,* m., pl. *dedhyow gōl, termyn dysquytha,* m., pl. *-yow d.*; to go on h., *havy, omdhysquytha*; make h., *golya*: **h.-maker,** n. *golyer,* m., pl. *-yoryon*; summer h., *havyas,* m., pl. *-ys.*
holy, a. *sans, benygys, hynwys*; of saints, days, etc., *gwyn*; h. man, *sans,* m., pl. *syns*; h. woman, *sanses,* f., pl. *-ow*: **-liness,** n. *sansoleth,* f., *benesykter,* m.
hollow, a. *cow, toll, tollek, gwak*; of voice, *ronk*: n. *cow,* m., pl. *-yow, dyppa,* m., pl. *-pys*; h. way, *keyforth,* f., pl. *-rdhow*; small valley, dell, *pans, gobans,* m., pl. *-ow, haun,* f., pl. *-ow*: v. *cowa.*
holly, n. *kelynen,* f., col. *kelyn*; h. grove, *kelynek,* f., pl. *-egy, -egow.*
hollyhock, n. *malowen lowarth,* f., col. *malow l.*
holm-oak, n. *glastanen,* f., col. *glastan.*
holt, n. *kelly,* f., pl. *-yow.*
homage, n. *omach,* m., **gwaso·nyeth,* f.; one who pays h., *o·majer,* m., pl. *-s.*
home, n. *trē,* f., pl. *-vow, olas,* f., pl. *-ow*; fixed h., *hendra,* f., pl. *-revow*; at h., *yn-chȳ, yn-trē*; to go h., *mōs trē*; from h., *a-drē*; h. with you! go h! *dhe-drē*! *kē dhe'th trē*!; welcome h! *wolcum yn-trē*!; I'll take them h., *my a-vyn aga dōn genef yn-chȳ*: **h.-bred,** a. *megys yn trē*: **-ly,** a. *sempel*: **h.-made,** a. *gwrēs yn trē*: **h.sick,** a. *hyrethek, morethek*: **h.sickness,** n. *hȳreth, moreth,* m.: **h. stead,** n. *tre(f),* f., pl. *-vow, treveth,* f., pl. *-ow*: **h.wards,** adv. *tu ha trē, dhe-drē.*
homicide, n., act or person, *dēnlath,* m.; person only, *denledhyas,* m., pl. *-ysy.*
homonym, n. *keshanow,* m., pl. *-hynwyn.*
hone, n. *agolen,* f., pl. *-now.*
honest, a. *lēn, lēl*: **-ly,** adv. *gans lendury, hep flows, hep fraus, hep wow*: **-y,** n. *lendury, leldury, lelder,* m.
honey, n. *mēl,* m.; my h., endearment, *ow melder,* m. or f.; h.-comb, *crȳben mēl,* f., pl. *-now m.*; to gather h., *mēla* (inf. only); h.-yielding, *melek*: **-ed,** a. *melys*: **h.dew,** n. *melgowas,* f., pl. *-osow*: **h.suckle,** n. **gwythvosen,* f., col. *gwȳthvos* (*gwyfos*).
honour, n. *gordhyans, brȳ, worshyp, rēouta,* m., *enor, onour,* m., pls. *-ys, -s*; to mention with h., *kywhethla*; to bring h., *gül worshyp* (*dhe*[2]); h. bright, *re'm lēouta, er ow fȳth, er dha lēouta*: v. *onoura, enora, gordhya*; by mention, *kywhethla*: **-able,** a. *wordhy, a vrȳ, a brȳs, enorys*; h. mention, *kywhethlans,* m.: **-orary,** a. *hep wober, drē enor.*
hood, n., of monk, †*cügol,* m., pl. *-low, hot,* m., pl. *-tys*; for riding, *hük,* f., pls. *-ys, hücow*: **-ed,** a. *cügolek*; h. crow, *brān Marghas Yow,* f., **fraw,* m., pl. *-as*: **h. wink,** v. *tulla, cüdha fās* or *lagasow dēn aral, gül dhodho bōs "margh-dall."*
hoof, n. *carn,* m., pl. *-ow*: **-ed,** a. *carnak.*
hook, n. *bagh,* m., pl. *-ow*; fish h., *hȳk,* m., pl. *-gow, hygen,* f., pl. *-now*; bill-h., **gwydhyf,* m., pl. *-yvow*; reaping h., *cromman,* m., pl. *-ow*; furze h., *cromman-eythyn*; h.-rod, *gwelen-hȳk, -hygen,* f.: v. *bagha, hygenna.*
hoop, n. *kelgh,* m., pl. *-ow.*
hooping-cough, n. *pās garm,* m.
hoot, n. *üs,* m., pl. *-ow, üjow, ullyans,* m.; I don't care a h., *ny-rōf oy*: v. *üja, hüa, ullya*: **-er,** n. *üjer,* m., pl. *-joryon*: **-ing,** a. *üjek.*
hop, n. *lam,* m., pl. *-mow*: v. *lamma, lemmel, cronogas, lefanjas.*
hop, n., bot., *pensak,* col., *hopysen,* f., col. *hopys*; h. garden, *hopysek,* f., pl. *-egow, -egy.*
hope, n. *trest,* m., *govenek,* m., pl. and abst. *-ygyon, gwaytyans,* m.; in the h. that, *mar*[4]: v. *gwaytya, fydhya, trestya*; I should h. so! *po Dew dyfen*!: **-ful,** a. *lün a waytyans*; promising, *lün a dhedhewadow*: **-fulness,** n. *gwaytyans,* m.: **-less,** a. *hep* or *drēs gwaytyans, dywaytyans*; a h. muddle, *kemysk drēs y dhygemysky.*

hopper, n., frog, toad, etc., *lefans*, m., pls. *lefyns, lefanjas*; h. of mill, **kern*, f., pl. *-yow*.
horde, n. *lu*, m., pl. *-yow, rūth*, f., pl. *-ow*.
horehound, n. †*les-lōs*, m.
horizon, n. **gorwel*, m.
horn, n., of animal or wind-instrument, *corn*, m., pls. *kern, kernow*; battle h., *cascorn*, m., pl. *-kern*; little h., *kernyk*, m., pl. *-ygow*; Gorsedd h., *Corn Gwlās*: **h.-blower,** n. *kernyas*, m., pl. *-ysy*; **h.-book,** primer, n. *lyver corn*: **-ed,** a. *kernek*; single h., *cornak, ūncorn*: **-less,** a. *mōl*.
hornet, n. *whyrnores*, f., pl. *-ow*.
horror, n. *scrüth*, m., pl. *-ow, üth, üthekter*, m.: **h.-stricken,** a. *üth ganso*; to be h., *kemeres scrüth*: **-rible,** a. *vȳl, scrüthüs, üthek, scrüth* or *üth y weles* or *y glewes, grysyl*: **-bly,** adv. *bylen, vȳl, üthek, dyflas*: **-rify,** v. *gorra scrüth yn*.
horse, n. *margh*, m., pl. *mergh* (*an vergh*), group pl., *merghas, marghas* (*an varghas*), *stēda*, m., pl. *-dys*; riding h., *hobba*, m., pl. *-bys*; war-h., *casvargh*, m., pl. *-vergh*: **h. back,** n. *keyn margh*; on h., *war geyn margh*: **h.-block,** n. *marghven*, m., pl. *-veyn*: **h.-breeder,** n. *mager mergh*: **h.-cloth,** n. *gorheras-margh*, m., **pallen margh*, f., **keynlen*, f., pl. *-now*: **h.-collar,** n. *mongar*, f., pl. *-ger, mongaren*, f., pl. *-now*: **h.-fly,** n. *sudronen*, f., pl. *-now*, col. *sudron*: **h.-hair,** n. *rünen margh*, f., col. *rün m.*: **h.-hide,** n. *marghken*, m.: **h. leech,** n. *gēl margh*, f., pl. *-as m.*: **h.load,** n. *saw*, m., pl. *-yow*: **h.man,** n. *marghak* (*marrek*), m., pl. *-ghogyon, marghoger*, m., pl. *-goryon*: **h.-mackerel,** n. *scad*, m., pl. *-dys*: **h.manship,** n. **marghogeth*, m.: **h.-pond,** n. *marghbol, pol margh, marghlyn, lyn marghas*, m.: **h.-race,** n. *resekva mergh*, f.: **h.-radish,** n. *marghredyk*, m.: **h.shoe,** n. *horn margh*, m., pl. *hern m.*: **h.tail,** n., bot., *lost margh*, m.: **h.-tamer,** n. *temprer-margh*, m., pl. *-roryon-m.*: **h.-woman,** n. *marghoges*, f., pl. *-ow*.
hose, n. †*hosan*, f., pl. *-ow*, col. *hōs*; stocking, *loder*, m., pl. *-drow*: **h.-pipe,** n. *pȳb heblyth*, f.: **-sier,** n. *gwerther lodrow* or *hōs*, m., pl. *-oryon l., h.*
hospice, n. **spyty*, m., pl. *-ow*.
hospitable, a. *hēl*.
hospital, n., **spyty*, m., pl. *-ow*; esp. for lepers, *clavjy* (*clojy*), m., pl. *-ow*.
hospitality, n. *gwestva*, f., *helder*, m.
host, n., army, *lu*, m., pl. *-yow, ōst*, m., pl. *-ys, nerth*, m., pl. *-ow*; of house, *ōst*, m., pl. *-ys*; eccl., *Corf Crȳst y'n Oferen*: **-stel,** n. *ostel*, f., pl. *-yow*: **-stelry,** n. *ostlery*, m.: **-ess,** n. *ostes*, f., pl. *-ow*.
hostage, n. *gwystel*, m., pl. *-tlow*.
hostile, a. *contraryüs, ave·l escar*: **-ility,** n. *cās, envy*, m.
hot, a. *tom, pōth*; ardent, *gwresak*; sultry, **tesak*; very h., *brōs*; to make h., *tomhē·*: **h.-house,** n. *tomjy*, m., pl. *-ow*: **-ness,** n. *pothter, potvan, tomder*, m.
hotel, n. *ostel*, f., pl. *-yow*.
hound, n. *kȳ*, m., pl. *cün, hond*, m., pl. *hons*, **helgy*, m., pl. *-gün*; as terms of abuse, *hond, kȳ*; large running h., ‡*gwylter*, m.; scent h., *rech*, m., pl. *-ys*; gase-h., grey-h., *mylgy*, m., pl. *-gün, rēsky*, m., pl. *-scün, grēont(d)*, m., pl. *-ons, kȳ hȳr*, m., pl. *cün hȳr*.
hour, n. *ür*, f., pl. *-yow*; in reckoning time, *owr*, m., pl. *-ys*; within an h., *a-jȳ dhe owr*; h's. time, *ürwyth*, f., pl. *-yow*; any h., *neb-ür*: **h.-glass,** n. *ürweder*, m., pl. *-drow*.
house, n. *chȳ* (in compounds *-jȳ, -tȳ*), m., pls. *-ow, treven, trevow*; dwelling h., *chȳ-anneth, trygva*; cow h., *bowjy*; calf h., *lughty*; mill-h., *melynjy*: v. *annedhy*; of cattle, etc., *crowya*: **h.-breaking,** n. *terry chȳ*, m.: **housed,** a. *annedhys, y'n harber*: **h.hold,** n. *mēny*, m., *tȳlu*, m., pl. *-yow, tyegeth*, m., pl. *-ow*, †*coscar*, †*goscor*, col.: **h.holder,** n. *tȳak*, m., pls. *-yogyon*, †*-yogow, pen-tylu*, m.: **h. leek,** n. **bewvyth*, f.: **h.maid,** n. *maghteth*, f., pl. *meghty-thyon*: **h.wife,** n. *be·nenvās* (*ben'vās*), *gwre'ty*, f., pl. *gwrageth chȳ*.
hovel, n. *crow*, m., pl. *-yow*.
hover, v. *trenyja*, **bargesy*.
how, adv. *fatel*², *fatla*; h. is he? *fatel yu ganso*? *pyth yu y jēr*?; I don't know h., *ny-won fatla*; h. . . . and h. . . ., *fatel*² . . . *ha del*² . . .; h. many, *pes, py lȳes, py sül*; h. much, h. great(ly), h. many, *pygemmys*; how long, *pygemmyshēs*; h. often, *pygemmys prȳs, py lȳes termyn* or *gwyth*; h., exclam., before adj., with *ellas*! *myr*! etc., *ha*; h., exclam. before v., *ass(a)*², particle, as h. tired I am! *ass-oma squyth*! etc.: **-ever,** adv., h. great he were (lit. though he were ever so great), *kyn fē* (*vȳth*) *mar vrās*; h., nevertheless, conj. *bytege·ns*.

howl, n. *üs, üj,* m., pl. *-jow*: v. *ūllya, üja*: **-er,** n. *üjer,* m., pl. *-joryon*: **-ing,** n. *ūllyans,* m., *üvva,* f.
hoyden, n. *scowt,* f., pl. *-ys.*
hubbub, n. *hubbadrylsy, hubbadullya,* **hūb,* **ūb,* m., *kedry·n,* f.
huddle, v. *kemysky,* **gwasca*: **-d up,** a. *gyllys yn gron.*
hue, n. *lyw,* m., pl. *-yow.*
hug, v. *gwrynya, strotha*; affectionately, *byrla, chersya*: n. *gwrynyans, strothans,* m.
huge, a. *brās drēs ēghen,* ‡*üthek brās,* ‡*hūjes.*
hulk, n.: see **hull.**
hulking, a., h. person, *quallok,* m., pl. *-ys.*
hull, n. *corf gorhel,* m., pl. *-ow gorholyon.*
hullo! int. *ow!, how!*
hum, v. *whyrny, sȳa*: n. *sȳ,* m.: **hummer,** n. *whyrnor,* m., pl. *-yon,* f. *-es,* pl. *-ow.*
human, a. *dēn, mabden,* **dēnyl,* **dēnüs*; h. race, *kynda mabden, dēnsys,* m.: **-e,** a. *whēk, whar, kerenjedhek*: **-ity,** n., human kind, *dēnsys, mabden,* m.; sense of h., *denseth,* m.: **-ize,** v. *wharhē·.*
humble, a. *whar, hüvel*; h. or base, *ysel*; to be h., *omhüvla*: v. *hüvelhē·*: **-d,** a. *drēs dhe yselder.*
humbug, n. *tull,* m.; person, *tullor,* m., pl. *-yon,* f. *-es,* pl. *-ow, falsgwas,* m., pl. *-wesyon.*
humerus, n. **pa·lather-brēgh,* m., pl. *-lether b.*
humid, a. *glyp,* **lȳth*: **-ity,** n. *lythter.*
humiliate, v. *huvelhē·, gül bysmē·r dhe*[2], *shamya*: **-d,** a. *drēs dhe yselder*: **-ation,** n. *yselder, shām, bysmē·r,* m.: **-ity,** n. *hüvelder,* m., *hüvelsys,* f.
humour, n. **humor, jolyfta,* m.: **-ous,** a. *frēth, jolyf.*
hump, hunch, n. *bothan,* m., pl. *-now, both,* f., pl. *-ow*: **h.-back,** n. *bothak,* m., pl. *-ogyon*: **h.-backed,** a. *bothak, crom y geyn,* **keyngrom.*
hundred, a., n. *cans,* m., pl. *-ow*; h. times, *canquyth*; two h., *deu cans*; three h., *try-hans*; h. thousand, *cansvyl,* m., pl. *-yow*; h.-pound weight, *canspüns,* m.; h.-fold, *cansplēk*; county division, *keverang* (for *kevran*), f., pl. *-ow*; h. court, h. men, †*cangour,* m.; chief of h. court, †*pencan-gour,* m.: **-th,** a., n. *cansves*: **-weight,** n. *canspōs,* m.
hung, a. *yn crok.*
hunger, n. *nown,* m.; extreme h., *ewl (awel), e. bōs* or *dhe vōs* f., *esow,* m.: **-ry,** a. *nownek, ewlek, gwak*; I am h., *yma·nown dhym, ewl dybry a-m-büs.*
hunt, v. *chassya, helghya (hely(a))*: n. *helgh (hel),* m., **hel(gh)va,* f.: **-er,** n. *helghor,* m., pl. *-yon, helghyas,* m., pl. *-ysy, helghyer (helyer),* m., pl. *-yoryon, honter,* m., pl. *-s*; horse, **helvargh,* m., pl. *-vergh*: **-ing,** n. **he(gh)lva,* f.; to go h., *sportya*: **-ing-dress,** n. **helwysk,* m.: **-ing-horn,** **hel-gorn,* m., pl. *-gern*: **-sman**: see **-hunter.**
hurdle, n. *clōs,* f., pl. *-ojow.*
hurl, v. *deghesy, tewlel*: **-er,** n. *towlor,* m., pl. *-yon*; in game, *hurlyas,* m., pl. *-ysy*: **-ing,** n., game, *hurlya,* m.; to play at h., *hurlya.*
hurricane, n. *hagerawel, enawel,* f., **cor-wyns,* **herdhwyns,* m.
hurry, n. *hast, tōth, rē a dōth*: v. *fystyna, dehelghya, stēvya.*
hurried, a. *hastyf*: **-ly,** adv. *war, yn* or *gans hast.*
hurt, v. *droga, golȳa,* **glosa, pystyga, brewy, myshevya, gül dregyn, shyndya, hurtya*; smart, *lesky, payna*: n. *pystyk,* m., pl. *-ygow, dregyn,* m., *drōk,* m., pl. *-ogow, brew,* m., pl. *-yon, myshyf,* m., pl. *-evys*: **-ful,** a. *drōk.*
husband, n. *dremā·s, gour,* m., pl. *gwēr, gorty,* m., *coth, gourgoth,* m., pl. *gwērgoth, prȳas,* m., pl. *-yosow*; bad h., *gwan-worty, tebel-wour,* m.: **-man,** n. *trevesyk,* m., pls. *-ygyon, -ejygyon, tȳak,* m., pls. *-yogyon, -yogow,* **ameth,* m., pl. *emyth*: **-ry,** n. **amethyans,* m.: v., to h. one's resources, *gwytha y byth.*
hush, v. *tewel*; int. *taw! teweugh! whyst! gās dha glap!*
husk, n. *plysken,* f., pl. *-now,* col. *plysk, üsyn,* m., pl. *üsyon,* col. *üs, cūth,* f., pl. *-ow,* **maskel,* f., pl. *-sclow*; full of h's., *üsak*: v. *plysca, dyblysca*: **-less,** a. *dyblysk, dyüs*: **-y,** a., of voice, *hōs,* †*crek, ronk.*
hussy, n. *flownen,* f., pl. *-now, scowt,* f., pl. *-ys.*
hustle, v. *fysky, fystyna, chassya.*
hut, n. *crow,* m., pl. *-yow*; ancient h., *crellas,* m.
hutch, n. *argh,* f., pls. *-ow, erghy.*
hybrid, a. *kemyskryth*: n. *mȳl* or *losowen k.*
hydromel, n. *medheklyn,* m., †*bragas,* m.
hydrophobia, n. *connar,* f.
hymn, n. **hympna,* m., pl. *-nys*: **-book,** n. **hympner, lyver hympnys,* m.

hypocrisy, n. *fekyl lavarow,* pl. *fekyl chēr, fayntys, *ypocrysy,* m.: **-ite,** n. *dēn fals,* m., pl. *tüs fals, *ypocryt,* m., pl. *-ys*: **-itical,** a. *fekyl.*
hysterics, n. *cleves an brȳs, fowt omrewlya,* m.: **-ical,** a. *claf hy brȳs, rē ēs hy müvya, gwan hy omrewlya.*

I

I, pron. *mȳ*; suffixed *-vȳ, -ma, -a*; stressed, *-avȳ·, -mavȳ·.*
ice, n. *rew, †yey, clēghȳ,* m.: **-cicle,** n. *clōghȳ,* m., pl. *clēghȳ*: **-cy,** a. *yeyn, rewys, †ōr.*
idea, n. *tybyans,* m., *cusül,* f., pl. *-yow, consay·t,* m.; a most erroneous i., *poynt brās a gamdybyans*; quick to get i.s, *jolyf a dhesevos*: **-l,** a. *a-dhevȳ·s, gwella, perfyth*; opposite to "real." *a'n spyrys*: n. *govenek ughel, whans,* m.
identical, a. *keth, hevelep*: **-ity,** n. *hevelepter,* m.
idiom, n. *yēth,* f., pl. *-ow, tavas,* m., pl. *-ow, ‡tavaseth, lavar specyal ün yēth*: **-atic,** a. *herwyth gȳs an yēth.*
idiot, n. *bobba,* m., pl. *-bys, ydyot* (*‡edyak*), m.: **-ic,** a. *goky, fol*: **-ocy,** n. *gokyneth, folneth,* m.
idle, a. *trüfyl, dȳek, wast, syger, üfer*: v. *crowdra, sygera*: **-ness,** n. *dȳegy, dȳekter, sygerneth,* m.: **-r,** n. *losel, lorel,* m., pl. *-s.*
idol, n. *ymach a dhew fals, *ȳdol,* m., pl. *-ys, boba·n,* m., pl. *-ys*; he is the people's i., *an düs keth a-n-gorth, yma· kepa·r ha dew dhe'n bobel*: **-ater,** *gordhyer ymajys, ȳdolys,* m., pl. *-yoryon y.*: **-atry,** n. *gordhyans ymajys.*
if, conj., of unlikely events, *a*[4]; of likely events, i. so be, what i., i. only, i. but, *mar*[4] (*s*), *mara*[4](*s*); of an alternative, *hag a*[4], *ha mar*[4].
igneous, a. *tanek, a dān*: **-nite,** v. *gorra tān yn.*
ignoble, a. *gal, vylen, sempel.*
ignominy, n. *bysmē·r, mewl, vȳlta, vy·lyny,* m.: **-ious,** a. *vȳl, *methüs.*
ignore, v. *bōs hep aswon*; he i's. that, *ny-vyn aswonvos,* or *myras orth, henna*: **-ramus,** n. *pen cōk, †talsōgh,* m.: **-rance,** n. *ny·cyta, fowt skȳans,* m.: **-rant,** a. *dyskȳans*; I am i. of it, *ny-wōn travyth anodho.*
ilex, n. *glastannen,* f., col. *glastan.*
ill, a., bad, *drōk, tebel*; sick, *clāf*; i. person, *clāf,* m., pl. *clevyon*; make i., *grevya*; i. at ease, *anēs*: n. *drōk,* m., pl. *-ogow*; to do i., *camwül*; to report i. of, *drok-gerya*: **-ness,** n. *grefons,* m., *drōk,* m., pl. *-ogow, cleves,* m., pl. *-vejow*: **i.-born,** a. *drōk* or *tebel -genesyk*; also i.b. person, m., pl. *-ygyon*: **i.-bred,** a. *drōk y vegyans*: **i.-clad,** a. *ternōth*: **i.-deed,** n. *camwythres, gwan-ober, drok-ober, tebel-wrȳans, camwrȳans,* m.: **i.-doer,** n. *drok-oberor,* m., pl. *-yon*: **i.-fated,** a. *anfüsek*: **i.-favoured,** a. *hager*: **i.-health,** n. *yēghes gwan,* m.: **i.-luck,** n. *anfüs,* f., *hapdrōk,* m.: **i.-natured,** a. *drōk y gnās*: **i.-omen,** n. *tebel-gōl,* f., *sȳn drōk,* m.: **-ed,** a. *anfüsyk*: **i.-pleased,** a. *drōk-pȳs*: **i.-repute,** n. *drōk-gēr,* m.: **i.-scented,** a. *messe·nt*: **i.-timed,** a. *mēs a'y dermyn, gwrēs y'n gwetha prȳs*: **i.-tongued,** a. *drōk y davas, hy thavas, aga thavas,* etc., *‡drokdavasek*: **i.-treat,** v. *tebel-dȳghtya, drokhandla*: **i.-turn,** n. *tebel dorn, drōk-tro,* m.: **i.-use,** v. *drok-handla, tebel dȳghtya, deffola*: **i.-will,** n. *attȳ, envy* (*avy*), m., *drok-vrüs,* m.
illegal, a. *erby·n lagha.*
illegible, a. *na-yller y rēdya.*
illiterate, a. *lēk, dydhysk.*
illuminate, v. *golowy, *lymna, *enlu·myna*: **-ation,** n. *golowys,* m., abst. *golowyjyon.*
illusion, n. *hüs,* m., *tarosvan,* m., pl. *-now*: **-ary,** a. *tarosvanüs.*
illustrate, v. *delynya, dysquedhes*: **-ation,** n. *delynyans, dysquedhyans,* m., pl. *-ow*: **-trious,** a. *splan, mür y vrȳ.*
image, n. *hevelepter,* m., *hevelep,* m., pl. *-ebow, ymach,* m., pl. *-ajys*; grotesque i., *boba·n* (M.E. *babewin*): **-ry,** n. *y·majery,* m.: **-gine,** v. *tyby, desevos, desmygy*: **-ginary,** a. *a'n tybyans*: **-ation,** n. *ynjyn,* m., pl. *-nys, tybyans,* m.; poetic, **awen,* f.
imbecile, a. *gwan y skȳans*: n. *fōl,* m., pl. *felyon,* f., *-es,* pl. *-ow, bobba,* m., pl. *-bys, penpyst,* m.
imbibe, v. *eva, *sugna.*
imitate, v. *gül warle·rgh*: **-ation,** n. *hevelepter,* m.; in i. of, *del o gwrēs gans, warle·rgh.*
immaculate, a. *dynam.*
immaterial, a. *dygorf*; it is i., *ny-vern.*
immature, a. *tender yn ōs, dyathves*: **-ity,** n. *newyth,* m.
immeasurable, a. *dyvusür.*
immediate, a. *trom, desempys*: **-ly,** adv. *dystough, adhystough, dyson, dewha·ns, adhewha·ns, desempys, a-dhesempys, ‡mēs a dhorn, prest, knak* (*stak*) *omma, kens es*

hedhy, hep lettya, hep namoy·let, hep hokkya, hep ardak, war-nuk, yn by- an-by; i. following, *ow-tegensewa.*
immemorial, a. *drēs cōf dēn.*
immense, a. *brās drēs musür*: **-sity,** n. *braster drēs musür,* m.
immerse, v. *sedhy, gorthroghya, gorra yndan dowr*: **-sion,** n. *sēth,* m., pl. *-edhow.*
imminent, a. *ow-tegensewa*; to be i., *degensewa, scon dhe sewya.*
immoderate, a. *drēs musür.*
immodest, a. *dyveth.*
immoral, a. *camhensek.*
immortal, a. *prest a-vew, hep deweth,* **dyvarow*: **-ity,** n. *bewnans hep deweth,* m.
imp, n. *bucca,* m., pl. *-ukkyas, dyawlyk,* m., pl. *-ygow, map an pla,* m., pl. *mebyon an p.*
impair, v. *apērya, gül dregyn dhe²*, *gwethhē·.*
impart, v. *rȳ, dysky.*
impartial, a. *ewn, lēl*: **-ity,** n. *ewnder, lelder,* m.
impassable, a. *hep forth, na-yllyr y dremena.*
impatience, n. *fowt perthyans,* m.: **-nt,** a. *dyberthyans, tēr, na-gar godhevel.*
impeach, v. *cuhüda*: **-er,** n. *cuhüdhor,* m., pl. *-oryon, cuhüdhyas,* m., pl. *-ysy,* †*cuhüdhojak,* m., pl. *-ogyon*: **-ment,** n. *cuhüdhans,* m., pl. *-ow.*
impede, v. *spralla, ancombra, lettya*: **-diment,** n. *spral,* m., pl. *-low, ancombrynsy,* m.; in speech, *stlaveth,* m.
impel, v. *herdhya.*
impend, v. *degensewa.*
impenetrable, a. *tew, na-yllyr y dhewana.*
imperative, a. it is i., *rēs porres yu.*
imperfect, a. *nammys, scant nag-yu perfyth, a-fyll a'y vōs perfyth, nag-yu dȳen*: **-ion,** n. *nam, fäll,* m.: **-ly,** adv. *yn ran.*
imperial, a. *a'n emperoreth.*
imperishable, a. *nefra na-wra pedry, a-bȳs nefra, a-dhür bys vyken.*
impersonate, v. *omwül* or *gwary bōs.*
impertinence, n. *camworthyp, fara dyveth,* m.: **-nt,** a. *tōnt*; to be i., *tontya, scornya*: **-ntly,** adv. *yn-tōnt*; to reply i., *camwortheby.*
impetus, n. *herdhyans,* m.: **-tuous,** a. *gwyls,* **fysk, ter*; to be i., *tēry*: **-ly,** adv. *yn-fēn, ave·l tüs (pyth) fol*: **-osity,** n. **fysk.*
impiety, n. **ansansoleth, fowt revrons,* m.: **-ious,** a. *ungrassyes,* **dyrā·s,* **ansans, hep revrons.*
implacable, a. *na-yllyr y dhyserry.*
implement, n. *toul,* m., pl. *-ys*: v. *collenwel.*
implore, v. *pysy.*
imply, v. *rȳ dhe grysy*; that i's., *drē henna yth-yu.*
impolite, a. *dyscortes, anwhēk.*
import, v. *drȳ y'n pow*: n. *da yu drēs y'n pow*; meaning, *styr,* m., pl. *-yow*: **-ance,** n. *prȳs, brȳ, roweth,* m.; it is of no i., *travyth ny-vern, na fors*: **-ant,** a. *bysy, a vrȳ, a brȳs, a-vern, dhe lēs*; it is i. for you to be careful, *bysy yu dheugh bones wār.*
importune, v. *ynnȳa*: **-nate,** a. *bysy.*
impose (upon), v. *tulla, hüda*: **-sing,** *bryntyn*; of size, *mür drēs ēghen*: **-sition,** n., penalty, *pȳn, bēgh,* m.; palming off, *supposyans,* m.; impost., *trübyt,* m.
impossible, a. *unpossybyl*; it is i., *ny-ȳl bōs*; it is i. to, *ny-yllyr*: **-bility,** n. *tra na-ȳl bōs,* m., pl. *taclow n. y. b.*; thing never done, *ancothvos,* m.
impostor, n. *faytour,* m., pl. *-s, hüder,* m., pl. *-oryon, falsgwas,* m., pl. *-wesyon.*
impotent, a. *dyallos, dynerth,* †*anvēn, dyspuyssant.*
impracticable, a. *na-yllyr y wül.*
imprecation, n. *mollath,* f., pl. *-lothow,* ‡*mollethyans,* m.
impress, v. *pryntya, ympryntya,* **gwasca*: **-ion,** n., track, *ōl,* m., pl. *-ow*; seal, *sēl,* f., pl. *-yow, ympryntyans,* m.: **-ive,** a. *ow-mōs y'n golon, owth-amüvya yn-town*: **-iveness,** n. *solempnyta,* m.
imprison, v. *prysonya*: **-ment,** n. *prysonyans,* m.
improbable, a. *na-ȳl bōs gwaytyes*; it is i. that he will come, *scant ny-ȳl dōs*: **-bility,** n. *tra üs dh'y dhowtya* or *nag-üs dh'y waytya.*
impromptu, a. *hep y barüsy, nag-yu darbarys, hep bōs gwrēs parys.*
improper, a. *ancoth,* †*camhensek, erby·n onester, na-dhego·th*: **-riety,** n. *ancothfos,* m.
improve, v. *gwellhē·, amendya*: **-ment,** n. *amendyans,* m., pl. *-ow.*
improvident, a. *dybreder*: **-ence,** n. *fowt provya* or *preder.*
improvise, v. *gül hep defnyth ewn, hep darbary.*
imprudence, n. *fowt preder*: **-ent,** a. *dybreder,* †*anfür.*
impudence, n. *fara tōnt*: **-ent,** a. *tōnt, dyveth*; be i., *tontya.*
impulse, n., mental, *müvyans,* m.; physical, *herdhyans,* m.: **-sion,** n. *herdhyans,* m.:

-sive, a. **fysk,* **tēr*; to be i., **tēry, bōs ber y breder*: **-sively,** adv. *hep preder, rē a-poynt.*
impunity, a., with i., *hep payn* or *pȳn, hep godhaf bōs punsys ragtho.*
impure, a. *mostys, afla·n, aflanyth*: **-rity,** n. *mostethes, aflanythter,* m.
impute, v. *cuhüdha*; falsely, *supposya.*
in, prep. *yn, y'*; i. two, *yntra deu*; within, *a-berth yn, a-jȳ dhe*[2]; a rogue i. a thousand, *sherewa yn-mysk mȳl*; with parts of body, *a*[2]; i. which, whom, etc., *may*[5]*(th)*: adv. *a-jȳ, yn-chȳ, yn-trē, a-berveth*; let him i., *gās e dhe entra*; who is i.? *pyu üs yn-trē?*; i. me, etc., *ynnof,* etc.; i. myself, *ynnof-vȳ ow honen.*
inability, n. *fowt gallos, dyfrethter,* m.
inaccessible, a. *na-yllyr dhodho hedhes, drēs hedhes.*
inaccuracy, n. *fowt composter,* m.: **-ate,** a. *nag-yu kewar* or *compes.*
inadvertent, a. *dyswār*: **-ly,** adv. *drē wall, a'y anvoth.*
inane, a. *goky, gwak.*
inanimate, a. *dyenef (dyena), hep bewnans.*
inarticulate, a. *omlavar,* †*aflavar,* †*stlaf.*
inasmuch as, conj. *pan*[2], *a-ban*[2], *par del*[2], *yn mar vür del*[2].
inattention, n. *gwall, fowt attendyans,* m.: **-ive,** a., he is i., *ny-rē scovarn, ny-vyn attendya.*
inaugurate, v. *dalleth, fundya*: **-tion,** n. *dalleth, fundyans,* m.
inborn, a. *ynno genys.*
incandescent, a. *gwyn drē domder,* **gwyn-flam.*
incantation, n. *sōn,* m., pl. *-ow,* †*gorhan,* f., pl. *-ow*: see **enchant.**
incapable, a. *antȳthy, hep gallos,* **dyallos*; he is i. of it, *ny-yl gül henna, ny-sēf y wül yn y allos*; i. person, *evreth,* m., pl. *-edhyon, pylyak,* m., pl. *-yogyon.*
incarnation, n. *yncarnasyon,* m., *kemeres kȳk, mōs ha bōs dēn,* infs.
incense, n. *yncens,* †*enkys,* m.
incentive, n. †*garthow, pȳgans,* m.; our i. was . . ., *an pyth esa orth agan trēlya dhodho o . . .*
incessant, a. *hep powes, hep hedhy*: **-ly,** adv. *anhedhek, prest, hep powes, hep hedhy, pup ür-oll.*
inch, n. *mesva,* f., pl. *-vedhy*; every i. a knight, *marghak a-dhevȳ·s.*
incident, n. *cās, wharfedhyans,* m.: **-ally,** adv. *ynwe·th, drē hap.*
incipient, a. *ow-talleth, yn kensa dalleth.*
incision, n. *trēgh,* m., pl. *-ow.*
incite, v. *ynnȳa, müvya, sordya, pȳga*: **-ment**: see **incentive.**
incline, v. *plegya, ynclynya, stümma*; lean, *posa*: n. **goleder,* f., pls. *-drow, -dry*: **-nation,** n. *plegadow,* m., *stüm,* m., pl. *-mow*; desire, *lüst,* m., pl. *-ys, whans, bōth,* m.: **-ned,** a., disposed, *plegadow, parys*; they do as they are i., *y a-sew aga bōth-y.*
include, v. *comprehendya, synsy ynno, rekna* or *kemeres warba·rth*: **-usion,** n. *synsyans*: **-usive,** a. *synsys* or *reknys warba·rth.*
incoherent, a. †*stlaf, dyskevelsys y lavarow.*
income, n. *rent,* m., pl. *-ys.*
incomparable, a. *hep par(ow).*
incompetence, n., *fowt gallos,* m.: **-ent,** a., he is i. to do so, *ny-ȳl* or *drēs y allos yu yndella gül.*
incomplete, a., it is i., *nyns-yu dȳen, cowal* or *perfyth, nyns-yu gwrēs yn-tȳen,* or *cowlwrēs.*
inconclusive, a. *na-ȳl conclūdya.*
inconsistent, a. *dygesson, brottel, ow-trēlya y gowsesow.*
inconstant, a. *brottel, fekyl.*
incontinent, a. *na-ȳl omrewlya, dyrewl*: **-ly,** adv. *dewha·ns, desempys.*
inconvenience, n. *dysē·s, ancombrynsy,* m. **-ent,** a. *a-annȳ·, na-dheseth.*
incorporate, v. *ünya, gül bōs corf*: a. *gwrēs bōs corf.*
incorrect, a. *dygompes, cam, nag-üs ewn*: **-ness,** n. *dygomposter, fowt kewerder,* m.
incorrigible, a. *trüs*; he is i., *nyns-yu dh'y gesky*; i. person, *drōk-ebol.*
increase, v. *encressya (cressya), moghhē·*: n. *encressyans, tevyans,* m.
incredible, a. *na-yllyr y, nag-üs dh'y, grysy*; i. thing, *aneth,* m., pl. *-ow.*
incredulity, n. *dyscryjyans,* m.: **-lous,** a. *dyscryjyk*; i. persons, *dyscryjygyon.*
incriminate, v. *cably, cuhüdha*: **-ting,** a. *ow-trȳ cabel.*
incubate, v. *covȳa*: **-tion,** n. *covȳans,* m.
inculpate, v. *cably.*
incur, v. *omgemeres, tenna warnodho.*
indebted, a., owing gratitude, *synsys*; owing money, *yn kendon.*
indecency, n. **dysonester, fara dyveth,* m.: **-ent, indecorous,** a. **dysonest*; i. person, *scaf a'y lygyon,* m.

indeed, adv. *yn prōf, hep whethel, hep gӯl, hep gow (heb ow), defrӯ·, yn-tefrӯ·, fest, dhe wӯr, yn-whӯr, dyogel, yn-tyogel, ywy·s*; i. I should not, *ny-wrüssen nēs*; Ohi. ! *ӯa* ! *yē* !
indefatigable, a. *hep squythder, na-yllyr y squytha.*
indefinite, a. *nag-yu dyblans*: **-inable,** a. *hep form, na-ӯl bōs gorrys yn geryow.*
indemnify, v. *gwytha rak coll, attylly, dyffres, gül restoryta dhe*[2]: **-nity,** n. *atta·l, sawment, dyffresyans,* m.
indent, v. *gül bōs dynsak*: **-ure,** n. *ambos,* m., pl. *-ow, gwarak üs trēghys yntra dyw gans trēgh dynsak,* f.
independence, n. **rӯthsys,* m.: **-ent,** a. *ow-sevel a'y honen, dystak, rӯth dywostyth.*
index, n. *menegva,* f., pl. *-ow*; i. finger, *bӯs a-rak* (*b. rag*).
India, n. *Eynda,* f.: **-n,** a. *Eyndek,* (*a*) *Eynda*; I. file, *yn ün rew.*
indicate, v. *kevarwedha, dysquedhes*: **-tion,** n. *tokyn,* m., pl. *-knys, sӯn,* m., pl. *-ys, arweth,* f., pl. *-edhyow, kevarwedhyans,* m., *menek,* m., pl. *-egow, dysquedhyans,* m.: **-tor,** n. *kevarwedhor,* m., pl. *-yon, dysquedhyas,* m., pl. *-ysy.*
indict, v. *cuhüdha*: **-ment,** n. *cuhüdhans,* m.
indifference, n. *mygylder, clorder,* m.; sloth, *sygerneth,* m.: **-nt,** a. *mygyl, clōr, syger, *dywhans*; to become i., *mygla*; I am i., *pynӯ·l vo, fors ny-rof* or *ny-m-dür.*
indigence, n. *esow,* m.: **-nt,** a. *boghosek, ethomek*; i. person, *pylyak,* m., pl. *-yogyon.*
indigestion, n. *drōk tor, drōk *gōans,* m.
indignant, a. *serrys*: **-ation,** n. *sōr,* m.
indigo, n. *glesyn Eynda.*
indirect, a. *gwӯüs, cam, nag-yu ewn*: **-ly,** adv. *drē forth cam, d. f. wӯüs*; he goes i. to his object, *ef a dh'y borpos yn ün wӯa* or *y. ü. scolkya.*
indiscreet, a. *nag-yu dōth, anfür, dybreder, drok-avӯsyes*: **-ly,** adv. *hep fürneth, yn-tybreder*: **-tion,** n. *folneth, anfürneth, fowt preder,* m.
indispensable, a. *a-rēs porres, na-yllyr y hepcor.*
indisposed, a. *nebes clāf*: **-ition,** n. *cleves scaf.*
indisputable, a. *dyogel, nyns-üs dh'y dhys-pūtya.*
indistinct, a. *tewl, *dysclēr*; of speech, *stlaf*: **-ly,** adv., of seeing, *yn-tewl*; of speaking, *yn-stlaf, yn ün stlevy*: **-ness,** n., of sight, *tewlder,* m.; of speech, *stlaveth,* m.

individual, n. *dēn,* m., pl. *tüs*; every i., *pup onen, kettep onen, k. pol, k. pen, k. mappro·n, mēster ha maw, mowes ha maw*: a. *y honen,* etc.: **-ity,** n. *gnās,* f.: **-ly,** *onen hag onen, yn kettep pen.*
indolence, n. *dyekter, sygerneth,* m.: **-t,** a. *dӯek, syger.*
induce, v. *tenna, dynya*: **-ment,** n. *dynyans, tenvos,* m.
induct, v. *gorra yn stallasyon*: **-ion,** n., the i., *an gorra y. s.*
indulge, v. *bōs rē güf dhe*[2]; i. in, *omrӯ dhe*[2].
industrious, a. *dywysyk*: **-ry,** n. *dywysygneth,* m.; an i., *gwӯth,* m., pl. *-yow, ober,* m., pl. *-ow.*
ineffectual, -ficient, a. *üfer, mothow, na-wra lēs, nag-yu 'vas.*
inequality, n. *dygomposter, fowt bōs parow,* m.
inert, a. *dyfrēth, antӯthy, †dycreft*: **-ness,** n. *dyfrethter,* m.
inevitable, a. *na-yllyr y avodya* or *goheles.*
inexpert, a. *hep creft, †dycreft, *dydhysk.*
infallible, a. *byth na-fyll*: **-bly,** adv. *hep fall*(*adow*).
infamous, a. *drōk-geryes, meth y henwel*: **-y,** n. *drōk-gēr, bysmē·r, meth,* m.
infant, n. *flēghyk,* m., pl. *-ghesygow, flogh bӯghan,* pl. *fleghes v., map omlavar* or *aflavar,* m., pl. *mebyon o., a., meppyk,* m., pls. *-ygow, mebyonygow, baby,* m., pl. *-ow*: **-ncy,** n. *flogholeth,* m.: **-icide,** n. *floghlath,* m.: **-ile,** a. *kepa·r ha flogh, *floghyl.*
infantry, n. *soudoryon trōs,* pl.
infatuated, a. *hüdys, müskegys*: **-ation,** n. *hüs, muskegyans,* m.
infect, v. *venymya, posnya, hasa cleves*: **-ion,** n. *venym, hās cleves,* m.: **-ious,** a. *venymys, a-yllyr y gemeres.*
infer, v. *supposya, tenna*: **-ence,** n. *an pyth üs tennys,* m.
inferior, a. *lē, ysella, gweth*: n. *lē y grē*: **-ity,** n. *yselder, gwethter,* m.
infernal, a. *yffarnak*; i. regions, *yffarnow,* pl.
infertile, a. *sēgh, dyfyth*; of seeds, *cōk.*
infest, v. *tropla, bōs pla.*
infidel, n. *dyscryjyk,* m., pl. *-ygyon*: **-ity,** n. *fowt lelder, dyslelder, dyscryjyans,* m.
infinite, a. *hep fӯn, h. deweth, h. worfen.*
infirm, a. *gwan, clāf, †anyagh*: **-ary,** n. **spyty,* m.; for lepers, *clavjy* (*clojy*), m.: **-ity,** n. *gwander, ‡gwanegreth, gref, cleves,* m.

inflame, v. *dywy, enawy*; of sore, *scaldya, *ynflamya, *fakly*: **-mmable,** a. *helo·sk*: **-mmation,** n. *losk*, m., *fakel*, f., pl. *-clow, *tanyjyon, *ynflamyans*, m.

inflate, v. *whetha, whethfy*: **-ion,** n. *whethfyans*, m.

inflict, v. *gorra* (*war*^{2}), *rӯ*; i. grief, torture, *ankenya, payna*: **-ion,** n. *kessydhyans*, m., pl. *-ow*.

influence, v. *müvya, dynya*: n. *roweth, gallos*, m.: **-ntial,** a *gallosek, mür y roweth*; i. person, *dēn a vrӯ, rowtor*, m,. pl. *-s*.

inform, v. *gwarnya, deryvas*: **-ation,** n *deryvadow*, m.: **-er,** n. *cuhudhor*, m., pl. *-yon*.

infrequent, a. *na-dhē namenough*: **-ly,** adv. *boghes venough, anvenough*.

infringe, v. *tremena drēs, deffola*: **-ment,** n. *mōs drēs*, inf.

infuriate, v. *serry yn-frās*: **-ting,** a. *a-drē connar, ow-cül bōs sōr fol*.

infuse, v. *trōtha, godrotha*: **-sion,** n. *godroth* m.

ingenious, a. *ynjyn*: **-nuity,** n. *ynjyn*, m.

ingenuous, a. *hep tull na gӯl*.

inglorious, a. *hep enor*.

ingratitude, n. *fowt aswon grās*, m.

ingredient, n. *ran*, f., pl. *-now, elven*, f., pl. *-now*.

inhabit, v. *tryga, annedhy, kevannedhy, bōs trygys*: **-ant,** n. *tryger*, m., pl. *-oryon*: **-ation,** n. *trygva*, f.

inhale, v. *tenna anal, anella*: **-ation,** n. *anellans*, m.

inherit, v. *e·ryta*: **-ance,** n. *ertons* (*e·rytons*), *ertach* (*e·rytach*), m., pl. *-ajys*.

inhuman, a. *dygnās, hep denseth, garow*: **-ity,** n. *fowt denseth, garowder*, m.

iniquity, n. *sherewynsy, sherewneth, camhenseth, *anewnder, dewlüjy*, m.: **-tous,** a. *hager, drōk, cam drēs ēghen*.

initial, a. *kensa*: n., i. letter, *lytheren vrās, l. tāl, kensa lytheren*, f., pl. *-now*: **-ate,** v. *dalleth*; of bards, *degemeres, *urdha*: n. *barth noweth*, m.: **-ative,** n., take the i., *gül dalleth*.

inject, v. **skӯtya* (*yn*): **-ion,** n. **skӯtyans*, m.

injudicious, a. *nag-yu dōth, anfür*.

injunction, n. *gorhemmyn*(*adow*), *dyfen*(*nadow*), m.

injure, v. *myshevya, deffola, pystyga, shyndya, apērya, gül dregyn dhe*^{2}, *brewy*: **-rious,** n. *drōk, cam, *damajyes*: **-ry,** n. *brew*, m., pl. *-yon, myshyf*, m., pl. *-evys, pystyk*, m., pl. *-ygow, cam*, m., pl. *-mow, dregyn, drocoleth, brewvan*, m.

injustice, n. *camhenseth, fowt ewnder*, ‡*anjustys, falsury*, m.

ink, n. *ynk*, m.; i.-well, i. pot, *padel-ynk*, f., pls. *-llow, -lly-y*.

inland, a. *aberveth y'n pow, yn crēs an tӯr*.

inlet, n. *logh*, f., pl. *-ow, brēgh an mōr*, f.; piece let in, *darn üs gorrys yn tra aral*.

inmate, n. *tryger*, m., pl. *-oryon*; i.s., *mēny chӯ*, m.

inmost, a. *downa, d. aberveth, nessa dhe'n crēs*; i. thought, *cowsys*, m., pl. and abst. *-sesow, -jejyow*.

inn, n. *tavern*, m., pl. *-yow*: **i.-keeper,** n. *tavernor*, m., pl. *-yon, -our*, pl. *-s, ōst* (*an chӯ*), m., pl. *-ys*, f. *-es*, pl. *-ow*.

innate, a. *ynno genys*.

inner, innermost: see **inmost.**

innocence, n. *gwyryonsys*, m.: **-nt,** a. *glan, y·nocent, gwyryon, gwergh, hep drōk*.

innovate, v. **nowedhy, chanjya, drӯ taclow noweth dhe*^{2}: **-tion,** n. **nowedhyans*, m., pl. *-ow, tra noweth*, m., pl. *taclow n.*: **-tor,** n. **nowedher*, m., pl. *-oryon*.

innumerable, a. **dynyver, drēs aga myvera*.

inoffensive, a. *hep drōk, whar, clōr, *dydhrōk*.

inopportune, a. *mēs a'y ewn brӯs*: **-ly,** adv. *yn gwetha prӯs*.

inquest, n. *whythrans yn kēn ancow*, m.

inquire, v. *govyn*: **-ry,** n. *govynnadow, whythrans*, m., pl. *-ow, questyon*, m., pl. *-s*.

inquisition, n. **ynquysysyon, apposyans, whythrans*, m.: **-itive,** a. *a-gar whylas, a-whyla gothvos rē*: **-itor,** n. *ynquy·sytor*, m., pl. *-yon, apposyer*, m., pl. *-yoryon*.

insane, a. *varyes, dyskӯans, müscok, müskegys, mēs a'y rewl*, †*gwan a skӯans*: **-nity,** n. *müscotter, müscogneth*, m.

inscribe, v. *scryfa*: **-iption,** n. *scryfa*, m., pl. *-vadhow*.

insect, n. *prӯf*, m., pl. *pryves*.

insecure, a. *deantel*: **-rity,** n. *fowt sawder*.

insensible, a. *clamderys*: **-bility,** n. *clamder*, m.

insert, v. *gorra yn*: **-tion,** n. *tra üs gorrys yn tra arel*.

inside, prep. *a-berveth yn, aberth yn, a-jӯ dhe*^{2}: adv. *a-berveth, a-jӯ, y'n chy*: n. *an tu a-berveth*, m.

insidious, -ly, a., adv. *yn dan gēl*.

insight, n. *golok lym*, m.

insignia, n. *sӯnys, toknys, *arwedhyow*, pl.

insignificance, n. *fowt brȳ* or *styr*: **-nt,** a. *sempel, dystyr, hep brȳ* or *styr.*
insincere, a. *gow, fals, *dywyryon, fekyl, nag-yu gwȳr*: **-rity,** n. *falsury,* m.
insipid, a. *melys, dysawor, dyflas, *anvlas, üfer*: **-ity,** n. *üfereth, fowt blas, *anvlas,* m.
insist, v. *ynnȳa, ērya, bōs bysy*: **-ence,** n. *ynnȳadow*: **-ent,** a. *bysy*: **-ently,** adv. *hep hedhy.*
insolence, n. *tōnt-fara, despy·t, garowder,* m.: **-nt,** a. *despytys, tōnt*: **-ntly,** adv. *yn-tōnt.*
insomnia, n. *fowt cusca, anhün,* m.
insomuch as, adv. *a-ban*[2], *par del*[2], *yn mar vür del*[2].
inspect, v. *whythra, myras glew* (*orth*): **-ion,** n. *whythrans,*: **-or,** n. *whythror,* m., pl. *-yon.*
inspire, v. *anella, gorra spyrys yn, enawy gans an spyrys*: **-ration,** n. **awen,* f., *gweres drē an spyrys, *spyryseth,* f.
instability, n. *brottelder,* m.
install, v. *ynstallya, gorra yn stallasyon*: **-ation,** n. *stallasyon,* m.
instalment, n. *ran,* f., pl. *-now.*
instance, n. *sampel,* m.; for i., *rak sampel, yn dysquedhyans.*
instant, n. *tuch, pols, prȳjwyth,* m.; this i., *knak omma*: a. *desempys*; the 5th i., *an pympes a'n mȳs-ma*: **-aneous,** a. *trom, desempys*: **-ly,-aneously,** adv. *a-dhesempys, a-dhystough, a-dhewha·ns, war* or *yn ün lam, ketto·th ha'n gēr.*
instead, adv. *yn lē*; i. of him, *yn y lē* (*-ef*); i. of, between adjs., *yn-dar.*
instep, n. *conna trōs,* m.
instinct, n. *gnās,* f., *gothvos drē gnās*: **-ive,** a. *a-dhē drē gnās*: **-ively,** adv. *drē gnās, hep bōs dyskys.*
institute, institution, n. *fundyans,* m., pl. *-ow*: v. *fundya.*
instruct, v. *dysky, kevarwedha*: **-ion,** n. *dyscans,* m.; i.s. sent, *danvonadow,* m.: **-or,** n. *dyscajor,* m., pl. *-yon.*
instrument, n. *dafar musyk, mayn,* m.: **-al,** a., he was i. in getting it done, *drē y vayn y-fē gwrēs*: i. music, *menestronthy,* m.
insufficient, a. *rē nebes*; it was i., *nyns-o lowr.*
insular, a. *enesek*: **-ity,** n. *ynder,* m.
insult, v. *despȳtya, arveth*: n. *despȳ·t,* m.
insure, v. *dyogely, sürhē·*: **-rance,** n. *dyogelyans, sürheans,* m.
insurrection, n. *sordyans,* m.
intact, a. *dȳen, *dywall, hep y apērya.*
intellect, intelligence, n. *skȳans,* m.: **-ual, -nt,** a. *skyansek.*
intemperance, n. *medhowynsy,* f., *fowt temprans, medhowenep,* m.: **-ate,** a. *dyglōr, drēs musür.*
intend, v. *jujja, mynnes, tewlel, ervȳra*; we i. to strike, *yma· war agan towl knoukya*: **-ntion,** n. *porpos, bōth, mynnas, brȳs, ente·nt,* m.; it is my i. to, *ervȳrys* or *avȳsyes ōf dhe*[2], *y-fynnaf*: **-ntionally,** adv. *der ente·nt, a borpos.*
intense, a. *tyn, mür, brās, crēf*: **-sity,** n. *nerth, braster,* m.: **-ive,** a. *specyal, dywysyk.*
inter, v. *encledhyes*: **-ment,** n. *encledhyas,* m.
intercede, v. *pysy gans, bōs mayn yntra*: **-cession, -cessor,** n. *mayn,* m.
intercept, v. *contrewaytya, dalghenna, lettya*
intercourse, n. *tremenyans, cowethyans, *daromres,* m.; talk, *kescows,* m.
interdependent, a., they are i., *omsewya y a-wra, y a-bōs an ȳl war y gȳla.*
interdict, v. *dyfen*: **-ion,** n. *dyfennadow,* m.
interest, def., v. *dür*; that does not i. me, *a henna ny-m-dür man*; if you are i.ed, *mara 'th-tür*: n. *lēs, bern,* m.; i. on money lent, **oker,* m.: **-ing,** a. *mür y-lēs, mür y vern, a-dāl y avȳsya.*
interfere, v. *mellya, yntramellya*: **-nce,** n. *mellyans,* m.
interim, n. (*yn*) *kettermyn,* m.
interior, a. *a-berveth, war-jȳ*: n. *parth a-jȳ, perveth,* m.
interlude, n. *ynterlüt,* m., pl. *-üdys.*
interminable, a. *hep deweth, nefra na-vyn bōs fynsys.*
intermingle, v. *kemysky, kesomgemysky.*
intermission, n. *spȳs, powes,* m.
intermittent, a. *a-dhē hag ā, na-bȳs saw rak sēson*; i. fever, *cleves sēson.*
internal, a. *a-berveth, a-jȳ.*
international, a. *ynter pow ha pow, *kesgwlasek.*
interpret, v. *styrya, glossya, trēlya*: **-ation,** n. *styr,* m., pl. *-yow*; **glossa,* m., pl. *-sys, styryans,* m., pl. *-ow.*
interrogate, v. *apposya, examnya*: **-tion,** n. *govynnadow, apposyans, examnasyon,* m.: **-ative,** a. *ow-covyn.*
interrupt, v. **goderry, astel*: **-tion,** **godor,* m.
interval, n. *spās,* m.
intervene, v. *dyberth yntra, dōs yntra*: **-ntion,** n. *mayn,* m.; but for his i., *na-vē ef.*

interview, v. *omweles*: n. *omwel*, m., pl. *-ow*.
interweave, v. **kesplethenna*, *plethy*: **-vable,** a. *hebleth*: **-woven,** a. *gwȳes*, *plethennys warbarth*; supple cords i. with thongs, *kerdyn gwethyn yn-mysk cronow*.
intestate, a. *hep gasa kemyn*.
intestine, n. *colon*, m., pl. *-yow*.
intimate, a. *ogas*, *kēr*; of knowledge, *down*; i. friend, *specyal brās*: v. *derȳvas*, *nōtya*: **-tion,** n. *deryvadow*, *aswonvos*, m.
into, prep. *yn*, *aberth yn*; i. the hands (of), *yntra dywla*.
intone, v. *tonya*: **-nation,** n. *tōn*, m., pl. *-yow*.
intoxicate, v. *me·dhowy*: **-d,** a. *medhow*, *me·dhowys*: **-ting,** a. *crēf*, *a-wra me·dhowy*: **-tion,** n. *me·dhowsys*, *me·dhowynsy*, ‡*me·-dhowenep* (*medhewnep*), m.
intractable, a. *gorth*, *stordy*; i. person, *drok-ebol*, m.
intrepid, a. *heb own*, *dyown*.
intricate, a. *gwȳüs*, **complek*, *kemyskys*: **-cy,** n. *keskelmyans*, m.
intrigue, n. *bras*, *towl*, *cast*, m.
introduce, v. *gül dhe aswon*, *comendya*, *gorra aberveth yn*, *dhe*²: **-ction,** n. *comend-yans*, m.
intrude, v. *omherdhya yntra* (*ter*): **-usion,** n. *omherdhyans*, m.
inundate, v. *dewraga*, *lȳva*: **-tion,** n. *lȳf*, m., pls. *-ow*, *-yvyow*, **reverthy*, m., pl. *-ow*.
invade, v. *dōs yn pow gans nerth*: **-asion,** n., as inf.
invalid, a., ill, *clāf*; of no force, *hep gallos drē lagha*: n. *clāf*, m., pl. *clevyon*, *dēn gwan*, m., *benen wan*, f., pl. *tüs wan*.
invaluable, a. *mür y brȳs*, *drüth drēs musür*.
invariable, a. *nefra na-janj*, *hep trēlva*.
inveigle, n. *flattra* (*-rya*), *tulla*, *hüda*, *dynya*: **-ment,** n. *antel*, f. *dynyans*, m., *trayn*, m., pl. *-ys*.
invent, v. *cafos*, *desmygy*, *devȳsya*: **-tion,** n. *desmyk*, m., pl. *-ygyon*, *devȳ·s*, m., pl. *-ys*, *jyn*, m., pl. *-nys*, ‡*vensyon*, m., pl. *-s*: **-ive,** a. *ynjyn*: **-or,** n. *devȳsour*, m., pl. *-s*.
inventory, n. *rōl pythow-chȳ*, f., pl. *-yow p*.
invert, v. *trebüchya*, *omwheles*, *gorra* or *trēlya y ben dhe woles*: **-sion,** n. *trebüchyans*, m.
invertebrate, a. *y geyn hep mellow*.
invest, v. *gorra arghans* (*dhe*²): **-ment,** n. *mona gorrys dhe wayn*, col.
investigate, v. *studhya*, *whythra*, *whylas*, *aspȳa glew yn*: **-tion,** n. *whythrans*, m.: **-tor, invigilator,** n. *whythrer*, m., pl. *roryon*.
invigorating, a. *a-rē nerth*, *a-grefhē·*.
invincible, a. **dydrȳgh*, *na-yllyr y drȳghy*.
invisible, a. **dywēl*, *mēs a wēl tüs*.
invite, v. *gelwel*; to feast, *kyfvewya*: **-tation,** n. *galow*, *kyfvewyans*, m.
invoke, v. *gelwel*, *pysy*, *crȳa* (*war*²): **-ocation,** n. *galow*, m.
involuntary, -rily, a., adv. *a'y anvoth*.
involve, v. *magly*, *omvagly*, *mayla*; entail, *drȳ ganso*.
inward, a. *a-berveth*; i. thought, *cowsys*, m., pl. and abst. *-esow*: **-ly,** adv. *war-jȳ*, *ynno-ef y honen*, etc.: **-s,** adv. *wor'tu a-berveth*.
ire, n. *sōr*, m.: **-rate,** a. *serrys*, *sor dhodho*.
Ireland, n. *Ywerdhon*, f.: **-rish,** a. *Ywer-dhonek*, *Gwydhalek Ywerdhon*: n., I. language, *Gwydhalek*, m.: **-rishman,** n. *Gwydhal*, m., pl. *-as*: **-rishwoman,** n. *Gwydhales*, f., pl. *-ow*.
iris, n., flower, *elestren*, f., col. *elester*; of eye including pupil, *bew an lagas*.
iron, n. *horn*, m., pl. *hern*; tungstate of i., *call*, m.; i. ochre on rockface, *callen*, f., pl. *-now*; ferruginous earth, *gossen*, f.; flat-i., n. **horn* or *levner dyllas*: a. *hornek*: v. *hernya*, *levna*: **i.-bearing,** a., i.b. ground, *hornek*, f., pls. *-egy*, *-egow*: **i.clad,** n. *lester hoberjon*, m., pl. *lystry h.*: a. *gwyskys yn horn*: **i.-foundry,** n. **tethva horn*, f., **tethla* or **tethty*, *horn*, m.: **i.monger,** n. *hornor*, m., pl. *-yon*, *gwerther dafar horn*, m., *-thoryon d. h.*: **i.-mould,** n. *nam horn*, m.: **i.-ore,** n. *mūn horn*, m..
irrational, a. *müskegys*, *hep rēson*, †*gorbollak*.
irregular, a. *dygompes*, *nag-yu ewn* or *leven*, *erby·n rewl*: **-ity,** n. *dygomposter*, m.
irresolute, a. *dyfrēth*, *owth-hokkya*.
irrevocable, a. *drēs galow*, *na-yllyr y janjya*.
irrigate, v. *dowra*: **-tion,** n. *dowrans*, m.
irritate, v. *serry*: **-tion,** n. *sōr*, m.
island, n. *enys*, f., pl. *enesow*; near i., *ragenys*, f., pl. *-nesow*: **-er,** n. *enesek*, m., pl. *-sogyon*: **-slet,** n. *enesyk*, f., pl. *-ygow*.
isolate, v. *dyberth*; i.d place, *enys*, f., *tyller kernwhylly*, m.: **-tion,** n. *dyberthva*, f.
Israel, n. *Ebbrow*, f.: **-ite,** n. *Yedhow*, m., pl. *-ewon*: **-itish,** a. *Yedhowek*.
issue, v. *dyllo*, *tardha*, *resek*, *danvon*, etc., *yn-mēs*: n. *dyllans*, m.; progeny, *yssew*, m., *hās*, col.; end, *deweth*, m., *fynweth*, f.
isthmus, n. *rōs*, f., pl. *-yow*, *conna tȳr*, *cüldyr*, **yndyr*, m., pl. *-yow*.

it, pron., as for **he, she, him, her,** etc.: **-s,** pron., as for **-his, hers**: **-self,** pron. *y honen*, m., *hy honen*, f.
Italy, n. *Ytaly*, f.: **-lian,** a., n. *Ytalek*, m., f. *-eges*, pl. *-ow*; I. language, n. *Ytalek*, m.
itch, v. *debrenna, cosa*; hanker, *sȳ*: n. *trosken*, m.: **-ing,** n. *cos, cosva*, f., *debron*, m.; fig. *sȳans, fancy*, m.
item, n. *poynt*, m., *tra*, neut.
ivory, n. *dans olyfans*, m.
ivy-bush, n. *ydhyowen*, f., col. *ydhyow*; place covered in i., *ydhyowek, -yowenak*, f., pls. *-egy, -egow*; covered in i., *ydhyowek*; i. berry, *grünen ydhyow*, f., col. *grün y.*; ground-i., *ydhyow dōr.*

J

jabber, v. *clappya*: n. *clap*, m.
jackass, n. *margh-asen*, m., pl. *-as.*
Jack-in-the-pulpit, n. *scaf a'y lygyon*, m.
jackdaw, n. *chogha*, m., pl. *-ghys, chōk, chōca*, m., pl. *-ōkys.*
jacket, n. *jerkyn*, m., pl. *-ys, pows*, **crȳspows*, f., pl. *-yow.*
jacksnipe, n. *dama-kȳogh*, f., pl. *-as.*
jade, n. *margh ūsyes, casek u. f.*, m.; wench, *moren*, f., pl. *moronyon, scowt*, f., pl. *-ys*: **-d,** a. *lafüryes, squythys, fethys.*
jagged, a. *dynsak.*
jam, n. *kyfyth*, m., pl. *-yow*, **jam*, m.
January, n. *mȳs-Genver*, m.; J. 1st, *Calan G., dē- Halan G.*
janitor, n. *porther*, m., pl. *-thoryon*, †*darrajor*, m., pl. *-yon.*
jar, v. *cryghylly*: n., jolt, *jag*, m., pl. *-gys*; a deuce of a j., *jag an pla.*
jar, n., vessel, *stēn*, m., pl. *-ys, sēth*, m., pl. *-ow*; large salting j., *bosseth* (*bussa*), m.
jaundice, n. *cleves melen*, m.: **-d,** a. *e·nvȳes.*
javelin, n. *gu*, m., pl. *-yow.*
jaw, n. †*grüth*, f., pl. *-üdhyow*, **awen*, f., pl. *-now*; j.s, *dywen*, d.: v. *gērya*, **tavasa*: **j.-bone,** n. *challa, chal*, m., pl. *-lys*, **carvan*, f., pl. *-ow.*
jay, n. **kegyn*, f., pl. *-as.*
jealous, a. **ōdhüs*, **gorvynnek*; he is j. of, *ef a-borth avy orth, yma· dhodho avy a²*: **-y,** n. *avy*, **ōth*, **gorvyn*, m.
jeer, v. *gēsya, gül gēs a², scornya*: n. *gēs*, m., *scorn*, m.
jelly, n. *cowlesen*, f., col. *cowles*: **j.-fish,** n. *morgowl(es)*, m.
jeopardize, v. *peryllya, gorra yn peryl*: **-dy,** n. *peryl*, **juparty.*
jerk, v. *squychya*: n. *squych*, m., pl. *-ys*; with a j., *war squych.*
jest, v. *scornya, gēsya*; j. at, *gül gēs a²*: n. *gēs, whethel wherthyn*, m.: **-er,** n. *gēsyer*, m., pl. *-yoryon, whethler wharth*, m., pl. *-loryon w.*
jet, n. *styf*, f., pl. *-yvow*; mineral, *mēn du.*
jetty, n. *cay*, m.
Jew, n. *Yedhow*, m., pl. *-dhewon*: **-ess,** n. *Yedhowes*, f., pl. *-ow*: **-ish,** a. *Yedhowek.*
jewel, n. *tegen*, f., *tegyn*, m., pls. *-now, jowal*, m., pl. *-welys*: **-ler,** n. *gwerther tegynnow*, **joweller*, m., pl. *-s*: **-lery,** n. *tegynnow*, pl.
jingle, v. *tynkyal*: n. *gwers a-wra tynkyal*; governess car, *car scaf dywrōs.*
job, n. *gwȳth*, m., pl. *-ow, whēl*, f., pl. *-yow, ober*, m., pl. *-ow.*
jocular, a. *lowenek, scaf y gows*: **-ity,** n. *gēs, lowender, scafter*, m.
jog, v., trudge, *trettya, trosya*; jolt, *herdhya, cryghylly, shakya*: n., shake, *jag*, m., pl. *-gys.*
join, v. *junnya, omjunnya dhe², kyjya*; carpentry, *scarfa, framya*; j. in one, *junnya dhe onen*; j. battle, *mellya*: **-er,** n. *sēr-pren*, m., pl. *sery-p., carpenter*, pls. *-toryon, -s, junnyour*, m., pl. *-s*: **-t,** n. *mel*, m., pl. *-low, kevals*, m., pl. *-yow, lȳth*, m., pl. *-yow, junt*, m., pl. *-ys*; joining, *junnyans*, m.; j. of flail, *kevren*, f., pl. *-now*; j. of meat, *ran kyk*, f.: prefix, *kes-, kev-*: **-ted,** a. *mellek*: **-tly,** adv. *warbar·th, kekefry·s.*
joist, n. *jȳst*, m., pl. *-ys*, †*keber*, f., pl. *-bryow.*
joke, v. *gēsya, gül gēs, kewsel yn ün wherthyn*: n. *gēs*, m., *cows wherthyn, wharthüs, lavar frēth.*
jolly, a. *lowenek, jolyf*: **-lity,** n. *lowender*, **jolyfta*, m.
jolt, n. *jag*, m., pl. *-gys*: v. *cryghylly.*
jonquil, n. *fȳonen*, f., col. *fȳon.*
jostle, v. *herdhya* (*erby·n*).
jot, n. *jēt*, m., *tam*, m., pl. *tymmyn, banna*, m., pl. *-ow, -how*; after neg., *man*; were I to break his commandment one j., *mara quren terry ün jēt y gomōndment.*
journal, n. **jornal*, m., pl. *-s*: **-ism,** n. *scryfa-newodhow*, m.: **-ist,** n. *scryfer newodhow*, m., pl. *-oryon n.*
journey, n. *kerth, vȳaj* (*-ach*), m., pl. *-ys, hens*, m., pls. *-y, -yow, henjy*: **j. work,** n. *dēdhwȳth*, m.: **j.man,** n. *dēdhwȳthor*, m., pl. *-yon*: v. *lafürya, vȳajya*; on foot, *travalya.*
joust, n. *jūst*, m., pl. *-ys*: v. *jūstya.*

Jove, n. *Jovyn*, m.
jovial, a. *lowenek, prest parys dhe vōs lowen.*
jowl, n. *challa* (*chal*), m., pl. *-lys*; jawbone, *ascorn an c.*, m.
joy, n. *lowena*, f., *lowender, joy*, m.: **-ful,** a. *hüth, hüdhyk, lowen, lowenek*; to be j., make j., *lowenhē·*: **-fulness,** n. *hüthter*, m.: **-less,** a. *drōk y jēr*, etc., *tryst*; to my j., *gwyn ow bys.*
jubilant, a. **gormoledhus.*
judge, v., n. *juj*, m., pl. *-jys, juster*, m., pl. *-s, brüsyas*, m., pl. *-ysy*, †*brüsyth*, m., pl. *-ydhyon*: v. *jujja, brüsy*: **-ment,** n. *brüs*, f., pl. *-ow, brüsyans*, m., pl. *-ow, dōm*, m.; bad j., *drōk-vrüs*, f.; day of j., *dēth deweth, d. brüs.*
judicious, a. *für, dōth.*
jug, n. *podyk*, m., pl. *-ygow, pycher*, m., pl. *-s.*
juggle, v. *juglya*: **-r,** n. *juglour*, m., pl. *-s*: **-ry,** n. **juglery*, m.
juice, n. *sūgan*, m.: **-less,** a. *sēgh*: **-ciness,** n. *ērder*, m.: **-cy,** a. **sugnek, ēr.*
July, n. *mȳs-Gortheren*, m.
jumble, v. *kemysky*: n. *kemyskys*, m.
jump, v. *lamma, lemmel*; j. about, *terlemmel, lappya*: n. *lam*, m., pl. *-mow*: **-er,** n. *lappyor*, m., pl. *-yon*, f. *-es*, pl. *-ow.*
junction, n. *ünyans*, m.; of waters, *kemper*, m., pl. *-prow*, †*kendefryon.*
June, n. *mȳs-Metheven*, m.
jungle, n. *gwylfos, dyfythcōs*, m.
junior, a. *yowynca*; j.s, *pobel yowynk*, f.
juniper, n. **merewen*, f., col. *merew.*
junk, n. *gorhel Cathay*; rope, *lovonow*, or *taclow, cōth nag-yu 'vās.*
junket, n. *lēth godrothys*, m.
Jupiter, n. *Jovyn*, m.
jurisdiction, n. *danjer, arlottes*, m.
juror, n. *tȳyas*, m., pl. *-ysy.*
jury, n. *an deudhek dēn*: **-man,** n. *dēn a'n deudhek*, m.
just, a. *ewnhensek, ewn, lēl, gwyryon, a-dhevy·s, just*: adv., exactly, *poran*; only, *ünwyth*; j. about, with a., *ogas*, with v., *namna(g)*; j. now, j. before, *namnyge·n*; only j., freshly, *noweth, a-dhewedhes*; j. now, *agensow, degensow, solabrȳ·s*; j. as, *kepa·r del*[2]; j. as much as I like, *dhe'm devȳ·s*; j. right, *a-dhevȳ·s*; j. like that, *yn-ketella, yndella kettep onen*; j. like this, *poran yn-ketelma*: **-ice,** n. *ewnder, lelder*, m., *gwȳr vrüs*, f.: **-iciary,** n., judge, *justys*, m., pl. *-yow, juster*, m., pl. *-s*: **-ifiable,** a. *a-yllyr y avowa*: **-ification,** n. *ewnans*, m.: **-y,** v. *ewna*; of one's action, *avowa*: **-ly,** adv. *quyt, yn-ewn*; prefix. *ewn-, lēn-.*
jut out, v. *sevel yn-rak, omherdhya yn-mēs.*
jut, n. *el*, f., pl. *-yow*: **-ting,** a. *elek, *balek.*
juvenile, a. *yowynk* (*yonk*).

K

kale, n. *cawlen*, f., col. *cawl*; sea-k., *morgawlen*, f., col. *mōrgawl.*
keel, n. *keyn lester*, m., pl. *-ow lystry.*
keen, a. *tyn, fȳn, ahas, lym*: **-ness,** n. *lymder, tynder*, m.
keep, v. *gwytha, synsy*; k. on, *pēsya, bōs bysy*; k. down, *compressa*; k. from, *lettya a*[2]; k. a promise, *kewera dedhewys*; k. house, *synsy chȳ, bōs annedhys*; k. to that! *byth na-ās henna!*: **-er,** n. *gwythyas*, m., pl. *-ysy*: **-sake,** n. *covath, cofro*, m.
ken, v. *medra, aswon, gweles*: n. *gweles, gothvos, convedhes.*
kennel, n. *kȳjȳ*, m., pl. *-ow, cünjȳ*, m., pl. *-ow*; gutter, *shanel*, m.
kerchief, n. *lȳen*, m., pl. *-enyow, *coverchyf*, m., pl. *-yvys.*
kern, v., to harden, of grain, *grünya.*
kernel, n. *sprüsen* (*spüsen*), f., pl. *-now*, col. *sprüs* (*spüs*), **bewesen*, f.
kestrel, n. *tygry* (*tykery*), m., pl. *-as, cryshōk*, m., pl. *-ys.*
kettle, n. *chek*, m., pl. *-kys, caltor*, f., pl. *-yow*; tea-k., *chek tē.*
kettledrum, n. *naker*, m., pl. *nacrys.*
kex, n. *gwelen-gegys*, col., *keser*, m., pl. *-ow.*
key, n. *alwheth, dyalwheth*, m., pl. *-edhow* (*whe'ow*); small k., *dyalwhedhyk*, m., pl. *-dhygow*; fasten with a k., *alwhedha*; open with a k., *dyalwhedha*: **k.-hole,** n. *tollalwheth*, m., pl. *tell-a.*
kick, v. *potya*; k. against, *offendya*: n. *pōt* (*pūt*) m., pl. *-ow, *towl eskys*, m., pl. *-ow e.*
kid, n. *myn*, m., pl. *menas*, dim., *mynen*, f., *mynyk*, m., pls. *-ygow, menasygow*; child, *meppyk*, m., pls. *-ygow, mebyonygow, myrghyk*, f., pl. *myrghesygow, flēghyk*, m., pls. *fleghesygow, -ghygow.*
kidney, n. *loneth*, f., pl. *-y*; k. bean, *faven Frynkek*, f., col. *fa(f) F.*
kill, v. *ladha*: **-ing,** n. *lath*, m., *lathva*, f.: **-er,** n. *ladher*, m., pl. *-dhoryon*, f. *-dhores*, pl. *-ow, ledhyas*, m., pl. *-ysy.*
kiln, n. *forn*, f., pl. *-ow*; lime k., *forn lȳm*; brick k., *forn meyn-prȳ*; potter's k., *forn lystry-prȳ*; k.-tender, *forner*, m., pl. *-noryon.*

kin, n. *cothmens*, pl. *ēghen*, f.; next of k., *neshevyn*, m. and col., *car nessa*, m., pl., *kerens, n.*

kind, n. *par*, m., pl. *-ow, ēghen*, f., *kynda*, m., *sort*, m., pl. *-ow*; suffix, *-rȳth*, f.; of dress, *sewt*, m.: a. *da, cüf, debone·r, whēk, whegoll*; k. person, *densa*, m.; k. regards, *gorhemmynadow a'n gwella.*

kind-hearted, a. *colonnek, whēk y golon.*

kindle, v. *dywy, gorra tān yn, enawy, cüna.*

kindlings, n. *scommow*, pl.

kindly, a. *hegar, whēk, kerensedhek.*

kindness, n. *whekter, cüfter, caradewder*, m.; a k., *dader, torn da*, m.; if we can do you a k., *mara kyllyn dheugh gül da*; for k. sake, *paramou·r.*

kindred, n. *ēghen*, f., *neshevyn*, col. *kerens*, pl.

kine, n. *gwarthek*, **byw*, col. *bughas*, pl.

king, n. *myghte·rn*, m., pl. *-eth*: **-ly,** a. *rȳal*, ‡*myghternyth*: **-ship,** n. *myghternsys*, m.: **-dom,** n. *gwlascor*, f., pl. *-ow*, **myghternas*, f., pl. *-nosow*, †*revaneth*, m.: **k.fisher,** n. *pyscador an myghte·rn*, m., pl. *-as an m.*

kink, n. *dōl*, f., pl. *-ow.*

kinsman, n. *neshevyn*, m. and col., *car*, m., pl. *kerens.*

kiss, v. *amma dhe*^{2}, *baya, drȳ* or *rȳ bay*: n. *am*, m., pl. *-mow, bay*, m., pl. *-ow*, †*cüssyn*, m., pl. *-now*; give me a k., *doro dhym dha vay.*

kitchen, n. *kegyn*, f., pl. *-ow*; k. garden, *erbyer*, m., pl. *-s, losowek*, f., pls., *-egow, egy*; k. maid, *kegyn-vyrgh*, f., pl. *-es.*

kite, n. *scowl*, m., pl. *-as*; toy, **sarf nyja*, f., pls. *syrf, n.*

kith, n. *ēghen*, f., *cothmens*, m., pl.; k. and kin, *tȳlu ha tȳthy.*

kitten, n. *cathyk*, m., pls. *-ygow, -thasygow.*

knack, n. *prat*, m., pl. *-tys, wrynch*, m., pl. *-ys, cast*, m., pl. *-ys*, **hyk*, f., pl. *-ygyon.*

knacker, n. *kyger mergh*, m., pl. *-goryon*, m.

knapsack, n. *sagh keyn*, m., pl. *-ow k.*

knapweed, n. *pederow-pronter*, pl.

knave, n. *drōk-pollat*, m., pl. *-ys, drōkwas*, m., pl. *-wesyon, drōk-coscar*, col. *knava*, m., pl. *-vys, sherewa*, m., pl. *-wys, jaudyn*, m., pl. *-s, atla*, m., pl. *-lyon, lorel, brybour*, m., pl. *-s*: **-ry,** n. *tull, sherewynsy*, m.

knead, v. **tosa*: **-ing-trough,** n. **new tōs*, f., pl. *-yow t.*

knee, n. *glyn*, m., pl. *-yow*, d., *deulyn*, †*clyn*, m., d. *deuglyn*; shipbuilding, *esker*, f., pl. *-yow*; knock-k.d, *glyngam*; point of k., *penglyn*, m., d. *pendeulyn*: **k.-pan, k.-cap,** n. **padel-penglyn*, f., pls. *-llow, lly, -p.*, *crogen an glyn*, f., pl. *cregyn an deulyn.*

kneel, v., on both k.s, *mōs war* or *dhe, ben deulyn*; on one k., *m. w.* or *d. ben glyn*; he knelt, *ef ēth dhe ben y dheulyn.*

knell, n. *clogh an marow*, m.

knife, n. *collel*, f., pls. *kellyl, kellylly*; sheath-k., †*kethel*, f., pl. *-ly*; large sheath-k., *collan*, f., pl. *-ow*; curved k., *collel gam*, f.; small k., pen-k., *kellyllyk*, m., pl. *-ygow.*

knight, n. *marghak* (*marrek*), m., pl. *-ghogyon* (*-regyon*); k.-service, *ago-marghogyon*, f.; land so held, *agottyr*, m.: **-hood,** n. **margho·gȳeth*, f., *che·valry*, m.; head of knightly order, *pen an che·valry*, m.

knit, v. *gwȳa* (*war naswedhow*); k. the brows, *plegya tāl, p. an dheuabrans*: **-ting,** n. *gwȳas nasweth*, m.; k. needle, n. *nasweth gwȳa*, f., pl. *-edhow g.*

knob, n. **clopen*, m., **talpen*, m., pl. *-now*: of door, etc., *dorn*, m., pl. *-ow*, **knoppa*, m., pl. *-pys*: **k.-stick,** n. *cūlbren*, m., pl. *-yer.*

knock, v. *bonkya, frappya, knoukya, tuchya, squattya, gweskel*: n. *bonk*, m., pl. *-ys, squat*, m., pl. *-tow, knouk*, m., pl. *-kys, whaf*, m., pl. *-fys, what*, m., pl. *-tys*: **-er,** n. *morthol darras*, m., pl. *-ow darrajow*: **k.-kneed,** a. *glyngam.*

knoll, n. *rȳn*, m., pl. *-yow, towan*, m., pl. *tewennow, tolgh, godolgh*, m., pl. *-ow.*

knot, n. *colm*, m., pl. *-ow, colmen*, f., pl. *-now*; slip-k., hangman's k., *colm-rē*: v. *kelmy*: **-less,** a. *dygolm*: **-ty,** a. *colmek, ynno lȳes colm*; fig., *cales y gonvedhes*: **k.-grass,** n. **mylgolm*, **canscolm*, m.

know, v., k. how, understand, *gothvos*; recognise, *aswon, aswonwos*; k. about, *gothvos a*^{2}; be in the k., *bōs pryveth gans*: **-ing,** a. *skentyl*, †*cal*: **-ingly,** adv. *a'y wothvos*: **-ledge,** n. *skentoleth, skȳans, gothvos, aswonvos, dyscans*, m.; to have k. of, *gothvos*: **-n,** a. *gothvedhys, cōth*; to make k., *nōtya, derȳvas.*

knuckle, n. *mel dorn*, m., pls. *-low d., -low an dheudhorn*, **mygorn*, m., pl. *-ow*: **k.-bones,** n., game, *nawmen.*

L

label, n. *tokyn, t. stak*, m., pl. *toknys* (*stak*): v. *staga tokyn war*^{2}.

labial, labiate, a. *gwēusek.*

laboratory, n. *whēlva*, f., pl. *-ow.*

labour, n. *whēl,* m. or f., pl. *-yow*; task, *ober,* m., pl. *-ow*; work, travail, childbirth, *lafür,* m.; hard l., *whēl crēf*: v. *lafürya, gonys, obery*: **-er,** n. *gonysyas,* m., pl. *-ysy*: **-ing,** n. *lafüryans,* m.: **-orious,** a. **lafürüs.*

laburnum, n. **chaynys owr.,* pl.

labyrinth, n. **mylhentall,* m., **kerdroya,* f.

lace, n. *lās,* m., pl. *-ys*: v. *lāsya.*

lacerate, v. *squardya.*

lack, n. *dyfyk,* m., pl. *-ygyow, fowt, gwall,* m., pl. *-ow*; extreme l., *esow,* m., †*dyo·dhenes,* f.: v. *fyllel, bōs fowt dhe²*, *bōs hep.*

lackey, n. *gwas chy̆,* m., pl. *-wesyon c., coscar, goscar,* col. **chambrour,* m., pl. *-s.*

lad, n. *pollat,* m., pl. *-ys, maw,* m., pl. *mebyon*; l.s, *coscar,* col.

ladder, n. **scül,* f., pl. *-yow.*

laden, a. *bēghyes, cargys.*

ladle, n. *lo,* f., pl. *-yow, l. vras*: v. *kemeres gans lo.*

lady, n. *arlodhes,* f., pl. *-ow, benen jentyl,* f., pl. *-es j.*; l. of the house, *mam-ty̆lu,* f.: **l.ship,** n. **arlodheseth,* m.: **l.-bird,** n. *bughyk-Dew,* f., pl. *-ygow-D.*: **L.Day,** n. *degol Marȳa mȳs-Mērth*: **L.'s-tresses,** n. *plēth-Marȳa,* f.

lag, v. *trȳnya, draylya*: **-gard,** a. *hell, lent·*; l. person, *draylyer,* m., pl. *-yoryon*; the l., *an hella.*

lair, n. *fow,* f., pl. *-ys,* **growethva,* f., pl. *-ow.*

laity, n. *lēskys,* m., *an düs lēk*; clergy and l., *lettrys ha lēk.*

lake, n. *logh,* f., pl. *-ow, lyn,* f., pl. *-now, stagen,* f., pl. *-now.*

lamb, n. *ōn,* m., pls. *-en, ēnas, ōnes,* f., pl. *-ow*; paschal l., *ōn Pask,* m.; **-kin,** n. *ōnyk,* m., pl. *enygow*: **-skin,** n. *ōngen,* m.; hand reared l., ‡*hobba,* m. or f., pl. *-bys.*

lame, a. *cloppek, mans, evreth, evredhek,* †*clof*: **-ness,** n. **clofny,* m.

lament, v. *kȳny, ola, gül drem war²*, *mornya,* **galary*: n. *drem,* m., **kȳnvan,* m.: **-able,** a. *trüethek, morethek*: **-ation,** n. *olva,* f., *galarow,* abst., pl., *dughan,* **kȳnvan,* m.

lamina, n. *laun,* m., pl. *-ow,* **scanten,* f., pl. *-now,* col. *scant*: **-ted,** a. *launek,* **scantek.*

Lammas, n. *Calan* or *dē-Halan Est,* m.

lamp, n. *lugarn,* m., pl. *lugern, golow-lester,* m., pl. *-lystry*; train-oil l., *chylla,* m., pl. *-ys*; l. post, *golowbren,* m.; l. wick (rag), *būben,* f., pl. *-now,* (rush), *porven,* f., pl. *-now.*

lamprey, n. *mornader,* f., pl. *-drys.*

lance, n. *gu,* m., pl. *-yow*: v. *gȳa*: **-r,** n. *gȳer,* m., pl. *-yoryon.*

land, n. *tȳr,* m., pl. *-yow, tyreth,* m., pl. *-ow*; region, *bro,* f., pl. *-yow*; country, county, *pow,* m., pl. *-yow*; nation, *gwlās,* f., pl. *-ow*; the L.'s End, *Pen an Wlās*; the Promised L., *an Tyreth a Dhedhewadow*; l. pared and burnt, *grond bȳten*: v. *tȳra, dōs yn tyreth, londya*; l.ing-place for boats, etc., *porth,* m., pls. *-ow, perth*; l.ing-stage, *cay,* m., pl. *-ys*: **l.-farthing,** n., 30 English acres, quarter of Cor. acre, *ferdhyn-tȳr,* m.: **l.lady,** n. *ostes,* f., pl. *-ow*: **l.lord,** n. *ōst,* m., pl. *-ys*; of property, *perghenek,* m., pl. *-ogyon, perghen,* m., pls. *-nas, -now*: **l.lubber,** n. *tȳror,* m., pl. *-yon, dēn an tȳr fest*: **l.owner,** n. *perghenek tȳr,* m., pl. *-ogyon-t. perghen,* m., pls. *-nas, -now*: **l.-rail,** n. **crekyar,* f., pl. *-yēr*: **l.scape,** n. *vu, lywans pow,* m.: **l.sman,** n. *tȳror,* m., pl. *-yon*: **l.-yard,** n. *lēs,* m.

lane, n. *bownder,* f., pl. *-yow, stretyn,* m., pl. *-now*; green l., *for'las,* f.

language, n. *ȳeth* (‡*eyth*), f., pl. *-yow, tavas,* m., pl. *-ow,* **tavaseth,* m.; traditional l., *henyēth,* f., pl. *-ow*; mode of speech, **cowsans,* m.

languid, a. *dyfreth, gwanek*: **-ness,** n. *dyfrethter, gwanegreth,* m.

languish, v. *gwanhē·, fyllel, mōs pür glāf.*

languor, n. *gwander, gwanegreth,* m.

lanky, a. *hȳr, tanow, cül,* **ysylȳek.*

lantern, n. *lugarn,* m., pl. *-gern, lantern,* m., pl. *-s*; a lighted l., *lantern gans golow.*

lap, n. *barlen,* f., pl. *-now, lappa,* m., pl. *-pys*: v. *mayla*; to hold in l. or apron, **barlenna*; to l. milk, etc., *lapya*: **-pet,** n. *lappa,* m., pl. *-pys, plēk,* m., pl. *-egow.*

lapse, n. *gwall,* m., pl. *-ow, fowt,* m., pl. *-ow*; during the l. of time, *a-jȳ dhe broces a dermyn*: v. *fyllel, codha, tremena, slynkya.*

lapwing, n. *cornwhylen,* f., pls. *-las, kernwhyly,* col. *cornwhyl.*

larceny, n. **ladrynsy,* m.

larch, n. *gwedhen larch,* f., col. *gwȳth l.*

lard, n. †*blonek,* †*mehyn,* m.

larder, n. *spens,* m., pl. *-ys.*

large, a. *mür, brās, larch, efan*; at l., *dhe wary.*

lark, *awhesyth,* m., pl. *-ydhas*; escapade, *prat,* m., pl. *-tys, gwary coynt*: v. *hyga.*

larynx, n. **aval-brȳansen,* m.

lash, n., stroke, *lash,* m., pl. *-ys*; thong, etc., *cron,* m., pl. *-ow, corden,* f., pl. *kerdyn*: v., bind, *kelmy*; thrash, *scorjya.*

lass, n. *mowes*, f., pl. *-wysy*, *moren*, f., pl. *-ronyon.*
lassitude, n. *squythans, dyfrethter*, m.
last, v. *pēsya, dürya, paragh*: **-ing,** a. *a-bȳs, a-dhür*: **-ly,** adv. *y'n deweth, dewetha.*
last, a., adv. *dewetha*; l. night, *nyhewer*; till late l. night, *bys yn newer gorthewer*; at l., *dhe-hēs, oteweth, wosteweth, worteweth*; finally, *gordheweth.*
latch, n. *cacha*, m., pl. *-chys*, **clyket*, m., pl. *-tys*: v. *cachya, fastya gans clyket*: **l.-key,** n. *alwhedhyk*, m., pl. *-ygow.*
late, a. *dewedhes, hole·rgh*; to make l. for, *lettya a*[2]; of l., *a-dhewedhes*; the l. . . ., *an . . . üs tremenys*: **-ly,** adv. *agensow, degensow, a-dhewedhes, solabrȳ·s*: **-r,** a. *dewetha*: **-st,** a. *an dewetha*; the l. news, *newodhow noweth.*
lath, n. *latha*, m., pl. *-thys, lasa*, m., pl. *-sys.*
lather, v. *sebony, ewony*: n. *ewon seban*, col.; of horse, *whēs ewonek margh.*
Latin, a. *Latyn, -nek*: L. language, *Latynek*, m.; teacher of L., *latymer*, m., pl. *-s.*
latitude, n. *efander, lēs*, m.
latten, n. *brest*, m.
latter, a. *dewetha*; the l., *an pyth üs cows anodho dewetha, nep üs henwys nessa*: **-ly,** adv. *a-dhewedhes, agensow, degensow.*
lattice, n. *clōs*, f., pl. *-ojow.*
laud, v. *gormel, lawa, laudya*, **canmel*: n. *gormola, lawa*, m.
laugh, v. *wherthyn*; hoot, *üja*; l. at, *gül gēs a*[2], *scornya gans*: n. *wharth*, m.: **l.able,** a. *wharthüs*: **-ing-stock,** *scorn*, m.; the l.-s. of all the county, *scorn oll a'n pow*; to make a l.-s. out of, *scornya gans, gül gēs a*[2]: **-ter,** n. *wharth*, m.; to be overcome with l., burst out l.-ing, *bōs codhys* or *dyeskynnys yn wharth.*
launce, n., sand-eel, *lavyn*, m., pl. *-yon*; l.-crook, *fynegler*, m., pl. *-ow*; to use a l.-c., *fynegly.*
launch, v. *herdhya scath dhe-vēs, dyeskynna gorhel noweth y'n mōr, mōra*; of missile, *tewlel*: n. **lonch*, m., pl. *-ys.*
launder, v. *golghy ha hernya dyllasow*: **-dress,** n. *golgheres*, f., pl. *-ow*: **-dry,** n. *golghty*, m., pl. *-ow.*
laurel, n. *lōrwedhen*, f., col. *-wȳth*; l. wreath, *curün lōrwȳth*, f., pl. *-now l.*; to crown with l., *lōrya.*
lavatory, n. *golghva*, f., pl. *-ow.*
lavender, n. **lavant*, m.
lavish, a. *rē hēl*, **gorhēl*, **gorfalsterek*: v. *rȳ rē* (*a*[2]).
law, n. *lagha*, m., *-ghys*, **rēth*, f., pl. *-yow*; religious l., *lay*, f., pl. *-es*: **l.-abiding,** a. *ow-synsy lagha*: **l.ful,** a. *lāfyl, herwyth lagha*: **l.fulness,** n. *fara lāfyl*, m.: **l.less,** a. **dylagha, erby·n lagha*: **l.lessness,** n. *fara dylagha*, m.: **l.suit,** n. *kēn*, m.: **l.yer,** n. *dēn an lagha*, m., pl. *tüs an l.*
lawn, n. *lawns*, m., pl. *-yow, glesyn*, m., *glasen*, f., pl. *-now, glasyjyon*, m.
lax, a. *logh, lows.*
lay, v. *gorra*; l. eggs, **dedhwy*; l. aside, *hepcor*; l. hands on, *tewlel dywla war*[2], *settya dalghennow yn*; l. it down! *gās e dhe wrowedha!*; l. off! *ho! do way!*; l. down life, *dascor bewnans*: a. *lēk*: n. *ton, gwyndon*, m. or f., pl. *-yow*; summer l., *havrak*, f., pl. *-vegow*: **-er,** n. *gwyscas*, m., pl. *-cosow, gwely*, m., pl. *-yow*: **-man,** n. *lēk*, m., pl. *legyon, tüs lēk.*
lazar-house, n. *clavjy, clojy*, **lo·verjy*, m., pl. *-ow.*
laziness, n. *dyegy, dyekter, sygerneth*, m.: **-y,** a. *dȳek, syger, lows.*
lea, n. *ton, gwyndon*, m. or f., pl. *-yow.*
lead, n. *plom*, m.; black-l., *plom du*; red-l., *plom rüth*; l. line, *plemmyk*, m., pl. *-ygow*; l. pencil, *plüven blom*: **-en,** a. *plom, plomek.*
lead, n., for an animal, *lesha*, m., pl. *-shys*: v. *hembronk, gorra, lēdya*, **blȳnya*; led by my hand, *yn ow dorn*: **-er,** n. *hembrynkyas*, m., pl. *-ysy, pen*, m., pl. *-now, ledyor*, m., pl. *-yon, gwelhevyn*, m. and col. †*gwa·-lather*, m., pl. *gwe·lyther*: **-ership,** n., under his l., *ganso hembrynkys, yn y sōth*: **-ing,** a. *pen-, chȳf-*; l. people, *gwelhevyn.*
leaf, n. *delen*, f., pl. *delyow*, col. *dēl*; of book, etc., *folen*, f., pl. *-now*, †*pythyonen*, f., pl. *pythyon*, ‡*lȳven*, f., pl. *-now*, †*aden*, f., pl. *edyn*; three l.d, *tyrdelen*; to put out l.s, to burst into l., *glasa, dēlya*: **-less,** a. *dydhēl*: **-y,** a. *delennek, delyowek, dēlek*: **-let,** n. *delennyk*, f.; of paper, *folennyk, lyvennyk*, m., pl. *-ygow.*
league, n., 3 miles, *try myldȳ·r*, m.; union, *ünyans*, m., pl. *-ow.*
leak, v. *sygera, dyllo dowr, devera*: n. **dowr-fals*, m., pl. *-aljow*: **-age,** n. *sygerans*, m.: **-y,** a. *tellek.*
leal, a. *lēl.*
lean, v. *posa*, **stümma*; l. downwards, *posa war-nans*; l. backwards, *posa war-dhelergh*; l. forwards, *posa war-rak*; l. to one side,

posa a'n ȳl tenewan; l. against, *scōdhya*; to l. something, *gorra dhe bosa*: **-ing,** n. *plegadow, stüm*, m.; I have a l. towards, *tennys ōf dhe²*.

lean, a. *cül, tanow, pen ha garen*: **-ness,** n. *cülder, tanowder*, m.

leap, v. *lamma, lemmel, lappya*: n. *lam*, m., pl. *-mow*: **-er,** n. *lappyor*, m., pl. *-yon, lappyores*, f., pl. *-ow*.

learn, v. *dysky*; l. from him, *d. ganso*: **-ed,** a. *skentyl, lettrys, gwenwhys, dyskys brās, skyansek, *hedhysk*; the l., *clerjy*, m.: **-er,** n. †*dyscor*, m., pl. *-yon*: **-ing,** n. *clerjy, lyen, dyscans, *dysk*, m.

lease, n. *set*: v. *settya*.

leash, v. *leshya*: n. *lesha*, m., pl. *-shys*; l. hound, **lȳmer*, m., pl. *-s*.

least, a. *lȳha*; at l., *dhe'n lȳha*; not in the l., with neg., *tra y'n bys, man*.

leather, n. *croghen*, f., *lether*, m.: **l.-jacket,** n. *prȳf-dor*, m., pls. *pryves-d*.

leave, v., l. off, l. alone, give l. to, *gasa*; l. it alone, *gās e, na-wra ganso mellya*; l. me alone, *gās crēs dhym*!; l. off wrangling, *gās dhe-vēs stryvya*; l. it to me, *gās vy dh'y wül*; to l. one-another, *kescar*; l. by will, *kemmynna*; l. off! *sāf*! *do way*!; l. out, *gasa mēs*.

leave, n. *cümyas, lecyans, gront*, m.; by your l., *drē dha vōth*; to give l. to him to go, *rȳ* or *grontya cümyas dhodho a vōs*; to take l., *gasa farwel, g. cümyas, g. bennath gans, kemeres cümyas*; ask l., *pysy cümyas*.

leaven, n. *gwēl*. m,

leavings, n. *godhas*, m., pl. *-dhojyon, growjyon, re·menant*, m., *soras*, col., pl. *soresyon. penynnow*, m., pl.; bit left over, *penyn*, m., pl. *-now*.

lechery, n. *drok-whans*, m.

lectern, n. **letryn*, m.

lecture, v. *pregoth*: n. *pregoth*, m., pl. *-gowthow, redyans*, m., pl. *-ow*: **-er,** n. *pregowther*, m., pl. *-thoryon*.

ledge, n., rock, *lēgh*, f., pl. *-ow*; board, shelf, *estyllen*, f., pl. *-now*.

leech, n. *gēl*, f., pl. *-as*; doctor, *medhek*, m., pl. *-ygyon*; horse-l., *gēl margh*.

leek, n. *kenynen*, f., col. *kenyn, porren*, f., col. *pōr*; wild l., *gothkenyn*, col.; l. garden, l. bed, *kenynek*, f., pls. *-egow, -egy*.

leer, v. *scrynkya*.

lees, n. *godhas*, m., pl. *-dhojyon*.

left, a. *clēth*; on his l., *a-glēth dhodho*; on the l., *a-glēth*; on the l. of, *a-glēth dhe²*; call in driving, **asow*!: **l.-handed,** a. *cledhek*; l.-h. person, *cledhek*, m., pl. *-egyon, *cledhyas*, m., pl. *-ysy*.

leg, n., shank, *ber*, f., pl. *-row, fer*, f., pl. *-ow*, d. *dywver*; l. and thigh, *gar*, f., pl. *-row*, d. *dywar*, †*esker*, m. pl. *-yow*, d. *dywesker*; of furniture, *trōs*, m., pl. *treys*; with bare l.s, *fer-nōth*; with crooked l's., *gargam*: **-ged, -gy,** a. *garrek*.

legacy, n. **kemynro*, m., pl. *-how*.

legal, a. *a lagha*.

legate, n. *cannas*, f., pl. *-ow*.

legend, n. *hēn-whethel*, m., pl. *-thlow*: **-ary,** a. *herwyth hēn-whethel*.

legion, n. *lȳjyon*, m., pl. *-s, lu*, m., pl. *-yow*.

legislate, v. *gül laghys*: **-tion,** n. *settyans l.*, m.: **-tor,** n. *gwrȳer laghys*, m., pl. *-yoryon l.*

legitimate, a. *gwȳr, herwyth lagha*.

leisure, n. *sygerneth, termyn gwak*, m.: **-ly,** adv. *yn-lent, yn-syger, hep fysky, ow- mōs war gam*.

lemon, n. *lȳmaval*, m., pl. *-low*: **-ade,** n. **dewas lȳmaval* (*-low*), m.

lend, v. *cola* (*orth*), **lēna, *prestya*; l. an ear, *rȳ scovarn*.

length, n. *hēs, hȳrder*, m.; at l., time, *oteweth, worteweth, dhe-hēs*; position, *a-hēs*; to what l., *pygemmys hēs*; of equal l., *kehē·s*; of the right l., *ewn-hēs*: **-en,** v. *hyrhē·, ystynna, gül bōs hyrra*: **-y,** a. *hȳr*: **-ways,** adv. *a-hēs*.

lenient, a. *cüf, parys dhe² wodhevel*: **-cy,** n. *cüfter, godhevyans*, m.

Lent, n. **Corawys*, m.: **-en,** a. **Corawys*; l. fare, *bōs hep kȳk*.

leopard, n. **lewpart*, m., pl. *-as*.

leper, n., separated l., *dēn* or *clāf dyberthys*, m., pl. *tüs* or *clevyon dhyberthys, clāf*, m., pl. *clevyon*, †*cla·vorek* (*clavrek*), m., pl. *-egyon, lover*, m., pl. *-vryon, leper*, m., pl. *-s*: **-prosy,** n. *lovryjyon, claver*, m., *cleves-brās, c.-mür*, m.; to get l., **lovry*: **-prous,** a. **lovrek*.

less, a., adv. *lē*; the l., *dhe lē*; grow l., *dōs ha bōs lē, dyfygya*; in l. than a week, *a-jȳ dhe seythen*; l. than two years old, *yn-dan deu vlōth*; any l., *nalē, byth dhe lē*: **-en,** v. *lehē·, tanowhē·*; of fire, flood, etc., *slakya*: **-er,** a, *lē*, ‡*byghanna*.

lesson, n. *dyscans, dysquedhyans*, m., pl. *-ow, dyscas*, m., pl. *-cosow, ober*, m., pl. *-ow*.

lest, conj. *na²-, ma na²-, rak na²-, rag own na²-, rak dowt na²-*, with subj.

let, v. *gasa, lavasos*; l. blood, *dyllo gōs*; l. go, *dyllo, delyfr*(*y*)*a*; l. a house, *settya chȳ*; l.

be! *sa! sa! do way!*; l. alone, *gasa, gasa crēs dhe*²; l. off, forgive, *favera*; l. us go, *dün ahanan, dün alemma, gwren-ny mōs.*

lethargic, a., l. person, †*cuscador desempys,* m., pl. *-yon dhesempys*: **-gy,** n. †*hün desempys,* m.

letter, n. *lyther,* m., pl. *-ow* (pl. used also of one l.), *scryven-danvon*; l. of alphabet, *lytheren,* f., pl. *-now*: **-ed,** a. *lettrys.*

lettuce, n. **letysen,* f., col. *letys,* **lethygen,* f., col. *lethyk.*

level, a. *gwastas, compes, leven*; l. with, *compes gans, kehē·s ha*: v. *composa, levenhē·.*

lever, n. *colpes,* m., pl. *-ys.*

leveret, n. *scovarnak vȳghan, s. yowynk,* f., pl. *-nogas bȳghan, y.*

Leviathan, n., as name of a devil, *Lawethan.*

Levite, n. **Levyas,* m., pl. *-ysy.*

levity, n. *scafter,* m.

levy, n. *toll,* f., pl. *-ow*: v. *tolly, gorra toll war*², *cuntell.*

lexicon, n. *gērlyver,* m., pls. *-lyfrow, -lyfryow.*

liable, a. *kelmys* or *synsys drē lagha*; apt to suffer, *gostyth*; make oneself l. for, *omgemeres rak*: **-bility,** n. *kendon,* f.

liar, n. *gowek,* m., pl. *-ygyon,* †*gowleveryas,* m., pl. *-ysy, myngo·w,* m.

libel, n. *cabel,* m.: v. *cabla*: **-lous,** a. *cablüs.*

liberal, a. *larch, hēl, brās,* **lybral*; the l. arts, *an seyth scȳens lybral*: **-ity,** n. *larjes, helder,* **lybralta,* m.

liberate, v. *dyllo, delyfr(y)a,* **rȳthhē·*: **-ation,** n. *lyfrēson, delyfr(y)ans,* m.

liberty, n. **rȳthsys,* **franchys,* **ly·berta,* m.; at l., *dhe wary, frank,* **dygabester.*

library, n., building, *lyverjy,* m., pl. *-ow*; room, etc., *lyverva,* f., pl. *-ow*: **-rian,** n. *gwythyas lyverva,* m., pl. *-ysy l.,* f. *-yades,* pl. *-ow, lyfror,* m., pl. *-yon,* f. *-es,* pl. *-ow.*

licence, n. *lecyans, cümyas, spās,* m.: **-ense,** v. *rȳ cümyas* or *lecyans, gasa spās.*

lichen, n. *kewny,* col.; to become covered with l., *kewnȳa*; covered with l., *lōs, melen, kewnȳek.*

lick, v. *lapya,* ‡*lykkya.*

licorice, n. **lycorys, gwrȳth whēk,* col.

lid, n. *gorher,* m., pl. *-yow*; to put on the l., *gorhery.*

lie, v., l. down, *growedha*; lying down, *a'y wroweth,* etc.

lie, n. *gow,* m., pl. *-yow, whethel,* m., pl. *-thlow*: v., tell l.s, *leverel gow,* †*gowleverel.*

liege, n. *sojeta,* m. and col., pl. *-tys, lȳch,* m., pl. *-ys, -ȳjys*; l. lord, *arluth lȳch*; l. knights, *marghogyon-kēth.*

life, n. *bewnans,* m.; state of l., *bew,* m.; all my l., *yn ow dedhyow, hedra vȳma bew*; bring back to l., *drȳ dh'y vewnans*; come back to l., *dasvewa, dasserghy dhe vew*: **-less,** *dyvewnans, marow*: **l.boat,** n. *scath-sawya,* f., pl. *-ow-s*: **l.time,** a. *densys, bewnans,* m., *üs,* f.: **l.-work,** n. *obereth,* m.

lift, v., l. up, *drehevel, sevel*: n. *drehevyans,* m.; he gave me a l. to town, *ef a-m-gorras bys y'n drē*; elevator, *jyn-yskynna,* m., pl. *-nys y.*

light, v., candle, lamp, etc., *enawy*; fire, etc., *gorra tān yn, cüna*; l. up, *golowy, dywy*; of eyes, etc., *lugerny*: a., bright, *gwyn, glan, golow*; of weight, etc., *scaf*: n. *golow,* m., pl. *-ys*: **-en,** *golowy, lughesy*; make or grow l., *golowhē·*; of weight, *scafhē·*: **-ly,** adv. *yn-scaf*: **-ness,** n. *golewder,* m.; of weight, *scafter,* m.: **l.-footed,** a. *scaf y drōs*: **l.-hearted,** a. *hüth y golon, dygüth*: **l.-house,** n. *golowjy,* m., pl. *-ow*: **l.ning,** n. *lughes,* col., *golowys,* m.; forked l., *lughes gam*; flash of l., *lughesen,* f., pl. *-now*: **-s,** n. offal,, *skevens,* m., pl.: **l.-vessel,** n. *golow-lester,* m., pl. *g.- lystry.*

like, v. *cara*; if you l., *mar mynnough*; I l., *y-plēk dhym, da yu genef, pȳs da ōf(a*²*)*; I've got something you'll l., *yma· genaf dhe'th plēsya*: **-able,** a. *caradow*: **-ableness,** n. *caradewder,* m.: **liking,** n. *kerensa,* f., *grē,* m.

like, adv. *kepa·r ha, ave·l*; l. him, etc., *avello,* etc.; l. this, with v., *yn-ketelma*; with n., *a'n par-ma*; l. that, with v., *yn-ketella*; with n., *a'n par-na*; just l., *kepa·r y'n bȳs ha*; just l. this, *y'n keth vaner-ma*: a. *haval, kehaval* (*dhe*², *orth*), *hevelep*: n., the l., of things, *taclow a'n par-na*; of people, *y hynsa*; his l., *y gowetha, y barow*; one l. this, *onen a'n par-ma* or *a'n keth sort-ma*: **-ly,** a. *a-ȳl bōs, üs dh'y waytya,* **gwyrhaval*; it seemed l. that we should be, *yn hevelep ny a-vedha*; it is not l., *nyns-üs dh'y waytya, ny-vȳth del hevel*: **-lihood,** n. *chōns,* ‡*lyklod,* m.: **-ness,** n. *hevelep,* m., pl. *-ebow, hevelepter,* ‡*havalder,* ‡*hevelenep,* m.; in the l. of men, *y'n hevelep dhe* or *a düs*: **-wise,** conj. *kefrȳ·s, kekefrȳ·s, ynwe·th, gensy,* (*ha*)*gensy-oll.*

lilac, n. **laylok,* col.

lily, n. *lylyen,* f., pl. *-now,* col. *lyly*; l. of the valley, **losow an Hāf.*

limb, n. *lӯth,* m., pl. *-yow, ēsel,* m., pl. *ysyly;* l. of tree, *scoren,* f., pl. *-now,* col. *scor;* large of l., **ysylyek.*
limber, a. *heblӯth, plӯth.*
limbo, n. *lymbo,* m.
lime, n. *lӯm,* m.; l. tree, *owrwernen,* f., col. *owrwern;* l. fruit, *lӯmaval,* m., pl. *-low;* l. kiln, *forn lӯm,* f., pl. *-ow l.;* l.-stone, *mēn lӯm.*
limit, n. *fӯn,* f., pl. *-yow, cūr,* m., pl. *-ow, ōr,* f., pl. *-yon:* v. *settya fӯn dhe*².
limp, v. *cloffy, cloppya, lympya:* n., a man with a l., *dēn a-glop, cloppek,* m., pl. *-pogyon:* **-ing,** a. *cloppek.*
limp, a. *gwan, lows, lӯth.*
limpet, n. *brennygen,* f., col. *brennyk;* l.-shell, *crogen,* f., pl. *cregyn;* out of shell, *lagas davas,* m., pl. *-ajow deves;* to gather l.s, *brennyca* (inf. only).
linden, n.: see **lime** (tree).
line, n. *lӯnen,* f., *lӯnyn,* m., pl. *-now, rew,* m., **rybyn,* m.; race, *lӯn,* m., pl. *-ow, lynyeth;* in l., *yn rew, yn ün rew;* hard l.s! *cales luk!;* rope, *lovan,* f., pl. *-vonow:* **l. up,** v. *rēsa:* **-eage,** n. *devedhyans,* m., *lynaja,* m., *lynyeth,* f.; of high l., *genys an gōs ughel.*
linen, n. *lyn,* m.; l. cloth, *lӯen,* m., pl. *-enyow;* fine l., *sendal,* m.: **l.-draper,** n. *lyennor,* m., pl. *-yon.*
ling, n., fish, *lenes,* f., pl. *-ow;* plant, *menkek,* m., pl. *-egow, grük,* col.
linger, v. *strechya, lettya, tarya, dylatya an termyn:* **-ing,** a. *hӯr, a hӯr-dermyn, lent.*
linguist, n. *yēthor,* m., pl. *-yon.*
link, n. *mel chayn,* m., pl. *-low c., kevren,* f., pl. *-now:* v. *junnya, gorra mel dhe vel.*
linnet, n. *lynek,* m., pl. *-egas;* green l., greenfinch, *melenek,* m., pl. *-egas.*
linseed, n. *hās lyn,* col.; l. oil, *oyl lyn,* m.
lint, n. *lӯen squerdys,* m.
lintel, n. *pen an darras,* m., pl. *-now an darrajow, *clavel,* m,. pl. *-ys.*
lion, n. *lew,* m., pl. *-as, lӯon,* m., pl. *-s, gothfyl-lonek,* m., pl. *-as-l.:* **-ess,** n. *lewes,* f., pl. *-ow, lӯones,* f., pl. *-ow.*
lip, n. †*gwēus,* f., pl. *-ow,* d. *dyw-wēus, gwelf,* f., pl. *-lvow,* d., *dyw-welf, gwelven,* f., pl. *-now, mӯn,* m., pl. *-yon;* having thick l's., *gwēusek.*
liquid, n. *lyn,* m.: a. *glyp, dowrak:* **-quefy,** v. *tedhy:* **-quor,** n. *dewas,* f., pl. *-wosow, gwyras,* f., pl. *-rosow, lycour,* m., pl. *-s;* l. not including wine, *syker,* m.; as a gift, †*las,* m., pl. *-ow;* stale l., *dewas cōth;* strong l., *dewas crēf;* malt-l., *dewas vrag.*
lisp, v. †*stlevy:* **-er,** n. †*stlaf,* m., pl. *stlevyon:* **-ing,** a. †*stlaf:* n. †*stlaveth,* m.
lissom, a. *heblyth.*
list, n. *rōl,* f., pl. *-yow;* for jousting, *lyst,* m., pl. *-ys;* desire, *lüst,* m., pl. *-ys;* selvedge, bandage, *lysten,* f., pl. *-now.*
listen, v., l. to, *goslowes* (*orth*).
litany, n. *letany,* f.
literal, a. *gēr rak gēr, herwyth an lytheren.*
literary, a. *lӯenak;* l. person, *dēn lettrys,* m., pl. *tüs l.:* **-ate,** a. *lettrys:* **-ature,** n. *lӯen,* m.
lithe, a. *heblyth.*
litter, n., vehicle, *grava,* m., pl. *-vathow;* bedding for live-stock, **gwasarn,* m.; horse-borne l., *grava-deuvargh;* mess, *stroll,* m.; of pigs, etc., **toras,* m.
little, a. *bӯghan, münys;* suffix, *-yk, -yn,* f. *-en;* a l. while before, *ün prӯs* or *pols kens:* adv. *boghes, nebes;* l. did we think, *nebes esen ow-tyby:* n., a l., *boghes,* m., *nebes,* m.
live, v. *bewa;* l. together, *kesvewa;* l. again, *dasvewa;* to l. on food, *bewa orth;* dwell, *tryga, bos annedhys* (*yn*); as long as I l., *yn ow bewnans, hedra vӯma bew:* **-lihood,** n. *bewnans, pega·ns,* m.: **-liness,** n. **bewder, scafter,* m.: **-ly,** a. *bew, bewek, jolyf:* **-ving,** a. *bew, yn-few;* dwelling, *trygys, annedhys;* l. flesh, *bew,* m.
liver, n., anat., *avy,* m.; a good l., *densa a'y gonversasyon:* **l.wort,** n. *kewny,* col.
lizard, n. *pedrevan,* f., pl. *-now,* †*gwedresyf,* f., pl. *-yvas, peswar-paw,* m., pl. *-as, sergh-war-glegar,* m.
lo! int. *otta! awo·tta!;* before vowel, *ot! awo·t!*
load, n. *bēgh* (*bē*), m., pl. *-yow, carg,* m., pl. *-ow, sawgh* (*saw*), m., pl. *-yow:* v. *carga, bēghya, *sawghya:* **-ed,** a. *lün, cargys.*
loaf, n. *torth,* f., pl. *-ow.*
loafer, n. *losel,* m., pl. *-s, dēn wast,* m., pl. *tüs w.*
loan, n. *ro war wystel, *erlegeth, *lendyans, *prest.*
loath, a. *ow-trӯna;* nothing l., *hep ardak;* I am l. to do that, *pōs* or *cās yu genef gül henna:* **-some,** a. *hegas, dyflas:* **-someness,** n. *last,* m.: **loathe,** v. *casa;* food, *dyflasa;* I l. insects, *cās yu genef pryves:* **-ing,** n. *cās,* m.
lobster, n. *legest,* m., pl. *-y.*
local, a. *a'n lē, a'n drē,* etc.: **-ity,** n. *tyller,* m., pl. *-yow, lē,* m., pl. *-ow, pow a-dro,* m.

lock, n. *hesp*, m., pl. *-ow, floren*, f., pl. *-now*: v. *alwhedha*; l.ed up, *yn-dan alwheth*.
lock, n., of hair, *cüdyn*, m., pl. *-now*.
locomotive, n. *margh-tān*, m., pl. *mergh-t*.
locust, n. *cülyek-reden askellek*, m., pl. *-yogas n. a*.
lode, n. *gōth mūn*, f., pls. *-ow, gwythy m.*; counter-l., *trōen*, f., pl. *-now*: **-stone,** n. **tenven*, m., pl. *-veyn, mēn-ten*, m., pl. *meyn-t*.
lodge, v. *tryga, ostya*: **-r,** n. *tryger*, m., pl. *-oryon, ostyas*, m., pl. *-ysy*: **-ment,** n. *godref, -dra*, f., pl. *-evy, trygva*, f., pl. *-ow, lojja*, m.: **-ging,** n. *erberow*, m., pl. *-ys, gwest*, f., *harber*, m., pl. *-ys*: **-ging-house, -gings,** *gwesty*, m., pl. *-ow*; to provide l., *annedhy*.
loft, n. *talyk*, m., pl. *-ygow, soler*, m., pl. *-yow*; corn-l., *ȳsla*, m., pl. *-lēow*: **-iness,** n. *ughelder*, m.: **-y,** a. *ughel*.
log, n. *pren*, m., pls. *-yer, prynner*, †*trēgh*, m., pl. *-ow*, **kef*, m., pl. *-yon*; for fire, *etew*, m., pl. *-y*.
logan-berry, n. *mōren Logan*, f., col. *mōr L.*
logan or **logging rock,** *mēn omborth* (*amber*), m.
logic, n. *rēson*, m., pl. *-s, lojyk*, m.: **-al,** a. *herwyth rēson*.
loin, n. *lōn*, f., *clün*, f., pl. *-yow*, d. *dywglun*.
loiter, v. *crowdra, lettya, strechya, tarya*: **-er,** n. *crowdrer*, m., pl. *-roryon, sevylyak*, m., pl. *-yogyon*.
loll, v. *sevel yn-lows, posa yn-tȳek*.
London, n. *Loundres*, f.
loneliness, n. *hȳreth*, m.; of place, *ünykter*, m.: **-ly,** a. *hyrethek, dyfȳth, dygoweth*; of place, *pell dyworth tüs*; l. place, *tyller kernwhyly*.
long, a. *pell, hȳr*; how l., *pygemmys prȳs* or *hēs*; before l., *kens nep-pell*; as l. as, of time, *spās, hedra vo*; of length, *kehēs ha*; it is not l. ago, *nyns-yu nep-pell*; for l., for a l. time, *soladhē·th*; a l. time, *pellder*, m.; a tedious l. time, *hȳrneth*, f.; all day l., *drēs an jēth*; l. ago, *solabrȳ·s, nans-yu pell*; not l. ago, *whath nyns-yu pell*; it was l. in coming, *pell o hep dōs*: **-er,** a. *pella*; (not) any l., *na fella*: **-ish,** a. **hȳryk*: **l.-boat,** n. *scath hȳr*, f., pl. *-ow h.*: **l.evity,** n. **hȳrōs*, m.: **l.-stone,** n. *menhȳr*, m., pl. *-yon, hyrven*, m., pl. *-veyn*: **l.-suffering,** n. *godhevyans, perthyans*, m.
long, v., l. for, *whansa, yeuny rak, bōs whansek dhe*[2], *bōs mal dhodho, bōs tryst warle·rgh*; to l. to do it, *bōs debron dh'y dhywvrēgh hag ef mar bell hep y wül*: **-ing,** n. *yeunes*, m., pl. *-ow, sȳans, whans*, m., pl. *-ow, hȳreth, yeunadow*, m.: **-ing,** a. *whansek, hyrethek*.
look, v. *myras*; l. at, *whythra*; l. out for, *aspȳa*; l. for, *whylas*; l. after, *gwytha*; l. out, be careful, *gorra* or *kemeres wȳth* or *gorwytha* (*na*[2]), *bōs wār, avȳsya*; l. out! *kemer* or *gor wȳth dhys dha honen*!: n. *mȳr*, m., *golok*, f., **trem*, f.; aspect, *tremyn*, m., *fysmant, semlant*, m., pl. *-ns*; to take a l. at, *myras ün wolok orth*; l. for (expect), *gwaytya*: **l.-ing-glass,** n. *gwēder-myras*, m., pl. *-drow-m, myrour*, m., pl. *-s*: **l.-out,** n., at head of ship, *brennyas*, m., pl. *-ysy*; l. place, *golva*, f., pl. *-ow*; l. place, building, **gōljy*, m., pl. *-ow*; headland, *penolva*, f., pl. *-ow*; that's his l., *avȳsyens-ef a henna*.
loop, n. *cabester*, m., pl. *-trow*, **tagell*, f., pl. *-ow*; running l., *colm-rē*, pl. *-ow-r., sygen*, f., pl. *-now*: **l.-hole,** n. **tardhell*, f., pl. *-ow*; in defences, *toll sēth*, m., pl. *tell s*.
loose, a. *lows*; of animals, etc, *dygabester*: **-ness,** n. **lowsethes*, m.: **-n,** v. *lowsel, lowsya, dyllo*, **dysclena*.
lop, v., trees, *skethry, dybenna, dyscora*; hang limply, *lowsel*: n. *skether*, m., pl. *-throw*: l. eared, *lows y scovarn*: **-ping,** n., twig, **gwresken*, f., col. *gwresk*.
loquacious, a. *tavasek*.
lord, n. *arluth*, m., pl. *-lydhy*: v., to l. it, *lordya*: **-ship,** *arlottes*, m.
lose, v. *kelly*; in contest, *fyllel*; l. the way, *sawthanas*, ‡*myskemeres an forth*: **-able,** a. *hegoll*.
loss, n. *coll*, m., †*colles*, m., *collva*, f., pl. *-ow, meth*, m., pl. and abst., *mothow*; danger of l., **argoll*, m.; without l., **dygoll*: **-st,** a. *kellys*; to be l., *mōs dhe goll*; easily l., *hegoll*.
lot, n. *ran*, f., pl. *-now, shara*, m., pl. *-rys*; to cast l.s., *tewlel pren*; such a l. of, *kemmys*: **-tery,** n. **gwary dall*, m.
loud, a. *ughel, heglew*.
lounge, v. *sevel* or *esedha attē·s* or *yn-lows*: n. *esethva*, f., pl. *-ow, powesva*, f., pl. *-ow*.
louse, n. *lewen*, f., col. *low*: **-sy,** a. *lowek*.
lout, n. *lowt*, m., pl. *-ys, lorden*, m., pl. *-s, lobba*, m., pl. *-bys*.
lovage, n., bot., †*gwyles*, col.
love, v. *cara*; l. dearly, *lüf-cara*; l. truly, *ewn-gara*: n. *kerensa*, f.; for l.s sake, *par amour*; l. oneself, one-another, *omgara*: **-vable,** a. *hegar, caradow*: **-ableness,** n.

caradewder, m.: **-r,** n. *carer*, m., pl. *-roryon, cares*, f., pl. *-ow, keryas*, m., pl. *-ysy, keryades*, f., pl. *-ow*; as term of endearment, *cüf-colon*: **-making,** n. *profyans kerensa, sergh, omgara*, m.: **-sick,** a. *clāf drē gerensa*: **-ing,** a. *cüf, caradow, kerenjedhek*: **-ing-kindness,** n. *dader, cüfter, kerensa*, f.
lovely, a. *tēk, hegar*: **-liness,** n. *tekter*, m.
low, a. *down, ysel*; of speech, manners, etc., *bylen, mylüs*: **-er,** v. *yselhē·*; of tide, etc., *bassya*: **-er,** a. *ysella*; in place names, †*ys*; to become l., *bassya*: **-est,** a. *an ysella*; in place names, *ysa*: **-ness,** n. *yselder, downder*, m.: **l.-born, l.-bred,** a. **yselgenesyk, kēth*; l-b. person, *ploswas*, m., pl. *-wesyon, mapgal*, m., *myrgh g.*, f.: **l.land,** n. *yseldyr*, m., pl. *-yow, tenow·* (†*tnow*), m., pl. *-y, strās*, m., pl. *-ow, tyrnans*, m.: **l.-water,** n. *tryg(k) yselvor*, **marvor*, m.: **-liness,** n. *yselder, hüvelder*, m.: **-ly,** a. *ysel, hüvel, whar*: **L. Sunday,** n. *an Pask bȳghan*, m.
low, v. *bedhygla*.
loyal, a. *lēl, lēn*: **-ty,** n. *lelder, leldury, lendury, lēouta*, m.
lozenge, a., diamond shape, **losanj*, m.; sweet, *tam whēk*, m.
lubber, n. *lobba*, m., pl. *-bys*.
lubricant, n. *üras*, m., pl. *-esow*: **-ate,** v. *üra*.
lucid, a. *splan, clēr*: **-ity,** n. *splander, clērder*, m.
luck, n. *fortyn, luk, hap*, m.; bad l., *mewl*, m.; good l! *god spēda*!; ironically, *goda chōns re-th-fo*!; worse l. for him, *er y wew, goef*!; worse l! *soweth*!; bad l., *meschō·ns, cales luk*!; bad l. to him, *re-n-jeffo mewl*!; a bit of bad l., *drok-lam* (*droglam*), m., pl. *-mow*: **-ily,** adv. *drē hap* (*da*), *y'n gwella prȳs*: **-y,** a. *gwynvȳs*, †*füsyk*; l. chap! *gwyn y vȳs*!
lucrative, a. *a-drē mür a vona, a-drēl dhodho dhe lēs*.
ludicrous, a. *wharthüs, dh'y scornya*.
lug, v. *draylya, tenna yn-fēn*.
luggage, n. *fardhellow*, m., pl.
lugworm, n. *kenak*, m., pl. *-nogas*.
lukewarm, a. *mygyl*, **godom*; to grow l., *mygla*: **-ness,** n. *mygylder*, m.
lull, v. *coselhē·, spavenhē·, lulla*: n. *spaven* (*span*), m., *spavnell* (*spanell*), f., pl. *-ow*.
lullaby, n. *hüngan*, f., pl. *-ow*.
lullay, n., to sing l., *lull ha lay*.
lumbago, n. *drōk dywglün*, m.
lumber, n. *dafar dydhefnyth*, m.; wood, *prynner trēghys*, m., pl.: v. *ancombra*.
luminous, a. *golow, a-dhewyn*. **golowek*,
lump, n. *pryl*, m., pl. *-yon, tam*, m., pl. *tymmyn, pellen*, f., pl. *-now, pȳs*, m., pl. *-ys*.
lunacy, n. *muscotter*, m.: **-nar,** a. *a'n lōr*, **lorek*: **-atic,** n. *muscok*, m., pl. *-cogyon*, **lōrek*, m., pl. *-rogyon*: a. *muscok*, †*badüs*, **lōrek*.
lunch, n. *crowst*, m., pl. *-ys, lȳ, lȳf*, f., pl. *lyfyow, tam bōs*, m.: v. *lyfya, dybry* or *kemeres crowst*.
lungs, n. *skevens*, m., pl.
lurch, v. *omrolya, trebüchya*: n. *rōl*, f., pl. *-yow*.
lure, n. *hüs, dynyans, trayn*, m.: v. *dynya, hüda*.
lurid, a. *gwan y lyw, üthek*.
lurk, v. *scolkya, tēghy, omgeles, contrewaytya*: **-ing,** n. *tēgh*, m.; l. place, *godēgh*, m.
lust, n. *drok-whans, tebel-ewl*, f., pl. *-ow, lüst*, m., pl. *-ys*.
lustre, n. *splander, golewder*, m.
lusty, a. *crēf, mür y nerth, corfek*.
lute, n. *gyttern* (*gyttren*), m., pl. *-s*.
luxuriance, n. **gorthevyans*, **gorfalster, lanwes*, m.: **-nt,** a. †*fȳthüs*, **gorfals*: **-ate,** v. **gorthevy*, **gordevy*.: **-rious,** a. *mür attē·s, pür rych*, **gorfalsterek*: **-ry,** n. **gorlanwes, plēsour hag ēs*; a l., *tam dēnty*, m., pl. *tymmyn d.*
lye, n. *troth*, **lysyow*, m.
lying, a., untruthful, *gowek, myngow*: n., falsehood, *gowegneth*, m.
lying, a., recumbent, *a'y wroweth*, etc.: n., l. posture, *groweth*, m.
lying-in, n. *gwelyvos*, m.
lymph, n. *lyn*, m.
lyric, n. *cān* **delynnek* or **lȳrek*, f., pl. *-ow t., l.*: **-al,** a. **telynnek*, **lȳrek*.

M

machine, n. *jyn*, m., pl. *-nys*: **-ry,** n. *jynwȳth*, m.
mackerel, n. *brȳthel* (*brȳel*), m., pl. *-thylly* (*brylly*); boiled head of m., *scogyn*, m., pl. *-now*.
mad, a. *müs, müscok, fol, mēs a'y rewl*, †*gorbollak*; as a dog, *conneryak*; become, drive m., *muskegy, connery*; gone m., *gyllys fol, muskegys, dōtyes, varyes*; to act like one m., *dōtya*: **-den,** v. *müskegy, varya*: **-house,** n. *foljy*, m., pl. *-ow*: **-man,** n. *muscok*, m., pl. *-ogyon, fol*, m., pl. *felyon, foles*, f., pl. *-ow*; raving, sleepless m., †*fol tergusca*: **-ness,** n. *muscotter*, ‡*muscogneth*, m.
madam, n. *madama*, f., pl. *-mys*.

magazine, n. *lyver termyn*, m., pl. *-vrow t.*; store, *gwythva*, f., pl. *-ow*.
maggot, n. *contronen*, f., col. *contron*; **-ty,** a. *contronek*; to become m., *kentreny*.
magic, n. *hüs, tebel art, pystry*, m.; to work m., *hüda, pystrya*: **-al,** a. *hüdol*: **-ian,** n. *hüder*, m., pl. *-oryon*, †*hüdol, pystryor*, m., pl. *-yon*, f. *-es*, pl. *-ow*.
magistrate, n. *justys*, m., pl. *-yow*.
magnanimous, a. *brās*, or *hēl, y vrȳs*.
magnet, n. *tenven*, m., pl. *-veyn*.
magnificence, n. *rȳelder, müreth, braster*, m.: **-nt,** a. *rȳal, bryntyn*, ‡*brās-oberys, gay*.
magnify, v. *mürhē·, moghhē·*.
magnitude, n. *myns, braster*, m.
magpie, n. *pȳasen*, f., col. *pȳas*.
Mahomet, n. *Mahom*, m.: **-an,** n. *Sarsyn*, m., pl. *-s*: a. *Sarsynek*.
maid, n. *maghteth*, f., pl. *meghtythyon*; chit, etc., *moren*, f., pl. *moronyon*; girl, *mowes*, f., pl. *-wysy*; virgin, *gwerghes*, f., pls. *-ow*, *-ghysy*; daughter, *myrgh*, f., pl. *-es*: **-en,** n., see **maid**: a. *gwergh, noweth*: **-enhair fern,** n. *gols an Werghes*, col.: **-enhood,** n. *gwerghsys*, f.: **-servant,** n. *maghteth*, f., pl. *meghtythyon*; bondmaid, †*kēthes*, f., pl. *-ow*.
mail, n., coat of m., **caspows*, f., pl. *-yow*, *cota-mayl*, m.; post-bag, chain armour, *mayl*, m., pl. *-ys*; letters, *lytherow*, pl.
maim, v. *evredhy*: **-ed,** a. *evreth, evredhek, mans*; m. persons, *evreth, -edhek*, pls. *-edhyon, -edhygyon*.
main, a. *mür, chȳf*; with might and m., *oll dh'y allos*: **-land,** n. *tȳr mür*, m.: **-ly,** adv. *kens oll, yn kensa lē, drēs oll*: **-mast,** n. *gwern vrās*, f.: **-sea,** n. *keynvor, mōr brās*, m.
maintain, v. *mentēna, synsy*; with supplies, *sostena*; support, *scodhya*; m. opinion, *gwytha, synsy*: **-tenance,** n. *mentons*, m.
majesty, n. *braster*, **müreth*, m.: **-tic,** a. *mür, ughel, splan, rȳal, brās*.
major, a. *brassa, moyha*: n., in rank, **major*, m., pl. *-s*: **-ity,** n. *an ran vrassa*, f.; attain m., *dōs dhe ōs, bōs tevys dhe dhēn*.
make, v. *gül* (*güthyl, grüthyl*), *formya*; m. ready, *darbary, gül parys*; m. up tales, *whethla*; m. up for, *attylly, astevery*; m. up one's mind, *bōs ervȳrys*; m. known, *nōtya, derȳvas*; m. out, *convedhes, dyscernya*; pretend, *gül wȳs*; m. one go, *gül dhodho mōs, y gonstrȳna dhe vōs*: n. ‡*gwra*, m.: **-believe,** n. *gül-wȳs*, inf.: **-r,** n. *formyer, gwrȳer*, m., pl. *-yoryon, formyas*, m., pl. *-ysy*: **-ing,** n. *gwrȳans*, m.; m.s, *defnyth*, m., pl. *-yow*, ‡*gwra*, m.: **-shift,** n. *towl a-serf fowt gwell*, m.: a. *a-servyo*.
malady, n. *drōk*, m., pl. *-ogow, cleves*, m., pl. *-vejow*.
malcontent, a. *drōk-pȳs, drōk-lowen*.
male, n. *gorow*, m. and col., *gorryth*, m., *gour*, m., pl. *gwēr*; m. and female, *gorow ha benow, gorryth ha benenryth*: prefix. animals, *gour-*; birds, *cülyek-*.
malediction, n. *mollath*, f., pl. *-lothow*, ‡*mollethyans*, m.
malefactor, n. *cam*, m., pl. *-mow, drok-oberor*, m., pl. *-yon*.
malevolent, a. *drōk y gnās*, ‡*drokbrederys*.
malice, n. *attȳ, spȳt, avy* (*envy*), **drogeth*, m.; to bear m. against, *perthy avy orth*: **-cious,**a. *spȳtys, e·nvyes,drōk y gnās*,‡*drok-brederys*: **-ciously,** adv. *yn-spȳtys*.
malign, v. *cably gans cam, drok-vrüsy*: **-ant,** a. *spȳtys*, †*camhensek*; the m. spirit, *an tebel ēl, Malan*: **-ity,** n. *attȳ, anfüsy*, m.
malkin, n. **scübylen forn*, f., pl. *-now f.*
mall, mallet, n. *morben*, m., pl. *-now*.
mallow, n. †*malowen*, f., col. *malow*.
malt, n. *brāg*(*k*), m.; m. sprouts, *skyl brāg*, col.; m. grains, *sēg*(*k*), m.; m. liquor, *dewas brāg*, m.; **-house,** n. *bragva*, pl. *-ow*, *brakty*, m., pl. *-ow*: v. *bragy*: **-ster,** n. *brager*, m., pl. *-oryon*.
maltreat, v. *drōkhandla, tebel-dȳghtya, deffola*.
mamma, mammy, n. *mam gēr*, **mammyk*, f., pls. *-ygow, -mowygow*.
man, n. *dēn*, m., pl. *tüs, gwas*, m., pl. *gwesyon, gour*, m., pl. *gwēr, gorryth*, m.; m. of war, *gorhel bresel*, m., pl. *-holyon b.*; a good m., *densa*, m.; m.-at-arms, *dēn*, pl. *tüs, arvow*: **-ful,** a. **gouryl*: **-fully,** adv. *ave·l dēn, manly*: **-hood,** n. *densys*, m.: **-kind,** n. *map-dēn, mabden, densys*, m.: **-ly,** a. *ave·l dēn*: **-servant,** n. *paja*, m., pl. *jys, boya*, m., pl. *-yes, gwas-chȳ*, m., pl. *-wesyon-c.*: **-slaughter, -slayer,** n. *dēnlath*, m. and pl., **-slayer,** *denledhyas*, m., pl. *-ysy*.
manage, v. *gül, rewlya*; m. by oneself, *omweres*; m. a house, *synsy chȳ*; I'll m. to be there, *my a-wra may fȳma ena*: **-able,** a., of animal, **hewar, dōf*: **-ment,** n. *rewl*, f., pl. *-ys, conduyk*, m.: **-er,** n. *rewler*, m., pl. *-oryon*; bad m., *gwan-dȳak*, m., pl. *-yogyon, g.-wycor*, m., pl. *-yon*.

mandible, n. *challa,* m., pl. *-lys, gēn,* **awen,* f., pl. *-now,* d. *dywen.*

mane, n. *mong,* m., pl. *-ow, mongen,* f., pl. *-now.*

mange, n. *lovryjyon cün,* m.: **-gy,** a. *lovrek,* †*clavrek.*

manger, n. **presep,* m., pl. *-ebow.*

mangle, v. *hakkya*; clothes, *rolya lyennow*: n. *rolyer dyllasow, mangel,* m., pl. *-s.*

mania, n. *connar,* f.: **-c,** n. †*conneryak,* m., pl. *-yogyon.*

manifest, a. *ape·rt,* **hewel*: v. *dysquedhes*: **-ation,** n. *dysquedhyans,* m., pl. *-ow.*

manifesto, n. *derȳvas, -vadow,* m.

manifold, a. *lȳesplēk.*

manikin, n. *dēnyk,* m., pl. *tüsygow.*

maniple, n., vestment of priest, †*stōl-lüf,* f.

manipulate, v. *handla, dȳghtya*: **-tion,** n.

manner, n. *maner,* f., pl. *-ow, gȳs,* m., pl. *-yow, ēghen,* f., *forth,* f., pl. *-dhow*; of life, thought, etc., *conversasyon,* m.; in this m., *yn-ketelma*; in that m., *yn-ketella*; in some m., *war nep cor*: **-s,** n. *fara,* m., *manerow,* f., pl.; good m., *cortesy,* m.

manor, n. *maner,* m., pl. *-oryow*; m. house, *manerjy,* m.

mansion, n. *plās,* m., pl. *-ow, ostel,* f., pl. *-yow, -s.*

mantelpiece, n. *estyllen-chymbla,* f., pl. *-now-c., clavel,* f., pl. *-ys,* **astell an olas,* f.

mantle, n. *pal,* m., pl. *-ys, mantel,* f., pl. *mentylly.*

manual, n. †*cowethlyver,* m., pl. *-lyvrow*: a. *-dywla.*

manufacture, v. *gül*: n. *gwrȳans,* m.: **-r,** n. *gwrȳer,* m., pl. *-oryon.*

manure, n. *teyl,* m.; particularly of fish-m., *mon,* m., **cardeyl,* m.; m. heap, *teylek,* f., pl. *-egy, pȳl-teyl,* m., pl. *-yow-t.*: v. *teyla.*

manuscript, n. *dornscryfa,* m.; m. book, *scryflyver,* m., pl. *-frow.*

many, a. *lȳes, lower* (both with sing. n.), *lower a*[2], *mür a*[2], *cals*; m. a one, *lȳes hüny* ‡*lower onen*; how m., *py-sül, py lȳes, pygemmys*; not m., *namü·r, nep lȳes* (with neg.); as m. as, *kemmȳ·s, kenyver* (both with *ha* before n., *del* before v.), *myns, sül*; as m. times as, *pesquyth may*[5]; twice, six times, etc., as m., *deugemmȳ·s, whēghkemmȳ·s,* etc.; so m., *kemmȳ·s, kenyver*; m. coloured, *lȳes lyw*; m. sided, *lȳes tu*: n. *lȳes, cals,* m.; m. saw them, *gans lȳes y-fons gwelys.*

map, n. *mappa,* m., pl. *-pys.*

maple, n. **gwynyolen,* f., col. *gwynyol,* **scawen gwragh,* f., col. *scaw g.*

mar, v. *shyndya, hagry.*

maraud, v. *rafna, pylla*: **-er,** n. *rafner, pyller,* m., pl. *-oryon,* **prēdhor,* m., pl. *-yon.*

marble, n. *marbel,* m.

March, n. *mȳs-Mērth,* m.

march, v. *kerdhes*: n. *kerth soudoryon,* m.; music, **tōn kerth*; on the m., *yn hens, ow-kerdhes.*

mare, n. *casek,* f., pl. *-sygy.*

margin, n. *glan,* f., pl. *-now, amal,* m. or f., pl. *emelow, ōr,* f., pl. *-yon, mȳn,* m., pl. *-yon*: **-al,** a. *war an oryon* or *emelow.*

marigold, n. †*les-an-gōk,* m.; corn-m., *bothen,* f., pl. *-now, blejen an drevas,* f.

marine, a. *mōr, morek*: **-er,** n. *marner,* m., pl. *-s, dēn mōr,* m., pl. *tüs m.,* **moror,* m., pl. *-yon*: **-itime,** a. **morek, an mōr.*

mark, n. *sȳn,* m., pl. *-ys, pryk,* m., pl. *-kys, merk,* m., pl. *-ys, ōl,* m., pl. *-ow, nos,* m., pl. *-ow*; up to the m., *dhe squȳr*: v. *merkya, sȳna, nosa*; notice, *avȳsya.*

market, n. *marghas,* f., pls. *-ow, -ajow, fēr,* m., pl. *-yow*; m. place, *tyller-marghas,* m., pl. *-yow-m,* **marghasla,* m., pl. *-lēow*; m. house, *chȳ-marghas,* m., pl. *-ow-m.*; m. town, *trē-varghas,* f., pl. *trevow-m.*; m. woman, **marghaswrēk,* f., pl. *-wrageth*: v. *marghasa*: **-er,** n. *marghad(j)or,* m., pl. *-yon, marghad(j)ores,* f., pl. *-ow.*

marksman, n. *medror,* m., pl. *-yon.*

marmalade, n. **marmelada,* **kyfyth owravallow,* m.

marram-grass, n. *morhesk,* col.

marriage, n., state of, *kesvewnans,* **pryosoleth,* m.; ceremony, *marȳach,* m., pl. *-ajys, demedhyans,* m.: **-ied,** a. *demedhys,* with *gour* or *benen,* †*prȳas*; m. person, *prȳas,* m. and f., pl. *-yosow, kespar,* m., and f., pl. *-ow*: **-ry,** v., be married, *demedhy, marȳa.*

marrow, n., in bone, *mēr,* m., ‡*marou,* m.; vegetable m., *pompyon,* m., pl. *-s*; m. plants, *losow pompyon,* pl.

marry! int. *rē Varȳa*!, *'Arȳa*! *'Rȳa*!

Mars, n. *Mērth,* m.

marsh, n. *gwern,* f., pls. *-ow, -y, heskyn,* m., *kenegen,* f., pls. *-now, heskek, bronnek, kenak, kersek,* f., pls. *-egow, -egy, porf,* col., *tȳr devrak,* m.: **-y,** a. *gwernak, devrak, dowrak.*

marten, n. †*yewgen,* f., pl. *-as.*

martial, a. *breselek.*

martin, n., house m., ‡*chȳcok,* f., pl. *-ogas, gwennol chȳ,* f., pl. *-nyly c.*
martyr, n. *merther,* m., pl. *-yon,* f. *-es,* pl. *-ow,* ‡*martyr,* m., pl. *-s*: **-dom,** n. **mer-therynsy,* f.: **-ize,** v. *mertherya.*
marvel, n. *aneth, marth, marthüs,* m., pl. *-ow, marthüsy,* m., pl. **barthüs*: v. *kemeres marth*; I m., *marth a-m-büs*: **-lous,** a. *marthys, barthüsek, aneth*: **-lously,** adv. *marthys.*
masculine, a. *gorryth*; prefix, *gour-.*
mash, v. *brewy, glüsa*: n. *brows,* m.
mask, n. *vȳsour,* m., pl. *-ys*: v. *cüdha.*
mason, n. *trēghyas meyn,* m., pl. *-ysy m., mason,* m., pls. *-s, -ys*: **-ry,** n. *menwȳth,* m.
masque, n. *gwary gȳs,* m., pl. *-ow g.*
mass, n. *pellen,* f., pl. *-now,* **tysk,* m. or f., pl. *-scow, bush,* m., pl. *-ys, gron,* m.; gone into a m., *gyllys yn gron.*
mass, n., sacrament, *oferen,* f., pl. *-now*; high m., *oferen-brȳs*; low m., *oferen-vyttyn*; midnight m., **pelgens,* m.
massacre, v. *ladha, moldra*: n. *lathva,* f.
massive, a. *tew, brās, corfek.*
mast, n. *gwern,* f., pl. *-ow*; one-, two-, three-, four-, five-m.er, *gorhel ün, dyw wern* and *tȳr, peder, pymp gwern,* m.; fore-m., *gwern a-rak*; main-m., *gwern vrās*; mizzen-m., *gwern a-dhelergh*: **-less,** a. *dywern.*
master, n. *mēster,* m., pl. *mestrysy* (*-yjy*), *arluth,* m., pl. *-lydhy*; owner, *perghen,* m., pls. *-nas, -now*; school-m., *mēster mebyon*; m. of house, *gorty, gour an chȳ*; m. and man, *mēster ha maw*: v. *maystry, gül maystry, bōs trȳgher war*[2]: **-ly,** a. *a dhorn mēster, a'n gwella*: **-piece,** n. *gwȳth-mēster,* m., pl. *-yow m.*: **-stroke,** n. *maystry, towl bryntyn,* m.: **-y,** n. *maystry, mestrynsys,* m.
masticate, v. *dynsel.*
mastiff, n. **gwylter,* m., pl. *-tras,* **gavelgy,* m., pl. *-gün.*
mat, n. *strayl,* m., pl. *-yow*; rush m., †*strayl e·lester*; sand-rush m., *strayl morhesk,* jocularly, *pan-ledan Pyran.*
match, n., equal, *coweth,* m., col. *-a, par,* m., pl. and abst. *-ow, equal,* m., pl. *-s*; bout, *fyt,* m., pl. *-tys*; m. to strike, **tan-bren,* m., pl. *-yer*; m. box, **box-tanbren,* m., pl. *-ys-t.*; to play, make a m., *gül fyt a*[2]: v. *comparya, fyttya*: **-less,** a. *hep par*(*ow*): **-stick,** n. **tanbren,* m., pl. *-yer*: **-wood,** n. *scommow,* m., pl.
mate, v. *parya, cowethya*: n. *par,* m., pl. and abst. *-ow, coweth,* m., col. *-a,* f. *-es,* pl. *-ow, mata,* m., pl. *-ys, cothman,* m., pl. *-mens*; familiar friend, husband, *cōth,* m.; m. in marriage, *prȳas,* m. and f., pl. *-ȳosow*; workman's m., *darbarer,* m., pl. *-roryon*; of ship, *brennyas,* m., pl. *-ysy.*
mater-familias, n. *mam-tȳlu,* f., pl. *-mow-t.*
material, n. *defnyth,* m., pl. *-ydhyow*; m.s, *dafar,* m., col.: a. *a vater*; important, *a-rēs*; not spiritual, *a'n bȳs-ma.*
maternal, a. *mam, a vam,* **mamol*; m. relative, *car aba·rth mam*: **-nity,** n. **mamoleth,* f.
mathematician, n. *calcor,* m., pl. *-yon*: **-ics,** n. *skȳans rekna,* m., *musüro·nyeth,* f., **awgrym.,* m.: **-ical,** a. *a rekna.*
matrimonial, a. *prȳosyl*(*-sol*): **-ny,** n.: see **marriage.**
matron, n. *mam-tȳlu,* f., *ben'vas* (for *benen-vas*), f., *gwrēk,* f., pl. *gwrageth.*
matter, v., it m.s, *vern, dür,* def. v.s used mostly in neg.; it does not m., *ny-vern*; no m., *ny-rēs fors, na fors*; no m. for that, *nyns-üs fors awo·s henna*; it doesn't m. to me, *ny-m-dür, ny-rōf* or *wraf, fors, ny-rēs dhym fors, dhym ny-amont man*; what is the m. with? *pandr' a-wher dhe*[2]?; what does it m.? *pan goll üs awo·s henna*?; more strongly, *anodho ny-rōf oy, cala,* etc., *anodho travyth ny-m-dür*; hear, if it m.s to thee, *clew, mara-th-tür.*
matter, n. *tra,* neut., pl. *taclow, cās,* m., *substans,* f., *mater,* m., pl. *-s, defnyth,* m., pl. *-yow, pyth,* m., pl. *-ow*; the whole m., *oll an sampel*; importance, *fors,* m.; no m., *nyns-üs fors, na fors.*
matting, n. *strayl,* m., pl. *-yow.*
mattock, n. *pygal-havrak,* f., pl. *-golow-h.*
mattress, n. **colghes,* f., pl. *-ow.*
mature, a. *athves* (*a'ves*): v. *athvejy, dōs ha bōs athves, dōs dhe ōs*: **-rity,** n. *athvetter,* m.
maul, v. *tebel-dȳghtya, deffola,* **badhy.*
Maundy Thursday, n. *Cablys, dē-Yow Hablys,* m.
maw, n. *glas,* m., *cowl,* m., pl. *-ow*: **-worm,** n. **lenkeren,* f., col. *lenker.*
maxim, n. *poynt a skȳans, lavar für,* m.
May, n. *mȳs-Mē,* m.; M. Day, *Cala' Mē, dē-Hala'Mē*; m.-tree, *spernen wyn,* f., col. *spern gwyn*; sycamore, *sycamorwedhen,* f., pl. *-wȳth*; m. game, *gwary Cala'Mē.*
may, v., I m., *my a-ȳl, y-hallaf*; m. it be, *re-bo*; come what m., *dens a-dheffo*; be that as it m., *bedhens henna del ȳl bōs.*

mayor, n. *mēr*, m., pl. *-as*: **-ess,** n. *mēres*, f., pl. *-ow.*
mayweed, n. *fenokel cün*, m.
maze, n. **kēr-Droya*, **mylhentall*, m.
me, pron., suffixed, *-vy*; emph. *-avȳ·*, *-mavȳ·*; infixed, *-m-*; combined with preps., of m. *ahanaf*; to m., *dhym*, etc.; with inf. *ow*³ (lit. my); he saw m., *ef a-wrük ow gweles*; seeing m., *orth ow gweles.*
mead, n. *mēth*, m.; m. and ale mixed, †*bragas*, m.: see **metheglin.**
meadow, n. *büthyn*, m., pl. *-yow*, *prās*, m., pl. *-ow*; with stream, *dōl*, f., pl. *-ow.*
meagre, a. *tanow*, *cül*: **-ness,** n. *tanowder*, *cülder*, m.
meal, n. *prȳs*, m., pl. *-yow*, *-yjyow*, *bōs*, †*sant*, m.; flour, *blēs*, m.; m.-time, *prȳs-bōs*, m.; picnic or workplace m., *crowst*, m., pl. *-ys.*
mean, v. *styrya*, ‡*sygnyfya*, ‡*mēnya*; m. to do so, *tewlel*, or *ervȳra yndella gül*; what do you m.? *pandr' a-vynnough-why leverel?*; I m. to get it, *my a-vyn porres y gafos*: **-ing,** n. *styr*, m., pl. *-yow*, ‡*sygnyfyans*, m., pl. *-ow*: **-ingless,** a. *hep styr-vyth.*
mean, a. *ysel*, *gwan*; ungenerous, *pȳth*; m. person, *caughwas*, m., pl. *-wesyon*: **-ly,** adv. *ysel*, *yn-pȳth.*
means, n., agency, *mayn*, ‡*maynys*, m.; materials, *dafar*, m.; property, *substans*, f., *pega·ns*, m.; by all m., *awo·s ēghen*; it was by no m. so, *nyns-o man*; by m. of, *drē*, by some other m. *drē nep forth aral*; by fair m. or foul, *drē dekter po drē hakter.*
meantime, -while, n., in the m., *ha henna ow-cortos*, *hedra vȳen ow-cortos*, *y'n keth termyn*, ‡*yn kettermyn-na.*
measles, n. *cleves rüth*, m., *an vregh gough*, f.
measure, n. *musür*, m., pl. *-ow*, *scantlyn*, m., pl. *-s*, *keheseth* (*-eja*), m., pl. *-edhow*; span, **rewhans*, m.; corn m., *croder-croghen*, m., pl. *-drow-c.*; of full m., *da*, *cowal*; beyond m., *drēs musür*: v. *musüra*: **-ment,** n. *musürans*, m., pl. *-ow.*
meat, n., food, *bōs*, m.; flesh, *kȳk*, m., pl. *-ygow*; hunt or beg for m., *kycca* (inf. only).
mechanic, n. *jynnor*, m., pl. *-yon*: **-al,** a. *drē jyn*: **-nism,** n. *jyn*, m., pl. *-nys*, *jynwȳth*,
medal, n. *medal*, m., pl. *-lys*; commemorative m., *bath cōf*, m., pl. *-ow c.*: **-list,** n. *gwaynyer* or *synser medal*, m.
meddle, v., m. with, *attamya*, *mellya* (*orth*): **-r,** n. *mellyer*, m., pl. *-yoryon*: **-some,** a. *a-gar mellya.*
mediaeval, a. *a'n osow crēs.*
mediate, v. *bōs mayn yntra deu*: **-tion, -tor,** n. *mayn*, m.
medical, a. *medhek*: **-cinal,** a. *medhek*, *losowek*: **-cine,** n. *medhekneth*, m., *medhy·-gȳeth*, f., *losowen*, f., pl. *losowys*; science of m., *fysek*, f., *art f.*, m.
meditate, v. *predery*, *ombredery*: **-tion,** n. *preder down ha hȳr*, m.
medium, n. *mayn*, m.; of m. size, *nanȳ·l brās nā bȳghan.*
medlar, n. **merys*, m., pl. *-yow*, **aval tȳn-doll*, m.; m. tree, **meryswedhen*, m., col. *-wȳth.*
medley, n. *kemysk*, m., **cabül*, m., pl. *-yow*, **cabülva*, f.
medusa, n. *morgowl*, m., pl. *-ow*, col. *-es.*
meek, a. *whar*, *clōr*, *hüvel*, *se·rvabyl*: **-ness,** n. *clōrder*, *hüvelder*, m.
meet, v. *dyerbyn*(*a*), *metya orth*; fall in with, *metya gans*, *cafos*, *dōs* or *mōs*, *erby·n*; m. together, *omgafos*, *omguntell warba·rth*: **-ing,** n. *cuntell*, m., *cuntelles*, f., pl. *-ow*, *cuntellyans*, m., pl. *-ow*, *cuntellva*, *kesva*, f., pl. *-ow*; bardic m., *gorseth*, f., pl. *-edhow*; m. of waters, *kendevryon*, pl.; m. of lands, *kendorow*, pl.
meet, a.: see **fitting, proper, right.**
megalith, n. *mēn brās*, m., pl. *meyn b.*: **-ic,** a. *drehevys a veyn brās*; m. burial chamber, *cromlegh*, f., pl. *-yow*; stone circle, *dōns meyn*, m.; longstone, *menhyr*, *hyrven.*
melancholy, a. *morethek*, *tryst*: n. *preder*, m., abst. *-ow*, *moreth*, *trystys*, m.
mellow, a. *athves*: **-ness,** n. *athvetter*, m.
melodious, a. *whēk y glewes* **melodyes*: **-y,** n. **melody*, m., pl. *-s*, **ȳlow*, m., *tōn*, m., pl. *-yow.*
melon, n. *pompyon whēk*, m., pl. *-s w.*
melt, v. *tedha*: **-ed,** a. *tēth*: **-er,** n. *tedher*, m., pl. *-dhoryon*: **-ing,** n. *tēth*, m.; m. pot, *tethlester*, m., pl. *-lystry.*
member, n., of body or society, *ēsel*, m., pl. *ysyly*; limb, etc., *lyth*, m., pl. *-yow*; joint, *junt*, m., pl. *-ys*; of guild, *mysterden*, m., pls. *-s*, *-dyns*; privy m.s, *lygyon*, m., pl.: **-ship,** n. *eseleth*, m.
membrane, n. *kennen*, f., pl. *-now.*
memento, n. *cofro*, m., pl. *-how*, *tra üs ow-trȳ cōf*, neuter, *covath*, m.
memory, n. *covath*, m., *cōf*, m., pl. *covyon*, *cofva*; beyond m., *drēs cōf dēn*; within living m., *a-jȳ dhe dermyn whath üs perthys anodho cōf*, *a-jȳ dhe gōf dēn*: **-rable,** a. *hegof*, *a-dāl y gofhē·*: **-randum,** n. *cofscryf*,

m.: **-rial,** n. *covath,* m., *cofva,* f., *mēn,* or *drehevyans, cōf,* m.
menace, n. *godros,* m., pl. *-ow*: v. *godros.*
menagerie, n. *mȳlva,* f., *gothfyljy,* m., pl. *-ow.*
mend, v. *ewna, gwellhē·*; stitch, *gwrȳas*; stitch coarsely, *crafa.*
menhir, n. *menhyr,* m., pl. *-yon, hyrven,* m., pl. *-veyn.*
menial, n. *gwas,* m., pl. *gwesyon, servyas,* m., pls. *-ysy, -yjy*: a. *kēth.*
mental, a. *a'n cowsys, a'n brȳs*: **-ity,** n. *forth-tyby,* f.: **-ly,** a. *yn y vrȳs.*
mention, v. *campolla, meneges*; m. with honour, *kywhethla*: n. *menek,* m.
menu, n. *rōl vytel,* m.
mercantile, a. *marghajorek.*
merchant, n. *marghajor,* m., pl. *-yon,* f. *-es,* pl. *-ow, marchont,* m., pl. *-ons*: **-man,** n. *gorhel marchont,* m., pl. *-holyon m.*: **-andise,** n. *marchondys,* m., *gwara,* col., **marghajoreth,* m.
mercy, n. *truēth, tregereth, mercy,* m.: **-ciful,** a. *truēthek,* **tregerethüs, mercyabyl*: **-ciless,** a. *dydruēth, dybyta.*
Mercury, n. *Mergher*; metal, *arghans bew,* m.
mere, n. *lyn,* f., pl. *-now, logh,* f., pl. *-ow.*
mere, a. *sempel, pür*: **-ly,** adv. *ünwyth, ‡ynünyk*; it is m. foolishness, *nyns-yu lemen,* or *marnas, folneth.*
meridian, n. *hanterdēth,* m.
merit, v. *tylly, dyndyl, deleth* (def. v.), *prena,* **goberna*: n. **delys,* m., pl. *-yjow*: **-orious,** a. *a brȳs, wordhy.*
mermaid, n. *morvoren,* f., pl. *-ronyon.*
merry, a. *lowenek, dygüth, hüdhyk, hüdhyk y golon, mery*; make m., *omlowenhē·*; as m. as a lark, *maga fery avel hōk* (hawk): **-iment,** n. *lowender,* m.
mesh, n. *magel,* f., pl. *-gow, maglen,* f., pl. *-now*; to catch in a m., *magly.*
mesmerism, n. **sōngusk,* **hüscusk.*
mess, n. *stroll, mostethes,* m.; food, *lommen,* f., pl. *-now, †sant,* m.; make a filthy m., *scumbla*: **-mate,** n. *coweth mōs,* m., pl. *-a m.*; his m., *onen a'y vōs*: **-y,** a. *strollek.*
message, n. *negys,* m., pls. *-sow, -syow, messach,* m., pl. *-ajys, cannas,* f., pl. *-ow, danvonadow,* abst. pl., *gēr,* m., pl. *-yow*; to go with a m., *mōs negys*: **-senger,** n. *negesyth,* m., pl. *-ydhyon, messejer,* m., pls. *-s, -ys, cannas,* f., pl. *-ow.*
metal, n. *mūn,* **olcan,* m.: **-lic, -liferous,** a. *mūnek*; m. ground, *mūnak,* f., pl. *-egy.*
meteror, n. *steren codha,* f., pl. *-now c.*: **-ite,** n. *mēn cowas,* m.
meter, n. *jyn-musüra,* m., pl. *-nys-m.*
metheglin, n. *medheklyn, mēth,* m.
method, n. *forth,* f., pl. *-dhow, maner,* f., pl. *-ow*; m. advised, *cusül,* m., pl. *-yow, ‡trāda,* m., pl. *-ys*: **-ical,** a. *rewlys.*
meticulous, -ly, a., adv. *dour.*
metric, -al, a. **metryk.*
metropolis, n. *mamdra,* f., pl. *-drevow, pencyta,* m., pl. *-tys.*
mettle, n. *spyrys,* m.; let's try his m., *gwren assaya py par gwas yu.*
mew, v. **myowal.*
Michael, n. *Myghā·l,* m.: **-mas,** n. *degol* (*dugol*)- *Myghā·l, Gōl M.,* m.
microbe, n. **corbrȳf,* m., pl. *-yves.*
microscope, n. *gwēder moghhē·,* m., pl. *-drow m.*: **-pic,** a. *münys drēs ēghen.*
mid-, a. *crēs, hanter-*: **-afternoon,** n. *hanterdohajē·th*: **-day,** n. *ha·nterdēth,* m.: **-night,** n. *ha·nternōs,* f.: **-summer,** n. *Golowan* (for *Gōl Jowan*), m.; m. eve, *Nōs Golowan,* f., *Crēs an Hāf,* m.: **-way,** adv. *dhe hanter an forth* (*yntra . . . ha . . .*).
middle, n. *crēs, perveth,* m.: a. *crēs, a-berveth.*
midge, n. *gwybesen,* f., col. *gwybes.*
midst, n. *crēs,* m.; in our m., *y'gan mysk, yntredhon.*
midwife, n. *gwelyvedhes,* f., pl. *-ow.*
mien, n. *chēr, semlant,* m.
might, n. *gallos, crefter, nell, nerth,* m.; with all my m., *oll dhe'm gallos, gans oll ow nell*: **-y,** a. *crēf, gallosek, barthüsek.*
might, v., I m., *my a-ylly, my a-alsa, y-hyllyn, y-halsen.*
migrate, v. *dyvrōa, omexylya, tremena*: **-tion,** n. *tremen,* m., pl. *-yow*; m. to another country, *dyvrōans,* m.
milch-kine, n. *gwarthek-godra,* col.
mild, a. *clōr, whar, dōf*; weather, *mygyl*: **-ness,** n. *clōrder, wharder, mygylder,* m.
mildew, n. *kewny,* col.; to become m.d, *kewnya, lōsy*: **-ed,** a. *lōs.*
mile, n. *myldȳ·r,* m., pl. *-yow*; **-stone,** n. *mēn myldȳ·r,* m., pl. *meyn m.*
milfoil, n. *†mynfel,* m.
military, a. *bresel, breselek*: **-tia,** n. **treflu,* m., *gwythysy trē,* m., pl.: **-tiaman,** n. *ēsel an *treflu, gwythyas trē,* m., pl. *-ysy t.*

milk, n. *lēth*, m.; curdled m., *lēth cowlys*; with rennet, *l. godrethys*; raw m., *lēth crȳf*; scalded m., *lēth cüdhys*; fresh m., *levryth*, m.; skimmed m., *lēth dydhehen*; first m. of cow, *godrak*, *kellēth*, m.: v. *godra*: **-er,** n. *godrer*, m., pl. *-roryon*, f. *-es*, pl. *-ow*: **-house,** n., dairy, *lēty*: **-less,** a. *hesk*, *dylēth*; to go m., of cow, *hesky*: **-maid,** n. *lēthores*, f., pl. *-ow*, *lēthwrēk*, *lēthvyrgh*, f., pl. *-wrageth*, *-vyrghes*: **-man,** n. *gwerther lēth*, m., pl. *oryon-l.*, *lēthor*, m., pl. *-yon*: **-y,** a. *lēthek*: **-weed, -wort,** n. *losow lēth*, col.

mill, n. *melyn*, f., pl. *-yow*; wind-m., *melyn-wyns*, *m. -gwyns*; water-m., *melyn-dhowr*, *m. -dowr*; tucking-m., fulling-m., *melyn-droghya*, *m.-troghya*; bolting m., *melyn-saya*; hand m., *brow*, f., pl. *-yow*; m. house, *melynjy*, m., pl. *-ow*, *chyvelyn*, m.; m.-pond, *crün* (*crēn*) *melyn*, m., pl. *-yow m.*, *polvelyn*, m.; m.stone, *mēn-melyn*, m., pl. *meyn-m.*; m.wheel, *rōs-melyn*; wheel-pit, *polrōs·*: v. *mala*: **-er,** n. *melynor*, m., pl. *-yon.*

millennium, n. *mylvledhen*, f.

millepede, n. *myldrōs*, m.

millet, n. *myllen*, f., col. *myll*; m. field, *myllek*, f.

milliner, n. **penwyskwrēk*, f., pl. *-wrageth*, *mylanor*, m., pl. *-yon*, f. *-es*, pl. *-ow*: **-y,** n. **penwyscas benenes*, m.

million, a., n. *mylvyl*, f., pl. *-yow*, *mylyon*, m.: **-aire,** n. *mylyonayr*, m., pl. *-ys*: **-th,** adv., n. *mylvylves.*

milt, n. *lēthan*, m., *an vam*, f.

mimic, v. *gül warlergh*, **mȳmya*, *gwary an appa*: n. *mȳm*, *appa*, m., pls. *-ys*, *-pys*: **-ry,** n. **mȳmyans*, m.

mince, v. *dyvynya*; not to m. matters, *ow-leverel dhe blemmyk*: **-meat,** n. *kȳk dyvynys*, **brewgyk*, m.

mind, v., take care, *gwaytya*, *gwytha*, *gorwytha*, *bōs wār*; take notice, *avȳsya*, *gül vrȳ a*²; guard, *gwytha*; object, *sconya*; m. out! *war*! *waryeugh*! *byth war*! *kemer wȳth dhys dha honen*!; m. you don't, *gwayt na-wrylly*; never m., *na fors*, *ny-vern*; I don't m., *ny-synsaf poynt*, *ny-m-dür*; if you don't m., *yndella mar peugh plēsyes*, *mar ny-th-tür henna*: **-ed,** a. *ervȳrys*; to be m., *mynnes*: **-ful,** a. *avȳsyes*, *wār*; to be m., *gorquytha.*

mind, n. *brȳs*, m., pl. *-yow*, *cowsys*, m., pl. *cowsesow*, *cowjejyow*; of one m., *ünver*, *kescolon*; to my m., *orth ow brȳs*; keep in m., *perthy cōf a*²; to make up one's m., *bōs avȳsyes* or *ervȳrys*; to change one's m., *trēlya cowsys*, *t. y gowsesow*; to make him change his m., *gül dh'y gowsys trēlya.*

mine, n. *whēl*, m. and f., pl. *-yow*; open working, *coffen*, f., pl. *-now*, *whēl-stok*, *laun*, m., pl. *-ow*, *mungleth*, m., pl. *-edhyow*; m.working, *gonys*, m.; tin m., *pol-stēn*, *whēl-stēn*, m.; streamwork, "moor-work," *whēl-hāl*; tin-pit, "shovel-work," *whēl bal*, *bal*; coal-m., *pol-glow*, *whēl-glow*; ancient tin-work, *whēl Yedhewon*; m.-waste, refuse, *atal*, col.; ancient, *atal Sarsyn*: v. *palas*: **-r,** n. *dēn bal*, m., pl. *tüs b.*; tin m., *stennor*, m., pl. *-yon*; m.-labourer, *spalyer*, m., pl. *-s*; coal m., *palor glow*, m., pl. *-yon g.*; on tribute system, *trübytor*, m., pl. *-yon.*

mine, poss. pron., it is m., *my-a-n-pew*, *dhymmo-vy yth-yu*, *ef a-long dhymmo -vy*; it is not m. to say, *nyns-yu ragof-vy leverel.*

mineral, n. *mūn*, m.; m. waters, *dowr* **ewonek*, *d. whethvys*: **-bearing,** a. *mūnek*; m.b. ground, *mūnak*, f., pls. *-egy*, *-egow.*

mingle, v. *kemysky.*

miniature, a. *bȳghan*, *münys*: n. **portrayans* or *lywans münys war dhans olyfans.*

minion, n. *dēn kēth*, m., pl. *tüs k.*

minister, v. *menystra*, *servya*: n. *menyster*, m., pl. *-trys*: **-try,** n. *menystry*, m.: **-tration,** n. *menystrans*, m.

minor, a. *lē*: n. *map yn-dan ōs*, m., pl. *mebyon yn-d.-o.*: **-ity,** n. **yowynkys*, *yowynkneth*, m.; he is still in his m., *nyns-yua whath devedhys dhe ōs.*

minster, n. *eglos managhty*, *peneglos*, f., pl. *-lysyow.*

minstrel, n. *menestral* (*menstrel*), m., pl. *-s*, *barth*, m., pl. *byrth*, *bardhes*, f., pl. *-ow*: **-sy,** n. *menestrouthy*, m.

mint, n., bot., *menta*, f.; coining, **batty*, m.: v. *bathy*: **-age,** n. *batho·rȳeth*, f.: **-er,** n. *gwas bathor*, m., pl. *gwesyon b.*

minus, adv. *hep*; less by, *lē a*².

minute, n. **mynysen*, f., col. *mynys.*

minute, a. *münys*, *pür vȳghan.*

miracle, n. *maystry*, *myrakyl* (*myrkyl*), m., pl. *-raclys*, *marthüs*, m., pl. *-ow*, *marthüsy*, m., pl. and abst. *-üjyon*; m. play, *gwary-mȳr*, *g. myrakyl*, m.: **-culous,** a. *marthys*, *barthüsek.*

mire, n. *lȳs*, *pol*, m.; a m., *lysek*, f.

mirk, n. *tewlder*, *tewlgow* (*tewolgow*); m. and morn, *mo ha myttyn*: **-y,** a. *tewl*, *comolek.*

mirror, n. *gwēder, g. myras,* m., pl. *-drow-m., myrour,* m., pl. *-s.*
mirth, n. *lowender, wherthyn,* m.
mis-, prefix *cam-, mys-*: **-adventure,** n. *drok-lam, droglam,* m., pl. *-mow*; in sense of accident, *gwall,* m., pl. *-ow, meschō·ns,* m.: **-apprehend,** v. *fyllel attendya, camgemeres, ‡myskemeres*: **-nsion,** n. *ancombrynsy, ‡myskemeryans,* m.: **-behave,** v. *tebel-fara, camomdhō·n*: **-viour,** n. *tebelfara,* m.: **-call,** v. *tebelhenwel*: **-carriage,** n. *meth,* m., pl. *mothow*: **-cellaneous,** a. *a bup sort*: **-chance,** n. *gwall,* m., pl. *-ow, meschō·ns,* m.: **-chief,** n. *mewl,* m., *dregyn,* f., *myshyf,* m., pl. *-evys, drok,* m., pl. *-ogow*: **-ievous,** a. *a-wra dregyn*: **-conduct,** v., m. oneself, *camomdhō·n, camwül*: n. *camwȳth,* m.: **-creant,** n. *tebelgryjyk,* m., pl. *-ygyon, bylen,* m.: **-deed,** n. *camwȳth,* m., pl. *-yow, tebel-wrȳans, drok-ober,* m., pl. *-ow*: **-demeanour,** n. *gwan-ober,* m., pl. *-ow*: **-doing,** n. *camwȳth,* m., pl. *-yow*: **-fortune,** n. *hap drōk, meschō·ns,* m.: **-giving,** n. *dowt, own,* m.: **-hap,** n. *droklam, droglam,* m., pl. *-mow*: **-judge,** v. *camvrüsy*: **-lay,** v. *kelly*: **-lead,** v. *sawthanas*: **-manage,** v. *camrewlya, bōs gwandȳak*: **-ment,** n. *camrewlyans,* m.: **-name,** v. *camhenwel, gelwel dēn mēs a'y hanow*: **-place,** v. *gorra mēs a'y lē*: **-print,** v. *cambryntya*: n. *cambryntyans,* m., pl. *-ow*: **-prise,** v. *dysprēsya*: **-pronounce,** v. *camleverel*: **-nunciation,** n. *camleveryans,* m.: **-rule,** n. *gwan-rewl,* f.: **-statement,** n. *camlavar,* m., pl. *-ow, derȳvas gow,* m.: **-take,** v. *fyllel convedhes, camgemeres, †myskemeres*: n. *fowt,* m., pl. *-ow, camgemeryans, ‡myskemeryans,* m., pl. *-ow*; m. in speaking, *camlavar,* m.: **-n,** a., to be m., *camdyby*: **-trust,** v. *dowtya, mystrestya*: n. *mystrest, dowt,* m.: **-understand,** v. *fyllel attendya, camġemeres, ‡myskemeres*: **-use,** v., ill-treat, *tebel-dȳghtya*; make wrong use of, *gül defnyth drōk a*²: n. *tebeldȳghtyans.*
miser, n, *†craf,* m., pl. *-evyon, †synsyas, *erbysyas,* m., pl. *-ysy*: **-ly,** a. *crefny.*
misery, n. *gew,* m., pl. and abst. *-ow, ponvos,* m.; state of m., *ponvotter, dysē·s,* m., *anfüs,* f., *anken,* m., pl. *-yow, cās, govyjyon,* m., *†dyodhenes,* f.: **-rable,** a. *trūan, morethek, drōk y jēr, ponvosyk*: **-bly,** adv. *trūan, yntrūan.*
Miss, n. *Mēstres, Mestresyk,* f.

miss, n. *meth,* m., pl. *mothow*; without a m., *hep fall*: v. *kelly, fyllel, bōs meth*; feel want of, *yeuny rak, bōs tryst warle·rgh*; fail to hit, *fyllel a weskel*; m. the train, *kelly an trēn*; m. the point, *sawthanas*: **-ing,** a., it is m., *nyns-üs omma, y-fyll, kellys yu.*
missal, n. *lyver-oferen,* m., pl. *lyfrow-o.*
missel-thrush, n. **traskel,* m., pl. *tryskly, *tresklen,* f., col. *treskel.*
mission, n. *cannaseth,* f., pl. *-ow*; m. house, **cannaty,* m., pl. *-ow, tyller cannas,* m.: **-ary,** n. *cannas an Eglos,* f., pl. *-ow.*
missive, n. *†scryven danvon,* f., pl. *-now d.*
mist, n. *newl, lewgh,* m.; thick, *cowas-newl,* f., pl. *-osow n.*; bank of m., *newlen,* f., pl. *-now*; m. free, *dynewl*: **-y,** *newlek, lewghek.*
mister, Mr., n. *mēster,* m., pl. *-strysy.*
mistletoe, n. **ughelvar,* m.
mistress, n. *mēstres,* f., pl. *-ow, arlodhes,* f., pl. *-ow.*
mite, n. *temmyk,* m., pl. *-ygow, tymmynygow, myjyn,* m., pl. *-now*; grub, *†gowdhan,* m., pl. *-as*; ½-farthing, *mȳta,* m., pl. *-tys.*
mitigate, v. *sewajya, lehē·, scafhē·*: **-tion,** n. *lehēans.*
mitten, n. *manek hep besyas,* f., pl. *-egow h. b.*
mitre, n. *mytour,* m., pl. *-s.*
mix, v. *kemysky, cabūly*: **-ed,** a. *yn-kemyskys*: **-ture,** n. *kemysk, kemyskyans,* m.
mizen, n., sail, *gōl a-dhelergh*; m. mast, *gwern a-dhelergh,* f.
moan, v. *kȳny, üja, crȳa "egha·n!"*: n. **kȳnvan, crȳ galar.*
moat, n. *clēth* (*c. castel*), *polglēth,* m., pl. *-edhyow*(*c.*), m.
mob, n. *rūth,* f., pl. *-ow*: v. *drokhandla, pyltya, settya war*².
mock, v. *scornya, gēsya, gül gēs a*²: **-ery,** n. *scorn, gēs,* m.
mode, n. *forth, maner,* f.; m. of life, *conversasyon,* m.
model, n. *hevelep mūnys, patron,* m.: v. *shapya, formya*; m. oneself on, *omformya warle·rgh.*
moderate, v. *tempra*: a. *clōr*; be m! *kē war dha gam!*: **-ly,** adv. *war gam, war aga ham,* etc., with imperative; make less outcry! *crȳ war dha gam!* help yourself m., *kemer lowr, saw hep kemeres rē*: **-tion,** n. *clōrder, musür,* m.; in m., *nanȳl rē na whath rē nebes.*
modern, a. *a'gan dedhyow-ny, a'n ōs noweth.*
modest, a. *hüvel, ysel, clōr, methek*: **-y,** n. *hüvelsys, meth,* f.

modify, v. *trēlya, chanjya*: **-fication,** n. *trēlyans, chanjyans*, m.
moist, a. *glyp*, **lȳth*: **-en,** v. *glybya*, **lȳtha*: **-ness,** n. *lȳthter*: **-ure,** n. †*glybor*, **glēgh*, m.
molar, n. **kyldans*, m., pl. *-dyns*.
molasses, n. *mola·s*, m.
mole, n. *gōth*, f., pl. *-dhas, go'dhor*, f., pl. *godhas dor*; on skin, **plüstren*, f., pl. *-now, merk genesygeth*; to catch m.s, *godhessa* (inf. only): **-hill,** n. *pȳl gōth, p. go'dhor*, m., pl. *-yow g.*
mole, n., breakwater, *bak*, m., pl. *-kys, mōrglēth*, m., pl. *-edhyow*.
molest, v. *despȳtya, tropla, mellya orth* or *gans*.
mollify, v. *medhelhē·*.
molten, a. *tēth*.
moment, n. *cors*, m., pl. *-ow, pols, prȳs*, m., *pryjwyth*, m., pl. *-yow, teken*, f., pl. *-now*; at this m., *lemmyn, nans-* (definite particle used before vowels in *bōs*); importance, it is of no m., *travyth ny-vern*: **-arily,** adv. *ün lam, ün prȳs, ün cors, pols, tuch*, ‡*rak teken*: **-ous,** a. *mür y-vern, awos ēghen a-dāl y attendya*.
momentum, n. *hedhyans, müvyans*, m.
monarch, n. *myghte·rn* (*mytern*), m., pl. *-eth*: **-y,** n. *myghternsys*, m.
monastery, n. *managhty*, m., pl. *-ow*: **-stic,** a. *managhek, meneghek*; m. land, *meneghek*, f.
Monday, n. *dē-Lün*, m.
money, n. *arghans, mona*, col. (followed by pl. pron.); piece of m., *mona*, m., pl. *-nyes*, †*bath*, m., pl. *-ow*; m.-changer, †*bathor*, m., pl. *-yon*, **arghanser*, m., pl. *-oryon*; m.-lender, **okerer*, m., pl. *-s*.
mongrel, a. **kemyskryth*.
monk, n. *managh*, m., pl. *menegh*: **-ish,** a. *managhek*: **m.-fish,** n. *morvanagh*, m., pl. *-venegh*.
monkey, n. †*sym*, m., pl. *-as*.
monochrome, a. *ünlyw*: **-olith,** n. *mēn ünyk*, m., pl. *meyn u.*; upright m., *menhyr*, m., pl. *-yon*: **-ic,** a. *gwrēs a veyn ünyk, ünmēnek, a ün mēn*: **-ologue,** n. *cows ün dēn, omgows*, m.: **-otonous,** a. **ündon, hep chanj*: **-ony,** n. *fowt chanjya*, **ündoneth*.
monster, n. *tebel vest*, m., pl. *-as*, **üthfyl*, m., pl. *-as*, †*enke·nethel* (**ankenel*), m., pl. *-ethlow*: **-strosity,** n. *üthekter, hakter*, m., *best*, etc., *tebel formyes*: **-strous,** a. *dygnās, üthek, drēs kynda, dyflas, formyes yn-cam*.
monstrance, n. *howl an sacrement*.
month, n. *mȳs*, m., pl. *-yow*; m.'s time, *mysquyth*, m.; m.'s end, *penvȳs*, m.; before three m.s are up, *kens pen tremmys*: **-ly,** a. *pup mȳs* (*-oll*), *mȳsek*.
monument, n. *pül-, mēn-, ymach-cōf*, m., pls. *-yow-, meyn-, -chys-c.*: **-al,** a. *pür vrās*; of graves, *a veyn-cōf*.
mood, n. *chēr*, m.; in angry m., *sōr dhodho*: **-y,** a. *drōk y jer*.
moon, n. *lōr*, f.: **-beam,** n. *golowyn lōr*, m., pl. *-now l.*: **-light, -shine,** n. *lōrgan*, m.: **-rise,** n. *drehafva an lōr*, f.: **-struck,** a. *fol*, †*badüs*, **lōrek*.
moor, v. *tewlel ancar, synsy lester gans lovan dhe'n tȳr*: **-ings,** n. *ancarva*, f., *pol*, m., pl. *-low*.
moor, n. *hāl*, f., pl. *-low, rōs*, f., pl. *-yow, gūn*, f., pl. *gonyow*: **-land,** n., m. part of property, *gūnran*, f.
Moor, n. *Sarsyn*, m., pl. *-s*: **-ish,** a. *Sarsynek*.
moorhen, n. *lagyar*, f., pl. *-yēr*.
mop, n. *scübylen*, f., pl. *-now*: v. *sēgha*.
mope, v. *dughanhē·, kemeres dughan*, **mūtya*.
moral, n. *dyscas*, m.; m.s, *manerow*, pl.: a. †*ewnhensek, da*: **-ity,** n. *ewnder, onester*, m.: **morale,** n. *colon* (*dha*).
morass, n. *gwern*, f., pls. *-ow, -y, lȳsek, kersek*, f., pls. *-egow, -egy*.
morbid, a. *morethek*, †*anyagh*: **-ity,** n. *cleves an brȳs*.
more, a., adv. *moy, kēn*; something m., *kēn tra*; a little m., *nebes moy*; anything m., *kēn*; nothing m., *tra nahē·n*; any m., no m., *byth moy, bys voy, nahē·n, nēs* (with neg.); once m., *arta, whath*; the m. . . ., the m. . . ., *sül voy . . ., dhe voy . . .*; no m., *namoy·*; what is m., *ynwe·th, moy es henna*: **-over,** adv. *kefrȳ·s, gensy, gans hemma, gans henna, yn prōf, drēs henna, ha, pella, yn prōf*.
morn, n. *myttyn*, †*bora*, m.: **-ing,** n. *myttyn*, m., pl. *-ow*; m. from 9 to 12, *kensewha*; in the m., *myttyn*; this m., *hedhyu vyttyn*; yesterday m., *dē vyttyn*; tomorrow m., next m., *ternos vyttyn*; before m., *kens* (*es*) *vyttyn*; on Friday m., *dē-Gwener vyttyn*; Easter m., *dē-Pask vyttyn*; the time of m., **myttynwyth*; early in the m., *ava·r myttyn*: **-ing-star,** n. *Berlewen*, f.
morose, a. *asper, trūan, trenk*: **-ness,** n. *aspe·ryta, trenkter*, m.

morphia, n. *losow cusca,* col. **cuskles,* m.

morrow, n. *morow,* f.; on the m., *a'n vorow, ternos*; to-m., *avorow.*

morsel, n. *pastel,* f., pl. *-llow, tam,* m., pl. *tymmyn, sūben,* f., pl. *-now, dyvyn,* m., pl. *-yon.*

mortal, a. *a-verow,* **marwyl*: n. *sojeta ancow,* m, pl. *-tys a.*: **-ity,** n. *mernans,* m., **marwoleth,* f.

mortar, n. *lȳm ha prȳ,* m.; for pounding, *lester brewy,* m.

mortgage, n. *gāja-mernans,* **marow-wystel,* m.: v. *gājya war vernans, marow-wystla.*

mortise, n. *morter, toll-tenon,* m.

mortification, n. *podrethes,* m.; disappointment, *sōr, tull,* m.: **-fy,** v. *tulla, serry*; m. the flesh, *omvertherya, ombayna* or *gwanhē· an kȳk, yndella gül na-vo rē fors y natur.*

mortuary, n. *marowjy,* m., pl. *-ow.*

mosquito, n. *gwybesen,* f., col. *gwybes.*

Moslem, n. *Sarsyn,* m., pl. *-s*: a. *Sarsynek.*

moss, n. *kewny,* col., *mūs, best,* m.; piece of m., *kewnȳen,* f., pl. *-now*; to collect m., *kewnȳa* (inf. only): **-y,** a. *kewnȳek.*

most, a. *moyha*; at m., *dhe'n moyha*: **-ly,** adv. *del yu ūsyes, moyha, yn-fenough*; they are m. foreigners, *brassa ran anedha yu estrenyon*; he is m. there, *namnag yu pupprys ena.*

mote, n. *motta,* m., pl. *-tys, breghy,* pl.

moth, n. *tykky-dew nōs,* m., pl. *-as n.*; m. grub, *gowdhan,* m., pl. *-as, prȳf dyllas,* m., pl. *-yvas d.*

mother, n. *mam,* f., pl. *-mow, dama,* f., pl. *-myow*; m.-in-law, †*wheger,* f., pl. *-grow,* **dama dha*; nursing m., *mammeth,* f., pl. *-ow*; m. church, *mameglos,* f.; of same m., *ünvam*; m. tongue, *mamyēth,* f.; m. land, *mamvro,* f.; m. of pearl, *askel,* f.: **-hood,** n. *mamsys,* m., **mamoleth,* f.: **-ly,** a. *mam, kepa·r ha mam,* **mamyl.*

motion, n., in debate, *müvyans,* m.; movement, *gwayans,* m.; to set in m., *müvya,* **keflesca*: **-less,** a. *hep gwaya.*

motive, n. *kēn,* m., *skyla, achēson* (*chēson*).

motley, a. *lȳes-lyw*: n. *dyllas l. l., dyllas Cala Mē.*

motor-car, n. *car-tān,* m., pl. *kerry t.*

mottle, v. **brytha*: **-d,** a. †*bryth.*

motto, n. *lavar,* m., pl. *-ow.*

mould, v. *formya*: n., soil, *gweras, prȳ,* m.; fungus, *kewny, cusk,* m.; shape, *form,* m., pl. *-ys,* †*furf,* f., pl. *-vyow*: **-board,** n. **whelder,* m.: **-y,** a. *lōs, kewnȳek*; to go m., *lōsy.*

moult, v. *mūtya, tewlel plüf.*

mound, n. *knogh, tolgh,* m., pl. *-ow, pȳl,* m., pl. *-yow, crük,* m., pl. *-ügyow, tomen,* f., pl. *-now*; small m., *crügell,* f., pl. *-low, crügyn,* m., pl. *-now.*

mount, v. *yskynna*: n. *mont* (*mownt*), m.; steed, *stēda,* m., pl. *-dys*: **-ing block,** n. *mēn-yskynna,* m., pl. *meyn-y,* **marghvēn,* m., pl. *-veyn.*

mountain, n. *meneth,* m., pl. *-nydhyow*: **-eer,** n. *menedhor,* m., pl. *-yon, menedhyas,* m., pl. *-ysy*: **-ous,** a. *menedhek*: **m.-ash,** n. *kerdhynen,* f., col. *kerdhyn*; m.a. berry, *keren,* f., col. *kēr.*

mountebank, n. *medhek fals,* m., pl. *-ygyon f., pomster,* m., pl. *-s.*

mourn, v. *kȳny, dughanhē·,* **galary, mornya*: **-er,** n. *kȳner,* m., pl. *-oryon, mornyer,* m., pl. *-s,* **galaror,* m., pl. *-yon*: **-ful,** a. *tryst, morethek, trūesy*: **-ing,** n. *galarow,* pl., abst. *kȳnvan, mornyng,* m.; dress, **galarwysk,* m., pl. *-as.*

mouse, n. *logosen,* f., col. *logas*; to m., catch m., *legessa* (inf. only): **-r,** n. *legessa,* m., pl. *-syon.*

moustache, n. **mȳnvlew,* col.

mouth, n. *ganow,* m., pl. *-ow, mȳn,* m., pl. *-yon*; of river, *aber,* m., pl. *-ow*; m.-ful, **ganowas,* m., pl. *-esow*; crooked m.d, *mȳngam*; large m.d, **ganowek*; m.-piece, *ganow,* m.

move, v. *müvya*; goods, house, *dyannedhy, chanjya chȳ*; m. along, *kerdhes*; m. about, *remüvya,* †*sommys*: **-ables,** n. *mebyl,* col. *dafar,* m., *taclow,* pl.: **-ment,** n. *müvyans,* m.

mow, v. *trēghy gora,* **falghas*: **-er,** n. *trēgher gora, falghor,* m., pl. *-yon.*

mow, n. *crük,* m., pl. *-ügyow*; of corn, *crük ȳs*; round topped, *c. bar-mōl*; pointed, *c. pedrak*: **mowhay,** n. **ȳslan,* f., *garth an deys,* m.

much, a. *mür, mür a²,* *lower, polta* (*pols da*); as m. as, *py sül a²-, myns del², kemmy·s del²* (before v.), *kemmȳ·s ha* (before n. or pron.); not m., *namü·r*; how m., *py sül, pygemmys*; too m., *rē, rē a²*; m. better, etc., *polta gwell,* etc.; that is as m. as to say, *hen yu dhe styrya*; thus m., ‡*an gemmyn-na*; make m. of, *gül mür a².*

muck-heap, n. *pȳl-teyl,* m., pl. *-yow-t.*

mucus, n. *pūr,* m.

mud, n. *lȳs, pol, lūb,* m.; estuary m., *lȳs hayl,* m.; to spatter clothing with m., *cagla*: **-dy,** a. *plos, lūbys, strollek, caglys, lȳsak*; m. place, *lȳsek,* f., pls. *-egy, -egow.*
muddle, n. *kemysk,* m., *cabūlva,* f.; a hopeless m., *k. drēs y dhygemysky, ancombrynsy a'n pürra*: v. *müskegy, kemysky.*
muffle, v. *cüdha, megy*: **-r,** n. **gūdhūgen,* f., pl. *-now.*
mug, n. *dewaslester,* m., pl. *-lystry.*
mugwort, n. †*lōsles,* m.
mulberry, n. *moren,* f., col. *mōr*; m. tree, *mōrwedhen,* f., pl. *-wyth,* †*morbren,* m., pl. *-nyer.*
mule, n. *mūl,* m., pl. *-as,* f. *-es,* pl. *-ow*: **-ish,** a. *maga gorth ave·l mūl.*
mullein, n. **gwlanyk,* m.
mullet, n. †*mēyl,* m., pl. *-ly*; red m., *mēyl rüth*; to catch m., *mēylessa* (inf. only).
multiply, v. *encressya, gül bōs moy, moghhē·, palshē·, *lyeshē·.*
multitude, n. *lu,* m., pl. *-yow, rūth vür,* f., pl. *-ow mür, nyver brās.*
mumble, v. *kewsel yn ün hanas,* †*stlevy*: **-r,** n. †*stlaf,* m., pl. *-levyon, hanajer,* m., pls. *-yoryon, -joryon*: **-ing,** a. †*stlaf*: n. †*stlaveth,* m.
mumps, n. **pensagh,* m.
munch, v. *dynsel.*
mundic, n. *poder,* m.
municipal, a. *a'n drē, a'n vurjysy*: **-ity,** n. **burjeseth,* m.
munificence, n. **hēlsys,* f., **hēlder,* m.: **-t,** a. *hēl.*
munitions, n. *dafar lathva, d. bresel,* m.
multigraph, v. †*lȳes-scryfa.*
mural, a. *fōs, a'n* †*parwys.*
murder, n. *lathva,* f., pl. *-ow, moldra, denlath,* m.: v. *dystrewy, moldra, ladha*: **-er,** n. *moldrer,* m., pl. *-oryon, denlath,* m., *denledhyas,* m., pl. *-ysy.*
murk, n.: see **mirk.**
murmur, n., complaint, *son,* m., pl. *-yow, crothval,* m.; light m., *hanas,* m., pl. *-ow, hanajen,* f., pl. *-now*; m. raised, *son,* m., pl. *-yow*: v. *hanaja, hanas, crothvolas* (*croffolas*).
muscle, n. *keher,* m., pl. *-ow*; small m., *keheryn,* m., pl. *-now*: **-cular,** a. *keherek.*
muse, v. *ombredery,*: n. **awen,* f.
museum, n. *gwythty,* m., pl. *-ow.*
mushroom, n. *scavel-cronek,* f., pl. *-low-c.*
music, n. *menestrouthy, *mūsyk, *ȳlow,* m.: **-al,** a. **ȳlow, a*vūsyk*: **-ian,** n. **mūsy·cyen, menstrel,* m., pl. *-s, *ylewyth,* m., pl. *-wydhyon.*
mussel, n. *mesclen,* f., col. *meskel*; to gather m.s, *mescla* (inf. only).
must, v., you m., I m., etc., *bysy yu dheugh, rēs yu dhym,* ‡*my a-dāl,* etc.
mustard, n. **kedhow, *senefa,* m.; m. pot, *padel *kedhow,* f.
muster, v. *cuntell*: n. *cuntellyans,* m.
musty, a. *messe·nt, flērys, -yüs.*
mutate, v. *trēlya, chanjya*: **-ion,** n. *trēlyans,* m.
mute, a. *omlavar,* †*aflavar, *dylavar.*
mutilate, v. *hakkya, dyfasya*: **-d,** a. *evreth, evredhek*; m. person, *evredhek,* m., pl. *-ygyon, evreth,* m., pl. *-edhyon.*
mutiny, n. *gustel,* m., pl. *-tlow*: v. *gustla, sordya erby·n pen.*
mutter, v. *crothval* (*-volas*), †*stlavy*: n.: see **murmur.**
mutton, n. *kȳk-davas, mols, molskyk,* m.; m. chop, *golyth davas,* m., pl. *-yn d.*
mutual, a. *an ȳl dh'y gȳla, a'n dheu du*; prefix, *om-, kes-*: **-ly,** adv. *an ȳl,* or *pup onen-oll, dh'y gȳla, an ȳl hy-bēn*; prefix, *om-, kes-.*
muzzle, n. *gwelf,* f., pl. *-lvow,* d., *dyw-welf, mȳn,* m., pl. *-yon*; black of m., *mȳndu*; long of m., *mȳnek.*
my, poss. pron. *ow*[3], *'w*[3], (after prep. or conj. only) *am, 'm.*
myrrh, n. *myr,* m.
myrtle, n. *myrtwedhen,* f., col. *-wȳth.*
myself, pron. *my ow-honen*; m. I cannot go, *mōs my ny-allaf*; for m., *ragof ow honen.*
mystery, n. *mystery, *kevrȳn, *rȳn,* m., pl. *-yow*; guild, *myster,* m., pl. *-ys*: **-rious,** a. **kevrȳnek, tewl*: **-tic,** a. **kevrȳnek, mystycal*: **-tify,** v. *müskegy, ancombra, kemysky.*
myth, n. **myth,* m., pl. *-ys, whethel pagan,* m., pl. *-thlow p.*: **-ology,** n. *studhyans whethlow, *mytholojy,* m.

N

nag, n. *hakney,* m., pl. *-s, rounsyn,* m., pl. *-as.*
nag, v. *gērya, bōs prest ow-crothvolas*; stop n.ging! *gās dha son!*
nail, n. *kenter,* f., pl. *-trow*; finger or toe n., *ewyn,* m., pl. *-as*; having n.s, *ewynek*; great n., bolt, †*ebyl horn*: v. *kentra, kentrewy, takkya.*

naked, a. *nōth, yn-nōth, lom, lom-nōth*; half-n., *ternōth*; n. oats, *pylas*, m.: **-ness,** n. *nōtha*, f., *lomder*, m.
naker-shell, n. *askel*, f., pl. *eskelly*.
name, n. *hanow*, m., pl. *hynwyn*; in the n. of, *aba·rth*; to call someone n.s, *gelwel dēn mēs a'y hanow*; good n., *hanow da*, †*gerda*; ill n., *gwan-hanow*: v. *henwel, gelwel, crȳa*: **-less,** a. *dyhanow, gesys hep y henwel, hep hanow*: **-ly,** adv. *hen yu*: **-sake,** n. *onen a'n keth hanow*; he is my n., *keshenwys yu genef-vȳ*.
nap, n. *nappa*, m., pl. *-pys*: v. *nappya, cusca pols*.
nape, n. *kyl, pol-kyl*, m., *gwar*, f., pl. *-row*; on his n., *war bol y gyl*.
napkin, n. *lȳen*, †*lȳen-dywlüf* or *-dywla*, m., pl. *-yow-d*.
narcissus, n. **fȳonen*, f., col. *fȳon*.
narrate, v. *leverel, derȳvas*: **-tive,** n. *whethel*, m., pl. *-thlow, drolla*, m., pl. *-lys, deryvadow*, m.
narrow, a. *cül, yn*; n.-minded, *cül y vrȳs*: **-ness,** n. *ynder, cülder*, m.
nasal, a. *a'n frygow*.
nastiness, n. *last, plosethes*, m.: **-ty,** a. *plos, plosek, mür y last, dysawor, hegas*.
nation, n. *ke·nethel*, f., pl. *-thlow, gwlās*, f., pl. *-ow, nasyon*, m., pl. *-s*: **-al,** a. *gwlasek, kenethlek, an nasyon*: **-ality,** n. **kenethlegeth*, m.: **-alize,** v. **kenethlegy*.
native, a. *genesyk, tȳthyak*: n. *genesyk*, m., pl. *-ygyon, trevesyk dōr*, m., pls. *-ygyon, -ejygyon d*.
Nativity, n. *Nadelek*, m.
nature, n. *natur, substans*, f., *kynda*, m.; human n., *natureth*, m., *gnās, nās*, f.; to modify, affect n., **nāsya*; against n., *erby·n natur*; of ill n., *drōk y gnās*: **-ral,** a. *genesyk, herwyth kynda*; n. feeling, *natureth*, m.; n. history, *skȳans an creatoryon*, m.:**- ralist,** n. *naturor*, m., pl. *-yon*: **-rally,** adv. *herwyth kynda*; of course, *hep mar, ny-rēs y leverel, yn sür, yredy*.
naughty, a. *drōk*: **-tiness,** n. *drokter, tebel fara*, m.
nautical, a. *morek, a'n mōr, a lystry*.
navy, n. *lu lystry*, m., pl. *-yow l., lystry bresel*: **-val,** a. *an mōr, morek, a'n lu-lystry*; n. war, *bresel war vōr*.
nave, n. *corf eglos*, m.; of wheel, **both*, f., pl. *-ow*.
navel, n. *bēgel*, m., pl. *-yow*.
navigate, v. *lewyas gorhel*: **-tion,** n. **navygasyon*, m.: **-tor,** n. *lewyth*, m., pl. *-ydhyon*.
nay, neg. particle *nag-yu*, etc., repeating v. of question; in late use, ‡*nā*.
neap-tide, n. *marvor, yselvor, tryg*, m.
near, a. *ogas*: prep. *ogas dhe*²; n. me, *yn ow ogas*; n. at hand, *rybon, omma yn ogas, a-ogas*; n. to me, *ogas dhym, rybof*: v. *nēshē·, nessa*: **-er,** a., adv. *nēs, yn-nēs*: **-est,** a. *nessa*: **-ly,** adv. *ogas dy* (*ogasty*, ‡*ogatty*) (ending clause), *ogas ha* (with n.), *namna*² (*g*) (with v.), *ogas* (with a.): **-ness,** n. *bōs ogas*, e.g., because of its n., *awo·s y vōs ogas*.
neat, a. *glanyth*, **kempen*: **-ness,** n. *glanythter*, **kempensys*, m.
neatherd, n. *bügel lothnow*, m., pl. *-eth*(*-a*) *l*.
nebula, n. *newlen stēr*, f., pl. *-now s*.
necessaries, n. *pega·ns, dafar*, m.: **-rily,** adv. *porres*; not n., *ny-sew bos henna gwȳr, ny-rēs bos yndella*: **-ry,** a. it is n., *rēs yu*; it is most n., *rēs porres yu*: **-situate,** v. *gül bōs rēs*: **-sity,** n. *rēs*, m., *ethom*, m., pl. and abst. *-mow*; indigence, *esow*, m.; of n., *porres*.
neck, n. *conna*, m., *gwar*, f., pl. *-row*; of corn harvest, *penyar*, m.; crying the n. *ow-carma p. y.*: **-cloth,** n. *lȳen conna*, m., pl. *-enyow c.*: **-lace,** n. **kelghen*, f., pl. *-now*: **-let,** n. †*delk*, m., pl. *-lcow*: **-tie,** n. *colm conna*, **güdhügen*, f.
necromancer, n. *pystryor*, m., pl. *-yon*, **nygromancer*, m., pl. *-s*: **-y,** n. *tebel-art*, **nygromans*, m.
need, n. *rēs, ethom, esow*, m.: v., I n., *yma· ethom dhym a*² . . .; I n. to be, *rēs yu dhym bōs* . . .; as well as n. be, *mar dha del rēs*; what n. have we to be, *pyth yu an ethom dhyn-ny bōs*: **-ful,** a., requisite, *bysy*: **-less,** a. *üfer, hep bōs anodho ethom, na-rēs*: **-s,** adv. *porres*; n. must, *nyns-üs nagha*: **-ments,** n. *pega·ns*, m.: **-y,** a. *ethomek*; n. person, *ethomek*, m., pl. *-mogyon*.
needle, n. *nasweth* (*najeth*), f., pl. *-edhow*; n.work, *gwyth-nasweth*, m.; n. eye, *crow n.*, m., pl. *crewow*, n.: **n.-fish,** n. *mornasweth*, f., pl. *-edhyow*.
ne'erdowell, n. *losel-was*, m., pl. *-wesyon, drok ebol*, m.
nefarious, a. *drōk, hager*.
negative, n. **negeth, an nagha*, m.: a. *negedhek, a-nagh*.

neglect, n. *dysprēsyans, gwall, scul,* m., *sculva,* f., *lowsethes,* m.: v. *gasa dhe goll, dysprēsya*; to be n.ed, *mōs* or *bōs gesys dhe goll*: **-ful,** *lows, logh, scullyak, *gwallek.*
negligence, -ent,: see **neglect, -ful.**
negotiate, v. *bargenya, spēdya negys*: **-tion,** n. *negys, bargen,* m.
negro, n. *dēn du,* m., pl. *tüs du*: **-gress,** n. *benendhu,* f., pl. *-es du*:
neigh, n. *gryghȳas,* m.: v. *gryghȳas, üja.*
neighbour, n. *kentrevak,* m., pl. *-ogyon, kentrevoges,* f., pl. *-ow, neshevyn,* m. and col.; thy n., *dha hynsa,* m. and col. *dha gescrystyon,* m., pl. *-stonyon*: **-hood,** n., in the n., *a-ogas, y'n pow a-dro*: **-ing,** a. *ogas*; of people, *kentrevak.*
neither, pron. *ny . . . nanȳ·l*; n. did he . . ., *na byth moy ny-wrük . . .*; n. . . . nor . . ., *nanȳ·l. . . . na . . ., na . . . na . . .*; n. one nor the other, *na'nȳ·l na'y gȳla.*
neophyte, n. *cathecu·mynys,* m.
nephew, n. *noy,* m., pl. *-ens.*
nereis, n. *prȳf mor,* m., pl. *-ves m.*
nerve, n. *gȳewen,* f., col. *gȳew*: **-vous,** a. *ownek, ēs y vüvya*: **-vousness,** n. *own, preder, dowt,* m.
nest, n. *nȳth,* m., pl. *-ow*: v. *nȳthy(-ya)*: **-ing,** n., n. place, **nȳthva,* f., pl. *-ow*; to go birds' n., **nȳthowa* (inf. only): **-le,** v. *omgüdha, omnȳthy.*
net, n. *rōs,* f., pl. *-ow*; small n., *rosyn,* m., pl. *-now*; draw-n., **tenrōs,* f., pl. *-ow*; to cast n., *tewlel rōs*: **-work,** n. *rōswȳth,* m.
Netherlands, n. *an Yseldyryow,* m. pl., *Pow Ysel,* m.
nettle, n. *lynasen,* f., col. *lynas*; n. bed, *lynajek,* f., pls. *-egy, -egow*: v. *serry.*
neuter, a. **nepryth.*
never, adv. *nefra, byth, termyn-vȳth, bys vyken, bynary, bynytha, yn y ōs, nēs,* etc., with neg.; n. again, *vynytha* (with neg.); n. a bit, etc., *mal bew dam,* etc.; n. a one, *nagonen-vȳth* (with neg.); may he n., *byner re*[2] (with subj.); that he may n., *vynytha na*[2] (with subj.).
never-failing, a. *byth na-dhyfyk* or *na-fyll.*
nevertheless, adv. *bytege·ns, ‡bytedhewetha, ‡bytelē·, na-whath, a'y wosa.*
new, a. *noweth*; brand n., *noweth splan, n. flam*; n. born, *noweth genys*; n. come, *noweth devedhys*: **-ly,** adv. *noweth, a-noweth*: **-ness,** n. **nowethsys, *nowetter,* m.
news, n. *newodhow,* m. pl., *‡nowedhys,* m.
newt, n. *peswar-paw,* m., pl. *-as, pedrevan an dowr,* f., pl. *-now a. d., †gwedresyf,* f., pl. *-yvas.*
New Year, n. *Bledhen Noweth,* f,; N. Y's. D., *Calan Genver, dē-Halan Genver,* m.
next, a. *nessa*; n. time, *nessa*; n. day, *ternos*; what n.? *fatel vyth lemmyn*?
nib, n. *mȳn-plüven,* m., pl. *-yon-p.*
nibble, v. *dynsel, dastynsel.*
nice, a. *tēk, whēk, da, dēnty, jentyl*; a n. problem, *mater tykly.*
nick, n. *trogh,* m., pls. *-ow, treghyon*; of time, *war nuk, y'n ewn dermyn, y'n gwella prȳs.*
nickname, n. **leshanow, *füg-hanow,* m., pl. *-hynwyn*: v. **leshenwel.*
niece, n. *nȳth,* f., pls. *-ow, -as.*
niggard, n. *†synsyas,* m., pl. *-ysy*: **-liness,** n. *crynder,* m.: **-ly,** a. *pȳth, crȳn, degē·s y dhorn, crefny.*
nigh, a., adv. *ogas, a-ogas, yn-nēs, ryp*; well n. (before v.), *namna*[2]; to draw n., *dōs nēs, nessa, neshē·.*
night, n. *nōs,* f., pl. *-ow*; this very n., *haneth yn nōs*; n. time, n. of feast, etc., *nōswȳth,* f., pl. *-yow*; by n., during the n., *yn-nōs, dyworth an nōs, nōswȳth*; every n., *pupnōs*; last n., *nyhewer, yn-newer*; n. before last, *kens nyhewer*; to-n, *haneth*; tomorrow n., *avorow dhe nōs*; good-n., *Dew re-dharbarro,* or *Dew roy, nōs da dheugh*! (*Durnostadha*); n. watch, *gōlva,* f., pl. *-ow*: **-ly,** adv. *pupnōs-oll*: **-fall,** n. *gorthewer,* m.; at n., *dyworth an nōs* (*dworenō·s*): **-ingale,** n. **ēos,* f., pl. *-ow,* dim., *ēosyk,* f., pl. *-ygow*: **-jar,** n. **churra-nōs,* m., **troȳller,* m., pl. *-loryon, *nedher,* m.: **-mare,** n., screaming, *hünlef* (*hülla*), m.; with tethered sensation, *stak,* m.: **-shade,** n., deadly, black, *morel,* m., woody, *scaw cough,* col.
nimble, a. *scaf, üskys, stryk*: **-ness,** n. *scafter, strykter,* m.: **-ly,** adv. *üskys, ynscaf*; the more n. wilt thou go, *dhe scaffa yth-ēth.*
nine, a., n. *naw*; n.-fold, *nawblēk*: **-th,** a., n. *nawves, nawes*: **-pin,** n. *kȳl,* m., pl. *-ys*; game of n.s, *gwary-kȳlys,* m.: **n. stones,** n., game, *nawmen,* m.: **-teen,** a. *nawnjēk*: **-th,** a., n. *nawnjegves*: **-ty,** a., n. *peswarügans ha dēk, dēk ha peswar-ügans*: **-ieth,** a., n. *degves ha peswar-ügans.*
nip, v. **gwasca, brathy*: n. **gwask,* f., pl. *-scow, brath,* m., pl. *-ow.*

nipple, n. *tethen*, f., pl. *-now*, *tēth*, f., pl. *-ow*, d. *dywdeth(en)*.
nit, n. *nedhen*, f., col. *nēth*.
no, neg. particle, a., adv., there is no bread, *nyns-üs bara*; I have n. bread, *nyns-üs dhym bara*, etc.; in n. way, *cammen-vȳth* (with neg.); n. more, *namoy·*; n. less, *nalē·*; n. longer, *na³ fella*; n. matter, *nyns-üs* or *na, fors*; it is n. good, *nyns-yu 'vās*; interj. ‡*na* (late only; in M. Corn. neg. reply repeats v. of question, *yu gwyr?—nag-yu. üs bara genough? nag-üs. a-vynta mōs? na-vynnaf*, etc.); is there or n.? *üs po nag-üs?*; n. wonder I am . . ., *nyns-yu marth kynth of*. . . .
noble, a. *bryntyn, gay, nobyl, rȳal*: n., n.man, *pensevyk*, m., pl. *-ygyon*, †*ughelor*, m., pl. *-yon*, *dēn rȳal*, m., pl. *tüs r.*, *nobyl*, m., pl. *-blys*, *bryntyn*, m., pl. *-yon*: n., n.woman, *pensevyges*, f., pl. *-ow*, *benen vryntyn*, f., pl. *-es bryntyn*: **-bility,** n. *bryntynsys, pensevygyans, nobylta*, m.; of class, *tüs nobyl, bryntynyon*, pl.
nobody, n., pron. *nagonen*, *denvyth* or, stressed, *dēn-vȳth*, *nep-dēn*; n. at all, *dēn y'n bȳs* (all with neg. v.); n. speaks, *nygows denvyth*.
nocturnal, a. *nōs, drēs nōs, drē nōs*.
nod, v. *pendroppya, gasa y ben dhe ynclynya*: n. *droppyans an pen, ynclynyans*, m.
noddle, n. *clopen*, m., pl. *-now*.
noise, n. *son*, m., pl. *-yow*, *trōs*, m., pl. *-ow*, **hūb*, m.; great or continuous n., *hubbadrylsy, hubbadullya*, m.; monotonous n., *drylsy*, m.; to make a n. about, *whetha corn, gül mür a "glewyeugh" a-dro dhe²*: **-less,** a. *hep son, dydrōs*: **-y,** a. *mür y drōs*.
noisome, a. *plosek, hegas*: **-ness,** n. *last, plosethes*, m.
nomad, n. *gwandryas*, m., pl. *-ysy*.
nom-de-plume, n. **leshanow, füg-hanow*, m., pl. *-hynwyn*.
nominal, -lly, a., adv. *orth y hanow*: **-ate,** v. *henwel, gelwel*: **-d,** a. *henwys *henwesȳk, *gelwesyk*: **-ation,** n. **henwesygeth*, f., *hanwans*, m.
nonconformist, n. **dyssentyer*, m., pls. *-yoryon, -s*: **-ity,** n. **dyssent, -yans*, m.
nondescript, a. *coynt, estranj*.
none, pron. *-vȳth* (after n. with neg. v.), *nagonen* (with neg.).
no-one, n., pron.: see **-nobody.**
nonplus, v. *conclūdya*.
nonsense, n. *flows*, m., *whethlow*, pl. *folneth, gokyneth*, m.; to talk n., *flattra, -trya*: n! *tetyvaly! gās dha flows! a gans dha whethlow!*: **-ical,** a. *fōl, goky*.
noodle, n. *fōl*, m., pl. *felyon, foles*, f., pl. *-ow, pen-pyst*, m., pl. *-now-p*.
nook, n. *sorn*, m., pl. *sernow, skyl*, m., pl. *-yow, bagh*, f., pl. *-ow, kyl*, m., pls. *-yow, -yer, corn*, m., pl. *kernow, cornel*, f., pls. *-ly, -low*, ‡*cornet*, m., pl. *-tys*.
noon, n. *hanterdēth*, m.
noose, n. *cabester*, m., pl. *-trow*, **tagell*, f., pl. *-ow*, **croglath*, f., pl. *-ow, crokken*, f., pl. *-now, colm rē*, m., pl. *-ow r.*
nor, conj. *na(g), na ny-²* (with v.); neither he n. I did it, *nag ef na my ny-n-gwrük*; n. yet a, *byth moy*.
normal, a. *ūsyes*.
north, n. and a., *North*, **Clēth*, m.
nose, n. *frygow*, pl. (lit. nostrils), *trōn*, m., pl. *-ow*; turn up his n. at, *fȳa, dysprēsya*: **-stril,** n. *fryk*, m., pl. *-ygow*.
nostalgia, n. *hyreth*, m.: **-ic,** a. *hyrethek*.
not, adv. *ny²(ns)-, na²(g)-*; n. one, n. any, n. a, *nagonen*; were it n. for, *na-vē*; and if n., *ha kēn*; it is yours and n. mine, *dheughwhywhȳ· yu, ha nyns-yu dhymmo-vȳ*; n. at all, *cammen*; Tom came (and) n. Frank, *Tubby o a-dheth, ha nyns-o Franky* (not *na* (*nep*), which is used only before adjs., as n. before, *na hens*; n. much, *namü·r*; n. many, *nep lȳes*; all with neg. v. to complete them).
notable, a. *notyes, mür y hanow*: **-bly,** adv. *kens oll*.
notary, n. *dustünyer dhe'n sēl*, m., pl. *-oryon d. s.*
notch, n. *trogh*, m., pl. *-ow, būlgh*, m., pl. *-ow*; on the n., *war nuk*: v. *trēghy, būlgha, crybba*.
note, n. *scryven danvon*, f., pl. *-now d., nōtyans*, m., pl. *-ow*; take n. of, *avȳsya*; n. of music, *nōta*, m., pl. *-tys*; a man of n., *dēn a vrȳ*: v. *avȳsya, nōtya*: **-d,** a. *geryes da, nōtyes, mür y hanow, kywhethlys*: **-book,** n. †*coweth-lyver*, m., pls. *-lyfrow, -lyfryow*.
nothing, n., pron. *travyth* (with neg. v.); that's n., *nyns-yu henna man*; there's n. else for it, *nyns-üs nahē·n*.
notice, n. *avȳsyans*, m., pl. *-ow*: v. *merkya, attendya, bos avȳsyes a², avȳsya, gül vrȳ a²*: **-able,** a. *hewel*: **-ification,** n. *avȳsyans, gwarnyans*, m.: **-ify,** v. *rȳ avȳsyans, gwarnya*.
notion, n. *consayt, tybyans*, m.

notoriety, n. *drōk-ger,* m.: **-rious,** a. *drōk-geryes, drōk-aswonys.*

notwithstanding, conj. *awo·s, a'y wosa, bytege·ns, na-whath, yn despȳ·t dhe²*.

noun, n. *hanow,* m., pl. *hynwyn.*

nourish, v. *maga, pesky,* **norsya*: **-ing,** a. *a-vāk*: **-ment,** n. *megyans, pask, sosten,* m.

novel, a. *noweth*: n. **novel,* m., pl. *-ys, lyver whethel*: **-ist,** n. *scryfer novelys,* m., pl. *-oryon n.*: **-ty,** n. **nowedhynsy,* m.; a n., *tra noweth,* m., pl. *taclow n.*

November, n. *mȳs-Du, mȳs-Du ken Nadelek,* m.

novice, n. **dallether,* m., pl. *-oryon*; eccl., *cathecū·mynys,* m., *lenes noweth,* f., pl. *maplȳen noweth,* m., pl. *lenesow n., mebyon-l. n.*

now, adv. *lemmyn, y'n ür-ma, y'n tor-ma, prest, omma*; definite part., *nans-*; what n? *fatel vȳth lemmyn*?; from n. on, *alemma rak*; n. and then, *trawythyow,* ‡*war ürow.*

nowadays, adv. *y'n dēdhyow-ma.*

nowhere, adv. *lē-vȳth, tyller-vȳth, nep plās* (all with neg. v.).

nowise, a. *forth-vȳth, cammen-vȳth, nep maner* (all with neg. v.).

noxious, a. *drōk, anyagh.*

nozzle, n. *trōn,* m., pl. *-ow.*

nucleus, n. *sprüsen, hasen,* f., pl. *-now,* col. *sprüs, hās,* **bewesen,* f., pl. *-now.*

nude, a. *nōth, lom*: **-ity,** n. *notha,* f.

nuisance, n. *pla,* m., pl. *-ow, bal,* f., pl. *-ow, ancombrynsy,* m.; person, *fyslak,* m., pl. *-logyon, map an pla,* m., pl. *mebyon an p.*

null and void, a. *gwak, üfer*; made n., *defendyes*: **-ify,** v. *dyswül.*

numb, a. *crom*; to go n., *cromma, clamdera*: **-ness,** n. *clamder,* **marder*; in fingers, *gwynrew, ewynrew,* m.

number, v. *rekna, nyvera*: n. *nyver,* m., pl. *-ow, nomber,* m., pl. *-s,* **rȳf,* m., pl. *-ȳvow, myns,* m., *parcel,* m., pl. *-s*: **-less,** a. *dynyver, drēs aga nyvera.*

numeral, n. *nyveren,* f., pl. *-now*; Arabic n., *n.* **awgrym*: **-ation,** n. **awgrym*: **-ical,** a. *nyverek*: **-ous,** a. *pals, lȳes,* **lyesek, mür a²*, *mür y nyver.*

numskull, n. *clopen,* m., pl. *-now.*

nun, n. *managhes,* f., pl. *-ow, lēnes,* f., pl. *-ow*: **-nery,** n. **lēnjy,* m., pl. *-ow.*

nuptial, a. *pryosol, -demedhyans*: **-s,** n. *demedhyans,* m.

nurse, n. **mageres,* f., pl. *-ow,* **norys,* f., pl. *-ys*; wet n., *mammeth,* f., pl. *-ow*; hospital n., *clavjyores,* f., pl. *-ow*; sick n., *gwythyas clevyon,* m., pl. *-ysy c.,* f. *-yades,* pl. *-ow c.*: v., n. the sick, *gwytha clevyon*; n. the young, *maga, mēthy,* **norsya*: **-ry,** n. **floghva,* f., pl. *-ow*; for animals or plants, *magla,* m., pl. *-lēow, magva-losow,* f., pl. *-ow-l.*, *plansva,* f.: **-ing,** n. *mēth,* m.

nurture, n. *megyans, norter,* **magereth,* **mak,* m.: v. *maga,* †*mēthryn.*

nut, n. *knofen,* f., col. *know*; walnut, *knofen Frynk*; beech-n., *knofen faw*; pig-n., earth-n., *keleren,* f., col. *keler*; abounding in n.s, *knowek*; to gather n.s, *knowa* (inf. only); metal n., *knofen horn,* etc.: **-crackers,** n. **gevel-know,* f., **tardher-know,* m.: **-grove,** n. *knowek,* f., pls. *-egow, -egy, kelly-gnowek, kelly-gnow, kelly-gnowwyth,* f., pls. *-ow -g.*:. **-meg,** n. *knofen muscat Eynda,* f., col. *know m. E.*: **-shell,** n. *plysken knofen,* f., col. *plysk-know.*

nutriment, n. *megyans, vytel,* m.: **-itious,** a. *a-vāk, lün a vegyans, da dhe grefhē·,* or *dhe besky.*

nuzzle, v. *mȳnya.*

O

O! int. *A²*!; of dismay, *Ogh*!

oak, n. *derowen,* f., pl. *-now,* col. *derow,* †*dar,* m., pls. †*dery, derow*; evergreen o., *glastanen,* f., col. *glastan*; o. grove, *derowek,* f., pls. *-egow, -egy*; o. timber, *pren derow,* m.; place where single o. trees grow, *derowennek,* f., pl. *-egy*: **-en,** a. *derow*: **-web,** n. *whȳl derow,* m., pl. *-as d.*

oakum, n. *carth,* m., pl. *-yon.*

oar, n. *rēf,* f., pl. *revow*: **-sman,** n. *revador,* m., pl. *-yon.*

oat, n. *kerghen,* f., col. *kergh*; naked o.s, *pylas,* m.; as groats, *whyjyon,* pl.; o. field, *kerghek,* f., pl. *-egy*; o. grass, *kerghwels,* m.; o.meal, *brunyon*; of naked o., *whyjyon,* pl.; o.-land, *kerghtyr,* m.: **-en,** a. *a gergh.*

oath, n. *lȳ,* m., pl. *-ow, tȳ,* m., pl. *-ow*; false o., *gow-lȳ,* m.; to take an o., *lȳa, tȳ.*

obdurate, a. *aflythys.*

obedience, n. *gostythter, obayans,* m.: **-nt,** a. *gostyth, hüvel, se·rvabyl.*

obeisance, n. *plegyans,* m.; to make o., *omblegya.*

obey, v. *obaya, bōs gostyth dhe²*, *sewya bōth,* ‡*hüvla*; to o. a command, *gül warlergh gorhemmyn.*

object, v. *sconya, trӯnya*; o. to, *sconya a²* (with inf.); I o. to that, *nyns-yu da genef henna*: n. *tra*, neuter, pl. *taclow*; aim, *towl*, m., pl. *-ow*: **-tion,** n. *rēson a-drüs*, m., *danjer*, m. (with *perthy, hep*); raise an o. to, *nagha*: **-tionable,** adj. *hegas, casadow, vӯl.*

oblation, n. *oblasyon*, m., pl. *-s.*

obligation, n. *kendon*, f., *ambos, synsyans*, m., pl. *-ow*: **-tory,** a. *a-rēs.*

oblige, v. *kelmy, constrӯna*; to please, *plēkya dhe²*: **-d,** a. *kelmys, synsys*; I am o. to go, *rēs porres yu dhym mōs*: **-ging,** a. *hegar, plegadow, prest parys.*

obliterate, v. *defendya dhe-vēs*: **-tion,** n. *defendyans hep gasa ol-vӯth.*

oblivion, n. *ancof*, m.; to go into o., *mōs dhe goll.*

obnoxious, a. *casadow, hegas.*

obscene, a. *plos, *lyk*; o. person, *caughwas*, m., pl. *-wesyon, scaf a'y lygyon*: **-nity,** n. *plosethes, dysonester, vӯlta*, m.

obscure, v. *tewlhē·, cüdha, keles, dysclērya*: a. *tewl, cüdhys, dysclēr*: **-rity,** n. *tewlyjyon*, m., *tewolgow*, abst. pl.

obsequious, a. **gorhüvel.*

observe, v. *whythra, synsy, nōtya, avӯsya, attendya, aspӯa*; keep, *gwytha, synsy*; say, *leverel*: **-vance,** n. *ūsadow*, m., *solempnyta*, m., pl. *-tys, rewl*, m., pl. *-ys*: **-ant,** a. *a-wra nōtya, lym y lagas*: **-ation,** n. *nōtyans*, m.; remark, *lavar*, m., pl. and abst. *-ow*: **-atory,** n. **mӯrjy*, m., pl. *-ow, *obse·rvatry*, m.

obsession, n., by evil spirits, *drogattӯ·*, m.

obsolete, a. *gyllys mēs a üs, tremenys an gӯs anodho, hēn.*

obstacle, n. *let, ancombrynsy*, m.; there is no o., *nyns-üs travyth a-drüs an hens.*

obstinacy, n. *gorthter*, m.: **-ate,** a. *stordy, pen-cales.*

obstreperous, a. *mür y drōs, *dyrewl, ow-cül hubbadullya.*

obstruct, v. *lettya, ancombra*: **-tion,** n. *let, ancombrynsy*, m.

obtain, v. *cafos, gwaynya*; be prevalent, *dōn rewl.*

obvious, a. *ape·rt, hewel, ēs y weles*; to be o., *omdhysquedhes*: **-ly,** adv. *ape·rt, splan yu.*

occasion, n. *treveth, torn*, m., *gwyth, tro*, f., pl. *-yow*; need, *rēs*, m.; cause, *kēn, achēson (chēson), occasyon*, m.; when there is o., *pan vo rēs*; on many o.s, *lӯes treveth*; on this o., *yn tor' -ma*; without o., *hep kēn*: **-al,** a. ‡*trawythys*: **-ally,** adv. *trawythyow, par termyn.*

occiput, n. *pol-kyl, kylben*, m.

occupant, n., of house, *nep üs ynno trygys* or *annedhys, *annedhyas*, m., pl. *-ysy*: **-pation,** n., work, *whēl*, m. and f., pl. *-yow, galwans*, m.; of site, *annedhyans*, m.: **-pied,** a. *bysy*: **-pier**: see **occupant**: **-py,** v. **kevannedhy*, ‡*occūpӯa*; o. position, *lenwel lē*; o. seat, *kemeres*; o. oneself with, *omrӯ dhe².*

occur, v. *wharfos, darfos, codha*; it o.s to me, *ow brӯs dhym yma· ow-tōn*: **-rence,** n. *wharfedhyans*, m.

ocean, n. *mōr brās*, m., **keynvor, *downvor*, m., **gwylgy*, f.

ochre, n. *prӯ melen*; iron-o. on face of rock, *callen*, f., pl. *-now*; red o., †*meles*, m.

October, n. *mӯs-Hedra*, m.

octopus, n. *collel-lēsa*, f., pl. *kellyl-l.*

oculist, n. *medhek lagasow*, m., pl. *-dhygyon l.*

odd, a. *coynt*; of numbers, *dybarow*: **-ity,** n. *coyntys*, m.

odious, a. *hegas, casadow.*

odour, n. *odor*, m., pl. *-s, ēth*, m., pl. *-ow, sawor*, m., pl. *-yow, saworen*, f., pl. *-now*; bad o., *flēr, flērynsy*, m.; person with bad o., *flērys, flēryüs*, m.: **-orous,** a. *saworek*; unpleasantly o., *flērys.*

of, prep. *a²*, (with *govyn, gothfos*) *orth.*

off, a. *y'n tu* or *war an tu a-vēs*; o. hind leg, *gar a-dryf y'n tu a-vēs*: adv. *a-bell, alemma, dhe-vēs*; go o., *mōs quyt*; leave o., *gasa dhe-vēs*; take o., *dy'sky dhe vēs*: prep. *dywar²*, *a-dhywar²*, *dyworth*; stand o.! *saf yn-nēs a-denewan!*; right o., without stopping, *kens es hedhy, hep let, ketto·th ha'n gēr*; o. from, *dhywa·r*; a little way o., *pols alemma*; let's be o., *dün alemma, dün ahanan*; carried o. by, *gyllys gans*; set o. on journey, *dalleth kerth*; of trap, etc., *dyllo.*

offal, n. *mon*, m., *colodhyon, scullyon*, pl.

offence, n. *pēgh, pēghadow*, m., *pēghas*, m., pl. *-ghosow, trespas, offens*; take o. at, *serry orth*; commit o., *gül trespas*: **-end,** v. *pēgha, sclandra, serry, camwül, gül trespas dhe², offendya*: **-ended,** a., be o. with, *dyflasa, serry orth*: **-ender,** n. *pēghador*, m., pl. *-yon, pēghadores*, f., pl. *-ow*: **-ensive,** a. *hegas*: n., military, *omsettyans*, m.

offer, v. *profya, *kynnyk*; to o. up, *offrynna, -nya*: n. *kynnyk*, m., pl. *-ygow, profyans*,

m.: **-ing, -tory,** n. *offryn,* m., pl. *-now, offrynnyans,* m.
off-hand, adv. *hep cortesy,* ‡*mēs a dhorn.*
office, n. *offys,* m., pl. *-ys*; employ, *sōth,* f., pl. *sodhow*; place, *offys,* m., **sothva,* f.; take o., **sodha*: **-r,** n. *offyser,* m., pl. *-s,* **sodhak,* m., pl. *-dhogyon*; o. of the law, executioner, *tormentor,* m., pls. *-s, -ys*: **-cial,** a. *offysyal*: n. *o·rdenary,* m., pl. *-s*: **-ciate,** v. *gonys, collenwel solempnyta.*
off-scourings, n. *carthyon, scübyon,* pl.
offspring, n. *hēnath, ascor, yssew,* m., *flēghes,* pl., *hās,* col., *lynyeth,* †*agh,* f., pl. *-ow.*
often, adv. *menough, yn-fenough, lȳes* or *lower gwyth, l. torn, l. tro, l. treveth*; as o. as . . ., *pesquyth may* . . .; not o., *namenough* (with neg.).
ogre, n. †*enke·nethel* (*ankenel*), m., f. *-thles,* pl. *-ow.*
oh! int. *A*! *ay*! *hay*!; of dismay, etc., *ogh*!
oil, n. *oyl,* m., pl. *-ys*; olive o., *olew,* m.: v. *üra*: **-y,** a. *oylek, ürys*: **-cloth,** n. *len-oyl,* f.
ointment, n. *yly,* m., pl. *ylȳow, üras,* m., pl. *-resow, unyent,* m., pl. *-ns, o·nyment,* m., pl. *-ns.*
old, a. *cōth, hēn,* as prefix and in expressions, *tüs hēn, yowynk ha hēn*; fig., *lōs*; grow o., *cothhē·*; of woman, **gwraghya*; o. age, *cōthny, hēnys*; o. fellow, *cōthwas,* m., pl. *-wesyon*; o. woman, *gwragh,* f., pl. *-as*; o.-fashioned, *a'n vaner gōth, a'n gȳs cōth, gyllys mēs a'n gȳs*; o.-wife, fish, *dama gōth,* f.
olive, n. *olyf,* m. and col., *grünen-olew,* f., col. *grün olew*; o. tree, †*olewbren,* m., pl. *-nyer, olew-wedhen,* f., col. *-wȳth*; o. oil, *olew,* m.; Mount of O.s, *Meneth Olyved, Meneth Olyf*; o. grove, *olew-wydhek,* f., pls. *-egy, -egow.*
omelet, n. *crampedhen oyow,* f., col. *crampeth o.*
omen, n. **cōl,* f., **arweth,* f., pl. *-edhyow*: **-minous,** a. *ow-* **tarogan drōk.*
omit, v. *gasa mēs*: **-ission,** n. *gwall,* m., pl. *-ow.*
omnipotence, n. *ollgallos, ollgallosekter,* m.: **-ent,** a. *ollgallosek, lün-gallosek.*
omniscience, n. *gothvos puptra,* **oll-skentoleth,* m.: **-ent,** a. *a-wōr puptra,* **ollskentyl.*
on, prep. *yn, war*[2]; o. which, etc., *may*; with days of the week, no prep. or *dhe*[2], ‡*war*[2]; oaths, *er, tan*: adv. *yn-rak, rak dodho.*
onager, n. †*asen gwyls,* m., f. *a. wyls,* pl. *-as g.*
once, adv. *ünwyth*; o. more, *arta*; formerly, *kens*; at o., *sket, scon, desempys, a-dhesempys, dyson, dystough, a-dhystough, prest, wharē·, yn cot-termyn*; all at o., *war-not.*
one, a. *ün*: n., pron. *onen*; person, *dēn*; every-o., *pup, pup-onen, pup hüny, pup dēn-oll*; many a o., *lȳes hüny, lower onen*; another o., *kēn onen*; a large o., *onen brās* or (f.) *vrās*; not a single o., *nagonen y'n bȳs* (with neg.); o. of the fruits, *ran a'n frutys*; o. another, *an ȳl y gȳla, an ȳl hybē·n*; the o. prevents the other, *an ȳl a-let y gȳla*; o. by o., *onen hag onen, dybarow*; o. eyed, *ün y lagas,* ‡*ünlagasek*; only o. of these boys will go, *nyns-a marnas an ȳl maw omma*; o. of these, *onen a'n rē-ma*; o. day I'll repay you, *ün jēth a-dhē ma-n-talvedhaf dheugh.*
oneself, pron. *y honen*; prefix to verbs, *om-.*
onion, n. *onyonen,* f., col. *onyon.*
only, a. *ün, ünyk*: adv. *ünsel, ünwyth, yn-ünyk*: conj. *saw, lemen, mēs, marnas*; o. one knows it, *ny-n-gor marnas onen.*
onset, onslaught, n. *omsettyans*; of illness, *shora,* m., pl. *-ys.*
onward(s), adv. *yn-rak, rak dodho.*
ooze, v. *sygera*: n. *lȳs,* m.
opaque, a. *tew.*
open, a. *efan, rȳth, yn-ygerys,* **ygor, a-lēs, splan, ape·rt,* ‡*ōpyn*: v. *ygery, dygēa,* ‡*ōpya*; o. out, **efany*; lay o., *dyscüdha*; o. wide, *lēsa*: **-ing,** n. **ygor*; gap, *būlgh,* m., pl. *-ow, aswy* (*ajy*), f., pl. *-ow*; o. out, *lēsans,* m., pl. *-ow*: **-ly,** adv. *a-wēl dhe bup den-oll, yn-ygerys, ape·rt,* ‡*opyn-*; o. cultivated land, *mēsek,* f., pls. *-egow, -egy*: **-ness,** n. **rȳthsys, efander,* m.
opera, n. *gwary-cān* or *-kenys,* m., pl. *-yow-c., k.*: **-tic,** a., o. society, *cowethas gwaryow-kenys.*
operate, v. *obery*: **-tion,** n. *gwȳthres, ober,* m., pl. *-ow*; surgical o., **medhegwȳth*: **-tive,** n. *creftor,* m., pl. *-yon, yn ober*: a., o. words, *geryow a vertu*: **-tor,** n. *oberor,* m., pl. *-yon.*
opine, v. *tyby*: **-nion,** n. *tybyans,* m., *brüs,* f., pl. *-ow, cusül,* f., pl. *-yow, avȳ·s,* m., *cowsys,* m., pl. and abst. *-sesow, prederyans,* m.; form an o., *ervȳra, jujja*; in my o., *dhe'm tybyans-vȳ, orth ow brüs-vȳ*; better o. excepted, *saw gwell avȳ·s*: **-nionated,** a. *gorth.*

opium, n. *_cuskles_, m., _losow cusk_, col.

opponent, n. _escar_, m., pl. _yskerens_, _contrary_, m., pl. _-s_.

opportune, -ly, a., adv. _yn prȳs da_, _a-dermyn_, _y'n gwella prȳs_: **-nity,** n. _tro_, f., pl. _-yow_, _spās_, _torn_, _chons_, m.

oppose, v. _settya_ (_orth_, _dhe_², _erby·n_), _sevel_, _kewsel_ (_erby·n_): **-d,** a. _contraryüs_, _gorth_; o. to, _erby·n_: **-site,** prep. _a-dal_, _dhera·k_, _a-drüs_; the o., _an contrary_; in the o. direction, _drēs keyn_: **-sition,** n. _offens_, _strȳf_, _let_, m.

oppress, v. _bēghya_, _grevya_, _compressa_, *_gorthrȳghy_; o. with work, _gwȳtha_: **-ion,** n. _poster_, _posyjyon_, _compressans_, m.: **-ive,** a. _pōs_, *_bēghüs_: **-or,** n. _compressor_, _trȳgher_, m., pl. _-oryon_.

optical, a. _a'n wolok_, _a'n gweles_; o. illusion, _hüs an dheulagas_, m., _tull golok_: **-ician,** n. *_optysyan_, m., pl. _-s_, _medhek an wolok_, m.

option, n. _dewys_, m.; if there is no o., _mar ny-ȳl bōs kēn_: **-al,** a. _herwyth dewys_.

opulence, n. _pythow_, pl. _rychys_, m. and pl., _mür a bȳth_: **-ent,** a. _rych_, _dhodho mür a bȳth..._

or, conj. _py_, _po_, _bo_; emphatic, _na_; o. else, _kēn_, _bokē·n_, _bonȳ·l_, _kēn maner_; o. yet, _byth moy_.

oral, -ly, a., adv. _war anow_, _gans y anow_.

orange, n. *_owraval_, m., pl. _-low_; colour, _rüthvelen_.

oration, n. _areth_, f., pl. _-yow_, _pregoth_, m., pl. _-gowthow_: **-or,** n. _arethyor_, †_da·thelor_, m., pl. _-yon_: **-tory,** n., chapel, _oratry_, m., pl. _-s_; speaking, _arethyo·rȳeth_, f.

orb, n. _pēl_, f., pl. _-yow_, _pellen_, f., pl. _-now_.

orbit, n., of planet, etc., †_resekva_, f., *_whelva_, f., pl. _-ow_, *_kelghtro_, m.; of eye, _pol lagas_, m., pl. _-low an dheulagas_.

orchard, n. _aval-lōn_, m., pl. _-ow_, _avallennek_, f., pl. _-egow_, _-egy_, _lowarth gwȳth_, m., pl. _-ow g._

orchestra, n. _menestrouthy_, m.

orchis, n. _blejen rüth an gōk_, f.

ordain, v. _o·rdena_ (_orna_); priest, _rȳ ordys dhe_².

ordeal, n. _prōf_, m., pl. _-ovow_, _prevyans_, m., pl. _-ow_.

order, v. _o·rdena_, _erghy_, _gorhemmyn_, _charjya_, _comōndya_, _dȳghtya_; o. about, _contrōlya_: n. _gorhemmyn_, m., pl. _-ow_, _gorhemmynadow_, m., _comōndment_, m., pl. _-ns_, _rewl_, f., pl. _-ys_; arrangement, _aray·_, m.; o. of service, _o·rdenal_, m., pl. _-ys_; o. of knighthood, _ordyr_, m., pl. _-drys_; holy o.s, _ordys_, pl.; set in o., _ewna_, _o·rdena_ (_ordna_, _orna_), _rewlya_, _araya_, *_kempenna_; give o.s, †_brennya_; in o., _yn ün rew_; in o. to, _awo·s_, _rak_; in o. that, _rak_ (_may_): **-ly,** a. _kewar_, _rewlys_, *_kempen_: n. _offyser anjēth_.

ordinance, n. _o·rdenans_, m., _gorhemmyn_, m., pl. _-ow_.

ordinary, a. _ūsyes_, _sempel_, _kemyn_, _kēth_.

ordination, n. _sacrans_, m.

ordnance, n. _gonnys mür_, pl.

ordure, n. _caugh_, _teyl_, _mon_, m.

ore, n. _mūn_, m.

organ, n. _organ_, m., pl. _-s_: **-ic,** a. *_organek_: **-ism,** n. _creatur bew_, *_organeth_, m.: **-ist,** n. _gwaryer war an organ_, m., pl. _-yoryon w. o._, *_organyth_, m., pl. _-ydhyon_.

organize, v. _formya_.

Orient, n. _Howldrehevel_ (_-drevel_), m.: **-al,** a. _a'n H._

orifice, n. _ganow_, m., pl. _-ow_, _mȳn_, m., pl. _-yon_.

origin, n. _dallethfos_, _devedhyans_, _dalleth_, m.: **-al,** a. _kensa_, _a'n dalleth_: n., o. text, _kensscryf_, _mam-scryf_, m.; he is an o., _coynt yu_: **-ate,** v. _dalleth_.

ornament, n. _tegyn_, m., _tegen_, f., pl. _-now_, v. _tekhē·_, _afȳna_, ‡_adorna_: **-ed,** a. _tekhēs·_, _afȳnys_, ‡_adornys_: **-al,** a. _tēk_, _rak afȳna_.

orphan, n. _omdhevas_, m., pl. _-ow_, _omdhevades_, f., pl. _-ow_: a. _omdhevas_: v. _omdhevasy_: **-age,** n. _omdhevatty_, m., pl. _-ow_.

orpine, n. *_cansewyn_.

orthography, n. _lythere·nȳeth_, f., ‡_scryfacomposter_, m.

oscillate, v. _gwaya yn-rak ha war-dhelergh_: **-ion,** n. _lesk_, m., pl. _-scow_, _shakyans_, _gwayans_, m.

osprey, n. _ēr an mor_, _morēr_, m., pl. _-as_.

ostentation, n. _gōth_, _rȳelder_, m., _dysquedhyans gwak_, _d. üfer_, *_bobans_: **-tious,** a. _gothys_, _a-gar omdhysquedhes yn-prowt_.

ostler, n. _paja-mergh_, m., pl. _-ys-m._

ostrich, n. *_strüs_, m., pl. _-yow_.

other, pron. _aral_; the o., _y gȳla_, _hy-bē·n_: a. (after n.) _aral_, pl. _erel_ (before n.), _kēn_; no o. (with neg.), _nahē·n_: **-s,** pron. _rē-erel_; with poss. prons., _hynsa_, m.: **-wise,** adv. _kēn_, _pykē·n_, _pokē·n_, _kēn maner_; with neg. _nahē·n_.

otter, n. _dowrgȳ_, m., pl. _-gün_, f., _dowrast_, pl. _-ysty_.

ought, v., I o., *y-talvya dhym, y-coth* or *y-tegoth dhym,* ‡*my a-dāl*; as one o., *del degoth, del yu devar.*

ounce, n. **ūns,* m., pl. *-yow.*

our, pron. *agan*; contractions, *'gan, 'an*: **-s,** pron., a. *dhyn-ny*; it is o., *ny a-n-pew, yma·dhyn-ny,* stressed, *dhyn-nynȳ·*: **-selves,** pron. *ny agan-honen, nynȳ·.*

oust, v. *gorra yn-mēs, herdhya a'y lē, kemeres lē ün aral drē nell.*

out, adv. *mēs, yn-mēs*; of fire, etc., *marow*; o. of doors, *mēs* or *yn-mēs a jȳ, mēs a'n chȳ*; o. upon thee! *fȳ dhyso*!; before the week is o., *ken penseythen*; get o! *kē dhe-vēs*!; I can't get o. of it, *ny-allaf y avodya*: **o. of,** prep. *mēs* or *yn-mēs a*², *adar*; an o. o. the way place, *tyller cornwhyly*: **-break,** n. *tarth,* m., pl. *-rdhow*: **-cast,** n. *gal,* m., pl. *-ow, atla,* m., pl. *-lyon*: **-cry,** n. *garm,* f., pl. *-ow, crȳ,* m., pl. *-ow, üs,* m., pl. *üjow,* **ünva,* f.: **-do,** v. *tremena, trȳghy, gül moy age·s*: **-doors,** adv. *mēs a'n chȳ, mēs a jȳ*: **-er,** a. *pella, war vēs*: **-fit,** n. *aparell, dafar, hernes,* m.: **-fitter,** n. *gwerther dyllas*: **-grow,** v. *gordevy, tevy moy age·s, tevy drēs*: **-house,** n. *crow,* m., pl. *-yow*: **-landish,** a. *ancoth, astranj, tramor*: **-law,** n. *atla,* m., pl. *-lyon, outlayer,* m., pl. *-s, dyvrēs,* m., pl. *-ow*: v. *dyvrōa*: **-lawed,** a. *dyvro*: **-lay,** n. *cost,* m.: **-let,** n. *aswy (ajy),* f., pl. *-ow*: **-line,** n. *lynen,* f., pl. *-now*: v. **lynenna*: **-live,** v. *bewa pella age·s*; he has o.d his son, *whath yn-few yu wosa merwel y vap-ef*: **-look,** n. **golokva,* f., *vu,* m.; our o., *an wolok a-ragon*: **-post,** n. **gwythysy a-vēs,* pl.: **-pour,** v. *denewy, dyllo, dyscarga*: **-pouring,** n. **denow,* m.: **-right,** a., of speech, *heb y dȳ, dhe blemmyk*; of action, *hep nam, glan*: **-set,** n. *dalleth (-fos),* m.; at the o., *ow-talleth an forth*: **-side,** n. *tu a-vēs,* m.: a. *a-vēs, war-vēs*: prep. *a-vēs dhe*², *wor-tu a-vēs dhe*²: adv. *adar, mēs a jȳ, mēs a'n chȳ*: **-skirts,** n. *oryon pella,* pl.: **-spoken, -ly,** a., adv. *frēth, hep tȳ-vyth na gow-lȳa, heb y dȳ, dhe blemmyk, hep hokkya*: **-spread,** a. *dysplewyes, a-lēs*: **-standing,** a. *mür y vrȳ, ow-sevel yn-rak*; unpaid, *üs whath dh'y bē, nag-yu pēs, hep gober*: **-stretched,** a. *a-hēs, ystynnys*; lying o., *a'y wroweth, ow-crowedha a-hes*: **-ward, -s,** adv. *a-vēs*; with motion, *dhe-vēs, yn-mēs*: **-ly,** adv. *a-vēs, war-vēs*: **-wit,** v. *dyssaytya, tulla.*

outrage, v. *deffola*: n. *deffolans, outray, hagerober,* m.: **-ous,** a. *drōk drēs ēghen*: **-ously,** adv. *gans outray.*

ouzel, n. *molgh (mola),* f., pl. *-as.*

oval, a. **hȳrgren*: n. **hȳrgelgh,* m., pl. *-ow.*

ovate, n. **ovyth,* m., pl. *-ydhyon.*

ovation, n. *trübyt a vrȳ, wolcum bryntyn,* m., *garm gormola, f.*

oven, n. *forn,* f., pl. *-ow.*

over, prep. *drēs, a-ugh*; finished, *dü, dewedhys*; prefix *gor-*; too much, *rē*; o. there, *eno, enos, -nos, yn-hans (hons)*; all o., *drēs . . . -oll, pup tenewan*: **-abound,** v. *bōs rē*: **-abounding,** a. *rē*: **-balance,** v. *omdhysevel, omwheles, trebüchya*: **-bearing,** a. *hautyn, ow-cül maystry*: **-board,** adv. *mēs a'n lester*: **-burden,** v. *compressa, bēghya rē*: **-careful,** a. *rē y breder, rē war, rē avȳsyes*: **-cast,** a. *comolek*: **-charge,** v. *gorlenwel*; price, *govyn rē, settya rē ughel y brȳs*: **-colour,** v. **gorlywa*: **-come,** v. *fetha, overcummya*; be o. by, *bōs trȳghys gans*: **-cook,** v. *gorbarüsy, rostya* or *bryjyon rē*: **-do,** v. *gül rē*: **-dose,** n. *ran rē vrās a vedhy·gȳeth*: **-draft, -draught,** n. *ten rē vrās*: **-draw,** v. *tenna rē*: **-due,** a. *a-dhelergh, hep pē a-dermyn*: **-eager,** a. *rē whansek, rē *dēr*: **-eat, -feed,** v. *quoffy, *gorbesky*: **-fill,** v. *gorlenwel*: **-full,** a. *gorlenwys, gorlün*: **-flow,** v. *fenna, *reverthy, *gorlȳva*: n. *lȳf,* m., pl. *-ow (-yvyow), fen,* m., pl. *-now*: **-fond,** a. *serghak*; be o., *sergha*: **-fondness,** n. **sergh,* m.: **-generous,** a. *rē hēl, gorhēl*: **-grow,** v. *gordevy, gorthevy,* ‡*overdevy*: **-growth,** n. *gordevyans, gorthevyans,* m.: **-hang,** v. *cregy drēs*: **-haul,** v., examine, *whythra*: see **overtake**: **-head,** adv. *a-ughof, a-ughon, a-van, a-wartha, drēs an gwȳth, d. agan pen,* etc.; from o., *a-wartha,* ‡*a-o·verbyn*: **-hear,** v. *wharfos clewes, clewes yn-dan gēl, c. drē hap*: **-heat,** v. *tomma rē, *gordomma*: **-joyed,** a. *lowen drēs musür*: **-land,** adv. *drēs tȳr*: **-lap,** v. **gorhüdha*; they o., *an ȳl a-güth y gȳla*: **-load,** v. *bēghya rē, *gorharga*: **-look,** v. *myras drēs*; excuse, *ascūsya*; miss, *fyllel gweles* or *avȳsya*: **-lord,** n. *gwarthevyas,* m., pl. *-ysy*: **-night,** adv. *drēs nōs*; it was prepared o., *darbarys o dē dhe nōs*: **-power,** v. *trȳghy, fetha, gül maystry war*²: **-powering,** a. *rē allosek, pōs*: **-rate,** v. *synsy rē*: **-d,** a. *rē synsys, rē y 'vrȳ es del yu y brȳs*: **-rule,** v. *sconya, maystry*: **-d,** a. *sconyes y lavarow*: **-run,** v. *resek drēs*: **-seas,** adv. *drēs an mōr*: a.

tramor: **-seer,** n. *chŷf-warden* (*war*²), m., pl. *-s, avŷsyer*, m., pl. *-yoryon*: **-shadow,** v. *tewlel skēs war*² or *drēs*: **-sight,** n. *gwall*, m., pl. *-ow, fyllel gweles*: **-sleep,** v. *cusca rē hŷr*: **-take,** v. *cachya, metya gans*: **-throw,** v. *domhel, omwheles, dysevel, confundya*: n. *pervers, terryjy*, m.: **-turn,** v. *omwheles*: **-weening,** a. *ow-tesevos rē*: **-whelm,** v. *trŷghy, gorhery, büdhy, domhel*: **-whelming,** a. *üthek, drēs ēghen*: **-whelmingly,** adv. *yn-tŷen, bys yn domhel*: **-work,** v. *lafürya rē, gwŷtha*: **-worked,** a. *gwŷthys ysel, squythys, lafüryes*.

owe, v. *tylly, bōs yn kendon*: **-wing,** a. *ynkendon dhe*²; unpaid, *dhe bē*; o. to, *drē, awo·s, rak*(*g*), *drefen*.

owl, n. *ūla*, m., pl. *-lys*, **cowan*, f., pl. *-as*.

own, v. *pew* (no inf.), *perghenna*; confess, *avowa, meneges*: **-er,** n. *perghenek*, m., pl. *-ogyon, perghen*, m., pls. *-nas, -now*: **-erless,** a. *dyberghen*, (*gesys*) *war an kē*: **-ership,** n. *perghenogeth*, m., *perghe·nŷeth*, f.

own, a. *honen* with poss. pron.; it is his o., *dhodho y honen yma·*; my o. house, *ow chŷ ow honen*, etc.; in their o. language, *yn aga yēth-y aga honen*.

ox, n. *ojyon*, m., pl. *oghen*; yoke o., †*ēal*, m.; young o., *denewes*, m., pl. *-wys*: **o.eye daisy,** n. *caja vrās*, f.

Oxford, n. *Resoghen*, m.

oyez! int. *oye·th*! o.! o.! this is to give notice! *oye·th or*! *oye·th ynwe·th sŷ*! *glewyeugh*!

oyster, n. *estren*, f., col. *ester*; o. catcher, sea-pie, *mōrbŷasen*, f., col. *mōrbŷas*; o. bed, *estrek*, f., pls. *-egy, -egow*.

P

pace, n., step, *cam*, m., pl. *-mow*; measurement, *pās*, m., pl. *-ys*; at a great p., *tōth mēn, t. brās*; at a slow p., *yn-cosel, hell*; go at your own p., quietly, *kē war dha gam*: v. *trōsya, kerdhes war gam*.

pacific, a. *cosel, quŷet*; the P. Ocean, *an Mor a Grēs*: **-fy,** v. *dyserry, coselhē·, hebaskhē·*.

pack, v. *trussa, mayla, fardella*: n. *fardel*, m., pl. *-low*; of people, etc., *bagas*, m., pl. *-ow*: **-age, -et,** n. *fardel*, m., pl. *-low*; p.ship, *lester trümach*, m.: **-ing,** n., to go p., *trussa*: **-saddle,** n. **strother*, f., pl. *-yow*.

pact, n. *ambos*, m., pl. *-ow*.

pad, n. *clowt*, m., pl. *-ys, queth*, m. or f., pl. *-ow*; stuffed saddle, straw p. for pack-horse, *dafar*, m.: v. *clowtya*.

paddle, v. *revya*; with feet, *troghya treys*: n. *rēf*, m.,, pl. *-evow*; wooden scraper, etc., **rothel*, f., pl. *-thlow*.

padlock, n. *floren crok*, f., pl. *-now c*.

pagan, n. *pagan*, m., pl. *-ys, dyscryjyk*, m., pl. *-ygyon*: **-ism,** n. *paga·nŷeth*, f.

page, n., of book, *folen, lyven*, f., pl. *-now*, †*pythyonen*, f., pl. *pythyon*, †*enep*, m., pl. *-ebow*.

page, n., boy, *boya*, m., pl. *-yes, paja*, m., pl. *-ys*.

pageant, n. *pajont*, m., pl. *-ns, gwary-mŷr*, m., pl. *-yow-m*.

pail, n. *buket*, m., pl. *-tys*, **kelorn*, m., pl. *-ow*; milking-p., *buket godra*.

paillasse, n. *gwely-cala*, m., pl. *-yow-c*.

pain, n. *galar*, m., pl. and abst., *-ow, anken*, m., pl. *-yow, pystyk*, m., pl. *-ygow, pŷn, payn*, m., pl. *-ys, glōs*, f., pl. *-ow*; mental p., *ponvos*, m., *ponow*, abst. pl.; state of mental p., *ponvotter*, m.; without p., *dyalar*; to take p.s, *bōs dywysyk*; to inflict p., *ankenya*: v. *payna*, **ankenya*, **glosa, pystyga*; smart, *lesky*: **-ful,** a. *tyn, ankensy, ahas*; p. matter, *ponvos*, m.: **-fully,** adv. *yn-tyn*: **-less,** a. *dyalar, dybayn*.

paint, n. *color*, m., pl. *-s, lyw*, m., pl. *-yow* **pēnt*, m., pl. *-ys*: v. *lywa*, **pēntya*, **lymna*, **portraya*: **-er,** n. **lymner*, m., pl. *-s, lywor*, m., pl. *-yon, pēntyer*, m., pl. *-yoryon*; of boat, *lovan scath*: **-ing,** n. *lywans*, m.; a p., **pēntur*, ‡*pyctur*, m., pl. *-ys*.

pair, n. *copel*, m., pl. *-plow*; of people, *deu dhēn*; the p., *an dheu*; in p.s, *deu ha deu, orth coplow*; married p., *deudhen, deubrŷas, pryosow*; p. of arms, hands, eyes, etc., *dywvrēgh, dywla, deulagas*, etc.: v. *parya*, **copla, ombary*.

palace, n. *lys*, f., pl. *-ow, palys*, m., pl. *-ys*; bishop's p., *lys epscop*, f., *epscopty*, m.

palanquin, n. *grava*, m., pl. *-vathow*.

palate, n. *stefnyk*, f.; taste, *blas*, m.: **-table,** a. *blesys da*.

pale, n., post, *styken*, f., pl. *-now*.

pale, v. *dōs ha bōs gwyn, gwanhē·*: a. *glas, dyslyw, gwynnyk*; of face, *gwyn, gwan y lyw*: **-llid,** a. *dyslyw*: **-llor,** n. *fowt lyw*, m.

palfrey, n. *palfray*, m., pl. *-s*.

paling, palisade, n. *kē stykennow*, m., **pülgē*, m., pl. *-ow*.

pall, n. **gelerlen*, f., pl. *-now, pal*, m., pl. *-ys*.

palm, n., of hand, *palf,* f., pl. *-vow, tor an dorn,* f., pl. *-row an deudhorn*; tree, *palm,* m., pl. *-ys*; to p. off, *supposya*; P. Sunday, *dē-Sül Blejyow*: **-istry,** n. *pomstry,* m.

palpitate, v. *lemmel, lamma, terlemmel*: **-tion,** n. *lamma an golon,* m.

palsied, a., *paljyes*: **-sy,** n. *paljy,* m.; person with p., *paljy,* m., pl. *-on*: v. *paljya.*

palter, v. *hokkya.*

paltry, a. *pylyak, boghosek, ysel, gal.*

pamper, v. *chersya rē, *gorbesky.*

pamphlet, n. *lyfryk,* m., pls. *-ygow, -owygow.*

pan, n. *padel,* f., pls. *-lly, -llow*; iron p., *padel horn*; small p., *padelyk,* m., pl. *-ygow*; warming p., *padel-tomma*; knee-p., *padel penglyn*: **-cake,** n. *crampethen,* f., pl. *-now,* col. *crampeth*; to go begging p.s, *crampetha* (inf. only).

pandemonium, n. *dera·y, hager-drōs, hubbadullya,* m.

pane, n. *quarel,* m., pl. *-s, squȳr gwēder,* m.

pang, n. *glōs,* f., pl. *-ow*; p.s of childbirth, *lafür,* m.

panic, n. *own fol, üth,* m.; to be seized with p., *kemeres üth, bōs ownekhē·s.*

panier, n. *panyer,* m., pl. *-s.*

pant, v. *dyena, anella yn-cales.*

pantry, n. *spens,* m., pl. *-ys, †talgell,* f., pl. *-ow.*

pap, n. *pot gwyn, †yōs,* m.

papacy, n. *pabeth,* m.: **-al,** a. *a'n Pap, pabek.*

paper, n. *pāper,* m., pl. *-yow*; sheet of p., *folen,* f., pl. *-now, †pȳthyonen,* f., pl. *pȳthyon.*

parable, n. **parabolen,* f., pl. *-now.*

parade, n. *omdhysquedhyans,* m.; broad walk, *kerthva,* f.: v. *kerdhes yn rȳelder, omdhysquedhes.*

paradise, n. *pa·radys (-dhys),* f.

paradox, n. **gow gwȳr,* m.

paragon, n. *patron perfythter, dēn hep par,* m.

parallel, a. **keslȳnek*: **-ogram,** n. *fygūr pedrak hȳr.*

paraffin, n. *oyl mēn,* m.

paralyse, v. *paljya*: **-sis,** n. *paljy,* m., person with p., *paljy,* m., pl. *-on.*

paramount, a. *ughella, pen-*; lord p., *gwarthevyas,* m., pl. *-ysy*; lady p., *gwarthevyades,* f., pl. *-ow.*

parapet, n. *fōs gwytha,* f., pl. *-ow g.*

paraphernalia, n. *pega·ns, dafar,* m.

parasite, n. *lo·senjer kēth, creatur a-vew drē aral, †oleker,* m., pl. *-s.*

parasol, n. *howl-len,* f., pl. *-now, *skēs-howl,* m.

parcel, n. *fardel,* m., pl. *-low.*

parch, v. *desēgha, *crasa*: **-ed,** a. *sēghys, desēghys, *cras.*

parchment, n. *parchemyn,* m.; sheet of p., *parchemynen,* f., pl. *-now*; of p., *parchemynek.*

pardon, n. *gyvyans, ‡pardon,* m.: v. *gava dhe*[2], *‡pa·rdona.*

pare, v. *dyrüsca, pylya, cot-trēghy*: **-ings,** n. *pylyon,* pl., *rüsk,* col.

parents, *kerens, tas ha mam, sȳra ha dama*: **-tage,** n. *lynyeth,* f., *gōs,* m.

parish, n. *plu,* f., pl. *-yow*: **-ioner,** n. *dēn an blu,* m., pl. *tüs an b.*, **pluak,* m., pl. *-uogyon,* f. *-uoges,* pl. *-ow*; his fellow p., *y gespluak, dēn (benen, flogh) y blu-ef.*

park, n. *clōs,* m., pl. *-ow, park mür,* m., pl. *-rcow m.*; car p., *park kerry tān,* m.; deer p., *kery,* m., pl. *-s*: v., cars, etc., **parkya.*

parliament, n. *seneth,* m., pl. *-edhow, parlament,* m., pl. *-ens.*

parlour, n. *parleth,* m., pl. *-edhow, hēl,* m., pl. *-ow.*

parochial, a. *plu, a'n blu.*

parrot, n. *popynjay,* m., pl. *-s.*

parry, v. *goheles, omwytha rak.*

parsley, n. **persyl,* col.

parsnip, n. *panesen,* f., col. *panes.*

parson, n. *pronter,* m., pl. *-yon, person,* m., pl. *-ys*: **-age,** n. *pronterjy, personjy,* m., pl. *-ow.*

part, n. *ran,* f., pl. *-now, parth,* f., pl. *-ow, darn,* m., pl. *-ow, part,* m., pl. *-ys*; in p., *part*; for my p., *dhe'm part-vȳ*; on the p. of, *a-barth*; in two p.s, *yntra dyw ran*: v. *ranna, kescar*; go away, *dyberth*; p. with, *dascor.*

partake, v. *kemeres ran*; to p. with him in, *bos kevrennek ganso a*[2]: **-r,** n. *kevrennek,* m., pl. *-nygyon.*

partial, a. *yn ran*; biassed, *ow-fa·vera, owplegya dhe*[2]: **-ity,** n. *fa·verans, dewys,* m.

participate, v. *kemeres ran, kevranna*: **-ant, -ating,** a. *kevrennek*: **-ator,** n. **kevrannor,* m., pl. *-yon.*

particle, n. *tam,* m., pl. *tymmyn, temmyk,* m., pls. *-ygow, tymmynygow*; p.s, *manylyon,* pl.

particular, a. *kens oll*; a p. thing, *ün dra*; in

p., *kens oll*: **-ly,** adv. *kens oll, spe·cyly*: n. *poynt*, m.; in every p., *yn pup poynt.*

parting, n. *dybarth*, f.; of roads, *forth dybarth*, f.

partisan, n. *holyer*, m., pl. *-yoryon.*

partition, n. *fōs dybarth*, f., pl. *-ow d.*; act, *rannans*, m., *dybarth*, f.

partly, adv. *part, yn ran.*

partner, n. *kescoweth*, m., pl. *-a*, **cowethyas*, m., pl. *-ysy*: **-ship,** n. *kescowethas*, f., pl. *-ow.*

partridge, n. *grügyar*, f., pl. *-yēr*, dim., *grügyeryk*, m., pl. *-ygow*; cock p., ‡*cülyek grüglon*, m., pl. *-yogas g.* **coryar*, f., pl. *-yēr.*

party, n. *kyfvewy, bagas, party, parcel*, m.: **-ti-coloured,** a. *deulyw.*

pass, v. *tremena, passya*: p. over, **trüsy*; come to p., *wharfos*; hand, reach, *hedhes, ystynna*: n. *aswy* (*ajy*), f., pl. *-ow*, **cülforth*, f., pl. *-dhow*; permit, *tokyn cümyas*, m.: **-able,** a. *heforth, da lowr*: **-er-by,** n. *tremenyas*, m., pl. *-ysy*: **-age, -ing,** n. *tremenva*, f., pl. *-ow*, *tremenyans*, m.; act of p., *tremen*, m., pl. *-yow*; free p., *forth lan*; p. between buildings, *scoch-forth*, f., pl. *-ordhow*; p. beneath a stage for actors, *conveyour*, m.; p. over water, sea p., *trēth, trümach*, m.: **-enger,** n. *tremenyas*, m., pl. *-ysy*; by water, *trēthyas*, m., pl. *-ysy.*

passion, n., suffering, *passyon*, m.; rage, *sōr*, m.: **-ate,** a. *ow-lesky y golon, sōr dhodho*: **-ive,** a. *ow-codhevel*, **godhevüs.*

Passover, n. *dē-*, or *bōs, Pask*, m.

past, adv. *drēs*: a. *tremenys, passyes*: n. *termyn a-vē, t. üs tremenys* or *passyes, t. res-ēth.*

paste, n. *glüs*, m.; dough, **tōs*, m.; to make into p., *glüsa*, **tosa.*

pastime, n. *gwary*, m., pl. *-ow, sport*, m., pl. *-ys*; he only does it for a p., *ny-n-gwra lemen rak gül dhe'n termyn tremena.*

pastor, n. *bügel*, m., pl. *-eth(-a)*; eccl., *menyster*, m., pl. *-trys*: **-al,** a. *bugelek*; p. staff, *bagyl*, f., pl. *-glow.*

pastry, n. **pāst*, **pastyas*, m.; p.-cake, *whȳogen, hogen*, f., pl. *-gas, fūgen*, f., pls. *-now, -gas*: **-ty,** n. *pasty*, m., pl. *-s.*

pasture, n. *glaswels*, m., †*clün*, m., pl. *-now, pōr, gwerwels, porwels, porla*, m., *porva*, f.; common p., *prās*, m., pl. *-ow*; revived p., *aswels*, m.; winter p., *gwavwels*, m.: v. *pory.*

pat, v. *frappya yn-scaf, tava, handla, chersya*: n. *what*, m., pl. *-tys*: a. *parys.*

patch, n. *clowt*, m., pl. *-ys*; p. of garden, *splat*, m., pl. *-tys*; p.-work, *clowtwȳth*, m.; p.-hook, **gwydhyf*, m., pl. *-yvow*: v. *clowtya.*

pate, n. *top an pen*, †*dywolewyth, pāt*, m.; by my p., *re'm pāt*; broken p., *pen-cough*, m.

paten, n. †*gorher*, m., pl. *-yow.*

patent, a. *efan, ape·rt, opyn-welys*; letters p., *lytherow ape·rt*: v. **patentya.*

paterfamilias, n. *pen-tȳlu*, m.

paternal, a. *ave·l tās, a dās, tasek*; in relationship, *aba·rth tās*: **-nity,** n. *tasegeth*, m.

paternoster, n., prayer, *pader, pater*, m.; bead, *pader*, m., pl. *pederow.*

path, n. *forth*, f., pl. *fordhow, hens*, m., pl. *-y*, †*trulergh*, m., pl. *-ow*; p. to church, *for' eglos* (*fryglos*), f.: **-finder,** n. *fordhor*, m., pl. *-yon.*

pathos, n. *müvyans dhe drūeth, an pyth üs ow-müvya dhe byta*: **-thetic,** a. *trūethek, pytethüs, ow-müvya dhe byta.*

patience, n. *cosoleth, perthyans, godhevyans*, m.; herb, *tavolen wherow*, f., col. *tavol w.*: **-nt,** a. *hebask, cosel*: n. *godhevyas*, m., pl. *-ysy*, f. *-vyades*, pl. *-ow, dēn clāf, benen glāf.*

patriarch, n. **treftas*, m., pl. *-ow*, †*ugheldas*, m., pl. *-ow*, **patryargh*, m., pl. *-as, -yergh.*

patriot, n. **gwlasçarer*, m., pl. *-roryon*: **-ic,** a. **gwlascar*: **-ism,** n. **gwlaskerensa*, f.

patrol, n. *gwythysy kerth*, pl.: v. **patrolya, kerdhes war wȳth.*

patron, n. *tasek*, m., pl. *-sygyon*: **-age,** n. **tasegeth*, m.: **-al,** a. *tasek*: **-ise,** v. *bōs tasek dhe*[2]; offensively, *omdhōn yn-ughel orth.*

patter, v., say prayers, **pederewa*, **padera*; with feet, *kerdhes yn ün frappya*; of feet, *frappya treys*; chatter, etc., *kewsel yn-scaf, clattra, clappya*: n. *clap*, m.

pattern, n. *patron*, m., *squȳr*, m., pl. *-ys, scantlyn*, m., pl. *-s*; of behaviour, *sampel, dēn parfyt*, m.

paunch, n. *tor*, f., pl. *-row, bolghen, pengasen*, f., pl. *-now.*

pauper, n. *boghosek*, m., pl. *-sogyon.*

pause, v. *hedhy, lettya, powes*: n. *powes*, m.

pave, v. *caunsya*: **-ed-way, -ment,** n., cobbles or sets, *cauns*, m., pl. *-ys*; flags, *forth lēghveyn.*

pavilion, n. **pavylyon*, m., pl. *-s.*

paw, n. *paw*, m., pl. *-yow*, d., *deubaw*: v. **pawa, ploshandla, mostya.*

pawn, v. *gwystla, gasa yn gaja*: n. *gwystel, gaja,* m.

pawnbroker, n. **okerer rak gaja,* m., pl. *-oryon r. g.*

pay, v. *pē, tylly*; p. for, *prena*; p. out, *pē dhe*[2]; still to p., outstanding, *dhe bē*; p. tithe, *degevy*; p. off, *aquӯtya*; p. attention to, *gül vrӯ a*[2], *nōtya, avӯsya, rӯ scovarn dhe*[2]: n. *gober,* m., pl. *-brow,* **tal,* m., pl. *-ow*: **-ment,** n. *payment,* m., pl. *-ns.*

pea, n., seed or plants, *pӯsen,* f., pl. *-now,* col. *pӯs*; to set p. sticks, *scorenna pӯs*: **-scod,** n. *cūth-pӯs,* f., pl. *-ow-p.*

peace, n. *crēs,* f.; quiet, *cosoleth,* m.; p.! *gās* (pl. *geseugh*) *crēs*! *pēs*!; to hold one's p., *tewel*: **-ful,** a. *cosel,* ‡*quӯet.*

peach, n. *aval *gwlanek,* m., pl. *-low g.*

peacock, n. *payon,* m., pl. *-as*; p. hen, *paynes,* f., pl. *-ow.*

peak, n. *col,* m., pl. *-ow, ban,* m. or f., pl. *-now, crӯb,* f., pl. *-ow, top,* m., pl. *-yow, topyn,* m., pl. *-now.*

peal, v. *kesseny clēgh*: n. *kessenyans clēgh,* m.; of thunder, *bom taran*; of laughter, *bom wharth, tarth w.*

pear, n. *peren,* f., pl. *-now,* col. *pēr*; p.-tree, *gwedhen pēr,* f., col. *gwӯth p.,* †*pērbren,* m., pl. *-nyer*; p. orchard, *pērlan,* f., pl. *-now.*

pearl, n. *perl,* m., pl. *-ys.*

peat, n. *towarghen,* f., col. *towargh, kesen,* f., pl. *kesow.*

pebble, n. *būlyen,* f., pl. *būlyow,* col. *būly*; pebbly, *būlyek*; p. ridge, *būlyek,* f., pl. *-egow.*

peck, v. *pyga*: n. *ēth quart.*

peculiar, a. *coynt, dybarow*: **-ity,** n. *coyntys,* m.

pecuniary, a. *arghans, a vona.*

pedal, n. *trōsla,* m., pl. *-ow*: v. *trōsya.*

peddle, v., wares, *trōsya, gwyca*: **-dlar,** n. *trōsyer,* m., pl. *-yoryon, gwycor,* m., pl. *-yon.*

pedestal, n. *trōs,* m., pl. *treys, goles,* m.

pedestrian, n. *kerdher,* m., pl. *-oryon, travalyer,* m., pl. *-yoryon*: a. *war drōs.*

pedigree, n. **petygrew,* m., pl. *-s,* †*aghow,* f., pl.

peel, n. *rüsken,* f., col. *rüsk, ken,* m., no pl., *pyl,* m., pl. *-yon, plysken,* f., pl. *-now,* col. *plysk*; of baker, *pāl forn,* f., pl. *-yow f.*; having p., *rüskek*: v. *dyrüsca, pylya.*

peep, v. *myras, gӯky*: n. *golok,* f.; let's take one p. at him, *myryn orto ün wolok.*

peer, v. *whythra, myras* or *aspӯa glew* (*war*[2], *orth*).

peer, n. *dēn nobyl,* m., pl. *tüs n.*; fellow, *coweth,* m., col. *-a, par,* m., pl. *-ow*; his p.s, *y hynsa, y barow, y gowetha*: **-age,** n. *bryntynsys, stāt-ughel,* m.: **-less,** *hep par, hep parow, sompēr.*

peevish, a. *nebes sērrys, crowsek, ēs y serry.*

peewit, n. *cornwhylen,* f., pls. *-las, -ly, kernwhyly*: col. *-whyl.*

peg, n. *pyn,* m., pl. *-nys, ebyl,* m., pls. *-yow, -yon*: v. *pynna, ebylya.*

pelisse, n., of fur, †*pellyst ken,* m., pl. *-ow k.*

pellet, n. *pellennyk,* f., pl. *-ygow, -nowygow.*

pellicle, n. *kennen,* f., pl. *-now.*

pellitory, n. **lesparwys,* **fōslys,* m.

pelt, v. *pyltya.*

pelt, n. *ken,* m., no pl.

pen, n., for writing, *plüven,* f., pl. *-now*; enclosure, *corlan,* f., pl. *-now*: v., write, *scryfa*; shut in, *degēa*: **-manship,** n. *scryfa plüven,* m.

penal, a. *pӯn, payn*; p. servitude, *gwaso·n-ӯeth, pӯn,* f., *kethneth,* m.: **-ty,** n. *pewas, pӯn, payn,* m.

penance, n. *penys, ankenek, penans,* m.; long p., *hӯrbenys,* m.; do p., *penys*: **-itential,** a. *ankenek*: **-tentiary,** n., religious, *penytty,* m., pl. *-ow*; reformatory, *pryson amendyans,* m.

pencil, n., brush, *pyncel,* m., pl. *-s*; lead, *plüven-blom,* f., pl. *-now plom.*

pending, a. *ow-cortos.*

penetrate, v. *dewana, gwana, telly, cropya, pychya, entra*: **-ion,** n. *gwan,* f.: **-ing,** a. *lym*; pain, *glew.*

penguin, n. **beraskel,* f., pl. *-las.*

peninsular, n. *gorenys,* f., pl. *-nesow, enys,* f., pl. *enesow, rōs,* f., pl. *-yow.*

penis, n. *cal,* m.; of animal, *caster,* m.

penitence, n. *edrek, edrega,* m.: **-nt,** a. *codhys yn edrek, cüdhyjyk.*

penknife, n. *kellyllyk,* m., pl. *-ygow.*

penny, n. *dynar,* m., pl. *-nerow*; p. piece, *deneren,* f., pl. *-now*; a p.worth of bread, *bara rag ün dynar.*

pennywort, n. **crampeth mowysy,* col.

pension, n. *pensyon,* m., pl. *-s*: **-er,** n. *pensyoner,* m., pl. *-s.*

pensive, a. *tryst, prederüs.*

Pentecost, n. *Pencast,* m.

penultimate, a. *an dewetha saw onen.*

penury, n. *esow,* m.

people, n. *tüs*, f., *pobel*, f., pl. *-blow*; retinue, *coscar*, col. *mēny*, m.: v. *pobla*.
pepper, n. **püber*, m.
peradventure, adv.: see **perhaps.**
perceive, v. *convedhes, gweles, aswon*: **-ceptible,** a. *hewel*: **-ception,** n. *gweles, clewes*, m.
perch, n. **trüspren*, m., pl. *-nyer, gwelen*, f., pl. *-lyny*: v. *esedha, desedha, cluttya*.
perchance, adv.: see **perhaps.**
peremptory, a. *hep argya, ow-cül maystry*: **-orily,** adv. *gordhewyth*.
perfect, a. *flowr, hep nam, dȳen, perfyth, cowal, pür, parfyt*: v. *cowlwül, gül perfyth, obery*: **-tion,** n. *perfythter*; fulfilment, *keweras*, m., *cowlwrȳans*, m. ‡*perfeksyon*: **-ly,** adv. *yn- perfyth, hep nam, yn-tȳen*: prefix *cowl-, fȳn-*.
pefidious, a. *fals, dyslēl, fekyl*: **-dy,** n. *bras, traytury, trayson, falsury, treghury*, m.
perforate, v. *telly, gwana*: **-d,** a. *toll, tellek*: **-tion,** n. *toll*, m., pl. *tell*; eye of needle, socket, *crow*, m., pl. *crewow*.
peform, v. *obery, gül, collenwel*; habitually, *ūsya*; as actor, *gwary*: **-ance,** n. *obereth*, m., *gwrȳth*, f., *gwythres*, m.; dramatic p., *gwary*, m., pl. *-ow*: **-er,** n., in a play, *gwaryer*, m., pl. *-yoryon*, f. *-ores*, pl. *-ow*.
perfume, n. *sawor*, m., pl. *-yow, ēth*, m., pl. *-ow, odor*, m., *saworen*, f., pl. *-now*; artificial, *dowr ēth whēk*: **-ier,** n. *gwerther dowrow ēth whēk*.
perhaps, adv. *martesen, par hap, par chōns*; p. it is, *y-hȳl bōs*.
peril, n. *peryl*, m., pl. *-yow*; at my p., *yn ow feryl-vy*; to be in p., *peryllya*: **-ous,** a. *deantel*.
period, n. *termyn*, m., pl. *-yow, sēson*, m., pl. *-s, ōs*, m., pl. *-ow, spās, spȳs*, m.: **-ical,** a. *dhe sēson settyes*: n. *lyver termyn, l. sēson*, m., pl. *lyfrow, -ryow t., s.*: **-ically,** adv. *trawythyow, a dermyn dhe dermyn*.
perish, v. *merwel, pedry, mōs dhe goll, dōs dhe dravyth, storvya, *persya*: **-able,** a. *a-ȳl pedry*.
periwinkle, n., mollusc, *gwȳghen*, f., pl. *gwȳghas*, col. *gwȳgh*; plant, **pervynk*, m., pl. *-ys*.
perjure, v. *gow-lȳa*: **-er,** n. *gow-lȳer*, m., pl. *-ȳoryon*: **-ry,** *gow-lȳ*, m.
permanent, a. *fast, a-sēf, a-bȳs*.
permeate, v. *gwana* or *sygera drē*[2].
permission, n. *cümyas, lecyans*, m.; to give p. to do . . ., *rȳ cümyas a wül* . . .; with your p., *drē dha vōth* or *gümyas*: **-sable,** a. *lafyl, a-levesyr*: **-mit,** v. *gasa, rȳ cümyas a*[2], *godhaf (-dhevel), grontya, lavasos*: n. *lecyans*, m.
pernicious, a. *drōk, tebel*.
perpendicular, a. *serth*.
perpetual, a. *hep powes, hep hedhy, nefra a-bȳs, a-dhür, hep let, gwāf ha hāf*: **-ly,** adv. *pup-ür, prest, byketh, vyketh, yn y dhēdhyow, ow dēdhyow*, etc., *pup termyn, pup nōs ha dēth*: **-ate,** v. *gül dhe bēsya, cofhē·*.
perplex, v. *ancombra, müskegy*: **-ity,** n. *ancombrynsy*, m.
perquisite, n. *waja*, m., pl. *-jys*.
persecute, v. *tormentya, tropla, helghya, plāgya*: **-tion,** n. *tormentyans*, m.: **-tor,** n. *tormentor*, m., pl. *-s, helghyas*, m., pl. *-ysy*.
perseverance, n. *dywysygneth, dywysykter*, m.: **-re,** v. *pēsya gans ober, obery* or *sevel yn-tewysyk, mōs yn-rak, contynewa (yn)*: **-ing,** a. *dywysyk*.
persicaria, n., spotted p., **lagas du*.
persist, v. *perthy, paragh, gleny (orth), pēsya (gans)*: **-tence,** n. *perthyans*, m.
person, n. *dēn*, m., pl. *tüs, person*, m., pl. *-s, corf*, m., pl. *-ow, body*, m., pl. *-s*; a single p., *ün body*; other p.s, *rē erel, kēn rē*; come in p., *dōs y honen*: **-al,** a. *prȳva, pryveth*: **-ally,** adv., in expressing opinion, *ow-kewsel ragof ow honen*; speak p. with him, *kewsel orth y anow*.
perspective, n. *gwēl*, m. or f., *vu*, m.
perspire, v. *whēsa*: **-ration,** n. *whēs*, m.; his brow is (covered with) p., *whēs yu y dāl*; covered all over with p., *whēs pup goth oll ha lyth*.
persuade, v. *gül, tenna, trēlya* or *drȳ dhe*[2], *dynya*: **-asion,** n. *tenvos, dynyans*, m.
pert, a. *frēth, tōnt*; to be p., *tōntya*; p. girl, *flownen*, f., pl. *-now*.
pertain, v. *pertaynya, longya*.
perturb, v. *müvya (amüvya), dystempra, serry*: **-bation,** n. *dystemprans, sōr*, m.
peruse, v. *rēdya*: n. *rēdyans*, m.
perverse, a. *trüs, dygnā·s, gorth, drēs keyn*; p. talk, *trüsyon*: **-ly,** adv. *trüs*: **-sity,** n. *trüster*, m.: **-vert,** v. *sawthanas, trēlya dyworth* or *yn-mēs a fȳth*: n. *negedhys*, m., pl. *-ysyon*.
pest, n. *pla*, m., pl. *-ow, plāg*, m., pl. *-ys, bal*, f., pl. *-ow*; p.! *mal! a-barth an pla!*: **-er,** v. *annȳa, ancombra, spralla, plāgya, vexya*:

-erer, n. *fyslak*, m., pl. *-logyon*: **-ilence,** see **pest**: **-ilent,** a. *a'n pla.*
pestle, n. **horth brewy*, m.
pet, n. *mȳl dōf*; of child, etc., *whegyn*, m., pl. *-now, whegen*, f., pl. *-now, melder*, m.: v. *chersya, dȳghtya yn whegyn.*
petal, n. *delen blejewen*, f., pl. *dēl blejyow.*
petition, n. *pysadow, petysyon*, m., *govenek*, m., pl. *-ygyon, desȳr*, m.: v. *pysy*: **-er,** n. *petysyoner*, m., pl. *-s.*
petrel, n. *edhen Peder, e. hager-awel*, f., pl. *-ydhyn P., h.*
petrify, v. *trēlya yn mēn.*
petrol, -eum, n. *oyl mēn*, m.
petticoat, n. **golesen*, f., pl. *-now*; p. trousers, of fishermen or sailors, *raglen*, f., pl. *-now.*
petty, a. *bȳghan*: prefix **cragh-.*
pew, n. *esethva*, f., pl. *-ow.*
phantasm, -tom, n. *tarosvan*, m., pl. *-now, skēs*, m., pl. *-ow, spyrys*, m., pls. *-yon, -yjyon.*
pheasant, n. *fesont*, m., pl. *-sons.*
phenomenon, n. *nep tra a-omdhysqueth, marth*, m., pl. *-ow*: **-al,** a. *üthek, marthys.*
philanthropic, a. *da orth tüs*: **-pist,** n. *car mabden*, m., pl. *kerens m.*: **-py,** n. *dader, cüfter* or *kerensa orth mabden*, f.
philologist, n. *yēthor*, m., pl. *-yon*: **-gy,** n. *skȳans yēthow, *fylolojy*, m.
philosopher, n. **fylosofer*, m., pl. *-s, dēn für*, m., pl. *tüs f., dēn skȳansek, d. skentyl*, m., pl. *tüs s.*: **-phic,** a. *skȳansek*: **-phy,** n. **fylosofy, skȳans*, m.
phosphorescence, n. *mordan*, m.: **-nt,** a. *mordanek.*
photograph, n. **fotograf*, m., pl. *-ys*: v. **fotografya.*
phrase, n. *lavar*, m., pl. *-ow.*
physic, n. *medhy·gȳeth*, f., *medhekneth*, m., *fysek*, f.: **-ian,** n. *medhek*, m., pl. *-ygyon, fysycyen*, m., pl. *-s*: **-al,** a. *a'n corf*: **-ics,** n. *skȳans natur*, m.: **-iognomy,** n. *fysmant*, m., pl. *-mens.*
pick, v., fruit, flower, *terry, cuntell*; choose, *dewys*; p. up, *kemeres yn-ban.*
pick, n. *pygal*, f., pl. *-golow.*
pickle, v. **kyfythya*; in brine, *salla, *hylyenna*: n. **kyfyth wherow, k. gwȳn fyllys*, m., pl. *-yow w.*; brine, *dowr sal, *hylyen*, f.
picnic, n. *crowst*, m., pl. *-ys.*
pickpocket, n. *squychyer porsys*, m., pl. *-yoryon p., porslader*, m., pl. *-dron.*
picture, n. **pyctur*, m., pl. *-s, *portrayans*, m., pl. *-ow, lywans, *delynyans*, m.; motion p.s, *gwaya-mȳr*, m.
pie, n. *pasty*, m., pl. *-s*: see **magpie.**
piece, n. *tam*, m., pl. *tymmyn, pȳs*, m., pl. *-ys, dral*, m., pl. *-yow, darn*, m., pl. *-ow*; small, *brewyonen*, f., col. *brewyon, dyjyn*, m., pl. *-now*; long, *sketh*, m., pl. *-ow*; p. of land, *pastel (a) dȳr*, f. ,pl. *-low tȳr*: **-meal,** a., adv. *tam ha tam, orth tymmyn.*
pied, a. *brȳth, du ha gwyn, deulyw.*
pier, n. *cāy*, m., pl. *-ys.*
pierce, v. *gwana, dewana, pychya, telly, gȳa, tardra*; p. through with, *mōs* or *dōs drē gans*: **-d,** *toll, tellek*: **-cing,** a. *lym, tyn*; of pain, *glew*: n. *gwan*, f.
piety, n. *dader, lēl-wonys orth Dew, sansoleth*, m.
pig, n. *hogh*, m., pl. *-as*, col. *mogh*; young p., *†banow*, m. or f., pls. *-as, -newy*; porker, *porghel*, m., pl. *-ly*; three p.s, *try lon-hogh, t. l.-mogh*; smallest p. of litter, *pyg bȳghan, pyg-gwyn*; sucking p., *porghellyk*, m., pl. *-ygow*: **-let,** n. *porghellyk*, m., pl. *-ygow*: **-sty,** n. *crow-mogh*, m.: **-wash,** n. *bōs mogh*, m.
pigeon, n. *colom*, f., pl. *-as, colomen*, f., pl. *-nas*; wood p., *colom* or *colomen cōs, cüdhan*, f., pl. *-as*; p. house, *colomyer*, m., pl. *-s, *colomjy*, m., pl. *-ow*; p. hole, *toll colom*, m., pl. *tell c.*
pike, n. *pȳk*, m., pl. *-ys, gu*, m., pl. *-yow*; fish, *dynsak dowr*, m., pl. *-sogas d.*
pilchard, n. *hernen*, f., col. *hern*; salted p., *fūmado*, m., pl. *-s*; decayed p., *pesak*, m., pl. *-sogas.*
pile, n. *graghell*, f., pl. *-low, bern*, m., pl. *-yow, das*, f., pl. *deys, crük(g)*, m., pl. *-ügyow*; small, *crügell*, f., pl. *-low, crügyn*, m., pl. *-now*; rock p., *carn*, m., pl. *-ow*; heap, plenty, *cals*, m.; post, *pül*, m., pl. *-yow*; of arrow, *pȳl*, m., pl. *-ys*; of carpet, *blew*, col.: v. *gorra yn bern, crügya, graghella, berna, dasa.*
pilfer, v. *ladra*: **-er,** n. *lader*, m., pl. *-dron, brȳbour*, m., pl. *-s.*
pilgrim, n. *perghyryn (pryeryn)*, m., pl. *-as*, f., *-es*, pl. *-ow, palmor*, m., pl. *-yon*: **-age,** n. *perghyrynsys (pryerynsys)*, m.
pill, n. *pellennyk*, f., pls. *-nowygow, -ygow.*
pillage, v. *pylla, ladra.*
pillar, n. *pyllar*, m., pl. *-s, post mēn*, m., pl. *-ow, m.*
pillory, n. **pylory*, m., pl. *-s, carghar pen*, m.: v. *carghara.*

pillow, n. *plüvak*, f., pl. *-vogow*.
pilot, n. *lewyer*, m., pl. *-oryon*, *lewyth*, m., pl. *-ydhyon*, *lewyador*, m., pl. *-doryon*: v. *lewyas*.
pimpernel, n. **brathles*, m.
pimple, n. *curȳak*, m., pl. *-ȳogas*.
pin, n. *pyn*, m., pl. *-nys*; larger, *ebyl*, m., pls. *-yow*, *-yon*; wooden p., *ebyl pren*; iron p., *ebyl horn*; game with p.s, *pen-ha-mȳn*, m.: v. *pynna*, *ebylya*.
pinafore, n. *raglen*, f., pl. *-now*.
pincers, n., pair of p., *pynsor*, m., pl. *-s*, *gevel*, f., pl. *-yow*; pliers, forceps, *gevel vȳghan*.
pinch, n. **gwask*, f., **pyncha*, m., pl. *-chys*; at a p., *fowt gwell*, *yn ethom*, *pan vo rēs*: v. **gevelya*, **pynchya*, *settya crok yn*.
pine, v. *omwethhē·* (*warlergh*), **nēghy*: **-ing,** a. *morethek*: n. *moreth*, m.
pine, n. *saben*, f., col. *sap*, *gwedhen pȳn*, f., pl. *gwȳth p.*, †*pȳnbren*, m., pl. *-yer*, *sybwedhen*, f., col. *sybwȳth*; p. cone, p.-apple, *aval saben*, m., pl. *-low s.*; p. needle, *nasweth saben*, f., pl. *-wedhow s.*
pine-end, n. *punyon*, m., pl. *-s*.
pink, a. *gwynrüth*; flower, **jylofer*, m., pl. *-s*; sea p., *tam ōn*, m., *bryton*, m., pl. *-s*.
pinnacle, n. *pynakyl*, m., pl. *-aclys*.
pint, n. **pȳnta*, m., pl. *-tys*.
pious, a. *dywysyk*, *sans*, **sansyl*.
pip, n. *sprüsen* (*spüsen*), f., pl. *-now*, col. *sprüs*; full of p.s, *sprüsek*.
pipe, n. *pȳb*, f., pl. *-ow*; tube, *pȳbel*, f., pl. *-low*; small p., *pȳben*, f., pl. *-now*; whistle, †*whȳb*, †*whybonol*, **whythell*, f., pl. *-ow*; cry, *gwȳgh*, m., pl. *-ow*: v. *pȳba*, *whythella*; cry, **gwȳghal*: **-er,** n. *whybanor*, m., pl. *-yon*, *pȳber*, m., pl. *-boryon*, *pȳbyth*, m., pl. *-ydhyon*: **-fish,** n. *mornasweth*, f., pl. *-edhow*, *prȳf-malan*, m., pl. *prevyon-m*.
piracy, n. *morladrynsy*, m.: **-ate,** n. *morlader*, m., pl. *-ladron*; viking, †*ancryjor* (*ancredor*) *mōr*, m., pl. *-oryon m*.
piscina, **pysyn*, m., pl. *-ow*.
piss, v. *pysa*: n. *pysas*, m.
pit, n. *pol*, m., pl. *-low*, *toll*, m., pl. *-tell*, *pyt*, m., pl. *-tys*; small p., *dyppa*, m., pl. *-pys*; deep p., *pol down*; p. of hell, *pyt yffarn*; clay p., *pol prȳ*, *pyt prȳ*; china-clay p., *pyt prȳ gwyn*, m.; p. of the stomach, *pol an golon*.
pit-a-pat, adv. *tys ha tas*.
pitch, v. *gorra*, *settya*, *pychya*; throw, *tewlel*; pay with p., *pega*: n. *pēk*, m.; degree, *pryk*, m.; attain that p., *dōs dhe'n pryk-na*; for cricket, etc., *gwaryva*, f.
pitcher, n., vessel, *pycher*, m., pl. *-s*; p.ful of clean water, *pycher dowr glan*.
pity, n. *tregereth*, f., pl. *-ow*, *pyta*, *pyteth*, *trüeth*, m.; a p., *dȳeth*, *trüeth*; it is a great p. for you, *trüeth* or *dȳeth mür yu ahanas*; it would be a p. for it to be lost, *trüeth vȳa y vōs kellys*; it is a p., *dȳeth yu*; it would be a p. for him, *anodho dȳeth vȳa*; to take p. on, *kemeres trüeth*, *pyta*, *tregereth* a^2 or war^2; what a p.! *tru*! *ass-yu dȳeth*!; more's the p.! *soweth*! *hen yu dhe voy pyta*!: v. *kemeres trüeth*, *rūthy*: **-teous,** a. *trüethek*, *trüan*: **-teously,** adv. *yn-trüan*: **-tiful,** a. *trüethek*, *trüan*, *pytethüs*; p. state of affairs, *trüeth*, *tebel-stüth*: **-iless,** a. *dybyta*.
pivot, n. *pen ēghel*, m., pl. *-now eghelyow*.
pizzle, n. *skytlen*, f., pl. *-now*.
place, n. *lē*, m., pl. *-ow*, *tyller*, m., pl. *-yow*; mansion, *plās*, m., pl. *-ow*; p. at table, **plas*, m., pl. *-yow*; seat, *eseth*, *esethva*, f., pls. *-edhow*, *-ow*; abiding p., *trygva*, f., **trygla*, m.; p. where one belongs, *tyller tȳthy*; sequestered p., *argel*, f., pl. *-ow*; without a p., **dylē·*; put in p., *desedha*; take p., *wharfos*; in his p., *yn y lē*: v. *gorra*, *settya*, *desedha*.
placid, a. *whar*, *clōr*, *hebask*, **dysōr*.
plague, n. *pla*, m., pl. *-ow*, *plāg*, m., pl. *-ys*, *bal*, f., pl. *-ow*; p. on . . . ! *mal bew* . . . !: v. *plāgya*.
plaice, n. *lȳth*, f., pl. *-as*.
plain, n. *gūn*, f., pl. *gonyow*; of playing-place, *plēn*, m., pl. *-ys*: a. *efan*, *rȳth*, *compes*, *leven*, *gwastas*, *nōth*, *plēn*, *sempel*, *splan y weles*: **-ly,** adv. *ape·rt*, *efan*, *yn-splan*, *hep afȳna*; without doubt, *hep dowt*, *hep mar*; to speak p., *leverel hep tȳ-vyth na gow-lȳa*, *dhe blemmyk*.
plaint, n. *plēnta*, m., pl. *-tys*; to make a p., *plēntya*: **-iff,** n. *plēntyer*, m., pl. *-yoryon*, **plēntyf*, m.; to act as p., *plēntya*: **-ive,** a. *trüethek*, *trüan*, *tryst*.
plait, n. *plēth*, f., pl. *-ow*, d. *dywbleth*; p.ed work, *plēthwȳth*, m.; fine p., *plethen*, f., pl. *-now*: v. *plethenna*, *plēthy*, ‡*plattya*.
plan, n. *towl*, m., pl. *-ow*, *cusül*, f., pl. *-yow*, *porpos*, m., pl. *-ys*; sketch, *ten*, m., pl. *-now*; make p.s, *tewlel towl*; we are p.ning to strike, *yma· war agan towl knoukya*; carried out according to p., *spēdyes dour dhe borpos*: v. *devȳsya*, *cusülya* (‡*consylya*), *ervȳra*, *tewlel towl*.

plane, n., carpenter's, *playn*, m., pl. *-ys*, **rask*, f., pl. *-ow*; aerop., *jyn-nyja, jyn-ebren*, m.: v. *playnya, *rasca.*

planet, n. *steren gwandra*, f., pl. *-now g.*, col. *stēr g., planet*, m., pl. *-tys.*

plank, n. *plynken*, f., pl. *-now, estyllen*, f., pl. *-now, astell*, f., pl. *estyll, plank*, m., pl. *-ys*: v. *astella, plankya.*

plant, n. *plans*, m., pl. *-ow, losowen*, f., col. *losow*, pl. *losowys*; to gather p.s, *losowa* (inf. only): v. *plansa*; disseminate, *plontya*; p. crop, *gonys*: **-ation,** n. *lowarth gwȳth, dōr plynsys*, m.: **-er,** n. *plansor*, m., pl. *-yon.*

plantain, n. *ledan-les*, m., pl. *-losow*, †*hen-ledan*, col.

plaster, n. **plaster*, m.: v. **plastra.*

plate, n. *plāt*, m., pl. *-ys*; p. armour, *arvow plāt*; p. or place at table, *plas*, m., pl. *-yow*; p. of metal, *laun*, m., pl. *-ow*; p. rack, **lystryer*, m., pl. *-yow*: v., p. with metal, *launya.*

plateau, n. *gwastattyr*, m.

platform, n. *soler*, m., pl. *-yow*, **arethva*, f., *mynk*, f., pl. *-ncow.*

plausibility, n. *fekyl-chēr*, ‡*gwȳrhevelepter*, m.: **-ble,** a. *fekyl, a-yllyr y grysy, a-hevel bōs da*, ‡*gwȳrhevelep.*

play, n. *gwary*, m., pl. *-ow, sport*, m., pl. *-ys*: v. *gwary*; on instruments, *pȳba, fylla, whetha*, etc.: **-er,** n. *gwaryer*, m., pl. *-yor-yon*, f., *-yores*, pl. *-ow*: **-ful,** a. *jolyf, gwarȳek*: **-house,** *gwaryjy*, m., pl. *-ow*: **-thing,** n. *tegen*, f., pl. *-now.*

plea, n. *clēm*, m., pl. *-ys, pysadow*, m., *gove-nek*, m., pl. *-nygon.*

plead, v., p. a cause, *gül clēm*, †*dathla* (*dala*), *plēntya*, **plēdya.*

pleasant, a. *mery, whēk, tēk, hebask*, ‡*plēsont*: **-ness,** n. *whekter, tekter*, m.: **-ry,** n. *gēs*, m.

please, v. *plēkya, plēsya*; p., if you p., *mar* (*mara*) *plēk* (*dheugh*), *drē*, or *mars yu, dha vōth, mar peugh-why plēsyes*; p., pray, *praydha, y praya, dha bysy*; I am p.ed with it, *pȳs da ōf anodho*: **-d,** a. *plēsyes, pȳs da, prowt, contentys*; I am p., *da yu genef*; I am not p.ed with you, *genes nyns-ōf contentys*: **-ing,** a. *jentyl, hegar, *dydhan*: **-ure,** n. *plesour, lüst*, m., pl. *-ys, fancy, tekter, whekter, *solas*, m.; I take p. in that, *da yu genef henna*; at your p., *dhe'th plegadow, dhe'th vōth.*

pledge, n. *gwystel*, m., pl. *-tlow, gaja*, m., pl. *-jys, plȳght*, m., pl. *-ys*: v. *gasa yn gaja, gwystla, plȳghtya*: **-r,** n. *gwystlor*, m., pl. *-yon.*

plenipotentiary, n. *cannas lün-gallosek*, f., pl. *-ow l.*: a. *lün-gallosek.*

plenty, n. *lanwes, cals, stoff, plenta*, ‡*tomals, palster*, **gorfalster*, m.; p. of, *lowr*, ‡*luk* (used as a.): **-tiful,** a. *pals, lün*: **-ifulness,** n. *lanwes*, m.

pliable, -ant, a. *heblyth, plyth, gwethyn.*

pliers, n., pair of p., *gevel vȳghan*, f., pl. *-yow bȳghan.*

plight, n. *stüth*, m., pl. *-yow, plȳt*, m., pl. *-ys*; sorry p., *tebel-stüth, drok-stüth.*

plod, v. *trōsya, lafürya.*

plot, v. *tewlel, cusülya*, **brasy*, ‡*plottya*: n., treachery, *bras*, m.; plan, *cusül*, f., pl. *-yow, towl*, m. pl. *-ow*; p. of ground, *splat*, m., pl. *-tys, shara*, m., pl. *-rys*; small p., *erewyk*, m., pl. *-ygow, pastel dȳr*, f., pl. *-llow tȳr*: **-ter,** n. *tewler towlow*, m., pl. *-loryon t.*, **brasyer* m., pl. *-yoryon*, ‡*plot-tyer*, m., pl. *-yoryon.*

plough, n. *ardar* (*a·radar, arjar*), m., pl. *erder* (*e·reder*); p.-tail, *dorn ardar*, m., pl. *-ow a.*, **pa·lather*, m., pl. **pe·lether*; p.-staff, **carthpren*, m.; p.-share, *sogh*, m., pl. *-yow*; p.-land, tilth, **ar*, m.: v. *aras*; p. together, *kevaras*; p. lightly, *fynegly*: **-ing,** n. *ar*, m.; joint p., *kevar*, m.: **-man,** n. †*ara·deror*, m., pl. *-yon.*

plover, n., peewit, lapwing, *cornwhylen*, f., pls. *-las, kernwhyly*, col. *cornwhyl.*

pluck, v. *tenna, squychya*; fruit, flowers, *terry*; feathers, *dyblüva.*

pluck, n., courage, *colonnekter, colon dha*, m.; butchery, *e·nether*, col.: **-y,** a. *colonnek.*

plug, n. *ebyl*, m., pls. *-yow, -yon, stoppyer*, m., pl. *-s*: v. *ebylya, prenna, stoppya.*

plum, n. *plūmen*, f., pl. *-now*; p. tree, *gwedhen plūmen*, f., pl. *gwȳth p.*, †*plūmbren*, m., pl. *-nyer*; p. stone, *mēn plūmen*, m., pl. *meyn plūm*; p. pudding, *pellen fyges*, f., pl. *-now f.*

plumb, a., adv. *dhe blemmyk*: v. *prevy gans plemmyk*: **-er,** n. *gwȳthor plom*, m., pl. *-thoryon p.*: **-line,** n. *plemmyk*, m., pl. *-ygow, lynen plom*, f.

plume, n. *plüven*, f., pl. *-now*, col. *plüf*: v. *plüvya*: **-mage,** n. *plüf*, col.

plummet, n. *plemmyk*, m., pl. *-ygow.*

plump, a. *tew*: **-ness,** n. *tewder*, m.

plunder, n. **prēth, pray*, m., *pythow rafnys, p. ledrys*, pl.: v. *pylla, robbya, rafna, ladra*:

-er, n. *robbyor,* m., pl. *-yon, rafner,* m., pl. *-noryon, lader,* m., pl. *-dron.*
plunge, v. *troghya;* p. right under water, **gorthroghya, sedhy*: n. *sēth,* m., pl. *sedhow*: **-r,** n. *sedhor,* m., pl. *-yon.*
plural, a. **lȳesek*: **-ity,** n. **lyester,* m.
plush, n. *paly fals,* m.
ply, v. *mōs ha dōs, *daromres, lafürya yn-frēth.*
ply, n. *plēk,* m., pl. *-egow*: three-p., *trȳflēk.*
pneumatic, a. *ayrek.*
poach, v. *ladra helgyk* or *gām*: **-er,** n. *lader helgyk, l. gām,* m., pl. *ladron h., g.*
pock-mark, n. *pocca,* m., pl. *pokkys*: **-ed,** a. *tellek, *gwenenek.*
pocket, n. *poket,* m., pl. *-tys;* bosom as receptacle, *ascra,* f.: v. *gorra yn ascra* or *poket.*
pod, n. *cūth,* f., pl. *-ow, plysken,* f., pl. *-now,* col. *plysk, *maskel,* f., pl. *-sclow;* rounded seed p., **bolghen,* f., col. *bolgh*: v. *plysca, *mascla, dyblysca.*
poem, n. **bardhonek,* m., pl. *-nogow, cān,* f., pl. *-ow.*
poet, n. *barth,* m., pls. *byrth, berdhyon, bardhes,* f., pl. *-ow, *prydyth,* m., pl. *-ydhyon, prydydhes,* f., pl. *-ow*: **-aster,** n. **cragh-varth,* m., pl. *-vyrth*: **-tic,** a. **prydydhek, *bardhonek*: **-try,** n. **bardho·nȳeth, *prydy·dhȳeth,* f.; piece of p., **bardhonek,* m., pl. *-nogow;* to write p., **prydydhy.*
point, n. *mȳn,* m., pl. *-yon, blȳn,* m., pl. *-ow, poynt,* m., *pȳk,* m., pl. *-ygow, col,* m., pl. *-ow;* of tool, *brōs,* m., pl. *-ojow;* pitch, degree, *pryk,* m., pl. *-kys;* of land, *pen,* m., pl. *-now, trōn,* m., pl. *-ow, penrȳn,* m., pl. *-yow;* extreme p., *penwyth,* m.; p. of death, *enewores,* m.; p. blank, *a poynt;* on the p. of, *parys dhe*[2]; at this p., *y'n ür-ma, omma*: v., indicate, *dysquedhes, poyntya, meneges;* sharpen, *lemma, blȳnya*: **-ed,** a. *lym.*
poise, n. *antel,* f., *omborth, *kespōs,* m.: v. *antel, omberthy, kespōsa.*
poison, n. *venym, poyson, †gwenyn,* m.: v. *posnya, venyma, †gwenyna*: **-er,** n. *posnyer,* m., pl. *-s, †gwenyn-rȳas,* m., pl. *-ȳesy*: **-ious,** a. *venymys, †gwenynek.*
poke, n. *pok,* m., pl. *-kys*: v. *pokkya*: **-r,** n. *pokkyer,* m., pl. *-s;* fire-iron, *gwelen-tan,* f.
pole, n. *gwelen,* f., pl. *-lyny,* col., *gwēl, pren,* m., pls. *-yer, prynner, lorgh,* m., pl. *-ow, pül,* m., pl. *-yow;* of cart, *gwelen-car,* f.; North P., *pen-ēghel North a'n bȳs;* South P., *pen-ēghel Sōth a'n bȳs.*
polecat, n. *†yewgen,* f., pl. *-as.*
Pole-Star, n. *an Steren,* f.
policeman, n. *gwythyas crēs,* m., pl. *-ysy c.*
policy, n., prudence, *fürneth,* m.; of government, *rewl menystrans,* m.
polish, v. *gül dhe splanna, *lentry, *polsya;* p. with wax, *cōra*: n. *splander,* m.: **-ed,** a. *splan, *lenter, *polsys.*
polite, a. *cüf, jentyl, cortes*: **-ness,** n. *cüfter, cortesy, jentylys,* m.
politic, a. *‡polytyk, für.*
political, a. *gwlasek*: **-ician,** n. *dēn gwlasek,* m., pl. *tüs wlasek*: **-ics,** n. *gwlasegeth,* m.
poll, n. *pen,* m., pl. *-now;* vote, **votyans*: v. *trēghy, knyvyas;* vote, **vōtya.*
pollack, n. **polak,* m., pl. *-logas;* young p., *dojel,* m., pl. *-las.*
pollen, n. *pon* or *blēs blejyow,* m.: **-linate,** v. *scullya p.* or *b. war*[2].
pollute, v. *mostya, deffola, *loshē·*: **-tion,** n. *mostethes, plosethes, lastethes,* m.
polypody fern, n. *redenen gwȳth,* f., col. *reden g., *marghreden,* col.
pomegranate, n. **grünaval,* m., pl. *-low.*
pomp, n. *rȳelder, gōth, solempnyta, *bobans,* m.: **-ous,** a. *gothys, stātly.*
pond, n. *pol,* m., pl. *-low, lagen, stagen,* f., pl. *-now, lyn,* f., pl. *-now;* little p., *pollen,* f., pl. *-now;* cow-p., *lyn-vugh,* m.; cattle p., *grēlyn, pol-lon,* m.; horse-p., *pol-margh, p. mergh, marghbol;* duck-p., *pol-heyjy;* goose-p., *pol-gōth, p.-godhow;* fish p., *†pysklyn;* toad p., *pol-cronogow;* tadpole p., *pol-penynnow;* frog-p., *pol-lefans;* mill p., *polvelyn;* dammed p., *crün, polgrün,* m.; clear p., *pol pür;* dirty p., *pol strong;* salt p., *pol-holan, p.-hyly;* full of p.s, *lynak, polak*: **-weed,** n. *kellyn,* m., **dowrles,* m.
ponder, v. *ombredery, studhya down.*
ponderous, a. *pōs, mür y bōs.*
poniard, n. *cledha bȳghan,* m., pl. *-dhevyow b., dagyer mōn,* m., pl. *-s m.*
pool, n.: see **pond.**
poop, n. *†aros,* m., pl. *-yow, castel a-dhelergh,* m., pl. *-stylly a.*
poor, a. *boghosek, trüan, gwan;* one who is p., *boghosek,* m., pl. *-sogyon;* to make p., *boghosekhē·*: **-ness,** n. *boghosogneth,* m.
poor-cod, n., power, fish, *gwyber,* m., pl. *-bras.*
poorly, a. *nebes clāf, gwanek.*
pop, n. *crak,* m., pl. *-kys;* with a p., *crak!*: v. *dyllo crak.*
Pope, n. *Pap,* m., pl. *Pabow, an Tassens,* m.

poplar, n. †*ēthlen,* f., col. *ēthel*; p. grove, *ēthlek,* f., pl. *-egy.*
poppy, n. †*myll,* f., pl. *-as,* **rosen-mogh,* f., pl. *-now m.,* col. *rōs, m.*; opium p., *losow cusk.*
populace, n. *pobel, tüs,* **gweryn,* f.
popular, a. *a'n bobel, geryes da,* **gwerynek, kerys gans an bobel*; p. vote, *bōth an bobel, comen voys*: **-larity,** n. *kerensa an bobel,* f.: **-late,** v. *pobla*: **-lation,** n. *pobel,* f., pl. *-blow, trygoryon,* m., pl.: **-lous,** a. *poblek.*
porcelain, n. *prȳ chēny,* m. and col.
porch, n. *porth,* m., pl. *-ow*; church-p., *portal an eglos.*
porcupine, n. *sort mür,* m., pl. *-as m.*
pore, v., p. over, *myras glew* (*orth*), *whythra bysy* (*war*[2]).
pore, n. *toll whēsa,* m., pl. *tell w.*: **-rous,** a. *tellek.*
pork, n. *kȳk mogh, k. porghel,* m.: **-er,** n. *porghel,* m., pl. *-lly.*
porphyry, n. *mēn-elven,* m.
porpoise, n. *morhogh,* m., pl. *-as,* col. *morvogh, porpus,* m., pl. *-pesow.*
porridge, n. *yōs kergh,* m.
porringer, n. *scüdel,* f., pls. *-low, -ly.*
port, n. *porth,* m., pls. *-ow, perth*; p. hole, cargo p., *port,* m., pl. *-ys.*
portable, n. *heborth, hedhō·n, a-yllyr y dhōn.*
portcullis, n. *porth-horn,* m., pl. *-ow-h.*
portent, n. *marthüs,* m., pl. *-ow, marthüsy,* m., pl. *-thojyon,* **ragarweth,* f.
porter, n. *porther,* m., pl. *-thoryon,* f. *-es,* pl. *-ow.*
portion, n. *darn,* m., pl. *-ow, ran,* f., pl. *-now, shara,* m., pl. *-ys, part,* m., pl. *-ys, kevran,* f., pl. *-now*; heritage, *ertach,* m., pl. *-ajys.*
portly, a. *brās y gorf, tew,* **corfak,* ‡*berryk.*
portmanteau, n. *mayl,* f., pl. *-ys,* **portmantel,* m., pl. *-s, sagh-hük,* m., pl. *sēghyer h.*
portrait, n. *portrayans, delynyans,* m., pl. *-ow, hevelep,* m., pl. *-ebow*: **-tray,** v. *portraya, delynya.*
portress, n., door-keeper, *portheres,* f., pl. *-ow.*
Portugal, n. *Portyngal,* f.: **-guese,** a. *Portyngalek.*
position, n. *lē,* **safla,* m., pl. *-ow*; state, *stüth, condysyon,* m.; rank, *degrē·, grē, roweth,* m.; posture, *sāf,* m.
positive, a. *hep nam, sür, certan*; a p. nuisance, *pla pür, p. hep nam*: **-ly,** adv. *hep nam, gordheweth.*
possess, v. *perghenna, pew* (def. v.): **-ion,** n. *perghenogeth, da, possessyon,* m.; take p. of, *kemeres, degemeres*; take up p., *sēsa*: **-or,** n. *perghen,* m., pl. *-nas, -now.*
possible, a. *a-ȳl bōs, possybyl*; if p., *mara kyller*; it is p., *y-hȳl bōs,* neg., *ny-ȳl bōs*; to be p. for one to do it, *sevel yn gallos dēn y wül*; if p., *mara kyllyr*: **-bly,** adv. *martesen, par hap.*
posse, n. *nerth,* m., pl. *-ow.*
post, n. *pül,* m., pl. *-yow, post,* m., pl. *-ow, pos,* m., pl. *-sys, styken,* f., pl. *-now*; p.-bag, *mayl,* m., pl.*-ys*: v. *postya*: **-age,** n. **lyther-doll,* m.: **p.-card,** n. *carten post,* f.: **p.-horn,** n. *trybeth,* m., pl. *-edhow*: **-master,** n. **postvester,* m., pl. *-trysy*: **-man,** n. **lytherwas,* m., pl. *-wesyon*: **-office,** n. **lytherva,* f., pl. *-ow.*
post-, prefix. *warle·rgh* (after n.).
posterior, n. *tȳn,* f., pl. *-yon, dywbedren,* d.
posterity, n. *hēnath,* m.
postpone, v. *hokkya, dylātya, rȳ dēth hyrra dhe*[2]: **-ment,** n. *hokkyans, dylātyans,* m.
postcript, n. *gēr warle·rgh, tam üs scryfys a-wosa* or *warle·rgh an lyther.*
posture, n. *maner omdhō·n*; erect p., *sāf,* m.; lying p., *groweth.*
pot, n. *seth,* m., pl. *-ow, pot,* m., pl. *-tow*; large, two-handled p., *pēr-seth,* m.; small p., *podyk,* m., pl. *-ygow*; earthen p., *pot prȳ*; iron p., *pot horn*; large p. for salting, etc., *bosseth* (*bussa*), m.; for storing butter, *bosseth amanyn* (*bussa 'manyn*), m.; p. for boiling, stewing, etc., †*caltor,* f., pl. *-yow,* ‡*caudarn,* m., pl. *-s, pēr,* m., pl. *-row, chek,* m., pl. *-kys.*
potato, n. *patata,* m., pl. *-tys,* **aval-dōr,* m., pl. *-low-d.*
potency, n. *nerth, gallos, crefter,* m.: **-ent,** a. *nerthek, gallosek, crēf*: **-entate,** n. *pen pow,* m.
potion, n. *dewas,* f., pl. *-wosow, ten,* m., pl. *-now, draght,* m., pl. *-ys.*
potsherd, n. *crym,* m., pl. *-yon.*
pottage, n. *brōs, cowl, yskel,* m.; mess of p., *lommen cowl,* f.
potter, n. *gwȳthor prȳ,* m., pl. *-thoryon p., potor,* m., pl. *-yon*: **-y,** n. *prȳwyth,* m., *lystry prȳ,* pl.; workplace, *prȳwythva,* f., pl. *-ow.*
pouch, n. *pors,* **jypser,* m., pl. *-ys.*
poulterer, n. *gwerther yēr,* m., pl. *-thoryon y.*: **-try,** n. *yēr,* pl.
pound, v. *brewy,* **medha.*

pound, n., sterling or weight, *püns*, m., pl. *-ow*; weight, *pōs*, m., pl. *-ow*.
pound, n., enclosure, *gwythva-lonnow*, f., pl. *-ow-l*.
pour, v. *devera, denewy, scullya*; p. back, *astevery*; p. out, *dyscarga, dyllo*.
pout, v. *gül mowys, camma dywwēüs*.
pout, n., fish, *bothak*, m., pl. *-ogas, lagater*, m., pl. *-tras*.
poverty, n. *boghosegneth*, m.; extreme p., *esow, anken*, m.
powder, n. **polter, pon*, m.
power, n. *nerth, nell, mestrynsys, maystry, danjer, gallos, fors, vertu, power*, m.; p.s, order of angels, *potestas*, m.; get, hold, in one's p., *cafos yn danjer*; that is not in thy p., *ny-sef henna y'th hallos*: **-ful,** a. *gallosek, nerthek, mēn, stowt, puyssant*: **-less,** a. *dynerth, dyallos, dyfrēth, antȳthy, dyspuyssant*.
pox, n. *pokkys*, pl., **bregh*, f.
practice, n. *ūsadow, ūs, ‡practys*, m.: **-tise,** v. *ūsya, omassaya, ‡practysya*: **-tical,** a. *hewül, drē ober*: **-lly,** adv., it is p. certain, *namnag yu sür, ogas sür yu*.
praise, n. *gormola, gologhas*, m.; in ejaculation, Praise Him! *dh'y lawa*! *prays*, m., pl. *-ys*.
prance, v. *terlemmel*.
prank, n. *prat*, m., pl. *-tys, gwary üfer*, m., pl. *-yow ü*.
prate, n. *clap*, m., *gerennow*, f. pl.: v. *clappya, clattra, gērya*.
prattle, v. *clappya kepa·r ha flogh bȳghan*: n. *clap flēghes, *mabyēth*.
pray, v. *pysy, *pederewa, *padera*; p. to, *pysy orth* or *war*²; p. God, *pysy Dew*; p. for person, *pysy rak, gans*; p. for pardon, *pysy gyvyans*; I p. you to, *my a-th-pȳs a*²; p., prithee, *y praya, dha bysy, drē dha vōth, yndella mar peugh plēsyes*: **-er,** n. *pysadow, orēmus*, m.; the Lord's P., *an Pader* (*Pater*), m.; p. for dead, *‡serēn*, m., pl. *-ys*. **-ing,** n. *pysadow*, m.
pre-, prefix *rag-*.
preach, v. *pregoth*: **-er,** n. *pregowther*, m., pl. *-thoryon*: **-ing,** n. *pregoth*, m.
precarious, a. *deantel*: **-ly,** adv. *deantel*.
precaution, n. *rakpreder, avȳ·s*, m.; take p.s, *bōs war, gorquytha, darwar* (def. v.): **-ary,** a. *a breder kens*.
precede, v. *blȳnya, mōs kens, mōs a-dhera·k, ragresek*: **-nce,** n., to take p. of, *mōs a-rak*: **-nt,** n. *ūs, üs dh'y sewya, sampel* (*kens*), m.: **-ding,** a. *ow-mōs kens, a-vē kens leverys, scryfys*, etc.
precentor, n. *penkenyas*, m., pl. *-ysy*.
precept, n. *gorhemmyn, poynt a skȳans*, m.
precincts, n., bounds, *oryon*, pl.; in its p., *yn y ogas, a-dro dhodho, a-jȳ dh'y oryon*.
precious, a. *drüth, mür y brȳs, kēr, precyous*.
precipice, n. *clegar*, m., pl. *-grow, serthals*, f., pl. *-yow, lamleder*, f., pl. *-drow*: **-itous,** a. *serth, clegerek, ledrüs, crakkya-conna*.
precipitate, v. *herdhya, tewlel, fystyna*: a. *rē a poynt*.
precise, a. *dyblans, precyous, harth, ewn, kewar*: **-ly,** adv. *precyous, hardlych, poran, pür gewar*: **-sion,** n. *ewnder, kewerder*, m.; with p., *hardlych*.
precocious, a. *für kens y dermyn, cōth drēs y ōs, *ragathves, rē a-brȳs*: **-city,** n. **ragathvetter*.
precursor, n. *ragresor*, m., pl. *-yon*.
predatory, a. *ow-whylas pray*.
predecessor, n. *dēn esa kens*, m., pl. *tüs e. k.*; my p.s, *an rē-na esa kens y'm lē-vy*.
predicament, n. *plȳt, tebel-stüth, ancombrynsy*, m.; in such a p., *yn plȳt an par-ma*.
predict, v. *profüsa, *dargana, *darleverel*: **-ion,** n. *profüsans*, m., **dargan*, f.
predisposed, a. *parys, plegadow*: **-sition,** n. *plegadow*, m.
predominant, a. *moyha, a-drȳgh*: **-nate,** v. *bōs moyha, trȳghy, maystry, gwarthevya*.
pre-eminent, a. *kens pup-oll, ughella*.
preface, n. *raglavar*, m., pl. *-ow, kens-scryf, rakscryf*, m., pl. *-ow*: v.
prefer, v., promote, *avonsya*; I p., *gwell yu genef*: **-able,** a. *gwell, dh'y dhewys*: **-ence,** n. *dewys, an pyth yu gorrys kens*: **-ment,** n. *avonsyans, remosyon*, m.
prefix, n. **rag-gorrans*, m.: v. **rag-gorra*.
prehistoric, a. *kens covath, kens y·story*: **-ory,** n. *termynyow* or *taclow kens y·story*.
prejudicate, v. *ragvrüsy*: **-ice,** n. *ragvrüs*, f.: **-icial,** a. *a-wra dregyn, üs ow-shyndya*.
prelate, n. *perlet*, m., pl. *-ys*.
preliminary, a. *kensa*; p. work, *ober darbar*: n. *darbaryans*, m.
prelude, n. *raglavar*, m., pl. *-ow*.
premature, a. *kens y ewn-dermyn, rē scon, rē a-var, r. a-dermyn, r. a-brȳs*.
premeditate, v. *raktewlel, rakpredery*.
premises, n. *chȳ*, m., *trē*, f.; on the p., *y'n chȳ, yn-trē*.
premium, n. *payment*, m., pl. *-ys, gober*, m., pl. *-brow*.

preparation, n. *darbar, dafar,* m.: **-re,** v. *darbary, dȳghtya, parüsy, araya, ‡fyttya, ‡dafar*: **-ed,** a. *parys*; to be p.d, *ombarüsy.*
preposition, n. *ragēr,* m., pl. *-yow.*
prepossessing, a. *hegar.*
preposterous, a. *drēs rēson, drēs ēghen, drēs kynda.*
prerogative, n. *gwȳr,* m., pl. *-yow.*
prescience, n. *ragaswonvos,* m.
prescribe, v. *gorhemmyn*: **-iption,** n. *gorhemmyn,* m., pl. *-ow.*
presence, n. *golok,* f., *‡presens,* m.; in my p., *y'm lok, dhe'm lok*; in p. of, *dherak, a-dherak, a-rak, a-wēl dhe*[2]; into the p. of gentlemen, *yn fās arlydhy*; because of his p., *awo·s y vōs ena.*
present, v. *rȳ*; to benefice, *avonsya, presentya*: n. *ro,* m., pls. *-ow (-how), presont,* m., pl. *-ons*: **-ation,** n., act, *rȳans,* m., pl. *-ow*: a. *omma, ena*; at the p. time, at p., *y'n ür-ma, y'n jēth hedhyu.*
presentiment, n. *ragown,* m.
presently, adv. *wharē·, scon, tōth da, totta·, a ver spȳs.*
preserve, v. *sawya, gwytha, mentēna*; foods, *kyfytha*: n., food, *kyfyth,* m., pl. *-yow*; game p., *tȳr helghya,* m.: **-vation,** n. *sawder, sawment, gwȳth, gwythyans,* m.
preside, v. *rewlya, *caderya*: **-nt,** n. *†lewyth,* m., pl. *-ydhyon, pen-rewler,* m., pl. *-loryon, *pre·sydent,* m., pl. *-ns.*
press, v. *posa, gwasca*; urge, *ynnȳa*; p. on, *ynnȳa war*[2]: n. *gwask,* f., pl. *-scow*; clothes, printing, cheese p., *g. dyllas, pryntya, kēs*: **-ing,** a. *bysy, a-rēs porres, *tēr*; p. business, *ober na-yllyr y asa pols hep gül*: **-ure,** n. *ynny, ynnȳadow, pōs,* m., *gwask,* f.
prestige, n. *roweth, worshyp,* m.
presume, v. *lavasos, bedha, desevos*: **-mption,** n. *ref,* m.; audacity, *bolder,* m.: **-mptious,** a. *mür y ref.*
presuppose, v. *raktyby*: **-ition,** n. *raktybyans,* m.
pretence, n. *fās, fayntys, falsury, ‡gül-wȳs,* m.: **-nd,** v. *facya, fēcla, dolo·s, mākya, ‡gül wȳs, dyssembla*: p. to be, *omwül*: **-nsion,** n. *fās,* m.
pretext, n. *cavanscüs,* m.; on the p. of, **war skēs.*
pretty, a. *tēk.*: **-iness,** n. *tekter, je·ntylys,* m.
prevail, v. *trȳghy, cafos an dorn ughella, gül dhe blegya, ‡prevaylya*; p. upon, *tenna, dynya*: **-ing,** a. *ūsyes.*
prevent, v. *gwytha na*[2], *gwytha worth, lesta, lettya*: **-tion,** n. *let,* m.
previous, -ly, a., adv. *kens.*
prey, v., p. on, *gül pray a*[2], **prēdhya war*[2]; p. on mind, *gwethhē·*: n. *pray, *prēth,* m.
price, n. *prȳs,* m., pl. *-yow, gwerth,* f., *cost,* m., pl. *-ys*; p. one shilling, *talvedhys* or *gwerthys a ün sols*: v. *settya prȳs war*[2], **prȳsya, talvos*: **-less,** a. *drēs prȳs.*
prick, n., point, *†brōs,* m., pl. *-ojow*; hurt, *gwan,* f., pl. *-ow;* of thorns, *gwan spern, g. drēn;* v. *gwana, pyga, brōsa*: **-le,** n. *eythen,* f., pl. *-now, drēn,* m., pl. *dreyn.*
pride, n. *gōth, ughelder,* m.
priest, n. *pronter,* m., pl. *-tyryon,* col. *prontereth, oferyas,* m., pl. *-ysy, ‡coggas,* m.; chief p., **arghoferyas,* m., pl. *-ysy*; parish p., *hembrynkyas plu,* m., pl. *-ysy p.*: **-ess,** n. *oferyades,* f., pl. *-ow*: **-ly,** a. *ave·l pronter, pronterek*: **-hood,** n. *clerjy,* m.; order, *prontereth,* m.; because of his p., *rag y glerjy, drefen y vōs pronter.*
prim, a. *methek, *kempen.*
primary, a. *kensa, pen-*; elementary, **elvennek.*
prime, n., of life, *Gwaynten ōs,* m.; in his p., *yn flowr y ōs, yn crēs y nerth*: a. *gwella, bryntyn, flowr.*
primer, n. *lyver-corn, kensa lyver,* m.
primrose, n. **bryallen,* f., pl. *-now,* col. *bryally.*
prince, n. *pryns,* m., pl. *-ncys, pensevyk,* m., pl. *-ygyon*: **-cess,** n. *prynces,* f., pl. *-ow, pensevyges,* f., pl. *-ow.*
principal, a. *pry·ncypal, kensa*; prefix, *pen-, chȳf-*: **-ity,** n. *pensevygeth,* f., *pryncy·pyta,* m., pl. *-tys.*
principle, n. *lagha,* m., pl. *-ys, dyscas,* m.
print, n. *ōl,* m., pl. *-ow, prynt,* m., pl. *-ys*: v. *pryntya, ympryntya*: **-er,** n. **pryntyer,* m., pl. *-yoryon*: **-ing,** n. **pryntyans, ympryntyans,* m.; p.-office, **pryntjy,* m.; p.-press, *gwask pryntya,* f.
prior, a., adv. *kens*: n. **prȳor,* m., pl. *-ys*: **-ity,** n. *kensa lē,* m.; that must be given p., *rēs yu gorra henna kensa*: **-ess,** n. **prȳores,* f., pl. *-ow*: **-ry,** n. *prȳorjy,* m., pl. *-ow.*
prison, n. *pryson,* m., pl. *-yow*: **-er,** n. *prysner,* m., pl. *-s.*
prithee, int. *y praydha, y praya.*
private, a. *pryva, pryveth*; p. soldier, *soudor kēth,* m., pls. *-yon, -drys k.*; in p., *yn-pryva.*
privation, n. *esow, *esewes, anken, dyvotter,* m.

privet, n. *skeswedhen,* f., pl. *-wȳth.*
privilege, n. *gwȳr specyal,* m.
privily, adv. *yn-pryva, pryveth:* **-ity,** n. *pryveta,* m.: **-y,** a. *pryva, pryveth;* p. seal, *sēl pryva,* f.
prize, n. ***prȳs,* m., pl. *-yow, gober,* m., pl. *-brow, weryson,* m., pl. *-s:* v. *synsy mür y brȳs;* be p.d by, *bōs drüth dhe*[2].
probability, n. *hevelepter,* m.: **-ble,** a. *a-ȳl bōs, dh'y waytya, gwȳrhaval:* **-ly,** adv. *del hevel, hep mar.*
probation, n. *prevyans,* m.
probe, v. *cropya, gwana.*
probity, n. *lēouta (louta), ewnder,* m.
problem, n. *colm dh'y dhygelmy,* ***problem,* m., pl. *-s.*
procedure, n. *cusül,* f., pl. *-yow, forth a wül,* f., pl. *-dhow a. w.*
proceed, v. *mōs, mōs yn-rak, lafürya:* **-ings,** n. *gwythresow,* pl.
proceeds, n. *gwayn, gober,* m.
process, n. *forth,* f., pl. *-dhow, gwythres,* ‡*proces,* m.: v.
procession, n. *processyon,* ***keskerth,* m.; in p., *yn processyon, yn ün rew.*
proclaim, v. *derȳvas, avowa:* **-amation,** n. *avȳsyans, deryvadow, gwarnyans, galow,* m.
procrastinate, v. *hokkya, dylātya:* **-ion,** n. *dylātyans,* m.
procure, v. *cafos, provya.*
prodigal, a. *scullyak, rē hēl,***gorhēl:* **-ity,** n. *sculva,* f., *larjes,* ***gorhelder,* m.
prodigious, a. *barthüsek, üthek, brās drēs ēghen.*
prodigy, n. *marthüs,* m., pl. *-ow, marthüsy,* m., pl. *-thojyon, marth,* m., pl. *-ow, tra 'varth, t. marthüsy,* f.
produce, v. *dōn, drȳ, denythy:* n. *trevas,* f., pls. *-ow, -vajow, ascor,* m.: **-ction,** n. *an pyth üs gwrēs,* m.
profanation, n. ***dysacrans,* m.: **-ne,** a. *ungrassyes, lēk, erby·n layes,* ***dyrās,* ***ansans:* v. *deffola,* ***dysacra:* **-nity,** n. *cows drōk,* ***ansansoleth,* m.
profess, v. *omrȳ, omwül, omdhysquedhes,* ‡*professya:* **-ion,** n. *galow,* ***galwesygeth,* m.; declaration, *derȳvas,* m.: **-ional,** a. *orth y* ***sōth,* *drē* ***alwesygeth:* **-or,** n. *dyscajor,* ‡*professor,* m., pl. *-yon.*
proffer, v. *profya.*
proficiency, n. *skentoleth, skȳans,* m.: **-t,** a. *skyansek, dyskys.*
profile, n. ***profȳl,* *hanter fās,* m.
profit, n. *lēs, prow, gwayn, dader,* m.: v. *gwaynya;* it will not p. us, *ny-dāl dhyn, ny-gan-bȳth prow anodho, ny-drēl dhyn dhe lēs:* **-able,** a. *dhe-lēs;* be p. to, *gül servys dhe*[2]: **-less,** a. *üfer,* ***dylēs.*
profound, a. *down:* **-dity,** n. *downder,* m.
profuse, a. *rē hēl, scullyak:* **-sion,** n. *helder, lanwes, palster,* m.
progeny, n. *lynyeth,* f., *hās,* col., *flēghes,* pl., *hēnath, yssew,* †*lyth,* m., †*agh,* f.
programme, n. ***program,* m., pl. *-mys.*
progress, n. *avonsyans, spēda, kerth,* m.; royal (summer) p., ‡*havy:* v. *mōs yn-rak, kerdhes, spēdya, sowyny.*
prohibit, v. *dyfen, defendya:* **-ion,** n. *dyfen, dyfennadow,* m.
project, n. *towl,* m., pl. *-ow, cusül,* f., pl. *-yow:* v. *sevel yn-mēs;* plan, *ervȳra, tewlel:* **-ile,** n. *arf tewlys,* f., pl. *arvow t.:* **-ion,** n. *corn,* m., pl. *kernow,* ***balek,* m., pl. *-logow,* †*el,* f., pl. *-yow.*
proletariat, n. ***gweryn,* f.
prolific, a. *üs owth-encressya, mür y ascor.*
prolix, a. *hȳr.*
prologue, n. *raglavar,* m., pl. *-ow.*
prolong, v. *hȳrhē·, ystynna, dylātya.*
promenade, n. *kerthva,* f., pl. *-ow:* v. *kerdhes, rōsya.*
prominent, a. *ughel, hewel:* **-nce,** n. *ban, lē ughel, ughelder, sevyans,* m.; p. men, *tüs a vrȳ.*
promise, n. *ambos,* m., pl. *-ow, dedhewadow,* m., *dedhewys,* f., *promys,* m., pl. *-mesys, plȳght,* m., pl. *-ys:* v. *ambosa, dedhewy, promysya:* **-ing,** a. *lün a dhedhewadow, a-ȳl yn-ta spedya, a-sowen del hevel.*
promissory, a., p. note, *scryven dedhewy,* m.
promontory, n. *pentȳ·r, penrȳ·n, rȳn,* m., pl. *-yow, pena·rth, garth,* f., pl. *-ow, rōs,* f., pl. *-yow.*
promote, v. *avonsya, müvya, scōdhya:* **-tion,** n. *avonsyans, remōsyon,* m.
prompt, a. *a-brȳs, frēth, dewh·ans, trom:* **-er,** n. *o·rdenary,* m., pl. *-s:* **-itude, -ness,** n. *frethter, tromder,* m.: **-ly,** adv. *a-poynt;* over-p., *rē a-poynt.*
prone, a. *a'y wroweth, a-hēs;* p. to, inclined, liable to, *gostyth* or *parys dhe*[2].
prong, n. *forgh,* f., pl. *fergh(y);* three-p.d, *tȳrforgh.*
pronoun, n. ***rag-hanow,* m., pl. *r.-hynwyn.*
pronounce, v. *leverel,* ***tonya;* p. on. *rȳ brüs war*[2], *gērya a-dro dhe*[2]: **-d,** a. *crēf:* **-nunciation,** n. *leveryans,* m.

proof, n. *prōf,* m., pl. *-ovow.*
prop, n. *pül,* m., pl. *-yow, jȳst,* m., pl. *-ys*: v. *settya pül dhe*[2], *synsy.*
propaganda, n. *plontyans,* m.
propagate, v. *plontya, denythy*: **-tion,** n. *denythyans,* m.
propensity, n. *whans,* **dewha·ns,* m.
proper, a. *lēl, gwyw, poran, ewn, onest, compes, mās*; it is p., *y-teleth, y-coth, y-tegoth*; his p. place, *y dyller tȳthy*; as is p., *del deleth, del gōth, del degōth*: **-ly,** adv. *drē gomposter, drē vaner dha, yn-fās, lēl-.*
property, n. *da,* m., *pȳth,* m., pls. *-ow, taclow, substans,* f., *possessyon,* m., *mebyl,* col.
prophet, n. *profüs,* m., pl. *-y*: **-ess,** n. *profüses,* f., pl. *-ow*: **-etic,** a. *profüsek*: **-ecy,** n. *profüsans,* m., pl. *-ow*: **-esy,** v. *profüsa.*
propitiate, v. *dyserry*: **-tious,** a. *plegadow*: **-tion,** n. *hebasca,* f., *dyserryans, dewhelans, ankenek,* m.
proportion, n. *kehavalder,* **kemusür, myns,* m.; in p., *orth an myns*; of fine p.s, *gwrēs yn-ta*: v. **kehesy,* **kemusüra, ranna.*
propose, v. *mynnes, ervȳra, müvya,* **kynnyk*; we don't p. to go far, *ny-jujjyn mones neppell*: **-sal, -sition,** n. *müvyans,* m., **kynnyk,* m., pl. *-ygow.*
proprietor, n. *perghenek,* m., pl. *-ogyon, perghen,* m., pls. *-nas, -now*: **-ship,** n. *perghenogeth,* m.
propriety, n. *onester, composter, dy·nyta,* m.
prosaic, a. **dyawen.*
proscribe, v. *dyfen, dyvrōa.*
prose, n. *yēth plēn,* f., **prōs,* m.
prosecute, v. *cuhüdha, sewya*: **-ion,** n. *cuhüdhans,* m.: **-or,** n. *cuhüdhor,* m., pl. *-oryon, cuhüdhyas,* m., pl. *-ysy,* †*cuhüdhojak,* m., pl. *-ogyon.*
prospect, n. *gwēl,* m. or f., pl. *-ow, vu,* m., pl. *ys*; fig., *gwaytyans,* m.: v. *whylas mūn*: **-ive,** a. *yn termyn a-dhē*: **-or,** n. *whyler,* m., pl. *-oryon.*
prosper, v. *sowyny, spēdya*: **-ity,** n. *sowynyans,* m., *spēda,* f., †*füs,* f., **berth,* m.: **-ous,** a. *sowyn,* †*kevothak.*
prostrate, a. *a'y wroweth, a-hēs, omwhelys dhe'n dōr*: **-ion,** n. *squythans,* m.
protect, v. *dyffres, gwytha, bōs scōs dhe*[2], **dywalla*; p. from, *gwytha rak*: **-ion,** n. *gwȳth, dyffresyans,* m.; fig., *scōs,* m.: **-or,** n. *gwythyas, dyffresyas,* m., pl. *-ysy.*
protest, n. *crothval*: v. *leverel erby·n, crothvolas, gül crothval, cows a-drüs.*
Protestant, n. *Protestant,* m., pl. *-ans.*
protract, v. *ystynna, hȳrhē·, dylātya*: **-ion,** n. *ystynnans,* m.
protrude, v. *sevel yn-rak, omherdhya mēs*: **-usion,** n. *omherdhyans,* m.
protuberance, n. *both,* f., pl. *-ow.*
proud, a. *gothys, stowt, prowt*; p. girl, *flownen,* f., pl. *-now.*
prove, v. *prevy*; p. oneself, *ombrevy.*
proverb, n. *lavar coth,* m., pl. *-ow c.*
provide, v. *provya, o·rdena* (*orna*), *darbary, dȳghtya,* ‡*dafar*: **-nce,** n. *Dew, darbaryans, ragavȳ·s, fürneth,* m.: **-r,** n. *darbarer,* m., pl. *-oryon*: **-ision(s),** n. *bōs, dafar, pega·ns, sosten, provȳans,* m.; provided that, conj., *mar*[4](*s*).
province, n. *pow,* m., pl. *-yow*: **-cial,** a. *a'n pow.*
provisional, a. *rak tro, a-wra servya.*
provoke, v. *serry, annȳa, pȳga, sordya,* ‡*provochya*: **-ocation,** n. *serryans,* m.
prow, n. *pen a-rak,* †*flūr-rak,* m.
prowess, n. *maystry, roweth,* m.
prowl, v. *whylas pray, crowdra*: **-er,** n. *crowdrer,* m., pl. *-roryon.*
proximity, n. *ogas,* **nester,* m.
proxy, n. *kemerer lē dēn aral*; by p., *drē gannas.*
prudence, n. *fürneth, dothter,* m.: **-nt,** a. *für, dōth, skyansek.*
prudish, a. *methek drē fayntys.*
prune, v. *dyvarra, dyscorenna, skethry*: **-ning,** n., cut twig, **gwresken,* f., col. **gwresk,* pl. *-scow*: **-ning-knife,** n. *collel gam, c. lowarther,* f.
prune, n. *plumen sēgh,* f., pl. *-now s.*
pry, v. *whylas glew*; p. into, *whythra.*
psalm, n. *salm,* m., pl. *-ow*: **-ter,** n. *sautour,* m., pl. *-s, lyver salmow*: **-tery,** n. *sautry,* m., pl. *-s.*
pseudonym, n. **leshanow,* **fük-hanow,* m., pl. *-hynwyn, hanow-scryfa.*
pshaw, int. *tetyvaly*!
pubes, n. *kethorva,* f.: **-erty,** n. **kethe·rȳeth,* f.
public, a. *a'n bobel, a-rak tüs*: n. *an bobel, an düs,* f.; in p., *a-rak* or *a-wēl tüs*: **-ly,** adv. *a-dhera·k an bobel, a-rak tüs, a-wēl dhe bup dēn-oll.*
publication, n. *dyllans,* **publysyans,* m.: **-ish,** v. *gorra a-lēs, publysya, dyllo*; p. false reports, *dolō·s*: **-isher,** n. *dyller lyvrow,* m., pl. *-loryon l.,* **publysyer,* m., pl. *-s.*
public-house, n. *tavern,* m., pl. *-yow, dewotty,* m., pl. *-ow.*

publicity, n. *deryvadow, avȳsyans,* m.
pudding, n. **pudyn,* m., pl. *-s*; bag p., *pellen,* f.; hasty p., †*yōs, pot gwyn,* m.; black p., *gosogen,* f.
puddle, n. *pollen,* f., pl. *-now, lagen,* f., pl. *-now.*
puff, v. *whetha, whyfla, pyffya*; p. up, *hothfy, whedhy*: n. *wheth,* m., pl. *-ow*: **-ed-up,** a. *omwhethys, prowt.*
puffin, n. *pōpa,* m., pl. *-pys, nath,* m., pl. *-as.*
pugnacious, a. *a-gar omlath.*
pule, v. **pȳpya, crȳa yn-whan.*
pull, n. *ten,* m., pl. *-now*; backwards p., *kylden,* m., pl. *-now*: v. *tenna, hālya*; p. back, *kyldenna*; p. down, *tenna dhe'n dōr*; p. together, *kestenna*: **-ing,** n. *ten,* m., *tenva,* f.
pullet, n. *mabyar,* m. or f., pl. *-yēr.*
pulley, n. *rōs,* f., pl. *-ow, r.-lovan.*
pulp, n. *bewesen,* f., *glüs,* m.; to make into p., *glüsa.*
pulpit, n. ‡*gogell,* f., pl. *-ow,* ‡*purcat,* m.
pulse, n., peas, beans, lentils, *pȳs, fāf, gweg-bȳs,* col.
pulse, n., heart-beat, **pols,* m.; to find the p., *tava an gwȳthy*: **-sate,** v. *lamma, *polsa.*
pulverise, v. *mala dhe bon, brewy münys.*
pumice-stone, n. *mēn pumys, m. scaf,* m.
pump, n. **pump,* m., pl. *-ys*: v. **pumpya.*
pumpkin, n. **pompyon,* m., pl. *-s.*
punch, n. *boxas,* m., pl. *-xesow, bom,* m., pl. *-myn, squat,* m., pl. *-tow*: v. *boxesy, squattya*; p. hole, *telly, gwana.*
punctilious, a. *precyous*: **-ly,** adv. *dour*: **-tual,** a. *a-poynt, a-dermyn, war nuk*: **-tually,** adv. *a-dermyn, a-brȳs*: **-tuate,** v. *poyntya, dyberth lavarow*: **-tuation,** n. *poyntyans, dyberthva lavarow,* f.: **-ture,** n. *toll,* m., pl. *-tell, gwan,* f., pl. *-ow, tellyk,* m., pl. *-ygow*: v. *telly, gwana*: **-d,** a. *toll, tollek, tellek.*
pungent, a. *lym, tyn, wherow*: **-ncy,** n. *wherowder, tynder, lymder,* m.
punish, v. *kessydhya, punsya, pē dhe*[2], *rȳ pewas a dhrocoleth*: **-ment,** n. *kessydhyans, pȳn,* m., *payn,* m., pl. *-ys*; inflict p. on, *dyala.*
puny, a. *gwan, dynerth, *ydhyl.*
pupil, n. *dyskybel,* m., pl. *-blon*; of eye, *bew an lagas, map l.,* m.
puppet, n. *popet,* m., pl. *-tys.*
puppy, n. *colyn,* m., pl. *kelyn*; little p., *kelynyk,* m., pl. *-ygow.*
purchase, v. *prena*: n. *pren,* m.; hold, *dalghen,* f., pl. *-now*: **-r,** n. *prener,* m., pl. *-noryon.*
pure, a. *pür, tēr, gwergh, glan, fȳn*: **-rity,** n. *glander, *püreth,* m.
purge, v. *purjya*: n. *purjyans,* m.
purple, a., n. *purpur, glasrüth, rüdhlas,* m.
purport, n. *styr, vertu,* m.
purpose, n. *mynnas, towl, ente·nt,* m., *porpos,* m., pl. *-ys, cās,* m.; for the p., *rag an cās*; to no p., *yn-üfer*; p. of his mind, *bōth y vrȳs*; for the p. of, *rak, awo·s*; on p. to, *a-borpos dhe*[2]; to that p., *dhen p.-na*: v. *mynnes, bōs ervȳrys dhe*[2], ‡*porposya*: **-ly,** adv. *a-borpos.*
purse, n. *pors,* m., pl. *-ys.*
pursue, v. *sewya, helghya*: **-r,** n. *helghyas,* m., pl. *-ysy*: **-uit,** n. *helgh, helghyans,* m.
pursuivant, n. **pursevont,* m., pl. *-ns.*
purulent, a. *podrethek, lynak.*
purvey, v. *provya.*
pus, n. *lyn,* m.
push, v. *pokkya, herdhya, pyltya*; p. off, *herdhya dhe-vēs*; swing, etc., *lesca*: n. *pok,* m., pl. *-kyow, herdhyans,* m.
put, v. *settya, gorra*; p. in a claim, *pottya quarel*; p. together, *junnya*; p. out, *drȳ* or *gorra yn-mēs*; light, etc., *dyfüdhy, megy, ladha,* ‡*gorra dhe varow*; p. to sea, *mōra*; p. on, clothes, *gwysca, omgwetha*; shoes, *arghenna*; p. off, remove, *dy'sky*; postpone, delay, *dylātya, hokkya, lettya*; p. up with, *perthy orth, godhevel*; p. before, †*raggorra*; p. forth, *ystynna*; p. in order, *o·rdena*; p. to death, *gül marow.*
putchook, n., incense, *costa,* m.
putrefaction, -ridity, n. *podrethes,* m.: **-rify,** v. *pedry*: **-rid,** a. *podrethek, pedrys.*
puzzle, v. *ancombra, müskegy*: n. *ancombrynsy,* m.: **-ling,** a. *a-ancomber, maglys, na-wodher pandra gül anodho.*

Q

quack, v. **quakkya*; give q. remedies, *pomstrya*: n. *quak,* m., pl. *-kys*; q. doctor, *pomster,* m., pl. *-s, *cragh-vedhek,* m., pl. *-dhyvyon*: **-ery,** n. *pomstry,* m.
quadruped, a. *peswartrōsek*; q. animal, *mȳl peswar y dreys.*
quagmire, n. *lȳs lenky,* m.
quail, v. *plynchya.*
quail, n. †*trynk,* f., pl. *-ncas.*
quaint, a. *coynt*; q. thing, *coyntys,* m.: **-ness,** n. *coyntys,* m.

quake, v. *crenna, deglena, crȳsya*: **-king,** n. *crȳs*, m., pl. *-yow*; q. grass, **crȳswels*, col.
Quaker, n. *Crenner*, m., pl. *-noryon.*
qualification, n. *composter, gwywder*, m.; what are his q.s? *fatel yua gwyw?*: **-fy,** v. *tempra, ewna, gül bōs gwyw.*
quality, n. *gnās*, f., *prȳs*, m.
qualm, n. *glōs*, f., pl. *-ow.*
quandary, n. *ancombrynsy*, m.
quantity, n. *myns, cals*, m.; in verse, *keheseth*, m.; great q., *showr, lower*, m.; small q., *boghes, nebes*, m.
quarantine, n. **quarantȳn*, m.; in q., *dyberthys.*
quarrel, v. *bōs yn strȳf* (*orth*), *kedrynya, stryvya, argya, omdhal*: n. *dalva*, f., *quarel*, m. **tryn, kedryn*, f., *strȳf*, m., pl. *-ow*: **-er,** n. *strȳfor*, m., pl. *-yon*, f., *-ores*, pl. *-ow*: **-some,** a. *a-gar strȳf*; q. person, *strȳfor*, m.
quarry, n. *menglēth*, m., pl. *-edhyow*: **-man,** n. *mengledhyor*, m., pl. *-yon.*
quarry, n., prey, *pray*, m.
quart, n. *quart*, m., pl. *-ys.*
quarter, n. *quartron* (*-ton*), m., pl. *-ys*; region, *quarter*, m., pl. *-trys*; q.s, *e·rberow*, m.; mercy, *trūeth*, m.: v. *quartrona*: **-ly,** adv. *pup trȳ mȳs*: **q.-sessions,** n. *brüslys trȳ mȳs*, f.: **-tet,** n. *pe·swarden*, m.: **-tern loaf,** n. *torth quartron*, f.
quartz, n. *can-tȳr, candȳr*, m.
quaver, v. *whybya, crenna*: n. *whybyans, cren*, m.; music, **quāver*, m., pl. *-s.*
quay, n. *cay*, m., pl. *-ys.*
queen, n. *myghternes*, f., pl. *-ow*, †*revanes*, f., pl. *-ow*: **-ly,** a., adv. *bryntyn, ave·l myghternes.*
queer, a. *astra·nj, coynt.*
quell, v. *fetha, megy, coselhē·*; outbreak of fire, *dyfüdhy.*
quench, v., thirst, *dysēgha*; fire, *dyfüdhy*: **-ing,** n. *dysēghans, dyfüdhyans*, m.
quern, n. *brow*, f., pl. *-yow.*
querulous, a. *dyscontentys, ow-kȳny.*
query, v. *govyn*: n. *govyn, govenek, govynnadow*, m.
quest, n. *whylas*, m.
question, v. *govyn, examnya*: q. thoroughly, *apposya*: n. *govynnadow, govyn*, m., *questyon*, m., pl. *-s*: **-able,** a. *dowtys.*
quick, a. *üskys, scaf, scon, snel, quyk, fast, stryk*; the q. and the dead, *an bew ha'n marow*: n. *bew*, m.; to the q., *bys y'n bew*: **-en,** v. *bewhē·*: **-ly,** adv. *üskys, fast, quyk, yn-scaf, yn-scon, yredy, prest, dewha·ns, a-dhewha·ns*; very q., *tōth da, totta·, tōth brās, tōth mēn, gans mür a dōth, a verdermyn*; as q. as possible, *mar scon del yllyr*: **q.sand,** n. *trēth-lenky*, m., *trēth bew*, **lonktrēth*, m.: **q.silver,** n. *arghans bew*, m.
quiescent, a. *cosel, tawesek.*
quiet, a. *cosel, dyson*; to be q., *tewel, powes*; be q! *taw sy! taw dha vȳn! gas dha son! syns dha glap!*: n. *powes, cosoleth, calmynsy*, m.: **-en,** v. *coselhē·, spavenhē·*, **destewel*: **-ly,** adv. *yn-cosel, clōr, hep whetha corn, war gam, w. dha g.*, etc.: **-ness,** see **-quiet.**
quill, n. *plüven, quyllen*, f., pl. *-now.*
quillet, n. *pastel-dȳr*, f., pl. *-llow tȳr.*
quilt, ‡*kewlet*, m., pl. *-tys*, **colghes*, f., pl. *-ow.*
quince, n. **quyn*, m., pl. *-ys.*
quinsy, n. **squynancy*, m.
quire, n. **quayer*, m., pl. *-ys.*
quit, v. *gasa, quytya*: **-tance,** n. *aquytyans*, m.
quite, adv. *glan, quȳt, pür, clēr, poran, cowal, yn-perfyth*; prefix, *cowl-.*
quits, a. *compes* (*gans*), *aquytyes, omaquytyes.*
quiver, v. *deglena, crenna*: n. *cren*, m.
quiver, n., for arrows, *gōn sethow*, f., pl. *-ow s.*
quoit, n. *coyt*, m., pl. *-ys.*
quotation, n. *devyn*, m., pl. *-now*: **-te,** v. *devynnes, alejya*; to q. his own words, *drē y anow ee·f*; but what need is there to q., *saw pan ethom yu a alejya?*
quoth, v. *yn-meth*, pl. *yn-medhans* (3 pers. only).

R

rabbit, n. *conyn*, m., pl. *-as*; to hunt r.s, *conynessa* (inf. only); r. skin, *conyngen*, m.; r. warren, *conery, godegh-conyn*, m.
rabble, n. *tüs kēth*, m., pl. **rascayl*, m.
rabid, a. *conneryak*: **-bies,** n. *connar*, f.
race, n. *ke·nethel*, f., pl. *-thlow, lȳm*, m., pl. *-ow*, †*agh*, f., pl. *-ow*, **hyl*, m.; human r., *lynyeth mapden*, f., *kynda mapden*, m.; r. course, *resekva*, f., pl. *-ow*; r. horse, *resekvargh*, m., pl. *-vergh*; tide r., *frōs*, †*rēs*: v. *resek, chassya*: **-r,** n. **rēsor*, m., pl. *-yon*, **resegyth*, m., pl. *-ydhyon*: **-cial,** a. *kenethlek.*
rack, v. *tenna, tormentya*: n. *rastel*, f., pl. *-lly, restel*; torture, *jyn tormentya*: **-ed,** a. *yn-ten.*
racket, n. **raket*, m., pl. *-tys*; noise, *trōs, hubbadullya*, m.

radiance, n. *golewder, golowyjyon, splander, golowys,* m.: **-nt,** a. *golow, splan, owtewynya.*
radish, n. *redyk,* m., pl. *-ygow.*
raft, n. **scath-clōs,* f., pl. *-ow-c.*
rafter, n. *styll,* m., pl. *-yow,* †*keber,* f., pl. *-brow.*
rag, n. *pyllen,* f., pl. *-now, skethen,* f., pl. *-now, clowt,* m., pl. *-ys*: **-ged,** a. *pyllenek, skethennek,* **pylyonek.*
ragamuffin, n. *tellek,* m., pl. *-ygyon, brȳbour, losel,* m., pl. *-s, pylyak,* m., pl. *-yogyon.*
rage, n. *coler, sōr brās,* m., *connar*: v. *serry yn-frās, connery.*
ragwort, n. †*maderē· brās,* m., **owr y dāl,* m.
raid, v. *ewhȳas*: n. *ewhȳans, omsettyans,* m.
rail, v. *raylya, deraylya, gēsya, gül gēs* (a^2).
rail, n. *pren,* m., pl. *-yer, pül,* m., pl. *-yow, clethren,* f., pl. *-now,* col. *clether*: **-ing,** n. *kē pülyow,* m., pl. *-ow p.* **rayl,* m., pl. *-ys.*
railway, n. *forth-horn,* f., pl. *-rdhow h., hens-horn,* m., pl. *-sy h.*
raiment, n. *dyllas,* m., pl. *-ajow, gwysk,* m., pl. *-scow.*
rain, n. *glaw,* m.; r.drop, *glawen, dagren,* f., pl. *-now*; r. storm, *cowas,* f., pl. *-wosow*; it threatens r., *yma· ow-degensewa cowas*; gather to r., *glūthenna*: v. *gül glaw*; it is r.ing, *yma·'n glaw ow-codha, yma· ow-cül glaw*: **-bow,** n. *gwarak an glaw,* f., pl. *-regow a. g., camneves,* f. (‡*camdhavas,* m.): **-ing, -y,** a. *glawek*; r. weather, *kewer lyp.*
raise, v. *drehevel, sevel*; r. strife, *sordya bresel*; rear, bring up, *maga*; r. up again, *dastrehevel, gül dhe dhasserghy*; exalt, *exaltya*; be r.d, strife, etc., *sordya*: **-ing,** n. *drehevyans,* m.
raisin, n. *fygesen an howl,* f., col. *fyges a. h.,* **fygesen Malyk,* f., col. *fyges M.*
rake, n., garden r., *racan,* m., pl. *-ow*; hay r., **rastel,* f., pls. *-lly, restel*: v. **ratha, racanna.*
rally, v. *dascuntell*; r. round, *resortya dhe²*: n. *dascuntellyans,* m.
ram, n. *horth,* m., pl. *-rdhas*: v. *herdhya*: **-mer,** n., hand-r., *horben,* m., pl. *-now.*
ramble, v. *gwandra, rōsya*: **-r,** n. *rōsyer,* m., pl. *-yoryon, gwandryas,* m., pl. *-drysy.*
rampart, n. *fōs,* f., pl. *-ow, scons,* m., pl. *-ys, gwal,* m., pl. *-low.*
ranatra, n., water insect, *peswar-paw,* m., pl. *-as.*
rancid, a. *crēf y vlas, mousak, trēlyes.*
random, a. *dyrewl*; at r., *hep medra, whymwham.*
range, n., series, *stüs,* f., pl. *-ow*; reach, *lēs, gallos,* m.; cooking r., **slabba,* m., pl. *bys.*
rank, n. *degrē·,* m., pl. *-ys, dy·nyta,* m., pl. *-tys, ordyr,* m., pl. *-drys, roweth stāt, grē,* m.; high r., *stāt-ughel*; row, *rew, renk,* m.; men of high r., *tüs ughel*: v. *o·rdena,* **renkya.*
rank, a. *mousak*; of growth, *gwyls*; r. treachery, *traysonpür*; grow r., *gorthevy, gordevy.*
ransack, v. *whylas glew, pylla.*
ransom, n. *daspren, raunson,* m.: v. *dasprena, raunsona*: **-er,** *dasprenyas,* m., pl. *-ysy.*
rant, v. *predheges*: **-er,** n. *predhegor,* m., pl. *-yon.*
rap, n. *pethyk,* m., *knouk,* m., pl. *-kys*; I don't give, care, a r. for him, *anodho ny-rōf oy, ny-settyaf gwel-gala,* etc.
rapid, -ly, see **quick, -ly**: **-ity,** n. *toth, scafter,* m.
rapine, n. **ravyn,* m.
rapt, a. *rafsys, gyllys y ena mēs a'y gorf*: **-ure,** n. *rafsyans, gwynvȳs, tranjyak,* m., *lowena,* f.
rare, a. *trawythys, tanow,* **dybals*: **-bit (Welsh),** n. *kēs pebys,* m.: **-ly,** adv. *boghes-venough, namenough, scant* (with neg.): **-ity,** n. *tanowder,* m.; object, *tra scant nag-üs kefys,* m., pl. *taclow s. n.-u. k.*
rascal, n. *atla,* m., pl. *-lyon, drōkwas, harlotwas,* m., pl. *-wesyon, drōk-coscar,* col., *drōk-pollat,* m., pl. *-ys, gal,* m., pl. *-ow, knava,* m., pl. *-vys, lorel, gadlyng,* m., pl. *-s, sherewa,* m., pl. *-wys, harlot,* m., pl. *-los, jawdyn,* m., pl. *-s, cam,* m., pl. *-mow*: **-ly,** a., prefix, *drok-, harlot-*: **-ity,** n. *harlotry,* m.
rash, a. *dybreder, dyswar*: **-ness,** *fowt preder,* m.
rash, n. *tarth,* m.
rasher, n. *golyth mogh,* m., pl. *-yon m.*
rasp, n. **rathel,* f., pl. *-low,* **lȳf,* f., pl. *-yvyon*: v. **ratha,* **rathella.*
raspberry, n. **avanen,* f., col. *avan,* **mōren rüth,* f., col. *mōr r.*
rat, n. *logosen vrās,* f., col. *logas brās*; r. infested place, *logosek,* f., pls. *-egy, -egow*: **-catcher,** n. *legessa,* m., pl. *-syon.*
rate, n. *prȳs, cost,* m.; assessment, *toll,* f., pl. *-ow*; at the r. of, *herwyth, worth myns a²*; at that r., *drē henna, mars yu gwȳr henna*; at any r., *yn nep cās, pyna·k a-wharfo*; going at a great r., *ow-mōs tōth brās*; first-r.,

bryntyn: v., scold, *gerya, tavasa*; value, *synsy, talvos*.

rather, adv., sooner, *kens, kensa*; somewhat, *nebes*; I had r., *gwell vȳa genef*; r. than you should be vexed, *kens del vy serrys*; the r., *dhe gens*; but r., between adjs., *yn-dar*.

ratify, v. *fasta, fasthē·*: **-fication,** n. *fasthēans*, m.

ratio, n., according to the r., *worth an myns*.

ration, n. *ewn-ran*, f., pl. *-now*: v. *ewn-ranna*.

rattle, n., instrument, **rüglen*, f., pl. *-now*; sound, *son*, m., pl. *-yow*; death r., *ronk, renkyas*, m.: v. *cryghylly, dasseny, *rügla*.

ravage, v. *rafna, pylla, deffola*.

rave, v. *müskegy, mōs yn müscogneth, connery*.

raven, n. †*marghvran*, f., pl. *-vrȳny, brān vrās*, f., pl. *brȳny brās*.

ravenous, a. *nownek brās, dhodho ewl vrās dybry*; I am r., *nown blȳth a-m-büs*.

ravine, n. *keynans*, m., pl. *-ow*.

ravish, v. *rafsya*: **-ing,** a. *mür y dhelȳ·t*.

raw, a. *ēr, crȳf, hep y barüsy*.

ray, n. *golowyn*, m., pl. *-now, golowys an howl*, m., *dewyn*, m., **sethen*, f., **lagasyn*, m., pls. *-now*.

ray, n., fish, *raya*, m., pl. *-s, carlȳth*, f., pl. *-ow*; starry r., *grȳja*, m.; cuckoo-r., *calamajȳna*, m.; spotted r., *tāl dywy*.

raze, v. *dyswül dhe'n dōr*.

razor, n. **alsen*, f., pl. *-now*; r. fish, *kyllygen*, f., pls. *-ygy, -ygys*, col. *kyllyk*.

re-, prefix *as-, das-*, causing special mutations.

reach, v. *drehedhes, drȳ yn-mēs, hedhes, ystynna*: n., of water, *efander dowr*, m.; out of r., *na-yllyr drehedhes dhodho*.

react (to), v. *gül fara* (a^2): **-ion,** n. *fara*, m.

read, v. *rēdya*; well r., *hedhysk*: **-er,** n. *rēdyor*, m., pl. *-yon*, f. *-res*, pl. *-ow*: **-ing-desk,** n. **letryn*, m., pl. *-ys*.

ready, a. *parys*; a r. answer, *gorthyp frēth*; r. for that day, *erby·n an jēth-na*; to make r., *parüsy*; make or get r., *fyttya dhe²*, *gül parys*; r. made, *gwrēs hag oll*: **-dily,** adv. *redy, yredy, sür-redy, pür barys, hep ynny, hep awhe·r, prest*; the more r., *dhe gens*: **-diness,** n. *mal*, m.; in r., *parys*.

real, a. *gwȳr, lēl, a'n bȳs-ma*: **-ity,** n. *gwȳryoneth*, m., *taclow an bȳs-ma*.

realise, v. *aswonvos, convedhes*.

really, adv. *hep fraus, hep wow* (*heb ow*), *hep flows, hep whethel, defrȳ·, yn-tefrȳ·, yntyogel, yn-whȳr*; sarcastically, *yē*!

realm, n. *gwlascor*, f., pl. *-ow*.

ream, n. **rȳma*, m., pl. *-mys*.

reanimate, v. *gül dhe dhasvewa, dasenawy*: **-ion,** n. *dasvewnans*, m.

reap, v. *myjy*: **-er,** n. *myjer*, m., pl. *-oryon, myjwas*, m., pl. *-wesyon*, †*myjyl*, m., pl. *-ow*: **-ing-hook,** n. *cromman*, m., pl. *-ow*.

reappear, v. *dewheles, dōs yn golok* or *omdhysquedhes arta*.

rear, v., bring up, *maga, drehevel, mēthryn*; of horse, *sevel* or *omdrehevel war y dreys a-dhelergh*: a. *delergh*; in the r., *a-dhelergh, helergh*; in his r., *war y lergh*; towards the r., *wor' tu delergh*: **-ed,** a. *denys, megys, drehevys*: **-er,** n. *mager*, m., pl. *-goryon*.

reason, n. *skyla, kēn, prak, praga*, m., *rēson*, m., pl. *-s*; motive, *achēson*, m., pl. *-ys*; intellect, *skȳans*, m., pl. *-ys*; for that r., *rag henna*; to be a r., *skyla* (def. v.): v. *argya, dyspūtya, rēsna, campolla, *polla*: **-able,** a. *dōth, herwyth rēson*: **-ing,** n. *argument*, m., pl. *-ns, rēson*, m., pl. *-s*.

rebel, n. *rebel*, m., pl. *-s, omsevyas*, m., pl. *-ysy*: v. *omsevel, gustla, rebellya*: **-lion,** n. *rebellyans*, m.: **-lious,** a. *gorth, a-wra omsevel*.

rebind, v. *daskelmy*.

rebirth, n. *daskenesygeth*, m.: **-born,** a. *daskenys*.

rebound, v. *daslemmel*.

rebuild, v. *dastrehevel, dassevel*: **-t,** a.

rebuke, n. *kereth*, f., *reprēf, rebük*, m.: v. *rebükya, keredhy, reprēfa*, ‡*chekkya, chastȳa*.

rebuy, v. *dasprena*: **-er,** n. *dasprenyas*, m., pl. *-ysy*.

recall, v. *perthy cōf a²*, **ascōfhē·*; call back, *gelwel trē*.

recant, v. *nagha* or *trēlya cowsesow*.

recede, v. *kyldenna, omdenna*.

receive, v. *degemeres, kemeres, receva*; as guest, *yntertaynya*: **-ceipt,** n. *aquytyans*, m.: **-ceptacle,** n. *dafar*, m., *lester*, f., pl. *lystry, vessyl*, m., pl. *-s*: **-ception,** n. *kemeryans, degemeryans*, m.; of guests, *yntertaynment*, m., pl. *-mens, recevans*, m.; favourable r., *kemeryans da*: **-cipient,** n. *degemerer*, m., pl. *-oryon*.

recent, a. *a-dhewedhes, noweth*; the most r. news, *an newodhow dewetha*: **-ly,** adv. *a-dhewedhes, agensow, degensow, nyns-yu nep-pell*; less r., *nyns-yu mar bell*.

recess, n. *kyl*, m., pls. *-yow, -yer, skyl*, m., pl. *-yow*.

reciprocal, a. *pup y gȳla, an ȳl y gȳla*; before vbs., *om-*^{2}, prefix: **-te,** v. *rȳ kemmȳ·s.*
recitation, n. *dyth,* m., pl. *-ys, devyn,* m.,
reckless, a. *dybreder, hep rach.*
pl. *-now*: **-te,** v. *kewsel dyth, devynnes, derȳvas.*
reckless, a. *dybreder, hep rach.*
reckon, v. *amontya, nyvera, rekna, acontya* (*comptya*); count on, *jujjya*: **-ing,** n. *reken,* m., pl. *-knys, acontyans,* m.
recline, v. *growedha, posa.*
recluse, n. *ancar,* m., pl. *-coryon.*
recognise, n. *convedhes, aswon*: **-ition,** n. *aswonvos,* m.
recoil, v. *trebüchya, kyldenna*: n. *kylden,* m.
recollect, v. *ombredery, perthy cōf a*^{2}, **ascofhē·*; I r., *yma· cōf dhym*: **-ion,** n. *covath,* m., *cōf,* m., pl. *-covyon*; to lose r., *gasa an covath.*
recommend, v. *comendya*: **-ation,** n. *gēr da, comendyans,* m.
recompense, n. *gober,* m., pl. *-brow, pewas, weryson,* m.: v. *tylly, rewardya, gobra.*
reconcile, v. *gül bōs ünverhē·s*: **-iation,** n. *kessenyans, ünverhēans,* m.
reconnoitre, v. *aspȳa.*
reconstruct, v. *daswül, dastrehevel*: **-ion,** n. *daswrȳans, dasformyans,* m.
record, n. *covath,* m., pl. *-ow, record,* m., pl. *-ys*; gramophone r., *sonscryfa,* m.: v. *cōfhē·, recordya*: **-er,** n. *covathor,* m., pl. *-yon*; flute, *recordya,* m., pl. *-dys.*
recount, v. *derȳvas, dasnyvera.*
recourse, n., to have r. to. *mōs dhe*^{2}, *gül defnyth* or *whylas gweres a*^{2}.
recover, v., health, *omwellhē·, sawya, yaghhē·*; get back, *cafos arta, daskemeres, dascafos,* **reke·vera*; cover again, *gorhery arta, rȳ gorheras noweth dhe*^{2}: **-y,** n. *restoryta, rekevrans,* m.
recreant, n. *negedhys,* m., pl. *-yjyon.*
recreation, n. *gwary, dydhana,* m.
recruit, n. *soudor noweth,* m., pl. *-yon n.*
rectangle, n. *fygur peswar corn,* m.: **-gular,** a. *pedrak, peswarcornek.*
rectify, v. *composa, ewna.*
rector, n. *pronter,* m., pl. *-tyryon,* **rector,* m., pl. *-yon*: **-y,** n. *pronterjy, rectorjy,* m., pls. *-ow.*
recumbent, a. *ow-crowedha, a'y wroweth.*
recur, v. *wharfos arta, dewheles*: **-rence,** n. *dōs arta.*
recusant, n. *negedhys,* m., pl. *-yjyon.*

red, a. *rüth*; blood r., *cough, gosrüth*: **-den,** *rüdhya, coughhē·*: **-dish,** a. *rüdhyk.*
redeem, v. *prena, dasprena, ‡redēmya*: **-ed,** a. *dasprenys*; to be r., *prena*: **-er,** n. *dasprenyas,* m., pl. *-ysy*; R., *Sylwador, Savyour, ‡Redēmyer,* m.: **-ption,** n. *daspren, prena, ‡redempsyon,* m.
red-headed, a. *pen-rüth.*
rediscover, v. *dascafos.*
red-ochre, n. *†meles,* m.; r.-o. paint, ruddle, *†lyw meles,* m.
redouble, v. *deublegya, moghhē·* or *encressya dywwyth.*
redoutable, a. *mür dh'y dhowtya, üthek.*
redoubt, n. *lē kēryes* or *scons a-rak.*
redress, n. *remedy, ewnans, ewnder,* m.: v. *ewna.*
redstart, n. **tyngough,* m., pl. *-as.*
reduce, v. *lehē·, gül bōs lē*; r.d, to ashes *leskys dhe lüsow*; r.d to penury, *gyllys ysel rag esow*: **-uction,** n. *lehēans,* m.
redwing, n. *sevellak,* m., pl. *-legas.*
reed, n. *corsen,* f., pl. *-now,* col. *cors, kers, kenen,* f., col. *kēn, penrüthen,* col. *-rüth*; thatching r., *cala to*; bundle of thatching r., *orren,* f., pl. *-now*; r. bed, *kenak,* f., pls. *-negy, -negow*; r. swamp, *kersek,* f., pls. *-egy, -egow*; r.-grown, a. *kersek.*
reef, n. *crȳb,* f., pl. *-ow*; of sail, *plēk,* m., pl. *-egow.*
reek, n. *mōk,* m.; of smell, *flēr,* m.: v. *megy, flērya*: **-ing,** *a-vēk, flērys.*
reel, n. **rolbren,* m., pl. *-nyer*: v. *mōs a-derdro*; wind, *trēlya, trōyllya.*
re-establish, v. *dasformya, dassevel.*
reeve, n. *mēr,* m., pl. *-as.*
refectory, n. *†bewdern,* m.
refer to, v. *campolla, meneges, kewsel a*^{2}.
referee, n. *brüsyas,* m., pl. *-ysy, brüsor,* m., pl. *-yon.*
reference, n. *campollans,* m.; character, *dustüny da.*
refill, v. *astevery, daslenwel*: n. *asteveryans, daslanwes,* m.
refind, v. *dascafos.*
refine, v. *pürhē·, afȳna.*
reflect, v. *dastewynya, gül hevelep*; consider, *ombredery, predery*: **-ion,** n. *hevelep,* m., pl. *-ebow, skēs,* m., pl. *-ow.*
reform, v. *amendya, gwellhē·*; form again, *dasformya*: **-ation,** n. *dasformyans,* m.
refractory, a. *stordy, gorth.*
refrain (from), v. *hepcor, sparya, sevel orth, powes hep, omwytha rak, omdenna.*

refrain, n. *pen-pusorn,* m., pl. *-sernow*; to sing the r., *pusornas.*
refresh, v. *dysēgha, dysquytha*: **-ment,** n. *megyans, crowst, bōs ha dewas, sosten,* m.
refuge, n. *harber, clōs,* m., pl. *-ys, scovva,* f., pl. *-ow, cüth,* m.; religious, *meneghy, meneghyjy, teghyjy,* m., pl. *-ow*: **-gee,** n. †*fōesyk,* m., pl. *-ygyon.*
refund, v. *astevery, pē arta*: n. *asteveryans,* m.
refurbish, v. *dasclanhē·.*
refusal, n. *nagh, sconyans,* m.: **-se,** v. *nagha, sconya*: **-ser,** n. *negedhys,* m., pl. *-yjyon,* **negeth,* m., pl. *-ydhyon.*
refuse, n. *sersyow, scübyon,* pl. *atal,* col.
refute, v. *conclūdya.*
regain, v. *daskemeres, dascafos,* **rekevra.*
regal, a. *rȳal, bryntyn.*
regale, v. *gōlya.*
regard, n., consideration, *fors,* m.; esteem, *brȳ, grē, rē·outa,* m.; in my r., *a-m-govys-vy*; with r. to, *yn-kever*; pay r. to, *gül vrȳ a*[2]; kind r.s, *gorhemmynadow a'n gwella*: v., think, *predery*; look at, *whythra*; esteem, *gül vrȳ a*[2], *regardya, synsy*; as r.s me, *y'm kever*: **-ing,** prep. *yn-kever*: **-less,** a. *dybreder*; r. of, *hep predery a*[2].
regency, n. *rewl yn lē myghte·rn,* m.: **-t,** n. *rewler y. l. m.,* m., pl. *-loryon y. l. m.*
regenerate, v. *dastenythy, daskenethly*: a. *daskenesyk*: **-tion,** n. *dastenythyans, daskenesȳgeth,* m.
regiment, n. **caslu,* m., pl. *-yow.*
region, n. *bro,* f., pl. *-yow, cōst,* m., pl. *-ys, pow,* m., pl. *-yow, ranvro, randȳr,* f., pl. *-yow, quartron,* m., pl. *-ys, pastel-vro,* f., pl. *-llow-bro*; wooded r., **argōs*; sea r., **arvōr.*
register, n. *cōflyver,* m., pl. *-vrow, cōfrol,* f., pl. *-yow, record,* m., pl. *-ys*: v. *cōfscryfa*: **-trar,** n. *cōfscryfor,* m., pl. *-oryon*: **-try,** n. *cōflyverva,* f.
regret, n. *edrek, edrega, govyjyon, moreth, cüth,* m.; cause for r., *dȳeth*: v., I r., *cüth a-m-büs, drok yu genef, codhys ōf yn edrek, yma· edrek dhym*: **-able, -ful,** a. *morethek, cüdhyjyk*: **-fully,** adv. *yn moreth, cüth dhodho, yn-forethek.*
regular, a. *ewn, compes, rewlys*; a r. thief, *lader pür, lader hep nam*: **-ity,** n. *ewnder, composter,* m.: **-ate,** v. *rewlya, o·rdena, governya*: **-ation,** n. *rewl,* f., pl. *-ys, rewlyans,* m.: **-ator,** n. *rewler,* m.
rehearsal, n. *assayans, dasleveryans,* m.: **-se,** v. *omassaya, dasleverel rannow gwary.*
reign, v. *rēgnya, rewlya*: r. together, *kesrēgnya*: n. *rewl, rēgnyans,* m.; during the r. of that king, *ha'n myghtern-na ena rēgnyes.*
reimburse, v. *atylly*: **-ment,** n. *atta·l,* m.
rein, n. *fron,* f., pl. *-now*: v., to r. in, *frona.*
reinforce, v. *confortya, crefhē·, socra*: **-ment(s),** n. *socor,* m.
reiterate, v. *leverel yn-fenough.*
reject, v. *denagha, sconya, hepcor, tewlel dhe-vēs, dastewlel*: **-ion,** n. *sconyans,* m.
rejoice, v. *dydhana, lowenhē·, omlowenhē·, hüthhē·, rejoyca*: **-ing,** n. *lowender, hüdhykter,* m., *joy,* m., pl. *-es.*
rejoin, v. *metya arta*; reply, *gortheby*: **-der,** n. *gorthyp,* m., pl. *-ebow.*
rejuvenate, v. *dasyowynkhē·, gül bōs yowynk arta.*
relapse, v. *dascodha*: n. *dascoth,* m.
relate, v. *leverel, derȳvas*; connect, *ünya*: **-tion,** n., report, *deryvadow,* m.; kin, *car,* m., pl. *kerens*; paternal, maternal r.s, *kerens abarth tās, mam*; near r., *car ogas*; very near r., *pür ogas car*; my nearest r.s, *ow gōs nessa*; r.s, *tüs, ēghen,* f., *neshevyn,* col. *nessa,* m., pl.; in r. to, *yn-kever*: **-tive,** a. *yn-kever, herwyth*: n.: see **relation.**
relax, v. *lowsel, dysquytha*; abate, *coselhē·, lehē·*; from worry, *dyserry*: **-ation,** n. *powes,* m., *powesva,* f.
release, v. *dyllo, delyfrya,* ‡*relēsya*; r. from obligation, *aquytya*; r. from trap, **dyvagly*: n. *delyfrans, lyfrēson,* **gores,* m.; of soul, *enewores,* m.
relent, v. *rūthy, dyserry*: **-less,** a. *dybyta.*
relevant, a. *a-dheseth, a-long.*
reliable, a. *dyogel, lēn, lēl, gwyryon*: **-ance,** n. *trest, crejys, kyfyans, fydhyans,* m., *fȳth,* f.
relic, n. **crēr,* m., pl. *-yow.*
relief, n. *hebasca,* f., *dyffrēsyans, gweres, remedy*: **-ieve,** v. *hebaskhē·, dyffres, socra, sewajya, gweres.*
religion, n. *cryjyans, relyjyon,* m., *fȳth,* f., *lagha,* m., pl. *-ghys, lay,* f., pl. *-es*: a. *cryjyk, sans.*
relinquish, v. *dascor, hepcor, gasa.*
reliquary, n. *crērva,* f., pl. *-ow.*
relish, n. *blas, sawor,* m.: v. *blasa, sawory.*
reluctance, n. *anvōth,* m.: **-t,** a. *hell*; to be r., *trȳnya, perthy danjer*; I am r. to, *dȳeth*

mür yu dhym, pōs yu genef (*gül*, etc.): **-tly,** adv. *a'y anvōth.*

rely on, v. *fydhya yn, trestya, kyfy, omscodhya war*².

remain, v. *sevel, tryga, gortos, remaynya*: **-der,** n. *remenant,* m., pl. *-ns, an ran aral,* f., *an pyth üs gesys,* m.: **-s,** n. *remanans,* m., pl.; ruins, *magoryow,* f., pl. *crellas,* m.; human r., *corf marow,* m.

remake, v. *daswül.*

remand, v. *danvon arta yn-dan wȳth.*

remark, n. *lavar,* m., pl. *-ow*: v., observe, *nōtya, avȳsya*; say, *leverel*: **-able,** a. *coynt, marthys, dh'y nōtya*; r. thing, *aneth,* m., pl. *-ow.*

remedy, n. *yly,* m., pl. *-ow, sawment,* m., pl. *-mens, losowen,* f., pl. *-wys, medhy·gȳeth,* f., *gweres, cür, remedy,* m.: v. *gwellhē·, sawya, gweres.*

remember, v. *perthy cōf a*², *cofhē·, remembra a*²; I r., *yma· cōf dhym a*²; they wish to be r.ed to you, *ymons-y ow-corhemmyn dheugh-why*: **-brance,** n. *cōf, covath,* m., *cofva,* f., *remembrans, recordasyon,* m.

remind, v. *cofhē·, drȳ dhe gōf, remembra dhe*².

remiss, a. *lent, logh, lows*; to be r. towards, *bōs dȳek yn-kever.*

remit, v. *dewheles, tylly, danvon*; pardon, *gava*: **-mission,** n. *remedy, dewhelans, gyvyans,* m.

remnant, n. *remenant,* m., pl. *-ns, penyn,* m., pl. *-now.*

remonstrance, n. *crothval, plēnta, clēm,* m.: **-ate,** v. *plēntya, crothvolas* (*croffolas*), *gül crothval war*².

remorse, n. *edrega, edrek, moreth,* m.: **-ful,** *dhodho edrek, morethek*; he was r., *edrek a-n-kemeras*: **-less,** a. *dydrüeth, dybyta.*

remote, a. *pell, down y'n pow.*

removal, n. *remōsyon,* m.: **-ve,** v. *remüvya, gorra mēs a'y lē, *dylēa*; clothes, *dy'sky.*

remunerate, v. *rȳ gober* or *weryson, *gobra, tylly, rewardya*: **-ion,** n. *gober,* m., pl. *-brow, weryson,* m.

rend, v. *squardya, dyswül, terry, skethenna, *regy.*

render, v. *tylly*; r. powerless, etc., *gül bōs dyfrēth,* etc.: **-ing,** n. *trēlyans, rȳans,* m.

renegade, n. *negedhys,* m., pl. *-yjyon.*

renew, v. *daswül, *nowedhy, gül arta, *nowethhē·, *dasnowethhē·*: **-al,** n. *daswrȳans, *nowedhyans,* m.

rennet, n. *cowl,* m.; decotion of yellow bedstraw, *godroth,* m.

renounce, v. *nagha, hepcor, dascor*: **-unciation,** n. **hepcor* (*-yans*), m.

renovate, -tion,: see **renew, -al.**

renown, n. *hanow da, gēr da, brȳ,* m.: **-ed,** a. *gēryes da, mür y hanow, kywhethlys.*

rent, n., tear, *squard,* m., pl. *-yow*; money, *rent,* m., pl. *-ys*: v. *rentya*; a. *squerdys.*

repair, v. *ewna, daskewera*; r. the loss, *astevery an coll*: **-aration,** n. *atta·l,* m.; make r., *gül amendys.*

repast, n. *prȳs-bōs, prȳs,* m., pl. *-yow.*

repay, v. *atylly, aquytya, tylly*; God r. you! *Dew tal dhyso*! *Dew re-dallo* (*Durdala*) *dheugh-why*!: **-ment,** n. *atta·l,* m.

repeal, v. *defendya*: n. *defendyans,* m.

repeat, v. *dasleverel, leverel* or *gül arta*: **-ed, -edly,** a., adv. *menough, arta hag arta.*

repel, v. *pellhē·, gorra dhe'n fo, gül dhe gyldenna.*

repent, v. *codha yn edrega, repentya, kemeres edrek*; I r., *edrek a-m-büs, yma· edrek dhym*; you'll r. it, *ty a-n-ōl*; to cause to r., *drȳ dhe vōs cüdhyjek, cüdhyjykhē·*: **-ance,** n. *edrega, edrek, cüth, *cüdhyjygeth, *repentons,* m.: **-ant,** a. *cüdhyjyk, repentys*; he was r., *edrek o dhodho, e. a-n-kemeras.*

repetition, n. *dascows,* m.; because of its r., *awo·s y vōs gwrēs arta.*

repine, v. *omwethhē·.*

replace, v. *collenwel lē*; put back, *gorra yn y lē arta.*

replenish, v. *lenwel, collenwel, astevery.*

replete, a. *lün, gwalghys, lenwys*: **-tion,** n. *quoff, gwalgh, *gorlanwes,* m.

reply, n. *gorthyp,* m., pl. *-thebow*: v. *gortheby*; r. pertly, *camwortheby.*

report, n. *derȳvas, deryvadow, danvonadow,* m., *gēr,* m., pl. *-yow*; noise, *son,* m., pl. *-yow, tarth,* m., pl. *-rdhow*; he is of good r., *gēryes da yu, anodho yma· nōtyes mür dhader*: v. *danvon, meneges, derȳvas, nōtya*: **-ing,** n. *derȳvadow,* m.

repose, n. *powesva,* f., *powes, cusk,* m.: v. *powes, cusca, *dysquytha.*

represent, v. *dysquedhes*; r. others, *bōs cannas, mōs yn lē rē erel*: **-ation,** n. *dysquedhyans, fygūr,* m.; make r.s, *dysquedhes kēn*: **-ative,** n. *cannas,* f., pl. *-ow.*

repress, v. *compressa, frona, dova, tempra, megy*: **-ion,** n. *compressans,* m.

reprieve, n. *spās,* m.: v. *grontya spās.*

reprimand, n. *keredhyans,* m., *kereth,* f.: v. *kesky, keredhy, shyndya.*
reprint, v. **dasprynty a*: n. **daspryntyans,* m.
reproach, n. *kereth,* f., *vylyny, bysmē·r, mewl, reprē·f, rebü·k,* m.: v. *cably, keredhy, blamya, reprēfa, sclandra, chastya, rebükya.*
reprobate, n. *emskemünys,* m.: v. *reprēfa, emskemünya*: a. *ungrassyes, dyrās.*
reproduce, v. *denythy, gül moy an keth sort*: **-ction,** n. *denythyans,* m.; copy, *equal, ymach, havalder,* m.
reproof, -prove: see **reproach.**
reptile, n. *prȳf,* m., pl. *prevyon.*
republic, n. **republyk,* m.
repudiate, v. *nagha, sconya, dyflasa*: **-tion,** n. *nagh, sconyans,* m.
repugnance, n. *cās,* m.; extreme r., *glōs,* f., pl. *-ow*: **-nt,** a. *dyflas, hegas, dysawor, casadow*; that is r. to me, *cās yu genef henna.*
repulse, v. *pellhē·, fetha a-dhyworth, gorra dhe'nfo*: n. *pellhēans,* m.: **-sive,** a. *casadow, fest hager*: **-siveness,** n. *hakter,* m.
reputation, n. *brȳ, hanow,* m.; good r., *hanow da, gērda,* m.: **-table,** a. *worthy*: **-te,** v. *henwel, kywhethla*: n. *worshyp,* m.: **-ted,** a. *brüsys*; he is r. to be, *y-tybyer y vōs.*
request, n. *govynnadow, desȳr, gorholeth, requyryans,* m., *govenek,* m., pl. *-nygyon*: v. *requȳrya, govyn, desȳrya.*
require, v. *dervyn, requȳrya, govyn, erghy, *gorholy*; I r. it, *bysy* or *rēs yu dhym y gafos*: **-ment,** n. *gorholeth,* m.
requisite, a. *bysy, a-rēs, requȳryes*: **-tion,** n. *gorholeth,* m.
requital, n. *aquytyans,* m.; harsh r., *drog-gras,* m.: **-te,** v. *aquytya, tylly.*
rescue, v. *delyfra, gweres, sawya*: n. **rescous,* m.
research, n. *studhyans,* m., *whylas,* inf.
resemblance, n. *hevelep, hevelepter, ‡hevelenep, ‡havalder,* m.: **-ble,** v. *bōs haval, favera, hevelly*; they greatly r. one another, *pür haval yns an ȳl dh'y gȳla*: **-bling,** a. *haval.*
resent, v. *serry orth*; we r. that, *ny a-sōr rak bōs henna gwrēs*: **-ful,** a. *serrys, sōr dhodho*: **-ment,** n. *sōr,* m.
reserve, v. *gwytha, gorra a-denewan*; he is r.ed, *omrewlys yu, gwell yu ganso tewel es leverel*: n. *an pyth üs gwythys, omwyth.*
reservoir, n. *crün,* m., pl. *-yow, crünva,* f., pl. *-ow, pol-grün,* m., pl. *-low-g.*
reside, v. *annedhy, tryga, bōs trygys*: **-nce,** n. *trygva,* f., pl. *-ow, chȳ,* m., pl. *treven, anneth,* f., pl. *-edhow, *annethva,* f.; in place-names, *bōs,* f., pl. *-sow*: **-nt,** n. *tryger,* m., pl. *-oryon*: **-ding,** a. *trygys, annedhys, a-dryk, ow-tryga.*
resign, v. *dascor, omdenna*: **-ation,** n. *omdennans,* m.; submission, *omblegyans,* m.
resist, v. *sevel* or *settya orth, offendya*; r. verbal attack, etc., *gül defens*: **-ance,** n. *offens, defens,* m.
resolute, a. *harth, stowt, colonnek.*
resolution, n. *cusül,* f., pl. *-yow, ervȳrans, determyans, mynnas crēf,* m.
resolve, v. *ervȳra, cusülya, determya, conclūdya.*
resonant, a. *heglew.*
resort, n., place, *resort,* m., pl. *-ys*; as a last r., *oteweth, fowt gweres aral*: v. *resortya, repayrya.*
resound, v. *dasseny.*
resource, n. *devys,* m., pl. *-ys, jyn,* m., pl. *-nys, towl,* m., pl. *-ow*: **-ful,** a. *jolyf a dhesevos, a-wōr lȳes cast.*
respect, n. *revrons, brȳ, worshyp, rē·outa,* m.; way, *maner,* f., pl. *-ow*; in r. of, *yn-kever*; in every r., *yn pup poynt* or *ēghen*; pay r. to, *gordhya*; with r. to him, *a'y wovys-ef*: v. *gül vrȳ a*[2], *enora, synsy*: **-ability,** n. *worshyp, onester,* m.: **-able,** a. *onest, wordhy*: **-ful,** a. *hüvel, ow-cül vrȳ*: **-ing,** prep. *yn-kever*; r. him, *a'y wovys-ef, yn y gever-ef*: **-ive,** a., they went their r. ways, *y ēth pup a'y du*: **-ively,** adv. *yn kettep pen, yn kever an ȳl ha'y gȳla.*
respiration, n. *tenna ha dyllo anal, anellans,* m.: **-ory,** a. *a'n anal*: **-re,** v. *anella.*
respite, n. *spās,* m.; without r., *anhedhek, hep hedhy* or *powes.*
resplendent, a. *splan, golow, ow-terlentry.*
respond, v. *gortheby*: **-nse,** n. *gorthyp,* m., pl. *-ebow.*
responsibility, n. *charj,* m., pl. *-ys, omgemeryans,* m.; I will take the r. for it, *my a ragtho*; to take r. for, *omgemeres rak*: **-ble,** a., be, make oneself r. for, *omgemeres rak, mōs rak*; r. people, *tüs a-yllyr ynna fydhya.*
rest, n. *powes, cosoleth, dysquyth,* m., *powesva,* f.; the r., others, *an rē erel, kēn rē, an rememant,* m., *an ran aral,* f.; all the r. of them, *oll aga hynsa*: v. *powes, hedhy, *dysquytha*; of spear, *restya*; r. on, against, *posa war*[2], *orth*: **-ful,** a. *cosel*: **-ing-place,** n. *powesva, trygva, growethva,* f.: **-less,** a. *hep powes, dybowes, ‡fyslak*: **-lessness,** n. *fowt powes.*

restaurant, n. *chȳ-dybry, *bōsty,* m., pl. *-ow.*
rest-harrow, n. **tag-ardar,* m.
restitution, n. *resto·ryta, dascor,* m.
restoration, n. *resto·ryta, *dastrehevyans,* m.: **-re,** v. *restorya, *dastrehevel, dascor, *astevery*; r. to life, *drȳ dh'y vewnans, gül dhodho dasvewa*; r. his wits, *drȳ dhodho y skȳans, y dhrȳ dh'y skȳans.*
restrain, v. *frona, lettya, ‡chekkya*: **-t,** n. *fron,* f., pl. *-now, let,* m.
restrict, v. *strotha, settya fȳn dhe*[2]: **-ion,** n. *let,* m., pl. *-tys, fȳn,* f., pl. *-yow.*
result, n. *sewyans, deweth,* m.; as a r., *drē henna*: v. *sewya, omsewya, dewedha, wharfos.*
resume, v. *dalleth arta, daskemeres.*
resurrect, v. *gül dhe dhēn dasserghy*: **-ion,** n. *dasserghyans,* m.
resuscitate, v. *dasvewa, gül dhe dhēn dasvewa*: **-ation,** n. *dasvewnans,* m.
retail, v. *dasquertha, gwertha yn rannow, yn shoppys*: r. price, *prȳs shoppa, p. drē ran,* m.: **-er,** n. *gwycor,* m., pl. *-yon, dasquerther,* m., pl. *-thoryon.*
retain, v. *gwytha, synsy*: **-er,** n. *o·majer,* m., pl. *-s, dēn-coscar,* m., pl. *tüs c.*; r.s, *tüs kēth,* f., *mēny,* m.
retake, v. *daskemeres.*
retaliate, v., speech, *gortheby*; action, *venjya*: **-tion**: see **revenge.**
retch, n. *wheja*: **-ing,** n. *whejans,* m.
retie, v. *daskelmy.*
retinue, n. *coscar,* col., *mēny,* m., †*tȳlu,* m., pl. *yow.*
retire, v. *mōs war-dhelergh, kyldenna, omdenna*: **-ment,** n. *kylden, omden,* m.
retort, n. *gorthyp,* m., pl. *-thebow*; chemistry, *gwēder cam,* f.: v. *gortheby.*
retrace, v., r. one's steps, *sewya olow y dreys.*
retract, v. *denagha, omdenna*: **-ion,** n. *nagh,* m.
retreat, v. *mōs* or *fȳa dhe'n fo, kyldenna, tēghy, mōs war-dhelergh*: n. (*mōs, fȳa, dhe'n*) *fo,* m., *tēgh, kylden, clōs,* m.; place of r., *teghyjy,* m., *argel,* f., pl. *-ow.*
retrench, v. *lehē·, berhē·* or *trēghy dhe-vēs cost, *erbysy.*
retribution, n. *dȳal, venjyans,* m.; certain r., *sür-gessydhyans,* m.
retrieve, v. *cafos arta, dascafos*: **-er,** n. *kȳ dowr,* m., pl. *cün d.*
retrospect, n. *golok war-dhelergh,* f.: **-ive,** a., **-ively,** adv., *ow-myras war-dhelergh.*
return, v. *dewheles, dōs* or *mōs trē*; give back, *dascor, restorya, danvon* or *rȳ trē*; of mechanism, etc., *trēlya, trebüchya*: n. *dascor,* m.; in r., *yn atta·l*; make r. to, *aquytya.*
reunion, n. **dasünyans,* m.: **-nite,** v. **dasünya.*
reveal, v. *dyscüdha, dysquedhes, dysclosya*: **-velation,** n. *dysquedhyans,* m.
revel, n. *gōl,* m., pl. *-yow*: v. *gōlya, omlowenhē·*: **-ry,** n. *gōlyans,* m.
revenge, n. *dȳal, drog-grās, hardygrās, yflagrās, venjyans,* m.; sudden r., *trom-dȳal,* m.; to take r. on, *dȳala, venjya, kemeres dȳal war*[2], etc.: v. *dȳala*; be r.d on, *gül, tewlel, tylly* or *kemeres dȳal war*[2], *venjya*: **-ful,** a. *a-gar dȳala, *venjyabyl.*
revenue, n. *rent,* m., pl. *-ys.*
reverberate, v. **dasseny*: **-tion,** n. **dassenyans, dasson,* m.
revere, v. *gordhya*: **-nce,** n. *revrons,* m.: **-nd,** a. *revrond.*
reverse, v. *trebüchya, kyldenna, gül mōs war-dhelergh, trēlya an pyth üs a-wartha dhe woles*: n., r. side, *kyl,* m., pls. *-yow, -yer, *gorthenep,* m.; upset, set-back, *pervers, kylden,* m., *anfüs,* f.; on the r. side, *a-barth a-woles*; the r. side, *an tu aral,* m.
revert, v. *trebüchya, trēlya, mōs war-dhelergh.*
review, v. **dasqueles*: n., of soldiers, *dasquel,* f. or m.; critique, *tybyans,* m.; journal, *jornal,* m., pl. *-s.*
revile, v. *cably, mylyga, tebel-henwel.*
revise, v. *ewna, amendya*; r. it, *myras arta orto.*
revival, n. *dasvewnans, dasserghyans,* m.: **-ve,** v. *dasvewa, dasserghy*; actively, *gül dhe dhasvewa.*
revoke, v. *omdenna, terry, defendya.*
revolt, n. *gustel,* m., pl. *-stlow, sordyans,* m.: v. *gustla, sordya erby·n rewl*: **-lution,** n. *gustel,* m., pl. *-tlow, *revolūsyon*; turn, *tro, trēlyans a-dro,* m.
revolting, a. *hegas, casadow, dyflas, pür hager y weles* or *glewes.*
revolve, v. *trēlya, mōs a-dro.*
reward, v. *tylly, rewardya, gobra, ‡talvesa*: n. *gober,* m., pl. *-brow, pewas,* m., *weryson, reward,* m., pl. *-ys*; get as a r., *dyndyl*; to be r.ed by, *bōs rewardyes a-dhyworth.*
reynard, n. *lostek,* m., pl. *-togas.*
rhetoric, n. **re·toryk,* m.
rheumatism, n. **rem,* m., *cleves ysyly,* m.: **-tic,** a. **remüs, claf a'y ysyly.*

rhinoceros, n. *üncorn*, m., pl. *-kern*, **tron-gornvyl*, m., pl. *-as*.
rhubarb, n. **trenkles*, m., **tavol Turkey*, col.
rhyme, n. *rȳm*, m., pl. *-ys*: v. *rȳmya*.
ribald, a. *plos*: **-ry,** n. *ploswas*, m., pl. *-wesyon*.
rib, n., body or boat, *asen*, ‡*asowen*, f., pl. *asow*.
ribbon, n. †*snod*, m., pl. *-ys*, **ryban*, m., pl. *-ys*.
rich, a. *rych*, †*golüsak*, †*kevothak*; the r. powerful man, *an rych gallosek*; of tin ore, *scof*; r. tin lode, *scoven*, f., pl. *-now*: **-es,** n., *rychys*, m., *pythow*, pl.
rick, n. *bern*, m., pl. *-ow*, *das*, f., pl. *-deys*; r.yard, **ȳslan*, f., pl. *-now*.
rickets, n. *lēghow*, pl.
rid, v. *delyfrya*: **-dance,** n. *delyfryans*, m.
riddle, n., sieve, *ryder*, *croder*, m., pl. *-drow*, **rydel*, m., pl. *-low*; puzzle, *desmyk*, m.: v. *crodra*, *rydra*; r. with holes, *telly*: **-d,** a., with holes, *tellek*.
ride, v., on horseback, *marghogeth*; r. forth, *ewhȳas*; r. in car, etc., *mōs yn car*, etc.; r. cycle, *marghogeth war vargh horn*: **-r,** n. *marghak*, m., pl. *-ghoryon*, **marghoger*, *-gor*, m., pl. *-goryon*, **marghoges*, f., pl. *-ow*, *ewhȳas*, m., pl. *-ysy*.
ridge, n. *crȳb*, f., pl. *-ow*, *trüm*, *drüm*, m., pl. *-yow*, *keyn*, m., pl. *-ow*, *mujoven*, f., pl. *-now*; of rick, *plēth*, f., pl. *-as*; of roof, *crȳb an chȳ*, *keyn an to*, m.; r.-beam, *nenbren*, m., pl. *-yer*.
ridicule, n. *scorn*, *gēs*, m.: v. *scoryna*, *gēsya*, *gül gēs a*[2], *gül bōs scorn oll a'n pow*: **-lous,** a. *wharthüs fōl*.
rifle, v. *pylla*.
rifle, n. *gon*, m., pl. *-nys*.
rift, n. *fals*, m., pl. *-lyow*.
rig, n. **takyl*, *taclans*, *gwysk*, m., pl. *-scow*: v. *tacla*, *gwysca*: **-ging,** n. **takyl*, m., *lovonow-gorhel pup ēghen*, pl.
right, a. *ewn*, *compes*, *kewar*, *gwyw*, *gwȳr*, *a-dhevȳ·s*; very, quite, *pür*, *poran*, *fest*; set r., *amendya*, *gorra dhe gür*; come r., *dōs dhe gür*; r. away, at once, *pür-dhewha·ns*; that's r., you are r., *gwȳr a-leverough*; it serves you r., *da aquytys ough*; r. in the middle, *poran*, *ewn* or *prest y'n crēs*; just the r. thing, *pyth a dhevȳ·s*; r. up to, *fast bȳs yn* or *dhe*[2]: v. *ewna*, *composa*: n. *gwȳr*, *ewnder*, m.; r. (hand), *dȳghow*, *dyghow-barth*, f.; r.-handed person, **dȳghowyas*, m., pl. *-ysy*; on the r., *a-dhȳghow(dhe*[2]); to have a r. to, *pew* (def. v.); by r.s, *a lagha*; you have no r. to speak, *nyns-yu dheugh* or *ragough-why kewsel*: **-eous,** a. *gwyryon*: **-eousness,** n. *gwyryoneth*, m.: **-ful,** a. *tȳthyak*; r. place, *tyller tȳthy*.
rigid, a. *tyn*, *serth*, **dywethyn*: **-ity,** n. **serthter*, **dywethynder*.
rigorous, a. *garow*, *cales*, *strayt*: **-our,** n. *caletter*, *serthter*, m.
rill, n. *goveryk*, m., pl. *-ygow*, *gwythen*, f., pl. *-now*.
rim, n. *mȳn*, m., pl. *-yon*, **cans*, m., pl. *-ow*; of wheel, **cammek*, f.
rind, n. *rüsken*, f., col. *rüsk*, *ken*, m. (no pl.).
ring, n., circle, **kelgh*, m., pl. *-ow*; finger r., *bysow*, m., pl. *-ewow*, †*modrewy*, f., pl. *-ow*; sound, *son*, m., pl. *-yow*: v. *seny*.
ringdove, n. *colomen cōs*, f., pl. *-nas c*.
ringleader, n. *pen-strȳfer*, m., pl. *-foryon*.
ringworm, n. **darwesen*, f., col. *darwes*.
rinse, v. *golghy*.
riot, n. *gustel*, m., pl. *-tlow*, *deray·*, m., pl. *-ys*: v. *gustla*.
rip, n. *squard*, m., pl. *-yow*: v. *squardya*, **regy*.
ripe, a. *athves*: **-n,** v. *athvejy*: **-ness,** n. *athvetter*, m.
ripple, n. **crȳgh*, m., pl. *-yon*: v. **crȳghy*: **-d,** a. **crȳgh*.
rise, v. *drehevel*, *sevel*, *yskynna*; r. sheer, *serthy*; of tide, *morlenwel*, *dōs*; r. again, *dasserghy*: n., of ground, *godolgh*, m., pl. *-ow*, dim. *godolghyn*, m., pl. *-now*; of tide, *morlanow*, m.: **-sing,** n. *yskynyans*, *dre-hevyans*, *drehafva*, f.
risk, n. *peryl*, m., pl. *-yow*: v. *peryllya*.
rite, n. *solempnyta*, m., pl. *-tys*, **devos*, f., pl. *-ow*.
rival, n. *kestrȳfor*, m., pl. *-yon*: v. **gorvyn-nes orth*: **-ry,** n. **gorvyn*, *kestrȳf*, m.
rive, v. *falsa*.
river, n. *avon*, f., pl. *-venow*, *ryver*, m., pl. *-s*; r. estuary, *hayl*, m.; r. mouth, †*aber*, m., pl. *-ow*.
rivet, n. **gorthkenter*, f., pl. *-trow*, *ryvet*, m., pl. *-tys*: v. **gorthkentrewy*, **ryvetya*: **-er,** n.
rivulet, n. *gover*, m., pl. *-ow*: see **rill.**
roach, n. †*talek*, m., pl. *-ogas*.
road, n. *forth*, f., pl. *-rdhow*, *hens*, m., pls. *-y*, *-yow*; old r., disused, *henforth*, f., pl. *-rdhow*; parting of r.s, *forth dybarth*; high-r., *forth-vür*; through r., *forth lan*; rail-r., **forth-horn*: **-side,** n., by the r., *ryp an forth*: **-stead,** n. *ancarva*, f., *lojja lystry*, m.

roam, v. *gwandra, rōsya.*
roan, a. *gell kesten.*
roar, n. *üs,* m., pl. *üjow, bedhyglans,* m.: v. *tarenna, bedhygla, üja*; of wind, *whyfla*: **-ing,** n., as wind or fire, *whyflyn, ow-whyfla.*
roast, v. *rōstya*; r. meat, *golyth,* m., pl. *-yon.*
rob, v. *ladra, robbya, pylla, rafna*: **-ber,** n. *lader,* m., pl. *-dron, robbyor,* m., pls. *-s, -yon,* **gwyll,* m., pl. *yow, ladres,* f., pl. *-ow*: **-bery,** n. *ladrans,* **ladrynsy,* m.
robe, n. *pows,* f., pl. *-yow*: v. *gwysca pows.*
robin, n. *rüdhak,* m., pl. *-ogas,* **bronrüth,* m.
robust, a. *crēf,* **nerthek.*
rock, v. **lesca, gwaya yn-rak ha war-dhe-lergh*: **-ing,** n. *lesk,* m., pl. *-ow*: r. chair, *cadar lesk,* f.
rock, n., great, *carrek,* f., pl. *carrygy*; r. or stone, *mēn,* m., pl. *meyn*; flat r., *lēgh,* f., pl. *-ow*; r. mass, bed-r., *carn,* m. or f., pl. *-ow*; r. pile, *carneth,* f., pl. *-edhow*; to clear away r.s, *dyveyna*: **-ery,** n. *lowarth meynek,* m.: **-y,** a. *carnak, carregek, meynek*; r. ground, *carnak, meynek,* f., pls. *-egy, -egow*; mass of loose r.s, *rajel,* m.
rockling, n., three-bearded r., *plumsūgan,* m., pl. *plumsūgas, plumsūgesen,* f., pl. *plumsūgas, penvagas,* m.; five-bearded r., *pen-barfüs,* m., pl. *-y, bonny,* m., pl. *-as.*
rod, n. *gwelen,* f., pl. *-lyny,* col. *gwēl, lorgh,* m., pl. *-ow*; also r. of land, 9-ft, sq.
roe, n., of fish, soft, *lethan,* m.; hard, *grün,* col.; r.-buck, *yorgh,* †*cōsyorgh,* m., pl. *-as*; hind, *yorghes,* f., pl. *-ow*; r. fawn, *yorghyk,* m., pl. *-ghesygow.*
rogue: see **rascal.**
roker, n., ray fish, †*rocha,* m., pl. *-chys.*
roll, n. *rōl,* f., pl. *-yow*: v. *rolya*: **-er,** n., wood, *rōlbren,* m., pl. *-yer*; stone, *rōlvēn,* m., pl. *-veyn.*
Roman, n. *Roman,* m., pl. *-as*: a. *Romanek.*
romance, n. *whethel,* m., pl. *-thlow, aneth,* m., pl. *-ow,* **romans,* m.: **-r,** n. *whethlor,* m., pl. *-yon*: **-ntic,** a. **romantek.*
Rome, n. *Rōm,* f.
romp, n. *gwary garow,* m.; person, *gyglot,* m. and f., pl. *-s*: v. *gwary yn-harow.*
rood, n. *crows,* f., pl. *-ow.*
roof, n. *to,* m., pl. *-(h)ow,* †*nen,* m., pl. *-now,* †*nenbren,* m., pl. *-nyer*; of mouth, *stefnyk,* f., *gorheras an ganow,* m.; r. frame, *clōs chȳ,* f., pl. *-ojow c.*; r. tree, *nenbren,* m., pl. *-nyer*: v. *tȳ, gorra to war*[2]: **-er,** n. *tȳor,* m., pl. *-yon*: **-less,** a. *hep to,* **dysto,* **dydo.*
rook, n. *bran-drē,* f., pl. *brȳny-trē*: **-ery,** n. *trē-vrȳny,* f.
room, n. *rōm,* m., pl. *-ys,* †*stevel,* f., pl. *-yow*; space, *spās, lē,* m.; make or leave r. for, *gasa spās dhe*[2]; to have plenty of r., *cafos y ēs*: **-y,** a. *efan.*
roost, v. *cluttya.*
root, v. **terghya,* **türya,* **fynegly*; to take r., *gwrȳdhya*; to up-r., *dywrȳdhya*: n. *gwredhen,* f., pl. *-now, gwrȳdhyow,* col. *gwrȳth*;
rope, n. *lovan,* f., pl. *-vonow*; fine, *lovanen,* f., pl. *-now*; r.s end, *lost lovan,* m., pl. *-ow lovannow*: **-maker,** n. *rōper,* m., pl. *-s.*
rose, n. *rosen,* f., pl. *-now,* col. *rōs,* †*brȳlūen,* f., pl. *-now,* col. *brȳlu*; dog-r., *rosen-kȳ*; r. noble, *rosa-noblen,* f., pl. *-now*: **-bush,** n. *rōslōn,* m., pl. *-ow*: **-y,** a. *lyw rōs.*
rostrum, n. *arethva,* f.
rot, n. *poder, podrethes,* m.; in sheep, *poth,* m.; dry-r., *cusk,* m.; **brynder*; don't talk r., *gas dha flows, taw gans dha whethlow!*: v. *pedry, lȳtha*; with dry-r., *cusca,* **brȳna*: **-ten,** a. *poder, podrethek, podrek, bryn*; of fish, *pesak*; r. part of anything, *podrethes,* m.: **-ter,** n. *podryn,* m.
rotation, n. *mōs a-dro,* inf.; in r., *herwyth rōl, tro*: **-te,** v. *mōs* or *trēlya a-dro.*
rough, a., wind, weather and general, *garow, hager*; of sea, *tonnek*; of men, *anwhēk, smat*: **-en,** v. *garowhē·*: **-ness,** n. *anwhekter, hakter, garowder,* m.: **-ly,** adv. *yn-harow.*
round, n. **kelgh,* m., pl. *-ow*: a. *cren, rond*; r. topped, *mōl*; r. shouldered, **gwargren*: adv. *a-dro, a-dro dhe*[2]; all r., *yn-kerghyn, a bup tu, a bup parth*; r. about, *a-drē-dro*: **-ed,** a. *crom*; r. body, *pellen,* f., pl. *-now*: **-ness,** n. *crender,* m.
rouse, v. *dyfüna, sordya, omsevel*; r. emotions, *gül sevel*; were I r.d, *pan vena fol ha garow.*
rout, v. *gorra dhe'n fo*: n. *rūth,* f., pl. *-ow,* **gustel,* m., pl. *-tlow.*
routine, n. *whēl pupteth-oll,* m., pl. *-yow p.o.*
rove, v. *gwandra*: **-r,** n. *gwandrer,* m., pl. *-roryon.*
row, v. *revya*: n. *tro revya,* f.: n., line, *rew, renk,* m., pl. *-yow, rēs,* **stüs,* f., pl. *-yow*: **-er,** n. *revador,* m., pl. *-yon.*
row, n., dispute, *dalva,* f.; noise, *frōs, trōs,* m., pl. *-ow, hubbadullya,* m.;
rowan, n. *kerdhynen,* f., col. *kerdhyn*; r. berry, *keren,* f., col. *kēr.*
rowel, n. **rosyk-kentryn,* m.

row-hound, n., fish, *mōrgy*, m., pl. *-gün*.
royal, a. *rȳal*, ‡*myghternyth*: **-ty,** n. *myghternsys*, *rē·outa*, m.; payment, *toll war vūnow*, m.
rub, v. *ruttya*; r. out, *defendya dhe-vēs*: **-ber,** n. **glüs gwethyn*, *ruttyer*, *defendyer*, m.
rubbish, n. *plosethes*, m., *scullyon*, *scübyon*, pl., *atal*, col.; nonsense, *flows*, *üfereth*, m.: int. *tety valy*!: **-y,** a. *scübelek*.
ruby, n. *rūby*, m., pl. *-s*.
rudder, n. *lew*, m., pl. *-yow*.
ruddle, n. †*meles*, *lyw-meles*.
ruddy, a. *rüdhyk*.
rude, a. *garow*, *dyscortes*, *dydhysk*, *anwhēk*: **-ness,** n. *dyscortesy*, *garowder*, *ancothvos*, *anwhekter*, m.
rudimentary a. *kensa*, *elvennek*.
rue, n. †*rūta*: v. *ola*, *bōs edrek dhe*[2]; you shall r. it, *why a-n-ōl*.
ruffian, n. *aflythys*, m., pl. *-yjyon*, *bylen*, m., pl. *tüs vylen*.
ruffle, v. *crȳghy*; annoy, *serry*, *dystempra*: n. *crȳgh*, m.: **-d,** a. *crȳgh*; of temper, *serrys*.
rug, n. †*strayl*, m., pl. *-yow*, *len*, f., pl. *-now*; r.s, *hüdhes*, f. and col.
rugged, a. *garow*.
ruin, n. *terros*, m., pl. and abst. *terryjy*, *myshyf*, m., pl. *-evys*; of buildings, *magor*, f., pl. *-yow*: v. *dystrewy*, *shyndya*, *do·mhel*, *myshevya*, *dyswül*.
rule, n. *rewl*, f., pl. *-ys*, *go·vernans*, m.; measure, *scantlyn*, m., pl. *-s*: v. *rewlya*, *lordya*, *governya*, *rowtya*; r. as paramount, *gwarthevya*; r. lines, **lȳnya*, **lynenna*: **-r,** n. *rewler*, m., pl. *-oryon*, *rewlyas*, m., pl. *-ysy*, *rowtor*, m., pl. *-s*, *pen-rewler*, m., pl. *-oryon*, **pentern*, m., pl. *-ow*, †*gwa·lather*, m., pl. *gwe·lyther*; straight-edge, **lynenner*, *lynyer*, m.
rum, n. *dowr tom molas* (*lollas*), m.
rumble, v. *trēlya gans trōs*, *rolya*, *tarenna a-bell*, **gromyal*: n. *trōs trēlya*, m.: **-ling,** a. *sōn taran*, *rolyans*.
ruminate, v. **dasknȳas*.
rummage, v. *whylas*, *türya*.
rumour, n. *son*, m., pl. *-yow*, *gēr*, m., pl. *-yow*, *whethel*, m., pl. *-low*; to spread r.s, *plontya whethlow*: **-ed,** a., it is r., *y-leveryr*, *yma· son anodho*.
rump, n. *tȳn*, m. or f., *dywbedren*, d. f.
rumple, n. *crȳgh*, m.: v. *crȳghy*, **fowssya*: **-d,** a. *crȳgh*.
run, v., general, *resek*; of living creatures, *ponya*; of water, *devera*; r. slowly, trickle, *sygera*, **govery*; r. before, **ragresek*; r. together, **kevresek*; r. away, *dyank*, *mōs dhe'n fo*, *fȳa dhe'n fo*; r. him through with a spear, *düs* or *resek dredho gans gu*; r. through (on spit, etc.), *berya*; r. house, *synsy chȳ*; r. to seed, *hasa*; r. out or short of, *bōs gyllys hep*: **-away,** n. †*fōesyk*, m., pl. *-ygyon*: **-let,** *laca*, m., pl. *lakkys*: **-ner,** n. *resor*, m., pl. *-oryon*, **resegyth*, m., pl. *-ydhyon*: **-ning,** n. *resek*, inf.; a. *rē*; r. knot, *colm rē*.
rupture, n. *tor*, *squard*, m., pl. *-yow*, *torva*, f., pl. *-ow*: v. *terry*, *squardya*.
rural, a. *pow*, *a'n pow*.
ruse, n. *cast*, m., pl. *-ys*, **kyldro*, f., pl. *-yow*.
rush, v. *fysky*, *stēvya*; of water, **frōsa*: n., action, **fysk*, m., *frōs*, m., pl. *-ow*.
rush, n., bot., *bronnen*, f., col. *bron*, *porven*, f., pl. *-now*, col. *porf*; sand r., *morhesk*, col., *bronnen mōr*, f., *cors mōr*, col.; r.-light, *kenak*, m., pl. *-ogas*; r. wick, *porven*, f.; r.-grown place, *porf*, f., *bronnek*, f., pl. *-egy*.
russet, a. **rüdhlos*.
rust, n. *gossen*, f., *call*, m.: v. **gossenna*, *mōs ha bōs call* or *callek*: **-y,** a. **gossenek*, **callek*.
rustic, a. *trevesyk*, *a'n pow*: n. *trevesyk*, m., pl. *-ygyon*, *dēn an pow*, pl. *tüs a. p.*; jocularly, **mager mogh*, m., pl. *-goryon m.*, *trēgher būlük*, m., pl. *-ghoryon b*.
rustle, v. **sȳa*, **rustla*.
rut, n. *ōl rōs*, m., pl. *olow rosow*, **rosla*, m., pl. *-leyow*.
ruth, n. *trüeth*, *pyta*, m., *tregereth*, f.: **-less,** a. *dybyta*, *dydrūeth*, *hep rūthy*.
rye, n. *sügalen*, f., col. *sügal*; r. land, *sügaldyr*, m.; r.field, *sügalek*, f., pls. *-egow*, *-egy*: **-grass,** n. *ȳvrē*, col.

S

Sabbath, n. *Sabot*, *dē-Sül*, m.; ere the S., *kens dōs Sabot*.
sack, v. *pylla*, *rafna*; put in s., *sagha*: n. *sagh*, m., pl. *seghyer*, *tygen*, f., pl. *-now*; corner of s., *bogen*, f., pl. *-now*: **-cloth,** n. *ȳscar*, *canfas garow*, *saghlen*, m., *saghlyen*, f.; s. garment, *saghwysk*, f.: **-ing,** n. *pan sagh*, *ȳscar*, m.
sacrament, n. *sacrement*, m., pl. *-mens*.
sacred, a. *sans*, *hynwys*, *sacrys*, *benygys*.
sacrifice, v. *offrynna*, *sacry·fȳa*, ‡*sacry·fysa*: n. *fa·cryfys*, m., pl. *-ys*, *offryn*, m., pl. *-now*, *oblāsyon*, m., pl. *-s*.

sacrilege, n. **sa·crylych*, m.
sad, a. *trūesy, morethek, trūethek, tryst, yeyn*: **-den,** v. *lenwel gans moreth, trysthē·, cüdhy*: **-ly,** adv. *trūan, yn-t., yn-trūethek*: **-ness,** n. *posyjyon, trystans, trystys*, m.
saddle, n. *dȳber*, m., pl. *-brow*: v. *dȳbra*; s. bow, *gwarak an dȳber*, f.; pack s., †*strother*, f., pl. *-yow*: **-r,** n. *dȳbror*, m., pl. *-yon.*
safe, a. *salow, dyogel, saw*: n. **cofyr saw*, m., pl. *-frow s.*: **-guard,** n. *gwȳth*, m., *scōs*, m., pl. *-ojow*: v. *gwytha*: **-keeping,** n. *sawment*, m.: **-ty,** n. *sawment, sawder, dyogeleth*, m.; place of s., *e·rberow*, m., pl. *-ys.*
saffron, n. *safron* (*safern*), m.
sagacious, a. *für, fēl, dōth*: **-city,** n. *fürneth, felder*, m.: **-ge,** a. *dōth*: n. *dōth*, m., pl. *-yon.*
sage, n., herb, **sauja*, col.
sail, n. *gōl*, m. or f., pl. *-yow*: v. *mora, gōlya*: **-or,** n. *marner*, m., pl. *-s, dēn mōr*, m., pl. *tüs m.*, **moror*, m., pl. *-yon.*
saint, n. *sans*, m., pl. *syns*, f. *-es*, pl. *-ow, dēn Dew*, m., pl. *tüs D., dremā·s*, m.; as title, *Sen, Synt*, m., pl. *-tys, Synta*, f., pl. *-tys*; All S.s, *an Ollsyns*; ancient prefix, *To-*: St. John's wort, *losowen SynJowan*, f., col. *-ow S. J.*: **-liness,** n. *sansoleth*, f.: **-ly,** a. *sans, sansyl*: s. person, *densa*, m.
sake, n. *kerensa*, f.; for the s. of, *er, awo·s, aba·rth*; for all s.s, *awo·s ēghen, awo·s an bȳs.*
salad, n. *bōs erbys crȳf*, m., *losow-lēth, beler*, etc., col.
salamander, n. *pedrevan an dowr*, f., pl. *-now a. d.*, **salamander*, m,, pl. *-drys.*
salary, n. *gober*, m., pl. *-brow, waja*, m., pl. *-jys, arfeth*, m., pl. *-edhow.*
sale, n. *gwerth*, f.: **-able,** a. *hewerth, a-yllyr y wertha*: **-sman,** n. *gwerther*, m., pl. *-thoryon.*
saline, a. *holanek*, ‡*sal.*
saliva, n. *trew*, **halow*, m.
sallow, a. *melenyk.*
sallow, n. *helygen wyn*, f., col. *helyk gwyn.*
sally, v. *mōs mēs gans nerth, ewhȳas, omsettya war*², *gül dera·y war*²: n. *omsettyans*, m.
salmon, n. †*ēok*, m., pl. *ēogas, sowman*, m., pl. *-mens.*
salt, n. *holan*, m.; s.-pan, s.-pond, *pol-holan*, m.; s.-cellar, *salyour*, m., pl. *-s*; s. water, *hyly, dowr sal*, m.; rock s., *holan mēn*; sea s., *holan mōr*; s. once used, *holan cōth*: v. *salla*: a. *sal*, **holanek*: **-ed,** a. *sellys*: **-er,** n. *holaner*, m.,pl.*-noryon*: **-ing-pot,** n. *bosseth* (*bussa*), m.: **-less,** a. *dyholan, hep holan.*
salutation, n. *dynerghyans, salujyans*, m.: **-te,** n. *dynergh*, **salus, salujyans*, m.: v. *dynerghy, salujy.*
salvage, n. *an pyth üs sawyes*, m., **salvay·*, m.: v.
salvation, n. *sylwyans, salvasyon*, m.
salve, n. *yly*, m., pl. *ylyow, üras*, m., pl. *-resow, sawment*, m., pl. *-mens*: v. *sawya, ylȳa.*
same, a. *keth*; in the s. way, *y'n keth vanerma*; that s., *an keth henna*; in the s. direction, *y'n ünforth*; all the s., *bytege·ns, awo·s henna.*
samphire, n. *fenokel mōr*, m.
sample, n. *sampel, patron*, m.: v. *sampla.*
sanctified, a. *hynwys*: **-fy,** v. *sona, ughelhē·, sacra, benyga.*
sanction, n. *cümyas*, m.: v. *rȳ cümyas.*
sanctity, n. *sansoleth*, f.
sanctuary, n. *sentry, meneghy*, m., pl. *-ow, meneghyjy*, m., pl. *-yow.*
sand, n. *trēth*, m., pl. *-ow*; grain of s., **tewesyn*, m., pl. *-now*, col. *tewas*; s. patch, *trethen*, f., pl. *-now*; s. beach, *trēth*; coarse s., *grow*, col.; scouring s., *growdyr*, m.; s. hill, *towan*, m.,pl. *tewennow*, ‡*bank*, m., pl. *-ncow*; consisting of s. hills, *tewennek*; to gather s., *tewessa* (inf. only); s.-hopper, *morwhannen*, f., col. *-whyn, whannen mōr*, f., col. *whyn m.*: **-y,** a. *trēthek*, **tewesek.*
sandal, n. *sandal*, m., pl. *-ys.*
sand-eel, n. *lavyn*, m. or col., pl. *-yon.*
sandpiper, n. *kȳogh mōr*, f., pl. *-ghas m.*
sane, a. *yagh y vrȳs, dhodho y ewn skȳans*: **-ity,** n. *yēghes brȳs*, m.
sanguinary, a. *gosek*: **-ne,** a. *gosek, lün a waytyans* or *fȳth.*
sap, n. *sūgan*, m.: v. *sūgna*: **-py,** a. *sūgnek, ēr.*
sapling, n. *glaswedhen*, f., col. *-wȳth.*
sapper, n. *soudor pāl*, m., pl. *-yon p.*
sapwood, n. **gwynyn*, m.
Saracen, n. *Sarsyn*, m., pl. *-s*: **-ic,** a. *Sarsynek.*
sarcasm, n. *gēs, lavar asper*, m.: **-stic,** a. *wherow, asper, leverys yn gēs.*
sarcophagus, n. *logel*, f., pl. *-low, bēth mēn*, pl. *bedhow m.*
sash, n. *grügys pan, owrlyn, paly*, etc., m., pl. *-ow.*
Satan, n. *Satnas* (*Sa·ttanas*), m.
satchel, n. **jypser*, m., pl. *-s.*
satiate, v. *gwalgha, quoffy*: **-iety,** n. *gwalgh, quoff*, m.
satin, n. *paly*, m.

satire, n. *gēs, scorn,* m.: **-irical,** a. *leverys yn gēs* or *scorn*: **-irize,** v. *scornya.*
satisfaction, n. *lowender,* m.; to thy s., *dhe'th plegadow*: **-tory,** a. *da lowr, dhe blegadow*: **-fied,** a. *pȳs da, plēsyes, ‡contentys*: **-fy,** v. *collenwel bōth, ‡contentya*; s. hunger, *terry nown*; I am not s.ed that it is so, *ny-won dhe-wȳr y vōs yndella.*
saturate, v. *sūba, glybya*: **-ion,** n. *sūbans, glybyans,* m.
Saturday, n. *dē-Sadorn,* m.
sauce, n. *sows,* m., pl. *-ow*: **-pan,** n. *padeldorn,* f., pls. *-llow, -lly, -d.*: **saucer,** n. *padelyk,* m., pl. *-ygow, †scala,* m., pl. *-ys,* **sowser,* m., pl. *-s.*
saucy, a. *tōnt*: **-cily,** adv. *yn-tōnt*; to reply s., *camwortheby, tōntya.*
saunter, v. *kerdhes yn-syger, rōsya, crowdra.*
sausage, n. **selsygen,* f., pl. *-now,* col. *selsyk*; s. meat, *kȳk-selsyk.*
savage, a. *gwyls, garow*: n. *dēn gwyls.*
save, v. *sylwel, sawya, dyffres* (from, *a*²), *gwytha* (from, *rak*); s. up, *gorra yn-ban*: s. money, *†erbysy*: prep., conj., *marnas, mas, lemen, saw*; s. only, *saw ünsel*: **-ings,** n. *arghans erbysys, †erbys,* m.: **-iour,** n., S., *Sylwyas,* m., pl. *-wysy, Sylvador* (*‡Salvador*), m., pl. *-yon, *Savyour,* m., pl. *-s.*
savour, n. *sawor,* m., pl. *-yow, blas,* m.: v. **sawory, blasa*: **-less,** a. *dyflas*: **-y,** a. *saworek.*
saw, n. **hesken,* f., pl. *-now, *lȳf,* f., pl. *-yvyow*: v. **heskenna, *lȳvya*: **-dust,** n. *blēs hesken,* m.
saxifrage, n. **tor-mēn, *mēndarth,* m.
Saxon, n. *Saws,* m., pl. *-on,* f. *-es,* pl. *-ow*; Anglo-S., *Sawsnek Cōth*: a. *Sawsnek.*
say, v. *leverel, cows, kewsel, medhes* (def. v.): s. again, *dasleverel*; he s.s, *yn-meth-ef*; as they s., *del leveryr*; from what you s., *drē dha ēr*; that is to s., *hen yu dhe styrya* or *leverel*: **-ing,** n. *dyth,* m., pl. *-ys, lavar,* m., pl. *-ow, gēr,* m., pl. *-yow.*
scab, n. *cragh,* m., pl. *creghy, creven, trosken, *cramen,* f., pl. *-now*: **-by,** a. *cragh, lovrek*; s.-head, term of abuse, *pen-crēghy,* m.
scabbard, n. *gōn,* f., pl. *-ow.*
scabious, n. *pen-glās,* m., pl. *-now-g.*
scaffold, n. *mynk,* f., pl. *-ncow, *scaffot,* m., pl. *-ys*: **-ing,** n. **scaffotys,* pl., *tymberwȳth,* m.
scald, v. *scaldya.*
scale, n. **scanten,* f., pl. *-now,* col. *scant, ken,* m. (no pl.); in music, *scül,* f.; pair of s.s, *mantol,* f., pl. *-yow, *balans,* m., pl. *-ys*; fish s.s, on clothing, *golowylyon,* pl.: **-y,** a. *kenak, *scantek.*
scale, v. *scülya, crambla yn-ban.*
scalp, n. *croghen pen,* f., pl. *crēghyn pennow.*
scalpel, n. *collel chyrurjyon,* f., pl. *kellyl c.*
scamp, n. *drokwas,* m., pl. *-wesyon.*
scamper, n. *ponya yn ün fysky*: **-ing,** a. *scurel-wyrly.*
scandal, n. *bysmē·r, sclander, drōk-gēr, whethel plos,* m.; s. party, *scavel an gow,* f.: **-ize,** v. *sclandra, drok-gerya, gül bysmē·r dhe*²: **-ous,** a. *droktavasek, meth y glewes.*
scantiness, n. *tanowder,* m.: **-ty,** a. *scant, tanow.*
scantling, n. *scantlyn,* m., pl. *-s.*
scapegrace, n. *scullyak,* m., pl. *-yogyon.*
scar, n. **crȳthen, clēsen,* f., pl. *-now, ōl goly,* m.
scarce, a. *scant, trawythys, tanow*: **-ly,** adv. *scant, scantlowr, yn-fās*; with neg., *namür*: **-city,** n. *tanowder, esow,* m.
scare, v. *gorra own yn*; he was s.d, *own a-n-jeva.*
scarecrow, n. *bucca,* m., pl. *bukkyas.*
scarf, n. *lȳen conna,* m., pl. *-yow c., *gūdhūgen,* f., pl. *-now*; carpentry, *scarf,* m., pl. *-ys*: v. *scarfa.*
scarlet, a. *cough, rüth*; s. fever, **cleves cough.*
scarped, a. *serth.*
scathing, a. *tyn, ow-shyndya.*
scatter, v. *scullya, dyberth, kescar, ‡scattra, *dysparplya*; broadcast, *tewlel a-lēs*: **-brain,** n. *pen-bronnen,* m.: **-brained,** a. *scaf y ben*: **-ed,** a. *dybals, kescar, *dysparplyes*: **-ing,** n. *sculva,* f.
scene, n. *vu,* m., pl. *-ys, gwēl,* m. or f., pl. *-ow*: **-ry,** n. *vu, tekter an pow,* m., **golokva,* f.
scent, n. *ēth,* m., pl. *-ow, ēthen,* f., pl. *-now, sawor,* m., pl. *-yow, saworen,* f., pl. *-now*: **-ed,** a. *saworys*; ill-s.ed, *messe·nt, flērys.*
sceptic, n. *dyscryjyk,* m., pl. *-jygyon*: **-al,** a. *dyscryjyk*; be s., *dyscryjy*; he is s. about it, *y-fynsa gothvos moy anodho.*
sceptre, n. *gwelen myghte·rn, g. rȳal, g. †revaneth,* f., pl. *-lyny, m. r.*
scheme, n. *towl,* m., pl. *-ow*: v. *tewlel towl.*
school, n. *scōl,* f., pl. *-yow*; s.house, *scōljy,* m., pl. *-ow*; s.-boy, *scoler,* m., pl. *-loryon*; s.-girl, *scolores,* f., pl. *-ow*; s.-master, *mēster mebyon,* m., pl. *mestrys m.*; s.-fellow, *kescoler,* m., pl. *-oryon*; s. of fish, *hēs,* f., pl. *-ow, hevva,* f.: **-olar,** n. *scoler,* m., pl.

-loryon, scolhȳk, m., pl. *-ygyon*: **-liness, -ship,** n. *scolhȳksys*, m., *scolo·rȳeth, scolhy·gȳeth*, f., *lȳen*, m.
scilicet, adv. *hen yu dhe styrya.*
science, n. *scȳens*, m., pl. *-ys*; the seven liberal s.s, *an seyth scȳens lybral*: **-ntific,** a. *scȳensek.*
scion, n. **ymp*, m., pl. *-ys.*
scissors, n., pair of, *gwelsow bȳghan*, m., pl. *-sevyow b.*, **sysours*, pl.
scoff, v. *sconya, gēsya*; s. at, *gül gēs a*[2]: **-er,** n. *gēsyer*, m., pl. *-yoryon, dyscryjyk*, m., pl. *-ygyon.*
scold, v. *godros, raylya, deraylya, keredhy, gērya, omdhal, *tavasa*: **-ing,** n. *kereth*, f., *godros*, m.: a. *tavasek.*
scope, n. *spās, gallos, lē*, m.; of tether, *stak*, m.
scorch, v. *gorlesky, potha*: **-ing,** a. *pōth*: n. *potvan*, m.
score, n., 20, *ügans*; reckoning, *scot*, m., pl. *-tys, reken*, m., *-knys*; games, **scōr*, m.: v. furrow, *fynegly*; games, **scōrya.*
scoria, n. *ken*, m., *soras*, col., *remanant mūn tedhys*, m.
scorn, n. *despȳ·t, scorn, dysprēsyans*, m.: v. *scornya, fȳa, dysprēsya, ‡kemeres yn dys-day·n*: **-ful,** a. *despȳtys, lün a scorn.*
scorpion, n. *scorpyon*, m., pl. *-s.*
Scot, n. *Alban*, m., pl. *-as*, f. *-es*, pl. *-ow, Gwydhal Alban*, m., pl. *-as A.*; *Gwydhules A.*, f., pl. *-ow A.*: **-ch, -tish,** *Albanek*: **-land,** n. *Alban*, f.
scoundrel, n. *tebelwas*, m., pl. *-wesyon, sherewa*, m., pl. *-wys, bylen*, m., pl. *tüs vylen.*
scour, v. *glanhē·, scūrya, *cartha, *püra, *scartha*; s. the plain, *resek drēs an ūn*: **-ings,** n. *scübyon, *carthyon*, pl.; s.sand, *growdyr*, m.
scourge, n. *scorja*, m., pl. *-ys, whyp*, m., pl. *-pys, scübylen*, f., pl. *-now*: v. *scorjya, whyppya.*
scout, v. *aspȳa*: n. *aspȳas*, m., pl. *-esy, aspȳer*, m., pl. *-yoryon.*
scowl, n. *plēk tāl*, m.: v. *plegya tāl.*
scramble, v. *crambla.*
scrap, n. *dral*, m., pl. *-yow, tam*, m., pl. *tymmyn*, dim. *temmyk*, m., pls. *-ygow, -mynygow, teken*, f., pl. *-now, myjyn*, m., pl. *-now, pastel*, f., pl. *-llow*: v. *gorra a-denewan, tewlel dhe scul.*
scrape, v. *cravas, *cravellas, gravya, *ratha*; s. off skin, *dyrüsca*; s. a pig, *dyrüna*: n. *cravas*, m.; get into a s., *codha yn tranjyak*: **-r,** n. **cravell*, f., pl. *-ow, collel gravya*, f., pl. *kellyl g.*; wooden s., **rothel*, f., pl. *-thlow.*
scratch, v. *cravas, scravynyas*: n. *cravas*, m.
scream, n. *garm ughel*, f., pl. *-ow u, üs*, m., pl. *üjow, scrȳs*, f., pl. *-ȳjow*: v. *üja, scrȳja, crȳa* or *garma ughel.*
scree, n. *rajel*, m.
screech, v.: see **scream.**
screen, n. *skew, *skrȳn*, f., pl. *-yow, goskes*, m., **goskeslen*, f., pl. *-now*: v. *goskesy, skewya.*
screw, n. **screw*, m., pl. *-ys, kenter tro*, f., pl. *-trow t.*; s. bolt, *ebyl tro*, m., pl. *-yow t.*: v. **screwya.*
scribble, v. *scryfa hep rach, *gwanscryfa*: n. *scryfa treys-kelyon*, m.
scribe, n. *scryfa*, m., pl. *-oryon, scryvynyas*, m., pl. *-ysy*; biblical, *‡scrȳba*, m., pl. *-bys.*
scrimmage, v. **skyrmsya*: n. **skyrmys*, m., pl. *-yjys.*
scrip, n. *scryp*, m., pl. *-pys.*
Scripture, n. *Scryptor*, m., pl. *-s*; the S.s, *an Scryptor Benygys*, m., *an Lyfryow*, pl.
scroll, n. *rōl-scryfa*, f., pl. *-yow-s.*
scrub, v.: see **scour.**
scrub, n., bushes, *prysclowek*, f., pls. *-egy, -egow, prysclowwȳth*, col.
scruple, n. *danjer, preder, own, dowt*, m.: v. *hokkya, perthy danjer*: **-ulously,** adv. *gans lendury, dour, yn pup poynt.*
scrutinize, v. *whythra bysy*: **-ny,** n. *whythra*, inf., *whythrans*, m.
scuffle, n. *omdowl*, m., pl. *-ow*: v. *omdewlel.*
scullion, n. *gwas kegyn*, m., pl. *gwesyon k.*
sculpt, v. *gravya, trēghy mēs a vēn*: **-or,** n. *gravyor*, m., pl. *-yon, y·majer*, m., pl. *-s*: **-ure,** n. *gravyans*, m., pl. *-ow, y·majery*, m., pl. *-s.*
scum, n. *ken, lastethes*, m.; green s. on water, *kellyn*, m., *kewny*, col.; to become covered with s., *kenna, kewnya*: **-my,** a. *kenak, kellynak.*
scurf, n. *cragh*, m., pl. *creghy, clavor*, m., *cresten*, f., pl. *-now*: **-urvy,** a. *cragh*; leprous, *cla·vorek, lovrek*; s. fellow, *pylyak, pen-pyllys*, m.: n. *cleves* or *drōk mōr*, m.: **-urvily,** adv. *yn-fylen*; s. treated, *vȳl dȳghtys.*
Scilly, n. *Syllan*, f.; S. Isles, *Enesow S.*, f., pl.
scythe, n. *falgh*, f., pl. *fylghyow*: v. *falghas.*

sea, n. *mōr*, m., pl. *-ow*; open s., *mōr dyfȳth*, **keynvor*; calm s., *spaven mōr*; rough s., *hager-vōr*; to s., *dhe'n mōr*; to put to s., *mōra*: **-board,** n. *morrep*, m., *morlan*, f.: **-man,** n. *marner*, m., pl. *-s*, *moror*, m., pl. *-yon*, *dēn mōr*, m., pl. *tüs m.*, **morwas*, m., pl. *-wesyon*: **-rover,** n. *morlader*, m., pl. *-ledron*, *ancryjor* (†*ancredor*) *mōr*, m., pl. *-yon m.*: **-shore,** n. *trēth*, m., pl. *-ow*, *als*, m., pl. *-yow*: **-side,** n. *morva*, *morlan*, f., *morrep*, m.: **-water,** *hyly*, m.

sea-eagle, n. *morēr*, *ēr an mōr*, m., pl. *-as*, *eras a. m.*

seagull, n. *gwylan*, f., pl. *-as*, *gulla*, m., pl. *-lys*; black-headed g., *scrawyk*, m., pl. *-ygow*.

sea-holly, n. *morgelynen*, f., col. *-lyn*, *kelyn mōr*, *k. trēth*, col.

sea-horse, n. *morvargh*, m., pl. *-vergh*.

sea-kale, n. *morgawlen*, f., col. *morgawl*, *cawl mōr*.

seal, n., animal, *rün*, m., pl. *-as*, *lugh ogo*, m., pl. *-y o.*

seal, n., impression, *sēl*, f., pl. *-yow*; privy-s., *sēl pryva*: v. **selya*: **-ing-wax,** n. **cōr sēlya*, m.

seam, n., stitching and mining, *gwrȳ*, m., pl. *-yow*: **-less,** *hep gwrȳ*: **-stress,** n. *gwryadores*, f., pl. *-ow*, †*sewyades*, f., pl. *-ow*.

sea-mew, see **seagull.**

sea-pie, n., bird, *morbȳasen*, f., col. *-byas*.

sea-pink, n. *tam-ōn*, m., col. *losow t.*

search, v., s. for, *whylas*, *whythra*; s. out, *aspȳa*: n. *whythrans*, m.; after a long s., *wosa whylas pell*: **-ing,** a. *lym*, *glew*.

sea-sedge, n., marram grass, *morhesk*, col.

sea-serpent, n. *morsarf*, f., pl. *-syrf*.

seasick, a. **mōrglaf*, *dhodho cleves an mōr*: **-ness,** n. *cleves an mōr*, m.

season, n. *sēson*, m., pl. *-s*, *termyn*, m., pl. *-yow*, *prȳs*, m., pl. *-yow*.

sea-swallow, n. **morwennol*, f., pl. *-nyly*.

seat, n. *eseth*, f., pl. *-edhow*, *esethva*, f., *sedhek*, m.; country s., *plās*, m., *trygva*, f.; head-quarters, *penplas*; throne, see, *sē*, m., pl. *-ys*; posterior, *tȳn*, *eseth*, m.: v. *gorra dhe esedha*; s. oneself, *esedha*, *mōs dh'y eseth*.

sea-urchin, n. *sort*, m., pl. *-as*.

seaweed, n. *goumman*, m.; grass-wrack, *kewny mōr*, col.

seaworm, n. *prȳf mōr*, m., pl. *prevyon m.*

seclude, v. *gwytha yn-cüdhys*, s. oneself, *omdenna dyworth tüs*: **-d,** a. *a-denewan*, *yn-dan gēl*, *y. d. güth*: **-sion,** n. *covva* (*cüthva*), f., *cüth*, *kēl*, m.

second, a., n. *secu·nd*, *nessa*; with *an ȳl* as "first," *y gȳla*: n. *secu·nd*: v. *scodhya*, **ȳla*: **-ary,** a. *ysella*, *lē y lēs*: **-hand,** a. *cōth*, **dasquerthys*: **-ly,** adv. *nessa*, *y'n nessa lē*.

secrecy, n. *keladow*, m.: **-et,** a. *cüth*, *pryva*, *pryveth*, *kēl*: n. *tra gelys*, **rȳn*, **kevrȳn*, m., pl. *-yow*; to keep s., *keles*: **-tly,** adv. *yn pryveth*, *yn pryva*, *worth golow nōs*, *yn-dan gēl*, *a-dryf tüs*.

secretary, n. *scryvynyas*, m., pl. *-ysy*, f. *-yades*, pl. *-ow*.

sect, n. *ran a gryjyans*, f., *henwans*, m.

section, n. *trogh*, m., pls. *-ow*, *trēghyon*, *trēgh*, m., pls. *-ow*, *-yon*, *ran*, f., pl. *-now*.

secular, a. *lēk*.

secure, v. *kelmy*, *takkya*, *crafa*, *fastya*, *dyogely*, *-elhē·*; obtain, *gwaynya*, *cafos*: a. *dyogel*, *saw*, *fast*: **-rity,** n. *sawment*, **dyogeleth*, ‡*sekerder*, m.; guarantee, *meugh*, m., pl. *-yow*, *gaja*, m., pl. *-jys*, *gwystel*, m., pl. *-tlow*; from fear, *dyagha*, m.

sedan chair, n. *cadar dhegys*, f.

sedate, a. *dōth*, **hebask*.

sedentary, a. **sedhek*.

sedge, n. *hesken*, f., col. *hesk*; s., iris, etc., loosely, *elestren*, f., col. *elester*.

sediment, n. †*godhas*, m., *cūthow*, f., pl.

sedition, n. *bras*, m.: **-ious,** a. *dyslēn*.

seduce, v. *tenna*, *hüda*, *tulla*, *sawthanas*, *dynya*: **-r,** n. *tullor*, m., pl. *-yon*: **-tion,** n. *tenvos*, m.

see, v. *gweles*, *myras*; mentally, *convedhes*; s. beyond, *gweles pella es*, *gorweles*; s.! *otta*! *awotta*! before vowel, *ot*! *awo·t*!; s. here, *otomma*!; s. there, *ot ena*!; s. that you do, *gwayt may whrylly*; s.ing that, *pan*[2], *aba·n*[2].

see, n. *epscobeth*, m., pl. *-ow*, *sē*, m., pl. *-ys*, *stalla*, m., pl. *-lys*; apostolic s., *sē Abostol*.

seed, n. *hasen*, f., pl. *-now*, col. *hās*; s. bed, *hasek*, f., *sprüsek*, f., pls. *-egow*, *-egy*; run to s., *hasa*: v. *hasa*; sow s., *gonys hās*: **-ed, -y,** a. *hasek*: **-ling,** n. *plansyk*, m., pl. *-ygow*.

seek, v. *whylas*: **-er,** n. *whyler*, m., pl. *-loryon*.

seem, v. *omwül*, *hevelly*; it s.s to me, *my a-dyp* or *syns*, *dhym del hevel*; how is he s.ing? *pyth yu y jēr*?; ask how he s.s, *govynneugh paha·n plȳt ymava*: **-ingly,** adv. *yn hevelep*, *del hevel* or *hevelly*.

seemly, a. *onest*, *semly*: **-liness,** n. *onester*, m.

seep, v. *sygera*.

seethe, v. *bryjyon, tythya, sygera*: **-thing,** n. *bryjyon*, m.
segregate, v. *dyberth*: **-tion,** n. *dybarth, dyberthva*, f.
seine-boat, n. *scath-rōs*, f., pl. *-ow r.*: **s.-net,** n. *rōs-sayn*, f., pl. *-ow-s.*
seize, v. *dalghenna, sēsya, settya dalghen yn, synsy, cachya*; take possession of, *degemeres*; s. together, *lathya*: **-zin,** n. *sēsans*, m.; to take or give s., *sēsa*: **-zure,** n. *dalghen*, m.; stroke, *shora*, m., pl. *-ys, towl gōs*, m.
seldom, adv. *boghes-venough*; with neg., *namenough*.
select, v. *dewys*: **-ion,** n. *dewys*, m.
self, n. *honen* (s. and pl.); himself, etc., *y honen*, etc.; as reflective prefix to verbs, *om-*:**-ish,** a. *crefny, pȳth*; to be s., *omgara rē, whylas y byth y honen*: **-ishness,** n. *omgerensa, kerensa y honen*, f.: **-willed,** a. *gorth, stordy*.
sell, v. *gwertha*; s. for, *gwertha a*[2]: **-er,** n. *gwerther*, m., pl. *-thoryon*.
selvedge, n. *lysten*, f., pl. *-now*.
semblance, n. *hevelepter*, m., *lyw*, m., pl. *-yow, semlant*, m., pl. *-ns*.
semen, n. *hās*, col.
semicircle, n. **hantergelgh*, m., pl. *-ow*.
seminary, n. *scōl*, f., pl. *-yow, colјy*, m., pl. *-ow*.
senate, n. *seneth*, m., pl. *-edhow*: **-tor,** n. *senedhor*, m., pl. *-yon*; s.s, *tüs hēn*, f.
send, v. *danvon, gorra*; s. for, *danvon warle·rgh*; s. to say, *danvon*; s. forth, *dyllo*; s. far away, *pellhē·*: **-er,** n. *dyller, danvoner*, m., pls. *-loryon, -noryon*.
seneschal, n. *rennyas*, m., pl. *-ysy, styward*, m., pl. *-s*.
senior, a. *henavak, cotha, hēna*: n. *henavak*, m., pl. *-vogyon, tüs hēn*, f.
sensation, n. *clewes amüvyans*, m.; cause a s., *sordya son, gül bōs marth*: **-al,** a. *marthys, a-vyn amüvya tüs*.
sense, n., meaning, *styr*, m., pl. *-yow*; wisdom, *skȳans*, m., pl. *-ow*; that doesn't make s., *nyns-yu rēson henna*; common s., *skȳans da*; brought to his s.s, *drēs dh'y skȳans*; out of his s.s, *mēs a'y rewl* or *skȳans*; the 5 s.s, *skȳansow gweles, clewes, blasa, sawory, ha tava*: v. *clewes, aswonvos*: **-less,** a. *dyskȳans, hep rēson*; unconscious, *clamderys*: **-sibility,** n. *fȳnder*, m.: **-sible,** a. *für, dōth*: **-itive,** a. *fȳn*.
sentence, v. *brüsy, jujјya*: n. *lavar, cows*, m. pl. *-ow*; judgment, *brüs*, f., pl. *-ow*.
sentiment, n. *tybyans, sȳans*, m.: **-al,** a. *whar y golon, rē ēs y amüvya*.
sentinel, sentry, n. *golyer*, m., pl. *-yoryon*.
separate, v. *ranna, kescar, dyberth*; disentangle, *dygemysky*; s. combatants, *dyberth yntra stryforyon*; s. threads, *früdha*: a. *dyblans, dyberthys*: **-ly,** adv. *dyblans, dybarow, orto y honen*: **-tion,** n. *kescar*, m., *dybarth, dyberthva*, f.; s. of roads, *forth dybarth*, f.
September, n. *Gwyngala, mys-G.*, m.
sepulchre, n. *bēth*, m., pl. *bedhow, logel*, f., pl. *-low*: **-pulture,** n. *enclathva*, f.
sequel, n. *an pyth üs ow-sewya* or *holya, *hol*, m.
sequestered, a. *y'n ȳl tu*; s. place, *argel*, f., pl. *-ow, kēl*, m., pl. *-ow*.
seraph, n. *se·rafyn*, m., pl. *-ys*: **-ic,** a. *ave·l* or *se·rafyn*.
serene, a. *hebask, clōr, whar, cosel*: **-nity,** n. *calmynsy, cosoleth*, m.
serf, n. †*kēth*, m., pl. *-yon*, †*tȳthyak*, m., pl. *-yogyon*.
serge, n. *saya*, m.
sergeant, n. *serjōnt*, m., pl. *-jōns*.
series, n. *rew, *kevrēs*, m., **stüs*, f., pl. *-ow*; in a s., *yn rew*.
serious, a. *trüesy, tryst, bysy, sevür, sad, hep wharth*; s. illness, *cleves drōk*: **-ly,** adv. *defrȳ·, yn-tefrȳ·*; s. wounded, *tebelwolȳes*: **-ness,** *sevüreth*, m.
sermon, n. *pregoth*, m., pl. *-gowthow, homyly*, m., pl. *-s*.
serpent, n. *sarf*, f., pl. *syrf, serpont*, m., pl. *-ns*: **-ine,** n., rock, *sarfvēn, mēn sarfek*, m.
serum, n. *lyn*, m.
serve, v. *gonys, servya, menystra*; treat, serve up, *dȳghtya*; take service, **sodha*; be useful, *bōs dhe lēs* or *weres*; s. purpose, *servya*; it s.s him right, *yn-ta ef re-n-dyndylas*; that will not s., *ny-vyth 'vas henna*: **-vant,** n. *servyas*, m., pl. *-ysy*, f. *-vyades*, pl. *-ow, servont*, m., pl. *-ns, gonesek*, m., pl. *-sogyon, paja*, m., pl. *-jys, maw*, m., pl. *coscar, gwas*, m., pl. *gwesyon, gwas-whēl*, m., pl. *gwesyon-w.*; maids, *maghteth*, f., pl. *meghtythyon, mowes*, f., pl. *-wysy*: **-ver,** n. *servyas*, m., pl. *-ysy*; tray, *servyour*, m., pl. *-s*: **-vice,** n. *gwrȳth*, f., *servys*, m., pl. *-ys, gonys*, m., *gonesegeth*, f., *sōth*, f., pl. *sodhow*; knight s., *ago-marghogyon*, **f.**; religious, *oferen*, f., pl. *-now, servys*, m., pl. *-ys*; to do s., *servya*,

gül servys; it will be of little s. to him, *y-fyth boghes dh'y weres*; employ s.s of, *arfeth*; dinner s., *dafar kynyow*, m.: **-viceable,** a. *'vās, dhe lēs*: **-ing-boy,** n. *paja*, m., pl. *-jys, boya* ,m., pl. *-yes*: **-ving-man,** n. *gonesek*, m., pl. *-sogyon, dēn whel*, m., pl. *tüs w.*: **-vitors,** n. *tüs kēth*: **-vitude,** n. **gwaso·nȳeth*, f., **kēthneth*, m.: **-vile,** a. *kēth, ysel, *gwasek*; s. person, **gwasek*, m., pl. *-sogyon, tüs ysel.*

session, n. **esethvos*, m., pl. *-ow*; place of s., *sedhek*, m., pl. *-egow.*

set, v. *gorra, settya*; of posts, *stykenna*; of sail, *ystynna*; put in place, arrange, *desedha*; of sun, *sedhy*; s. upon, *settya* or *deghesy war*[2]; s. going, *lesca, dalleth*; s. free, *dyllo, delyfrya, dygargharа*; s. out, *mōs yn hens*; s. oneself to, *mākya*; s. before, **raggorra*; s. foot on, *tewlel paw yn*; s. fire to, *gorra tan yn*; s. trap, *antel*; s. off trap, **dyantel, dyllo*; s. about it, *gonys a-dro dhodho*; s. right, *amendya*: n., s. of people, *bagas, para, party*, m.; tea s., *dafar tē*; collection, *cuntellyans*, m.; mining, etc., *set*, m., pl. *-tys*: **-ter,** n. *ydhyngy*, m., pl. *-gün*: **-ting,** n. *gorrans*, m.; of sun, *sedhas*, m.

set-back, n. *let, kylden*, m.

set-square, n. *squȳr*, m., pl. *-ys.*

settle, v. *tryga, gül *trevesygeth, kevannedhy*; decide, *jujja, ervȳra*; s. argument, *conclūdya*; s. accounts, difference, *rekna gans*: **-d,** a., of person, *trygys*; of place, *poblys*: **-ment,** n. *trevesygeth*, m., *trygva*, f., pl. *-ow*; agreement, *ambos*, m., pl. *-ow*, **kevambos*, m., pl. *-ow*; s. of debt, *atta·l, *tāl, payment*, m., pl. *-mens.*

seven, a., n. *seyth*; s. times, *seythquyth*: **-fold,** a. *seythplēk*: **-th,** a., n. *seythves*: **-teen,** a., n. *seytek*: **-teenth,** a., n. *seytegves*: **-ty,** a., n. *dēk ha tryügans, tryügans ha dēk*; until 70 times 7, *bys yn dēk ha tryügansgwyth seythgwyth*: **-tieth,** a., n. *degves ha tryügans.*

sever, v. *trēghy yntra deu, dyberth.*

several, a., many, *lȳes, lower*; s., but few, *nebes*; s. particular, *dybarow, dyblans, ‡several.*

severe, a. *ahas, garow, tyn, cales, *sevür*: **-rity,** n. *hardygrās, garowder, sevüreth*, m.

Severn, n. *Havren*, f.

sew, v. *gwrȳas, †sewa*; s. roughly, *crafa*: **-er,** n. *gwrȳador*, m., pl. *-yon*, f. *-es*, pl. *-ow, †sewyas*, m., pl. *-ysy*, f. *-yades*, pl. *-ow.*

sewer, n., drain, *dowrglēth*, m., pl. *-edhyow, carthpȳb*, f., pl. *-ow.*

sex, n. *rȳth*, f.; male s., *gorrȳth*; female s., *benenrȳth.*

sexton, n. *dēn an clogh*, m., pl. *tüs an clēgh, palor bedhow*, m., pl. *-yon b.*, **sacrystan*, m., pl. *-s.*

shabby, a. *cōth* or *ūsyes y dhyllas, pyllenek.*

shackle, n. *cargh·ar*, m., pl. *-ow*: v. *carghara.*

shad, n. *keynak*, m., pl. *-nogas*; allice s., *dama'n hern*, f.

shade, n. *skēs, goskes, goscotter, hüth*, m., *scovva*, f.; the s.s, the abode of the dead, **annown*, m.; s.-trees, *goskejwyth*, col.: v. *goskesy, skewya*: **-ded,** a. **skēsek, goskesys, *goskesek, yn-dan skēs*: **-dow,** n. *skēs*, m., pl. *-ow, goskēs*, m., pl. *-ow*: **-dowed,** a. *goskesys, *goskesek*: **-dowy,** a. **skēsek*: **-dowy,** a. *goskesek.*

shaft, n. *gwelen*, f., pl. *-lyny*, col. *gwēl, *pa·lather (palar)*, m., pl. *pe·lether (peler)*; of spear, etc., *sheft*, m., pl. *-ys*; of cart, *brēgh*, f., pl. *-ow*, d. *dywvrēgh*; of ox-cart, *gwelen-car*, f.; mine s., *shafta*, m., pl. *-tys, pol-stēn*, m.

shag, n. *shagga*, m., pl. *-gys*; nicknames, *spylgarn*, m., pl. *-as, trēn y gōta*: **-gy,** a. *blewak, garow y vlew, dygrȳbys*; of cloth, **pannek*; s. headed, *penvagas.*

shake, v. *crenna, deglena, crȳsya, cryghylly, shakya*: n. **-king,** n. *crēn*, m., pl. *-now, crȳs*, m., pl. *-yow, jag*, m., pl. *-gys.*

shale, n. *lēghen danow*, f., pl. *-now tanow.*

shallot, n. *onyonen ewynek*, f., col. *-yon e.*; clove of s., *ewyn*, m., pl. *-as.*

shallow, a. *bās*; to become s., *bassya*: n. *basdowr, dowr bās, bāsla*, m.: **-ness,** n. *baster*, m.

sham, a. *fals, fekyl, fük*: v. *fükya, omwül bōs*: n. *fük*, m., pl. *-yow, fayntys*, m.

shame, n. *meth*, f., *bysmē·r, shām*, m.; for s.! *rak meth*! *rak shām*! *fȳ dhyso*!: v. *deffola, shamya, shyndya, gorra meth yn, gül bysmē·r dhe*[2]: **-ful,** a. *dyflas, vȳl, vylen, methüs*: **-less,** a. *dyveth.*

shank, n. *esker*, f., pl. *-yow*, d. *dywesker, garen*, f., pl. *-now, ber*, f., pl. *-row*, d. *dywver, fer*, f., pl. *-ow.*

shanny: see **blenny.**

shape, n. *form*, f., pl. *-ow, †furf*, f., pl. *-vyow, fygur, ‡rōth*, m., *shāp*, m., pl. *-ys*: v. *formya, shapya*: **-ly,** a. *tēk, †fythüs*: **-less,** a. *hep form.*

shard, n. *darn pot prȳ*, m., pl. *-ow pottow p.*

share, n. *ran*, f., pl. *-now, kevran*, f., pl. *-now, dōl, trübyt*, m., pl. *-ys, shara*, m., pl. *-rys, part*, m., pl. *-ys*; let each appropriate his s., *kemerens pup ran a'y du*; that's enough for my s., *lowr yu henna dhe'm part-vy*: v. *ranna, kevranna*: **-rer, s.-holder,** n. *kevrennek*, m., pl. *-nogyon, kevrannor*, m., pl. *-yon*.

shark, n. *sharca*, m., pl. *-rkys, morvlȳth*, m., pl. *-ȳdhas, -ȳdhy*; blue s., *morast*, f., pl. *-ysty*; bottle-nosed s., *porgh-bügel*, m.

sharp, a. *lym*; s. of taste, *trenk, wherow*; acute, *glew, tyn, ahas, sherp*; clever, *connek*; of sight, *lagasek*; s. pointed, *skethrak*: **-en,** v. *lemma*: **-ly,** adv. *yn-tyn, sherp*: **-ness,** n. *lymder*, m.

shatter, v. *brewy, terry dhe dymmyn*, **syga*.

shave, v. *dyvarva, trēghy barf*: **-n,** a. *dyvarvys, trēghys y varf*; s. headed, *blogh*: **-vings,** a. *scommow playnyes*, **raskyon*, **rasclyon*, m., pl.

shawl, n. *whytel*, m., pl. *-tlys*, **gwarlen*, f., pl. *-now*.

shawm, n. *salmus*, m., pl. *-ys*.

she, pron. *hȳ*, suffixed, *-y*; emphatic, *hyhȳ·*, suffixed, *-yhȳ·*, *homma, honna*.

sheaf, n. *manal*, f., pl. *-low*; gleaner's s., *tysken*, f., pl. *-now*; to make into sheaves, *manala*.

shear, v. *knyvyas*: **-er,** n. *knyvyor*, m., pl. *-yon*: **-s,** n., pair of s., *gwelsow*, m., pl. *-sevyow*: **-ing,** n. *knyvyans*, m.

shearwater, n., bird, *scüthen*, f., pl. *-as*.

sheath, n. *gōn*, f., pl. *-ow*: **-e,** v. **gōna, gorra yn gōn*: **s.-knife,** n. *collel gōn*, f., pl. *kellyl g.*, †*kethel*, f., pl. *-ly*.

shed, v. *devera, scullya, dyllo, denewy*; of garment, etc., *gasa dhe godha*; s. blood, *scullya lyn*.

shed, n. *crow*, m., *skyber*, f., pls. *-yow*; against rain, *glawjy, cowotty*, m., pl. *-ow*; cattle s., *bowjy*, m.; cart-s., *carjy*, m., pls. *-ow*; goat s., *crow an gever*, m.

she-devil, n. *dyawles*, f., pl. *-ow*.

sheep, n. *davas*, f., pl. *deves*, separative pl. *devysyow*; little s., *davasyk*, f., pl. *devesygow*; to hunt for s., *devyja* (inf. only); s. dog, *kȳ deves*; s.-worrying dog, *devyjor*, m., pl. *-yon*; s. rot, *pōth*, m.; s. dung, *cagal*, m.: **-ish,** a. *kepa·r ha davas*: **-cote,** n. *devetty, davatty*, m., pl. *-ow, bowjy deves*, m., pl. *-ow d.*: **s. fold, s.-pen,** n. *corlan*, f., pl. *-now*: **s.-skin,** n. *molsken*, m., *croghen davas*, f.: s. cloak, †*pellyst-gour*, m., pl. *-ow-tüs*: **s.-span,** n. *spral, pral*, m., pl. *-low, sprallyer*, m., pl. *-ow*.

sheer, a., steep, *serth, crakkya-conna*; utter, *pür, ewn*.

sheet, n., paper, *folen*, f., pl. *-now, pythyonen*, f., pl. *pythyon, lȳven*, f., pl. *-now*; linen s., *lȳen*, m., pl. *-enyow, lȳen-gwely*, m.; winnowing s., *nothlen*, f., pl. *-now*.

shelf, n. *estyllen*, f., pl. *-now*, col. *estyll*.

shell, n., of egg or nut, *plysken*, f., pl. *-now*, col. *plysk*; of fish, *crogen*, f., pl. *cregyn*; bomb, **tanbellen*, f., pl. *-now*; having a s., *crogennek*; having s.s, *cregynnek*; to gather s.s, *cregynna* (inf. only): v. *dyblysca, plysca*; bomb, **tanbellenna*: **-less,** a. *dyblysk*.

shell-fish, n. *bōs-tryg*, m., *puskes crogennek*, pl.; to gather s., *mōs dhe dryg*.

shelter, n. *goskes, goscotter, harber, sclew*, **godor*, **clejor*, m. *skew*, f.; place of s., *scovva, goscovva*, f., *e·rberow, kēl*, m.; s. against rain, *cowotty, glawjy*, m., pl. *-ow*; tree giving s., *cleswedhen, goskejwedhen*, f., col. *-wȳth*: v. *goskesy, skewya, sclewya*, **clesa*: **-ed,** a. *skēsek, goskesek, skewys, skewyek*: **-ing,** a. *clēs*.

shepherd, n. *bügel deves*, m., pl. *-eth(-a) d.*: v. *bügelya*: **-ess,** *bügeles*, f., pl. *-ow*.

sheriff, n., high s., *mēr an pow*, †*ughelvēr*, m., pl. *-as*.

shield, n. *scōs*, m., pl. *-ojow*; coat of arms, *scochon*, m., pl. *-s, cōta arvow*; buckler, *costen*, f., pl. *-now*: v., see **protect**: **s.-bearer,** n. **scoswas*, m., pl. *-wesyon*.

shift, v. *remüvya, gwaya, chanjya, trēlya*: n., garment, *crȳs*, m., pl. *-yow*; dodge, *cast*, m., pl. *-ys*; change, *trēlva*, f.; of work, *torn*, **cōr*, m., pl. *-ys*: **-y,** a. *fēl, coynt, ynjyn, a-wōr lȳes cast*.

shilling, n. *sols*, m., pl. *-ow*.

shilly-shally, v. *hokkya*.

shin, s.-bone, n. *el-esker*, f., pls. *-lyow, -yow*, d. *elyow dywesker*.

shine, v. *terlentry, splanna, dewynya, golowy*, **lentry, howlya*; s. back, *dastewynya*: n. *dewyn*, m., pl. *-now, can*, m.; star-s., *stērgan*; moon-s., *lōrgan*; **-ning,** a. *splan*, **lenter*.

shingle, n., board, *astell*, f., pl. *estyll*; stones, *būly*, col.

ship, n. *gorhel*, m., pl. *-holyon, lester*, m., pl. *lystry*; steam-s., *gorhel-tān*; s.-wreck, *gorhel terrys*, ‡*gwrek*, m., pl. *-ys, torva lester*, f.: **s.-wright,** n. *sēr lystry*, m., pl. *syry l.*: v. **lestra, gorra yn gorhel*.

shire, n. *pow,* m., pl. *-yow.*
shirt, n. *crȳs,* m., pl. *-yow, hevys,* m., pl. *-yow.*
shiver, n. *crēn,* m., pl. *-now, scrüth,* m., pl. *-ow, crȳs,* m., pl. *-yow*: v. *crenna, cryghylly, crȳsya, deglena, scrütha.*
shoal, n., of fish, *hevva,* f.; shallow, *dowr bās, bāsla,* m.
shock, v. *gül üth dhe*², *fetha drē veth*; be s.ed, *bōs dyegrys, dyflasa, kemeres meth*: n., impetus, *herdhyans,* m., *bom,* m., pl. *-myn*; surprise, etc., *scrüth,* m., *drok-glos,* f.: **-ed,** a. *dyegrys*: **-ing,** a. *vȳl, dyflas, üthek, üth y weles*: **-ingly,** adv. *vȳl, üthek.*
shock, n., of corn, *bern,* m., pl. *-yow*; of hair, etc., *bagas,* m., pl. *-ow*: **s.-headed,** a. *penvagas.*
shoe, n. *eskys,* f., pl. *eskyjyow*; low s., †*pawgen,* m., pl. *-now*; s.s, footwear, *arghennas,* m.; horse-s., *horn margh,* m., pl. *hern m.*: v., s. horse, *hernya*; s. person, *arghenna*: **-less,** *dyeskys, dyskyjyow, dyarghen(as)*: **s.maker,** n. †*keryor,* m., pl. *-yon, eskyjyas,* m., pl. *-ysy*: **s.smith,** n. *hernyor,* m., pl. *-yon.*
shoot, v. *tenna*; with arrow, *setha*; s. net, *tewlel rōs*; of plants, *tevy, *egyna, *ympya*: n. **egyn,* m., pl. *-now, skyllen,* f., pl, *skyl, lows,* m., pl. *-ow*; of water, *pystyl,* m., *pȳbel,* f., pl. *-low*: **-er,** n. *tenner,* m., pl. *-noryon, sethor,* m., pl. *-yon.*
shop, n. *gwerthjy,* m., pl. *-ow, shoppa,* m., pl. *-pys*: v. *prena gwara.*
shore, n. *als,* f., pl. *-yow, morva,* f., *glan,* f., pl. *-now*; prop, *jȳst,* m., pl. *-ys, pül,* m., pl. *-yow*: v. *settya pül dhe*².
short, a. *ber, cot*; go, come, or fall s., *fyllel*; in s., *war ver lavarow, war nebes lavarow*; s.-cut, *scoch-forth,* f., pl. *-rdhow, cot-hens,* m., pl. *-njy*; s.-sighted, *ber y wolok*; s.-winded, *ber y anal*; s. wind, *ber-anal,* m.; s. time, *tuch, pols,* m., *teken,* f.: **-en,** v. *berhē·, cotthē·*: **-ly,** adv. *a ver spās, yn cot-termyn, a dermyn ber, kens nep-pell*: **-ness,** n. *berder, cotter,* m.; s. of breath, *ber-anal.*
shot, n. *ten,* m., pl. *-now*; tavern bill, *scot,* m., pl. *-tys*; *reken,* m., pl. *-nys*; bullet, *pellen gon,* f., pl. *-now g.*; like a s., *sket*; within bow s. of, *a-jȳ dhe den gwarak a*²; he's a good s., *tenner da yu.*
shoulder, n. *scōth,* f., pl. *-odhow,* d. *dywscoth*; s. blade, *ascorn-scōth,* m., pl. *eskern-s.*; broad s.ed, *scōdhak*: v. *scodhya.*
shout, n. *crȳ,* m., pl. *-ow, garm,* f., pl. *-ow, galow,* m.: v. *garma, crȳa, predheges, gelwel, hūa, lēfa*; s. out to, *crȳ war*²: **-er,** n. *garmor,* m., pl. *-yon*: **-ing,** n. *garm,* f., *hubbadrylsy, hubbadullya,* m.
shove, n. *pok,* m., pl. *-kyow*: v. *herdhya, pokkya.*
shovel, n. *pāl,* f., pl. *-yow, rēf,* f., pl. *revow*; fire-s., *rēf tān*: v. *palas*: **-ler,** n. *palor,* m., pl. *-yon*; f. *-es,* pl. *-ow.*
show, n. *dysquedhyans, mȳr,* m.; play, *gwary,* m., pl. *-yow*; make a s. of, *mākya, omwül*: v. *dysquedhes*; s. forth, *derȳvas*; s. oneself up, *ombrevy*; s. oneself, *omdhysquedhes*; s. the way, *gedya*: **-y,** a. *splan y lyw.*
shower, n. *cowas,* f., pl. *-wosow*: v. *devera, dyllo, scullya* or *gül cowas glaw*: **-y,** a. *cowesek.*
shrew, n. **logosen mȳn-hogh,* f., col. *logas m-h.,* **whystel, whystlen,* f., pl. *whystlas*; woman, *tebelvenen, tebelwrēk,* f.
shrewd, a. *fēl, fȳn, connek*: **-ness,** n. *felder,* m.
shriek, n. *scrȳs,* f., pl. *-yjow, üs,* m., pl. *üjow*: v. *üja, scrȳja.*
shrike, n. *edhen kyger,* f., pl. *ydhyn k.*
shrill, a. *tyn, yeyn, pür ughel.*
shrimp, n. *bȳbyn-būbyn,* m., pl. *-as.*
shrine, n. *bēth-mēn, tyller sans,* m., *scrȳn,* f., pl. *-yon,* **crērva,* f.
shrink, v. *omdenna, lehē·*; in fear, *plynchya*; shrunken, *gyllys yn gron*: **-ing,** n. *plynch, omdennans,* m.
shrive, v. *assoylya*; s. oneself, *yēs*: **-en,** *yessē·s, assoylyes.*
shrivel, v. *desēgha, gwedhra, crȳghy.*
shroud, n. *lȳen-bēth,* m.: v. *cüdha, mayla.*
shrouds, n., of ship, *lovonow gwern,* pl.
Shrovetide, n. *Enes,* m.; Shrove Tuesday, *dē-Merth Enes.*
shrub, n. *prysken,* f., col. *prysk*: **-bery,** n. *prysclowek,* f., pls. *-egy, -egow.*
shrug, n. *scrüth,* m., pl. *-ow*: v. *scrütha, sevel dhywscoth.*
shudder, n. *scrüth,* m., pl. *-ow, crēn,* m., pl. *-now*: v. *scrüth, kemeres scrüth, deglena, crenna.*
shuffle, v. *draylya treys*; s. cards, *kemysky.*
shun, v. *goheles, sconya, avodya, nagha.*
shunt, v. *herdhya a-denewan, dyberth.*
shut, v. *degēa*; s. in, s. up, *kēas*; s. up! *gās dha sōn! syns dha glap! taw tavas!*: a. *clōs, kēs, degē·s*: **-ter,** n. *kēas fe·nester,* m., pl. *-ow fenestry, gorher,* m., pl. *-yow*; person, *kēer,* m., pl. *-ēoryon.*
shuttle, n. *gwennol,* f., pl. *-nyly.*

shy, a. *methek,* **gohelüs*; to be s. of, *goheles*: v., start aside, *scüsy, plynchya*; apt to s., *skēsek*: **-ness,** n. *meth,* f.

sick, a. *clāf*; s. person, *clāf,* m., pl. *clevyon*; become s., *mōs yn-clāf*: **-ly,** a. *gwan, yn-clāf,* †*anyagh*: **-ness,** n. *cleves,* m., pl. *-vejyow,* ‡*gwanegreth,* m.

sickle, n. *cromman,* m., pl. *-ow, fals,* m., pl. *fylsyow.*

side, n. *tu,* m., pl. *-yow, tenewan,* m., pl. *tenwennow*; of country, *amal,* m. or f., pl. *emlow, e·melow*; upright s., *glan,* f., pl. *-now*; of opponents, *party,* m.; on every s., *a bup tu, a bup parth*; on the hinder s., *wor' tu delergh*; close by my s., *poran ryp ow thenewan* or *scōth*; on one s., from his s., etc., *a'n ȳl tenewan* or *tu*; one on each s. of him, *onen dhodho a bup tu*; on this s. of, *a'n barth-ma dhe*[2]; from one s. to the other, *a ün tenewan dh'y gȳla*; reversed s. by s., *pen ha tyn*; on the s. of, *a-barth*; by thy s., *rybos-sy, ryp dha scōth* or *denewan*; take the s. of, *assentya* or *kewsel gans*: **-long,** a. *dhe-denewan*; a s. look, *golok a gorn y lagas*: **-ways,** adv. *a'n ȳl denewan, a-denewan, ha'y denewan yn-rak.*

sideboard, n. *bord lystry,* m.

siege, n. *omsettyans,* m., *esethva,* f.

sieve, n. *ryder,* m., pl. *-drow*; coarse s., *rydel,* m., pl. *-low, croder,* m., pl. *-drow*; large s., *casyer,* m.: v. *crodra.*

sift, v. *crodra, rydra*; finely, *saya, serjya, dylewghya*: **-er,** n. *crodrer,* m., pl. *-roryon.*

sigh, n. *hanas,* m., pl. *-ow, hanajen,* f., pl. *-now*: v. *hanaja.*

sight, n. *gwēl,* m. or f., pl. *-ow, vu,* m., pl. *-ys, golok,* **trem, sȳght,* m.; sense, *golok, gweles, sȳght,* m.; take s., aim, *medra*; in s. of, *a-wēl dhe*[2], *yn sȳght dhe*[2]; in my s., *yn ow golok*; at first s., *dhe'n kensa vu.*

sign, n. **arweth,* f., pl. *-wedhyow, sȳn,* m., pl. *-ys, tokyn,* m., pl. *toknys*; trace, *ōl,* m., pl. *-ow*: v., to make a s., **arwedha*; s. name, **sȳna, scryfa hanow*: **-gnal,** n. *sȳn,* m., pl. *-ys*; s. station, *arwethva,* f.: v. **arwedha, gül sȳn*: **-ature,** n. *hanow scryfys,* m., pl. *hynwyn s.*: **s.-board,** n. *bord arweth, bord hanow,* m., pls. *-ys a., hynwyn*: **s.post,** n. *post kevarweth, p. hanow,* m., pl. *-ow k., h.*

significance, n. *styr,* m., pl. *-yow,* ‡*sygny-fyans,* m.: **-nt,** a. *splan y styr,* **arwedhek*: **-cation,** n. *styr,* m., pl. *-yow*: **-ify,** v. *styrya,* **arwedha,* ‡*sygnyfya.*

silence, n. *taw,* m.: v. *gül dhodho tewel,* **destewel, megy*; in argument, *conclūdya*: **-nt,** a. **tawesek, dydrōs*; to be s., *tewel*: **-ntly,** adv. *hep gül son, hep whetha corn, hep gül gyk na myk.*

silk, n. *owrlyn,* m., **syjan,* m.; s. fabric, *paly,* m.: **-y,** a. *kepa·r hag owrlyn*: **s.-worm,** n. *pryf owrlyn,* m., pl. *-yves o.*; to take s., *gwysca gon hȳr an lagha.*

silly, a. *fol, goky*; s. fellow, *bobba,* m., pl. *-bys.*

silver, n. *arghans,* m.; s. smith, *gwȳthor a.,* m., pl. *-yon a.*; s.-bearing ground, *arghan-sek,* f., pls. *-egy, -egow*: v. *arghansa*; s. over, *gorarghansa*: **-y,** a. *splan ave·l, arghans, arghansek.*

similar, a. *hevelep, kehaval, haval dhe*[2] or *orth*: **-ity,** n. *hevelepter,* m.: **-ly,** adv. *yndella*: **-itude,** n. *hevelep,* ‡*hevelenep,* m.

simmer, v. *sygera.*

simony, n. *symo·nȳeth,* f.

simple, a. *sempel*; noble and s., *bryntyn ha kēth*; learned and s., *lettrys ha lēk*; to gather s.s, *losowa* (inf. only): **-ton,** n. *goky,* m., pl. *-es,* ‡*cobba,* m., pl. *-ys,* †*edyak,* m., pl. *-s.*: **-plicity,** n. **sempleth,* m.: **-plify,** v. *sempelhē·, ēshē·.*

simultaneous, a. *y'n keth termyn*: **-ly,** adv. *oll warba·rth, war ün wyth, war-not*; s. with, *warbar·th ha . . ., ketto·th ha'n gēr.*

sin, n. *pēgh,* m., no pl., *pēghas,* m., pl. *-gho-sow, peghadow,* m., abst.: v. *pēgha, gül pēgh, camwül*: **-ful,** a. *drok, lün a bēgh*: **-less,** a. *dybēgh*: **-ner,** n. *peghador,* m., pl. *-yon,* f. *-es,* pl. *-ow*: **-ning,** n. *pēgh, peghadow,* m.

since, conj. *pan, aba·n*[2], *par del*[2], *aba·n vē*; s. many years, *nans-yu lȳes bledhen*: adv. *wosa henna*; long s., *solabrȳs, soladhēth.*

sincere, a. *gwyryon, gwȳr, lēl, lēn, hep tull na gȳl*: **-rity,** n. *gwyryoneth, lendury, lelder,* m.

sinecure, n. *benfys hep cür enevow,* m.

sinew, n. *gȳewen,* f., col. *gȳew, skenna,* m., pl. *-ys,* dim. *skennyn,* m., pl. *-now.*

sing, v. *cana*; in concert, **caroly, kescana*: **-er,** n. *caner,* m., pl. *-oryon,* f., *-canores,* pl. *-ow, kenyas,* m., pl. *-ysy,* f. *kenyades,* pl. *-ow*: **-ing,** n. *kenys,* m., pl. *-nesow.*

singe, v. **golesky.*

single, a. *ün, ünyk*; unmarried, *yowynk, dydhemeth*; with neg., *nagonen*; s.-minded, *ünver*; s. heartedly, *kescolon*; a s. moment, *ün prȳs* or *tuch*; there's not a s. one, ‡*nyns-üs ün onen.*

singular, a. *ünyk, coynt*: **-ity,** n. *coyntys, ünykter,* m.
sink, v. *sedhy, codha, büdhy*; s. a hole, *polly, telly*: **-ing,** *sēth,* m., pl. *sedhow, sedhas,* m.: n., plumbing, *toll-dowr,* m., pl. *tell-d.*
sip, v. *eva, glybya mȳn, eva lemmyk ha lemmyk*: n. *lemmyk,* m., pl. *-ygow, lommowygow.*
sippet, n. *sūben,* f., pl. *-now.*
sir, Sir, n. *syrra, syr, Syr,* m., pl. *syrys, arluth,* m., pl. *-lydhy*: **-e,** n. *sȳra,* m., pl. *sȳryow.*
sister, n. *whōr,* f., pl. *wheryth,* dim. *whoryk,* f., pl. *wherythygow*: s. in law, *whōr drē lagha*; half s., *hanter whōr.*
sit, v. *esedha* (*sedha*); you s. there all day long, ‡*yth-esough-why owth-esedha war agas lost oll an jeth*: **-ting,** a. *esedhys, a'y eseth*: n., s. posture, *eseth,* f.; session, *esethvos,* m.
site, n. *lē,* m., pl. *-ow, tyller,* m., pl. *-yow.*
situated, a. *ow-sevel, desedhys*: **-tion,** n. *lē,* m., pl. *-ow*; state, *stüth,* m., pl. *-yow.*
six, a., n. *whēgh*; s. days, *wheddyth,* m.: **-fold,** a. *wheghplek, wheghkemmy·s*: **-pence,** n. *whednar,* m. (for *whēgh dynar*): **-th,** a., n. *wheghes, wheghves* (*wheffes*) **-teen,** a., n. *whetek*: **-th,** a. *whetegves*: **-ty,** a., n. *trȳügans*: **-tieth,** a., n. *trȳügansves.*
size, n. *braster, myns,* m.; glue, *glüs,* m.
sizzle, v. *tythya, whybana.*
skate, v. **skȳtya,* **slynk-resek*: n. **skȳta,* m., pl. *-tys,* **eskys slynk-resek,* f., pl. *eskyjyow s.-r.*; fish, *talver,* m., pl. *-as, morgath,* f., pl. *-as, carlyth,* f., pl. *-ow, carlyth trȳlost,* f.; long-nosed s., *mȳnek,* m., pl. *-nogas.*
skeet, n. **skȳt,* m., pl. *-ys.*
skein, n. **cüden,* f., pl. *-now.*
skeleton, n. *corf, eskern,* f., pl. *-ow, corf gyllys yn eskern,* f., pl. *-ow g. y. e.*
sketch, v. *lynenna, tenna*: n. *ten,* m., pl. *-now.*
skewer, n. *kȳkbren,* m., pl. *-yer.*
skill, n. *connek, sleyneth,* m.: **-ed,** a. *skentyl, gwenwhys*: **-lful,** a., *connek, ynjyn, sley.*
skim, v. *resek yn-scaf drēs*; milk, *dydhehenna*; in digging, **gobalas.*
skin, n. *croghen,* f., pl. *crēghyn, ken,* †*hē,* m. (no pl.), *knēsen,* f., col. *knēs*; thin s., *kennen,* f., pl. *-now*; s. of fruits, etc., *maskel,* f., pl. *-sclow*; turf, etc., *tonnen,* f., pl. *-now*: v. *dyscroghenna, dygroghenna, pylya, dyrüsca*: **-less,** a. *dygroghen, dyscroghen*: **-ner,** n. *cronor,* m., pl. *-yon*: **-ny,** a. *cül, kenak.*
skip, v. *terlemmel*: n. *terlam,* m., pl. *-mow.*
skirmish, v. **skyrmsya*: n. *deray·,* **skyrmys,* m.
skirt, n. **losten,* f., pl. *-now*: v. *mōs ryp.*
skit, n. *scowt,* f., pl. *-ys*; burlesque, *scryfa scaf*: **-tish,** a. *skēsak,*
skittle, n. *kȳl,* m., pl. *-ys*; game of s.s, *gwary-kȳlys,* m.
skua, n., bird, *gwagel,* f., pl. *-as.*
skulk, v. *scolkya, tēghy, goheles.*
skull, n. *crogen,* f., pl *cregyn*; for distinction from "shell," *c. an pen*; thick s., **clopen,* m.; of animal, *penpral,* m.
sky, n. *nēf,* m. or f., pl. *nevow, ebren* (*ebron*), f.; patch of blue s., *lagas,* m., pl. *-ow.*
skylark, n. *awhesyth,* m., pl. *-ydhas.*
skylight, n. *fe·nester-to,* f., pl. *-nestry-t.*
slab, n. *lēgh,* f., pl. *-ow, leghven,* m., pl. *-veyn.*
slack, a. *lows, lent, lak*; s. person, *caughwas,* m., pl. *-wesyon*: **-en,** v. *lowsel, slakya,* **dyestynna*: **-ness,** n. *lowsethes,* m.
slag, n. *atal mūn tedhys,* m.; tin, *pylyon,* pl.
slake, v. *dysēgha, slakya*; s. lime, *ladha.*
slam, v. *deghesy gans mür a drōs ha nell.*
slander, n. *sclander, cabel,* m.: v. *sclandra, cably.*
slang, n. *yēth ysel,* f.; strip of land, *lȳn,* f., pl. *-yow.*
slant, n. *leder,* f., pls. *-drow, -dry*: v. *ledry*: **-ing,** a. *ledrek.*
slap, n. *squat,* m., pl. *-tow, stewan,* m., pl. *-now, what,* m., pl. *-tys, whaf,* m., pl. *-fys*: v. *squattya, frappya, stewanny*: **s.-dash,** a. *whym-wham.*
slash, v. *hakkya, trēghy*: n. *lash,* m., pl. *-ys, trogh,* m., pls. *-ow, trēghyon.*
slate, n. *lēghen,* f., pl. *-now*; s. rock, *kyllas,* col.; s. slab, *lēghven,* m., pl. *-veyn*: **-r,** n. *tȳor,* m., pl. *-yon, trēghyas lēghennow,* m., pl. *-ysy l.*
slaughter, n. *lath,* m., *lathva,* f., †*ar,* f., pl. *-ow,* **arva,* f.; s.-house, **latty,* m.: v. *ladha.*
slave, n. †*kēth,* m., pl. *-yon,* f. *-es,* pl. *-ow, kēthwas,* m., pl. *-wesyon*; attached to soil, †*tȳthyak,* m., pl. *-yogyon*; s.-ship, s.er, *lester kēthyon*: **-ry,** n. **kēthneth,* m., **gwaso·nȳeth,* f.: **-ish,** a. **gwasek, ysel.*
slaver, n., slobber, **glavor,* m.: v. **glavorya.*
slay, v. *ladha*: **-er,** n. *ledhyas,* m., pl. *-ysy.*
sledge, n. *car slynkya,* m., pl. *kerry s.*; s.-hammer, *slodya,* m., pl. *-yes.*
sleek, a. *leven*; of hair, *plattyes.*
sleep, n. *hün, cusk, cuscas,* m.: v. *cusca,* **hüna*; s. heavily, *cusca pōs*; s. badly, *ter-*

gusca; s. face downwards, *cusca war y dor*, *agathor*, etc.; when not s.ing, *a-dhyfüna*: **-er,** n. *cuscador* (*-jor*), m., pl. *-yon*, f., pl. *-ow*: **-iness,** n. *whans hün*, *posyjyon*, m.; sudden s., †*hün desempys*: **-ing,** n. *hün*, m.: **-less,** a. *dyfün*, **dygusk*: **-lessness,** n. *dyfüna*, *fowt cusca*, m.: **-y,** a. *hünek*; unseasonably s. person, *hünek*, m., pl. *-nogyon*, †*cuscador desempys*, m.; I am s., *yma· dhym whans cusca*, *yma· hün orth ow grevya.*

sleet, n. *dowrērgh*, **glybērgh*, **ērghlaw*, m.

sleeve, n. †*brēghal*, m., pl. *-ellow*: **-d,** a. *brēghelek.*

sleight, n. *sleyneth*, *connyng*, *sotelneth*, m.

slender, a. *cül*, *mōn*, *tanow*; make or become s., *monhē·*, *tanowhē·*: **-ness,** n. *cülder*, m.

sleuth, n. *hellerghyas*, m., pl. *-ysy.*

slice, n. *skethen*, f., pl. *-now*, *trēgh*, m., pl. *-ow*: v. *skethenna*, *trēghy.*

slide, v. *slynkya*: n. *slynk*, m.

slight, a. *boghes*, *scaf*, *tanow*, *gwan*, **ydhyl*; insult, *dysprēsyans*, m.: v. *dysprēsya*: **-ly,** adv. *boghes*, *nebes*, *yn-scaf.*

slim, -ness: see **slender, -ness.**

slime, n. *lȳs*, *slȳm*, *lūb*, m.; s. of slug or snail, **lȳs melwhes*: **-my,** a. *lȳsak*; to make s., *lūba.*

sling, v. *tewlel*: n. **towlbren*, m., pl. *-yer*: **-stone,** n. **mēn towlbren*, **m. labedha*, m.

slink, v. *scolkya*, *cramyas*, *mōs yn-dan gēl.*

slip, v. *trebüchya*, *slynkya*, *resek*, *dyank*, ‡*slyppya*; let s., *dyllo*: n. *slynk*, m.; s. of land, *lȳn*, f., pl. *-yow*: **-knot,** n. *colm-rē*, m., pl. *-ow-r.*: **-per,** n. †*whybanor*, *eskys chȳ*, m.: **-pery,** a. *slynk.*

slit, n. *fals*, m., pl. *-ljow*, *squard*, m., pl. *-ys*: v. *falsa*, *squardya.*

sloe, n. **yrynen*, f., pl. *-yryn.*

slop, v. *scullya*: **-s,** n. *scullyon*, *golghyon*, pl.

slope, n. *leder*, f., pls. *-drow*, *-dry*, *rȳn*, m., pl. *-yow*, *ryll*, m., pl. *-yow*: v. *ledry*: **-ing,** a. **ledrek.*

sloth, n. **dȳegy*, m.: **-ful,** a. *dȳek.*

slough, n. †*lagen*, f., pl. *-now.*

sloven, n. *lavrak*, m., pl. *-rogyon*, *scübelak*, m., pl. *-logyon*: **-ly,** a. *dȳek*, *lows*, *plos.*

slow, a. *lent*, *cosel*, *hell*, *syger*, **ara*(*f*); of wits, *pensogh*: **-ness,** n. *sygerneth*, m.

slow-worm, n. †*anaf*, m., pl. *-avas.*

slug, n. *melwhesen* (†*melwhen*), f., col. *melwhas*; large spotted s., *melwhesen velen*; black s., *melwhesen dhu*; small s., *glüthvelwen*, f., pl. *-wes*; to catch s.s, *melwhessa* (inf. only): **-gish,** a. *dȳek*, *syger*; s. person, *caughwas*, m., pl. *-wesyon*: **-gishness,** n. *sygerneth*, *dyekter*, m.

sluice, n. *darras dowr*, **flosyet*, m.

slumber, n. *hün*, *cusk*, m.: v. *cusca*, *hüna.*

slush, n. *lȳs*, m.; snow, *tedhergh*, m.

slut, n. *lavroges*, *scübeloges*, f., pl. *-ow.*

sly, a. *fēl*, †*cal*: **-ness,** n., *felder*, *calder*, m.

smack, n. *squat* (*scat*), m., pl. *-tow*, *what*, m., pl. *-tys*; boat, *cok*, m., pl. *cūcow*; taste, *blas*, m.: v. *squattya*, *rȳ what*, *frappya.*

small, a. *münys*, *bȳghan.*

small-pox, n. *pokkys-münys*, pl.

smart, n. *glōs*, f., *losk*, m.: v. *lesky*, **glōsa*: a. *fȳn*, *jolyf*, *frēth*; painful, *tyn*; spruce, *brāf*: **-ly,** adv. *shērp*, *yn-tyn*; s. dressed, *afȳnys.*

smash, n. *torva*, f.; with a s., *squat*!: v. *brewy*, *terry dhe dymmyn.*

smear, v. *droküra*, *mostya*; with clay, *prȳa*; s. colours, *dyslywa*: n. *drokürans*, *dyslywans*, m.

smell, v., perceive s., *clewes*, *sawory*, *blasa*, **mousa*; give out s., *rȳ ēth*, *mousegy*, *flērya*: n. *blas*, m., pl. *-ow*, *sawor*, m., pl. *-yow*, *ōdor*, m., pl. *-s*, *smyllyng*, m.; bad s., *flēr*, *flērynsy*, *droksawor*, m.; sense of s., *clewes* or *skȳans ēth*, m.: **-y,** a. *mousak*, *flērys.*

smelt, v. *tedha*: **-er,** n. *tedher*, m., pl. *-oryon*: **-ed,** a. *tedhys*, *tēth*; of tin, *gwyn*: **-ing,** n. *tēth*, m.

smile, n. *wharth*, **mynwharth*, **gwenwharth*, m.: v. *wherthyn*, **gwenwherthyn*, **mynwherthyn.*

smite, v. *brewy*, *gweskel*, *squattya*, *frappya*, *cronkya.*

smith, n. *gōf*, m., pls. *-ves*, *-vyon*; s.s mate, *gwas-gōf*, m., pl. *gwesyon-g.*, *-goves*; s.s apprentice, *map-gōf*, m., pl. *mebyon-goves*; black s., *gōf*, *gōf du*; shoe-s., *ferror*, m., pl. *-yon*: **-y,** n. *govel*, f., pl. *-yow.*

smithereens, n. *skethrygow*, *tymmynygow*, **dernowygow*, pl.

smock, n. *hevys*, m., pl. *-yow*: v. *cryghwrȳas*: **-ing,** n. **hevyswȳth*, *gwrȳas crȳgh*, *g. crȳben mēl*, m.

smoke, n. *mōk*, m.; a s. of tobacco, *tuch -pȳb*, m.: v. *megy*; s. tobaco, *tuchya pȳb.*

smooth, a. *leven*, *gwastas*, *compes*, *plattyes*, *smōth*; hairless, *blogh*; of manner, *cosel*: v. *composa*, *levenhē·*, *levna*, *plattya*, *coselhē·*: **-ly,** adv. *yn-leven*, *smōth*: **-ness,** n. *levender*, *composter*, m.; of sea, †*spaven*, m., *spavnell*, f., pl. *-ow.*

smother, v. *megy*, *taga*; s. fire, *dyfüdhy.*

smoulder, v. *sygera, lesky yn ün sygera.*

smudge, v. *mostya, dyslywa.*

smuggle, v. **franklondya, londya yn-dan gēl, dyscarga da *dydoll*; s.d, **franklondyes*: **-r,** n. *gwycor frank, g. *dydoll*, m., pl. *-yon d.*: **-ling,** n. *chyffar frank, c. cüth*, m.

smut, v. *dūa*: **-s,** n. **hü·dhygel, hylgeth*, m.

snail, n. †*melwhen*, f., col. *melwhes*, †*melwhy-oges*, f., pl. *-ow, bulho·rn*, m., pl. *-as*; to catch s.s, *melwhessa* (inf. only).

snake, n. *gorthfyl*, m., pl. *-as, sarf*, f., pl. *syrf*; s.-stone, *mylprȳf*, m.: **-y,** a. *sarfek, gwȳüs.*

snap, n. *crak*, m., pl. *-kys*; as interj. *crak! knak! squat!*: v. *crakkya, squattya.*

snare, n. *maglen*, f., pl. *-now, crokken*, f., pl. *-now, croglath*, f., pl. *-ow, magel*, f., pl. *-glow*, ‡*trayn*, m., pl. *-ys*: v. *cachya, bagha, magly*: **-ing,** n. *antel*, f.

snarl, n. *scrynk, deskernyans*, m.: v. *scrynkya, deskerny.*

snatch, n. *squych*, m., pl. *-ys*: v. *kȳbya, cachya dhe-vēs, *skyvly.*

sneak, v. *scolkya*; tell tales, *kewsel adryf tüs*: n. **scolk*, m., pl. *-ys, *kylgy*, m., pl. *-gün.*

sneer, v. *scornya*; s. at, *gül gēs a*[2].

sneeze, v. *strewy*, ‡*rahaya*: n. *strew*, m., pl. *-yow*: **-wort,** n. *strewles*, m.

sniff, v. **frony, *mousa, *frygwhetha*: n. **frygwheth*, m., pl. *-ow.*

snipe, n. *kȳogh*, f., pl. *-as, gavar- hāl*, f., pl. *gever-h.*; jack-s., *dama-kȳogh*, f.

snivel, v. *mēry*: n. *pūr*, m.: **-ler,** n. *merek*, m., pl. *-rogyon*: **-ling,** a. *goverek, merek, purek.*

snore, v. *renky, whyrny*: n. *ronk, renkyas*, m.: **-r,** n. *renkyer*, m., pl. *-yoryon, renkyas*, m., pl. *-ysy.*

snort, v. *renky, *frony*: n. *renkyas, ronk*, m.

snot, n. *pūr*, m.: **-ty,** a. *purek.*

snout, n. *trōn*, m., pl. *-ow.*

snow, n. *ērgh*, m.; s. flake, *plüven-ērgh*, f., col. *plüf-e.*: v. *gül ērgh*: **-y,** a. *ērghek*: **-drop,** n. *blejen ērgh*, f., pl. *-jyow-ē.*

snub, v. *keredhy*: n. *keredhyans*, m.

snuff, n. *pon strewy*, m.; of candle, *pen cantol*, m.: v., s. out, *megy, ladha*: **-ers,** n., pair of s., *gevel cantol*, f., pl. *-yow c.*

snuffle, v. *kewsel drē an frygow*: **-ly,** a. *merek.*

snug, a. *mür attē·s, cüdhys, clōs, *cles*; to make s., *cüdha yn-clōs*: **-gle,** v. *omgüdha yn clōs, omjersya.*

so, adv. *mar*[2], *del*[2]; s. that, *may*[5], *rak may*[5], *par may*[5]; thus, *yndella, y'n for'-ma, y'n for'-na*; just s., *y'n ketella, y'n ketelma*; eh, what, is that s.? *ay, dar, yndella vyth-hy*?; s. be it, *yndella re-bo, ha bedhens*; s. much, *kemmȳ·s*; s. and s., *map y dhama*; an illness s. severe that he will die of it, *cleves mar ahas ha dredho ef dhe verwel*; conj. *ytho·, rag henna*; and s., *ha gans* or *rag henna.*

soak, v. **glēghy, *sūba, *sēgy*; to put to s., *gorra yn *glēgh.*

soap, n. *seban*, m.; v. *sebony.*

soar, v. *nyja ughel, yskynna y'n ayr.*

sob, v. *ola*: n. *olva*, f., pl. *-ow.*

sober, a. *dyvedhow*; serious, *tryst, sad, dōth*: **-briety,** n. *dyvedhowder, sevüreth*, m.

sociable, a. *a-gar cowethas.*

social, a. *a'n düs, a gowethyans*; convivial, *lowen, a gyfvewy.*

society, n. *cowethas*, f., pl. *-ow.*

sock, n. †*pawgen*, m., pl. *-now.*

socket, n. *morter*, m.; for helve, *crow arf*, m.; eye s., *pol lagas*, m., pl. *-low l.*

sod, n. *towarghen*, f., col. *towargh, tam*, m., pl. *tymmyn.*

soda, n. **soda*, m.

sofa, n. *gwely dēth*, m., pl. *-yow d.*

soft, a. *medhel* (‡*medel*), *cosel, lȳth, blüth, medhew*: **-en,** v. *medhelhē·, blüdhya, lȳth, coselhē·*: **-ly,** adv. *yn-cosel*: **-ness,** n. *medhelder*, m.

soggy, a. *devrak.*

soil, n. *gweras, prȳ, dōr*, m., pl. *-ow*: v. *mostya*: **-ed,** a. *lōs, mostyes* (*-tys*).

sojourn, v. *tryga*: n. *trygva*, f., *gortos*, inf.

Sol, n. *Soly*, m.

solace, n. *hebasca*, f., *confort, *solas*, m.: v. *confortya, chersya, hebaskhē·.*

solan-goose, n. *sethor*, m., pl. *-as.*

solder, n. **soder*, m.: v. **sodra.*

soldier, n. *soudor*, m., pls. *-yon, -drys*; horse s., *marghak* (*marrek*), m., pl. *-ogyon.*

sole, n., of foot, †*gothen*, ‡*gothen-trōs*, f., pl. *-thnow*, d. *dyw-wothen, goles-trōs*, m., pl. *-ow t.*, d. *deuwoles t.*; of shoe, *gothen* or *goles eskys.*

sole, n., fish, **garlythen*, f., col. **garlyth.*

sole, a. *ünyk, ün.*

solecism, n. *ancothfos*, m.

solemn, a. *sad, sevür, solempna*: **-ity,** n. *sevüreth, solempnyta*, m.

solen, n. *kyllygen*, f., pls. *-ygy, -ygys*, col. *kyllyk.*

solicit, v. *govyn, pysy*: **-ous,** a. *prederüs*: **-ude,** n. *fyenasow*, abst. pl. *preder, bern*, m.

solicitor, n. *dēn an lagha*, m., pl. *tüs a. l.*

solid, a. *cales, crēf, fast*: **-arity,** n. *ünvereth,* m.: **-ify,** v. *crefhē·, fasthē·, caleshē·*; clot, *moly*; curdle, *cowla*: **-ity,** n. *crefter, caletter,* m.

soliloquize, v. *kewsel orto y honen, omgewsel*: **-quy,** n. *omgows,* m.

solitariness, n. *ünykter,* m.: **-tary,** a. *dygoweth, ünyk, y honen-oll*: **-tude,** n. *dyfȳth, tyller clōs, *ünygeth,* m.; in s., *y honen.*

soluble, a. *hedēth*: **-ution,** n., chemical, *tedhans, tēth,* m.; of problem, *desmygyans, desmyk,* m.

solve, v. *assoylya, desmygy.*

solvency, n. *gallos dhe dylly,* m.: **-t,** a. *a-ȳl tylly.*

sombre, a. *du, tewl*: **-ness,** n. *duder, tewolgow,* m.

some, a. *nebes, neppyth a²*; pron. *ran, rē, nep-part, darn*; s. of them, *rē* or *ran anedha*: adv. *nep*: **-body,** pron. *nebonen, nep-onen, nep dēn*; s. else, *kēn onen*: **-day,** adv. *ün jēth a-dhē*: **-how,** adv. *nep maner, nep forth, war nep cor*: **-one,** see **somebody**: **-thing,** pron. *neppyth, nep-tra, nebes, ün dra*: **-time,** adv. *neb ür, nep prȳs*: **-times,** adv. *trawythyow, ‡war-ürow*: **-what,** adv. *neppyth, nebes*; prefix, *go-*: **-where,** adv. *nepplas, nep-lē*; s. else, *kēn tyller.*

somersault, b. *cryghlam,* m.; to turn a s., *cryghlemmel.*

Somerset, n. *Gwlās an Hāf,* f.

son, n. *māp (mab),* m., pl. *mebyon*; s.-in law, *düf,* m., pl. *devyon*; dearly beloved s., *maprās*; His only-begotten S., *y ün Vab-ef*; the S. of Man, *Map an Dēn, ‡an Map a Dhēn.*

song, n. *cān,* f., pl. *-ow*; in choir, *cürgan,* f. pl. *-ow*: **-ster,** n. *canor,* m., pl. *-yon*: **-stress,** n. *canores,* f., pl. *-ow.*

soon, adv. *wharē·, yn-scon*; very s., *dystough, a-dhystough*; as s. as (before v.), *kettel²*; (before n.), *ketto·th ha*; as s. as ever, *bys pan²*; so s., *mar gwyk* or *scon*; I would as s., *mar dha vȳa genef*: **-er,** adv. *kens, kensa*; the s., *dhe sconna, dhe gens*; no s., *nahe·ns* (with neg.).

soot, n. *hylgeth, *hü·dhygel (hüdhyl),* m.: **-y,** n. *hylgethek, *hüdhyglek, du.*

soothe, v. *coselhē·, dyserry, hebaskhē·.*

soothsayer, n. *†cōlyak,* m., pl. *-yogyon,* f. *-yoges,* pl. *-ow, *darganor,* m., pl. *-yon.*

sop, n. *sūben,* f., pl. *-now.*

soprano, n. *trebyl,* m.

sorcerer, n. *pystryor, †hüdol,* m., pl. *-yon, †gorhenyas,* m., pl. *-ysy*: **-ess,** n. *pystryores, †gorhenyades,* f., pl. *-ow*: **-ry,** n. *pystry, tebel-art, *nygromans,* m.

sordid, a. *plos, gal.*

sore, a. *clāf, tyn, brew*; to be s. after a beating, *cosa*: n. *gwenen,* f., pl. *-now, podrethes, goly,* m., pl. *-ow, brew,* m., pl. *-yon*; full of s.s, *podrethek.*

sorrel, n. *tavolen-wherow,* f., col. *tavol-w.*; wood-s., **bara an gōk,* m.

sorrow, n. *awhē·r, cavow, cüth, govyjyon, trystans, trystys, moreth, dughan, edrega, edrek,* m., *galar,* m., pl. and abst. *-ow*: v. *kȳny, bōs cüdhys, *galary*: **-ful,** a. *cüdhys, tryst, trūesy, yeyn, morethek, trūethek, lün a voreth*: **-ry,** a. *morethek, cüdhyjyk*; I am s., *edrek* or *cüth a-m-büs, drōk yu genef, edrek dhym yma·*; to be or make s., *dughanhē·*; to make s., *cüdhy, cüdhyjykhē·*; you'll be s. for that, *ty a-ōl henna*; I should be very s. to break it, *dȳeth fest vȳa dhym y derry.*

sort, n. *ēghen,* f., *par,* m., pl. *-ow, sort,* m., pl. *-ow, kynda,* m.; in some s., *war nep cor*; any s. of, *ēghen a²*: v. **sortya, *assortya, dygemysky.*

soul, n. *enef, ena,* m., pl. *-evow*; by my s., *re'm ena* or *sowl.*

sound, n. *trōs,* m., pl. *-ow, sōn,* m., pl. *-yow*; without the slightest s., *hep gyk na myk*; s. advice, *cusül stowt* f.: v. *seny*; s. together, *kesseny*; s. a trumpet, *üscana*; s. instruments, *cana, gül dhe gana*; test depth, *prevy gans plemmyk, whylas an goles*: a. *yagh, salow, saw*: **-ing,** a. ,well-s., *heso·n*; harsh-s., *garow, dygesso·n*; depth, *downder a-yllyr y brevy,* m.

soup, n. *cowl, yskel,* m.

sour, a. *trenk, wherow, *sür*; s. milk, *lēth cowlys*; to make s., *trenkhē·*: **-ish,** *godrenk, *skyldrenk*: **-ness,** n. *whe·rowder, trenkter, *sürny,* m.

source, n. *penfenten,* m., pl. *-tynyow, pengover,* m., pl. *-ow.*

South, n. *dȳghow, Sōth,* m.; S.-West, *Sōth-West*; s. country, *dȳghowbarth,* f.: **-ern,** a. *a'n Sōth, a'n barth dyghow.*

southernwood, n. *†dyghowles,* f.

souvenir, n. *cofro,* m., pl. *-how.*

sovereign, n. *myghte·rn,* m., pl. *-eth, sovran,* m., pl. *-s*; coin, *püns sterlyn,* m., pl. *-ows*: a. *sovran, rȳal*: **-ty,** n. *sovranta, myghternsys,* m.

sow, v., s.seed, *gonys hās, *hasa*; s. broadcast, *gonys hās a-lēs, gorthewlel*: **-er,** n. *gonader,* m., pl. *-doryon, haser,* m., pl. *-oryon.*
sow, n. *banow,* f., pls. *ba·nowas, by·newy,* d. *by·newyk*; s. for breeding, *gwȳs,* f., pl. *-y.*
sow-thistle, n. *losowen lēth, *lethegen,* f.
space, n. *spās, efander,* m.; empty s., *gwakter,* m.; short s., while, *pols, tuch, lam,* m.: **-ious,** a. *efan, ledan.*
spade, n. *pāl,* f., pl. *-yow.*
Spain, n. *Spayn,* f.: **Spaniard,** n. *Spanyer,* m., pl. *-s*: **-ish,** a. *Spaynek*; lang., *Spaynek,* m.
span, n. *dornva,* f., pl. *-vedhy*; of inches, **rewhans,* m.; for sheep, etc., *spral,* m., pl. *-low, sprallyer,* m., pl. *-s*: v., measure, *musüra, *rewhansa*; s. sheep, *spralla.*
spangle, v. *sterenny*: **-d,** a. *sterennek*: **-s,** n. *golowylyon,* pl.
spaniel, n. *spanyol,* m., pl. *-ys, kȳ Spayn,* m., pl. *cün S.*
spar, n. *pren,* m., pl. *-yer*; fluor s., *can, candȳr,* m.
sparable, n. *sparbyl,* m., pl. *-s.*
spare, a., thin, *tanow, cül*; of wheel, room, etc., *gwythys erby·n ethom, drēs an pyth a-rēs*: of s. diet, *nebes y vōs ha sosten*: v. *hepcor, sparya, †erbysy*: **-ingly,** *yn-tanow, boghes.*
spark, n. *elven,* f., pl. *-now, gwrȳghonen,* f., col. *gwrȳghon*; s. of fire, **tannen,* f., pl. *-now*: **-le,** v. *terlentry, glyttra, gwrȳghony, elvenny, sterenny*: **-ling,** a. *elvennek, gwrȳghonek, ow-clyttra.*
sparrow, n. *golvan,* m., pl. *-as*; hedge s., *golvan-gē*: **s.-hawk,** n. **spar-hōk,* m., pl. *-ys.*
spasm, n. *glōs,* f., pl. *-ow, squych,* m., pl. *-ys*; to move in s.s, *squychya.*
spatter, v. *lagenna, scullya*; with dirt, *cagla*: **-dashes,** n. *poltrygas,* m., pl. *-gosow.*
spatula, n. **spadel,* f., pl. *-low.*
speak, v. *cows, kewsel, medhes, ‡clappya*; s. under one's breath, *hanas*: **-er,** n. *leveryas,* m., pl. *-ysy, cowser,* m., pl. *-soryon*; public s., **arethyor,* m., pl. *-yon*: **-ing,** n. *cows, ‡cowsans, ‡tala,* m.
spear, n. *gu (gew),* m., pl. *-yow*; *spēra,* m., pl. *-ys*; boar-s., *hoghwu,* m., pl. *-yow*: v. *gȳa, gwana.*
special, a. *specyal*: **-ly,** adv. *kens oll, drēs ēghen, mür dhe voy, specyly*: **-ity,** n. **specyalta,* m.
species, n. *ēghen,* f., *kynda,* m.
specimen, n. *ēqual,* m., *sampel,* m., pl. *-plys, ran,* f., pl. *-now*; finest s., *flowr,* f., pl. *-ys.*
specious, a. *fekyl.*
speck, n. *nam,* m.: **-le,** v. *brȳtha*: n. *brȳthen,* f., pl. *-now,* col. *brȳth*: **-led,** a. *brȳth*; of fowl, *‡speckyar.*
spectacle, n. *gwary-mȳr,* m.: **-tator,** n. *myrer,* m., pl. *-oryon*: **-tacles,** n. *spectaklys, *golokwedrow,* pl.
spectre, n. *tarosvan,* m., pl. *-now, skēs,* m., pl. *-ow.*
speculate, v. **aventurya*; meditate, *predery*: **-tion,** n. **aventur,* m., pl. *-ys, vȳaj,* m., pl. *-ys*: **-tor,** n. **aventuryer,* m., pl. *-yoryon*: **-tive,** n. **aventuryes.*
speech, n. *cows, lavar,* m., pl. *-ow*; oration, *areth,* f., pl. *-yow*; long, noisy s., *predhek,* m., pl. *-egow*; language, *ȳeth,* f., pl. *-ow, tavas,* m., pl. *-ow*; to make a s., *arethya*: **-less,** a. *omlavar, †aflavar.*
speed, n. *tōth, crȳs,* m., *speda,* f.; at great s., *gans mür a dōth* or *grȳs, tōth brās, t. mēn, t. da, totta·*; good s., *spēda dēk*; God s.! *God spēda dhys*!: v. *spēdya, tothya*; give success, *gweres, gwellhē·, spēdya*: **-ily,** adv. *yn cottermyn, a ver-dermyn, a ver-spas, war, yn* or *gans hast, yn-scon, quyk*: **-y,** a. *snel, üskys.*
spell, v. **spellya, *lytherenna, *syllaby*: n. *sōn,* m., pl. *-ow*; of time, *cors,* m., pl. *-ow, prȳjwyth,* m.; s.-binder, *hüder,* m., pl. *-doryon*; s.-breaker, *peller,* m., pl. *-loryon*; s.-bound, *yn-dan hüs*: **-ing,** n. **lythere·nȳeth,* f.
spence, n. *spens,* m., pl. *-ys.*
spend, v. *spēna*: **-thrift,** n. *scullyak,* m., pl. *-ogyon*: **-nt,** a., exhausted, *squythys*; finished, *dü(dē)*; of money, *spēnys.*
spew, v. *wheja.*
sphere, n. *pēl,* f., pl. *-yow, pellen,* f., pl. *-now*: **-rical,** a. *crēn, rond.*
spice, n. *spȳsa,* m., pl. *spȳcys*: **-y,** a. *blesys da, spȳcek.*
spider, n. **kefnysen,* f., col. *kefnys*; s.'s web, *gwȳas-kefnysen*: **s.-crab,** n. *gevryk,* m., pl. *-ygow, gryll vor,* m., pl. *-as v., tragesort,* m., pl. *-as, canker hȳr y baw.*
spigot, n. *canel,* m., pl. *-lys.*
spike, n. *kenter,* f., pl. *-trow, brōs,* m., pl. *-ojow*; fine, *drēn,* m., pl. *dreyn*; of flower, *tos,* m., pl. *-ow*; s.-nail, *spȳk,* f., pl. *-ygys*: v. *berya, kentra, gwana*: **-y,** a. *drēnak*; of flower, *tosak*: **s.nard,** n. *spȳknard,* m.
spill, v. *scullya, *gorscullya, gasa dhe godha*: n., fall, *coth,* m.

spill, n. *ebyl, paper trēlyes yn pyb drōyllek,* m., pls. *-yow.*
spin, v., yarn, thread, etc., *nedha*; twist, turn, etc., *nedha trēlya*; s. round, *trōyllya, *rosella*; s. out, *strechya*; of time, *dylātya*: n. *trōyll,* f., pl. *-yow*: **-ner,** n. *nedher,* m., pl. *-dhoryon,* f., *-dhores,* pl. *-ow*: **-ning-wheel,** n. *torna,* m., pl. *-nys.*
spinach, n. **spynach,* m.
spindle, n. *gwerthys,* f., pl. *-yjow*; s. tree, *gwedhen-gwerthyjow,* f., col. *gwȳth-g.*; s. whorl, **rosellen,* f., pl. *-now.*
spine, n., backbone, *eskern* or *mellow an keyn*; thorn, *drēn,* m., pl. *dreyn.*
spinney, n. *spernek, dreynek, spynek,* f., pls. *-egy, -egow, dreyngos, dreyscos,* m., pl. *-ow.*
spinster, n., unmarried woman, *benen* or *myrgh dhybrȳas,* f., pls. *-es dybrȳas.*
spiral, n. *trōyll,* f., pl. *-yow*: a. *trōyllek.*
spire, n. *pül,* m., pl. *-yow, blȳn clēghty,* m., pl. *-ow c.*
spirit, n. *spyrys,* m., pl. *-yon*; evil s., *drōk-spyrys, tebel-edhen,* f., pl. *t.-ydhyn*; s.s, alcohol, *dowr tom,* m., *gwyras,* f., pl. *-rosow*: **-ed,** a. *colonnek*: **-ual,** a. *spyrysek*: **-ualism,** n. *spyryse·gȳeth,* f.
spit, n., for roasting, *bēr,* m., pl. *-yow*: v., transfix, *berya.*
spit, -tle, n. *trew, trewyas, *halow,* m.: v. *trewa.*
spite, n. *despȳ·t, spȳt, attȳ·, avy, envy, yflagrās,* m., *myken, drok-vrüs,* f.; in s. of, *yn despȳ·t* or *spȳt dhe*², *awo·s*; out of s. to, *yn attȳ· dhe*²: v. *despȳtya, spȳtya*: **-ful,** a. *spȳtys, e·nvyes.*
splash, n. *cabūly, scullya dowr, lagenna, lagya*; s. violently, *plowghya*: n. *lagyans, trōs dowr, plowghyans,* m.: **-ing-stone,** n. *cabūlen,* f., pl. *-now.*
splay, v. *dysplewyas*: **-ed,** a. *plat, ledan, dysplewyes*: **-footed,** a. *trōs-plat, plat y dreys.*
spleen, n. *an vam,* f.; spite, *attȳ·,* m.
splendid, a. *rȳal, splan, gay, bryntyn, stātly, gwyn*: **-dour,** n. *rȳelder, splander, braster, can, golowyjyon, golowys, *splanyjyon,* m.
splint, n. *skethren, †dysclȳen,* f., pl. *-now.*
splinter, n. *scommyn,* m., pl. *scommow, brows,* f., pl. *-yon, skyryonen,* f., pl. *skyryon, skethren,* f., *skethryk,* m., pls. *-ygow, -rowygow, skether,* m., pl. *-thryow*: v. *skethry*: **-ed,** a. *skethrak, squattyes dhe scommow.*
split, v. *squardya, falsa*: n. *fals,* m., pl. *-ljow, squard,* m., pl. *-yow.*
spoil, v. *namma, apērya, dyswül, pylla*: n. *pray,* m.
spoke, n. *brēgh, rōs,* f., pl. *-ow r., asen rōs,* f., pl. *asow r.*
spoke-shave, n. *raskel,* f., pl. *-clow.*
spokesman, n. *cowser, leverer,* m., pls. *-soryon, -roryon.*
sponge, n. *spong,* m., pl. *-ow.*
spontaneous, a. *hep ynny* or *ynnȳadow, a'y vōth y honen.*
spoon, n. *lo,* f., pl. *-yow*: **-ful,** n. **lōyas,* f., pl. *-yesow*; a s. of, *lün ün lo a*².
sport, n. *gwary,* m., pl. *-ow, sport,* m. pl., *-ys*; mockery, *gēs,* m.: v. *sportya, gwary*: **-ive,** a. *gwarȳek, jolyf*: **-sman,** n. *sportyer,* m., pl. *-s, helghyer,* m., pl. *-yoryon.*
spot, n. *nam,* m., pl. *-mow, brythen,* f., pl. *-now,* col. *brȳth*; pimple, etc., *curȳak,* m., pl. *-ȳogas, brēgh,* m., pl. *-ow*; place, *tyller,* m., pl. *-yow, lē,* m., pl. *-yow*; on the s., *y'n plās, stak* or *knak omma*: v., mark, *brytha, namma*: **-less,** a. *dynam, tēk, glan*: **-ted,** a. *bryth, brythennek*; of fowl, *spletyar*: **-ty,** a. *gwenenek.*
spouse, n. *prȳas,* m. or f., pl. *-ȳosow, deubryas, kespar,* m. and f., *pl. -ow.*
spout, n. *pystyl,* m., pl. *-low, styf,* f., pl. *-yvow*; of kettle, *conna,* m.; of pitcher, *gwēus,* f.: v. **pystylya, styfa.*
sprain, v. *trēlya, tenna, *syga*: n. *trēlyans,* m.
sprat, n. **spratta,* m., pl. *-tys, *hernen vȳghan,* f., col. *hern byghan.*
sprawl, v. *omlēsa, omdhysplewyas.*
spray, n., branch, *baren,* f., pl. *-now*; water, *ewon,* col., *mōrlewgh,* m.: v. *scullya.*
spread, v. *dysplewyas, lēsa, omlēsa*; of liquid, *fenna*; s. with butter, *amanynna*; s. straw, manure, etc., *scullya*; s. tales, *plontya whethlow*: n. *lesans,* m.; of water, *fen,* m.: a. *a-lēs.*
spree, n. *gwary medhow* or *fol,* m.
sprig, n. *baren,* f., pl. *-now.*
sprightly, a. *jolyf.*
spring, n. *fenten,* f., pl. *-tynyow*; leap, *lam,* m., pl. *-mow*; elastic device, **sprynga,* m., pl. *-ys, *torgh,* m., pl. *-tergh*: v. *lamma, lemmel, tardha*; s. back, *trebüchya*; s. up, *sordya, tevy, dastevy.*
Spring, n. *Gwaynten,* m.
springe, n. *crokken, *croglath,* f., pl. *-ow, *tagvaglen,* f., pl. *-now.*
sprinkle, v. *scullya dowr*: **-ling,** n. *scullyans,* m.

sprite, n. *spyrys,* m., pl. *-yon.*
sprout, n. *skyllen,* f., col. *skyl, lows,* m., *egyn,* m., pl. *-now;* Brussels s.s, **cawlenygow,* pl.: v. *tardha, tevy, glasa, egyna;* of leaves, *dēlya;* of malt, *bragy.*
spruce, a. *jolyf, glanyth, *kempen.*
spruce, n. *sprūs, gwedhen sprūs,* f., pl. *gwȳth s.*
spume, n. *ewon,* col.; s. flake, *plüven ewon, ewonen,* f., pl. *-now:* v. *ewony:* **-my,** a. *ewonek.*
spur, n. *kentryn,* m., pl. *-now:* v. *kentrynna;* s. on, *rȳ kentryn dhe²:* **s.-dogfish,** n. *drēnak,* m., pl. *-ogas.*
spurge, n. *flamgōs,* m.
spurious, a. *gow, fals, supposyes.*
spurn, v. *potya, dysprēsya, sconya.*
spy, v. *aspȳa, whythra:* n. *aspȳas,* m., pl. *-esy, aspȳer,* m., pl. *-ȳoryon, aspȳ·,* m., pl. *-es.*
spy-glass, n. *gweder-aspȳa,* m., pl. *-drow-a.*
squadron, n. *†lu lystry,* m., pl. *-yow l.*
squalid, a. *lōs, dyflas, plos.*
squall, n., storm, *cowas,* f., pl. *-osow, towl gwyns,* m., pl. *-ow g.:* v. *crȳa, üja:* **-ling,** *üs, üjans, crȳans,* m.
squalor, n. *plosethes, lastethes, mostethes, vylta, yselder boghosogneth,* m.
squander, v. *wastya, kescar, spēna yn-üfer, scullya a-les.*
square, a. *pedrak:* adv., come s., *dōs dhe sqūyr:* n., figure, *fygur pedrak;* of town, *plēn,* m.; set-s., *squȳr,* m., pl. *-ys.*
squash: see **squeeze.**
squat, a. *plat, ysel:* v. *plattya;* on property, *annedhy hep lecyans.*
squeak, n. **gwȳgh,* m., pl. *-yow:* v. **gwȳghal, *pȳpya.*
squeal: see **squeak.**
squeeze, v. *gwrynya, gwasca, strotha:* **-d,** a. *strōth.*
squid, n. *styfak,* m., pl. *-fogas.*
squint, n. *camlagas,* m.: v. *camlagasa:* **-ing,** n. *camlagajek, cam y lagas.*
squire, n. *squȳer,* m., pl. *-yon, scōswas,* m., pl. *-wesyon.*
squireen, n. **cragh-dēnjentyl,* m., pl. *c.-tüs-jentyl.*
squirm, n. *plynchya, omwen.*
squirrel, n. **gwywer,* m., pl. *-as, *scürel,* m., pl. *-ys.*
squirt, n. **skȳt,* m., pl. *-ys, *styf,* f., pl. *-yvow:* v. **skȳtya, *styfa.*

stab, n. *pych,* m., pl. *-ys, gwan,* f., pl. *-ow:* v. *pychya, gwana, cropya.*
stability, n. *faster, crefter,* m.: **-able,** a. *fast, crēf, sad.*
stable, n. *marghty,* m., pl. *-ow, stābel,* m., pls. *-blyow, -blys;* s.-boy, *paja-mergh,* m., pl. *-ys m.:* v. *gorra yn stābel.*
stack, n. *das,* f., pl. *deys, bern,* m., pl. *-ow:* v. *berna, dasa.*
staff, n. *lorgh,* m. or f., pl. *-ow, bat,* m., pl. *-tys, füst,* f., pl. *-ow;* of management, etc., *mēny,* m.
stag, n. *carow,* m., pls. *kervys, *ker·ewy:* **s.-hound,** n. *carowgy,* m., pl. *-gün.*
stage, n. *gwaryva,* f., pl. *-ow;* mining, etc., *soler,* m., pl. *-yow;* s.manager, *o·rdenary,* m., pl. *-s.*
stagger, v. *trebüchya, settya yn-tyberthys:* **-ed,** a. *dyegrys, dyberthys.*
stagnant, a. *crünys, marow:* **-nation,** n. *marder,* m.
staid, a. *sad, dōth.*
stain, v. *dyslywa, namma:* n. *dyslywans, nam,* m.: **-less,** a. *dynam.*
stair, n. **stayr,* m., pl. *-ys, *deres,* m., pl. *-yow, *grȳs,* m., pl. *-ys.*
stake, n. *pül,* m., pl. *-yow, styken,* f., pl. *-now;* wager, *gwystel,* m., pl. *-tlow:* v. *stykenna;* wager, *gwystla, kessynsy.*
stake-net, n. *kydel,* m., pl. *-lys.*
stale, a. *cōth, trenk, pedrys, fyllys, marow:* **-ness,** n. *trenkter, marder,* m.
stalk, n. *garen,* f., pl. *-now, gar,* f., pl. *-row;* grass s., *gwelsen,* f., pl. *-now,* col. *gwels;* straw s., *gwelen-gala,* f., col. *gwēl cala.*
stalk, v. *dōs ogas dhe vylas yn ün scolkya;* walk stiffly, *kerdhes yn-serth.*
stall, n. *stalla,* m., pl. *-lys.*
stallion, n. *margh *kellek,* m., pl. *mergh k.*
stalwart, a. *mēn, stowt, stordy, colonnek, smāt.*
stamina, n. *nerth, genesyk* m.
stammer, v. *hokkya yn cows, kewsel yn ün hokkya:* **-er,** n. *†crek,* m., pl. *-gow.*
stamp, n. *stampa,* m., pl. *-pys;* of feet, *stank,* m.; postage s., *stamp lyther:* v. *stankya, trettya;* of tin, *stampya.*
stampede, v. *gwylsya, omwylsya, resek own ynna:* n. *†resekva ownek,* f.
stance, n. *sāf, tryk,* m.
stand, v. *sevel;* last, *pēsya;* put up with, *perthy;* s. upright, *sevel a'y sāf, *serthy;* s. up! *saf yn-ban! yn sol!;* s. out against, *sevel orth, ērya;* s. by, support, *mentēna;*

s. aside! *seveugh nēs a-denewan*!; s. off! *saf a-vēs*!; to s. off, *avodya*; make a s., *sevel, gortos*: n. *sāf*, **safla*, m.; s., holder, *synser*, m.: **-ing,** a. *a'y sāf, sevylyak*; s. up, *sevys, yn-sol*; s. pool, *lagen*, f.: n. *sāf*, ‡*sevyans*, m.; importance, *prӯs*, m., pl. *-yow*: **-still,** n. **gorsaf*, m.

standard, n. *baner*, m., pl. *-ow*; pattern, etc., *sqūyr*, m., pl. *-ys*; s. bearer, *baneror*, m., pl. *-yon*; it's not up to s., *ny-dhē dhe sqūyr, nyns-yu da lowr*.

stannous, a. *stenys*.

star, n. *steren*, f., pl. *-now*, col. *stēr*, d. *sterennyk*, m., pls. *-ygow, -nowygow*; s.-shine, *stērgan*, m.; bright with s.s, *sterennek, stērgannek*; falling s., *steren codha*; fixed s., *steren stak*; the Pole-s., *an Steren*; the Morning S., *Berlewen*, f.; s. on horse's brow, **bal*, m.: **-light,** n. *stergan*, m.: **-lit,** a. *stergannek*: **-ry,** a. *sterennek*.

starboard, n. *tu dyghow*, m.; to s., *wor' t.d.*

starch, v. **starchya, serthy*: n. *glüs serthy*, **starcha*, m.

stare, v. *lagata, myras stark* (*war*[2]): n. *tremyn settyes*, m.: **-r,** n. *lagasek*, m., pl. *-sogyon, lagater*, m., pl. *-toryon*: **-ing,** a. *lagasek*.

starfish, n. *pymp-bӯs* (*pympӯs*), m., pl. *-a*.

stark, a. *serth*; s. madness, *folneth pür*; s. naked, *lom-nōth*.

starling, n. *trōs*, m., pl. *treyjy, trojen*, f., pl. *-nas*.

start, v. *dalleth*; s. a journey, *dalleth an forth, mōs y'n hens*; s. to bite or cut loaf, fruit, etc., *attamya*; s. back, *plynchya*: n. *dalleth*, m.; flinch, *plynch*, m., pl. *-ys*; at the s., *y'n kensa lē, wostalleth*.

startle, v. *amüvya, sawthanas*: **-ling,** a. *üthek, marthys*.

starvation, n. *dyvotter, nown, esow*, m.: **-ve,** v. *merwel drē nown*: with cold, *storvya*: **-veling,** n. *nownek*, m., pl. *-negyon*: **-ving,** a. *nownek*.

state, n., political, *an Stāt*, m., **kywsys*, f.; condition, *stüth, plӯt, poynt, chēr*, m.; station, *stāt*, m., pl. *-ys, roweth*, m.; s. of mind, *chēr*, m.; in a bad s., *tebel y stüth, yn gwan cās*: v. *derӯvas*: **-ment,** n. *derӯvas*, m.: **-sman,** *den an Stāt*, m., pl. *tüs an S.*

stateliness, n. *dy·nyta*, m.: **-ly,** a. *stātly, mür y rē·outa*.

station, n. *stasyon*, **gorsaf*, m.; rank, *degrē·*, m.; high s., *stāt ughel*, m.

stationary, a. *hep gwaya, sevylyak*.

stationery, n. *dafar scryfa*, m.

statue, n. *ymach*, m., pl. *-ajys*, **delow*, f., pl. *-ow*.

stature, n. *ughelder, hӯrder*, m.

status, n. *grē, prӯs*, m.

staunch, a. *lēn, stanch*: v. *stanch-üra, stoppya*.

stave, n. *asen*, f., pl. *asow*.

stave off, v. *gwytha a-bell, lettya*.

stay, v. *tryga, sevel, gortos, remaynya*; hinder, *lettya*; s. a short time. **godryga, sojornya*: n. *trygas, tryk*, **godryk*, m., *strech*, m., pl. *-ys*; of vessel, **stay*, m., pl. *-ys*; without s., *hep let nȧ strech*; s. sail, *gōl* **stay*.

steadfast, a. *lēn, stedfast*, **ferf, sad*: **-ness,** n. *lendury, ferfter*, m.

steady, a. *sür, crēf, gwastas, sad*; s. on! *kē war gam*!: **-dily,** adv. *war* (*dha*) *gam*, etc.

steak, n. *golyth bowyn*, m., pl. *-yon b., trēgh bowyn*, m., pl. *-ow b.*

steal, v. *ladra*; s. away, etc., *scolkya, goheles*: **-ing,** n. *ladrans*, m.

stealth, n., by s., *yn-dan gēl, a-dryf tüs, yn ün scolkya*: **-y,** *ave·l lader*: **-ily,** adv. *clōr*; to go s., *mōs yn ün skolkya*.

steam, n. *ēthen*, f.: v. *ēthenna, rynny*: **s.-boat,** n. *gorhel -tān*, m., pl. *-holyon-t.*: **s.-engine,** n. *jyn-tān*, m., pl. *-ys-t.*: **s.-locomotive,** n. *margh-tān*, m., pl. *mergh-t.*

steed, n. *stēda*, m., pl. *-ys*.

steel, n. **dür, metol*, m.

steep, a. *serth, crakkya-conna, ledrek*; s. place, *clegar*, m., *leder*, f.: **-ness,** n. *serthter*, m.

steep, v. *troghya, glybya, sūba*, **glēghy*; s. malt, *sēgy*.

steeple, n. *tour, clēghtour, clēghty, cloghty*, m., pl. *-ow, pül*, m., pl. *-yow*.

steer, v. *lewyas*: **-sman,** n. *lewyer*, m., pl. *-oryon, lewyth*, m., pl. *-ydhyon, lewyader*, m., pl. *-oryon*.

steer, n. *lon* (*lothen*), m., pls. *-now, lothnow, denewes*, m., pl. *-wys*.

stem, n. *gar*, f., pl. *-ow, garen*, f., pl. *-now, gwelen*, f., pl. *-lyny*, col. *gwēl*; of tree, **kelf*, m., pl. *-yow, bēn*, m., pl. *-ow*; of cherry, etc., *lost*, m.

stench, n. *flēr*, m., pl. *-yow*.

step, v. *kerdhes*: n. *cam*, m., pl. *-mow, stap*, m., pl. *-pys*, †*grath*, m., pl. *-adhow*; stair, **grӯs*, m., pl. *-ys*, **deres*, m., pl. *-yow*; s. in direct descent, in rank, etc., *degrē·*, m., pl. *-s*: **-ping-stones,** n. **sarn*, f., pl. *-ow*.

step-, prefix, in relationship, **lēs-*; s.father, †*altrow*, m., pl. *-on*, **lestās*, m., pl. *-ow*; s. mother, †*altrewan*, f., pl. *-neth*, **lesvam*, f., pl. *-mow*; s. son, †*els*, m., pl. *-yon*, **lesvap*, m., pl. *-vebyon*; s. daughter, †*elses*, f., pl. *-ow*, **lesvyrgh*, f., pl. *-es*; s. brother, **lesvroder*, m., pl. *-vreder*; s. sister, **les-whoer*, f., pl. *-wheryth*; s. child, **lesflogh*, m., pl. *-flēghes*.

sterile, a. *anvab*; of cattle, *hesk*; if still giving milk, *gawnagh*; of seeds, nuts, etc., *cōk*: **-ility,** n. *anvabeth*, m.

sterling, a. *bryntyn*; of money, *sterlyn*.

sterm, a. *asper, garow*.

stern, n. *delergh*, m., †*aros*, m., pl. *-yow*.

stew, n. *brōs, yskel*, m.: v. *bryjyon yn-cosel* or *yn-syger*.

steward, n. *styward*, m., pl. *-s*, *mēr-bōs*, m., pl. *-as-b.*, †*rennyas*, m., pl. *-ysy*; house or estate s., *mērdra*, f., *mērjy*, m.

stick, v. **glüsa, glena* (*orth*); s. fast, *tevy, kyjya*: **-y,** a. *glüjek*.

stick, n. *pren*, m., pl. *-yer*; rod, *gwelen*, f., pl. *-lyny*; staff, *lorgh*, m., pl. *-ow*; cudgel, *bat*, m., pl. *-tys*; branch, twig, *baren*, f., pl. *-now*; stake, *styken*, f., pl. *-now*; s.s for fuel, *cünys*, col.; to gather s.s, *cünyssa* (inf. only); to give one the s., *y bē yn-dan onnen*.

stickleback, n. **keyndreynek*, m., pl. *-nogas*.

stickler, n. **stȳghtler*, m., pl. *-s*, *brüsyas*, m., pl. *-ysy*.

stiff, a. *serth, dywethyn*; of behaviour, *gorth, serth y war*; rigid, tight, *tyn*: **-en,** v. *serthy*: **-ness,** n. *serthter*, m.

stifle, v. *megy, taga*: **-ling,** n. *tāg*; it is s. hot, *tam lowr yu dh'agan megy*.

stile, n. *trap*, m., pl. *-pys*, *step*, m., pl. *-pys*, **lamva*, **camva*, f.

still, adv. *prest, whath, hogen*, ‡*stella*: a. *cosel*; to be s., *powes, tewel*: v. *spavenhē·, coselhē·*: **-ness,** n. *calmynsy, spaven*, m., *spavnell*, f., pl. *-ow*.

still, n., for distilling, *lester* **styllya*, m., pl. *lystry s.*

stimulant, n. *pyger*, m., pl. *-goryon*; drink, *dewas crēf*: **-ate,** v. *pyga, kentrynna*.

sting, n. *brōs*, m., pl. *-ojow*, *gwan*, f., pl. *-ow*, *pȳk*, m., pl. *-ygow*: v. *pyga, brōsa, gwana*.

stingy, a. *pȳth, crefny*; s. person, †*synsyas*, m., pl. *-ysy*.

stink, n. *flēr, flērynsy*, m.: v. *mousegy, flērya*: **-ard, -er,** n. *flērys, flēryüs*, m.: **-ing,** *flērys, flēryüs, mousak*.

stint, v. *sparya, sconya*; without s., *hep let, hep hedhy*.

stipulate, v. *ambosa*: **-ion,** n. *ambos*, m., pl. *-ow*.

stir, v. *müvya, omwen, kemysky, remüvya, gwaya, pyga*, ‡*styrrya*; s. up, *cabūly*; of strife, *sordya*; slime, *trelūba*: n. *frōth, müvyans, son*, m.: **-rer,** n., implement, *spadel*, f., pl. *-low*; one who bestirs himself, *cabūler*, m., pl. *-loryon*.

stirrup, n. *gwarthowl*, f., pl. *-ow*; s. cup, *dewas an darras*, m.

stitch, n. *gwrȳ*, m., pl. *-ow*; knitting s., *magel*, f., pl. *-glow*; rough s., *crāf*, m., pl. *-ow*; pain, *pystyk*, m., pl. *-ygow*; line of s.s, seam, *gwrem*, m., pl. *-yow*; s. of land, *lȳn*, f., pl. *-yow*: v. *gwrȳas, brōsya*; roughly, *crafa*: **-er,** n. *gwrȳador*, m., pl. *-yon*, *gwrȳadores*, f., pl. *-ow*, †*sewyas*, m., pl. *-ysy*, *brosyth*, m., pl. *-ydhyon*, f., *-ydhes*, pl. *-ow*: **-ing,** n., sewing, *brōsyans*, m.; line of s., *gwrȳ*, m., pl. *-ow*.

stoat, n. *conna-gwyn*, m., pl. *-as*.

stock, n., tree, *bēn*, m., pl. *-ow*, *trēgh*, m., pl. *-ow*, **kelf*, m., pl. *-yow*, *stok*, m., pl. *-kys*; goods, *stoff, da*, m.; lineage, *lynyeth*, f., *devedhyans*, m.; bees, *mam-gwenyn*, f., pl. *-mow-g.*: v. *provȳa, stoffya*.

stockade, n. *kē stykennow, pülgē*, m., pl. *-ow*.

stocking, n. *loder*, m., pl. *-drow*.

stocks, n. *cargharow pen*, m., pl. *stokkys*, m., pl.; to put into the s.s, *carghara*.

stoker, n. *fōgor*, m., pl. *-yon*, *forner*, m., pl. *-noryon*.

stole, n. *stōl*, f., pl. *-yow*.

stolid, a. *talsogh, pentew*.

stomach, n. *cowl*, m., pl. *-ow*, *pengasen*, f., pl. *-now*, *sagh bōs* m., pl. *-ow b.*, *glas*, m.; of animal, esp. pig, *agen*, f.

stone, n. *mēn*, m., pl. *meyn*, *an veyn*; thin, flat s., *lēghen*, f., pl. *-now*; s. with hole in it, *tollven*, m., pl. *-veyn*; rounded s., *būlyen*, f., pls. *-now*, *būlyow*, col. *būly*; building s., *mēn whēl*; little s., *meynyk*, m., pl. *-ygow*; s. malady, *manteth*, m.; s. cutter, *trēghyas meyn*, m., pl. *-ysy m.*; s. like, *mēnek*; to clear away s.s, *dyveyna*: v. **labedha, tewlel meyn orth*: **-s throw,** n. *hēs ün towl mēn*: **-work,** n. *mēnwȳth*, m.: **-y,** a. *mēnek, mēn, meynek*; s. ground, *meynek*, f., pls. *-egy*, *-egow*.

stonechat, n. *chekker*, m., pl. *-eccras*.

stonecrop, n. *bewles*, m.

stool, n. *scavel*, f., pl. *-low*; small, *tuttyn*, m., pl. *-now*; three-legged s., *scavel trythros*, **escammys*, m., pl. *-ow*; foot-s., *scavel-drōs*.

stoop, v. *ynclȳnya*; to cause to s., *stopya*: **-ing,** a. **gwargrom*.

stop, v. *lettya, stoppya, sevel, hedhy, astel, cessya, powes, gortos, tryga*; s. him! *gwra dhodho gortos!*; s. where you are! *saf yn-nēs! seveugh nēs!*; s. your noise, *gās dha sōn!*; s. it! *gās crēs! do way!*; s. doing, *cessya hep gül*; s. a gap, *gorra spern dhe aswy*: n. *trygas, strech, ardak*, m.; without a s., *hep let na strech*: **-gap,** n. *neppyth a-lanow aswy*: **-page,** n. *stoppyans, lestyans*, m.: **-per,** n. *stoppyer*, m., pl. *-s.*

store, n. *gwythva*, f., *gwythty*, m., pl. *-ow, stoff*, m.; household s., *stoff chȳ*, m.; for fuel, *cünyjek*, f.: v. *gwytha, *stoffya*: **-keeper,** n. *gwythyas stoff*,m., pl. *-ysy s.*

stork, n. **whybon*, f., pl. *-as, †stork*, m., pl. *-ys.*

storm, n. *hager-awel*, f., pl. *-low, †enawel*, f., *teweth*, m.: **-beaten,** a. *tewedhak*: **-y,** a. *garow, hager*; s. weather, *hager-awel*, f.

story, n. *whethel*, m., pl. *-thlow, drolla*, m., pl. *-lys*; tell s.s, *whethla*: **s.-teller,** n. *whethlor*, m., pl. *-yon*; liar, *gowek*, m., pl. *-wygyon, †gowleveryas*, m., pl. *-ysy.*

stout, a. *stowt*; fat, *tew*; brave, *colonnek*; hardy, *smat.*

stove, n. *forn*, f., pl. *-ow.*

straddle, v. *rambla, *gavlya*: **-ling,** a. *ramblys, *gavlak.*

straggle, v. *gwandra pup a'y du, bōs dyberthys.*

straight, a. *compes, ewn, poran*; upright, *serth, a'y sāf*: **-edge,** *lȳnyer*, m., pl. *-s*: **-forward,** a. *hep fayntys na falsury, *dydro*: **-forwardly,** adv. *dhe blemmyk*: **-en,** v. *composa, ewna*: **-ness,** n. *ewnder, composter*, m.: **-way,** adv. *desempys, a-dhesempys, scon, sket, dewha·ns, kens es hedhy, straft, hep hokkya, dystough, a-dhystough*; s. thither, *y'n ewn forth dȳ.*

strain, v. *tenna rē*; joint, *dyskevelsy*; sift, *crodra, *sythla*: n. *tenva*, f.; breed, *hās*, m.; music, **tōn*, m.: **-ed,** a. *yn-ten*: **-er,** n. *croder*, m., pl. *-drow, *sythel*, m., pl. *-thlow.*

strait, a. *harth, yn, tyn, *strōth, strayt*: **-ly,** adv. *yn-tyn, hardlych, straytly.*

strait, n. *cülvor, mor yn*, m.; in great s.s, *yn tebel stüth.*

strand, n. *trēth*, m., pl. *-ow, als*, f., pl. *-yow*; s. of rope, *corden*, f., pl. *kerdyn*: **-ed,** a. *tewlys war an als, gesys gans an mōr.*

strange, a. *ancoth, coynt, reveth, marthys*; foreign, *astranj, *estrennek*; s. thing, *aneth*, m., pl. *-ow, coyntys*, m.: **-ness,** n. *ancothvos, stranjnes*, m.: **-r,** n. *estren*, m., pl. *-yon*, f. *-es*, pl. *-ow, dēn ancoth*, m., pl. *tüs a., perghyryn* (*pryeryn*), m., pl. *-as, alyon*, m., pl. *-s.*

strangle, v. *taga, *lyndaga*: **-gulation,** n. *tāk, *lyndak*, m.

strap, n. *crōn*, m., pl. *-ow, *lethren*, f., pl. *-now*: v. *strotha*; beat, **lethrenna, scorjya.*

strategem, n. *ynjyn*, m., pl. *-nys, wrynch, cast*, m., pl. *-ys, bras*, m.

stratum, n. *gwely*, m., pl. *-ow*; soft s. between lodes, *flüken*, f., pl. *-now.*

straw, n. *gwelen-gala*, f., pl. *-lyny-cala*, col. *gwēl c., cala*; s. bedding, *cala gwely*, col.: **-berry,** n. *syvyen*, f., col. *syvy, moren-cala*, f., col. *mōr-c.*; to gather s.s, *syvya* (inf. only).

stray, v. *gwandra, sawthanas, ‡errya, mōs yn* or *dhe stray*: **-er,** n. *gwandryas*, m., pl. *-ysy.*

streak, n. *lȳn*, m., pl. *-ow, *lynen*, f., pl. *-now, *rybyn*, m.: v. *brytha, *lynenna*: **-ed,** a. *brȳth, *lynennys.*

stream, n. *frōs, gover*, m., pl. *-ow, strēth*, f., pl. *-ow, laca*, m., pl. *lakys, goth* (*gwȳth*), f., pl. *gwythy, nonnen*, f., pl. *-now, strēm*, m., pl. *-ys, ryver*, m., pl. *-s*; place with s.s, *goverek, gothek* (*gwythek*), *dowrak*, f., pls. *-egy, -egow*: v. *devera, denewy, dewraga, *frōsa*: **-er,** n. *strēmour*, m., pl. *-s*: **-let,** n. *gothen* (*gwythen*), f., pl. *-now, goveryk*, m., pl. *-ygow*: **-work,** n., for tin, *whēl-hāl*, m., pl. *-yow-h., hāl*, f., pl. *-low.*

street, n. *strēt*, m., pl. *-ys*, dim. *strētyn*, m., pl. *-now.*

strength, n. *nerth, nell, crefter, fors*, m.: **-en,** v. *crefhē·, confortya, *nertha.*

strenuous, a. *mēn, nerthek*: **-ly,** adv. *yn-fēn.*

stretch, v. *tenna, ystynna, antel, strechya*; s. apart, *dysplewyas*; s. out, *trȳnya*; of time, *dylātya*: n. *ten*, m., pl. *-now*; full s., *keheseth* (*keheja*), m., pl. *-edhow*: **-ed,** a. *tyn*; of body, *a-hēs, yn-tyn*; of arms, *a-lēs*: **-er,** n. *grava*, m., pl. *-thow*; carpentry, *ten*, m., pl. *-now*: **-ing,** n., of body, *keheseth* (*keheja*), m.

strew, v. *scullya.*

stricken, a. *tuchys, gwyskys.*

strict, a. *harth, fast, *strōth, tyn, strayt*: **-ly,** adv. *yn-tyn, hardlych, dour, fast, straytly*: **-ness,** n. *lymder, tynder*, m.

stride, n. *lam*, m., pl. *-mow, lam hȳr*, m., pl. *-mow h., *gaul*, f., pl. *-ow*: v. *lemmel, lamma, kerdhes hȳr y gam, k. yn-prowt.*

strife, n. *bresel*, m., pl. *-yow, strȳf, stryvyans*, m.

strike, v. *gweskel, squattya* (*scattya*), *knoukya, frappya, tuchya, ‡clowtya*; s. violently, *deghesy*; go on s., *sconya ober*; of clock, *seny*: n. *hedhyans, nagh ober*, m.: **-ing,** a. *coynt, mür dh'y nōtya.*

string, n. *corden*, f., pl. *kerdyn, lynen*, f., pl. *-ow, lovanen*, f., pl. *-now*; s. of onions, *plethen onyon*, f.; attachment, such as tongue-s., **stagell*, f., pl. *-ow*; harp-s., *corden harp* or *†telyn*: v., of bow, *antel.*

stringent, a. **strōth, harth*: **-ly,** adv. *dour*, pl. *hardlych.*

strip, v. *lomhē·, stryppya, dystryppya, pylya*; s. off clothes, *omdhy'sky, dy'sky*; s.ped naked, *stryppys yn-nōth*: **-ping,** n. *pyl*, m., *-yon.*

strip, n. *skethen*, f., pl. *-now, sketh*, m., pl. *-ow*; selvedge, *lysten*, f., pl. *-now*; of land, *lȳn*, f., pl. *-yow.*

stripe, n. *lynen*, f., pl. *-now*; blow, *strocas*, m., pl. *-cosow, strekys*, m., pl. *-kesow*: **-d,** a. *brȳth*; brindled, *labol.*

stripling, n. *dēn-yowynk*, m., pl. *tüs-y.*

strive, v. *stryvya, o·mdhal*; s. against, *offendya.*

stroke, n. *strocas*, m., pl. *-cosow, strekys*, m. pl. and abst. *-kesow, lash*, m., *bommen*, f., pl. *-ow, towl*, m., pl. *-ow*; hand s., **palvas*, m., pl. *-vosow*; s. of luck, *towl chōns*; s. for s., *tys ha tas*: v. *handla, tava, chersya*, **palva.*

stroll, v. *rōsya, gwandra, kerdhes a-dhe-dro*: n. *rōsyas, gwandrans*, m., *tro kerdhes*, f.: **-er,** n. *gwandryas*, m., pl. *-ysy, rōsyer*, m., pl. *-yoryon.*

strong, a. *stowt, crēf, mēn, †cadarn*: **-ly,** adv. *yn-fēn, yn-crēf.*

strong-box, n. *argh*, f., pls. *-ow, erghy, cofyr crēf*, m., pl. *-frow c.*

strop, n. *crōn*, m., pl. *-ow*, **faskel*, m., pl. *-low, raw*, f., pl. *-yow*; razor s., **lethren lemma*, f.; of withy, *†gusen*, f., pl. *-now*: v. *lemma.*

structure, n. *gwrȳans, ‡gwra*, m., *form*, f., pl. *-ow.*

struggle, n. *strȳf*, m., pl. *-ȳvow, bresel*, m., pl. *-yow, omdow·l*, m., pl. *-ow, omlath*, m., pl. *-dhow*: v. *omlath, omdewlel, stryvya, omwen*, **gwenel.*

strumpet, n. *hora*, f., pl. *-ys, gast*, f., pl. *gysty.*

strut, v. *kerdhes yn-hautyn.*

strut, n., carpentry, *latha*, m., pl. *-ys.*

stub, n. *stok*, m., pl. *-kys.*

stubble, n. *sowlen*, f., col. *sowl*; field of s., *sowlek*, f., pls. *-egow, -egy*; s.-goose, *sowlwōth*, f., pl. *-odhow*: **-bly,** adv. *sowlek, garow.*

stubborn, a. *stowt, gorth, stordy, cales y ben*; s. person, *pen-cales*, m., pl. *-now c., drōkebol*, m.: **-ness,** n. *ēr, gorthter*, m.

stud, n. **both*, f., pl. *-ow*, **boton*, m., pl. *-now*; of horses, *grē*, f., pl. *-yow.*

student, n. *scoler*, m., pl. *-loryon*, f. *-lores*, pl. *-ow, †scolhȳk*, m., pl. *-hygyon*, f. *-hyges*, pl. *-ow, studhyer*, m., pl. *-yoryon*; fellow-s.s, *kesscolhygyon*: **-dious,** a. **dyskesyk*; s. persons, *-ygyon*: **-dy,** v. *studhya*: n. *studhyans*, m.; workroom, *gwȳthva*, f.

stuff, n. *defnyth*, m., pl. *-ydhyow, stoff, stok*, m., *pyth*, m., pls. *-ow, taclow*; nonsense, *üfereth*, m.: v. **gwalgha*, **stoffya*, **sagha.*

stumble, v. *trebüchya, omdhysevel.*

stump, n. *†trēgh*, m., pl. *-ow, †stok*, m., pl. *-kys*, **kef*, m., pl. *-yon, ‡stubba*, m., pl. *-bys.*

stun, v. *gül dhe glamdera*; with noise, *bodhara*; with surprise, *sawthanas*: **-ned,** a. *dyegrys*; to be s., *clamdera.*

stunt, v. *lettya a'y devy*: **-ed,** a. *lettys y devyans*; s. person, *†cor*, m., pl. *-as*; s. trees, *prysclowwyth*, col.

stupefied, a. *†badüs*; to become s., *clamdera*: **-fy,** v. *sawthanas, dyegry*: **-por,** n. *clamder*, **bad*, m.

stupendous, a. *marthys brās, üthek.*

stupid, a. *goky, †dycreft, †talsogh*, **pensogh*, *†dyskȳans, †badüs*: **-ity,** n. *gokyneth, folneth*, m.

sturdy, a. *stordy, crēf.*

sturgeon, n. **sturjyon*, m., pl. *-s.*

stutter, v. *hokkya, †stlevy*: n. *†stlaveth*, m.

sty, n. *crow-mogh*, m., pl. *-yow-m.*

style, n. *forth*, f., pl. *-dhow, maner*, f., pl. *-ow, gȳs*, m., pl. *-yow*; in some s., *war nep cor*: v., s. oneself, *omhenwel.*

suave, a. *hebask, cosel, whēk.*

subdue, v. *fetha, tempra, dova.*

subject, n. *mater*, m., pl. *-s*, **testen*, f., pl. *-now*; s. to ruler, *sojeta*, m., pl. *-tys*; s.-matter, *defnyth*, m., pl. *-yow*: a. *gostyth, kēth*: v. *gorra yn-dan²*: **-ion,** n. *gwaso·nyeth*, f.

sublime, a. *ughella, ughel a-ughon*, **gorughel.*

submerge, v. *sedhy, büdhy, lȳva, troghya*; s. oneself, *omsedhy, omvüdhy.*

submission, n. *plegyans, hüvelder*, m.: **-ive,** a. *gostyth, hüvel, whar, se·rvabyl*: **-mit,** v. *lavasos, obaya, omblegya.*

subordinate, a., s. to, *yn-dan*[2], *yn lē grē es*: n. *sojet*, m., pl. *-tys*: v. *gorra yn-dan*[2], *g. yn lē lē* or *grē*.
subscribe, v. *rȳ mona dhe*[2], **rakprena*: **-ription,** n. **rakpren*, *ro a vona*, **subscrypsyon*, m.
subsequent, a. *a-sew*, *warle·rgh*: **-ly,** adv. *wosa henna*, *a'y wosa*.
subside, v. *codha yn y honen*; of storm, *spavenhē·*: **-nce,** n. *coth*, m.; of sea, *spaven*, m., pl. *-vnow*.
subsidize, v. *scodhya gans arghans*: **-dy,** n. *arghans gweres*, *kynweres*, m.
subsistence, n. *pega·ns*, *megyans*, *sosten*, m.
subsoil, n. *cothen*, f., *grond*, m., pl. *-ys*; gravelly s., *growdyr*, *rabmen*, m.
substance, n. *substans*, f., *pyth*, m., pl. *-ow*, *tra*, m., pl. *taclow*, *stoff*, *mater*, m., *defnyth*, m., pl. *-ydhyow*.
substantial, a. *crēf*, *brās*, *mür*, *gwȳr*: **-tiate,** v. *prevy*.
substitute, v. *gorra yn lē*, *supposya*, **gorthry*: n. *tra supposyes*, *kemerer lē un aral*: **-ion,** n. *chanjyans*, *supposyans*, m.
subterfuge, n. *keladow*, *wrynch*, *cavanscüs*, m.
subtle, a. *sotel*, *fēl*, *fȳn*, *connek*: **-ty,** n. *sotelneth*, **so·tylta*, m.: **-tilize,** v. *sotla*.
subtract, v. *kemeres dywo·rth*, *tenna mēs a*[2]: **-ion,** n. *kylden*, *ten yn-mēs*, m.
suburb, n. **randra*, **mēstra*, f.; s.s, *lēow a-dro dhe'n cyta*: **-an,** a. (*a'n*) **randra*, *a-dro dhe'n cyta*.
subvert, v. *do·mhel*, *omwheles*.
subway, n. **keyforth*, *hens yn-dan an dōr*.
succeed, v. *sowynny*, *spēdya*, *gallos*; come after, *dōs warle·rgh*: **-cess,** n. *sowynyans*, m., *sowena*, *spēda*, f.; without s., *penhelygen*: **-cessful,** a. *sowyn*, †*füsek*; to make s., *spēdya*, *fortynya*: **-cession,** n. *rew*, **hōl*, m., pl. *-yow*; of ruler, *dōs dhe'n trōn*: **-sively,** *yn ün rew*, *yn rew*: **-sor,** n. *sewyer*, *holyer*, m., pl. *-yoryon*, *sewyas*, m., pl. *-ysy*.
succour, n. *kynweres*, *gweres*, *socor*, m.: v. *socra*, *gweres*.
succulent, a. *ēr*.
such, pron. *sül*; s. as will, *sül*, *myns* or *kemmy·s a-vynno*: a. *a'n par-na*, *a'n keth sort-na*; s. a high house, *chȳ mar ughel*; it's s. a long way! *Dew, hyrra forth yu*!
suck, v. *dēna*, *sugna*: **-ing-pig,** n. *porghellyk*, m., pl. *-ygow*.
suckle, v. *rȳ bron dhe*[2], **bronna*: **-lings,** n. *an rē münys ow-tēna*.
sudden, a. *desempys*, *trom*: **-ly,** adv. *desempys*, *a-dhesempsys*, *dystough*, *a-dhystough*, *dewha·ns*, *a-dhewha·ns*, *marthys scon*, *cot*, *yn-trom*: **-ness,** n. **tromder*, m.
suds, n. *golghyon*, m., pl. *dowr ewon seban*, m.
sue, v. *sewya drē lagha*, *pysy*.
suet, n. *sōf*, m.
suffer, v. *godhevel*, *godhaf*, *lavasos*, *perthy*, *gasa*, ‡*suffra*: **-er,** n. **godhevyas*, m., pl. *-ysy*, f. *-ades*, pl. *-ow*, *clāf*, m., pl. *clevyon*: **-ance,** n. *lecyans*; on s., *drē lecyans*, *hag ef levesys*: **-ing,** n. *pȳn*, m., *torment*, m., pl. *-ns*, *galar*, m., pl. *-ow*; long s., *hȳr-wodhevyans*, m.
suffice, v. *servya*, *bōs lowr*: **-cient,** a., n., **-ly,** adv. *lowr*.
suffocate, v. *megy*, *taga*: **-tion,** n. **tāk*, m., **megva*, **tagva*, f.
suffrage, n. *gwȳr dhe vōtya*, m.
sugar, n. **sugra*, m.: v. **sugra*, *whekhē·*.
suggest, v. *cusülya*, *gorra yn brȳs*: **-ion,** n. *cusül*, f., pl. *-yow*, *avȳ·s*, m.
suicide, n. *omladhans*, m.; person, *omladher*, m., pl. *-oryon*; to commit s., *omladha y honen*.
suit, v. *desedha*, *servya*: n. *dyllas*, m., pl. *-ajow*, *sewt*, m.; s. of law, *kēn*, m.: **-ability,** n. *composter*, m.: **-able,** a. *gwyw*, *'vās*, *onest*; it is s., *y-cōth*, *y-teleth*.
suitor, n. †*tanter*, m., pl. *-toryon*.
sulk, v. *mūtya*, *serry*: **-y, sullen,** a. *serrys*, *ow-mūtya*.
sully, v. *mostya*.
sulphur, n. **loskven*, m.: **-ous,** a. **loskvenek*.
sultan, n. *sodon*, m., pl. *-ys*; the S. of Turkey, *an Turk Brās*: **-a,** n. *sodones*, f., pl. *-ow*; fruit, *fygesen sodones*, f., pl. *fyges s*.
sultry, a. *pōs*, **tesak*: **-triness,** n. *poster*, m.
sum, n. *sum*, m., pl. *-mys*, *summen*, f., pl. *-now*, *reken*, m., pl. *reknys*.
summary, n. *derȳvas cot*, m.
Summer, n. *Hāf*, m., pl. *Havow*; duration of s., **havwyth*, *havas*, m.; s. visitor, tripper, etc., **havyas*, m., pl. *-ysy*; s. holiday, *havyans*, m.; to take s. holiday, excursion, etc., *havy*; s. dwelling, *hewas* (†*havos*), m.; s.y, of s., **havek*.
summit, n. *bar*, m., pl. *-ow*, *gwartha*, m., pl. *-avyon*, *mujoven*, f., pl. *-now*, *top*, m., pl. *-yow*, dim. *topyn*, m., pl. *-now*, *pen*, m., pl. *-now*, *crȳben*, f., pl. *-now*.

summon, v. *gelwel*, **sompna*: **-s,** n. *galow*, **somons*, m.: **-ner,** n. **sompnour*, m., pl. *-s*.
sump, n. *sump*, m., pl. *-ys*.
sumptuous, a. *rych*, *bryntyn*, †*fȳthüs*.
sun, n. *howl*, m., pl. *-yow*; to warm in the s., s.-bathe, **tesy*, *omdesy*, *omhowla*, *eva an howl*; s.s heat, **howldes*, m.: **-beam,** n. *golowys an howl*, m.: **-dial,** n. *üryor howl*, m.: **-light,** n. *golow an howl*, m.; in full s., *yn lagas an h.*: **-ny,** a. **howlek*, **tesak*, *tom*: **-rise,** n. *howldrehevel*, m.: **-set,** n. *howlsedhas*, m.: **-shine,** n. *dewynyans* or *splander a. h.*: **-stroke,** n. *towl a. h.*, m.
Sunday, n. *dē-Sül*, m.; S. time, on a S., *Sülwyth*, *dhe Sül*; on S. morning, *dē-Sül vyttyn*.
sundew, n. *eyles*, m.
sundry, a. *lȳes ēghen*, *lower kynda*.
sup, n. *swynnen*, f., pl. *-now*, *lemmyk*, m., pl. *-ygow*, *lommen*, f., pl. *-now*: v. *cona*, *sopya*, *eva*: **-per,** n. *cōn*, f., pl. *-yow*, *soper*, m., pls. *-s*, *-ow*, *bōs soper*; s.-time, *prȳs soper*, m.
super, a. *pür*, †*ugh-*.
superabundance, n. *rē*, *gorlanwes*, **gorfalster*, m.: **-nt,** a. *rē a*², **gorfals*; to be s., *bōs rē*.
superb, a. *bryntyn*, *splan*, **gorwyw*.
supercilious, a. *gothys*, *hautyn*.
superficial, a. *bās*, *scaf*, *wor'ton*, *hep whȳlas down*.
superfine, a. *fȳn* or *tēk drēs ēghen*.
superfluity, n. *rē*, *gwalgh*, m.: **-uous,** a. *rē*, *drēs ethom*.
superhuman, a. *drēs densys*, *drēs gallos mabden*.
superintend, v. *myras war*², *avȳsya*: **-ant,** n. *avȳsyer*, m., pl. *-yoryon*.
superior, a. *gwell*, *ughella*, *trȳgh*: s. to, *gwell age·s*, *pen war*²; n. *pen*, m., pl. *-now*, *trȳgher*, m., pl. *-ghoryon*; s.s, *pennow tüs*, †*gwelhevyn*: **-ity,** n. *trȳgh*, *stāt ughella*, m.
superlative, a. *ughella*.
supernatural, a. *drēs natur*, *drēs kynda*.
supernumerary, a. *drēs nyver*, *a-rēs* or *üs usyes*.
superscription, n. *penscryfa*, *superscrypsyon*, m.
supersede, v. *settya aral yn y lē*, *kemeres lē* or *holya ün aral*.
superstition, n. *crysyans cōth*, *üfer* or *woky*, *falscrysyans*, **hegoleth*, m.: **-ious,** a. *hegol*, *rē barys dhe grysy*.
supervise, v. *avȳsya*, *myras war*²: **-sor,** n. *avȳsyer*, m., pl. *-yoryon*.
supple, a. *heblyth*, *gwethyn*; comp., *gwethna*; to make s., *gwethynhē·*: **-ness,** n. **gwethynder*, *gwethneth*, m.
supplement, n. *ystynyans*, m., pl. *-ow*, *ran aral*, pl. *-now erel*: v. *moyhē·*, *ystynna*, *gorra moy dhe*².
suppliant, -icant, n. *pysador*, m., pl. *-yon*: **-icate,** v. *pysy*: **-ication,** n. *pysadow*, *desȳ·r*, m., *govenek*, m., pl. *-ygyon*.
supply, v. *rȳ*, *darbary*, *collenwel*, *provya*; food, *so·stena*, *cafos*, *mēthy*; mill, furnace, etc., *bōsa*; s. a loss, *astevery coll*: n. *stoff*, m.; good s., *lanwes*, *cals*, m.: **-lier,** n. *provyer*, m., pl. *-yoryon*.
support, v. *scodhya*, *mentēna*, *confortya*; hold, *synsy*; endure, *perthy*: n. *confort*, *scodhyans*, *porth*, m.: prop, *pül*, m., pl. *-yow*, *jȳst*, m., pl. *-ys*: **-er,** n. *mentēnour*, m., pl. *-s*, *scodhyer*, m., pl. *-yoryon*.
suppose, v. *tyby*, *desevos*, *supposya*: **-sition,** n. *tybyans*, m., pl. *-ow*, **desef*, m., pl. *-evyow*.
suppuration, n. **gōr*, m., pl. *-ow*: **-te,** v. **gory*.
suppress, v. *compressa*, *defendya*, *lettya*: **-ion,** n. *compressans*, m.
supremacy, n. *trȳgh*, *gorughelder*, *brassa gallos*, m.: **-me,** a. *rȳal*, *ughel*, *trȳgh*, *gorughel*.
surcoat, n. *surcot*, f., pl. *-tys*, *pows*, f., pl. *-yow*.
sure, a. *dyogel*, *sür*; I'm not s., *ny-wōn yn-fās*, *scantlowr ny-wōn*; I feel s., *trest a-m-büs*, *gōn lowr*; for s., *dhe-wȳr*; make s., *dyogelhē·*; to be s., *yn-tefry*, *hep nep mar*: **-ly,** adv. *yredy*, *sür*, *sürly*, *yn sür-redy*, *yntyogel*, *certüs*: **-ty,** n. *gwystel*, m., pl. *-tlow*, *meugh*, m., pl. *-yow*, *gaja*, m., pl. *-ys*, **sürta*, m.; to go s., *gwystla*, *meughya*; of a s., *a-plȳght*.
surf, n. *mōrdarth*, m., *ewon*, col.; sound of s., *mōrdrōs*, m.
surface, n. *ton*, m. or f., *enep*, m., pl. *-ebow*, ‡*bejeth*, *ken*, m.: v.
surfeit, n. *rē*, *gwalgh*, m.
surge, n. *whethfyans an mōr*, *gwayans yn tonnow*: v. *tonna*, *whethfy*.
surgeon, n. **chyrurjyen*, m., pl. *-s*, **lüfvedhek*, m., pl. *-ygyon*, **chyrurjery*, m.; place, **medhekva*, f.
surly, a. *drōk y gnās*, *kepa·r ha brathky*.
surmount, v. *trȳghy war*².
surname, n. *hanow-tās*, m.

surpass, v. *tremena, trȳghy, passya*: **-ing,** a. *flowr, gwella, drēs puptra.*
surplice, n. †*cams,* f., pl. *-ow,* **oferengrȳs,* m., pl. *-yow.*
surplus, n., a s. of, *rē a*²: see **superabundance.**
surprise, n. *marth,* m., pl. *-ow, sawthan,* m.: v. *sawthanas*; I am s.d at, *yma* · *marth dhym a*²: **-ing,** a. *reveth, marthys*; it is s. to me that you don't go, *mür a varth yu genef-vy na-wrēta mōs*: **-ingly,** adv. *marthys, ynfarthys.*
surrender, v. *omrȳ, obaya, hepcor, dascor*: n. *omrȳans, obayans,* m.
surreptitious, -ly, a., adv. *ave ·l lader, yndan güth, orth golow nōs.*
surround, v. *bōs, dōs* or *mōs a-dro, settya* or *omsettya a-dro dhe*²: **-ing,** adv. *yn-kerghyn*: **-ings,** n. *an pow a-dro,* m.
survey, v. *myras orth, musüra tȳr*: n. *musürans, vu,* m., *golok,* f.: **-or,** n. *musürer,* m., pl. *-oryon.*
survival, n. *düryans*; a s., *nep a-dhür drēs y hynsa*: **-ve,** v. *bewa wosa, tryga, dürya* or *gortos yn-few.*
suspect, v. *tyby, drōkdyby, dowtya*: a. *dowtys*: n. *onen üs dh'y dhowtya.*
suspend, v. *cregy*; s. work, *astel.*
suspense, n. *preder, hokkyans,* m., *fyenasow,* abst. pl.; in s., *ow-cortos gothvos*: **-sion,** n. *crōk,* f., pl. *-ogow.*
suspicion, n. *gorthgrēs (gorgys), skēs,* m., pl. *-ow, dowt,* **drokdybyans,* m.: **-ious,** a. *skēsek, mür y dhowt*; I am s. of him, *yma* · *skēs dhym anodho.*
sustain, v. *perthy, synsy, so ·stena*; s. a cause, *synsy quarel*: **-tenance,** n. *sosten, pega ·ns, megyans,* m.
sutler, n. †*mēthor,* m., pl. *-yon.*
suzerain, n. *gwarthevyas,* m., pl. *-ysy,* f. *-ades,* pl. *-ow*: **-ty,** n. *gwarthevyans,* m.
swaddle, v. *mayla (-lya)*: **-ling-band,** n. *lysten,* f., pl. *-now*: **s.-clothes,** n. *quethow mayla,* pl.
swagger, n. *maystry,* m.: v. *maystry, gül maystry, lordya.*
swale, v. *golesky grūgek* or *eythynek.*
swallow, v. *lenky*; s. down, *collenky,* **terlenky,* **daslenky*: n., throat, *lonk,* m.
swallow, n., bird, *gwennol,* f., pl. *-nyly*; house-martin, ‡*chycok,* f., pl. *-ogas.*
swamp, v. *büdhy,* **lȳva,* **gorthroghya*: n. *kersek, kenak,* f., pls. *-egow, -egy, gwern, corswern,* f., pls. *-ow, -y, cors,* f., pls. *-ow, kersy*: **-y,** a. *gwernak, dowrak.*
swan, n. *alargh,* m., pl. *elergh(y), swan,* m., pl. *-nys.*
sward, n. *ton,* m. or f., pl. *-now, lawns,* m., pl. *-njyow.*
swarm, n. *hēs,* f., pl. *-ow*; first s., **kenshēs,* f.; 2nd s., **tarowhēs*; 3rd s., **losthēs*: v. *tewlel hēs, hēsya,* **muryonna*: **-ing,** n. *hevva,* f.: a. *ow-hēsya, yn hēs.*
swath, n. *dram,* m., pl., *mow.*
swathe, v. *mayla (lya)*: **-ing-band**: see **swaddling-band.**
sway, v. *rowtya, rewlya, governya*; rock, *lesca*; wave, *swaysya, gwevya*: n., rule, *governans, roweth, gallos, rewl,* m.
swear, v. *lȳa, tȳ*; s. falsely, *gow-lȳa*: **-er,** n. *tȳas,* m., pl. *-ȳesy, lȳor,* m., pl. *-yon.*
sweat, n. *whēs,* m.; his brow is covered with s., *whēs yu y dāl*: v. *whēsa*: **-ing,** a. *owwhēsa.*
sweep, v. *scüba*: n., man, *scüber chymblys,* m., pl. *-boryon c.*: **-er,** n. *scüber,* m., pl. *-boryon*: **-ing,** n. *scüb,* m., pl. *-yon*: **-stake,** n. **kescaja,* m.
sweet, a. *whēk, whēgoll, melys*; s. one, s.ing, *whegyn,* m., pl. *-now, whegen,* f., pl. *-now, whēk,* m., pl. *-egow*; s. course of meal, s.s, *bōs whēk, whēgow*: **-est,** a. *whēgoll*: **-en,** v. *sugra, whēkhē* ·: **-ish,** a. *melys*: **-ness,** n. *melder, whekter, melyster,* m.
sweetheart, n. **keryas,* m., pl. *-ysy,* f. *-ades,* pl. *-ow, defnyth prȳas*; my s., *ow melder, ow herensa, myrgh ow holon,* etc.
swell, v. *hothfy, whedhy, whethfy*; from surfeit, *quoffy*; grow higher, *sevel*: n., of sea, *hothfyans, whethfyans, sevel, mōs garow*: **-ing,** n. *bothan,* f., pl. *-now, wheth, whedhyans, whethfyans,* m.
swift, n., a. *üskys, scaf,* ‡*strȳk*: **-footed,** a. *scaf y drōs*: **-ly,** adv. *üskys, yn-scaf, tōth mēn*: **-ness,** n. *tōth, scafter,* m.
swift, n., bird, *gwennol dhu,* f., pl. *-nyly du.*
swig, v. *collenky*: n. *swynnen,* f., pl. *-now.*
swim, v. *nyja y'n dowr*: **-mer,** n. *nyjer,* m., pl. *-joryon*: **-ming,** n. *nyj,* m.
swindle, v. *gül falsury, hyga, fükya*: n. *falsury,* **hyk,* f., pl. *hygyon,* **fük,* m., pl. *-yow*: **-r,** n. *faytour,* m., pl. *-s, tullor,* m., pl. *-yon.*
swine, n. *hogh,* m., pl. *-as,* col. *mogh*: **-herd,** n. *bügel mogh,* m., pl. *-eth (-a),* m.: **-fever,** n. *terthen mogh,* f.

swing, v. *swaysya, lesca,* **keflesca*: n. *lesklovan,* m., pl. *lescow-l.*; s. gate, **lyjyet,* m., pl. *-tys.*
swingle-tree, n. *cambren,* m., pl. *-nyer.*
switch, v. *trēlya, squychya*; beat, *cronkya gans gwelen*: n. *gwelen,* f., pl. *-lyny,* col. *gwēl*; for electricity, **squychyer,* m., pl. *-s.*
swoon, n. *clamder,* m.; v. *clamdera.*
sword, n. *cledha,* m., pl. *-dhevyow* (*-dhedhyow*): **-sman,** n. *cledhevyas,* m., pl. *-ysy, cledhyer,* m., pl. *-yoryon, cledhevor,* m., pl. *-yon*: **-stroke,** n. **cledhevas,* m., pl. *-esow.*
syllable, n. **syllaben,* f., pl. *-now.*
symbol, n. *sȳn,* m., pl. *-s, tokyn,* m., pl. *toknys,* **arweth,* f., pl. *-wedhyow*: **-ic, -ical,** a. **arwedhek.*
symmetrical, a. **kemusür*: **-try,** a. **kemusürans,* m.
sympathy, n. *tregereth,* f., **kescodhevyans,* m.; I shall die in s. with thee, *genes my a-vȳth marow*: **-thetic,** a. *tregerethüs,* **kescolonnek*: **-thize,** v. **kescodhaf, -dhevel.*
symptom: see **symbol.**
synagogue, n. *synaga,* m., pl. *-gys.*
synod, n. *seneth,* m., pl. *-edhow.*
synonymous, a. **kesstyr*; they are s., *nynsüs dhedha saw ün styr.*
syringe, n. *skȳt,* m., pl. *-ys*: v. *skȳtya.*
system, n. *o·rdyr,* m., pl. *-drys, rewl,* m., pl. *-ys*: **-atic,** a. *rewlys, herwyth rewl.*

T

tabby, a. *brȳth.*
tabernacle, n. *scovva,* f., pl. *-ow,* **tabernakyl,* m., pl. *-aclys.*
table, n. *mōs,* f., pl. *-ow, tābel,* m., pl. *-blys*; list, *rōl,* m.; t.-top, *bord,* m., pl. *-ys*; t.-cloth, *lȳen mōs,* m.; t.-ware, *dafar,* m.
tablet, n. *lēgh,* f., pl. *-ow*; pill, **tablet,* m., pl. *-tys.*
tabor, n. *tabour,* m., pl. *-s.*
taciturn, a. *tawesek.*
tack, v., stitch, *crafa*; nail, *takkya*; naut., *trēlya cors*: n., stitch, *craf,* m., pl. *-ow*; naut., *corn goles a-rak a'n gōl, cors gōlya*; small nail, **kentryk,* m., pl. *-ygow.*
tackle, v. *settya dalghen yn*: n. *aparell,* m., *taclow,* pl.
tact, n. *dōthter, fürneth,* m.: **-ful,** a. *dōth, für.*
tadpole, n. *penyn,* m., pl. *-now, pen du,* m., pl. *-now d.*
tail, n. *lost,* m., pl. *-ow, tȳn,* f., pl. *-yon*; t.-end, *lost, penyn,* m.; t. of shirt, *losten,* f.; t. to t., **tȳn ha tȳn*; t. end up, *lost yn-ban, tȳn drēs pen*; big-t.ed, *lostek*; having three t.s, *trȳlost, trȳ y lostow*: **-less,** a. *dylost*: **-ings,** n., mine, *lost,* m.
tailor, n. *trēgher,* m., pl. *-ghoryon,* †*sewyas,* m., pl. *-ysy*: v. *trēghy, gül dyllasow.*
taint, v. *pedry, mostya*: n. *podrethes,* m.
take, v. *kemeres, degemeres, receva*; t. with one, *drȳ, gorra*; t. care of, *gorra wyth a*[2]; t. care to, *gorra wyth dhe*[2]; t. place, *wharfos, darfos, bōs* (*bones*); t.! *tan*! *taneugh*!; t. away, *dōn yn-mēs, dōn dyworth*; t. with, *dōn gans*; t. off clothes, *dy'sky dyllas*; t. oneself off, *trussa*; I don't t. wine, *gwȳn ny-ūsyaf*; t. off, *tenna mēs*; t. to, *tenna dhe*[2]; t. that! *hava that*!; t. up eagerly, **tēry*; be t.n by, *mōs gans*; t.n up, *bysy*; let's t. it away, *dün ganso*; t. by surprise, *sawthanas*; t. leave, *gasa cümyas*; t. hold of, *settya dalghen yn, dalghenna, synsy*; t. care, *gwaytya, gorquytha, bōs war*; t. off guard, *contrewaytya*; how did he t. the news? *pana fara a-wrug-e a'n newodhow?*
tale, n. *whethel,* m., pl. *-thlow,*‡*drolla,* m., pl. *-ys,* ‡*tala,* m., pl. *-lys*; rumour, *kywhethel,* m., pl. *-thlow*; to tell t.s, *whethla, cuhüdha*; t. teller, *cuhüdhor,* m., pl. *-yon, cuhüdhyas,* m., pl. *-ysy,* †*cuhüdhojak,* m., pl. *-jogyon, whethlor,* m., pl. *-yon,* f. *-es,* pl. *-ow.*
talent, n. *ro,* m., pl. *-how, skȳans genesek,* m., **talent,* m., pl. *-ns*: **-ed,** a. *mür y rohow.*
talk, v. *kewsel, cows, talkya*: t. together, *keskewsel*; t. idly, *flattra*; t. noisily, *clattra*; jabber, *clappya, predheges*: n. *cows,* m., pl. *-ow*; idle t., *clap, flows,* m.: **-er,** n. *cowser,* m., pl. *-soryon, leveryas,* m., pl. *-ysy*; a great t., *predhegor,* m., pl. *-yon*: **-ative,** a. *tavasek.*
tall, a., *hȳr, ughel.*
tallow, n. *sōf,* m.
tally, n. *bōs kehaval* (*gans*).
talon, n. *ewyn,* m., pl. *-as,* **skyvel,* m., pl. *-vlow.*
tame, a. *dōf,* **dywoth*: v. *tempra, dōva, dōfhē·, wharhē·*: **-ness,** n. *doveth,* m:. **-mable,** a. *hedhōf.*
tamper, v. *mellya* (*gans*).
tan, n. **kyfȳth rüsk derow,* m.: v. **kyfȳthya crēghyn*: **-ned,** a. *kyfȳthys,* fig. *leskys gans an howl*; brown, **gell*: **-ner,** n. **kyfȳthyer crēghyn,* m., pl. *-yoryon c.*: **-yard,** n. *crēghynva,* f.

tang, n. *drokvlas, last,* m.; of blade, *tavas,* m.
tangible, a. *a-yller y dava.*
tangle, n. *dōl,* f., pl. *-ow, magel,* f., pl. *-glow, ancombrynsy,* m.: v. **cam-nedha,* **magly.*
tank, n. *dowrargh,* m., pl. *-ow.*
tankard, n. *crüskyn* (‡*knysken*), f., pl. *-now,* †*canna,* m., pl. *-nys, pot-dewas,* m., pl. *-tow-d.*
tantalize, v. *tormentya.*
tap, v., bore hole in, *tardra, attamya*; hit, *frappya yn-scaf*: n. *bom scaf,* m., pl. *-myn. s.*; of pipe, barrel, etc., *tap ha canel,* m., pl. *-pys ha canelys*: **-per,** n. *frappyer,* m., pl. *-yoryon.*
tape, n. **tāpa,* m.; broad, **ynkyl,* m.; t.-worm, **lenkeren,* f., pl. *-now.*
taper, v. *mōnhē·*: **-ing,** a. *mōn, mōn hy blȳn.*
taper, n. †*taper,* m., pl. *-prow.*
tapestry, n. *strayl,* m., pl. *-yow,* **tapȳt,* m., pl. *-ys.*
tapster, n. †*mēthor,* m., pl. *-yon.*
tar, n. **tar,* m.; coal-t., **tar du,* m.: v., pay with t., *gorra tar war*[2], *üra gans tar, duhē·*: **-red, -ry,** a. *duhē·s gans tar, tar warnodho.*
tardy, a. *lent, hell, dȳek.*
tares, n. *gwegas,* pl. *gwek,* col; in corn, *ȳvrē,* col., **drewk,* m.
target, n. *costen,* f., pl. *-now.*
tariff, n. *toll,* f., pl. *-ow.*
tarnish, v. *mostya,* **tarnsya*: **-ed,** a. *mostys,* **tarnsys.*
tarpaulin, n. **peglen,* f., pl. *-now.*
tarry, v. *strechya, tryga, tarya, gortos, lettya*: **-ing,** n. *let, strech,* m.
tart, a. *lym, wherow.*
tart, n. *tart,* m., pl. *-ys.*
task, n. *whēl,* m. and f., pl. *-yow, ober,* m., pl. *-ow, ran lafür,* f.
tassel, n. *crybell,* f., pl. *-ow, tos,* m., pl. *-ow.*
taste, n. *sawor,* m., pl. *-yow, saworen,* f., pl. *-now, blas,* m.: v. *blasa, assaya* ('*saya*), *sawory, tastya*: **-less,** a. *dysawor*: **-lessness,** n. **anvlas,* m.: **-ty.** a. *blesys da, saworek.*
tatter, n. *sketh,* m., pl. *-ow, skethen, pyllen,* f., pl. *-now, pyl,* m., pl. *-yon*: v. *früdha, skethenna, frēga*: **-ed,** a. *skethennek, pyllenek, pylyonek*: **-dermalion,** n. *frēgys,* m.
tattle, n. *whethel,* m., pl. *-thlow, clap,* m.: v. *clattra, whethla*: **-r,** n. *whethlor,* m., pl. *-oryon.*
taunt, v. *tōntya, scornya, blamya*: n. *blām,* m.: **-ingly,** adv. *yn ün tōntya* or *scornya.*
taut, a. *tyn, yn-ten, cowl-ystynnys.*
tavern, n. *tavern,* m., pl. *-yow, dewotty,* m., pl. *-ow.*
tawny, a. *rüthvelen,* **gell,* **gellrüth, melen, melen-cōr*: **-niness,** n. **gellder,* m.
tax, n. **toll,* f., pl. *-ow*; t.-collector, **tollor,* m., pl. *-yon*; t.-payer, *tyller toll,* m.: v. **tolly*: **-ation,** n. **tollans,* m.
tea, n. *tē,* m.; t.pot, *pot-tē,* m., pl. *-tow t.*; t. kettle, *chek-tē,* m., pl. *-kys t.*; t. party, *cuntell t.,* m.; t. things, *dafar t.,* m.; t. leaves, *cūthow,* pl.
teach, v. *dysky, dysquedhes*; t. him, *d. dhodho*: **-able,** a. *hedhysk*: **-er,** n. *dyscajor, dyscor,* m., pl. *-yon,* f. *-es,* pl. *-ow*: **-ing,** n. *dyscas,* m.
team, n. *para,* m., pl. *-ys*; of men, *party,* m., pl. *-s.*
tear, v. *squardya*; t. up, *frēga, skethenna*; t. down, *terry, dyswül*: n., rent, *squard,* m., pl. *-yow.*
tear, n. *dager,* m., pl. *-grow*; t.-drop, *dagren,* f., pl. *-now*; to shed t.s, *scullya dagrow, gül dh'y dhagrow devera,* **dagrewy*: **-ful,** a. *ow-tevera dagrow.*
teaze, v. *hyga, annȳa, serry*; t. out rope, etc., *früdha, crybella.*
teat, n. *tēth,* f., pl. *-ow, tethen,* f. pl. *-now.*
technical, a. *a greft*: **-ity,** n. *crefto·rȳeth,* f.: **-cian,** n. *creftor,* m., pl. *-yon.*
tedious, a. *hȳr*; t. time, *hȳrneth,* f.: **-ness,** n. *squythans, hȳrder,* m.
teem, v. *drȳ ascor, bōs lenwys*(a^2), *bōs pals*; pour, *denewy*: **-ing,** n. *lün, lenwys*(a^2), *ow-trȳ ascor pals.*
teetotal, a. *a-scon dewas crēf, dowr y dhewas*: **-ler,** n. *ever dowr,* m., pl. *-oryon d.*
telegram, n. **pell-scryven,* f., pl. *-now*: **-graph,** v. **pell-scryfa*: **-graphic,** a. **pellscryfys.*
telephone, v. **pellgewsel*: n. **pellgowser,* m.. **-ony,** n. **pellgows,* m.
telescope, n. *gwēder aspȳa,* m., pl. *-drow a.,* **pellweler,* m.: v.
televise, v. **pellvyras*: **-sion,** n. *pellwolok,* m.
tell, v. *leverel, derȳvas*; bid, *erghy*; I t. you, *jevodȳ·*; t. good of, *kywhethla*; I'll t. thee what, *my a-lever a'n cās dhys*; I can't t., *ny-wōn desmygy*; as we are told, *del leveryr*: **-er,** n. *leveryas,* m., pl. *-ysv.*
temerity, n. *ref, fās, bolder,* m.
temper, n., good t., *caradewder,* m.; bad t., *sōr,* m.: v. *tempra*; good t.ed, *nag üs ēs y serry.*

temperament, n. *gnās,* m.
temperance, n. *clōrder, temprans,* m.: **-ate,** a. *clōr, whar, mygyl.*
temperature, n. *tomder, yeynder,* m.
tempest, n. *hager awel,* †*enawel,* f.: **-uous,** a. *gwynsak, hager, garow, awelek.*
temple, n., anat., †*ēr,* m., pl. *-yow*; relig., *templa,* m., pl. *-ys.*
templet, n. *scantlyn,* m.
temporary, a. *drēs ün prȳs, prȳjwyth.*
tempt, v. *temptya, dynya*: **-ation,** n. *temptasyon,* m., *antel,* f. *dynyans,* m.: **-ing,** a. *whans y weles.*
ten, a., n. *dēk,* pl. *degow*; t. times, *dēgwyth*: **-fold,** *dēkplēk*: **-th,** a. *dēgves.*
tenacious, a., grasping, *craf*; sticky, *glüjek*; t. person, *synsyas,* m., pl. *-ysy*: **-city,** n. *synsyans, crefny, crefter,* m.
tenancy, n. *bargen,* **gobrenans,* m.: **-ant,** n. *kemerer,* m., pl. **gobrener,* m., pl. *-noryon*; of farm, *tȳak,* m., pl. *-ogow.*
tend, v. *plegya, pōsa,* **stümma*; care for, *gwytha*: **-ency,** n. *plegyans,* m., *stüm,* m., pl. *-mow.*
tender, a. *medhel*; painful, *tyn*; immature, *tender*; delicate, *blüth,* **lȳth*: **-ness,** n. *medhelder,* m,
tender, v. *profya*: n. *profyans,* m.
tendon, n. *gyewen,* f., col. *gyew.*
tenement, n. *chȳ,* m., pl. *-ow, bargen tȳr,* m., pl. *-ys t.*
tennis, n. **tennys,* m.
tenor, n. **tenor,* m., pl. **-s.**
tense, a. *ten, ynten*: **-sion,** n. *antel,* f., *tynder,* m., *tenva,* f.
tent, n. *tylda,* m., pl. *-ys, scovva,* f., pl. *-ow,* ‡*tenta,* m., pl. *-ys*; to pitch a t., *tyldya.*
tenure, n. *possessyon,* m.; feudal t., *agomarghogyon,* f., *fē,* m., pl. *-ys.*
tepid, a. *mygyl*; to grow t., *mygla*: **-ity,** n. *mygylder,* m.
term, n. *termyn,* m., pl. *-yow*; t.s, *ambosow,* pl.; on equal t.s, *quyt*; on good t.s with, *accordyes orth.*
terminate, v. *dewedha, gorfenna*: **-ion,** n. *deweth,* m., *dewethva, fynweth,* f.
terminus, n. **penhens,* m.
tern, n. *morwennol,* f., pl. *-nyly, scrawyk,* m., pls. *-ygow, -esygow.*
terrace, n. **terras,* m., pl. *-ys.*
terrestrial, a. *a'n norvȳ·s.*
terrible, a. *üthek, fell, garow*: **-bly,** adv. *üthek, yn-harow.*
terrific, a. *üthek, üth y weles* or *glewes*: **-fy,** v. *gorra ownyn,* **braweghy*; I am t.d, *yma·üth dhym, own brās a-m-büs, dyegrys ōf.*
terrier, n. **dorgy,* m., pl. *-gün.*
territory, n. *tȳreth,* m., pl. *-ow*: **-rial,** a. *tȳrethek.*
terror, n. *üth, üthekter,* m., **brawagh,* m., pl. *-ow*: **-ism,** n. *rewl drē üth,* m.
terse, a. *ber, cot*: **-ly,** adv. *war ver lavarow, ber y eryow, hep gül areth anodho*: **-ness,** n. *berder,* m.
tertian: see **fever.**
test, v. *prevy, trȳa, assaya* (*saya*); by questions, *apposya*: n. *prof, prevyans, assay,* m.
testaceous, a. *cregynnek.*
testament, n. *testament,* m.; will, *kemmyn,* m., pl. *-ow*; the Old and New T.s, *an Scryptors Coth ha Noweth*: **-stator,** n. *kemmynor,* m., pl. *-yon,*: **-trix,** *-es* f., pl. *-ow.*
testicle, n. *kell,* f., pl. *-yow,* d. *dywgell.*
testify, v. *dustünya, testa, desta*: **-timonial,** n. *dustünyans,* m.: **-mony,** n. *dustünya,* m., pl. *-yow.*
tether, n. *stak,* m., pl. *-agow*: v. *staga*; I am at the end of my t., *ny-wōn fatel gül nessa, stagys ōf.*
tetter, n. **darwesen,* f., col. **darwes.*
text, n. **testen,* f., pl. *-now*; Bible, *ran Scryptor Sans,* f., *test,* m., pl. *-ow*; original t., *mamscryf,* m.
textile, a. *gwȳes*: n. *gwȳas,* m.: **-ture,** n. *gwȳas,* m., *gwȳ,* f.
than, a. *es, age·s* (combines with prons.).
thank, v. *grassa, aswonvos* or *gothvos grās dhe*^{2}; t. you! *mür rās dheugh-why*! *y-whōn dhys mür rās*! *dheugh gro·mercy*! *Dew re-dallo dheugh-why*! (*Durdala dywy*), *Dew re-n-tallo dhys*; t. God,! *gras e dhe Dhew*! *dhe Dhew re-bo grassys*!; I t. God for it, *dhe Dhew y-n-grassaf*: **-ful,** a., I am t., *y-whōn grās, gōn* or *yth-aswonaf mür rās*: **-fulness,** n. *grassans,* m.: **-less,** a. *hep aswon* or *gothvos grās*: **-s,** n. *grās,* m., pls. *-sow, -sys*; many t., *gro·mercy, mür rās*: **-sgiving,** n. *grassans,* m.
that, a. *an . . . -na*; t. boy, *an maw-na*: pron. *henna,* f. *honna*; before, *yu, ō, hen,* f. *hon*: rel. pron. *a*^{2}-, neg. *na*^{2}-: conj. *may*^{5}(*th*), neg. *ma na*^{2}-; so t., in order t., *rak, rak may*^{5}, neg. *rak na*^{2}-; he says t. he is, *y-lever y vōs*; he says t. he will come, *y-lever y-tē*; he said t. he would come, *y-leverys y-to.*

thatch, n. *to cala,* m.: v. *tȳ gans cala* or *sowl*: t.ed house, *tȳ sowl,* m.: **-er,** n. *tȳor,* m., pl. *-yon*: **-ing reed,** n., unbroken straw, *cala to, sowl,* col.
thaw, n. *tēth, tedhans,* m.: v. *tedha.*
the, art. *an,* after prep. or conj. ending in vowel, *'n*; t. before comp. adjs., *dhe*²; t. more . . . t. less . . ., *sül voy*•. . ., *dhe lē* . . .
theatre, n. ***gwaryjy,* m., *gwaryva,* f., pl. *-ow*; open air t., *plēn an gwary,* m.
thee, pron. *ty*; suffixed, *-sy, -jy, -ta*; emphatic, *dhesȳ*•, *dhejȳ*•, *tejȳ*; infixed, *-th-* (*-d-*); with inf., *dha*²; with prep., *ahanas, ragos,* etc.; to "thee and thou" one, *tȳas.*
theft, n. *ladrans,* ***ladrynsy,* m.
their, pron. *aga*³; after prep. ending in vowel, *'ga*³: **-s,** pron. *dhedha*; it is t., *y a-n-pew, dhedha-y yma*•; it is not t. to say, *dhedha ny-long leverel.*
them, pron. *-y*; emphatic, *-ynsȳ*•; infixed, *-s-*; with infin., *aga*³; with prep., *anedha,* etc.; the three of t., *aga thrȳ*: **-selves,** pron. *ynsȳ*•, *y aga-honen*; of t., *anedha aga honen.*
then, adv. *ena, y'n ür-na* (‡*nenna*): conj. *ytho*•, ‡*dhanna.*
thence, adv. *alenna*; t.forward, *alenna-rak, wosa henna, a'n termyn-na.*
theologian, n. *dyvyn,* m., pl. *-ys*: **-ogy,** n. *skȳans Dew,* ***dyvy·nyta,* m.
theory, n. *tybyans,* m.: **-retical,** a. *drē dybyans.*
there, adv. *ena*; yonder, *eno, enos*; thither, *dȳ, dhȳ*; from t., *alenna*; over t., *enos, ynhans*; t. is, *yma*•; t. is the man! *ot, otta* or *awotta an dēn*!; see t.! *ot ena*!; see him t.! *ottensa enos*!: **-abouts,** adv. *ogas dȳ* (‡*ogasty, ogatty*): **-after,** adv. *wosa henna*: **-by,** adv. *gans henna, drē henna, dredhy*: **-fore,** adv. *rag-henna, ytho*•: **-in,** adv. *ynno,* f. *ynny*: **-of,** adv. *anodho,* f. *anedhy*: **-on,** adv. *warnodho,* f. *warnedhy*: **-upon,** adv. *gans henna, kettoth ha'n gēr*: **-with, -al,** adv. *gans henna, gensy.*
thermometer, n. *musürer tomder,* m.
these, pron. *an rē-ma*: a. *an . . . -ma*; t. men, etc., *an düs-ma,* etc.
they, pron. *y*; emphatic, *ynsȳ*•.
thick, a. *tew*; of voice, †*crek*; abundant, *pals* (after pl. or col. noun): **-en,** v. *tewhē*•: **-ness,** n. *tewder,* m.
thicket, n. *gwydhal* (*godhal*), m., pl. *-dhyly, pryskel,* m., pl. *-clow, cardhen,* f., pl. *-now, caswyth, tewgos, dreyngos,* m.
thick-head, n. *pen-brās, pen-tew,* m.
thief, n. *lader,* m., pl. *ladron, ladres,* f., pl. *-ow*: **-ve,** v. *ladra.*
thigh, n. *mordhos,* f., pls. *-ow, -ojow,* d. *dywvordhos.*
thimble, n. *bysgon* (*bysken*), f., pl. *-now*; silver t., *bysgon arghans.*
thin, a. *tanow, cül, mōn*; of fabric, *boll*; t. person, *sagh eskern, eskernek,* m., pl. *-nygyon*: v., t. down, t. out, *tanowhē*•: **-ness,** n. *cülder, tanowder,* m.
thine, pron. *dhys, dhyso, dhyso-jy, ragos*; it is t., *ty a-n-pew*; it is not t. to (kill, etc.), *nyns-yu ragos-sy* (*ladha,* etc.).
thing, n. *tra,* neut., pl. *taclow,* d. ‡*taclennow, pyth,* m., pl. *-ow*; like a mad t., *ave·l p.fol.*
think, v. *predery, tyby, desevos*; t. oneself to be, *omsynsy*; bet. oneself, *ombredery*: **-ing,** n., way of t., *brȳs,* m., *cowsys,* m., pl. *-sesow.*
third, a., n., **-ly,** adv. *tressa, y'n tressa lē*; t. day hence, *godreva,* f.
thirst, n. *sēghes,* m.: v. *bōs sēghes dhe*²: **-y,** a. *sēghes dhodho*; I am t., *yma*• *sēghes dhym*; a t. place, *sēghla,* m.
thirteen, a., n. *tredhek*: **-th,** a., n. *tredheg·ves.*
thirty, a., n. *dēk-warn-ügans*; **-ieth,** a., n. *degves-warn-ügans.*
this, pron. *hemma,* m., *homma,* f. (before *yu* or *ō, hem, hom*): a. *an . . . -ma*; t. man, etc., *an dēn-ma,* etc.
thistle, n. *ascallen,* f., col. *ascal*; sow-t., *ascallen mogh,* f., col. *ascal m.*; t. bed, t. ground, *ascallek,* f., pls. *-egy, -egow*: **-ly,** a. *ascallek.*
thither, adv. *dȳ, dhȳ, bys dȳ* (*bystȳ*), *dhe'n lē-na.*
thong, n. *crōn,* m., pl. *-ow.*
thorn, n. *drēn,* m., pl. *dreyn*; t. or t.-bush, *drēnen,* f., col. *dreyn, spernen,* f., col. *spern*, black t., *spernen dhu*; buck-t., ***spernen velen*; haw-t., *spernen wyn,* col. *spern du, melen, gwyn*; crown of t.s, *curün spern*; t. brake, *spernek, dreynek, drēnak,* f., pls. *-egy, -egow*: **-y,** a. *drēnak, dreynek, spernek.*
thornback, n. *raya,* m., pl. *-s,* †*rogha,* m., pl. *-s.*
thorough, a. *perfyth, lün, cowal, dȳen*: **-ly,** adv. *pür, yn-tȳen, hep nam*; prefix, *cowl-, lün-*: **-bred,** a. *sevys a wōs pür*: **-fare,** n. *forth lan,* f., pl. *-dhow glan.*
those, pron. *an rē-na*; all t. who, *kemmys a*²-, *sül a*²-, *myns a*²-: *an . . . -na*; t. old men, etc., *an düs cōth-na,* etc.

thou, pron. *ty*; suffixed, *-sy*, *-jy*; emphatic, *dhesȳ·*, *dhejȳ·*, *tejȳ·*: v., to "thou" one, *tȳas*.

though, conj. *kyn*[5](*th*): adv. *bytege·ns*, *awo·s henna*.

thought, n. *tybyans*, *preder*, m., pl. *-ow*, abst. *prederow*, *brȳs*, m., pl. *-yow*, *cowsys*, m., pl. and abst. *-sesow*, **desef*, m., pl. *-eyvow*: **-ful,** a. *prederüs*: **-less,** a. *dybreder*.

thousand, a., n. *mȳl*[2], f., pl. *-yow*; t.fold, *mylblēk*; t. years, *mylvledhen*, f.; t. years of age, *mylvlōth*, m.; t. times better, *mylwell*; t. times worse, *mylweth*; t. times, *mylwyth*; three hundred t., *tryhansvyl*: **-th,** a., n. *mylves*.

thrall, n., bondage, *danjer*, n.; slave, *kēth*, m., pl. *-yon*.

thrash, v. *cronkya*, *castȳga*, *stewanny*, **dorna*; of corn, *füsta*, ‡*drusha*: **-ing,** n. *castȳk*, *stewan*, m., *cosva*, f.; t.machine, *jyn-füsta*, m., pl. *-nys*, f.

thread, n. †*nüjen*, f., pl. *-now*, col. *nüs*, *lynyn*, m., pl. *-now*: v. **nüjenna*, *gorra drē grow nasweth*: **-bare,** a. *ūsyes bys yn nüjen*.

threat, n. *bras-lavarow*, pl. *bragyans*, m., *godros*, m., pl. *-ow*: **-en,** v. *godros*, *bragya*; impend, *degensewa*: **-ening,** a. *ow-tegensewa*, *hager*, *a-vrak*.

three, a., n., *trȳ*[3], f. *tȳr*[3]; t. times, *tergwyth*; t. fold, *tryflek*; t. cornered, **tryhornek*, *tryelyn*; t. times as much, *tryhemmy·s*; contracts to *tre-* in certain compounds, *tredden*, *treddeth*, *treffer*, *trelles*, *tremmyl*, *tremmys*, in which the numeral takes the accent, the initials of *dēn*, *dōth*, *fēr*, *bōs*, *mȳl*, *mȳs*, being doubled and their vowels being shortened; this applies only to special words; t. masted ship, *gorhel tȳr gwern*, m.

thresh, v. *füsta*, *drushya*: **-er,** n. *füster*, m., pl. *-storyon*, *drushyer*, m., pl. *-yoryon*.

threshold, n. *trüthow*, m.

thrice, adv. *tergwyth*.

thrift, n. *sparyans*, *sowynyans*, **erbys*, m.; sea pink, *tam-ōn*, *bryton*, m.: **-y,** a. *sowyn*; to be t., *sparya*, *sowyny*, **erbysy*; t. person, †*erbysya*, m., pl. *-ysy*.

thrill, v. *müvya*; figuratively, *gwana*, *gül dhe'n golon lamma*; t.ed, *hüdhyk y golon*: n. *lam*, m., pl. *-mow*, *müvyans*, m.: **-ing,** a. *a-vüf*, *ow cül dhe'n golon lamma*.

thrive, v. *sowyny*, *spēdya*: **-ing,** a. *sowen*: n. *sowynyans*, m., *sowena*, f.

throat, n. *lonk*, m., *brȳansen*, f., **gūdhūk*, m., pl. *-ügow*.

throb, v. *lemmel*, *lamma*: n. *lam colon* or *pols*, m., pl. *-mow c.*, *p.*: **-bing,** a. *ow-lamma*.

throne, n. *sē*, m., pl. *-ys*, *eseth*, f., pl. *-edhow*, *trōn*, *trōn-esedha*, m., pl. *-ys*, *-ys-e.*; bishop's t., *chayr* or *sē epscop*.

throng, n. *rūth*, f., *bagas*, m., pl. *-ow*, *bush*, m., pl. *-ys*: v. *hēsya*, *mōs yn ün tonek*.

throstle, n. *molgh* (*mola*), f., pl. *-as*.

throttle, v. *taga*, **lyndaga*.

through, prep. *drē*[2] (before vowel *der*): **-out,** prep. *drēs*: adv. *a'n ȳl pen dh'y gȳla*, *hēs-ha-hēs*.

throw, v. *tewlel*; t. open, *ygery*, *ōpya*; t. down carelessly, *tewlel dhe scul*; t. violently, *deghesy*; t. down, *dysevel*, *omwheles*; t. back, **attewlel*: n. *towl*, m., pl. *-ow*, *flynk*, m., pl. *-ys*.

thrush, n. *molgh-lōs*, f., pl. *-as-l.*

thrust, v. *herdhya*, *pokkya*; with point of weapon, *pychya*: n. *herdhyans*, m., *pok*, m., pl. *-kyow*; of pointed weapon, *pych*, m., pl. *-ys*.

thud, n. *bom*, m., pl. *-myn*.

thumb, n. *bȳs brās*, m., pl. *besyas b.*; nickname in finger game, *crakkya-lewen*.

thump, v. *cronkya*, **dorna*: n. *bom*, m., pl. *-myn*, *cronk*, m., pl. *-ys*, *tummas*, m., pl. *-ow*, **dornas*, m., pl. *-nesow*.

thunder, n. *taran*, f., pl. *-rennow*; t.-bolt, as figuratively, *crak-taran*, m.; as stone celt, *mēn-taran*, m.; t. clap, *crak taran*; t. cloud, *newl taran*, m.; t. storm, *kewer a daran*, f.; t. struck, *dyegrys*: v. *tarenna*, *gül taran*: **-er,** n. *tarenner*, m., pl. *-noryon*: **-ering,** n., of surf, *mōrdrōs*, m.: **-erous, -ry,** a. **taranek*.

Thursday, n. *dē-Yow*, m.; T. before Christmas, *dē-Y. Wyn*; Ascension Day, *dē-Y. Bask*; Maundy T., *dē-Y. Hablys*.

thus, adv., in that way, *yndella*, *yn-ketella*, *y'n for'-na*; in this way, *yndelma*, *y'n forma*; t. far, *bys y'n lē-ma*, *bys y'n ür-ma*.

thwack, a. *what*, m., pl. *-tys*.

thwart, n. *trüspren*, m., pl. *-nyer*: v. *lettya*: **-wise,** adv. *a-drüs keyn*, *drēs keyn*.

thick-thwack, adv. *tys-ha-tas*.

thy, pron. *dha*[2]; of t., etc., *a'th*[5], etc.: **-self,** pron. *dha honen*, *-dhejȳ·*, *myrgh dha dhama* or *vam*, *map dha dhama* or *vam*.

thyme, n. *tym*, m.

tick, v. *gül tys ha tas*: **-ing,** n. *tys-ha-tas*, m.; of bed, *lȳen gwely-cala*.

tick, n., insect, †*torogen*, f., col. *torak*.

ticket, n, **tokyn*, m., pl. *toknys*; t. inspector, *tokynner*, m., pl. *-oryon.*

tickle, v. *cosa, debrenna, dybry*: n. **-ling,** n. *debron*, m., *cos*, f., **cosva*, f.: **-lish,** a., difficult, *tykly*; sensitive, **hegos.*

tide, n. *lanwes mōr*, m., ‡*tӯd*, ‡*mor-tӯd*, m., pl. *-ys*; time, *prӯs*, m., pls. *-yow, -yjyow*; high t., **lanow*, **morlanow*, **reverthy*, m., pl. *-ow*; low t., *tryg, mordryg*, m.; flowing t., *lanwes, morlenwel*, m.; the t. is out, *tryg yu*; t. race, *frōs*, m.; neap-t., **marvor*, m.

tidings, n. *newodhow, danvonadow*, pl.

tidy, a. *glanyth*, **kempen*: v. *o·rdena, restry*, **kempenna*: **-diness,** n. *glanythter*, **kempensys*, m.

tie, v. *kelmy, fastya, fasta*: n. *colmen*, f., pl. *-now, colm*, m., pl. *-ow*, **stagell*, f., pl. *-ow*, **syg*, f., pl. *-yow*, **fask*, f., pl. *-scow*, **ēry*, m., pl. *-ow*; all t.d up together, *yn ün golmen*: **-beam,** n. *styll*, m., pl. *-yow.*

tiger, n. **tӯger*, m., pl. *-gras.*

tight, a. *tyn, fast, yn-ten*, **strōth*; water-t. *stanch*: **-en,** v. *strotha, tynhē·fastya, fasta*: **-ly,** adv. *fast, yn-tyn*: **-ness,** n. *tynder*, m.

tile, n. *prӯlēghen*, f., pl. *-now*: v. *tӯ* or *gorhery gans pryleghennow.*

till, v. *gonys*, **amethy*: **-age,** n. *gonys*, m., *trevas*, f., pl. *-ow*: **-er,** n. *gonysyas*, m., pl. *-ysy.*

till, prep. *bys, bys yn*; conj. *bys pan*[2], *bys may*[5], *erna*[2]*(g).*

tiller, n., naut., †*ebyl lew*, m., pl. *-yow l.*

tilt, v., lean, etc., *posa, ynclӯnya*; joust, *jūstya*: n. *tylda*, m., pl. *-dys*; to cover with a t., *tyldya.*

tilth, n. *trevas*, f., *gonys*, **ar*, m.

timber, n. *pren*, m., pls. *-yer, prynner, tymber*, m.

time, n. *prӯs, termyn*, m., pl. *-yow*; occasion, *treveth, gwyth, tro*, f., pl. *-yow*; short t., *cors, pols, torn, tuch*, m.; very long t., *hӯrneth*, f.; age, period, epoch, *ōs*, m., pl. *-ow*; clock t., *owr*, m., pl. *-ys, ür*, f., pl. *-yow*; life t., *üs, ōs, densys*; meal t., *prӯs bōs*; supper t., etc., *prӯs soper*, etc.; all the t., *prest, pup ür oll, pup nōs ha dēth*; at all t.s, *pup termyn, mo ha myttyn, ha dewedhes hag a-var*; at any t., *war nep tro, neb ür, nep-prӯs, yn jēth nag yn nōs*; at the same t. as, *warba·rth ha, kefrӯ·s* or *kekefrӯ·s ha*; at the same t., *y'n keth termyn* (‡*kettermyn*); at this t., *yn tor'-ma*; once upon a t., *kens*; at one t. . . . at another t. . . ., *an ӯl torn . . ., trēs aral . . .*; a short t. ago, *agensow*; a long t. ago, *nans-yu pell, soladhē·th*; in t., *a-dermyn*; in good t., *a-brӯs*; in t. to come, *termyn a-dhē*; in t. past, *yn termyn res-ēth* or *üs tremenys* or *passyes*; by the t. that was done, *erby·n bones gwrēs henna*; a third t., etc., *tressa treveth*, etc.; three t.s, etc., *tergwyth*, etc.; t. without end, *trank hep worfen*; what is the t.? *py ür yu? pyth yu an ür?*; seven t.s as much, etc., *seythkemmy·s*, etc.; it is t. to end, *prӯs yu dewedha* or *gül deweth*: **-ly,** a. *yn prӯs da, a-brӯs*: **-table,** n. *rōl termynyow*, m.

timid, timorous, a. *ownek.*

tin, n. *stēn*, m.; t. stone, *pryl*, m., pl. *-yon*; rich t., *scof*, m.; fine mealy t., *floren*, f.; inferior t., *relystyon, manylyon*, pl.; t.-working, *whēl-stēn, w.-hāl, w.-bal*, m. or f., pl. *-yow-b. s., h.*; t.-bearing, *stenak, stenys*; t. b. ground, *stenak*, f., pls. *-egy, -egow*; t. bound, *bownd*, m., pl. *-ns*; cutter of t. b., *tollor*, m., pl. *-yon*: **-ner,** n. *stenor*, m., pl. *-yon.*

tinder, n. *losk, defnyth golow*, m.: **-box,** n. *corn tān*, m., pls. *kern* or *kernow t.*

tinge, n. *lyw*, m., pl. *-yow*: v. *lywa.*

tingle, v. *lesky, cosa.*

tinker, n. *gwӯthor stēn*, m., pl. *-yon s.*

tinkle, v. **tynkyal.*

tint: see **tinge.**

tiny, a. *münys, pür vünys.*

tip, n. *blӯn*, m., pl. *-ow, mӯn*, m., pl. *-yon, topyn*, m., pl. *-now, tӯb*, m.; gift, *rō*, m., pl. *-how*: v. *rӯ gober*; t. up, *settya war y vӯn*; t. rubbish, *gwakhē·, dyllo, omwheles, tewlel dhe-vēs, scullya, dyscarga.*

tipsy, a. *hanter medhow*, **govedhow.*

tiptoe, n., on t., *war vesyas treys* or *y dreys*, etc.

tire, n. *bond rōs*, **cans rōs*; pneumatic t., *bond rōs whethys.*

tire, v. *squytha, annӯa (nӯa)*; t. out, *fetha*: **-d,** a. *squyth, squythys*, **blӯn*; t. out, *lafüryes*: **-dness,** n. *squythter, squythans*, m.: **-ing,** a. *a-squyth, a-annӯ·.*

tiresome, a. *hӯr, dyflas*; to be t., *annӯa.*

tissue, n. *gwӯas*, m.; t. paper, *paper tanow.*

tit, n., titmouse, **penglow*, m., pl. *-as*; blue-t., *pen-paly*, m., pl. *-as.*

tit-bit, n. *tam dēnty*, m., pl. *tymmyn d.*

tit-for-tat, adv. *tys-ha-tas*; you shall have t.-f.-t., *why a-gyf kemmy·s del rylly.*

tithe, n. *dēga,* m.; true t., *gwȳr-dhēga*; rectorial t.s, *manal,* f.; t. barn, *skyber-vanal,* f.: v., to pay or take t.s, *degevy.*

title, n. *tȳtel,* m., pl. *-tlys*; right, *gwȳr,* m.: **-tular,** a. *orth tȳtel, drē dȳtel.*

titmouse: see **tit.**

to, prep. *dhe*², *orth, yn*; towards, concerning, *yn kever*; in order t., *rak*; up t., even t., *bys, bys yn*; t. us, *bys dhyn*; t. it, *bys dȳ* (*tȳ*); t. and fro, *yn-rak ha wardhelergh, omma hag ena*; t. his woe, *er y wew.*

toad, n. *cronek,* m., pls. *-nogow, -nogas*; dark t., *cronek du*; light t., *cronek melen*; little t., *cronekyn,* m.; t. or frog, *lefans,* m., pls. *lefyns, -fanjas*: **-flax,** n. **lyn gōth,* m.: **-stool,** n. *scavel-cronek,* f., pl. *-low c.*

toast, n. *crasen,* f., pl. *-now,* col. *cras*: v. *crasa*; in drink, *eva dh'y yēghes da*: **-ed,** a. *cras*: **-ing-fork,** n. *forgh crasa,* f., pl. *fergh*(*y*) *c.*: **-rack,** n. **rastel crasennow,* m.

tobacco, n. *tobacco, bacca,* m.; t. pouch, *saghyk t.,* m.: **-nist,** n. *gwerther tobacco,* m., pl. *-oryon-t.*

to-day, adv., pres. and future sense, *hedhyu, y'n jēth hedhyu*; pres. or past tense, *hedhyu y'n jēth, dēdhwyth*; t. week, *dhe ben seythen,* ‡*an jorna-ma war seythen.*

toddle, v. *kerdhes cot* or *gwan y gam, rambla*: **-r,** n. *flogh üs ow-tysky kerdhes.*

toe, n. *bȳs trōs,* m., pl. *besyas treys* or *trōs.*

toffee, n. *clyjjy,* m., *whegow,* pl.

together, adv. *warba·rth, kefrȳ·s, kekefrȳ·s*; t. with, *gans*; all t., *oll warba·rth*; prefix, *kes-,* e.g., *kescana,* to sing t.

toil, v. *lafürya*: n. *laførryans, lafür, whēl crēf,* m.: **-er,** n. *lafüryer,* m., pl. *-yoryon*: **-some,** a. **lafürüs.*

token, n. *tokyn,* m., pl. *-knys*; fig. *ōl,* m., pl. *-ow,* **arwedhynsy, nōs,* m., pl. *-ow.*

tolerance, -ation, n. *perthyans, godhevyans,* m.: **-ate,** v. *perthy, godhaf, godhevel,* ‡*pēsya.*

toll, v. *seny clogh* or *gül dhe glogh cana yn-forethek.*

toll, n. *toll,* f., pl. *-ow*; t. house, *tolljȳ,* m., pl. *-ow*; t. keeper, †*tollor,* m., pl. *-yon*; t. place, **tollva,* f., pl. *-ow*; t. gate, **tollyet,* **tollborth,* m.

tomato, n. **aval kerensa,* m., pl. *-low k.*

tomboy, n. *flownen,* f., pl. *-now, gourvoren,* f., pl. *-ronyon.*

tomb, n. *bēth,* m., pl. *bedhow*; t. stone, *mēn bēth,* pl. *meyn bedhow*; t. chamber of prehistoric burial, *cromlēgh,* f., pl. *-yow.*

tomcat, n. *gourgath,* m., pl. *-as.*

tome, n. *lyver brās,* m., pl. *-vrow b.*

tomfoolery, n. *folneth, gokyneth, gwary Cala Mē,* m.

to-morrow, adv. *avorow*; day after t., *trenja*; t. morning, *ternos vyttyn.*

tomtit: see **blue tit**, under **tit.**

ton, n. *ügans-canspos,* **ton,* m.

tone, n. *tōn,* m., pl. *-yow*: v., t. down, *tempra.*

tongs, n. †*gevel,* f., pl. *-yow*; iron t., *gevel horn*; fire t., *gevel tān.*

tongue, n., also language, *tavas,* m., pl. *-ow*; having long t., *tavasek*; sharp t.d, *lym y davas.*

to-night, adv. *gorthewer, haneth yn-nōs, yn-nōs haneth, haneth dhe-nōs.*

tonsure, n. *pen blogh,* m.: **-d,** a. *blogh.*

too, adv. *rē*; also, *ynta·, gans henna, ynwe·th, magata·, kefrȳ·s*; t. much, *rē.*

tool, n. *toul,* m., pl. *-ys.*

tooth, n. *dans,* m., pl. *dyns*; front t., *dans a-rak*; back t., *dans a-dhelergh, kyldans*; t. brush, *scüber dyns*; t. pick, *pyger dyns*; t. drawer, *tenner dyns*; in the teeth of your opposition, *yn despȳ·t war dha dhyns*; to show the teeth, *deskerny,* ‡*grysla*: **-ed,** a., indented, *dynsak*: **-less,** a. *dydhyns, hep dans*: **-y,** a. *dynsak* (†*denjak*).

top, n. *gwartha,* m., pl. *-avyon, pen,* m., pl. *-now, top,* m., pl. *-yow,* dim. *topyn, blȳn,* m., pl. *-ow*; of ship, *top,* m., pl. *-pys*; of steep place, *tāl,* m., pl. *-yow*; on t., *a-wartha*; *a-barth a-wartha*; t.heavy, *rē bōs y ben.*

topic, n. *cās, mater,* m., *tra,* neut., pl. *taclow*: **-al,** a. *a'n lē, a'n mater, a'n termyn.*

topknot, n. *crybell,* f., pl. *-ow.*

topmost, a. *ughella.*

topple, v. *omdhysevel, omwheles.*

topsy-turvy, adv. *tȳn drēs pen, trēlyes an pyth a-wartha dhe woles, pen war woles ha goles war-van.*

torch, n. *torchen,* f., pl. *-now,* **fakel,* f., pl. *-clow,* **faklen,* f., pl. *-now.*

torment, n. *payn,* m., pl. *-ys, torment,* m., pl. *-ns*; harsh t.s, *cales-paynys*: v. *tormentya, payna*: **-or,** n. *tormentor,* m., pls. *-s, -ys.*

tormentil, n., bot., **seythdelen,* f.

torpid, a. *clamderys, dyvewnans*; t. person, †*cuscador desempys,* m.

torque, n. **torgh,* f., pl. *tergh.*

torrent, n. *frōs,* f., pl. *-yow, lȳf,* m., pl. *-yvyow, †keynres,* m., **reverthy,* m., pl. *-ow, lȳfwoth,* f., pl. *-wythy*; of rain, *hagergowas,* f., pl. *-wosow*: **-ial,** a. *ynfrōs, kepa·r ha lȳf Noy.*

tortoise, n. **cronek-ervys,* m., pls. *-nogow, -nogas-e.*; t. shell, *crogen cronek-ervys,* f.

torture, -r: see **torment, -or.**

toss, v. *tewlel, ‡tossya*: n. *towl,* m., pl. *-ow.*

tot, n. *banna gwyras,* m., pl. *-how g.*

total, n. *sum,* m., pl. *-mys, summen,* f., pl. *-now*: a. *cowal*: **-ly,** adv., prefix to v. *cowl-*; with adjective or p.p., *yn-tȳen, glan, cowal.*

totter, v. *trebüchya*: **-ing,** a. *parys dhe godha.*

touch, v. *tava, tuchya, handla*: n. *tuch,* m.; sense of t., *tava,* inf.: **-ing,** a. *trūethek, pytethüs*; adjacent, *fest ogas, ow-junnya nessa dhe*²: prep., concerning, *yn-kever*: **-y,** a. *skēsek, ēs y serry.*

tough, a. *gwethyn, cales, crēf, aflydhys*: **-en,** v. *caleshē·, gwethynhē·*: **-ness,** n. *caletter, gwethynder,* m.

tour, n. *tro,* f., pl. *-yow, vȳach a-dro*: v. *gül tro, vȳajya a-dro*: **-ist,** n. *vȳajyer,* m., pl. *-yoryon, gwandryas,* m., pl. *-ysy, *touryst,* m., pl. *-ys.*

tournament, tourney, n. *jūst,* m., pl. *-ys, tournay,* m., pl. *-s*: v. *jūstya.*

tow, v. *tenna lester po car*; t. rope, *lovan tenna,* f., pl. *-vonow t.*

tow, n. *carth,* m., pl. *-yon*: **-head,** n. *pen melen.*

towards, prep. *troha, wor' tu ha*; of behaviour, *yn-kever*; t. me, etc., *y'm kever,* etc.

towel, n. *towal,* m., pl. *-wellow, lȳen dywlüf* (*l. dywla*), m., pl. *-yow d.*

tower, n. *tour,* m., pl. *-ow.*

town, n. *trē* (*trēf*), f., pl. *-trevow*; t. council, *consel an drē,* m., *chyf-conslers an drē*; t. crier, *crȳer an drē,* m.; t. hall, *lys an drē,* f., *mērjȳ,* m.: **-sman,** n. *burjes,* m., pl. *-jysy.*

toy, n. *tegen,* f., *tegyn,* m., pls. *-now*; t. shop, **tegenjy,* m., pl. *-ow.*

trace, v. *hellerghy, holya, sewya olow*: n. *ōl,* m., pl. *-ow*; harness, **cadōn,* f., **syg,* f., pl. *-yow*; rope t., *raw,* f., pl. *-yow.*

track, v. *hellerghy, holya*: n. *ōl,* m., pl. *-ow*; way, *trēs,* m., pl. *-ow*; cart t., *carhens,* m., pl. *-y, rōsla,* m., pl. *-lēow*: **-er,** n. *hellerghyas,* m., pl. *-ysy*: **-less,** a. *hep forth, heb ōl.*

tract, n., land, *pastel,* f., pl. *-llow, pastel dȳr,* f., pl. *-llow tȳr, ran,* f., pl. *-now*; treatise, *lyvryk,* m., pl. *-ygow.*

tractable, a. *hebask, dōf.*

traction, n. *ten,* m.: **-engine, tractor,** n. *jyn-tenna,* m., pl. *-nys-t.*

trade, n. *myster,* m., *creft,* f., pl. *-ow, chyffar, *kenwerth,* m.: v. *gwertha ha prena, *kenwertha*: **-r,** n. *gwycor,* m., pl. *-yon*: **-sman,** n. *marchont,* m., pl. *-ns, gwycor,* m., pl. *-yon, creftor,* m., pl. *-yon, mysterden,* m., pl. *-dyns.*

tradition, n. *hengof,* m., pl. *-govyon*: **-al,** a. *a hengof, a-dhē dyworth tās dhe vap.*

traffic, n. *mōs ha dōs, *daromres,* m.; trade, *chyffar, *kenwerth,* m.

tragedy, n. *wharfos* or *darfos trūesy, droklam,* m.; dramatic, *gwary trūesy,* m., pl. *-ow t., trajedy,* m., pl. *-s*: **-gic,** a. *trūesy, morethek.*

trail, n. *ōl,* m., pl. *-ow*; v., to track, *hellerghy, holya*; to t. along the ground, *draylya, slynkya war dor a-hēs.*

train, v. *dysky, maga, mēthryn, gedya*: n., railway t., **trēn,* m., pl. *-ys*; of gown, *losten,* f., pl. *-now*; followers, *mēny, draylyoryon,* pl. *coscar,* col.; t. oil, *saym,* m.: **-er,** n. *dyscador,* m., pl. *-yon, gedyer,* m., pl. *-yoryon*; of horses, etc., *temprer,* m., pl. *-roryon, dover,* m., pl. *-voryon*: **-ing,** n. *megyans, dyscans.,* m.

traits, n. *tȳthy,* col. and abst.

traitor, n. *traytour,* m., pl. *-s, fals-gwas,* m., pl. *-gwesyon, brasyer,* m., pl. *-yoryon.*

tramp, v., trudge, *trōsya, crowdra, travalya*; stamp, *stankya*: n. *trōsyer, rōsyer,* m., pl. *-yoryon, crowdrer,* m., pl. *-roryon*; of feet, *stank,* m.

trample, v. *stankya, pōtya, trettya yn-dan dreys.*

trance, n. *clamder, tranjyak,* m.; to go into a t., *clamdera.*

tranquil, a. *cosel, dysōr, whar*: **-ity,** n. *calmynsy, cosoleth, dyagha,* m.: **-ize,** v. *coselhē·, dyserry.*

transact, v. *gül, collenwel*: **-ion,** n. *negys, chyffar, bargen,* m.: **-cribe,** v. *dascryfa*: **-iption,** n. *dascryf,* m.: **-ept,** n. **crows eglos,* f., pl. *-ow eglosyow*: **-fer,** v. *transformya, dōn, remüvya, gorra dhe lē aral*: n. *remüvyans, transformyans,* m.: **-figuration,** n. *trēlyans yn kēn form,* m.: **-fix,** v. *berya, gwana, pychya*: **-form,** v. *trēlya, dyheveleby* (*dyfeleby*), *chanjya, ‡transformya*: **-ation,** n. *trēlyans,* m., *trēlva,* f., *‡transformyans,* m., etc.: **-gress,** v. *pēgha,* *camwül, camdremena, mōs drēs dyfen, trespassya*: **-ion,** n. *peghadow, pēghas, trespas, camwyth,* m.: **-or,** n. *peghador,* m., pl. *-yon, camdremenyas,* m., pl. *-ysy*: **-it,** n. *tremenva,* f., pl. *-ow,* **tremen,* m., pl. *-yow*; in t., *hag ef war forth, ow-chanjya*: **-ion,** n. *tremenyans,* m.: **-ory,** a. *brottel, na-bȳs, a-fȳ, a-dremen, ow-mōs arta kens nep-pell*: **-late,** v. *trēlya, styrya, tenna mēs an ȳl yēth dh'y gȳla*; transfer, *transformya*: **-ion,** n. *trēlyans,* m.: **-or,** n. *trēlyer,* m., pl. *-yoryon*: **-lucent,** a. *glew, boll*: **-mission,** n. *danvonadow,* m.: **-mit,** v. *danvon*: **-parency,** n. *clērder, bollder, glewder,* m.: **-t,** a. *clēr, boll, glew*: **-pire,** v. *wharfos, darfos*: **-plant,** v. *trüsplansa*: **-port,** v. *gorra, carya, dōn*; with rapture, *rafsya*: n., by vehicle, *caryans,* m.; rapture, *rafsyans, tranjyak,* m.: **-ubstantiation,** n. *trēlva bara ha gwȳn yn Sacrament an Alter,* f.: **-verse,** a. *trüs.*

trap, n. *maglen,* f., pl. *-now*; vehicle, *car scaf*; t. door, *darras-lür,* m., pl. *-darrajow-l.*; to set a t., *antel*: v. *bagha, magly*: **-per,** n. *magler,* m., pl. *-loryon.*

trappings, n. *hernes,* m., *gwyscas margh,* m., pl. *-cosow mergh*; to put on t., *hernessya.*

trash, n. *plosethes,* m., *scullyon, carthyon, scübyon, masclow,* pl., *atal,* col.: **-y,** a. *nadāl man.*

travail, n. *lafür,* m.; of mind, *cüth,* m.: v. *bōs yn gwelyvos.*

travel, v. *vȳajya, lafürya*; on foot, *travalya*: n. *lafüryans, vyajyans,* m.; on foot, *travel,* m., pl. *-lys*: **-ler,** n. *tremenyas,* m., pl. *-ysy*; commercial t., *gwycor,* m., pl. *-yon*: **-ling,** n. *lafüryans,* m.

traverse, v. *tremena drēs, mōs a-drüs dhe²*.

travesty, n. *trēlyans yn gēs, hevelep goky,* m.

trawl, v. *pyskessa draylya*: n. *rōs draylya*, f.: **-er,** n. *cōk draylya,* m., pl. *cūcow d.*

tray, n. **servyour,* m., pl. *-s*; washing t., *trok,* m., pl. *-kys.*

treacherous, a. *fals* (*falj*), *fekyl*: **-ly,** adv. *yn-fals, falslych*: **-ery,** n. *trayson, bras, traytury* (*treghury*), m., *antel,* f.; a t., *poynt a falsury,* m.; to commit t., *brasy.*

treacle, n. *mola·s*; balm, **trȳakel,* m., pl. *-aclys.*

tread, v. *trettya, stankya, pōtya*: n. *stank,* m.; t.mill, *melyn treys,* f.

treadle, n. *trōsla,* m., pl. *-lēow.*

treason: see **treachery.**

treasure, n. *tresor,* m.: v. *tresorya*: **-er,** n. *tresoror, alwhedhor,* m., pl. *-yon, tresoryer,* m., pl. *-yoryon*: **-ry,** *arghow,* pl. **tresorva,* f.

treat, v. *dȳghtya, handla*; t. well, *favora, chersya*; t. badly, *tebel-dȳghtya, drokhandla*; t. medically, *bōs medhek dhe²*; negotiate, *spēdya negys, gül chyffar*: n. *gōl,* m., pl. *-yow*: **-ment,** n. *dȳghtyans,* m.: **-y,** n. *ambos,* **kevambos,* m., pl. *-ow.*

treble, a. *tryflek, trebyl*: n. *trebyl,* m.

tree, n. *gwedhen,* f., col. *gwȳth, pren,* m., pl. *-nyer*; hollow t., **keybren,* m.; dead t., *sēghen,* f., pl. *-now*; place grown with t.s, *gwȳdhek, gwedhennek,* f., pls. *-egow, -egy*; t.s for charcoal burning, *glowwȳth,* col.

trefoil, n. *tȳrdelen,* f., *mullyonen,* f., col. *mullyon*; bird's foot t., **mullyon melen,* col.

tremble, v. *crenna, deglena, scrütha, dascrenna*: n. *scrüth,* m., pl. *-ow, crēn,* m., pl. *-now*; all a-t., *yn-crēn*: **-r,** n. *crennor,* m., pl. *-yon*: **-ling,** a. *dyegrys, yn-crēn*: n., see **tremble.**

tremendous, a. *üthek, marthys brās.*

tremor: see **tremble.**

trench, v. *cledhya,* **rygolya*: n. *clēth,* m., pl. *-edhyow, cleys,* f., pls. *-ow, -eyjow,* **rygol,* m., pl. *-yow.*

trencher, n. *tallyour,* m., pl. *-s.*

trepidation, n. *scrüth, crēn, own,* m.

trespass, n. *camwyth, trespas,* m.: v. *camwül, trespassya, camdremena.*

tress, n. *cüdyn, plethen,* f., pl. *-now.*

trial, n. *prōf, experyans,* m.; trouble, *govyjyon,* m.; law, *brüs,* f., *trȳal,* m., pl. *-s*; attempt, *atte·nt, assay·,* m., pl. *-ys*; to make a t. of, *assaya* (*'saya*).

triangle, n. *trȳelyn, trȳhorn,* m.: **-gular,** a. *trȳelyn, trȳhornek.*

tribe, n. *ēghen,* f., *ke·nethel,* f., pl. *-thlow,* †*lȳth,* m., pl. *-ow,* ‡*trȳb,* m., pl. *-ys.*

tribulation, n. *govyjyon,* m., *galar,* m., pl. and abst. *-ow, anken,* m., pl. *-yow.*

tribunal, n. *sedhek,* m., *bar,* m., pl. *-ys, brüslys,* f., pl. *-yow.*

tributary, n. *avon maga,* f., pl. *-venow m.*

tribute, n. *trübyt,* m., pl. *-ys.*

trice, n., in a t., *yn ün lam, war nuk.*

trick, n. *prat,* m., pl. *-tys, ynjyn,* m., pl. *-nys, cast, wrynch,* m., pl. *-ys, hyk,* f., pl. *-ygyon*; treacherous t., *poynt a falsury,* m.; to play t.s, *hyga, gül prattys*: v. *tulla, hyga*: **-ery,** n. *tull, fayntys, traytury* (*treghury*), m.

trickle, v. *devera, sygera,* **deuny*: n. *sygerans,* m.

tricolour, a. *trylyw.*
trident, n. *forgh dyrforgh,* f.
trifle, n. *trüfyl,* m., pl. *-flys*; t.s, idle matters, *flows, üfereth,* m.: v. *scornya, *trüfla, *üfera*: **-ling,** a. *trüfyl, üfer, boghes.*
trigger, n. *tryger,* m.
trill, v. *whybya, dascrenna*: n. *whybyans,* m., pl. *-ow, dascren,* m., pl. *-now.*
trim, v. *tacla*: a. *glanyth, taclys yn-ta, *kempen.*
trinity, n. *Trynsys* (*-jys*), *Trynyta,* f.
trinket, n. *tegen,* f., *tegyn,* m., pls. *-now.*
trip, v., dance, *dōnsya, lappya*; stumble, *trebüchya, omdhysevel*; take a t., *vȳajya*: **-per,** n. *havyas, gwandryas,* m., pl. *-ysy.*
tripe, n. *clowt-bolghen* (‡*clot-boffen*), m. (translating M.E. "pawncheclowt"); **trȳpa,* m., pl. *-pys.*
triple, a. *tryflek*: **-t,** n. *onen a drȳ, m., o. a. dȳr,* f.; t.s, *denythyans tryflek,* m.
tripod, n. *trebeth,* m., pl. *-bedhow.*
triumph, v. *trȳghy, *gormoledha*: n. *gormola,* m.: **-ant,** a. *trȳgh, *vycto·ryes, *gormoledhüs.*
trivet, n. *trebeth,* m., pl. *-bedhow.*
trivial, a. *trüfyl, üfer, scaf.*
troop, n. *lu,* m., pl. *-yow, bagas, nerth,* m., pl. *-ow, rūth,* f., pl. *-ow, mēny,* m.
trooper, n. *marghak,* m., pl. *-ghogyon.*
trophy, n. *weryson, tokyn trȳgher,* m.
tropic, n. **tropyk,* m., **trova,* f., pl. *-ow*: **-al,** a. *a bowyow tom.*
trot, v. *ponya.*
trouble, v. *serry, dughanhē·, dysēsya, tropla, vexya, annȳa, ancombra*: n. *anken,* m., pl. *-yow, ponvos, ponvotter, sōr, dughan, cüth, awhe·r, cās,* m., *kedry·n, *tryn,* f., *trobel, anger,* m.: **-d,** a. *anēs, ponvosyk, morethek, dughanhēs*: **-some,** a. *a-annȳ·*; t. person, *fyslak,* m.; t. thing, *ancombrynsy,* m.
trough, n. *trok,* m., pls. *-kys, tregys, caun,* m., pl. *-ow, *new,* f., pl. *-yow.*
trousers, n. *lavrak hȳr,* m., pl. *-regow h.*
trout, n. *trüth,* m., pl. *-as.*
trowel, n. *lo mason,* f., pl. *-yow m.*; garden t., *lo balas,* f.
troy-weight, n. *pōs troy,* m.
truant, n. *scoler dyenkys,* m., pl. *-loryon d., mynchyer,* m., pl. *-yoryon*; to play t., *mynchya.*
truce, n. *powes,* m., *ambos powes hep omlath.*
truck, n. *trok,* m., pl. *-kys*; naut., *rōsyk,* f., pl. *-ygow, clopen tellys gwern.*
trudge, v. *trōsya* (*-jya*), *lafürya, travalya*: n. *travel,* m., pl. *-lys.*
true, a. *gwȳr, gwyryon*; prefix, *lēl-, lēn-*: **-ly,** adv. *yn-whȳr, dhe wȳr, yn tefrȳ·, defrȳ·, hep whethlow, hep flows. ve·rement*; prefix *lēl-, lēn-*; yours t., *dheugh-why yn-lēl.*
trumpet, n. *corn,* m., pl. *kern, trompa,* m., pl. *-pys,* ‡*trybeth,* m., pl. *-edhow,* †*hȳrgorn,* m., pl. *-gern,* †*tollcorn, *üscorn,* m., pl. *-kern*: v., sound t. blast, *üscana*: **-er,** n. *trompa,* m., pl. *-pys, trompour,* m., pl. *-s,* †*kernyas, hȳrgernyas,* m., pl. *-ysy,* †*barth hȳrgorn,* m., pl. *byrth h.*: **-ing,** n. *üs* (*üj*), m.
trundle, v. *rolya.*
trunk, n., of tree, *bēn,* m., pl. *-ow, *kelf,* m., pl. *-yow, *kef,* m., pl. *-yon*; box, *cofyr,* m., pl. *-frow*; of elephant, *trōn,* m., pl. *-ow*; of human body, *corf, c. hep pen nag ysyly,* m.
truss, v. *trussa*: n. †*grügys,* m., pl. *-ow,* †*trussa,* m., pl. *-ys*; of hay, etc., *bern,* m., pl. *-yow.*
trust, v. *cola orth, kyfy, fydhya yn, trestya* (*dhe*[2], *yn*); I t., *trest a-m-büs*: n. *crejys, kyfyans, fydhyans, trest,* m., *fȳth, *cōl,* f.: **-ful,** a. *hegol*: **-worthiness,** n. *lēlder, lēndury,* m.: **-worthy, -y,** a. *lēl, lēn, trēst.*
truth, n. *gwyryoneth, lēlder, gwȳrder, gwȳr, sōth,* m.: **-ful,** a. *gwȳr, gwyryon*; t. person, †*gwȳrleveryas,* m., pl. *-ysy, dēn ha ganso sōth.*
try, v. *prevy, assaya, whylas, profya, trȳa, tāstya*; t. a bout of, *gül fyt a*[2]: n. *atte·nt, profyans,* m.: **-ing,** a. *a-annȳ·, üs ow-prevy, cales.*
tub, n. *keryn,* f., pl. *-y, cüva,* m., pl. *-vys, kybel,* f., pl. *-low*; shallow t., †*bayol,* f., pl. *-yow.*
tube, n. *pȳb,* f., pl. *-ow, pȳben,* f., pl. *-now, tewel,* m., pl. *-ys*; of conduit, *pȳbel,* f., pl. *-low*: **-bular,** a. *pȳbennek.*
tuck, n., fold, *plēk,* m., pl. *-egow*: v. *plegya*; to full cloth, *troghya* (*trokkya*): **-er,** n., of cloth, *troghyer,* m., pl. *-yoryon.*
Tuesday, n. *dē-Mērth,* m.
tuft, n. **crybell,* f., pl. *-ow, tos, bagas,* m., pl. *-ow*: v. **crybella*: **-ed,** a. *tosak, penvagas.*
tug, v. *tenna, settya crok yn, halya*: n. *ten,* m., pl. *-now, crok,* f., pl. *-ogow*: **-boat,** n. **tenlester,* m., pl. *-lystry.*
tuition, n. *dyscans,* m.
tulip, n. *blejen *tu·lyfant,* f., pl. *-jyow t.*: see **turban.**

tumble, v. *trebüchya, codha, omwheles, dysevel, omdhysevel*; of acrobats, *lappya*: **-r,** n., acrobat, *lappyor*, m., pl. *-yon*, f. *-yes*, pl. *-ow*; glass, *gwedren*, f., pl. *-now.*
tumour, n. *calesen kўk*, f., pl. *-now k.*
tump, n. *bēgel*, m., pl. *-yow, tolgh, godolgh*, m., pl. *-ow*, dim. *godolghyn*, m., pl. *-now.*
tumult, n. *frōs, froth, gustel, deray·, trōs, tervans*, m.; to make a t., *gustla, tervy*: **-uous,** a. *mür y drōs.*
tun, n. *keryn*, f., pl. *-y, tonnel*, f., pl. *-low.*
tune, n. *tōn*, m., pl. *-yow*, **ȳlow*, m.: **-ful,** a. *whēk y dōn, lün a* **ȳlow.*
tungstate, n., of iron, *call*, m.
tunic, n. *pows*, f., pl. *-yow.*
tunnel, n. *forth yn-dan dōr*, f., pl. *-dhow y. d.*, **keyforth*, f., pl. *-dhow.*
turban, n. *tu·lyfant*, m., pl. *-ns.*
turbary, n. *towarghwȳth*, m., *towarghek*, f., pls. *-egy, -egow, pyt kesow*, m., pl. *-tys k.*
turbulent, a. *dyrewl*; of sea, *tonnek.*
turf, n. *ton*, m. or f., pl. *-yow, towarghen*, f., col. *towargh*; patch of growing t., *tonnen*, f., pl. *-now*; small tuft of t., *tomen*, f., pl. *-now*; peat-t. for fuel, *kesen*, f., pl. *kesow*; t. rick, *das kesow*, f., pl. *deys k.*
Turk, n. *Turk*, m., pl. *-ys*; the Grand T., *an Turk Bras.*
turkey, n., t. cock, *cülyek-Gyny*, m., pl. *-yogas-G., cok-Gyny*, m., pl. *-kys-G.*; t. hen, *yar-Gyny*, f., pl. *yēr-G.*
turmoil, n. *tervans*, m.; to make a t., *tervy*: see **tumult.**
turn, n. *tro*, f., pl. *-yow*, **trōen*, f., pl. *-now, stüm*, m., pl. *-mow, troÿll*, f., pl. *-yow*, **whēl*, f., *cors*, m., pl. *-ow, torn*, m., pl. *-ys*; backwards t., **kyldro*, f., pl. *-yow*; good t., *torn da*, m.; bad t., *tebel-dorn*, m.; clockwise t., *tro howl*; upside-down t., t. of events, *pervers*, m.; bout, *fyt*, m., pl. *-tys*; each in t., *an ȳl wosa y gȳla, pup war y dorn, oll yn rew*: v. *trēlya, troÿllya, stümma*; t. soil, *terghya, fynegly*; t. away from, *plynchya, dyflasa*; t. oneself into, t. out to be, *omwül*; t. out, *gorra mēs, dysagha*; t. over, *omwheles*; t. back, *dewheles*: **-er,** n. *troÿllyer*, m., pl. *-oryon*: **-coat,** n. *negedhys*, m., pl. *-yjyon*: **-ing,** n. *torn*, m., pl. *-ys, trēlyans*, m., *trēlva*, f., *stüm*, m., pl. *-mow.*
turnip, n. *turnypen*, f., col. *turnyp*, **ervynen*, f.,, col. *ervyn.*
turnstile, n. **camva-dro*, f., pl. *-ow-tro.*
turpentine, n. **terebentyn*, m.
turret, n. *touryk*, m., pls. *-ygow, -rowygow.*
turtle, n. **cronek-ervys mōr*, m., pl. *-nogas -e.*, m.; turn t., *trēlya goles war-van.*
turtle-dove, n. †*türen*, f., pl. *-now.*
tusk, n. *dans hȳr, dans olyfans, morvargh* or *bāth*, m., pl. *dyns o. m. b.*
tussle, v. *omlath, stryvya, batēlyas.*
tussock, n.: see **tuft**; t. grass, *fynny vür*, f.
tutor, n. *dyscador*, m., pl. *-yon.*
tut-tut! int. *tety-valy*!
twaddle, n. *clap goky, gokyneth*, m., *gerennow*, pl.
tweak, n. *crok*, f., pl. *-ogow, squych*, m., pl. *-ys*: v. *squychya, settya crok yn.*
tweezers, n. *gevel vȳghan*, f., pl. *-yow bȳghan.*
twelve, a., n. *deudhek*: **-lfth,** a., n. *deudhegves*; T. Day, *Dēgol Stūl*, m.; T. Night, *Gōl an Steren*, m.
twenty, a., n. *ügans*; t. fold, *ügansplek*; t. times, *ügansquyth*: t.one, a., n. *onen warn ügans*: a., 21 sheep, *ün dhavas warn ügans*: **-ieth,** a., n. *ügansves.*
twice, adv. *dywwyth.*
twig, n. *gwelen*, f., pl. *-lyny*, col. *gwēl, baren*, f., pl. *-now*: **-gy,** a. *barrek.*
twilight, n. *tewlwolow*, m.; morning t., **pelgens*, m.
twin, n. **gevell*, m., pl. *-as*, f. *-es*, pl. *-ow.*
twine, v. *omnedha, gwȳa*: n. *lynyn*, m., pl. *-now.*
twinge, n. *glōs*, f., pl. *-ow*; to cause a t., *glosa.*
twinkle, v. *terlentry, dewynya*: **-kling,** n. *dewyn*, m., pl. *-now*; in a t., *yn ün lam, a-jȳ dhe lam lagas, war nuk.*
twirl, v. *troÿllya, trēlya a-dro, gwȳa*: n. *tro*, f., pl. *-yow*, **neth*, m., pl. *-edhow*: **-ed,** a., three times t., *trȳthro.*
twist: see **twirl.**
twitch: see **tweak.**
twitter, -ing, n. *cān wan*, f.: v. *cana yn-whan.*
two, a., n. *deu*, f. *dyw*; t. at a time, *deu ha deu*[2]; t. fold, *deublek*; t. score, *deu ügans, deugans*; in t., *yntra deu, yntra dyw ran*; we t., *agan deu*; t. persons, *deudhen*; I don't give t.-pence for him, *anodho my ny-rōf oy, my ny-settyaf demma.*
type, n. *ēghen*, f., *sort*, m., pl. *-ow*; printing, *olow*, pl.; t.writer, *jyn-scryfa*, m., pl. *-nys-s*: **-ist,** n. *jyn-scryfer*, m., pl. *-oryon*, f. *-ores*, pl. *-ow.*
tyrannise, v. *gül maystry, rewlya yn türont*: **-ny,** n. *maystry*, m.: **-ant,** n. *türont*, m., pl. *-rons.*
tyre: see **tire,** n.

U

udder, n. *bron,* f., pl. *-now,* **sagh bugh,* m., pl. *sēghyer b.*
ugly, a. *hager,* comp. *haccra,* superl. *an haccra*; to make u., *hagry*: **-liness,** n. *hakter,* m.
ultimate, a. *dewetha, pella*: **-tum,** n. *dewetha gēr,* m.
umbrage, n. *sōr, skēs,* m.
umbrella, n. **glawlen,* f., pl. *-now.*
umpire, n. *mayn, *nomper,* m., pl. *-s.*
unabashed, a. *dyveth.*
unabated, a. *hep y lehē·.*
unable, a. *hep gallos, *dyallos*; I am u., *ny-allaf-vy, ny-wōn, nyns-üs y'm gallos.*
unadulterated, a. *pür, dyblans, dygemysk, -ys.*
unafraid, a. *dyagha, heb own*; I am u., *ny-m-büs own-vyth.*
unaided, a. *hep weres, drē y allos y honen,* etc.
unalarmed, a. *dyagha.*
unalloyed, a. *pür, hep kemysk, dygemyskys.*
unamiable, a. *hegas.*
unanimous, a. *ünver, kescolon*: **-ly,** adv. *kescolon.*
unarmed, a. *dyarf, hep arvow.*
unashamed, a. *dyveth.*
unassuming, a. *sempel, hüvel, na-omvōst.*
unattended, a. *hep coscar.*
unauthorized, a. *hep cümyas.*
unavoidable, a. *na-yllyr y woheles.*
unaware, a. *hep gothvos*; to take u.s, *sawthanas, contrewaytya.*
unbar, v. *dybrenna, dyvarya.*
unbelief, n. *dyscryjyans,* m.: **-r,** n. *dyscryjyk,* m., pl. *-jygyon*: **-ing,** a. *dyscryjyk.*
unbend, v. *lowsel, omwül, bōs hüvel*: **-ing,** a. *serth, anheblek.*
unbiassed, a. *hep rakvrüs.*
unbind, v. *dygelmy.*
unblemished, a. *hep nam, pür, dyblans.*
unbolt, v. *dyvarya, dybrenna*: **-ed,** a. *ygor, dyvaryes.*
unborn, a. *hep bōs genys, nag-üs genys.*
unbounded, a. *hep fyn.*
unbroken, a. *dyen, hep y derry.*
unbuckle, v. *dyvocla, dygelmy brōcha.*
unburden, v. *dyvēghya, dyscarga.*
unbury, v. *dysencledhyes.*
unbutton, v. **dyvotonna.*
uncanny, a. *astranj, marthys, drēs natur.*
uncastrated, a. **kellek.*
unceasing, a., **-ly,** adv. *hep hedhy, hep powes.*
unceremonious, a. *hep solempnytys*: **-ly,** adv. *war ver lavarow, hep argya.*
uncertain, a. *tykly*; I am u., *ny-wōn dhe-wȳr.*
uncharitable, a. *hep cheryta*: **-ness,** n. *fowt-c.,* m.
unchecked, a. *hep let, hep fron.*
uncircumcised, a. **dyenwosys.*
uncivil, a. *anwhēk y lavarow*: **-ized,** a. *gwyls, nag-yu wharhē·s.*
unclad, a. *dywysk, nōth.*
unclaimed, a. *gesys war an kē.*
uncle, n. *ewnter,* m., pl. *-tras.*
unclean, a. *plos, mostys, *aflan, *aflaneth*: **-ness** n. *plosethes, mostethes.* m,
unclose, v. *dygēa.*
uncoil, v. **dyderghy.*
uncomfortable, a. *hep confort*; I am u., *nyns-oma attē·s.*
uncommon, a. *tanow, astranj.*
uncommunicative, a. *tawesek.*
uncompromising, a. *stordy.*
unconcealed, a. *ape·rt, nag-üs kelys, *dygüth.*
unconditional, a., **-ly,** adv. *hep ambos-vyth.*
unconquered, a. *dydrȳgh.*
unconscionable, a. *üthek, erby·n pup rēson, drēs ēghen.*
unconstitutional, a. *erby·n rewl an stāt.*
unconstrained, a. *hep ynnȳadow, hep let, *dygabester.*
unconventional, a. *erby·n üsadow.*
uncooked, a. *crȳf, nag-us parüsys.*
uncouple, v. *dygopla.*
uncouth, a. *ancoth, coynt, astranj*: **-ness,** n. *ancothfos,* m.
uncover, v. *dyscüdha.*
unction, n. *untyans, ungys, üras,* m., pl. *-resow*; to administer u., *untya.*
uncultivated, a. *gwyls, gōth*; of land, *dyfȳth, wāst, cōth.*
undaunted, a. *dyown.*
undeceive, v. *dyscüdha tull.*
undecided, a. *hep bōs ervȳrys.*
undefiled, a. *gwergh, glan, hep mostya.*
under, prep. *yn dan*[2]; in oaths, *tan*: adv. *yn-dan*[2]; from u., *a-dhan*[2].
underbid, v. *profya lē age·s.*
undercharge, v. *govyn rē voghes.*
underclothing, n. *dyllas nessa (dhe'n groghen),* m.
undercurrent, n. *frōs yn-dan dowr,* m.
underdone, a. *hanter, crȳf.*
underfoot, adv. *yn-dan dreys* or *drōs.*
undergarment, n. *pows nessa,* f.

undergo, v. *perthy, godhaf.*
undergraduate, n. *studhyer,* m., pl. *-yoryon,* †*scolhȳk nag-üs whath* **gradhyes.*
underground, a. *yn-dan dōr.*
undergrowth, n. *pryskwȳth, prysk,* col.
underhand, a. *gans tull, fals, fekyl, yn-dan gēl* or *güth.*
underlie, v. *bos yn-dan²*: **-ying,** a. *üs yn-dan², a-woles.*
underline, v. *lȳnya yn-dan².*
undermine, v. *palas yn-dan²*; fig. *domhel.*
undermost, a. *ysella*; of clothing, *nessa.*
underneath, adv., prep. *yn-dan², a-woles.*
underpay, v. *tylly* or *pē rē nebes* or *rē voghes*: **-ment,** n. *payment nag-üs lowr,* m.
underpin, v. *scodhya yn-dan².*
underrate, n. *dysprēsya.*
undersell, v. *gwertha rak lē es.*
undersized, a. *rē vȳghan, lettys y devyans*; prefix *cor-*; of fish, *pen ha garen.*
understand, v. *convedhes, attendya,* ‡*understondya*: **-ing,** n. *convedhes,* m.; intelligence, *skȳans,* m.
undertake, v. *omgemeres*: **-r,** n. *omgemeryas,* m., pl. *-ysy*: **-ing,** n. *omgemeryans,* m., *vyaj,* m., pl. *-ys.*
undertow, n. *frōs yn-dan dowr.*
undervalue, v. *dysprēsya.*
underwear, n. *dyllas nessa.*
underwrite, v. *sürhe·, settya hanow dhe²*: **-r,** n.
underworld, n. *yffarnow,* pl. *bȳs Ancow,* m., *gwlās enevow,* f.; of society, *ran ysella mapden,* f.
undeserved, a. *hep kēn, hep y dhervyn* or *dhyndyl.*
undesirable, a. *nag-yu dh'y dhesyrya.*
undeviating, a. *ewn, compes, hep gwȳa* or *trēlya,* **dydro.*
undo, v. *dyswül, shyndya, dystrewy*; untie, *dygelmy, lowsya*: **-ing,** n. *dyswrȳans, anfüsy,* m.
undoubted, a. *gwȳr*: **-ly,** adv. *hep mar (vyth), yn-tyogel, yn-tefrȳ·, hep tull, fall, falladow* or *dhowt.*
undress, n. *dy'sky, omdhy'sky.*
undue, a. *rē a², nag-üs gwyw.*
undulate, v. **tonny, mōs yn-ban hag yn-nans kepa·r ha tonnow*: **-ion,** n. *gwayans kepa·r ha tonnow.*
unduly, adv. *rē, moy es del yua gwyw.*
undying, a. *nefra a-bȳs, dyvarow.*
unearth, v. *dysencledhyes*: **-ly,** a. *nag-yu a'n bȳs-ma.*
uneasiness, n. *anēs, skēs,* m.: **-sy,** a. *anēs, gyllys yn prederow, ownek.*
uneducated, a. *dydhysk.*
unemployed, a. *dywȳth, wast, hep whēl, dyober*: **-ment,** n. *fowt whēl,* m.
unending, a. *hep fȳnweth, nefra a-bȳs, dydheweth.*
unequal, a. *dybarow,* **dyspar*: **-led,** a. *nag-üs y bar, na-n-jeves par, hep par* or *parow, sompē·r, flowr.*
unerring, a. *hep sawthan, sür, compes.*
uneven, s. *dygompes,* **ancompes, garow*; bent, *crom*: **-ness,** n. *fowt levender* or *composter, garowder,* m.
uneventful, a. *cosel, hep wharfos travyth.*
unexampled, a. *hep parow, sompē·r.*
unexpected, a. *hep y waytya, nag-üs gwaytyes, trom*; u. thing, *coyntys, ancothvos,* m.
unfailing, a. *byth na-fyll, na-dhyfyk*; steadfast, *sad*: **-ly,** adv. *hep fall* or *falladow, pup termyn-oll.*
unfair, a. *cam,* **anewn*: **-ly,** adv., to play u., *gwary gans cam, fükya*: **-ness,** n. *cam,* **anewnder,* m.
unfaithful, a. *dyslēn, dyslēl.*
unfasten, v. *dygelmy,* **dylathya.*
unfathomable, a. *down drēs musür, hep goles,* **dywoles.*
unfavourable, a. *drōk, hep lēs*; u. to, *erby·n.*
unfeeling, a. *dynatur, smat, aflythys*: **-ly,** adv. *yn-harow.*
unfeigned, a. *gwȳr, hep fayntys.*
unfenced, a. *dygēs.*
unfettered, a. *hep spral, dyspral.*
unfilial, a. *na-dhegoth dhe vap.*
unfinished, a. *gesys hep y gollenwel.*
unfit, a. *na-dhegoth,* **anwyw*; poorly, *clāf.*
unflagging, a. *hep squytha.*
unfledged, a. *dyblüf.*
unfold, v. *dysplegya, dysplētya, lēsa*: **-ed,** a. *dyblēk*: **-ing,** n. *dysplegyans, lēsans,* m.
unfollowed, a. *hep sewya, hep y holya.*
unfortunate, a. *anfüsyk, tebel y stüth*; u.s, *anfüsogyon*; lepers, *tüs Dew*: **-ly,** adv. *yn gwētha prȳs, soweth.*
unfounded, a. *hep grond-vyth, üfer,* **dysēl.*
unfriendly, a. *ave·l escar, anwhēk.*
unfurl, v. *dysplegya, dysplētya, lēsa.*
unfurnished, v. *hep mebyl* or *pyth-chȳ, gwak.*
ungentle, a. *anwhēk, garow.*
ungentlemanly, a. *dyscortes, hep bōs jentyl, garow y vanerow.*
ungird, v. **dystrotha, dy'sky grügys.*
ungodly, a. *dyscrassyes, ungrassyes, dydhew.*

ungracious, a. *ungrassyes*: **-ly,** adv. *hep grās.*
ungrateful, a. *unkynda*; be u., *ankevy dader, drōk aquȳtya.*
ungrudging, a. *hep ardak, hep danjer.*
unguent, n. *unyent, onyment,* m.
unhampered, a. *ylyn, hep let.*
unhappily, adv. *soweth, yn awhē·r*: **-iness,** n. *moreth,* m., *anfüs,* f., *anfüsy,* m.: **-py,** a. *morethek, anfüsyk, dyscrassyes.*
unharmonious, a. **dygesso·n.*
unhealthy, a. *anyagh, gwanek.*
unheard of thing, n. **anclewvos.*
unheeded, a. *hep y nōtya*: **-ing,** a. *dybreder.*
unhesitating, a., **-ly,** adv. *hep hokkya.*
unhindered, a. *ylyn.*
unhinge, v. *dyvagha.*
unholiness, n. *ansansoleth,* m.: **-ly,** a. *hep sansoleth,* **ansans.*
unhook, v. *dyvagha.*
unhorse, v. *tewlel dywar geyn margh.*
unhurt, a. *hep drok-vyth, dybystyk, saw, salow.*
unicorn, n. *üncorn,* m., pl. *-kern.*
unification, n. *ünyans,* m.: **-fy,** v. *ünya.*
uniform, a. *a ün form, ün sewt*: n. *gwysk ün form, ün sewt,* m.: **-ity,** n. *hevelepter,* **ünformyans,* m.
unilateral, a. *worth ün tu, w. ün tenewan.*
unimpeded, a. *ylyn, hep let, hep spral, hep ancombrynsy.*
unimportant, a. *hep pōs*; it is u., *nyns-üs fors awo·s henna, ny-vern, nyns-yu dhe lēs.*
unimposing, a. *hep mür rēouta.*
uninfluenced, a. *hep bōs rewlyes (gans).*
uninhabited, a. *gwak, hep tüs, hep tryger-vytholl, dybobel, dyanneth.*
uninspired, a. *hep golow an spyrys,* **dyawen*: **-ing,** a. *na-wra lēs dhe'n spyrys, na-wra enawy.*
unintelligent, a. †*dyskȳans,* †*talsogh.*
unintentional, a. *gwrēs hep towl, nag-üs ervȳrys.*
uninteresting, a. *sēgh, dyflas, hep nep bern, hep lēs-vyth.*
uninterrupted, a. *hep let, hep powes.*
union, n. *ünyans, kesünyans,* m.
unique, a. *dybarow, hep par, hep parow, ünyk.*
unison, n. *ünson,* m.; in u., *kescolon, ünver*; music, *ünlēf, yn ünson.*
unit, n. *ün, ünsys,* m.
unite, v. *kesünya, ünya, omünya, kyjya, dōs* or *junnya dhe onen.*
unity, n. *ünsys,* m.
universal, a. *yn pup lē, a bup sort, a bup dēn-oll.*
universe, n. *u·nyvers, pup-oll üs gwrēs.*
university, n. *unyve·rsyta,* m., pl. *-tys.*
unjoint, v. *dyskevelsy.*
unjust, a. *cam,* †*camhensek,* **anewn*: **-ly,** adv. *gans cam.*
unkempt, a. *dygrȳbys.*
unkind, a. *anwhēk, dygüf, unkynda*: **-ly,** a. *dygnās, dynās, hep cüfter*: **-ness,** n. *fowt cüfter, anwhēkter,* m.
unknotted, a. *dygolm, hep y gelmy.*
unknowingly, adv. *hep y wothvos*: **-wn,** *nag-üs gothvedhys,* †*ancoth*; **u.** thing, *ancothfos,* m.
unlace, v. *dylasya.*
unlasting, a. *brottel, ber y dermyn.*
unlawful, a. *erby·n lagha.*
unlearned, a. *dydhysk, lēk.*
unleash, v. *dyllo,* **dylēshya.*
unleavened, a. *hep gwēl.*
unless, conj. *marnas (ma's)*; u. thou dost that, *marnas ty a-wra* or *na lē es ty dhe wül henna.*
unlettered: see **unlearned.**
unlike, a. *dyhevelep, dybarow*; to make u., *dyheveleby (dyfeleby)*: **-ness,** *dyhevelepter,* m.
unlikely, a. *scant na-ȳl bōs.*
unlimited, a. *hep fynweth.*
unload, v. **dyscarga,* **dyvēghya.*
unlock, v. *dyalwhedha*: **-ed,** a. *dyalwheth.*
unloose, v. *dyllo, lowsel, dygelmy.*
unlucky, a. *anfüsyk*; u. person, *anfüsyk,* m., pl. *-ygyon*: **-kily,** adv. *yn gwetha prȳs.*
unmake, v. *dyswül, dyswrüthyl, dyformya.*
unmarred, a. *hep nam, hep dyfowt.*
unmarried, a. *dybrȳas, dydhemeth, yowynk,* †*ankespar.*
unmask, v. *dyscüdha, dyskevra.*
unmatched, a. *dybarow, sompē·r, hep par (ow), flowr.*
unmentionable, a. *na-dhegoth y leverel, ny-rēs y gampolla, erby·n onester.*
unmerciful, a. *dydrüeth, dybyta.*
unmerited, a. *hep y dhyndyl.*
unmindful, a. *dybreder.*
unmitigated, a. *pür.*
unmixed, a. **dygemyskys.*
unnatural, a. *dygnās, dynā·s, dynatur, un-kynda, erby·n kynda, erby·n natur*: **-ly,** adv. *erby·n natur* or *kynda.*
unnecessary, a. *na-rēs, nag-üs ethom ano-dho*: **-rily,** adv. *hep bōs ethom.*
unobjectionable, a. *dyflam, da lowr.*

unobservant, a. *hep avȳsya, na-vyn nōtya.*
unobstructed, a. *hep y lettya.*
unoccupied, a. *syger, dȳek, wast, hep whēl;* of place, *nag-üs annedhys, hep bōs ynno denvyth.*
unopposed, a. *hep sevel erby·n.*
unorthodox, a. *cam y gryjyans, camgryjyk.*
unostentatious, a. *sempel, na-gar omdhysquedhes.*
unowned, *a. hep perghen.*
unpack, v. *dydrussa.*
unpaid, a. *hep pē, nag-üs pēs.*
unpalatable, a. *dyflas.*
unparalleled, a. *hep parow, dybarow, na-njeves par, nag-üs y bar, sompē·r.*
unperturbed, a. **dysawthan,*
unpin, v. *dybynna.*
unpleasant, a. *dyflas, anwhēk.*
unpopular, a. *cās, hep kerens.*
unpopulated, a. *dybobel, nag-üs poblys.*
unprecedented, a. *hep y haval, nefra na-vē kens.*
unpretentious, a. *ysel, hüvel, sempel.*
unprinted, a. *hep y bryntya.*
unprofitable, a. *nag-üs dhe lēs, na-wra lēs.*
unpromising, a. *hep dedhewy mür.*
unprotected, a. *dywyth;* from weather, *dywoskes.*
unprovided for, a. *gesys hep myras dhodho:* **u. with,** a. *hep.*
unqualified, a. *anwyw;*thorough, *hep nam, pür.*
unquestionable, a. *nag-üs dh'y dhowtya:* **-ly,** adv. *hep dowt.*
unravel, v. *dysplegya. dywȳa;* fig. *desmygy, dystrewy.*
unreal, a. *nag-yu gwȳr, astra·nj, tarosvanüs.*
unreasonable, a. *mēs a rēson, dyrēson;* he is u., *ny-amo·nt argya orto.*
unrebuked, a. *dygereth.*
unregenerate, a. *ungrassyes.*
unrelated, a. *dyblans;* by blood, *hep bōs ünwos.*
unrelenting, a. *dybyta, hep rūthy.*
unremitting, a. *hep powes, hep hedhy, dywysyk.*
unremunerated, -tive, a. *hep gober.*
unrepentant, a. *hep edrega, dyveth.*
unrest, n. *ancrēs,* m.: **-ing,** a. *hep powes.*
unrestrained, a. *frēth, yl,yn dygabester.*
unrig, v. *dydacla.*
unrighteous, a. *ungrassyes, camhensek.*
unripe, a. *crȳf, glās, anathves.*
unrivalled, a. *hep par, sompē·r, dybarow, hep parow, na-yllyr ganso comparya.*
unroll, v. *dyrolya.*
unroof, v. **dystȳ·, tenna to dyworth chȳ:* **-ed,** a. **dysto, dystȳes.*
unruly, a. *dyrewl, gwyls.*
unsaddle, v. **dydhȳbra.*
unsalted, a. *whēk, dyholan, hep holan* or *sal.*
unsatisfactory, a. *na-blēk dhe dhēn-vȳth:* **-fied,** a. *drōk pȳs.*
unsavoury, a. *dysawor, dyflas.*
unscathed, a. *yagh y groghen, hep pystyk, hep pystyga, maga saw ave·l pysk.*
unscrupulous, a. *na-wra rūthy.*
unseasonable, a. *mēs a'y dermyn* or *sēson.*
unseat, v. **dysedha.*
unseeing, a. *dall, hep gweles.*
unseemly, a. *dysonest, *anwyw.*
unshaken, a. *crēf, hep crenna.*
unsharpened, a. *nag-yu lemmys, *sogh, *dylym.*
unsheathe, v. *tenna mēs a'y wōn, nōthhē·, *dywōna.*
unsheltered, a. *hep goskes, dywoskes.*
unship, v. *dyscarga;* of mast, oars, etc., **dylēa.*
unshod, a. *dyeskys, dyarghen(as);* animal, *dyhorn.*
unsightly, a. *hager, üth y weles:* **-liness,** n. *hakter,* m.
unskilful, -lled, a. *dyskȳans, †dycreft.*
unmelted, a. **dydēth;* of tin, *du.*
unsmiling, a, **dywharth, sad y vysach.*
unsociable, a. *na-gar cowethas.*
unsophisticated, a. *sempel, hep tull na gȳl.*
unsound, a. *anyagh, poder, hep bōs dȳen, lün a fowtow.*
unspotted, a. *gwergh, glan, hep mostethes.*
unstable, a. *tykly, brottel, fekyl, gwan.*
unsteady, a. *tykly, brottel, deantel:* adv. *deantel, whym-wham.*
unstick, v. *dysclena.*
unstitch, v. *dywrȳa:* **-ched,** a. *hep gwrȳ, dywrȳes.*
unstinted, a. *hēl, hep fȳn, hep sparya.*
unstretch, v. *lowsel, *dyestynna.*
unsubstantial, a. *scaf, tanow ave·l ayr, tarosvanüs;* of textile, *boll.*
unsuccessful, a. *anfüsyk, hep sowynyans, pen-helygen.*
unsuitable, a. **anwyw;* it is u. for you, *ny-dheseth dheugh.*
unsullied, a. *pür, hep mostethes, gwergh.*

unsurpassed, a. *hep parow, sompē·r, hep par, dybarow, flowr.*
unsuspected, a. *hep bōs skēs anodho*: **-ting, unsuspicious,** *hep predery drōk.*
unswathe, v. **dysmayla.*
untainted, a. *pür, hep bōs mostyes, *dynam, hep pedry, gwergh.*
untamed, a. *gōth, gwyls, hep y dempra.*
untaught, a. **dydhysk.*
untaxed, a. *dydoll.*
untenable, a. *nag-yu dhe synsy.*
untended, a. *(gesys) war an kē.*
untether, v. **dystaga*: **-ed,** a. **dystak.*
unthread, v. **dynüjenna.*
untidy, a. *hep y dacla, dygempen*; u. person, *scübelek,* m., pl. *-logyon,* f. *-loges,* pl. *-ow.*
untie, v. *dyskelmy, dygelmy*: **-d,** a. *dygolm.*
until, prep., conj. *erna*[2]*(g), bys, bys dhe*[2]; before v., *bys-pan*[2] *bys-may*[5]: it was not u. then, *nys-o kens es henna.*
untilled, a. *dywonys*; u. field, *ton,* m. or f., pl. *-yow.*
untimely, a. *rē a-brȳs, mēs a'y* or *kens y dermyn.*
untiring, a. *hep squytha.*
unto, prep. *dhe*[2], *yn, bys yn, orth.*
untoward, a. *anfüsyk.*
untraceable, a. *hep ōl, na-yllyr y hellerghy.*
untramelled, a. *hep let, hep spral, dygabester.*
untroubled, a. *hep sōr, *dysōr, *dyancrēs, *dyanken.*
untrue, a. *gow, fals, fekyl, *anwȳr*: **-uth,** n. *gow, gowegneth, falsury,* m.: **-uthful,** a. *gowek, a-lever gow.*
untrustworthy, a. *nag-üs dhe fydhya ynno.*
untwine, untwist, v. *dysmayla (-lya) *dynedha, *dywȳa.*
unusual, a. *coynt, drēs ēghen, erby·n ūsadow*; u. thing, *coyntys,* m.
unveil, v. *dyscüdha.*
unwarrantable, a. *nag-üs dh'y warrantya, hep ascū·s.*
unwary, a. *dyswar.*
unwavering, a. *crēf, sad, hep gwaya.*
unwed: see **unmarried.**
unwell, a. *claf,* †*anyagh.*
unwholesome, a. *erby·n yēghes, na-vāk, *anyaghüs.*
unwieldy, a. *pōs, cales y vüvya.*
unwilling, a., I am u., *pōs yu genef, nyvynnaf*: **-ly,** adv. *a'y anvōth*: **-ness,** n. *anvōth,* m.
unwind, v. *dysmayla, *dystrēlya, *dywȳa.*
unwittingly, adv. *hep y wothfos.*
unwise, a. *dybreder,* †*anfür.*
unwonted, a. *nag-üs ūsyes, erby·n ūsadow, coynt.*
unworthiness, n. *fowt bōs gwyw, *anwywder,* m.: **-thy,** a. *a-fyll bōs gwyw, *anwyw*; to think u., *kemeres yn dysdayn.*
unwrap, v. *dysmayla.*
unyielding, a. *crēf, stowt, sad, dywethyn.*
up, prep. *a-van*; u. above, *a-barth a-wartha*; u. to, *bys, bys yn, bys dhe*[2]; u. in the tree, *y'n wedhen a-wartha*: adv. *yn-ban, warvan*; u. and down, *yn-ban hag yn-nans*; of standing, rising, etc., *a'y sāf, a'm sāf,* etc.; int., u.! *yn-sol! sāf yn-ban! sa' ban!*; u. from the ground, *a-dhywar lür.*
upbraid, v. *blamya, rebükya, keredhy.*
upbringing, n. *megyans,* m.
upheaval, n. *omwhelyans,* m.
uphill, adv. *war veneth, troha pen an meneth*; fig., u. work, *ober cales.*
uphold, v. *mentēna.*
upholster, v. *tacla, gorhery, cüdha*: **-y,** n. *taclans, gorherans,* m.
upkeep, n. *cost, mentons,* m.
upland, n. *ugheldyr,* m., pl. *-yow.*
uplift, v. *drehevel, müvya spyrys.*
upon, prep. *orth, war*[2], *war-ben*; of clothing whole body, *drēs*; of clothing parts of body, *a-dro dhe*[2]; in oaths, *tan, er, rē*[2]; live u., *bewa orth*; enough to l. u., *pega·ns dhe vewa*; u. the word, *kettoth ha'n gēr.*
upper, a. *gwartha, a-wartha, ughella.*
uppish, a. *tont.*
upright, a. *serth, a'y sāf*; morally, *gwyryon, ewn,* †*ewnhensek.*
upright, a. *serth, a'y sāf*; morally, *gwyryon,*
uprising, n. *sordyans, drehevyans,* m.
uproar, n. *trōs,* m.: see **tumult.**
uproot, v. *dywrȳdhya.*
upset, v. *dysevel, domhel, omwheles*; mentally, *dystempra.*
upshot, n. *deweth,* m.
upside-down, adv. *war y ben, ha'y ben awoles, trēlyes an pyth a-wartha dhe woles, trēlyes y ben dhe'n dōr ha'y dreys yn-ban*; to turn u.-d., *trebüchya.*
upstairs, adv. *war-van, yn-ban, drēs an stayrys*: n. *soler,* m., pl. *-yow.*
upwards, adv. *yn-ban*: look u.! *mȳr war-van.*
urban, a. *a'n drē.*
urbane, a. *cortes*: **-ity,** n. *co·rtesy, je·ntylys,* m.
urchin, n. *maw,* m., pl. †*mebyon, meppyk,* m., pl. *mebyonygow*; sea-u., *sort,* m., pl. *-as.*

urge, v. *ynnȳa*; u. onward, *kentrynna*: n. *ynny*, m.: **-ncy,** n. *ynnȳadow*, m.: **-nt,** a. **tēr*; it is u., *rēs porres yu*: **-ntly,** adv. *porres*; it is u. needed, *yma· ethom brās anodho*: **-ing,** n. *ynny, ynnȳadow*, m.

urinal, n. *pycher pysa*, m., pl. *-s p., urnel*, m.; of blue glass, *gwēder glās*, m., pl. *-drow g.*: **-ne,** n. *urȳn, pysas, trōth, dowr*, m.; to pass u., *pysa*.

us, pron. *ny*; suffixed, *-ny*; stressed, *nynȳ·*; to see u., *agan gweles*; infixed, *-n-, -gan-*; with preps. *ahanan*, etc.

use, v. *ūsya, gül defnyth a*²; treat, *dȳghtya*; ill-u., *tebel-dȳghtya*; u. up, *spēna*; u.d to . . . imperf. of vb. or *ūs re-bē genef* . . .: n. *defnyth, lēs*, m.; in full u., *bysy*; to be of u., *bōs dhe lēs*; it is of no u., *ny-amo·nt man, nyns-yu henna 'vās dhe dravyth*: **-sage,** n. *ūsadow, ūs*, m., *gȳs*, m., pl. *-yow*: **-d,** a. *ūsyes*: **-ful,** a. *'vās, dhe lēs, a-wra lēs*: **-fulness,** n. *lēs*, m.: **-less,** a. *üfer, nag-üs 'vās dhe dravyth, hep lēs-vyth*; it is u. to reason with him, *ny-amo·nt argya orto*; u. person, *pylyak*, m., pl. *-yogyon*.

usual, a. *ūsyes*: **-ly,** adv. *del yu ūsyes*.

usurer, n. **okerer*, m., pl. *-roryon*: **-ury,** n. **oker*, m.

usurp, v. *dalghenna lē ün aral, kemeres gallos gans cam*: **-er,** n. *türont*, m., pl. *-ns*.

utensil, n. *lester*, m., pl. *lystry*; u.s, *pega·ns, dafar*, m.

utilize, v. *ūsya, gül defnyth a*².

utmost, n., in spite of his u., *yn despȳt oll dh'y ēghen*; to the u., *dhe'n lan*: a. *pella*.

utter, v. *leverel*: **-ance,** n. *lavar, lēf, leveryans*, m., *lavarow*, pl.; impassioned u., *areth*, f., pl. *-yow, predhek*, m., pl. *-egow*.

utter, a. *cowal*; u. rubbish, *muscogneth pür*: **-ly,** adv. *hep nam, oll yn-tȳen, glan, yn pup ēghen, quyt ha glan*; as prefix, *cowl-*.

uttermost: see **utmost.**

V

vacancy, n. *lē gwak*, **gwagla, gwakter*, m.: **-nt,** a. *gwak*; make v., *ōpya*: **-cate,** v. *ōpya, gasa, gwakhē·*: **-cation,** n. *termyn gwak*, m.

vacuous, a. *gwak, hep styr*.

vacuum, n. *gwakter*, m., *gwagva*, f., **gwagla, spās gwak*, m.

vagabond, n. *scajyn*, m., pl. *-now, crowdrer*, m., pl. *-roryon, rosyer*, m., pl. *-yoryon, losel, lorel, faytour, brybour, gadlyng*, m., pl. *-s, gwandryas*, m., pl. *-ysy, atla*, m., pl. *-lyon*: a. *ow-quandra*.

vagina, n. *cons*, f.

vagrant: see **vagabond.**

vague, a, *dyslyw, newlek, dydhyblans*.

vain, a. *üfer, cōk, mogh, gwak*; conceited, *gothys*; v., person or thing, *cōk*, m., pl. *kegyon*.

vainglorious, a. *hautyn, owth-omvostya*.

valerian, n. *losow an gath*.

valiant, a. *colonnek, da y golon*: **-ly,** adv. *manerlych*.

valid, a. *da, herwyth lagha, crēf lowr, ewn*: **-ity,** n. *ewnder, dader*, m.

valley, n. *nans*, m., pl. *-ow*; small v., *gola·ns*, m., *teno·w*, m., pl. *-newyow, cūm*, m., pl. *-mow, de·veran*, m.; v. without river, *sēghnans, sēghteno·w*; deep v., *glyn*, m., pl. *-now, haunans*, m., pl. *-ow*; v. land, *tȳr-nans*, m.; v. of Hebron, *valy Ebron*.

valour, n., *colonnekter*, m., *colon dha*, f.

value, n. *prȳs* m., pl. *-yow, rās*, m., pl and abst. *-ow, brȳ*, m., *gwerth*, f., **talvesygeth*, m.: v. *synsy, talveja, talvos, gül vrȳ a*²: **-uable,** a. *drüth, a brȳs, mür y brȳs*, **talvesek*: **-uation,** n. *prȳsyans*, m.: **-ued,** a. *drüth, talvedhys*: **-ueless,** a. **dybrȳs*; it is v., *ny-dāl man*.

valve, n. †*gorher*, m., pl. *-yow*.

van, n. *kert tyldys*, m., pl. *-ys t.*

vane, n. *cülyek-gwyns*, m.

vanguard, n. *voward, pen lu lystry*, m.

vanish, v. *omdenna, avodya, mōs mēs a wēl tüs*, **vansya*.

vanity, n. *üfereth, goth, gwakter*, **va·nyta*, m.

vanquish, v. *trȳghy, fetha*.

vapid, a. *hep blas*.

vapour, n. *ēth*, m., pl. *-ow, ēthen*, f., pl. *-now, lewgh*, m.: **-ize,** v. *trēlya yn ēth*: **-s,** n. *shorys a voreth*.

varnish, v. **vernsya*.

vary, v. *changya, trēlya*: **-riable,** a. *fekyl, brottel, prest ow-chanjya*: **-iation,** n. *chānj*, pl. *-ys, dyffrans*, m.: **-iance,** n. *fowt bōs ünverhē·s*; at v., *hep bōs ünver, ow-stryvya*: **-iegated,** a. *lȳes lyw*, †*brȳth*, ‡*spekyar*, ‡*spletyar*: **-iety,** n. *dyffrans, sort, lȳester y ēghen*, m.: **-ious,** a. *lȳes ēghen, a bup sort* or *ēghen, dȳvers, dyffrans*.

vase, n. *lester tēk*, m., pl. *-lystry t.*; large, †*cafas*, m., pl. *-ow*.

vassal, n. *omajer,* m., pl. *-s, kēth,* m., pl. *-yon*; v.s, *tüs kēth,* pl. *coscar,* m.
vast, a. *efan, mür drēs ēghen*: **-ness,** n. *efander,* m.
vat, n. †*cafas,* m., pl. *-ow, keryn,* f., pl. *-y.*
vault, v. *lappya, lemmel drēs gans gweres dywla po gwelen*: **-er,** n. *lappyor,* m., pl. *-yon,* f. *-es,* pl. *-ow.*
vault, n., arch, *gwarak,* f., pl. *-regow*; cell, *dorgell,* f., pl. *-ow*: **-ed,** a. *cammys, crom.*
vaunt, v. *bostya, omvostya, bragya.*
veal, n. *kȳk-lugh,* m.
vear, n. *porghel,* m., pl. *-ly.*
veer, v. *trēlya, chanjya tu.*
vegetable, n. *losowen-dybry, l.-kegyn,* f., pl. *losowys-d., -k.,* col. *losow, erba,* m., pl. *-bys*; v. garden, *lowarth-kegyn,* pl. *-ow-k., erbyer,* m., pl. *-ys*; v. marrow, **pompyon,* m., pl. *-s.*
vehemence, n. *crȳs,* m.: **-nt,** a. **tēr*: **-ntly,** adv. *yn-frēth, yn-fēn, gans mür a grȳs.*
vehicle, n. *car,* m., pl. *kerry, kert,* m., pl. *-ys.*
veil, n. *cüdhlen,* f., pl. *-now, vayl,* m., pl. *-ys*: v. *cüdha, keles*; v.ed, *yn-dan gēl, cüdhys.*
vein, n. *gōth, gwȳth,* f., pl. *gwythy, gwythȳen,* f., pls. *-now, gwythȳ*; small v. of tin, *scoren,* f.: **-ed,** a. *gwythȳek.*
vellum, n. *lughgen, parchemyn fȳn,* m.; piece of v., *parchemynen,* f., pl. *-now*; a. *parchemynek.*
velocity, n. *crȳs, tōth, scafter,* **üskytter,* m.
velvet, a. and n., *paly,* m.
vendor, n. *gwerther,* m., pl. *-thoryon, gwycor,* m., pl. *-yon.*
veneer, v. **launya,* **venȳrya*: n. **launyans,* **venȳ·r,* m.
venerable, a. *mür y vrȳ, enorys*: **-ate,** v. *gordhya, enora, kywhethla*: **-ation,** n. *gordhyans,* m.
vengeance, n. *hardygras, dȳal, venjyans,* m.; to have v. on, *tylly, tewlel, kemeres* or *gül dȳal war*[2], *venjya war*[2], *dȳala.*
venison, n. *kȳk-ewyk, kȳk-carow, kȳk-gwȳls, helgȳk,* m.
venom, n. *venym,* †*gwenyn,* m.: **-ous,** a. *venymys,* **gwenynek.*
vent, v. *dyllo*: n. **tardhell,* f., pl. *-ow.*
ventilate, v. *rȳ gwyns dhe*[2]: **-tion,** n. *ayr,* m.: **-tor,** n. *toll-gwyns,* m., pl. *tell-g.*
ventriloquism, n. *lavar tor, tor-leveryans,* m.: **-ist,** n. †*torleveryas,* m., pl. *-ysy.*
venture, v. *bedha, lavasos, aventürya*; v. against, *arveth*; v. upon, *attamya*: n. *vȳaj,* m., pl. *-jys*; at a v., *drē ref.*
Venus, n., star, *Gwener,* f., *Berlewen,* f.
verb, n. *gēr,* m., pl. *-yow*: **-al,** a. *drē ēr*: **-ally,** adv. *war anow.*
verbena, n. **vervȳn,* f.
verbiage, n. *clap,* m., *gerennow,* pl.: **-bose,** a. *gēryak, tavasek*; to be v., *gērya, clappya rē.*
verdant, a. *gwēr, ow-clasa*; v. land, *gwerdhor, gwerdyr,* m.
verdict, n. *brüs,* f., pl. *-ow.*
verdure, n. *glasneth* (*glasny*), *gwerder,* m., *glāsen,* f.
verge, n. *glan,* f., pl. *-now, mȳn,* m., pl. *-yon.*
verify, v. *composa,* **gwȳrya, prevy yua gwyr po nag-yu.*
verily, adv. *yn-whȳr, dhe-wȳr, yredy, defrȳ·, certüs, ve·rement, hep fraus.*
verisimilitude, n. **gwyrhevelepter,* m.
veritable, n. *gwȳr*: **-ility,** n. *gwȳrder,* m.
verjuice, n. *aysel,* m.
vermilion, a. **vermayl.*
vermin, n. *lastethes, prȳf,* m., pl. *pryves, drōkvȳl,* m., pl. *-as*; to hunt for v., *pryvessa*: **-ous,** a. *pryvesek*; to become v., *pryvesy.*
vernacular, a. *genesyk, tȳthyak, a'n vro*: **m.** *tavas an pow, yēth an vro*; in the v., *y'gan yēth agan honen, yn yēth an bobel.*
verse, n. *gwers, vers,* f., pl. *-yow*: **-sicle,** n. *gwersygel, gwersyk,* f.: **-sification,** n. **gwe·rsȳeth,* f.: **-ify,** v. *gorra yn gwers, gül gwersyow.*
version, n. *trēlyans, derȳvas, form,* m.
vertebra, n. *mel keyn,* m., pl. *-low k.*; cervical, v., *m. kylben.*
vertex, n. *pen ughella, blȳn, topyn,* m.; of head, †*dywolewyth,* m.
vertical, a. *serth.*
vertigo, n. **pendro,* f.
very, a. and adv. *pür, ewn, fest*; the veriest, *an purra.*
vesicle, n. *whesygel,* f., pl. *-glow, whesygen,* f., pl. *-now.*
vespers, n. *prȳs-gwesper, gwesper,* m., pl. *-ow.*
vessel, n., utensil or ship, *lester,* m., pl. *lystry, vessyl,* m., pl. *-s,* †*cafas,* m., †*fȳol,* f.; ship, *gorhel,* m., pl. *-holyon.*
vest, n. *jerkyn,* m., pl. *-s,* **vesta,* m., pl. *-ys.*
vestibule, n. *portal,* m., pl. *-ys.*
vestige, n. *ōl,* m., pl. *-ow.*
vestments, n. *dyllas* or *gwysk an eglos*: **-ture,** n. *gwysk,* m., pl. *-scow, queth,* m. or f., pl. *-ow*: **-try,** n. *gwyskva,* f., *gwysktȳ,* m., pl. *-ow.*

vetch, n. *gwek*, col., pl. *-egas*, **gwegbȳs*, col.
veterinary, a. *rag yaghhē· mȳlas*: v., surgeon, n. *medhek enevalles*, m., pl. *-dhygyon e.*, **mȳlvedhek*, m., pl. *-dhygyon*.
vex, v. *annȳa* (*'nya*), *dystempra*, *tropla*, *despȳtya*, *spȳtya*, *serry*, *vexya*, **nēghy*, *angra*: **-ation,** n. *despȳ·t*, *sōr*, *anger*, *ponvos*, m.; state of v., *sōr*, *ponvotter*, **nēgh*, m.: **-ed,** a. *ponvosyk*, *serrys*.
viaduct, n. **ponsforth*, f., pl. *-rdhow*.
vial, n. †*fȳol*, f., pl. *-ow*.
vibrate, v. *crenna*, *dascrenna*: n. *crȳs*, m., pl. *-yow*, *crennans*, m.
vicar, n. *pronter*, m., pl. *-yon*, *vycar*, m., pl. *-s*: **-age,** n. *pronterjy*, *vycarjy*, m., pl. *-ow*.
vice, n. *cam*, m., pl. *-mow*, *camhens*, m., pl. *-y*, *drokwhans*, **drogeth*, m.
vice, n., tool, **byns*, f., pl. *-ow*.
vice-president, n. **yslewyth*, m., pl. *-ydhyon*.
vicinity, n. *ogas*, m.
vicious, a. *drōk y gnās*.
vicissitude, n. *tro*, f., pl. *-yow*, *pervers*, *torn*, m., pl. *-ys*.
victim, n. *sa·cryfys*, m., pl. *-ys*, *offryn*, m., pl. *-now*, **vyctym*. m., pl. *-s*.
victor, n. *trȳgher*, m., pl. *-oryon*: **-ious,** a. **trȳgh*, *vyctoryes*, **büdhek*, **büdhygyl*; to be v., *trȳghy*: **-y,** n. *trȳghans*, **büdhygoleth*, *vyctory*, m.
victualler, n. †*mēthor*, m., pl. *-yon*: **-ls,** n. *vytel*, *bōs*, *pega·ns dhe vewa*, m.
videlicet, viz., adv. *hen yu* (*dhe leverel* or *styrya*).
vie, v., v. with, *stryvya* or *comparya gans*, **gorvynnes*.
view, n. *golok*, f., *gwel*, m. or f., pl. *-ow*, *vu*, m., **gwelesva*, f.: v. *myras*, *gweles*: **v.-point,** n. **gwelva*, f.
vigil, n. *gōlyas*, m., *gōl*, m., pl. *-yow*, *gōlva*, f., *nōswyth*, f., pl. *-yow*, **gōlnos*, f.: **-ance,** n. †*hewolder*, m.: **-nt,** a. *ow-colyas*, †*hewol*.
vigour, n. *crefter*, *crȳs*, *nerth*, m.: **-orous,** a. *crēf*, *yagh*, *frēth*, *mēn*: **-ly,** adv. *yn-fēn*.
viking, n. *morlader an North*, m., pl. *-dron a. N.*, †*ancryjor mōr*, m., pl. *-oryon m.*
vile, a. *casadow*, *lōs*, *vȳl*, *gal*: **-ness,** *vȳlta*, *ha·rlotry*, *by·lyny*, m.
village, n. *treveglos*, f., pl. *trevow eglos*, *castel*, m., pl. *-lys*, *pendra*, f., pls. *-reven*, *-revow*, *tref*, f., pls. *-even*, *-evow*, *gwȳk*, f., pl. *-ygow*: **-er,** n. *trevesek*, m., pl. *-vejygyon*.
villain, n. *casadow*, m. or f., pl. *-yon*, *harlot*, m., pl. *-los*, *harlotwas*, m., pl. *-wesyon*, *vylen*, m., pl. *tüs v.*, *gal*, m.. pl. *-ow*, *sherewa*, m., pl. *-wys*: **-ous,** a. *bylen*, *vylen*: **-y,** n. *by·lyny*, *vy·lyny*, m.
villein, n. *bylen*, m., pl. *tüs vylen*, *tȳthyak*, m., pl. *-yogyon*.
vindicate, v. *mentēna*, *ewnhē·*: **-ion,** n. *ewnhēans*.
vindictive, a. *dydrüeth*; to be v. towards, *dȳala*.
vine, n. *gwȳnwedhen*, f., pl. *-wyth*, †*gwȳnbren*, m., pl. *-yer*: **-leaf,** n. *gwȳndhelen*, f., col. *-dhēl*: **-yard,** n. **gwȳnlan*, f., pl. *-now*.
vintage, n. *trevas gwynrün*, m.
viol, n. *fyl*, m., pl. *-lys*, †*harfel*, m., pl. *-low*; v. player, †*fyllor*, †*harfellor*, m., pl. *-yon*, f. *-es*, pl. *-ow*.
viola, n. **melyonen drylyw*, f., col. *melyon d.*
violate, v. *deffola*, *gül drēs*: **-ion,** n. *deffolans*.
violence, n. *garowder*, *nell*, *nerth*, m.: **-nt,** a. *garow*, *gwyls*, *fol*; to become v., *dōs ha mōs garow*, *fol*, etc.
violet, n. *melyonen*, f., col. *melyon*; v. bed, *melyonek*, f.: a. **glasrüth*, *lyw melyon*.
violin, n. *fyl*, m., pl. *-lys*, *crowd*, m., pl. *-ys*: **-ist,** n. †*fyllor*, m., pl. *-yon*, f. *-es*, pl. *-ow*, *crowder*, m., pl. *-s*.
viper, n. *nader*, f., pls. *nedras*, *-dron*.
virago, n. *gourvyrgh*, f., pl. *-es*, *gourvoren*, f., pl. *-ronyon*.
virgin, n. *maghteth*, f., pl. *meghtythyon*, *gwerghes*, f., pl. *-y*, *vyrjyn*, f., pl. *-s*: **-al,** a. *gwergh*: **-ity,** n. *gwerghsys*, f.
virginals, n. **vyrjynals*, pl.
virile, a. **gouryl*, *ave·l dēn*.
virtually, adv. *yn ober*, *ogas*.
virtue, n. *grās*, m., pls. *-sow*, *grassys*, *rās*, m., pl. and abst. *-ow*, *vertu*, m.; V.s, order of angels, *Vertutys*, m.; force, etc., *vertu*: **-uous,** a. *da*, *mās*, *glan*; v. man, *dremā·s*.
virulent, a. *spȳtys*, *venymys*, *wherow*.
viscount, n. **vyscont*, †*ughelvēr*, m., pl. *-as*, **ysyurl*, m., pl. *-ys*.
visible, a. *hewel*, *a-wēl dhyn*, etc., *a-wylyr*: **-ility,** n. *clērder*, m.
vision, n. *vesyon*, m.; dream, *hünros*, m., pl. *-ow*, **gwelesygeth*, f., abst., **gorweles*, m.; sense of v., *golok*, f., *gweles*, *sȳght*, m.
visit, v. **vysytya*, *mōs dhe vyras*, *omweles*: n. **vystya*, m., pl. *-tys*, *mōs* or *dōs dhe weles*: **-ation,** n. **vysytasyon*, m., **vysyter*, m., pl. *-s*, f. *-yores*, pl. *-ow*, *sojornour*, m., pl. *-s*; guest, *gwestor*, m., pl. *-yon*, *gwestē*, m., pl. *-tyon*; summer v., **havyor*, *havyas*, m., pls. *-yon*, *-ysy*.

vital, a. *bew, a vewnans*; it is v., *rēs porres yu*: **-ity,** n. *bewnans, nerth,* m.
vituperation, n. *dalva,* f., *omwodros,* inf.
vivacious, a. *bew, jolyf*: **-city,** n. *bewder,* m.
vivid, a. *bew, splan, golow.*
vixen, n. *lowernes,* f., pl. *-ow.*
viz.: see **videlicet.**
vocabulary, n. **gerva,* f., pl. *-ow,* **geryador,* m.
vocal, a. *a anow* or *drē lēf.*
vocation, n. *galow, galwans,* m.
vociferous, a. *prest ow-carma, ow-prèdheges.*
vogue, n. *gӯs,* m., pl. *-yow.*
voice, n. *lēf,* m., pl. *levow, voys,* m., pl. *-ycys,* ‡*tala,* m.
void, a. *gwak, voyd, hep vertu*; to make v., *gwakhē·*: n. **gwagla,* m., pl. *-lēow, gwak,* m., pl. *-agyon, gwakter,* m., *gwagva,* f., pl. *-ow*; to v. excrement, *caca, scumbla.*
volcano, n. *meneth tān,* m., **loskveneth,* m., pl. *-nydhyow*: **-nic,** a. **loskvenedhek.*
volition, n. *mynnas, bōth,* m.
volley, n. *cowas,* f., pl. *-wosow, hēs pellennow gon,* f., pl. *-ow p. g.*
voluble, a. *tavasek, frēth,* **gerennek,* **geryak, mür, hӯr* or *ughel y lavarow*: **-ility,** n. *frēthter,* m.
volume, n. *braster,* m.; book, *lyver,* m., pl. *-vrow.*
voluminous, a. *brās, mür, lӯes lyver ganso lenwys.*
voluntarily, adv. *hep ynny, orth bōth y vrӯs, hep awhē·r* or *ardak*: **-y,** a. *a'y vōth y honen.*
vomit, v. *wheja*: n. *whejans,* m.
voracity, n. *ewl vrās dybry* or *dhe vōs,* m.: **-ious,** *parys dhe lenky puptra, dhodho nown blӯth.*
vortex, n. *pollen troyllya,* f., **lonklyn,* m., pl.*-now.*
vote, v. *vōtya*: n. *vōta,* m., pl. *-tys*; popular v., *comen voys,* m.
vouch for, v. *mōs rak, afydhya.*
vouchsafe, v. *vossawya, lavasos, darbary, grontya.*
vow, v. *avowa, ambosa*: n. *ambos,* m., pl. *-ow.*
voyage, n. *vӯaj,* m., pl. *-ys, trēth,* m., pl. *yow*: on the v., *war drēth*: v. *vӯajya,* **trētha.*
vulgar, n. *ysel, kēth, gal*; the v. tongue, *yēth an wlās, y. an bobel*: **-ity,** n. *vylyny, fowt je·ntylys* or *onester,* m.
Vulgate, n. *an Lyfryow Latynek.*

W

waddle, v. *rambla,* **gwydyla.*
wade, v. *kerdhes y'n dowr* or *drē dhowr.*
wag, v. *shakya, gwevya.*
wage, n. *arfeth,* m., pl. *-dhow, gober,* m., pl. *-brow, wāja,* m., pl. *-jys*: v., w. war, *gwerrya, gustla bell.*
wager, n. *gwystel,* m., pl. *-stow, gāja,* m., pl. *-jys*: v. *kessynsy, gwystla,* **kenwystla.*
wagon, n. *kert peder rōs,* m., pl. *-ys p. r.,* **carven,* f., pl. *-y.*
wagtail, n. *stenor,* m., pl. *-yon.*
waif, n. *omdhevas,* m., pl. *-ow, omdhevades,* f., pl. *-ow, flogh kyllys* or *gesys,* m., *tra üs gesys war an kē,* neut.
wail, v. *hūla, kӯny, ola, üja*: **-ing,** n. *olva,* f., **kӯnvan,* m.
wain, n. *car,* m., pl. *kerry*; Charles's W., *car Arthur.*
wainscoting, n. **parwyswӯth pren,* m.
waist, n. *crēs, wāst, grügysla,* m.: **-coat,** n. **crӯspows,* f., *jerkyn,*
wait, v. *gwaytya, gortos, tryga*; w. at table, *tendya, servya*; lie in w. for, *contrewaytya*: w. in readiness, *ombarusy*: n. *gortos,* m.; the w.s, *canoryon* or *kenysy nōs,* m., pl.: **-er,** n. *tendyer, gwaytyer,* m., pls. *-yoryon*: **-ing room,** n. *rōm gortos,* m., pl. *-ys-g.*: **-ress,** n. *maghteth,* f., pl. *meghtythyon, servyades,* f., pl. *-ow.*
wake, v. *dyfüna*; watch, *gōlya*: n. *gōl,* m., pl. *-yow*: **-ful,** a. *dyfün*; to be w., †*tergusca*: **-king,** n. *gōlyas,* m.
wake-robin, n., wild arum, *scaf a'y lygyon,* m.
Wales, n. *Kembry,* f.
walk, v. *kerdhes,* ‡*walkya*; w. far, *travalya*; w. about, *rōsya, gwandra*; w. together, *keskerdhes*: n. *kerth,* m.; long w., *travel,* m., pl. *-lys*; stroll, *rōsyas,* m.; place to w., foot-w., etc., *forth,* f., pl. *-rdhow, trūlergh,* m., pl. *-ow, kerthva,* f., pl. *-ow*: **-er,** n. *kerdher,* m., pl. *-dhoryon,* f. *-es,* pl. *-ow*: **-ing,** n., way of w., *kerth, kerdhes,* m.; w.-stick, *lorgh,* m., pl. *-ow.*
wall, n. *fōs,* f., pl. *-ow*; house-w., *fōs-chӯ,* f.; earth and stone, field w., *kē,* m., pl. *-ow*; party-w., †*parwys,* m., pl. *-y*; rampart, †*gwal,* m., pl. *-low, fōs,* f., pl. *-ow*; of old ruins, *māgor,* f., pl. *-yow*: v. *drehevel fōs*; of fort, *kēry*: **-eye,** n., of horse, *lagas bysow,* m., pl. *-ow b.*: **w.-flower,** n. **blejen fosow,* f., pl. *-jyow f.*: **w.-hanging,** n. *gōl,* m. or

f., pl. *-yow*, *strayl*, m., pl. *-yow*, **tapȳt*, m., pl. *-ys*.

wallet, n. *tygen*, f., pl. *-now*.

wallow, v. *omdrēlya*, *omrolya yn lȳs*.

walnut, n. *knofen-Frynk*, f., col. *know-F*.

walrus, n. **morvugh*, f., pl. *-as*.

wan, a. *glās*, *gwyn*, **glaswyn*, *gwan y lyw*; to grow w., *glasa*.

wand, n. *gwelen*, f., pl. *-lyny*.

wander, v. *gwandra*, *rōsya*; go astray, *sawthanas*, *myskemeres y forth*: **-er,** n. *gwandryas*, m., pl. *-ysy*; pilgrim, *palmor*, m., pl. *-yon*, *perghyryn* (*pryeryn*), m., pl. *-as*, f. *-es*, pl. *-ow*.

wane, v. *gwanhē·*, *lehē·*.

want, v. *mynnes*, *desyrya*; lack, *fyllel a²*; as much as he w.s, *myns a-vynno*; I w. to, *my a-vyn*, *yma· whans dhym a²*; *yma· dhymmo mür dhesȳr a²*; I w. for nothing, *tra ny-fyll dhym*; I do not w. it, *my ny-m-büs ethom anodho*, *ny-vynnaf henna*; what do I w. of it? *pyth yu an ethom dhym anodho?*: n. *dyvotter*, *defowt*, *fowt*, *ewl* (*awell*), m., *ethom*, m., pl. and abst. *-mow*, *esow*, **esewes*, m., †*dyodhenes*, f.; in urgent w., *ethomek*; for w. of, *fowt*: **-ing,** a., find w., be w., *fyllel*.

wanton, n. *gyglot*, m. or f., pl. *-s*, *scowt*, f., pl. *-ys*: a. *dybreder*, *gwyls*: **-ly,** adv. *hep ethom*, *hep kēn*.

war, n. *bresel*, m. or f., *-yow*, *cās*, f., pl. *-ow*, *bell*, m.; to make w., go to w., *gwerrya*, *bresely*, *mōs dhe'n gās*: **-horse,** n. **casvargh*, m., pl. *-vergh*, *courser*, m., pl. *-s*: **-like,** a. **breselek*: **-rior,** n. *soudor*, †*casor*, m., pl. *-yon*, *breseler*, m., pl. *-loryon*, *breselyas*, m., pl. *-ysy*.

warble, v. *cana*, **telora*: **-r,** n. **telor*, m., pl. *-yon*.

warble-fly, n. *stut*, m., pl. *-tys*.

ward, n., of borough, *randra*, f.; separate room, **dyberthva*, **gwythva*, f.; care, charge, *gwyth*, m.: **-en, -er** n. *gwythyas*, m., pl. *-ysy*, *warden*, m., pl. *-s*.

wardrobe, n. **dyllasva*, *gwyskva*, f., pl. *-ow*; stock of clothes, *dyllajow*, m., pl.

ware, n. *gwara*, col.: **w.-house,** n. *chȳ gwara*, *c. stoff*, m., pls. *-ow g.*, *s.*, *treven g. s.*

warm, a. *tom*, *gwrēsak*; tepid, *mygyl*, *godom*; to get w., **dyanwesy*; w., fertile, field, *gwrēsen*, f., pl. *-now*: v. *tomma*, *dastomma*, *tesy*: **-ing-pan,** n. *padel-tomma*, f., pls. *-llow*, *-lly-t.*: **-th,** n. *tomder*, *gwrēs*, †*tēs*, **tomyjyon*, m.

warn, v. *gwarnya*: **-ing,** n. *gwarnyans*, m.; by example, *bysna*, m.

warp, v. *camma*, *cromma*; w. yarn, **stüvy*; w. a ship, *halya*: n. **stüf*, m., **stüven*, f., pl. *-now*; rope, *lovan*, f., pl. *-vonow*.

warrant, v. *warrantya*, *rȳ cümyas*; I'll w. it, *my a ragtho*: n. *warrant*, m.; w. of arrest, *capyas*, m.

warren, n. *godegh conyn*, *conery*, m.

wart, n. *gwenogen*, f., pl. *-now*.

wary, a. *fēl*, *wār*, *fȳn*; w. person, *lagasek*, m., pl. *-sogyon*: **-rily,** adv. *yn-fēl*: **-riness,** n. *fēlder*, *connyng*, m.

wash, n. *golghy*, *troghya*; w. oneself, *omwolghy*, *omdroghya*; w. over, **gorwolghy*: **-place,** n. *golghva*, f., pl. *-ow*: **-erwoman,** n. *golgheres*, f., pl. *-ow*: **-ing,** n. *golgh*, *omwolgh*: **-ing-pit,** n., for tin, *cowans*, m.: **-stand,** n. **bord omwolghy*, m., pl. *-ys o.*

wasp, n. *gūhȳen*, f., col. *gūhȳ*.

wassail, n. *wassel*, m.

waste, v. *scullya*, *wastya*, **üfera*, *gasa* or *tewlel dhe goll*; w. time, **gwybessa*; w. breath, *spēna gwyns*; lay w., **dyfȳthya*: n. *scul*, m., *sculva*, f.; w. land, *dyfȳthtyr*, m., *cothen*, f.; w. pipe, *pȳb wolghyon*, f.: a. *wāst*, *ynyal*, *cōth*, *dyfȳth*, *scullyes*: **-d,** a. *gesys dhe goll*, *tewlys dhe scul*: **-ful,** a. *scullyak*: **-fulness,** n. *scul*, m., *sculva*, f.: **-r,** n. *scullyak*, m., pl. *-yogyon*.

wastrel, n., person, *pyllyak*, *scullyak*, m., pl. *-yogyon*; land, *tȳr wāst*, m.

watch, v. *golyas*, *gwaytya*, *aspȳa*; w. over flocks, *bügelya*; w. over, *gwytha war²*: n. *gōl*, m., pl. *-yow*, *gōlyas*, m., pl. *-yosow*, night w., body of men, *gwythysy nōs*, m., pl.; w. place, *gōlva*, f., pl. *-ow*; timepiece, *üryor*, m., pl. *-ow*; be on the w., *gwaytya*; keep w., *gōlyas*: **-er,** n. *gōlyer*, m., pl. *-yoryon*, *gōlyador*, m., pl. *-yon*: **-ful,** a. *ow-cōlyas*, †*hewōl*; very w., †*ugh-hewōl*: **-fulness,** n. †*hewōlder*, m.: **-house,** n. *gōljy*, m., pl. *-ow*: **-ing,** n. *gōlyas*, m.: **-man,** n. *gōlyador*, m., pl. *-yon*, *gōlyer*, m., pl. *-yoryon*: **-word,** n. *arweth gōlyas*, f., pl. *-edhyow g*.

water, n. *dowr*, m., pl. *-ow*, *lyn*, m.; salt w., brine, *dowr sal*; sea w., *hȳly*, *dowr mōr*, m.; the sea, *mōr*, m., pl. *-ow*; dirty w., ‡*dowr a vostyon*; spring w., *dowr fenten*; well w., *dowr pȳth*; rain w., *dowr glaw*; w.ing place, *dowren*, f., pl. *-now*; confluence of w.s, *kendevryon*, pl.; running w., *dowr owresek*; pass w., make w., *pysa*; high w.,

low w.: see **tide**: v. *dowrhē·*, *dowra*, *devera*; my mouth w.s, *yma· ow ganow ow-tevera*.
water-board, n., of mill wheel, *pāl rōs*, f., pl. *-yow r.*
watercourse, n. *dowrhens* (*deverhens*), m.,. pl. *-y*, *aweth*, f., pl. *-edhow*.
watercress, n. *beleren*, f., col. *beler*.
water-diviner, n. *desmygyer dowr*, m., pl. *-yoryon d.*, f. *-es*, pl. *-ow*.
waterfall, n. *dowrlam*, m., pl. *-mow*.
watering-place, n. *dowren*, f., pl. *-now*; for cattle, *dowrva*, f., pl. *-ow*, *dowrla*, m., pl. *-lēow*.
waterless, a. *dydhowr*, *sēgh*.
water-lily, n. **scüdel dowr*, f., pls. *-low*, *-ly d.*, **alaw*, m., pl. *elew*.
waterman, n. *dowror*, m., pl. *-yon*.
water-pot, n. *canna dowr*, m., pl. *-nys d.*
waterproof, a. *stanch*; w. mackintosh, *cōta stanch*, m., pl. *-tys s.*
water-rail, n. *yeryk dowr*, f., pl. *-ygow d.*
water-side, n. *dorrep*, m., *dowrlan*, *glan*, f.
waterspout, n. *newldarth*, *comoldarth*, *trōyll dowr*, m.
water-tank, n. *dowrargh*, m., pl. *-ow*.
watertight, a. *stanch*.
water-way, n. *dowrhens*, m., pl. *-y*.
waterworks, n. *whēl-dowr*, m.
watery, a. *dowrak*, *devrak*, *lynak*; w. place, w. ground, *dowrak*, f., pls. *-egy*, *-egow*, *dowren*, f., pl. *-now*, *dowrla*, m., pl. *-lēow*.
wattle, n. *clōs*, f., pl. *-ojow*.
wave, n. *ton*, f., pl. *-now*; sea w., *mōrdon*, f., pl. *-now*; of hand, *sȳn*, m.; sound of w.s, *mōrdrōs*, m.: v. *gwevya*, *swaysya*, *gül sȳn*, **tonny*: **-y,** a. *tonnek*.
waver, v. *gwevya*, *hokkya*, *shakya*.
wax, n. *cōr*, m.; cake of w., **coren*, f., pl. *-now*: v. *moghhē·*, *encressya*; become, *dōs ha bōs*.
way, n. *forth*, f., pl. *-rdhow*, *trēs*, m., pl. *-ow*, *hens*, m., pls. *-y*, *-yow*; distance, *travel*, m.; room, space, *spās*, m.; a long w., *pellder*, *sketh*, m., pl. *-ow*; a little w., *pols*, m.; manner, *mayn*, *gȳs*, m., *maner*, *forth*, f., ‡*trāda*, m.; to be on one's w., *mōs y'n hens*; go one's w.s, *mōs y'n forth* or *dhe gerdhes*; on the w. (to), *kelmys dhe²*, *war an* or *y'n forth dhe²*; all the w. to, *bys yn*; in the same w., *kepa·r*; by w. of, *war²*, *drē²*; in some w., in any w., *war nep cor*; come such a long w., *dōs mar hȳr forth*; have your own w., *kemer dha rewl dha*, *honen*; go thy w.s! *y'th forth gwra mōs*! *kē dhe gerdhes*!; (in) this w., *yndelma*, *y'n for'-ma*; (in) that w., *yndella*, *y'n for'-na*; is that the w. of it? *yndella'vyth-hy?*; this w. and that, *whym-wham*; make w. for, *gasa spās dhe²*.
waylay, v. *contrewaytya*.
we, pron. *ny*; emphatic, *nynȳ·*.
weak, a. *gwan*, *medhel*, †*anvēn*, *gwak*, **ydhyl*; w. in the head, *gwan a skȳans*: **-ling,** n. *caughwas*, m., pl. *-wesyon*: **-ness,** n. *gwander*, ‡*gwanegreth*, m.: **-en,** v. *med-helhē·*, *gwanhē·*, *blüdhya*.
weal, n. *strocas*, *strekys*. m., pls. *-cosow*, *-kesow*: see **welfare.**
wealth, n. *pyth*, m., pl. *-ow*, *rychys*, *rychyth*, *da*, m.; worldly w., *pyth an bȳs*, m.: **-y,** a. *rych*, †*kevothak*, †*golüsak*.
wean, v. **dydhēna*.
weapon, n. *arf*, f., pl. *-arvow*; claw, fang, **skyvel*, m., pl. *-vlow*.
wear, v. *gwysca*; w. out, *ūsya*: n. *ūsyans*, m.; clothing, *dyllas*, m.; worse for w., *ūsyes*.
weary, a. *squyth*, *ūsyes*, *anēs·*, *annȳes*: v. *squytha*, *annȳa*: **-ried,** a. *squythys*, *ūsyes*, *anē·s*: **-rily,** adv. *yn-squyth*: **-riness,** n. *squythans*, *squythter*, m.: **-risome,** a. *a-wra squytha*.
weasel, n. *conna-gwyn*, m., †*lovennan*, f., pls. *-as*.
weather, n. *kewer*, *awel*, f.; heavy w., *teweth*, m.; w. dog, fragmentary rainbow, *lagas awel*, m., pl. *-ow a.*; fine w., **hynon*, f.: **-beaten, -ed,** a. *tewedhak*: **-vane, -cock,** n. *cülyek-gwyns*, m.
weave, v. *gwȳa*: **-r,** n. *gwȳador*, m., pl. *-yon*, f. *-es*, pl. *-ow*.
weazand, n. *brȳansen*, f., pl. *-now*.
web, n. *gwȳas*, m., *gwȳ*, f.; spider's-w., *gwȳas kefnysen*.
wed, v. *demedhy*: a. *prȳas*: **-ding,** n. *demedh-yans*, m.
wedge, n. *gen*, m., pl. *-ow*: v. *genna*.
Wednesday, n. *dē-Mergher*, m.; Ash W., *d.M. Lüsow*.
wee, a. *pür vünys*, *fest bȳghan*.
weed, n. *whennen*, f., pl. *-now*, col. *when*; w.s, **lastethes*; widow's w.s, *galarwysk gwedhowes*; seaw., *goumman*, m.: v. *whenny*: **-er,** n. *whennor*, m., pl. *-noryon*: **-y,** a. *whennek*: w. place, *whennek*, f., pls. *-egy*, *-egow*.
week, n. *seythen*, f., pl. *-now*; w.-day, *gwȳth*, m., pl. *-yow*, *dēth gwȳth*, *degwȳth*, m.; before the end of the w., *kens penseythen*;

today w., *an jēth-ma* (‡*jorna-ma*) *war seythen*: **-ly,** a., adv. *pup seythen* (*-oll*).
weep, v. *ola, devera* or *scullya dagrow*, ‡*hūla*: **-ing,** n. *olva*, f.
weever-fish, n. *calcar*, m., pl. *-cras*.
weevil, n. *whylen mȳn-mogh*, f., pl. *-whylas* m.
weft, n. **anwȳ*, f.
weigh, v. *mantolly, posa*; w. down, *grevya*: **-ing-machine,** n. *jyn-posa*, m.: **-t,** n. *pōs, poster*, m., pl. *-ow, wȳght*, m.; pound-w., *pōs*, m.; hundredw., *canspōs*, m.: **-less,** a. **dybōs*: **-ty,** a. *pōs*.
weir, n. *cores*, f., pl. *-ow, banken*, f., pl. *-now*.
welaway, int. *eghā·n*! *welawa·*!
welcome, a. *wolcum*; to be w. to, *bōs mal gans*: n. *dynargh, yntertaynment*, m.: v. *wolcumma, dynerghy, yntertaynya*.
welfare, n. *sowena*, f., *lēs*,m.
welkin, n. *ebren* (*-bron*), f.
well, n. *pȳth*, m., pl. *-ow*; surface w., *fenten*, f., pl. *-tynyow*; w. spring, *gover fenten*, m., pl. *-ow f.*: v. *resek, tardha*.
well, a., adv. *yagh, yn-yagh, saw, salow, yn poynt da*; to do w., etc., *yn-fās, mās, yn-ta* (*y'ta·*, *'ta*), *da*; to make, become w., *yaghhē·*; as w., *magata·*, *ynta·*, *ynwe·th, kefrȳ·s, kekefrȳ·s, gans hemma* or *henna*; as w. as, *kefrȳ·s ha*; as w. as I can, *gwella gallaf*; I know w. enough, *gōn lowr*; we may w. say it, *ny a-ȳl lowr y leverel*; I may w. be ..., *my a-ȳl bōs* ...; int. *wel*!: conj. *ytho·*: **w.-behaved,** a. *dōth*: **w.-being,** n. *yēghes, lēs*, m., *sowena*, f.: **w.-born,** a. *jentyl, genys a'n gōs ughel*: **w.-bred,** a. *mās y vegyans*: **w.-doer,** n. *masoberor*, m., pl. *-yon*: **w.-mannered,** a. *cortes, jentyl*: **w.-nigh,** adv. before v., *namna*²(*g*); before n., *ogas ha*; before a., *ogas*: **w.-read,** a. *gwenwhys, hedhysk*: **w.-spoken,** a. *mās y lavarow*.
Welsh, a. *Kembrek*: W. language, *Kembrek*, m.: **-man,** n. *Kembro*, m., pl. *-bryon*: **-woman,** n. *Kembres*, f., pl. *-ow*.
welter, v. *omrolya, omsūba*: n. *kemysk*, m.
wen, n. *gwenen*, f., pl. *-now*.
wench, n. *moren*, f., pl. *moronyon, mowes*, f., *mowysy, benewen*, f., pl. *-now*; low w., *myrgh gal*, f., pl. *-es g*.
werewolf, n. **gourvlȳth*, m., pl. *-ydhy*.
West, n. *Howlsedhas*, m., †*Gorlewen*, f., *West*, m.: a. **-ern,** a. *west, a'n Howlsedhas*: **-ward,** adv. *war'tu ha'n West*.
wet, a. *glyp*: v. *glybya*: n. *glybor*, m.: **-ness,** n. *glybor*, m.
wether, n., sheep, *mols*, m., pl. *mels, lon davas*, m., pl. *-now d*.
wet-nurse, n. *mammeth*, f., pl. *-ow*.
whack, n. *whaf*, m., pl. *-fys, what*, m., pl. *-tys, bom*, m., pl. *-myn*: v. *rȳ whaf* or *what*.
whale, n. †*mōrvyl*, m., pl. *-as*.
wharf, n. **cay*, m., **porthva*, f.
what, pron. *pyth, pandra*; that which, *an pyth, pyth*: a. *py, pan, pana*; w. for? *praga, prak*; w. is more, *yn-prōf*; w. now? *pyu an jawl üs wharfedhys*? *pandra vyth gwrēs*? *fatel vyth lemmyn*?; w. will become of us? *fatel vyth dyn*?; I don't know w. to do, *ny-won pyth whraf* or *pandr' a-wraf*; w. if there were ...? *fatla mar pedha* ...?; w.'s-his-name, *map y dhama, map y vam*; in w. state is he, *pahan·* (*pan*) *plȳt ymava*; w. a fine day! *Dew*! *tecca dēth yu hemma*! *ass-yu tēk an jēth*!: exclam. *pandra*!; expostulating, *dar*!: **-ever,** pron. *kekemmȳ·s, pypyna·k, puppyna·k, py-sül*; suffix, *-vyth, -vytholl*.
wheat, n., grain, *gwanethen, grünen gwaneth*, f., col. *gwaneth*; buck-w., *gwaneth Frynk*; w. land, *gwanettyr*, m.; w. field, *gwanethek*, f., pl. *-egy, -egow*: **w.ear,** n. bird, **tynwyn*, f., pl. *-as, chekker*, m., pl. *-eccras*.
wheedle, v. *flattra*.
wheel, n. *rōs*, f., pl. *-ow*: v. *rolya*; cog-w., *rōs dynsak*: **w.-barrow,** n. *grava-rōs*, m., pl. *-vathow r.*; **w.-pit,** n., of water-mill, *pol-rōs*, m., pl. *-low-r.*: **w.wright,** n. *sēr rosow*, m., pl. *-y r*.
wheeze, v. *whybana*.
whelp, n. *colyn*, m., pl. *kelyn*; of lion, *lewyk*, m., pls. *-ygow, -wowygow*: v. *kelyna*.
when, adv. *pan*², *p'ür*⁵, *may*⁵; w. I was going, *ha my ow-mōs*; w. I was a boy, *termyn may fēma maw, ha my maw*: **-ever,** *byth pan*², *pesquyth, puppyna·k, pypyna·k*.
whence, adv. *may*⁵, *a-blē*⁵, *a-byla*.
where, adv. *py tyller, py plās, py*⁵(*th*), *py lē, plē*⁵, *pyla, may*⁵, *yn lē may*⁵; w. is, *pyma*: **-abouts,** adv. *py plās, py tyller*: n. *trygva*, f.; I don't know his w., *ny-wōn pymava*: **-as,** conj. *pan*², *aba·n*², *ha bytege·ns*: **-at,** adv. *hag ena, ha gans henna*: **-by,** adv. *ganso* or *dredho may*⁵: **-fore,** adv. *prag, praga*; on which account, *rag henna*: **-in,** adv. *ynno may*⁵: **-of,** adv. *anodho may*⁵:

-upon, adv. *hag ena, ha gans henna*: **-ever,** adv. *py lē pyna·k, yn lē may*^{5}, *puppyna·k* (*-na·g-oll*),: **-with,** adv. *ganso may*^{5}: **-withal,** n. *pega·ns*, m.

whet, v. *lemma*: **-stone,** n. **agolen*, f., pl. *-now*.

whether, conj. *po, bo, mar*^{4}; w. he was or not, *esa po nag-esa.*

whey, n. *mӯth*, m.; cheese w., **kēsvӯth*, m.

which, interrog. pron. *pynӯ·l, py*; that w., *an pyth*; relative particle, *a*^{2}-; at, on, with, in, for, from, w. *may*^{5}: **-ever,** pron. *pynӯ·l pyna·g-oll, an ӯl y'n bӯs.*

while, adv. *hedra*^{2}, *whath-oll*, ‡*spās*, w. he slept, *hag ef ow-cusca*: n. *cors*, m., pl. *-ow*, *lam*, m., pl. *-mow*, *teken*, f., pl. *-now*, *prӯs*, m., pl. *-yow*, *prӯjwyth*, *pols*, *tuch*, m.; long w., *hӯrneth*, f.; for a long w. past, *solabrӯ·s*; a little w. ago, *agensow*: v., w. away time, *dylātya, spēna, strechya.*

whim, n. *sӯans*, m., pl. *-ow*; to carry out, have, their w.s, *gül a'ga sӯans*: v., take a w., *sӯ*: **-sical,** a. *sӯansek, ow-sewya y sӯans*: **-sically,** adv. *herwyth sӯans, whym-wham.*

whimper, v. *ola trüan, kӯny.*

whinchat, n. *chekker-eythyn*, m., pl. *-eccras-e.*

whine, v. *kӯny*: n. *kӯnyans*, m.

whinny, -ing, n. *gryghӯas*: v. *gryghӯas, üja.*

whip, n. *whyp*, m., pl. *-pys, scorja*, m., pl. *-jys*: v. *whyppa, scorjya*: **-ping,** n. *whyppyans, scorjyans*, m.

whir, v. *whyrny*: n. *whyrnyans*, m.

whirl, v. *troӱllya, rosella*, **forlya*: n. **trōen.* f., pl. *-now*: **-pool,** n. *lonklyn, pol-tro*, m,, pl. *-low-t.*, *pollen-troӱllya, lyn-tro*, f., pls. *-now-t.*: **-wind,** n. *corwyns*, m., pl. *-ow.*

whisk, v. *squychya*: n. *scübyllyk*, f., pl. *-ygow.*

whiskers, n., *boghvlew, mӯnvlew*, col.

whisky, n., Scotch, *dowr tom Alban*; Irish, *dowr tom Ywerdhon*, m.

whisper, n. *hanas*, m., pl. *-ow*: v. *hanaja, hanas, whystra.*

whistle, n. †*whyb*, f., pl. *-ow*, †*whybonol*, f., pl. *-ow*, **whythell*, f., pl. *-ow*; of reed, *whythell-gors*; of straw, *whythell-gala*; with mouth, **whyban*, m.: v. **whybana.*

whit, n., every w., *kettep tam*; with neg., *man, tam y'n bӯs*, m.

white, a. *gwyn*; pure w., *can*: n., colour or clothing, *gwyn*, m.; w. of eye, *gwyn an lagas*; w. of egg, *gwyn oy*; dressed in w., *gwyskys yn gwyn*: **-headed,** a. *pen-gwyn*: **-en,** v. *canna, gwynna, gwynhē·*: **-lead,** n. *plom gwyn*, m.: **-ness,** n. *can, gwynder*, m.: **-wash,** n. *lӯm gwyn*, m.: **-ting,** fish, n., *gwynnak*, m., pl. *-ogas*; w. pout, *bothak*, m., pl. *-thogas, lagater*, m., pl. *-tras*; powder, *gwyn*, m.: **-tish,** a. *gwynnyk, skylwyn.*

whither, adv. *py*^{5}(*th*), *plē*^{5}(*th*), *pyla, may*^{5}; of two places, *pynӯ·l.*

Whit Sunday, n. *Sül Gwyn, dē Fencast*, m.: **-suntide,** n. *Pencast*, m.

whittle, n., shoulder-shawl, *scōthlen, gwarlen*, f., pl. *-now*; knife, *collan*, f., pl. *-ow*: v. *trēghy dhe dymmyn* or *scommow.*

whiz, v. *whybana, whyrny.*

who, interrog. pron. *py, pyu*; w.? *p'yua?*; rel. *a*^{2}, *nep, sül*: **-ever,** pron, *nep, pypyna·k, puppyna·k, pyu-pyna·k, sül, kekemmӯ·s*; w. of us, *pyu ahanan-ny vyth-onen.*

whole, n., complete, *dӯen, cowal*; sound, *saw, salow*; the w. . . ., *oll an . . .*: n. *myns, oll*, m.: **-lly,** adv. *oll, cowal, yn-tӯen, a-hēs, yn-lan.*

wholesale, adv. *cowlwerth*: **-r,** n. **cowlwerther*, m., pl. *-oryon.*

wholesome, a. *da*, **yaghüs*: **-ness,** n. *dader*, **yaghüster*, m.

whom, pron.: see **who**: to, for, in w., *may*^{5} (*th*).

whooping-cough, n. **pas-garm*, **pas-tak*, m.

whore, n. *hora*, f., pl. *-ys*: **-son,** n. *horsen*, m., pl. *-s.*

whortleberry, n. **lüsen*, f., col. *lüs, ӯs du*, col.

whose, pron., w. is this? *dhe byu yu, pyu a-bew* or *pyu a-n-jeves hemma?*; big children w. health is good, *fleghes brās hag a-vo da aga yēghes.*

whoso, -ever, pron. *nep, sül, pyna·k, pyu-pyna·g-oll.*

why, adv. *praga, prak*; w. . . .? interj. expostulating, *dar?*

wick, n., rush, *porven*, f.; cotton, *būben*, f., pls. *-now.*

wicked, a. *drōk, tebel, trüs*; of w. ways, *camhensek*: w. person, *cam*, m., pl. *-mow*, *tebelwas*, m., pl. *-wesyon, sherewa*, m., pl. *-ys*; the w., *an debeles, an sherewys*: **-ly,** adv. *trüs, gans cam, yn-tebel*: **-ness,** n. *sherewneth, sherewynsy, cam, drōk, drokter, droktra, dewlüjy*, m.

wicker, n. *plēth gwēl*, f., *gwelwӯth, helygwӯth, basketwӯth*, m.

wicket, n., door, **darrajyk*, f., pls. *-ygow*, *-jowygow*.
wide, a. *ledan, efan*; w. open, *ygerys a-lēs*; w. awake, *pür dhyfün*; far and w., *drēs oll an pow, ogas ha pell*; to be w. of the mark, *sawthanas yn-mēs a bup for'*!: **-ly,** adv. *a-lēs, efan*: **-n.,** v. *ledanhē·, lēsa*: **-dth,** n. *lēs*, m.
widow, n. *gwedhowes*, f., pl. *-ow, gwrēk wedhow*, f., pl. *gwrageth gwedhow*: **-ed,** a. *gwedhow*: **-er,** n. *gour gwedhow*, m., pl. *tüs wedhow*: **-hood,** n. *gwedhowsys*, m.
wield, v. *synsy, handla*; w. a sword, *cledhya, cledhevya*.
wife, n. *gwrēk*, f., pl. *gwrageth, benen*, f., pl. *-es, prȳas*, f., pl. *-yosow*; house-w., *gwrē'ty, ben'vā·s*, f.: **-ly,** a. **gwrēgol*.
wig, n. *blew fals*, col. *†gols fals*, m.
wild, a. *gwyls, gōth*; of land, *yeyn, ynyal, dyfȳth, wast*; w. animal, *gōthfȳl*, m., pl. *-as*; w. cat, *coscath*, f., pl. *-as*; w. sheep, *gōthfols*, m., pl. *-fels*; w. dog, *gōthky*, m., pl. *-thcün*; w. horse, *gōthfargh*, m., pl. *-fergh*; w. pigs, *gōthfogh*: **-erness,** n. *dyfȳth, gwylfos, ynyal*.
wildfire, n. *tan gwyls*, m.
wile, n. *dynyans*, m., pl. *-ow, prat*, m., pl. *-tys, ynjyn*, m., pl. *-nys, bras, coyntys*, m.
wilful, a. *gorth*: **-ness,** n. *gorthter*, m.
will, v. *mynnes, desȳrya*; bequeathe, *kemmynna*; I w., *my a-wra, my a-vyn*; do as you w., *gwra myns a-vynny, gwra collenwel bōth dha vrȳs*; would that it were better, *my a-vynsa a peva gwell*: n. *mynnas*, m., *desȳ·r, devȳ·s*, m., pl. *-ys, bolunjeth, bōth*, m.; testament, *scryfa kemmyn*; with a w., *gans colon da, gans mal, gans bones mal*; just as you w., *poran dhe'th vōth dha honen*; when they w., *pan vo bōth gansa-y*; against his w., *a'y anvōth*; of one's own free w., *hep ynnȳadow*: **-ing,** a. *parys, se·rvȳabyl, *bolunjethek*; to be w., *mynnes*; if you are w., *agas bōth mars yu henna*; he is not w., *nyns-yu y vōth yndella*; I am w., *mal yu genef, parys ōf, my a-vyn*: **-ingly,** adv. *yn-assentys, yn-lowen, a'y vōth, hep ynny* or *ynnȳadow, gans bolunjeth* or *colon da, hep bern, hep awhē·r*: **-ingness,** n. *bōth, plegadow*, m.
Will o' the Wisp, n. **tān-nōs*, m.
willow, n. *helygen*, f., pls. *helygy, -gennow*, col. *helyk*; w. garden, *helyglowarth*, m.; w. catkin, *cath helyk*, f.; w.-grown place, *helygek*, f., pls. *-egy, -egow*: **w.-herb,** n. *helygles*, m.
willy-nilly, adv. *drē hakter po drē dekter, mynno kyn na-vynno, dh'y vōth py dh'y anvōth kyn fo, kyn na-vē da ganso*.
wily, a. *fēl, connek, sotel, coynt, ynjyn, wȳly*.
win, v. *dyndyl, pew*; in fight, *fetha, gwaynya, trȳghy*; I won the victory, *an vy·ctory ēth genef*; w. over from, *trēlya dywo·rth*: **-ner,** n. *fether*, m., pl. *-thoryon, trȳgher*, m., pl. *-ghoryon*: **-nings,** n. *gwayn, pewas*, m.
wince, v. *plynchya, omwen*: n. *plynch*, m., pl. *-ys*.
winch, n. *gwyns*, f., pl. *-ys*.
wind, v., meander, *gwȳa, trēlya, *gwydyla*: **-ing,** a. *gwȳüs, troȳllek*; w. stream, *camdhowr*, m.; w. valley, *camlyn*, m.; w. machine, *gyg*, m., pl. *-gys*.
wind, n. *gwyns*, m., pl. *-ow, awel*, f., pl. *-low*; icy w., **ōrwyns*, m.; whirlw., *gwyns a-dro*; be borne away by the w., *mōs gans an gwyns*; w. bag, **sagh wheth*, m., pl. *-ow w.*; short of w., *ber y anel, cot y wyns*: v., blow, *whetha corn*; scent, *clewes ēth a*[2]: **-storm,** *cowas gwyns*, f., pl. *-wosow g.*: **-swept,** a. *yeyn, hep goskes*: **-ward,** adv. *troha'n gwyns*: **-y,** a. *gwynsak, awelek*.
windfall, n. *frūt codhys*, m., pl. *-ys c., hap da*, m.
winding sheet, n. *lȳen-bēth*, m., pl. *-now b.*
windlass: see **winch.**
window, n. *fe·nester*, f., pl. *-try*; to make w.s, *fenestry*: **-ed,** a. *fenestrek*.
windpipe, n. *brȳansen*, f., pl. *-now*.
wine, n. *gwȳn*, m.; sweet, spiced, honeyed w., *pȳment*, m.; palled w., *gwȳn marow* or *fyllys*: **-glass,** **gwȳnwedren*, f.: **-merchant,** n. *gwȳnwerther*, m., pl. *-thoryon*: **-press,** n. **gwȳnwask*, m., pl. *-scow*: **-vat,** n. **gwȳngaun*, m., pl. *-ow*.
wing, n. *askel*, f., pl. *eskelly*: **-ed,** a. *eskellek*.
wink, n. *plynch*; he slept not a w., *ny-guscas tam* or *banna*: v. *plynchya, *gwynkya*; w. at, *kēas lagas orth*.
winkle, n. *gwȳghen*, f., col. *gwȳgh*.
winnow, v. *gwynsa, *gwynsella, *nothya*; sift, *crodra*: **-er,** n. *gwynsor*, m., pl. *-yon, *nothyer*, m., pl. *-yoryon*: **-ing fan,** *gwynsell*, f., pl. *-ow*: **-ing-sheet,** n. *nothlen*, f., pl. *-now*.
Winter, n. *Gwāf*, m., pl. *-avow*; duration of w., **gwavwyth*, m., pl. *-yow*: v. **gwavy*: **-dwelling,** n. *gwavas*, m.: **-pasture,** *gwavwels*, m.: **-try,** a. *gwavek*.

winze: see **winch.**
wipe, v. *sēgha, dēsegha.*
wire, n. **gwyver*, m., pl. *-vrow*; telegram, **pellscryf*, m.; w. netting, **gwȳas horn*: v., telegraph, **pellscryfa*: **-less,** a. *dywyver, war an ayr*: n. **pellgowser, dywyver, ayrgows*, m.
wise, n. *maner*, f., *gȳs*, m.; in no w., *cammen, yn nep maner*, with neg.
wise, a. *skȳansek, für, skentyl, gwenwhys, dōth*: **-acre,** n. *den für-goky*, m., pl. *tüs f.*, **cragh dēn skentyl*, m.: **-sdom,** n. *skentoleth (skyentoleth), skȳans, fürneth*, m.; w. tooth, *kyldhans*, m., pl. *-dhyns.*
wish, n. *bolunjeth, yeunadow, whans, bōth, mynnas, govenek*, m., pl. and abst. *-nygyon, desȳ·r, devȳ·s*, m., pl. *-ys*: v. *mynnes, yeuny, desȳrya*: **-ful,** a. *whansek, bolunjethek.*
wisp, n. *tos*, m., pl. *-ow.*
wistful, a. *hyrethek.*
wit(s), n. *connek, skȳans*, m.; out of his w., *varyes, mēs a'y rewl*; to w., *hem yu dhe styrya* or *leverel*: **-less,** a. *dyskȳans*; become w., *dōtya.*
witch, n. *gwragh*, f., pl. *-as, pystryores*, f., pl. *-ow*, †*colyoges*, f., pl. *-ow*; white w., ‡*peller*, m., pl. *-oryon*: **-ery, -craft,** n. *tebel art, pystry, hüs*, m.
with, prep. *gans, orth*; along w., *yn herwyth, warba·rth gans*; filled w. *lenwys a*[2]; a man w. a dog, *dēn ha ganso kȳ*; a woman w. a child in her arms, *benen hag yn hy dywvron flogh*; w. me, w. thee, etc., *genef, genes*, etc.
withal, adv. *gans-hemma, gans-henna, kekefrȳ·s, magata·.*
withdraw, v. *omdenna, mōs a'n ȳl tu, kyldenna*; w. statement, *nagha*: **-al,** n. *kylden, omdennans*, m.
wither, v. *gwedhra, crȳna, sēgha*, **gwewy*, **crebeghy*: **-ed,** a. *sēgh, crȳn, crebogh*, **gwew.*
withhold, v. *sconya, sparya, nagha, gwytha hep rȳ.*
within, prep. *yn, a-jȳ dhe*[2], *a-berth yn, a-berveth yn*: adv. *a-jȳ, yn chȳ, war-jȳ, a-barth a-iȳ, a-berveth.*
without, prep. *hep, adar*: adv., conj. *adar (ater), a-vēs, war-vēs, yn-mēs, mēs*; go w., *hepcor*; when he saw that he could not go w. having trouble from his associates, *pan welas na-ylly mōs, ma na-n-jeffa sōr dyworth y gowetha.*
withstand, v. *perthy, sevel orth.*
withy, n. *gūsen*, f., pl. *-now, helygen*, f., pls. *-helygy, -gennow*, col. *helyk*; w. bed, *helyglowarth*, m.
witness, n. *dustüny, test*, m., pl. *-ow, record*, m., pl. *-ys*; person only, ‡*tȳyas*, m., pl. *-ysy, dustüny*, m.: v., bear w., *dustünya, testa (desta)*; God w., *Dew (dhe'm) dustüny, Dew yn test.*
wittingly, adv. *a'y wothvos.*
witty, a. *lym y skȳans.*
wizard, n. *pystryor*, m., pl. *-yon, hüder*, m., pl. *-doryon*, ‡*podrek*, m., pl. *-rogyon*, †*colyak*, m., pl. *-yogyon.*
woad, n. †*glesyn*, **lywles*, m.
wobble, v. *trebüchya, crenna, bōs parys dhe godha.*
woe, n. *cüth, gew*, m.; interj. *tru*! *eghā·n*!; w. is me, etc., *govy*! etc., *go* with suffixed prons.: **-begone, -ful,** a. *morethek, tryst.*
wolf, n. *blȳth*, m., pl. *-ȳdhas (-es)*; she-w., *blȳdhes*, f., pl. *-ow*; w. hound, *blȳthky*, m., pl. *-thcün*: v., gobble, *collenky kepa·r ha blȳth*, **lewa.*
woman, n. *benen*, f., pl. *-es, benenrȳth*, f.; young w., *moren*, f., pl. *moronyon, mowes*, f., pl. *-wysy, myrgh*, f., pl. *-es*; old w., *gwragh*, f., pl. *-as*; little w., *benewen*, f., pl. *-now*; to seek, run after women. *benena* (inf. only); married w., *gwrēk*, f., pl. *gwrageth*: **-hood,** n. **benensys*, f.: **-ly,** a. **benenek.*
womb, n. *brȳs*, m., *tor*, f., pl. *-row.*
won, a. *gwaynyes*; be w. by, *mōs gans.*
wonder, n. *marth*, m., pl. *-ow, marthüs*, m., pl. and abst. *-ow, marthüjy*, m., pl. and abst. *-thejyon, aneth*, m., pl. *-ow*: v., I w. you are not ashamed to do that, *marth yu genef na-th-üs meth ow-cül henna*; I w. at, *marth a-m-büs a*[2], marth yu *genef a*[2], *yma· marth dhym a*[2]; I w. if it is true, *dowt dhym yma· na-vova gwȳr*; I w. who . . ., *yma·-dhym mür varthejyon pyu* . . .; no w. that it is . . ., *nyns-yu marth kyn fo* . . .: **-ful,** a. *marthys*: **-fully,** adv. *marthys, yn-farthys, wondrys*; he's w. clever, *marthys ef yu dēn für*: **-drous, -drously,** a., adv.: see **wonderful, -ly.**
wont, -ed, a. *ūsyes, herwyth ūsadow.*
woo, v. *whylas yn prȳas* or **pryosoleth, profya kerensa*, †*tanta.*
wood, n. *cōs*, m., pl. *-ow, gwȳk, coswyk, kellywyk*, f., pls. *-wygow*; small w., *kelly*, f., pl. *-ȳow, kellywyth*, f.; timber, *pren*, m.

firew., *cünys*; a piece of f.w., *cünyjen*, f., pl. *-now*; to pick up f.w., *cünyssa* (inf. only): see also **plank, beam,** etc.
woodbine, n. **gwythvosen*, f., col. *gwythvos*.
woodcock, n. *kevelek*, m., pl. *-logas*; to shoot w., *kevelecca* (inf. only).
woodcutter, n. *trēghyas gwȳth*, m., pl. *-ysy g*.
wooded, a. *cosak*; w. region, **argōs*.
wooden, a. *pren, a bren*.
wood-louse, n. **gwragh*, f., pl. *-as*.
woodpecker, n. **casek cōs*, f., pl. *-sygy c.*, **gegyn*, f., pl. *-as*.
wood-pigeon, n. *colomen cōs*, f., pl. *-nas c.*, *†cüdhan*, f., pl. *-as*.
wood-pile, n. *tasorn*, m., pl. *-sernow*; for fuel, *cünyjek*, f., pl. *-egy*.
woodwork, n. *gwȳth pren, prenwȳth*, m.: **-er,** n. *sēr pren*, m., pl. *-y p*.
woody, a. *cōsak*; of w. nature, *ave·l pren*.
wool, n. *gwlan*, col.: **-len,** a. *gwlanek, gwlan*; w. cloth, *pan*, m.: **-ly,** a. *gwlanek*: **-sack,** n. *Sagh Gwlān*, m.
word, n. *gēr*, m., pl. *-yow, geren*, f., pl. *-now*; mere w.s, *gerennow*, pl.; in a few w.s, *war ver lavarow, war nebes geryow*; a w. in favour of, *ger 'vas gans*; by his own w.s, *dre ȳ anow*; by w. of mouth, *war anow*; without another w., *hep na hyrra lavarow*; take my w. for it, *trest-jy dhymmo*.
work, n. *gwythres, gonys, lafür, ober*, m., pl. *-ow, gwȳth*, m., *whēl*, m. and f., pl. *-yow*; w.s, *obereth, ‡gwrythyans*, m.; good w., *da-ober*, m., pl. *-ow*: v. *gonys, lafürya*; w., w. at, *obery*; set w.ing, w. a machine, *gwȳtha*; to w. about it, *dhe wonys a-dro dhodho*: to w. by the day, **dēdhwȳtha*: **-day,** n. *dēgwȳth, gwȳth*, m.: **-er,** n. *†gwȳthor, †oberor*, m., pl. *-yon, gonesek*, m., pl. *-sogyon*; farm w., *gonysyas*, m., pls. *-ysy, -yjy*; field w., *†gonysyas erow*: **-house,** n. *oberjy*, m., pl. *-ow*: **-less,** a. *dywȳth*: **-man,** n. *oberwas*, m., pl. *-wesyon, gonysyas*, m., pls. *-ysy, -yjy, †gwȳthor, †oberor*, m., pl. *-yon, gwas-whēl*, m., pl. *gwesyon-w., †gonesek*, m., pl. *-sogyon*: **-manship,** n. *creft*, f.: **-people,** n. *†oberoryon*, pl.: **-shop,** n. *gwȳthva*, f., pl. *-ow, shoppa*, m., pl. *-pys, chȳ-whēl*, m., pls. *-ow, treven -w*.
world, n. *bȳs*, m.; the w., *an nōr, an norvȳ·s*, m.: **-ly,** a. *a'n bȳs-ma*.
worm, n. *kenak*, m., pl. *-ogas, prȳf*, m., pl. *pryves*; small w., *preven*, f., pl. *-now*; ring-w., **darwesen*, f., col. *darwes, ‡prȳf bysow*; intestinal w., *lenkeren*, f., col. *lenker*; flesh w., *†contronen*, f., col. *contron*; lug-w., *kenak*; timber-w., *prȳf pren*; silk w., *prȳf owrlen*; earth w., *būlügen*, f., col. *būlük, prȳf dōr*: **-eaten,** a. *pryvesek, tellek, tellys*: **-hole,** n. *toll prȳf*, m., pl. *-tell pryves*: **-cast,** n. *whejans būlügen*, m., pl. *-w. būlük*.
wormwood, n. *†fūelen, *wherowles*, f.
worn, a., w. thin, *boll*; w. out, *üsyes*; w. with toil, *lafüryes*; weather-w., *tewedhek*.
worry, n. *sōr, ponvos*, m., *preder*, m., pl. and abst. *-ow*: v. *annȳa* (*'nȳa*), *serry, despȳtya*; w. sheep, *devȳja* (inf. only).
worse, a. *gweth, lacca*; grow w., *gwetha*; make w., *gwethhē·*: **-n,** v. *omwethhē·*, *gwethhē·*: **-ness,** n. *gwethter*, m.: **-t,** a. *gwetha, an lacca*.
worship, n. *gologhas, gordhyans, lawa*, m.: v. *gordhya, gologhy*: **-ful,** a. *wordhy*.
wort, n., plant, as suffix, *-les*, m.; w. of malt, *dowr brag*, m.
worth, n. *prȳs, brȳ, rās, dy·nyta*, m.: a. *talvedhys*; to be w., *tylly*; it's not w. a straw, *ny-dāl oy, gwelen-gala, cath, bronnen*, etc.: **-ily,** adv. *manerlych, yn-whyw*: **-less,** a. *poder, cōk, dybrȳs, na-dāl man*; w. person or thing, *cōk*, m., pl. *kegyon*; w. person, *podryn*, m., *podrek*, m., pl. *-rogyon, pencok*, m., pl. *-now-c.*; *culyak, pylyak*, m., pls. *-yogyon*: **-y,** a. *gwyw, wordhy, a brȳs*.
wound, n. *brew*, m., pl. *-yon, goly*, m., pl. *-ow*: v. *deffola, golȳa, brewy*: **-ed,** a. *brew, golȳes*.
wrangle, v. *argya, dyspūtya, stryvya, debātya*; w. with, *dyspūtya cās orth*: n. *strȳf*, m., pl. *-ow*: **-r,** n. *strȳfor*, m., pl. *-yon*: **-ling,** n. *strȳf*, m., pl. *-ow, *cavyl*, m.; causing a w., *cavylek*.
wrap, v. *plegya, mayla* (*-ya*): **-er,** n. *maylyer, gwysk, queth*, m.: **-ping,** n. *maylyans, gorheras*, m.
wrasse, n. *gwragh*, f., pl. *-as*; blue w., *cūcū*, f., pl. *-as*.
wrath, n. *sōr*, m.
wreak, v., w. vengeance, *tylly* or *tewlel dȳal*.
wreath, n. *garlont*, f., pls. *-ow, -ons, *torgh*, f., pl. *tergh, *curünblēth*, f., pl. *-ow, curün delyow*, f., pl. *-now d.*: **-the,** v. *nedha, gwȳa, *terghy*.
wreck, n. *gorhel kellys, torva lester*, f., *‡gwrek*, m., pl. *-kys*: v. *dyswül, mōs dhe wrek*: **-age,** n. *scommow, browsyon*, pl.
wren, n. *gwrannen*, f., pl. *-as*.

wrench, v. *trēlya*: n. *tro*, f., pl. *-yow*; tool, **alwheth-screw*, m.

wrestle, v. *gwrynya, omdewlel*: **-r,** n. *omdowlor*, m., pl. *-yon, gwrynyer*, m., pl. *-yoryon*: **-ling-match,** n. *fȳt-omdowl*, m., pl. *-tys o.*

wretch, n. *anfüsyk*, m., pl. *-ygyon, canjeon*, m. or f., pl. *-s, casadow*, m. or f., pl. *-yon, prȳf*, m., pl. *prevyon, plos*, m., pl. *-yon, ploswas*, m., pl. *-wesyon*: **-ed,** a. *casadow, trūan, trūethek, tryst, morethek, ponvosyk*: **-ness** n. *ponvotter, moreth, trystans*, m.

wriggle, v. *omwen, gwenel, *gwydyla*: **-r,** n. *fyslak*, m., pl. *logyon.*

wright, n. *oberor*, m., pl. *-yon, ynjynor*, m., pl. *-yon.*

wring, v. *strotha, gwrynya.*

wrinkle, v. *crȳghy*: n. *crȳgh*, m., pl. *-ow, plēk*, m., pl. *plegow*: **-d,** a. *crebogh, crȳgh.*

wrist, n. *conna-brēgh*, m., pl. *-nahow-b.*, d. *deugonna-b.*

writ, n. *scryfa*, m., pl. *-vadhow, scryven*, f., pl. *-now*; w. of arrest, *capyas*, m.; Holy W., *an Lyfryow, an Scryptor Benygys.*

write, v. *scryfa*; w. by hand, *dornscryfa*; w. about, *scryfa a*² or *a-dro dhe*²; w. again, *dasscryfa*; w. to one another, *kesscryfa*: **-r,** n. *scryfer*, m., pl. *-foryon, scryfyas, scryvynyas*, m., pl. *-ysy*; clerk, *scryfwas*, m., pl. *-wesyon*: **-ing,** n. *scryf*, m., pl. *-yvow, scryven*, f., pl. *-now, scryfa*, m., pl. *-vadhow*; original w., *kens-scryf*, m.; hand-w., manner of w., *scryfa plüven*, m.; w. table, **bord-scryfa*, m., pl. *-ys-s.*

writhe, v. *camma, omgamma, omnedha, gwenel.*

wrong, n. *drocoleth*, m., *cam*, m., pl. *-mow*; do w., *gül cam* (*dhe*²), *camwül* (*camwrüthyl*), *tebel wül*: a. *cam, trüs*, prefix *cam-*, ‡*bad-*; w. headed, perverse, **pengam*; to go w., *drokfara, fyllel*; there's nothing w. with my striking, *my a-wysk hep blam*; all w., *drēs keyn*; that is w., *nyns-yu henna gwȳr*; in the w., *dhe vlamya*: **-doer,** n. *drōkoberor*, m., pl. *-yon*: **-doing,** n. *camwythres, tebelwrȳans*, m.: **-fully, -ly,** adv. *trüs, gans cam*; prefix *cam-.*

wrought, a. *oberys, gwrēs* (*gwrȳs*).

wry, a. *cam, cammys*; make a w. face, *omgamma mȳn*: **-neck,** n. **pengam*, m., pl. *-mas*: **-ed,** a. *cam y gonna, *pengam, *connagam.*

Y

yacht, n. *lester-gwary, l. hāf*, m., pl. *lystry g., h.*: v. *havy yn lester.*

yard, n., measure, *lath*, f., pl. *-ow, gwelen*, f., pl. *-lyny*; ½y., *kevelyn*, m., pl. *-now*; y. of sail, †*delē*, f., pl. *-lēyow, gwelen gōl*, f.; enclosure, *garth*, m., pl. *-ow, lan*, f., pl. *-now*; cattle y., *büarth*, m., pl. *-ow*; corn y., *ȳslan*, f.: **-arm,** n., naut., *pen gwelen gōl, pen delē*, m., pl. *-now g. d.*: **-stick,** *lath*, f., pl. *-ow.*

yarn, n. *nüs*, col., sing. *nüjen*; thread, *lynyn*, m., pl. *-now*; tale, *whethel*, m., pl. *-thlow, drolla*, m., pl. *-lys.*

yarrow, n. †*mynfel*, m.

yawn, v. *ygery ganow, *delevy gen, *dyanowy*: n. **delevy gen, ygeryans ganow*: **-ing,** a. *ygerys yn-ledan.*

ye, pron. *why*; emphatic, *whywhȳ·.*

yea! interj. *yē*! *yā*! (both sometimes derisive).

yean, v. **ona.*

year, n. *bledhen*, f., pl. *-dhynnow*; y. of age, *blōth*, m.; a y.'s time, *blodhwȳth* (*blydhy*), f.; in a y.'s time, *dhe ben ün vledhen*; before the end of the y., *kens penvledhen*; last y., *an vledhen üs tremenys, *warleny*; this y., *an vledhen-ma, *hevleny*; next y., *nessa bledhen, an vledhen a-dhē*; all the y. round, *drēs oll an vledhen*; if I live a y., *mara pydhaf bew bledhen*: **-ling,** n. **blothyas*, m., pl. *-ysy*: **-ly,** adv. *pup bledhen-oll, a'n vledhen.*

yearn, v. *yeuny, whansa*; I y. for, *hyrethek of warle·rgh, yma· whans brās dhym a*²: **-ing,** n. *yeunes, yeunadow, moreth, hȳreth, ewl* (*awell*), m.: a. *hyrethek, morethek* (*warle·rgh*).

yeast, n. *gwēl*, m., ‡*burmen*, f., col. *burm.*

yell, v. *üja, scrȳja, crȳa*: n. *üs* (*üj*), *scrȳs*, m.: **-ing,** n. **üvva*, f.

yellow, a. *melen*; tawny y., **rüthvelen*: **-ish,** a. *melenyk*: **-ness,** n. *melender*, m.: **-hammer,** n. **melenek eythyn*, m., pl. *-egas e.*, **penmelen*, m., pl. *-as.*

yelp, n. *harth, üs*, m., pl. *-ow*: v. *hartha, üja.*

yeoman, n. *yēman*, m., pl. *-s, *gour efan*, m., pl. *gwēr e.*; y. of the guard, *prȳva-gwythyas*, m., pl. *-ysy*: **-ry,** n. *yēmanry*, col.

yes, affirmative, ‡*yā*; in M. Cor. expressed only by repeating v. of question, e.g., will you? yes. *a-vynnough-why? mynnaf.*

yesterday, adv. *dē*; day before y., *dēgensetē·*, m.; y. evening, *nyhewer.*

yet, conj., adv. *whath, na-whath, bytege·ns, hogen, ‡stella*; nor y., *na byth moy*; or y., *byth moy*; more y., *moy ynta·*; he never y. came, *whath byth ny-dhüth.*

yew, n. *ewen*, f., col. *ew*; y. wood, *ewek*, f., pls. *-egow, -egy.*

Yiddish, n. *Yedhowek*, m.

yield, n. *hepcor, dascor, rȳ, omrȳ*; give way, *obaya, plegya*: n., offspring, *ascor*, m.; crops, *trevas*, f.

yoke, n. *yew*, f., pl. *-ow*; y.-bows, *gwaregow an yew*, f., pl.: v. *yewa*; y. together, *kevyewa, kesyewa.*

yolk, n. *melen oy*, m., pl. *melen oyow.*

yonder, a., adv. *yn-hans, hans* (*hons*), *eno, enos*; suffix *-nos, an chȳ-nos*, y. house.

you, pron. *why*; emphatic, *whywhȳ·*; before inf. *'gas, agas*; to teach y., *dh'agas dysky* (to please y., *dheugh plēkya*); infixed *-gas-, -s-.*

young, a. *yowynk* (*yonk*); y. man, *dēn yowynk*, m., pl. *tüs y.*, *‡yunker*, m., pl. *-s*; y. person, *flogh*, m., pl. *flēghes*; the y., *yowynkes*, m.

your, pron. *agas, 'gas*: **-self,** pron. *why agas honen, whywhȳ·*: **-s,** poss. pron. *dheughwhy*; it is y., *why a-n-pew, dheugh-why yth-yu.*

youth, n., state, children, *yowynkes*, m.; time, state, *newyth, yowynkneth, yowynksys*, m.; a y., *dēn yowynk*, m., pl. *tüs y.*, *gwas*, m., pl. *gwesyon, maw*, m., pl. *mebyon*, col. *coscar*: **-ful,** a. *yowynk, tender yn ōs*: **-fulness,** n. *yowynkneth*, m.

yule-log, n. *etew Nadelek*, m., pl. *-y N.*

Z

zeal, n. *dywysygneth, dywysykter*, **ōth, *gres*, m.: **-ot,** n. *dywysyk*, m., pl. *-ygyon*: **-ous,** a. *dywysyk, *gresys.*

zedoary, n., incense, *†costa*, m.

zenith, n. *ughelder ebren*, m., *an pryk ughella, an poynt üs a-ughon a-wartha.*

zephyr, n. *ēthen*, f., pl. *-now, awel glōr*, f., pl. *-low clōr.*

zest, n. *blas, *ōth*, m.

zither, n. *gyttern*, m., pl. *-s.*

zone, n. *grügys*, m., pl. *-ow, *kelgh*, m., pl. *-ow.*

zoo, n. **mȳlva, *gothfȳlva*, f., pl. *-ow*: **-logical,** *a vȳlas*; z. gardens, *lowarthow mȳlas*, pl.: **-logy,** n. *skȳans mȳlas*, m.: **-phyte,** n. *penvagas*, m.